CAPTAIN AMERICA

OFFI...
MARVEL UNIVERSE

W9-CHW-120

...EAD WRITERS/COORDINATORS
...ron Jensen, Al Sjoersdma & Stuart Vandal

...RITERS
*...ul Bourcier, Chris Buchner, Ronald Byrd, Russ
...appell, Michael Hoskin, Chris McCarver, Jacob
...ugemont, Robert J. Sodaro & Kevin Wasser*

...DITOR
...f Youngquist

...DITORS, SPECIAL PROJECTS
...nifer Grünwald & Mark D. Beazley

...SISTANT EDITORS
...ex Starbuck & Nelson Ribeiro

...DITORIAL ASSISTANTS
...eph Hochstein & James Emmett

...NIOR VICE PRESIDENT OF SALES
...avid Gabriel

...OOK DESIGN
...f Powell

...ODUCTION
...e Frontirre

...DITOR IN CHIEF
...xel Alonso

...UBLISHER
...n Buckley

...XECUTIVE PRODUCER
...lan Fine

*...cial thanks to George Olshevsky for starting it all and setting
...standard so high; Jimmy Petersson, Michael Fischer, Gerard
...Menemy, Michel and everyone else at the Marvel Chronology
...ject for appreciating what we get right and pointing out what we get
...ng; Spiderfan.org; the Marvel Appendix; Randy Scott, Christine
...lawski, Agnes Widder, Peter Berg, and the Michigan State
...iversity Special Collections Library; Jeff Nevins; Brian Hirsch; Jeff
...ristiansen; Jeph York; and the rest of the Handbook team.*

...APTAIN AMERICA CREATED BY
...e Simon & Jack Kirby

Welcome to the new *Official Index to the Marvel Universe*'s fifth collected edition, featuring Captain America!

Entry format: Credits include all the known creators. Where the cover artists are different from those handling the interior, we credit them separately. Pencilers and inkers are separate credits, unless the same person did both, whereby they are credited for "art." Feature Characters are the lead, often title, characters in the comic. Supporting Cast are the regular cast. Villains should be obvious. Guest Stars cover other heroes and major characters who turn up in the story, while Other Characters covers everyone else. When multiple characters have used a given codename, we identify which version the character is the first time they appear in a given title; thereafter, unless otherwise stated, all subsequent appearances can be assumed to be the same version. Locations/Items serves to list places plus unusual, unique, or significant equipment. The Synopsis covers the events depicted in the story. Flashbacks are placed in their own section for ease of reference and divided into four types (fb, dfb, pfb, & rfb) described in the Abbreviation Key. The Note section covers interesting information and anomalies that don't fit the other headings.

Chronologies: Along with telling you which characters turn up in which issues, we also try to let you know where they were beforehand, and where they go afterwards. After so many years of flashbacks and retroactive continuity (retcons), this can become a tricky process. For Feature Characters, we list, in order, all appearances between the issue being covered and the character's next appearance in the series. For all other reoccuring characters, we list their last and next appearances. However, so that readers can enjoy tracking a character's appearances both in the genuine historical order, and in the revised order created by the insertions of flashbacks over the years, we distinguish between real world and flashback-revised "chronologically" last and next appearances. We omit "next in" if the subsequent issue is that character's next appearance (or if the issue in question is their final appearance to date), and, for Supporting Cast, we omit "last in" if the previous appearance is within the last five issues of the same series. We also include characters' next and last "behind-the-scenes" appearances, if applicable. As confusion has arisen in the past over volume numbers, we distinguish between different volumes sharing the same cover title by including the publication year. Issue numbers with a slash and extra digit indicate later stories in the same issue; for example, 50/3 is the third story in issue 50.

...TAIN AMERICA: OFFICIAL INDEX TO THE MARVEL UNIVERSE. Contains material originally published in magazine form as AVENGERS, THOR & CAPTAIN AMERICA: OFFICIAL
...X TO THE MARVEL UNIVERSE #1-14. First printing 2011. ISBN# 978-0-7851-5097-8. Published by MARVEL WORLDWIDE, INC., a subsidiary of MARVEL ENTERTAINMENT, ! LC.

"Case No. 1: Meet Captain America" (8 pages)

CREDITS: Joe Simon (co-writer, c co-pencils), Jack Kirby (co-writer, pencils, c co-pencils), Al Liederman (inks), Syd Shores (c inks) (see NOTE)

FEATURE CHARACTER: Captain America (Steve Rogers, America's only Super-Soldier, 1st but chr last & also in Cap #255, '81 fb, also in ToS #63/2, '65, Cap #109, '69 fb, Av:In Ann #1, '08 fb, Cap:Re #2, '09, Next #9, '06 fb, Cap #270, '82 fb, MvPro #5, '10, bts in Cap:SoL #6/3, '99, Cap:SoL #7, '99, Cap #2, '05 fb, MSH #3, '90 fb, ToS #1, '95 fb, SR:SSol #1, '10 fb, Cap #2, '02 fb, BP #30, '01 fb, Cap Ann #13/2, '94 fb, Cap #25, '07 fb, Cap:SoL #7/2, '99, Cap #255, '81, Cap #303, '85 fb, Cap #12, '05 fb, Cap #215, '77 fb, Cap:SoL #12, '99 fb, next in Cap #109, '69 fb, Cap #26, '04 fb, Cap #14, '06 fb, Av #213, '81 fb, SR:SSol #2, '10 fb, Cap:SoL #12, '99 fb, ToS #63/2, '65, Cap #423, '94)

SUPPORTING CAST: Bucky (James Buchanan "Bucky" Barnes, Captain America's partner, 1st but chr last & also in Cap:SoL #12, '99 fb, also in ToS #63/2, '65, chr next in Cap #109, '69 fb)

VILLAINS: Heinz Krueger (1st but chr last & also in MvPro #4, '10, also in ToS #63/2, '65, Cap #109, '69 fb & Av:In Ann #1, '08 fb, dies, next in Cap:Re #2, '09 as corpse), Agent R (Lt. Cynthia Glass, Nazi double agent posing as FBI agent X-13, 1st but chr last in Cap Ann, '00 fb, also & next in ToS #63/2, '65, see NOTE), 3 spies

OTHER CHARACTERS: Dr. Abraham Erskine (as "Prof. Reinstein," 1st but chr last & also in Cap #255, '81 fb, also in ToS #63/2, '65, Cap #109, '69 fb, Av:In Ann #1, '08 fb, dies, next in Cap:Re #2, '09 as corpse, see NOTE), Gen. Chester Richard Phillips (1st but chr last & also in MvPro #4, '10, also in GSInv #1, '75 fb, also & next in ToS #63/2, '65), Franklin Delano Roosevelt (President of the United States, last in HT #3/3, '40, chr last in Cap Ann #8, '86 fb, chr next in ToS #63/2, '65, next in CapC #4, '41), J. Arthur Grover (FBI head, only app), Project: Rebirth employee, military officer, Grover's driver, several military recruits, Uncle Sam (on recruiting poster only), Adolf Hitler, Nazi soldiers (both on cover only)

LOCATIONS/ITEMS: Camp Lehigh (army base, Cap and Bucky's de facto HQ, 1st) inc Steve Roger's tent, Washington DC inc the White House, the Capitol & Project: Rebirth scientific facility within curio shop, American Muntions Inc. factory (destroyed); Captain America's steel shield (only appears in this issue), Prof. Erskine's Super-Soldier Serum (1st, called "the Wonder Serum" here), Project:Rebirth scientific equipment, Agent R's old-woman mask & pistol, Krueger's firearm

SYNOPSIS: After two officers report rampant fifth columnist presence in the US Army, President Roosevelt instructs FBI Director Grover to take them to a top-secret installation. At a curio shop, they follow Agent X-13 to a secret laboratory, where Prof. Reinstein injects Steve Rogers with his "wonder serum," causing the young man to immediately develop peak human strength and ability. One of the officers, revealing himself as a Nazi spy, kills Reinstein and destroys the wonder serum vial. Steve beats the spy, who flees and stumbles into laboratory equipment, where wire coils electrocute him. As the serum's sole beneficiary, Steve becomes Captain America and, over the next few months, captures a spy, prevents a dam explosion, and performs other heroic feats. As Pvt. Steve Rogers, he is assigned to Camp Lehigh, and after camp mascot Bucky Barnes discovers Steve's secret identity, Cap allows him to become his crimefighting partner Bucky.

NOTE: Contains "Table of Contents" (1 page) featuring Captain America, Bucky, Sando, Omar, saboteur, Rathcone, Death, Admiral Perkins, soldiers, Red Skull, & Nazis. Story followed by half-page ad to join Captain America's Sentinels of Liberty. Story called "Case No. 1: Meet Captain America Sentinel of Our Shores and Bucky…" on Contents page. Credits for many of the Golden Age issues are approximate and incomplete. Although the story's timeframe is given as 1941, subsequent chronological analysis places its events from Fall 1940 to March 1941. Although Cap #255, '81 shows that Captain America receives his indestructible disc-shaped shield and an altered costume with his cowl attached to his shirt before he takes Bucky as a partner (between pages 7 and 8 of this story), Cap is depicted with his original steel shield and costume throughout this issue. Erskine's Super-Soldier regimen consists of injection and oral serum with effects stabilized by "vita-rays," as clarified in Cap #255, '81; only the injection shown here. For a full chronology see sidebar following Cap #109, '69. Heinz Krueger named in Cap #109, '69. Reinstein renamed to Erskine in ToS #63/2, '65. Cap #255, '81 reveals "Reinstein" is a code name to fool enemy spies. NW #4, '90 reveals Steve Rogers was not the only participant in the Super Soldier Program. ACap #1-4, '91-92 retells this story, but only elements of it have been confirmed as in continuity; ACap #1, '91 reveals Agent R is a Nazi double agent & her name is Lt. Cynthia Glass & SR:SSol #1, '10 confirms it, her code name is revealed in ToS #63/2, '65, her rank "X-13" revealed here. Gen. Phillips' name is revealed as Chester in ACap #2, '91, Richard in Cap:Legend, '96 & surname in ToS #63/2, '65.

2ND STORY: "No Man But Captain America Could Solve the Riddle" (7 pages)

CREDITS: Jack Kirby, Joe Simon (writers, pencils), Al Liederman (inks)

FEATURE CHARACTER: Captain America (also in Cap:SoL #12, '99 fb)

SUPPORTING CAST: Bucky (also in Cap:SoL #12, '99 fb), Betty Ross (1st, FBI agent)

VILLAINS: Sando (Wolfgang Von Krantz, also in ToS #64/2, '65, see NOTE), 2 Nazis, saboteurs (bts, destroy Fort Bix and Hilltown Bridge)

OTHER CHARACTERS: Omar (Sando's pawn, also in ToS #64/2, '65), Fort Bix soldiers (some in Sando & Omar's crystal ball, many die), drivers on Hilltown Bridge (most die), theater employee, ticket seller, reporters, theatergoers

LOCATIONS/ITEMS: Camp Lehigh, Olympia Theater in Manhattan inc Sando's dressing room, Fort Bix, Hilltown Bridge (destroyed), US Munitions' Works (in crystal ball only); Nazis' guns, Sando's bomb, Omar's crystal ball, tanks (many destroyed)

SYNOPSIS: When Sando and Omar seemingly predict Fort Bix's decimation in their "see the future" act, Cap and Bucky investigate. The "seers" predict the destruction of Hilltown Bridge, which collapses before Cap and Bucky can intervene, but they forcibly confront Sando and Omar, who flee backstage. In Sando's dressing room they find two Nazis who, having already captured FBI agent Betty Ross, hold guns on them. After Sando reveals the "predictions" are part of a chain of disasters intended to destroy US morale, Cap and Bucky quickly defeat the gunmen. Sando pulls out a bomb, but Bucky hurls it out a window before it explodes, and all three criminals are captured.

NOTE: Story called "Case No. 2" on Contents page. Story retold in ToS #64/2, '65. Von Krantz's first name revealed in that story.

3RD STORY: "Captain America and the Chess-Board of Death" (16 pages)

CREDITS: Jack Kirby, Joe Simon (writers, pencils), Al Liederman (inks)

FEATURE CHARACTER: Captain America (also as chess piece)

SUPPORTING CAST: Bucky (also as chess piece), Sgt. Michael Thaddeus Duffy (Camp Lehigh drill sergeant, 1st but chr last in Cap:SoL #12, '99 fb)

VILLAINS: Rathcone (also as chess piece, only app), Kameleon (only app, Rathcone's second-in-command), Rathcone's spy ring (Number 3, Number 13 "Strangler", Number 15, & Fritz named)

OTHER CHARACTERS: Admiral Perkins (also as chess piece, dies), General Ellsworth (also as chess piece & in newspaper photo, dies), Major Fields, military lecture attendees, Death (symbolic splash page image only), Adolf Hitler (bust on cabinet only), bird (signifying Strangler's unconsciousness only)

LOCATIONS/ITEMS: Camp Lehigh inc Steve and Bucky's tent & Ellsworth's tent, Manhattan lecture hall, Rathcone's Peek Street hideout, Army HQ; Rathcone's cane, handgun, military/industrial maps of North and South America, chess board & chess pieces, Kameleon's short wave radio set, chandelier w/microphone, killers' knives & handguns

SYNOPSIS: Nazi spymaster Rathcone selects his targets, including Admiral Perkins, via a specialized chessboard. Steve and Bucky attend Perkins' scheduled lecture but the Admiral is found dead on stage. Cap and Bucky capture the escaping killer, but other spies kill him before he can talk. After General Ellsworth visits Camp Lehigh for an inspection, Sgt. Duffy assigns Steve and Bucky as guards, but Ellsworth too is slain by Rathcone's men. Rathcone next decides to capture Cap and Bucky alive, and spy Number 13 directs Bucky to Rathcone's hideout. Bucky is captured, but a note he left at Lehigh leads Cap there. He frees Bucky, and the pair defeat the entire spy ring, then summon the police.

NOTE: Strangler appears to know camp mascot Bucky Barnes is Cap's partner Bucky. This seems to be an early plot error, since nearly all subsequent stories take it for granted that no one knows the two Buckys are one and the same. Bucky reads "Marvel Comics" in his tent. Story called "Case No. 3, Captain America and the Chess-Board of Death" on Contents page. Sgt. Duffy's rank revealed next story, last name in CapC #4, '41.

4TH STORY: "Captain America and the Riddle of the Red Skull" (14 pages)

CREDITS: Ed Herron (writer), Jack Kirby (co-pencils), Joe Simon (co-pencils, inks)

FEATURE CHARACTER: Captain America (also in ToS #65/2, '65)

SUPPORTING CAST: Bucky (also in ToS #65/2, '65), Sgt. Duffy (also in ToS #65/2, '65)

VILLAINS: Red Skull (Johann Shmidt, top Nazi agent, 1st but chr last in MvPro #5, '10, chr next in ToS #66/2, '65, next in CapC #7, '41), Red Skull ("George Maxon," Nazi agent working with Shmidt, 1st, also in ToS #65/2, '65 as "John Maxon," next in CapC #3, '41) (both see NOTE) & their 4 henchmen (Slug named), Adolf Hitler (bts, promises "Maxon" post of Minister of all American Industry, last in SubC #1, '41)

OTHER CHARACTERS: Major Croy (dies), General Charles Manor (dies), Mildred Manor, two police officers, three FBI agents, Camp Lehigh soldiers, bomber plane pilots (bts, flying sabotaged plane, die), motorcyclist, Nazis (on splash page only)

LOCATIONS/ITEMS: Camp Lehigh inc Steve and Bucky's tent, Major Croy's home on Lower Broadway, General Manor's home, Red Skull's hideout; "Maxon's" bomber plane (destroyed), Major Croy's car, Red Skull's poison hypodermic & red-colored skull "calling card," Mildred Manor's pistol

SYNOPSIS: After Steve and Bucky drive him home, Major Croy is slain by the Red Skull. While police investigate, Cap and Bucky scout the area. Bucky finds the Skull's hideout and is captured, but Cap also finds it soon afterward, freeing Bucky and knocking out the Skull's underlings, although the Skull escapes. The next day, at Camp Lehigh, George Maxon of the Maxon Aircraft Corporation attends an army test of his latest bomber plane, which goes down in flames. That night, the Skull kills General Manor, but Manor's wife delays him long enough for Cap and Bucky to arrive. Following a fight, the Skull is unmasked as Maxon, who seemingly kills himself with his own poison.

NOTE: Story called "Case No. 4, The Fantastic Tale of the Red Skull" on Contents page. Story retold in ToS #65/2, '65 in which it is revealed that a Nazi agent took over Maxon's identity some time before. ToS #66/2, '65 reveals that the agent was not Johann Shmidt, the actual Red Skull, while OHMU HC #9, '09 reveals that both Skulls appear here with Shmidt coordinating the henchmen behind the scenes and Maxon working as the Skull out in the field. Johann Shmidt's name revealed in in Cap #298, '84.

5TH STORY: "Murder Ltd." (10 pages)

CREDITS: Joe Simon (co-writer), Jack Kirby (co-writer, art)

FEATURE CHARACTER: Hurricane (Makkari, also as "Mike Cury" and "Gabriel," also on Hurricane Cab Company insignia, last in RRC #1/3, '40 as "Mercury")

VILLAINS: Kro (as Pluto posing as Paul Sayden, "the Big Guy," last in RRC #1/3, '40), the Murder Mob (Kro's underlings; Piggy Perroni, Jake, Koky, Dum-Dum, & Trigger Bates named; Bates dies)

OTHER CHARACTERS: Police Commissioner Regan, District Attorney Nelson, cab driver, police, several masquerade ball attendees (as jester, bear, cowboy, others), Vanderpont butler, newsboy, murder victim (in newspaper photo only), bystanders, Chunky Lewis (criminal), Tim O'Leary (prospective murder victim) (both mentioned only)

LOCATIONS/ITEMS: Coast City inc Perroni residence, police department, & Vanderpont Estate; Hurricane Cab Co. taxi cab, criminals' guns, Kro's poison, Hurricane's detachable wings

SYNOPSIS: Hurricane visits Coast City, where Pluto's gangsters have committed several murders. Taking a cab to meet Piggy Perroni, Pluto's chief underling, Hurricane whimsically grants the cab super-fast flight, reaching his destination in seconds. Pretending to join Perroni's Murder Mob, Hurricane quickly tires of the charade and sends Perroni flying to the police, where he identifies Paul Sayden as the mob's boss. Sayden, in devil garb, attends a masquerade ball, where he slips a slow-strangling poison into the punch, but Hurricane, briefly in angel garb, intervenes.

6TH STORY: "Tuk, Caveboy, in Stories from the Dark Ages" (6 pages)

CREDITS: Joe Simon (co-writer), Jack Kirby (co-writer, art)

FEATURE CHARACTER: Tuk (1st, also in pfb)

SUPPORTING CAST: Tanir ("the Cro-Magnon," 1st)

VILLAINS: 2 Goreks ("Brain Eaters," both die), Attilan denizens (bts in pfb, exile Phadion and Rhaya)

OTHER CHARACTERS: Ak (last of the Shaggy Ones, also in pfb, dies), Phadion and Rhaya (Tuk's parents or guardians, pfb only, both die), Gholla the Woolly Horned (pfb only, dies), Kag the Lion-Wolf (pfb only), Gru the Lion (pfb only, dies), Cavegirl, lion-wolf (both in symbolic splash panel only)

LOCATIONS/ITEMS: The "rock country beyond the forest" inc Ak's cave & Ak's worship cave (pfb only), the shore (pfb only), the jungle; Tanir's bow & arrows, Goreks' spear & club, Attilan denizens' boat (pfb only)

FLASHBACK: Ak observes Phadion, Rhaya, and their infant son being exiled. Gholla attacks Phadion, and both die. Kag approaches, but Ak takes Rhaya and her child to safety. He lives with the two for a time until Gru kills Rhaya. Ak kills Gru, then relocates with the child, whom he names "Tuk" (p).

SYNOPSIS: On his deathbed, Tuk's surrogate father Ak reveals Tuk's origins. Following Ak's death, Tuk sets out on his own; attacked by Goreks, he kills one and is saved from the other by Tanir, who joins him on his adventures.

NOTE: Series takes place in 50,000 BC. Tuk's name means "Avenger" in the Shaggy Ones' language. Tuk's mission is to "reclaim a lost throne" at Attilan, "Island of the Gods." Phadion is apparently the rightful Attilan King. When he and his family are exiled, he declares "Kadir will fall!" Kadir is presumably the Attilan ruler who deposed him, but he/she is never seen. It is unclear if the Attilan mentioned here has any relationship to the city inhabited by the Inhumans 50,000 plus years later. Story pages numbered 1-4, 6, & 7.

TEXT STORY: "Captain America and the Soldiers' Soup" (2 pages)

CREDITS: Joe Simon, Jack Kirby (art)

FEATURE CHARACTER: Captain America

SUPPORTING CAST: Bucky

VILLAINS: Crusher and Slinky (only apps, criminals employed by "Baron") & their gang (arrested bts), "Baron" (criminal mastermind, mentioned only)

OTHER CHARACTERS: Camp Lehigh soldiers & sentry, colonel

LOCATIONS/ITEMS: Camp Lehigh inc cook house & Steve and Bucky's tent; poison bottle, Slinky's blackjack & knife

SYNOPSIS: Cap and Bucky prevent two criminals from poisoning Camp Lehigh.

NOTE: Story appears between 2nd and 3rd stories.

CAPTAIN AMERICA COMICS #2 (April 1941)

"Captain America and the Ageless Orientals Who Wouldn't Die!!" (15 pages)

CREDITS: Joe Simon (co-writer), Jack Kirby (co-writer, pencils), Reed Crandall (inks), Syd Shores (c inks)

FEATURE CHARACTER: Captain America

SUPPORTING CAST: Betty Ross (next in CapC #4/3, '41), Bucky, Sgt. Duffy

VILLAINS: Benson and Finley (criminal bankers, also in pfb, both die), the Walking Mountains (4 Tibetan giants, also in pfb, all die)

OTHER CHARACTERS: Thompson (FBI agent, dies), Camp Lehigh soldiers, police, cab driver, fireman, Manhattan bystanders (some die), Tibetan guide (pfb only), General Meade (bts, Camp Lehigh commander, visited by Betty Ross, see NOTE)

LOCATIONS/ITEMS: Manhattan inc Benson & Finley's bank w/basement torture room, tenement room, First National Bank, & other banks, Camp Lehigh inc KP tent, Tibet (pfb only); Captain America's steel-vibranium shield (1st but chr last in Cap #255, '81), Benson's cannon & gun, Camp Lehigh's multiple firearms, Betty's gun

FLASHBACK: Benson and Finley encounter the Walking Mountains in Tibet and learn that loud sounds can kill them (p).

SYNOPSIS: Under investigation for tax fraud, Benson and Finley set the Walking Mountains, whom the two brought from Tibet, against government agent Thompson. Soon after, Betty Ross finds Thompson dead. When Finley balks at the plan, Benson has the Mountains kill him as well, then sends two after Betty. Cap and Bucky protect Betty, but the giants escape. The next day, a Walking Mountain attacks Camp Lehigh and proves invulnerable to bullets. Bucky throws a hand grenade which does not injure the giant but nonetheless kills him. Benson sends the remaining three on a crime spree, looting banks and killing bystanders. Cap allows himself to be captured and brought to Benson, who reveals the Mountains' weakness. As Benson orders them to kill Cap, Bucky arrives and uses the cannon, whose sound kills all three Mountains. The blast starts a fire, in which Benson perishes.

NOTE: Contains "Table of Contents" (1 page) featuring Captain America, Bucky, Betty Ross, a Walking Mountain, Adolf Hitler, Hermann Göring, Nazi soldiers, Wax Man & Napoleon, Cleopatra, Knight and other wax figures. Story called "Captain America and the Mystery of the Deathless Monster" on Contents page. Story followed by 1 page ad to join Captain America's Sentinels of Liberty. Cap's steel-vibranium shield appears in virtually all subsequent Captain America appearances. General Meade is apparently already replaced by General Stevens in the 3rd Story.

2ND STORY: "Trapped in the Nazi Strong-Hold" (15 pages)

CREDITS: Joe Simon (co-writer), Jack Kirby (co-writer, pencils), Reed Crandall (inks), Al Gabriele (inking assist)

FEATURE CHARACTER: Captain America (also as "Granny"; also in Av #213, '81 fb, between panels 5 and 6 on page 15)

SUPPORTING CAST: Bucky (also as "Little Lord Fauntleroy"), Sgt. Duffy

VILLAINS: Adolf Hitler (next in YA #1, '41), Hermann Göring (last in SubC #1, '41, next in YA #1, '41) (both see NOTE), Agent 3-21 (impersonates Henry Baldwin, dies), at least 4 Nazi operatives (Fritz & Heinrich named), Nazi soldiers (many die) inc Stuka pilot

OTHER CHARACTERS: Henry Baldwin (only app, wealthy American financier), public speaker, speech attendees, airplane passengers, captain & crewman, Vichy France citizens, Buckingham Palace guard, London reporters & bystanders

LOCATIONS/ITEMS: Camp Lehigh, speech hall, Atlantic Ocean, outside Lisbon, Portugal, Vichy France, Germany inc Berlin hotel, Camp 22 in Black Forest, & Hitler's headquarters, London inc Buckingham Palace; Cap and Bucky's disguises, Nazi Stuka dive bombers, tank, cannon, & guns, spies' sedan, RAF planes, Baldwin's cane, Agent 3-21's cane

SYNOPSIS: After Henry Baldwin announces his intent to sign a financial support pact with Great Britain, Nazi agents abduct him. Disguised as an old woman and her grandson, Cap and Bucky take a plane to Europe to search for Baldwin. They spot Baldwin among the passengers, but although they fight his captors, he disappears again. Cap and Bucky travel from Portugal, through France, and into Germany. There Baldwin is held prisoner. Nazi Agent 3-21 has been impersonating him and Hitler orders him to repudiate the British pact at the signing, as Baldwin, and later sign with Italy instead, creating a propaganda victory. Agent 3-21, as Baldwin, publicly claims his abduction was a ploy to avoid enemies. The disguised Cap and Bucky travel to Britain to observe the pact ceremony, but Bucky recognizes 3-21's imposture, and Nazi agents kill their fellow spy. Cap and Bucky capture the killers, and a note on 3-21's person leads them to concentration camp Camp 22, in Germany's Black Forest, where Hitler and Göring are overseeing Baldwin's execution. Cap and Bucky halt the execution, then defeat the camp's soldiers, rescuing Baldwin.

NOTE: Hitler and Göring, as seen in this story and YA #1, may be impostors. Bucky defeats them both and a later newspaper headline reads, "Germans find Hitler and Goerring in Ashcan."

3RD STORY: "Captain America and the Wax Statue That Struck Death" (15 pages)
CREDITS: Joe Simon (co-writer), Jack Kirby (co-writer, pencils), Reed Crandall (inks), Al Gabriele (inking assist)
FEATURE CHARACTER: Captain America
SUPPORTING CAST: Bucky (also as wax mask), Sgt. Duffy
VILLAINS: The Wax Man (Dobbs, Mayor of city near Camp Lehigh, only app), the New Order (Wax Man's subversive organization; Captain Klotz, Fritz named; Fritz also as wax mask, Fritz dies)
OTHER CHARACTERS: Senator Keats (also as wax mask, dies), General Stevens (Camp Lehigh commander, apparently taking over from General Meade, see NOTE), a Lieutenant, Camp Lehigh soldiers (Joe named, several die bts), Casey, Mike, & one other police officer; Senator Thomas & several other Wax Man victims (all dead, severed heads only), Benedict Arnold, executioner, condemned criminal, Napoleon, Cleopatra, Knight, & other wax statues
LOCATIONS/ITEMS: Camp Lehigh inc stables & General Stevens' office, large city near Camp Lehigh inc Wax Man's Wax Museum base, Wax Man's underground factory beneath nearby forest; super-tanks w/anti-tank gun, rocket bomber, Wax Man's pistol and machete
SYNOPSIS: Senator Keats addresses Camp Lehigh regarding the Wax Man's spy ring. Minutes later, Steve and Bucky find Keats dead, suffocated within a wax mask. The next day, Wax Man's forces attack Lehigh with "super tanks," but Cap and Bucky seize control of one tank to disable most others, allowing soldiers to capture the tank crews. The next day, Wax Man's forces abduct Bucky; searching the city, Cap enters Wax Man's museum and allows himself to be captured. He and Bucky then quickly defeat Wax Man, unmasked as Mayor Dobbs.
NOTE: As with the Strangler in CapC #1/3, '41, the Wax Man appears to know camp mascot Bucky Barnes is Cap's partner Bucky. General Stevens is apparently replaced by General Haywood in CapC #5/2, '41.

4TH STORY: "Tuk, Caveboy, in the Valley of the Mist" (6 pages)
CREDITS: Jack Kirby (co-writer, pencils p 1 only), Joe Simon (co-writer, inks p 1 only), Al Avison (pencils), Al Gabriele (inks)
FEATURE CHARACTER: Tuk
SUPPORTING CAST: Tanir
VILLAINS: The Hairy Ones (1st, some die), the Witches of Endor (only app)
OTHER CHARACTERS: Eve (Princess of Atlantis, 1st), Amir (King of Crete, only app), Crete citizens (many as corpses), a pterodactyl-like bird (dies), single-horned apelike creature (on splash panel only), Toni the Elephant, Jimpo the Monkey (both mentioned only)
LOCATIONS/ITEMS: Crete (King Amir's city), the Valley of Mist (also as "the Valley of Endor") inc the Witches' citadel, the kingdom of Atlantis; Tuk's spear, Tanir's knife & bow and arrows, three vapor masks, Witches' acid & daggers
SYNOPSIS: Tuk and Tanir visit Crete to consult King Amir, but apelike Hairy Ones have conquered it. Tanir and Tuk kill several Hairy Ones, and the others flee. In gratitude, Amir provides directions to Atlantis. A giant bird attacks Tuk and Tanir as they pass through the Valley of Endor. Tanir slays it. Then, the two fall victim to the valley's "mists of sleep." The Witches of Endor abduct them as "permanent guests," but the two prevent the Witches from scarring their prisoner Princess Eve of Atlantis. The three, using "vapor masks" to survive the mists, escape and travel to the outskirts of Atlantis, where Eve hopes to reclaim the throne stolen by her uncle.
NOTE: The Witches of Endor mistakenly called "the Witches of Ender" once here. The relationship between Crete and Atlantis here and the historical, legendary, or actual lands of the same names is unclear.

5TH STORY: "Hurricane, Master of Speed" (10 pages)
CREDITS: Joe Simon, Jack Kirby (writers, art)
FEATURE CHARACTER: Hurricane (also as "Michael Gray")
VILLAINS: Kro (as "Pluto"), Kepiquoatzi (only app, Jivaro shaman), Axti (only app, Jivaro high priest, dies), Xelak (safari porter), Jivaro headhunters (many die)
OTHER CHARACTER: Dr. Ruth Holden (only app), Dr. Ralph Rand (only app), General Ortiz (dies), Juan (Ortiz's aide, dies), Dr. Clay (dies, as shrunken head here), pilot (bts, flying Ruth and Ralph's plane), safari guide & 5 porters, Amazon Rain Forest residents (many die), a boa constrictor (dies), monkey
LOCATIONS/ITEMS: Coast inc that of Medical Research, somewhere in the Amazon Rain Forest within Matto Grosso, Brazil; General Ortiz's

Holden and Rand's expedition to join Dr. Clay's medical efforts. Arriving by plane, the three enter the jungle with Xelek's safari group, most of whom eventually refuse to go further for fear of headhunters. While Hurricane investigates an attacked settlement, Xelek helps the Jivaros abduct Holden and Rand to a Mayan city, where Kepiquoatzi and Axti intend to sacrifice them. Hurricane intervenes, having discovered Dr. Clay was killed weeks before; he kills Kepiquoatl for the plague's antidote, then kills Axti to save Holden and Rand. Hurricane grants Rand temporary wings to fly Holden to safety, then destroys the Mayan city.

NOTE: Story called "Hurricane, Master of Speed in The Devil and the Green Plague" on Contents page. In this story, Hurricane transforms into a giant; since Eternals are not known to have this power, this may be attributed to artistic license. "Michael Gray" mistakenly called "Michael Jupiter" once here.

TEXT STORY: "Captain America and His Boy-Pal Bucky in Short Circuit" (2 pages)
CREDITS: Writer unknown
FEATURE CHARACTER: Captain America (next in Cap #423, '94)
SUPPORTING CAST: Bucky (chr next in Cap #423, '94)
VILLAINS: Herr Glotz and 3 gangsters (all die)
OTHER CHARACTERS: Pvt. Hank Weldon (Lehigh soldier)
LOCATIONS/ITEMS: Camp Lehigh inc Soldiers' Fun Shack & Canteen, nearby deserted mine; Steve's flashlight, gangsters' TNT & guns
SYNOPSIS: Investigating activity in an abandoned mine, Cap and Bucky discover Nazi operatives planting explosives beneath Camp Lehigh's recreation hall. The two intervene, and when one gangster sets off the explosives, the mine implodes, killing the criminals instead.
NOTE: Story appears between 3rd and 4th stories.

CAPTAIN AMERICA COMICS #3 (May 1941)

"The Return of the Red Skull" (17 pages)

CREDITS: Joe Simon, Jack Kirby (writers, pencils, co-inks), Al Avison (co-inks), Al Gabriele (co-inks), Alex Schomburg (c art)
FEATURE CHARACTER: Captain America
SUPPORTING CAST: Bucky, Sgt. Duffy
VILLAINS: Red Skull ("George Maxon," also in fb after CapC #1/4, '41, dies, see NOTE) & several dozen underlings inc power drill driver & "Gun Turret 5," Duffer and Midge (two criminals impersonating Captain America and Bucky, both die), 5 associates of Duffer and Midge inc carnival barker & ticket-taker
OTHER CHARACTERS: Major Douglas (dies) & several military conference attendees, Camp Lehigh soldiers, police dispatcher, Ebbets Field baseball players and spectators (some die), police riot squads, Manhattan residents (Bill & Bill named, thousands killed bts), Coney Island attendees inc kid fans of Cap and Bucky (Larry & Sandy named), Betty Ross (on cover only)
LOCATIONS/ITEMS: Camp Lehigh inc Hartley Hall, Major Douglas' home, Red Skull's abandoned subway tunnel base, BRT Subway System station, multiple Manhattan buildings (destroyed), Ebbets Field, Coney Island inc Duffer and Midge's back dressing room, alleyway, Duffer & Midge's gang headquarters, General Manor's home (in fb only); power drill plans, the Red Skull's Power Drill vehicle w/at least 5 gun turrets, gallows, red skull used as calling card, bomb, & electrically wired costume causing his "Touch of Death," Camp Lehigh firearms, police guns
FLASHBACK: The Red Skull, immune to his own poison, recovers from his supposed death.
SYNOPSIS: The Red Skull kills Major Douglas and steals the US government's plans to create a giant Power Drill vehicle. Manned by the Skull and his underlings, the vehicle wreaks havoc throughout Manhattan. The Skull attacks Ebbets Field, where Cap and Bucky try but fail to board the vehicle. When police riot squads gather, the Skull departs. Later, criminals Duffer and Midge impersonate Cap and Bucky to profit from a Coney Island appearance, only for Steve and Bucky to upstage them. Mistaking Duffer and Midge for the real Cap and Bucky, the Skull and his underlings capture and hang the pair. Catching up with the Skull, Cap and Bucky outfight his underlings. The Skull throws a bomb, but Cap throws it back, and the explosion destroys the Power Drill and kills the Skull.
NOTE: Contains "Table of Contents" (1 page) featuring Captain America, Bucky, Red Skull, Duffer, Midge, Hunchback, dead body, & Lenny. Story called "Case No. 1, Captain America and the Return of the Red Skull" on Contents page. Story followed by 1 page ad to join Captain America's Sentinels of Liberty. Although OHMU:U #6, '89 states that the Red Skull in YA #1, '41, his next appearance, is "probably also a Skull impersonator," OMHU HC #9, '09 reveals that Maxon did die in the explosion here, making the YA #1, '41 Skull a second impersonator. His identity has not been revealed. The real Red Skull, Johann Shmidt, does not appear again until CapC #7, '41.

2ND STORY: "The Hunchback of Hollywood and the Movie Murder" (17 pages)
CREDITS: Joe Simon (co-writer), Jack Kirby (co-writer, pencils), Bernie Klein, George Roussos (inks)
FEATURE CHARACTER: Captain America
SUPPORTING CAST: Bucky, Sgt. Duffy
VILLAINS: The Hunchback (Craig Talbot, only app), archer (Hunchback's hireling, dies)
OTHER CHARACTERS: Mark Carstine (movie producer, also in newspaper photo, dies), Parks (Carstine's assistant), Carol Young (actress), Goris Barloff (actor), McAllister (director), Hawkshaw Brogan (movie studio detective), Marie DeTerle (actress), Hannah (wardrobe woman), watchman (dies), jousting stunt man (dies), Camp Lehigh soldiers, actors, extras, cameraman, sound man & other movie crew members, Clark Gable, John Barrymore, Lon Chaney (prev 3 Hollywood actors, mentioned only), dead body (in symbolic splash page), 2 horses
LOCATIONS/ITEMS: Mark Carstine's Hollywood office, Camp Lehigh, movie location inc Ebony Castle w/dungeon, flimsy castle set, Goris Barloff's trailer, & Carol Young's trailer; medieval costumes and armor, filmmaking equipment, catapults, battering rams, scaling ladders, archer's bow and arrows, lances, Hunchback's spear, Barloff's hunchback wig & makeup, Castle's axe, swords & shields, Brogan's gun
SYNOPSIS: After Superstar Pictures producer Mark Carstine begins production on anti-dictatorship film "The Tyrant," the Hunchback kills him. Nonetheless, filming continues at Ebony Castle, located near Camp Lehigh, and several soldiers, including Steve and Bucky, are cast as extras. During a jousting scene, Steve's opponent is shot by an archer. Cap and Bucky capture him, but the Hunchback kills him before he can talk, then collapses part of a castle set on Cap and Bucky. Goris Barloff, playing a hunchback in the film, is suspected, but director McAllister

helps Barloff flee. Meanwhile, the Hunchback menaces actress Carol Young, then kills a watchman and seals himself in the castle. Steve rallies the film crew to besiege the castle, then, as Cap, has himself catapulted to a turret. Within the castle, he confronts actor Craig Talbot, whom he realizes is the killer Hunchback. As the two duel with swords, overconfident Talbot, an avowed Bundist, admits his crimes, including hiring the archer who was supposed to kill Steve because Carol was attracted to him. Talbot's confession complete, Cap quickly defeats him and turns him over to the police.

NOTE: Story called "Case No. 2, Captain America in The Hunchback of Hollywood and the Movie Murders" on Contents page. Camp Lehigh called "Fort Lehigh" here. Goris Barloff is an homage to horror actor Boris Karloff. Bucky calls Barloff, "Frankenstein" once. Karloff played the Frankenstein monster in 3 films.

3RD STORY: "The Queer Case of the Murdering Butterfly and the Ancient Mummies" (11 pages)
CREDITS: Joe Simon (co-writer), Jack Kirby (co-writer, pencils), Reed Crandall (inks)
FEATURE CHARACTER: Captain America
SUPPORTING CAST: Bucky
VILLAINS: The Butterfly (Dr. Vitrioli, dies) & his 5 underlings, Lenny (Vitrioli's super-strong assistant, only app)
OTHER CHARACTERS: 4 museum guards (2 die), plainclothes police sergeant & 4 policemen, VOX radio announcer, Bucky's teacher and fellow students, 2 Manhattan bystanders, Egyptians & horses (both in hieroglyphics only), tiger & African gorilla (both stuffed museum exhibits), a bat
LOCATIONS/ITEMS: Camp Lehigh inc Steve and Bucky's tent, State Museum inc Butterfly's hidden room, City Bank, VOX radio station; museum exhibits inc several Egyptian artifacts, dinosaur skeleton, multi-armed Kali statue equipped with speaker system, treasures of King Tut (Tutankhamun, 1341-1323 BC), Cleopatra's Diamond, & a sarcophagus and 2 mummies in the basement, Butterfly's winged costume & handgun, Lenny's knife, guards' guns, VOX microphone
SYNOPSIS: After museum curator Dr. Vitrioli receives valuable Egyptian relics, the Butterfly steals several, killing a guard. Following a police investigation, he returns to steal and kill again. When Bucky explores the museum, Vitrioli's assistant Lenny imprisons him in a sarcophagus. The Butterfly sends underlings to rob a bank, but Steve Rogers quickly defeats them. Concerned by Bucky's disappearance, Cap waits in the museum until after-hours. After outfighting Lenny, Cap battles the Butterfly, whom he knocks to the ground. Dying, the Butterfly, unmasked as Vitrioli, reveals Bucky's whereabouts, and Cap frees Bucky.
NOTE: Story called "Case No. 3, Captain America in the Mummy and the Butterfly Killer" on Contents page.

4TH STORY: "Tuk, Cave-Boy" (6 pages)
CREDITS: Joe Simon, Jack Kirby (writers), Mac Raboy (art)
FEATURE CHARACTER: Tuk
SUPPORTING CAST: Tanir
VILLAIN: Eve's uncle ("the Usurper," Atlantean King, only app)
OTHER CHARACTERS: Eve (final app), the Soothsayer, Atlantis' royal guards
LOCATIONS/ITEMS: The kingdom of Atlantis inc the Royal Palace w/North Gate, tunnel (in crystal only); Tanir's bow & arrows, Soothsayer's crystal ball, King's dagger, Royal Guard's armor, swords, & shields
SYNOPSIS: The Usurper's Soothsayer perceives Tuk, Tanir and Princess Eve approaching Atlantis. The Usurper seals the city. The three instead use a cave tunnel to reach a secret passage, emerging before the Usurper himself, who tries to attack with a dagger but is quickly outfought by Tuk and Tanir. The pair outfight several guards, and Tanir holds others at bay with his bow and arrows. When Eve's identity is revealed, the guards welcome her return, and she has the Usurper imprisoned. She offers Tuk and Tanir wealth, but they depart to continue searching for Attilan.
NOTE: Story called ""Tuk, Caveboy, in Atlantis and the False King" on Contents page. Both Atlantis and Attilan called "Island of the Gods" here. Attilan called "Attillan" here.

5TH STORY: "Amazing Spy Adventures: The True Story of the Bald-Head Message and How It Was Delivered" (2 pages)
CREDITS: Jack Kirby (co-writer, pencils), Joe Simon (co-writer, inks)
FEATURE CHARACTER: Istiaeus the Milesian (only app, a spy)
VILLAIN: King Darius (Darius I of Persia, Darius the Great: 550-486 BC)
OTHER CHARACTERS: Istiaeus' 2 servants, Darius' courtier, soldiers, & physician, 3 members of Milesian "council of chiefs," Milesian soldier
LOCATIONS/ITEMS: Persia inc Darius' city & Istiaeus' camp, Miletus inc council chamber; Darius' soldiers' spears and swords
SYNOPSIS: "In the days before the Greek rebellion," Istiaeus visits Darius' court. Suspecting him of espionage, Darius has him closely watched. One of Istiaeus' servants shaves his head supposedly to avoid the heat, then seemingly falls ill. After 2 months' care in Istiaeus' tent, the servant, his hair regrown, apparently recovers. Istiaeus asks that the servant be allowed to return home. After having the servant carefully searched for messages, Darius agrees. Back in Miletus, the servant's head is again shaved, revealing the message written on his skin: "Incite the Ionians to revolt."
NOTE: Story called "Amazing Spy Adventures: The True Story of the Bald-Head Message" on Contents page. The Milesians were the inhabitants of Miletus, a city in the Anatolia province of what is now Turkey.

FEATURE CHARACTER: Hurricane
VILLAINS: Kro (as "Pluto," posing as S. Devile "the Big Shot," chr next in MUni #4, '98, next in Et #1, '76), Scarface Rispoli (only app, Kro's aide) & his three men (Jerry named)

OTHER CHARACTERS: Police Commissioner Holt, Detective Bronson, railway investigators, Groton City's mayor, city officials, reporters, newsboy, train passengers (all die), bystanders

LOCATIONS/ITEMS: Groton City inc subway terminal, Rispoli residence, police station w/Holt's office, Rexal Hotel w/penthouse, & Fifth Avenue Subway Station; 2 "infernal death-boxes" (Deviant technology), subway trains, criminals' car & guns, Kro's "sleep-vapors" & decorative skulls, Kro's flying apparatus (bts, as Pluto, Kro demonstrates a power of flight he does not innately possess)

SYNOPSIS: Hurricane travels to Groton City, where Pluto has caused five subway wrecks within a week, with all passengers killed. At the latest scene, investigators discover a device, identical to devices found at previous wrecks, which Hurricane recognizes as "an infernal death-box," responsible for the passengers' deaths. Hurricane follows a Pluto underling to Scarface Rispoli. He quickly defeats the criminals present, and Rispoli reveals Pluto's penthouse location. Hurricane visits and Pluto renders him unconscious. At a new station's opening ceremony, Pluto plans to kill the mayor and officials aboard a train, but Hurricane, having recovered, arrives in time to prevent it. Hurricane and Pluto battle in the sky until Pluto flees.

NOTE: Story called "Hurricane, Master of Speed, in Satan and the Subway Disasters" on Contents page.

TEXT STORY: "Captain America Foils the Traitor's Revenge" (2 pages)

CREDITS: Stan Lee (writer)

FEATURE CHARACTER: Captain America

SUPPORTING CAST: Bucky

VILLAINS: Lou Haines (a "muscular giant" and ex-soldier, only app) and 2 accomplices

OTHER CHARACTER: Col. Stevens (1st, Camp Lehigh officer)

LOCATIONS/ITEMS: Camp Lehigh inc Steve and Bucky's tent & Stevens' tent; Haines' knife, accomplices' revolvers, Steve Rogers' checkers game

SYNOPSIS: After Lou Haines receives a dishonorable discharge from Col. Stevens, he returns with two others to kill Stevens, but Cap and Bucky defeat all three.

NOTE: Story appears between 2nd and 3rd stories. Story is Stan Lee's first known published comic work.

CAPTAIN AMERICA COMICS #4 (June 1941)

"Captain America and the Unholy Legion" (15 pages)

CREDITS: Joe Simon (co-writer), Jack Kirby (co-writer, pencils), Al Avison, Al Gabriele (inks), Alex Schomburg (c art)

FEATURE CHARACTER: Captain America

SUPPORTING CAST: Bucky

VILLAINS: The Unholy Legion (Herr Snupp & assorted beggars w/faked disabilities, only apps), German submarine commander & crew

OTHER CHARACTERS: Howard Baxter (president of Baxter Munitions Plant, dies), John L. Green (labor leader, dies), George & Mort (aircraft officials, both die), Kenny (Manhattan detective, as corpse), two Manhattan police officers, federal agent (dies), two Navy officers (Warren named), President Franklin D. Roosevelt (last in CapC #1, '41, chr last in Cap #423, '94, next in HT #5b, '41)

LOCATIONS/ITEMS: Manhattan inc Midtown street & Unholy Legion's town hall base w/cage and tunnel to river, other cities w/Baxter Munitions Plant & lecture hall, river, Camp Lehigh inc Steve and Bucky's tent, White House; Unholy Legion's knives, crutch-gun, poisoned apples, guns, swastika branding iron, noose, & machine gun, German sub w/weapons & torpedo, Bucky's Sentinel of Liberty badges, Der Fuehrer's Collection Box

SYNOPSIS: Across the country, the Unholy Legion, saboteurs disguised as beggars and indigents, kill US industrial leaders. In Manhattan, Steve and Bucky encounter a "legless" beggar whom they see run away soon afterward. Although Steve must return to camp, Bucky follows the beggar and, seeing several others enter an abandoned town hall building, suitably disguises himself and follows. When Legion members prove their identities via swastikas branded on their chests, Bucky is exposed as an intruder and captured. The Legion's leader Herr Snupp is prevented from torturing Bucky when Cap arrives. The Legion attacks, overwhelming Cap with sheer numbers before Bucky threatens them with a machine gun. Bucky imprisons the Legion, then joins Cap to chase Snupp, who meets a German sub. Cap and Bucky board, overcome the crew, and wreck the sub. Snupp flees back to the hall and frees his compatriots, but Cap and Bucky follow and defeat them all, leaving them for the FBI.

NOTE: Contains "Table of Contents" (1 page) featuring Captain America, Bucky, Ivan the Terrible, Betty Ross, counterfeiters, & ghouls. Story called "Case No. 1, Captain America and the Unholy Legion" on Contents page. The password to enter the Unholy Legion's meeting is "Down with Democracy."

2ND STORY: "Captain America and Ivan the Terrible" (9 pages)

CREDITS: Jack Kirby (co-writer, pencils, co-inks), Joe Simon (co-writer, co-inks), Al Avison (co-inks)

FEATURE CHARACTER: Captain America (also in Bucky's dream)

SUPPORTING CAST: Bucky (also in Bucky's dream), Betty Ross (in Bucky's dream only)

VILLAINS: Ivan the Terrible ("King of the Tartars") & his underlings (all in Bucky's dream only)

OTHER CHARACTERS: King Peter Ross & his followers, Grisha (servant), Wazira (King of the Africans), Siberian kingdom's subjects, horses & elephant, moat sharks (all in Bucky's dream only)

LOCATIONS/ITEMS: Camp Lehigh inc Steve and Bucky's tent, Siberian kingdom inc Ivan's castle w/dungeon, drawbridge, Ivan's throneroom, & balcony (in Bucky's dream only), King Peter's cave (in Bucky's dream only); Ivan's knife, swords, axes, lances, and other weapons (in Bucky's dream only)

SYNOPSIS: In his Siberian kingdom, Ivan the Terrible passes judgment on criminals, including Captain America and Bucky, who escape the dungeon with Betty Ross. The three join the forces of Betty's father, King Peter, rightful ruler of the kingdom, and retake the castle, forcing Ivan to abdicate. As the kingdom cheers, Bucky awakens in Camp Lehigh, for the adventure was only a dream.
NOTE: Ivan the Terrible, as seen in Bucky's dream, should not be confused with the historic figure Prince Ivan IV of Russia (1530-1584), aka "Ivan the Terrible." Since it is possible Cap and Bucky have met Betty Ross' father, "King Peter Ross" might be a dream-version of him. Story called "Case No. 2, Captain America and Ivan the Terrible" on Contents page.

3RD STORY: "The Case of the Fake Money Fiends" (10 pages)
CREDITS: Jack Kirby (co-writer, co-pencils), Joe Simon (co-writer, co-pencils, co-inks), Al Avison (co-inks)
FEATURE CHARACTER: Captain America (also as farmer)
SUPPORTING CAST: Bucky, Betty Ross, Sgt. Duffy
VILLAINS: The Counterfeit Gang (leader and at least 14 others, 3 disguised as "ghosts")
OTHER CHARACTERS: Pvt. Tom Peters & other Camp Lehigh soldiers, Hillsdale residents
LOCATIONS/ITEMS: Camp Lehigh inc Steve and Bucky's tent, Hillsdale inc "haunted house," deserted warehouse on outskirts, & sewers; counterfeit presses, counterfeiters guns, lapel flower that shoots water
SYNOPSIS: When ghosts are seen in a Hillsdale house, Cap and Bucky investigate and discover a counterfeiter's den, where some criminals impersonate "ghosts" to frighten away intruders. The two defeat the criminals and free Betty Ross, who had been captured while trailing the gang. She reveals the head counterfeiter has another lair in town but she doesn't know where. The next day, Cap, disguised as a farmer, receives counterfeit money from one criminal, upon whose car he secretly rides to find the lair. After Bucky joins him, they capture the criminals. Back at Camp Lehigh, the two are put on onion-peeling duty as punishment for their absence.
NOTE: Story called "Case No. 3, Captain America and the Fake Money Fiends" on Contents page.

4TH STORY: "Captain America in Horror Hospital" (13 pages)
CREDITS: Jack Kirby (co-writer, co-pencils), Joe Simon (co-writer, co-pencils, co-inks), Al Avison (co-inks)
FEATURE CHARACTER: Captain America (next in Cap:P #1, '10, YA #1, 41, ToS #66/2-68/2, '65, AllWin #1/3, '41, UXM #268, '90 fb, W:O #16, '07)
SUPPORTING CAST: Bucky (next in YA #1, '41), Sgt. Duffy (chr next in ToS #68/2, '65, next in AllWin #1/3, '41), Betty Ross
VILLAINS: Dr. Grimm (dies), Lomm and Igan (Grimm's henchmen, only apps), Gorro (Grimm's monster, dies), 3 theater-robbing criminals (Chuck & Willie named)
OTHER CHARACTERS: Pete (Camp Lehigh soldier), Miss Ray (nurse, dies), cab driver, theater doorman, Manhattan bystanders, 3 ghouls (on symbolic splash page only)
LOCATIONS/ITEMS: Manhattan inc Bijou theater, Grimm Private Hospital on Glenn Road w/Grimm's office and lab, Bucky's room, & airtight room, Camp Lehigh; Grimm's pistol, hospital apparatus inc a "glasso-metal" cage
SYNOPSIS: When Cap and Bucky pursue criminals, one strikes Bucky with a blackjack. Cap, as Steve, rushes Bucky to the nearest hospital, Grimm Private Hospital. Despite Dr. Grimm's strange demeanor, Bucky agrees to remain for observation. When his nurse goes missing, Bucky writes Steve a letter that "this is a case for Captain America." Seeing the letter, Grimm prepares for Cap's arrival. When Cap shows up, Grimm's insane henchman Igan traps them both in a hidden room and floods it with water. Cap escapes, but Grimm imprisons him, revealing he intends to drain both Bucky and Cap of blood to feed his "greatest experiment" Gorro. The next day, Betty Ross, investigating, applies as Grimm's nurse, but Grimm brings both her and Cap to his lab, where he and henchman Lomm prepare to drain Bucky. Cap frees Bucky, but Lomm releases the apelike Gorro, who almost kills Cap before Bucky shoots it. Grimm tries to throw Betty off a balcony, but Cap intervenes, and Grimm falls to his death.
NOTE: Cap presumably rescues Igan from drowning, but this is not shown. Story called "Case No. 4, Captain America in Horror Hospital" on Contents page. The Bijou is showing "Million Dollar Robbery," starring Humphrey Raft and George Bogart.

5TH STORY: "Tuk, Caveboy" (6 pages)
CREDITS: Joe Simon, Jack Kirby (writers), Reed Crandall (art)
FEATURE CHARACTER: Tuk
SUPPORTING CAST: Tanir
VILLAINS: Bonzo the Brute and his marauders (two die)
OTHER CHARACTERS: Woman w/baby & other village denizens (some die)
LOCATIONS/ITEMS: Village inc caves, jungle w/clearing, cliffs; Tanir's bow and arrows, Bonzo and marauders' clubs
SYNOPSIS: Tuk and Tanir arrive at a village terrorized by Bonzo the Brute's forces. When one villager dies protecting a woman and baby, Tanir kills the attacker with an arrow, a death the marauders attribute to magic. While Tuk takes the woman and baby to safety in the jungle, Bonzo captures Tanir, who claims his "magic stick" bow will be useless if he is tortured or killed. Bonzo instead forces him to join the marauders and sends him to attack Tuk. Instead Tanir reveals his intent to outwit Bonzo, killing the marauder sent to spy on them, and returning to the Brute.
NOTE: Story called "Tuk, Caveboy, and the Ogre of the Cave-Dwellers" on Contents page.

6TH STORY: "Hurricane, Master of Speed, in The Pirate and the Missing Ships" (7 pages)
CREDITS: Joe Simon, Jack Kirby (writers), Reed Crandall (art)

OTHER CHARACTERS: Steamship office clerk, police officer, automobile driver, newsboy, ocean liner crew and passengers, Manhattan bystanders, British officials and soldiers (pfb only)
LOCATIONS/ITEMS: Manhattan inc steamship ticket office, the Pirates' home island north of Hawaii (also in pfb), Pacific Ocean; ocean liner,

Pirates' ship, swords, & guns

FLASHBACK: In the late 16th century, the British exile pirate John Cruthers to an island. Seeking eventual revenge on society, Cruthers teaches piracy to the natives. On his deathbed, he urges them to one day rob and destroy ships (p).

SYNOPSIS: In the present, the Pirates finally leave their island home and quickly prey upon several steamships. Learning the ships all disappear north of Hawaii, Hurricane flies to the region and locates the Pirates' island, then finds the Pirates themselves attacking and boarding an ocean liner. Hurricane forces them back onto their ship, which he steers back to the island. He then summons a storm, killing the Pirates.

NOTE: Story called "Hurricane, Master of Speed, in The Pirate's Crime" on Contents page.

TEXT STORY: "Captain America and the Bomb Sight Thieves" (2 pages)
CREDITS: Stan Lee (writer), Jack Kirby (pencils), Al Avison (inks)
FEATURE CHARACTER: Captain America
SUPPORTING CAST: Bucky
VILLAINS: Monk & One-Eye (would-be thieves, only apps)
OTHER CHARACTERS: Sentinels of Liberty (1st, patriotic youth club of which Bucky Barnes is president; Pete Keller the "sergeant-at-arms," Joey, & Larry named), Professor Colby (only app)
LOCATIONS/ITEMS: Rooming house w/both Prof. Colby's apartment/lab and the Sentinels' meeting room; Colby's bomb sight, Monk and One-Eye's guns
SYNOPSIS: Monk and One-Eye follow a non-costumed Bucky to his Sentinel of Liberty meeting, which is next door to Professor Colby's room. Colby has developed a new bomb sight and the criminals want to sell it to dictators. As Pvt. Steve Rogers addresses the Sentinels, the criminals burst in, One-Eye holding the meeting attendees at gunpoint while Monk seeks Colby. Steve outfights One-Eye, then, as Cap, captures Monk.
NOTE: Story appears between 4th and 5th stories followed by Sentinels of Liberty ad (1 page). Back cover features Captain America and Bucky pin-up (Jack Kirby, art).

CAPTAIN AMERICA COMICS #5 (August 1941)

"Captain America and the Ringmaster of Death" (12 pages)

CREDITS: Jack Kirby (co-writer, co-pencils, c pencils), Joe Simon (co-writer, co-pencils, co-inks), Al Avison (co-inks), Syd Shores (c inks)
FEATURE CHARACTER: Captain America (also on Wheel of Death)
SUPPORTING CAST: Bucky (also on Wheel of Death), Sgt. Duffy (both last in AllWin #1/3, '41), Betty Ross (also on Wheel of Death)
VILLAINS: Ringmaster of Crime ("Ringmaster of Death," Fritz Tiboldt, 1st, chr next in XFor #-1, '97, next in MTIO #76, '81 fb) & the Circus of Death: Butch the Roustabout, Derko the Clown, the Missing Link, Omir the Snake Charmer, Rawal the Elephant Trainer, Spike the Roustabout, Tommy Thumb, the Trapeze Trio, Zandow the Strongman, barker, others (1st for all; Derko next in SubC #22, '47)
OTHER CHARACTERS: General Blaine (also on Wheel of Death, dies) & 2 subordinates, Defense Commissioner Newsome (also on Wheel of Death, dies), circus crowds, police, Omir's cobra, 2 tigers (one dies), Rajar & 2 other elephants, other Wheel of Death figures, circus creatures (on symbolic splash page only)
LOCATIONS/ITEMS: Ringmaster's Circus inc Ringmaster's tent, tiger cage, & Big Top, Camp Lehigh inc KP tent & Newsome's armory; Ringmaster's Wheel of Death and whip, other circus equipment, Omir's flute
SYNOPSIS: Steve and Bucky visit a circus run by the Ringmaster, a Nazi spy who chooses victims via a "Wheel of Death." Targeting circus attendee General Blaine, he forces midget Tommy Thumb to release a tiger. Steve, as Captain America, kills the tiger, but Blaine, mauled by the tiger, dies. Later, at Camp Lehigh, Steve discusses the incident with Betty Ross. Ringmaster sends several performers after Defense Commissioner Newsome, who is killed by Omir's cobra. Cap and Bucky intervene, but the performers escape, abducting Betty. Cap and Bucky head for the circus and find Ringmaster about to hang Betty. With quick trapeze work, Cap frees her while Bucky knocks out Ringmaster's underlings. The duo depart, leaving Betty to explain matters to the police.
NOTE: Contains "Table of Contents" (1 page) featuring Captain America, Bucky, Ringmaster, Derko, other circus creatures, Wheel of Death victims, Captain Okada, & Pepo Laroc. Butch and Rawal's names revealed in OHMU:U #1, '08. General Blaine mistakenly called "General Barnes" once here.

2ND STORY: "The Gruesome Secret of the Dragon of Death" (15 pages)
CREDITS: Jack Kirby (co-writer, co-pencils), Joe Simon (co-writer, co-pencils, co-inks), Al Avison (co-inks)
FEATURE CHARACTER: Captain America
SUPPORTING CAST: Bucky, Sgt. Duffy, General Haywood (Camp Lehigh's commanding officer, apparently replacing General Stevens, 1st, next in CapC #11, '42)
VILLAINS: Captain Okada (commander of the Dragon of Death, dies) & his crew (Hiroshi, Toshio named, several die)
OTHER CHARACTERS: Commander Phillips (1st, US Navy officer), Marie Phillips (Commander Phillips' daughter, only app), Anohu (islander), US sailors (Miller named), scouting plane pilots
LOCATIONS/ITEMS: Kunoa Island (near Hawaii) inc volcano & US naval base w/radio room & Haywood's quarters, Camp Lehigh inc Steve and Bucky's tent & General Haywood's office, Pacific Ocean; Dragon of Death (1st, Okada's giant dragon-shaped submarine, next in MUni #1, '98, similar submarine next in CapC #43, '44) w/armored barge, dynamite, & other apparatus, patrol boat Winfield, Anohu's fishing boat, US scouting planes, Navy utility transport plane, Toshio's canoe, row boat, escape craft
SYNOPSIS: General Haywood, scheduled to meet with Cmdr. Phillips at Kunoa Island Naval Base, instructs Steve and Bucky to accompany

him as orderly and messenger boy, respectively. Arriving, they learn Cmdr. Phillips' ship was reportedly swallowed by a sea dragon. Aboard the "Dragon," actually a monstrous submarine, Capt. Okada tortures Phillips for information. When Phillips remains unbroken, Okada's underlings abduct his daughter Marie. Cap and Bucky, observing Marie, follow them into the Dragon's "mouth." While they fight some of the crew, others take Marie to Okada's torture chamber, but after learning Cap and Bucky are aboard, Okada escapes on a barge. Okada's men plant dynamite in Kunoa's volcano, intending to flood the US fleet with lava, then depart in a second craft, leaving the barge itself laden with dynamite to block the fleet's escape. Cap boards the barge and steers it away. Although both volcano and barge explode, the fleet escapes the lava. Now in possession of the Dragon with Phillips, Bucky, believing Cap dead, uses the Dragon's cannon to blast Okada's escape craft, but Cap turns up alive.

NOTE: Haywood's decision to bring Steve and Bucky with him implies he either knows they are Cap and Bucky or is acting on advice from someone who does. Story called "Captain America and the Riddle of the Great Sea Dragon" on Contents page. Dragon of Death is taken into US custody following this story as revealed in MUni #1, '98. Camp Lehigh called "Fort Lehigh" here.

3RD STORY: "Captain America in Killers of the Bund" (10 pages)
CREDITS: Jack Kirby (co-writer, co-pencils), Joe Simon (co-writer, co-pencils, co-inks), Al Avison (co-inks)
FEATURE CHARACTER: Captain America
GUEST STARS: Young Allies (as Sentinels of Liberty here): Jeff, Tubby (both last in YA #1, '41, next in CapC #6, '41), Knuckles, Whitewash (both last in YA #1, '41, next in CapC#8/Text, '41, see NOTE)
SUPPORTING CAST: Bucky
VILLAINS: The Bund (1st, Herr Shnitzel "leader," Hans, & Fritz named; at least 4 die)
OTHER CHARACTERS: 2 other Sentinels of Liberty members, Heinrich Shmidt (1st, German-American), Bob Shmidt (1st, Heinrich's son and Bucky Barnes' friend), nurse, soda jerk, Sentinels of Liberty's fathers, US militia (both bts, raiding the Bund camp), Adolf Hitler (in picture on wall only)
LOCATIONS/ITEMS: Camp Lehigh inc Steve and Bucky's tent, Shmidt residence, hospital, Camp Reichland (Bund base) inc guardhouse, Sentinels of Liberty headquarters, Bund residence, diner, Shnitzel's cabin, 2nd Bund base; 5 Bund planes (all but one destroyed), Bund's sedan & firearms
SYNOPSIS: The Bund try to recruit Heinrich Shmidt. When he refuses, they beat him up. Shmidt's son Bob reports the crime to Steve and Bucky, who visit Shmidt in the hospital, then raid the Bund's Camp Reichland, beating up everyone present. The next day, Bucky Barnes and the Sentinels of Liberty spy on Bund members, some of whom capture Cap. Learning the Bund plan to spray Manhattan with sleeping gas, Cap escapes his captors and, seeing 4 planes take off, boards a fifth to pursue. He shoots down one plane and steers 2 more into crashing into each other; the fourth's pilot boards Cap's plane and they fight hand-to-hand, forcing Cap to knock the man to his death. Landing, Cap meets Bucky, and they return to Camp Reichland, where the Sentinels, their fathers, and US forces round up the Bund.
NOTE: Story called "Captain America and the Killers of the Bund" on Contents page. The Young Allies' names revealed as Jefferson Worthington Sandervilt ("Jeff"), Percival Aloysius O'Toole ("Knuckles"), Henry Tinkle ("Tubby") & Whitewash Jones ("Whitewash") in YA #1, '41 but amended to Geoffrey Worthington Vandergill, Pat O'Toole, Henry Yosef Tinkelbaum, & Washington Carver Jones respectively in YA #1, '09. OHMU HC #2, '09 changes Whitewash's 1941 name to Douglas Jones. Story followed by one page Sentinels of Liberty ad.

4TH STORY: "Captain America and the Terror That Was Devil's Island" (6 pages)
CREDITS: Jack Kirby (co-writer, co-pencils), Joe Simon (co-writer, co-inks), Al Avison (co-inks)
FEATURE CHARACTER: Captain America (next in CapC #21, '42 fb)
SUPPORTING CAST: Bucky (chr next in CapC #21, '42 fb)
VILLAINS: Pepo Laroc (only app, Devil's Island overseer), Durel (only app, Laroc's underling), 2 guards
OTHER CHARACTERS: Tom Jason (only app, fighter pilot, Steve and Bucky's friend), 3 sharks (2 die)
LOCATIONS/ITEMS: Devil's Island inc Laroc's office, small hut, & torture chamber, Camp Lehigh; Laroc's knife
SYNOPSIS: At Devil's Island, Steve and Bucky visit Tom Jason, a former French pilot imprisoned after Germany defeated France. As Cap and Bucky, they investigate the prison and find warden Pepo Laroc torturing Tom. Laroc drops Cap into a water-filled shark pit, but Cap, using one of his cowl's wingtips as a blade, kills 2 sharks and escapes a third. Resurfacing, he knocks out Laroc and frees Tom. Weeks later, Steve and Bucky learn Tom, now with the Greek Air Force, has shot down Nazi planes over Albania.
NOTE: Story called "Captain America and the Terror of Devil's Island" on Contents page. Last page has half-page story and half-page Marvel Mystery Comics #21, '41 ad. Cap's mask wings revealed as steel here.

5TH STORY: "Headline" Hunter, Foreign Correspondent" (5 pages)
CREDITS: Stan Lee (writer), Harry Fisk (art)
FEATURE CHARACTER: Jerry "Headline" Hunter (1st, foreign correspondent for Daily News)
SUPPORTING CAST: Ed (1st, London Star editor, next bts in CapC #6/5, '41, next in CapC #7/5, '41, see NOTE)
VILLAINS: Cooles (Ambassador Jordan's legal advisor, German operative, only app), his 4 underlings (all die), & his pilot, Nazi pilots (bts, only planes seen)
OTHER CHARACTERS: US Ambassador Jordan, Billings (Jordan's secretary), Crawford of the English War Relief Society, Winston Churchill (British Prime Minister, last in SubC #3, '41, next in HT #5b, '41), Londoners, office boy, newsboy, police, British soldiers, Daily News editor in New York (bts, on phone)
LOCATIONS/ITEMS: London inc London Star office (see NOTE), the US Embassy, & air raid shelter w/secret room, Berlin inc Grupp Munitions

reveals himself as the thief, and takes Hunter aboard his plane. In the air, Cooles ties Hunter to a bomb and releases it. However, Hunter hangs on to the plane's landing gear. Once Cooles' plane is over Berlin, Hunter, wriggling free, drops the bomb, destroying a factory. Blaming his underlings, Cooles kills most of them, but Hunter knocks him out and forces the pilot to return to London, where Hunter returns the documents.

NOTE: Headline Hunter identified as Daily News foreign correspondent in CapC #13/4, '42. The London star is identified in CapC#7/5, '41, revealed as part of Affiliated Press in CapC #10/3, '42 & later identified as New Londontown News (possibly a subsidiary) in CapC #13/4, '42. Ed's name is revealed in CapC #12/5, '42.

6TH STORY: "Tuk, Caveboy in Weird Stories from the Dark Ages" (4 pages)
CREDITS: Joe Simon, Jack Kirby (writers), Reed Crandall (art)
FEATURE CHARACTER: Tuk (last app)
SUPPORTING CAST: Tanir (last app)
VILLAINS: Bonzo the Brute (dies) & his marauders (some die)
OTHER CHARACTERS: A sabertooth tiger (dies), herd of mammoths
LOCATIONS/ITEMS: Village, jungle; Tuk and Tanir's bows and arrows, Bonzo & his marauders' clubs
SYNOPSIS: Bonzo prepares to torture Tanir, but Tuk, from afar, summons a sabertooth, whom Tanir kills, winning another chance to prove himself to Bonzo. Pretending he will smoke Tuk out of hiding, Tanir starts a forest fire, which sends mammoths stampeding toward Bonzo's men. Tuk and Tanir mount a mammoth, and Tuk kills Bonzo with an arrow as they ride from the scene. Dismounting, the two prepare for further adventure.
NOTE: The woman and child saved by Tuk in CapC #4/5, '41 have apparently been forgotten here. This is the last story of the series.

7TH STORY: "Hurricane, Master of Speed" (8 pages)
CREDITS: Stan Lee (writer), Charles Nicholas (art)
FEATURE CHARACTER: Hurricane (also as Harry Kane, reporter for the Star-Eagle)
VILLAINS: Nicolai ("Old Nick the Beggar," apparently a communist insurgent, only app), Horace Flinthart (dies) & his 2 underlings, 2 criminal financiers, 4 communist insurgents
OTHER CHARACTERS: Bank teller, bank guard, Flinthart's butler, storekeeper, Manhattan police, bystanders
LOCATIONS/ITEMS: Bank, Flinthart Mansion inc Flinthart's office w/trapdoor, rooming house, store, "dark hallway," hotel suite; counterfeit money, criminals' guns
SYNOPSIS: Repeatedly receiving counterfeit money from banks, Hurricane investigates retired financier Horace Flinthart, a longtime miser who recently donated millions to charity. Forcing his way into Flinthart's office as "Harry Kane," Hurricane is attacked by two hirelings but easily outfights them. Interrogated, Flinthart confesses to circulating counterfeit money. Shot by an underling, he only reveals the mastermind's name, "Nick," before dying. Apparently forcing an address from the underlings, Hurricane tracks down Nick and follows as Nick spreads counterfeit money at several stores, consults associates at a hotel, and finally meets with a communist ring, where, revealed as "Nicolai," he discusses the ring's plan to lead a revolution after the counterfeit money ruins the US economy. After fighting Nicolai's men, Hurricane summons the police.

TEXT STORY: "Captain America and the Ruby Robbers " (2 pages)
CREDITS: Stan Lee (writer), Jack Kirby (co-pencils), Joe Simon (co-pencils, inks)
FEATURE CHARACTER: Captain America
SUPPORTING CAST: Bucky, the Sentinels of Liberty (bts, departing meeting, Harry named)
VILLAINS: Two thieves (Muggsy named, only apps)
OTHER CHARACTERS: Jerry Briggs (1st, a Sentinel of Liberty), Mr. Briggs (Jerry's father, only app), Mr. Crowley (Mr. Brigg's employer, mentioned only)
LOCATIONS/ITEMS: Briggs residence; ruby
SYNOPSIS: Sentinels of Liberty member Jerry returns home after a meeting, There, Jerry's father, believing Captain America a hoax, forbids him from further attendance. When two criminals attempt to steal a ruby entrusted to Briggs' safekeeping, Cap and Bucky arrive and defeat the pair, convincing Briggs of his error.
NOTE: Story appears between 3rd and 4th stories.

CAPTAIN AMERICA COMICS #6 (September 1941)

"Captain America Battles the Camera Fiend and His Darts of Doom" (16 pages)

CREDITS: Jack Kirby (co-writer, co-pencils, c art), Joe Simon (co-writer, co-pencils, co-inks), Al Avison (co-inks)
FEATURE CHARACTER: Captain America
GUEST STARS: Young Allies (as Sentinels of Liberty members here): Jeff & Tubby (both next in CapC #8/Text, '41)
SUPPORTING CAST: Bucky (chr last in CapC #21, '42 fb) & other Sentinels of Liberty (Bucky's classmates)
VILLAINS: The Camera Fiend (Professor Lucius Hall, Bucky's teacher) & his underlings w/3 impersonating janitors at Bucky's school (Slug named)
OTHER CHARACTERS: Senior maritime officer (dies), Johnson (maritime officer), Bucky's classmates (several boys and girls, not Sentinels of Liberty), Sir Maitland Drake (British diplomat, dies), Britannia captain and crew (some die), Camp Lehigh soldiers, Camera Fiend victim (in symbolic splash panel only), Nazis, ax thrower (both on cover only), Dr. Jekyll and Mr. Hyde (as "Mister Jekyll and Hyde," mentioned only, by Cap to Prof. Hall)
LOCATIONS/ITEMS: Maritime Commission office, Camera Fiend's waterfront hideout, Bucky's school inc Hall's classroom & basement, New York Harbor inc Dock Five, Liberty Island w/Statue of Liberty, Camp Lehigh inc Steve & Bucky's tent; steamship Britannia, armored truck, British Crown Jewels, Camera Fiend's rubber mask & camera weapons w/poisoned needles, student cameras, erasers & sticks, Bucky's Sentinel whistle, coded trans-Atlantic cablegram, underlings' machine guns
SYNOPSIS: The Camera Fiend learns of the British Crown Jewels' arrival. He and his gang storm the Maritime Commission office to discover the ship bringing the Jewels. Steve and Bucky, assigned to guard the Jewels, arrive and, as Cap and Bucky, fight and lose to the criminals, who flee from police sirens. Later, at school , Bucky suggests to Professor Hall that the class take photos at the docks, where Steve, as a guard, awaits the steamship. When a British diplomat disembarks, the Fiend kills him from afar then reaches the Jewels with his gang. Cap and Bucky knock out the thugs, but the Fiend escapes without the Jewels. Soon after, Bucky boasts to his classmates that he can get photos of Cap. At Camp Lehigh, the Fiend switches Bucky's camera with one of his so that Bucky inadvertently shoots a poisoned needle at Cap while taking his picture. Cap defends himself with his shield. The next day, Cap accompanies Bucky to school, where Hall's camera shoots a poisoned needle at him, revealing Hall as the Fiend. Bucky and the Sentinels of Liberty take care of the thugs allowing Cap to knock out the Fiend.
NOTE: Contains "Table of Contents" (1 page) featuring Captain America, Bucky, & Dr. Nicolai Vardoff (also as Hangman). Story called "Captain America and the Camera-Fiend" on Contents page. This story depicts Bucky as a student and implies he is at most 14 while most modern wartime stories depict him as 16 or older and a high school dropout. Page 6 panel 6 shows the Camera Fiend observing the Brittainia's arrival even as he is still with his students as Hall on page 6 panel 7.

2ND STORY: "Meet the Fang, Arch Fiend of the Orient" (9 pages)
CREDITS: Jack Kirby (co-writer, co-pencils), Joe Simon (co-writer, co-pencils, co-inks), Al Avison (co-inks)
FEATURE CHARACTER: Captain America
SUPPORTING CAST: Bucky, Sgt. Duffy, Betty Ross
VILLAINS: The Fang (leader of San Francisco Chinatown criminal organization, 21, 1st, next in ToS #82, '66, see NOTE) & his organization inc the Hatchet-Men (Wong named), Chu Yin, & 2 torturers/executioners (Wong named, see NOTE), Baron Nushima (agent of "Asiatic aggressor nation")
OTHER CHARACTERS: Chan (Chinese delegate), Liang (Chan's assistant, dies), FBI agent, army officer, guardhouse guard, dragons (as statues only)
LOCATIONS/ITEMS: San Francisco inc Chinatown w/Fang's hideout, Camp Lehigh inc guest barracks & guardhouse, the Fang's Lotus Street hideout; Fang's sleeping vapor & torture devices, the Hatchet-Men's hatchets, swords & other weapons, executioner's sword, Steve & Liang's guns
SYNOPSIS: The Fang makes a deal with a foreign agitator to kill Chinese officials seeking a loan from the US, currently at Camp Lehigh and guarded by Steve and Bucky. There, the Fang floods the guest barracks with sleeping vapor. Steve falls unconscious while Bucky covers his face and fights the Fang's men. A Hatchet-Man stabs Liang, and the Fang departs with Bucky and Chan. The FBI holds Steve for questioning and Betty Ross reveals Chiang, before dying, overheard the Fang name his local hideout's address. Steve locates the Fang's hideout, where Betty has also been captured. The Fang orders Bucky's decapitation, but Cap interrupts and defeats the Fang and his men.
NOTE: Story called "Captain America Meets the Fang," on Contents page. The Fang appears as an hallucination in ToS #82, '66 revealing his death in the 1945 Hiroshima bombing. By being on the scene there, he is therefore bts in fbs in WoF #10, '58, ST #93, '62, TTA #33, '62, Logan #2, '08 & others and is presumably a component of the Everwraith, an astral embodiment of the victims of the Hiroshima and Nagasaki bombings as seen in Sun #1-3, '98. As in CapC#5/2, '41 the selection of Steve and Bucky for so important an assignment implies that someone involved with the selection process knows they are Cap and Bucky. The Fang's underling erroneously identifies Betty Ross as a Secret Service agent here. Judging by body type, there appear to be two underlings named Wong.

3RD STORY: "The Grim Reaper Deals with Crime" (6 pages)
CREDITS: Stan Lee (writer), Al Avison (pencils), Al Gabriele (inks)

only, man John Scott is accused of killing)
LOCATIONS/ITEMS: Courtroom, Chips Brant's apartment, prison inc John Scott's cell, warden's office, & gallows, Larry's apartment; Father Time's scythe (1st, see NOTE), 2nd scythe (see NOTE), Spike's blackjack, Brant's pistol, Larry's evidence papers, clock with skull motif

SYNOPSIS: When his father John is found guilty of murder, wealthy Larry Scott finds evidence to clear him but foolishly confronts the true murderer, Chips Brant, seeking a confession on the night of his father's execution. Brant's associate Spike blackjacks Larry, who is held for hours before escaping. He arrives at the prison with his evidence as his father is being hung. Obsessing over how time worked against him, Larry takes the costumed identity of Father Time to confront Brant and Spike whom he beats up and pins to the wall for the police, leaving a symbolic clock behind.

NOTE: Story called "Father Time" on Contents page. Splash page notes, "From the famous character created by Joe Simon and Jack Kirby as narrated to Stan Lee." Father Time's scythe appears in all subsequent stories. Father Time uses his scythe to pin Chips and Spike to the wall and yet leaves carrying a scythe, perhaps implying a 2nd collapsible scythe that he keeps somewhere on his person.

4TH STORY: "The Strange Case of Captain America and the Hangman: Who Killed Doctor Vardoff?" (16 pages)
CREDITS: Jack Kirby (co-writer, co-pencils), Joe Simon (co-writer, co-pencils, co-inks), Al Avison (co-inks)
FEATURE CHARACTER: Captain America
SUPPORTING CAST: Bucky
VILLAINS: The Hangman (Dr. Nicolai Vardoff, dies) & his 4 underlings, the "Gun Moll" (dies), gangsters (Butch named), Dino Cardi ("Man with the Monocle," criminal businessman, dies)
OTHER CHARACTERS: Major Crane (Camp Lehigh officer), Ludwig (Vardoff's assistant, dies), townspeople inc firefighters & lynch mob, several corpses (in morgue), Vardoff's investors (bts, on phone), Ka-Zar the Great (mentioned only, Bucky's reference to Cap when they swing from a tree)
LOCATIONS/ITEMS: Camp Lehigh inc Major Crane's office, town within driving distance of Camp Lehigh inc Vardoff's lab (destroyed), oak tree, city morgue, & Hangman's hideout at edge of town; Hangman's car, super silk, acid spray gun & acid beaker, Vardoff's safe & laboratory chemicals, super-silk formula documents, gangsters' firearms, underlings' guns & blackjack, Hangman & lynch mob's nooses
SYNOPSIS: Having perfected his super-silk formula, Vardoff is plagued by monocled businessman Dino Cardi, a "Gun Moll" offering mob protection, and others. That night, in Vardoff's lab, the masked Hangman and his gang kill a lab-coated figure, whom they hang with super-silk, leaving the lab to burn. Cap and Bucky arrive but Hangman uses a super-silk lasso to ensnare them. Soon after, Cap and Bucky enter the burning lab, finding the corpse. A mob, believing them arsonists, tries to hang them but they escape. Next day, the heroes sift through the lab, as does Vardoff's assistant Ludwig, who is strangled. In the next room, Cap and Bucky find the Moll and fight her gangster associates until they find Ludwig and the Moll hung. At the morgue, Cap examines the lab corpse; it has a glass eye, which Vardoff does not. Hangman lassos Cap and Bucky, planning to kill them with an acid spray gun, but they break free and defeat his underlings. Cap unmasks Hangman as Vardoff who admits he killed Cardi, the first victim, for rifling through his safe. Now repentant, Vardoff gives Cap his formula, then commits suicide by turning his acid gun on himself.
NOTE: Story called, "Captain America and the Hangman" on Contents page.

5TH STORY: "Headline Hunter, Foreign Correspondent, Battles the Engine of Destruction…" (5 pages)
CREDITS: Stan Lee (writer), Harry Fisk (art)
FEATURE CHARACTER: Headline Hunter
SUPPORTING CAST: Ed the editor (bts, on phone)
VILLAINS: Lord Wotonby (dies) & his factory employees (bts), two Nazis (both die)
OTHER CHARACTERS: Factory guard, pub bartender & waitress, five customers, British soldiers
LOCATIONS/ITEMS: London inc Headline's apartment & outskirts inc Lord Wotonby's factory & pub; the Engine of Destruction (unusually fortified and equipped tank), airplane (both destroyed), soldiers' weapons
SYNOPSIS: Headline investigates Lord Wotonby's factory. Suspicious of Wotonby, who was thrown out of Parliament for fascist organization membership, Headline makes inquiries and learns loud noises and rumbling sounds are frequently heard. After climbing over the factory's fence and entering through a window, he discovers a secret Nazi stronghold from which the "Engine of Destruction, " manned by Wotonby and two Nazis, speeds toward London, wreaking havoc. Headline steals a plane loaded with explosives and crashes it into the Engine, diving into a river to escape the explosion which destroys the Engine and its crew.
NOTE: Story called "Headline Hunter" on Contents page. Story followed by "Sentinels of Liberty Secret Club News" (1 page) w/ "A Message from Captain America," "Bucky's Column," & 2 puzzles featuring Captain America, Bucky, hidden spies, & Red Skull (prev 2 in puzzles only).

6TH STORY: "Hurricane, Master of Speed" (7 pages)
CREDITS: Stan Lee (writer), Charles Nicholas (art)
FEATURE CHARACTER: Hurricane (also as Harry Kane)
VILLAIN: The Menace (Mrs. Hagor's brother, as "Mr. Sander, the mining engineer")
OTHER CHARACTERS: Mrs. Hagor, Mr. Crowley (millionaire, dies), Mr. Valez (gambler), Miss Sleed (actress), young girl, young boy, police, mad dog, bats (in symbolic splash panel only)
LOCATIONS/ITEMS: Mrs. Hagor's rooming house; Menace's knife, police gun, advertisement sign reading "Eat at Rne's Best Food"
SYNOPSIS: While seeking lodgings, Harry Kane rescues a girl from a mad dog; the girl mentions Mrs. Hagor's rooming house where two murders have occurred. Intrigued, Kane rents a room from Mrs. Hagor and meets her tenants: Crowley, Valez, Sleed, and Sander. Soon afterward, Crowley is murdered and a note, signed "the Menace," warns Kane to leave. The police investigate, but Hurricane, wanting to solve the mystery alone, vibrates himself into invisibility until they exit. When Menace emerges from a hidden passage to attack Hurricane, the hero fights back, pursuing the murderer, who is revealed to be Sander, actually Mrs. Hagor's brother, trying to drive away tenants to seek $50,000 his father supposedly hid in the house. Hurricane throws the captive Menace to the police and departs.
NOTE: Story called "Hurricane" on Contents page.

TEXT STORY: "Trap for a Traitor" (2 pages)
CREDITS: Stan Lee (writer), Jack Kirby (pencils), Joe Simon (inks)
FEATURE CHARACTER: Captain America (next in AllWin #2/2 '41)
SUPPORTING CAST: Bucky (next in AllWin #2/2, '41)
VILLAIN: Bill Haynes (see NOTE)
OTHER CHARACTERS: Larry David (a Sentinel of Liberty), Gov. Herbert H. Lehman (bts, in newspaper article)
LOCATIONS/ITEMS: Larry David's house, Camp Lehigh, park; Bucky's Sentinels of Liberty badge, code, pad, & pen, Haynes' blackjack
SYNOPSIS: Shadowed by escaped criminal Bill Haynes, Bucky Barnes suspects he's been recognized as Cap's partner. Bucky leaves fellow Sentinel of Liberty Larry a message to forward to Steve. After following Bucky all day, Haines confronts and nearly strangles him when Cap arrives to save the day.
NOTE: Story called "Captain America and the Trap for a Traitor" on Contents page. Story appears between 4th and 5th stories. Bucky refers to Haynes as "the guy Cap and I caught a few months ago trying to murder Colonel Stevens." In CapC #3/Text, '41, Cap and Bucky save Colonel Stevens from Lou Haines; possibly "Bill Haynes" is actually Haines and Bucky has misremembered his name.

CAPTAIN AMERICA COMICS #7 (October 1941)

"Captain America and the Red Skull" (13 pages)

CREDITS: Jack Kirby (co-writer, co-pencils, c pencils), Joe Simon (co-writer, co-pencils, co-inks), Syd Shores (co-inks, c inks)
FEATURE CHARACTER: Captain America (also as "Harold" in play rehearsal)
SUPPORTING CAST: Bucky (also as "Slats" in play rehearsal), Sgt. Duffy, Betty Ross (also as "Clementine" in play rehearsal)
VILLAINS: Red Skull (Johann Shmidt, also as stagehand, last in CapC #1/4, '41, chr last in ToS #68/2, '65, chr next in Inv #5, '76, next in CapC #16/4, '42) & his mob, Hermann Kroft (dies), van Raat (both former Red Skull underlings)
OTHER CHARACTERS: Camp Lehigh soldiers inc Camp Lehigh Orchestra, play director, & lieutenant, Captain Craig (dies), General King, 4 former Skull henchmen, donkey (both on symbolic splash page only), John Barrymore (actor, mentioned only, Bucky sarcastically calls Steve "Barrymore")
LOCATIONS/ITEMS: Camp Lehigh inc theater & Gen. King's quarters, Brightone Arms Apartments inc Kroft's apartment, Red Skull's hideout, dock; theater costumes & props, Red Skull's pistol, whistle, stagehand disguise, poisoned baton, & red-painted skull, mob's guns, bicycle built for three
SYNOPSIS: The Red Skull kills ex-underling Kroft. Later, at Camp Lehigh, Duffy puts Steve and Bucky to work on a theater production set in the 1890s, with Betty Ross as leading lady. Soon after, orchestra conductor Captain Craig is killed with a poisoned baton. Cap and Bucky pursue a stagehand through the theater's catwalks, but release him when he appears innocent. Alone, the stagehand removes his disguise revealing himself as the Skull. Targeting America's best military experts, the Skull and his gang break into General King's quarters. Cap and Bucky defeat the underlings, but the Skull escapes with King, leaving a note implicating Cap in his crimes. Cap and Bucky escape and find the Skull departing with King by boat. Cap knocks the Skull overboard and he apparently drowns. King clears Cap's name, and the rehearsal continues.
NOTE: Contains Table of Contents (1 page) featuring Captain America, Bucky, and reproduced cover of YA #1, '41. Story called "Captain America in the Case of the Red Skull and the Whistling Death" on Contents page.

2ND STORY: "Death Loads the Bases" (15 pages)
CREDITS: Jack Kirby (co-writer, co-pencils), Joe Simon (co-writer, co-pencils, co-inks), Syd Shores (co-inks)
FEATURE CHARACTER: Captain America
SUPPORTING CAST: Bucky, Sgt. Duffy
VILLAINS: The Toad ("The Black Toad," Chuck McArthur, Badgers manager, 1st, apparently dies, see NOTE) & his gang (Charlie, Rocco named)
OTHER CHARACTERS: Bernard Riggley (Brooklyn Badgers owner, dies), Pops Grimes (Badgers trainer), the Brooklyn Badgers inc Adams (dies), Joey DiRaggio (dies), Myers (catcher) & Bill Rickey (pitcher), the Blue Sox (Mike named), 2 umpires, game attendees, game announcer (bts, voice only), "Death" (as umpire in symbolic splash panel only), baseball players (in newspaper photos only), Hank Weiss (mentioned only, in newspaper headline, "Hank Weiss Drafted")
LOCATIONS/ITEMS: Riggley's office, Brooklyn Badgers baseball stadium inc grandstand, Badgers' locker room & Toad's hidden room, Camp Lehigh inc KP tent; Steve's binoculars, Toad's blowgun, poison darts, & pistol, Charlie's bat, bomb disguised as baseball, gang's machine guns, Bucky's baseballs
SYNOPSIS: After Brooklyn Badgers' owner Riggley refuses manager McArthur's offer to buy a team interest, the Badgers play against the Blue Sox, with Steve and Bucky among the fans. When Badgers DiRaggio and Adams are killed during the game, Cap and Bucky search the stadium and find the Toad and associates. After a struggle, underling Charlie knocks the heroes out and the villains escape. The following night,

NOTE: Story called "Captain America in the Case of the Baseball Murders" on Contents page. The Toad next appears in an apparent dream sequence in CapC #18/2, '42.
3RD STORY: "Horror Plays the Scales" (13 pages)

CREDITS: Jack Kirby (co-writer, pencils), Joe Simon (co-writer, co-inks), Syd Shores (co-inks)
FEATURE CHARACTER: Captain America (next in AllWin #2/2, '41, MvPro #6-7, '10)
SUPPORTING CAST: Bucky, Sgt. Duffy
VILLAINS: The Fiddler ("The Mad Musician," Ulrich Kuster, Nazi operative using special-frequency musical notes as weapons, dies, see NOTE), 3 fake butlers (Harver & Hobbs named), Domestic Employment Agency employee
OTHER CHARACTERS: Senator Alvin Benson (dies), Inspector Grimes, police officer, radio announcer, radio booth worker, concert hall MC, Camp Lehigh soldiers, concert audiences, newsboy, Senator Lee (in newspaper photo only, dies), tailor, Senator Shores
LOCATIONS/ITEMS: Camp Lehigh inc Steve and Bucky's tent, Senator Benson's home, radio station booth, concert hall inc Fiddler's dressing room, Senator Lee's home, tailor shop, Domestic Employment Agency, Senator Shores' home at 135 Raven Street; Fiddler's violin, bow, sound-sensitive devices (at least 2 destroyed), & pistol, radio stations WLM and WOX
SYNOPSIS: While listening to a radio violin recital, Senator Benson dies in a mysterious explosion. Cap and Bucky investigate. Despite new butler Harver's interference, Cap uncovers a bomb fragment. Later, the Lehigh regiment attends the Fiddler's violin performance, where his "weird, unheard-of" notes, also broadcast over radio, leave the audience strained and confused. Just after, Senator Lee is reported dead in the same circumstances as Benson. Discovering both men had new butlers, Steve visits an employment agency for a butler job but is turned down, only for the next applicant, Hobbs, to receive a job with Senator Shores. That night, Shores turns on his radio and Hobbs attempts to withdraw, but Cap appears and delays him. The panicky butler admits the Fiddler is using his broadcast music to kill, via exploding sound-sensitive devices implanted in radios. Cap thwarts the plan. Meanwhile, the Fiddler captures Bucky and tries to drive him mad with his music. However, Bucky has cotton in his ears. The Fiddler plays more and more frantically, and dies, struck down by his own music.
NOTE: Story called "Captain America in Horror Plays the Scales" on Contents page. Fiddler's real name revealed in MAtlas #1, '07.

4TH STORY: "Hurricane, Master of Speed" (7 pages)
CREDITS: Stan Lee (writer), Ken Bald (pencils), Bill Ward (inks)
FEATURE CHARACTER: Hurricane
SUPPORTING CAST: Solidius X. "Speedy" Scriggles (cigar store owner who becomes Hurricane's crimefighting partner, 1st)
VILLAINS: Petro (racketeer, only app) & his two men (Mike named)
OTHER CHARACTER: Model (on Sat Eve Boast magazine cover only)
LOCATIONS/ITEMS: Scriggles Cigar Store, Petro's hideout; Speedy's car & Cigar Store merchandise inc Duke Pipes, Baldowski Cigars, Elwar Cigars, El Wardo Cigars, Chocopop Cigars, Sat Eve Boast magazines, & Tru Jacks Pipe Cleaners, Mike's car & blackjack, Petro's pistol
SYNOPSIS: When storekeeper Scriggles refuses to continue paying protection money to Petro, Petro's men beat him up and depart. Entering the store, Hurricane finds Scriggles, helps him to recover, waits until the gangsters return and gives them a super-fast beating. When the villains awaken and depart, Scriggles, nicknamed "Speedy" by Hurricane, follows them by car, with Hurricane behind him. At Petro's hideout, Hurricane again fights Petro's men. Petro draws a gun, but Scriggles knocks him down. After Hurricane knocks all three criminals out, Scriggles declares himself the hero's new right-hand man.
NOTE: Story called "Hurricane, Master of Speed, in Justice Laughs Last" on Contents page.

5TH STORY: "Headline Hunter, Foreign Correspondent" (5 pages)
CREDITS: Stan Lee (writer), Harry Fisk (art)
FEATURE CHARACTER: Headline Hunter
SUPPORTING CAST: Ed the editor (last in CapC #5/5, '41, last bts in CapC #6/5, '41)
VILLAINS: The Leader (Perry Reginald, masked Nazi, only app) & his Nazi operatives (Fritz named)
OTHER CHARACTERS: Mr. Reginald, London police officer, Central Criminal Court guard, American actor (dies)
LOCATIONS/ITEMS: London inc London Star office, Leader's hideout, Central Criminal Court ("Old Bailey") inc Reginald's cell, & River Thames; Nazis' pistol, blackjack, & brass knuckles
SYNOPSIS: In London, two Nazi operatives, intending to spoil UK/USA relations, kill a visiting American actor and thrust the murder weapon into bystander Reginald's hands. After Reginald's arrest, the killers report to their masked Leader. Headline, suspicious at Reginald's lack of motive, visits him in prison, as does the prisoner's cousin Perry. The two Nazis waylay Headline, dumping him in the river, but he quickly recovers and, clinging to their car's back, accompanies them to the Leader's hideout. After defeating the three, he unmasks the Leader as Perry.
NOTE: Story called "Headline Hunter, Foreign Correspondent, in Dust of Destruction" on Contents page. The Leader should not be confused with other wartime villains of that name seen in CapC #8-9, '41, USA #1, '41, MC #23, '41, and elsewhere.

6TH STORY: "Father Time in Race Against Doom" (7 pages)
CREDITS: Stan Lee (writer), Al Avison (pencils), Al Gabriele (inks)
FEATURE CHARACTER: Father Time
VILLAINS: Bank president, Joe & his associates (also in pfb, 1 in pfb only), Morristown District Attorney (also in pfb), criminal posing as detective (in pfb only)
OTHER CHARACTERS: Hal Saxson, defense attorney, judge, bailiff, jury, trial attendees, diners, DA's secretary, pharmacist, bank customer, bank teller (bts, helping customer), Gov. Herbert H. Lehman, state troopers, new District Attorney, bats, dragon (in symbolic splash panel only)
LOCATIONS/ITEMS: Larry's apartment, Morristown inc courthouse, prison w/Hal's cell, restaurant, DA's office, pharmacy, bank w/vault, hotel w/Larry's room, barn hideout on Morristown Road, clock tower, & Hal Saxson's shack (in pfb only), Governor's mansion; counterfeiting equipment, dictaphone, Father Time's phosphorous compound
FLASHBACK: Hal Saxson speaks to a supposed "detective" about a smear campaign against him on the ship, the Southern Princess, unaware a dictaphone is recording them. The recording ends up in the DA's hands (p).
SYNOPSIS: Larry Scott visits Morristown, where friend Hal Saxson is tried for murder. A Dictaphone seems to have recorded Hal's confession of murdering the Southern Princess' crew and stealing its gold cargo. Larry learns from Hal that the "confession" was part of a larger conversation

describing false allegations against him. After learning the local bank has counterfeit coins, Larry follows the bank president to a barn hideout where criminals are using the Southern Princess gold to forge coins. He photographs the criminals and takes the photo to the DA, whose disinterest convinces him he too is in on the scheme. Back at the barn, Father Time frightens the other criminals into confessing, recording it on the dictaphone. State troopers arrive to arrest all involved.

NOTE: Story called "Father Time in the Riddle of the Dictaphone Doom" on Contents page. Hal Saxson also called "Saxon" here. Story followed by "Sentinels of Liberty Secret Club News" (1 page) w/ "A Message from Captain America," "Bucky's Column," & 2 puzzles.

TEXT STORY: "A Message from Captain America" (2 pages)
CREDITS: Stan Lee (writer)
FEATURE CHARACTER: Captain America
SYNOPSIS: Addressing the reader, Captain America discusses Bucky, Betty Ross, Sgt. Duffy, Father Time, Headline Hunter, Hurricane, Speedy Scriggles, and the Sentinels of Liberty.
NOTE: Cap reveals here that Betty Ross was motivated to join the FBI after her father, a US army general, was murdered by a spy. While breaking the "fourth wall" to speak to the reader, Cap demonstrates knowledge of Father Time and Hurricane's origins that he would be unlikely to possess. Story appears between 2nd and 3rd stories.

CAPTAIN AMERICA COMICS #8 (November 1941)

"The Strange Mystery of the Ruby of the Nile and Its Heritage of Horror from the Personal Files of Captain America" (13 pages)

CREDITS: Jack Kirby (co-writer, pencils), Joe Simon (co-writer, co-inks), Al Gabriele (co-inks, c inks)
FEATURE CHARACTER: Captain America
SUPPORTING CAST: Bucky, Betty Ross, Sgt. Duffy
VILLAINS: Ra the Avenger ("The Pharaoh," Henry Sanders, only app, also in pfb)
OTHER CHARACTERS: Camp Lehigh soldiers (Jones named), Marina Bates, Mr. Bates (Marina's father, dies), Mr. Parker (Bates' partner, dies), Biggs (the Bates' butler), Operative Seven (FBI agent, bts on phone), Sanders' archeological assistants (in pfb only), Ra the Sun God & other Egyptian myth figures (as statues, in pfb only), King Tut (mentioned only, Cap refers to Ra this way), 2 Nazis (on cover only)
LOCATIONS/ITEMS: Camp Lehigh inc canteen, Bates Mansion & garden, Egyptian tomb at the mouth of the Nile (in pfb only); tomb's treasures (in pfb only), Ruby of the Nile (also in pfb), Ra's daggers & smoke-bombs, Betty's pistol, candlestick
FLASHBACK: In Egypt, Sanders explores an ancient tomb and discovers the Ruby of the Nile (p).
SYNOPSIS: Betty's friend Marina invites her to dinner, where her father and his partner Parker display a fabulous gem, the Ruby of the Nile. While Steve and Bucky keep watch outside, within, Sanders, from whom Bates and Parker bought the ruby, recounts that the gem is supposedly cursed. After Parker expresses his wish to keep the gem whole, Bates lingers, hoping to take it and have it cut into small stones without Parker's consent, and is strangled and stabbed by the costumed "Ra the Avenger." Hearing the action, Cap and Bucky burst in, but Ra escapes. Betty takes charge, but the lights briefly go out; when they are restored, the ruby is gone, taken by Cap for safekeeping. Presuming Parker has it, Ra stabs him but again flees from Cap and Bucky. Ra next attacks Betty, who contacts the FBI about her prime suspect, but Cap knocks him out after a brief fight and unmasks him as Sanders, as Betty suspected.
NOTE: Contains "Table of Contents" (1 page) featuring Captain America, Bucky, & reproduced cover of AllWin #2, '41. Story called "Captain America in the Strange Case of the Ruby of the Nile and its Heritage of Horror" on Contents page. The Egyptian tomb discovered by Sanders is described as "older than the Pyramids," the first of which was constructed circa 2630 BC; if true, this implies the pharaoh entombed within was Sekhemkhet (d. circa 2643 BC) or a preceding pharaoh.

2ND STORY: "From the Personal Files of Captain America: Murder Stalks the Maneuvers" (11 pages)
CREDITS: Jack Kirby (co-writer, pencils), Joe Simon (co-writer, co-inks), Al Gabriele (co-inks)
FEATURE CHARACTER: Captain America (next in CapC #9/2, '41)
SUPPORTING CAST: Bucky (next in CapC #9/2, '41), Sgt. Duffy
VILLAINS: Major Pierre Dumort (Gestapo agent posing as Free French Forces agent, only app) & his men, Fenton (traitorous Lehigh soldier)
OTHER CHARACTERS: Camp Lehigh soldiers (Clodd named) inc Number 2 Company (Sweeney named), guardhouse guard, Colonel Carter (Lehigh officer; commands "Whites"), Colonel Williams (commands "Blues"), US Army regiments divided into "Whites" and "Blues" (some die), Henri (Dumort's chauffeur)
LOCATIONS/ITEMS: Camp Lehigh inc 2 company barracks, Steve and Bucky's tent & guardhouse, maneuvers battlefield inc Col. Williams' tent, Whites' headquarters & communications tent, nearby forest, "distant hilltop" overlooking battlefield, Carter's home, Dumort's hideout; tanks, firearms, & other military equipment, Dumort's car, gas masks, Bucky's itching powder
SYNOPSIS: A bored Bucky uses itching powder to cause chaos, but Steve is blamed and sent to the guardhouse. When "Free French" Major

in the supposedly simulated battle and realizes real ammunition is being used. To try to stop the battle, Cap and Bucky capture Colonel Williams, "leaving him" to Steve and Bucky who bring him to Carter, whom Steve informs of the ammunition switch. Carter calls off the battle, and Steve discovers Dumort is behind the switch. Cap and Bucky defeat Dumort and his men, learning Dumort is actually a Gestapo agent.
NOTE: Story called "Captain America in Murder Stalks the Maneuvers" on Contents page.

3RD STORY: "Headline Hunter, Foreign Correspondent, in the Strange Riddle of the Plague of Death" (5 pages)

CREDITS: Stan Lee (writer), Harry Fisk (art)

FEATURE CHARACTER: Headline Hunter

SUPPORTING CAST: Ed the editor (next in CapC #10/3, '42)

VILLAINS: Herr Leader & his fifth column underlings (Frederich named, at least two die)

OTHER CHARACTERS: London police officer, plague victim (dies), London bystanders, Adolf Hitler (in painting over fireplace only), Death, farmers (both in symbolic splash panel only)

LOCATIONS/ITEMS: London inc Affiliated Press branch office editorial room, Herr Leader's farm house; Frederich's car, tractor with machine guns, plane with poison, rake, thug's blackjack, poisoned piece of bread

SYNOPSIS: Headline investigates a plague killing people throughout London. Overhearing two men speaking German, he hops a ride to their farmhouse hideout, but is caught eavesdropping. The boss, Herr Leader, boasts of poisoning food, causing the plague. Taking Herr Leader by surprise, Headline escapes to seize a machine gun-equipped tractor, with which he attacks. When Herr Leader dives at him in a poison-carrying plane, Headline uses a rake to vault onto it, releasing poison onto the Nazi agents before flying Herr Leader to Scotland Yard.

NOTE: Story erroneously called "Headline Hunter in Death in the Alps" on Contents page, which is the title of next issue's story. Story followed by Sentinels of Liberty Secret Club News (2 pages) w/"A Message from Captain America," "Bucky's Column," & 2 puzzles, featuring Captain America, Bucky, Mr. Bull the Dog Detective, Mr. Donkey, Mr. Squirrel, dog, white rabbit, 4 birds, boy (prev 7 in puzzles only).

4TH STORY: "Case of the Black Witch" (17 pages)

CREDITS: Otto Binder (writer), Jack Kirby (pencils), Joe Simon (co-inks), Al Gabriele (co-inks)

FEATURE CHARACTER: Captain America (next in CapTW:AB #1, '09 fb)

SUPPORTING CAST: Bucky (last in CapC #9/2, '41), Sgt. Duffy (chr next in CapTW:AB #1, '09 fb)

VILLAINS: The Black Witch (Mr. Feritt, attorney costumed as witch, dies) & his men (one dressed as a devil, 2 as ghosts, 5 as demons)

OTHER CHARACTERS: Karin Lee (only app), Camp Lehigh soldiers inc bugler, Jonathan Lee (Karin's uncle, mentioned only, died prior to story & left will), bats, serpents (in symbolic splash panel only), bird, demons (both as Hagmoor Castle carvings only), gargoyles, hobgoblins & other creatures (as monster images only)

LOCATIONS/ITEMS: Camp Lehigh inc Steve and Bucky's tent, Hagmoor Castle inc dungeon, control room & torture room, moat feeding into stream, adjoining moor; Black Witch's control console w/dials labeled "dummy monster dial" and "moving armor dial," movie projector labeled "movie ghost images," remote-controlled monster dummies and suits of armor, torture device, dagger, crossbow, mask & broom, his men's costumes, guns & other weapons, Jonathan Lee's will

SYNOPSIS: Hearing a scream from Hagmoor Castle, Cap and Bucky rescue Karin Lee from attackers. After Attorney Ferrit arrives, Karin explains that her uncle's will requires her to stay three nights in the castle, supposedly haunted by the Black Witch, to inherit it. Cap and Bucky return next evening, finding "nightmarish creatures" and animated suits of armor menacing Karin. While Cap and Bucky discover the armor to be empty, the "creatures" vanish. Next evening, Bucky heads for the castle and encounters Black Witch who throws him into a stream leading to a waterfall. Cap rescues him, noticing the river's oily residue. They hurry to Hagmoor Castle but are captured there. In a dungeon, Bucky breaks the aging chains and finds Black Witch's control room with remote-control dials and movie-projected creatures. Bucky uses the projections to scare the hoods torturing Cap and frees his partner. They interrupt Black Witch's attempt to murder Karin and drive the underlings into the castle's moat. Black Witch shoots a crossbow from the castle ramparts but the recoil throws him off balance for a fatal fall. Cap unmasks him as Ferrit, who wanted the property cheap because of the land's oil content.

NOTE: Story called "Captain America and the Mystery of the Black Witch" on Contents page. Black Witch's ability to fly while riding a broom is never explained, but presumably it too was trickery. Black Witch's attack of Bucky Barnes implies a realization that he is Cap's costumed partner Bucky. The 3 criminals at the story's start, who escape, are presumably members of Black Witch's gang seen at the story's end. When one thug proclaims, "Holy cats! It's Captain America," Cap replies, "It's not my Aunt Prissy, dimwit!" Presumably this is only an expression and Cap does not have an Aunt Prissy.

5TH STORY: "Hurricane, Master of Speed in Carnival of Crime" (7 pages)

CREDITS: Stan Lee (writer), Charles Nicholas (art)

FEATURE CHARACTER: Hurricane

SUPPORTING CAST: Speedy Scriggles (next in CapC #10/5, '42)

VILLAINS: Silky Saunders (crooked state fair manager, only app) & other state fair employees

OTHER CHARACTERS: Additional non-criminal state fair employees, state fair attendees, Prince the lion, two policemen, bus passengers, strong man, snake (both on fair posters only)

LOCATIONS/ITEMS: Hurricane and Speedy's apartment, State Fair inc rigged bottle game booth w/lead-weighted bottles, roller coaster, Prince's cage, trailers & tents, police station

SYNOPSIS: Hurricane and Speedy visit a state fair, where Speedy is cheated at a bottle game. The pair discover a roller coaster beam is rotting, but manager Silky Saunders tries to bribe them into silence. When this fails, Silky strikes Hurricane from behind, then cages him and Speedy with a lion. Hurricane outfights the lion and punches through the cage's lock, then runs up the roller coaster, saving a car from falling when the beam collapses. Hurricane puts Silky and company in a cage, taking them to the police.

NOTE: Story called "Hurricane: Carnival of Crime" on Contents page.

6TH STORY: "Father Time" (7 pages)

CREDITS: Stan Lee (writer), Al Avison (art)

FEATURE CHARACTER: Father Time

VILLAINS: 4 bank robbers, (only app, Mike & Mugsy named, see NOTE)

OTHER CHARACTERS: Two 6th National Bank employees & others (bts) (all die), police, emergency responder, 2 armed car guards (Joe named, both die), bystanders

LOCATIONS/ITEMS: 6th National Bank of New York inc vault, Larry Scott's apartment, Nickle Bank, robbers' hideout w/vault; armed car, robbers' machine guns & gas bombs, acetelene torch, bags of gold, clock stamp on wall

SYNOPSIS: Three men rob Larry Scott's bank, shoot one employee, knock Larry unconscious, and lock the other employees in the bank's vault. The police arrive but the captives suffocate before the vault can be opened. Later, Father Time stakes out the Nickle Bank and its arriving gold shipment. As expected, the trio show but overwhelm Father Time, take him to their hideout, and lock him in their own vault to suffocate. Having jammed the vault door with his scythe, however, Father Time escapes and captures the crooks.

NOTE: Story called "Father Time: Vault of Doom" on Contents page. Although there only appear to be 3 men commiting these crimes and Father Time catches 3 criminals at the end, page 6 panel 5 shows 4 criminals.

TEXT STORY: "The Young Allies Deal a Blow for Justice" (2 pages)

CREDITS: Stan Lee (writer)

FEATURE CHARACTERS: The Young Allies: Bucky, Jeff, Knuckles, Tubby, Whitewash (prev 4 next in YA #2, '42, see NOTE)

GUEST STAR: Captain America (chr next in UXM #268, '90 fb)

SUPPORTING CAST: Betty Ross

VILLAINS: "The Chief" & 3 criminals

LOCATIONS/ITEMS: Vacant house, Jeff's house, Camp Lehigh; chair, ropes & gag, criminals' guns, "Chief"'s white-hot poker

SYNOPSIS: Investigating a cry for help, Knuckles finds criminals holding Betty Ross prisoner and gathers the other Young Allies. After Bucky informs Steve of the situation, the five youths hurry to the house, where the trio's "chief" prepares to torture Betty to learn about the government's new super-torpedo. The five tussle with the criminals until Captain America arrives to quickly end the crisis.

NOTE: Story called "Young Allies Deal a Blow for Justice" on Contents page. The Young Allies are referred to only as "Sentinels of Liberty" in the story's body. Jeff's and Knuckles' real names are erroneously given as "Jefferson Van Smythe" and "Percy Bartwell" here.

CAPTAIN AMERICA COMICS #9 (December 1941)

"Captain America and the White Death" (11 pages)

CREDITS: Joe Simon (co-writer, co-pencils, co-title page art), Jack Kirby (co-writer, co-pencils, co-title page art, c pencils), Al Avison (co-pencils), George Klein (co-inks), Reed Crandall (co-inks, c inks)

FEATURE CHARACTER: Captain America

SUPPORTING CAST: Bucky

VILLAINS: The White Death (Manuel Perez, only app), Matthew Clinton (attorney)

OTHER CHARACTERS: Lucy Harrow, Jim Slade (dies), Mr. Harrow (Josiah's brother), Harrow's housekeeper, Harrow's butler (dies), Camp Lehigh sentry, Phillip Avery (dies), demon (as Harrow Mansion statue only), Josiah Harrow (mentioned only, eccentric millionaire recently deceased), loincloth and shroud-wearing villains (on cover only)

LOCATIONS/ITEMS: Camp Lehigh inc Steve and Bucky's tent, Lehigh City suburbs (see NOTE), inc Harrow Mansion & garden w/multiple hidden tunnels; White Death's daggers, Clinton's pistol, Bucky's "copy of Marvel Comics"

SYNOPSIS: Steve and Bucky discover a dead butler at Harrow Mansion and a note from the White Death claiming responsibility. Later, they return as Cap and Bucky to find Josiah Harrow's heirs -- granddaughter Lucy, son-in-law Manuel, and nephew Jim -- gathered for Attorney Clinton to read Harrow's will. The heroes find hidden tunnels in the mansion, as well as another relative, Phillip Avery, dead. Emerging into the mansion proper, they save Lucy from the costumed White Death, who escapes to kill Jim. Clinton and Manuel capture a latecomer, Josiah's brother, whom they accuse of being the White Death. Later, Cap and Bucky defeat the White Death but Clinton shoots at them, claiming he was targeting the White Death. Josiah's brother accuses Clinton, and Bucky unmasks the White Death as Manuel, whom Cap realizes worked with Clinton to kill fellow heirs and split the estate.

NOTE: Contains "Table of Contents" (1 page) featuring Captain America, Bucky & Black Talon. Story identified as "Case 1987-D" from Captain America's files. Title has exclamation point on Contents page. Lehigh City mentioned for the first time here.

2ND STORY: "Captain America and the Man Who Could Not Die" (13 pages)

CREDITS: Joe Simon (co-writer, co-title page art), Jack Kirby (co-writer, co-title page art, co-pencils), Al Avison (co-pencils), George Klein, Reed Crandall (inks)

FEATURE CHARACTER: Captain America (also in CapC #8/4, '41, CapC #9/1, '41, see NOTE)

SUPPORTING CAST: Bucky (also in CapC #8/4, '41, CapC #9/1, '41, see NOTE), Sgt. Duffy (chr last in CapTW:AB #1, '09 fb), Betty Ross

VILLAINS: Nick Pinto (gangster who survives two executions, dies) & his underlings (Muggsy, Red, Spike named), prison coroner (dies), trustee, Tony Scarlatti (dies), other criminals

hearse, special voltage reducer, coffin, prison guards' rifles, criminals' weapons, Pinto & Betty's guns, electrified fence

SYNOPSIS: Nick Pinto, supposedly executed, kills rival Tony Scarlatti. Pinto's secret return to the underworld sparks a crime wave. Cap and Bucky locate Pinto's hideout, as does Betty Ross, who is captured by Pinto's thugs. Cap rescues Betty and defeats Pinto. A month later, Pinto is again sent to the electric chair and executed. However, the on-the-take coroner, who previously tampered with the death switch during Pinto's earlier "execution, " again revives Pinto, this time using a special voltage reducer to simulate electrocution. The coroner escorts Pinto's "corpse" to his underlings, disguised as undertakers, but Cap and Bucky catch on. Betty, present for the execution, prevents Pinto's underlings from opening fire, while the coroner is shot down trying to escape. Pinto takes Betty hostage long enough to reach the prison fence, but a guard electrifies it, and Pinto is finally electrocuted.

NOTE: Story called "Captain America and the Man Who Would not Die!" on Contents page. The first half of this story occurs in the preceding month, contemporaneous with the events of #8. Steve and Bucky sing, "The Prisoner's Song (1924)" from the guardhouse.

3RD STORY: "Death in the Alps" (5 pages)
CREDITS: Stan Lee (writer), Warren Kremer (art)
FEATURE CHARACTER: Headline Hunter
VILLAINS: Herr Leader (hotel manager, dies), Hans and Fritz (Herr Leader's men, both die)
OTHER CHARACTERS: Henri (hotel clerk), von Groser (German refugee scientist), Schultz (refugee, dies), Death (in symbolic splash panel only)
LOCATIONS/ITEMS: Switzerland inc mountain, hotel & bobsled track; von Groser's skiing equipment (used by Headline), Hans' bobsled, Fritz's knife, Herr Leader's pistol
SYNOPSIS: In Switzerland, Nazi operatives kill a German refugee, then target anti-Nazi writer von Groser. Headline, looking for a story, meets von Groser whom the Nazis invite to go bobsledding. When Headline sees one has a knife, he pursues on skis, rescuing von Groser and knocking the bobsled off a ledge, killing the Nazis. The killers' boss, Herr Leader, holds Headline at gunpoint, but he strikes the Nazi with a ski and unmasks him as the hotel manager. The two struggle, and Headline flips Herr Leader over a ledge to his death.
NOTE: Story called "Headline Hunter and the Snowslide of Peril" on Contents page.

4TH STORY: "Captain America in the Case of the Black Talon" (18 pages)
CREDITS: Otto Binder (writer), Jack Kirby (co-pencils, co-title page art), Al Avison (co-pencils), Joe Simon (co-title page art), George Klein, Reed Crandall (inks)
FEATURE CHARACTER: Captain America (also in painting, next in AllWin #3/2, '41, YA #2, '41)
SUPPORTING CAST: Bucky (also in painting, next in AllWin #3/2, '41), Sgt. Duffy
VILLAINS: The Black Talon (Pascal Horta, artist, also in pfb, next in YA #2, '41) & his underlings (Red, Slugger named, some possibly next in YA #2, '41), Strangler Burns (pfb only, dies bts)
OTHER CHARACTERS: Rafael Miller (artist, also in painting, dies), Oliver Simms (artist, also in painting, dies), 2 policemen (Joe named), art gallery visitor, newsboy, newsstand vendor, Mr. Smith (newsstand patron), Dr. Steiner & 3 surgeons (both pfb only), Abraham Lincoln (in portrait only), Human Torch, Toro, crooks in flameproof suits (prev 3 on Human Torch comic cover only), 2 men, woman, demon (prev 3 in paintings only), man (in newspaper photo only), Michaelangelo & Leonardo da Vinci (both mentioned only by Sgt. Duffy as he hands Steve and Bucky paint brushes), lion (as statue only)
LOCATIONS/ITEMS: Lehigh art gallery, Camp Lehigh inc unpainted barracks, Miller's studio, Simms' studio, newsstand w/copies of Marvel Mystery Comics, Mystic Comics & Human Torch #3, Lehigh Public Library, Black Talon's home (also in pfb), hospital (pfb only); Black Talon's daggers, spiked flail & other weapons, underlings' firearms, paintings at Miller's studio, Simms' studio, art gallery & Black Talon's home
FLASHBACK: After artist Pascal Horta's right hand is crushed in a car accident, Dr. Steiner surgically attaches a new one, donated by condemned murderer Strangler Burns. Eventually driven mad by the transplant, Horta, as the Black Talon, vows to kill rival artists and paint their death scenes (p).
SYNOPSIS: After viewing the disturbing Black Talon painting in an art gallery, Steve and Bucky witness a strangulation in the window of an artist's studio. Investigating, they find Rafael Miller dead and his paintings slashed. The killer, Black Talon, almost strangles Bucky one-handed, then escapes. The next day, Talon and his underlings kill artist Oliver Simms, but Cap and Bucky intervene. They quickly outfight Talon's men, but Talon almost kills them before police arrive. At the library, Steve reads up on Pascal Horta's accident and suspects him of being the Talon. At Horta's house, however, Cap and Bucky find Horta hung, apparently dead. Encountering Talon's underlings, they defeat them. However, Horta is the Talon and has faked his death. He knocks them unconscious with a flail. Cap and Bucky awake as captives. As Talon paints them, Cap breaks his bonds. He and Talon prove almost evenly matched until Talon escapes, swearing vengeance.
NOTE: Story identified as "Case 241-B" from Captain America's files. Story called "Captain America and the Black Talon!" on Contents page.

5TH STORY: "Hurricane, Master of Speed" (7 pages)
CREDITS: Stan Lee (writer), Charles Nicholas (art)
FEATURE CHARACTER: Hurricane (also as "Harry Kane")
VILLAINS: X (John Smithers, owner & managing editor of Daily Star, dies) & his underlings (Spike named)
OTHER CHARACTERS: Brown (Daily Star city editor), policeman, bystanders
LOCATIONS/ITEMS: Midvale inc Daily Star building w/press room & Smithers' office; criminals' car & pistols
SYNOPSIS: Visiting Midvale, "Kane" rescues Daily Star editor Brown from four criminals who targeted him for anti-crime editorials. Given a reporter's job by Brown, Kane soon becomes Hurricane when attacked. He rousts a carful of criminals, and one confesses the crime wave is organized by "X," someone connected to the Star. Back at the office, X, in reality Star owner John Smithers, has his underlings capture Brown and Kane who becomes Hurricane and quickly outfights them. Hurricane confronts X in the press room, where the criminal falls into the printing rollers and dies.
NOTE: Story called "Hurricane, Master of Speed, in Crime Goes to Press!" on Contents page. Midvale's Daily Star, owned by Smithers, should not be confused with Manhattan's Daily Star, seen in multiple Captain America stories and elsewhere. Story followed by Sentinels of Liberty Secret Club News (1 page) w/"A Message from Captain America," "Bucky's Column" & "Sentinel of Liberty Secret Code" featuring Captain America & Bucky.

6TH STORY: "Father Time" (7 pages)

CREDITS: Stan Lee (writer), Al Avison (pencils), George Klein (inks)

FEATURE CHARACTER: Father Time

VILLAINS: Zarpo (insane inventor, dies) & 3 hired thugs

OTHER CHARACTERS: John Peters (government employee, dies), Senator Rogers (dies), 6 victims (in symbolic splash panel only)

LOCATIONS/ITEMS: John Peters' office & home, Zarpo's hideout, Senator Rogers' home; Zarpo's "bombs of doom" set to automatically detonate after 5 minutes in a person's presence

SYNOPSIS: When his "bombs of doom" are dismissed by government employee John Peters, Zarpo, with three hired thugs, blows up Peters' home shortly after Larry Scott departs. Larry, as Father Time, passes Senator Rogers' home, where one of Zarpo's underlings leaves another bomb. Father Time, unable to save Rogers, catches the hood, who reveals Zarpo's location. Hurrying there, Father Time is captured and left with another bomb, but he escapes. Fleeing, Zarpo throws a bomb that Father Time bats back with his scythe. It explodes, killing Zarpo.

NOTE: Story called "Father Time and the Bombs of Doom!" on Contents page.

TEXT STORY: "Dead Man's Ring" (2 pages)

CREDITS: Stan Lee (writer)

FEATURE CHARACTER: Paul Martin (dies)

OTHER CHARACTERS: Native American chief & tribe, Chief Little Eagle (mentioned only, died several years earlier), Will Smithers (mentioned only, trapper, killed by Martin)

LOCATIONS/ITEMS: The North Woods, hill; Martin's compass, gun, hunting knife, stolen map & stolen ring, tribe's spears, bows, arrows & sacrificial knife

SYNOPSIS: After killing Will Smithers for his map to Chief Little Eagle's buried gold, Paul Martin also absconds with Smithers' ring, to prevent his body from being identified. He travels through the woods for days before reaching the site where Little Eagle's tribe captures him. Doomed to be killed at midnight for his trespass, Martin cuts through his bonds while his captors sleep, but Smithers' ring falls from his pocket and clangs against a stone, awakening the tribe, who quickly kill him.

NOTE: Story appears between 3rd and 4th stories. Title has exclamation point on Contents page.

CAPTAIN AMERICA COMICS #10 (January 1942)

"Captain America, A Personal Account of His Smashing a Spy Ambush" (11 pages)

CREDITS: Jack Kirby (co-writer, co-pencils, co-title page art, c pencils), Joe Simon (co-writer, co-title page art), Al Avison (co-pencils), George Klein (co-inks), Reed Crandall (co-inks, c inks)
FEATURE CHARACTER: Captain America
SUPPORTING CAST: Bucky (last in AllWin #3/2, '41)
VILLAINS: Countess Mara (only app) & her Nazi assistants (Franz named), Nazi soldiers (Shultz named, most die) inc Klaus (7-foot hulking fighter)
OTHER CHARACTER: Adolf Hitler (in portrait only)
LOCATIONS/ITEMS: Mountain highway en route from Washington DC to Camp Lehigh, Countess Mara's castle-like base (partially destroyed) inc "Dungeon of Fire" & arsenal; army truck, Franz's motorcycle, Mara's hand grenade & gas gun, rapid-fire grenade gun
SYNOPSIS: Driving a truck to Camp Lehigh, Steve and Bucky halt when a woman collapses on the road. Steve sends Bucky for help, but the woman, Countess Mara, has faked the incident to hijack the truck. Steve defeats her men but Mara fells him with a grenade. The Nazis take the truck but Steve, as Captain America, seizes a motorcycle and he and Bucky follow to Mara's base. There, they fight through a small army to reach the truck, but Mara knocks them out with a gas-gun. When they recover, Mara reveals the truck's cargo, a rapid-fire grenade gun, then imprisons the pair in a dungeon whose walls spout flames. They escape through a ceiling panel and again fight the Nazis who flee to the base's arsenal. Mara fires the grenade-gun at Cap, but it rebounds from Cap's shield to the arsenal, destroying half the base and killing most of Mara's followers. She surrenders to Cap.
NOTE: Contains "Table of Contents" (1 page) featuring Captain America, Bucky, & reproduced cover of AllWin #3, '41. Story called "Captain America and the Spy Ambush" on Contents page.

2ND STORY: "Hotel of Horror" (13 pages)
CREDITS: Joe Simon (co-writer), Jack Kirby (co-writer, co-pencils), Syd Shores, Al Avison (co-pencils), George Klein, Reed Crandall (inks)
FEATURE CHARACTER: Captain America (also in newspaper photo)
SUPPORTING CAST: Bucky
VILLAINS: Netman ("Charley Boswell," only app, Nazi operative posing as Mayor's secretary, see NOTE) & his underlings inc robed fifth columnists (some die), 2 hotel desk clerks & bellhops
OTHER CHARACTERS: Gotham City's mayor, two mayoral aides, Miss Wallace (mayor's secretary), Gotham City police, Gotham City denizens inc local Sentinels of Liberty chapter, railroad porter, Rastus (train waiter), train passenger, hotel guest, firemen, military officer, Eddie "Rochester" Anderson (actor, mentioned only by Rastus), Seabiscuit (race horse, mentioned only by Bucky to horse)
LOCATIONS/ITEMS: Gotham City inc train station, mayor's office, 17th Precinct w/jail & Zaragon Hotel w/front desk, 13th floor Presidential suite, laundry chute, and Netman's underground base, Camp Lehigh inc Steve and Bucky's tent; train, WOZ Radio microphone, Netman's net, flaming brazier & daggers
SYNOPSIS: Invited to Gotham City's defense drive celebration, Cap and Bucky arrive by train. There, they meet supposed mayoral secretary Boswell, who escorts them out the back to the Zaragon Hotel's 13th floor Presidential suite. When Bucky goes downstairs, the desk clerk has the bellboys throw him out. Returning with a police officer, Bucky finds a different desk clerk, who claims there is no 13th floor. Later, Bucky learns that the mayor's real secretary is a woman. Meanwhile, Boswell, calling himself Netman, captures Cap and takes him to an underground hideout. Bucky, jailed as a nuisance, attaches a nearby wagon's chain to his cell's bars, then persuades the horse to pull them down. He returns to the hotel, where he takes a bellboy's place and confronts the desk clerk, who drops him through a trap door to Netman's lair. There, he watches as Netman's men kill a captive man, thinking him Cap, but one of the robed men reveals himself as Cap, having traded places with an underling. While Cap and Bucky outfight his men, Netman overturns a burning brazier to set the hotel aflame but Cap and Bucky emerge with Netman and attend the celebration as planned.
NOTE: Story called "Captain America and the Hotel of Horror" on Contents page. Netman also called "Net-Man" here. The name "Charley Boswell" is probably an alias. Gotham City is not to be confused with the home of the Caped Crusader. The "Register of Death" on the symbolic splash page contains, among others, the names "Stan Leeman" & "S. Shires," references to Stan Lee & Syd Shores.

3RD STORY: "Headline Hunter" (5 pages)
CREDITS: Stan Lee (writer), Warren Kremer (art)
FEATURE CHARACTER: Headline Hunter (next in CapC #12/5, '42)
SUPPORTING CAST: Ed the editor (next in CapC #12/5, '42)
VILLAIN: Will Jenks (Wilhelm von Logor, Gestapo agent undercover as reporter, only app)
OTHER CHARACTERS: Reginald Whitney (diplomat, only app), Barkley Hotel desk manager & bellboy, 2 taxi drivers (1 bts, spoken to by Headline), Affiliated Press employees (in symbolic splash panel only)
LOCATIONS/ITEMS: London inc Affiliated Press office & Barkley Hotel; press pass, bellboy uniform, Jenks' pistol
SYNOPSIS: Headline heads to the Barkley hotel for an exclusive interview with diplomat Reginald Whitney, carrying the necessary press pass. En route, rival reporter Jenks knocks Headline out and steals the press pass. Recovering, Headline dons a bellboy's uniform and enters the room while Jenks interviews Whitney, who reveals information that could damage Germany. Jenks, actually a Gestapo agent, prepares to kill Whitney, but Headline steps in and knocks Jenks unconscious.
NOTE: Story called "Headline Hunter Uncovers a Sinister Scoop!" on Contents page.

4TH STORY: "The Phantom Hound of Cardiff Moor" (16 pages)
CREDITS: Joe Simon (co-writer, co-title page art), Jack Kirby (co-writer, co-title page art, co-pencils), Al Avison (co-pencils), George Klein, Reed Crandall (inks)

FEATURE CHARACTER: Captain America (next in W:O #17-20, '07-08 fbs)
SUPPORTING CAST: Bucky (chr next in W:O #17, '07 fb), Betty Ross (next in CapC #13/3, '42), Sgt. Duffy
VILLAIN: The Hound (Mr. Murdock, also in fb as child)
OTHER CHARACTERS: Miss Primm (retired schoolteacher), Miguel Ramos (writer, dies), Mary Scott, Amos Willard (doctor) (only app for all, Murdock's neighbors), man who comes to Camp Lehigh for help, Camp Lehigh officer, guardhouse MP, army doctor, Murdock's parents & family dog (in fb only, years before), 2 eviction agents (fb only), 2 victims (1 in fb only), the Phantom Hound (Hound's trained dog, coated with luminescent paint, also in fb, dies)
LOCATIONS/ITEMS: Camp Lehigh inc Duffy's tulip garden, guardhouse & medical station, Cardiff Moor inc Cardiff Manor (also in fb), Mary Scott's home & hidden cave; Hound's blackjack, claws & pistol, threatening note
FLASHBACK: During Murdock's childhood, his family owns Cardiff Moor, its namesake manor, and a regal hound. When the Murdocks are evicted, Murdock's father swears his hound will destroy anyone who claims the land.
SYNOPSIS: When a man seeks the Army's help against the "phantom hound" of Cardiff Moor, Cap and Bucky investigate. After unsuccessfully pursuing the hound, they visit moor resident Murdock and neighbor Mary Scott. Outside, the hound chases Murdock's other neighbors – Ramos, Primm, and Willard but Cap hurls his shield to drive the beast away. After Murdock's house briefly goes dark, Cap finds a threatening note from "the Hound." Cap, Bucky and the others spread out to search the moor, but one person sneaks off to become the costumed Hound. Responding to the Phantom Hound's howl, Cap and Bucky meet the human Hound, who attacks them before fleeing. The two then find Ramos dead. When the Phantom Hound attacks Mary, Cap grapples with it and snaps its neck. The Hound holds them at gunpoint, but Cap disarms him and unmasks him as Murdock, who wanted his family's land all to himself.
NOTE: Story called "Captain America and the Phantom Hound!" on Contents page. Designated "No. 382-F" of Captain America's Personal Files. Story followed by "Sentinels of Liberty Secret Club News" (1 page) w/"Message from Captain America" & "Bucky's Column" featuring Captain America.

5TH STORY: "Hurricane" (7 pages)
CREDITS: Charles Nicholas (art)
FEATURE CHARACTER: Hurricane
SUPPORTING CAST: Speedy Scriggles
VILLAINS: The Masked Leader (Lionel van Devanter, secret owner of Gem Construction Company, only app), & his underlings inc Grant
OTHER CHARACTERS: Bill Slade (head of Star Construction), construction workers, construction site watchman, bystanders
LOCATIONS/ITEMS: van Devanter's office, construction site; constuction materials & tools, criminals' weapons, blowtorch, hacksaw, rivets
SYNOPSIS: Multimillionaire van Devanter gives a skyscraper contract to Bill Slade of Star Construction Co. The next day, Slade's rival, Grant of Gem Construction Co., harasses Slade's workers at the site, causing one to fall several stories. Speedy spots the falling man, and Hurricane rushes to save him. After reporting to his boss, the Masked Leader, Grant and his gang sabotage the site. Later, Hurricane and Speedy join the construction crew where Speedy interrupts Grant and company attempting to weaken the foundation. Hurricane quickly knocks out the criminals. The Masked Leader, observing the proceedings, flees, but Speedy catches him and unmasks him as Devanter, who confesses that, as secret owner of Gem Construction, he had set Slade up to fail. Weeks later, Star Construction completes the project.
NOTE: Story called "Hurricane, Master of Speed, and the Skyscraper Plot" on Contents page. Story allegedly takes place over a 3-month period.

6TH STORY: "Beware the Man Who Could Forecast Doom!" (7 pages)
CREDITS: Stan Lee (writer), Al Avison (pencils), George Klein (co-inks, see NOTE)
FEATURE CHARACTER: Father Time
VILLAINS: Yogi Zamor (Kurt Hausner, Nazi agent, dies) & henchman (dies)
OTHER CHARACTERS: General John Peters (dies), Mrs. Peters, Zamor's victims (generals, statesmen, financiers; all die), delivery man
LOCATIONS/ITEMS: Peters' home, Zamor's house, the S.S. Vacation, victims' homes, Larry's apartment; Zamor's crystal ball, clocks containing poison pellets, henchman's blackjack
SYNOPSIS: At his wife's insistance, General Peters visits fortune teller Yogi Zamor, who warns him of impending death at 8 PM the next day. The following day, Peters receives a package containing a clock and is found dead, the clock stopped at 8 PM. Over several days, more men die, with stopped clocks at the scene. Larry investigates Zamor. When Larry claims to be an ambassador, Zamor predicts his death the next day, at midnight. Later, Larry receives a clock and, as Father Time, confronts Zamor, whom he realizes killed using gas pellets released within the clocks at predetermined times. Faced with arrest, Zamor drops a gas pellet, thinking to kill them both, but Father Time uses his cloak to protect his face, avoiding the gas even as Zamor dies.
NOTE: Story called "Father Time and the Man Who Could Forecast Doom!" on Contents page. Co-inker w/George Klein is unknown. When consulting Zamor, Larry claims to have been appointed "ambassador to Algoslavia" which may be the only reference to this fictional nation. General John Peters should not be confused with government employee John Peters, who was killed in CapC #9/6, 41.

TEXT STORY: "All in a Day's Work" (2 pages)
CREDITS: Stan Lee (writer)
FEATURE CHARACTER: Perry Ashford (British Military Intelligence agent, only app, also in pfb)

High Command HQ (pfb only)), Panzer division's weapons
FLASHBACK: Weeks earlier, Mayvell gives volunteer Ashford his assignment (p).
SYNOPSIS: Sent to deliver the British High Command's joint secret plans to the Russian army, Perry Ashford spends days crawling through

marshlands, finally reaching enemy lines. A few hundred yards from the Kriper River, he is stopped by a Panzer detachment, whose commander holds him at gunpoint. Ashford quickly grabs the man's gun, uses him as a human shield, then hurls him at the Nazi soldiers; his enemies thus delayed, Ashford swims the Kriper to Russia and delivers the plans.

NOTE: Story appears between 3rd and 4th stories.

CAPTAIN AMERICA COMICS #11 (February 1942)

"The Case of the Squad of Mystery" (15 pages)

CREDITS: Al Avison (pencils, c art), George Klein, Al Gabriele (inks), Stan Lee (editor)
FEATURE CHARACTER: Captain America
SUPPORTING CAST: Bucky (chr last in W:O #20, '08 fb), Gen. Haywood (last in CapC #5/2, '41, next in AllWin #4/2, '42)
VILLAINS: 13 Nazi operatives impersonating the Sergeant & 12 soldiers of Camp Lehigh's 2nd Squad, 1st Platoon, Company B (only app, see NOTE), Herr Grotz (Nazi spy, manages Mariposa Cafe as cover) & his 3 waiters
OTHER CHARACTERS: The 13 actual members of 2nd Squad, 1st Platoon, Company B, Camp Lehigh soldiers inc Lieutenant in command of 1st Platoon (dies), visiting general, travelers aid employee, police operator (bts, called by Bucky), birds, Adolf Hitler (on symbolic splash page only)
LOCATIONS/ITEMS: Camp Lehigh inc Steve & Bucky's tent, 2nd Squad's tents & administration building, state capital inc Travelers Aid Bureau & Cafe Mariposa ("Mariposa Cafe," Nazi spy front w/underground dungeon); Cap's commandeered truck, Grotz's coat & rifle, waiters' sabers, soldiers' rifles, bayonets & targets
SYNOPSIS: Camp Lehigh holds competitive demonstrations and 2nd Squad, previously average, wins every one. A visiting general rewards the squad's sergeant, who nearly responds with a "Heil Hitler" salute before catching himself. Noticing this, Steve and Bucky investigate. First Platoon's commander also notices, and is killed when he confronts 2nd Squad. The assassin also shoots at Cap and Bucky, then escapes. Later, Cap and Bucky ask Camp Lehigh's general to transfer Steve Rogers to 2nd Squad. Once there, Steve overhears the sergeant and a soldier discuss how his presence "complicates" things. An attempt on Steve's life fails. Learning the 2nd Squad was on leave in the state capital, Cap and Bucky travel there and discover that a bald man directed them to Cafe Mariposa. There, Bucky removes the manager's toupee, exposing him as the assassin. He activates a trap door, sending Cap and Bucky to an underground dungeon, where the real 2nd Squad is imprisoned. They identify the manager as "big shot Nazi" Grotz who plans to have his imposters massacre Lehigh's soldiers. After Grotz departs, his underlings try to kill Cap and Bucky, who defeat them and use their keys to free the soldiers. They all hurry back to Lehigh, where they quickly defeat Grotz and the false soldiers.
NOTE: Contains "Table of Contents" (1 page) featuring Captain America, Bucky & reproduced cover of YA #2, '41. Story called "Captain America and the Squad of Mystery!" on Contents page. Nazi imposters called "the Sinister Squad" on Contents page only.

2ND STORY: "Captain America and the Feud Murders" (15 pages)
CREDITS: Al Avison (pencils), George Klein, Al Gabriele (inks)
FEATURE CHARACTER: Captain America
SUPPORTING CAST: Bucky, Sgt. Duffy
VILLAINS: George Brinner (impersonates Camp Lehigh MP) & his underlings
OTHER CHARACTERS: Pvt Lee Coger (dies), Pvt Jonce Rand (dies), 2 Camp Lehigh MPs, Forrest Coger & the Coger family (inc Lee's sister or cousin, see NOTE), Colonel Rand & the Rand family (inc Colonel's granddaughter Druscilla), NYV radio announcer, 2 NYV employees, telephone operator (bts, called by Brinner), Rands' horse, birds
LOCATIONS/ITEMS: Camp Lehigh inc guardhouse, Tennessee inc Raccoon Gulch, surrounding hill country, Coger and Rand shacks & Canyon City (mentioned only), NYV radio station; freight train, Cap's car, Brinner's knives & gun, hidden telephone in tree, Cogers' and Rands' rifles, Bucky's knife, bauxite (aluminum ore), Forrest's pitchfork (on splash page only)
SYNOPSIS: At Camp Lehigh, a fistfight breaks out between soldiers Lee Coger and Jonce Rand, members of two formerly feuding Tennessee families. Soon after, Steve, Lee and an apparent MP find Jonce killed with Bucky's knife, which Lee had borrowed and lost. The "MP" decides to arrest all three, but Lee, suspicious of the man's non-regulation gun, flees. Steve follows but Bucky is arrested. Radio reports reach Tennessee, where Lee's Uncle Forrest prepares for renewed feuding. Lee arrives but is killed with a knife in his back. Arriving minutes later, Cap is accused. Overcoming two Cogers, he meets the Rand clan. When a sniper shoots at Colonel Rand, the clan searches for him, leaving Cap guarded by rifle-toting Druscilla. George Brinner, a newcomer, flirts with Druscilla, allowing Cap to escape. He trips over bauxite, giving him a clue. Later, Brinner instructs two underlings to separately fire upon the Cogers and Rands. Cap intervenes having recognized Brinner as the false MP. Joined by an escaped Bucky, Cap stops the hirelings, one of whom confesses that Brinner intended the families to wipe each other out so he could claim the bauxite. The Cogers and Rands make peace. Brinner hurls a dagger, evidence that he killed Jonce and Lee, that Cap deflects. Forrest promises to send Brinner to Canyon City for trial, and Cap and Bucky return to Camp Lehigh.
NOTE: Title has exclamation point on Contents page. Lee and his female relation both call Forrest "Uncle" but it isn't stated what their relationship is to each other.

3RD STORY: "A Life at Stake!" (7 pages)
CREDITS: Stan Lee (writer), Charles Nicholas (art)
FEATURE CHARACTER: Hurricane (also as "Harry Kane," final golden age app; next, as "Frank Harper," in ToS #7, '60)
SUPPORTING CAST: Speedy Scriggles (last app to date)

VILLAINS: Lew Grey (dies) and 4 underlings

OTHER CHARACTERS: Florence Grey (heiress and Lew's cousin, only app), Pierre (Florence's chauffeur, dies), hotel doorman, Manhattan police officer, driver (bts, nearly colliding with Florence's car), 2 ducks, Louie de Lug (mentioned only, by gangster)

LOCATIONS/ITEMS: Manhattan hotel, Florence's townhouse inc cellar w/electric panel-board (destroyed), lake; Florence's car, criminals' car & tommy guns

SYNOPSIS: Out for a walk, "Kane" and Speedy see a woman's chauffeur shot, causing the car to speed uncontrollably. Kane pursues and stops the car, then offers his chauffeur services to the woman, Florence Grey. The next day, Kane, with Speedy as footman, drives Florence through town, but a car of gangsters follows. Hurricane subdues the gangsters, one of whom admits they work for Florence's cousin Lew, who will inherit the family fortune upon her death. When Hurricane confronts Lew, he flees to the cellar, threatening to blow up the house. Hurricane shoves Lew against a control panel, triggering the explosion, hurries Speedy and Florence to safety, then asks Florence on a date.

NOTE: Story called "Hurricane, Master of Speed, in A Life at Stake!" on Contents page. Story followed by "Sentinels of Liberty Secret Club News" (1 page) w/"Message from Captain America," "Bucky's Column," and "Special Notices to Sentinels" featuring Captain America & Bucky.

4TH STORY: "Father Time Battles The Scourge of Crime!" (6 pages)

CREDITS: Stan Lee (writer, see NOTE), Mike Sekowsky (art)

FEATURE CHARACTER: Father Time

VILLAINS: Peter Drew (Midvale DA), Nails Riggly (Midvale crime boss) & his underlings

OTHER CHARACTERS: Tom Bryant (Larry's friend, elected DA at end of story, also on campaign poster & newspaper photo), Bryant's aide (dies), 2 city officials, campaign crowd, hooded gunman (on symbolic splash page only)

LOCATIONS/ITEMS: Midvale (also "Midvale City," see NOTE), inc auditorium w/speaker's platform, Drew's apartment, Larry's hotel room & county jail, Larry's apartment; Drew & Riggly's guns, campaign signs, tomato, lead pipe

SYNOPSIS: Larry Scott visits Midvale, where his friend Tom Bryant is running for DA. As Bryant addresses an auditorium audience, current DA Pete Drew and crime boss ally Nails Riggly plot against him. A Riggly underling throws a tomato, provoking a riot. Scott, as Father Time, singles out the troublemaker, but as Bryant calls for order, another gangster strikes his aide dead with a lead pipe, which he shoves into Bryant's hand. Accused of murder, Bryant seems certain to lose, but Father Time, recognizing Drew as the obvious suspect, attacks him and Riggly. He quickly incapacitates both, then threatens Drew into signing a confession only minutes before voting begins. Bryant is freed and elected DA by a huge majority.

NOTE: The Midvale of this story may be the same as the Midvale of the Hurricane story in CapC #9/5, '41; if so, Nails and his gang may have been bts there. Stan Lee uses the pen name "Neel Nats" here. Story followed by "Do You Know?" (1 page), offering alleged facts about US naval ship-naming practices; supposed bomb inventor "Galen, Bishop of Munster," his bombs supposedly first used on March 24, 1580; polar bears; and Joshua A. Norton (1819-1880), self-proclaimed "Emperor of the United States." "Galen, Bishop of Munster" presumably refers to Prince-Bishop Christoph Bernhard Freiherr von Galen (1606-1678), who used bombs to besiege the Dutch city Groningen but neither invented bombs nor was alive in 1580 to use them.

5TH STORY: "Captain America Combats the Symphony of Terror!" (16 pages)

CREDITS: Syd Shores (pencils), George Klein (co-inks, see NOTE)

FEATURE CHARACTER: Captain America (next in CapC #22/3, '43, Cap #139, '71 fb, Inv #29, '78 fb)

SUPPORTING CAST: Bucky, Sgt. Duffy (both chr next in CapC #22/3, '43)

VILLAIN: Mephisto the Devil (Jacques Laval, costumed killer, dies; see NOTE)

OTHER CHARACTERS: Morton Friend (opera manager, dies), Miss Hale (Friend's secretary), Richard Thomas (opera singer, dies), Henri Defarge (opera singer, plays "Mephisto" role, see NOTE), police operator (bts, called by Miss Hale), Insp. Gribbon and Det. Finnegan, homicide squad members, coroner, police photographer, opera attendees, conductor, orchestra members, ticket vendor

LOCATIONS/ITEMS: Camp Lehigh inc Steve & Bucky's tent, Pike's Opera House ("the Grand Opera House") w/Friend's office, ticket office, auditorium & subterranean tunnels; PA system microphone, Mephisto's pistol, dagger, steel pike, piano & weight

SYNOPSIS: Opera house manager Morton Friend receives a letter threatening his life if he allows Richard Thomas to sing. He dismisses it, but an hour later, the costumed Mephisto kills him. Inspector Gribbon and Detective Finnegan arrive. Gribbon advises that the show go on. Steve and Bucky attend. During the first act, which Richard Thomas performs with Lily Renaud and Henry Defarge as "Mephisto," Thomas is shot dead. Gribbon informally deputizes Steve. When Gribbon mentions Thomas was shot in the chest, Steve points out the killer must have been in front of the footlights, and Gribbon immediately suspects the conductor. Cap and Bucky investigate a trap door leading to a cellar passageway, where they hear Lily's scream. They find the conductor, who tells them Lily was abducted by "Mephisto." Cap and Bucky follow the sound of Lily singing a literal command performance for Mephisto, who accompanies her on piano. He decides she must die if he can't have her but Cap and Bucky intervene. Mephisto flees, climbing a ladder to the surface. Cap and Bucky pursue. They encounter Defarge, still in costume, and accost him, but a dropped weight from a catwalk reveals the criminal Mephisto is above. The heroes climb up and Cap knocks Mephisto down. Mephisto identifies himself as Jacques Laval, who has long held unrequited love for Lily. He killed Richard after learning Lily was in love with him. He tries to escape, but a police officer shoots him down.

NOTE: George Klein's co-inker is unknown. An actor/villain using the name "Mephisto the Devil," but with different motivations, fights the Angel in SubC #20/4, '46. Another Mephisto, an alleged thought-projection, fights the Human Torch and Toro in CapC #67/2, '48. None of these should

TEXT STORY: "Broken Trust" (2 pages)

CREDITS: Stan Lee (writer)

FEATURE CHARACTER: Bob Slade (FBI agent, poses as "Spike Conroy")
VILLAINS: Gunner Sloan & his 3 men (Lefty Hogan & Lippy Jenks named)
OTHER CHARACTERS: Bank teller, 2 warehouse watchmen, police
LOCATIONS/ITEMS: Sloan gang's hideout, Slade's apartment, bank, warehouse, New York Treasury Building, garage; Sloan gang's black sedan, Gunner's wall map, acetylene torch, gang's revolvers, Slade's revolver, money, furs
SYNOPSIS: After he and his gang rob a bank of $300,000, Gunner Sloan, who attributes his success to a refusal to trust anyone, dismisses reports that FBI agent Bob Slade is on his trail. Directed by rumor, Gunner and company rob a warehouse of furs but are quickly surrounded by police. The criminals escape with help from Spike Conroy, who supposedly intended to steal the furs himself, and the grateful Gunner gives Conroy a share of the loot and accepts him into the gang. Later, Gunner plans his last and most spectacular job, to rob the New York Treasury Building. With Conroy as getaway driver, Gunner and company escape with the loot, but Conroy drives them to a garage where police are waiting, for Conroy, whom Gunner made the mistake of trusting, is Agent Slade.
NOTE: Story appears between 2nd and 3rd stories. Title has exclamation point on Contents page.

CAPTAIN AMERICA COMICS #12 (March 1942)

"The Terrible Menace of the Pygmies of Terror!" (20 pages)

CREDITS: Otto Binder (writer), Al Avison (pencils, c art), George Klein (co-inks, see NOTE), Stan Lee (editor)
FEATURE CHARACTER: Captain America
SUPPORTING CAST: Bucky (chr last in Inv #29, '78 fb), Sgt. Duffy (chr last in Cap #139, '71 fb, next in AllWin #4/2, '42)
VILLAINS: Dr. Crime ("Master of Evil," Dr. Edward Elmgren, scientist & would-be underworld leader, 1st, next in AllWin #7, '42), the Pygmies of Terror (4 criminals shrunk by Dr. Crime), Knuckles Samson (dies)
OTHER CHARACTERS: Camp Lehigh soldiers, Jim Barney (soldier of fortune), Prof. Gibbs (archaeologist), Paul Fung (scientist, dies), banker (dies), banker's cat, Dr. Crime's cat
LOCATIONS/ITEMS: Camp Lehigh, Dr. Elmgren's laboratory & home, theater, banker's home, Fung's home, Dr. Crime's hideout (see NOTE); Dr. Crime's shrinking fluid (see NOTE), fluid-shooting gun, blowgun, poisoned darts, notebook & "liquid smoke" vial, Pygmies' guns & clubs, needles
SYNOPSIS: After reading that an Amazon River expedition has returned with a valuable secret, Cap and Bucky stake out expedition head Elmer Elmgren's lab, where the expedition members – Elmgren, Barney, Gibbs, Fung – discuss their discovery, a fluid that shrinks humans. Hours later, criminal Knuckles Samson breaks into Elmgren's lab and tries to steal the fluid, only to be confronted by Dr. Crime, who kills him with a poisoned dart. Cap and Bucky burst in but Crime uses a vial of "liquid smoke" to cover his escape. The next morning, Steve and Bucky oversleep, and Sgt. Duffy assigns them to the soldiers' benefit play. Meanwhile, robbers infiltrate Crime's lab hideout. He hurls the shrinking fluid at them, reducing them to a foot high. As Crime's "Pygmies of Terror," they kill a rich banker and loot his home. Hearing the banker's death cry during the benefit, Cap and Bucky investigate. Bucky encounters the Pygmies, who knock him out, and escape. Later, the two consult Elmgren, who blames Paul Fung. Cap and Bucky confront Fung, but Crime kills him then shoots the heroes with shrinking fluid, taking them to his hideout and caging them with his hungry cat. Cap and Bucky outfight the cat and escape, quickly defeating the Pygmies. Crime returns with two more shrunken victims, but Cap and Bucky leap upon his shoulders and, threatening him with needles, force him to restore them to normal. Cap restores the captives, Gibbs and Barney, then unmasks Crime as Elmgren. Returning to the theater, Steve and Bucky find Duffy waiting for them to clean up.
NOTE: Contains "Table of Contents" (1 page) featuring Captain America & Bucky. Story called "Captain America and the Pygmies of Terror" on Contents page. When Knuckles Samson breaks in, he goes directly to the desk containing the shrinking fluid, implying he was hired by someone who saw Elmgren place it there, but this is never explained. It is unclear if Dr. Crime's "secret lair" is part of Elmgren's lab or in an entirely different lab. On the story's last page, Bucky erroneously refers to Prof. Gibbs as "Prof. Briggs" & Jim Barney as "Tim Barney." The soldiers' benefit play is "Florodora," a musical comedy by Leslie Stuart, Paul Rubens, Edward Boyd-Jones, and Jimmy Davis (as Owen Hall), first performed in 1899. Cap and Bucky encounter another user of shrinking technology, General Nikki, in USA #10, '43. Dr. Crime's shrinking fluid erroneously called "pygmy gas" on symbolic splash page. Co-inker w/George Klein is unknown.

2ND STORY: "Captain America in The Case of Rozzo the Rebel" (20 pages)
CREDITS: Al Avison (pencils), George Klein (inks)
FEATURE CHARACTER: Captain America (next in AllWin #4/2, '42, MvPro #7-8, '10, GSInv #1, '75, Cap #247, '80 fb, MvPro #8, '10 fb, Inv #1-4, '75-76, Consp #1, '98 fb, Inv #31, '78 fb, CapTW:AB #1, '09 fb)
SUPPORTING CAST: Bucky (next in AllWin #4/2, '42)
VILLAINS: Rozzo the Rebel (also in fb, ex-Oroco soldier, dies) & his underlings (Felipe named, all die)
OTHER CHARACTERS: President Alvaro (also in fb, president of Oroco), Camp Lehigh officer, reporters, Lotta (dancer), Club Cantina patrons, Club Cantina employees (manager, waiters, musicians), police officer, bellboy, Mayor Fiorello La Guardia (bts, lends car to President Alvaro), Alvaro & Rozzo's horses (fb only), Alvaro's rebel soldiers & horses (fb only), dictator's soldiers (fb only; dictator bts), bystanders, fish
LOCATIONS/ITEMS: Pier 22, Alvaro's hotel, Club Cantina, Mud-Hook Lake w/swamp & dock, Rozzo's Swamp Citadel inc cable car, watertight vacuumatic elevator, plastic glass-enclosed lookout tower, ammunition chamber, torture chamber, private vault with loot & invasion alarms, Oroco (South American nation, fb only) inc pampas, battlefield, rebel HQ & ruler's palace; Rozzo's car, boat, dagger, gun, blowtorch, swords, dummy & lead-weighted bolas, Alvaro's car, Cap's raft and poles, flower bomb (strong enough to kill 10 men), Oroco medal, boulder, Oroco soldiers' weapons (fb only)
FLASHBACKS: Ten years ago, Alvaro and Rozzo work as gauchos in Oroco. Alvaro leads rebel forces against Oroco's dictator, while Rozzo commands the dictator's army. When the rebels win, Alvaro allows Rozzo to leave for the USA.
SYNOPSIS: When Oroco's President Alvaro visits Manhattan, Steve and Bucky act as his guards. Rozzo the Rebel attacks with a lead-

weighted bola. As Cap and Bucky fight Rozzo's forces, Alvaro uses Rozzo's bolas to stop Rozzo from stabbing Cap. Later, Alvaro tells Steve and Bucky of his history with Rozzo. Soon after, Cap and Bucky accompany Alvaro to Club Cantina where Rozzo gives famed dancer Lotta a flower, actually a bomb, to toss to him. Cap, instinctively suspicious, catches it on his shield, where it explodes. Rozzo captures Alvaro and Lotta but Bucky overhears their destination, "the Swamp Citadel" north of Manhattan. They follow, discovering the Swamp Citadel is at Mud-Hook Lake's bottom, accessible by cable-car and then elevator. Within, Rozzo demands Alvaro share rulership of Oroco, threatening to torture Lotta with a blowtorch. Cap and Bucky burst in. During the battle, Rozzo's blowtorch expands a metal plate, letting the lake's water gush in. Cap and Bucky rescue Alvaro and Lotta. Rozzo's men drown but Rozzo escapes. Later, Rozzo sends a message challenging Alvaro to a rooftop duel. Alvaro agrees. They have a sword fight but Rozzo gives Alvaro a weak sword. Cap intervenes and Rozzo falls to his death. Alvaro asks Steve to give Cap a medal, Oroco's highest decoration for bravery.

NOTE: Story called "Captain America Defies Rozzo the Rebel!" on Contents page. Story identified as "Case 6310-B" from Captain America's files. Story contains Swamp Citadel diagram "drawn by Steve Rogers." Although Cap's shield's extraordinary impact-absorbing qualities were not formally established until the modern era, they are evident here when it absorbs the impact of Rozzo's flower bomb. Rozzo is erroneously identified as a "Mexican rebel" on page 12, panel 1. Oroco is next mentioned in MW:OFiles, '06, as the retirement site of Forja Seguidor, the "el Aguila" active during the Spanish Civil War.

3RD STORY: "The Imp" (6 pages)
CREDITS: Stan Lee (writer), Chad Grothkopf (art)
FEATURE CHARACTER: The Imp (a heroic antennaed humanoid with super-strength, able to grow from approx 2 mm tall to 6 inches, 1st)
SUPPORTING CAST: Jefferson "Jeff" Vandermeer (the man within whose ear the Imp lives, 1st)
VILLAINS: The Spider & his two underlings, the Monster of the Age
OTHER CHARACTERS: Police (some armored), townspeople, 2 horses, mayor (mentioned only, by Spider)
LOCATIONS/ITEMS: "The Imp's world" (1st, a comedic/quasi-medieval realm where everyone speaks in rhyming couplets, setting of all Imp stories) inc town with castle & bridge near sea; Spider's wagon, Monster's cage, police armor, lance & spear
SYNOPSIS: Criminal Spider releases the Monster of the Age to attack the Imp's town. Emerging from Jeff's ear, the Imp tickles the Monster into distraction. With Imp aboard, it flies away. The police pursue to capture it, as Spider wanted since he and his henchmen are now free to rob the town. Imp steers the Monster into the nearby sea, then leads the police back to town, where they arrest Spider and associates. The police seek to thank Imp, but he has returned to Jeff's ear.
NOTE: Story called "Introducing -- The Imp!" on Contents page. One citizen describes the Monster as "like a dragon from another world," indicating it is not typical of local fauna; its nature and origins are unrevealed.

4TH STORY: "Father Time: Nemesis of Evildoers" (7 pages)
CREDITS: Jack Alderman (art)
FEATURE CHARACTER: Father Time (next in YA #3, '42)
VILLAINS: Beretti & his underlings (Spike named)
OTHER CHARACTERS: Mary (young tenement dweller), Mary's father (dies), police, firefighters, bystanders, train motorman, Mary's neighbor
LOCATIONS/ITEMS: Manhattan slum inc Beretti's tenement building (destroyed), railroad yard, Dugan's warehouse (Beretti's waterfront base); trains, gangsters' car, Father Time's car, stone slab, thug's gun (on splash page only) & cudgel
SYNOPSIS: Father Time enters a burning building to rescue a man, whom he finds has been shot; outside, the man reveals before dying that he overheard building owner Beretti and his gangsters mention collecting fire insurance. The man's grieving daughter Mary spots Beretti and company in the crowd, and Father Time pursues them to a railroad yard. Taking him by surprise, they knock him out and tie him to the tracks. While he escapes, one of Beretti's thugs abducts Mary. When Mary's neighbor calls for help, a thug tries to silence her, but Father Time forces him to reveal Beretti's waterfront location. He arrives in time to prevent Beretti from dumping Mary, tied to stone, into the sea, then ties up Beretti and company.
NOTE: Story called "Father Time and the Flaming Horror!" on Contents page.

5TH STORY: "Headline Hunter" (5 pages)
CREDITS: Stan Lee (writer), Warren Kremer (art)
FEATURE CHARACTER: Headline Hunter
SUPPORTING CAST: Ed the editor
VILLAINS: Guy Stanford (editor of The Tattler, dies) & Nazi reconnaissance plane crew (bts), Nazis (splash page only)
OTHER CHARACTERS: London Star reporters & pressroom printers, London mob, radio shack broadcaster, pilots, outskirts resident
LOCATIONS/ITEMS: London inc Affiliated Press office & hospital, radio shack and tower on London's outskirts, airport; mob's clubs, rock thrown through window, chemically treated paper, millions of circulars, planes, Nazi reconnaissance plane, poison gas cloud, medal
SYNOPSIS: En route to work, Headline is pursued by an angry mob. At the office, Ed reveals Nazis attacked the British navy following Headline's story on navy maneuvers, and rival publisher Guy Stanford is accusing the London Star of providing the Nazis with inside information. Determined to prove their innocence, Headline leaves through the back to seek leads, eventually sighting a huge cloud rolling in from the English Channel. Using chemical paper, he discovers the cloud is poison, one he recognizes as slow-acting and preventable. He rushes to a

NOTE: Story called "Headline Hunter Fights the Silent Death!" on Contents page. Stan Lee uses pen name "Neel Nats" here. Story followed by "Sentinels of Liberty Secret Club News" (1 page) w/"Message From Captain America" in which Cap explains the title's format change to 2 "book-length" Cap stories instead of 3 shorter ones and notes Hurricane "has gone for a short vacation," to be replaced by the Imp, and "Bucky's

Column" in which Bucky requests Sentinel Clubs send in their addresses to be printed and offers a contest to complete a Captain America illustration, with $100 as first prize, featuring Captain America & Bucky.

TEXT STORY: "Timber!" (2 pages)

CREDITS: Writer unknown

FEATURE CHARACTER: Pat Cowley (lumberjack)

SUPPORTING CAST: "Old Man" Cowley (Pat's father, owner of timber land tract and Cowley lumber outfit)

VILLAINS: "Old Man" Corivan (rival lumberer), Lamson (Corivan's hireling)

OTHER CHARACTERS: Cowley's lumberjacks, nearby town's "authorities," Ames Lumber Company (bts)

LOCATIONS/ITEMS: The North Woods, inc Cowley lumber camp w/lumberjack quarters, log-raising engine & well, Corivan lumber camp, Red River, nearby town; logging equipment, buckets of water, brooms, shovels, Corivan's gun & dynamite

SYNOPSIS: The Cowley and Corivan logging outfits are competing for an Ames Lumber Company contract, but Cowley Sr. suspects Corivan will resort to unfair tactics. One night, Cowley's son Pat awakens to the smell of smoke and organizes the lumberjacks to extinguish a forest fire. Noticing recent hiree Lamson is the only lumberjack fully dressed, Pat correctly deduces he set the fire and dismisses him. Later, Corivan himself sneaks into camp, intending to dynamite the log-raising engine, but Pat, anticipating his visit, throws the dynamite into a well, then beats Corivan severely and has him arrested. A week later, the Cowley outfit wins the contract.

NOTE: Story appears between 3rd and 4th stories. The story twice notes people "still talk" about the events described, implying they occurred years before.

CAPTAIN AMERICA COMICS #13 (April 1942)

"The League of the Unicorn!" (20 pages)

CREDITS: Al Avison (pencils, c art), Syd Shores, George Klein (inks). Stan Lee (editor)

FEATURE CHARACTER: Captain America

SUPPORTING CAST: Bucky (last in AllWin #4/2, '42, chr last in Inv #31, '78 fb)

VILLAINS: Zong the King Unicorn ("King Zong," Burton J. Hargraves, railroad president, mercenary leader, & power-seeker, only app) & the League of the Unicorns (costumed mercenaries, Yen Soy named) inc a "giant" & laundryman

OTHER CHARACTERS: Prince Tsai Hoon (royal Chinese dignitary), Princess Yana (Tsai Hoon's wife), railroad tower guard (dies), baggage car attendant (w/additional train crew members bts), Lee City citizens inc mayor, reception committee, police & railway station crowd, renegade League member (dies), Prince Tsai Hoon's father (mentioned only), the original League of the Unicorn (a cabal of "master criminals of Asia" whom Tsai Hoon's father drove from China and whose modus operandi Zong appropriates for his League, mentioned only), Hideki Tojo (Japanese general & Prime Minister, on cover only)

LOCATIONS/ITEMS: Manhattan inc Chinatown, Black River drawbridge & railroad watchtower, Lee City inc railway station, Chinatown w/ Hara Sada Hand Laundry, Tsai's quarters & multiple abandoned tunnels below, the Bamore Mansion ("the Master Mansion," Zong's surface base, two miles outside Lee City on Route 29); luxury train, note tied to rock, Cap's Chinese garb and Tsai mask, Unicorns' horns, daggers & other weapons, Zong's horn, axe, lanterns, acid, grenade & mask, clock supposedly connected to explosives, laundryman's iron

SYNOPSIS: Steve and Bucky see a man gouged from behind by one of four horn-wearing "League of the Unicorns" members. The dying man tells them the Unicorns have been paid to disrupt US/China relations by killing the visiting Prince Tsai Hoon. At the Black River, the Unicorns commandeer the drawbridge controls to try to wreck the Prince's train. Cap and Bucky save the train, then board, report to Tsai and his wife Yana, and appoint themselves the couple's bodyguards. They arrive in Lee City where the mayor and railroad president Hargraves greet them. The Unicorns attack and abduct Yana and Bucky, whom they take to their leader, Zong, at Bamore Mansion. Zong sends a letter instructing Tsai to come if he values Yana's life but a disguised Cap goes in Tsai's stead. Eventually, Cap follows Zong and company to a Lee City laundry, finding the Unicorns' underground lair. He rescues Bucky but Zong escapes with Yana. Soon after, Hargraves appears, claiming to have been trailing the Unicorns. Cap sends Bucky to the police, then continues with Hargraves, losing sight of him and finding Zong again. Several fights ensue until Bucky arrives with the police. Cap defeats the Unicorns, then unmasks Zong as Hargraves who, seeing a great opportunity for profit, had revived the Unicorns.

NOTE: Contains "Table of Contents" (1 page) featuring Captain America, Bucky & Minuteman (on Defense Bond stamp). Story called "Captain America Battles the League of the Unicorn!" on Contents page. The terms "League of the Unicorn" and "League of the Unicorns" are used interchangeably. Lee City, of course, shares its name with writer Stan Lee. As the first Cap issue published following the Japanese attack on Pearl Harbor, the cover features a "Remember Pearl Harbor" symbol and is labeled, "All Out for America Issue!" while depicting Cap stepping across the Pacific, punching Japanese General Tojo and saying, "You started it! Now we'll finish it!" In spite of all the indications that the League, like Prince Tsai, are Chinese, page 8 panel 6 refers to them as "Japanese killers" while the Contents page states they come from "out of the dark recesses of barbarian Japan."

2ND STORY: "Polly Tix" (1 page)

CREDITS: Fred Schwab (writer, art)

FEATURE CHARACTER: Polly Tix ("Polly-Tix," an anthropomorphic parrot sailor)

SUPPORTING CAST: "Mrs. Polly" (Polly's wife), their 5 children (all anthropomorphic parrots)

OTHER CHARACTERS: Bill (Polly's fellow sailor, mentioned only), Lulu, Kate, Minnie, and other human women from Egypt, China, France, Spain, Brazil, Hawaii & elsewhere (in photographs or daydreams only)

LOCATIONS/ITEMS: Dock with tugboat, Tix home; photographs, club

SYNOPSIS: Polly Tix arrives home following a voyage. He tells his family it was a dull trip, but his wife, finding photographs of several women, suspects otherwise and angrily chases him into the night with a club.

NOTE: Not listed on Contents page.

3RD STORY: "The Lighthouse of Horror" (20 pages)

CREDITS: Al Avison (pencils), George Klein (inks)

FEATURE CHARACTER: Captain America (next in Inv #5-6, '76, MP #30, '76, Inv #7-15, '76-77, Inv Ann #1, '77, Av #71, '69, Inv #16, '77 fb, earlt:Book #1, '11 fb)

SUPPORTING CAST: Bucky (chr next in Inv #5, '76), Sgt. Duffy (last in AllWin #4/2, '42), Betty Ross (last in CapC #10/4, '42)

VILLAINS: The Looter ("the Head Looter," Mr. Phillips, pirate captain, only app) & his pirate crew

OTHER CHARACTERS: Lems (blind lighthouse watchman), captain and crew of steamship Good Cheer (all die), crew and passengers of steamship Albatross (all die), captain and crew of steamship Hesperia, radio announcer (bts, voice only), Minuteman (on Defense Bond stamp only)

LOCATIONS/ITEMS: Camp Lehigh inc Steve & Bucky's tent, Last Chance Lighthouse (on island off Atlantic Coast, a few hours' running distance from Camp Lehigh) inc secret elevator & adjoining subterranean passages; steamship Good Cheer (destroyed), steamship Albatross (destroyed), steamship Hesperia, Looter's cutlass & mask, pirates' weapons, valise with radioelectric transformer, Steve's radio, Lems' stool

SYNOPSIS: At the Last Chance Lighthouse, the Looter and company use a radioelectric transformer to shut off the light from afar. The steamship Good Cheer runs aground, and the Looter's forces rob it, killing all aboard. At Camp Lehigh, Steve receives a letter from Betty Ross, who will soon arrive on the steamship Albatross. When they hear radio reports of the Good Cheer's fate, Cap and Bucky investigate. Hours later, they swim to the lighthouse as the Albatross approaches. Onboard, Betty's fellow passenger, Mr. Phillips, begins proposing marriage, but the Looter's men shut off the lighthouse, and the Albatross runs aground. Cap and Bucky fight the Looter's men. Onboard, Phillips disappears and a pirate abducts Betty. The other pirates knock out Cap and Bucky. The Albatross is sunk with all hands and the pirates grab Bucky. Recovering, Cap enters the lighthouse, where attendant Lems attacks him, then flees into a subterranean passage. Cap captures Lems, who claims no knowledge of the shipwrecks. Meanwhile, Looter and company, within a nearby tunnel, threaten to kill Bucky but spare Betty. Cap arrives and rescues them but the Looter escapes and wrecks another ship, the Hesperia. Cap knocks out the Looter's men, whom the Hesperia's captain takes into custody, but Looter grabs Betty and returns to the lighthouse. Confronting Lems, Cap and Bucky learn he is blind and that, out of fear of losing his job, he shared the lighthouse's subterranean passages with Looter, who in turn kept his secret. Lems leads Cap and Bucky to a passage, at whose end they find and knock out Looter, unmasked as Phillips.

NOTE: Story called "Captain America Enters the Lighthouse of Horror!" on Contents page.

4TH STORY: "The Imp" (7 pages)

CREDITS: Stan Lee (writer), Chad Grothkopf (art)

FEATURE CHARACTER: The Imp

SUPPORTING CAST: Jefferson Vandermeer

VILLAIN: Dr. Sinn (only app)

OTHER CHARACTERS: 2 police officers, townspeople, Minuteman (on Defense Bond stamp only)

LOCATIONS/ITEMS: Dr. Sinn's castle inc laboratory w/scientific apparatus, town inc bank; "Black Magic" and other magic books, ropes, Imp's mirror

SYNOPSIS: Dr. Sinn magically grants himself superhuman strength and robs a bank. Jeff is present and summons the Imp from within his ear. Initially struck aside by Sinn, Imp rebounds and knocks him down. The bank customers bind Sinn, but he easily breaks their ropes, captures Imp, and returns to his castle lab. With a magic tome, Sinn casts a "dissolving" spell at Imp, who uses a mirror to reflect the spell back at him. Sinn shrinks into nothingness. When the townspeople break into the castle, the Imp departs.

NOTE: Contents page adds exclamation point to title. Dr. Sinn remarks that, "[of] all living human beings," only the Imp opposes him, implying the Imp, despite his appearance, is human (or as much so as any other denizen of his world). At story's end, the Imp "breaks the fourth wall" to address the "pals, guys and gals" who have sent him letters.

5TH STORY: "Headline Hunter" (5 pages)

CREDITS: Unknown

FEATURE CHARACTER: Headline Hunter (last app to date)

SUPPORTING CAST: Ed the editor (last app to date)

VILLAINS: Herr Horner (Nazi official, also in newspaper photo), Cramm (Gestapo agent)

OTHER CHARACTERS: Lord Danvers (publisher), Robbie & his associate (London outskirts denizens), army captain, 2 army guards (more bts), Scotland Yard officer (bts, on phone w/Lord Danvers), Adolf Hitler (mentioned only, by Horner), Sir Winston Churchill (mentioned only, by headline)

LOCATIONS/ITEMS: London inc Star office (w/printing press room in symbolic splash page only) & Lord Danvers' home, London outskirts, army HQ, deserted field & plane, Tower of London (mentioned only, by Headline); Horner's one-man plane (destroyed), pistol & parachute, guards' rifles

SYNOPSIS: While Headline interviews Lord Danvers, a major British publisher whose newspapers keep the public morale high, German official Herr Horner parachutes into England, claiming he wants to help the British against Hitler. Headline accompanies Danvers to interview Horner whom Danvers offers lodging at his home. The army posts guards there, but Gestapo agent Cramm slips past them to meet Horner, who plans to abduct Danvers to Germany, thus forcing his papers to cease printing anti-Nazi articles. Headline sees Cramm's entry and follows to confront both Nazis. However, Cramm knocks Headline out, and the Nazis abduct Danvers. When Headline recovers, he borrows a motorcycle and follows. At a deserted airfield, Headline rides the motorcycle over a rising-to-land-step Cramm, then quickly dismounts to knock out Horner

Patriot (Jeff Mace) encountered a similar false detector, Rodney Huss, in MC #24-25, '41. Story followed by "Sentinels of Liberty Secret Club News" (1 page) w/Message From Captain America exhorting the readers to "Remember Pearl Harbor" & Bucky's Column promising to "lick the tar out of the dictators," featuring Captain America & Bucky. Includes "Remember Pearl Harbor" symbol. Feature is listed as "Sentinels of

Liberty Club Page!" on Contents page.

6TH STORY: "Roddy Colt, Alias "The Secret Stamp," U.S. Defense Agent" (8 pages)
CREDITS: Don Rico (pencils), George Klein (inks)
FEATURE CHARACTER: The Secret Stamp (Roddy Colt, teenage Freetown Star delivery boy/defense bond salesman, 1st)
SUPPORTING CAST: Tom Colt (Roddy's younger brother, 1st, next in CapC #23/4, '43), Jerry Dash (Freetown Star reporter, 1st), Spud Sickles (Freetown News delivery boy and rival defense bond salesman, 1st)
VILLAINS: 2 gangsters, bank robber, fruit stand robber, 2 muggers
OTHER CHARACTERS: Mr. Williams (banker), 2 police officers, fruit stand vendor, woman rescued from drowning, blind mendicant, bystander, Minuteman (on Defense Bond stamp only)
LOCATIONS/ITEMS: Freetown (1st, setting of all Secret Stamp stories unless otherwise noted) inc Colt home, Freetown Star office, bicycle shop, Memorial Hospital (founded 1918), Mutual Bank of Freetown, dock, Williams' home & cemetery, gangsters' hideout at Swan Lake (several hours' drive from Freetown); gangsters' car, Roddy's bicycle (destroyed), Roddy's new bicycle with two-way radio, Spud's bicycle, defense stamps, Freetown Star & Freetown News (newspapers), gangsters' gun
SYNOPSIS: Roddy and Tom deliver newspapers by bicycle. A speeding car strikes Tom, breaking his leg. The 2 gangster occupants steal defense stamps that fall from the bike. Roddy's reporter friend Jerry drives Tom to Memorial Hospital, then buys Roddy a new bicycle with two-way radio, so he can report any news he encounters. Roddy takes the costumed identity of Secret Stamp to oppose crime and US defense program enemies. Over the following days, he foils crimes and rescues people. Roddy tries to scoop rival Spud by selling bonds to banker Williams but Williams, whose life has been threatened unless he leaves $10,000 at a nearby cemetery, kicks him out. That night, Williams leaves the money and the gangsters who hit Tom claim it, then catch Secret Stamp staking the cemetery out, throwing him and his bike into their trunk. Stamp uses his radio to summon Jerry, then later escapes, noticing the stolen stamps in the trunk. He bowls the 2 men over on his bike, marks one's forehead with a stamp, and departs as Jerry arrives with police. The following day, Williams buys $100 of stamps from Roddy. Spud claims to be the Secret Stamp, much to Roddy's amusement.
NOTE: Story called "The Secret Stamp!" on Contents page.

TEXT STORY: "Wild West" (2 pages)
CREDITS: Writer unknown
FEATURE CHARACTER: Grandpop Saunders (70-year-old rancher)
SUPPORTING CAST: Tom Saunders (Grandpop's grandson, in his 20s)
VILLAINS: Blackie Dione (also as Oliver Wentworth), mining corporation inc inspector (pfb only)
OTHER CHARACTERS: Sheriff, ranchers, Tom's 2 horses, Dione's hired horse, general store proprietor (bts, where Tom buys supplies), Billy the Kid & Jesse James (mentioned only, by Grandpop)
LOCATIONS/ITEMS: Saunders ranch & adjoining gold mine, Butlertown (about 5 miles from ranch) inc general store & hotel, multiple ranches; Tom's buckboard wagon, Dione's gun, legal papers, flashlight, letter & envelope
FLASHBACK: The mining corporation sends an investigator to the Saunders mine on the sly (p).
SYNOPSIS: Longing for the supposed excitement of the old west, Grandpop Saunders frequently tells tales of the era as if he experienced them. When his grandson Tom buys supplies in Butlertown, "Oliver Wentworth from New York," announces his intent to buy a ranch, and Tom takes him for a ride around the area. They return to the Saunders ranch, where the visitor surveys the area for two hours, making Tom suspicious. "Wentworth" is actually wanted murderer Blackie Dione from Chicago hired by a mining corporation who discovered signs of gold ore at the Saunders property's abandoned mine. Dione, having confirmed the mine's location, intends to claim it for himself and forces Grandpop and Tom at gunpoint to accompany him there, where he intends to force Grandpop to sign over ownership, then kill them both. Inspired by being in the situation he had so often bragged about, Grandpop attacks Dione, pummeling him into unconsciousness. Dione is arrested, and Grandpop has a true-life story to tell future listeners.
NOTE: Story called "Wild-West!" on Contents page. Story appears between 3rd and 4th stories. Story's events occur years prior to 1942, since Grandpop is said to have retold the events over "the remaining years of his life."

"Captain America Battles The Horde of the Vulture!" (19 pages)

CREDITS: Al Avison (pencils, c art), Syd Shores, George Klein (inks), Stan Lee (editor)
FEATURE CHARACTER: Captain America
SUPPORTING CAST: Bucky (chr last in FearIt:Book #1, '11 fb), Sgt. Duffy
VILLAINS: The Vulture (also as "Black Hawk," Hugh Bradley, Mojave Indian Agency trader & Japanese operative, only app) & the Vultures (also as "the Black Hawks" & the "Black Raiders," alleged Mojave warriors, supposed revival of pre-existing secret society, possibly disguised Japanese soldiers, only app), Japanese commander, sergeant, guard patrol & soldiers
OTHER CHARACTERS: Little Moose (see NOTE) & other Mojaves, Pete the Prospector, Camp Lehigh soldiers, Camp Mojave general, Lt. Stewart (dies), Stewart's horse, 2 hooded villains (on cover only)
LOCATIONS/ITEMS: Camp Lehigh, Camp Mojave (Arizona), Wampum Indian Camp, Pete's campground, "the Den of the Raiders" subterranean chamber beneath abandoned valley village, accessible by tunnel); remote-controlled "Aztec Idol" (destroyed), ammunition & supply trucks (one destroyed), duffle bag w/Cap & Bucky's costumes, Pete's pistol & camping equipment, Vultures' rifles, bows & arrows, Vulture's grenade, Japanese rifles
SYNOPSIS: Steve, Bucky and Duffy accompany an explosives supply convoy to Arizona's Camp Mojave. On the way, the Vulture and his men attack. Cap and Bucky drive them off. At Camp Mojave, Steve overhears businessman Bradley tell an officer about the Vultures' alleged roots as an "Indian secret society." Bradley offers to ferret out membership, but Cap proceeds on his own with Bucky. They contact their friend Little Moose, who reports mysterious activities in an abandoned village. Cap and Bucky investigate a campfire but find only would-be gold prospector Pete. The Vulture and his men capture all three and take them to a subterranean hideout. Bucky and Pete are shackled in a dungeon, but Cap escapes and returns to Little Moose's reservation, where Camp Mojave's Lt. Stewart reports that Moose, a Vulture mask planted in his possessions, has been arrested. Cap vouches for Moose and Stewart departs to summon backup from Camp Mojave, but a Vulture kills him. Meanwhile, Cap tells Moose's fellow Mojaves that the Vultures are "foreign sneaks" hiding behind "the name of the First Americans," and they agree to help. Meanwhile, Vulture's men place Bucky and Pete in a hole filling with water to drown them. Finding the hideout's entrance blocked, Cap scales a ladder and discovers Japanese soldiers. As the Mojaves fight the Japanese, Cap confronts Vulture, then frees Bucky and Pete. After Cap knocks out Vulture, the Japanese soldiers surrender, and Cap unmasks Vulture as Bradley.
NOTE: Contains "Table of Contents" (1 page) featuring Captain America, Bucky & Minuteman (on Defense Bond stamp). Little Moose's prior encounter with Cap, when Cap "saved [him] from wicked gangsters," is an untold story; this story is his only appearance. "Little Moose" is possibly a mistranslation of his name in the Mojave language, since there are no moose in Arizona. Hugh Bradley is the first of at least five presumably unconnected golden age villains to use the codename of "the Vulture," none of whom should be confused with Spider-Man's enemy Adrian Toomes or any of Toomes' imitators/successors. Story followed by "Captain America Brain Teasers" (1 page), featuring Captain America, Bucky, girl, rabbit, lion, mouse & goose (prev 5 in puzzles only). Feature called "Captain America's Puzzle Page" on Contents page and is written by A.W. Nugent w/spot illustrations by Al Avison & Syd Shores.

2ND STORY: "Captain America and the Petals of Doom!" (21 pages)
CREDITS: Al Avison (pencils), Syd Shores, George Klein (inks)
FEATURE CHARACTER: Captain America (next in Av #6, '64 fb, Inv #16-23, '77, Inv #25-28, '78, SgtF #13, '64, Cap #383/2, '91, DF:Av #2.4, '99, DF:Av #3.6, '00)
SUPPORTING CAST: Bucky (chr next in Inv #16, '77), Sgt. Duffy, Betty Ross
VILLAINS: The Yellow Claw (Capt. Rod Elliot, intelligence officer & master criminal, dies) & his underlings (some as "the Messengers")
OTHER CHARACTERS: Camp Lehigh soldiers, army camp's major (dies), dance attendees, Major Adams (dies), lieutenant (dies), 3 surgeons, ? nurses (more hospital personnel bts), Gen. Berry (dies), MPs, military ballgoers inc army and navy officers, musicians, singer, postman, Army lab analyst, butler, major & 3 other officers (Claw's earlier victims, all die), Captain Aquilino (mentioned only, Camp Eckley officer)
LOCATIONS/ITEMS: Camp Lehigh inc KP tent, Steve and Bucky's tent, dance hall, Adams' office & Lieutenant's office, other army camp, hospital, army lab, mansion, Yellow Claw's hideout, Yellow Claw's crime sites in major's office & exploded building, Camp Eckley (mentioned only); flower truck, Claw henchman's car, poisoned flowers, Yellow Claw's dagger, henchman's blackjack
SYNOPSIS: The Yellow Claw declares war on US defense, killing officers and destroying government facilities. Cap and Bucky spy Claw & his underlings killing an officer, stealing his plans. They pursue but MPs unknowingly interrupt, allowing the villains to escape. Back at Camp Lehigh, Steve is supposed to meet Betty at a dance, but Duffy assigns him and Bucky to KP. Duping Duffy, Steve attends the dance, finding Betty dancing with Captain Elliot, a recently assigned intelligence officer. Later, Cap and Bucky tackle two intruders, claiming to be messengers delivering flowers to Major Adams. The next day, Adams is reported dead, and the "messengers" enter a lieutenant's quarters. Steve and Bucky find the lieutenant dead and pursue, arriving at the Yellow Claw's hideout. They quickly defeat the villains, but Bucky smells the assembled flowers and collapses, poisoned. Cap rushes Bucky to a hospital, saving him. Retrieving a flower from the lieutenant's quarters, Steve has it tested to confirm it secretes poison. After Bucky leaves the hospital, the duo crash a military ball, warning that the flowers are poisoned. Elliot tries to shoot Cap but Betty stops him. When General Berry drops dead after smelling a flower, Betty realizes Cap's warning is true, but Yellow Claw has an underling abduct her, then sends Steve a note, ostensibly from Betty, implying she is eloping with Elliot. Later, Claw sends another note to Steve, threatening Betty's life. Cap and Bucky rescue Betty, kidnap the actress playing in the film of the same name. Although Elliot sends a warning letter to Steve Rogers, he is surprised when Cap and Bucky arrive shortly afterward, indicating the letter was indeed intended for Betty's friend Steve, not for Cap. Steve calls Duffy "Sour-Face Duffy" once here.

3RD STORY: "The Imp" (10 pages)

CREDITS: Stan Lee (writer), Chad Grothkopf (art)

FEATURE CHARACTER: The Imp (also as "the Demon of the Lake")

SUPPORTING CAST: Jefferson Vandermeer

VILLAINS: Gruesome Gus & his 2 "hired thugs"

OTHER CHARACTERS: Police officer, villagers, donkey, horse, alligator

LOCATIONS/ITEMS: City inc jail & Gus' hideout, Jeff's isolated house; wagon, thug's gun, Gus' begging cup and sign, Imp's "Demon of the Lake" figure

SYNOPSIS: Out for a walk one night, Jeff summons the Imp for company, but Gruesome Gus and his thugs abduct Imp and threaten to shoot Jeff if he follows. The next day, in a neighboring city, Gus binds Imp with a leash and passes him off as an undernourished child to collect money from sympathetic citizens. When Imp's leash breaks, he flees. Reuniting with Jeff, Imp distracts Gus so Jeff can beat him up, but the thugs overpower Jeff and take him to a river to feed him to an alligator. Imp, using a large branch with foliage that gives it a human shape, impersonates "the Demon of the Lake" and frightens the three so badly they seek safety in the city jail, where a police officer commends Jeff and Imp.

NOTE: Title has exclamation point on Contents page. Jeff's connection with the Imp appears to have become common knowledge between CapC#13/4 '42 and this story. It is unclear how Gruesome Gus could so easily capture the Imp, who has proven strong enough to escape people before. At story's end, the Imp declares he bought a savings stamp to "serve [his] country, " making his stories' setting even vaguer.

4TH STORY: "Elmer" (3 pages)

CREDITS: Mike Sekowsky (pencils), George Klein (inks)

FEATURE CHARACTER: Elmer (trouble-prone pre-adolescent)

SUPPORTING CAST: "Pop" (Elmer's father), Elmer's friend

OTHER CHARACTERS: Mr. Mason (bank president), police officer, Elmer's mother (mentioned only), Smith family, Jones family (both bts, Elmer puts letters in their mailboxes)

LOCATIONS/ITEMS: Elmer's house (damaged by explosion) & neighborhood, bank; chemistry set, love letters, "Crime and Criminals" book, advertisement for All Winners Comics (posted on fence)

SYNOPSIS: For Elmer's birthday, Pop gives him a dollar, but when Elmer buys a chemistry set, Pop declares it too dangerous and tells him to return it; Elmer sneaks the set to his room and mixes chemicals, inadvertently proving Pop right when he creates an explosion that sends them both flying from the house. Later, Elmer plays postman by delivering "old letters" from the attic, but Pop thrashes him after learning they were love letters he wrote when courting Elmer's mother. He subsequently reads about supposed criminal characteristics and tackles a man who fits the description, but his target is bank president Mason, who nearly has Elmer arrested.

NOTE: Title has exclamation point on Contents page.

5TH STORY: "The Secret Stamp" (7 pages)

CREDITS: Don Rico (pencils), George Klein (inks)

FEATURE CHARACTER: The Secret Stamp

SUPPORTING CAST: Spud Sickles, Jerry Dash

VILLAINS: Three-Man-Blitzkrieg: Mr. Lenz, Otto & one other (Nazi spies)

OTHER CHARACTERS: Mrs. Jones & Mr. Cane (Roddy's customers), police officer, Minuteman (on Defense Bond stamp only)

LOCATIONS/ITEMS: Mr. Lenz's house (on Cedar Road) & tunnel network beneath, Mrs. Jones' house, Mr. Cane's house, Freetown Star office; Roddy's bicycle & stamps, Spud's bicycle, Lenz's gun, lead pipe, dynamite plunger

SYNOPSIS: Mr. Lenz refuses to buy Roddy's defense stamps. Suspicious, Roddy, as Secret Stamp, stakes out Lenz's house. When two men visit, he follows them down a passage to an underground chamber, where Lenz waits. Lenz elaborates on the trio's planned "three-man blitzkrieg" to create panic by crippling Freetown's electric, gas, and water supply stations -- beneath which Lenz's tunnels lead -- as a test run for New York. Secret Stamp charges in but is distracted when Spud enters the chamber. Shot in the left arm by Lenz, Stamp feigns unconsciousness and is dumped outside while Spud is tied up. Stamp radios Jerry to report spies at Lenz's house. Rushing back inside, Stamp finds Spud, whom he leaves behind to pursue Lenz and company through the tunnel. There, Lenz and Otto prepare to set off dynamite charges beneath supply stations, but Stamp, armed with a lead pipe, knocks out Otto, dismantles the dynamite plunger, then knocks Lenz out, leaving "signature" stamps on both men's foreheads. He departs, leaving them for Jerry, the freed Spud, and the police.

NOTE: Title has exclamation point on Contents page. Story followed by "Sentinels of Liberty Secret Club News" (1 page) w/"Important Announcement!" & "Bucky's Column" featuring Captain America & Bucky.

TEXT STORY: "The Commandos!" (2 pages)

CREDITS: Writer unknown

FEATURE CHARACTERS: Captain Clive (Australian Forces officer) & his Commandos (at least 90 soldiers, in 3 units, under Clive's command)

SUPPORTING CAST: Clive's commanding officer, additional soldiers

VILLAINS: Two platoons of Japanese soldiers (all die)

OTHER CHARACTERS: "Wild Beasts" of British Malaya (bts, previously traversed jungle paths), the Commandos (a famous military unit, mentioned only, see NOTE)

LOCATIONS/ITEMS: British Malaya (see NOTE), British-held and Japanese-held regions; Japanese supply trucks (destroyed), both sides' pistols, grenades & axes

SYNOPSIS: Inspired by the Commandos' activities in German-occupied Norway, Clive forms his own units to penetrate enemy lines. After killing one platoon, they bomb a supply caravan, killing more enemy soldiers. Chopping down trees to block an enemy highway and leave it more open to aerial view, they return to their own sector.

CAPTAIN AMERICA COMICS #15 (June 1942)

"The Tunnel of Terror!" (20 pages)

CREDITS: Otto Binder (writer), Al Avison (pencils, c art), Syd Shores, Al Gabriele (inks), Stan Lee (editor)
FEATURE CHARACTER: Captain America
SUPPORTING CAST: Bucky (chr last in SgtF #13, '64), Betty Ross, Sgt. Duffy
VILLAINS: The Earthmen (Nazis impersonating Subterraneans), Fritz Krone (fifth column leader) & his bodyguard, fifth columnists & Bundists disguised as street cleaners, beggars, police & sailors (some die), Nazi soldiers (Moeller, von Bosh named), Nazi lieutenant (Krone's commanding officer, dies)
OTHER CHARACTERS: Foreman & tunnel workers, radio announcer, radio employee, Mayor Fiorello La Guardia, two mayoral aides, steamer captain (crew bts), US destroyer crew, US soldiers, Manhattan citizens inc crowd at Mayor's speech, Adolf Hitler (in photograph only)
LOCATIONS/ITEMS: Manhattan inc Grand Central Station, Times Square, restaurant, radio station, City Hall, Krone's hideout & Nazi officer's office at 250 Gabriele Towers, Governor's Island, East River & underground tunnels beneath it, Nazi subterreanean mine chamber with attached submarine refueling station & tunnel leading to Brooklyn waterfront warehouse (sign obscured, possibly "Teas & Spoons"), Liberty Island w/ Statue of Liberty; the Mary Ann (ferry), steamship, US destroyer, Earthmen's guns, Krone's machine gun, knife & tunnel map, Nazi officer's grenades, fifth columnists' clubs & knives, smoke-bombs, mines, pineapple grenades, floating periscopes, construction workers' explosives, naval depth charges, disguised Bundist's "The Wave of the Future" sign, air pump flywheel
SYNOPSIS: Fifth columnist Fritz Krone sends his men to spread fear as part of his plan to evacuate Manhattan. Steve, Bucky, and Betty Ross encounter several such defeatists. In Times Square, a fifth columnist uses smoke bombs to spread fear of a Nazi gas attack until Steve reveals the smoke is harmless. While Betty pursues the fleeing bomber, Bucky chases another columnist. Meanwhile, construction under the East River destroys a tunnel wall. Armored figures emerge and attack, causing a panic. The mayor appeals for Cap to investigate. Cap battles the "Earthmen," but is captured and taken underground to a Nazi torture chamber. Betty and Bucky chase their separate quarries, converging at a waterfront warehouse where they find mines, grenades, and a secret entrance to a Nazi arsenal and shooting gallery. The Nazis overpower them and take them underground to join Cap in a dungeon. Krone tells them that the underground construction broke into their underwater "mine chamber," and that his operatives, dressed as "Earthmen," emerged to scare the authorities away from investigating. He releases mines to explode in the East River, but Cap, Bucky, and Betty escape. In Manhattan, Krone's commanding officer spreads further destruction with grenades, but Cap and Bucky storm his office where a ricocheting bomb blasts him out his window to his death. A US destroyer arrives in the East River. Cap and Bucky help them target the Nazis' underground chamber with depth bombs. The Nazis are forced to the surface, where Manhattan citizens fight them. Cap fights Krone, who surrenders. Cap reminds the crowd not to believe planted rumors.
NOTE: Contains "Table of Contents" (1 page) featuring Captain America, Bucky & Minuteman (on Defense Bond Stamp). Story called "Captain America and the Tunnel of Terror!" on Contents page. In the final panel, Cap and Bucky sing, "Heigh-ho, heigh-ho, it's back to Sergeant Duffy we go," a take-off on the song "Heigh-Ho" from the Walt Disney film "Snow White and the Seven Dwarfs" (1937).

2ND STORY: "To the Land of Nod" (10 pages)
CREDITS: Stan Lee (writer), Chad Grothkopf (art)
FEATURE CHARACTER: The Imp
SUPPORTING CAST: Jefferson Vandermeer
VILLAINS: Morpheus ("god of sleep"), Nightmare (Morpheus' burro), the Moon-Mad Monster & 3 gnomes (Morpheus' creations), several trees animated by Moon-Mad Monster), sharks
OTHER CHARACTERS: Sir Reginald Lamp O'Lime (only app, Jeff's lamp, animated by Morpheus), the furniture army (Jeff's bed, bureau, & other furnishings, animated by Morpheus), elephant, bird (both Morpheus' creations)
LOCATIONS/ITEMS: City inc Jeff's house, forest, Morpheus' cloud; Morpheus' "nightmare dust," Sir Reginald's whip, gnomes' stewpot
SYNOPSIS: While the Imp and Jeff sleep, Morpheus amuses himself by tossing "nightmare dust" on Jeff. Morpheus' magic seemingly brings Jeff's furniture to life, but one item, a lamp calling itself "Sir Reginald Lamp O'Lime," calms the other furnishings. Observing from a cloud, Morpheus creates the Moon-Mad Monster, who, failing to notice the tiny Imp, targets Jeff and Sir Reginald, who run in different directions. The Monster brings nearby trees to life, and they capture both. Imp helps Sir Reginald free his hands, and the sound of his whip summons the furniture army to attack. As furniture and trees clash, Imp, Jeff and Sir Reginald flee. Morpheus creates gnomes who lasso the trio with their tails. Not wanting the fun to end so soon, Morpheus creates a shark-filled ocean around Imp and Jeff, but laughs so hard he falls to the ground. The impact "awakens" Imp and Jeff back at home.
NOTE: Story called "The Imp and His Nightmare!" on Contents page. It is unclear how much, if any, of the Imp and Jeff's encounter with Morpheus' forces occur in their objective reality instead of in a dream. The Imp enters Jeff's left ear to go to sleep but emerges from his right, literally going in one ear and out the other. Story followed by "Attention Americans" (2 pages), a special announcement asking readers to buy fewer comic magazines then donate that extra money to "Captain America's War-Fund." Cap will match the money and send it to President

3RD STORY: "The Invasion From Mars" (20 pages)
CREDITS: Bill Finger (writer), George Klein (co-inks) (see NOTE)

FEATURE CHARACTER: Captain America (next in AllWin #5/2, '42, Inv #29-37, '78-'79)

SUPPORTING CAST: Bucky, Sgt. Duffy (both next in AllWin#5/2, '42), Gen. Haywood (last in AllWin #4/2, '42)

VILLAINS: The Gool (Ludwig, Nazi operative disguised as Martian warlord) & his "Martians" (disguised Nazi operatives), Nazi transport ship crews (most die)

OTHER CHARACTERS: Camp Lehigh soldiers (many die), Gotham City mayor (dies), police (at least one dies), newsboy, radio announcer, drunk, Martha, her husband & son (prev 3 die), bystanders (at least 2 die), US navy ship crews, Orson Welles (mentioned only, by Martha's husband & Gool)

LOCATIONS/ITEMS: Gotham City inc City Hall w/mayor's office & roof, radio station & Martha's home (see NOTE); Camp Lehigh; army-commandeered ferries (all but one destroyed), Nazi transports, US navy ships, bus to Camp Lehigh (#2017), Martians' modified lugers, "red death ray machine" (spotlight with papier-mache shell), stilts, time-bomb (only 1 shown, all destroyed) & rays guns (symbolic splash page only)

SYNOPSIS: In Gotham City, a policeman pulls over a car driven by a 10-foot-tall Martian who runs over two people. On leave, Bucky tackles the Martian who quickly knocks him away. Bucky returns to Camp Lehigh, but neither Duffy nor Steve believe him until a Martian raids the camp. Martians appear throughout the city. One man, recalling Orson Welles' "War of the Worlds," scoffs at radio reports, but a Martian breaks in and kills him and his family. Cap and Bucky arrive but the Martian escapes, dropping a German luger disguised as a "Martian Gun." Cap sends Bucky to summon the army. "The Gool, Martian Warlord" & his men raid City Hall and force the mayor to order an evacuation. Cap intervenes, but the Martians overcome him. Gool kills the mayor, intending to use Cap to broadcast a surrender order. Leaving Cap bound, the Martians activate their "red death ray machine" on the roof, aiming it at army-commandeered ferries in the river. Some ferries explode but Bucky finds a time-bomb on his ferry and throws it out a porthole, saving the ship. Bucky fights his way to City Hall and rescues Cap. They knock out the "death ray" operators, discovering the machine is a fake to make people believe its "ray," not time-bombs, destroyed the ferries. Remembering the luger, Cap unmasks one Martian as a human on stilts and realizes the "invasion" is a Nazi plot. Re-entering City Hall, Cap and Bucky defeat the Martians. Cap broadcasts to US naval forces, who sink the Nazi ships, then announces the invasion's true nature to the relieved city.

NOTE: Story called "Captain America and the Invasion from Mars!" on Contents page. Penciler and George Klein's co-inker are unknown. "Gotham City" is perhaps Manhattan here, however "New York" is referenced here as if it is a different city and the murdered mayor is clearly not Fiorello La Guardia, who, furthermore, did not die in 1942. Genuine Martians attacked Manhattan in MC #3, '40, but were presumably never identified as such, explaining public skepticism here. Genuine Martians next appear in CapC #70, '49. Orson Welles misspelled "Wells" here.

4TH STORY: "The Secret Stamp" (7 pages)

CREDITS: Mike Sekowsky (pencils), Don Rico (title page pencils), George Klein (inks)

FEATURE CHARACTER: The Secret Stamp

SUPPORTING CAST: Spud Sickles, Jerry Dash

VILLAINS: Grandmaw (Nazi spy), Butch & his associate (Grandmaw's underlings)

OTHER CHARACTERS: Mary Sickles (Spud's sister, 1st), Mr. Corbey (Star subscriber), Minuteman (on Defense Bond stamps)

LOCATIONS/ITEMS: Sickles home, Mr. Corbey's house, "Old Walsey House" (spy base); Spud's Secret Stamp costume, Roddy's newspaper satchel, spies' whip & pistol, Freetown Star

SYNOPSIS: Jealous of Secret Stamp, Spud, with his sister Mary's sewing supplies, makes his own Stamp costume. Roddy, on his delivery rounds, overhears Grandmaw's spy ring plotting against Secret Stamp. That night, Grandmaw's agents encounter Spud dressed as Stamp. They easily knock him out and take him to their base where Spud fearfully confesses his imposture. Secret Stamp intervenes and allows himself to be captured to learn more. Elsewhere, Jerry Dash and Mary, searching for Roddy, hear Spud's cry for help. They burst in as a spy prepares to torture Secret Stamp. Dash knocks out one spy, and Secret Stamp the other. As Stamp departs, Dash prevents Grandmaw from escaping. The next day, Spud boasts to Roddy that he will be "helping" Secret Stamp from now on.

NOTE: Grandmaw also spelled "Grandma" here. Story followed by "Captain America Secret Club News (1 page) w/ "Message From Captain America!" & "Bucky's Column" (which solicits letters about the Imp), featuring Captain America & Bucky.

TEXT STORY: "The Secret of Lost River Cave" (2 pages)

CREDITS: Writer unknown

FEATURE CHARACTER: Dave (an 18-year-old rancher)

SUPPORTING CAST: Sam (Dave's older brother), Dave and Sam's mother

OTHER CHARACTERS: Mr. Lewis (general store owner), cattle, a bat, albino fish (7 die), Mr. Presser (mortgage holder on Dave's ranch, mentioned only), Dave's biology teacher (mentioned only), Mr. Lewis' brother (grocery chain owner, mentioned only)

LOCATIONS/ITEMS: Dave's family ranch inc ranch house, Elida (New Mexico) inc Lewis Grocery Store, Commanche Draw, Arias Arroyo, Lost River Cave w/Lost River within; Dave's pickup truck & flashlight, arroyo gages in road, coals for campfire

SYNOPSIS: Lacking money to pay the ranch mortgage, Dave's mother sends him to Elida to sell her diamond heirlooms. Partway there, rain-induced flooding blocks both Dave's path to Elida and the path back home. That night, he seeks shelter in Lost River Cave, from whose underground river he catches fish who have developed albinism and atrophied eyes. He cooks and eats some. The next morning, with the road clear, he drives into Elida and gives fish to general store owner Lewis. After tasting it, Lewis offers to pay Dave to bring more, which Lewis' brother can sell in the East. Dave agrees, pleased to have found a way to earn mortgage money.

NOTE: Story called "Secret of Lost River Cave!" on Contents page. Story appears between 2nd and 3rd stories.

"The Horror of the Seas" (20 pages)

CREDITS: Manly Wade Wellman (writer), Al Avison (pencils, c art), Syd Shores, George Klein (inks), Stan Lee (editor)

FEATURE CHARACTER: Captain America

SUPPORTING CAST: Bucky, Sgt. Duffy (both last in AllWin #5/2, '42), Betty Ross (next in YA #4, '42), Gen. Haywood

VILLAINS: The Hooded Horror (Nazi officer disguised as Laison King, also in pfb, only app) & the Followers of the Yellow Hoods ("the Hooded Horde," Nazi officers & operatives disguised as Laisons, also in pfb, many die), the Laisons (green-skinned Subterraneans, many die) inc the Laison King, the High Priest & assistant (only app), the Sea Monsters (Laisons' monstrous companions, many die, only app), diner counterman, Valley Port hotel manager, Viking captain & crew (in fb only)

OTHER CHARACTERS: The Laison Queen of centuries ago (the King's distant relative, fb only, only app) & Laisons & Sea Monsters of her era (fb only), Camp Lehigh soldiers, Eddie & Sally (abducted by Laisons, die), Littleton ticket vendor, bus driver (dies), bus passenger, diner patron, Vikings' descendants (fb only, many die), 2 FBI agents (killed bts a week prior to story), Lai-Son (also "Laison," the Laisons' goddess, as statue), miniature armored figure (hotel decoration), fish, birds (in fb only)

LOCATIONS/ITEMS: Camp Lehigh inc general HQ, Lehigh City train station, Littleton (train ride's distance from Lehigh City), Valley Port (also "Valleyport" & "Valley-Port," bus drive's distance from Littleton) inc hotel w/lobby and Betty's room, Hooded Horror's headquarters inc torture room & harbor, Satan's Reef, diner on road to Valley Port, the Kingdom of Lai-Son (subterranean city beneath Satan's Reef) inc undersea entrance with air-locks, passageway to inner sanctum, cells, private quarters of the Hooded Horror, musty passageway & Temple of Lai-Son, the Island of Lai-Son & Laison community beneath it (fb only), Vikings' descendants' town inc harbor (fb only); gold treasures, Viking ship, Laisons' duplicate Viking ship (prev 3 fb only), Eddie's car, bus (wrecked), High Priest's sword, flaming brazier & sacrificial altar, Hooded Horror, Laison King & Followers' maces, Nazis' firearms, dynamite, drugged coffee, counterman's cleaver

FLASHBACK: Vikings visit the Isle of Lai-Son, marry Laison women, but steal Laison treasures, and depart (see NOTE). The Laisons search for them for centuries, eventually finding the Vikings' descendants' town, where they kill men and abduct women. They build the Satan's Reef city beneath the sea, frightening off the Valley Port residents. Nazis investigate the deserted Valley Port. Their officer imprisons the King and, as the Hooded Horror, impersonates him (p).

SYNOPSIS: At Camp Lehigh, following a football game, Gen. Haywood assigns Steve to accompany Betty Ross to Valley Port to investigate multiple bus accidents. From Littleton, Betty takes a bus to Valley Port, and Steve, as Cap, follows. At a diner, the counterman drugs the driver's coffee. Soon after, the bus crashes. Cap pulls Betty and the dead driver from the wreck. Reaching Valley Port, Betty checks into a hotel, but the manager alerts the Hooded Horror, who sends his followers and Sea Monsters to capture her. Bucky, who has followed Cap, tries to rescue Betty but is captured, and both are taken to an underground city. Cap finds the captive Laison King, freeing and accompanying him to prevent the Laisons from sacrificing Bucky and Betty. When the King reveals the Nazis' deception, the High Priest declares all humans must die. Although Cap and company escape, the Laisons and Monsters massacre Hooded Horror's Nazis. The King directs Cap to dynamite the underwater city, but when Cap departs, reveals that the blast will kill Cap as he abducts Betty for his Queen. Bucky defeats the King, alerts Cap, and they escape as the city is destroyed.

NOTE: Contains "Table of Contents" (1 page) featuring Captain America, Bucky & Minuteman (on Defense Bond stamp). Story called "Captain America and the Horror of the Seas!" on Contents page. During their football game, Duffy, with unwitting irony, sarcastically calls Steve "All America." The goddess Lai-Son, worshipped by a subterranean race, may be one of the Gods of the Netherworld who were, as revealed in Av #306, '89, worshipped by the subterranean Gortokians. The Hooded Horror refers to Cap as the "greatest of [the USA's] heroes," a comparatively rare acknowledgement that Cap co-exists with other heroes. The Vikings who visited the Laisons may have arrived in the same exploration wave, circa AD 1000, as the Vikings seen in MCP #63/4, '90, who established the Vinland colony but were later slain or vampirized by Varnae. Although the Red Skull appears on the cover (fighting Cap & Bucky in his "terror chamber," with 2 underlings and a woman who may be Betty Ross present), the events depicted there bear no relation to the contents of the 4th Story.

2ND STORY: "Imp" (7 pages)

CREDITS: Stan Lee (writer), Chad Grothkopf (art)

FEATURE CHARACTER: The Imp (final app)

SUPPORTING CAST: Jefferson Vandermeer (final app)

VILLAINS: 8 pirates (only app)

OTHER CHARACTERS: Stan Lee & Chad Grothkopf (as splash page caricatures), Minuteman (on Defense Bond stamp)

LOCATIONS/ITEMS: Shore of land of Imp's town, "treasure isle" inc tree beneath which treasure chest is buried, Jeff's house; Jeff's rowboat, ship, spyglass, shovel & map, pirates' ship w/Jolly Roger & firearms, 2 other ships, treasure chest full of money bags and coins

SYNOPSIS: Imp and Jeff set sail to find a "treasure isle," unaware a pirate ship is following. Using a map, they find a treasure chest, which the pirates promptly claim at gunpoint, taking it and Jeff back to their ship. Stowing on board, Imp knocks the head pirate into the treasure chest. Blaming Jeff, the pirates have him walk the plank, but Imp intervenes, dropping the sail on the pirates. Imp and Jeff tie them up. Later, Imp and

3RD STORY: "Percy" (1 page)

CREDITS: Mike Sekowsky (pencils), George Klein (inks)

FEATURE CHARACTER: Percy (pre-adolescent boy, 1st, next in CapC #18/4, '42)

OTHER CHARACTER: Sally (pre-adolescent girl)

LOCATIONS/ITEMS: Percy's neighborhood inc open manhole; manhole cover, "Bijou To-Night" poster, Percy and Sally's roller skates

SYNOPSIS: Hoping to impress Sally, Percy performs skating tricks, but while skating backwards, he falls into a manhole.

NOTE: Story not listed on Contents page.

4TH STORY: "Red Skull's Deadly Revenge!" (24 pages)

CREDITS: Stan Lee (writer), Al Avison (pencils), Syd Shores, George Klein (inks)

FEATURE CHARACTER: Captain America (next in YA #4, '42, Inv #38-41, '79, Cap #11, '05 fb)

SUPPORTING CAST: Bucky (next in YA #4, '42), Sgt. Duffy

VILLAINS: Red Skull (also as archer, last in CapC #7, '41, chr last in SgtF #25, '65, also in YA #4, '42 fb, next in YA #4, '42, see NOTE), Brute Benson (dies), Duke Shores & Igor ("Man of a Thousand Nameless Terrors") (all past Skull hirelings, all possibly last, unnamed, in CapC #7, '41, Shores & Igor possibly next in YA #4, '42), 4 other henchmen (on symbolic splash page only)

OTHER CHARACTERS: Camp Lehigh soldiers, prison guards (1 dies), "Dr. Bat" (see NOTE), telegram carrier, army officer w/war plans, War Department officer & guard, 2 newsboys, costume shopkeeper (bts, sells costumes to Cap & Bucky), police officer (dies), 3 civilians (1 dies), farmer (as corpse, used by Skull to fake death, see NOTE), Minuteman (on Defense Bond stamp)

LOCATIONS/ITEMS: Camp Lehigh inc kitchen & Steve and Bucky's tent, archery range on Camp Lehigh's outskirts, prison & adjoining marshland, Manhattan inc Red Skull's hideout at 22 Black Road (possibly last in CapC #7, '41) w/dungeon & adjoining cemetery, City Bank, Benson, Shores & Igor's apartments, Dr. Bat's office, city hospital, US Defense office, War Department office, costume shop (# 620 on unidentified street), Star Air-Port, Red Skull's crime scenes throughout USA; Red Skull's plane, bow and arrows w/ropes, archer disguise & knife w/cord, 2nd plane (NC 67442), guard's key, Igor's drill, Benson, Shores & Igor's pistols, Cap's crime clippings & wallet, Cap & Bucky's storebought costumes, Bucky's file, defense plans & other government documents

SYNOPSIS: The Red Skull escapes prison, learns archery, then recruits former henchmen Shores, Igor, and Benson, killing Benson when he rebels. Cap and Bucky find Shores and Igor robbing City Bank, but while Cap defeats them, the Skull shoots Bucky with an arrow. Cap rushes his friend to a doctor, then returns to Camp Lehigh, unaware the Skull has followed. Consulting his files, Cap travels to the Skull's last known hideout, but the Skull takes him by surprise, pinning him to a dungeon wall with arrows and pounding him unconscious. Learning Cap's secret identity from his wallet, the Skull takes Cap's costume & shield. He embarks on a month-long nation-wide crime spree, during which he impersonates Cap to steal defense plans. Reports of the crime motivate the still-recovering Bucky to locate the Skull's hideout and free Cap. The two acquire replacement costumes and track the Skull and company to an airport. They make short work of Shores and Igor, but the Skull takes off in a plane. Cap and Bucky manage to cling to the plane's tail. While fighting Cap, the Skull falls, and Cap and Bucky land to find his corpse, with evidence he, not Cap, stole the plans.

NOTE: Story called "Captain America and the Red Skull's Deadly Revenge!" on Contents page. On page 4, many weeks pass between the Skull's escape in panel 3 and the shift to Camp Lehigh in panel 4, yet, oddly, the news of his escape does not reach Lehigh until those weeks have passed. The Skull's shirt emblem changes from a stylized "rising sun" to a swastika in mid-story. While Bucky recuperates in the hospital, his costume is apparently stored or stolen, since he must later acquire a new one. When the Skull pins Cap's arms to his dungeon's wall, he apparently pins him by the shirt sleeves concealed beneath Cap's gloves (if he had only pinned the gloves, Cap could slip out of them), demonstrating truly extraordinary marksmanship. When impersonating Cap, the Skull wears Cap's cowl over his skull mask and shields his lower face from observers rather than simply remove his Skull mask. The doctor's nameplate is slightly obscured by the Skull's bow but appears to say "Dr. Bat." The Skull's YA #4, '42 fb appearance takes place between panels 6 & 7 of page 24 of this story. As revealed in YA #4, '42, the Skull does not fall to his death, but unseen by Cap & Bucky, parachutes safely to the ground, kills a farmer, exchanges clothes with the corpse, leaves it to be mistaken for his own, and flees before Cap & Bucky land the plane, though why he leaves the evidence clearing Cap on the corpse is not known. Story followed by "Sentinels of Liberty Secret Club News" (1 page) featuring Captain America and listing the winners of the Captain America Coloring Contest.

5TH STORY: "The Secret Stamp" (7 pages)

CREDITS: Mike Sekowsky (pencils), Paul Reinman (inks)

FEATURE CHARACTER: The Secret Stamp

SUPPORTING CAST: Spud Sickles (next in CapC #18/7, '42), Jerry Dash

VILLAINS: Titus Locke (newspaper & tool works magnate), 2 reporters, Mr. Snull (ticket vendor), rabble rouser, lynch mob

OTHER CHARACTERS: Freetown's DA (1st), police scientist, police, grand jury, bystanders, Ella Wright (reporter, dies bts, in photos only), Minuteman (on Defense Bond stamp), Patrolman Moriarity (mentioned only, in newspaper)

LOCATIONS/ITEMS: Train station inc ticket booth, DA's office, police lab, intersection of Cross Lane & Martin Street, jail, meeting hall, Jerry's house, Lonely Oaks (lynching trees), Freetown Court House; train, Jerry's pistol (registration #W-455-623), watch, chain, wallet & other personal effects, Roddy's bicycle and newspapers (Freetown Star), Spud's newspapers (Freetown News), ticket stubs, noose

SYNOPSIS: The day after Jerry travels to Chicago, his co-worker Ellen Wright is found dead, and the News' owner Titus Locke, accusing Jerry of the crime, provides the DA with the recovered murder weapon, a pistol registered to Jerry. Spud finds Jerry's watch chain at the murder scene. Jerry is arrested upon his return, but Secret Stamp forces ticket vendor Snull to hand over Jerry's ticket stub, providing an alibi. Jerry is released, but a town meeting rabble rouser inspires vigilante action. A mob grabs Jerry to lynch him, but Secret Stamp dissuades them with a patriotic speech. Noticing one of Locke's reporters has Jerry's watch, Secret Stamp exposes Locke and company as the true culprits. Jerry reveals he visited Chicago to corroborate Ella's findings of Locke's war-profiteering and union-breaking activities. Locke kills Ella thinking she still has her notes, then frames Jerry and bribes Snull to withhold evidence.

NOTE: Title has exclamation point on Contents page. The story does not clarify how Locke acquired Jerry's pistol. Roddy Colt is incorrectly called "Ronny" on page 3, panel 5 and page 7, panel 9.

TEXT STORY: "Pacific Voyage" (2 pages)
CREDITS: Writer unknown
FEATURE CHARACTER: Narrator (also in pfb)
SUPPORTING CAST: Dick (narrator's friend, pfb only)
VILLAIN: An octopus (pfb only, dies)
OTHER CHARACTERS: Junk's former owner, Hong Kong quay bystanders, reporter & other Californians, flying fish & other types of fish (some die) (all pfb)
LOCATIONS/ITEMS: Hong Kong, Pacific Ocean inc small islet, California inc dock, newspaper office, "ruins of ancient towns, temples, volcanic mountains, and glamorous cities" (bts, narrator & Dick's tour destinations); Chinese junk/boat, narrator & Dick's money, supplies, sea coats, blankets, kerosene lamp, slickers & rain hats, matches, pole, knives, newspaper (all pfb)
FLASHBACK: Following a vacation in "the Orient," the narrator and Dick impulsively purchase an antiquated Chinese junk to sail back to the USA. After various travails -- including a storm, shipwreck upon an islet, and an octopus attack -- the two, on the seventh week of their voyage, reach California, where a newspaper reports on their accomplishment of crossing the Pacific Ocean on such a flimsy craft. Although declared heroes, the two decide nothing could persuade them to make the voyage again (p).
SYNOPSIS: The narrator thinks back to his Pacific voyage.
NOTE: Story title has exclamation point on Contents page. Story appears between 3rd & 4th Stories.

CAPTAIN AMERICA COMICS #17 (August 1942)

"The Monster from the Morgue" (12 pages)

CREDITS: Al Avison (pencils, assoc editor, c art), Syd Shores, George Klein (inks), Stan Lee (managing editor)
FEATURE CHARACTER: Captain America
SUPPORTING CAST: Bucky (last in YA #4, '42, chr last in Cap #11, '05 fb)
VILLAINS: Killer Kole (executed criminal whose brain is transplanted into a gorilla's body, only app, also in newspaper photo as human, dies), 2 gorillas (recruited from Wengler Brothers' Circus by Kole)
OTHER CHARACTERS: Dr. Thomas Austin (also in newspaper photo), Dr. Jason Weirdler (dies), Judge Hudson (also in newspaper photo, dies), Judge Basset (also in newspaper photo, dies), Judge Johnson (also in newspaper photo), nurses, medical school students & other observers, Wengler Brothers Circus employees inc ticket taker, Wilcox, Musser (both litigants before Judge Basset), attorney, cab driver, elevator operator, police, firefighters, reporters, bystanders, 3 bailiffs (2 in newspaper photo only), Dr. Frankenstein (mentioned only, by Bucky), Frankenstein's Monster (mentioned only, by Weirdler), 2 masked criminals (on cover only)
LOCATIONS/ITEMS: Camp Lehigh inc Steve & Bucky's tent, Manhattan inc Harkness Medical College w/Dr. Weirdler's office, Dr. Austin's office, Operating Room No. 2 & morgue, cemetery, Central Park, Judge Hudson's home inc bedroom, Dr. Weirdler's home, Municipal Courts Building inc General Sessions Courtroom, Judge Johnson's apartment building inc apartment & roof, Police HQ, & Wengler Brothers' Circus inc tents & gorilla cage; Austin's Elixir 23Y, "Doctor Austin's Mistake" tombstone, Kole's noose & knife, jar w/Kole's brain, Judge Basset's gavel
SYNOPSIS: Dr. Austin develops Elixer 23Y to resurrect the dead, with a dead circus gorilla as test subject, but rival Dr. Weirdler replaces the gorilla's brain with that of dead criminal Killer Kole so that, even if successful, Austin will discredit himself by creating a monster. Austin's experiment fails, and medical students clothe and bury the gorilla corpse, but a lightning bolt brings it to life: Killer Kole's mind controlling the gorilla's body. Answering his gorilla instinct, Kole breaks into Wengler Brothers' Circus and frees two gorillas who act as his underlings. Cap and Bucky investigate and defeat the gorillas, but Kole escapes and kills Judge Hudson, one of three jurists who sentenced him to death. The next day, he kills Judge Basset, escaping in a commandeered taxi. Cap and Bucky pursue him to Judge Johnson's apartment. Kole throws his knife at Cap, but Dr. Weirdler, repenting his actions, arrives and steps into the blade's path, dying from the wound. With police & firefighters at the scene, Kole leaps atop an extension ladder, where he and Cap battle. Caught in a stranglehold, Cap has no choice but to knock Kole several stories to the ground, killing him.
NOTE: Contains "Table of Contents" (1 page) featuring Captain America & Bucky. Story called "Captain America Combats the Monster from the Morgue!" on Contents page. Designated "Case 4472-F." Kole states that he remembers Cap from over a year before but provides no context for the remark; neither Cap nor Bucky show any sign of having encountered Kole before. Cap sings "The Man on the Flying Trapeze" here.

2ND STORY: "Rookie McQuirk" (5 pages)
CREDITS: Red Holmdale (writer/art)
FEATURE CHARACTER: Joe "Rookie" McQuirk (also called "Quirk," potato peeler pitchman turned soldier, only app)
SUPPORTING CAST: Mack (McQuirk's civilian friend), Sgt. Thunder (McQuirk's sergeant), Blackout (McQuirk's fellow soldier & tentmate)
OTHER CHARACTERS: Soldiers inc guards, street crowd
LOCATIONS/ITEMS: City inc recruitment office, army camp inc kitchen, guardhouse & McQuirk and Blackout's tent; train, handcar, tanks, artillery battery, rifles, McQuirk & Blackout's duffle bags, McQuirk's "Zipp the Wonder Potato Peeler" case/stand, draft notice, potatoes, dice
SYNOPSIS: Bored with his potato peeler job, McQuirk is thrilled to get drafted but finds himself peeling potatoes in the Army, although he briefly tricks Blackout into peeling some for him. McQuirk and Blackout anger Sgt. Thunder by disassembling an artillery battery, instead of a rifle as

3RD STORY: "Sub-Earthmen's Revenge!" (20 pages)
CREDITS: Al Avison (pencils), Syd Shores, George Klein (inks)
FEATURE CHARACTER: Captain America

SUPPORTING CAST: Bucky, Sgt. Duffy, Gen. Haywood (next in AllWin #6/3, '42)

VILLAINS: The Spook (Hans Knutte, reporter and Nazi agent, only app) and his Sub-Earthmen followers (some die), 3 fifth column arsonists, posse inc Millbrook sheriff, Clem, general store owner & others

OTHER CHARACTERS: Queen Medusa (only app) & the Sub-Earthmen (neanderthal-like Subterranean race ruled by Queen Medusa, some die, 1st, see NOTE), the Sub-Earthmen's steeds (giant wormlike creatures, 1st, see NOTE), Gen. Keller, Capt. Brooks (bts on phone), DFK radio announcer, soldiers from Camp Lehigh & Midwest camp (some die), reporters, soldiers in anti-Sub-Earthmen attack force (some die), Millbrook citizens (some die), the Satan in Satin (villain from untold story, mentioned only by Bucky), Queen Medusa's father and the "top world man" who taught him English (both deceased, mentioned only by Queen Medusa), the Red Skull, the Black Talon, Dr. Crime (mentioned only, by Spook), Human Torch (on cover of comic read by Bucky)

LOCATIONS/ITEMS: Millbrook (Midwest town) inc general store, sheriff's office w/jail & Radio Station DFK, adjacent army camp inc ammunition building & tents (destroyed), the Sub-Earthmen's Subterranean territory & hilltop encampment, Spook's cave; army's trucks, tanks, motorcycles & planes, posse's car & truck, supply trucks (wrecked), jeep, motorcycle (wrecked), Spook's machine gun, Sub-Earthmen's firearms, arsonist's machine gun, Clem's rifle, DFK microphone, issue of "Human Torch" (read by Bucky) and other comic books, shovel, pick

SYNOPSIS: As Midwest army maneuvers begin, reporter Hans Knutte criticizes the American soldiers. Soon after, explosions set the local camp ablaze. Cap and Bucky pursue the arsonists, who escape. The explosions damage the Sub-Earthmen's underground territory. Queen Medusa leads her race, astride their worm steeds, to the "Top World," emerging near Millbrook. They seek peace but Clem, a hunter, spies them, shoots, kills one and flees. In town, Steve and Bucky overhear Clem tell the locals his story and follow a posse that kills more Sub-Earthers. Cap and Bucky protect Medusa, but the sheriff arrests her. Later, the pair free her and escort her to her people in the hills. Later, the costumed Spook, a Nazi operative, offers to help Medusa conquer the "Top World." She refuses, but some Sub-Earthmen follow him and invade Millbrook, killing many. Soldiers mobilize against them. Cap and Bucky rescue Medusa from Spook's men, although Spook escapes. Leaving Bucky to protect Medusa, Cap departs, promising to stop the army, but Spook knocks him unconscious. When the army attacks, Spook leads his forces into battle. When Cap returns, he and Bucky overcome the Sub-Earthmen, then sue for peace on their behalf. The army withdraws. As reporters question Gen. Haywood, Cap recognizes Knutte's voice as the Spook. After one Cap punch, Knutte confesses.

NOTE: Story called "Captain America and the Sub Earthmen's Revenge!" on Contents page. The Spook is presumably in league with the arsonists, but this is never confirmed. The Sub-Earthmen might be the same as other hidden races in later Timely/Atlas stories; their wormlike steeds somewhat resemble another type of Subterranean fauna, the Kraawl, from FF #127, '72. Unlike her subjects, Queen Medusa has a human appearance, implying she is not entirely of the same species. Hans Knutte also spelled "Knute" here.

4TH STORY: "The China Road" (6 pages)

CREDITS: Jimmy Thompson (art)

FEATURE CHARACTER: The Fighting Yank (Bill Prince, only app)

VILLAINS: Ah Kee (Agent X5, Japanese spy disguised as Chinese interpreter, dies), other Japanese operative, Agent B7 (Japanese operative, bts, contacted by Ah Kee), Japanese soldiers

OTHER CHARACTERS: Prince's commanding officer, Chinese soldiers, truck drivers & civilians

LOCATIONS/ITEMS: China inc Win Weh Pass, Prince's CO's headquarters & enemy agents' tent w/radio equipment; Chinese convoy trucks, both armies' firearms inc machine guns, Japanese commander's sword, Ah Kee's dagger, wrench & signal mirror

SYNOPSIS: In China, US operative Fighting Yank accompanies a supply convoy, unaware his interpreter Ah Kee is a Japanese spy and has alerted the enemy of the convoy's route. The Japanese attack at Win Weh Pass, and during the battle, Yank slips among enemy forces and attacks them with a machine gun, forcing their withdrawal. Yank stops Ah Kee from sabotaging a truck, but Ah Kee knocks him out with a wrench and throws him off a cliff. The fighting resumes until Yank climbs back up to again rout the enemy, and Ah Kee commits hari-kari.

NOTE: Story called "The Fighting Yank" on Contents page. Regrettably, the Yank and his commander are openly contemptuous of their Chinese allies. The Yank is later referenced in USAgent #4, '93; he should not be confused with the Fighting Yank (Bruce Carter III), who was hinted to exist in the Marvel Universe in Av #92, '71.

5TH STORY: "Machine of Doom!" (12 pages)

CREDITS: Al Avison (pencils), Syd Shores, George Klein (inks)

FEATURE CHARACTER: Captain America

SUPPORTING CAST: Bucky, Sgt. Duffy

VILLAINS: Professor Clement Mott (insane scientist, dies), le Bull, Chico, Armand, & Pierre (all 4 Vichy operatives, all die, also in pfb); Vichy admiral (pfb only, called "Mon Chef" by le Bull), Vichy guard (pfb only)

OTHER CHARACTERS: Jensen (Mott's assistant, dies), radio announcer (voice only), Vichy France residents (pfb only)

LOCATIONS/ITEMS: Camp Lehigh, Murky Swamp inc Mott's island laboratory, Vichy France inc French Academy (pfb only), Manhattan, Burma inc Burma Road, ocean; Mott's inventions inc Cosmic Depressor, Gravity Retractor, electrical barrier (all destroyed), ships at sea, Vichy plane, Steve's car, Cap's glider, Mott's books (inc "The World of Atoms" & "Molecules for Destruction"), Mott's pistol, Vicky operatives' firearms & parachutes

FLASHBACK: Five days earlier, a Vichy Admiral orders le Bull & his men to parachute into Murky Swamp & seize Mott's Cosmic Depressor (p)

SYNOPSIS: Horrified by the war, Prof. Mott, in his quicksand-surrounded lab, decides to halt the evil by destroying the Earth. He prepares his Cosmic Depressor to disintegrate all matter within 48 hours. Meanwhile, Steve and Bucky drive near Murky Swamp. Their car tumbles in and Bucky is lost in the quicksand. Le Bull's forces parachute down, and Cap fights them. When Cap is caught in quicksand, they reach Mott who traps them between electrical bars. Escaping the quicksand, Cap returns two days later, via glider, and reaches Mott, who levitates him with a Gravity Detractor. The 48 hours up, people, objects, and buildings across the world begin gradual disintegration. Bucky, having survived in a subterranean tunnel, emerges from a trap door and punches Mott, who disintegrates entirely. Bucky shuts down the Compressor, but accidentally frees le Bull and company, knocking le Bull into a panel which shuts off the Retractor. Le Bull grapples with the Compressor controls before fleeing and sinking into quicksand. Cap and Bucky, pursuing, witness the lab exploding, killing le Bull's men.

NOTE: Story called "Captain America Defies the Machine of Doom!" on Contents page. The location of Murky Swamp (and nearby Camp Lehigh) is erroneously given as Florida. It is not known why Cap waited 2 days to resume his pursuit of le Bull, nor how Bucky survived for 2 days in a subterranean tunnel with no food or water. A radio announcement declares that "Except for Switzerland and Eire, the government of every nation of the world presses for a decision in this war," a dubious statement at best. According to Prof. Mott, cosmic rays strike all matter at a speed of 600 miles per second, and their speed is responsible for holding matter together; his Cosmic Depressor can accumulate cosmic rays and slow them to only 100 miles per second, thus causing matter to lose cohesion and disintegrate into dust.

6TH STORY: "The Secret Stamp" (7 pages)
CREDITS: Mike Sekowsky (pencils), Paul Reinman (inks)
FEATURE CHARACTER: The Secret Stamp (also dubbed "Kid Launcelot" by police officer)
SUPPORTING CAST: Jerry Dash (last app to date), Mr. and Mrs. Colt (Roddy's parents, 1st, next in CapC#21/5, '42)
VILLAINS: 2 "enemy aliens" (only app)
OTHER CHARACTERS: Freetown's DA, Mrs. Tompkins, Mr. Eckman (Vital Statistics Bureau chief), Miss Kemp (Roddy's teacher), Roddy's classmates, doctor, two police officers (Pat named), Snoopy (Eckman's dog), Charlie (Jerry's co-worker, bts on phone), police chief (bts on phone)
LOCATIONS/ITEMS: Freetown High School, Colt home, Tompkins home, Eckman home, DA's home, Criminal Courts Building inc police laboratory; enemies' car & pistol, 2 hypodermic needles, birth certificates, Roddy's bicycle, newspapers & defense stamps
SYNOPSIS: When Snoopy, Mr. Eckman's dog, shows up in the Colt yard, Roddy follows him back to Eckman's house and finds a man fleeing from the cellar. As Secret Stamp, he attacks the man, who escapes with another in their car. Inside the house, Secret Stamp finds Eckman in a stupor, along with birth certificates strewn about. Having followed Roddy, Jerry enters and finds a hypodermic, suspecting Eckman of dope addiction, then, finding isulin, of being a diabetic. As a doctor arrives, Secret Stamp finds another hypo outside. The two men return, seeking something they left behind but police, previously summoned, round them up. The next morning, Stamp takes the second hypo to the DA for prints. In class, Roddy asks his teacher about the Vital Statistics Bureau, where Mr. Eckman works, then returns, as Stamp, to the DA, who reveals the hypo yielded prints of "a much hunted enemy alien." The two realize the criminals sought birth certificates as false ID for sabotage work, using the hypo to drug the diabetic Mr. Eckman, and the DA has the pair turned over to the FBI.
NOTE: The DA refers to "the Ella Wright case" from CapC #16/5, '42. On page 3, panel 4, Secret Stamp is erroneously drawn as Roddy. The implication is that Mr. Eckman is a diabetic accounting for the hypo Jerry finds in the house but that the criminals dope Eckman with the hypo Secret Stamp finds outside. This, however, is never stated outright. Roddy & his classmates recite the Pledge of Allegiance here, saying "one nation, indivisible, with liberty and justice for all" since the phrase "under God" is not added until 1954. Story followed by "Sentinels of Liberty Secret Club News" (1 page) w/"Message from Captain America" &" Bucky's Column" featuring Captain America & Bucky.

TEXT STORY: "Situation Wanted: I Got an Action Story" (2 pages)
CREDITS: Mortimer Breen (writer)
FEATURE CHARACTER: "Mortimer Breen" (1st person narrator, pulp writer)
OTHER CHARACTERS: Wilbur (soda jerk), editor, artists, "Thunder" Wenczikowski (dubbed "Beefy Boy" & "Big Stuff" by narrator, East Jersey light-heavyweight boxer), "Thunder"'s manager (dubbed "Sharpey" by narrator), 2 police officers, "Irish" Farbstein (boxer mentioned by narrator), Brooklyn Dodgers & New York Giants (discussed by narrator & Wilbur), Michelangelo di Lodovico Buonarroti Simoni (Renaissance artist, mentioned by narrator), person to whom narrator relates his story
LOCATIONS/ITEMS: Magazine office, drug store inc soda fountain & prescription dept; Hartford Arena (mentioned by narrator); manager's .38 pistol, narrator's papers, pipe cleaners, pipe & malted milk, Thunder's parfait, officers' notebooks, 7-gallon water jar (destroyed), water pail, magazine rack, month-old issue of "Daring Deeds," additional drug store items, $100 bill
FLASHBACK: Assigned to write an action story, a writer, distracted by office workers, seeks solace at a soda fountain. A large man enters and orders a parfait, but the dish is shattered by a .38 bullet. The man seemingly departs, but after the police come and go, the narrator and Wilbur find him still in the store, throwing around items in frustration. The narrator tries to throw a large jar at the man, but it too is shot. He learns the big man is a boxer and the gunman his manager, who wants him to keep his weight down and thus literally shoots snacks out of his hands. The writer's careless mention of one of the boxer's defeats earns him a final knockout. Recovering, the writer still needs an action story idea and, his experience's applicability completely lost on him, he steals and edits a story from a rival magazine.
SYNOPSIS: Pestered as to where he got the plot of the story he is about to write, the narrator relates his recent adventure.
NOTE: Story not listed on Contents page. Story appears between 3rd & 4th Stories.

(September 1942)

"Bowling Alley of Death!" (15 pages)

CREDITS: Syd Shores (pencils), Don Rico (inks), Stan Lee (managing editor), Al Avison (c art, assoc editor)
FEATURE CHARACTER: Captain America
SUPPORTING CAST: Bucky (also as pin-boy), Sgt. Duffy
VILLAINS: Gigo (Peter G. Higorovitch, head of US arm of Holy Ring, former czarist general, only app) & several members of Holy Ring (secret order of anti-democracy Russian czarists, working for Nazis)
OTHER CHARACTERS: Camp Lehigh soldiers inc camp bowling team (Bob named) & gunners expert section team (1 dies), MPs, major, billiard players, librarian, library patron, 2 police officers
LOCATIONS/ITEMS: Camp Lehigh inc Steve and Bucky's tent, mess hall & other tents, Gigo's Recreation Parlor w/bowling alley & pool hall inc underground chamber, loading dock & freight elevator, library, Russian restaurant inc Holy Ring HQ, drug store, police station (88th Precinct); Gigo & his men's firearms & daggers, bowling balls inc trick balls with spring clamps in thumbholes, bowling pins (1 equipped with .22 caliber cartridge, launched by catapult), billiard balls & cues, silverware w/Holy Ring insignia, adhesive tape, vitriol bottle, Bucky's pin-boy clothes, Greek newspaper
SYNOPSIS: Steve and Bucky join other soldiers at Gigo's new bowling alley, but two are injured by bowling ball sabotage and a third, struck by a pin, is killed by a .22 caliber bullet. Steve gets Bucky to go undercover as a pin-boy, where he learns some balls are specially equipped to injure players. Hearing this, Steve tries to prevent a Major from bowling but, angered that a Private is interfering on Officer's Night, he calls the MPs. Steve escapes and, as Cap, prevents the Major's murder but Gigo and his men capture and take him into a secret passage. Bucky intervenes, helping Cap break free. Pursuing Gigo, they are struck down by a freight elevator. Gigo locks them beneath a bowling alley, with their heads visible to be struck by bowling balls, but the Major and MPs rescue them, although Gigo escapes. Noticing Gigo's thumb has left a "P" print on his bowling ball, Cap checks a library and learns the Greek letter Rho, which resembles a P, symbolizes the Russian Holy Ring. Finding a hideout at a Russian restaurant, Cap burns a "P" onto his thumb to show at the door, gaining entrance, and he and Bucky defeat the Ring members, including Gigo.
NOTE: Contains "Table of Contents" (1 page) featuring Captain America, Bucky & Minuteman (on Defense Bond stamp). Story called "Captain America and the Bowling Alley of Death!" on Contents page. Final panel of story features an ad reading, "Cap and Bucky will ask for Terry-Toons Comics at their newsstand. Will you?"

2ND STORY: "Captain America and the Tomb of Horror!" (12 pages)
CREDITS: Otto Binder (writer), Al Avison (art)
FEATURE CHARACTER: Steve Rogers (as Captain America in dream sequence only, next in GSInv #2, '05, Inv #1-4, '93, Mv #1, '94, ThorCp #1-2, '93, AllWin #6, '42, CapC #18/3, '42)
SUPPORTING CAST: Bucky Barnes (as costumed Bucky in dream sequence only, chr next in Inv #1, '93 fb, next in AllWin #6/2, '42), Sgt. Duffy (also in dream sequence, next in AllWin #6/2, '42)
OTHER CHARACTERS: Camp Lehigh soldiers, Prof. Harold Wembly (National Museum of New York archaeologist, also as the Black Talon in dream sequence), 3 camels, ants, the Horrors of the Nether World (over a dozen "demons, furies, werewolves, vampires," 2 resemble mummies, dream figures only), the Toad (as "the Black Toad," dream figure only), Betty Ross (as dream figure only), Frankenstein Monster (mentioned in caption only)
LOCATIONS/ITEMS: Egypt inc Pyramids (interior w/Tomb of Horror, Casket Chamber, iron maiden & other devices in dream sequence only), Tomb of Tut-Ka-Aamen (mentioned only); hieroglyphic
SYNOPSIS: In Egypt, following a 10 mile hike, Steve and Bucky are assigned by Duffy to be archaeologist Wembly's bodyguards while he seeks a priceless hieroglyphic tablet within a Pyramid. Exhausted, Steve and Bucky fall asleep outside. Steve apparently awakens as Wembly insists he and Bucky accompany him inside. After opening the Tomb of Horror to unleash demons, Wembly unmasks as the Black Talon. The demons overwhelm Cap and Bucky, and Talon takes them to the Casket Chamber, where the Black Toad, another Cap enemy, awaits. Duffy bursts in, knocking out Talon and some demons. Cap and Bucky recover and join the fight, and Duffy leads them to where Betty Ross is menaced by more demons. After her rescue, Betty reveals a romantic involvement with Duffy, much to Cap and Bucky's astonishment. When Duffy and Betty depart, the villains and demons resume the fight, and as Cap strikes Black Talon, Steve awakens to find it has all been a dream. Wembly having uncovered the hieroglyphic tablet, the trio return to Duffy.
NOTE: Story is actually 11½ pages long w/last half page containing ad reading, "But this is no dream - - Terry-Toons will be on sale soon!" Steve's dream inaccurately depicts Betty as his fiancee. Story followed by "A Special Message to the Boys and Girls of America from Henry Morgenthau, Jr. - Secretary of the Treasury!" (1 page) about defense stamps & featuring Minuteman (on Defense bond stamp).

3RD STORY: "The Mikado's Super-Shell!" (16 pages)
CREDITS: Al Avison (pencils), Syd Shores (inks)
FEATURE CHARACTER: Captain America (next in YA #5, '42)
SUPPORTING CAST: Bucky (last in AllWin #6, '42, next in YA #5, '42), Betty Ross (last in YA #4, '42, next in CapC #33/3, '43)
VILLAINS: Paw (large-handed Japanese genius), his two assistants & his two tigers (all die), Japanese soldiers (some die), 2 Japanese sailors, German spy
OTHER CHARACTERS: Camp Lehigh soldiers, USO dancers inc Steve's partner, 4 army officers, KING radio operator (voice only), Army pilots (most bts), Navy sub commander, USS Washington captain, sailors (some bts), 2 Japanese monks
LOCATIONS/ITEMS: Camp Lehigh (severely damaged), inc USO dance hall, dam 2000 miles from Camp Lehigh (destroyed), Army general HQ, Station KING w/radio tower, German spy's hideout, Japan inc Yokahama Harbor, temple & weapons complex inc Paw's chamber, Pearl Harbor; Weapon T-7 (long-range gun capable of dispatching shells across the Pacific Ocean, destroyed), Army planes inc flying fortress, USS

Washington (Navy ship), US Navy destroyer & sub, Japanese 2-man sub, tank & seaplane, Japanese soldiers' firearms, giant shell fragment, Paw's battleaxe & maces, monks' robes, Cap's machine gun & time bomb

SYNOPSIS: During Camp Lehigh's USO dance, a giant shell strikes the camp, but no aircraft is detected. Miles away, a dam undergoes a similar attack. Having received word from Betty Ross, in Japan on assignment, of a new weapon, Army officials send Cap and Bucky to retrieve her and destroy the weapon. A spy relays their mission to Paw, the weapon's genius inventor, who holds Betty prisoner. Following transport by plane, ship, and sub, Cap and Bucky hijack a Japanese sub and dock at Yokahama Harbor. They commandeer a tank to raid Paw's military complex, where they are taken captive. A gloating Paw brings them and Betty to see his gigantic long-range gun that can fire rockets into the USA. Cap breaks his bonds, grabs a machine gun and frees Bucky and Betty. Japanese soldiers storm the compound, and Cap reluctantly shoots them down. He sets a time bomb on the weapon, then leads Bucky and Betty up the weapon barrel. Paw meets them at the end, but Cap pushes him into the ocean. Cap and company then hijack a seaplane, taking off just as Paw's complex and weapon explode. The three rendezvous with a ship to return to the USA.

NOTE: Story called "Captain America and the Mikado's Super-Shell" on Contents page. In this story, Cap, although noting that he "hate[s] to do this," deliberately kills enemy soldiers for the first time. Betty reveals the plans for Paw's weapon are drawn on her back in invisible ink, a moderately risqué notion for the era. Story is actually 15¾ pages long. Final ¼ page contains ad reading, "Watch for Terry-Toons Comics."

4TH STORY: "Percy" (1 page)
CREDITS: Mike Sekowsky (pencils), George Klein (inks)
FEATURE CHARACTER: Percy (last app to date)
OTHER CHARACTERS: Performer in gorilla costume, sideshow barker, clown, circus attendees
LOCATIONS/ITEMS: Circus inc tents & cages; Percy's slingshot, performer's cudgel, circus equipment
SYNOPSIS: Visiting a circus sideshow, Percy slingshots an apparent caged gorilla, but the gorilla is a costumed performer who easily exits the cage and furiously chases Percy.
NOTE: Story not listed on Contents page.

5TH STORY: "The Fighting Fool!" (7 pages)
CREDITS: Don Rico (pencils), Al Gabriele (inks)
FEATURE CHARACTER: The Fighting Fool (Wade Huston, ex-ANZAC, Australia & New Zealand Army Corps, only app)
SUPPORTING CAST: Napoleon "Nap" Sack (ex-Free French Army member, only app)
VILLAINS: Herr Mongrel (only app, dies) & his Nazi underlings (all die)
OTHER CHARACTERS: ANZAC officer, steward (other ship crew bts), 3 police officers, truck drivers (bts, die), supply train crew (bts, most die), supply ship crew (bts, most die)
LOCATIONS/ITEMS: ANZAC general HQ, Australian waterfront w/dock, Manhattan inc apartment, waterfront w/dock & abandoned warehouse, Liberty Island w/Statue of Liberty, leading highway into New York, countryside outside New York w/train track; 2 trucks and train carrying food, supply ship (all destroyed), ship to USA, Mongrel & company's car, remote-controlled mines, firearms, blackjacks & explosives, Wade's piece of broken glass
SYNOPSIS: After being shot in both lungs while fighting Nazis, Huston recovers but is forcibly retired from ANZAC service. Wanting to fight Nazi spies, he takes a ship to the USA. En route, he rescues a passenger who falls overboard, Napoleon Sack, another would-be Nazi fighter, and the two decide to share adventures. Meanwhile, Herr Mongrel's spies are cutting off Manhattan's food supply by sabotaging trucks and train travel. Wade, whom Sack dubs "a Fighting Fool" for his eagerness for trouble, reads of the incidents, and he and Sack investigate. At the waterfront, they find Mongrel testing a remote-controlled mine, with which he destroys a supply ship. The duo fights well but is defeated. Mongrel ties them up in a warehouse, but Wade uses glass to cut his bonds and free Sack. The two set Mongrel's car speeding toward the Nazis. Its impact sets off the mines, killing the villains.
NOTE: Story title lacks exclamation point on Contents page. Final panel of story features ad reading, "The New Terry-Toons Comics as Sensational as Krazy Komics!"

6TH STORY: "Dippy Diplomat" (1 page)
CREDITS: Guy Blythe (writer, art)
FEATURE CHARACTER: Dippy Diplomat (diplomat from unidentified nation, 1st)
OTHER CHARACTERS: 2 movers
LOCATIONS/ITEMS: "Dippy's world" (a comedic version of Earth, setting of all Dippy Diplomat stories, see NOTE) inc Dippy's residence; "We Move Stuff Incorporated" truck, Dippy's possessions inc piano, table, chest, bureau, carpet & birdcage
SYNOPSIS: Moving to a new residence, Dippy helps the movers carry his possessions to their truck, but he wears himself out so much that they have to carry him to the truck as well.
NOTE: Story not listed on Contents page. "Dippy's world" may or may not be one of the comedic versions of Earth already presented in various humor features.

7TH STORY: The Case of the "Costumed Crook" Starring Roddy Colt, the Secret Stamp!" (6 pages)
CREDITS: Don Rico (pencils), Al Avison (inks)

clown, cowboy, gaucho, musketeer, pirate & others), Mr. Bruce (Roddy's customer), Minuteman (on Defense Bond stamp), dog (on billboard)
LOCATIONS/ITEMS: Freetown High School, Colt home, school principal's home, Mr. Bruce's house, criminals' hideout; Roddy's bicycle, newspapers & defense stamps, classmates' costumes, principal's safe w/jewels

SYNOPSIS: When the school holds a costume party at the principal's home, Roddy uses his costume to go as Secret Stamp. Two criminals, wanting to rob the principal, waylay Roddy and steal his costume, which one, Spike, wears as a party attendee. He finds the principal's safe, but Roddy, having recovered, sneaks in the back way and knocks him out. Reclaiming his costume, he lures the second criminal inside and knocks him out as well, then departs, returning to the party as uncostumed Roddy.
NOTE: Story called "The Secret Stamp" on Contents page.

8TH STORY: "Dippy Diplomat" (1 page)
CREDITS: Guy Blythe (writer, art)
FEATURE CHARACTER: Dippy Diplomat (next in CapC #20/5, '42)
SUPPORTING CAST: Mergetroide (Dippy's chauffeur, 1st, next in CapC #21/4, '42, see NOTE)
OTHER CHARACTERS: 2 diplomats, 2 police officers, 2 guards, zoo animals inc giraffe, 2 hippos, 2 zebras, 2 seals
LOCATIONS/ITEMS: Dippy's embassy inc bathroom w/tub, zoo; 2 police motorcycles, Dippy's limousine, pocket watch & globe, seal's ball
SYNOPSIS: Dippy and other diplomats visit the zoo. A seal's ball-balancing performance so impresses Dippy that, at home, he tries it himself, balancing a globe on his nose while in the bathtub.
NOTE: Story not listed on Contents page. Dippy's use of a globe as a plaything is reminiscent of a scene in Charlie Chaplin's film "The Great Dictator" (1940). Mergetroide named in CapC #21/4, '42. Story followed by "Sentinels of Liberty Page" (1 page) featuring Captain America, Bucky & the Red Skull in a contest for the reader to find the errors in the picture made by "our careless artist."

TEXT STORY: "The Yanks Are Coming!" (2 pages)
CREDITS: Writer unknown
FEATURE CHARACTER: Pvt. Pete Jones
VILLAINS: Japanese soldiers (many die) & engineers
OTHER CHARACTERS: US commander ("officer in charge"), US soldiers (some die), Australian soldiers, Australian civilians, narrator ("ordinary American boy," see NOTE)
LOCATIONS/ITEMS: US army camp, US port, Australian army camp, Pacific Ocean, Japanese-occupied island hundreds of miles off Australia inc jungle, hills & north shore w/Japanese military encampment (w/tents, lumber pile & dock); US transport ships, lifeboats, Japanese planes, US firearms & grenades, Japanese firearms
SYNOPSIS: Drafted into the army, Pete Jones accompanies his platoon to Australia, where they are assigned to break Japan's hold on a neighboring island. Penetrating jungle growth, Pete is given the honor of the first shot, as the soldiers attack the Japanese base, killing most enemy soldiers and accepting surrender from the survivors. The unit returns to Australia in triumph.
NOTE: Story not listed on Contents page. The narrator is not a character here but the story begins in first-person with the narrator stating, "Private Jones was an ordinary American boy, just as you and I." Story appears between 2nd and 3rd stories.

CAPTAIN AMERICA COMICS #19 (October 1942)

"The Crocodile Strikes! Case #A1625-R: Case of the Haunted Mansion!" (17 pages)

CREDITS: Al Avison (pencils, assoc editor, c art), Syd Shores (inks), Stan Lee (managing editor)
FEATURE CHARACTER: Captain America
SUPPORTING CAST: Bucky (last in YA #5, '42), Sgt. Duffy (last in AllWin #6/2, '42)
VILLAIN: The Crocodile (Freeman Mosher, gardener & criminal, only app)
OTHER CHARACTERS: Jane Crawford, Mrs. Crawford (her grandmother), Professor Ratcher (history professor, dies), Mose (butler), Thomas (servant, dies), southern Army camp's commanding officer, Army pilot, horse, owl, black cat, bats, Colonel Crawford (Crawford ancestor, mentioned only, writer of February 13, 1860 letter), Mosher (Freeman's ancestor) & his gang (mentioned only in 1860 letter), cavalier, Elizabethan (both in paintings only), 3 robed villains (on cover only)
LOCATIONS/ITEMS: Southern US Army camp w/stables & commanding officer's office, airport, forest swamp inc Crawford Mansion ("old plantation mansion") w/cellar, parlor, Jane's room, Ratcher's room, Mrs. Crawford's room & hidden passages; airplane, two-man parachute, mansion's suit of armor, large statue, grandfather clock & vault, family documents, Mosher's flashlight, Crocodile's daggers & pistol, bedpost w/ jewels, coffins (on cover only)
SYNOPSIS: In the South on maneuvers, Steve and Bucky test a new two-man parachute. The two are blown into a forest swamp ending up near a plantation mansion. There, they see a giant crocodile standing on two legs, who strangles a man, then departs. Steve and Bucky investigate the mansion. As Cap and Bucky, they return that night, where the Crocodile attacks, knocking both out. When they recover, they question the mansion's occupants: Mrs. Crawford, her granddaughter Jane, butler Mose, and Prof. Ratcher, who is compiling the Crawford family history. Gardener Mosher interrupts, claiming to have seen the Crocodile. Later, Crocodile attacks Mose, but Cap and Bucky intervene. Escaping, Crocodile later returns, and Cap knocks him into a grandfather clock, which hides a passage through which the villain escapes. He next threatens Jane, whom Cap and Bucky rescue. Soon after, Ratcher is found dead, but Cap peruses his documents and learns a treasure is concealed in Mrs. Crawford's room, where Crocodile is attacking. Cap identifies him as Mosher, descendant of a Civil War-era criminal, then knocks him out and unmasks him. He reveals the treasure, hidden in a post of Mrs. Crawford's bed.
NOTE: Contains "Table of Contents" (1 page) featuring Captain America, Bucky & Minuteman (on Defense Bond stamp). Story called "Captain America Fights When the Crocodile Strikes!" on Contents page. The title "Case of the Haunted Mansion" appears in the upper left margin of each page except splash page.

2ND STORY: "Human Torch" (7 pages)

CREDITS: Al Bellman (pencils), George Klein (inks)

FEATURE CHARACTER: Human Torch (last in MC #36, '42, chr last in Mv #1, '94, next in MC #37, '42)

SUPPORTING CAST: Toro (last in MC #36, '42, chr last in Mv #1, '94, next in MC #37, '42)

VILLAINS: Gordon Bell (see NOTE, former deep sea diver, killer plant user, also in pfb, only app) & his Bloodsuckers (several dozen tropical plants which grow from seeds to feet-long vines within seconds, some destroyed)

OTHER CHARACTERS: John A. Hart (treasure hunter, also in pfb bts, dies), police chief, woman (in portrait only), fish (in pfb only), ants (bts, mentioned by Torch), the "Devil" (on symbolic splash page only), Captain Flint (Long John Silver's parrot from Robert Louis Stevenson's "Treasure Island," mentioned only, by Torch), Captain William Kidd (mentioned only, Toro sarcastically calls Torch "Cap'n Kidd")

LOCATIONS/ITEMS: Hart's home w/swimming pool, surrounding countryside in which Torch and Toro picnic, police HQ, South American coast (in pfb only); Hart's ship (in pfb only), recovered sunken treasure (also in pfb), Gordon's diving suit (in pfb only), Hart's ring, portrait concealing treasure, Torch & Toro's picnic lunch, Gordon's waterproof seed sack

FLASHBACK: With Gordon as diver, Hart's expedition finds sunken treasure off a South American coastline (p).

SYNOPSIS: Torch and Toro's picnic is interrupted by a scream. Rushing to a nearby cottage, they find blood-sucking vines strangling John Hart. Although Torch burns the vines, Hart dies of blood loss. He and Toro wait until nightfall, when a man breaks into the cottage. Torch and Toro confront him, but he flees into a swimming pool. The two dive after him, but he releases seeds which quickly grow into vines, strangling Torch and Toro. Unable to flame on in the pool, Torch pulls Toro free, holding him out of the water. Toro regains his flame and rescues Torch. They destroy the vines and pursue the criminal, who has found hidden jewels, and quickly defeat him. He tells the treasure-hunting story, revealing he wanted the whole treasure for himself. Torch and Toro turn him over to local police.

NOTE: Story called "The Human Torch and the Vines of Doom!" on Contents page. Gordon's surname revealed in OHMU:HC #12, '10. Bloodsuckers possibly appear in later Timely/Atlas stories where people are victimized by bloodthirsty plants.

3RD STORY: "Your Life Depends on It! A Special Feature" (4 pages)

CREDITS: Stan Lee (writer), Al Avison (art)

FEATURE CHARACTER: Captain America

SUPPORTING CAST: Bucky

VILLAINS: 2 spies

OTHER CHARACTERS: Adolf Hitler, Hideki Tojo, 3 giant fire-breathing dogs, machinists, civilians, Axis Powers' victims, US soldiers, Japanese sailors & pilots (bts, in planes & ships), US pilots (bts) (all in imaginary images only, accompanying Cap's speech), Minuteman (on Defense Bond stamp)

LOCATIONS/ITEMS: Battlefields, Atlantic Ocean, Pacific Ocean, United States of America, factories, war room (all in imaginary images only, accompanying Cap's speech), police headquarters w/jail, hillside; Japanese airplanes, US airplanes, shells, enemy flags, war bonds (all in imaginary images only, accompanying Cap's speech)

SYNOPSIS: After Cap and Bucky capture two spies, Cap contemplates the dangers the USA faces from abroad and stresses the importance of buying war bonds to help the Allies defeat the Axis.

NOTE: Story called "Captain America in Your Life Depends on It! -- A Special Feature of Vital Importance!" on Contents page.

4TH STORY: "On to Berlin!" (24 pages)

CREDITS: Stan Lee (writer), Al Avison (pencils), Syd Shores (inks)

FEATURE CHARACTER: Captain America (next in CapC #20/6, '42, Cap:RW&B/6, '02 fb)

SUPPORTING CAST: Bucky (chr next in Cap #20/6, '42), Sgt. Duffy

VILLAINS: Adolf Hitler (also in portrait, last in YA #5, '42, next in MC #37, '42), Herr Demon (Gestapo head, only app), Kurt & his associate (spies), Gestapo officers (Hein named), German soldiers (many die)

OTHER CHARACTERS: General Spenser, US soldiers (some from Camp Lehigh) inc bugler, the Commandos (British soldiers), American Expeditionary Forces (AEF), War Ministry driver, War Ministry officials, reporters, British crowd, Berlin civilians, Scotland Yard representative (bts on phone), 2 officials (bts on phone), RAF pilots (bts in planes)

LOCATIONS/ITEMS: England inc dock, War Ministry offices, US army camp & English Channel, German Channel Coast inc lookout tower, Berlin inc Gestapo HQ; US Army transport ship Revenge, limousine, British commando barges, RAF planes, 2 bicycles, armies' firearms, German anti-aircraft gun, Gestapo's whips, firebrand, stake, firewood

SYNOPSIS: In England, US troops, including Steve and Bucky's regiment, arrive with well-known General Spenser. A limousine driven by Nazi spies abducts the General who is taken to Berlin. The real driver arrives, sparking an investigation. In Germany, Hitler oversees Spenser's interrogation. The British Commandos plan a rescue mission, and Duffy asks for volunteers to assist. Only Steve declines to volunteer, prompting Bucky to label him a coward. That night, the expedition departs. Steve, as Cap, swims the English Channel to join them. Although Nazi soldiers attack, Cap's arrival rallies the US and British soldiers to victory. Cap tells the soldiers he will rescue Spenser and departs, Bucky soon joining him. After hours of travel, the two enter Berlin, prompting Nazi soldiers to chase them. The city thus in confusion, Cap and Bucky head for Gestapo HQ, pausing to destroy a German anti-aircraft gun. At HQ, Spenser remains defiant, and Herr Demon is summoned to escalate the torture. Cap and Bucky burst in but are overwhelmed and imprisoned. Herr Demon boasts the Nazis will take Spenser to the Channel Coast and execute him before England's metaphorical eyes. Quickly escaping, the two arrive as Demon prepare to burn Spenser at the stake. The two are again outnumbered, but the Commandos in turn overwhelm the Nazis and rescue Spenser. To salvage Steve's reputation, Cap tells the Commandos "Steve Rogers" helped him get to Berlin. Later

"Spencer" here.

5TH STORY: "Roddy's Double Trouble" (7 pages)

CREDITS: Don Rico (art)

FEATURE CHARACTER: The Secret Stamp

VILLAINS: Spud Sickles (impersonates Secret Stamp, dubs himself "Napolean Spud Sickles," final app), Pete (also "Petey," Spud's friend, only app)

OTHER CHARACTERS: Jane (teenage girl), Bobby (Roddy's young friend), newsstand vendor, participants in "anti-American plot" (mentioned in headline, defeated shortly before this story), Minuteman (on Defense Bond stamp only)

LOCATIONS/ITEMS: Newsstand, costume store, Charles Street, Jane's house, other houses and buildings; fence on Charles Street, Roddy's bicycle, newspapers, war bonds, delivery bag, Spud's Secret Stamp costume, Freetown Star

SYNOPSIS: Irritated by Roddy's "goody-goody" nature, Spud hatches a plan with his friend Pete. First, Pete harasses Jane, and Spud, dressed as Secret Stamp, "saves" her. When Roddy, understandably curious, addresses "Secret Stamp," the latter claims to know what Roddy really does with the war bonds he's "supposed to be selling," alienating Jane from Roddy. After "Stamp" sweet-talks Jane and walks her home, Roddy follows and sees Spud unmask. Hatching his own plan, Roddy tells Jane she can learn "something very interesting" about Secret Stamp on Charles Street, then leaves Spud a note, daring him to meet her there. As "Stamp," Spud keeps the appointment, as does Jane, but Roddy, as the real Secret Stamp, shows up. Pete tries to help the fearful Spud, but the Secret Stamp quickly outfights them both, and Spud confesses his imposture. Jane dismisses Spud and, later, apologizes to Roddy.

NOTE: Story called "The Secret Stamp!" on Contents page. Spud previously impersonated Secret Stamp in CapC #15/4, '42, although he apparently destroyed the costume from that story in the interim, since he buys a new one here. Story followed by "Sentinels of Liberty Secret Club News" (1 page) w/"Cap Says" & "Bucky Says" featuring Captain America & Bucky. Although Cap promises that the Human Torch will be "appearing regularly," there is no Torch story next issue.

TEXT STORY: "Kid Patriotism Vs. the Reich"

CREDITS: Writer unknown

FEATURE CHARACTER: Bricks Lee (only app)

SUPPORTING CAST: Gramps Huston, Bricks' stickball club (Johnnsie, Smiley, Smitty named)

VILLAINS: Nazi U-boat crew (all die), Nazi spy (bts, his raft found)

OTHER CHARACTERS: US Navy seaplane crew, neighborhood children

LOCATIONS/ITEMS: New York inc Bricks' neighborhood w/schoolyard & adjacent beach, Atlantic Ocean; Nazi U-boat (destroyed), US Navy seaplane, 2 rowboats, buoy, rope, Nazi rubber boat w/leather-strap oarlocks & bellows, stickball equipment

SYNOPSIS: When Bricks' friends discover a spy's abandoned raft on the beach, local neighbor Gramps Huston suspects he is there to signal a U-boat. Bricks and his friends accompany Gramps at sea to watch for the spy's lights, but their two boats are separated. Bricks' crew encounters the U-boat itself. Bricks ties a buoy to the U-boat so that, even submerged, its presence can be detected. Later, a seaplane, with Gramps and crew, rescues Bricks' crew, and Bricks learns the buoy enabled the Navy to spot and destroy the U-boat.

NOTE: Story called "Kid Patriotism!" on Contents page. Story appears between 2nd and 3rd stories.

CAPTAIN AMERICA COMICS #20 (November 1942)

"The Spawn of the Witch Queen" (16 pages)

CREDITS: Al Avison (art), Stan Lee (managing editor), Syd Shore (assoc editor, c art)

FEATURE CHARACTER: Captain America

SUPPORTING CAST: Bucky (chr last in CapC #20/6, '42), Sgt. Duffy

VILLAINS: Spawn of the Witch Queen (Lawrence Thornton, aka Captain Tarleton, a resurrected mummy, "dies" and reverts to mummified form, only app) and his underlings (all die, Ankha and Ibi named)

OTHER CHARACTERS: US soldiers (some from Camp Lehigh), British soldiers, Colonel Fitzpatrick (dies), Barbec the Egyptian (British Intelligence agent, dies), Sir Gerald Thornton & servants (as corpses, died in 1941), Witch Queen (as mummified corpse), Isis (mentioned by Spawn), Anubis (mentioned in Book of Thoth), giant snake (dies), snake, 2 crocodiles (1 dies), bat (on splash page only), Nazi soldiers (on cover only)

LOCATIONS/ITEMS: Egypt inc pyramid w/Tomb of the Witch Queen, other pyramids & Sphinx, US/British army camp w/tents; army's rifles, Book of Thoth, Sir Gerald Thornton's diary, Witch Queen's altar, burning braziers, underlings' knives, Spawn's ropes, statues of Egyptian gods, sarcophagi, basket of wrappings, Nazi ammunition storehouse (on cover only)

SYNOPSIS: While Steve and Bucky are stationed in Egypt, Colonel Fitzpatrick is strangled. Cap and Bucky learn Fitzpatrick was studying the Tomb of the Witch Queen and the Book of Thoth, "the Bible of the ancient masters of black magic." Entering the tomb, Cap and Bucky are attacked by a giant snake. When Cap kills it, its death throes open a sealed room, containing the remnants of explorer Sir Gerald Thorton's second expedition. They find his diary that states that, in 1912, he and his expedition uncovered a mummified child, upon whom they performed rituals described by hieroglyphics, and a week later, found a living boy in the mummy's place that Sir Gerald adopted as his son Lawrence. A mummy-head apparation, identifying himself as the Witch Queen's son, warns Cap and Bucky to leave, but they continue to the inner tomb, where the masked Spawn of the Witch Queen and followers pray for the Witch Queen's revival. Spawn uses drugged smoke to incapacitate the two and prepares to entomb them as mummies, but Cap recovers. Unwrapping still-woozy Bucky, Cap rushes him outside, where Fitzpatrick's Egyptian servant Barbec and British officer Captain Tarleton have arrived. Cap returns to the tomb, but Spawn catches him in a noose. Recovered, Bucky finds Cap hung and cuts him down, but Cap's enhanced neck muscles prevent strangulation. The two find the Book of Thoth, but Spawn magically renders them immobile, then sets a crocodile on them. Barbec, revealed as a British intelligence agent, shoots the crocodile. The sound breaks the spell, and Cap burns the book, then punches out Spawn, unmasked as Tarleton, whom Barbec further identifies as the reborn mummy Lawrence Thornton. Spawn reverts to mummified form, but the gunfire's reverberations cause the tomb to collapse. Cap and Bucky escape, but Barbec is crushed beneath falling stones, as are the Spawn's underlings.

NOTE: Contains "Table of Contents" (1 page) featuring Captain America, Bucky & Minuteman (on Defense Bond stamp). Story called "Captain America and the Curse of the Witch Queen" on Contents page. Cap & Bucky next encounter a mummy in CapC #25/3, '43.

2ND STORY: "Sub-Mariner" (7 pages)
CREDITS: Carl Pfeufer (art)
FEATURE CHARACTER: Sub-Mariner (Prince Namor McKenzie, Atlantean, last in MC #36/2, '42, chr last in Mv #1, '94, next in MC #37/2, '42)
SUPPORTING CAST: Betty Dean (Namor's friend, last in HT #9/2, '42, next in MC #38/2, '42)
VILLAINS: Professor Holz (Nazi scientist, dies, only app) his men (all die) & his "Devil-Fish" (giant mutated manta rays, jellyfish, sharks, octopi, swordfish & others; some initially seen as normal sea life; one swordfish confirmed to die, others presumably die)
OTHER CHARACTERS: US Navy officers & sailors inc survivors of Devil-Fish attacks, fisherman, dead crews of 8 sunken ships, Holz's dentist (mentioned only)
LOCATIONS/ITEMS: US Navy Headquarters, Atlantic Ocean inc Holz's underwater laboratory w/fish tank & airlock (destroyed); US Naval ship (numbered "150"), 8 sunken merchantman ships, Holz's ray machine, Nazis' diving suits & gas gun, fisherman's boat
SYNOPSIS: In the Atlantic Ocean, giant fish wreck and sink several merchantman ships, cutting off supply lines. Betty Dean recruits Namor, who accompanies an outgoing ship. A giant swordfish attacks, but Namor snaps off its bill and impales it. The dead fish is magnetically drawn to an underwater Nazi base, Namor right behind, discovering Professor Holz and his men. Namor attacks, but a Nazi immobilizes him with a gas gun. Holz releases his latest mutated fish, intending to destroy New York Harbor. Recovering, Namor uses the base's magnetic force to recall the fish. As the fish batter the base, Namor withdraws, leaving Holz and company to die when the flooded base explodes in a short circuit.
NOTE: Story called "The Sub-Mariner" on Contents page. Namor's claim to have never seen such giant fish before indicates that, at this stage of his life (he is nearly 22), he is still unfamiliar with various monstrous fish-creatures that, in later years, he encounters and even commands. Namor next encounters Axis-created sea monsters in AllSel #2/5, '43.

3RD STORY: "The Case of the Killer Shylock!" (7 pages)
CREDITS: Don Rico (art)
FEATURE CHARACTER: The Secret Stamp
VILLAINS: Charles "Cherry" Chwatt (loan shark, only app) & 2 underlings, Curly (counterman at Cherry's candy store)
OTHER CHARACTERS: James White, Mrs. White (James' wife), Toddy White (James' son), elderly woman, police
LOCATIONS/ITEMS: Chwatt's candy store, White home, James White Meat Market (advertising "Fancy Fowl"), hospital, Moderne Garage w/"car elevator," city dump (bts, James White found there); cherries, phone booth (destroyed), Chwatt's gun, Stamp's note
SYNOPSIS: When butcher James White, client of loan shark Chwatt, disappears, Secret Stamp investigates. At Chwatt's candy store, from a phone booth, he watches Chwatt and his thugs threaten an elderly woman, but before he can intervene, the phone rings, alerting Chwatt and company to his presence. They rush the booth, and Stamp calls the police, prompting the criminals to flee. White is found beaten up at the city dump. Later, in the hospital, he agrees to testify. After bullying Chwatt's employee Curly for an address, Secret Stamp confronts Chwatt at the Moderne Garage, where he knocks out the loan shark and his thugs. Secret Stamp leaves a note for the police and departs.
NOTE: Story called "The Secret Stamp and the Killer Shylock" on Contents page.

4TH STORY: "The Fiend That Was the Fakir!" (15 pages)
CREDITS: Al Avison (art)
FEATURE CHARACTER: Captain America (next in AllWin #7/2, '42, USA #6, '42, CapC Spec #1, '09, Cap Ann, '98 fb, CapC #21, '42)
SUPPORTING CAST: Bucky, Sgt. Duffy (both next in AllWin #7/2, '42), General Haywood (last in AllWin #6/2, '42, next in CapC #24, '43)
VILLAINS: The Fakir (high priest, "King of Bowhanee," rebel & fanatic, dies, only app) & the Gangees (the Fakir's followers from "fanatical hill-tribes," some die), 2 Japanese pilots
OTHER CHARACTERS: US soldiers from Camp Lehigh (some die) inc buglar, renegade Gangee, Bengal tiger (dies), wild elephants, Kali (mentioned by Fakir), Bowhange ("god of the Gangees," mentioned by Fakir), cobra (on splash pages only)
LOCATIONS/ITEMS: Benares, India, inc US army camp w/tents on Ganges River bank, 2nd US army camp w/tents, Gangee cave stronghold & Ganges River w/temple of Kali; bridge, bandages & altar, soldiers' rifles, Gangees' rifles & swords, Fakir's sword & dagger
SYNOPSIS: General Haywood leads his troop to India, which Japan is preparing to invade in conjunction with the Fakir's Gangee saboteurs. After receiving arms from the Japanese, the Fakir leads a raid on the army camp. The soldiers fight back, and Cap and Bucky join the fray. When Fakir attacks Cap, Cap pursues him but is led into the path of a Bengal tiger. While Cap fights and finally kills the tiger, the soldiers defeat the Gangees, but Bucky is concerned by Cap's absence. Picking up the Fakir's trail, Cap arrives at the Gangee stronghold and finds the Fakir within Kali's temple. The Gangees attack, overwhelming him. The Fakir binds Cap and, as Haywood's soldiers march into the hill country, leaves Cap to burn to death while he leads the Gangees into action. A rogue Gangee, siding with the USA, frees Cap, who hurries to the battlefield, dodging an elephant stampede. Cap and Fakir fight hand-to-hand, and Cap knocks his enemy down a ravine, where he is impaled on Bucky's bayonet. With their leader dead, the Gangees surrender.
NOTE: Story called "Captain America Battles the Fakir" on Contents page. When Bucky Barnes expresses concern over Steve's disappearance, Haywood's casual reaction implies an awareness of Steve's secret identity. Cap & Bucky return to India in CapC #34, '44. General Haywood is without his mustache here. Bucky & the soldiers sing, "Goodbye Mama (I'm Off to Yokohama)" (1942) by Teddy Powell and his orchestra.

OTHER CHARACTERS: Cat, goat, giant koala, puma, donkey, bear, fish (all as mounted heads on Dippy's wall only), moth (in newspaper only)
LOCATIONS/ITEMS: Dippy's embassy residence inc closet & stairway; newspaper, fur coat, 3 other coats
SYNOPSIS: After reading an advertisement which advises people to store their furs, Dippy stores his fur coat in his trophy room, containing

several mounted heads, all also "furry."
NOTE: Story not listed on Contents page.

6TH STORY: "The Case of "The Clammy Things"" (13 pages)
CREDITS: Al Avison (art)
FEATURE CHARACTER: Captain America (next in Cap:RW&B/6, '02 fb, CapC #20, '42)
SUPPORTING CAST: Bucky (between CapC #19/4-20, '42)
VILLAINS: Dr. Destiny (Dr. Jorlstead, dies, only app), Dr. Purvis (Jorlstead's assistant, also as Dr. Destiny, dies), the "Things" (mutated humans, spindly, 20-foot-tall, near-mindless monsters, called "Clammy Things" in title only, see NOTE)
OTHER CHARACTERS: Adam Leeds ("Lord High Mayor of London," see NOTE), high constable, other London officials, newsboy, London bystanders
LOCATIONS/ITEMS: London inc Leeds' office, Buckingham Subway Station w/multiple public and hidden passageways inc Dr. Destiny's lab, Leeds' office & Jorlstead Historic Scientific Museum, Jorlstead's car, Dr. Destiny's pistol, comics inc Krazy Komics & Terry-Toons
SYNOPSIS: In London, strange spindly "Things" abduct city officials. On leave, Cap and Bucky charge into action, but the "Things" overwhelm them. The two feign unconsciousness and are taken to the "Things"' creator, Dr. Destiny, who intends to conquer first London and then the world. Cap and Bucky escape, but the "Things" pursue, and at Bucky's suggestion, the two heroes take separate tunnels. Cap hears the "Things" capture Bucky and rushes back. While he fights the "Things," Destiny abducts Bucky, although Cap strikes Destiny's wrist with his shield. Cap hurries to the surface and consults Dr. Jorlstead, brilliant scientist and acting mayor. Jorlstead and assistant Dr. Purvis accompany Cap to search the tunnels. When Cap separates from the others, Destiny shoots at him from a hidden passage, but Cap knocks him out and unmasks him as Purvis. Using the passage, Cap finds Destiny's lab, where the "Things" await. Since they only act under instructions, Cap realizes Purvis was not truly Destiny. He fights past the "Things" to where Destiny holds Bucky. Destiny flees, then Jorlstead enters the lab and reveals where the missing officials are held. Cap, noticing his shield's mark on Jorlstead's wrist, realizes Jorlstead is Destiny. Cap knocks him sprawling and Destiny lands against electric cables which kill him. Cap and Bucky lead the officials to the surface.
NOTE: Story called "Captain America Trapped by the Clammy Things" on Contents page. The actual Lord Mayor of London in 1942 was Sir Samuel Joseph (1888-1944). After Cap knocks out the "Things" during his second visit to the subway station, they disappear from the story, their fate unrevealed.

7TH STORY: "Dizzy Doodles" (1 page)
CREDITS: Lou Paige (writer, art)
FEATURE CHARACTERS: Pedestrian, sailor, pipe-smoker, 2 baby carriage users, doctor, medal collector, 2 fishermen, bricklayer, soldier disguised as tree, elderly man, department store salesman, department store customer, tire salesman, sheet salesman, ghost (member of Ghost Union 23), two soldiers, Bill & his neighbor
OTHER CHARACTERS: Man trapped in cement, cat, bird, bicyclist, dog, bystander, sleeping youth
LOCATIONS/ITEMS: Sailor's home, doctor's office, pond, elderly man's home, department store, tire store, ghost's home, Bill's apartment building; pedestrian's shoes, sailor's spyglass, pipe smoker's pipe, baby carriage, doctor's saw & medicine bottle, medals, fishing pole, cement & trowel, camouflage tree, elderly man's birthday cake & fan, hand mirror, tires, sheet, soldier's eyepatch, Bill's alarm clock
SYNOPSIS: Various people experience humorous or whimsical moments.
NOTE: Story not listed on Contents page. Story followed by Sentinels of Liberty Secret Club News (1 page) w/"Cap Says" & "Bucky Says," featuring Captain America & Bucky.

TEXT STORY: "Two Dangerous Surprises" (2 pages)
CREDITS: Writer unknown
FEATURE CHARACTERS: Jimmy (age 17) & Tom (his older brother)
VILLAINS: Miller & Woods (only app)
OTHER CHARACTERS: Spanish explorers & Taos Indians (in fb only), Jimmy & Tom's grandfather (mentioned only, died prior to story), J. Edgar Hoover (mentioned by Jimmy)
LOCATIONS/ITEMS: Jimmy & Tom's family's smokehouse (constructed over an adobe pueblo, see NOTE) inc back room, 19th century adobe pueblo (in fb only); Jimmy's boots, Miller & Woods' guns, ax, spade, rope & map, hams, empty gunnysacks, hay, metal box w/gold doubloons (also in fb), watermelon wrapped in newspaper
FLASHBACK: In 1845, Taos Indians fight and capture Spanish explorers, holding them in their pueblo. At night, the Spaniards bury their gold but the Indians run them out of the country before they can retrieve it.
SYNOPSIS: On Jimmy's 17th birthday, Tom takes him to the family smokehouse for a surprise treat, but both are surprised when they meet two criminals there. The criminals knock in part of the floor and dig, claiming Spanish gold is buried beneath. Tom quietly directs Jimmy's attention to a bundle, which Jimmy kicks into the digging pit, knocking down both men. After tying up the criminals, the brothers see they excavated a metal box of gold doubloons, which by law belongs to the brothers' family. Tom opens the bundle, finding a watermelon that was Jimmy's intended surprise, and the two enjoy the treat, jokingly offering some to the angry criminals.
NOTE: The presence of a Taos pueblo indicates the story occurs in New Mexico. Taos Indians misspelled "Toas" here. Story appears between 4th & 5th stories.

CAPTAIN AMERICA COMICS #21 (December 1942)

"The Creeper and the 3 Rubies of Doom!" (19 pages)

CREDITS: Syd Shores (pencils, c art, assoc editor) Vince Alascia (inks), Stan Lee (managing editor)
FEATURE CHARACTER: Captain America (also in fb between CapC #5/TEXT, '41 & CapC #6, '41)
SUPPORTING CAST: Bucky (also in fb between Cap #5/TEXT, '41 & CapC #6, '41; last in USA #6, '42, chr last in Cap Ann, '98 fb), Sgt. Duffy (last in AllWin #7/2, '42)
VILLAINS: The Creeper (Ambassador John Lissom, master spy, also in fb months ago & in dfb, only app, see NOTE) & his men (Eric named, 4 also in fb, 2 in dfb), Nazi delegate in Alslavia, Adolf Hitler (also as drawing in Creeper's note, in fb between AllWin #1/3, '41 & USA #1/3, '41), Nazi soldier w/Hitler (in fb only), Nazi sub crew (bts, take Creeper to USA, fb only)
OTHER CHARACTERS: King Dane the Fifth (king of Alslavia, only app), reporters, President Franklin D. Roosevelt (last in Mystic #6/4, '41, chr last in GSInv #2, '05, next in YA #7, '43), army officers, newsboy, HLK radio announcer, US government officials, Alslavian crowd (Serge named), J. Edgar Hoover (bts), FBI agents (bts), prison guard (dies, fb only), George Washington (as bust & painting)
LOCATIONS/ITEMS: Alslavia (last in MC #22, '41, described as "last neutral country in Europe") inc Royal Palace, Camp Lehigh, Lissom's office, Washington DC inc USO headquarters & Canteen, Creeper's subterranean hideout, 2nd hideout in old Elby haunted house inc electric eye devices & dungeon, Convention Hall, White House inc Oval Office, New York City, Liberty Island w/Statue of Liberty, Midvale Arsenal, prison (prev 4 in fb only); Nazi sub (fb only), three-gem Alslavian ruby ring, 3 separated rubies, Creeper's pistol, notes, burning poker, HLK radio microphone
FLASHBACK: Months before, the Creeper departs Germany to wreak havoc in the USA. After inflicting nationwide death and destruction, he is captured by Cap and Bucky, but escapes from prison. Lisson uses built-up shoes in his disguise of the Creeper (d).
SYNOPSIS: King Dane, pledging loyalty to the Allies, gives Ambassador Lissom his nation's historic three-gem ruby ring to wear when signing the USA's treaty with Alslavia. Later, the Creeper steals the ring, without whose symbolism Alslavia may not accept the treaty. Discovering the Creeper's men robbing a USO headquarters, Cap and Bucky knock them out but allow one to escape. He leads them to the Creeper's hideout, where they defeat the criminals. One shows them the first ruby's hiding place and directs them to the second at another hideout. There, the Creeper imprisons them but Cap escapes his bonds and hurries to the treaty signing without freeing Bucky. At the signing, Cap defeats the Creeper unmasking him as Lissom. Cap returns to the hideout disguised as the Creeper and sends the henchmen to the hall, where the FBI await, and President Roosevelt himself dons the ring to sign the treaty.
NOTE: Contains "Table of Contents" (1 page) featuring Captain America, Bucky & Minuteman (on Defense Bond stamp). Story called "Captain America Battles the Creeper" on Contents page. Contrary to the story's description of Alslavia as "last neutral nation in Europe," Spain, Sweden and Switzerland officially remained neutral throughout World War II. In the interim between flashback and main story, the Creeper implicitly killed and took over the identity of John Lissom. The Creeper's second note, thrown into Lissom's office while Lissom is present, is presumably thrown by an underling. The 3rd ruby is evidently on the Creeper's person, allowing Cap to claim it after the fight.

2ND STORY: "The Cobra Strikes" (9 pages)
CREDITS: Don Rico (pencils), Al Gabrielle (inks)
FEATURE CHARACTER: Human Torch (last in HT #10, '42, next in AllWin #7, '42)
SUPPORTING CAST: Toro (last in HT #10, '42, next in AllWin #7, '42)
VILLAINS: The Cobra (Albri Leiricgrie, costumed kidnapper, next in MKSM #9, '05 fb, 1st) & 3 underlings
OTHER CHARACTERS: The South American ambassador, Manhattan police officer, 2 motorcycle officers, 2 police officers in unidentified state, 2 South American officials, Manhattan bystanders, South American crowd
LOCATIONS/ITEMS: Manhattan inc Broadway, Cobra's cave hideout in unidentified state, South American nation inc state building; ambassador's limousine, 2 police motorcycles, Cobra's torture device, asbestos cloth & ropes, underlings' machine gun, gas & pistol
SYNOPSIS: When criminals abduct a South American ambassador, Torch and Toro pursue, but the driver projects gas from the car, rendering both unconscious. Police revive Torch minutes later, but Toro remains unconscious. Furious, Torch follows the car's tracks for hours, finally reaching a cave several states away. Within, he finds the Cobra and henchmen preparing to torture the ambassador for war plans. Torch quickly frees the ambassador, but the man is recaptured when Cobra snares Torch in asbestos cloth. Toro, having recovered soon after Torch's departure, arrives to fight the criminals, giving Torch time to free himself. Police arrive to arrest the criminals, and the ambassador is saved.
NOTE: Story called "The Human Torch Versus the Kidnapping Cobra" on Contents page. Cobra's real name revealed in OHMU:HC #5, '08; he should not be confused with Herr Cobra from HT #14/4, '43, or with Modern Era Cobras Klaus Voorhees (1st in JIM #98, '63), James Lardner (1st in MP #21, '80), or Piet Voorhees (1st in WTig #1, '07). Inasmuch as the Torch can fly hundreds of miles per hour, the Cobra's henchmen's car must have been specially constructed to move at even greater speeds to be able to outrun him after only a few minutes.

3RD STORY: "Satan and the Sorcerer's Secret!" (16 pages)
CREDITS: Al Avision (art)
FEATURE CHARACTER: Captain America (also in Balthar's crystal ball)
SUPPORTING CAST: Bucky

couple's house, criminal hideout on waterfront, abandoned bait-man's hut, several coastal cities (bts); the Light of Evil, Balthar's mystic tome, crystal ball, chair, table, candle & note

SYNOPSIS: Sequested on Bald Mountain to study black magic, Balthar is visited by Satan himself, who claims the time is right for evil to conquer the world, although he must first defeat Earth's greatest champion. Charging Balthar to find this champion, Satan grants him superhuman power and departs. Spying Cap in his crystal ball, Balthar seeks him in several cities, killing any who fail to help him. Learning of this, Cap and Bucky set out to find him. Eventually Balthar seeks out waterfront criminals for help but Cap and Bucky, anticipating this move, interrupt. The two quickly defeat the criminals, but Balthar retreats. When Cap and Bucky catch some sleep before resuming the chase, Balthar hypnotizes and abducts Bucky, knowing Cap will follow. Cap catches up as Balthar nears Bald Mountain, and Bucky overcomes his spell and returns to Cap. Reaching his cave, Balthar turns a magically deadly stare on the two, but Cap reflects it with his shield, and Balthar dies. Satan challenges Cap for the fate of the world but, after hand-to-hand combat, admits he cannot defeat Cap's indomitable will and withdraws.
NOTE: Story called "Captain America Defies the Sorcerer" on Contents page. An alleged "Satan" was last in MC #34/6, '42, an alleged "Satan" is next in AllWin #8, '43.

4TH STORY: "Dippy Diplomat" (7 pages)
CREDITS: Guy Blythe (writer, art)
FEATURE CHARACTER: Dippy Diplomat (next in CapC #24/4, '43)
SUPPORTING CAST: Swizzlestick (Dippy's assistant, 1st, next in CapC #24/4, '43), Mergetroide (last in CapC #18/8, '42, next in CapC #25/5, '43)
VILLAINS: Agent 123 ("Bud," designation revealed in CapC #25/5, '43) & his associate (spies, 1st, next in CapC #24/4, '43)
OTHER CHARACTERS: 6 diplomats, 3 police officers
LOCATIONS/ITEMS: Dippy's embassy inc bedroom, golf course, store w/marquee; speed cop warning sign, Dippy's limousine, 3 police motorcycles, golf clubs, golf balls, golf paraphernalia, exploding golf ball, exploding pencil, autograph book, Dippy's pocket watch, treaty, champagne, glasses, fountain pen, ink
SYNOPSIS: Scheduled to sign a treaty with the USA, Dippy first plays golf, unaware of two spies, intent on sabotaging the treaty. They try to kill Dippy with an exploding golf ball, but he hits it farther than expected and the explosion leaves him unharmed. The spies follow Dippy back to the embassy and, "seeking an autograph," offer him an exploding pencil. The explosion hurls him into his own bedroom, but he soon recovers and joins his fellow diplomats downstairs. A breeze blows the treaty outside, and when Dippy pursues, the spies attack him. Swizzlestick intervenes, knocking the evildoers out. After signing the treaty, Dippy toasts Swizzlestick's bravery but inadvertently drinks from an inkwell.
NOTE: Story called "Dippy Diplomat Fights the Sinister Spies" on Contents page.

5TH STORY: "The Case of the Silent Hermit" (7 pages)
CREDITS: Don Rico (art)
FEATURE CHARACTER: The Secret Stamp
SUPPORTING CAST: Mr. & Mrs. Colt (last in CapC #17/6, '42, final app)
VILLAINS: The Hermit (Mr. Schores, spy, only app)
OTHER CHARACTERS: Police officer, Adolf Hitler (mentioned by Hermit), Minuteman (on Defense Bond stamps only)
LOCATIONS/ITEMS: Hermit's home, Colt home, police headquarters, defense plant; Roddy's delivery bag, jackknife, newspapers & war bonds, Hermit's short wave radio set & pistol
SYNOPSIS: On his delivery rounds, Roddy tries to sell war bonds to Mr. Schores, aka "the Hermit," who claims destitution. At home, Roddy's father offers to employ Schores at his defense plant. Roddy returns to Schores' house but sees him using a short wave radio set. Schores catches him at gunpoint, boasts that Mr. Colt's plant will blow up the next day, locks Roddy in a closet, then leaves on an errand. As Secret Stamp, Roddy picks the closet lock, then hides upon Schores' return. When Schores enters the closet, Stamp locks him in, and Schores shoots through the door until out of ammo. Stamp releases him, binds him in radio wire, and threatens him until he reveals a time bomb is in the plant. Secret Stamp takes Schores to the police, who find the bomb.
NOTE: Story called "The Secret Stamp and the Silent Hermit" on Contents page. The Hermit has evidently been a fixture in Freetown for some time, implying he was not sent by the Nazis but recruited by them. On page 6, Secret Stamp threatens to gouge out the Hermit's eyes if he doesn't talk, an unusually brutal tactic for a costumed hero, even by wartime standards. Story followed by "Sentinels of Liberty Secret Club News" (1 page) w/"Cap Says" & "Bucky Says" featuring Captain America, Bucky & the 50 winners of the Captain America Picture Contest from CapC #18, '42 including "Alexander Toth, Jr.," noted comic artist Alex Toth (1928-2006). This is the last "Sentinels of Liberty" page.

TEXT STORY: "Catch That Firebug!" (2 pages)
CREDITS: Writer unknown
FEATURE CHARACTER: Mickey Forrest (age 13)
SUPPORTING CAST: Lt. Malone (police detective)
VILLAINS: Matches Birken (arsonist), Duke Haney (criminal, bts, employs Birken)
OTHER CHARACTERS: Police inspector, Chicago FBI agents (mentioned by Malone), fire commissioner, code experts (both mentioned by inspector), Mickey's teacher (mentioned by Mickey)
LOCATIONS/ITEMS: Mrs. Murphy's boarding house inc Birken's room, hamburger diner, Police HQ, Nelson Warehouse (bts, arson target); Birken's black car, envelope with coded letter, police copy
SYNOPSIS: When known arsonist Matches Birken returns to his old boarding house, Mickey Forrest informs Lt. Malone, who asks the youth to delay Birken until he arrives. The police suspect Birken is the recipient of Duke Haney's coded letter. Mickey finagles his way into Birken's room, where he notices a typewriter. When the police arrive, Birken escapes. Malone finds the original letter, which Mickey, recognizing the code as a classroom typing exercise, decodes as an address and the day's date. Malone sends men to the address, and Birken is caught red-handed.
NOTE: Story title has no exclamation point on Contents page. Story appears between 3rd & 4th stories.

CAPTAIN AMERICA COMICS #22 (January 1943)

"The Vault of the Doomed! " (12 pages)

CREDITS: Al Avison (pencils), Syd Shores (inks, c art, assoc ed), Stan Lee (editor, art director)
FEATURE CHARACTER: Captain America (next in CapC #25-26, '43 fbs, MFan #5/2, '82 fb)
SUPPORTING CAST: Bucky (chr next in CapC #25, '43 fb)
VILLAINS: Dr. Eternity (Nazi operative disguised as spirit guide, only app), his 2 hunchback assistants, 5 Nazi spies (Schultz named)
OTHER CHARACTERS: Congressman Barlow (dies), woman visiting Dr. Eternity about her dead son, Sam (Barlow's chauffeur), Judge Cohn (as corpse only), John Barlow (Congressman Barlow's brother, as illusion only), army truck driver (bts, driving truck that Steve and Bucky ride on), police (bts, take the villains into custody between panels), US & Japanese soldiers (on cover only)
LOCATIONS/ITEMS: Washington DC inc hotel room & Congressman Barlow's office, the Vault of the Departed Spirits (Dr. Eternity's establishment, near Camp Lehigh) inc cellar seance room w/ television projector, adjacent graveyard & subterranean tunnel linking crypt and vault; army truck, Dr. Eternity's crystal ball (on symbolic splash page only), dagger & letter, hunchback's noose, spies' pistols
SYNOPSIS: Congressman Barlow receives a letter from Dr. Eternity, who claims Barlow's deceased brother John has contacted him. To his superstitious chauffeur Sam's distress, Barlow meets with Eternity. Another client, a woman, arrives, frightening Sam, whose scream draws Cap and Bucky to investigate. Inside, his brother's apparition warns Barlow he must "come to the world of the spirits" that night, and Barlow collapses dead. Cap and Bucky rush in, but Eternity's assistant knocks out Bucky and brings him to Eternity's seance room. There Eternity claims the female client's dead son's spirit is trapped within Bucky. The woman rejects Eternity's claims, and he draws a dagger. Cap bursts in, but another assistant snares him in a noose. Outside, two Nazi spies, Eternity's employers, arrive and take Sam prisoner. The criminals lock Barlow's corpse, Cap, Bucky and Sam in a subterranean crypt. Tied up and forgotten, the female client escapes and releases the men. Cap and Bucky quickly knock out the criminals, unmasking Dr. Eternity as a wanted Nazi, and turn them over to police.
NOTE: Contains "Table of Contents" (1 page) featuring Captain America, Bucky & Minuteman (on Defense Bond stamp). Story called "Captain America and the Vault of the Doomed!" on Contents page. Barlow's cause of death is unexplained.

2ND STORY: "Human Torch in the Sabotage of the Supply Trains" (7 pages)
CREDITS: Harry Sahle (pencils), Carl Pfeufer (inks)
FEATURE CHARACTER: Human Torch (last in MC #39, '43, next in YA #6, '43, MC #40, '43)
SUPPORTING CAST: Toro (last in MC #39, '43, next in YA #6, '43)
VILLAINS: The Beak (railroad saboteur, only app) & his men
OTHER CHARACTERS: Russian captain & crew, seaport workers, American General Staff official, radio operator, army guards, engineer, railroad firemen, 2 army officers, FBI agent, second train's crew (bts), dog
LOCATIONS/ITEMS: Russian seaport, American General Staff office, National City inc Beak's apartment building & railroad depot, railroad tunnel, mountain cave; hijacked train (Shultz & Phutz RR) w/ cargo, second train, Beak's gang's cars, explosives, scrap cargo, fake tracks & crates, Beak's vapor gun & binoculars, 1000 rounds of 75 mm anti-tank ammunition (removed & replaced with scrap bts), Russian ships
SYNOPSIS: When supply shipments from the USA to Russia are mysteriously intercepted and scrap substituted for supplies, a US government official asks Torch and Toro to investigate. The two set out for National City, the most likely site for shipment interception. There, Nazi saboteur Beak has already targeted another train. When the train enters a tunnel, Beak gasses it, rendering those aboard unconscious so his men can drive the train down a secret track. However, hidden in a freight car, Torch and Toro resist the vapor's effect and confront Beak who uses a vapor gun to knock them out. Beak brings Torch and Toro along when the train pulls into a hidden trainyard for supply replacement. They recover and trap Beak and company in a "freight car" sculpted out of fire, then rendezvous with a second train to explain the proceedings.
NOTE: Entitled "The Human Torch and the Train of Terror!" on Contents page. The name of the seacoast city from which the investigated ship is scheduled to depart is redacted in dialogue, replaced with a "Censored" to lend an air of authenticity.

3RD STORY: "Captain America Battles the Reaper! The Man the Law Couldn't Touch!" (15 pages)
CREDITS: Al Avison (pencils), Al Gabriele (inks)
FEATURE CHARACTER: Captain America (next in Cap #139, '71 fb, see NOTE)
SUPPORTING CAST: Bucky, Sgt. Duffy (both chr last in CapC #11/5, '42, chr next in Cap #139, '71 fb, see NOTE)
VILLAINS: The Reaper (Gunther Strauss, charismatic spy, also in newspaper photo, only app, dies, see NOTE) & his 3 employees, Nazi followers, Adolf Hitler (last in HT #5B, '41, next in AllWin #4/5, '42), Joseph Goebbels (chr last in SagaSM #5, '89, chr next in HT #8, '42, next in MC #42/2, '43), high-ranking Nazi officials, Nazi soldiers, jewel thief
OTHER CHARACTERS: Police chief & his assistant, police sergeant, police officers, state attorney, defense attorney, judge, teacher, 2 students (more bts), 4 "great minds" contemplating how to counter Reaper, radio announcer, Miss Plentiplump, Madison Square Garden crowd, radio listeners across USA (most bts), multiple crowds, German crowd, Emperor Hirohito (mentioned only, by Reaper)
LOCATIONS/ITEMS: Berlin inc the Krolloper building, Camp Lehigh inc Steve and Bucky's tent, Manhattan inc Madison Square Garden, Municipal Building w/ police chief's office, courtroom, schoolroom, "great minds" office, apartment building w/ Reaper's office & Miss Plentiplump's

prosecution. As Reaper's ideas spread, Cap and Bucky confront him at his office, and Reaper's employees attack. Although Cap and Bucky quickly knock them out, Reaper calls the police and swears out a warrant. When Cap and Bucky depart through a window, they inadvertently crash through another tenant's window, and she too files charges. Later, while Bucky works elsewhere, Cap watches Reaper call upon his followers to revolt against the government. Cap challenges Reaper's anti-American sentiments, but the villain's followers overwhelm him. The mob marches on City Hall, but Bucky distracts them, displaying documentation that Reaper is a foreign agitator, while Cap confronts Reaper alone. Reaper flees into the subway. When Cap grabs his scythe, Reaper panics, landing on the track's third rail and electrocuting himself.

NOTE: Story called "Captain America Battles the Reaper!" on Contents page. Inv #10, '76 reveals this story occurs earlier than originally indicated, circa mid-1941. Reaper's real name revealed in MAtlas #1, '08. Cap and Bucky called "the Dynamic Duo" once here.

4TH STORY: "Captain America Wears the Cobra Ring of Death!" (18 pages)
CREDITS: Al Avison (pencils), Al Gabriele (inks)
FEATURE CHARACTER: Captain America (next in YA #6, '43, Cap:SoL #2-4, '98, Cap #43, '08 fb, Cap #46, '09 fb, bts in Truth #4, '03, Truth #6, '03 fb, Cap #5, '05 fb, Cap #50, '09 fb)
SUPPORTING CAST: Bucky (chr last in MFan #5/2, '82 fb, next in YA #6, '43), Sgt. Duffy
VILLAINS: The Ring (Bundist leader, dies, only app), Toto (Ring's muscular "Mongolian" assistant), several dozen bundists (Kumpf named)
OTHER CHARACTERS: Camp Lehigh soldiers temporarily transferred to Washington DC (Callahan, Campbell, Hanes named), Hugo (curio shop owner, dies), Senator Ralph (dies), General Lang (Camp Potomac's commanding officer, dies), 3 MPs, 2 jewelers (others bts), Mike's Lunch Room counterman, senators & senate attendees, bystanders, Billy Mitchell (Army General, "father of the US Air Force," mentioned only by Senator Ralph), cobra (on ring & in caption only), figures in portraits on Capitol Building's walls
LOCATIONS/ITEMS: Washington DC inc Capitol Building w/Senate chamber, Hugo's curio shop at 50 River Street, jewelers, curio shops (some bts), Mike's Lunch Room, Camp Potomac w/Barracks A, General Lang's home & river dock, Shoal Island inc Ring's hideout w/dungeon, Camp Vaterland; 2 motorboats, Ring's car & gun, cobra rings equipped w/ strychnine fangs, Toto's spiked club, spies' guns & clubs
SYNOPSIS: Senator Ralph collapses and dies mysteriously. Kumpf reports the death to his leader, the Ring. The next day, Steve finds General Lang dead, a cobra ring on his finger. MPs arrest Steve, but he escapes with the ring. Laying low, he gets Bucky to seek the ring's source. The search leads to Hugo, a curio shop owner whom the Ring has intimidated into providing the shop as a hideout. The Ring and associates emerge from the back and overwhelm Bucky. Muscular Toto hurls Hugo through a display window, leaving him for dead. Cap, who Bucky had called before entering the shop, arrives and Hugo identifies Ring's other hideout on Shoal Island before dying. Cap bursts in there, but Toto strikes him from behind. Cap and Bucky are imprisoned together. While Ring sends Kumpf to distribute cobra rings to important figures, Cap and Bucky escape. They defeat the bundists, but Ring and Toto depart by boat. Following, Cap defeats Toto, forcing him to reveal the rings' secret and Ring's destination, Camp Vaterland, which Bucky has already infiltrated in disguise, wearing the cobra ring. The Nazis spot him but, before they can attack, Cap bursts in and orders Bucky to discard the ring. Bucky complies, then the two outfight the bundists. Only Ring remains, and when Cap knocks him down, he brushes against the discarded ring and dies, for the rings kill by strychnine. After warning the men on Kumpf's list of recipients, the two return to Camp Potomac.
NOTE: Story called "Captain America and the Ring of Death!" on Contents page. Presumably Senator Ralph was wearing a cobra ring when he died, but this is never clearly stated. The circumstances in which Steve is cleared of suspicion for General Lang's murder are not mentioned. Story followed by "Next Month" (1 page) preview of CapC #23, '43 featuring Captain America, Bucky & Turtle-Man.

5TH STORY: "War Bond Vengeance" (7 pages)
CREDITS: Don Rico (pencils), Vince Alascia (inks)
FEATURE CHARACTER: The Secret Stamp
VILLAINS: Several Nazi stormtroopers (Fritz, Hans named)
OTHER CHARACTERS: Carson Bells (actor, also in Daily Bugle photo, only app), Roddy's classmates (Red named), actors & actresses participating in National Hollywood Actors War Bond Campaign inc Bells' hired extras, representative of Bells' movie company, Freetown mayor, Freetown reporters, ambulance crew, Hollywood reporters & photographer, movie studio head, Freetown citizens
LOCATIONS/ITEMS: Freetown inc City Hall, school, Colt home & garage, Hollywood inc movie studio office, Green Run Saw Mill w/buzz-saw platform; Nazis' sedan, Roddy's bicycle, speaker's platform & microphone, radio, Nazis' guns
SYNOPSIS: At a war bond rally, Nazi storm-troopers abduct actor Carson Bells. The crowd presumes the abduction is faked, but Roddy suspects otherwise. On bicycle, he pursues the abduction car but is outpaced. Returning, Roddy tries to tell the crowd, but they scoff at him. As Secret Stamp, he spends hours searching, pausing to nap at the Green Run Saw Mill. Meanwhile, the public realizes the abduction is genuine and Bells' studio offers a one million dollar reward for his return. Later, Secret Stamp awakens to find the Nazis at the mill, where they demand Bells, tied to a buzz-saw platform, write his studio for a $500,000 ransom. When he refuses, they start the saw, but Stamp intervenes, freeing Bells and defeating the Nazis. The two return to Freetown with their captives. The next day, Bells' movie company presents Secret Stamp's "best friend" Roddy with a million-dollar check, which he donates to the war bond drive.
NOTE: Entitled "War Stamp Vengeance!" on Contents page. Carson Bells is an homage to Orson Welles. Bells mistakenly called "Wells" once here. Secret Stamp describes himself as a "one-man vigilante committee," the term "super hero" having not yet been popularized.

TEXT STORY: "The Missing Ear" (2 pages)
CREDITS: Writer unknown
FEATURE CHARACTER: Jackie Coloney (high school student & grocery clerk, only app)
SUPPORTING CAST: Red Coloney (treasury agent & Jackie's father, also as "Chicago Red" & "Red Clyde," counterfeiter)
VILLAINS: Bull Darwin, Jake & Slippery (counterfeiters, only app), Joe Tomasci (Chicago racketeer, mentioned by Bull)
OTHER CHARACTERS: Federal agents, traffic cop, Alexander Hamilton (depicted on ten dollar bills)
LOCATIONS/ITEMS: Harvey's Grocery Store, Bull's garage hideout, farmhouse hideout w/basement; Slippery's car, Red's car (gray coupe w/Illinois license plate), tool table, engraving instruments, printing press, paper stacks, paper cutter, cash register, counterfeit ten dollar bills
SYNOPSIS: When Jackie realizes a customer has given him a counterfeit ten dollar bill, he leaps onto his car's running board. The customer Jake, punches him and pulls him inside as his colleague, Slippery, drives away. At their garage hideout, the counterfeiters rendezvous with their

boss Bull, who has been joined by apparent Chicago engraving man Red Clyde. Slippery notes that Jackie resembles Red, but Red scoffs at this then seemingly intimidates Jackie into revealing he recognized the counterfeit ten because Hamilton's portrait lacks a left ear. The gang takes Jackie to a more remote hideout where the counterfeiting equipment is kept. Red takes Jackie outside to apparently kill him. Slippery, suspicious, follows. A shot rings out and Slippery re-enters, wounded, followed by Red, Jackie and federal agents. Red is actually a treasury agent and Jackie's father, having earlier told Jackie how to recognize a counterfeit ten in the first place.

NOTE: Story erroneously called "The Missing Car!" on Contents page. Story appears between 3ʳᵈ & 4ᵗʰ stories.

CAPTAIN AMERICA COMICS #23 (February 1943)

"The Mystery of the 100 Corpses!" (17 pages)

CREDITS: Syd Shores (art, assoc editor) Stan Lee (editor, art director)
FEATURE CHARACTER: Captain America
SUPPORTING CAST: Bucky (last in YA #6, '43, chr last in Cap #50, '09 fb), Sgt. Duffy
VILLAINS: Dr. Izan (Nazi spymaster, also as conventional doctor, only app) & his men (all die, Gioco named), at least 100 Nazi spies, Nazi pilots (bts, some die)
OTHER CHARACTERS: Doctor & investigator, man (dies), his wife and son, 2 FBI agents, US pilots (bts), over 100 corpses (all former patients of Dr. Izan), Betty Ross, Nazi agents & soldiers (prev 3 on cover only)
LOCATIONS/ITEMS: Camp Lehigh inc Steve and Bucky's tent, other tents & mess hall, adjacent stone quarry inc pool, Manhattan inc city morgue, apartment building & city power plant, Izan's "house of death" on outskirts of town w/basement morgue; Nazi planes, US planes (both bts), hearse, Izan's pistol, face disguise, stone-crushing machine & trident (splash page only)
SYNOPSIS: Steve and Bucky discover dozens of corpses at a quarry's pool. The man responsible, Izan, shoots at them. They tackle him as Cap and Bucky but Izan escapes. Authorities determine the pool's 99 victims died of natural causes. When Cap and Bucky meet a boy crying for his dying father, they find the "father" recovered, yet a hearse transports his doctor and a corpse. Cap and Bucky follow the doctor to a hideout, where he unmasks as Izan. They attack, but Izan escapes, killing his own men in the process. At the quarry, Cap and Bucky find Izan with over 100 spies who have assumed the identities of the quarry victims, most of whom are air raid wardens. The spies detect and overwhelm the two, whom Izan leaves in a stone-crushing machine, but Cap gets Bucky to kick a rock into a gear, shutting it off. Izan and company light up Manhattan for a Nazi air raid, but Cap and Bucky confront them at a power plant, where Cap punches Izan into a console, short-circuiting the plant and throwing the city into darkness. FBI agents arrive, reporting that US planes intercepted the Nazi planes.
NOTE: Contains "Table of Contents" (1 page) featuring Captain America, Bucky & Minuteman (on Defense Bond stamp). Story called "The Mystery of the Hundred Corpses!" on Contents page. Dr. Izan should not be confused with Izan from MC #28, '42. Dr. Izan refers to Cap as "the man of steel," a nickname more commonly associated with DC Comics' Superman. "Izan" is, as Bucky points out, "Nazi" spelled backwards.

2ND STORY: "Terror at the Shipyards!" (7 pages)
CREDITS: Unknown
FEATURE CHARACTER: Human Torch (next in HT #11, '43, MC #41, '43)
SUPPORTING CAST: Toro (last in MC #40, '43, next in HT #11, '43)
VILLAINS: Mr. Hefler (spy & Calbin Ship Yards manager, only app), 3 spies (Joe named)
OTHER CHARACTERS: Government truck driver, shipyard officials & crowds, shipyard investigator, 2 government agents, ceremonial bottle wielder, radio announcer (voice only)
LOCATIONS/ITEMS: Calbin Ship Yards inc Hefler's office, docks w/Hyde-Ballory S.S. dockhouse, The Great White Way dockhouse & other dockhouses, Manhattan inc Torch & Toro's apartment, spies' hideout; Budweiser Beer ad, crane, ships (at least one damaged), government truck (license US 6-090), Hefler's radio control apparatus, spies' firearms, asbestos suits, "foamite" guns, remote-controlled TNT-loaded boats (one destroyed), asbestos straitjackets, bottle cases, nitroglycerin-filled champagne bottles, grenade & guns (both on splash page only)
SYNOPSIS: After spies switch cargo on a government truck, Torch and Toro attend a ship launching, where the ceremonial bottle explodes upon striking the ship, which Torch and Toro save from sinking. After saving a second ship, the two consult shipyards manager Hefler. Later, the spies open fire on Torch and Toro, who melt the bullets and pursue. They enter the spies' hideout, but the spies use "foamite" to extinguish their flames, bind them in straitjackets, and depart. Using his teeth, Toro unties Torch, who then frees him, and they return to the shipyard, where multiple ships have launched. They prevent a remote-controlled TNT-loaded boat from sinking one ship. Torch leads Toro to Hefler's office, which overlooks the entire shipyard, finding Hefler allied with the spies. They knock the gang out and turn them over to government agents.

3RD STORY: "Captain America Battling the Deadly Snapper" (15 pages)
CREDITS: Otto Binder (writer), Al Avison (pencils), Syd Shores (inks)
FEATURE CHARACTER: Captain America
SUPPORTING CAST: Bucky, Sgt. Duffy
VILLAINS: The Turtle-Man (also "the Turtle Man," "the Snapper" & "the Strangler," "Rocks" Rico, criminal using bulletproof shell-costume, only app) & the Swamp Killers (dozens of escaped killers), "Killer" Bane (joins Swamp Killers)
OTHER CHARACTERS: Camp Lehigh soldiers, chain gang inmates, prison guards, several parade participants & observers (some die),

followed by guards and hounds, pursue Bane into Swamp Sinister, where the gigantic, bulletproof Turtle-Man offers protection and his giant turtles delay Kane's pursuers. Cap and Bucky make it past, but Turtle-Man downs them and escapes. Later, Turtle-Man brings Kane to the hideout of his gang, the Swamp Killers, all freed convicts. That night, Steve and Bucky attend a Mardi Gras parade, as do the Killers, disguised as float riders. At Turtle-Man's command, they rob and kill, drawing Cap and Bucky who capture several Killers. The rest, including Turtle-Man, escape into the swamp by boat. Cap and Bucky follow, using vines to swing past alligators. Turtle-Man, withdrawn into his shell to resemble a boulder, takes them by surprise, hurling them into quicksand. Cap uses his shield to cut down a tree branch, which the two climb to freedom. At the hideout, they take the Killers by surprise and defeat them, including Turtle-Man, revealed as criminal "Rocks" Rico in a costume. Prison guards take the whole gang into custody.

NOTE: Title listed with exclamation point on Contents page. Turtle-Man only called "Snapper" in the title.

4TH STORY: "The Case of the Bund's Bonds!" (7 pages)
CREDITS: Don Rico (art)
FEATURE CHARACTER: The Secret Stamp (next in USA #7/5, '43)
SUPPORTING CAST: Tom Colt (last in CapC #13/6, '42, last app to date)
VILLAINS: The All-Out Americans Club (4 Nazi spies/counterfeiters, hired saboteurs (bts, spies channel money to them)
OTHER CHARACTERS: Girl & her father (bts, forced to buy bonds), 2 Riverdale police officers, Freetown citizens, Riverdale citizens, Freetown citizen's son (US soldier stationed in Iceland, mentioned only), Minuteman (on Defense Bond stamp only), Adolf Hitler (in framed picture only)
LOCATIONS/ITEMS: Grocery store, apartment building, Grimes mansion & well underneath, Riverdale (neighboring town); police wagon, spies' car, engraving plates, gun, money, ropes, & Nazi flag
SYNOPSIS: The All-Out Americans Club sells war bonds at half-price, but Roddy grows suspicious when several low-income residents buy $100 bonds. After a girl tells him the Club forced her father to buy, Secret Stamp hitches a ride on the Club car to their abandoned mansion hideout. Hearing that the bonds are counterfeit and the money intended for Nazi saboteurs, Secret Stamp bursts in but is struck from behind. The Nazis leave him in a death trap, in which engraving acid will gradually dissolve the ropes holding him suspended over an ancient well. They depart for nearby Riverdale. Escaping, Stamp sends the Riverdale Police a code message over telephone wires, warning them of the Nazi counterfeiters. He arrives in Riverdale just as police close in on the Nazis, himself tackling the fleeing leader.
NOTE: Story called "The Bund's Bonds!" on Contents page. Since Secret Stamp arrived at the hideout on the spies' car and not via his bicycle, it is unclear how he traveled from the hideout to Riverdale.

5TH STORY: "The Idol of Doom!" (17 pages)
CREDITS: Al Avison (pencils), Syd Shores (inks)
FEATURE CHARACTER: Captain America (next in USA #7, '43)
SUPPORTING CAST: Bucky, Sgt. Duffy (both next in USA #7, '43)
VILLAINS: Prince Ba'rahm (criminal mystic, dies, only app) & his men (Frog named, all die), Shao the Dwarf (Ba'rahm's assistant, dies, only app), Mr. Brady (attorney & Ba'rahm's secret employer, dies)
OTHER CHARACTERS: Camp Lehigh soldiers, Mrs. J. Wallinger (also in newspaper photo, dies), woman (found dead), Mrs. Dale (wealthy socialite), Syd & Bill (fishermen), Vince & Frank (yachtsmen), Brotherhood of Magicians employee, bank manager, newsboy, cab driver, bystander, Decka (presumed god, "Master of Fire and Water," invoked by Ba'rahm, as idol), "the Unholy Serpent" and "the Muted Satan" (names invoked by Ba'rahm, possibly aliases for Decka)
LOCATIONS/ITEMS: Camp Lehigh inc partially constructed airport, Manhattan inc Brotherhood of Magicians office, city bank & office building w/Brady's 14th floor office, Snake River inc ore dock w/Prince Ba'rahm's adjacent warehouse hideout (destroyed), subterranean tunnel to multiple chambers beneath Decka idol; Ba'rahm's rowboats, Syd & Bill's boat, Vince & Frank's boat, gold case w/calling card, Shao's knife, hammer & poker, Brady's briefcase & pistol, gang member's blackjack
SYNOPSIS: Steve and Bucky observe a turbaned man and a woman out on Snake River at night. When the man chants to "Decka," the pair's boat is encircled by flame, then disappears. Steve and Bucky dive in, finding only the card case of "Prince Ba'rahm, Oriental Mystic." Days later, the woman's body is found. Soon another woman's body surfaces; both are identified as wealthy society women. A third woman, Mrs. Dale, arranges for her wealth to be claimed by a third party bearing her signature, then visits Ba'rahm. Meanwhile, Steve and Bucky consult Brady, the dead women's attorney, who directs them to Ba'rahm. Ba'rahm's underlings overwhelm the heroes, who are bound and taken to an underground machine room. Cap and Bucky escape and knock out their captors. Through a telescope, they see Ba'rahm and Mrs. Dale on the river and Cap realizes the machinery pumps oil into the river to create the burning circle, then sucks the rowboat into the room. Shao the Dwarf knocks out Cap and Bucky. When Ba'rahm returns, he takes them to another chamber, opens a river valve, and leaves them to drown. Reviving, Cap and Bucky swim up the gushing pipe and reach the river's surface. They break into Ba'rahm's seance room, where Mrs. Dale is unconscious. They knock out Ba'rahm and company, but a masked man, Ba'rahm's employer, enters. Struck by Cap's shield, the man burns his hand on an incense brazier, which he topples, setting the warehouse ablaze. Cap and Bucky escape with Mrs. Dale, leaving Ba'rahm and company behind. Back in Manhattan, Cap and Bucky confront Brady, whose burned hand identifies him as Ba'rahm's employer, having sent his clients to be bamboozled into signing fortunes over to Ba'rahm, who promised them eternal life but killed them instead. Brady draws a pistol but, stumbling, crashes through his window, falling to his death.
NOTE: Cap misidentifies Ba'rahm as a "Hindu." At story's end, Cap provides exposition on Brady & Ba'rahm's scheme, although how he gained such information is not depicted.

TEXT STORY: "Head Hunters' Stew" (2 pages)
CREDITS: Writer unknown
FEATURE CHARACTER: Diego Smith (also in pfb)
SUPPORTING CAST: Bill Glammis (pilot, also in pfb)
VILLAINS: Head hunter tribe inc chief/shaman dubbed "Monk" by Diego
OTHER CHARACTERS: Judd A. Smith (ornithologist & Diego's father, pfb only), Mrs. Smith (Diego's mother, pfb only)
LOCATIONS/ITEMS: Brazil inc jungle w/ headhunter tribe's village & Bahia (pfb only); Bill's plane (also in pfb), Diego's pocket knife & parachute, tribe's poison-tipped arrows, spears & torches, Monk's feathered headdress, white panther-fur cape, staff topped with shrunken human head & silver bracelet

FLASHBACK: 3 days earlier, Diego departs his parents' Bahia home to return to US boarding school via Bill's plane. When the plane suffers engine trouble over the tribe's village, Diego parachutes to safety, erroneously believing the plane to have crashed when Bill in fact repairs the engine and lands safely, only to be captured (p).

SYNOPSIS: Attacked by spear-carrying tribesmen, Diego is seemingly saved when their chief intervenes. In the tribe's village, Diego receives food and shelter, only to gradually realize his hosts intend to decapitate and eat him. He releases a second victim, an imprisoned man who proves to be Bill, his pilot. The two find the plane and escape.

NOTE: Story not listed on Contents page. First page of story appears between 3rd & 4th stories, second page appears after 5th story.

CAPTAIN AMERICA COMICS #24 (March 1943)

"The Vampire Strikes" (20 pages)

CREDITS: Al Avison (pencils), Syd Shores (inks, c art, assoc editor), Stan Lee (editor, art director)
FEATURE CHARACTER: Captain America
SUPPORTING CAST: Bucky, Sgt. Duffy (both last in USA #7, '43), Gen. Haywood (last in CapC #20/4, '42, next in AllWin #8/2, '43)
VILLAINS: Count Varnis (500-plus year old vampire, also as bat, only app), Varnis' butler (vampire, only app)
OTHER CHARACTERS: Private Joe Dawson (also briefly as vampire, only app), Camp Lehigh non-coms & soldiers, bats, Black Dragon Society (on cover only)
LOCATIONS/ITEMS: Camp Lehigh inc non-com mess hall, Vampire Mountain (also "Vampire's Mountain") w/Count Varnis' house inc dining hall and bedrooms, adjacent cemetery w/tomb containing coffins and tunnel connected to house; army truck, searchlight, hammer & nails, boulder, Varnis Jewels (bts, mentioned by Varnis)

SYNOPSIS: Duffy sends Steve, Bucky and their friend Joe to place a searchlight atop Vampire Mountain. As the three drive upward, an avalanche falls behind them. Steve and Bucky clear the road while Joe continues on to set up the light, where a vampire attacks him. Hearing Joe's scream, Cap and Bucky rush to find the vampire drinking Joe's blood. Cap pulls him off, but he escapes as a bat. The two bring Joe to a nearby house, where its owner, Count Varnis, greets them and insists they stay the night. Later, the vampire visits Joe and drinks more blood. Cap finds Joe dead, but when he brings Varnis to investigate, Joe is gone. Later, after meeting with the vampire, who is Varnis himself, Joe, now a vampire, attacks Bucky, but Cap intervenes, and Joe flees. At Camp Lehigh, Steve and Bucky report Joe's disappearance to Duffy, who goes to Vampire Mountain himself and is imprisoned by Varnis. When Cap and Bucky return, Varnis traps them and takes them to a tomb where Varnis' butler and Joe await, holding Duffy prisoner. Varnis ties the two heroes down, declaring they and Duffy will provide sustenance so the vampires can feed during the day in hope of building up sunlight resistance. When the vampires depart, Cap, Bucky, and Duffy escape their bonds. They attack the returning vampires who flee outside. Cap blocks the tomb's entrances. The vampires weaken as dawn approaches. Varnis leaps from a cliff but lands in a tree, impaled by a branch. With Varnis' death, the butler collapses into dust, and Joe reverts to normal.

NOTE: Contains "Table of Contents" (1 page) depicting Captain America, Bucky & Minuteman (on Defense Bond stamp). Haywood is erroneously identified as a colonel here. Varnis does not turn to dust upon being staked, implying the branch did not fully kill him; in any event, both he and his butler are presumably revived, along with all of Earth's other vampires, by the events of Blade #12, '07.

2ND STORY: "Human Torch Solves the Monument Murder" (7 pages)
CREDITS: Unknown
FEATURE CHARACTER: Human Torch (next in AllWin #8, '43, MC #42, '43)
SUPPORTING CAST: Toro (last in MC #41, '43, next in AllWin #8, '43)
VILLAINS: Eric (Ward's stepbrother; sculptor & Nazi, dies, only app)
OTHER CHARACTERS: Mr. Ward (supervisor), Mt. Rushmore workers (one dies), company doctor, George Washington, Thomas Jefferson, Theodore Roosevelt, Abraham Lincoln (as sculpted faces on Mt. Rushmore), Sub-Mariner (in framed photo only)
LOCATIONS/ITEMS: South Dakota inc Black Hills w/Mt. Rushmore National Monument & workers' shack, Manhattan inc Torch & Toro's apartment; Mt. Rushmore ladders, hanging baskets, & other mountain apparatus, Eric's pistol & silencer, Ward's pistol

SYNOPSIS: As the Mt. Rushmore monument nears completion, Torch and Toro agree to use their flames to clean the mountain's base of scrap rock. Soon after their arrival, a worker near Roosevelt's face falls to his death, and a gunshot wings Toro. Torch finds supervisor Ward quarreling with an armed worker. When Torch disarms the man, Ward draws a gun, identifying the man as his stepbrother Eric. Toro disarms Ward, and Torch pursues Eric, whom he finds planting dynamite by Roosevelt's face. When Torch intervenes, Eric falls, pulling the explosives with him. They explode, killing him. Ward admits his stepbrother was a refugee Nazi, although Ward knew nothing of his scheme, and Torch and Toro get to work clearing debris.

NOTE: Story called "Mt. Rushmore Memorial" on Contents page. Although the story states the monument took 15 years to complete, in the real world construction occurred from October 4, 1927 to October 31, 1941, or 13 years. No one died during construction.

3RD STORY: "Meet the Eel of Horror Harbor" (18 pages)
CREDITS: Syd Shores (art)
FEATURE CHARACTER: Captain America (next in Cap #616/6, '11, AllWin #8/2, '43, Cap:ME #1, '94)
SUPPORTING CAST: Bucky (chr next in Cap #616/6, '11), Sgt. Duffy (both next in AllWin #8/2, '43)

LOCATIONS/ITEMS: Camp Lehigh, United Shipyard inc foundry & adjacent Horror Harbor, Eel's cliffside hideout inc eel pit & octopus chamber, war bond booth; ship, speedboat, 2nd boat (bts), 2 diving helmets, 2 spears, wrench & other workers' equipment, large quantities of fish oil, christening bottle

SYNOPSIS: Steve and Bucky take jobs at United Shipyard to investigate launch sabotage. As Cap and Bucky, they enter a nearly completed ship and find workers coating the interior with fish oil. When they inquire, the workers attack. Cap and Bucky defeat them, allowing one to escape, following him into the shipyard's foundry where more workers attack. Eventually snared by a lasso, the pair surrender so as to be taken to the workers' leader, the fishlike Eel at his hideout within coastal cliffs. Eel drops them into a pit of hungry electric eels, then departs to finish his ship-sinking preparations. While Cap fights back the eels, Bucky finds a stone passage through which to escape. Later, the empty ship launches, and Cap and Bucky board it. The Eel's giant octopus, attracted by the fish oil, attacks the ship. Cap and Bucky, in diving helmets, submerge to fight the octopus, who eventually captures them, returning them to the Eel's hideout where Cap instructs Bucky to clear the passage to the eel pit. They lure the octopus into probing the passage, and the eels shock it to death. Cap and Bucky then defeat the Eel and company.

NOTE: Story called "The Eel of Horror Harbor" on Contents page.

4TH STORY: "Dippy Diplomat" (8 pages)
CREDITS: Guy Blythe (writer, art)
FEATURE CHARACTER: Dippy Diplomat
SUPPORTING CAST: Swizzlestick
VILLAINS: Agent 123 & associate (last in CapC #21/4, '42), 2 criminals (only app)
OTHER CHARACTERS: Armor-wearing armored truck driver, bank teller, bank president, 2 demolition workers, 2 police officers, cow, Agent 123's associate's mother (mentioned only)
LOCATIONS/ITEMS: Dippy's embassy, railroad station, bank, barn in rural area, police station & jail; armored truck (license 55-3), police truck w/ tires, driver's armor, crates, explosives
SYNOPSIS: Dippy and Swizzlestick claim a million dollars worth of war bonds at the railroad station, where an armored truck, driven by an armored man, awaits them. Meanwhile, Agent 123 and his associate seize a bank president's office, intending to abscond with the bonds. At the station, two other criminals hijack the truck, with Dippy, Swizzlestick and the armored driver inside. They drive to the bank, intending to steal a bank key to acquire the bonds the next day. They carry in a crate labeled "war bonds," not realizing Dippy and company are within. Confronted by Agent 123 and associate, the hijackers drop the crate, releasing Dippy and company. The two criminal pairs fight, but Swizzlestick and the armored driver knock out all four. Outside, the truck rolls away. Dippy's group and the criminals pursue. Just as a demolition crew blows up a road, the truck hits a boulder and careens upward, suffering four flat tires. Dippy tries to claim tires from a parked truck, not realizing it belongs to the police, who jail Dippy, Swizzlestick, and the driver.
NOTE: Story called "Blondes of a Different Color" on Contents page. Although the four criminals are shown pursuing the runaway truck, they vanish from the story before catching up with it.

5TH STORY: "The Secret Stamp in The Mystery of the Song of the Wind" (7 pages)
CREDITS: Don Rico (art)
FEATURE CHARACTER: The Secret Stamp
VILLAINS: Mike Shultz (spy & Apex foreman, only app) & other spies
OTHER CHARACTERS: Thomas "Tom" Trimble (Roddy's classmate, boy scout), Miss Jones (Roddy's teacher), Roddy's classmates (all but 2 bts), Apex workers, 2 police officers, Minuteman (on Defense Bond stamp only)
LOCATIONS/ITEMS: Miss Jones' classroom, Freetown library, spies' hideout inc garage, Apex Aircraft Plant No. 4; Roddy & Tom's bicycles, 2nd spy's car, ultra violet lamp, "Song of the Wind" (book), Tom's library pencil
SYNOPSIS: Miss Jones assigns Roddy and Tom to work as librarians. One patron returns the book "Song of the Wind," which is immediately checked out by another. Suspicious, Roddy follows the second patron home, where the man reads the book under an ultra violet lamp. Tom has also tracked the man. Returning later, Roddy finds Tom's bicycle there but Tom and the man's car are gone. Finding Tom's pencil, Roddy sees that it points to the Apex Aircraft Plant. He calls the police and, as Secret Stamp, hurries to the plant. There, Foreman Shultz pretends to cooperate but, boasting that a bomb will soon destroy the plant, locks Secret Stamp in an underground room, where Tom is imprisoned. Tom reveals that spies use "Song" to send messages, literally written between the lines, that can only be read by ultra violet light. Secret Stamp climbs atop boxes to tap out morse code. Plant workers find him and Tom. After the police arrive, Stamp finds and disposes of the bomb, which Shultz claims Stamp planted himself. However, Tom uses the book and lamp to prove Shultz's culpability.
NOTE: Story called "The Mystery of the Song of the Wind" on Contents page.

TEXT STORY: "A Nosey Guy" (2 pages)
CREDITS: Writer unknown
FEATURE CHARACTER: Lieutenant Peter "Pete" Wilson (also as "Steve," see NOTE)
OTHER CHARACTERS: Commander Bill Ryder, Todd Winters, Mel Griffin & other members of Wilson's crew, Ryder's 2 associates, villagers (bts), clipper plane's skipper, crew & passengers inc 2 children & Ryder's mother, Ryder's girl friend (mentioned only)
LOCATIONS/ITEMS: US military base, adjacent village inc hotel, cliffs w/signal fire; transport ship, clipper plane, steamer, Wilson's plane (bts)
SYNOPSIS: Lt. Wilson, a transport pilot, frequently clashes with commanding officer Ryder because Ryder thinks Wilson is too nosey, causing him to go off schedule unnecessarily. Wilson leads his transport ship on a mission but diverts to investigate a signal fire, discovering a damaged clipper plane and its crew and passengers, some injured. Wilson repairs the clipper and flies it to safety. He expects Ryder to give him grief over diverting the mission, but Ryder, whose mother was among the passengers, instead gives him a 10-day leave and tells him "being a nosey guy pays dividends after all."
NOTE: Story not on Contents page. Pete's name changes to "Steve" midway through the story. Story appears between 3rd & 4th stories.

"The Princess of the Atom" (21 pages)

CREDITS: Ray Cummings (writer), Syd Shores (pencils, c art), Vince Alascia (inks)
FEATURE CHARACTER: Captain America (also in fb between CapC #22, '43 & CapC #26, '43 fb)
SUPPORTING CAST: Bucky (also in fb between CapC #22, '43 & CapC #26, '43 fb; last in AllWin #8/2, '43, chr last in Cap:ME #1, '94), Sgt. Duffy (last in AllWin #8/2, '43)
VILLAINS: Togaro (1st, "Atom World" green race leader) & his 7 underlings (4 die) (all fb only)
OTHER CHARACTERS: Frank Ferrule (Steve & Bucky's friend), Dianne Ferrule (Princess of Mita & Frank's adopted sister), Ahlma (Mitan woman), Alt (Mitan man) (1st for all), Ezra & Foley (Maine residents, only app), reporter, newsboy, male and female radio listeners, radio announcer (voice only), Maine residents (many die), freighter crew (all die), roach (grown to giant size, dies), ant (all fb only), Mr. & Mrs. Ferrule, the King & Queen of Mita (prev 4 mentioned only), US & Japanese soldiers (on cover only)
LOCATIONS/ITEMS: Maine coast inc Ferrule bungalow w/lab, airfield, Maine town, Birds' Nest Island (also "Bird's Nest Island"), newsroom, wood particle "realm," radio listeners' home (all in fb only), Army camp at maneuvers location, Mita (a planet within the Atom World, mentioned only); airplane w/ mounted gun & bombs, Frank's boat, meteorite fragment containing entrance to the Atom World, size-changing drugs, Foley's rifle, sulphuric acid bottle, chemical jars inc tanide solution & sulphuric acid, Bucky's Flit squirter, additional lab items (all in fb only), Bucky's guitar (also in fb), Steve's files
FLASHBACK: At Birds' Nest Island, off Maine's coast, Steve and Bucky picnic with Frank Ferrule and his adopted sister Dianne, whom Frank's parents found as an infant. Later, the group returns to the mainland Ferrule home, but Dianne vanishes. Further up the coast, four giants, hundreds of feet tall, wreak havoc, sinking ships and killing hundreds. Cap and Bucky commandeer a plane and attack. With so many lives at stake, they have no recourse but to kill the giants via strafing and bombing. Cap and Bucky visit Frank, where a mysterious man warns them away from Birds' Nest Island. They nonetheless return and find two women only inches tall, Dianne and a younger woman, Ahlma, who identifies Dianne as princess of Mita, a planet within an "Atom World" on a meteorite fragment on Birds' Nest Island. Mita is threatened by Togaro, leader of a neighboring green skinned race. For her safety, Dianne's parents, Mita's king and queen, sent her to Earth as an infant. The king and queen dead, Ahlma asks Dianne to return to Mita, where Togaro has stolen recently developed drugs to easily shrink and grow. Cap and Bucky realize the giants were Togaro's men and the mystery man Togaro himself. Unnoticed, a tiny Togaro climbs onto Cap and accompanies the group to Frank's father's lab, where they synthesize additional size-changing drugs. Togaro feeds some to a roach, which grows to giant size and attacks the group until they overwhelm and kill it. Spotting Togaro, Cap and Bucky shrink and pursue him into a wood particle's cellular structure. A fight ensues, but when Togaro starts growing, Cap does the same, and the fight moves back into the lab proper, where Togaro knocks Cap unconscious and flees. Cap and Bucky return to normal size, move the "Atom World" meteorite fragment to the lab and hire local men Ezra and Foley to guard it. When a Mitan man, Alt, appears to report Togaro's forces are readying an attack, Cap, Bucky, Dianne, Ahlma, and Frank shrink to accompany him to the Atom World. Togaro's underlings raid the lab. Foley throws an acid bottle at them, but a drop falls into the fragment, where, to the shrunken humans, it is a deadly flood.
SYNOPSIS: Steve and Bucky recall their encounter with Togaro.
NOTE: First issue to lack a Table of Contents. Story continues in CapC #26, '43 making it the only golden age Captain America story to extend over two issues. Designated "Case No. 1745-A." Scripter Ray Cummings (1887-1957) is the author of "The Girl in the Golden Atom" (1922) and used that novel's premise in this story. When Dianne disappears, she is presumably abducted by Togaro and subsequently rescued by Ahlma, who then explains her true origins, but this is not explicitly stated. Although a radio announcer describes the giants as "100 feet tall," they are clearly far larger, since one of them snaps a freighter in two with his bare hands. As made clear in the next issue, by the time Cap and company relocate the rock fragment, Togaro has already re-entered the Atom World. On page 20, one of Togaro's underlings is erroneously identified as Togaro himself.

2ND STORY: "The Films of Death" (7 pages)
CREDITS: Harry Sahle (pencils), Gustav Schrotter (inks)
FEATURE CHARACTER: Human Torch (next in YA #7, '43, MC #43, '43)
SUPPORTING CAST: Toro (last in MC #42, '43, next in YA #7, '43)
VILLAINS: Von Bacht (Gestapo spy, only app) & 2 underlings, Gestapo officer, concentration camp guards (one dies), Heinrich Himmler (Nazi Germany's Reichsführer-SS, 1st but chr last in Blaze #9, '95 fb, next in SubC #10/2, '43)
OTHER CHARACTERS: 2 Russian prisoners, Russian soldiers, theater owner, theater projectionist, usherette, theater attendees, Manhattan bystanders, concentration camp victim (on posters only), federal agents (bts, arrest Nazi agents), Bobby Ross (the "Buffalo Murderess," news photo only), Gash (news photo only), man ("Lloy..."; probably "Lloyd") & woman on movie poster, snake (on symbolic splash page only), Hamilton, Yukon Torpey (both boxers), Kapitan, Hughes, Everett, Fitzsimmons (prev 4 judges), Jordan (WAACS member), Playboy Fisk, Shrotter (prev 9 mentioned in newspaper headlines only)
LOCATIONS/ITEMS: Manhattan inc Torch and Toro's apartment, theater inc projection room and owner's office, von Bacht's hideout & theater owner's home w/basement, Nazi concentration camp, Russian battle zone, Gestapo headquarters; von Bacht's short-wave radio set, Nazi film camera & Russian captive's film (plus 2 copies), theater projection camera & reels

copy, are waiting within, and they quickly defeat the spies.
NOTE: Story followed by "Captain America's Fun Page" (1/2 page), w/quiz and puzzle featuring Captain America and six Nazi saboteurs.

3RD STORY: "The Murdering Mummy and the Laughing Sphinx!" (17 pages)
CREDITS: Syd Shores (art)
FEATURE CHARACTER: Captain America (next in YA #7, '43, Cap #600/4, '09 fbs, CapC #26/3, '43)
SUPPORTING CAST: Bucky (next in YA #7, '43), Sgt. Duffy
VILLAINS: The Mummy (Karr, also as Professor Jameson, 1st, next in YA #18/3, '45), Modebl the Demon, gong striker, other mummies (prev 3 in dream sequence only)
OTHER CHARACTERS: Red (Bucky's friend, possibly last in CapC #6, '41), 3 army officers (1 dies), 2 army engineers (1 dies), hunter (dies), librarian, library patron, Skip (hunter's dog), radio announcer (voice only), John Conte (priority board official, dies bts), police officers (bts, arrest Mummy), female mummy (as exhibit display only)
LOCATIONS/ITEMS: Camp Lehigh inc Steve and Bucky's tent, barracks & guardhouse, woods off north road, Manhattan inc officer's and engineer's offices & library inc Egyptian room (Room 210); Modebl's throne, gong & blood filled skull w/pen (all in dream sequence only), Egyptian relics, Mummy's sword, chain w/Sphinx pendant inc opium vial & parchment within, translation scrap
SYNOPSIS: When the Mummy, conducting a murder campaign along the eastern seaboard, kills six victims in one night, Cap and Bucky investigate. They find a recent victim, along with a paper scrap, an Egyptian passage in which Modebl the Demon recommends seeking "the sphinx who laughs." The two find the Mummy targeting world leaders so Modebl may rule. The Mummy pushes Cap off a cliff and almost strangles Bucky before letting him live to spread word of Cap's death. However, Cap survives by hanging on with the Mummy's sphinx pendant, which he grabbed in the struggle. Later, Bucky investigates the pendant's inscription at a library, meeting Prof. Jameson. The inscription reads "The key to all is the laughing sphinx." Outside, Bucky meets his friend Red, an archaeology student who mentions Jameson recently discovered Modebl's tomb. That night, Cap and Bucky head for the library to confer with Jameson but find the Mummy instead. The sphinx pendant is struck in battle and opens its mouth - or "laughs" - to reveal a hidden vial, with a message claiming answers will be provided to he who drinks it. Cap takes a sip and finds himself in a dream of Modebl's court, surrounded by attacking mummies. Modebl proclaims Cap himself will "carry the curse of the mummy," but as Cap fights his opponents, he awakens, shocked at the powerful reaction to just a sip. The heroes return to the library in time to see Jameson transform into the Mummy. Cap knocks him out and turns the Mummy over to police. Cap tells Bucky that Jameson drank an entire vial of potion when he discovered Modebl's tomb, turning him into the Mummy.
NOTES: As in CapC #20, '42, Cap demonstrates unusual respect for and knowledge of Egyptian magic. Karr inquires as to whether Cap is "he...the mightiest one of all," language similar to that used to describe Cap by Balthar and "Satan" in CapC #21/3, '42. Cap describes the vial's contents as "concentrated opium...a couple of drops of [which] would eat away [one's] whole brain." Cap attributes Jameson's transformation to "lycanthropy," which should only apply to werewolves. Presumably he means Jameson/Karr is a "weremummy."

4TH STORY: "The Mystery of the Air-Mail Marker" (7 pages)
CREDITS: Carl Pfeufer (pencils), Gustav Schrotter (inks)
FEATURE CHARACTER: The Secret Stamp (next in USA #8/7, '43)
VILLAINS: Henry Smith ("Smith, the Missing Link," sailor and spy, only app), 3 spies
OTHER CHARACTERS: Teddy (Roddy's young friend), Bill (Teddy's brother), stationery store vendor, Pat's Hotel desk clerk & patrons, police (Clancy named), train passengers, Minuteman (on Defense Bond stamp only)
LOCATIONS/ITEMS: Colt home, train station, W. 45th Street, stationary store, Teddy's house, Pat's Hotel on the waterfront inc Room 777; train, Bill's car, Smith's luger w/ silencer, spies' firearms, envelopes
SYNOPSIS: Roddy accompanies his friend Teddy to to meet Teddy's brother Bill, an injured returning sailor. Bill mentions the seeming coincidence that his ship suffered sabotage following each letter from Teddy and recalls giving the letters' envelopes to Henry Smith, a fellow sailor and supposed stamp collector also on leave in Freetown. Based on Roddy's suspicions, Bill visits Smith's hotel to retrieve the envelopes, but Smith pulls a gun on him, then admits the Nazis sent him messages concealed on Teddy's envelopes. Secret Stamp, having followed Bill, bursts in to knock Smith down, but three fellow spies arrive. Fortunately, Teddy arrives with police officers, who arrest the lot. Secret Stamp departs, but as Bill and Teddy drive away, Roddy runs after for a ride, his presence prompting Bill to suspect his secret.
NOTE: Story reveals Freetown is located on a waterfront, and thus in a coastal state.

5TH STORY: "Dippy Diplomat" (8 pages)
CREDITS: Gus Blythe (writer, art)
FEATURE CHARACTER: Dippy Diplomat (last app to date)
SUPPORTING CAST: Swizzlestick (last app to date), Mergetroide (last in CapC #21/4, '42, last app to date)
VILLAINS: Agent 123 & associate (last app to date), Agent 456 (also as valet "Guff," only app)
OTHER CHARACTERS: The Minister from Skullduggery (only app), child on tricycle, air raid wardens, air raid shelter occupants, pier guard, US Coast Guard captain & sailor, 2 customs officers, ocean liner crew & passengers (bts, off-panel), dog, fish
LOCATIONS/ITEMS: Dippy's embassy, Agent 123's hideout, air raid shelter, Pier 58 and adjoining bay inc customs office, jail; Dippy's limo, tricycle, tugboat, USCG ship, ocean liner, air raid siren, Dippy's walking stick, Minister's passport
SYNOPSIS: Agent 123 instructs Agent 456 to prevent Dippy from meeting with the Minister from Skullduggery to discuss a treaty. 456 tries twice to incapacitate Dippy but fails. After Dippy and company depart, 123 and associate hijack a tricycle to pursue. When an air raid drill is called, Dippy's limo pulls over. The spies precede Dippy to Pier 58, where the Minister will arrive. Replacing a guard, 123 directs Dippy's limo into the bay, then boards an arriving ocean liner and steals the Minister's passport. When Dippy and company swim to the dock, they are arrested for sneaking into the country. The Minister is arrested for lacking a passport. Agent 123 and associate's self-congratulatory mood is broken when they find Dippy and the Minister, eager to discuss the treaty, locked in the same cell.

TEXT STORY: "Jinx Mutt" (2 pages)
CREDITS: Writer unknown
FEATURE CHARACTERS: Chris (young kennel employee), "the Mutt" (Chris' dog)
VILLAIN: A razorback sow (dies)

OTHER CHARACTERS: Tom (kennel manager), Mr. Coates (prospective dog purchaser), Marjorie Coates (Coates' young daughter), Jerry (kennel employee, mentioned only), Mr. Anderson & Mr. Clover (dog purchasers, mentioned only), Marjorie's nurse (mentioned only), sow's brood, quail, kennel dogs (bts)

LOCATIONS/ITEMS: Village "close to the coast range" inc kennels, adjacent field and forest; Chris' gun

SYNOPSIS: When Mr. Coates seeks a dog as a companion for his daughter Marjorie, he notices Chris' "Mutt," but Tom denigrates the dog as a unmanageable runt. Stung, Chris takes the Mutt hunting, but the dog senses trouble and wanders off, eventually encountering the also wandering Marjorie, whom he befriends. When a wild razorback sow happens by, she charges the two, and Mutt kills the sow, protecting Marjorie. Tom and Coates are impressed, and Coates offers to buy Mutt, but Chris declines.

NOTE: Story appears between 3rd & 4th stories.

CAPTAIN AMERICA COMICS #26 (May 1943)

"The Princess of the Atom, Part II" (25 pages)

CREDITS: Ray Cummings (writer), Syd Shore (pencils), Vince Alascia (inks), Alex Schomburg (c art)
FEATURE CHARACTER: Captain America (only in fb between CapC #25, '43 fb & MFan #5/2, '82 fb)
SUPPORTING CAST: Bucky (only in fb between CapC #25, '43 fb & MFan #5/2, '82 fb)
VILLAINS: Togaro (dies) & his followers (3 from CapC #25, '43, 300 more in Microverse inc size-change ship's crew, most bts, Greer named, all in fb only)
OTHER CHARACTERS: Princess Dianne (Dianne Ferrule), Frank Ferrule, Ahlma, Alt (dies), Alt's crew (bts, die), thousands of Mitans (most bts, all die), Maine citizens (many die), Ezra & Foley (mentioned only) (all in fb only), Nazi undersea workers, shark (both on cover only)
LOCATIONS/ITEMS: "The Atom World" (1st, a Microverse) inc planet with portal to and from Earth w/Togaro's encampment, Mita (Dianne, Ahlma, & Alt's native planet) inc city of Mita, other populated districts, mountain stream and Togaro's mountain stronghold (destroyed), Mita's star, & additional planets and stars, one or more Maine towns (all in fb only), Nazi underwater base (on cover only); meteorite fragment containing entrance to the Atom World, Frank's lab & boathouse (destroyed), Alt's size-change ship (destroyed), Togaro's size-change ship, size-changing drugs, acid (all in fb only), S.S. Columbia (on cover only)
FLASHBACK: Faced with the acid flood, Cap grows large enough to carry his friends to safety, then, shrinking, joins them through the portal to the Atom World where they board Alt's space size-change ship. Unnoticed, a tiny Togaro hitches a ride on Bucky. As the ship travels, Togaro grows and takes the women hostage. Cap and Bucky shrink to sneak onto Togaro who ties Dianne and Ahlma to his belt, unaware of the heroes' presence. When the ship lands on Mita, Togaro grows to immense size and heads for his mountain stronghold. Cap and Bucky untie the women, but only Cap and Dianne escape. In Mita's city, they rejoin Frank and Alt. Togaro's size-change ship, crewed by his men, arrives at Togaro's stronghold, where it grows gigantic. Noticing Dianne's absence, Togaro declares Ahlma his servant but remains unaware of Bucky. His ship soon dwarfs Mita itself, which falls from orbit. Meanwhile, Cap, as a giant, places thousands of Mitans into Alt's ship, which barely escapes before the planet falls into its sun. Togaro captures Bucky and plans to conquer Earth. When Togaro's ship lands near the portal, Bucky and Ahlma shrink and escape. The Mitan ship crashes on the portal-world; only Cap, Dianne, and Frank survive. They join Bucky and Ahlma, and make the return trip to Earth, but Togaro's three comrades, having stolen the meteorite "containing" the Atom World, guard it in Frank's boathouse. The heroes evade detection and escape. Togaro's men enter Earth, becoming giants. Cap and Bucky fight wave after wave of giant warriors, repeatedly growing themselves to dwarf their opponents. Finally only Togaro himself, now thousands of feet tall, remains. Cap grows to the same size. Togaro catches Cap in a wrestling hold, but Cap breaks free and pummels him with blows, knocking him into a cliff. Apparently struck dead, Togaro shrinks into nothingness. Back to normal, Cap and Bucky bid farewell to Frank, Dianne, and Ahlma.
NOTE: The entire story is a continuation of the flashback begun in CapC #25, '43 and never returns to the present. This story marks the first appearance of a "microverse" in a Marvel Comics story. With Togaro apparently dead, his followers presumably retreat back to the "Atom World," or possibly automatically shrink back after being rendered unconscious, but this is not explicitly stated. Togaro's size-change ship is repeatedly referred to as "a Togaro ship," implying "Togaro" is also the name of his forces, or perhaps of his race.

2ND STORY: "Deposits of Death" (7 pages)
CREDITS: Harry Sahle (pencils), Al Bellman (inks)
FEATURE CHARACTER: Human Torch (next in HT #12, '43, SubC #23/3, '47 fb, MC #44, '43)
SUPPORTING CAST: Toro (last in MC #43, '43, next in HT #12, '43)
VILLAINS: Herr von Richter (saboteur & Hitler lookalike, also as "Edward Hamilton," dies, only app) & 3 underlings
OTHER CHARACTERS: City National Bank president, CNB employees & customers (some die), ambulance crew, police officer, Builder's Bank employees & customers (bts), Manhattan bystanders, Adolf Hitler (in photograph only)
LOCATIONS/ITEMS: Manhattan inc City National Bank (destroyed), von Richter's hideout, Torch and Toro's apartment & Builder's Bank inc Vault Number 1334; von Richter's car, Torch's guard uniform, Torch & Toro's money, deposit slips
SYNOPSIS: Making a deposit, Torch and Toro are caught in a bank explosion, the fifth one in a month. They clear a path to safety but are unable to save everyone. Realizing the explosion came from the vault, Torch asks the bank president for recent deposit slips. Meanwhile, at his hideout, the bomber, Nazi saboteur von Richter, tells his men that the bank explosions will motivate people to keep their wealth at home, where criminals

...banks, where he tackles him. Von Richter's men enter the fray, as does Toro, and the saboteurs are soon defeated. Von Richter flees in a car, but Torch retrieves the bomb and throws it into the car, where it explodes and kills the Nazi.

3RD STORY: "Captain America and the Russian Hell-Hole" (24 pages)

CREDITS: Syd Shores (pencils), Al Alascia (inks)

FEATURE CHARACTER: Captain America (next in CapC #29, '43 fb, USA #8, '43, Cap:FA #1, '10 fb, bts in CapBiB, '76, Kid #3, '43, Cap:Who #1, '10 fb)

SUPPORTING CAST: Bucky (last in YA #7, '43, chr next in CapC #29, '43 fb, next in USA #8, '43), Sgt. Duffy (next in USA #8, '43)

VILLAINS: Nazis inc iceberg fleet commander, pilots, soldiers & sailors (most bts, some die), a wolf pack (at least one dies)

OTHER CHARACTERS: Camp Lehigh soldiers & other army personnel (most bts, some die), tramp steamer captain & crew (bts), Josef Stalin (last in HT #5a, '41, chr last in Inv #33, '78, chr next in SgtF #51, '68, next in HT #14/5, '43), Col. Nem, Capt. Petrovitch, Russian intelligence officers, 2 Russian intelligence operatives (referred to as "KBX," die), Russian soldiers & sailors, "Lapp" villagers (see NOTE), 2 reindeer, 2 sled dogs, chicken, "a man-eating rabbit" (mentioned by Bucky to distract guard)

LOCATIONS/ITEMS: The Atlantic Ocean, Soviet Union inc Murmansk, KBX base, Lapp village & Moscow w/military intelligence HQ inc radio room and the Kremlin; Nazi aircraft carriers disguised as icebergs w/planes (most destroyed), Nazi sled convoy & ships (many destroyed), Nazi boat, Russian boats, ships & artillery, US Army convoy ships, tramp steamer inc deck gun, reindeer sled, Bucky's rifle, Russian parkas, Nazis rifles, skis & poles, guard's keys, KBX map

SYNOPSIS: In an army convoy, Steve, Duffy, and their outfit sail for Russia. Bucky comes along, working in the tramp steamer's galley. Nazi planes attack the convoy, and the steamer sinks, but Steve and Bucky commandeer a Nazi plane. Hours later, Cap and Bucky crash land in northern Russia. They hike inland and see Nazi soldiers pin down and shoot two Russian soldiers, both of whom are intelligence operatives. One dying Russian tells Cap, "October...icebergs...map." Donning the dead men's parkas, Cap and Bucky find a German supply convoy, heading for an apparent iceberg. Sighted, the two surrender to learn more. They are taken within an "iceberg," a shell housing a Nazi aircraft carrier and planes. The commander imprisons them, and Bucky finds a map in his parka, which indicates a pending Nazi attack on Murmansk. Cap and Bucky escape, sabotage the ship's radio room, and commandeer a boat to escape the "iceberg." Once outside, they flee on skis. Locating the Russian operatives' shack, they radio Moscow, remembering the codeword "October" to prove their story's validity, and warn them of the impending "iceberg" attack. After escaping a wolf pack, they receive food and rest at a Lapp village but are again captured and imprisoned on the iceberg commander's ship, which leads the invasion fleet. During battle with the alerted Russians, the ship is struck and quickly takes in water. Chained in a cell, Cap and Bucky expect to die until a dead guard floats by allowing them to obtain his key. Escaping through a torpedo tube, they are rescued by Russian sailors. Days later, Cap and Bucky are honored at the Kremlin, guests of Stalin himself.

NOTES: Axis forces previously used seagoing vessels (Japanese submarines) disguised as icebergs in SubC #9, '43. Coincidentally, Captain Petrovitch resembles the Black Widow's ally Ivan Petrovitch (1st in AA #1, '70). The Russian intelligence agency is presumably the GRU (Glavnoye Razvedyvatel'noye Upravleniye, "Main Intelligence Directorate"). The story's depiction of Murmansk as a vital wartime supply center is accurate, as is the city's placement near regions inhabited by "Lapps," more correctly called "Sámi." Murmansk was invaded by Nazi forces in June-September 1941 as part of Germany's Operation Silver Fox. Its invasion in 1943, by iceberg-ships or anything else, is strictly a Marvel Universe event. When preparing to build an ice shelter, Cap references Uncle Tom's Cabin, by Harriet Beecher Stowe, first published in 1852.

4TH STORY: "The Secret Stamp and the Ration Book Counterfeits" (4 pages)

CREDITS: Jack Alderman (art)

FEATURE CHARACTER: The Secret Stamp

VILLAINS: Stumpy Logan, Weasel Waxton & their men

OTHER CHARACTERS: Johnson of the FBI, 2 police officers, pool hall patrons, 2 of Roddy's customers (Mr. Warren named), FBI phone caller (bts, tipped FBI about Stamp's fight), Minuteman (on Defense Bond stamp only)

LOCATIONS/ITEMS: Freetown's Main Street inc pool hall & gas station, the US capitol (in symbolic last panel); Roddy's cart and "Buy War Stamps Here!" sign, Stumpy's printing press, Weasel's pistol

SYNOPSIS: Stumpy Logan, suspected crime ring leader, buys $100 worth of war bonds from Roddy. Initially impressed, Roddy learns counterfeit gas ration books are being sold by a local gang. Guessing this to be the source of Logan's largesse, Roddy, as Secret Stamp, investigates and finds Logan's counterfeiting operation. He knocks out Logan and his gang, then turns them over to a visiting FBI agent.

NOTE: The Secret Stamp's cowl is red in this story. Roddy's claim that Stumpy's gang is "the only local gang" in Freetown, implying he has driven out all others, appears to be accurate, since in his subsequent appearances he encounters only solo criminals. The Secret Stamp mentions he may publicly reveal his true identity when the war is over.

TEXT STORY: "Bonus to Boot" (2 pages)

CREDITS: Writer unknown

FEATURE CHARACTERS: Jack & Ned (2 young war bond salesmen)

VILLAIN: A robber

OTHER CHARACTERS: Mr. Arnold (elderly wealthy man)

LOCATIONS/ITEMS: The Arnold estate inc rooms, cellar, shrubbery & path to house; Mr. Arnold's walking stick & bag of money, robber's gun, Ned's flashlight

SYNOPSIS: Jack and Ned visit Mr. Arnold but are turned away by a surly thug whose demeanor rouses suspicion. The two sneak in through the cellar, where they find Arnold tied up. After freeing him, they take the intruder, a robber, by surprise. The robber draws a gun, and a stray bullet grazes Jack. The encounter moves into the basement, where Arnold downs the robber with his walking stick. Learning Jack and Ned are selling war bonds, Arnold promises to buy several and to will their subsequent value to local boys, including his two rescuers.

NOTE: Story appears between 2nd and 3rd stories.

"North of the Border" (25 pages)

CREDITS: Syd Shores (pencils, assoc editor), Vince Alascia (inks), Vince Fago (managing editor), Alex Schomburg (c art)
FEATURE CHARACTER: Captain America
SUPPORTING CAST: Bucky (last in USA #8, '43, chr last in Cap:Who #1, '10 fb)
VILLAINS: Baron von Hartmann (spy & ex-consular attache, only app) & his spy ring members
OTHER CHARACTERS: Ramona "Ramon" Bedoin, General Bedoin (Canadian Army officer, Ramona's father, also in newspaper photo), 3 Canadian government officials, 2 army guards (die), landlady, dog sled driver, bystanders, 7 huskies, President Franklin D. Roosevelt, Prime Minister Winston Churchill, Prime Minister acKenzie King, Adolf Hitler (all 4 mentioned only), Nazi soldiers (on cover only), Russian tank corps, airplane pilots (both bts on cover only)
)CATIONS/ITEMS: Quebec City inc Parliament building, Chateau Frontenac w/Steve & Bucky's room, Dufferin Terrace, "lower city" w/133 ie Carteret, Chambers A Lours (rooms for rent, street #129) inc Cap's room, St. Lawrence River, von Hartmann's island hideout accessible by bridge; spies' pistols, von Hartman's knife & torch, Russian tanks, airplanes, Cap's motorcycle (prev 3 on cover only)
'NOPSIS: In Quebec City, where Steve and Bucky are on furlough, Baron von Hartmann's spies abduct General Bedoin for war plan ormation. Steve and Bucky encounter von Hartmann's men harassing a youth, Ramon, and drive them away. Ramon, carrying $20,000, uncooperative and flees, dropping a note ordering war plans to be brought to 133 Rue Carteret. Recognizing the connection to Bedoin, Cap d Bucky find the address and the youth keeping watch. Bucky returns to the hotel, while Cap confronts "Ramon," actually Ramona Bedoin, e general's daughter, who hopes to ransom her father's freedom. Cap is captured but Ramona escapes. Left locked in by von Hartmann, io mentions an island hideout, Cap uses a candle to send morse code to Bucky, who responds until von Hartmann's men abduct him. mona frees Cap, and the two check the hotel, where Bucky leaves a message directing them to the island. A blizzard breaks out, and Cap mmandeers a dog sled to reach the hideout, where a bound Bucky hurls himself into the fire to protect Gerneral Bedoin, burning off his bonds it as Cap arrives. The two defeat von Hartmann and company. Ramona is reunited with her father.
)TE: Table of Contents (1 page) returns for this issue and the next, featuring Captain America, Bucky & Minuteman (on Defense bond stamp). eve & Bucky sing a variation of "Jingle Bells" here.

ID STORY: "The Man-Hole of Death!" (7 pages)
REDITS: Paul Reinman (pencils), Al Bellman (inks)
ATURE CHARACTER: Human Torch (next in AllWin #9, '43, MC #45, '43)
IPPORTING CAST: Toro (last in MC #44, '43, next in AllWin #9, '43)
LLAIN: The Sewer-Man ("Sloppy Joe," only app, dies)
'HER CHARACTERS: Chase Stewart (finance clerk, dies), police officer, messenger (dies), Sewer-Man's 4 other victims (as corpses, 3 e), Everett & "Ghandi" (in newspaper headlines only), "Barlow Lemon" (in newspaper photo only)
)CATIONS/ITEMS: Manhattan inc financial district w/bank, furniture store, Spruce Street and Sewer-Man's domain beneath Torch and o's apartment; Sewer-Man's weighted "snake whip," brass knuckles, makeshift bomb & flame-retardant powder
'NOPSIS: Five people have been abducted in the financial district, prompting Torch and Toro to patrol. When a weighted rope pulls a essenger into a manhole, Toro signals Torch, then follows, only to be doused with flame-retardant powder by the abductor, Sewer-Man. Torch ds Sewer-Man hurling Toro into a rapid sewer current, rescues him and provides artificial respiration. Sewer-Man throws a makeshift bomb them, but Torch deflects it. Fleeing, Sewer-Man falls into the current. Torch allows it to carry the murderer away. Torch and Toro recover the len money; days later, Sewer-Man's drowned body is found.
)TE: Story entitled "The Man Hole of Death" (without hyphen & exclamation point) on Contents page. The Sewer-Man may be connected to Sewer Men, an inbred sewer-dwelling criminal community apparently wiped out by the Vision in MC #36/4, '42.

.D STORY: "Blitzkrieg to Berlin!" (22 pages)
REDITS: Syd Shores (pencils), Vince Alascia (inks)
ATURE CHARACTER: Captain America (next in AllWin #9/2, '43, Cap #615.1, '11 fb)
IPPORTING CAST: Bucky (next in AllWin #9/2, '43)
LLAINS: Adolf Hitler ("Shicklegruber," last in HT #12/2, '43), Herr Wolf & his fellow spies (Fritz named), Captain Huntzel & his sub crew (most), Nazi soldiers & workers (many bts, most die), 2 cowled Nazis torturers (symbolic splash page only)
'HER CHARACTERS: Pierre Leroux (dies), French prisoners (Henri, Philippe, Jacques named), Camp Lehigh soldiers (most bts), USO rformers (bts), chained prisoner (symbolic splash page only)
)CATIONS/ITEMS: USO circus tent, Herr Wolf's hideout w/dungeon (destroyed), tavern, Long Island beach, Berlin inc Hitler's "castle" underground factory inc dungeon equipped with sliding floor w/flames beneath (destroyed), Nazi airfield, Atlantic Ocean; Huntzel's submarine 17), giant submarine (destroyed), German bomber plane (commandeered by Cap and Bucky), Nazi staff car, Cap's motorcycle, Nazis' tols, rifles, gas & dynamite, Herr Wolf's catapult device w/daggers, Pierre's explosives & detonator, branding iron (symbolic splash page y)

carrying hundreds of tanks and planes. Thrown into a dungeon, Cap and Bucky are rescued by Pierre Leroux, one of a group of escaped ench prisoners. He takes Cap and Bucky to the sub factory where he and other French prisoners set explosives. Cap and Bucky volunteer to detonate them. The prisoners knock them out and carry them to safety while Pierre takes the suicide mission. Shot by Nazi troops, the dying Pierre sets off the detonator and destroys the factory. After bidding farewell to the prisoners, who plan to continue fighting in Germany, Cap and Bucky commandeer a Nazi bomber plane and depart.

NOTE: Title lacks exclamation point on Contents page. Although Hitler speaks as though he has never met Cap and Bucky before, he met them in CapC #2/2, 42, unless the Hitler in that story was an impostor. He also chr met them in Inv #16, '77. Hitler presumably departed the factory before it was destroyed. Cap & Bucky called "the Dynamic Duo" here.

4TH STORY: "Roddy Colt Steps Out" (6 pages)
CREDITS: Vince Alascia (pencils), Don Rico (inks)
FEATURE CHARACTER: The Secret Stamp (next in USA #9/7, '43)
VILLAIN: Jones (USO chapter treasurer, thief)
OTHER CHARACTERS: Freetown USO chapter president, members (Joe named), Air Raid Warden (ARW) leader & messengers (Jackie Bill named), actors in play (see NOTE), softball players, audience members, Minuteman (on Defense bond stamp only)
LOCATIONS/ITEMS: Freetown inc air raid warden post, ballfield & Town Hall w/auditorium and stage; costumes, stage equipment, Secret Stamp's mirror
SYNOPSIS: Roddy learns $5000 has been stolen from the USO treasury. The USO is reluctant to involve police lest public morale is damaged. To collect additional funds, Roddy suggests staging a play, with himself "impersonating" Secret Stamp, enacting the USO theft. During the play Roddy, as Secret Stamp, prepares to "identify the thief," bluffing to draw the culprit out. It works as Jones, the USO treasurer, shoots at him from the audience, striking a mirror set up by Stamp instead. Jones is caught, and the USO president finds Roddy tied up backstage, convincing everyone that Secret Stamp "took his place" on stage.
NOTE: Although it might be presumed the play's actors are Roddy's fellow ARW messengers, this is not specified.

TEXT STORY: "Swell Guy" (2 pages)
CREDITS: Writer unknown
FEATURE CHARACTER: William Cortlandt (retired businessman & Nazi agent, only app)
SUPPORTING CAST: Ted (newsboy, only app)
VILLAINS: The Nazis (mentioned only)
LOCATIONS/ITEMS: Cortlandt's mansion inc garage, library & workshop w/desk, adjacent town & river; Cortlandt's files & shortwave radio set
SYNOPSIS: William Cortlandt, who has been providing the Axis with carefully acquired military intelligence via radio, congratulates himself on his "farsightedness" in joining the Nazi cause. When newsboy Ted delivers Cortlandt's newspaper, he professes a desire to become a "respected citizen" like Cortlandt and hopes that Cortlandt will share his "wisdom" so Ted can better understand world events, including Nazi atrocities, upon which Cortlandt has not allowed himself to dwell. Shamed by Ted's faith and admiration, Cortlandt resolves to destroy his files and radio set.
NOTE: Story not listed on Contents page. Story appear between 2nd & 3rd stories.

CAPTAIN AMERICA COMICS #28 (July 1943)

"The Challenge of the "Mad Torso"" (23 pages)

CREDITS: Syd Shores (pencils, assoc editor), Vince Alascia (inks), Vince Fago (managing editor), Alex Schomburg (c art)
FEATURE CHARACTER: Captain America
SUPPORTING CAST: Bucky (last in AllWin #9/2, '43, chr last in Cap #615.1, '11 fb), Sgt. Duffy (last in USA #8, '43)
VILLAINS: The Mad Torso (cyborg scientist, only app, dies), Dr. Roerich, Carl & 2 other sanitarium guards, 2 Torso operatives, Ol' John the Hermit, Adolf Hitler (next bts in CapC #30/4, '43), Josef Goebbels (last in MC #42/2, '43, next in CapC #31, '43), Hermann Goering (last in AllWin #8, '43, next in CapC #31, '43), Benito Mussolini (last in USA #5, '42, next in YA #9, '43), Emperor Hirohito (last in YA #7/3, '43, next in YA #8/3, '43), Nazi soldiers (some on cover only), Mad Torso's spies (bts, existence presumed by Nazis)
OTHER CHARACTERS: Camp Lehigh soldiers, Robert Winters (rubber industrialist) & his chauffeur, 2 railroad yard workers, conductor, Westown train station manager, 12 industrialists (Mad Torso's prisoners), "ape-men" (Mad Torso's experimental subjects, die), gray-skinned man in suit (on cover only)
LOCATIONS/ITEMS: Camp Lehigh inc Steve and Bucky's tent, Nazi HQ in Berlin, Roerich Sanitarium inc Roerich's office & padded cell, Westown train station, Ol' John's monastery w/belfry & organ, Mad Torso's mountain citadel/laboratory inc transparent dome w/mountain view, elevator, electrical apparatus, control panels, cages, desk & portable dynamo, Nazi fortress inc 5000 lbs. pressure death device (on cover only), cable car between monastery & citadel, Nazi soldiers' guns, sanitarium guards' pistols, Mad Torso's letters, Torso operatives' knives
SYNOPSIS: The Axis leaders accept the Mad Torso's offer to undermine the Allies and kill Captain America. First, Torso abducts US industrialists and shuts down war plants. Steve and Bucky receive a Torso letter, for the villain knows their secret identities, announcing his intent to abduct industrialist Robert Winters, whom Cap and Bucky track to Dr. Roerich's sanitarium. Roerich drugs and imprisons the two, but they escape, and Roerich confesses Winters was shipped away in a crate. Following a second letter, Cap and Bucky find Winters and a third letter, directing them to Westown and deranged John the Hermit. In an abandoned monastery, John traps them and drops a fourth letter, noting the next clue is the belfry. Cap dives into a raging river hundreds of feet below and returns to free Bucky. In the belfry, they find a cable car system between the monastery and a mountain citadel. There, they meet the Mad Torso, who, rendered limbless by an American bomb, wears electrically charged mechanical arms and legs. He shows them his human subjects mutated into ape-like beings, and the abducted industrialists. Bucky encourages

orso to talk while Cap sweeps him from the steel floor, weakening his now ungrounded electric charge. Bucky takes the industrialists to safety. ap carries the Torso to his desk, where he repowers himself with a portable dynamo, grabs the returning Bucky and flees up a mountain. When s climb requires both hands, Torso throws Bucky to Cap, then falls, starting an avalanche which destroys his citadel and apparently kills him. OTE: Contains Table of Contents (1 page) featuring Captain America, Bucky & Minuteman (on Defense bond stamp). Next Tales of Contents age appears in CapC #59, '46. The Mad Torso's name is rendered in quotation marks throughout the story. On page 18, the Torso is erroneously ›lored as if his head is also made of metal. John the Hermit wears a strange cap, implying the Torso may be mentally controlling him.

ND STORY: "Black Voodoo Murders!" (7 pages)
REDITS: Unknown
EATURE CHARACTER: Human Torch (next in MC #46, '43)
UPPORTING CAST: Toro (last in MC #45, '43, next in YA #8, '43)
ILLAINS: Karl (butler & "voodoo" user, only app), two African warriors (on symbolic splash page only)
THER CHARACTERS: Fred von Kirsten (German refugee & African explorer), Sally von Kirsten (Fred's daughter), Seth Jensen (government mployee, dies), 2 police detectives, boa constrictor (dies)
OCATIONS/ITEMS: Von Kirsten home, servant's quarters inc Karl's room; Karl's blowgun & darts, witch doctor drum, African artifacts inc ▪ears, masks, mummy case & stuffed gorilla, stolen German airplane designs, warriors' machete & spear (on symbolic splash page only)
YNOPSIS: German refugee von Kirsten meets with Jensen to offer the USA stolen German airplane designs, but Jensen drops dead. ›n Kirsten telephones Torch. When Torch and Toro arrive, the police are present, having determined Jensen died of a rare tropical drug. ›ro suspects von Kirsten's butler Karl, but Torch suspects daughter Sally, who secretly removes the designs. Torch follows her and is struck ▪ a poison dart from the servant's quarters. He burns the poison out of his system, then burns his way into Karl's room, filled with "voodoo" araphernalia. Karl, hiding in a mummy case, beats a "witch doctor's drum" to weaken Torch, then releases his pet boa constrictor. Toro enters, ▪capitates the snake and forces Karl to emerge. A Nazi operative, Karl confesses to poisoning Jensen and extorting Sally's cooperation by reatening her father.
OTE: Title on Contents page has no exclamation point.

RD STORY: "The Vultures of Violent Death" (22 pages)
REDITS: Syd Shores (pencils), Vince Alascia (inks)
EATURE CHARACTER: Captain America (next in USA #9, '43, Cap #262, '81 fb, FallSon:IM, '07 fb)
UPPORTING CAST: Bucky (next in USA #9, '43), Gen. Haywood (last in AllWin #8/2, '43, next in CapC #30/3, '43)
LLAINS: The Pa-Pi-Ru-Guan chief (dies), the Birdmen (Pa-Pi-Ru-Guan warriors who ride giant birds, some die), Japanese officer (called ‣elestial Commander" by soldier, dies), Japanese soldiers & pilots (some bts, most die)
THER CHARACTERS: 3 US Army officers, radio operator, 6 captive pilots (Higgins, Kelly named), giant birds (some die), giant ape (dies), everal hundred" crocodiles (all die)
OCATIONS/ITEMS: Pa-Pi-Ru-Gua island inc river & volcano of same name w/Japanese air base inc barracks and prison hut, Solomon ands inc Allied field HQ & Steve and Bucky's tent; birdmen's clubs, shields, spears, & swords, giant birds' bridles & saddles, Japanese ▪ldiers' rifles, 2-handed samurai sword, artillery machine gun
YNOPSIS: In the Solomon Islands, General Haywood assigns Cap to search by plane for a hidden Japanese base. Bucky tags along. ▪eir plane is shot down, and they parachute to the island Pa-Pi-Ru-Gua. There, the natives capture them and fly them, via giant birds, to ▪e Japanese base, within the island's volcano. The base commander wants the two executed, but the island's Chief offers freedom if Cap ▪mpletes the three trials of Ru-Gu-Ri-Bi: trials of strength, of water, and of fire. Cap and Bucky are imprisoned with captive US pilots, with whom ▪ap shares an escape plan. The next day, in the trial of strength, Cap defeats a giant ape. Meanwhile, the prisoners knock out their guards, arm emselves and pile bombs together. For his second trial, Cap braves a riverful of crocodiles, then fights his way to a plane readied by Bucky and ▪e prisoners. Aboard the plane, Cap and crew set off the piled bombs, igniting the volcano, which destroys the Japanese base and all within. OTE: General Haywood directly gives Cap assignments and orders for the first time. Haywood notes the Japanese base's efforts have evented the Allies from liberating New Guinea; the base's destruction notwithstanding, New Guinea remained under Japanese control until ▪d-1945. Haywood investigates another South Pacific island secretly under Japanese influence, Sulaharua, in his next appearance. Although ▪ap's shield is apparently confiscated by the Birdmen, his retrieval of it is not depicted. Although the story mentions a third test, "the fiery path ▪ Tua-Ru-Pa-Pi," Cap escapes before undergoing it.

XT STORY: "The Imperfect Crime" (2 pages)
REDITS: Writer unknown
EATURE CHARACTER: Cleve (general store employee, thief)
IPPORTING CAST: Pop Andrew (Cleve's employer), Skat (Cleve's sheepdog)
THER CHARACTERS: Sheriff Pringle ("Pringy"), Charlie Skinner (local youth), Lem Rainier, Glendale residents
OCATIONS/ITEMS: Glendale (country village) inc Pop's store, Pop's 2-story house & Cleve's home; Pop's money
YNOPSIS: Cleve, accompanied by his dog Skat, steals his employer's life savings, believing he left no clue behind. Later, the sheriff visits ▪eve's home. He "arrests" not Cleve but Skat, who left distinct paw prints. Unwilling to let his dog be locked away, Cleve confesses, as the sheriff ▪pected.
OTE: Story appears between 2nd and 3rd st...

"The King of the Dinosaurs" (19 pages)

CREDITS: Syd Shores (pencils), Vince Alascia (inks), Alex Schomburg (c art)
FEATURE CHARACTER: Captain America (also in fb between CapC #26/3, '43 fb & USA #8, '43)
SUPPORTING CAST: Bucky (also in fb between CapC #26/3, '43 & USA #8, '43; last in USA #9, '43; chr last in FallSon:IM, '07 ft
VILLAINS: Iguanodon (Olaf Olsen, brain transplanted in dinosaur body, also as human, dies), Professor Schultz (scientist & Nazi sympathizer, dies), Nazi saboteurs
OTHER CHARACTERS: Erda Olsen (defense plant worker), Greneker Antarctic Expedition, museum visitors, museum employees (bts), Blainesville workers (most bts, some die), townspeople (bts, some die), 2 radio announcers (voices only), US Army troops, sled dogs, Nazi commander & 4 soldiers, 5 Free French Underground members (prev 3 on cover only)
LOCATIONS/ITEMS: Pennsylvania inc Ramapo Hills area w/US Army camp, town w/Widmyer Museum inc Schultz's office & exhibits, Schultz's underground lab, tunnels leading to cave & old house & Blainesville w/Blainesville Munition Works & Blainesville Junction Railroad Station (both destroyed), Antarctica, Camp Lehigh inc Steve & Bucky's tent, Free French Underground HQ (on cover); Schultz's operating table, lab equipment, pistol, knife & "globes of living tissue," saboteurs' pistols, dog sled, Nazis' firearms (on cover)
FLASHBACK: Three months ago, the Greneker Antarctic Expedition, including Schultz and his assistant Olaf, discover an iguanodon, frozen in suspended animation. Steve and Bucky hear of the find on the radio.
SYNOPSIS: Steve and Bucky attend Widmyer Museum's display, where Bucky overhears Schultz extolling "master race" rhetoric. That night, Schultz and Nazi saboteurs abduct Olaf to an operating room. Days later, the Iguanodon comes to life, escapes the museum, and hides in the Ramapo Hills. Cap and Bucky meet Olaf's sister Erda who is concerned for her missing brother. Knowing about Schultz's secret lab, Erda takes the heroes there. The Iguanodon confronts them. Erda trips, and the Iguanodon lumbers off without harming her, giving Cap a "gruesome" insight. Within the lab, Erda mentions Schultz was a brain specialist in Germany. The saboteurs attack Cap and Bucky, while Schultz abducts Erda. Outside, Cap and Bucky see the Iguanodon destroy a munitions factory. Cap, to Bucky's astonishment, speaks to the Iguanodon, addressing it as "Olaf" and explaining how Schultz is using him to harm the USA. The Iguanodon, controlled by Olaf's transplanted brain as Cap deduced, heads for Schultz's hideout. There, Cap frees Erda, and the Iguanodon hurls Schultz over a precipice to his death, then throws himself over. Cap tells Erda her brother died exposing Schultz and serving the USA.
NOTE: The iguanodon, a perfectly preserved dinosaur found in Antarctica, is almost certainly an escapee from the Savage Land, last in MM #22/6, '41. A radio announcer's reference to the iguanodon as a "million year[s] old" is a gross underestimation; iguanodons died out during the Early Cretaceous Period some 120 million years ago. Blainesville spelled "Blainsville" on munitions works sign.

2ND STORY: "Carnival of Doom" (7 pages)
CREDITS: Harry Sahle (art)
FEATURE CHARACTER: Human Torch (next in HT #13, '43, MC #47, '43)
SUPPORTING CAST: Toro (last in MC #46, '43, next in HT #13, '43)
VILLAINS: The Devil Dancers (3 Gestapo agents, Rudolf named, all die), Heinrich (Gestapo agent, dies)
OTHER CHARACTERS: "Hitler," "Goebbels" (dies) & "Goering" (dies) (actors), "conquered people" (ballet performers), ballet attendees, orchestra members, stagehands (bts)
LOCATIONS/ITEMS: Manhattan inc Torch & Toro's apartment, Kort Theatre inc auditorium; catwalks, Devil Dancers' pitchforks, Devil Dancer's pistol, Heinrich's grenade, sandbags
SYNOPSIS: Torch and Toro prepare to attend "Ballet Gestapo," a performance satirizing Nazism. A would-be assassin throws a bomb from their fire escape, then falls to the ground, his dying words that he was to "keep [Torch] from Gestapo." Torch and Toro attend the ballet, which is disrupted when two "dancers," actually Nazis, kill the actors satirizing Goebbels and Goering. Torch flies to the stage, but a third "dancer," on the catwalk, knocks him down with a sandbag. Soon, the three Nazis are on the catwalk, threatening to shoot into the audience. Torch and Toro hold back, and the three swing from ropes, intending to escape. Torch burns the ropes, and the three fall to their deaths.
NOTE: One Devil Dancer shows near-superhuman strength in lifting and throwing a 1000-lb sandbag.

3RD STORY: "The Case of the "Phantom Engineer"" (12 pages)
CREDITS: Syd Shores (pencils), Vince Alascia (inks)
FEATURE CHARACTER: Captain America
SUPPORTING CAST: Bucky
VILLAINS: Phantom Engineer (Peter Blakemann, district traffic manager, Nazi spy, only app), the Ghost Crew (disguised Nazis)
OTHER CHARACTERS: Dora Thomas (Comet engineer's daughter), Midtown station ticket vendor, Midtown residents, Mr. Thomas (engineer), Comet crew (most bts), soldier & government official passengers (most bts)
LOCATIONS/ITEMS: Midtown inc Peconic & Western railroad station, Wreck Canyon & railroad tracks, Morleyville (neighboring town, mentioned), Jamestown (Steve & Bucky's destination, mentioned); the Comet (passenger train), handcar, the Ghost Crew's radium-dipped ropes, giant film projector w/wide angle lens, train whistle operated by tank of compressed air & "ghost train" (projected image), Cap's flares
FLASHBACK: Many years ago, a train wreck kills almost all of the crew and passengers. The ghost train is later seen running on the track.
SYNOPSIS: While Steve and Bucky wait for a train, the Phantom Engineer appears, proclaiming he'll wreck any train that passes through Wreck Canyon and frightening the ticket vendor, who calls his supervisor, Peter Blakemann. Local townspeople demand the trains be stopped, but the Comet, carrying troops and government officials, cannot be delayed. Cap and Bucky search for the Engineer but instead find Nazi saboteurs in glowing robes, intending to impersonate ghosts. They quickly knock them out, then see a "ghost train" on the tracks, "heading" for the Comet. Realizing the "train" is a projected image, Cap and Bucky find the projector, manned by more Nazis. The two make short work of them, but one boasts the tracks have been sabotaged. By handcar, Cap and Bucky rush to the scene. The Phantom Engineer boards the

oving handcar, but Cap punches him so hard the villain's mask breaks, revealing Blakemann. Using flares to signal the Comet's engineer, ap averts the crash.

TH STORY: "The Case of the Headless Monster" (13 pages)
CREDITS: Syd Shores (pencils), Vince Alascia (inks)
EATURE CHARACTER: Captain America (next in CapTW:AB #1, '09 fb)
SUPPORTING CAST: Bucky, Sgt. Duffy
VILLAIN: The Headless Monster ("the Headless Thing," Jonathan Torgson, disfigured dwarfish man in super-strong exoskeleton, dies)
OTHER CHARACTERS: 2 Pocano residents, Mary (found dead), city official, 4 cops, radio announcer, Tunnel of Love ticket vendor, newsboy, ain crew & passengers (100 in all, bts, all die), amusement park staff & visitors (bts, some die), other victims (bts), bystanders
LOCATIONS/ITEMS: Pennsylvania inc Ramapo Hills area w/Pocano Country town (1 house destroyed), Glen Caves, US Army camp, orgson's house and passage to Glen Caves w/pool, railroad tracks & Playground Amusement Park w/roller coaster (wrecked) and Tunnel of ove w/mirror maze, train (destroyed), Torgson's exoskeleton, Headless Monster's "head" (symbolic splash page only)
SYNOPSIS: Cap and Bucky hunt the Headless Monster, a spectral figure guilty of arson and murder. They find it, but after a struggle, the Monster flees into a cave, where Cap and Bucky find wealthy Jonathan Torgson, who claims the Monster abducted him. The next day a newspaper publishes the Monster's challenge for Cap to confront him at Playground Amusement Park. Cap and Bucky arrive as a roller coaster rashes, its beams damaged by the Monster's metal fingernails. They check the Tunnel of Love, where he waits in a mirror maze, setting fire o the place and departing. After Cap and Bucky escape, a newsboy relays a message from Torgson, who claims the Monster has threatened im. At Torgson's house, they find a secret door into a cave. The Monster pushes them into a pool hundreds of feet below. Emerging, they fight e Monster and unmask him as an exoskeleton-wearing Torgson. Proclaiming he became the Monster to get the respect he never received, e scales the cave's walls, then deliberately falls to his death.

EXT STORY: "Hoodlum" (2 pages)
CREDITS: Writer unknown
EATURE CHARACTER: Sam Yankey (middle-aged police officer)
SUPPORTING CAST: Red Rawlins (local youth)
VILLAINS: Steve & his gang (Mike named), Tony (milk station manager)
OTHER CHARACTERS: Several police officers
LOCATIONS/ITEMS: Neighborhood inc refinery, police HQ, gang's condemned warehouse base; milk trucks & cans, gasoline, oil drums
SYNOPSIS: Concerned that Red Rawlins is getting involved with a gang, Officer Sam Yankey confronts the gang's leader Steve but is struck rom behind just as Red shows up to apparently work with the gang. They tie Yankey up, but he escapes and tracks them to a gasoline-muggling operation at a milk station. Struck down again, he awakens to more officers arriving and learns Red tipped them off to the crime.
NOTE: Story appears between 2nd & 3rd story.

CAPTAIN AMERICA COMICS #30 (September 1943)

"The House of the Laughing Death" (17 pages)

CREDITS: Syd Shores (art)
FEATURE CHARACTER: Captain America
SUPPORTING CAST: Bucky
VILLAINS: The Silent Killer ("the Laughing Death," James Carlin, also as "Miss Green," only app, dies), Dr. Carlin (James' brother, dies), Arthur Blaine (John Blaine's nephew)
OTHER CHARACTERS: John Blaine (financier), Dora Blaine (John's daughter), police commissioner, coroner, sanitarium nurse, police officer, sanitarium patients, Pleasantmere townspeople (bts), corpse of 4th victim, Death (in symbolic splash page only), snake, cultists (both on cover only)
LOCATIONS/ITEMS: Pleasantmere inc Carlin Sanitarium w/Room 42 (Blaine's), Room 48 (Cap & Bucky's) & ellar, adjacent US Army camp inc Steve and Bucky's tent, cultists' citadel (cover only); Silent Killer's blowgun, curare, darts, oxygen cylinders with breathing mask & coffin-like box, Dr. Carlin's dagger, Bucky's guitar, cultists' swords (cover only)
SYNOPSIS: After four patients die mysteriously at Carlin Sanitarium, Dora Blaine, her father a patient, places an ad pleading for Cap's help. Upon arrival, Cap and Bucky meet Dr. Carlin and housekeeper Miss Green. They observe Dora's cousin Arthur speaking with Carlin about taking care" of his uncle. Cap and Bucky stay the night, and Bucky suffers sudden insanity. Realizing the room is being gassed, the two escape nd find Arthur in the corridor. They pursue, but a robed man, the Silent Killer, intervenes. However, Bucky captures Arthur, who confesses to iring Dr. Carlin to kill Dora's father, who is missing. They capture Dr. Carlin but the Silent Killer shoots him with a poison dart. Dying, he identifies he Killer as his brother James, who extorted his involvement. In the cellar, Cap and Bucky find a compression cylinder of pure oxygen and ecognize it as the gas used to induce madness and eventual death. When they find the Killer about to gas John Blaine, Cap defeats him. Under he hood he finds Miss Green, actually James Carlin in a wig. Carlin kills himself with a poison dart.
NOTE: Steve says he met James and Dora Blaine years before; Dora's request for Cap's help implies he met them as Cap, not as Steve.

ND STORY: "The Nazi Cleaver" (8 pages)
CREDITS: Al Fagaly (pencils), Al Bellman (inks)
FEATURE CHARACTER: Human Torch (also impersonates Hans over radio, next in AllWin #10, '43, AllSel #1/2, '43, MC #48, '43)
SUPPORTING CAST: Toro (last in MC #47, '43, next in AllWin #10, '43)
VILLAINS: Nazi black marketeers ("the Chief," Fritz Bruck, Hans, Luther & 5 others, all die)
OTHER CHARACTERS: FBI official, butcher, morgue attendant, cop, newsboy, Manhattan bystanders, Mr. Fairbanks (Chicago Meat Packing Company executive), several butchers (questioned by Torch bts), slaughterhouse workers (bts), family of 6 (die bts), corpses, cattle (some die)

LOCATIONS/ITEMS: Manhattan inc FBI HQ, butcher shop & morgue, Chicago inc slaughterhouse, shack (destroyed), tree w/concealed radio, Chicago Meat Packing Company w/Fairbanks' office, "the Chief's" hideout, abandoned railroad yard & tracks; racketeer's gun

SYNOPSIS: When a family dies from poisoned black market meat, Torch and Toro head for Chicago, the criminals' operations center. At a slaughterhouse, Torch suspects seemingly cooperative night foreman Fritz Bruck; following Bruck, they hear him discussing sabotage with underlings Hans and Luther. They confront the marketeers, but Bruck flees and detonates a bomb, killing his own men. Finding the ring's hidden radio, Torch impersonates Hans and contacts "the Chief," who tells "Hans" the marketeers will rendezvous at a railroad yard, where cattle will be shipped. Torch and Toro surprise the remaining marketeers, who flee, but the two start a cattle stampede that kills them all.

NOTE: Story followed by "Make-Believe Magic" (1 page), describing five tricks, featuring magician.

3RD STORY: "The Curse of the "Yellow Scourge"" (15 pages)

CREDITS: Syd Shores (pencils), Vince Alascia (inks)

FEATURE CHARACTER: Captain America

SUPPORTING CAST: Gen. Haywood (last in CapC #28/3, '43), Sgt. Duffy (both next in AllWin #10/2, '43), Bucky

VILLAINS: Medicine Man (Japanese agent impersonating Tu-Ra-Bi-Ka, dies), Japanese pilots, sailors & soldiers (prev 3 bts) & 2 officers

OTHER CHARACTERS: Chief Nar-Ku-Ra (dies), Nar-Ku-Ra's son (becomes chief), Tu-Ra-Bi-Ka (witch doctor), Sulaharuans (many die) Captain Burke, 4 army officers, Allied base commander

LOCATIONS/ITEMS: Sulaharua (South Pacific island) inc chief's hut, medicine man's hut, prison cave, sacrificial fire dance area w/stakes incomplete Japanese army base (bts) & US army base (replacing Japanese base), US Army South Pacific base; PT boat, Japanese ship & 2 planes, Sulaharuan spears, shields, torches & war canoe, Medicine Man's gas tanks, nozzle & gas mask, Japanese officer's pistol

SYNOPSIS: Sulaharua, formerly a neutral island, has allied with Japan after US soldiers seemingly bring a "curse" that kills the natives. Arriving to investigate, Cap and Bucky are attacked by Sulaharuans. When the Medicine Man Tu-Ra-Bi-Ka approaches, heroes and natives alike collapse, but only Cap and Bucky awaken, which Chief Nar-Ku-Ra deems proof of the "curse." When Cap points out Tu also survived, the Chief falls dead, and the two heroes are imprisoned with US officers. A native youth, the dead Chief's son, is also imprisoned. The boy knows of a secret exit, and the officers distract guards so the heroes and the Chief's son can escape. Bucky sprains an ankle and must be left behind. Enraged, Tu ties Bucky and the officers to stakes and prepares to burn them in "the fire of Pulorigu," but Cap finds Japanese soldiers in Tu's hut along with the real Tu-Ra-Bi-Ka; the other man is a Japanese impersonator, using gas to kill Sulaharuans and blame the USA. The Chief's son kills the impostor, and the Sulaharuans drive out the Japanese. Weeks later, the US is allowed to build an army base on the island.

NOTE: In Haywood's last appearance, CapC #28/3, '43, he also investigated an island secretly under Japanese influence, Pa-Pi-Ru-Gua.

4TH STORY: "The Saboteur of Death!" (12 pages)

CREDITS: Syd Shores (art)

FEATURE CHARACTER: Captain America (next in AllWin #10/2, '43, MCP #39/4, '90 fb, Cap:RWB/3, '02 fb, Cap&FT #1, '11, AllSel #1, '43 USA #10, '43, YA #9, '43, CapTW:AB #1, '09 fb, Cap:RWB/2, '02, Cap #616/3, '11 fb)

SUPPORTING CAST: Bucky (next in AllWin #10/2, '43)

VILLAINS: Von Broot ("top Nazi sabotage agent," only app) & his men (some die, Hans named), Herr Professor & another scientist, Adolf Hitler (bts, sends written instructions to destroy convoy, also in a photograph, last in CapC #28, '43), poisonous snakes

OTHER CHARACTERS: Camp Lehigh soldiers (Company B, some die), US army officer, Ambassador Kirk, diplomat (dies), convoy ships crews, Nazi sub officer (symbolic splash page only)

LOCATIONS/ITEMS: Barabia inc US Army camp w/Steve & Bucky's tent & officer's tent, adjacent town w/US embassy, shack (destroyed) & von Broot's sewer hideout inc lab & connecting tunnels w/seaside exit; troop convoy, seaplane w/ammunition, mines (destroyed), saboteur's flashlight & hypodermic needle, von Broot's pistol & explosive plunger, Hitler's note (see NOTE), booby trap, Nazi sub (on symbolic splash page)

SYNOPSIS: In Barabia, a booby trap decimates Steve's unit. An officer assigns him to track saboteur von Broot. In a nearby town, Cap and Bucky find a saboteur attacking a diplomat, and turn the villain's hypodermic needle on himself, killing the man. The dying diplomat gives Cap and Bucky a communique for US Ambassador Kirk, from whom Cap and Bucky learn von Broot's underground hideout location, where the saboteurs keep snakes to provide poison. Once there, Cap and Bucky knock out several Nazis, but von Broot escapes, leaving a note from Hitler himself to mine Barabia's harbor to destroy troop ships. Commandeering a seaplane, Cap and Bucky set off the mines before the ships get too close. Returning to von Broot's hideout, they prevent von Broot and company from blowing up the local army camp and capture them.

NOTE: Barabia is a coastal nation; its location is not specified. The officer's singling out of Steve to pursue von Broot implies awareness that Steve and Cap are one and the same. Hitler's note to von Broot is written in English.

TEXT STORY: "The Blackout Detective" (2 pages)

CREDITS: Writer unknown

FEATURE CHARACTER: Ted Morf (Alhambra Apartments employee)

VILLAINS: Duke Blackwood (wanted criminal), Wiggins (unemployed actor), Philip McCree (Shakespearean actor)

OTHER CHARACTERS: Det. Dick Purcell, Det. Jackson Coles, Mr. Boston (Alhambra Apartments manager), plainclothesmen, police officers, state's attorney, Fario Musso (Hialeah Club owner, mentioned only)

LOCATIONS/ITEMS: Alhambra Apartments inc lobby, elevators, Room 809, adjoining room & basement, Union Square, City Hall; briefcase

SYNOPSIS: Believing an Alhambra guest to be criminal Duke Blackwood, Ted Morf calls the police, who are seeking Blackwood for stealing $40,000 from the Hialeah Club. Instead, they find Wiggins, who claims the room is his, but Ted, noticing mud on Wiggins' shoes, correctly guesses he entered through the fire escape. The police find a passage from Blackwood's room to Philip McCree's, previously seen leaving with a package. While Ted prepares the hotel for a wartime blackout, police track McCree to Union Square, but his package is empty. At City Hall, Wiggins and McCree confess to being Blackwood's accomplices. Ted arrives and tells the police and DA that Blackwood is trapped in the hotel. During his preparations, Ted found Blackwood's footprints at the basement door and locked him in. The grateful DA offers Ted a job.

NOTE: Story appears between 2nd story & "Make-Believe Magic."

CAPTAIN AMERICA COMICS #31 (October 1943)

"The Terror of the Green Mist!" (18 pages)

CREDITS: Syd Shores (pencils), Vince Alascia (inks), Alex Schomburg (c art)
FEATURE CHARACTER: Captain America (also impersonates Col. Erik Moltke)
SUPPORTING CAST: Bucky (last in YA #9, '43, chr last in Cap #616/3, '11 fb), Sgt. Duffy (last in AllWin #10/2, '43)
VILLAINS: Fungi (monstrous Nazi scientist, dies), Adolf Hitler (chr next in SgtF #48, '67, next in HT #14/4, '43), Josef Goebbels (last in CapC #28, '43, next in AllWin #12/5, '44), Hermann Goering (last in CapC #28, '43, next in HT #15, '44), Nazi soldiers inc dirigible crew (Carl named), Gestapo (Col. Erik Moltke named), Hitler Youth member
OTHER CHARACTERS: US soldiers (some die), army camp commanding officer, Porsden citizens, train passengers (bts), radio announcer (bts, Cap receives radio report on green mist attack), Army radio operator bts, radioed by Cap), Birds, Betty Ross, Japanese soldiers & scientist (prev 3 on cover only)
LOCATIONS/ITEMS: US Army camp w/Steve and Bucky's tent, Commanding Officer's tent & adjacent farm, skies over California, France inc railroad station & wood and river bordering open field, Germany inc Hitler's Berlin headquarters, Porsden & Fungi's ruined castle w/wine vault, lab and surrounding swampland, Japanese fortress (on cover only); army plane, Nazi dirigible, Hitler's letter, German train & car, collapsed humanoid membranes containing green mist, mist tanks, Nazi firearms, Nazi soldier's axe, army air raid rifles & bazookas, parachutes, Cap & Bucky's rifles, Fungi's lab equipment, Japanese torture rack, firearms, medical instruments & flag (on cover only)
SYNOPSIS: Days after Hitler consults a Nazi scientist, a monstrous figure parachutes into a US army camp but disintegrates under gunfire. The next day, green mist dissolves surrounding farmland into mud masses which spread across the countryside. Anticipating a California attack, Cap and Bucky fly there and locate a camouflaged dirigible. They board it and find Nazi soldiers preparing "collapsed membranes," figures containing the matter-dissolving green mist, under command of Nazi scientist Fungi, a plant-being similar to the membranes. When Fungi orders the dirigible back to Germany, Cap and Bucky overpower several Nazis and remain undetected in the dirigible's tail cabin for 12 hours until a captive sounds an alarm, forcing them to escape by parachute, then board a train for Porsden, where Fungi's mists are manufactured. In Porsden, Hitler and Fungi address a crowd. Spotted by Fungi, Cap and Bucky escape by car. They force the driver to direct them to Fungi's base, but Fungi traps them. To learn the mist's secrets, Cap and Bucky surrender. Imprisoned, they learn only Fungi himself can manufacture the mist, and Cap vows the scientist must die. Easily escaping, Cap chases Fungi into a lab where broken glass pierces Fungi's body, which emits green mist and deflates. Cap and Bucky return to the USA via Fungi's dirigible.
NOTE: On page 3, panel 3, Bucky carelessly calls Steve "Cap" while both are still in army fatigues. Hitler's note states multiple fungi creatures have simultaneously parachuted into the USA, but no additional havoc is reported. While disguised as Nazi soldiers at story's end, Cap and Bucky continue to wear their masks, but this may be attributed to artistic license.

2ND STORY: (7 pages)
CREDITS: Al Bellman (art)
FEATURE CHARACTER: Human Torch (next in MC #49, '43)
SUPPORTING CAST: Toro (between MC #48-49, '43)
VILLAINS: Kriss "Gabby" Lout (also as Mrs. Fagan, only app), Nazi operative, cowled pointed-eared Nazi (on symbolic splash page only)
OTHER CHARACTERS: G-2 workers inc Col. Little (G-2 head), Col. Dennis (dies), Capt. Clark (dies) & other officers (some die), G-2 switchboard operator, FBI agents, doctors, repairmen (bts, off-panel), government employees (bts)
LOCATIONS/ITEMS: Washington DC inc G-2 (Army Intelligence Corps) offices & Gabby's house w/secret passage maze and 40-foot deep tank; Gabby's poisoned pins, poison bottle, detonator, mop, bucket, broom & club-footed shoes, Mrs. Fagan's dress & wig, G-2's telephones, coded teletype machine & operator's switchboard, giant drill, molten lava (both on symbolic splash only)
SYNOPSIS: When G-2 officers are found dead, Torch and Toro investigate. Noticing each victim clutches a telephone receiver, Torch discovers the earpieces contain poisoned pins which embedded themselves in the victims' skulls. After questioning the G-2 building's employees, Torch suspects janitor Gabby Lout, whose home he and Toro visit. Mrs. Fagan, claiming to be Gabby's landlady, tells them Gabby snuck out, with back rent unpaid. Torch finds pins and poison in Gabby's room, then unmasks "Mrs. Fagan" as Gabby himself. Gabby flees through a secret panel, and the two pursue, but suction pulls them into a 40-foot deep muddy tank which douses their flames. After a torturous climb, they emerge as Gabby and a Nazi plan to blow up the White House. Torch and Toro chase the pair through an intricate tunnel maze, knocking out the saboteurs before they can carry out their plan.
NOTE: Page 2, panel 4's caption states two staff members are dead, but panel 5 shows three. The origin of the network of tunnels and apparatus beneath Gabby's house is unrevealed.

3RD STORY: "Let's Play Detective!: Can You Solve the Mystery of the Locked Door?" (1 page)
CREDITS: Al Bellman (writer, art)
FEATURE CHARACTER: Mike Trapp (police detective, 1st, next in AllSel #2/6, '43, AllWin #11/5, '43, CapC #34/5, '43)
VILLAIN: The Parks Arms' janitor (only app)
OTHER CHARACTERS: Police officers, Mr. Thornton, Mrs. Thornton (dies)
LOCATIONS/ITEMS: Parks Arms Hotel inc Thorntons' apartment, police station; janitor's pass key (see NOTE)
SYNOPSIS: After Mr. and Mrs. Thornton quarrel publicly, a janitor reports Mrs. Thornton's murder. Trapp and associates investigate, and Trapp concludes the janitor himself is the murderer. The janitor confesses to attempting to steal Mrs. Thornton's diamond, then killing her when she surprised him.
NOTE: The "Let's Play Detective" feature is a brief mystery story with the mystery's solution printed upside down in the main character's word balloon in the final panel; it appears monthly from CapC #34, '43 until CapC #41, '44 and then sporadically until CapC #71, '49. Trapp is

erroneously called "Chief" in this story; per the majority of his stories, he is a high-ranking detective but not the police chief. Trapp concludes the janitor is guilty because, although the Thorntons' apartment was locked, he nevertheless knew about the murder, but the janitor, as stated in the story, has a key to every apartment and could thus easily have unlocked the door to find Mrs. Thornton's body and then re-locked it before summoning the police, so Trapp's "deduction" is flawed.

4TH STORY: "The Canal of Lurking Death" (14 pages)
CREDITS: Sid Greene (pencils), Jack Alderman (inks)
FEATURE CHARACTER: Captain America
SUPPORTING CAST: Bucky
VILLAINS: Nazi sub captain & his boatman (both die), Nazi sub officers, soldiers, sailors (most bts, most die) & pilots (bts, in planes)
OTHER CHARACTERS: Command post officer, British patrol boat crew, 2 British soldiers, Chatham officer, RAF pilots (bts, in planes), Dutch woman (on symbolic splash only)
LOCATIONS/ITEMS: England inc "secret service command post," waterfront, English Channel & Chatham w/home guard post, Nazi sub base near Holland coast inc guard bridge (destroyed), subterranean canals, sub elevators, dry dock, guard house, windmills (#2 Windmill, the torpedo depot, named) & bomb shelter; Nazi subs (some concealed under false barges, most destroyed), Nazi planes, sub captain's motorboat (destroyed), Nazis' rifles, torpedos, time bomb fuses, ammunition boxes & grenades, British patrol boat w/guns, RAF planes, Cap's seaplane, British soldiers' rifles, Cap & Bucky's pistols, English Channel steel nets (bts, entangle Nazi sub), Bucky's mace (on symbolic splash only)
SYNOPSIS: Assigned to locate and destroy a secret Nazi sub base, Steve and Bucky catch a ride on a patrol boat whose crew detects a Nazi sub. They board it before it submerges, capture its captain, and force him to continue to the base. Near Holland's coast, the sub enters a channel leading to a subterranean canal. The captain secretly broadcasts orders to warn the base about Cap. Met by soldiers, Cap and Bucky fight but are defeated and tortured inside a windmill. When Allied planes arrive, the Nazis leave them to be bombed, but the base remains undetected. Cap and Bucky escape their bonds. Later, at a torpedo supply depot, they reset torpedos to explode in twelve hours. When the sub captain appears, they take him hostage and accompany him and his boatman to a rendezvous point thirty miles from England. Nazi planes bomb the boat, killing the captain and boatman, but Cap and Bucky escape. With four hours before the torpedos explode, Cap swims the 30 miles in two hours to reach Chatham. After apprising British officers, he takes a seaplane to recover Bucky, and they join RAF planes in attack formation. The Nazi subs explode, directing the planes to the hidden base, which they destroy.
NOTE: The command post officer delivers Cap and Bucky's mission directly to Steve and Bucky, indicating he knows their secret identities. Later, the two change to their costumed identities in front of a patrol boat crew, implying several people at the post know their secret. Cap swims 30 miles to the English coast but must later return to retrieve Bucky, reminding the reader that Cap has near-superhuman endurance, essential for such a swim, while Bucky does not.

5TH STORY: "The Coughing Killer" (13 pages)
CREDITS: Al Gabriele (pencils), Vince Alascia (inks)
FEATURE CHARACTER: Captain America (next in CapC #76, '54 fb)
SUPPORTING CAST: Bucky (chr next in CapC #76, '54 fb)
VILLAINS: The Cougher ("the Coughing Killer," Nazi spy, dies) & his underlings (Mueller (dies), Schmit, Weasel named)
OTHER CHARACTERS: Dorothy Sheridan (actress, dies), Admiral Smathers (ship building program head), 2 stagehands (more bts), 2 police officers (more bts, one dies bts), desk sergeant, crane operator, theater attendees, launch attendees, US Navy sailors (2 seen, more bts), doctor, canary (dies), Adolf Hitler (mentioned by Cougher)
LOCATIONS/ITEMS: Manhattan inc theater, police HQ, waterfront saloon, abandoned subway tunnel w/Cougher's hideout within, Steve and Bucky's hotel room & shipyard; ship, crane, scenery truck, Cougher's box of "cough drops" containing tiny poisoned darts, Cougher & his underlings' artillery, Bucky's machine gun & ammo (on symbolic splash only)
SYNOPSIS: After taking control of a sabotage ring, the Cougher targets a war bond rally that Steve and Bucky attend. There, Cougher kills actress Dorothy Sheridan, then flees while his men, disguised as stage hands, delay pursuit. Steve and Bucky nevertheless catch them all but Cougher escapes jail. At Cap's request, the police allow an underling to escape, and Cap and Bucky follow him to an abandoned subway tunnel. There, they attack Cougher and his men, but a cave-in pins them down and Cougher captures them. Gloating, Cougher demonstrates, on a "miner's canary," how he kills via special cough drops, then locks Cap and Bucky at the tunnel's end in a chamber separated from the bay by a few feet of ceiling, there to die by cave-in or asphyxiation. Unable to dig past the chamber's steel door, Cap causes a cave-in and fights gushing water torrents to emerge in the bay with Bucky. They hurry to a ship launching platform and prevent Cougher's assassination attempt on Admiral Smathers. While Bucky knocks out Cougher's underlings, Cougher flees up ship rigging, then climbs a crane, Cap right behind. Cougher means to dive and swim for safety, but the crane's operator, distracted by the spectacle, mishandles the controls. The crane arm suddenly swings and Cougher falls to his death.
NOTE: Mueller, whom the Cougher kills, supposedly secretly worked with the FBI. Cougher mentions the saboteurs had previously "smash[ed] a few machines," implying they may have appeared in earlier stories. Dorothy Sheridan's name is a portmanteau of actresses Dorothy Lamour and Ann Sheridan. While imprisoned underground, Cap and Bucky carelessly allow a candle to continue burning even though this will use up oxygen more quickly.

TEXT STORY: "Loose Lips!" (2 pages)
CREDITS: Writer unknown
FEATURE CHARACTERS: Andy, Ben (2 civilian test drivers)
VILLAINS: Ike, Oscar, Tony (spies)
OTHER CHARACTERS: Capt. Richards (Military Police officer) & other MPs, Hawkshaw the Detective (comic strip character mentioned, Ben sarcastically calls Andy "Hawkshaw")
LOCATIONS/ITEMS: US Army proving ground & adjacent woods, spies' cottage; "water baby" (experimental land/water vehicle), Andy's

alopy, spies' sedan, Oscar's gun, Tony's gun

SYNOPSIS: Employed by the army, test driver Andy grows concerned over fellow driver Ben's apparent flippant attitude toward necessary secrecy. Observing two suspicious-seeming men with whom Ben spoke earlier, Andy follows them to a cottage and overhears their plan to manipulate Ben to gain army secrets. When Ben arrives, Andy tries to stop him, and the two tussle before the spies interrupt. When they threaten Andy, Ben turns on them, and the encounter is ended by military police, whom Ben, aware all along of the spies' intention, directed to the scene.

NOTE: Story appears between 2nd & 3rd stories.

CAPTAIN AMERICA COMICS #32 (November 1943)

"Captain America Battles the Menace of the Murderous Mole-Man!" (13 pages)

CREDITS: Otto Binder (script), Jimmy Thompson (pencils), Al Bellman (inks), Syd Shores (c art)
FEATURE CHARACTER: Captain America
SUPPORTING CAST: Bucky (chr last in CapC #76, '54 fb)
VILLAINS: The Mole ("the Mole-Man," only app) & his underlings, German pilots (bts, some die)
OTHER CHARACTERS: Sir Winston Churchill (British Prime Minister, last in SubC #3, '41, chr last in GSInv #2, '05, chr next in SgtF #41, '67, next in Battle #27/2, '54), British officer, British soldier, 2 air raid wardens, 2 bobbies, Churchill's servants, dignitaries, London citizens (many die), Allied soldiers, Japanese pilots (bts, in airplanes) (both on cover only)
LOCATIONS/ITEMS: London inc Tower of London w/air raid shelter, boiler room and Mole's "secret dungeon hideout," restaurant, London Defense Area Command HQ, RAF landing field, Churchill's #10 Downing Street residence, Mole's #21 Wenksley East base w/tunnel to dungeon hideout & other buildings (several destroyed bts); British planes, German planes (bts), bombs, Mole's pistol & note, underlings' clubs, Japanese planes, Allied ships (both on cover only)
SYNOPSIS: When Nazi bombers attack London, Steve and Bucky, sightseeing atop the Tower of London, head for shelter but inadvertently enter the boiler room, where the Mole's operatives open fire. Later, Steve and Bucky learn two dozen buildings were damaged or destroyed, although only six planes bombed London. As Cap and Bucky, they return to the Tower and find a dungeon hideout, where Mole's men again attack and withdraw. During a subsequent air raid, Cap and Bucky, via RAF plane, observe the bombings. Using an anonymous note, Mole lures Cap and Bucky into a trap but, realizing this, they take the Mole's underlings by surprise, forcing one to take them to Mole's central hideout. There, they find a bomb, one of several Mole has planted throughout London to simulate successful air bombings. More underlings capture them, and Mole ties Bucky to the bomb, then takes Cap to the basement of Churchill's home, which Mole plans to destroy. Cap hits a light switch, and the blinded Mole inadvertently shoots an underling. Knocking out Mole, Cap hurries to the surface and both defuses the Churchill bomb and rescues Bucky. Churchill himself congratulates the heroes on their bravery.
NOTE: The Mole should not be confused with Herr Mole from CapC #34/4, '44, the Mechanical Mole from MystC #1/2, '44, the Mole Men from AllSel #6, '45, the Mole from BlonPhan #22, '49, or the Mole Man from FF #1, '62.

2ND STORY: "Captain America versus Ali Baba and His Forty Nazis" (16 pages)
CREDITS: Ken Bald (pencils), Vince Alascia (inks)
FEATURE CHARACTER: Captain America
SUPPORTING CAST: Bucky, Sgt. Duffy
VILLAINS: Ali Baba (Nazi operative in Iraq, only app, called "Alee Babee" by Duffy) & "His Forty Nazis" (named thus only in title, actually several hundred Iranian, Iraqi, & Turkish criminals, Yousef named, some die), Nazi colonel
OTHER CHARACTERS: US Army soldiers (some die), US Army captain, Yanni (Turkish Intelligence agent, dancer), 4 Baghdad city officials, Allied officer, Baghdad firefighters, cafe employees & patrons, Solina (mentioned by Ali Baba operative who swears "By the black beard of Solina")
LOCATIONS/ITEMS: Iraq inc Baghdad w/oil refinery, military camp, radio station, Red Cross hospital (see NOTE), business district inc Ali Baba's cafe w/tunnel to city outskirts & Ali Baba's castle hideout w/subterranean region; Ali's trucks & oil drums, Ali Baba's men's knives, scimitars, rifles & grenades
SYNOPSIS: Organizing arsonists, kidnappers, murderers, and thieves into a terrorist unit, Ali Baba leads a Baghdad crime spree. US forces, including Steve and Bucky's unit, place the city under martial law. While searching Ali's cafe for an escaped assassin, Steve thinks dancer Yanni is signaling him. When Cap and Bucky return, Yanni pushes Cap out of gunfire's path, then flees after promising to send a message. Cap and Bucky outfight Ali's men, returning later to observe Yanni's act as she tap-dances in Morse code. Catching on, Ali sends his men to kill her, but Cap and Bucky rescue her. Yanni reveals she is a Turkish Intelligence agent and tells Cap that Ali will seize a radio station to spread false riot alarms and lure soldiers into action, leaving the camp unprotected. Yanni leads them to Ali's fortress, where Ali's men overpower them. Ali boastfully says his men will enter the camp in oil drums as part of a supply shipment, then imprisons his enemies in a steel-doored cavern. Bucky accidentally opens it by saying "Open Seame." Too late to stop the broadcasts, Cap and Bucky find Ali's trucks en route and hurl Ali's own grenades, igniting the oil drums and killing most within.
NOTE: Steve and Duffy are on unusually friendly terms in this story. The story states several times that Ali Baba is disguising his Nazi operation as a "holy war" to drive the Allies out of Iraq, but nothing indicates that anyone in his unit has actually been deceived on this point. Although the Red Cross is mentioned, it should more likely be its sister agency, the Red Crescent, that would be stationed in predominantly Muslim Iraq. Baghdad mistakenly spelled "Bagdad" thoughout story.

3RD STORY: "The Talons of the Vulture!" (16 pages)

CREDITS: Syd Shores (pencils), Vince Alascia (inks)
FEATURE CHARACTER: Captain America (also in Joan's thoughts, next in CapTW:AB #1, '09 fb)
SUPPORTING CAST: Bucky, Sgt. Duffy, Gen. Haywood (last in AllWin #10/2, '43)
VILLAINS: The Vulture (Nazi slave labor camp commandant, only app, dies), Jacques (Joan's brother, French traitor, dies), Nazi soldiers (many die), Nazi train crew (bts)
OTHER CHARACTERS:, Joan (French guerilla leader, nicknamed "Miss Wildcat"by Cap, also in Cap's thoughts), French guerilla fighters (3 separate units, Roul named in 3rd unit, many die), US Army officer, French guerilla general, enslaved Frenchmen & women (some die), Dracula (mentioned by Bucky as nickname for Duffy), giant vulture (symbolic splash only)
LOCATIONS/ITEMS: England inc US Army camp, the Savoy (French province in western Alps, called "the Savoie Haut" here) inc 3 French guerilla camps, Vulture's slave labor camp, Camp Lehigh; Allied transport plane (destroyed), Nazi train, Nazi & rebels' firearms, Vulture's machine gun & whip
SYNOPSIS: In the Alps, Cap and Bucky deliver supplies to French guerillas and depart, only to see the guerillas, attempting to liberate a train of French slave laborers, ambushed by the Vulture's troops. Cap and Bucky strafe the Nazis, allowing the guerillas to free the prisoners, but their plane catches fire and crashes. Vulture's men capture Cap and Bucky with the Vulture deciding to take them to Hitler himself. Vulture's train resumes travel, but the two soon escape. Reaching another French camp, they are almost shot by rebel leader Joan before her general vouches for them. Cap, Bucky, Joan and others travel to Vulture's labor camp, where Cap and Bucky allow themselves to be captured. After Vulture futilely tortures Cap, he and Bucky are locked up with French prisoners, including Joan's brother Jacques. The next day, after Joan's capture, both Cap and Jacques are to be "tortured," but when Cap escapes, he finds Jacques, a traitor, dining with Vulture. Cap frees the prisoners and all escape. Back at camp, Joan, learning of Jacques' betrayal, shoots him dead. Days later, Steve, back in the USA, and Joan, in France, contemplate each other romantically.
NOTE: The Vulture should not be confused with Hugh Bradley from CapC #14, '42, Cap's enemy Ottokar Meltzer from AllSel #1, '43, the Torch's enemy from AllWin #10, '43, Lorna the Jungle Queen's enemy from Lorna #4/4, '53, the Torch's enemy Isidoro Scarlotti from YM #26, '54, or Spider-Man's various Vulture enemies.

4TH STORY: "Mind Smasher!" (7 pages)
CREDITS: Al Gabriele (pencils), Al Bellman (inks)
FEATURE CHARACTER: Human Torch (next in HT #14, '43, MC #50, '43)
SUPPORTING CAST: Toro (next in HT #14, '43)
VILLAINS: Professor Fear (Nazi scientist, only app), 4 hired criminals
OTHER CHARACTERS: Atlas security guard (dies), police (bts)
LOCATIONS/ITEMS: Manhattan inc Atlas Electrical building, neighborhood w/ Prof. Fear's hideout inc "mind smasher" (name only used in title, destroyed) & police HQ (bts); Ajax Moving truck, motor, Prof. Fear's helmet & vacuum hood, criminals' guns (one melted)
SYNOPSIS: Torch and Toro disrupt a robbery, capturing two criminals, but two others escape with a stolen motor. While Toro takes the captives to the police, Torch tracks the criminals to a neighborhood but arrives too late to see which house they enter. Within one, they deliver the motor to Prof. Fear and demand payment. Fear, pretending to "test" the motor, activates a device that sends "super-sonic sound waves" into the criminals' brains, forcing them to obey commands. Torch enters but Fear traps him in a vacuum hood to prevent flaming. Before Fear can use his device on Torch, Toro, having an address from his captives, crashes in, destroying the machine and freeing Torch, who knocks out all three enemies.
NOTE: Prof. Fear should not be confused with the Blazing Skull (Mark Todd)'s enemy Dr. Fear from MystC #8/6, '42, nor with Daredevil (Matt Murdock)'s various Mr. Fear enemies.

TEXT STORY: "The Tomb of Death" (2 pages)
CREDITS: Writer unknown
FEATURE CHARACTER: Scoop Gorden (Manhattan reporter, mistaken for Sandro by Prof. James)
SUPPORTING CAST: Jerry Wayne (young cameraman, mistaken for Debo by Prof. James)
OTHER CHARACTERS: Professor James (archaeologist), Pedro (Prof. James' assistant), villagers, Bodeo ("prophet of the Ancient Gods," as preserved corpse) & 8 disciples (Debo, Sandro named, as preserved corpses), Scoop & Jerry's boss (mentioned only)
LOCATIONS/ITEMS: Bolivia inc village, adjacent land & Tomb of Bodeo w/burial chamber and cup chamber; Jerry's camera, Tomb's ebony burial slabs, Cup of the Gods & pedestal, James' knife
SYNOPSIS: In Bolivia to cover the excavation of ancient prophet Bodeo's grave, newspapermen Scoop and Jerry interview Prof. James, who shows them the unearthed "Cup of the Gods." James' assistant Pedro warns that the Cup curses any who drink from it, as Bodeo did, but James defies the curse and drinks. Later, during the village's Carnival ceremony, James behaves manically, shrieking and dancing. The next day, Scoop and Jerry find James' hut in a shambles, the Cup gone. With Pedro, they enter Bodeo's tomb where the deranged James, believing he is Bodeo, claims the gods demand blood sacrifice. He attacks Pedro, but Scoop intervenes. As the pair struggle, Jerry throws his camera at the madman, who falls and strikes his head. "We came to get a story and we certainly got it," Scoop tells Jerry.
NOTE: Story appears between 2nd and 3rd stories.

"Meet --- "Mother Wong"" (18 pages)

CREDITS: Al Avison (pencils), Syd Shores (inks), Alex Schomburg (c art)
FEATURE CHARACTER: Captain America
SUPPORTING CAST: Bucky, Sgt. Duffy (next in AllSel #2, '43), Gen. Haywood
VILLAINS: Japanese officers, Japanese soldiers (some die)
OTHER CHARACTERS: Mother Wong (120-year-old Chinese sage & spy, only app) & her 4 giant retainers (Chu Min & Ti Po named, 2 die), US soldiers (at least 21 die, also on cover), Lee (Chinese guide), Burmese guide (dies), guide's wife, Chiang Kai-Shek (mentioned), Burmese monkeys, Buddha (as statue), Nazis (cover only)
LOCATIONS/ITEMS: Southern China inc mountain near China/Burma border & emergency camp, Burma inc Burmese guide's hut, jungle, Falls of Jhadore, ledge, bridge & Mother Wong's temple (destroyed) w/courtyard, wall, dungeon, cave and connecting tunnel, Brenner Pass (cover only); US Army truck convoy inc firearms, supplies & crated planes (bts) mostly destroyed), Mother Wong's tent, mines, battle plans & jiao/litter, retainers' scimitars, Bucky's machine gun, Japanese weapons
SYNOPSIS: Along the China/Burma border, Japanese forces attack a US convoy. Mother Wong, a Chinese sage whose seeming defection demoralizes the locals, accompanies them. Entering Burma, Cap and Bucky persuade a guide to track Wong's party. Enemy soldiers kill the guide but Cap and Bucky locate Wong's hidden temple where her hulking retainers overwhelm them. Isolating the pair, supposedly so she can torture them, Wong reveals she is a spy, having gained Japan's confidence to gather information and deflect schemes. Overhearing her, the Japanese soldiers open fire, killing two retainers. The remaining two help Cap and Bucky rescue Wong. Having planted mines in her temple, she entrusts the heroes with stolen battle plans and prepares to die, but Cap dissuades her and is himself shot while leading the others to safety before the temple explodes. Mother Wong tends Cap's wounds, and, remaining dedicated to undermining the Japanese, departs with her surviving retainers.

2ND STORY: "The Human Torch Meets the Japanese Beetle" (7 pages)
CREDITS: Unknown
FEATURE CHARACTER: Human Torch (next in AllSel #2/2, '43, AllWin #11, '43, MC #51, '44)
SUPPORTING CAST: Toro (last in MC #50, next in AllSel #2/2, '43)
VILLAIN: The Beetle ("the Japanese Beetle," evil scientist, also in fb "years ago," only app, dies)
OTHER CHARACTERS: Janice Perry (Torch's secretary, only app), Magu (scientist, also in fb "years ago"), Henry & his wife, Henry's doctor, Japanese beetles (some die), 2 large insects, large spider
LOCATIONS/ITEMS: Manhattan inc Torch's new office & Henry's home, countryside south of Manhattan inc "the Castle of Death" (the Beetle & Magu's lab, also in fb) w/trap door pit and beetle pit; Torch's almanac, Magu's bag, net & ring containing poison, Beetle's scientific apparatus
FLASHBACK: Magu becomes a scientist. Later, he and his partner move into the Castle of Death.
SYNOPSIS: Teasing the Torch about new secretary Janice, Toro is bitten by a Japanese beetle and becomes weak. Bystander Henry, also bitten, faints. After the two recover, Torch and Toro trace the beetles' likely migration path and meet dwarf scientist Magu, who reveals his fellow researcher, a Japanese scientist dubbed the Beetle, bred the poison beetles, whose venom sickens in small doses and kills in large doses. The two accompany Magu to his castle, but Beetle captures them, and Janice, who had come to question him. Torch and Toro escape and stop Beetle from lowering Janice into a pit of poisoned beetles. Magu hurls Beetle into the pit to die from his own insects' bites.

3RD STORY: "The All-American Fighting Trio Battle…The Master of the Killer Mongoose!" (14 pages)
CREDITS: Ken Bald (pencils)
FEATURE CHARACTER: Captain America
SUPPORTING CAST: Bucky, Lt. Betty Ross (now in the WACs [Women's Army Corps], last in CapC #18/3, '42, next in CapC #44/3, '44)
VILLAINS: Mongoose Master (Nazi agent, only app), his 6 underlings (Pepe named, dies) & Leibschen (trained mongoose, dies)
OTHER CHARACTERS: WAC captain, 3 WAC soldiers, US Army soldiers, medic, Tunisian townspeople, dog, giant cobra (splash only)
LOCATIONS/ITEMS: Tunisia inc city w/hotel, "native quarter" taxidermist shop and adjacent alley, Tunis inc US Army post and bridge, & US Army camp; military plans (cut into pieces & mostly swallowed), Mongoose Master's stuffed owl, mounted tiger head, animal skins, whips & gas gun, Betty's pistol & lipstick, underlings' rifle, WACs' firearms & baseball bats, Bucky's knife
SYNOPSIS: In a Tunisian alley, Steve and Bucky chance upon thugs attacking two WACs. They intervene, finding one of the WACs is Betty Ross. Later, the WACs memorize and destroy the military plans the thugs sought. Mongoose Master, the thugs' leader, accompanied by his mongoose Leibschen, leads the next attack, gassing the women. Betty leaves a scrawled message, "thing that fights snak[es]." Cap and Bucky return to the alley where Master invites them into his shop as Betty and another WAC are smuggled out. Realizing Betty's message referred to Master's mongoose, Cap kills Leibschen, but Master traps them with a trick floor and escapes with the two WACs. Cap and Bucky find the other two WACs, and the four escape. Cap and Bucky pursue Master, rescuing Betty and her associate. Arming themselves with bats, the other two WACs catch up with Cap's group, stranded by engine trouble and under fire. The four WACs outfight and capture Master and his remaining men.

4TH STORY: "The Symbol of Doom" (12 pages)
CREDITS: Mike Sekowsky (pencils), Jack Alderman (inks)
FEATURE CHARACTER: Captain America (next in AllSel #2, '43, AllWin #11/2, '43)
SUPPORTING CAST: Bucky (next in AllSel #2, '43)
VILLAINS: Symbol of Doom (Japanese saboteur, dies), 3 "assistant Symbols" (all die), train "Symbol" (dies), Japanese soldiers (some die)
OTHER CHARACTERS: US Army soldiers (most die), 2 train engineers (both die), train crew (bts, most die), "Symbol" in newspaper photo

LOCATIONS/ITEMS: Mountain region, railroad trestle, emergency camp w/Steve and Bucky's tent, abandoned copper mine w/2 adjacent shacks, Willows Arms Plant (bts, destroyed); Symbol's transport plane (destroyed) & explosives, US Army troop train (destroyed), Symbols explosive belts, Japanese soldiers' rifles & daggers, parachutes

SYNOPSIS: Aboard a troop train, Steve, Bucky and other soldiers discuss the Symbol of Doom, who has staged four sabotages, apparently dying and returning each time. When the Symbol appears on the track, Steve and Bucky exit to investigate. The train explodes, killing all aboard. Cap and Bucky search the wreckage and are fired on by Japanese soldiers. They track the soldiers to an abandoned mine. There, Symbol ambushes them. Captured, the heroes learn the "Symbol" identity is used by multiple operatives, explaining the seeming "resurrections." The true Symbol, with three others, takes them onto a suicide-mission plane. Cap and Bucky escape by parachute as Symbol blows up the plane.

TEXT STORY: "Mission Accomplished" (2 pages)
CREDITS: Writer unknown
FEATURE CHARACTER: Mike (US Army pilot)
SUPPORTING CAST: Lt. William "Bill" Peterson ("Butch," US Army pilot)
VILLAINS: Nazi shocktrooper & soldiers (some die)
OTHER CHARACTERS: Pierre & his son, Snyder (US invasion leader, bts) & his men (bts, some die)
LOCATIONS/ITEMS: France inc woods, valley, hills, church, Pierre's house & Nazi fortress (others bts) w/searchlights, ammo dumps & anti-aircraft artillery; Mike & Bill's US recon plane (bts, wrecked), US invasion ships (bts), Mike's grenades & cord, US & Nazi armies' weapons
SYNOPSIS: Mike and injured Bill, survivors of their plane's crash, have received smuggled food from Pierre while recovering. When Pierre goes missing, Mike investigates and finds Pierre and son held captive by a Nazi shocktrooper. Capturing the trooper and donning his uniform, Mike infiltrates a Nazi fortress to leave grenades in an ammunition dump, then escapes before the fortress explodes. US forces invade, and Mike returns to Bill to await rescue.
NOTE: Story appears between 2nd & 3rd stories. Story followed by "Captain America Badges Have Gone to War!" (1/2 page), featuring Cap & Bucky informing readers that the badges are no longer available, their metal being used in ammunition.

CAPTAIN AMERICA COMICS #34 (January 1944)

"The Cult of the Assassins!" (16 pages)

CREDITS: Zac Gabel (writer), Syd Shores (pencils, c art), Vince Alascia (inks)
FEATURE CHARACTER: Captain America
SUPPORTING CAST: Bucky (last in AllWin #11/2, '43), Sgt. Duffy (last in AllSel #2, '43, chr next in Cap #219, '78 fb, next in CapC #36, '44), Gen. Haywood (misidentified as a major, next in CapC #36, '44)
VILLAINS: Kali ("Daughter of Kali", Princess Ramasi, Japanese agent, dies) & her Dacoits (most die)
OTHER CHARACTERS: Montley (British Indian Intelligence head), Sir Archibald Wavell (Earl Wavell, British Viceroy of India, see NOTE), Wavell's secretary (dies), US soldiers (most bts), India dignitaries, native informant (bts, directs Cap and Bucky to Ramasi's fortress), female human sacrifice (as corpse), Kali (goddess, as sacrificial idol), lions (as statues), Nazi officer & soldiers, Dutch woman (prev 3 on cover only)
LOCATIONS/ITEMS: India inc Viceroy's House in Delhi w/reception area and Viceroy's office, US Army camp w/Steve and Bucky's tent, Dacoit fortress (destroyed) w/giant Kali idol, human sacrifice platform, pedestal, braziers & trees, Nazi fortress (cover only); Kali's dagger, guns & ammunition, Dacoits' silken nooses, map (depicts India, Arabian Sea, Indian Ocean, Ceylon, Bay of Bengal), US firearms, Nazi machine guns, daggers & net (prev 3 on cover only)
SYNOPSIS: In India, Steve and Bucky act as guards at a government function. One guest, Princess Ramasi, feigns fainting spells to distract attendees while her Dacoit operatives attempt to assassinate the Viceroy. Steve and Bucky tend to her. Her men murder the Viceroy's secretary by mistake. Ramasi flees. Cap and Bucky arrive at Ramasi's fortress where she, as Kali, conducts human sacrifice. There, they rescue intelligence operative Montley, who reveals Kali is a Japanese agent who revived the Dacoit cult for an anti-Allies uprising. Kali captures the three but, recognizing Cap as Steve, with whom she's fallen in love, doesn't kill them. Hoping Cap will join her, she tells him her plans of a simultaneous countrywide Dacoit revolt. Cap rejects her. Still unwilling to kill him, Kali flees, leaving the heroes to fight her Dacoits. She commits hara-kiri on the sacrificial altar, throwing the Dacoits into a frenzy which knocks over flaming braziers. As Cap, Bucky and Montley escape, the fortress burns, killing all within.
NOTE: Dacoits are chr next in MKF #18, '74. Sir Archibald Wavell (1883-1950) remained India's Viceroy until February 1947. Princess Ramasi misidentifies Steve as a major. Steve, paraphrasing Shakespeare, tells Sgt. Duffy to "rave on McDuffy."

2ND STORY: "Captain America in The Stage of Death!" (12 pages)
CREDITS: Vince Alascia (pencils), Bob Powell (inks)
FEATURE CHARACTER: Captain America
SUPPORTING CAST: Bucky
VILLAIN: The Great Rosso (Rossi, insane disfigured ex-tenor, only app, dies)
OTHER CHARACTERS: Patrolman Casey (dies), police, 2 opera singers (others bts), opera house manager, opera attendees, T. Caboto ("The Great Caboto," tenor, as corpse)
LOCATIONS/ITEMS: Manhattan inc Central Opera House w/stage, auditorium, balcony, elevator shaft & Rosso's sub-basement lair; Rosso's blackjack, dagger, pipe organ, coffin, "The Man in Gray" painting and other stolen artwork & sandbags (splash only)
SYNOPSIS: Steve and Bucky attend the opera. There, a corpse is thrown from above the stage; the month's third victim of the deformed Great Rosso. That night, Patrolman Casey hears Rosso playing a pipe organ. When he investigates, Rosso kills him. Cap and Bucky arrive, Rosso hurls Casey's body to them. Cap and Rosso struggle, but Rosso escapes. Splitting up, the heroes pursue. Rosso takes Bucky below, but Cap

llows. Rosso reveals the opera company accused him of crimes and fired him. Disfigured in a train accident, he returned for revenge. When Cap punches Rossi into a coffin, the lid slams, driving the madman's dagger into his chest, killing him.
NOTE: The opera partially performed is Georges Bizet, Henri Meilhac & Ludovic Halévy's "Carmen" (1875).

3RD STORY: "Invasion Mission!" (13 pages)
CREDITS: Ken Bald (pencils), Jimmy Thompson (inks)
FEATURE CHARACTER: Captain America (next in USA #11, '44)
SUPPORTING CAST: Bucky (next in USA #11, '44)
VILLAINS: Herr Captain (Gestapo chief), Nazi soldiers (some die)
OTHER CHARACTERS: "Signorina" (female Italian spy), male Italian spy (dies), 2 Allied officers, submarine captain, Italian officers & general (bts, arrested by Nazis), sub crew (bts), Allied invasion fleet crews (most bts)
LOCATIONS/ITEMS: Italy inc Allied HQ (southern Italy), Gestapo HQ, town w/wayside inn, Nazi base in abandoned mill, Nazi castle fortress, bridge, & beach (central Italy), Adriatic Sea; submarine, invasion fleet (mostly bts), firearms, shells, male spy's bicycle
SYNOPSIS: In Italy to investigate Nazi activity near an upcoming Allied invasion's site, Cap and Bucky outfight a Nazi patrol, then make contact with a female Italian spy, who directs them to a second spy who is later shot by Nazis. Cap and Bucky pursue the Nazis to their base but are captured as is the female spy. When the trio escapes, "Signorina" directs them to a second base, where the Nazis have a battery of guns trained on the invasion site. Cap commandeers one gun and fires on the others, enabling the invasion to succeed.
NOTE: Story followed by "Bucky Builds for Victory" (1 page), featuring Bucky who demonstrates how to make a toy "automatic tommy gun."

4TH STORY: "The Mad Mole's Folly!" (7 pages)
CREDITS: Jimmy Thompson (pencils), Al Gabriele (inks)
FEATURE CHARACTER: Human Torch (also as "Hans"; next in MC #52, '44)
SUPPORTING CAST: Toro (also as "Fritz," between MC #51-52, '44)
VILLAINS: Herr Mole (only app, see NOTE), Otto Heinkle (dies), Reich, 4 Nazi saboteurs, Herr Blitz (mentioned, see NOTE)
OTHER CHARACTERS: Peter Lauber (German-American factory worker, dies), Mrs. Lauber, FBI agents (Kennedy named), police (Casey named), 2 plant workers (others bts), plant president (bts), Nazi soldier, captive woman (both splash page only)
LOCATIONS/ITEMS: Connecticut inc Hartford w/Hartford Cannon Plant, Lauber home, woods, & Herr Mole's hideout (destroyed) w/basement and sub-cellar; saboteurs' electrically-controlled glass vats w/gaseous mist dispenser, bomb constructed w/"new type of dynamite," & chloroform-soaked rags, Heinkle's dagger, Mole's chemical apparatus (splash page only)
SYNOPSIS: German agent Heinkle kills Lauber, a German-born cannon plant worker who refuses to join Herr Mole's sabotage ring. The Torch and Toro happen by and attack Heinkle, who flees. Later, Torch poses as a plant worker and convinces Heinkle to "recruit" him and identify the saboteurs' hideout. Torch and Toro invade the place, but Mole, after killing Heinkle for his incompetence, boasts a bomb has been set at the plant. The Nazis chloroform Torch and Toro, whom Mole places in spinning vats. Police and FBI raid the hideout, arresting the saboteurs and rescuing Torch and Toro who retrieve the bomb from the plant and use it to destroy the now-empty hideout.
NOTE: See NOTE for CapC #32, '43, regarding Mole's name. As "Hans," Torch claims to have worked for "Herr Blitz" blowing up Pacific Coast factories, producing photos to corroborate his story; presumably Torch battled Blitz in an untold story, gaining knowledge of his activities.

5TH STORY: "Let's Play Detective" (2 pages)
CREDITS: Allen Bellman (art)
FEATURE CHARACTER: Mike Trapp
SUPPORTING CAST: Officer Ryan (1st, Trapp's frequent co-investigator)
VILLAIN: Mr. Casey (businessman)
OTHER CHARACTERS: Detective, policeman, cab driver, warehouse watchman (corpse), Mr. Smith (Casey's business partner, mentioned)
LOCATIONS/ITEMS: Police HQ, Casey & Smith Warehouse inc Casey's office
SYNOPSIS: After a phone call from Casey, Trapp and Ryan find him tied up at his warehouse, where the watchman has been killed. Casey claims he was struck from behind by a man who bound him and stole bonds and securities but that he managed to knock the phone off the desk and call the police. Trapp realizes a bound man could not have dialed the phone, however, and Casey confesses to fakery, theft and murder.
NOTE: Story followed by "Wake Up, Americans!" (1 page), a plea to buy War Stamps, signed by Martin Goodman & featuring Cap.

TEXT STORY: "Greedy Grab" (2 pages)
CREDITS: Writer unknown
FEATURE CHARACTER: Porkey Blake
SUPPORTING CAST: Chet & Kelly
OTHER CHARACTERS: Andy Carson (constable, postmaster, justice of the peace, game warden, judge, jury) & his posse, Old Jed Jenkins (prospector, dies), Clem Baker (landowner, mentioned), crickets
LOCATIONS/ITEMS: Rural area inc criminals' cabin, Jenkins' cabin, Clem Baker's place (mentioned), woods & river; gold nuggets, cigarette packet, Chet's revolver, Carson's single-action service gun, posse member's rifle
SYNOPSIS: Following a payroll heist, Porkey and his fellow criminals hole up in a cabin in a remote "hillbilly" community that doesn't even carry Porkey's favorite cigarette brand. Craving action, Porkey kills prospector Jenkins, steals his gold, opens a cigarette pack, and lights up. When Constable Carson accuses Porkey, Chet pulls a gun, but Carson's posse intervenes. When Porkey asks how he gave himself away, Carson reveals that he found the top wrapping of Porkey's cigarette pack, a brand not sold in the area.
NOTE: Story appears between 2nd & 3rd stories. Story followed by "Captain America Badges Have Gone to War!" (1 page), an expansion of the feature from CapC #33, '43, featuring Cap & Bucky.

CAPTAIN AMERICA COMICS #35 (February 1944)

"The Gargoyle Strikes!" (16 pages)

CREDITS: Syd Shores (pencils, c art), Vince Alascia (inks)
FEATURE CHARACTER: Captain America
SUPPORTING CAST: Bucky (chr next in Cap #219, '78 fb) (last in USA #11, '44)
VILLAINS: The Gargoyle (Count Georges Tarragh, also in pfb) & his Nazi underlings, Nazi U-boat crew (bts)
OTHER CHARACTERS: Colonel Grant, Sir Anthony Hutchins (British diplomat), Anne Hutchins (Sir Anthony's daughter), Seminole Indians, US Army soldiers & officer, Paris ball attendees, British skeet shooters, Munich celebrators, Manhattan baseball patrons, beachgoers, jockeys & horse, Manhattan newsboy, radio announcer, citizens reacting to Nazi acts (prev 10 in pfb only), fish, bystanders (on splash page), Japanese torturer, soldiers & two temple guards, 2 tortured soldiers, temple idol & worshippers (prev 6 on cover)
LOCATIONS/ITEMS: Paris (France), England, Munich (Germany), beach, race track, "big cities of Europe & America" (bts), New York baseball park (all in pfb only), South Florida inc Seminole camp w/adjacent woods, hotel, bayou island hideout, US Army camp & airport, Manhattan inc Gargoyle's hotel suite (also in pfb), Japanese temple (on cover); abandoned tanker ship (50 miles off Florida coast, 26 degrees, 31', 40" north, 118 degrees, 10', 12" west), Gargoyle's boats, helicopter & incendiary bombs, Anne's compact, Sir Anthony's microfilm, latitude/longitude note
FLASHBACK: Count Georges Tarragh, amnesiac masked mystery man, builds a reputation as "the Gargoyle," a debonair adventurer. No one knows that he's a monstrous hairy creature under his mask. He decides to help the Nazis, hoping to seize power for himself (p).
SYNOPSIS: In a Florida Seminole village, Steve and Bucky arrange for diplomat Sir Anthony Hutchins and his daughter Anne's arrival. Seeking Sir Anthony's microfilmed secrets, Gargoyle bombs the village and abducts him. Cap and Bucky discover Anne's room has been searched. They follow Gargoyle's underlings and find a note leading them and Anne to Gargoyle's abandoned tanker HQ. While Bucky and Anne are abducted, Cap boards the ship. Gargoyle realizes Sir Anthony's microfilm is hidden in Anne's compact. Cap frees Bucky, and they defeat the underlings. Gargoyle flees in a helicopter but Cap causes it to crash. He turns Gargoyle over to the army.

2ND STORY: "Mystery of the Horrible Hermit!" (7 pages)
CREDITS: Jimmy Thompson (pencils), Al Gabriele (inks)
FEATURE CHARACTER: Human Torch (next in HT #15, '44, MC #53, '44)
SUPPORTING CAST: Toro (next in Kid #5, '44)
VILLAINS: Fritz von Arnheim (Nazi spy, also as Herman the Hermit), Nazi prisoners of war, Nazi operative in St. Louis (others bts)
OTHER CHARACTERS: Herman the Hermit (Civil War veteran), US Army Capt. & Lt., steamboat crew, POW camp soldiers & staff (most bts)
LOCATIONS/ITEMS: Mississippi River & adjacent levy, POW camp, Black Peak inc Herman's home w/underground vacuum chamber, Nazis' St. Louis hideout, Randolph Hwy; steamboat, Nazi guns, von Arnheim's disguise
SYNOPSIS: Along the Mississippi River, Torch and Toro stop Nazis POWs from escaping. A few evade capture, as does the jailbreak's leader, identified as local recluse Herman the Hermit. At Herman's home, the leader lures Torch and Toro into a vacuum chamber, where they lack air to flame on. The real Herman releases them. They capture the remaining POWs and unmask the fake Hermit as a top Nazi spy.

3RD STORY: "The Steel Mask" (15 pages)
CREDITS: Otto Binder (script)
FEATURE CHARACTER: Captain America (next in Cap #219, '78 fb)
SUPPORTING CAST: Bucky
VILLAIN: The Steel Mask ("the Man in the Steel Mask," "Germany's ace agent")
OTHER CHARACTERS: Professor Dix (archaeologist), Susan Dix (Prof. Dix's daughter), Mayan descendants, villagers, poisonous snakes
LOCATIONS/ITEMS: American Southwest inc Mayan temple w/passageways & US Army camp, subterranean Mexico/USA tunnel, Mexican village; Brazen Champion (giant robot, destroyed), temple's torture wheel, Nazi firearms, ammunition, powder keg & grenades, Mayan clubs
SYNOPSIS: Steve and Bucky are on patrol near the US/Mexican border. Archaeologist Dix and daughter Susan explore a Mayan temple, discovering the Brazen Champion, a gigantic bronze idol. Steel Mask, alleged Mayan high priest, demands Dix translate hieroglyphics to "bring the idol to life." Susan flees. Her cries attract Cap and Bucky, but Steel Mask knocks them out and escapes with Dix and Susan. Cap and Bucky find German ammunition in a chamber; Steel Mask seals them in and releases poisonous snakes, but Cap and Bucky escape. With the Brazen Champion activated, Steel Mask rallies Mayan-descended locals to rebuild the Mayan Empire. They attack a village with the Brazen Champion, but Cap and Bucky destroy the Champion with grenades. Cap unmasks Steel Mask as a Nazi spy, and the locals disperse.

4TH STORY: "The Case of the Horror Money!" (12 pages)
CREDITS: Syd Shores (pencils), Vince Alascia (inks)
FEATURE CHARACTER: Captain America (next in Cap #219, '78 fb)
SUPPORTING CAST: Bucky (chr next in Cap #219, '78 fb)
VILLAINS: Peter Stromboli (Engraving Department Manager & Nazi spy, also as "L.K. Waters of the Waters Department Stores"), the Money Bandits (Nazi operatives, Fritz & Karl named, one as cab driver)
OTHER CHARACTERS: Ezra Jenkins (engraver), Gloria Jenkins (cigarette girl & Ezra's granddaughter), engravers, gatehouse guard (dies), White Cat night club patrons, 3 Washington DC detectives, Pierrie (White Cat club employee), bank clerk & customers, police, L.K. Waters (financier, mentioned), Adolf Hitler (in photo on cave wall), bystanders (on splash page)
LOCATIONS/ITEMS: Washington DC inc US Bureau of Engraving w/engraving tools, guardhouse, White Cat Night Club, Police HQ, hospital, Washington Monument (splash only) & 2nd National Bank, Virginia inc Camp Lehigh w/Steve and Bucky's tent & Money Bandits' cave w/ engraving tools & duplicate money; Money Bandits' firearms, knife, wrench & blackjacks, Bucky's jelly bean chewing gum

SYNOPSIS: Steve and Bucky work as guards at the US Bureau of Engraving. Engraver Ezra Jenkins receives a note claiming his granddaughter Gloria is in danger. Gloria gets the same message about Ezra and heads for the bureau. Ezra meets her outside, still carrying a $1000 engraving. Nazis knock out Steve and Bucky, kill the guard & abduct Ezra and Gloria. Days later, duplicate $1000 bills flood the USA, endangering the economy. Realizing the counterfeiters must be the Jenkins' abductors, Steve and Bucky stake out a bank, then trail "L.K. Waters," the only customer using a $1000 bill. Nazis ambush them, knocking out Cap and abducting Bucky to their cave hideout, where they hold Ezra and Gloria. Following Bucky's jelly bean trail, Cap finds the cave, defeats the Nazis and unmasks Waters as Ezra's boss Peter Stromboli.

NOTE: Story followed by "Magic Quiz" (1 page), featuring a boy magician demonstrating 5 tricks.

5TH STORY: "Let's Play Detective: The Mystery of the Scarlet Skull" (2 pages)
CREDITS: Al Bellman (art)
FEATURE CHARACTER: Mike Trapp
SUPPORTING CAST: Detective Ryan (formerly Officer Ryan)
VILLAINS: Peter Van Stone (Gordon's nephew), Red Lacy (gambler), the Scarlet Skull Gang (imprisoned gang) (both mentioned only)
OTHER CHARACTERS: Gordon Van Stone (Peter's uncle), Jennings (Gordon's butler), Scarlet Skull (on ransom note), Helen (Peter's girlfriend, mentioned in diary)
LOCATIONS/ITEMS: Gordon's home, Greenwood Cemetery, Sing Sing prison (mentioned); Peter's diary, ransom note, Trapp's note
SYNOPSIS: After refusing to loan money to his gambler nephew Peter, Gordon Van Stone receives a ransom note from "the Scarlet Skull Gang," demanding $50,000 for Peter's return. Knowing the Scarlet Skulls are in prison, Trapp searches Peter's room, finds his diary and notices both it and the ransom note misspell the word "receive." At the drop site, Trapp leaves a note instead of money, and Peter turns himself in.
NOTE: Identified as Case #752. Trapp and Ryan are apparently private detectives in this story.

TEXT STORY: "Good Luck Story" (2 pages)
CREDITS: Writer unknown
FEATURE CHARACTER: Eddie "Ed" Dayton (reporter)
VILLAINS: 2 enemy operatives
OTHER CHARACTERS: Colonel Brandon, Ryder (government technician), hotel desk clerk, army sergeant, soldiers, hotel bystanders
LOCATIONS/ITEMS: North woods boomtown inc hotel w/Room 14 and lobby, operatives' shack, Eddie's shack & adjacent US Army base; soldiers' machine guns, Ryder's suitcase & gun, operatives' gun & hunting knife
SYNOPSIS: Desperate for a story, Eddie watches two men check up on newcomer Ryder, whom Eddie suspects of illegal activity. Eddie grabs Ryder, a government employee, slugs him and ties him up. Eddie confronts the other two men, but soldiers intervene. Col. Brandon confirms who Ryder is. Unable to write the story lest vital information be leaked, Eddie resigns himself to being fired. Brandon offers him an army position.
NOTE: Story appears between 4th & 5th stories.

CAPTAIN AMERICA COMICS #36 (March 1944)

"The Blood of Doctor Necrosis" (16 pages)

CREDITS: Syd Shores (art, c art)
FEATURE CHARACTER: Captain America (also as "Digger" & "Yank")
SUPPORTING CAST: Bucky (chr last in Cap #219, '78 fb), Sgt. Duffy (last in CapC #34, '43, chr last in Cap #219, '78 fb), Gen. Haywood (erroneously identified as a colonel, last in CapC #34, '44)
VILLAINS: Dr. Necrosis (Nazi scientist & white gangrene victim, also as Death on splash page, dies) & his underlings, Japanese soldiers (many die)
OTHER CHARACTERS: US soldiers, Australian soldiers (some bts, some die for both), Capt. Roberts (medical officer), US Army doctor (others bts), Mary Knowles (Red Cross nurse, Gen. Knowles' daughter), 2 Australian police officers, Brisbane bystanders, Gen. Knowles (mentioned), leucopedesis germs (bts, see NOTE), Adolf Hitler, Hermann Goering, Josef Goebbels, Heinrich Himmler, Nazi soldiers (prev 5 on cover)
LOCATIONS/ITEMS: South Pacific island inc village, dressing station & base hospital, Brisbane (Australia) inc Red Cross building w/Necrosis' lab and operating room; US, Australian & Japanese soldiers' rifles, underlings' firearms, Necrosis' laboratory & operating room equipment, Cap & Bucky's plane, Nazi planes, Hitler's car, Nazis' motorcycles and firearms, Bucky's rifle (prev 5 on cover)
SYNOPSIS: In the South Pacific, Steve and Bucky's unit seize an enemy-held village. Wounded soldiers receive plasma. Steve and Bucky drive them through enemy lines to a hospital where they find the wounded have contracted leucopedesis, or white gangrene, from the plasma. Learning thousands have been similarly afflicted, Cap and Bucky fly to Brisbane, Australia, the plasma's origin point. They meet Dr. Necrosis, a rare, disfigured survivor of white gangrene, and his assistant Mary Knowles. Necrosis later captures Cap and Bucky. In his operating room, Necrosis prepares Mary for a blood exchange, explaining that white gangrene is curable with a serum based on Mary's rare blood type; previous attempts to identify someone with that type created the tainted plasma. Cap and Bucky escape, knocking Necrosis onto broken glass which pierces his heart. Mary reveals she can create a cure for the stricken soldiers from her notes.
NOTE: "Leucopedesis" is not a disease, but the passage of white blood cells through unruptured capillary walls and into surrounding tissues.

2ND STORY: "Meet the Director of Death!" (7 pages)
CREDITS: Jimmy Thompson (pencils), Al Gabriele (inks)
FEATURE CHARACTER: Human Torch (next in AllSel #3/2, '44, AllWin #12, '44, MC #54, '44)
SUPPORTING CAST: Toro (last in MC #53, '44, next in AllSel #3/2, '44)
VILLAINS: "The Director of Death" (named in title only, pyromaniac/ex-stuntman, Nazi agent (both die)

OTHER CHARACTERS: Hollywood police chief, firefighters, ambulance attendants, injured man, murder victim (dies), Hollywood bystanders, Grant Films Inc. (mentioned only), several skeletal figures, captured woman (both on splash page only)

LOCATIONS/ITEMS: Hollywood inc Police HQ, Pixy Pictures studio (arson site), hospital, "film site" building, "Director"'s house inc asbestos-lined garage & highway w/curve; "Director"'s truck, sedan (destroyed) & mask, film

SYNOPSIS: In Hollywood, Torch and Toro discuss recent arson/murder cases with the police chief. At one scene, they find the targeted building's walls filled with film, making it extra flammable. Later, they observe a film crew at work as a man is pushed from a building. Toro, thinking the scene was real, follows two men in a movie truck. They pull into an asbestos-lined garage, locking Toro and the truck within. Police determine the arson victims all once worked with a disgruntled ex-stuntman. Torch finds the criminals, the ex-stuntman and his Nazi associate, who depart in a fireproof car. Torch frees Toro and follows, but an exhaust leak in the tightly sealed car knocks the men out and they drive over a ledge.

3RD STORY: "Let's Play Detective" (1 page)
CREDITS: Al Bellman (art)
FEATURE CHARACTER: Mike Trapp (next in AllSel #3/5, '44, Kid #4/3, '44)
SUPPORTING CAST: Detective Ryan
VILLAIN: A bellhop
OTHER CHARACTERS: Hotel manager, Henry Ricard (as corpse)
LOCATIONS/ITEMS: Hotel inc Ricard's room; bellhop's watch, gun
SYNOPSIS: Playboy Henry Ricard is found dead in a hotel, a smoking gun at his side. Trapp and Ryan question a bellhop, who recalls that he heard the gunshot at 10:15. Trapp checks the bellhop's watch, which is stopped at 9:00, meaning he lied. The bellhop confesses.
NOTE: Trapp and Ryan are apparently policemen again.

4TH STORY: "The Strange Mystery of the Leopard Woman!" (16 pages)
CREDITS: Unknown
FEATURE CHARACTER: Captain America
SUPPORTING CAST: Bucky
VILLAINS: Leopard Woman (Countess Kyra, Nazi operative) & her Nazi underlings (one dies), Elsa (Kyra's housekeeper), Eric (Elsa's brother)
OTHER CHARACTERS: William "Bill" Sands (New York Water Commissioner), Mrs. Sands (Bill's wife), Mrs. Van Loan (society matron), Mr. Raczkowski (Polish diplomat), garden party guests, reservoir guards (1 seen, others bts, all die), Leopard Woman's 4 black panthers
LOCATIONS/ITEMS: Manhattan inc Sands and Van Loan apartments & garden, Countess Kyra's mansion w/boat house, Ashaka Reservoir inc power plant; Leopard Woman's whip & panther cage, map, Countess Kyra's cigarette holder & cigarette
SYNOPSIS: Steve and Bucky guard a diplomat at a society garden party, where Leopard Woman abducts Water Commissioner Sands. They pursue but Nazi saboteurs delay them. Finding a map of the Ashaka Reservoir and neighboring mansions, Cap and Bucky investigate and meet Countess Kyra who lures them into a locked room, uncaging two panthers to occupy them. Kyra, as Leopard Woman, takes Sands to the reservoir to poison Manhattan's water. Escaping the panthers, Cap and Bucky stop her. Leopard Woman vanishes into the night.

5TH STORY: "The General of Death!" (12 pages)
CREDITS: Unknown
FEATURE CHARACTER: Captain America (next in USA #12, '44, AllSel #3, '44, AllWin #12/2, '44, Cap #600/2, '09 fb, Av/Inv #1-12, '08-09)
SUPPORTING CAST: Bucky (next in USA #12, '44), Sgt. Duffy
VILLAINS: General von Savage (Nazi officer, dies), Gestapo chief, Emil & Hans (Nazi torturers), Nazi soldiers (most bts, many die)
OTHER CHARACTERS: General Matson, Major Kirby, Captain Gorely, Lieutenant Dalton (dies) (all US Army Intelligence), Barrack A soldier (voice only), French Guerilla Unit 8 (Raoul named), Major Kompts (panzer division head, mentioned only)
LOCATIONS/ITEMS: Vichy France inc French guerilla HQ, Nazi HQ w/von Savage's office and torture chamber & Sector 3 w/Nazi building, tunnel under English Channel (destroyed), England inc Army Intelligence office & Barrack A; explosives truck (destroyed), Nazi tanks and trucks (most destroyed), torture wheel, soldiers' rifles & dynamite
SYNOPSIS: Lt. Dalton sends a message from Vichy France regarding Nazi troop movement, but is interrupted. Army Intelligence sends Steve and Bucky to investigate. In France, Nazi soldiers capture Cap and Bucky. Gen. von Savage, in charge of the troop movements, sends them to his torturers, who are just finishing with Lt. Dalton. Cap and Bucky escape but Dalton dies. Cap forces a Nazi soldier to reveal von Savage's plan to attack England through a tunnel built beneath the English Channel. Commandeering an explosives truck, Cap and Bucky hurry through the tunnel, with von Savage and his invasion force close behind. As the two near the English side, the truck blows a tire and crashes. Attaching a fuse to the truck's cargo, Cap and Bucky surface in England, just as the fuse goes off, killing von Savage and most of the invasion force.

TEXT STORY: "Eight Lives Lost" (2 pages)
CREDITS: Writer unknown
FEATURE CHARACTER: Spike (US sailor & ex-cowpuncher),
SUPPORTING CHARACTERS: Narrator, Phil (both US sailors)
VILLAINS: Nazi sub captain & crew (some bts, all die)
OTHER CHARACTERS: "The Old Man" (Emily Green's captain), & crew members, convoy ship & destroyer crews (bts)
LOCATIONS/ITEMS: Atlantic Ocean; Emily Green (convoy ship), convoy ships, destroyers, Nazi sub (destroyed), Spike's lasso & knife
SYNOPSIS: Former cowboy Sailor Spike has evaded death eight times, but his shipmates were not always as fortunate. His presence on the Emily Green troubles the crew. When the ship is damaged, Spike's jinx seems in effect. A Nazi sub interrupts repairs. The Nazi captain approaches by boat. Spike lassoes him and hauls him over a spar, confusing the Nazis long enough to gun them down and destroy the sub. Spike's jinx is broken.
NOTE: Story appears between 3rd & 4th stories.

"The Chambers of Dr. Agony" (14 pages)

CREDITS: Vince Alascia (pencils), Bob Powell (inks), Alex Schomburg (c art)
FEATURE CHARACTER: Captain America
SUPPORTING CAST: Bucky (chr last in Av/Inv #12, '09), Gen. Haywood
VILLAINS: Dr. Agony (Conrad Meer, Nazi scientist & torturer, dies), Tula (Agony's mutated panther, dies)
OTHER CHARACTERS: Mr. Morley (govt administrator) & his driver, corpse, torture victims (on splash only),
US & Nazi soldiers (on cover only)
LOCATIONS/ITEMS: US Army Camp inc Admin. Office of Occupied Territories w/nearby gully, Dr. Agony's
subterranean base; Dr. Agony's torture equipment, pain immunity serum, heated cage & dagger, Cap's mace (on
splash only), Nazi & US firearms, Cap's missile, Bucky's flamethrower (prev 3 on cover only)
SYNOPSIS: Searching for missing administrator Morley, Steve and Bucky find a black panther dragging a corpse whose face is frozen in pain.
When they follow the panther, Dr. Agony opens a shaft, dropping them into his underground torture chamber, where his pain-immune panther
Tula's purring mesmerizes them. Agony, who is using a captured Morley to test his pain immunity serum, binds Bucky to a rack, but Cap steps
on Tula's tail, halting her purr and ending the mesmerism. Agony drops a heated cage over Cap. Bucky lures Tula to bite through one of his
restraints, escapes and deactivates the cage. Bucky and Agony fight. Tula attacks Cap, knocking him into a light switch. Blinded by the light,
Tula mistakenly attacks Agony, who stabs her; unable to feel pain, she kills him before expiring. Steve and Bucky return to base with Morley.
NOTE: Morley erroneously refers to Haywood as "Colonel." Dr. Agony's real name revealed in MAtlas #1, '07.

2ND STORY: "The Seven Sons of Satan" (13 pages)
CREDITS: Syd Shores (art)
FEATURE CHARACTER: Captain America
SUPPORTING CAST: Bucky, Sgt. Duffy
VILLAINS: The Seven Sons of Satan (7 Japanese brothers, 3 die, all also in pfb, 1st also as snake charmer) & their father (pfb only, dies)
OTHER CHARACTERS: Gen. Montbatten, US soldiers, giant four-armed figure (on splash only), cobra, elephants, 2 mice
LOCATIONS/ITEMS: India inc city w/adjacent US Army camp inc munition dump, India-Burma border territory & nearby ruins w/tower and
dungeon; Sons' daggers, flamethrower, sword, mist pills & torpedo, satanic statue (on splash only)
FLASHBACK: A dying Satanist declares his sons "the Sons of Satan", telling them how to use "black magic" against "the white race" (p).
SYNOPSIS: In India, Steve and Bucky rescue General Montbatten from a killer cobra, then pursue the cobra's master, a disguised Japanese
agent, who inadvertently falls on his own dagger. As he dies, he declares himself "a Son of Satan" and promises to return stronger than ever.
That night, Cap and Bucky prevent a torpedo from detonating their camp's munition dump, tracing it to the Son of Satan, seemingly alive and
stronger than before. When soldiers approach, he commits suicide, claiming he will return again. Cap and Bucky witness the man's apparent
spirit depart his body. Later, they again encounter the Son of Satan, who is electrocuted. Meeting him once more, Cap and Bucky realize their
current opponent is brother to the three earlier Sons. Three more Sons join the fight and capture them. Cap and Bucky break their bonds and
knock out all four. Finding mist pills on them, Cap realizes a similar pill was the source of the supposed spirit seen earlier.

3RD STORY: "Let's Play Detective: The Blackout Murder Case" (1 page)
CREDITS: Al Bellman (art)
FEATURE CHARACTER: Mike Trapp
SUPPORTING CAST: Det. Ryan
VILLAIN: Charley Dane
OTHER CHARACTERS: Policeman, landlady, Moe Barton (stoolie, bts, as corpse), Phil Dane (Charley's brother, mentioned only)
LOCATIONS/ITEMS: Midtown Manhattan inc rooming house & Police HQ; knife (bts, kills Barton)
SYNOPSIS: Moe Barton is murdered during a blackout. Trapp and Ryan question his landlady and tenant Charley Dane, who claims a green-
suited masked man ran from Barton's room. Realizing Dane couldn't have seen such details during the blackout, Trapp arrests Dane.
NOTE: Story followed by "Urgent! Sentinels of Liberty! A Vital Message from Captain America!" (1 page) with Cap asking the reader to join the
wartime waste paper drive, featuring Captain America & Bucky.

4TH STORY: "Frozen Death" (15 pages)
CREDITS: Otto Binder (script), Al Gabriele (pencils), Vince Alascia (inks)
FEATURE CHARACTER: Captain America (next in Cap #219, '78 fb, Cap #600/2, '09 fb, CD #8, '95 fb)
SUPPORTING CAST: Bucky (chr next in Cap #219, '78 fb), Sgt. Duffy
VILLAINS: Red Skull (last in AllWin #12/2, '44, chr next in Cap Ann #9/2, '90 fb, see NOTE), Nazis (some die, Gratz, Hans, Heinler named)
OTHER CHARACTERS: Inuit girl, US soldiers, torture subject (dies), Inuit girl's father (bts, Skull's prisoner), 3 mastiffs (1 dies)
LOCATIONS/ITEMS: Red Skull's tropical Arctic island (destroyed) inc prison & lab, surrounding sea; US Army plane (destroyed), turbine
which "collects the energy from the aurora australis" (see NOTE), torture device, Nazi artillery & firearms, US firearms, Bucky's machine gun
SYNOPSIS: From a tropically heated Arctic island, the Red Skull's men shoot down a transport plane carrying Steve, Bucky and Duffy. Nazi
soldiers bring them before Red Skull, who is accompanied by an Inuit girl. When Steve and Bucky loudly insult him, the Skull separates them for
special treatment, strapping Steve into a deathtrap, but he escapes and frees Bucky. Red Skull starts up his aurora-powered turbine to destroy
all Allied countries' machinery but Cap forces him to flee, and shuts down the turbine, setting up a chain reaction. The Inuit girl, only helping the
Skull because he holds her father prisoner, leads the Skull into one of his own pit traps. Cap falls into the pit, but defeats Red Skull with judo.
Cap and Bucky release the American prisoners, and they escape by boat as the chain reaction destroys the island.

NOTE: This is Red Skull's last confirmed golden age appearance; later ones feature impersonators or remain unexplained. The Skull is shown here as a white-haired, mustached man, whom Cap recognizes as the real Skull. Presumably Skull's turbine draws energy from the Arctic's aurora borealis, rather than, as stated, Antarctica's aurora australis.

5TH STORY: "Flaming Steel!" (7 pages)
CREDITS: Charles Nicholas (pencils), George Klein (inks)
FEATURE CHARACTER: The Human Torch (next in MC #55, '44, CapC #45/2, '45, CapC #38/2, '44)
SUPPORTING CAST: Toro (next in MC #55, '44)
VILLAIN: "The Wizard Welder" (Pop Kunz, welder turned saboteur)
OTHER CHARACTERS: Mr. Clark (superintendent of King Shipyards), Jackson (Clark's assistant), King Shipyards workers
LOCATIONS/ITEMS: King Shipyards inc Clark's office & acetylyne gas shack, Manhattan inc Torch & Toro's apartment; ships, Pop's gun
SYNOPSIS: When acetyline explosions plague the King Shipyards, superintendent King contacts Torch and Toro. A ship explodes minutes after their arrival & the employees walk off. Torch and Toro volunteer as welders, and King gets Pop Kunz, his oldest employee, to instruct them. However, Pop is the saboteur, and he traps Torch inside a ship boiler. Pop tries to similarly seal in Toro at gunpoint, but Toro knocks the gun away, then releases Torch. The two capture Pop and the shipyard employees return to work.

TEXT STORY: "Tried at Sea" (2 pages)
CREDITS: Writer unknown
FEATURE CHARACTER: Sailor aboard the Margaret Kenny (as narrator)
SUPPORTING CAST: Karl (German-born sailor), Skeet (sailor)
VILLAINS: U-Boat crew (bts, in sub, all die)
OTHER CHARACTERS: "The Old Man" (Margaret Kenny's captain), Margaret Kenny crew members (some die)
LOCATIONS/ITEMS: South American port, Atlantic Ocean; Margaret Kenny (freighter, destroyed), U-Boat (destroyed), rowboats
SYNOPSIS: When German youth Karl joins the Margaret Kenny's crew, other sailors suspect him of being a spy. In the wake of a storm, Skeet, the most suspicious sailor, almost fights Karl, but a Nazi sub fires on the ship. The sailors fire back, but when the ship is damaged, all abandon ship in rowboats except Karl who strafes the sub, sinking it. Rejoining the others, Karl curses the sub crew and Hitler in both German and English, cementing camaraderie with Skeet and the other sailors.
NOTE: Story appears between 3rd & 4th stories.

CAPTAIN AMERICA COMICS #38 (May 1944)

"Captain America in Castle of Doom!" (17 pages)

CREDITS: Syd Shores (pencils), Vince Alascia (inks), Alex Schomburg (c art)
FEATURE CHARACTER: Captain America
SUPPORTING CAST: Bucky (chr last in Cap #219, '78 fb), Gen. Haywood (next in CapC #40, '44), Sgt. Duffy
VILLAINS: Honorable Leader (dies) & Japanese soldiers (most die, some also as escaped POWs in pfb)
OTHER CHARACTERS: Death Valley Pete, Sparks (FBI agent, dies), FBI chief & agent (others bts), Pvt Perkins (as corpse), US pilot, mechanic, reporter, US Army officer & soldier (prev 5 in pfb only), Japanese pirates, captive woman, bats (prev 3 on cover only)
LOCATIONS/ITEMS: Washington DC inc FBI HQ, Nevada inc US Army camp, Death Valley inc oil pipeline, Pete's castle w/plane factory/base (destroyed), hidden mine, plane factory (pfb), ammunition dump (pfb); Japanese rifles, Hon. Leader's ancestral statues, Pete's club & explosives, Cap's machine gun, pirates' clubs, firebrands & brazier (prev 4 on cover)
FLASHBACK: Over 100 POWs escape from internment. Authorities discover airplane part thefts at factories and munitions dumps (p).
SYNOPSIS: At a camp near Death Valley, Haywood assigns Steve and Bucky to drive FBI agent Sparks to investigate sabotage at an oil line, where truck tracks are found. Sparks believes the incident is tied to the POW escapes and plane part thefts. A plane strafes them, killing Sparks. Steve and Bucky hide until the plane runs out of ammunition and departs. They follow the truck tracks to local eccentric Death Valley Pete's castle, now controlled by Japanese operatives and converted into a hidden plane base. Cap and Bucky are taken prisoner, and the Japanese Honorable Leader boasts that their planes, indistinguishable from US aircraft, will attack US cities, before locking them up with Death Valley Pete. They escape, with Pete leading them to his hidden mine and its explosives cache. As Japanese soldiers prepare for takeoff, Cap boards the first exiting plane and seizes control, firing upon and destroying the other planes. Once Cap escapes, Pete blows up the castle, destroying all within. Cap and Bucky promise to keep Pete's mine a secret.
NOTE: Story followed by "Urgent! Sentinels of Liberty! A Vital Message from Captain America!" (1 page)

2ND STORY: "Murder for Profit!" (7 pages)
CREDITS: Al Avison (pencils), Al Bellman (inks)
FEATURE CHARACTER: Human Torch (next in MC #56, '44)
SUPPORTING CAST: Toro (chr last in CapC #45/2, '45, next in Kid #6, '44)
VILLAINS: The Dagger (food bootlegger & war profiteer) & his underlings (2 die)
OTHER CHARACTERS: Russ Morgan (farmer, dies), Mary Morgan (Russ' wife), Morgans' son & daughter
LOCATIONS/ITEMS: Happy Corner (farming community) inc Morgan farm, Dagger's camouflaged warehouse; Dagger's car (destroyed), pistol & powder sprayer, underlings' pistols, Torch and Toro's hoes
SYNOPSIS: Torch and Toro are investigating war profiteer Dagger when two of Dagger's men shoot Russ Morgan for his refusal to sell his goods at extorted low prices. Torch and Toro pursue the getaway car, which crashes. One dying criminal reveals where Dagger's camouflaged

valley warehouse is. Torch and Toro destroy the trucks and trap Dagger's men in flames. Dagger stops them momentarily with crop-killing powder, but when he tries to escape, they destroy his car.

3RD STORY: "Frozen Death" (13 pages)
CREDITS: Don Rico (pencils), Al Gabriele (inks)
FEATURE CHARACTER: Captain America
SUPPORTING CAST: Bucky
VILLAINS: Cellmen (artificially evolved amoeba-creatures, Amoebus named w/3 Cellmen splitting from Amoebus, all die), Japanese scientist (dies), officers (most die) & pilots (most bts, Maj. Yuki named, some die)
OTHER CHARACTER: US Army pilot
LOCATIONS/ITEMS: Arctic Circle inc subterranean Arctic jungle w/Japanese base within volcano crater (destroyed); US Army transport plane & supplies, Japanese planes (some destroyed), firearms, grenades, explosives & lighter
SYNOPSIS: Steve and Bucky's supply plane is shot down near the Aleutian Islands; while the pilot repairs the plane, they set out for an Allied base. Bucky falls through an ice crevice, and Steve jumps after him, finding the floor unexpectedly warm. The ice gives way and they fall into a volcano-heated hidden jungle. A Japanese scientist, riding a giant humanoid "Cellman," greets them. The heroes attack, but their blows merely split the creature into two, then four Cellmen, who capture them. The scientist explains he discovered the jungle ten years before and created Bucky seizes grenades and attacks, but the explosions only create more Cellmen. Imprisoned, the two use a lighter for illumination and discover flames can disintegrate the Cellman. Using torches to panic the Cellmen, they attack the soldiers, with Bucky shooting the scientist. They blow up the ammunition dump, triggering the volcano, then return to the plane, where the pilot has completed repairs.
NOTE: The jungle's origins are unrevealed. The Cellmen resemble the Goons from E.G. Segar's Thimble Theatre comic strip (later Popeye).

4TH STORY: "Captain America Fights the Peril of the Past!" (14 pages)
CREDITS: Otto Binder (script), Syd Shores (pencils), Vince Alascia (inks)
FEATURE CHARACTER: Captain America (also as Hercules & Sir Amerigo in screening of Cap's "memories")
SUPPORTING CAST: Bucky (also as Buckalaag & Bucky the Squire Boy in screening of Cap's "memories")
VILLAINS: Dr. Emil Natas (criminal mastermind & saboteur, also as Phao Na Tash & Diablo Natas in Cap's "memories," dies) & his Black Gang
OTHER CHARACTERS: Buckalaag's fellow slaves, villagers in AD 1313 inc innkeeper & inn patrons, Sir Amerigo & Bucky the Squire Boy's horses, Phao Na Tash's fellow overseers (all in screening of Cap's "memories"), police, medieval criminals (on splash only)
LOCATIONS/ITEMS: Egypt inc pyramids, construction site & village (all Cap's "memories"), Manhattan, Dr. Natas' office (13 Gravesend Ave, N.R. Metropole 23, ph: Endicott 6085); Phao Na Tash & overseers' whips, spears & arrows, Hercules' shield, Diablo Natas' stolen gold, Sir Amerigo's sword & shield (all Cap's "memories"), Natas' memory retrieval apparatus w/screen, cyanide & pistol, Black Gang's guns
SYNOPSIS: When Cap and Bucky defeat the Black Gang, one member drops Dr. Emil Natas' card. Suspecting him of leading the Gang, Cap and Bucky visit him, but he captures them, and declares he has fought them in two previous lives. Using an exotic apparatus, he apparently retrieves Cap's buried memories of past incarnations and projects them on a screen, showing Ancient Egypt where Phau Na Tash was defeated by Hercules and Buckalaag, then AD 1313 when Diablo Natas lost to Sir Amerigo and Bucky the Squire Boy. Freeing himself, Cap punches Natas across the room where a cyanide bottle falls in his face. Predicting a fourth meeting, in reincarnations centuries hence, Natas dies.
NOTE: If Natas' claims are true, while Cap's "Hercules" incarnation isn't the Olympian Heracles, it might be the "Hercules" in DarMys #6, '40 whose power was granted to Marvel Boy (Martin Simon Burns) and, perhaps, to Marvel Boy (Martin Oksner Burns) in USA #7/3, '43.

5TH STORY: "Let's Play Detective: The Mystery of the Coin" (1 page)
CREDITS: Al Bellman (art)
FEATURE CHARACTER: Mike Trapp
SUPPORTING CAST: Officer Ryan (last app)
VILLAIN: Lucky Adams (gambler)
OTHER CHARACTERS: Burton Lorr (criminal lawyer, bts, murder victim), Lorr's secretary, Earl Cartwell (Lorr's former business partner)
LOCATIONS/ITEMS: Burton Lorr's home, Police HQ; Adams' two-headed coin
SYNOPSIS: Investigating Burton Lorr's death, Trapp questions Lorr's secretary, ex-business partner Earl Cartwell, whom Lorr owed money, and gambler Lucky Adams, who had an appointment with Lorr. At the murder scene, Trapp finds a two-headed coin. Figuring only a gambler would carry such a coin, Trapp arrests Adams, who confesses.
NOTE: Back in uniform, Ryan has apparently been demoted back to officer.

TEXT STORY: "The Sarge's Song" (2 pages)
CREDITS: Writer unknown
FEATURE CHARACTER: Pete (narrator)
SUPPORTING CAST: Cpl. Williard ("Will"), Sgt. Humphrey ("Hump")
VILLAINS: Axis pilots (bts, some die)
OTHER CHARACTERS: US Army soldiers (some die, Mike Hanrahan, Michaels named)
LOCATIONS/ITEMS: US Army supply depot inc barracks, sickbay, oil dump & adjacent river w/wharves; Axis planes, Humphrey's notes
SYNOPSIS: Will's singing cheers the men in his barracks, but Sgt. Humphrey, nearly twice his size, considers him an unmanly nuisance. Later, Will learns Humphrey spends spare time writing music. Shortly after Humphrey quarrels with Will, Axis bombers attack the base. Will, Pete, and other soldiers spend hours firefighting. Humphrey, seriously wounded, is confined to sickbay, and sends for Will. He gives a song he has written to Will, who sings it for him. Humphrey recovers, cheered by hearing his work performed, and the two men become friends.
NOTE: Story appears between 3rd & 4th stories.

"Terror of the Ghost Harpoon" (15 pages)

CREDITS: Syd Shores (pencils), Vince Alascia (inks), Alex Schomburg (c art)
FEATURE CHARACTER: Captain America
SUPPORTING CAST: Bucky
VILLAINS: Ghost Harpooner (mad fisherman, dies), Silas ("the Mate," dies), 4 crew members in Silas' pay
OTHER CHARACTERS: Molly (Moby Dick owner), Tom (Moby Dick captain), Moby Dick crew members, Fluke and Fin patrons, aged sailor, motorboat owner, doctor (bts, tells Molly that Tom will recover from the attack), Jed (Molly's deceased father, mentioned), Herman Melville (mentioned, see NOTE), birds, Death (splash only), 7 Japanese operatives, 2 power plant employees (both on cover only)
LOCATIONS/ITEMS: Nantucket (Massachusetts) inc the Fluke and Fin Inn w/Steve and Bucky's room & dock, Atlantic Ocean, Boulder Dam Power Plant No. 1 (on cover only); the Moby Dick (Molly's ship), motorboat, Steve & Bucky's car (license # DL 1356) & fishing equipment, Ghost Harpooner's harpoons, Silas' knives, Japanese weapons, Bucky's baseball bat (both on cover only)
SYNOPSIS: In a Nantucket Inn on a fishing vacation, Steve and Bucky find ship owner Molly quarreling with sailors over crewing the Moby Dick, upon which "the Ghost Harpooner" has killed Molly's father and others. Sailor Silas offers to be first mate. A harpoon is flung in and a half-mad old fisherman blames the ghost. That night, Steve and Bucky intervene when Silas and others attack Molly's captain Tom. The next day, Cap and Bucky catch up to the Moby Dick, sailing with Molly as captain. Aboard, Silas' sailors attack them but they quickly defeat them. They overhear that another sailor has died, seemingly confirming the curse. Silas offers to buy the ship at a low price. Realizing Silas is behind the deaths, Cap and Bucky intervene, but the crazed fisherman, allied with Silas but wanting to destroy the ship, enters, flings his harpoon, then leaps to a watery death. Cap battles Silas in the ship's rigging, where the Mate falls and dies.
NOTE: Steve notes that Nantucket is where Herman Melville (1819-1891) worked on his novel Moby-Dick.

2ND STORY: "Let's Play Detective" (1 page)
CREDITS: Al Bellman (art)
FEATURE CHARACTER: Mike Trapp
SUPPORTING CAST: Pepper Burns (police photographer, 1st)
VILLAIN: Miss Walton (Cyrus' secretary)
OTHER CHARACTERS: Coroner, Cyrus Crane (as corpse), Peter Crane (Cyrus' half-brother), Cyrus' butler
LOCATIONS/ITEMS: Manhattan inc Crane's home; Cyrus' clock, letter opener & will
SYNOPSIS: Wealthy Cyrus Crane is murdered. The coroner places time of death at 8:00. Trap questions Miss Walton, Peter, and the butler. When Walton claims to have heard Crane arguing with another man at 9:00, Trapp arrests her. Later, he learns Crane changed his will to leave his entire estate to Walton.
NOTE: Trapp is again identified as a private detective.

3RD STORY: "Riders of Death" (13 pages)
CREDITS: Otto Binder (script), Jimmy Thompson (pencils), Ken Bald (inks)
FEATURE CHARACTER: Captain America
SUPPORTING CAST: Sgt. Duffy (chr next in ToS #69/2, '65, next in CapC #42/4, '44), Bucky
VILLAINS: The Death Riders (motorcycling arsonists) inc leader
OTHER CHARACTERS: Henry Crawford (Crawford Bomber Plant owner), Mary Crawford (Henry's daughter), Lt. Jim Hale (Mary's fiancé), minister, 60,000 town citizens inc firefighters, plant workers & guards (most bts, some die)
LOCATIONS/ITEMS: US Army camp & adjacent town (several bldgs destroyed) inc Crawford Bomber Plant, minister's home, and Death Riders' hidden base; Death Riders' truck, motorcycles, torches, machine guns & binoculars, plant workers' tools
SYNOPSIS: On leave, Steve and Bucky observe Lt. Hale marrying Mary Crawford which is interrupted when hooded motorcyclists set houses aflame. Cap and Bucky capture one and unmask him as a Japanese operative who declares the Death Riders plan to destroy the Crawford Bomber Plant, where "long-range skymaster bombers" are under construction. Cap and Bucky pursue the others but they vanish. Despite the disaster, Hale is determined to marry Mary that night, but the Riders return to abduct Mary and her Bomber Plant owner father, then vanish again. Cap, Bucky, & Hale visit the plant where the Riders attack. Plant workers help defeat them, and Cap, Bucky and Hale don Riders' robes to infiltrate them. Near the earlier vanishing point, they find a black truck, camouflaged by darkness, which ferries them to the Riders' secret cliffside base. Once inside, the trio attack the Riders and free the Crawfords.

4TH STORY: "Rockets of Doom" (12 pages)
CREDITS: Mike Sekowsky (pencils), Al Bellman (inks)
FEATURE CHARACTER: Captain America (next in AllSel #4, '44, BP #21, '06 fb, BP #1, '05 fb, MCP #6/3, '08, USA #13, '44, YA #12, '44)
SUPPORTING CAST: Bucky (next in AllSel #4, '44)
VILLAINS: Carl von Brummel (Nazi scientist, dies), Rocket Shell Submarine crew (most bts, all die), Nazi supply ship crew (most bts), Nazi pilots & underlings (Hans named), Adolf Hitler (also in photo, last in AllWin #11/5, '44, chr last in SgtF #59, '68, next in Kid #5/2, '44)
OTHER CHARACTERS: US Army colonel, police, bystanders, US destroyer crew (bts, pick up Cap & Bucky), Death (splash only)
LOCATIONS/ITEMS: Manhattan, Camp Lehigh, Shore Airfield, Hitler's Berlin HQ; von Brummel's Rocket Shell Submarine (diagram indicates radio control room, firing tube, shell compartment w/rocket shells, engine room & release mechanism), Nazi ship (both destroyed), unmarked Nazi plane, US Army plane (damaged), US destroyer, von Brummel's failed "Big Bertha" gun (mentioned)
SYNOPSIS: Hitler and scientist von Brummel discuss their failure to create a "rocket-gun" big enough to launch shells across the Atlantic. They

decide to try "Master Plan #2" instead. A month later, rocket shells strike Manhattan. When Cap and Bucky investigate, they find von Brummel and company gloating. The heroes attack, but the Nazis flee. Cap and Bucky borrow an army plane to search for a Nazi sub and are shot down by an unmarked Nazi plane. A Nazi ship captures them. The ship transfers giant rocket shells to a sub. The heroes realize this, not a "Big Bertha" gun, is the source of the attacks. Escaping, they board the sub, knock out von Brummel and lock the controls. Unable to escape its firing tube, the rocket explodes, destroying the sub. A US destroyer picks up Cap and Bucky.
NOTE: Story followed by "Urgent! Sentinels of Liberty! A Vital Message from Captain America!" (1 page)

5TH STORY: "Let's Play Detective: The Case of the Talking Crystal Ball" (2 pages)
CREDITS: Al Bellman (art)
FEATURE CHARACTER: Mike Trapp
SUPPORTING CAST: Pepper Burns
VILLAIN: Pettibone (Mrs. van Aster's butler)
OTHER CHARACTERS: Mrs. van Aster, masquerade ball attendees (1 as devil)
LOCATIONS/ITEMS: Mrs. van Aster's home inc ballroom; Mrs. van Aster's $500,000 diamond necklace, Pettibone's pistol, crystal ball
SYNOPSIS: Mrs. van Aster hires Trapp to provide security at her masquerade party, where she wears an expensive diamond necklace. During the party, someone steals the necklace from her. Trapp, having pre-treated the necklace with a special dye, sees traces on Pettibone's hands. Pettibone draws a gun, but Trapp knocks him out.
NOTE: Trapp is again a private detective here.

6TH STORY: "The Human Torch in Tarbu's Mission of Death" (7 pages)
CREDITS: Jimmy Thompson (pencils), Allen Simon (inks)
FEATURE CHARACTER: Human Torch (next in AllSel #4/2, '44, MC #57, '44)
SUPPORTING CAST: Toro (last in MC #56, '44, next in AllSel #4/2, '44)
VILLAINS: Prof. Tarbu (false spiritualist, dies) & his 3 underlings (one dies)
OTHER CHARACTERS: Mrs. Blair, Janet Blair (Mrs. Blair's daughter), Jim Blair (US Marine & Mrs. Blair's deceased son, as image), 2 morgue attendants, coroner, bus & car drivers (bts, in vehicles)
LOCATIONS/ITEMS: Manhattan inc Tarbu's home, Torch and Toro's apt & Janet's hospital room; Tarbu's glass cylinder & séance table
SYNOPSIS: When Tarbu convinces Mrs. Blair, via a false image of her deceased son, to entrust him with her money, her daughter Janet consults Torch and Toro. Tarbu's underling shoots Janet through Torch's window. When Toro pursues, the shooter runs into traffic, to his death. Torch and Toro visit Tarbu. He gases them, placing them in a glass cylinder, intended to rotate at a killing speed. Toro swings at Tarbu, accidentally knocking a gem from his turban, which fortuitously grates against the cylinder's revolving base, stopping it. The two escape and, while they tackle the underlings, Tarbu backs through a window, falling to his death.
NOTE: Although Janet claims to have proof Tarbu's vision of Jim was fake, she never provides it. Torch and Toro next encounter a criminal spiritualist, Swami Krishna, in HT #31/3, '48.

TEXT STORY: "On the Square" (2 pages)
CREDITS: Writer unknown
FEATURE CHARACTER: Junior Waring (15-year-old first aid instructor)
SUPPORTING CAST: Dr. Schauf (dean of Central City's doctors, head of Advisory Public Health Committee & school board chair)
VILLAINS: Slick Welsh (also as "Dr. Glenndon," con man) & associate (poses as chauffeur)
OTHER CHARACTERS: Chief of Police Hartman, police, reporter, first aid class instructors & students, city employees, bystanders, the Mayor (mentioned), Dr. Forbes (John Millerton Med College president, mentioned)
LOCATIONS/ITEMS: Central City inc high school gym, City Hall, Gem City Bank, State Bank & hotel (prev 3 mentioned), Hannibal garage (mentioned, see NOTE), Welsh's rented limo, first aid equipment, black bag full of nearly $10,000 in cash & checks
SYNOPSIS: Visitor Dr. Glenndon's condescension alienates Dr. Schauf and his protégé Junior Waring; supposedly seeking funds for a Central City Clinic, he takes over Schauf's first aid class as a fund-raising event. Via careful remarks, Junior and Schauf trick Glenndon into displaying medical ignorance, then warn the police. After collecting donations, Glenndon tries to leave, but the police chief, having learned his true identity of con man Slick Welsh, arrests him.
NOTE: Story Story appears between 3rd & 4th stories. Dr. Schauf mentions Central City is near Hannibal, implying story is set in Missouri.

CAPTAIN AMERICA COMICS #40 (July 1944)

"The Jester of Death!" (12 pages)

CREDITS: Syd Shores (pencils, c art), Vince Alascia (inks)
FEATURE CHARACTER: Captain America
SUPPORTING CAST: Bucky (last in YA #12, '44), Gen. Haywood
VILLAIN: The Jester of Death (Johnnie Pinkham, dies but see NOTE)
OTHER CHARACTERS: Bryce (House of Pranks owner), Belton (dies), Swanton (dies), partygoers, Jester's 3 dogs, alligators, devils (as wall decorations) (both on splash only), Japanese soldiers (cover only)
LOCATIONS/ITEMS: The House of Pranks inc arsenic bar, pitching room, control room w/viewing screen, subbasement w/cell & elevator; Jester's pistol, arsenic, torture wheel, collapsible barbed wire fence & electrical bars, Japanese arsenal, explosives-filled US jeep, Bucky's pistol (prev 3 on cover only)
SYNOPSIS: Steve and Bucky accompany Haywood to the House of Pranks, run by Haywood's friend, notorious jokester Bryce. There, the

masked Jester invites Belton, a guest, to partake of his arsenic bar. The poison is real and Belton dies but the others presume he is playing along. Realizing the truth, Cap and Bucky pursue the partygoers and find Jester has another guest, Swanton, tied to a torture wheel, killing him. Cap and Bucky pursue Jester but enter a trick room, where the floor heaves, then drops them into a subbasement. They find the real Bryce imprisoned and free him. Meanwhile, Jester pins Haywood to a wall with electrical bars, but Bryce shows Cap and Bucky a secret entrance to surprise him. Cap unmasks Jester as Johnnie Pinkham, seeking vengeance on Bryce and the others for a traumatic college prank. He flees but falls down an elevator shaft to his apparent death.

NOTE: Cap (William Nasland) and Bucky (Fred Davis) fight a Jester in CapC #65/4, '48; since Pinkham's "death" is not confirmed, the two Jesters may be one and the same. Haywood is again misidentified as a colonel.

2ND STORY: "Human Torch vs the Bloody Assassin" (7 pages)
CREDITS: Jimmy Thompson (pencils)
FEATURE CHARACTER: Human Torch (next in HT #16, '44, MC #58, '44)
SUPPORTING CAST: Toro (last in MC #57, '44, next in Kid #7, '45)
VILLAINS: Herr Loeder (head Nazi operative) & 5 underlings (Franz, Fritz, Ricky named)
OTHER CHARACTERS: Gen. Mershing (military chief of staff) & his bodyguards (one dies, others bts), ceremony attendees
LOCATIONS/ITEMS: Washington DC inc Washington Park & Nazis' southside hideout w/torture chamber, Falcon Aircraft Plant; Justice (aircraft), Nazis' airtight glass cylinder (broken), iron maiden, bed of nails, blackjacks & spray guns, Franz's knife, Ricky's pistol (destroyed)
SYNOPSIS: Arriving for an aircraft christening ceremony led by Gen. Mershing, Torch and Toro find a bodyguard dead, killed so a Nazi can replace him. Seeing the fleeing killer, Franz, they pursue. However, Franz, Herr Loeder and others, set a trap, sealing Torch and Toro in an airtight cylinder to asphyxiate them. The heroes topple the cylinder against an iron maiden's spikes, breaking it. After capturing Loeder and company, they head to the ceremony, where Torch incinerates would-be assassin Ricky's gun and captures him.
NOTE: Gen. Mershing's name is derived from Gen. John J. "Black Jack" Pershing (1860-1948). Story reprinted in AllWin #16/2, '45; the only Torch story printed twice in the 1940s. Story followed by "Urgent! Sentinels of Liberty! A Vital Message from Captain America!" (1 page)

3RD STORY: "Captain America in the Auction of Death" (16 pages)
CREDITS: Unknown
FEATURE CHARACTER: Captain America
SUPPORTING CAST: Bucky, Gen. Haywood
VILLAINS: The Keeper of the Flash (asst lighthouse keeper, dies), Adolf Hitler (last in Kid #5/2, '44, chr next in SgtF #66, '69, next in MC #58, '44), Josef Goebbels (last in Kid #5/2, '44, next bts in CapC #49, '45 fb), Herman Goering (last in Kid #5/2, '44, next in CapC #49, '45 fb), Emperor Hirohito (last in SubC #11, '43) & his aide, Nazi general, 3 operatives & sub crew (some bts, most die), Japanese officer, 2 operatives & sub crew (most bts, most die)
OTHER CHARACTERS: Lighthouse keeper (dies), President Franklin D. Roosevelt (last in MC #54/4, '44, chr last voice only in SgtF #66, '69, chr next in Cap Ann '01) & his aide, Gen. Miles, 1 Russian & 2 US Army officers
LOCATIONS/ITEMS: Rock Island ("Auction Island") w/lighthouse & cave, Washington DC inc White House, US Army camp, Berlin inc Nazi HQ, Tokyo inc Imperial Palace, Wondmere Island (bts, destroyed); PT boat, Nazi sub, Japanese sub, meteor (all destroyed), military boats (bts), Keeper's club & "flash" (weapon powered by meteor fragment), Nazi & Japanese firearms, bidder's knife
SYNOPSIS: A meteor lands near Rock Island's lighthouse, The keeper discovers a fragment can channel sunlight into devastating power. The keeper's assistant kills him and fashions the fragment into a crude weapon, "the flash," then offers it for sale to both Allies and Axis. FDR assigns Cap and Bucky to prevent the Axis from purchasing it. Hitler plots to buy it without Japan's knowledge, while Hirohito makes similar plans regarding Germany. The day before the scheduled auction, Cap, Bucky, a U-Boat & Japanese sub arrive at Rock Island. While the enemy captains quarrel over their early arrivals, Cap and Bucky make for shore. Annoyed at their early arrivals, the Keeper of the Flash destroys both subs. The covert bidders escape by raft, defeat Cap and Bucky and imprison them in a cave. The following morning, Germany and Japan's official bidders arrive, as do Russians and Americans including General Miles. The covert bidders try to steal the flash, as Cap and Bucky escape. A Nazi bidder stabs Keeper for the flash, but Cap grabs it. Deeming the weapon too dangerous, General Miles uses it to disintegrate the meteor, and Bucky hurls the flash out to sea.

4TH STORY: "Captain America in The Mystery of the Floating City" (16 pages)
CREDITS: Otto Binder (script)
FEATURE CHARACTER: Captain America (next in Cap Ann #9, '90 fb, Cap Spec, '06 fb)
SUPPORTING CAST: Bucky (chr next in Cap Ann #9, '90 fb), Gen. Haywood (next in Cap #42/4, '44)
VILLAINS: Nazi officer (dies) & 1000 Nazi soldiers (most bts, some die)
OTHER CHARACTERS: Lyander (Floating City rebel leader), Floating City's million citizens inc 100 rebel fighters (most bts, some die), US officers & soldiers, "deep sea monster" (dies), Adolf Hitler (in photograph)
LOCATIONS/ITEMS: East Coast US Army base inc CO's office, the Floating City (built 1,000 years ago by a race trying to cross the ocean) inc rebel HQ, palace w/sub pool & Nazi lounge; US planes, Nazi subs, planes & firearms, rebel weapons & pontoon shoes, torpedo
SYNOPSIS: Investigating bomber planes' disappearances, Cap and Bucky fly a plane over the Atlantic and find the Floating City, whose weapons fire upon them. Cap manages a water landing. Men using pontoons to walk on water lead them to the City. Their leader, Lyander, explains that outsiders, Nazis, have conquered the City. Cap and Bucky join Lyander's resistance movement and reconnoiter within the palace, discovering a U-Boat-filled submarine bay. They attack the Nazi soldiers but are captured. The chief Nazi summons a "pet" sea monster to devour them, but they escape into a sub and destroy the creature with a torpedo. They resurface just as Lyander's rebels retake the palace. Confessing the Axis leaders hoped to use the City as a hiding place after losing the war, the chief commits suicide. Cap and Bucky promise to keep the Floating City a secret.
NOTE: The introductory narrative claims that Cap and Bucky were sworn to secrecy and that "the editors of [Captain America Comics]" take the responsibility for revealing it. Story reprinted in AllWin #16/3, '45; the only Cap story printed twice in the 1940s.

TH STORY: "Let's Play Detective" (1 page)
CREDITS: Al Bellman (art)
FEATURE CHARACTER: Mike Trapp
SUPPORTING CAST: Pepper Burns
VILLAIN: Mr. Ranes (playwright)
OTHER CHARACTERS: Actor, actress, Brenda Kane (actress, bts, as corpse), theater employees (bts)
LOCATIONS/ITEMS: Manhattan inc theater & Police HQ; Ranes' blackjack, Brenda's letters
SYNOPSIS: Trapp investigates actress Brenda Kane's death. He finds hidden letters in her dressing room but the killer sneaks in, knocks him on the head and steals them. Playwright Ranes and others enter the room to find him. Ranes remarks on the blow on his head. Presuming only his attacker would know how he was injured, Trapp arrests Ranes, who confesses that Brenda was blackmailing him.

TEXT STORY: "Periscope Ahead" (2 pages)
CREDITS: Writer unknown
FEATURE CHARACTER: Sgt. Bob Keating (blimp radio operator)
VILLAINS: Nazi U-Boat crew (all die)
OTHER CHARACTERS: Capt. Esmond (blimp captain), Johnny Keating (Streckfus radio operator & Bob's brother) & other Strekfus crewmembers (about a dozen survivors, others die bts), blimp crew inc navigator, steersman & bombardier
LOCATIONS/ITEMS: Northern Atlantic Ocean; US Army blimp w/radio set & conical canvas water-enveloping anchor, US supply ship Streckfus, U-Boat (both destroyed), Nazi weapons, blimp "ash can" bomb & rubber raft
SYNOPSIS: When a U-Boat attacks the Streckfus, the blimp commanded by Esmond and served on by Keating speeds to respond. They anchor near the destroyed ship and find a handful of survivors, including Keating's brother Johnny, in the water. Rescue operations are interrupted when the U-Boat attacks. Injured, Esmond passes command to Keating, who orders the blimp into action despite still being anchored. The blimp destroys the U-Boat, and an impressed Esmond decides Keating should be promoted to command his own blimp.
NOTE: Story appears between 3rd & 4th stories.

CAPTAIN AMERICA COMICS #41 (August 1944)

"Captain America in The Killer Beasts of Notre Dame" (14 pages)

CREDITS: Vince Alascia (art), Alex Schomburg (c art)
FEATURE CHARACTER: Captain America
SUPPORTING CAST: Bucky (chr last in Cap Spec, '06 fb)
VILLAINS: Herr Governor (Vichy official, dies), the Gargoyles ("the Killer Beasts," 20 luminescent-costumed French psychopaths, all die), Nazi officers & soldiers (Maj. Schwam named, some die)
OTHER CHARACTERS: French Underground leader & members (most bts, some die), Parisian citizens (some die), Adolf Hitler (in photograph), the Hunchback of Notre Dame (mentioned by Bucky), gargoyles (as statues), US soldiers (most bts, in tanks, cover only), Japanese soldiers (some die, cover only)
LOCATIONS/ITEMS: Vichy Paris inc Herr Governor's office, Cathedral of Notre Dame & nearby insane asylum, French shore; Nazi & underground members' firearms, Nazi whips & leashes, Cap & Bucky's motorcycle, TNT kegs, firearms, Cap's machine gun, Bucky's grappling line & flamethrower (prev 6 on cover only)
SYNOPSIS: After Herr Governor takes charge of Vichy France, monstrous Gargoyles kill Parisians but not Nazis, who claim to be unable to see them. The French Underground contacts Cap for help. When he and Bucky arrive in Paris, a Gargoyle attacks. While Cap grapples with him, Bucky fights a black-clad Nazi, near-invisible in the darkness. At the Cathedral of Notre Dame, Cap and Bucky follow soldiers to a chamber, where black-clad Nazis cage and control the Gargoyles, actually murderous lunatics. Cap and Bucky are captured and taken to the Cathedral's bell tower, where Herr Governor ties them to the bell clapper to be battered when the bell rings at midnight. Cap escapes, stops the bell ringer, and frees Bucky. When the Nazis return, Cap and Bucky feign death, then attack. The Gargoyles, inadvertently released, fall upon their captors as French underground members swarm the Cathedral. Herr Governor flees to the roof where the underground leader fires from below, killing him. The Gargoyles and their handlers kill each other. Cap, Bucky, & the underground retreat before Nazi reinforcements arrive.
NOTE: Following this issue, the title changes to bimonthly publication.

2ND STORY: "Human Torch Versus Berlin's Mistress of Death!" (7 pages)
CREDITS: Al Bellman (pencils)
FEATURE CHARACTER: Human Torch (next in AllWin #13, '44, DarMys #9, '44, MC #59, '44)
SUPPORTING CAST: Toro (last in MC #58, '44, next in AllWin #13, '44)
VILLAINS: Elsa (Nazi spy, dies, see NOTE), Bernhart & Franz (spies, both die), Lisbon Nazi agent (mentioned)
OTHER CHARACTERS: FBI colonel, Thomas "Tommy" Malone (merchant marine, dies), telephone operator, Quill of Local 205 of the Maritime Union (both bts, on phone w/Torch), Elsa's victim, Nazi soldier (both on symbolic splash only), police (bts, notified by Torch)
LOCATIONS/ITEMS: Manhattan inc Elsa's brownstone, FBI office, Brooklyn Bridge & East River; Nazis' truck, fireproof glass coffin (both destroyed) & liquid asbestos guns, Elsa's machine gun, Nazi's knife, Tommy's dog tags, Nazi dungeon (symbolic splash only)
SYNOPSIS: Elsa lures Tommy Malone to be killed by her fellow agents, who abscond with his dog tags. When Torch and Toro investigate, Elsa claims a fence obscured her view. Torch notices the fence is too low to do so. Later, Torch and Toro consult the FBI and learn a Lisbon Nazi agent is smuggling reports on US ships via sailors' dog tags. The two fly to Elsa's home but are captured. The Nazis place them in a fireproof glass coffin and drop them into the East River but Torch and Toro heat the glass to such a high temperature that it breaks on contact with the water. Torch's fireball blows out a tire on the Nazis' truck which goes out of control on the Brooklyn Bridge, killing the three spies.

NOTE: Elsa's last name is erroneously given as "Bernhart" in OHMU : HC #5; this is actually the name of one of her accomplices.

3RD STORY: "Captain America and The Murder Brain" (15 pages)
CREDITS: Vince Alascia (pencils), Jack Binder (inks)
FEATURE CHARACTER: Captain America
SUPPORTING CAST: Bucky
VILLAINS: The Brain ("Tiger" Duncan, "the Murder Brain," condemned killer, destroyed) prison doctor (controlled by Duncan)
OTHER CHARACTERS: Prison warden, guards (some bts, 4 die bts), chaplain, executioner, execution witness & medical attendant, District Attorney (dies), DA's butler (bts, slugged by doctor), Judge Dale (dies), police, gun-toting criminal (on splash only)
LOCATIONS/ITEMS: Prison inc death chamber, medical lab, prison cemetery & warden's office, US Army camp, Manhattan inc prison doctor's home w/lab, DA & Dale's homes; Tiger's pistol, doctor's pistol, rope, knife & thermometer, guard's gun, Brain's glass container
SYNOPSIS: Condemned criminal "Tiger" Duncan escapes prison, but Cap and Bucky recapture him. Vowing vengeance against Cap and others, Duncan is electrocuted, but during the autopsy, the prison doctor finds Duncan's brain virtually unharmed. The brain compels the doctor to preserve him in his home lab, then compels the doctor to shoot the DA. The prison warden, on the phone with the DA, hears the killing and recognizes the doctor's voice as Duncan's. Later, the doctor strangles Judge Dale. Investigating, Cap and Bucky find a broken thermometer and return to the prison to question the doctor who, his face now resembling Duncan's, attacks the warden. Cap intervenes. The doctor escapes home; Cap and Bucky in pursuit. There, Duncan directs the doctor to shoot them, but a misfire strikes his jar, finally killing him.
NOTE: Cap mentions that the affair cost the doctor his life. Story inspired by Curt Siodmak's 1942 novel, "Donovan's Brain."

4TH STORY: "Let's Play Detective: The Case of the Hit and Run Monster" (2 pages)
CREDITS: Al Bellman (art)
FEATURE CHARACTER: Mike Trapp (next in CapC #46/5, '45)
SUPPORTING CAST: Pepper Burns (next in CapC #46/5, '45)
VILLAIN: John Whalen
OTHER CHARACTERS: Spike Ruggers, Roger Billingsgate Jr., Marion Tyler, Marion's mother, bystander, police
LOCATIONS/ITEMS: Manhattan inc Marion's neighborhood & Police HQ; Whalen's car
SYNOPSIS: When young boy Marion Tyler runs into the street, a driver hits him, then speeds away. A bystander reads all but the last number of the car's license plate. Trapp interviews three men whose cars' licenses match the first six. When Trapp mentions the victim's name, Marion, two presume the child is a girl. Only Whalen presumes "Marion" is a boy, identifying him as the driver. Pepper reports that Marion is recovering.

5TH STORY: "Captain America in The School of Horror" (15 pages)
CREDITS: Vince Alascia (pencils), Al Gabriele (inks)
FEATURE CHARACTER: Captain America (next in MUni #1-3, '98, Cap:RW&B/4, '02, CapTW:AB #1, '09 fb, Cap #109, '69 fb, SecWs #17 '11 fb, Cap:Re #1, '09, Order #7, '08 fb, Siege:Cap #1, '10 fb, Cap #616/3, '11 fb, ToS #69/2-71/2, '65, Cap #25, '07 fb, Cap&Crb #1, '11 fb, Hulk #284, '83, AllWin #13/2, '44, Cap #616/8, '11, USA #14, '44)
SUPPORTING CAST: Bucky (chr next in MUni #1, '98 fb)
VILLAINS: The Schoolmaster (Sanderson, Carver's partner, also in pfb1 & pfb3, dies) & his students, Mickey the Goon (leading class demonstration), John W. Carver (Greystone Building owner, also in pfb1-3, dies)
OTHER CHARACTERS: Mary Carver (John Carver's wife, also in pfb2), chauffeur, police (some in pfb1), Mr. Conway (Mickey's intended victim), bystanders, Greystone tenants (Jim, Frank, Stevenson Manufacturing employee, others, some die, all in pfb1), moving men (pfb1)
LOCATIONS/ITEMS: Manhattan inc Greystone Building (also in pfb1 & pfb3) inc Schoolmaster's classroom (on top floor), students' firearms, nooses, cement mixer (pfb3 only)
FLASHBACK: Greystone building residents get notes threatening their deaths. When several are killed, the rest move out (p1). Greystone owner Carver enters the building to try to learn the truth (p2). Years before, Carver buries his partner Sanderson alive in the building's cement foundation. Sanderson escapes and hides away in a secret room (p3).
SYNOPSIS: Soon after entering his building to investigate (in pfb2), John Carver falls to his death. His widow tells Steve and Bucky the building's history. That night, Cap and Bucky investigate and find a hidden room where the Schoolmaster instructs criminals on torture and murder. The criminals capture them. The Schoolmaster orders them hung, but Cap gets free & rescues Bucky. They defeat the criminals but the Schoolmaster finesses Cap into falling out a window. Cap catches a flagpole and vaults himself back, knocking Schoolmaster down and unmasking him as Sanderson, Carver's former partner. Sanderson explains his grudge, adding that the experience prompted him to open his criminal school. He then hurls himself out a window to his death.

TEXT STORY: "Defense Witness" (2 pages)
CREDITS: Writer unknown
FEATURE CHARACTER: Andy (would-be sailor)
OTHER CHARACTERS: Chris Turner (Andy's friend, discharged from US Army), Andy's father and mother, sailor, recruitment official, recruitment office employees, passengers, bystanders
LOCATIONS/ITEMS: City inc subway station, building w/US Navy recruiting office & docks, small town inc Andy's house; freighters, tugboat, sailor's billy club & gun, Andy's bag, Andy's mother's knitting
SYNOPSIS: Against his parents' wishes, Andy applies to the US Navy, but because he is underage, cannot join without consent. Returning home, Andy fails to convince his mother. Chris Turner, recently discharged from the army, visits and agrees with Andy's perspective. Later, Andy's father reveals he invited Chris in hope he could convince either Andy or his mother of the other's viewpoint. Andy remains resolute. Perhaps his mother will change her mind.
NOTE: Story appears between 2nd & 3rd stories.

"Tojo's Terror Masters" (18 pages)

CREDITS: Vince Alascia (art), Alex Schomburg (c art)
FEATURE CHARACTER: Captain America
SUPPORTING CAST: Bucky
VILLAINS: Gen. Yokima (invasion force leader, dies), Japanese soldiers (most bts, many die) inc "Major" & "Captain," Japanese secret service chief & agents
OTHER CHARACTERS: Gen. Douglas MacArthur (US Army Supreme Commander, Southwest Pacific Arena, last in AllWin #8/2, '43, chr next in WI #4, '77, next in Battle #26, '54), US soldiers (most bts, "Sparks" named) inc "Colonel," sub captain & sub crew (most bts), Chinese guerrillas (Tein Lin, Wang named, see NOTE) w/leader, birds, 4 bank guards (2 die), 4 bank robbers, bank customer (prev 3 on cover only)
LOCATIONS/ITEMS: Manchuria-Russia border, Chinese guerrilla HQ, South Pacific island inc US Army base w/Operations Room, barracks & MacArthur's quarters, Japan inc Tokyo w/Yokima's HQ, Mt. Fuji w/invasion base and sea plane base, Minami Torishima "Marcus Island") inc "escape hatch" base & munitions shed, 2nd Nat'l Bank (street address #5, on cover only); Japanese underground train destroyed), sea plane, US sub, Japanese & US firearms, Marcus Island explosives, Yokima's sword (symbolic splash only) Armored Bank Service truck, guards & robbers' firearms, Bucky's baseball bat (prev 3 on cover only)
SYNOPSIS: Receiving reports of Japanese forces massing for an all-out US invasion, Gen. MacArthur sends Cap and Bucky to investigate. A sub takes them to Japan where soldiers overpower and take them to Gen. Yokima, who boasts that millions of Japanese troops will invade the USA the following day. Outfighting their guards, Cap and Bucky escape with Yokima's plans, which direct them to a secret Mt. Fuji base, where Yokima's forces have tapped the volcano's gas to propel a train carrying Yokima and his troops through an underground tunnel leading to the USA. Arriving too late, Cap and Bucky steal a plane and fly to the tunnel's emergency escape hatch at Marcus Island. They enter the tunnel and pack it with explosives. The hurtling train strikes and set offs the explosives, killing all on board.
NOTE: Wang called Yang once here.

2ND STORY: "The Human Torch vs the Spy-Master of the Third Reich!" (7 pages)
CREDITS: Al Bellman (art)
FEATURE CHARACTER: Human Torch (next in MystC #1/2, '44, MystC #2/3, '44, HT #17, '44, MC #60, '44)
SUPPORTING CAST: Toro (last in MC #59, '44, next in MystC #1/2, '44)
VILLAINS: Lambert (Carlsbad Plant manager) & 3 underlings
OTHER CHARACTERS: Sam Gleason (FBI agent, see NOTE), plant guard (bts)
LOCATIONS/ITEMS: FBI office, Carlsbad Plant, woods, Lambert home; tree w/ asbestos rope, stolen plans, Lambert's flashlight & note; spies' guns, hydraulic torture device (both on splash only)
SYNOPSIS: Gleason asks Torch and Toro to investigate Carlsbad Plant, where plans are being photographed and smuggled out. There, they spot a man in the blueprint room, but he evades them. Finding a note implicating Lambert, they travel to his home. Lambert and his men spring a trap on Torch and Toro, hanging them from a tree with an asbestos rope. After the spies depart, Torch easily burns the tree instead. Freed, the two speed to the plant and capture the spies.
NOTE: Gleason is identified as "chief" of the FBI, a position actually held by J. Edgar Hoover (1895-1972).

3RD STORY: "Waters of Death!" (10 pages)
CREDITS: Vince Alascia (pencils)
FEATURE CHARACTER: Captain America
SUPPORTING CAST: Bucky
VILLAIN: Ichthyologist (also as party-goer who suggests they all go for a swim, dies)
OTHER CHARACTERS: JT Fleming (millionaire, dies), partygoers (John named), octopus (dies, see NOTE), man-of-war (dies), fish
LOCATIONS/ITEMS: US Army camp w/nearby road, Fleming estate inc indoor basement pool, ichthyologist's shack; octopus, man-of-war, & fish tanks (man-of-war tank shattered), Steve & Bucky's rifles, ichthyologist's pistol
SYNOPSIS: A car suffers a flat tire near Steve and Bucky, on guard duty. The driver, millionaire JT Fleming, claims the tire was sabotaged, the latest of several mishaps following notes threatening to kill him. The next night, Cap and Bucky stake out Fleming's party, where he dies while swimming in his basement pool. Investigating, Cap discovers a poisonous man-of-war that stung Fleming. Cap and Bucky withdraw and watch as a man, an ichthyologist, catches the man-of-war in a tank. They follow him to his shack to renew the fight, during which the ichthyologist falls into his octopus tank and is severely mangled. The killer tells them Fleming's previous close calls were coincidental accidents but admits sending the notes since Fleming once denied him expedition funding, then dies.

4TH STORY: "The Baron of Horror Castle" (10 pages)
CREDITS: Syd Shores (pencils), Vince Alascia (inks)
FEATURE CHARACTER: Captain America (next in SecAv #11-12, '11 fbs, Cap:Re #2, '09, Cap Ann '01, ToS #75/2, '66 fb, Cap #25, '07 fb, ToS #77/2, '66 fb, Cap#3, '05 fb, Cap #49, '09 fb, Cap #37, '08 fb, Cap:Re #1, '09, Cap:DMR #2, '02 fb, Cap #26, '04 fb, IM #73, '03 fb)
SUPPORTING CAST: Bucky (chr next in Cap Ann '01 fb), Sgt. Duffy (last in CapC #39/3, '44, chr last in ToS #70/2, '65), Gen. Haywood (last in CapC #40/4, '44, next in CapC #44, '45)
VILLAINS: Baron of Horror Castle (dies) & his underlings (Fritz named, one dies)
OTHER CHARACTERS: 2 US Army officers, "piraya" fish (bts)
LOCATIONS/ITEMS: European US Army camp, Horror Castle inc dining hall, fish pool & battlement; Baron's medieval swords, shields,

maces, helmets & knives

SYNOPSIS: Haywood selects Steve and Bucky for guard duty when he and other officers dine with the Baron of Horror Castle. There, the Baron drugs his guests, planning to abduct them to Germany. Noticing the sudden silence, Cap and Bucky investigate but are captured. The Baron kicks them into a piranha pool, then absconds with his captives to a waiting plane, but Cap breaks his bonds and rescues Bucky. Cap hurls the Baron's own spear to halt the plane. Back at his castle, with the heroes in pursuit, Baron foolishly tries to hurl a cannonball at Cap, but its weight topples him off the battlement to his death.

TEXT STORY: "Bottle Neck" (2 pages)
CREDITS: Writer unknown
FEATURE CHARACTER: Dennie (machine shop foreman)
OTHER CHARACTERS: Gregg (junior mechanic), Ted Carter (new foreman), Andy & other machine shop workers, gas pump attendant, front gate guard, Captain Wright (mentioned)
LOCATIONS/ITEMS: Machine shop, Gregg's neighborhood; US Army trucks, grease guns
SYNOPSIS: Dennie quarrels with Gregg over his frequent absences. The immediacy of the machine shop's army vehicle work is lost on Gregg, who resents being moved to more "menial" grease pit work due to greater need. When Gregg calls in "sick," Dennie drives to his neighborhood to further lecture him on their work's importance. The next day, Gregg comes to work to find Dennie in the grease pit. He has promoted Ted Carter to foreman and demoted himself to spur production. Moved by Dennie's dedication, Gregg becomes a more diligent worker.
NOTE: Story appears between 2nd & 3rd stories.

CAPTAIN AMERICA COMICS #43 (December 1944)

"Captain America in The Shadows of Death!" (16 pages)

CREDITS: Vince Alascia (pencils), Al Bellman (inks), Syd Shores (c art)
FEATURE CHARACTER: Captain America
SUPPORTING CAST: Bucky (chr last in Cap #26, '04 fb)
VILLAINS: The Shadow Monster (Karl Shaffer, dies), Nazi agents (all die)
OTHER CHARACTERS: John Shaffer (Karl's uncle, silhouette painter, dies), Blakely (Shaffers' butler, dies), sheriff, young baseball players inc Red McIntyre (dies), Meadow Brook residents (Jones mentioned), 2 govt geologists (die), US Army major, mural figures, bats, 6 criminals (cover only)
LOCATIONS/ITEMS: Meadow Brook (New England) inc sheriff's office, Jones' house, quarry w/Zorite, underground river & Shaffer estate, Mechanicsville, Johnson Falls (adjacent towns, both mentioned only), Ajax Powder Works & adjacent building (on cover only); Shadow Monster's truck (wrecked), Steve & Bucky's motorcycle, Nazis' spear, knife & magic lantern projector, Shaffer's mural, American Mining Journal clipping, criminals' mace & guns (on cover only)
SYNOPSIS: Returning to camp, Steve and Bucky investigate a call for help but arrive too late to save a youth from the Shadow Monster, who has been terrorizing Meadow Brook. They also meet two government geologists, in the area for secret prospecting. Later, Cap and Bucky find the geologists dead, killed by the Monster, whose trail leads to the Shaffer estate, home of Karl and his uncle John. Inside, the Monster attacks, as do two Nazi agents. Cap and Bucky fight them off, then find Shaffer's butler, dying, clutching an article on Zorite, a rare metal. Cap realizes both geologists and Nazis are seeking a Zorite deposit, with the Monster murdering to conceal its discovery. Soon after, the Monster traps Cap and Bucky in a flooded quarry tunnel but they quickly escape, discovering Zorite traces. On the surface, they find John, dying & dressed as the Monster, intended as a decoy. They spot the real Monster and Nazis, fleeing by truck, board it, and unmask the Monster as Karl, who steers the truck over a cliff. Cap and Bucky leap to safety as their enemies perish. They report the Zorite discovery to authorities.

2ND STORY: "Mystery of the Wingless Bat!" (7 pages)
CREDITS: Jack Alderman (art)
FEATURE CHARACTER: Human Torch (next in AllSel #5/2, '45, DarMys #10/2, '44, MC #61, '45)
SUPPORTING CAST: Toro (last in MC #60, '44, next in AllSel #5/2, '45)
VILLAINS: Herr Bat (Nazi saboteur, dies), Franz & associate (Herr Bat's henchmen)
OTHER CHARACTERS: Major Brant, US Army soldiers & pilots (most bts, many die), news vendor, bystanders
LOCATIONS/ITEMS: Table-Top Mesa inc US Army Glider School (partially destroyed) w/field headquarters, Herr Bat's hideout, nearby town inc newsstand; planes (many destroyed), Herr Bat's balloons, explosives, control/map console, flame-dowsing bombs & asbestos straitjackets, Nazis' guns (on splash only)
SYNOPSIS: After learning the Glider School was bombed without any planes being detected, Torch and Toro offer assistance. When a second attack occurs, Torch and Toro spot a remote-controlled balloon carrying TNT that they follow to a mountain shack, Herr Bat's base. When the heroes enter, the Nazis dowse their flames, bind them in asbestos straitjackets and depart to release more balloons. Toro uses his teeth to untie Torch, who frees Toro. The two defeat Bat's underlings, then inadvertently kill Bat by setting off an explosive balloon.

3RD STORY: "The Death That Came from Nowhere!" (10 pages)
CREDITS: Vince Alascia (art)
FEATURE CHARACTER: Captain America
SUPPORTING CAST: Bucky
VILLAINS: Baron Hitso ("Japan's greatest scientist," also on televisor, dies), Japanese soldiers & pilots (all die)
OTHER CHARACTERS: Staff headquarters officer, Allied Intelligence officer, soldiers (most bts, many die)
LOCATIONS/ITEMS: Luoki Island inc staff HQ (destroyed) & munitions sheds, Allied base inc intelligence HQ, Baron Hitso's mountain lab (destroyed); Hitso's remote-controlled piloted rocket shells inc Shell 8, control panel inc televisor & note, Allied televisor, firearms
SYNOPSIS: Baron Hitso's radio-controlled shells bomb Allied-controlled Luoki Island, killing many. Hitso warns the next barrage will strike the

island's ammunition sheds. Cap and Bucky crash their plane into the shell, detonating it in mid-air. Military intelligence locates Hitso's mountain lab. Cap and Bucky travel there and discover the shells are piloted by kamikaze soldiers, making them far more maneuverable than remote control alone. Hitso's soldiers capture them and Hitso places Bucky in Shell 8. Cap escapes, defeats Hitso & uses Hitso's controls to steer Shell 8 to safety. He sets the other shells to return to Hitso's lab. He and Bucky depart as the lab is destroyed.

NOTE: Both Hitso and Allied intelligence possess "televisors" through which they can communicate via screen. Story followed by "An Important Message to the Boys and Girls of America! From General Arnold, Commanding General, US Army Air Forces" (1 page), in which Gen. HH Arnold urges "every young man and woman of pre-military age who has been filling a summer war job to return to school this autumn," featuring Gen. Arnold (in photo) & Minuteman (on war bond stamp) and "Teen-Age Girls!!! Enter the Miss America Magazine Contest!!" (1 page) featuring Miss America (in photo).

4TH STORY: "The Sea Dragon!" (10 pages)
CREDITS: Vince Alascia (pencils), Jack Alderman (inks)
FEATURE CHARACTER: Captain America (next in AllSel #5, '44, AllWin #14/2, '44, Cap #12, '05 fb, Cap #15, '06 fb, CapTW:PoD #1, '10, CapTW:OZP #1, '08, IM #73, '03 fb)
SUPPORTING CAST: Bucky (next in AllSel #5, '44), Sgt. Duffy (next in AllWin #14/2, '44)
VILLAINS: Dr. Yokotio (Japanese scientist, dies), Japanese sailors (some bts, many die)
OTHER CHARACTERS: US Army soldiers (most bts, many die), transport ship captain & crew, convoy ship crews (bts, many die)
LOCATIONS/ITEMS: Pacific Ocean inc island; the Sea Dragon (submarine, destroyed), transport ship (damaged), convoy ships (destroyed), firearms, Cap's machine gun (splash only)
SYNOPSIS: An apparent sea dragon attacks an army convoy. Cap and Bucky fire upon it without effect. When Bucky falls into the dragon's mouth, Cap dives in after him. They discover the "beast" is a machine, piloted by Dr. Yokotio and his crew. As Cap and Bucky fight Yokotio's sailors, the Sea Dragon spirals out of control. When Yokotio accidentally bumps a control panel, the Dragon's "jaws" open to flood the interior. Cap and Bucky escape just as the vehicle explodes.
NOTE: Despite Dr. Yokotio's claim that the Sea Dragon is "the only [mechanical monster] of its kind in existence," it is very similar to the Dragon of Death from CapC #5/2, '41.

TEXT STORY: "The Black Fortune" (2 pages)
CREDITS: Writer unknown
FEATURE CHARACTER: Chris
VILLAINS: 2 would-be black marketeers (1 in corpse-like makeup)
OTHER CHARACTERS: Mike (Chris' friend), Winters (warehouse's former owner, mentioned), birds, rats (bts, heard scurrying)
LOCATIONS/ITEMS: Hilly area inc abandoned warehouse; rubber supply
SYNOPSIS: Chris and Mike visit an old warehouse, entering through a rear window. Inside, they split up, and a cadaverous man frightens Chris. Mike investigates and finds a second man upstairs. Chris inadvertently sets off a booby trap and a beam falls, knocking out the cadaverous man. Mike explains the criminals wanted to steal the warehouse's abandoned rubber supply for the black market and planned to scare intruders into their booby trap.
NOTE: Story appears between Gen. Arnold message & Miss America contest.

CAPTAIN AMERICA COMICS #44 (January 1945)

"Captain America in The Prophet of Hate!" (15 pages)

CREDITS: Vince Alascia (pencils), Al Bellman (inks), Alex Schomburg (c art)
FEATURE CHARACTER: Captain America
SUPPORTING CAST: Bucky (chr last in IM #73, '03 fb), Sgt. Duffy (last in AllWin #14/2, '44), Gen. Haywood (last in CapC #42/4, '44)
VILLAINS: The Prophet of Hate (Japanese operative posing as long-dead warrior) & his disciples (1 dies) inc bull-roarer assassin
OTHER CHARACTERS: US soldiers, "disbeliever" (dies), the true Prophet of Hate (as mummified corpse), Flo (Duffy's girlfriend, mentioned, writes letter asking Duffy why he isn't yet a hero), 9 criminals (cover only)
LOCATIONS/ITEMS: India inc Allied army base & Tomb of the Prophet, town (on cover only); disciples' spears, knives & swords, Prophet's bull-roarer (near-invisible noose), soldiers' rifles, true Prophet's golden sword, Flo's letter, incomplete bridge, cable car, criminals' firearms & detonator box, Bucky's whip & mace (prev 6 on cover only)
SYNOPSIS: In India, the Prophet of Hate, a supposed resurrected swordsman destined to lead his disciples against "the white race," stirs an anti-Allies uprising. Cap and Bucky infiltrate the Tomb of the Prophet and find the true Prophet's mummified corpse. The living Prophet's disciples capture them. The prophet demonstrates his supposed power by seemingly causing a man's death with words. Cap and Bucky are imprisoned, as is Duffy, who challenged the Prophet earlier, hoping to achieve heroism to impress his girlfriend back home. The trio escapes and fights the disciples. Duffy is knocked unconscious. The Prophet uses his "power" on Cap, who feels himself choking, but Bucky discovers a nearly invisible noose thrown by an accomplice and rescues Cap who unmasks the Prophet as a Japanese spy. The deceived disciples vow to kill him. Cap and Bucky give Duffy credit for unmasking the Prophet, getting him back in his girlfriend's graces.
NOTE: Cap and Bucky last visited India in USA #14, '44; their successors (William Nasland and Fred Davis) visit India in CapC #50/3, '45.

2ND STORY: "The Human Torch Vs. the Bandit Murder Gang!" (7 pages)
CREDITS: Al Bellman (pencils), Bob Powell (inks)
FEATURE CHARACTER: Human Torch (next in HT #18, '45, MC #62, '45)
SUPPORTING CAST: Toro (last in MC #61, '45, next in HT #18, '45)
VILLAINS: The Bandits ("the Bandit Murder Gang"): "Boss," Duke & 1 other (all die)
OTHER CHARACTERS: Police Chief Ryan, 2 policemen (die)
LOCATIONS/ITEMS: Manhattan inc Bandit hideout, bank, police HQ, Farmers Exchange Bank & sewers; glass dome apparatus w/asbestos

gum, Bandits' guns & TNT

SYNOPSIS: Hearing an explosion and gunshots, Torch and Toro fly to a bank where two policemen lie dead and a wrecked vault stands empty, with no sign of how the criminals entered. Two more bank robberies occur with the same MO. At one, Torch finds a hole in the vault floor and realizes the Bandits tunnel up inside then blow the vault door to confuse investigation. Torch and Toro follow a sewer passage to the Bandits' hideout but are trapped in a glass dome filled with cooling, constricting asbestos gum. Realizing the dome is cooling along with the asbestos, Torch super-heats the glass, which explodes outward, freeing them. They attack the Bandits in the sewers below another bank. The Bandits panic and flee into the vault, where their own explosives kill them.

3RD STORY: "The Graveyard of Ships" (13 pages)
CREDITS: Vince Alascia (art)
FEATURE CHARACTER: Captain America
SUPPORTING CAST: Betty Ross (last in CapC #33/3, '43, chr next in Cap:P #1, '10, next in CapC #61/5, '47, also in fb1 prior to main story), Bucky
VILLAINS: The Creatures (East Shipping Co. Inc.'s owner & gang members, also in fb2 prior to fb1), other gang members
OTHER CHARACTERS: Theater attendees, Henry Morgan crew inc stokers & engineers (others bts), dock employees (bts), surviving sailor (fb1 only), hospital attendant (fb1 only)
LOCATIONS/ITEMS: Manhattan inc theater, East Shipping Co. Inc. office, hospital (fb1 only) & docks, Sea of Weeds, (piece of the Sargasso Sea, also in fb2), Creatures' island base (mentioned); Henry Morgan (cargo ship), survivor's ship (destroyed, fb2 only), "Sole Survivor of Marine Disaster Tells Harrowing Tale" (newsreel), crates of bricks, owner's pistol
FLASHBACK: Betty Ross interviews the sole survivor of a sea attack (1). A cargo ship stalls in the Sea of Weeds and begins to sink. Octopus-like Creatures board, killing all but one sailor (2).
SYNOPSIS: Steve and Bucky see Betty Ross interview the survivor in a movie newsreel. Cap and Bucky find Betty undercover at the shipping company, where criminals attack, escaping with Betty and the shipping company owner. Directed by one captured criminal, they secretly board the Henry Morgan before it departs, finding Betty and the owner imprisoned in the hold. They learn the ships contain phony cargo so their owners can collect insurance while keeping their goods. Suddenly, the owner pulls a gun, handcuffs the three, and leaves them to be drowned when the ship's hatches are opened. By the time Cap breaks his handcuffs, the ship is sinking in the Sea of Weeds. He swims underwater to close the valves. The attacking Creatures, carelessly speaking English, board the ship, but Cap, Bucky and the crew overpower them and expose them as men in costumes. Cap unmasks the lead Creature as the owner.

4TH STORY: "Midnight Means Murder" (9 pages)
CREDITS: Vince Alascia (pencils), Al Gabriele (inks)
FEATURE CHARACTER: Captain America (next in Cap/NF:OthW, '01, WX #14, '03 fb, SW #42, '82 fb)
SUPPORTING CAST: Bucky (chr next in Cap/NF:OthW, '01), Gen. Haywood (next in AllSel #6, '45)
VILLAINS: The Black Hand (Gregory Smith, aircraft plant manager) & his underlings (1 dies)
OTHER CHARACTERS: Lt. Jensen (dies), Army board of inquiry, US soldiers, lab scientist, plant worker, Manhattan bystanders
LOCATIONS/ITEMS: US Army camp inc Army Intelligence HQ, Manhattan inc experimental lab (destroyed), Black Hand's hideout, aircraft plant & nearby abandoned tower; P-31 model plane, underlings' pistols, Steve & Bucky's rifles, underling's watch, Jensen's watch (bts)
SYNOPSIS: When intelligence agent Lt. Jensen literally explodes outside camp, Cap and Bucky pursue a car containing terrorist Black Hand and his associates but they escape. Learning Black Hand seeks information on bomber prototype P-31, Cap and Bucky visit an experimental lab, but Black Hand's explosions destroy it. While Bucky rescues a scientist, Cap glides the plane model out of the burning building. Black Hand allows a rebellious employee to depart, then kills him by transmitting "explosive radiations" to his watch, the same method he used on Jenkins. Later, manager Gregory Smith reports Black Hand has threatened to destroy his plant if P-31 construction continues. That night, Black Hand and company plant explosives, but Cap and Bucky intervene. Cap overpowers and unmasks Black Hand as Smith.

TEXT STORY: "Two Dangerous Companions" (2 pages)
CREDITS: Writer unknown
FEATURE CHARACTER: Charlie (17-year-old camper)
VILLAINS: Frey & Smidt (escaped POWs)
OTHER CHARACTERS: Sheriff, Charlie's horse, radio announcer (voice only)
LOCATIONS/ITEMS: New Mexico inc Rocky Mountain pine forest w/stream, nearby town w/sheriff's office, Fort Rona internment camp & Mescalero ("Mescelero") Indian Reservation (both mentioned); Charlie's water bottle, radio, bear traps & pistol, Frey's pistol
SYNOPSIS: After setting a bear trap at a stream, Charlie is captured by escaped German POWs. Charlie allows his water bottle to spill, requiring the three to seek more. He leads the POWs to the stream, catching one in the bear trap and knocking down the other. He marches both to the sheriff at gunpoint.
NOTE: Story appears between 3rd & 4th stories.

CAPTAIN AMERICA COMICS #45 (March 1945)

"Captain America in Dynamos of Death" (12 pages)

CREDITS: Vince Alascia (art), Alex Schomburg (c art)
FEATURE CHARACTER: Captain America
SUPPORTING CAST: Bucky (chr last in Cap/NF:OthW, '01)
VILLAINS: The Skeletons of Glowing Death (criminals in fluorescent costumes, some die), power plant superintendent (Skeletons' boss, dies)
OTHER CHARACTERS: Police (3 die bts), theatrical district bystanders (at least 2 die), power plant maintenance crew (as corpses), 5 bank robbers, train engineer (both on cover only)
LOCATIONS/ITEMS: Manhattan inc Skeletons' hideout, theatrical district, Biijou theater, jewelry store & power

plant; Skeletons & police firearms, train, robbers' guns, Third Nat'l Bank money satchel, Bucky's lasso (prev 4 on cover only)

SYNOPSIS: Manhattan is plunged into darkness, and glowing "skeletons" embark on a wave of robbery and murder. Cap and Bucky interrupt the spree, but the Skeletons flee. Tracing the blackout to the power plant, Cap and Bucky find the maintenance crew dead. They watch the plant superintendent confer with the police, who authorize a replacement crew. However, the "crew" are some of the Skeletons, wearing luminescent costumes under long raincoats. Cap and Bucky attack, but are defeated. The superintendent ties the two to an emergency dynamo, which will activate when main power shuts off, electrocuting them but Cap uses his teeth to tear loose a power cable, preventing their deaths. He and Bucky escape. Cap knocks the superintendent into a main dynamo just as Bucky reactivates the main power, inadvertently killing him. The police capture or kill the remaining Skeletons.

2ND STORY: "The Human Torch Versus the Walking Corpse" (7 pages)
CREDITS: Al Gabriele (pencils), Jimmy Thompson (inks)
FEATURE CHARACTER: Human Torch (next in CapC #38/2, '44, see NOTE)
SUPPORTING CAST: Toro (chr last in MC #55, '44, chr next in CapC #38/2, '44, see NOTE)
VILLAINS: The Walking Corpse (Det. Brady, Slasher's brother, impersonates Slasher), Slasher (convicted killer, dies, also as corpse)
OTHER CHARACTERS: Police chief, Det. Van, Judge Roemer (dies), DA Hogan, jurors (some bts), desk sergeant, police officer, 2 prison guards, minister, executioner, radio announcer (voice only), Roemer's butler (bts, finds Judge's body), Peter Moonie (1916-1944, name on tombstone), skeleton (on splash page)
LOCATIONS/ITEMS: Prison w/death chamber, Manhattan inc Judge Roemer's home, DA Hogan's home, cemetery & police HQ; prison electric chair, Walking Corpse's pistol, knife & sleeping gas vials, Slasher's tombstone & severed left hand
SYNOPSIS: Following his execution, Slasher apparently rises from the grave, to kill Judge Roemer, who sentenced Slasher to death. A knife with Slasher's prints are found. One detective, Brady, disdains the notion of Slasher's return. Torch and Toro fly to DA Hogan's home and rescue him from the killer, who indeed appears to be Slasher, but the killer escapes. Torch and Toro exhume Slasher's grave, discovering the corpse is missing its left hand, explaining the fingerprints' source. Hurrying to police HQ, they prevent "Slasher" from killing the DA and jurors. Toro unmasks him as Brady, secretly Slasher's brother.
NOTE: Slasher's tombstone lists "Born Nov 1900 Died Feb 1944," placing this story out of publication order.

3RD STORY: "Captain America in The Thing in the Swamp!" (18 pages)
CREDITS: Vince Alascia (art)
FEATURE CHARACTER: Captain America
SUPPORTING CAST: Bucky, Sgt. Duffy (next in CapC #47/3, '45)
VILLAINS: The Monster ("the Thing in the Swamp," Hans, von Kaulus' assistant, dies), Maj. von Kaulus (Nazi pilot & expert saboteur, dies), 2 Nazi officers
OTHER CHARACTERS: US pilots (most bts) & soldiers (bts), Kelly (factory guard, dies), 2 other factory guards, factory workers (most bts), cutter crew (most bts), German citizens (bts, several die), mosquitoes
LOCATIONS/ITEMS: Germany inc bombed city & Nazi HQ, "a southern state" inc coast, Keecheebee Swamp w/shack, industrial city w/ Beacon Aircraft factory & US Army camp, Atlantic Ocean; US Army planes, von Kaulus' plane (wrecked), Beacon bomber planes (2 destroyed), von Kaulus' pistol & knife, guards' pistols
SYNOPSIS: Accompanied by Hans, von Kaulus flies to the USA to bomb Beacon Aircraft, source of improved bombers, but is shot down by a US plane. Crashing in the Keecheebee Swamp, Hans dies but von Kaulus witnesses the swamp's chemicals revive and turn him into a bulletproof Monster. The two travel to Beacon Aircraft, where the Monster carries out sabotage and murder. He and von Kaulus return to the swamp. Hearing of the incident, Cap and Bucky explore the swamp and find them. The Monster overpowers Cap and von Kaulus knocks out Bucky. After recovering, the heroes pursue as von Kaulus and the Monster depart in a stolen bomber. Cap and Bucky commandeer a plane. Hans leaps onto their plane in mid-air. Cap collides the plane with von Kaulus'. Cap and Bucky parachute away as the crash presumably kills von Kaulus and the Monster.

4TH STORY: "The Human Beast!" (8 pages)
CREDITS: Vince Alascia (pencils), Al Bellman (inks)
FEATURE CHARACTER: Captain America (next in AllWin #15/2, '45, AllSel #6, '45, AvCl #5/2, '07 fb, Cap #26, '04 fb, AllSel #7, '45, USA #15, '45, Cap #32, '00 fb, WS:WK #1, '07 fb, CapC #48/3, '45, Cap #50, '09 fb)
SUPPORTING CAST: Bucky (next in AllWin #15/2, '45)
VILLAINS: The Cat Woman (dies) & 3 underlings
OTHER CHARACTERS: Cab driver (bts), Cat Woman's victim (as corpse)
LOCATIONS/ITEMS: Manhattan inc office building & Cat Woman's hideout; Cat Woman's knife & gun
SYNOPSIS: Investigating gunshots, Cap and Bucky find the Cat Woman robbing a 10th floor office. Cap grabs her, and she seemingly surrenders, but when Cap relaxes his grip, she bites through his glove and vaults out a window. Cap and Bucky pursue but a man gets in their way, delaying them until she escapes. Realizing the man is Cat Woman's accomplice, the two follow him to her hideout. They outfight her underlings, but she flees by car. When the heroes board the car's running boards, she crashes the car, perishing in flames.

TEXT STORY: "Conqueror" (2 pages)
CREDITS: Writer unknown
FEATURE CHARACTER: Andy (US Army Medical Corpsman)
OTHER CHARACTERS: German woman, wounded man, sniper, old man, Captain Ranger (mentioned)
LOCATIONS/ITEMS: Devastated German village inc church, surrounding woods inc trail, ravine & cave; Andy's medical kit, sniper's rifle, woman's revolver, shell fragment

SYNOPSIS: Trailing behind his unit, Andy tracks gunfire to a village church's tower, where he disarms and binds a sniper. Later, he spies and follows a figure into the woods. Confirming there are people hiding there, he returns to the church, where a young woman holds him at gunpoint. She takes him to the cellar, where her group's leader suffers from a shrapnel wound. After Andy tends the man's wound, the woman allows him to depart and assures him that the German locals will trust him.

NOTE: Story appears between 3rd & 4th stories.

CAPTAIN AMERICA COMICS #46 (April 1945)

"Captain America in Invitation to Murder!" (18 pages)

CREDITS: Stan Lee (writer), Vince Alascia (art), Alex Schomburg (c art)
FEATURE CHARACTER: Captain America
SUPPORTING CAST: Bucky (chr last in Cap #50, '09 fb)
VILLAINS: Silas Matison's lawyer, butler & housekeeper (both die), Mrs. Matison (Silas' widow, dies)
OTHER CHARACTERS: Silas Matison's brother & nephew, Silas Matison (deceased multi-millionaire, mentioned), concentration camp prisoners, 2 Nazi officers, 3 Nazi soldiers (prev 3 cover only)
LOCATIONS/ITEMS: Matison estate inc library & wine cellar, nearby road, cliff & beach, concentration camp inc crematorium (cover only); mannequin, conspirators' firearms & knives, mace (splash only) Nazi firearms (cover only)

SYNOPSIS: Steve and Bucky see a figure fall off a cliff and find two men there. They take them to a nearby mansion, where Silas Matison's will has just been read leaving the bulk of his estate to his wife, brother and nephew with the survivors standing to inherit the share of anyone who dies. The wife is missing but the others deny wrongdoing. Cap and Bucky return to the cliff and find the "body" is only a mannequin. Matison's butler attacks them but is easily outfought. Cap and Bucky follow him to the wine cellar, where the true mastermind, Matison's lawyer, emerges, as do Matison's widow and housekeeper, all scheming to get the brother and nephew executed for murder, so the widow can later "resurface" and claim the entire inheritance. The lawyer kills the butler and housekeeper to avoid splitting the loot. The lawyer and widow march Cap and Bucky to the cliff to shoot them. With precision timing, the heroes avoid the bullets but play dead. When the killers approach, Cap charges the lawyer, whose gun fires, killing the widow. He and Cap fall over the cliff, but both survive. Cap captures the lawyer. The brother and nephew decide to donate the widow's share to the war fund.

2ND STORY: "The Five Traitors from Berlin!" (7 pages)
CREDITS: Paul Reinman (pencils), Carmine Infantino (inks)
FEATURE CHARACTER: Human Torch (next in HT #19, '45, MC #64, '45)
SUPPORTING CAST: Toro (last in MC #63, '45, next in Kid #8, '45)
VILLAINS: Bluhm & 5 Nazi operatives (Emil named), 5 high-ranking Nazis
OTHER CHARACTERS: US Secretary of State (see NOTE), Jare Barry (State Dept employee, dies), FBI agents, Washington DC police chief, Jarvis (Barry's butler), ship arrival announcer (voice only)
LOCATIONS/ITEMS: Washington DC inc Sec of State's office & Barry's home, Manhattan inc Nazis' hideout & Pier 7 of North River; Holmshaven (Swedish ship), Nazis' firearms, blackjacks, & forged list, Barry's list
SYNOPSIS: A Nazi operative shoots Barry dead and replaces a passenger list for the Swedish ship Holmshaven with a forgery. Torch and Toro investigate the shots, but the killer escapes. The arriving Secretary of State tells them that the Nazis, in order to sneak high-ranking Nazis into the USA, have added names to the forged list, but there is no way to tell which ones. Torch plants a false story in the newspapers that the ship is arriving ahead of schedule. At the dock, Nazi Emil waits for the escapees. When the ship's true schedule is announced, Emil departs, Torch and Toro following. They capture the Nazi operatives, then force leader Bluhm to accompany them to the dock. Five arriving Nazis greet Bluhm, and Torch and Toro capture them.
NOTE: This is noted artist Carmine Infantino's second inking job for Timely/Marvel. In early 1945, the US Secretary of State was Edward Stettinius Jr. (1900-1949).

3RD STORY: "Captain America vs The Shadow of the Monster!" (10 pages)
CREDITS: Vince Alascia (art)
FEATURE CHARACTER: Captain America
SUPPORTING CAST: Bucky
VILLAINS: Butch Cantwell (also as "Captain America," gangster) & his gang (4 men, Runty named)
OTHER CHARACTERS: Police Chief Harvey Magruder (see NOTE), Jack (soldier) & girlfriend, police (some bts), 4 Boy Scouts, FBI agents (bts, seeking Cap), radio announcers (voices only)
LOCATIONS/ITEMS: Manhattan inc Cantwell's hideout & police HQ, US Army camp; Cantwell's bulletproof Captain America costume & shield, gangsters' pistols, police firearms
SYNOPSIS: Gangster Butch Cantwell, wearing a bulletproof version of Cap's costume, frames Cap for multiple crimes. The real Cap and Bucky patrol the city in search of the impostor but find only police and FBI agents on the hunt for Cap. Finally, Cap and Bucky visit Chief Magruder, whom Cap convinces to distribute an offer to withhold charges against Cap unless he commits a crime proven to be his work. As anticipated, Cantwell arrives, intent on killing Magruder to "prove" Cap guilty. Cap and Bucky quickly capture him.
NOTE: Unidentified police chiefs of various descriptions appeared throughout several golden age stories. Whether or not any of them were Chief Magruder is undetermined.

4TH STORY: "The Mystery of the Puff-Adder Skulls!" (8 pages)
CREDITS: Vince Alascia (pencils), Al Bellman (inks)

FEATURE CHARACTER: Captain America (next in Inv #1-4, '10-11 fbs, Cap:Re #2, '09, Cap #601, '09 fb, SpSM #17, '04 fb)
SUPPORTING CAST: Bucky (chr next in Inv #1, '10 fb)
VILLAINS: The Snake Skulls ("the Master" & 2 others), 4 hirelings (1 poses as butler & chauffeur)
OTHER CHARACTERS: Bank manager, doctor, PL Ramsey (dies), Cyrus S. Little (bts, off-panel), Little's secretary, Evan Ruyt & Steven Hart (names on target list), W. Buston & JM Smathers (names on target list, killed prior to story), bystanders, puff-adder (splash panel only)
LOCATIONS/ITEMS: Manhattan inc bank, Little's office & Snake Skulls' house w/Chamber of the Snake Skulls, US Army camp; hireling's knife & tablet, Master's servants' scimitars, vapor-dispensing snake skulls
SYNOPSIS: At a bank, Steve and Bucky see PL Ramsey collapse and his butler flee with his money. They overtake him but a second man attacks, punching Bucky down. After Bucky is treated for a bloody nose, Cap and Bucky find Ramsey dead and a tablet dropped by the butler, listing wealthy men, the first two recently dead and the third Ramsey himself. Cap and Bucky visit the office of the fourth intended victim, Cyrus Little, and find him dying in a limo, chauffeured by the butler. Three other criminals accompany him, but Cap and Bucky outfight all four, then take Little for medical care. After interrogating the criminals, Cap and Bucky visit the Snake Skulls' house, where "the Master" greets them. When Cap staggers, Master reveals he and Bucky have been breathing will-robbing vapor. Luckily, Bucky's injured nose prevents him from inhaling enough to be affected. He breaks a window to admit fresh air, clearing Cap's mind. After defeating Master and company, the heroes learn the organization had used vapor-emitting skulls to mesmerize their targets into withdrawing large sums. However each victim had a weak heart and the vapor induced cardiac arrest.

5TH STORY: "Let's Play Detective: The Case of the Forged Check!" (1 page)
CREDITS: Al Bellman (art)
FEATURE CHARACTER: Mike Trapp (also as "Elmer Thomas," next in CapC #48/4, '45)
SUPPORTING CAST: Pepper Burns (last in CapC #41/4, '44, next in CapC #48/4, '45)
VILLAIN: "Pop" (clerk & forger)
OTHER CHARACTERS: Mr. Gould (firm manager), male clerk, female clerk
LOCATIONS/ITEMS: Manhattan inc Gould's firm & police HQ; Pop's blotter
SYNOPSIS: Businessman Gould reports one of his clerks has forged his signature on a check and cashed it. Trapp poses as a fellow clerk. Finding a reversed forged signature on "Pop's" blotter, Trapp exposes him as the forger and arrests him.

TEXT STORY: "Too Smart to Live" (2 pages)
CREDITS: Writer unknown
FEATURE CHARACTER: Captain Jess Gaynor (US Army pilot)
VILLAINS: Everett Parsons & Paul (Axis agents)
OTHER CHARACTERS: US Army pilots (in Jess' thoughts)
LOCATIONS/ITEMS: Town inc booby-trapped building; Parsons' gun
SYNOPSIS: Returning home after action overseas, Gaynor is captured by Parsons and his midget employer Paul, who briefly poses as Parsons' son. Gaynor overpowers Parsons but is taunted by Paul over the building's loudspeakers. Gaynor forces Parsons to guide him through any traps. Parsons falls through a trap door, and when Paul emerges to investigate, Gaynor knocks him out.
NOTE: Story appears between 2nd & 3rd stories.

CAPTAIN AMERICA COMICS #47 (June 1945)

"Captain America Versus the Crime Dictator" (20 pages)

CREDITS: Stan Lee (writer), Vince Alascia (art), Alex Schomburg (c art)
FEATURE CHARACTER: Captain America
SUPPORTING CAST: Bucky (chr last in Cap #601, '09 fb)
VILLAINS: Crimorto ("the Crime Dictator," apparently dies), the Criminal Convention ("murderers, cutthroats, thieves, madmen" from "the four corners of the earth," at least 13 die)
OTHER CHARACTERS: Young woman, her parents & family dog (dies), firefighters, doctor, Crimorto's victims inc train crew & passengers (both bts, in train), radio announcer (voice only), bystanders, bats, Nazi soldiers (cover only)
LOCATIONS/ITEMS: Criminal conference location, Manhattan, US Army camp, 3 cities (1 w/burning building), countryside w/train tracks, young woman's house & adjoining houses, Crimorto's castle w/drawbridge atop jagged rock mass (destroyed), Steve & Bucky's home, Nazi rocket base (cover only), train (destroyed), fire engine, Crimorto's scythe (splash only), cloak & teleporting mist, criminals' firearms, knives & clubs, V-5 rockets, Nazis' firearms, Bucky's bazooka (prev 3 on cover only)
SYNOPSIS: Wanting crime and death to "rule the universe," Crimorto gathers a criminal army and launches a nationwide crime wave, his ultimate goal Cap's death. Searching for a lead, Cap and Bucky arrive at a house, where three criminals attack a family. One abducts a young woman and flees. Cap and Bucky pursue into a Crimorto-created mist, which teleports all to Crimorto's castle. There, Cap and Bucky find the woman unconscious with Crimorto standing over her. Eight armed criminals surround them and attack. Cap and Bucky punch through them to follow Crimorto and his victim to the castle roof. When Crimorto drops her over the side, Cap catches her. Crimorto shoots lightning bolts at Cap, who orders Bucky to take the woman to safety. She tells Cap that Crimorto's cloak is his power source. Cap removes the cloak, but this causes the castle to crumble. Cap escapes. Although Crimorto appears to be dead, Cap has his doubts.

2ND STORY: "Horror in Room 1705" (7 pages)
CREDITS: Al Gabriele (art)
FEATURE CHARACTER: Human Torch (next in AllSel #8/3, '45, DarMys #11/2, '45, MC #65, '45)

SUPPORTING CAST: Toro (last in MC #64, '45, next in AllSel #8/2, '45)

VILLAINS: Percy the Puppet (diminutive criminal posing as puppet), Prof. Kilgory (puppeteer)

OTHER CHARACTERS: Mrs. H. van Spoon (wealthy widow, dies), Mr. Gary (dies), 3 female hotel guests, boardwalk patrons, barker, puppet show attendees, police officers (bts, summoned after Mrs. van Spoon's death)

LOCATIONS/ITEMS: Atlantic City (New Jersey) inc boardwalk w/theater & Bittler Hotel w/Room 1705 and Torch, Gary and Kilgory's rooms; Percy's knives, Kilgory's lead pipe, Mrs. van Spoon's jewelry, Percy & girl puppets

SYNOPSIS: Torch and Toro take in Prof. Kilgory's puppet show on Atlantic City's boardwalk. Later, at the pair's hotel, Mrs. van Spoon is murdered and her jewels stolen. Searching for the killer, Torch and Toro alight on the roof, but a large man knocks them out with a pipe. When they revive, they find another guest slain. Finding small footprints, Torch realizes the killer is a small man, the pipe-wielder his accomplice. At the theater, Torch checks Kilgory's puppets and finds that the most popular one, Percy, shows no sign of use. Back at the hotel, they raid Kilgory's room, but Kilgory knocks Toro out, and a second "Percy the Puppet," actually a little person, lunges at Torch with a knife. Torch dodges, and Percy inadvertently stabs Kilgory. Torch knocks Percy out, then calls for a police ambulance.

NOTE: Torch depicted in pajamas with the same color scheme as his costume.

3RD STORY: "Captain America Battles the Monster of the Morgue!" (17 pages)

CREDITS: Vince Alascia (pencils), Al Bellman (inks)

FEATURE CHARACTER: Captain America (next in AllSel #8, '45, USA #16, '45, Cable&Dp #45, '08, Cap&FT #1, '11, CapTW:BA #1, '09, Cap #616/4, '11 fb)

SUPPORTING CAST: Bucky (next in AllSel #8, '45), Sgt. Duffy (last golden age & chr app, next in ToS #63, '65 chr before CapC #1, '41, his grave seen in YA #1, '09), Gen. Haywood (next in AllSel #6, '45)

VILLAINS: The Morgue Master (Prof. Todt, "cleverest saboteur in the Reich," poses as undertaker, dies) & 5 underlings (4 die)

OTHER CHARACTERS: Morgue attendant (dies), US Army colonel & soldiers (some bts, several die), supply ship crews & stevedores (bts, most die), firefighters, ferry crew & passengers (some die), fireboat captain & crew, dead bodies

LOCATIONS/ITEMS: Manhattan inc Nazis' waterfront dive basement HQ, pier & city morgue, US Army camp w/hospital; supply ships, ferry, motor launch, fireboat, Nazis' truck, Morgue Master's knife, scalpel & gas pistol, Nazis' firearms, Bucky's pistol, magnetic mechanisms (bts, placed on bodies to attract them to steel ships)

SYNOPSIS: An explosion at a pier kills several soldiers and civilians. Haywood sends Steve and Bucky to the morgue to identify any soldiers' bodies, possibly including the missing Duffy. While there, Steve and Bucky intervene in a conflict between the morgue attendant and Prof. Todt, a supposed undertaker but secretly a Nazi saboteur. The attendant tells them Todt has claimed corpses with no relatives. Steve and Bucky later return to the morgue to find the attendant murdered with Todt and his men loading corpses onto a truck. The Nazis depart for a second pier attack. Cap and Bucky escape and follow, but the Nazis have already departed by ferry, using the corpses, laden with explosives, as floating mines for sabotage. Cap and Bucky convince a fireboat captain to pursue. Bucky uses the fireboat's hose to force Todt and company into the ferry's engine room, where the boilers heat the water into a steam explosion that kills them. The next day, Steve and Bucky visit Duffy, located and hospitalized.

TEXT STORY: "AWOL" (2 pages)

CREDITS: Writer unknown

FEATURE CHARACTER: Pvt Tim Callaway

VILLAINS: Japanese soldiers (some die), Japanese bomber pilots (bts, in Zeros)

OTHER CHARACTERS: King (messenger collie), Major Traymore, Captain Stanton (Tim's CO), Tim's fellow soldiers (most bts, some die), Traymore's troops, doctor, patients, Queenie (messenger dog, dies)

LOCATIONS/ITEMS: Kotyo (Pacific island) inc US Army base hospital, kennels, cavern & Japanese machine gun nest; LST Landing Ship, Japanese bombers, Japanese & US firearms, message

SYNOPSIS: Hospitalized after a battle wound, Tim still craves action. Maj. Traymore promises to delay his evacuation. Later, Tim and messenger dog King reconnoiter without permission. They find Queenie dead, carrying a message requesting reinforcements for a surrounded Captain Stanton. Tim sends the message with King, single-handedly seizes an enemy machine gun nest & reunites with his outfit, leading some soldiers to the nest, from which they mow down the enemy. Again wounded and hospitalized, Tim is commended for his bravery and initiative.

NOTE: Story appears between 2nd & 3rd stories. Story is set in September.

CAPTAIN AMERICA COMICS #48 (July 1945)

"The Mark of the Satyre!" (16 pages)

CREDITS: Vince Alascia (pencils), Al Gabriele (inks), Alex Schomburg (c art)

FEATURE CHARACTER: Captain America (next in CapC #48/5, '45)

SUPPORTING CAST: Bucky (last in Kid #8, '45, next in CapC #48/5, '45)

VILLAINS: The Satyre (Bret Labale, Pierre's nephew, see NOTE)

OTHER CHARACTERS: Pierre Labale (wax figures owner, dies), Paul Cowles ("Oaffley," Eastern Petroleum Inc. geologist, dies), sheriff, Jed (deputy), Widow Barclay, Ma Perkins, Job Stuart (both as corpses), Halton citizens, cows, wax figures inc devil, hunchback, Napoleon, knights, torture victims, criminal in electric chair & satyre, imp, tortured woman (both on splash only), 4 criminals (2 masked, cover only), 2 subway attendants & bystanders (both on cover only)

LOCATIONS/ITEMS: Halton (Pennsylvania) inc general store, farm, Stuart home, sheriff's office, Widow Barclay's home w/Cowles' room & Labale estate w/chamber of horrors (wax museum) and torture chamber (splash only), Camp Lehigh (mentioned, see NOTE), 42nd Street Times Square subway station (cover only); Pierre's wheelchair, Satyre's machete & nooses, Cowles' sand vial, torture wheel, iron maiden, mace, imp's sword (prev 4 on splash only), subway train, Independent Subway money satchel (both on cover only)

SYNOPSIS: En route to Camp Lehigh, Cap and Bucky find a dead man. They pursue the murderer, a demonic "satyre" who disappears near a mansion. In nearby Halton, where the Satyre has been committing murders for days, they learn the victim is Paul Cowles, geologist. The mansion, owned by local eccentric Pierre Labale, contains a private wax museum, including a near-century old Satyre statue. After checking Cowles' rented room and finding a sand sample, Cap and Bucky visit the Labale estate, meeting Pierre and his nephew Bret. They find the Satyre statue missing. Soon after, Satyre kills Pierre. Cap locates a secret passage where Satyre catches them in nooses, leaving them to hang, but Cap frees himself and Bucky. They interrupt Satyre setting the museum aflame. Cap knocks him out and unmasks him as Bret. Cap demonstrates the rotating wall which allowed the Satyre statue to seemingly disappear. He explains Satyre has been killing people to drive them from Halton since Cowles discovered oil in his sand sample.

NOTE: Title returns to monthly status. Camp Lehigh's location is implied to be in or near Pennsylvania here. Bret also spelled "Brett" here.

2ND STORY: "The Human Torch vs the Collector of Death" (7 pages)

CREDITS: Al Gabriele (art)

FEATURE CHARACTER: Human Torch (next in MC #65, '45, Twelve #1, '08, YM #24, '53, SagaHT#3, '90, WI #4, '77, Cap Ann #6, '82)

SUPPORTING CAST: Toro (last in Kid #8, '45, next in MC #65, '45)

VILLAINS: Danbury Fawcett ("the Collector of Death," insane art collector) & 8 hirelings (Bugs named)

OTHER CHARACTERS: 3 police officers (more bts), Clive Anderson (millionaire art collector, mentioned), telephone operator (bts, locates Fawcett's address), horses (as statue & painting), Rodin's the Thinker (statue), Rembrandt van Rijn (in painting), other men and women in paintings and busts, museum guard, bystander (both on splash only)

LOCATIONS/ITEMS: Manhattan inc Torch & Toro's apartment, Long Island inc Anderson estate, criminal hideout on Slate Street, Corner Drugstore, Fawcett estate; paintings, statues, hirelings' firearms, ladder & knife (melted) (both splash only)

SYNOPSIS: While investigating several portrait thefts, Torch and Toro visit art collector Clive Anderson's estate and capture several art thieves, who direct them to the gang's hideout. There, one gang member provides their buyer's phone number, and Torch traces it to reclusive art collector Danbury Fawcett who locks them in a windowless asbestos room, turns on carbon monoxide gas, and departs. Toro plugs the gas pipe. When Fawcett returns, the two feign death, then overpower him.

3RD STORY: "The Corpse That Wasn't There" (9 pages)

CREDITS: Al Gabriele (art)

FEATURE CHARACTER: Captain America (next in Cap #50, '09 fb, see NOTE)

SUPPORTING CAST: Bucky (chr last in WS:WK #1, '07 fb, chr next in Cap #50, '09 fb, see NOTE)

VILLAINS: Laird Carson (Matilda Carson's uncle & guardian) & his hirelings

OTHER CHARACTERS: Matilda Carson (heiress, also in newspaper photo, dies), driver for Inter City Cab Co. (ph CH2-3465), morgue attendant, Matilda's parents (in newspaper photos only)

LOCATIONS/ITEMS: Manhattan inc morgue, Matilda's apartment (10th floor, #4-J), Clarion newspaper office w/morgue & Carson's home; Matilda's purse & ID, mannequin, Carson's blackjack, cordials

SYNOPSIS: Steve and Bucky spot a man assaulting a woman, but the assailant escapes and the woman dies as Cap and Bucky rush her to the hospital. While Cap and Bucky seek a morgue attendant, the woman's body is stolen, but her purse is left behind, allowing Cap and Bucky to learn her identity, Matilda Carson, and her address. Visiting her apartment, the two are blackjacked by an assailant. Later, they check newspaper files and learn Matilda would have gained control of her dead parents' estate the following day. Realizing Matilda's uncle Laird Carson, the estate's administrator, is the culprit, the two confront him at his home. After fighting Carson's hired thugs, Cap reveals he has deduced the details of Carson's plan: with Matilda's death reported but her body stolen, he would retain the estate's control until she was declared dead seven years later. Breaking down, Carson admits Matilda's body is in his basement.

NOTE: Story's events set on the night of January 2, placing this out of publication order.

4TH STORY: "Let's Play Detective: The Case of the Clutching Claw!" (2 pages)

CREDITS: Al Bellman (art)

FEATURE CHARACTER: Mike Trapp (next in CapC #51/4, '45)

SUPPORTING CAST: Pepper Burns (last in CapC #46/5, '45, next in CapC #51/4, '45)

VILLAINS: The Clutching Claw (William Grayston, banker)

OTHER CHARACTERS: Ken Kennedy (attorney), "Fingers" Farrell (pickpocket), John Roy (dept store magnate, mentioned), 2 victims (die, 1 also in newspaper photo), earlier victim (dies bts), Jim Godwin (mentioned only, left $100,000 to 6 friends)

LOCATIONS/ITEMS: Manhattan inc police HQ & Kennedy residence; Grayston's wallet (bts)

SYNOPSIS: During the mysterious Clutching Claw's murder spree, attorney Kennedy informs Trapp the victims were, like himself, heirs to a $100,000 inheritance to be distributed soon; two additional heirs remain, Grayston and Roy. Trapp plants a story that Kennedy will be leaving town soon, then persuades pickpocket "Fingers" Farrell to impersonate Kennedy. At Kennedy's home, Clutching Claw attacks but escapes when Trapp appears. However, Farrell lifted the killer's wallet, revealing him to be Grayston.

5TH STORY: "Captain America Battles Colosso and His Murder Marionettes!!!" (10 pages)

CREDITS: Vince Alascia (pencils)

FEATURE CHARACTER: Captain America (also as marionette on splash, next in Cap:SoL #12, '99 fb, SecWs #18, '10 fb, Cap #259, '81 fb, Cap #237, '79 fb, Cap #241, '80 fb, FallSon:IM, '07 fb, Inv #7, '05 fb, Cap:SoL #7/2, '99, SagaHT #2, '90, Cap:SoL #12, '99 fb, Nam Ann #1/2, '91 fb, Twelve #1, '10, Cap Ann #13, '94, ToS #72/2, '65 fb, ToS #79/2, '66 fb, Cap:MoT #1, '11, Cap #26, '04 fb, Cap:SoL #12, '99, Av #56, '68, Cap #4, '05 fb, Cap:Re #4, '10, Av #4, '64 fb, Cap #6, '05 fb, Cap #220, '78 fb, Cap #215, '77 fb, MSaga #1, '85, Cap:SoL #11, '99 fb, Av #4, '64, beginning his modern career)

SUPPORTING CAST: Bucky (also as marionette on splash, last in CapC #48, '45, chr next in Cap:SoL #12, '99 fb, see NOTE)

VILLAINS: Dr. Colosso (super-strong showman, dies), the Marionettes (3 diminutive criminals disguised as puppets, 1 dies), Colosso's Native American assistant, other assistants (bts)

OTHER CHARACTERS: Bell County sheriff, 2 deputies, bank watchman, doctor, fair attendees

LOCATIONS/ITEMS: Bell County inc fairgrounds, Bell County Bank & doctor's office, nearby town, bridge over ravine; Colosso's truck, trailer, pistols, actual puppets & strength formula

SYNOPSIS: A trail of robberies and murders follows a traveling puppet/medicine show, with which Cap and Bucky catch up in Bell County. The two interrupt a bank robbery carried out by Colosso's employees. When the bank's watchman is hospitalized, he makes disjointed remarks about "puppets." Since Colosso was at the fairground during the robbery, no link can be proven. Later, Cap and Bucky observe Colosso's "Marionettes," little men posing as puppets, emerge from a secret door in their trailer. When Cap and Bucky confront Colosso in the back of his truck, a Marionette drives it away. As Cap and Colosso fight, the driver loses control and crashes off a bridge. Cap and Bucky leap to safety.

NOTE: Per Av #4, '64's revelation that Cap and Bucky were MIA shortly before the war's end, and WI #4, '77's dating of that event, this is the final golden age appearance of Steve Rogers as Captain America and of James Barnes as Bucky, both of whom are presumed killed prior to CapC #49, '45 in which William Nasland ("the Spirit of '76") becomes Captain America and Fred Davis becomes Bucky.

TEXT STORY: "Cooked to a T" (2 pages)

CREDITS: Writer unknown

FEATURE CHARACTER: Hap Kingston (discharged US Army cook, also in pfb)

VILLAINS: Mike "The Chink" Wadsley (also in pfb), Mike's gang (pfb only)

OTHER CHARACTERS: Old Man Peters (grocer, also in pfb), police (pfb only)

LOCATIONS/ITEMS: Hap's home, Peters' grocery (also in pfb); Mike's revolver, Hap's kettle of stew

FLASHBACK: Years before, Mike and his delinquent gang rob Peters' store. Hap turns them in. Sentenced to prison, Mike swears vengeance. Hap graduates high school, takes a job with Peters, and enters the army. He receives a leg wound and is discharged (p).

SYNOPSIS: Hap returns to his hometown and learns Mike escaped prison two months before. Later, Mike visits, gun in hand, but Hap calmly offers him stew. After Mike eats, he collapses, and Hap informs him the stew is poisoned just enough to incapacitate him. He has been cooking such stew every day for two weeks, waiting for Mike to appear. Hap escorts Mike to the sheriff's office.

NOTE: Story appears between 3rd & 4th stories.

THE "DEATH" OF CAPTAIN AMERICA & BUCKY

Assigned to guard a top secret Allied drone plane (Cap:MoT #1, '11), Captain America and Bucky stop some Nazis from breaking into its hangar (Cap #26, '04 fb & Cap:SoL #12, '99) as Baron Zemo sneaks inside (Av #56, '68). As Zemo activates his Humanoid Cap and Bucky ambush the Nazi, battling both him and the giant android. Bucky is knocked out when the Humanoid throws him against a wall, Cap is shot in the back by Zemo when he checks on his partner (Cap:SoL #12, '99 & #56, '68). Redressing the heroes in standard army dress, Zemo ties Cap and Bucky to the drone plane for transport (Av #56, '68). Cap wakes up on a secret Nazi island in the English Channel to see Zemo torturing Bucky, and is tortured in turn (Cap #4, '05 fb). Cap wakes up while Zemo brags and frees himself from his bonds, he unties Bucky and they grab a motorcycle as Zemo launches the drone plane (Cap:SoL #12, '99, Cap:Re #4, '10 & Av #4, '64 fb). Catching up to the plane Bucky, jumps from the bike, followed by Cap. Bucky tries to defuse the plane as Cap loses his grip, Bucky's arm becomes caught and the plane explodes (Cap:MoT #1, '11, Cap #6, '05 fb, Cap:Re #4, '10, Cap:SoL #12, '99 & Av #4, '64 fb). As Cap falls into the English Channel (Cap:Re #4, '10, Cap #220, '78 fb & Av #4, '64 fb) Bucky falls as well, missing an arm (Cap #11, '05 fb). Zemo escapes (WI #5, '77) and broadcasts his defeat of Captain America, heard by Colonel Karpov who's aboard an experimental Soviet submarine near Dover (Cap #8, '05 fb). Captain America is fished out of the English Channel and brought aboard General Dekker's submarine. As Cap meets the General the sub speeds off to Newfoundland. At Dekker's fortress Cap breaks free and retrieves his shield. When he tries to escape by plane he's shot down, bathed in nerve gas, crashes in the Atlantic off the coast of Newfoundland (Cap #220, '78 fb), and begins to freeze (Cap #215, '77 fb). Meanwhile, the Soviets find Bucky's body (Cap #8, '05 fb).

Though reports of Captain America and Bucky's death make it to the newspapers (Cap #155, '72 fb), President Truman asks the Spirit of '76, William Naslund, to become the new Captain America (Cap #215, '77 fb). Truman tells the Invaders that Cap and Bucky have died, and introduces them to the new Cap, and the new Bucky, Fred Davis (WI #4, '77 & SagaHT #3, '90). After the war ends, the Invaders stay together under the name All-Winners Squad, but Naslund dies in 1946 saving Congressional candidate John F. Kennedy from the android Adam-II. The Patriot, Jeff Mace, takes his place as the new Captain America and destroys Adam-II (WI #4, '77, Cap #215, '77 fb & Cap:P #1, '11). In 1950 Mace is forced to retire and later marries Betty Ross (Cap:P #4, '11) and is replaced himself in 1954 by William Burnside, a college professor who took the name Steve Rogers, and his student Jack Munroe as Bucky (YM #24/2, '54 & Cap #155, '72 fb). The pair are eventually driven insane by improper use of the Super Soldier Serum and placed into suspended animation (Cap #155, '72 fb). Meanwhile, Barnes is studied and revived by Soviet scientists, but he has amnesia. He's eventually given a robot arm and becomes the Winter Soldier, a Cold War Soviet assassin, and is put into suspended animation when his usefulness is over (Cap #11, '05 fb). In the modern day, Captain America is found by his wartime ally Namor, the Sub-Mariner and is revived by the Avengers (Cap:Re #3, '09, Av #4, '64, FallSon:IM, '07 fb, Av:EMH #1, '05, Cap #13, '03 fb, MAv #20, '09 fb, Cap:MoT #1-2, '11 & Av:EMH #2, '05).

CAPTAIN AMERICA COMICS #49 (August 1945)

"The League of Hate" (15 pages)

CREDITS: Vince Alascia (art), Alex Schomburg (c art)
FEATURE CHARACTER: Captain America (William Nasland, chr last in Cap Ann #6, '82, see NOTE)
SUPPORTING CAST: Bucky (Fred Davis, chr last in Cap Ann #6, '82, see NOTE)
VILLAINS: The League of Hate (over 200 Nazi operatives, many impersonating wounded US soldiers, most bts, "Bill Summers" & 3 others die, also in fb1, "some months ago," as Nazi soldiers, 3 in dfb), Captain Vergelhaupt ("Jim Mason," League of Hate Middlevale ringleader, also in fb1), Adolf Hitler (only in fb1 between Kelly #26/4, '54 fb & SVTU #17, '80 fb, see NOTE), Josef Goebbels (bts in fb1 to 1st app after CapC #40/3, '44), Hermann Goering (only in fb1 to last app after CapC #40/3, '44), Heinrich Himmler (only in fb1 between SubC #10/2, '43 & AWC #98, '93 fb as Zyklon)

OTHER CHARACTERS: Tommy Weston (blind veteran, also in dfb, dies), graveyard watchman, Middlevale Mayor (also in dfb), police inc chief, coroner, radio announcer, Middlevale residents (many bts) inc lynch mob, FBI agent (voice only), Garabaldi (Polish-American), Grabosky (Jewish-American), Kelly (Catholic-American), Levin (African-American) (prev 4 Weston's dead army buddies, mentioned), birds, saboteurs & as reserve guards (both on cover only)

LOCATIONS/ITEMS: Middlevale (Alabama) inc church graveyard, Yolla Tailor shop, Mayor's office, gas station, town hall, Vergelhaupt's deserted barn hideout, "Middle Town" Jail (see NOTE), police HQ w/morgue, radio broadcast station, RR trestle & Mayor's home (in dfb), Germany (in fb1 only), US Air Force Gas Reserve (on cover only); League's wireless, gun & knife (both on splash only), Comet Limited (train), Nazi rifles & machine gun (fb1 only), Vergelhaupt's crutches, lynch mob's battering ram & club, Mayor's rifle (in dfb), Weston's cane, saboteurs' firearms, TNT kegs, TNT packets & detonator, Bucky's whip (prev 5 on cover only)

FLASHBACK: Hitler and "his unholy trio" inspect 200 specially trained young Nazis, who are intentionally maimed to impersonate wounded US soldiers and spread dissension and racism in the USA (1). League of Hate members bring Tommy Weston's body to the Mayor's house where they shoot him with the Mayor's gun (d).

SYNOPSIS: In Middlevale, "wounded veterans" Jim Mason and Bill Summers lead a group blaming foreigners for their troubles. Blind veteran Tommy Weston denounces them and calms the townspeople. Later, when Steve and Bucky arrive to visit Weston, they find him dead, supposedly shot by the mayor, who has no memory of doing so. Although Mason and Summers' war records seem above reproach, Cap suspects them. He requests FBI information, then checks Weston's body and finds the cause of death was a knife wound. The FBI reports similar vandalism/vigilantism in other towns, all led by wounded veterans. A Nazi operative overhears and warns Mason, actually Nazi Captain Vergelhaupt and the others to flee. They try to run down Cap and Bucky but crash. All but Mason die. Later, Cap exposes the League of Hate's activities in a nationwide broadcast.

NOTE: Av #4, '64 reveals Rogers and Barnes were both lost, presumed KIA, shortly before the war in Europe ended; WI #4, '77 confirms William Nasland, formerly the Spirit of '76 (1st in Inv #14, '77) & Fred Davis, a New York Yankees' batboy who once stood in for Bucky (1st in MPr #30, '76), replaced them. Pinpointing the changeover point, WI #4, '77 shows a dispatch dated April 18, 1945 reporting "Captain America and Bucky killed in action," depicts Adolf Hitler's death on April 30, 1945, and has President Truman introducing the new Captain America & Bucky to the Invaders "not long afterward." This story's start date is given as June 1945, placing it after those events. All post-CapC #48 Captain America apps are presumed to be Nasland up to CapC #58, '46. All post-CapC #48 Bucky apps are presumed to be Davis up to CapC #71, '49. Since this retcon occurs far after the publication of these issues, the characters will still be referred to as Steve and Bucky in their civilian IDs in the stories' synopses. Middlevale's state identified in OHMU:HC #11, '09. This is Adolf Hitler's final appearance in a Timely comic book. Hitler declares the League of Hate will be sent not only to the USA but to several nations; nothing is known of the League's non-US-based efforts. Vergelhaupt's name, literally translated, means "Gel Head." Middlevale Jail mistakenly called "Middle Town" Jail here.

2ND STORY: "The Gem of Destruction" (7 pages)
CREDITS: Carmine Infantino (pencils), Al Bellman (inks)
FEATURE CHARACTER: Human Torch (next in HT #20, '45, MC #66, '45, DarC #12/3, '45, AllSel #9/2, '45)
SUPPORTING CAST: Toro (last in MC #65, '45, chr last in Cap An #6, '82, next in HT #20, '45)
VILLAINS: Rheims (jewel thief & killer, dies) & 3 underlings (Mendoza named)
OTHER CHARACTERS: Peter Meershaum (diamond cutter), Mrs. Meershaum (Peter's mother), police chief, Mrs. Meershaum's maid, Queen's previous possessor (dies), Brazilian gem dealer (dies), Kimberly Brazilian cab driver (bts, in cab), Jan Bruttick (as corpse), Brazilian bystanders, Blue Angel waiter & customers
LOCATIONS/ITEMS: Brazil inc airport & Place de la Junta w/Santos Gem Co., New Jersey highway, Manhattan inc Torch & Toro's apartment, police HQ, Mrs. Meeshaum's home & Blue Angel (bistro on South Street) w/upstairs; Kimberly Queen (5000 carat uncut diamond), Rheims' pistol
SYNOPSIS: In Brazil, a man steals a priceless diamond, the Kimberly Queen. Later, in New Jersey, Torch and Toro find a corpse, identified as diamond cutter Jan Bruttick. In Manhattan, they meet Mrs. Meershaum, who claims her son Peter, also a diamond cutter, is missing, although family friend Rheims doubts foul play. Learning Kimberly Queen is an uncut diamond, explaining the need for a cutter, Torch and Toro visit Mrs. Meershaum's home but find her absent. The maid reports she and Rheims departed for the Blue Angel bistro. Flying there, Torch and Toro find Rheims holding Peter and his mother hostage. Rheims flees but falls down stairs. Dying, he confesses to stealing the gem, to killing Bruttick when the latter refused to cooperate, and to abducting Mrs. Meershaum to extort Peter's gem-cutting cooperation.
NOTE: The splash depicts Rheims wearing a cowl.

3RD STORY: "Captain America Versus Diavolo and His "Symphony of Death"" (14 pages)
CREDITS: Vince Alascia (art)

FEATURE CHARACTER: Captain America
SUPPORTING CAST: Bucky
VILLAINS: Diavolo (criminal leader, as skull-like figure on splash, dies), false organ grinder, 3 additional underlings
OTHER CHARACTERS: Tony (organ grinder), Tony's wife, Maria (Tony's daughter), Jimmy (Tony's son), police (1 dies) inc inspector, 2 messengers (1 dies), financial district bystanders, slum district residents, cab driver (bts, in cab), monkey
LOCATIONS/ITEMS: Manhattan inc financial district w/Wall Street and Federal Hall, Diavalo's hideout, "Steve" & "Bucky's" apartment, police HQ, slum district w/Tony's apt (324 Minetta Lane); hand organ w/silenced gun, Diavalo's knife, police & gang's firearms, Tony's hand organ, messenger pouches
SYNOPSIS: A messenger and police escort are killed, shot at close range, but no shots are heard. Steve and Bucky find the messenger's pouch stolen, then are distracted when a young woman, Maria, attacks an organ grinder, demanding information about her father. Diavalo covertly observes the proceedings. When Maria departs by cab, Steve hears her give her address. Diavalo and his men visit Maria's family to further intimidate her, but Cap and Bucky intervene. Taking Maria's brother Jimmy hostage, Diavalo departs. At his hideout, Diavalo ties up Jimmy alongside Jimmy's organ grinder father, Tony. Cap and Bucky question Tony's neighbors and learn he vanished weeks ago. A Wall Street cop reports Tony vouched for the current organ grinder and Cap realizes Diavalo forced Tony to cooperate so the replacement could operate without suspicion. Seeing the replacement grinder near another messenger and police guard, Cap and Bucky save them from the grinder's bullets, fired via a specially made organ. When Diavalo, observing, flees, police shoot him. Tony and his family are reunited.

4TH STORY: "Captain America in Murder by Proxy!" (8 pages)
CREDITS: Vince Alascia (pencils)
FEATURE CHARACTER: Captain America (next in USA #17, '45, AllSel #9, '45)
SUPPORTING CAST: Bucky (next in USA #17, '45)
VILLAINS: The Boss (district attorney) & 5 underlings
OTHER CHARACTERS: Jim (DA's assistant), Jim's fiancée (DA's niece), Jennings (DA's assistant, dies), doctor, police, bystander
LOCATIONS/ITEMS: "A thriving New England town" inc hospital w/Jim's fifth floor room and fire escape, road to Maine Woods, Washington DC inc US Capitol (splash only); Steve & Bucky's car, criminals' car, criminal's knife, Boss' axe (splash only) & gun, criminal's gun, cash box (both splash only)
SYNOPSIS: En route to a Maine Woods vacation, Steve and Bucky are run off the road by a speeding car, in which three criminals hold two DA assistants hostage. Cap and Bucky stop the car and knock out the criminals. One hostage, Jennings, is dead, but Cap rushes the other, Jim, to a hospital. The DA's niece, Jim's fiancée, tells Cap the two men had learned the local crime boss' identity. The DA places guards at the hospital, but Cap finds the rear unguarded. Later, thugs break into Jim's hospital room, attacking "Jim" and immobilizing "the DA's niece." The pair are actually Cap and Bucky in disguise. They quickly defeat the thugs, then lure in and capture the Boss, the DA himself.

TEXT STORY: "Shipwreck" (2 pages)
CREDITS: Writer unknown
FEATURE CHARACTERS: Sykes, Butch Valentine (Alma Mary shipmates, both also in pfb)
OTHER CHARACTERS: Island natives, Alma Mary's crew (in pfb only, Steve Anderson, Worth named, all die), sea gulls, crabs
LOCATIONS/ITEMS: 2 islands, ocean; Alma Mary (ship, in pfb, destroyed), lifeboat (wrecked), Valentine's raft
FLASHBACK: A storm hits and the Alma Mary sinks. Sykes finds a lifeboat and rescues one man from the sea: Valentine, the shipmate he considers worthless.
SYNOPSIS: The lifeboat washes ashore on a small island without food and water. Sykes forces Valentine to live on the other side of the island. Later, Sykes falls and breaks his leg. Valentine cares for him. Feverish and delirious, Sykes comes to on another island with friendly natives and plenty of food. He learns Valentine built a raft and transported them. Sykes discovers Valentine isn't so worthless after all.
NOTE: Story appears between 3rd & 4th stories.

CAPTAIN AMERICA COMICS #50 (October 1945)

"Captain America in The Walking Dead" (17 pages)

CREDITS: Vince Alascia (pencils), Al Bellman (inks), Alex Schomburg (c art)
FEATURE CHARACTER: Captain America (next in CapC #50/4, '45)
SUPPORTING CAST: Bucky (last in Kid #9, '45, next in CapC #50/4, '45)
VILLAINS: Peter Anzel (undertaker & Japanese operative) & his underlings (4 as "Walking Dead")
OTHER CHARACTERS: John Porter (germ weapon inventor, dies), Laura Porter (John's sister), Constable Jonas, Ralph & his wife (both witness "Walking Dead"), Lawnmere residents, dog, Joan Blair ("our beloved daughter"), John Smith (both names on tombstones), cattle (die), sheep (bts, die w/cattle), bats, 5 peak-capped men, gorilla-like creature, woman captured by gorilla, bystander, dove, gargoyle (prev 6 on cover only)
LOCATIONS/ITEMS: Porter estate, Lawnmere Cemetery w/mausoleum, town of Lawnmere inc Anzel's mortuary, US Army camp inc "Steve" & "Bucky's" tent, neighborhood inc church, bell tower & building w/gargoyle (on cover only); John's plane & locket (destroyed), crematory furnace, coffins, Japanese operatives' knives & guns (splash only), peak-capped men's pistols, club, dagger & lasso (on cover only)
SYNOPSIS: When wealthy John Porter dies, his sister Laura, per his wishes, buries him in a secret location in Lawnmere Cemetery with a locket containing his deadly germ formula. Japanese agents, posing as walking corpses, search the cemetery. Undertaker Peter Anzel organizes a posse, but the "corpses" frighten the townspeople away. Cap and Bucky arrive but Laura refuses to reveal John's burial place. The

o follow her when she goes to retrieve the locket to re-hide it, but so do hooded Japanese agents, who find a secret mausoleum passage. ‍e group's ring leader finds John's secret crypt and the locket. Cap follows and tackles him, the locket destroyed in the struggle. Unmasking ‍e ringleader as Anzel, Cap and Bucky turn him over to local police.

‍OTE: Upon capturing Anzel, Cap advises Constable Jonas to be sure his prisoner, singular, reaches the FBI safely; apparently Anzel's ‍nderlings successfully fled.

‍ND STORY: "The Case of the Mad Sculptor" (7 pages)
‍REDITS: Ken Bald (pencils), Bob Powell (inks)
‍EATURE CHARACTER: Human Torch (next in MC #67, '45, WI #4, '77, MKSM #9, '05 fb)
‍UPPORTING CAST: Toro (last in Kid #9, '45, next in MC #67, '45)
‍ILLAINS: The Mad Sculptor (Chris Ramsay, sculptor & murderer, dies), 2 henchmen (both die)
‍THER CHARACTERS: Mr. & Mrs. Beasley, Beasleys' daughter, Jim Russell (as corpse), demons (as ice sculptures)
‍OCATIONS/ITEMS: Manhattan inc Torch & Toro's apartment, Lake Placid inc Mad Sculptor's Snow Mountain castle; Mad Sculptor's ice ‍culptures, "quick-freezing snow" & knife, henchmen's clubs
‍YNOPSIS: The Beasleys ask Torch and Toro to rescue their daughter from Chris Ramsey, the man accused of killing her fiancé Jim Russell. ‍he pair fly to Ramsey's Snow Mountain studio, where they stop the Mad Sculptor from killing the woman. She leads them to Jim's frozen ‍orpse, made into a statue, but Sculptor's employees club Torch and Toro. Placing the heroes in his garden, the Sculptor covers them with ‍uick-freezing snow, making them ice statues. Sculptor starts an avalanche to bury the two, but Torch revives, burns straight down to escape ‍e ice and flies up from underground to free Toro as the avalanche falls. The villains panic and fall from the mountain top to their deaths.

‍RD STORY: "Captain America in The Mystery of the Eyes of Death!" (12 pages)
‍REDITS: Vince Alascia (art)
‍EATURE CHARACTER: Captain America (next in Nam Ann #1/3, '91, WI #4, '77, SagaSM #5, '89, MKSM #9, '95, fb)
‍UPPORTING CAST: Bucky (chr next in WI #4, '77), Gen. Haywood (last in CapC #47/3, '45, last app to date)
‍ILLAINS: Puri Genrami (Indian spy for Japan, dies) & 5 underlings (Yori named), Japanese pilot (bts, in plane)
‍THER CHARACTERS: US soldiers (2 temporarily blinded), US pilot (temporarily blinded), medic, India city residents, Genrami's horse, ‍eath (splash only)
‍OCATIONS/ITEMS: India inc US Army camp & city w/Genrami's office and Myriad of Mirrors; Japanese plane, US plane (destroyed), "Steve" ‍ "Bucky's" rifles, black light machine, US Army's machine guns, Genrami's men's swords, spears & club, Genrami's treated mirror & 10,000 ‍irrored ornaments (bts)
‍YNOPSIS: In India, some US soldiers are suddenly stricken blind. Learning the blinded soldiers visited Genrami's Myriad of Mirrors, Cap and ‍ucky confront Genrami, whose underlings club them from behind. Genrami elaborates that his mirrors are treated with "Trilite," which induces ‍elayed blindness. After the soldiers visited the Myriad, he contacted Japanese forces with the best attack time. He locks Cap and Bucky in the ‍yriad, where even if they avoid blindness by keeping their eyes shut, the air will soon run out. Cap starts a fire, whose smoke covers the Trilite ‍lowing Bucky and him to open their eyes and escape. They force Genrami's underlings to reveal the blindness can be reversed by a "black ‍ht machine," then return to camp, where Genrami is selling mirrored novelty items to better spread blindness. When Cap and Bucky pursue ‍m, he tries to use a mirror treated for instant blindness, but stumbles, blinds himself, and falls from a cliff. Cap and Bucky use the black light ‍achine to cure the blinded soldiers.

‍TH STORY: "Captain America Battles the Leopard and His Killer Mob!" (8 pages)
‍REDITS: Vince Alascia (art)
‍EATURE CHARACTER: Captain America (next in CapC #50/3, '45)
‍UPPORTING CAST: Bucky (next in CapC #50/3, '45)
‍ILLAINS: The Leopard (Lasco Vincenti, see NOTE) & his Killer Mob
‍THER CHARACTERS: Warden, prison guard, doctor, police scientist, police, murder victim (dies, more bts), leopard (splash only)
‍OCATIONS/ITEMS: State Penitentiary, multiple crime sites in various cities, hospital, police HQ inc lab & radio room, Leopard's abandoned ‍arn hideout; Leopard's electric beam guns w/battery packs, tank of explosives & whip (splash only), Bucky's scrap metal
‍YNOPSIS: Released after fifteen years' imprisonment, the Leopard leads his men in a nationwide crime wave, using electric beam guns. ‍hen Cap and Bucky rush into action, Leopard blasts Cap's shield aside and zaps Bucky, seriously injuring him. While Bucky is hospitalized, ‍ap finds the beam chanced to strike scrap metal in Bucky's pocket. Within the metal he finds a liquid-filled capsule, the "bullet" through which ‍e gun's effect is achieved. Cap has his shield treated with lead coating, then visits Leopard's hideout. Their beams unable to penetrate Cap's ‍hield, the criminals flee, but Cap easily captures them.
‍OTE: Leopard's real name revealed in OHMU:HC #11, '09.

‍EXT STORY: "Bulldozer" (2 pages)
‍REDITS: Writer unknown
‍EATURE CHARACTER: Narrator (construction worker)
‍THER CHARACTERS: Clancy (construction foreman), Bill Ames (camp medic), Pete, Turner, other construction workers
‍OCATIONS/ITEMS: Construction camp, road, river; makeshift bridge (destroyed), bulldozers, explosives
‍YNOPSIS: When young Clancy becomes foreman, Turner, who had hoped for the job, fights him. Clancy proves surprisingly strong and ‍urner, out of surprise, fights unfairly, alienating him from the crew. Later, Clancy drives a bulldozer across a bridge, which breaks, sinking him ‍to the river, but Turner rescues him, squaring accounts.
‍OTE: Story appears between 3rd & 4th stories.

CAPTAIN AMERICA COMICS #51 (December 1945)

"Captain America in Mystery of the Atomic Boomerang!" (16 pages)

CREDITS: Vince Alascia (art), Alex Schomburg (c art)
FEATURE CHARACTER: Captain America (next in CapC #51/5, '45)
SUPPORTING CAST: Bucky (next in CapC #51/5, '45)
VILLAINS: Prof. Scio Rudo (Japanese scientist, dies), Japanese soldiers (some die)
OTHER CHARACTERS: 2 US Army officers (1 on cover only), soldiers (some die), 8 criminals & 8 torturers (on cover only)
LOCATIONS/ITEMS: Pacific island inc US Army camp & Rudo's underground cave base, castle (on cover only); army firearms, Rudo's "atom-water" & gun, Bucky's magnifying glass, criminals' torture device & firearms (on cover only)

SYNOPSIS: On a recently taken island, mysterious explosions decimate US forces. Cap and Bucky encounter the culprits, Prof. Rudo and his soldiers. They trail Rudo to his hidden lab but are captured. Revealing his "atom-water" explodes once evaporated by sunlight, Rudo binds them outside, splashes them with the liquid, and leaves them to die by explosion. Using a magnifying glass to burn his ropes, Cap frees Bucky and they escape the explosion to again confront Rudo. To keep the atom-water formula secret, Rudo kills his own men, then flees to his lab and perishes when atom-water remnants, left by Cap, explode.

NOTE: Prof. Rudo's first name given in OHMU:HC #11, '09. At story's end, the commanding officer states the USA has "just perfected" the atomic bomb, placing the story's action circa late July 1945.

2ND STORY: "Killer from the Grave" (7 pages)
CREDITS: Carmine Infantino (art)
FEATURE CHARACTER: Human Torch (next in HT #21, '45, AllWin #17/3, '45)
SUPPORTING CAST: Toro (chr last in WI #4, '77, next in HT #21, '45)
VILLAINS: Danny King (killer), Dr. Hack (Freedmore director & King's accomplice)
OTHER CHARACTERS: Police Chief Bolton, Lem (police detective), Rufus King (Danny's uncle, dies), Freedmore nurse & guard, police newsboy, Manhattan bystanders, 5 criminals, bird (both on splash only)
LOCATIONS/ITEMS: Manhattan inc police HQ, Freedmore State Hospital, State Hotel (Rm 23) & cemetery (splash only), police & Danny's pistols, police fingerprint cards, criminals' firearms (splash only)

SYNOPSIS: After Rufus King is murdered, Torch and Toro suspect his nephew Danny, whom King had committed to an asylum. They learn Danny died months before, with Freedmore's Dr. Hack completing the death certificate and arranging for the burial. Police find the killer's car upon whose steering wheel Danny's thumbprint is found. Torch realizes that, by law, a doctor can neither complete a death certificate nor arrange for burial without consulting relatives, and he and Toro fly to Freedmore and confront Hack, who admits faking Danny's death. Learning Danny's location, Torch and Toro easily capture him.

NOTE: The date of Danny's "death," January 2, is stated to have been "three months ago," indicating the story occurs in late March or early April.

3RD STORY: "The Fraternity of Fat Fellows!" (10 pages)
CREDITS: Vince Alascia (pencils)
FEATURE CHARACTER: Captain America (next in AllWin #17/2, '45)
SUPPORTING CAST: Bucky (last in CapC #51/5, '45, next in AllWin #17/2, '45)
VILLAINS: The Chameleon (Breese, Mortimer's assistant, also in pfb) & his underlings (2 die), the Fraternity of Fat Fellows (Chameleon's accomplices, pfb only)
OTHER CHARACTERS: Jonathan Mortimer (mortician, also in pfb), 77 Dunhill Lane superintendant, corpses
LOCATIONS/ITEMS: Manhattan inc 77 Dunhill Lane (also in pfb), restaurant, Mortimer's Mortuary w/underground chamber, bridge & bank, Chameleon's conveyor belt & furnace, criminals' firearms
FLASHBACK: Breece tells Mortimer about the Fraternity of Fat Fellows, a foundation to benefit portly men, and Mortimer joins the club (p).

SYNOPSIS: Investigating the disappearance of the Fraternity of Fat Fellows who previously met at 77 Dunhill Lane, mortician Jonathan Mortimer is manhandled by the building super until Steve and Bucky intervene. Suspicious of what seems an overly elaborate prank, Cap and Bucky visit Mortimer's mortuary, which is next to a bank. Criminals in a hearse attempt a drive-by shooting, but Cap and Bucky thwart them. One admits they were hired by the mysterious Chameleon. Back at the mortuary, Cap and Bucky question Mortimer, who mentions his assistant Breese constructed a new storage room during his Fraternity absences. Cap and Bucky visit the room, which includes a tunnel to the bank, but Chameleon and company knock them out and tie them to a furnace conveyor belt. Cap grips an exposed wire in his teeth to short-circuit the belt and the furnace burns their ropes. When the criminals return from the bank, Cap and Bucky capture them, unmasking Chameleon as Breese.

4TH STORY: "Let's Play Detective: The Case of the Accusing Hand!" (1 page)
CREDITS: Al Bellman (art)
FEATURE CHARACTER: Mike Trapp (last in CapC #46/5, '45, next in CapC #57/4, '46)
SUPPORTING CAST: Pepper Burns (last in CapC #46/5, '45, next in CapC #58/2, '46)
VILLAIN: Dr. Keller
OTHER CHARACTERS: Nurse Mary Richards, Hansen (intern)
LOCATIONS/ITEMS: City Hospital inc Keller's office
SYNOPSIS: Dr. Keller informs Trapp the hospital's radium supply has been stolen, and Hansen and Richards are suspects. Once all three are

the same room, Trapp has Pepper turn out the lights. The darkness reveals a glow around Keller's hand, proving he most recently handled the radium and is thus the thief.

TH STORY: "Captain America in The Case of the Blonde Bombshell!" (10 pages)
CREDITS: Vince Alascia (art)
FEATURE CHARACTER: Captain America (next in CapC #51/3, '45)
SUPPORTING CAST: Bucky (next in CapC #51/3, '45)
VILLAINS: Captain Catti (Japanese officer, dies), Japanese soldiers
OTHER CHARACTERS: Fluffy Flair (USO entertainer), Fluffy Flair impersonator, USO entertainers & workers (most bts), US officers & soldiers (most bts)
LOCATIONS/ITEMS: Pacific island inc US Army camp & Catti's cave; USO plane, Catti's smoke bomb & knife (splash only), Japanese firearms, impersonator's wig, Cap's dime
SYNOPSIS: USO entertainers, including popular performer Fluffy Flair, visit Steve and Bucky's Pacific island camp. When Captain Catti abducts Flair, Cap and Bucky pursue, finding her lost shoe. Catti takes her to a cave hideout, and a Flair double emerges to meet Cap and Bucky, but Cap realizes the shoe is not her size. He and Bucky storm the cave but are overpowered. Catti gloats that the impersonator will send coded messages to the Japanese via dance motions, then seals the heroes in a locked room. Cap uses a dime to unscrew the door's hinges. Bucky rescues the real Flair while Cap fights and kills Catti. The heroes return Flair to camp and expose the impostor, who was forced to cooperate due to Japanese threats to her brother.
NOTE: The island in this story may be the island from the issue's 1st story.

TEXT STORY: "Manhunt" (2 pages)
CREDITS: Writer unknown
FEATURE CHARACTER: Henry
VILLAIN: Hawkins
OTHER CHARACTERS: Will Clayton, horse, pack-horse
LOCATIONS/ITEMS: "A part of the world where few white men had ever gone" inc Henry's camp, adjacent woods, stream, hills & valley; Hawkins' revolver, Henry's carbine, Clayton's rifle
SYNOPSIS: Hired as guide, Henry accompanies Hawkins to search for former business partner Clayton. In the hills, Henry spots Clayton and follows him back to camp, where Clayton threatens Hawkins, who shoots him. Henry disarms Hawkins, who is revealed as an escaped prisoner seeking vengeance on Clayton, who had been instrumental in getting him convicted for murder before retiring to the area.
NOTE: Story appears between 4th & 5th stories.

CAPTAIN AMERICA COMICS #52 (January 1946)

"The Case of the Telepathic Typewriter" (12 pages)
"Chapter 2: Captain America in Beauty and the Beast" (15 pages)

CREDITS: Bill Finger (writer), Vince Alascia (art), Alex Schomburg (c art)
FEATURE CHARACTER: Captain America
SUPPORTING CAST: Bucky (last in AllWin #17/2, '45)
VILLAINS: Am the Horrible (radio drama monster given life by listeners' belief, dies), Allen Slake (radio writer, dies), Viljem ""Jigger" Jones (noted criminal, 1st, next in AllWin #18/2, '46, see NOTE) & 2 underlings (both die)
OTHER CHARACTERS: Dorothy Roberts (Daily Globe reporter), WMGP employees, program director, studio audience & voice actors (Carleton named, one plays "Kenneth"), radio announcers (voices only), 2 switchboard operators, Milton & fellow radio comedian, police, bank guards (1 dies), observatory scientist (dies), millions of radio listeners (most bts, Joe named), bystanders (some die), birds, bats, Orson Belles (radio provocateur, mentioned), 6 criminals, 3 soldiers (both cover only)
LOCATIONS/ITEMS: Manhattan inc WMGP radio station w/program director's office, switchboard and studio, "Steve" & "Bucky's" apartment, National Bank, abandoned subway tunnel, Jones' waterfront hideout & Ace Radio store, Slake's mountain studio, mountain observatory w/ telescopes, Limestone Caverns, radio listeners' homes, US Vault facility (cover only); Jones' blimp w/sand ballast, police & gang's firearms, Bucky's scout-knife, Slake's telepathic typewriter, radios, Ronkers Diamond (bts, stolen by Am), Atomic Bomb Experiment No. 1, criminals' firearms (both on cover only)
SYNOPSIS: Allan Slake's radio character Am, "the monster with a soul," captivates millions of listeners, whose collective thought waves bring him to life. Materializing in the WMGP radio studio, he runs amok in Manhattan, killing several but sparing reporter Dorothy Roberts, to whom he is drawn. Cap and Bucky battle Am, but Slake, hearing reports of Am's rampage, realizes he can control Am via the "telepathic" typewriter on which he typed his scripts. As he types out actions, Am carries them out. Realizing the potential for wealth and power, Slake seizes a mountain observatory to watch Am's reign of havoc. Am returns to the observatory, seizes Slake's typewriter for himself, kills Slake and later abducts Dorothy, claiming Limestone Caverns as his domain. Dorothy suggests Am, tormented by his own ugliness, capture criminal Jigger Jones, ostensibly so people will consider him heroic but actually in hope the police will follow him. The ploy fails, and Jones suggests Am earn Dorothy's love via jewels and furs, which Am steals. Cap and Bucky follow Am back to the caverns, where Jones tries to betray Am and take the loot. Am thrashes him and kills Jones' men. Following Cap's advice, Dorothy convinces Am to bring her the typewriter. While Am fights Cap and Bucky, Dorothy, feeling sorry for Am, reluctantly types, "Am dies." Am falls into a bottomless pit. Cap hurls the typewriter after him.
NOTE: Jigger Jones' first name revealed in OHMU:HC #11, '09.

2ND STORY: "The Human Torch Vs. the Cat-Man" (7 pages)

CREDITS: Al Bellman (art)

FEATURE CHARACTER Human Torch (next in MC #68, '46)

SUPPORTING CAST: Toro (last in HT #21, '45, next in YA #18, '46)

VILLAINS: Cat-Man (Peter Blake, inventor, Thorton Kennedy's step-son; see NOTE)

OTHER CHARACTERS: George Wilson (Kennedy Wilson Steamship Lines co-owner), Thorton Kennedy (Wilson's partner, dies), Kennedy's butler, hotel manager

LOCATIONS/ITEMS: Manhattan inc hotel w/Room 1209, Kennedy estate inc Cat-Man's secret lab, Wilson home; Cat-Man's fire extinguisher, billy club, machete (splash only), lead/asbestos coating & acid bath, Western Union telegram

SYNOPSIS: Torch and Toro confront the costumed Cat-Man after he strangles Thorton Kennedy, but he blinds them with a fire extinguisher and escapes. They inquire at Kennedy's home, where Cat-Man knocks them unconscious and takes them to his private lab. He seals the pair in asbestos, then lowers them into a specially-prepared acid bath. Torch and Toro flame on at the precise second the acid melts the asbestos, but before it burns them. They capture Cat-Man and unmask him as Peter Blake, Kennedy's adopted son and heir.

NOTE: Torch battles a (presumably) different Catman in CapC #60/3, '47.

3RD STORY: "The Hermit's Heritage!!" (10 pages)

CREDITS: Vince Alascia (pencils), Al Gabriele (inks)

FEATURE CHARACTER: Captain America

SUPPORTING CAST: Bucky (next in YA #18, '46)

VILLAINS: Lefty & his gang

OTHER CHARACTERS: Hugo Pergody (sculptor & hermit), Montmorency, Percival & 1 other (hoboes), art gallery guard, tour guide, gallery patrons

LOCATIONS/ITEMS: Manhattan inc art gallery & Lefty's hideout, woods inc Hugo's tree & hoboes' camp; Hugo's statue, gang's pistols & tear gas bomb, hoboes' stewpot

SYNOPSIS: After befriending reclusive sculptor Hugo Pergody, three hoboes visit an art gallery, where Cap and Bucky capture art thieves, although one, Lefty, evades their notice. The hoboes discuss the revelation that one of Pergody's statues is now worth a fortune. Overhearing, Lefty decides to buy the statue cheap from the unknowing Pergody, but Cap notices his interest. That night, Lefty and henchmen approach Pergody who offers to give them the statue for free until the hoboes tell him of its value. Cap and Bucky intervene and defeat the criminals. Pergody decides to sell the statue and use the money to build a home for unfortunates such as the hoboes.

TEXT STORY: "Future Alliance" (2 pages)

CREDITS: Writer unknown

FEATURE CHARACTER: Murdock (fur trapper)

VILLAIN: Pierre "the Half-Breed"

OTHER CHARACTERS: Spook (wild dog), Trading Post denizens, Charlie Michaelson (trapper, as corpse), Mounted Police (bts, tracking Pierre), sled dogs

LOCATIONS/ITEMS: Canada inc Trading Post, hunting camp, Murdock's home, adjacent forest, cavern, valley & gully; furs, Pierre's hunting knife & carbine

SYNOPSIS: Murdock spends days trying to befriend a wild dog, dubbed "Spook." Notorious criminal Pierre shoots Spook, who retreats into the woods to recover. Angered, Murdock pursues Pierre, and the two struggle until Pierre pulls a knife. Spook appears and attacks Pierre, allowing Murdock to triumph.

NOTE: Story appears between 2nd & 3rd stories.

CAPTAIN AMERICA COMICS #53 (February 1946)

"Robe of Evil" (12 pages)
"The Robe of Evil, Chapter 2" (12 pages)

CREDITS: Vince Alascia (pencils), Al Gabriele (inks), Alex Schomburg (c art)

FEATURE CHARACTER: Captain America

SUPPORTING CAST: Bucky (last in YA #18, '46)

VILLAINS: The Robe ("The Robe-Master of Evil," "Snatch," Hammer Riley's lookout man, dies) & the Empire of Crime ("the Empire of Evil," "almost half a million" criminals in Robe's service, most bts, some die), Hammer Riley (gang leader, dies) & his Killer Mob (4 join Empire of Crime), "the Prince of Darkness" (in fb1) & his "evil hosts" (bts in fb1), Hyskos (in fb2), Pergamum (in fb3), de Signy (in fb4)

OTHER CHARACTERS: Police Captain Wilson, Manhattan police (1 dies), San Francisco police (some die), costume shop proprietor, man & daughter (buy Robe of Evil), demons (as costumes), Manhattan bystanders (2 die), San Francisco bystanders, spokesman responding to Robe's ultimatum (voice only), an angel (in fb1), Egyptian soldiers & citizens (in fb2), Roman centurions & senators, crocodiles (prev 3 in fb3), French citizens, (in fb4), 6 burglars (cover only)

LOCATIONS/ITEMS: Manhattan inc bank, Killer Mob's hideout, costume shop, police HQ, Moreau's jewelry store & bonds shop, Chicago inc police HQ, San Francisco inc police HQ & radio shop, Robe's castle, "fiery pits" (in fb1), Egypt (in fb2), Rome (in fb3), France (in fb4); Robe of Evil (also in fbs 1-4), Robe's wireless, police & criminals' firearms, criminals' clubs, interrogation spotlight, angel's sword (in fb1), Egyptian spears & shields (in fb2), guillotine (in fb4), Bucky & burglars' firearms (cover only)

FLASHBACK: Long ago, "when the world was emerging from chaos," the "Prince of Evil" wears the Robe of Evil while he and his hosts fight he forces of good and are cast into "the Fiery Pit of the Nether Regions" (1). Circa 5000 BC, Egyptian conqueror Hyksos wears the robe, conducting a reign of terror until put to death (2). In Rome of 200 BC, Pergamum wears the robe and leads his tribe in a murdering spree until put to death (3). In 19th century France, robber chief de Signy wears the robe until guillotined (4).

SYNOPSIS: When lookout man Snatch's cowardice allows Cap and Bucky to capture some Killer Mob members, Hammer Riley thrashes and dismisses him. Snatch steals a package containing an apparent replica of the mystic Robe of Evil. Donning it, Snatch becomes the super-powerful Robe, takes over Riley's Mob and defeats Cap and Bucky. After killing Riley, Robe embarks on a nationwide crime wave. In San Francisco, Robe, now served by thousands, issues an ultimatum: Disband all forces of law and order, or his Empire of Evil will devastate the USA. Robe has Cap and Bucky captured and brought to him. When his ultimatum is refused, Robe battles Cap, who having realized Robe's power depends upon his victims seeing his garment's mystic light, keeps his eyes closed and overcomes him. Frightened, Robe flees. Cap reaches for him, grasping only the robe as Snatch falls from a window to his death. His followers surrender. Cap burns the Robe of Evil.

2ND STORY: "The Killer Who Died Twice!" (7 pages)
CREDITS: Paul Reinman (pencils), Carmine Infantino (inks)
FEATURE CHARACTER: Human Torch (next in MC #69, '46)
SUPPORTING CAST: Toro (between MC #68-69, '46)
VILLAINS: Werner (part-owner of Harrison Steel Co., dies), Steve Lars (Harrison Steel Co. foreman)
OTHER CHARACTERS: Mr. Walker (part-owner of Harrison Steel Co.), Harrison Steel workers (most bts, Mike named), Werner's wife (mentioned)
LOCATIONS/ITEMS: New Jersey inc Harrison Steel Co. mill & Werner's home, Manhattan inc Torch & Toro's apartment; molten vats (#3 Ded), asbestos suits
SYNOPSIS: At Harrison Steel, Werner seemingly falls into a molten steel vat, but Walker suspects foul play, because a fall would have resulted in molten spatter, and there is none, suggesting Werner was lowered while unconscious. He consults Torch and Toro, who come to the mill. When the vat is drained, Torch finds no trace of Werner's asbestos suit. Realizing Werner's death has been faked, Torch and Toro trail Lars, who meets with Werner. The men return to the mill and try to kill Walker, but Torch and Toro intervene. Werner stumbles into the vat and truly perishes. Lars reveals their intention to kill Walker so the factory would be inherited by the "dead" Werner's wife.

3RD STORY: "Murder Etched in Stone!" (13 pages)
CREDITS: Vince Alascia (pencils)
FEATURE CHARACTER: Captain America (also as bust, in fb prior to chr 1st in Inv #14, '77, & as chesspiece in splash panel)
SUPPORTING CAST: Bucky (also as chesspiece in splash panel)
VILLAINS: Ivor the Sculptor, his head servant & 5 "Indian" servants
OTHER CHARACTERS: Inspector Grady (head of homicide), police (Officer Hogan named), Mr. Drew (city councilman, also as bust) & his daughter (also as statue and chesspiece in splash panel), Drew's butler & doctor, jail matron, 2 city councilmen, Os-So-Me-Lim ("Mighty Angel of the Image of Death," mentioned by Ivor's servants), figures (as statues, masks & paintings)
LOCATIONS/ITEMS: Manhattan inc police HQ, Ivor's penthouse studio at 21193 Park Ave, City Hall & Drew home w/bedroom, swimming hole (fb only); Ivor's lamp, hammer, chisel & statues, servants' clubs & knives, chessboard, pistol (both on splash panel only)
FLASHBACK: As a youth, Cap dives into a swimming hole and sails a sailboat, both beneath a hot sun.
SYNOPSIS: Cap and Bucky accompany Inspector Grady when Miss Drew reports Ivor the Sculptor is "killing" her father. At Ivor's studio, they find him carving a marble bust of Mr. Drew, which Miss Drew believes is causing his current illness. Grady reveals that, years before, Ivor was accused of similarly killing two city councilmen who rejected his work but was acquitted. Cap and Bucky interview two other councilmen. When Cap claims Ivor is sculpting their busts, they admit Ivor had stricken them ill but relented when they paid him. Believing Ivor's threat is purely psychological, Cap and Bucky return to his studio, but his servants overpower them. Ivor completes a Cap bust, seemingly inflicting deadly pain on him. In his delirium, Cap recalls childhood experiences involving strong sunlight. Bucky breaks free of Ivor's servants, cuts Cap's bonds, and fight the servants until Cap revives and helps end the battle. Recalling his hallucinations, Cap deduces Ivor's victims' lamps were fitted with chemically-treated bulbs that emitted concentrated "actinic rays" which inflict illness.
NOTE: Without prompting, Bucky notes that he and Cap were on a case in South America at the time of Ivor's earlier murders five years before; since Nasland and Davis were not Cap and Bucky five years before, there seems no current explanation for Davis' claim.

TEXT STORY: "Practice Makes Perfect" (2 pages)
CREDITS: Writer unknown
FEATURE CHARACTER: Ted Manners
OTHER CHARACTERS: Jim Manners (ranch owner, Ted's older brother), Slim Hannagan, Steve & other cowhands, black stallion, filly & other horses, stampeding cattle
LOCATIONS/ITEMS: Ranch inc house & corral, desert, hills, cliffs, valley
SYNOPSIS: After taking a cowhand job at his brother's ranch, Ted is determined to prove his horsemanship. Initially thrown from a filly, he tries again during the other cowhands' absence, and when a cattle stampede approaches, he steers it to safety, proving himself.
NOTE: Story appears between 1st & 2nd stories.

CAPTAIN AMERICA COMICS #54 (March 1946)

"The Big Guy!" (12 pages)

CREDITS: Stan Lee (writer), Vince Alascia (pencils), Al Avison (inks), Alex Schomburg (c art)
FEATURE CHARACTER: Captain America (also in Cupie's thoughts)
SUPPORTING CAST: Bucky
VILLAINS: The Big Guy (Alvin Martinike, diminutive gangster, see NOTE), Cupie (bouncer, Big Guy's girlfriend, also in her own thoughts), Dinosaur (Big Guy's mastiff/steed), Big Guy's gang (Joe, Mike, Pete named), 5 non-aligned criminals
OTHER CHARACTERS: Furniture salesman, bar & grill patron, 8 masked criminals, actress, sound technician, cameraman, 2 stagehands (prev 5 on cover only)
LOCATIONS/ITEMS: Manhattan inc furniture store, jewelry shop, smokestack, underworld bar, bar and grill, Big Guy's hideout, lab w/atom smasher & Wheat Exchange Bank (mentioned), movie set (Stage 3) (cover only); tractor crane, Big Guy's spring-powered stone fist & parachute/hat, gang's firearms, Cupie's club, Cap's catnip, cameras (1 labeled "Technicolor"), criminals' firearms (both on cover only)
SYNOPSIS: Cap and Bucky interrupt a jewelry robbery undertaken with a crane by members of the Big Guy's gang, renowned for performing "big" crimes. The gangsters escape. Learning where Big Guy's girlfriend Cupie works, Cap kisses her. As anticipated, Big Guy sends his underlings to capture Cap and Bucky. They bring Cap before Big Guy, a diminutive mastermind who strikes Cap with a large stone fist device, then sets his dog Dinosaur on Bucky. Gloating, Big Guy claims his next big job will involve tiny things. Cap releases catnip to madden Dinosaur allowing Bucky and him to escape. Realizing Big Guy's heist is to steal silver from an atom smasher, Cap and Bucky reach the atomic lab shortly after the gang. Big Guy climbs to the roof and parachutes to a getaway car. For separate reasons, both Big Guy and Cupie, recalling Cap's kiss, hope to encounter Cap again.
NOTE: The Big Guy is a rare villain who escapes Cap and Bucky to remain free at story's end. Big Guy's real name revealed in OHMU:HC #11, '09.

2ND STORY: "The Wish of Death!" (7 pages)
CREDITS: Bill Finger (writer), Carmine Infantino (art)
FEATURE CHARACTER: Human Torch (next in HT #22, '46, MC #70, '46)
SUPPORTING CAST: Toro (next in HT #22, '46)
VILLAINS: Baxter ("Hugo White," murdering hunchback), the Rocky Blane Counterfeit Gang
OTHER CHARACTERS: Manhattan & Jersey City police, Baxter's neighbors & landlord (dies), Baxter's other 2 victims (die bts) & extortion victims (Otis named), Otis' brother (bts, dies)
LOCATIONS/ITEMS: Manhattan inc 10th Street tenement building (Baxter's Apt 12, also Apts 11 & 13), Torch and Toro's apartment & police HQ, Jersey City inc bank, apartment building w/"White's" apartment & Silver Lake Park; Baxter's electric apparatus w/electrified gloves
SYNOPSIS: When Baxter quarrels with his landlord, he wishes the man dead. The landlord drops dead from heart failure and Baxter develops a deadly reputation. With his "wish of death," he kills two other men, both perishing of heart failure. Torch and Toro confront him, but Baxter escapes. Relocating to New Jersey as "Hugo White," Baxter extorts people into paying him to stay alive. Torch and Toro track him down, but Baxter's touch drops them, and he leaves them for dead. Realizing Baxter uses an artificial electrical shock to kill by inflicting heart failure, Torch and Toro find him meeting with his latest victim and destroy his apparatus. The police arrest him, and his victims' payments are returned.
NOTE: Story followed by "Paige's Looney Page" (1 page), featuring Joe Mush, sleeper, father & son, Mrs. ABC, Mr. XYZ, man w/tilted hat, the Nut family (6 people), digger, teacher, cat, Mr. ABC, Mrs. XYZ (bts), Mr. & Mrs. XYZ's baby, family (father, mother, child), dog & digger's wife in comic vignettes (Lou Page, writer/art).

3RD STORY: "Scarface and the Script of Death" (14 pages)
CREDITS: Bill Finger (writer), Vince Alascia (pencils), Al Bellman (inks)
FEATURE CHARACTER: Captain America
SUPPORTING CAST: Bucky
VILLAIN: Scarface (Bel Commings, also as "Larry Shore," actor & screenwriter, dies)
OTHER CHARACTERS: Jerry Small (producer), Sonja Blake (actress, also as "Jenny" in film, dies), Jeff Crain (actor, also as "Walter" in film), Lake Wood (actor, also as "Scarface" in film, dies), Tommy (stagehand), director, cameraman, additional film crew members, bat
LOCATIONS/ITEMS: Hollywood, (California), inc Colossal Pictures Inc. studio w/Small's office & newspaper office, Mad Mountain inc Tarrymore Castle w/dungeon; cameras, stage lights, set backgrounds inc Set 4, props, Scarface's club, gun, knife & spring-powered lasso, Shore's wallet, 4 skulls (splash only)
SYNOPSIS: In Tarrymore Castle, Jerry Small's crew films "The Death of Scarface." An actress' scream draws Cap and Bucky to investigate, and they remain to observe. The Scarface character, supposedly played by Lake Wood, kills the actress, and Lake himself is found dead, making Scarface's identity a mystery. When writer Larry Shore is seemingly attacked, Cap checks a nearby wallet and finds a 1934 news clipping on actor Bel Commings, who formerly worked with Small and the others. Back in Hollywood, Cap checks newspaper back editions to learn Commings, disfigured in a fire, blamed his co-workers, and Cap suspects Commings is Scarface. At the castle, Small agrees to act as bait to lure Scarface, but Scarface traps Cap and Bucky instead, binding them in a flooded dungeon to drown. Cap and Bucky escape and prevent Scarface from killing Small. Scarface falls to his death. Cap unmasks him as Commings, AND Larry Shore, who faked his own earlier attack.

4TH STORY: "Murder Mountain!" (10 pages)
CREDITS: Vince Alascia (pencils)

FEATURE CHARACTER: Captain America

SUPPORTING CAST: Bucky (next in YA #19, '46)

VILLAINS: Dr. Weerd (Irwin Hawes, island governor) & his underlings (2 die), George Harris (volcanologist, dies)

OTHER CHARACTERS: US Army officer, island inhabitants, geologists (bts, off-panel)

LOCATIONS/ITEMS: Pacific island inc Mt. Oku Sama, bay, Dr. Weerd's volcano hideout, Gov. Hawes' office & Harris' lab; Harris' lava exciter, gang's firearms

SYNOPSIS: Steve and Bucky accompany geologists to a Pacific island, where the volcano Oku Sama has apparently reactivated. When criminals attack the geologists, Cap and Bucky weigh in until a burst of volcanic steam kills the crooks. Their leader, Dr. Weerd, presumes the incident will end government investigation, but Cap correctly suspects the volcanic activity is man-made. When he and Bucky question volcanologist George Harris, more gunmen knock them out. They awaken to find Harris gone. Cap recommends the island as a US base to draw out the crooks, but when Oku Sama seemingly erupts, Governor Hawes orders the island evacuated. Cap and Bucky find Weerd's hideout, with Harris dead, an apparent suicide implying he was the criminal mastermind. However, Cap pursues and unmasks Weerd as Hawes, who used Harris' "exciter" to simulate the volcanic activity, in order to claim secret silver deposits.

NOTE: Governor Hawes' first name revealed in OHMU:HC #11, '09.

NEXT STORY: "Cub-Reporter" (2 pages)

CREDITS: Writer unknown

FEATURE CHARACTER: Larry (cub reporter)

VILLAINS: Winky Malloy (con man), Mamie (maid)

OTHER CHARACTERS: Chris Fadden, Eddie Wells (both reporters), Harry Robinson ("the chief," Evening Standard managing editor), Gloria Bolitho (stage actress), Royal Hotel desk clerk, police, "Murder in Three Acts" cast

LOCATIONS/ITEMS: Evening Standard office, Royal Hotel inc Room 1005, Olympia Theater; Mamie's revolver, ropes, gag, carpet

SYNOPSIS: Larry's fellow reporters give him a "tip" about Gloria Bolitho being blackmailed. Not realizing the "assignment" is a prank, Larry goes to Bolitho's hotel and finds her bound and gagged in preparation for abduction. Larry literally pulls the rug out from one of the criminals, acquiring her gun until police arrive. Grateful, Gloria accompanies Larry to the newspaper office, to the shock of his would-be hoaxsters, and editor Robinson promotes him to feature writer.

NOTE: Story appears between 3rd & 4th stories.

CAPTAIN AMERICA COMICS #55 (April 1946)

"The Hands of Sensitivo!" (13 pages)

CREDITS: Bill Finger (writer), Vince Alascia (pencils, c art), Frank Borth (inks)

FEATURE CHARACTER: Captain America (in pfb only)

SUPPORTING CAST: Bucky (in pfb only, last in Kid #10, '46)

VILLAINS: Sensitivo (Andrew, "Handy" Andy, large-handed criminal, in fb1 years before & in pfb) & the Crime Company (Trigger named, dies) (in pfb only)

OTHER CHARACTERS: Anders (artist/collector, also in pfb), police chief, Margie Hawes (manicurist & Trigger's girlfriend, dies), guard (prev 3 in pfb), Margie's landlady (bts in pfb, find's Margie's body), Sensitivo's parents (fb1 only), Sensitivo's classmate (voice only, in fb1), Sensitivo's employer (bts, in fb1), Edgar Allan Poe (1809-1849), Charles Dickens (1812-1870) (both authors, both mentioned only), 12 counterfeiters (cover only)

LOCATIONS/ITEMS: Manhattan inc building with Rare Books shop and Turkish bath gym, Margie's home and beauty shoppe, Sensitivo's abandoned glove factory hideout on riverfront, police HQ w/lab (all in pfb), Anders' studio (also in pfb), hospital, high school gym & office (prev 3 in fb1 only), counterfeiter den (on cover only); Cap's infrared bulb & infrared filter-goggles, Margie's manicuring tools, kid leather & pigskin articles (from Sensitivo's hands), gang's firearms, Sensitivo's hand grenade (all in pfb), Anders' collection of hand sculptures & pictures (also in pfb), counterfeiters' printing presses & firearms (both on cover only)

FLASHBACKS: Born with unusually large hands, in childhood Andrew learns his extra-sensitive fingers can "hear" through walls by telegraphing sound vibrations to his brain. As an adult, he uses his power to become a successful criminal (1). Cap and Bucky break up the Crime Company's Rare Books robbery. Sensitivo, opening the vault, "hears" Cap and Bucky's approach and shoves Bucky out a window. Cap rescues Bucky, but Sensitivo and company depart. When Sensitivo grumbles about breaking a fingernail, henchman Trigger takes him to his girlfriend Margie for a manicure. When Margie accidentally cuts Sensitivo's finger, he kills her. Cap researches Sensitivo and learns he never commits crimes at night. Meanwhile, Margie's manicuring tools' residue leads Cap and Bucky to Sensitivo's hideout. When Cap mentions Margie's death, Trigger turns on Sensitivo, who shoots him, then escapes. Dying, Trigger whispers a clue. Cap and Bucky get hand-casting artist Anders to lure Sensitivo in. Cap, having realized from Trigger's whisper that Sensitivo suffers from astereognosis and cannot recognize objects by touch, has Anders' studio darkened, panicking Sensitivo. Using infra-red goggles to see, Cap and Bucky quickly defeat Sensitivo (p).

SYNOPSIS: Artist Anders tells the Sensitivo story.

NOTE: Sensitivo also called "Sensitivio."

2ND STORY: "Just What the Doctor Ordered" (12 pages)

CREDITS: Allen Simon (pencils), Al Bellman (inks)

FEATURE CHARACTER: Captain America

SUPPORTING CAST: Bucky

VILLAINS: Boss, Lefty, & 2 others, 2 delinquents,

OTHER CHARACTERS: Patsy Perkins (young tomboy), Mr. & Mrs. Perkins (Patsy's parents), doctors, police radio announcer, pilots, airport workers, Patsy's Aunt Sarah (mentioned only), Death (splash only)

LOCATIONS/ITEMS: Manhattan suburb inc Perkins home, Manhattan inc State Hospital, police HQ, Cy's Laundry, criminals' hideout & airport; Patsy's bicycle, criminals' firearms & blackjack, serum packets

SYNOPSIS: During an epidemic, a gang steals vital serum samples. Cap and Bucky interrupt one theft, but the criminals escape. To evade discovery from a police search, the gang pay runaway tomboy Patsy Perkins to deliver the serum on her bicycle to "a sick friend" at their hideout. A stranger to the city, Patsy searches for the address and literally runs into Cap and Bucky, who take her there and wait outside for her. Within Patsy finds the gang, having preceded her there. Concerned, Cap and Bucky burst in, but the gang ends the fight by taking Patsy hostage. While the gang members depart to intercept an airport serum shipment, their leader holds Cap and Bucky at gunpoint, but Patsy distracts him then knocks him down with judo. Cap and Bucky capture the other criminals, saving the serum, and Patsy, given pause by her dangerous day, returns home.

NOTE: Serum thefts from "most of the...hospitals" in Manhattan hints at a far larger organization than the four criminals seen here, but this is not addressed.

3RD STORY: "The Rest Home Mystery!" (7 pages)
CREDITS: Mike Sekowsky (pencils)
FEATURE CHARACTER: Human Torch (next in MC #71, '46)
SUPPORTING CAST: Toro (last in Kid #10, '46, next in MC #71, '46)
VILLAINS: Dr. Malwow, Ed Owens, 3 hirelings
OTHER CHARACTERS: Dr. Allen, George Whitton (dies), rest home employee (voice only, more bts), morgue guard (bts, Toro distracts him while Torch examines Walter's body), town citizens, Walter Owens (as a corpse), 12 ghoulish faces (splash only)
LOCATIONS/ITEMS: Town inc morgue & Riverside Rest Home w/pump shack and underground passage; steamroller roller, Owens' gas bombs, Malwow's gun, Allen's "eye serum" (bts, used on Walter, cures Ed)
SYNOPSIS: Torch and Toro interrupt a lynch mob attacking Dr. Allen, whom Ed Owens accuses of killing his brother Walter while trying to cure him of blindness. Torch checks the town morgue and finds Walter's true cause of death, a skull base injection. Learning Walter received treatment at Riverside Rest Home, Torch and Toro question its head, Dr. Malwow. George Whitton, disguised as a blind patient, leaves the heroes a note requesting a meeting. Later, a seemingly runaway roller kills Whitton, with Malwow nearby. Torch and Toro discover a nearby shack, where Malwow's associates are tapping a secretly discovered oil line. An armed Malwow enters, along with his confederate Ed Owens, who, like his brother, is struck blind. Upon learning both Walter and Whitton were killed for learning about the oil operation, Torch persuades Owens to restore Allen's reputation by undergoing his sight-restoration treatment. He agrees and regains his sight before being imprisoned.
NOTE: George Whitton's reason for investigating Riverside Rest Home is not provided.

4TH STORY: "The Merry Widow Murders!" (12 pages)
CREDITS: Vince Alascia (art)
FEATURE CHARACTER: Captain America
SUPPORTING CAST: Bucky
VILLAIN: The Merry Widow Murderer (Myron Delasco, insane actor, also in newspaper photo, dies)
OTHER CHARACTERS: Sidney Saunders (director), actress, cameraman, tour guide, tour members, 2 victims (die), police, bystanders
LOCATIONS/ITEMS: Hollywood inc movie studio, "Steve" & "Bucky's" hotel room & clock tower, mountain road; Bucky's disguise, Delasco's scissors & script
SYNOPSIS: After filming is complete on "The Merry Widow Murderer," Myron Delasco, the title role actor, crashes his car and sustains head injuries. Believing himself to actually be the Merry Widow Murderer, he kills a woman. Hearing her scream, Cap and Bucky respond, but the Murderer escapes. Cap confirms the crime's similarities to the film's fictional crimes. That night, Bucky, disguised as a woman, acts as decoy, luring the Murderer to attack. Cap moves in but the Murderer knocks him down and flees up a fire escape with Bucky. Remembering that, in the film, the Murderer always halted in his tracks at the stroke of midnight, Cap turns a tower clock ahead, then yells, "Cut!" The confused Murderer stumbles from a rooftop to his death.
NOTE: "Steve" and "Bucky's" Hollywood hotel room is erroneously described as their "apartment."

TEXT STORY: "House of Mystery" (2 pages)
CREDITS: Writer unknown
FEATURE CHARACTER: Narrator
VILLAIN: A poisoner (as a ghost)
OTHER CHARACTERS: 4 poisoning victims (as ghosts), spiders (bts)
LOCATIONS/ITEMS: New England state inc narrator's estate, 2 paths, brook & abandoned house; wine bottle (broken), 4 goblets, old letters (burned)
SYNOPSIS: The narrator ventures into an abandoned house and, when a storm breaks out, falls asleep near a fireplace, then wakens to watch four ghosts demand poisoned wine from a fifth, the man who poisoned them years before and is now tormented by it. Not noticing the narrator, the poisoner pours the wine, and the ghosts drink and fall as if poisoned again. Determined to break the spell, the poisoner throws the wine bottle at the fireplace, narrowly missing the narrator, who faints. He awakens to find the storm has stopped. Departing the house, he tries to convince himself the experience was a dream...until he notices his shirt is damp with wine.
NOTE: Story appears between 2nd & 3rd stories.

"The Casbah Killer!" (15 pages)

CREDITS: Don Rico (pencils), Rick Dowd (inks), Syd Shores (c art)
FEATURE CHARACTER: Captain America (also in photos & in Sari's thoughts)
SUPPORTING CAST: Bucky
VILLAINS: Miguel Juan Gonzales Lopez-Iruli ("Mike Reilly," hotel owner, entrepreneur & hijacker) & his henchmen
OTHER CHARACTERS: Sari ("Casbah girl"), Pepe Ris (informant, dies), US government official, Algiers police, Reilly's staff inc bellhop, cook & handyman, truck drivers (1 dies, others bts), brass band, Algiers citizens inc Casbah denizens, horse, 8 art thieves & robed figure (as statue) (both on cover only), Casbah creature (in splash panel only)
LOCATIONS/ITEMS: Washington DC inc government office, Atlantic Ocean, Algiers inc airport, Hotel America w/Cap and Bucky's room & Mike's office, RR yards, docks & the Casbah, the Metropolitan Museum of Art (cover only), hijackers' car & firearms, Mike's gun, truck convoy, Casbah denizens' knives & guns, Met artwork (cover only), Casbah creature's knife (in splash panel only)
SYNOPSIS: Assigned to investigate food & medicine hijackers, Cap and Bucky travel to Algiers and are greeted by exuberant Mike Reilly, hotel owner, politico, and devotee of all things American. A car full of gunmen attempt an assassination, but Cap and Bucky easily defeat them. At Reilly's Hotel America, the heroes receive warnings from "Casbah girl" Sari, who is secretly in love with Cap, and informant Pepe Ris. After learning their assailants escaped police custody, Cap and Bucky follow a supply convoy to the docks, where the hijackers attack. The two follow them into the Casbah, where the locals attack them as law and order representatives. Sari leads them to safety. Back at Hotel America, the hijackers kill Ris, but Cap, recognizing the criminals as Americans, realizes Americophile Reilly is the head hijacker. Reilly's underlings surround them. Sari distracts the crooks long enough for Cap and Bucky to overpower and defeat them.

2ND STORY: "A Name for an Old Doll!" (12 pages)
CREDITS: Vince Alascia (pencils), Syd Shores (inks)
FEATURE CHARACTER: Captain America (in pfb only)
SUPPORTING CAST: Bucky (in pfb only)
VILLAINS: 3 gambling syndicate members (in pfb only)
OTHER CHARACTERS: Newsstand Nelly (news vendor), Rocky Norris (boxer), Nelly's neighbors (2 men, 1 woman), Slugger Shloop (boxer, dies), boxer (Rocky's opponent), boxing match attendees, Manhattan bystanders (all in pfb only), narrator
LOCATIONS/ITEMS: Manhattan inc Broadway district (also in pfb) w/Nelly's newsstand and apartment, boxing arena, drugstore & equipment warehouse (prev 5 in pfb); criminals' firearms & blackjacks, Nelly's newspapers & change belt (all in pfb)
FLASHBACK: Teased for her lack of family, news vendor Nelly impulsively claims prize-fighter Rocky Norris is her son. During Rocky's fight with Slugger Shloop, gambling syndicate members with money on Slugger shoot at Norris but inadvertently kill Shloop. Cap and Bucky pursue the criminals, who lose themselves in a crowd. Later, gambling syndicate members attack Norris, but Cap and Bucky intervene. Nelly takes Rocky, an orphan, as a boarder, and the two form a familial bond. When the syndicate threatens to kill Nelly, Rocky agrees to take a dive, but Nelly, not knowing of the threat, dissuades him. The gamblers shoot at Nelly, but Cap and Bucky pursue and defeat them. Nelly survives when the bullet strikes her change belt, and she and Rocky officially adopt each other as mother and son (p).
SYNOPSIS: The narrator tells the story of Nelly & Rocky.
NOTE: Story is an homage to the work of Damon Runyon (1880-1946) w/the narrator speaking in the vernacular of Runyon's stories.

3RD STORY: "The Case of the Chiming Tree" (7 pages)
CREDITS: Carmine Infantino (art)
FEATURE CHARACTER: Human Torch (next in MC #72, '46, HT #23, '46, MC #73, '46, AllSel #10/2, '46, AllWin #18/3, '46)
SUPPORTING CAST: Toro (between MC #71-72, '46)
VILLAINS: Dude (ex-policeman), John Grant (gem appraiser, dies) & his men
OTHER CHARACTERS: Fred Flanders (traveling poet, dies), Mrs. Grant, policeman, Prof. Thornton (metallurgist, as corpse), information clerk (bts, directs Torch & Toro to Thornton's office), the "Bank Killers" (mentioned, captured by Torch and Toro just prior to this story), dead figures (splash only)
LOCATIONS/ITEMS: New Mexico town inc Grant Appraisers (225 Rocco St.), police HQ & Metallurgical Institute w/Thornton's office, Stony Gulch w/petrified forest; diamond tree, Thornton's almanac, Dude's badge, Flanders' wallet & diamond, Grant's card, hood's gun (on splash only)
SYNOPSIS: Passing through a southwestern town, Torch and Toro find Flanders dying and gasping about a "chiming tree." Finding a diamond and address card on him, Torch and Toro, accompanied by alleged detective Dude, visit John Grant, whose wife reports Flanders intended to visit Prof. Thornton. Torch and Toro find Thornton dead as an explosion wrecks his office, then see he had been researching nearby ghost town Stony Gulch. In an adjacent petrified forest, Torch and Toro find criminals harvesting a "diamond tree," a natural rarity where Flanders found the diamond. Torch and Toro capture the criminals, who confess to killing Flanders and Thornton. Grant arrives, threatening to kill his own wife unless the heroes cooperate, but Dude shoots him. Torch then punches out Dude, who, by coming directly to the diamond tree, proved his involvement with the criminals.

4TH STORY: "Murder on the Campus!" (9 pages)
CREDITS: Al Gabriele (pencils), Charles Nicholas (inks)
FEATURE CHARACTER: Captain America (also as "America," next in AllSel #10, '46, AllWin #18/2, '46)

SUPPORTING CAST: Bucky (also as "Captain Bucky," next in AllSel #10, '46)
VILLAINS: 3 counterfeiters ("Boss" named)
OTHER CHARACTERS: Prof. Squiggins (absent-minded physics prof), Jim Cole (US Treasury agent), football coach, football game attendees, football players, the Human Torch, Toro, Sub-Mariner (prev 3 mentioned by Squiggins, mistakes Cap & Bucky for them)
LOCATIONS/ITEMS: Squiggins' home, counterfeiters' house (next door to Squiggin's home), Cumulus College inc football stadium & gym; Squiggins' umbrella, counterfeiters' pistols, dagger, counterfeiting equipment & money
SYNOPSIS: En route to deliver a lecture, absent-minded Prof. Squiggins blunders into the house next door, where counterfeiters are trying to intimidate a college football coach into spreading their fake money. They shoot at Squiggins, who flees and bumps into Cap and Bucky, in town for the charity football game. They drive off the criminals, but Squiggins offers only a befuddled explanation about machinery and money, then departs. Next day, at the game, the counterfeiters force the coach to switch charity donations with counterfeit money. Remembering Squiggins' remarks, Cap and Bucky find him. Squiggins idly mentions seeing the counterfeiters in the gym, intending to kill the coach. Cap and Bucky interrupt and, with Squiggin's inadvertent help, defeat the counterfeiters.

TEXT STORY: "The Last Frontier" (2 pages)
CREDITS: Writer unknown
FEATURE CHARACTER: Jeff Wilcox (in fb only, years before narrated story)
VILLAINS: "Red-hands" Roarke (outlaw, dies) & his fellow outlaws (some die) (all in fb only)
OTHER CHARACTERS: City Museum director, scientific expedition members, boat crew (bts, take expedition to Australia), outlaws' horses (some die), Australian fauna (all in fb only), narrator
LOCATIONS/ITEMS: City Museum, Australia inc Darwin & unexplored region (all in fb); expedition's station wagons, carbines, cameras & additional equipment, outlaws' revolvers (all in fb)
FLASHBACK: Craving adventure, Jeff joins a scientific expedition to unexplored areas of Australia. When Roarke's outlaws set upon the expedition, Jeff leads the members in circling their vehicles "stagecoach style" and shooting down the outlaws.
SYNOPSIS: Narrator tells Jeff's story that "is often spoken of whenever explorers gather to recall the adventurous tales of their profession."
NOTE: Story appears between 2nd & 3rd stories. Story begins "weeks" prior to June and concludes the following August.

CAPTAIN AMERICA COMICS #57 (July 1946)

"Death on the Downbeat" (13 pages)

CREDITS: Al Avison (pencils), Jim Mooney (inks), Vince Alascia (c art)
FEATURE CHARACTER: Captain America
SUPPORTING CAST: Bucky (last in AllWin #18/2, '46)
VILLAINS: The Crooner ("the Jive-Killer," criminal impersonating famous singer), "Doc" (Crooner's accomplice, "Swoon King's" private doctor, dies)
OTHER CHARACTERS: The Crooner ("the Swoon King," the actual famous singer, not in on the scheme, also on posters), Crooner's band inc sax player, bull fiddle player & 2 others, police inc inspector, Dr. Wells (plastic surgeon, dies) & his secretary (bts), autograph seekers, theater audience (1 dies), train passengers & crew (most bts), pin-up girl (on Bucky's tent wall), 10 criminals (on cover only), demonic face (on splash only)
LOCATIONS/ITEMS: Wells' surgery room, US Army camp inc "Steve" & "Bucky's" tent, Manhattan inc police HQ, theater w/dressing room & train station; train, band's instruments, extra bull fiddle case, Crooner's knives & gun, Doc's revolver, autograph books, criminals' firearms & blackjack (both on cover only)
SYNOPSIS: A man undergoes plastic surgery, then kills the surgeon. Later, the Crooner, a national singing sensation, is accused of jewel robberies during the time he was seen on stage. At a later performance, while the Crooner sings, Cap and Bucky see him robbing audience members and realize there are two Crooners. The criminal Crooner shoots a robbery victim and escapes. When the real Crooner, his private doctor, and his band depart by train, Cap and Bucky jump on. When Cap inquires about an extra bull fiddle case, Doc pulls a revolver, and the criminal Crooner double emerges from the case. Cap loosens an upper berth, knocking down Doc. Crooner throws a knife at Cap but strikes Doc instead, killing him. He climbs to the top of the moving train, but Cap pursues and knocks him out.

2ND STORY: "The Monkey's Curse!" (9 pages)
CREDITS: Vince Alascia (art)
FEATURE CHARACTER: Captain America
SUPPORTING CAST: Bucky
VILLAINS: Bill Summers, 4 criminals
OTHER CHARACTERS: Police, Louise & friend, museum employees & patrons (most bts), 3 monkeys (in symbolic splash panel & on trinket)
LOCATIONS/ITEMS: Manhattan inc store, Summers' apartment & museum; "Speak Evil, See Evil, Hear Evil" monkey trinket, museum's paintings & statues, wooden revolver, whittling knife
SYNOPSIS: Cap and Bucky fight thieves, knocking one out. Bill Summers finds a monkey statue near the fallen thief. Reading the statue's "curse" that the bearer must commit three crimes, Summers becomes obsessed with following its instructions. The next day, he steals paintings from a museum. Cap and Bucky pursue, arriving at Summers' apartment, where they see him expound to the statue, then carve a wooden revolver. After Bill leaves, Cap and Bucky examine the monkey statue, then follow. When Summers attempts to rob two women, Cap and Bucky tackle him. Summers insists he must break the curse, but Cap, noting the act of taking the statue itself was a crime, points out that he's already committed three crimes. He then shows the statue's "Ajax Novelty Co." label, proving it a mere trinket rather than a cursed item.
NOTE: Bill Summers should not be confused with the League of Hate member who used the same name in CapC #49, '45.

3RD STORY: "The House That Haunts" (7 pages)
CREDITS: Bill Finger (writer), Carmine Infantino (art)
FEATURE CHARACTER: Human Torch (next in MC #74-75, '46)
SUPPORTING CAST: Toro (last in AllWin #18/3, '46, next in MC #74, '46)
VILLAINS: Dr. Marshal, Amy Lynn, Slug & associate
OTHER CHARACTERS: Amos Grayson (apartment house owner), 2 policemen ("Sergeant" named), Grayson's tenant (also in portrait), Daily Bulletin city editor & employee, Bob Duncan (Bulletin reporter/photographer, as corpse), 7 ghoulish figures (splash only)
LOCATIONS/ITEMS: Manhattan inc Torch & Toro's apartment, Grayson's building w/Room 1A (Marshal's apt) and 2A (Duncan's apt), Daily Bulletin office & Amy's home; Slug & associate's pistols (firing blanks only), Marshal's metal tube, zono-chemical & time bomb, tenant's altered portrait, Duncan's photographic plates
SYNOPSIS: Torch and Toro investigate Grayson's apartment building, where furnishings mysteriously change color. While checking Dr. Marshal's office, they notice two fleeing thugs and pursue. When Amy Lynn walks into the thugs' gunfire, Torch rescues her, but the thugs' escape. Checking Amy's fiancé Bob Duncan's apartment, they find him dead, with ruined photographic plates. Calling his editor, Torch learns Duncan was trailing a blackmail ring. Torch and Toro trace an electrical line from Duncan's dark room to Marshal's office, where they find high-radiation x-ray tubes which Marshal used to kill Duncan and ruin his photos, causing the building's color changes. Marshal knocks the two unconscious, seals them in a metal tube, and leaves them to die via timebomb. Police arrive, release the heroes and defuse the bomb. Having deduced Amy's involvement, Torch and Toro check her home, where the blackmailers have gathered. The two burst in and capture the lot.

4TH STORY: "Let's Play Detective: Passport to Murder" (1 page)
CREDITS: Al Bellman (art)
FEATURE CHARACTER: Mike Trapp (last in CapC #51/4, 45)
VILLAIN: Earl Sachett
OTHER CHARACTERS: Policeman, radio announcer (voice only), "Eyes" Skyler, "Red" Lacy (bts, murder victim)
LOCATIONS/ITEMS: Manhattan inc police HQ & Golden Dice Nightclub (bts, where "Red" is killed), Skyler's mountain hideaway (mentioned); Sachett's forged passport
SYNOPSIS: After nightclub owner and ex-criminal Lacy is murdered, Trapp questions two of his past associates, Sachett and Skyler. When Sachett offers his passport to prove he was in Cuba during Lacy's murder, Trapp, knowing US citizens do not require passports to visit Cuba, realizes Sachett is lying and arrests him.
NOTE: Story followed by "Now You Can Be the Editor!" (1 page), in which readers are invited to tell Stan Lee what they like and dislike about CapC, featuring Captain America, Bucky, & Stan Lee.

5TH STORY: "Beware the Medicine Man!" (12 pages)
CREDITS: Bill Finger (writer), Bob Powell (pencils), George Klein (inks)
FEATURE CHARACTER: Captain America (also as marionette on splash)
SUPPORTING CAST: Bucky (also as marionette on splash, next in MC #75/4, '46)
VILLAINS: Jig Baker, Stalk, & 2 others
OTHER CHARACTERS: Doc Spiel (pitchman/watchman/salesman), Thomas "Tommy" Spiel (Doc's young son), Mr. Lamont (aluminum magnate) & his butler, Mytown Herald editor, sheriff, judge & residents, other town's residents inc town constable, news vendor, 2 newstand customers, sales demo attendees, Lamont Aluminum Products manager, Chief Atchooblessyou (medicine man, mentioned by Spiel, presumably fictitious)
LOCATIONS/ITEMS: Town, Manhattan inc "Out-of-Town Newspapers" newsstand, Mytown inc Mytown Herald office, courtroom, Stalk's shack, Lamont estate and aluminum plant & fairgrounds, city inc Lamont Aluminum Products display stand; Tommy's ventriloquist dummy costume, semaphore flags (B, R, J singled out), bottles of Doc Spiel's Cure All, frying pan, puppet stage (splash only)
SYNOPSIS: Via newspaper ad, Jig Baker's associate Stalk invites him to Mytown for criminal opportunities. Seeing the message, Cap and Bucky also travel to Mytown, where pitchman Doc Spiel has been arrested and is threatened with losing custody of his son Tommy unless he obtains honest employment. Lamont, owner of the aluminum plant which Stalk has singled out for Baker's attention, gives Spiel a watchman job, and Baker extorts Spiel's cooperation by kidnapping Tommy. When Cap and Bucky perform at Lamont's charity auction, Spiel uses signal flags to send Cap the message "J.B." -- "Jig Baker." That night, Spiel admits Baker and company into the plant, but Cap and Bucky await them and, with Spiel's assistance, defeat them. Lamont adopts Tommy as a godson, and Spiel puts his oratory skills to work as a salesman.

TEXT STORY: "Date with Danger" (2 pages)
CREDITS: Writer unknown
FEATURE CHARACTER: Larry (7-year veteran trucker)
VILLAINS: Froggy & Joe
OTHER CHARACTERS: Slim (gas station attendant), Buck & Willie (Larry's friends), motorcycle cop
LOCATIONS/ITEMS: Joe's Diner inc gas pumps, Bald Mount, fur processing plant, Bigville (both mentioned), Larry's diesel truck (destroyed) & trailer, furs, Froggy's pistol, Larry's pistol
SYNOPSIS: When Froggy hijacks Larry's furs-transporting diesel truck, Larry stops for gas and instructs the attendant to fill the truck's tank with high octane gas; soon afterward, the gas, as Larry expected, reacts disastrously with the truck's diesel engine, causing an explosion which knocks out the unprepared Froggy. Tipped off by the attendant, police arrive to arrest Froggy.
NOTE: Story appears between 2nd & 3rd stories.

CAPTAIN AMERICA COMICS #58 (September 1946)

"Crime on Cue" (10 pages)

CREDITS: Al Avison (pencils), Frank Borth (inks), Alex Schomburg (c art)
FEATURE CHARACTER: Captain America (also as carved figure on splash)
SUPPORTING CAST: Bucky (also as carved figure on splash, last in MC #75/4, '46)
VILLAINS: The Statue of Death (Peter Sazlo, woodcarver, also in fb years before)
OTHER CHARACTERS: Police commissioner, police, female customer, blacksmith (dies), magician (also on posters), Mr. Mercy (china shop owner), news vendor, bystanders (some on cover only), Bijou ticket taker, theater attendees, rabbit, Romany ("gypsy") man (fb only), Buddha (as statue), William Shakespeare (c. 1564-1616, mentioned, Sazlo's inspiration), 7 masked criminals (on cover only)
LOCATIONS/ITEMS: Sazlo's shop & well, blacksmith shop, Bijou w/magician's dressing room, Mercy's Quality China Shop, Europe (in fb), bank w/flagpole, drug store, neighboring businesses (prev 3 on cover only), Statue of Death (actual statue, w/time bomb, destroyed), Sazlo's sword & pistol, Shakespeare pages, Shakespeare volume, carving tool (both on splash only), criminals' helicopter & firearms (on cover only)
FLASHBACK: In Europe, Sazlo's carvings sell well but he spends most of his time reading Shakespeare.
SYNOPSIS: When his work is rejected by potential customers, woodcarver Sazlo vows to avenge the insult and prove himself superior to the USA's crimefighters. Naming himself after his favorite work, the Statue of Death, he places a newspaper ad quoting Shakespeare as a clue to his first murder. Although Cap deciphers the clue, he and Bucky arrive too late to save the Statue's victim, a blacksmith. A second Shakespeare quote leads them to a theater, where they stop the Statue from killing a magician, and the third to a china shop, where Statue leaves them a trail of Shakespeare pages to follow. Reaching the villain's shop, they tackle what seems to be their foe but is actually the genuine statue, containing a time bomb, on the ledge of a well, into which they fall. Bucky leaps for the ledge but misses. However, he pulls down a roped bucket, and the two climb the rope to escape the bomb's blast, then capture Statue.

2ND STORY: "Let's Play Detective: Dead Man Talks" (1 page)
CREDITS: Al Bellman (art)
FEATURE CHARACTER: Mike Trapp (next in CapC #60/4, '47)
SUPPORTING CAST: Pepper Burns (last in CapC #51/4, '45, next in CapC #60/4, '47)
VILLAINS: Carlos & Louie
OTHER CHARACTER: "Big Chips" Malone (gambler, as corpse)
LOCATIONS/ITEMS: Manhattan inc police HQ & Malone's apartment; Malone's pistol, Carlos' pistol (bts, murder weapon)
SYNOPSIS: Trapp investigates "Big Chips" Malone's shooting death, which his fellow gamblers claim was in self-defense since he drew a gun first during a poker game. Noticing that, although Malone wears his gun holster on his right shoulder, his pistol is in his right hand, Trapp realizes the gun was planted after Malone's death. He arrests the pair, who killed Malone over a gambling debt.

3RD STORY: "The Sportsman of Crime!" (12 pages)
CREDITS: Al Avison (art)
FEATURE CHARACTER: Captain America
SUPPORTING CAST: Bucky
VILLAINS: Sportsman (Sonny Fenton, sports promoter, also in dfb, also impersonates Jim Gates) & 3 underlings, 4 convicts
OTHER CHARACTERS: Jim "Pearly" Gates (paroled criminal, impersonated by Sportsman, also in dfb, mentioned as 5'9", 155 lbs), warden, prison guard, Mr. Martini (sports commissioner), police inc commissioner, Red-Caps (4 polo players), Blues (4 polo players, Hotchkiss named), baseball commission employee, Vandervine family, hockey players, rink maintenance workers, cashier, polo, hockey & steeplechase attendees, polo ponies, police dispatcher (voice only), golfer (as statue)
LOCATIONS/ITEMS: Prison inc warden's office, Manhattan inc Sportsman's hideout, polo field, baseball box office, Martini's office, police HQ, Monroe Oval Arena, Outboard Motor Steeplechase pier, river, "Steve" & "Bucky's" apartment & Fenton's home (also in dfb); polo mallets & balls, golf bags & clubs, hockey sticks, pucks, ice skates, gas masks, TNT pellets, firearms, Fenton's toupee, nose plugs & false uppers, motor-driven surfboards
FLASHBACK: Gates goes to Fenton demanding the money he owes him. Fenton captures Gates and uses a toupee, nose plugs, and false teeth to impersonate him (d).
SYNOPSIS: After criminal gambler Gates is released from prison, he apparently recruits fellow criminals to rob sporting events. The gang, with Sportsman as leader, raid a polo match, dressed as polo players and riding horses. Cap and Bucky interrupt their robbery of the attendees, and pursue the fleeing felons on horseback, but Sportsman, who Cap recognizes as Gates, and company escape. After an encounter at a hockey arena, the heroes visit sports promoter Fenton's home. They find Gates, imprisoned and impersonated by Fenton, to set him up to blame for Sportsman's crimes. When Sportsman and company rob an outboard motor steeplechase, Cap and Bucky outmaneuver them on motor-driven surfboards and capture them.

4TH STORY: "The Wax Doctor!" (7 pages)
CREDITS: Carmine Infantino (art)
FEATURE CHARACTER: Human Torch (also as wax figure)
SUPPORTING CAST: Toro
VILLAINS: The Wax Doctor (Elena King, artist, also as wax figure), Harold King (Elena's brother)
OTHER CHARACTERS: Allen Waite, Jim Hargrave (both artists), police sergeant, telegram messenger, bartender, cafe patrons, Anthony

Lane (mentioned, died weeks before), men (as wax figures & masks)

LOCATIONS/ITEMS: Manhattan inc cafe, Elena's apartment, police HQ, cemetery, Wax Doctor's hideout/studio & Jim's apartment; Wax Doctor's wax cauldron, vapo-cloud bomb, smoke bomb & gun (on splash only), Jim's satchel of fake money

SYNOPSIS: Elena King tells fellow artists Allen and Jim that mutual friend Anthony Lane, having supposedly gone insane, has threatened to use a serum to change her into wax unless she pays him. The following day, Allen and Jim find Elena seemingly transformed. Receiving a similar letter, Allen contacts Torch and Toro, who meet him at police HQ. Although Allen pays the money, Jim, also threatened, refuses, and Torch convinces him to leave phony money. The Wax Doctor claims the "ransom" and immobilizes Torch with "vapo-gas." Toro, awaiting Torch's signal, finds a wax Torch. However, the Wax Doctor actually transports the Torch to a hideout, leaving a wax statue in his place. Toro traces Wax Doctor's discarded vapo-gas can to the hideout. Torch and Toro find the two villains threatening Jim and capture them, unmasking them as Elena, who made up dead Anthony Lane's involvement and faked her own death, and her brother Harold.

4TH STORY: "The House of Hate!" (13 pages)

CREDITS: Don Rico (pencils), Syd Shores (inks)

FEATURE CHARACTER: Captain America (next in AllWin #19, '46, WI #4, '77, dies, as corpse in Cap #215, '77 fb & Cap:P #1, '10, see NOTE)

SUPPORTING CAST: Bucky (next in AllWin #19, '46)

VILLAINS: The House of Hate (mansion imbued w/evil quasi-sentience, destroyed), Keys & Piggy (racketeers, both die)

OTHER CHARACTERS: Mark & Doris Smith (recently married couple), Derek Devens (actor, dies), bus driver (dies), Jason Tombs (as recorded voice, died 1/13/31), Tombs family members & victims (fb only, years before), disembodied heads (on splash only)

LOCATIONS/ITEMS: Road w/washed-out bridge, House of Hate w/bedrooms & gameroom; bus, Keys & Piggy's pistols, sword, gramophone w/recording cylinder, kerosene lamp, gun, knife, noose (prev 3 in fb)

FLASHBACK: Tombs family members, possessed by the house, commit murder.

SYNOPSIS: A washed-out bridge halts a bus, and its passengers, including Cap, Bucky and suspected criminals Keys and Piggy, take shelter at a hilltop mansion. Once there, the bus driver and passenger Derek Devens quarrel. Devens kills the driver with a sword from off the wall. Attacking Cap and Bucky, he falls against the blade and dies. Mark and Doris Smith, also go mad and attack each other. Cap locks them in separate rooms. Cap and Bucky quarrel. Seeing this, Keys and Piggy speak to them, stoking anger and resentment. The heroes fight but soon regain their senses. Cap stumbles against a gramophone that plays a recording in which Jason Tombs tells of a murder in a fit of rage during the house's construction, states that every Tombs family generation in the house was marked by hate and violence, and leaves this warning before committing suicide. Cap and Bucky pursue Keys and Piggy. The house catches fire from a shattered kerosene lamp. Keys and Piggy lapse into madness and kill each other. Cap and Bucky rescue the Smiths. With the House's destruction, the couple's love returns.

NOTE: Per modern continuity, this is William Nasland's final appearance as Captain America in this title. He next appears as Cap in AllWin #19, '46, his final golden age appearance, then dies in WI #4, '77, leaving Jeff Mace, the Patriot, to become Captain America.

TEXT STORY: "Melody for Murder" (2 pages)

CREDITS: Writer unknown

FEATURE CHARACTER: Chic "Maestro" Rand (police detective & opera lover)

VILLAIN: Orchestra flautist

OTHER CHARACTERS: Detective Tim Ryan, Enrico Mardi (opera singer, dies), police inc 2 detectives, opera house director, opera performers, conductor & orchestra members, opera attendees

LOCATIONS/ITEMS: Police HQ, opera house; orchestra's instruments, flute/pistol

SYNOPSIS: At a performance of Carmen, Detective Rand sees singer Mardi shot and killed. Determining the shot came from the orchestra pit, he instructs the orchestra to re-play the music from when the shot was fired. Rand's opera expertise enables him to notice a flautist has two flutes, one of which is a concealed gun. The flautist confesses he killed Mardi because the singer caught him stealing before the performance.

NOTE: Story appears between 3rd & 4th stories.

CAPTAIN AMERICA COMICS #59 (November 1946)

"The Private Life of Captain America!" (16 pages)

CREDITS: Stan Lee (writer & editorial and art director), Jack Binder (pencils), George Klein (inks), Al Sulman (editor), Syd Shores (art associate, c & "Secret Files" art)

FEATURE CHARACTER: Captain America (Jeff Mace, last in MC #74/4, '46 as the Patriot, chr last in Cap:P #1, '10, see NOTE)

SUPPORTING CAST: Bucky (Fred Davis, last in MC #78/4, '46)

GUEST STAR: Captain America (Steve Rogers, in rfb and fb1 during CapC #1, '41, see NOTE)

VILLAINS: The Fire Bandits (criminals who arrange fires & rob targets dressed as firemen)

OTHER CHARACTERS: Snipe Gooligan (student in "Steve's" class, 1st, next in CapC #61/2, '47), "Steve's" students, other Lee School students, Henry Hawley (Lee School principal), Mrs. Gooligan (Snipe's mother), apartment house residents (mother & daughter), fire marshal, firefighters, autograph seekers, news vendor, police, worm, Dr. Abraham Erskine (as "Prof. Reinstein"), Heinz Krueger (Nazi spy), Bucky (James Buchanan Barnes), General Chester Phillips, army officer, J. Arthur Grover (prev 6 in rfb only), Abraham Lincoln (in picture on classroom wall), villainous faces (on splash only)

LOCATIONS/ITEMS: Manhattan inc Lee School (1st) w/"Steve's" classroom and Hawley's office, "Steve" and "Bucky's" apartment, "fashionable apartment house" (burning building), Snipe's apartment, Tiger Sweet perfume plant, police HQ & newsstand, Project: Rebirth scientific facility within curio shop (in fb1 & rfb), Camp Lehigh (in rfb); Snipe's salesbook, darts, top, pea shooter, marbles & perfume sample, Fire Bandits' firearms, & perfume bottles w/acid and incendiary fluid, "Reinstein's" super-soldier serum & equipment, Krueger's pistol (both in rfb only)

FLASHBACK: Prof. Reinstein transforms Steve Rogers into a super-soldier. A Nazi spy kills Reinstein (CapC #1, '41). Steve strikes the spy, then flees (1, see NOTE). Steve becomes Captain America. When Bucky Barnes discovers his secret identity, Cap takes him as a partner (CapC #1, '41).

SYNOPSIS: Steve accepts a teaching job at Lee School and Bucky becomes a student. They meet mischievous student Snipe, who sells Tiger Sweet perfume after school. When an apartment house catches fire, Cap and Bucky find three "firefighters" attempting to rob an apartment. One Fire Bandit turns a hose on the heroes to cover an escape. With the fire under control, Cap and Bucky consult the fire marshal, who reveals five previous fire sites were similarly burgled. The next day, Steve and Bucky see Snipe talking to the Bandits. Realizing Snipe has sold perfume at every fire site, Cap and Bucky head for the perfume distributor. Snipe also makes the connection and confronts the Bandits. Cap and Bucky arrive and fight the criminals, while Snipe sets off the building's sprinklers, bringing firefighters who join the heroes. Later, Cap reveals the perfume bottles conceal acid and incendiary fluid, designed to start the fires.

NOTE: Contains "From the Secret Files of Captain America" (1 page), a Table of Contents featuring Captain America, Bucky, "Steve Rogers," "Bucky Barnes," & reproductions of the 4 stories' splash pages. WI #4, '77 reveals Jeff Mace took over as Captain America from the deceased William Nasland in late 1946; thus, per modern continuity, "Steve Rogers" is actually Mace from this story until CapC #74, '49. Principal Hawley's postcard to "Steve" is dated Feb. 1, 1946 indicating the story takes place over several days in February 1946; however, since, per modern continuity, William Nasland held the Captain America identity at that time, this date must be attributed to story error. "Steve" acts as geography teacher in this story. The flashback implies that, after becoming a super-soldier, Steve fled the government, but this can be interpreted as him briefly departing the room, as depicted in Next #9, '06 fb. Flashback also incorrectly depicts "Reinstein" himself giving Steve the "Captain America" codename, which was not selected until months later. Since, per modern continuity, the Cap/"Steve" in this story is not actually Steve Rogers, his appearance in flashback qualifies him as a Guest Star.

2ND STORY: "Pennies from Heaven!" (12 pages)
CREDITS: Syd Shores (pencils), Vince Alascia (inks)
FEATURE CHARACTER: Captain America (also in newspaper photo)
SUPPORTING CAST: Bucky (also in newspaper photo)
VILLAINS: The Modern Robin Hood (Joshua Blaine, weapon collector), Little John & Friar Tuck (Modern Robin Hood's accomplices)
OTHER CHARACTERS: Peter Pinchtight (wealthy miser), reporter, tenement district residents, street sweeper, bystanders, Lee School students (Tommy named), Abraham Lincoln (in picture on classroom wall), Liberty (on coins), birds
LOCATIONS/ITEMS: Manhattan inc Lee School w/"Steve's" classroom, tenement district, Sedgeham Towers w/Blaine's penthouse (# 42), Pinchtight residence inc basement, department store (street # 68); Blaine's weapon collection inc bow, arrows, 2 quivers, swords & spears, Little John's bat, Friar Tuck's staff, coins
SYNOPSIS: Over several days, the Modern Robin Hood hurls thousands of dollars in change upon the tenement district, winning residents' devotion. When Robin and associates extort miser Pinchtight to "give to the poor," Cap and Bucky intervene, but the criminals escape. The next day, the heroes visit the tenement district, where Robin again hurls money to the streets. Cap and Bucky catch the crooks but the tenement dwellers step in the way so that Robin and his men can escape. Seeking info on Robin's arrows, Cap and Bucky visit weapon expert Joshua Blaine's apartment, where Robin shoots an arrow with a note into the room, demanding Blaine "donate to the poor." Cap and Bucky defeat Little John & Tuck, but Robin escapes. When Blaine returns, Cap, noticing Blaine's decorative quiver lacks arrows, realizes Blaine is Robin, who kept half of what he stole for himself. Cap captures him.
NOTE: "Steve," described as a substitute teacher, teaches medieval history here.

3RD STORY: "The Case of the Borrowed Eyes" (7 pages)
CREDITS: Carmine Infantino (art)
FEATURE CHARACTER: Human Torch (also as butler & Swami's voice, next in HT #25, MC #79, '46, AllWin #21, '46, AllWin Spec #1, '09, Cap:P #2, '10, MC #80, '47)
SUPPORTING CAST: Toro (last in MC #78/4, '46, next in HT #25, '46)
VILLAIN: Ed Fallon ("Count de List," man w/hypnotic power from eye transplants)
OTHER CHARACTERS: Police (Sgt. Heneker named), Marge (Fallon's girlfriend), 3 doctors, nurse, hospital receptionist, Fallon's robbery victims, Rajah Swami Sabini (mentioned, deceased, Fallon receives his eyes), party voices (on phonograph), five people's eyes (on splash only)
LOCATIONS/ITEMS: Manhattan inc General Hospital w/operating room, police HQ, Central Park, Marge and Fallon's apartments, van Allister 5th Ave mansion & 536 E. 6th (Fallon's former address, mentioned); Fallon's chemical spray, trunk, phonograph w/record, Braille hospital handbook
SYNOPSIS: At General Hospital, blind Ed Fallon receives a new set of eyes, donated by renowned occultist Rajah Swami Sabini. The eyes grant Fallon sight and mesmeric power, which he uses to hypnotize and rob people. Later, Torch and Toro find Fallon robbing a victim in Central Park. Fallon mesmerizes the heroes into immobility and escapes but drops a Braille hospital handbook, leading Torch and Toro to General Hospital where they learn his name. They set a trap with a fake society party, but Fallon dowses their flames with chemical spray and locks them in a trunk. While they escape, Fallon reveals his new power and wealth to his girlfriend Marge, who criticizes him for using such power for evil. He almost strikes her, but a ghostly voice reprimands him and threatens to take back the eyes. The voice belongs to Torch, who swoops in and knocks out the distracted Fallon.

4TH STORY: "House of Hallucinations!" (7 pages)

CREDITS: Syd Shores (pencils), Allen Simon (inks)

FEATURE CHARACTER: Captain America (next in AllWin #21, '46, AllWin Spec #1,'09, Cap:P #2, '10, MC #80/5, '47)

SUPPORTING CAST: Bucky (also in dfb, next in MC #79/4, '46)

VILLAINS: The Great Amazo (magician, also in dfb) & 3 underlings (1 on splash only)

OTHER CHARACTERS: Tommy Colman (one of Steve's students), Jim Markham (theatre producer, also in dfb)

LOCATIONS/ITEMS: Manhattan inc Lee School w/"Steve's" classroom, Amazo's "house of hallucinations" (street # 21) w/basement; Amazo's 2 suits of armor, swords, smoke bomb, hook & prop gun (shoots flower bouquet), Tommy's fishing pole, underling's pistol (on splash only)

FLASHBACK: Amazo uses trap doors and secret passages to make Markham, Bucky, & himself disappear (d).

SYNOPSIS: Concerned about Tommy Colman's low grades, Steve and Bucky visit his supposed home, where a man curtly dismisses them. Suspicious, Cap and Bucky return to the house, where they see the man, the Great Amazo, and two assistants forcing another man into a large basket, which Amazo then stabs with swords. The two burst in, but Amazo reveals the basket is empty. He then uses a tablecloth to seemingly make Bucky disappear, then disappears into smoke himself. An armored assistant knocks Cap out & takes him to the basement, where Bucky and the basket victim, producer Jim Markham, are held captive; Markham for canceling Amazo's stage act. Cap escapes his bonds to knock out the assistants. Amazo draws a prop gun by mistake and is quickly punched out.

NOTE: Tommy Colman should not be confused with Tommy from the 2nd story.

TEXT STORY: "Lost Island" (2 pages)

CREDITS: Writer unknown

FEATURE CHARACTER: Steve Galway (writer/artist, also in fb during WWII)

VILLAINS: 6 head-hunters (more bts, 5 die), Italian soldiers (some die, in fb only)

OTHER CHARACTERS: Cruise ship crew & guests, 2nd island inhabitants, Galway's fellow US soldiers (in fb only), shrunken heads

LOCATIONS/ITEMS: Atlantic Ocean, West Indies inc 2 islands, wartime Italian front (in fb); cruise ship (sinks), lifeboats, headhunters' boat, pitch cauldrons, stakes, blowgun, poisoned darts & feathers, Italians' machine gun & additional firearms (in fb)

FLASHBACK: In Italy during WWII, Steve Galway rescues fellow soldiers from an enemy patrol by distracting the enemy long enough to seize a machine gun and kill them.

SYNOPSIS: Steve takes a West Indies cruise to gather information for a book, but a storm wrecks the ship. The crew and passengers escape by lifeboats that drift in different directions. When Steve's lifeboat runs aground, he scouts the area and finds shrunken human heads. Returning to the beach, he discovers the other passengers gone, abducted by headhunters. Remembering his wartime experiences, Steve acquires a blowgun with poisoned darts and kills five headhunters, then captures a sixth, who leads the survivors to a friendlier island. There the passengers reunite with additional survivors and the headhunter is arrested.

NOTE: Story appears between 2nd & 3rd stories.

CAPTAIN AMERICA COMICS #60 (January 1947)

"The Human Fly!" (12 pages)

CREDITS: Mike Roy (pencils, c inks), Al Avison (inks), Al Sulman (editorial associate), Syd Shores (art associate, "Secret Files" art), Stan Lee (managing editor, director of art), Vince Alascia (c pencils)

FEATURE CHARACTER: Captain America

SUPPORTING CAST: Bucky (last in MC #80/5, '47)

VILLAINS: The Human Fly (Hy Heale, window washer & Hi-Low Window Washing president)

OTHER CHARACTERS: "Steve's" students, the Human Fly (Mike Galen, circus performer), Vera (circus performer & Mike's girlfriend), ringmaster, clown, circus attendees, office worker (on building's 30th floor), night watchman, Galen's opera house supervisor, opera patrons, John Moth (lighthouse keeper), woman (on cover only)

LOCATIONS/ITEMS: Circus inc Big Top & Galen's dressing room, Manhattan inc skyscraper w/30th floor, penthouse, clock tower, opera house, Hi-Low Window Washing Co. offices & water tower (cover only), Shoal Island w/lighthouse; Cap's helicopter, Human Fly's suction discs, lighthouse food stash inc molasses

SYNOPSIS: Steve, Bucky, and students attend the circus, where "Human Fly" performer Mike Galen nearly dies in a fall and loses his nerve for heights. The next night, Steve and Bucky see a Human Fly climbing a skyscraper. Cap and Bucky investigate, but the Fly kicks Cap off the building and escapes. After questioning Galen's girlfriend, Cap and Bucky, via helicopter, spot the Fly breaking into a penthouse. When the Fly parachutes to the ground, Bucky jumps after him. The Fly uses Bucky to break his fall and escapes. Suspecting Galen, Cap and Bucky track him to an opera house, presuming he plans robbery, but Galen has taken a backstage catwalk job to reaccustom himself to heights. He tells Cap and Bucky a window washer stole his spare costume. At Hi-Low Window Washing, they find a news clipping about a lighthouse keeper's valuable stamp collection. They reach the lighthouse shortly after the Fly, who trips over a food stash and gets stuck in molasses, allowing Cap to unmask him as Hi-Low president Hy Heale.

NOTE: Contains "From the Secret Files of Captain America" (1 page), a Table of Contents featuring Captain America, Bucky, "Steve Rogers," "Bucky Barnes," & reproductions of the 4 stories' splash pages.

2ND STORY: "The Last Case of Inspector Leeds!" (12 pages)

CREDITS: Mike Sekowsky (pencils), Al Avison (inks)

FEATURE CHARACTER: Captain America

SUPPORTING CAST: Bucky

VILLAINS: Broadway Lil Carter, Rocky Rhoads (also in photo), Sheik Moline (Schooner Club owner) his 2 bodyguards & 4 henchmen, 4

Schooner Club employees

OTHER CHARACTERS: Inspector Leeds (dies), female student (others off-panel in classroom), Sure Life employee, morgue attendant, police inc desk sergeant, dogs, drifter (mentioned, killed w/gunshot to the face so Lil could identify his body as Rocky)

LOCATIONS/ITEMS: Manhattan inc Lee School w/"Steve's" classroom & "Steve" & "Bucky's" apartment, Leeds' home, Broadway Lil's apartment, Main Street, Schooner Club inc gaming room w/pool tables & Sheik's office, Sure Life Insurance Co., city morgue, police HQ; crooks' firearms, knives & blackjacks, Lil's knife & $50,000 check, Rocky's signet ring & gun, duplicate ring (on corpse), Leeds' journal

SYNOPSIS: Retired police detective and insurance investigator Leeds, known for solving every case, supposedly commits suicide, his journal citing his failure to solve criminal Rocky Rhoads' death. Cap and Bucky tackle the case, questioning Rhoads' girlfriend Broadway Lil, but gambler Sheik Moline interrupts. After outfighting Sheik and his bodyguards, Cap and Bucky visit Sheik's Schooner Club gambling house where they find a $50,000 check from Lil to Sheik, implying Lil hired Sheik to kill Rhoads. Revisiting Lil's apartment, Cap sees Lil has kept Rocky's ring and photo, suggesting she still loves him. At the morgue, Cap learns Rhoads was killed by a shotgun blast to the face, leaving him unrecognizable, and was found wearing his ring. Cap and Bucky follow Lil to the Schooner Club and find Rocky Rhoads, alive and well, having faked his death to collect insurance. Cap gives credit for solving the case to Leeds, whom he believes was killed by Rhoads because he discovered the truth.

NOTE: Story begins on a Saturday.

3RD STORY: "The Catman Murders!" (7 pages)

CREDITS: Carmine Infantino (pencils)

FEATURE CHARACTER: Human Torch (also as "Jim Ames, writer," next in SenSH #22, '90)

SUPPORTING CAST: Toro (also as "Jim Ames' brother," chr next in SenSH #22, '90)

VILLAINS: The Catman (Kindly Hand asylum patient, also on Wanted poster on splash, dies; see NOTE), Dr. Francis (Kindly Hand doctor, also as "Dr. Kale")

OTHER CHARACTERS: Police (Fred named) inc chief, 5 "claw murder" victims (3 bts, 1 on splash only, all die), nurse, 2 fishermen, surviving victim, his daughter (mentioned), cat, Dr. Kale (mentioned)

LOCATIONS/ITEMS: Manhattan inc police HQ, alley, General Hospital w/victim's room & Kindly Hand Charity Hospital w/basement and Francis' office, adjoining bay; fishing schooner, Francis' Dr. Kale mask, gun & 2Q8 explosive

SYNOPSIS: At the police chief's request, Torch and Toro investigate "the claw murders" and find the killer, a costumed Catman, who escapes, his latest victim still alive. Hospitalized, the victim identifies his life insurance policy beneficiary as humanitarian Dr. Kale. Learning Kale is also beneficiary to other victims, Torch and Toro visit his hospital and meet Dr. Francis. Later, they find "Kale" providing instructions to Catman, a mental patient devoted to Kale. Catman delays them while "Kale" escapes. The heroes find Francis in his office but Toro finds a Dr. Kale mask and realizes Francis has been impersonating Kale. Francis threatens to blow up the hospital. Thinking he is protecting Kale, Catman tackles Francis, and both fall through a window into a nearby bay. Catman dies. Torch and Toro turn Francis over to the police.

NOTE: Torch battles a Cat-Man in CapC #52/2, '46. While the two similarly named villains appear to be different people, since this issue's Catman is not seen unmasked, it is feasible that he is CapC #52's Peter Blake, committed rather than imprisoned after capture, with his interest in felines now full blown insanity.

4TH STORY: "Let's Play Detective: The Case of the Careless Killers" (1 page)

CREDITS: Al Bellman (art)

FEATURE CHARACTER: Mike Trapp

SUPPORTING CAST: Pepper Burns (last in CapC #58/2, '46)

VILLAINS: Richard (Christy's nephew) & Christy's niece

OTHER CHARACTERS: Christy (middle-aged woman, dies), Christy's lawyer (mentioned)

LOCATIONS/ITEMS: Manhattan inc Christy's home; sleeping pills, gardenias

SYNOPSIS: An ailing woman's nephew and niece give her a sleeping pill overdose, then remove petals from the gardenias they brought their aunt to imply they have not visited her in days. When Trapp investigates, he realizes that gardenias, which never shed petals, have been tampered with, and confronts the two with their lie.

5TH STORY: "The Big Fight!" (10 pages)

CREDITS: George Klein (pencils)

FEATURE CHARACTER: Captain America (next in SenSH #22, '90)

SUPPORTING CAST: Bucky (chr next in SenSH #22, '90)

VILLAINS: "Hatchetface" (criminal leader) & 7 henchmen (Butch named), 5 delinquents

OTHER CHARACTERS: Roundhouse Kelly (janitor & 1918 boxing champ), Tim Kelly (Roundhouse's son), police, Kid Gloves contenders, boxing match attendees, referee, gym employees, boxing commission member (others bts, award Cap $500), storekeeper, customer, woman & child bystanders, fur truck driver (bts, truck attacked by Hatchetface's men), Death, screaming woman (both on splash only)

LOCATIONS/ITEMS: Manhattan inc downtown store, Lee School w/gymnasium, Kelly apartment, gym w/phone booth, boxing arena w/dressing rooms & "Hatchetface's" hideout, Highway 8 near bridge; Knight's Fine Furs truck, criminals' firearms, delinquents' clubs, barbells, punching bags

SYNOPSIS: Bucky helps young Tim Kelly against delinquents who mock Tim's father. Tim introduces Bucky to his father, Roundhouse Kelly, ex-boxing champion turned janitor. Bucky hurries to join Cap in action but arrives to find the criminals, fur thieves, already defeated. Cap declares the real target is the criminals' boss, "Hatchetface." Later, Bucky enters a Kid Gloves boxing contest to win money for Lee School athletic equipment, but Tim enters as well, wanting money to help Roundhouse open a gym. The two become the finalists. The day of the match, "Hatchetface" tries to bully Tim into throwing the fight. "Hatchetface" and company return that night to re-emphasize their point, but Cap and Bucky defeat them, with Roundhouse knocking out "Hatchetface." Spraining his ankle in the fray, Bucky loses the match to Tim, who wins the money, but the boxing commission rewards Cap an equal amount for preventing "Hatchetface's" involvement.

NOTE: Hatchetface's name is rendered in quotation marks throughout the story.

TEXT STORY: "Evidence on File" (2 pages)

CREDITS: Writer unknown

FEATURE CHARACTER: Nick Banion (police detective)

VILLAIN: Charlie Green (Palomar Café owner)

OTHER CHARACTERS: Dinsmore Grogan (bartender), Banion's co-worker (bts, looks up gun's serial number), sheriff, coroner (both mentioned), gambler (as corpse)

LOCATIONS/ITEMS: Palomar Café & surrounding grounds; 2 roulette wheels, card & dice tables, Green's .38 revolver (bought 10 years ago) & keys, Banion's pistol, 5-cell flashlight, handcuffs & forensics kit w/5-vt light, camera, flashgun, bulbs, bottles of reagenters inc copper sulphate, hydrochloric acid and distilled water

SYNOPSIS: Detective Banion investigates a murder at the Palomar Café, known for illegal gambling. He finds a pistol with its serial numbers filed off, of which café owner Charlie Green claims ignorance. However, Banion uses his car's forensics kit to excavate the numbers. Calling them in, he learns the pistol belongs to Green, who killed a patron who won too much.

NOTE: Story appears between 2nd & 3rd stories. The name "Palomar Café" implies the story takes place in California.

CAPTAIN AMERICA COMICS #61 (March 1947)

"The Red Skull Strikes Back" (12 pages)

CREDITS: Al Avison (pencils), Syd Shores (inks), Vince Alascia (c pencils), Mike Roy (c inks)

FEATURE CHARACTER: Captain America

SUPPORTING CAST: Bucky (chr last in SenSH #22, '90)

VILLAINS: The Red Skull (also as electrician, possibly dies, see NOTE), 3 death row inmates

OTHER CHARACTERS: Prison warden, prison guards (Bob named), City Hospital administrator, truck drivers, 2 paramedics (1 bts, off-panel), bystanders, captured woman, 5 additional Red Skull underlings (both on cover only)

LOCATIONS/ITEMS: State Prison inc warden's office, condemned row, death chamber & adjacent swamp, city inc General Hospital w/administrator's office, lake, dam & power plant inc water outlet #3 and power room, "Steve" & "Bucky's" apartment; Red Skull's swamp boat, electrician truck, mine detector, grappling hook, pistol & handcuffs, convicts' firearms, electric chair, guards' billy clubs, drug shipments (bts, stolen by Skull), underlings' guns (on cover only)

SYNOPSIS: Red Skull frees three death row inmates, who become his henchmen in a medicine-stealing crime spree. Planting a news story about a penicillin shipment, Cap and Bucky lure Red Skull and company into a trap. When the Skull and one henchman flee to a nearby dam in their swamp boat, Cap and Bucky lasso it and water-ski behind on Cap's shield. When the crooks reach a water outlet, Red Skull floods it, rendering the heroes unconscious. The Skull ties them to the power room's arc poles, intending to electrocute them. Cap breaks an insulator, stopping the charge, then breaks free and fights the criminals. Bucky escapes and pitches in. Red Skull flees to the dam's top. Cap catches up, and they struggle until the Skull falls over the edge.

NOTE: At the story's beginning, Cap initially believes the Red Skull is already dead. Since Jeff Mace, as Patriot, accompanied Cap on a mission which seemingly resulted in the Red Skull (Johann Shmidt)'s death in Cap Ann #13, '94, this belief is understandable. Since Shmidt is in suspended animation at this time, and the communist Red Skull (Albert Malik) has not yet debuted, it is unclear who the Red Skull in this story is; he may be George Maxon (last in CapC #3, '41) or another Shmidt impersonator.

2ND STORY: "The Bullfrog Terror!" (12 pages)

CREDITS: Al Avison (pencils), Syd Shores (inks)

FEATURE CHARACTER: Captain America

SUPPORTING CAST: Bucky

VILLAIN: The Bullfrog (Kelsey Riordan, gangster)

OTHER CHARACTERS: Snipe Gooligan (also in newspaper photo, last in CapC #59, '46), "Steve's" students, Yvonne (actress, also in newspaper photos), producer (bts, hosts party), Dan (PR man, impersonates Bullfrog), costume ball attendees, hotel employees, police, reporter, bystanders, bullfrogs (1 as biology chart)

LOCATIONS/ITEMS: State penitentiary & adjacent marshes w/Bullfrog's hideout & frog well, river, Manhattan inc Lee School w/"Steve's" classroom, hotel & "Steve" and "Bucky's" apartment; producer's yacht, Yvonne's Green Lake Emerald necklace, Bucky's autograph book, Bullfrog's coiled springs

SYNOPSIS: Escaping prison, Riordan invents coiled spring boots and becomes the costumed criminal Bullfrog. He tries to steal an emerald necklace from French actress Yvonne, whose autograph a smitten Bucky, accompanied by Snipe, is seeking. Bucky drives Bullfrog away, but Snipe finds the necklace and Yvonne considers him a hero. Suspecting the incident is a publicity stunt, Cap visits a costume ball on Yvonne's producer's yacht. A fake Bullfrog does interrupts the party, but so does the real one, who evades Cap and departs. While Cap pursues him underwater, Bullfrog swims to a well near his hideout, where Bucky is hunting frogs to bring Yvonne who expressed a taste for frogs' legs. Bullfrog attacks Bucky, whose shout draws Cap. Cap defeats Bullfrog and Bucky brings frogs to Yvonne but finds the appalled actress is actually a Brooklynite who fakes her French mannerisms.

NOTE: Bullfrog's coil-boots are nearly identical to those developed many years later by Daredevil's enemy Leap-Frog (Vincent Patilio), in DD #25, '67. "Steve" is a biology teacher in this story. "Bucky's" quest for autographs continues in the 5th story.

3RD STORY: "The Green Mask Killer!" (7 pages)

CREDITS: Carmine Infantino (art)

FEATURE CHARACTER: Human Torch (next in HT #26, '47, MC #81, '47)

SUPPORTING CAST: Toro (chr last in SenSH #22, '90, next in HT #26, '47)

VILLAIN: The Green Mask Killer (Silas Stevens)

OTHER CHARACTERS: Hillary King (writer), Ellabella Wilkins (King's landlady), police (2 bts, posted at King's room) inc desk sergeant, Roger Hatch (attorney & King's uncle, as corpse), Richard Alton (Hatch's law partner, as corpse), King's neighbors, Hatch's neighbors (bts, phone police), duplicate Green Mask Killers, hanged man (both on splash only)

LOCATIONS/ITEMS: Manhattan inc King's rooming house (446 W. 83rd), police HQ, Hatch's home (1002 West End), Alton's home (12 Sutton) & Stevens' apartment (across the court from King's room); Green Mask Killer's gun, & atomizer w/"ethero fumes," King's typewriter & "The Green Mask Killer" manuscript, Hatch's torn letter

SYNOPSIS: After frustrated writer Hillary King threatens his uncle, wealthy attorney Roger Hatch, King's landlady reports him to the police. Torch and Toro agree to investigate. They find Hatch dead and pursue the murderer, the Green Mask Killer, who uses a water tank to deluge them and flees. They fly to King's rooming house but find him absent. Torch checks King's unfinished manuscript, in which a fictional Green Mask Killer kills his uncle, then his uncle's business partner. They subsequently find Hatch's partner dead. Later, Torch and Toro return to Hatch's home, where they find a blackmail letter. The Green Mask Killer blasts them with sleeping fumes and recovers the letter. Deducing the true killer, Torch and Toro return to King neighbor Silas Stevens' apartment, where the Killer menaces the writer. Torch unmasks him as Stevens, who reveals Hatch and Alton were blackmailing him, explaining that, as a lip reader, he could see King through his window talking aloud while writing his story, leading him to model his murders after King's tale.

4TH STORY: "Let's Play Detective: Stop That Swindle!" (2 pages)
CREDITS: Al Bellman (art)
FEATURE CHARACTER: Mike Trapp
VILLAINS: Roscoe & Krane (garage owners)
OTHER CHARACTER: Dugan (soldier)
LOCATIONS/ITEMS: Manhattan inc Acme Garage & Trapp's office, Camp Kind, TN (mentioned, return address on envelope); papers, forged envelope
SYNOPSIS: When garage owners falsely claim a returning soldier sold them the car he only placed in storage, the soldier seeks Trapp's help. The garage owners show Trapp a stamped envelope in which they supposedly received the soldier's signed bill of sale, but Trapp, knowing that servicemen can mail letters postage-free, confronts them about the lie, and they pay the soldier four times what the car is worth.
NOTE: Trapp is again identified as a private detective.

5TH STORY: "Death Enters...Laughing!" (10 pages)
CREDITS: Stan Lee (writer), Syd Shores (art)
FEATURE CHARACTER: Captain America (next in MC #81/5, '47)
SUPPORTING CAST: Bucky, Betsy Ross (also as "Marie Antoinette," last in CapC #44/3, '45, chr last in Cap:P #2, '10, next in MC #81/5, '47, see NOTE)
VILLAINS: Laughing Boy (merry yet sadistic criminal, also in fb1 as infant, fb2 as young boy & fb3 as reform school youth) & 3 henchmen
OTHER CHARACTERS: "Steve's" students, Susan Dane (actress, also as "Marie Antoinette," in fb2 & in newspaper photo), movie director, cameramen, other film crew members, Laughing Boy's mother, truck driver (voice only, driving truck in accident), accident victim (dies), bystanders (prev 4 in fb1), teacher, student (dies) (both in fb2), reform school guards, Laughing Boy's reform school roommate (dies) (both in fb3)
LOCATIONS/ITEMS: Manhattan inc Lee School w/"Steve's" classroom, Laughing Boy's hideout, "Steve" and "Bucky's" apartment, Betsy's apartment, "French Revolution" movie set inc Susan's dressing room, Bastille set, school (in fb2), reform school (in fb3); movie cameras, microphones & stage lights, Laughing Boy's gun & knife (on splash only), henchmen's firearms, guillotine, Betsy's spiked shoe, "Bucky's" autograph book, Marie Antoinette Jewels, baby carriage (in fb1), guards' billy clubs (in fb3)
FLASHBACK: As an infant, the future Laughing Boy sees a man killed in an accident and laughs (1). As a youth, he pushes another boy out a window to his death. Susan Dane reports him, and Laughing Boy promises vengeance (2). Sent to reform school, Laughing Boy knocks out his roommate with a hammer (3).
SYNOPSIS: Learning of Bucky's book of movie star autographs, Laughing Boy and henchmen steal it, then use it to forge checks, robbing the stars. Suspecting Laughing Boy will seek more autographs, Cap and Bucky travel to Hollywood, as does Betsy Ross, who is vacationing with Susan Dane, now an actress. Laughing Boy, seeking vengeance for Susan's actions years before, abducts her. Cap and Bucky pursue and prevent him from guillotining her on a French Revolution set. He flees up a set wall but, losing his balance, is reduced to sobbing for help. Cap turns him over to police. Later, after Bucky has acquired many more star autographs, the three depart Hollywood.
NOTE: Betty Ross is called "Betsy Ross" through the rest of her appearances. "Steve" is a psychology teacher here.

TEXT STORY: "Nine Points of the Law!" (2 pages)
CREDITS: Writer unknown
FEATURE CHARACTER: John S. McClure
VILLAIN: Wes Miller (gunman, Full House Bar owner, dies)
OTHER CHARACTERS: Stationmaster, hotel clerk & wife, Full House Bar patrons (Wilson named) inc rancher & cowpuncher, Rimrock residents, Big John McClure (McClure's father, mentioned, died 15 years before)
LOCATIONS/ITEMS: Rimrock (Kansas) inc train station, feed store/Aurora Hotel inc Room #10, Full House Bar, Circle O Ranch (mentioned); McClure's suitcase, 2 .44s, short-barreled .38 & document, Miller's two .45s, additional firearms
SYNOPSIS: John McClure arrives in Rimrock, where Wes Miller killed the town's sheriff, John's father, and claimed his ranch 15 years before. In a saloon, McClure awaits a confrontation with Miller, who soon arrives. When McClure claims his father's ranch, Miller draws his gun, but McClure kills him with a hidden gun.
NOTE: Story appears between 2nd & 3rd stories. Followed by "Captain America Fun Page" (1 page), featuring Captain America, Bucky & puzzles.

CAPTAIN AMERICA COMICS #62 (May 1947)

"The Kingdom of Terror!" (12 pages)

CREDITS: Otto Binder (writer), Al Avison (pencils), Syd Shores (inks, c art)
FEATURE CHARACTER: Captain America (also on dartboard & newspaper photo)
SUPPORTING CAST: Bucky (last in MC #81/5, '47), Betsy Ross
VILLAINS: The Black Baron (Old Man Rumford's former butler), Queenie (Old Man Rumford's former maid) & their Crime Club inc bellboy & waiters, Barney Bates (wanted crook) & other guests
OTHER CHARACTERS: Armed messenger, cab driver, Peerless Paper employee, Old Man Rumford (deceased, mentioned, built bomb shelter), police, Amazon women (cover only)
LOCATIONS/ITEMS: Lee School, Rumford mansion (88 Dorchester Drive) inc Crime Club (entrance through door in a tree) w/clothes closet, dining room, gaming room, Black Baron's office & bunk room, Peerless Paper Company; bellhop & crooks' guns, Amazon spears (cover only)
SYNOPSIS: Cap and Bucky pursue crooks who disappear on the Rumford mansion grounds. Bucky finds a dropped calling-card advertising the Crime Club, including "hide-out facilities." Cap, Bucky, and Betsy determine that the card was printed by the Peerless Paper company who confirm a recent delivery to the Rumford Mansion. There, they find a secret door in a tree, take an elevator underground, encounter the Crime Club bellboy stationed at the entrance and stuff him in a closet. Cap finds a coat and hat and infiltrates the club, confronting the Black Baron, the club's owner. Baron's men capture him. Baron explains that the Club is an old bomb shelter built by Old Man Rumford. Once Rumford died, Baron, Rumford's butler and Queenie, his maid, started their business. Before the crooks can execute Cap, Bucky, undercover in the bellboy's outfit, intervenes. Betsy arrives with the police to mop up.
NOTE: Betsy becomes a teacher at Lee School. The Crime Club rates are one third of the haul plus $100 a day for expenses. Story followed by "Captain America Fun Page" (1 page) featuring Captain America, Bucky & puzzles.

2ND STORY: "The Dance of Death!" (10 pages)
CREDITS: Otto Binder (writer), Syd Shores (pencils), Al Avison (inks)
FEATURE CHARACTER: Captain America
SUPPORTING CAST: Bucky, Betsy Ross (next in MC #82/5, '47)
VILLAINS: Signor Zagana & his gypsy troupe
OTHER CHARACTERS: Mrs. Thorndyke (wealthy socialite), Tinka (Yvonne Thorndyke, Mrs. Thorndyke's daughter), Mickey (Lee School student), Thorndyke's chauffeur, Thorndyke party guests, gypsy's horses
LOCATIONS/ITEMS: Lee School, Thorndyke estate, gypsy camp; gypsy wagon & knives, Tinka's tambourine & knife
SYNOPSIS: Cap and Bucky take Betsy to Mrs. Thorndyke's Ball. There, a gypsy troupe performs. While they play, their leader Zagana robs the mansion. Tinka, Zagana's daughter, disapproves of crime but supports her father. When Cap and Bucky tackle Zagana, Tinka steps in the way. Unwilling to strike a woman, Cap lets the gypsies escape, then lets Tinka escape as well in order to follow her to the gypsy camp. Aware of this, Tinka tips Zagana off. The gypsies capture Cap and Bucky and use them to show off their knife-throwing abilities, surrounding the heroes with blades. Betsy slips into camp and tells Tinka that her birthmark reveals she is actually Mrs. Thorndyke's daughter, kidnapped as an infant. Just as Zagana throws a knife directly at Cap's heart, Tinka deflects it with a knife throw of her own. Cap and Bucky mop up the gypsies and Tinka, in reality Yvonne Thorndyke, is reunited with her mother.

3RD STORY: "The Case of Blank Benny!" (7 pages)
CREDITS: Carmine Infantino (art)
FEATURE CHARACTER: Human Torch (next in MC #82, '47, HT #27, '47, SubC #23/3, '47)
SUPPORTING CAST: Toro (between MC #81/4-82, '47)
VILLAINS: Pruella & Priscilla Elton (Benny's sisters) & 3 criminals
OTHER CHARACTERS: "Blank Benny" Elton, car driver, pharmacist, gem store clerk, Police Inspector Drake, policeman
LOCATIONS/ITEMS: Manhattan inc drug store, Elton home at 8 West Street, gem shop, police HQ, 515 E. 50th St. & Central National Bank; hat w/"Sisel" written in hatband, sodium-terzum-chemo solution ("knockout"), hypo, ampule containing insulin, Ajax Safe Company safe, Elton sisters' rifles (both on splash)
SYNOPSIS: Torch and Toro find autistic Blank Benny standing in the middle of the street. Soon after, three crooks arrive and abduct him. Torch and Toro visit Benny's elderly sisters Pruella & Priscilla. When Torch finds "colored glass" on Benny's bedroom floor, the sisters describe Benny's love for such baubles, leading the heroes to a gem store that was recently robbed where a hat was found with the name "Sisel" in the band. Torch determines that "Sisel" is actually an address, 515 E. 50th. They travel there and find the crooks with Benny. Captured and placed in a safe, Torch and Toro escape by using the combination "Sisel." The pair find insulin ampules, looking like colored glass, and realize that the crooks are injecting Benny with insulin to bring his autistic "special talent" to the fore: safecracking. They find the crooks and Benny at a bank with Benny using his talents, unaware it is wrong. Captured, the crooks reveal that Pruella & Priscilla rented Benny out for part of the take.

4TH STORY: "Melody of Horror!" (12 pages)
CREDITS: Stan Lee (writer), Syd Shores (pencils), Al Avison (inks)
FEATURE CHARACTER: Captain America (next in MC #82/5, '47, Cap:P #2, '10)
SUPPORTING CAST: Bucky (next in MC #82/4, '47)
VILLAINS: The Mad Musician (Boris Dumarr, violinist, Prof. Carlotti's former star pupil, also as dummy) & his men
OTHER CHARACTERS: Professor Carlotti (Lee School music teacher), Rosa Dell (violinist, Prof. Carlotti's star pupil), Jim (Rosa's fiancé), Town Hall audience, MC & stage manager, Elizabethan and Conquistador figures (as dummies)

LOCATIONS/ITEMS: Manhattan inc Lee School & Town Hall w/Cap's box, Boris' Box, prompters' box and backstage dressing room; Carlotti's Stradivarius, substitute violin, sandbag

SYNOPSIS: Professor Carlotti invites Steve and Bucky to Town Hall to hear his star pupil Rosa Dell play his Stradavarius. Also there are Boris Dumarr, the jealous former star pupil and Jim, Rosa s fiancé who doesn t want her to have a musical career. As Rosa plays, the masked Mad Musician threatens her from the prompter's box, scaring her into fleeing the stage. Cap, suspecting Boris, checks his theater box but sees him sitting in it. He turns his suspicions to the missing Jim. In the ensuing confusion, the Musician steals the Stradavarius, substituting an inferior violin that screeches when Rosa plays. Cap and Bucky pursue the Musician, retrieving the Stradavarius. Rosa takes the stage a third time as the Musician attempts to drop a sandbag on her. Cap captures him, revealing him as Boris, who had placed a dummy in his seat in his box. Rosa becomes the hit Professor Carlotti expected. Jim returns and professes his love for her no matter what she decides to do.

5TH STORY: "Let's Play Detective: Gangster's Greed" (1 page)
CREDITS: Al Bellman (art)
FEATURE CHARACTER: Mike Trapp (last app to date, see NOTE)
SUPPORTING CAST: Pepper Burns
VILLAINS: Joey Morgan & his gang (bts, aided in the robbery)
OTHER CHARACTERS: Police
LOCATIONS/ITEMS: Police HQ inc Trapp's office, post office (in newspaper photo only)
SYNOPSIS: The Post Office is robbed of money order blanks. Trapp suspects criminal Joey Morgan. Hauling Joey in, he finds a money order for $150 in his possession. Joey claims his cousin paid off a debt but Trapp knows that the Post Office doesn't make out money orders for more than $100. Joey confesses.
NOTE: Mike Trapp is a policeman again here. Skip McCoy takes over the "Let's Play Detective" feature in CapC #66/3, '48.

TEXT STORY: "Science Pays Off!" (2 pages)
CREDITS: Writer unknown
FEATURE CHARACTER: Larry Denning (police scientist)
VILLAIN: Joe Durkin
OTHER CHARACTERS: Bull Maher (Larry's partner), desk sergeant, patrolman, jewelry store clerk, ambulance intern, Remmy (pool hall proprietor), pool hall idlers
LOCATIONS/ITEMS: Police HQ inc lab, Martier's jewelry store, Remmy's pool hall inc club room; Larry's microscope & gun, woolen thread, Bull's blackjack & Smith and Wesson .38, Joe's gun
SYNOPSIS: Larry and his partner Bull argue over the best police techniques. Larry believes in science while Bull believes in the old "rubber hose" methods. Called to a robbery at Martier's jewelry store where a clerk was shot, Larry finds a woolen thread from a suit. Bull, playing a hunch, goes to Remmy's pool hall to interrogate recently-released con Joe Durkin. Bull tricks Joe into revealing his guilt but has no evidence… until Larry scientifically proves that the thread came from Joe's suit.
NOTE: Appears between 2nd and 3rd stories.

CAPTAIN AMERICA COMICS #63 (July 1947)

"Captain America vs. the Tenpins of Terror!" (10 pages)

CREDITS: Stan Lee (writer), Syd Shores (pencils, c inks), Vince Alascia (inks, c pencils)
FEATURE CHARACTER: Captain America
SUPPORTING CAST: Bucky (last in in MC #82/5, '47, chr last in Cap:P #2, '10), Betsy Ross
VILLAINS: Rip Van Winkle (Hubert Van Poole, Mayda's cousin) & his gnomes (hired thugs), Don Juarez (fence)
OTHER CHARACTERS: Mayda Van Poole (Betsy's wealthy friend), bird (stuffed, in Mayda's home), cat (on The Kaatskills' knocker), caged woman (on cover only)
LOCATIONS/ITEMS: Manhattan inc Lee School & Van Poole home, The Kaatskills (abandoned inn), Don Juarez's shop; Mayda's rare stamps, old coins inc pebble money of Tagali natives & 1st editions inc Rip Van Winkle book, Rip's gun, net & dynamite, gnomes' bowling balls & pins
SYNOPSIS: Betsy Ross' friend Mayda Van Poole agrees to display her rare stamps, coins and 1st editions to help raise funds for Lee School. Her indolent cousin Hubert thinks she shouldn't loan them out to "any riffraff that walks in." At the school auditorium, Betsy and Mayda set up the Exhibit of Van Poole Collection. Just as Mayda shows Betsy her Rip Van Winkle 1st edition, Rip himself enters, accompanied by 4 gnomes, and robs them. Cap and Bucky intervene but Rip abducts Mayda and escapes. Overhearing Rip proclaim, "Off to the Catskills!" Cap deduces that the crooks are hiding out in The Kaatskills, an abandoned inn. Cap and Bucky enter to find the gnomes bowling. Rip captures them in a net and sets dynamite. Announcing he's taking Mayda's collection to the fence Don Juarez, Rip departs. Cap and Bucky get free and extinguish the dynamite. Mayda leads them to Don Juarez's shop where they defeat the gang and unmask Rip as Cousin Hubert.

2ND STORY: "The Parrot Strikes!" (13 pages)
CREDITS: Stan Lee (writer), Syd Shores (pencils), Jack Binder (inks)
FEATURE CHARACTER: Captain America (next in MC #83/5, '47)
SUPPORTING CAST: Bucky (next in MC #83/4, '47), Betsy Ross
VILLAINS: Mr. Polly & his men, Figaro (Mr. Polly's parrot)
OTHER CHARACTERS: Joan Chawson & her father (building contractors), Captain Salters (ship captain, dies), John Lee, Linda Shores, Ann Smith (prev 3 teachers, mentioned as moving to Lee School's new wing, see NOTE)
LOCATIONS/ITEMS: Manhattan inc Lee School w/half-built new wing and Chawson Contractor hut & docks w/freight loading building,

abandoned rock quarry; Mr. Polly's knife, crooks' guns, lumber, Joan's blank check

SYNOPSIS: Joan Chawson, Betsy's school friend, and her father are the contractors for Lee School's new wing. They tell Betsy, Steve and Bucky that the lumber they need to complete the job is coming in on a ship today. They all decide to meet it. Meanwhile, at the docks, Mr. Polly, a peanut-eating gang leader who resembles a parrot, kills the ship captain and his men load the lumber on trucks. Cap and Bucky intervene but the crooks escape. The next day, Polly's parrot Figaro delivers a note to the Chawsons, telling them to "bring a blank check" if they want the lumber. Steve convinces them to comply. Polly leads Betsy and Joan to an abandoned quarry; Mr. Polly's hideout. Cap and Bucky follow and fight the crooks but Polly buries them under the lumber, then departs. Freeing themselves, Cap and Bucky follow the trail of Polly's peanut shells and capture the crook and his gang.

NOTE: Two of the mentioned teachers are named for writer Stan Lee and penciler Syd Shores.

3RD STORY: "The Threat of the Asbestos Lady!" (7 pages)
CREDITS: Stan Lee (writer), Al Avison (pencils)
FEATURE CHARACTER: Human Torch (next in MC #83, '47, HT #28, '47)
SUPPORTING CAST: Toro (last in SubC #23/3, '47, next in MC #83, '47)
VILLAINS: Asbestos Lady (Victoria "Vicky" Murdock, Killer Murdock's twin sister, 1st but chr last in MKSM #9, '05 fb, next in HT #27, '47) & her 3 men (Jacques, Smiley, Lifter, all Killer Murdock's friends), Killer Murdock (dies)
OTHER CHARACTERS: Paula Goddit (actress), prison guards, police inc dispatcher (voice only)
LOCATIONS/ITEMS: Penitentiary inc gallows, shack on Old Simms Road (gang's hideout), Manhattan inc Torch and Toro's apartment; Asbestos Lady's asbestos suit, ray gun & glass cage, police & gang's guns, police axe
SYNOPSIS: After witnessing the execution of Killer Murdock, his twin sister vows revenge on Torch and Toro who captured him. Collecting Killer's three friends Jacques, Smiley, and Lifter as her gang, she dons an asbestos costume and becomes Asbestos Lady. The gang kidnaps actress Paula Goddit to lure Torch and Toro to their hideout, releasing her soon after their arrival. Paula tells the Torch that she was held in a nearby shack. When Torch and Toro enter, Asbestos Lady traps them in a fireproof glass cage. However, Paula summons the police. They round up the gang except for Asbestos Lady who escapes.
NOTE: Asbestos Lady's first name revealed in HT #27, '47.

TEXT STORY: "Diamond in the Rough" (2 pages)
CREDITS: Writer unknown
FEATURE CHARACTER: Dodge Cottrell (store detective, 1st, but chr last in CapC #72/TEXT, '49 fb, next in CapC #72/TEXT, '49)
VILLAIN: Anthony J. Caruthers (ring thief)
OTHER CHARACTERS: Carrol (department store manager), jewelry department clerk, store customers
LOCATIONS/ITEMS: Department store inc jewelry department & Carrol's 4th floor office; rings
SYNOPSIS: After Anthony J. Caruthers looks at some jewelry department rings, the clerk notices one is missing. He summons store detective Dodge Cottrell who takes Caruthers in a crowded elevator to the store manager's office. There, Cottrell searches Caruthers thoroughly but finds no ring. Caruthers threatens to sue and Cottrell escorts him out of the store, again taking a crowded elevator. Suddenly realizing the truth, Cottrell takes Caruthers back to the manager's office, by the stairs this time, then demands the ring. Caruthers, who had planted the ring on Cottrell in the elevator up and retrieved it in the elevator down, gives it up and surrenders.
NOTE: Story appears between 1st & 2nd stories.

CAPTAIN AMERICA COMICS #64 (October 1947)

"Sparkles Strikes Back!" (12 pages)

CREDITS: Stan Lee (writer), Vince Alascia (pencils), Ken Bald (inks), Al Avison (c pencils), Syd Shores (c inks)
FEATURE CHARACTER: Captain America
SUPPORTING CAST: Bucky (last in MC #83/5, '47), Betsy Ross (also as "Joan of Arc")
VILLAINS: Sparkles LaBelle (jewel thief), Cracker McGillis & their gang
OTHER CHARACTERS: Mrs. Monitawks (wealthy socialite), Jimmy Monitawks (her son), masquerade ball MC & guests inc "King Arthur" and Colonial patriot, car & cab drivers, doorman
LOCATIONS/ITEMS: Manhattan inc Monitawks' penthouse, Lee School w/auditorium & Sparkles' hideout; kornerupine rubies, gangs' guns
SYNOPSIS: Sparkles LaBelle, well-known jewel thief, is lying low as Mrs. Monitawks' maid but can't resist going after her employer's kornerpine rubies when she wears them to the Lee School masked ball. Sparkles has her gang set a fire, trying to rob Mrs. Monitawks in the confusion but Betsy Ross, in a Joan of Arc costume, stays with the wealthy woman. When Betsy leaves to get water, Sparkles slugs her and takes her costume, then robs Mrs. Monitawk framing Betsy with the crime. Wise to it all, Cap and Bucky follow Sparkles and her gang to their hideout, then to Mrs. Monitawk's home. While Cap and Bucky stop the gang, Betsy gets her revenge by tripping Sparkles.

2ND STORY: "Diamonds Spell Doom!" (11 pages)
CREDITS: Ken Bald (pencils), Al Gabriele (inks)
FEATURE CHARACTER: Captain America
SUPPORTING CAST: Bucky
VILLAINS: King Leer (Crown Colony Club owner, also in pfb) & his gang inc "Angel" (chief bouncer), Mitzi (cigarette girl, also in pfb) & "clumsy" waiter (in pfb)
OTHER CHARACTERS: Dean Thorp (Lee School Dean), Sylvia Thorp (Dean's niece, Gaylord Jewelry Company employee, also in pfb), Mr.

Gaylord (in pfb), Crown Colony Club guests (some in pfb), woman in powder room (in pfb), doorman, police

LOCATIONS/ITEMS: Manhattan inc Lee School w/"Steve's" classroom and Dean Thorp's office, Crown Colony Club w/powder room (in pfb), Leer's office and penthouse & Gaylord Jewelry (in pfb); necklace, imitation necklace, Leer's battleaxe & sword, Mitzi's cigarette tray, waiter's soup

FLASHBACK: Sylvia Thorp, instructed by Mr. Gaylord to wear a $22,000 necklace to promote his store, dines at the Crown Colony Club. A "clumsy" waiter spills soup on her and a cigarette girl, Mitzi, takes off the necklace, while helping her tidy up. When Sylvia returns to work, her boss tells her that the necklace is a fake and demands she pay for it within three days or be arrested (p).

SYNOPSIS: Cap and Bucky find Dean Thorp considering the theft of school funds to help his niece Sylvia. They accompany Sylvia to the Crown Club and search King Leer's office for the necklace but are caught. Leer takes them to his penthouse where he has Cap fight his bouncer "Angel." Cap wins and the necklace is found in Mitzi's cigarette tray. Leer confesses that when he learned Gaylord would display the necklace at his club, he had an imitation made, had the waiter dump soup on Sylvia and instructed Mitzi to switch the necklace.

3RD STORY: "Death is the Highest Bidder!" (7 pages)
CREDITS: Mike Sekowsky (pencils), Paul Reinman (inks)
FEATURE CHARACTER: Human Torch (next in MC #84, '47, HT #29, '47)
SUPPORTING CAST: Toro (last in HT #28, '47, next in MC #84, '47)
VILLAINS: Carl Correll (Johnson's assistant at Elite Furs), Hubert (west coast detective hired by Correll) & their men
OTHER CHARACTERS: Anne Richards, Jimmy Richards (Anne's brother, mentioned), Mitzi Miles (deceased, model at Elite Fur Company, mentioned), police, auction attendees, auctioneer, Mr. Johnson (Elite Fur owner)
LOCATIONS/ITEMS: Manhattan inc Mitzi's apartment building (#6), Gavelle Auction House, Elite Fur Company, Correll's home w/basement, police HQ & corner of 5th Ave and 34th Street (symbolic splash only); Mitzi's ashtray w/false bottom, "liquid special" (citric acetate, used for cleaning furs), letter in false bottom, guns (on splash)
SYNOPSIS: Anne Richards, whose brother Jimmy is accused of killing fur model Mitzi Miles, asks Torch and Toro for help. Finding out that Mitzi's effects are up for auction, they and Anne attend. Torch has Anne bid on any item that is commanding higher bids than its value. Anne buys an ashtray for $30 but is attacked afterward by a man who repels the Torch with citric acetate, a liquid used in fur cleaning. The man steals the ashtray. Visiting Elite Furs, Torch and Toro get on the trail of employee Carl Correll who had a fur-stealing scheme going with Mitzi, revealed in a letter kept in the false bottom of Mitzi's ashtray. When Mitzi wanted more money, Correll killed her. Torch and Toro defeat him and he confesses.

4TH STORY: "Terror at the Fair!" (12 pages)
CREDITS: Ken Bald (pencils), Al Avison, Syd Shores (inks)
FEATURE CHARACTER: Captain America (next in MC #84/4, '47, BlonPhan #16/2, '47, Cap:P #2, '10)
SUPPORTING CAST: Bucky (next in MC #84/4, '47), Betsy Ross (next in Cap #66, '48)
VILLAINS: Acrobat ("city of 1960" creator) & his men
OTHER CHARACTERS: Future Fair goers, Gloria DeVille (young society social worker and sponsor of the Future City exhibit) & her prize judges, birds, policeman, house-wrecking machine inventor, Maze of Madness ticker taker, performers, birds
LOCATIONS/ITEMS: Future Fair inc Future City models building, Acrobat's performance area, Maze of Madness & race track; Acrobat's water tank, Lee School's model city of the future, "future house wrecker machine" exhibit, racing car, envelope w/$10,000
SYNOPSIS: Cap, Bucky, and Betsy sponsor Lee School's exhibit of the model city of the future. When a thug hears sponsor Gloria Deville say that Lee School will win the blue ribbon, he tells his boss, the Acrobat who tries to set fire to the exhibit, fighting Cap and temporarily abducting Betsy. Soon after, he grabs Gloria, snatching an envelope in her possession. Cap captures the Acrobat, unmasking him as the thwarted inventor of the model "city of 1960." The envelope contains $10,000 in prize money, as Gloria tells the winners she plans to "promote future cities built according to your model." Gloria hands the money to Betsy who announces it will go to the Lee School lunch fund.
NOTE: A later Acrobat impersonates Cap in ST #114, '63.

TEXT STORY: "Recruit" (2 pages)
CREDITS: Writer Unknown
FEATURE CHARACTER: Johnny Walsh (policeman)
VILLAINS: Ducky Donaldson & his 3 assistants (Mike named)
OTHER CHARACTERS: Mary (policewoman, Johnny's girlfriend), "Peg" Donaldson (Ducky's kid brother, deceased, mentioned)
LOCATIONS/ITEMS: Warehouse, police HQ, Mary's house, cemetery inc Peg's grave; Mary & Johnny's .38s, gang's sub-machine gun & other guns
SYNOPSIS: Going on a tip that killer Ducky Donaldson is lying wounded in a warehouse, policeman Johnny Walsh walks into a trap. Ducky tells Johnny he is getting revenge for Johnny killing his kid brother and plans to take him past police headquarters, then past his girlfriend Mary's house to kill her in a drive-by until finally killing him at his brother's grave. As they drive past Mary, waiting outside for their date, Johnny puts up a fight, disrupting the plans and saving her. At the cemetery, Ducky prepares to kill Johnny but Mary who observed Johnny in the car, appears and shoots him. "Too bad," Johnny says, "You picked on a policewoman."
NOTE: Story appears between 2nd & 3rd stories.

"When Friends Turn Foes!" (12 pages)

CREDITS: Syd Shores (pencils, c art), Ken Bald (inks)
FEATURE CHARACTER: Captain America
SUPPORTING CAST: Bucky (last in MC #84/4, '47)
VILLAINS: Chief (Grace) & her Crime Syndicate (last under the King's leadership in MC #25, '41, next under Butcher's leadership in YM #24, '53 fb, Digger Dolan named)
OTHER CHARACTERS: Lee School teacher & students, police inc desk sergeant & dispatcher (voice only), Sam's Beds' desk clerk, 3 flophouse patrons (2 voices only), tropical fish, "Gats" Morgan & mob (mentioned, previously defeated by Cap & Bucky), "Bullets" Bronson (mentioned, previously shot at Cap)
LOCATIONS/ITEMS: Manhattan inc Lee School, World Wide Camera Factory, nightclub, "Steve" & "Bucky's" apartment, police HQ, Elysium Tropical Fish Co. (bts, robbed by Syndicate), Granever Blvd., Sam's Beds & Syndicate warehouse base on Grover Street; Grace's gun, Syndicate members' firearms & blackjack, threatening note
SYNOPSIS: While Cap romances Grace, who hopes to convince him to give up crimefighting, Bucky, on his own, fights Crime Syndicate members, who have been directed to increasingly unpredictable crimes by their female Chief. When Bucky confronts Cap about his seemingly frivolous behavior, Cap strikes him and informs him their partnership is over. Despondent, Bucky departs. Later, Cap, despite Grace's resistance, captures Crime Syndicate members as Bucky, at a flophouse, overhears a conversation about a Crime Syndicate meeting and investigates. Syndicate members capture him. The Chief orders a quick death for him, but Cap intervenes, and Bucky gladly fights by his side. The Chief flees by car, but Cap unmasks her as Grace, whom he followed to the meeting place, suspecting her from the start. Later, Cap reveals he distanced himself because the Syndicate threatened to kill Bucky, and the two crimefighting partners are reconciled.
NOTE: Sam's Beds are 25 cents, cash in advance.

2ND STORY: "Meet the Matador!" (12 pages)
CREDITS: Al Avison (pencils), Syd Shores (inks)
FEATURE CHARACTER: Captain America
SUPPORTING CAST: Bucky
VILLAINS: The Matador (dies) & 2 henchmen
OTHER CHARACTERS: Lolita Despana (Lee School student), "Steve's" students, Simpson (pawnbroker, dies), James Ortell (wealthy collector), his daughter & butler, Hernán Cortés ("Hernando Cortez," 1485-1547, mentioned, brought jeweled crown to Spain), Matador's matador ancestor (dies), his "adored one," her suitor, King Charles I of the Spanish Empire (1500-1558, bts, gives crown to matador) (prev 4 in fb only), bull (splash only)
LOCATIONS/ITEMS: Manhattan inc Lee School, Simpson's pawnshop, Lolita's home (37 Hillcrest Dr., destroyed) & Ortell's Castle, Spain (in fb only); Cortez Crown (also in fb) inc separated diamond & ruby, Matador's fencing sword (broken), narcotic gas vial, blackjack & firebomb, Simpson & henchmen's pistols, pawnshop merchandise inc bass drum (broken), antique gun, bow & arrow, Ortell's collection inc Cortez helmet, 2 fencing swords (fb only)
FLASHBACK: In 16th century Spain, the King bestows the Crown of Cortez upon Matador's ancestor who gives it to his beloved. The woman betrays him for another, and her suitor stabs the matador in a duel. Dying, he curses the woman and the Crown
SYNOPSIS: Following Steve's lecture on Hernando Cortez, student Lolita Despana reveals she owns the jeweled Crown of Cortez. Meanwhile, the Matador, who believes the Crown is rightfully his, robs a pawn shop for one Crown gem. Cap and Bucky appear, but Matador knocks them out with narcotic gas and escapes. They trace the gem's sale to Lolita, who admits she sold it and another to finance her education. She entrusts the Crown to Steve. Learning the other buyer was James Ortell, Cap and Bucky visit and find Matador, who again flees, seemingly drowning in Ortell's castle moat. The next day, Bucky receives a note supposedly from Lolita requesting the Crown's return. When he brings it, the Matador captures him, then uses a fire bomb to set Lolita's home aflame. Cap, having found the forged note, arrives, frees Bucky, then battles Matador in the burning house. The fire consumes Matador but Cap escapes with the Crown.

3RD STORY: "Death Swings a Bat!" (6 pages)
CREDITS: Ken Bald (pencils), Bob Oksner (inks)
FEATURE CHARACTER: Human Torch (next in MC #85, '48, CitV #1, '01 fb, Cap:P #2-3, '10)
SUPPORTING CAST: Toro (last in HT #29, '47, next in MC #85, '48)
VILLAINS: Coach Lamson (Typhoon coach), Ed Crums (Typhoon equipment manager, dies), Nick & his henchmen
OTHER CHARACTERS: Jack Bartley (Typhoons' star hitter, #7), Donna Carter (Jack's fiancée), hotel desk clerk, policeman, radio announcer (voice only), Tropic Typhoons (bts, off-panel, Charlie named), Southern Sluggers (bts, off-panel), Typhoon assistant coach (bts, takes over managing game), baseball game attendees, Sparks (Jack's dog, dies), Death (splash only), Brown (mentioned, see NOTE)
LOCATIONS/ITEMS: Florida inc Sea View Hotel w/Rm 300, Fairfield Park w/locker room, criminals' shack & police HQ; henchman's pistol, lockers (some destroyed), bats (1 poisoned), balls inc spiked ball (splash only)
SYNOPSIS: In Florida following a case, Torch and Toro take an impromptu vacation. At their hotel, they chase off gangsters threatening star baseball player Jack Bartley, who refuses to throw a game. Next day, they accompany Bartley to the ballpark, where Bartley's dog Sparks dies after licking Bartley's bat, revealing the handle is coated with acid. Torch and Toro confront equipment manager Ed Crums, but before they can question him, Bartley's girlfriend Donna is attacked and calls for help. After checking on Donna, who reports Bartley's disappearance, they find Crums dead. When Coach Lamson shows knowledge of Crums' wounds, Torch and Toro follow him to a criminal hideout, catch him and the other crooks, and rescue Bartley.
NOTE: At the story's beginning, Torch and Toro have recently completed "the Brown forgery case"; whether "Brown" refers to the forger, the

victim, or someone else is unrevealed.

4TH STORY: "The Menace of Mirth!" (12 pages)
CREDITS: Syd Shores (pencils), Ken Bald (inks)
FEATURE CHARACTER: Captain America (next in MC #86/4, '48, AllWin #1/3, '48, CitV #1, '01 fb, CapC #66/4, '48)
SUPPORTING CAST: Bucky (next in MC #86/4, '48)
VILLAINS: The Jester (also as balloon) & 2 henchmen
OTHER CHARACTERS: Dorothy Graham (gag-writing contest winner), Martha van Dozier (radio gag-writing contest sponsor), radio employee, radio announcer, Elwell Cluyon (bts, pays ransom to Jester) & his Mongolian dog (in newspaper photo & bts, kidnapped by Jester)
LOCATIONS/ITEMS: Manhattan inc Jester's hideout, Lee School w/radio station and radio tower, ceremony hall & "Steve" and "Bucky's" apartment, river; Jester's nitrous oxide/laughing gas bomb, Jester-faced balloon w/magnesium flare, Steve's collector's edition "Joe Miller's Jests, or the Wit's Vade-Mecum" (1739), henchmen's guns, van Dozier's Hen's Egg Diamond
SYNOPSIS: When Dorothy Graham wins Lee School's radio gag-writing contest, costumed criminal and sore loser Jester starts a crime spree. When Steve, with Bucky, awards Dorothy the prize money, Jester steals it. Cap and Bucky pursue but Jester uses laughing gas on them and escapes. Later, when Dorothy visits Steve's apartment, Jester blinds them with a magnesium flare balloon, then steals Steve's rare collector's item jokebook. When the contest's sponsor, Martha van Dozier, joins Dorothy for a radio broadcast, Jester tries to steal her Hen's Egg Diamond, but the scenario is a trap, and Cap and Bucky quickly disarm Jester's henchmen. Jester flees onto the radio tower but almost falls. Rescued by Cap, he surrenders.
NOTE: The Jester may be Johnnie Pinkham from CapC #40, '44.

5TH STORY: "Hey, Look" (1 page)
CREDITS: Harvey Kurtzman (writer, art)
FEATURE CHARACTER: Junior elevator operator
OTHER CHARACTERS: Senior elevator operator, 8 elevator passengers, "Hey, Look" eyes
LOCATIONS/ITEMS: Building inc elevator
SYNOPSIS: An elevator operator shows his subordinate how to handle a new elevator, warning him not to give it "too much juice." After passengers board, the subordinate sends the elevator up but indeed gives it "too much juice," sending himself and the elevator's ceiling upward while the passengers and the elevator's floor remain stationary.

TEXT STORY: "Adventure in the Night" (2 pages)
CREDITS: Writer unknown
FEATURE CHARACTERS: Phil Blake & Harry Wilson (young campers)
OTHER CHARACTERS: Mr. Wilson (Harry's father), Mr. Blake (Phil's father) (both in fb, weeks before), Mrs. Wilson & Mrs. Blake (bts, supply food), black panther, Mr. Blake's friends (both in Mr. Blake's story), wild cat, river rats (both in boys' imaginations), screamer (possibly woman or child)
LOCATIONS/ITEMS: Manhattan inc brownstone tenement roof campsite, Maine inc Moosehead Lake & Bangor (both in Mr. Blake's story only); fishing tent, charcoal burner, WWI mess kit, coffee pot, scout axe
FLASHBACK: Mr. Blake claims that he once hunted a black panther at Maine's Moosehead Lake. When Mr. Wilson insists that black panthers are not found in North America, Blake tells him this one had escaped from a Bangor circus.
SYNOPSIS: Phil and Harry camp out, their heads filled with Mr. Blake's stories of the wild. Late at night, a scream awakens them. Peering out of their tent, they see "luminous eyes" and decide wild cats are after their food. They stow the food, stoke up a fire in their burner and stand guard all night. Finally the sun rises and the boys feel safe enough to sleep...in their tent held up by a clothesline on the tar paper roof of a Manhattan brownstone tenement.
NOTE: Story appears between 3rd & 4th stories.

CAPTAIN AMERICA COMICS #66 (April 1948)

"Golden Girl!" (12 pages)

CREDITS: Stan Lee (writer), Syd Shores (pencils, c art), Ken Bald (inks)
FEATURE CHARACTER: Captain America (also in Cap:P #2-3, '10, next in CapC #67/3, '48)
SUPPORTING CAST: Bucky (last in CapC #66/3, '48, chr last in Cap:P #2, '10, also in Cap:P #2-3, '10, next in CapC #71, '49), Golden Girl (Betsy Ross, last in CapC #64/4, '47, also in Cap:P #3, '10, next in CapC #67/3, '48)
VILLAINS: Lavender (also bts in Cap:P #2, '10, also in Cap:P #3, '10) & 2 henchmen (also bts in Cap:P #2, '10, also in Cap:P #3, '10, Pete named on cover, see NOTE)
OTHER CHARACTERS: Doctor, policeman, night watchman (dies), platina mink-wearing woman, her husband (mentioned, used connections to buy stolen fur), Mme. Fifi (furrier, bts, robbed by Lavender), fences & wholesalers (bts, traced by Golden Girl back to Lavender), female mannequin
LOCATIONS/ITEMS: Manhattan inc perfumery w/store room, hospital w/Bucky's room, Betsy's apartment, "Steve" & "Bucky's" apartment, Mme. Fifi's Furrier shop & Lavender's hideout; Lavender's knife & perfume bottles, Lavender & her henchmen's firearms, Cap & Betsy's fencing swords, crate of ambergris, furs inc platina mink
SYNOPSIS: Cap and Bucky interrupt Lavender's perfumery robbery. Lavender shoots Bucky and escapes. Cap hurries Bucky to a hospital, where he survives but remains weakened. Accustomed to having a crimefighting partner, Cap approaches Betsy Ross, to whom he reveals his secret identity. After days of training, Betsy, as Golden Girl, joins Cap in action, but when the pair encounter Lavender and company, Golden

Girl's overeagerness to help Cap allows the criminals to escape. Days later, Betsy chances upon a lead, and she and Cap trace Lavender to her hideout, defeating the criminals. Cap and Golden Girl visit Bucky in the hospital. Bucky promises to be back in action soon but, in the meantime, gives his blessing to Betsy.

NOTE: Per Cap:P #3, '10, Lavender leads henchmen named Blackie, Deke, Joey, Lem, & Mutt. Which, if any, of these is the 2nd henchman here is unrevealed.

2ND STORY: "Tusks of Terror!" (7 pages)
CREDITS: Unknown
FEATURE CHARACTER: Human Torch (next in Cap:P #3, '10, HT #30, '48, MC #86, '48)
SUPPORTING CAST: Toro (last in MC #85, '48, chr next in Cap:P #3, '10, next in HT #30, '48)
VILLAINS: Prester Jim (jungle outlaw, dies) & 3 henchmen (2 white, 1 black)
OTHER CHARACTERS: Lois Rivers, Dan Rivers (ivory trader, Lois' father and Torch & Toro's friend, dies), expedition bearers/porters, Manuguay residents, Dinah (Rivers' pet elephant, dies), other elephant
LOCATIONS/ITEMS: Manhattan inc Torch & Toro's apartment, Republic of Côte d'Ivoire ("Ivory Coast") inc Manuguay seaport, Rivers' home (destroyed), San Dwana River & the Elephants' Graveyard (a few miles from river mouth, next in MysT #18/4, '54), Prester Jim's raft, whip & firearms
SYNOPSIS: Torch and Toro travel to the Ivory Coast to visit their friend Dan Rivers. With Dan away ivory hunting, the two meet his daughter Lois. That night, Dan returns astride family elephant Dinah. Shot by jungle criminal Prester Jim, Dan reveals he discovered the famed Elephants' Graveyard, supposed source of great ivory caches, then dies. Informed of this by an eavesdropper, Prester Jim tries to abduct Lois and force her to lead him to the Graveyard, but Torch and Toro drive him off. The two accompany Lois on an expedition to find the Graveyard. When they camp for the night, Prester Jim abducts Lois. Dinah, following, catches up to Prester Jim and crushes him, even as his henchmen shoot her. Torch and Toro arrive and knock out the henchmen. With Lois, they follow the dying Dinah to the hidden elephants' graveyard, a lake of quicksand from which no one will extract any ivory.

3RD STORY: "Let's Play Detective: The Case of the Hermit's Fortune!" (1 page)
CREDITS: Al Bellman (art)
FEATURE CHARACTER: Skip McCoy (police detective, 1st, next in Blackst #2/3, '48, MC #86/3, '48, AllWin #1/3, '48, Ideal #2/3, '48, ComMys #2/3, '48, LawLose #4/4, '48, BlonPhan #20/5, '48, CapC #69/3, '48)
VILLAIN: Harry Cranford
OTHER CHARACTERS: Sam Hicks, Hank the Hermit (as corpse)
LOCATIONS/ITEMS: Hank's shack w/broken window & adjoining woods, police HQ; footprints, spider web
SYNOPSIS: Hank the Hermit is murdered and his shack ransacked for money. Cranford claims he saw Hicks rob Hank, then break through a window to flee into the woods, with Cranford chasing after him. However, McCoy notices the window has a spider web across part of it, proving it has been broken for some time, and only one set of footprints leads into the woods, disproving Cranford's claim of a chase. McCoy arrests Cranford, who confesses.
NOTE: Story followed by "Stamp News" (1 page, Kent B. Stiles, writer) & 3 gag panels.

4TH STORY: "Swords of the Cavaliers!" (6 pages)
CREDITS: Unknown
FEATURE CHARACTER: Captain America (next in CapC #66/1, '48)
SUPPORTING CAST: Bucky (chr last in CitV #1, '01 fb, chr next in CAP:P #2, '10, next in CapC #66/1, '48)
VILLAINS: The Cavalier (Prof. Wagstaff, Lee School teacher), two additional Cavaliers (Wagstaff's underlings)
OTHER CHARACTERS: Patricia Walker (heiress), Patricia's father (mentioned, apparently deceased), Masked Cavalier (in duplicate painting only)
LOCATIONS/ITEMS: Lee School inc Prof. Wagstaff's office, Walker mansion inc picture gallery & grandfather clock; Cavaliers' rapiers, Wagstaff's medieval artifact collection, "The Masked Cavalier" (painting, bts, in a special vault awaiting the auction), duplicate painting (destroyed), additional swords (splash only)
SYNOPSIS: Patricia Walker plans to sell her father's most valuable painting, the "Masked Cavalier," and donate the proceeds to Lee School. Meanwhile, two costumed cavaliers seemingly rob Prof. Wagstaff until Bucky intervenes. When the fight moves into the hallway, Steve pushes Patricia to safety, but she complains about the manhandling and withdraws her donation offer. The Cavaliers escape. Later, at the Walker mansion, Cap and Bucky make short work of two cavaliers, but a third steals the supposed painting. Cap and Bucky unmask him as Wagstaff; the earlier incident actually a training session that Bucky mistook for a robbery. The painting is ruined in the fight but Patricia reveals it to be a duplicate. With the true "Masked Cavalier" safe, Patricia again agrees to sell it and donate proceeds to Lee School.
NOTE: Story begins on a Saturday. Story followed by "Unsolved Mysteries" (1 page), a featurette presenting the mysteries of "Devil's Footprints," "Three English Sparrows," & "The James Chester," featuring a priest, 3 residents of South Devon, England, 3 sparrows, & the ship James Chester.

TEXT STORY: "Vacation for Murder" (2 pages)
CREDITS: Writer unknown
FEATURE CHARACTER: Adam Mortimer (police detective)
VILLAIN: Perry Van Smythe
OTHER CHARACTERS: Mrs. Bishop (wealthy woman, dies), Lee Bishop (her daughter), Jeb Harris (hotel tennis & archery instructor), Mr. Connor (hotel manager), hotel guests, dead man, man holding gun (hand only) (both in illustration only)
LOCATIONS/ITEMS: Hotel w/lake, tennis court & archery range; bows & arrows, gun (in illustration only)

SYNOPSIS: Detective Adam Mortimer is on vacation. He observes fellow guest Mrs. Bishop quarrel with her daughter Lee over her choice of suitors. Lee is in love with sports instructor Jeb Harris, but Mrs. Bishop believes blueblood Perry Van Smythe is a better match. Soon after, Mrs. Bishop is found murdered in her room, an arrow through her heart. Mortimer notices that, although Mrs. Bishop was claustrophobic, the room's window is closed, its sash cord cut. Realizing the murderer knew the victim would open the window upon entering, he discovers Perry was with Lee on the archery range but misfired badly, having to retrieve his arrow from the woods. He accuses Perry of shooting Mrs. Bishop from the woods when she opens her window, claiming his prints are on the arrow. Without thinking, Perry claims he removed the fingerprints, confirming his guilt.
NOTE: Story appears between 1st & 2nd stories.

CAPTAIN AMERICA COMICS #67 (July 1948)

"The Secret Behind the Mirror!" (10 pages)

CREDITS: Syd Shores (pencils), Vince Alascia (inks), Charles Nicholas (c art)
FEATURE CHARACTER: Captain America (next in MC #87/4, '48)
SUPPORTING CAST: Golden Girl (last in CapC #67/3, '48, next in MC #87/4, '48)
VILLAINS: Denton "Doc" Smith and Cecil Babylon (jewel thieves)
OTHER CHARACTERS: Mr. Zrr ("mischief man" of Dimension Zee), Andrew (mirror maker, shop owner), Sally (Andrew's granddaughter), Zachary Brown (Universal City Diamond and Gold Buying Center president), Buying Center employee, would-be mirror purchaser, Universal City bystanders, Justice Officer of Zee, Dimension Zee denizens (some die), "the Boss," Mac, & one other gunman (prev 3 on cover only)
LOCATIONS/ITEMS: Universal City inc Universal Diamond Center, Andrew's home/mirror shop & Universal City Diamond and Gold Buying Center inc Brown's office, Dimension Zee (dimension of imp-like race) inc Justice Officer of Zee's office & gold-paved streets, the Great Divide (barrier between Earth & Dimension of Zee), criminal hideout (on cover only); dimensional portal mirror (broken), Doc & Babylon's pistols, Cap's portable seismograph, crooks' 2 machine guns & pistol (both on cover only)
SYNOPSIS: Cap and Golden Girl pursue jewel thieves Doc Smith and Babylon to Universal City. The crooks hide in Andrew's mirror shop and inadvertently enter a mirror portal to Dimension Zee. There, they convince Mr. Zrr, a "mischief man" who has befriended Andrew and granddaughter Sally, to sell some of Zee's commonplace gold on Earth for cash. Considering the experience a simple diversion, Zrr cooperates. When Cap and Golden Girl investigate, Zrr scatters cash so bystanders delay them, then returns to Zee. Cap, who has been tracking seismograph readings that don't stem from earthquakes, finds their source at the mirror portal. He and Golden Girl enter and find Zrr, despondent because Doc and Babylon have introduced gambling, hostility, and murder to his formerly peaceful realm. He helps Cap and Golden Girl capture the crooks and return his dimension to normal. Cap and Golden Girl return Doc and Babylon to Earth but Andrew voluntarily stays behind. The mirror falls and breaks, severing the dimensional link.
NOTE: Doc and Babylon's full names revealed in OHMU:HC #8, '09.

2ND STORY: "Design for Death!" (6 pages)
CREDITS: Bob Oksner (art)
FEATURE CHARACTER: Human Torch (also in Sparks' dream, next in HT #32, '48, MC #87, '48, AllWin Spec #1,'48)
SUPPORTING CAST: Toro (also in Sparks' dream last in MC #86, '48, next in HT #32, '48)
VILLAIN: Mephisto (Ted Sparks' dream-form, in dream only)
OTHER CHARACTERS: Ted Sparks (crime stories writer), Peggy (Sparks' girlfriend, also in photo), Brenda Coleman (socialite), Karen Warren (opera singer), Taffy Cavanaugh (cover girl), opera singer (as "Don Juan"), Taffy's banker, circus benefit attendees, opera patrons, Manhattan bystanders (prev 8 in dream only)
LOCATIONS/ITEMS: Manhattan inc Ted's Greenwich Village 5th floor apartment, Central Square Garden, opera house (both in dream only); Ted's typewriter, skulls, skeleton hat rack, red ink, fishing pole & "The Monster at Large" pages, Mephisto's rapier & trapeze, Don Juan's stage sword (prev 3 in dream only), Mephisto's knife (on splash panel only)
SYNOPSIS: Troubled by his girlfriend Peggy's seeming neglect, Ted melodramatically complains to his friends Torch and Toro that Peggy told him she was too busy to mend his socks. Attempting to channel his emotions into crime fiction, Ted falls asleep and imagines himself as super-villain Mephisto. Chased by Torch and Toro, Mephisto romantically pursues various women, all of whom reject him. As the dream Torch and Toro close in, Ted awakens, then reconciles with Peggy who arrives and reveals that she was too busy because she knitted him a new pair of socks.
NOTE: See NOTE for CapC #11/5, '42.

3RD STORY: "The Singer Who Wanted to Fight!" (8 pages)
CREDITS: Syd Shores (pencils), Vince Alascia (inks)
FEATURE CHARACTER: Captain America (next in CapC #69, '48 fb)
SUPPORTING CAST: Golden Girl (next in CapC #67/1, '48)
VILLAINS: Killer Casey (leading heavyweight boxing contender, see NOTE), Hawk Martin (Killer's manager)
OTHER CHARACTERS: Scotti Warren ("spaghetti tenor," singer), Martha (Papa Lenori's waitress & Scotti's girlfriend), Rocky Gonzales (boxer), Papa Lenori's customer & waiters, autograph seeker, referee, boxing arena employees, 2 pianists, gym patrons, boxing & theatre audiences, boxers (in photos on Casey's dressing room wall)
LOCATIONS/ITEMS: Manhattan inc Papa Lenori's (restaurant), Lee School, boxing arena w/dressing rooms and ring, Callahan's Gym & theatre; Killer's chloroform bottle, resin & boxing gloves
SYNOPSIS: While Steve and Betsy dine at Papa Lenori's, Scotti Warren, a singer who longs for greater success, confronts boxer Killer Casey

hen Casey harasses Scotti's girlfriend Martha. After knocking Casey down through a fluke, Scotti decides to abandon singing for boxing. A
month later, he has become a boxing sensation, unaware Casey and manager Hawk are setting him up for Casey to defeat him, with them
profiting from built-up odds. When Cap and Golden Girl fail to dissuade Scotti, Cap spars with him, deliberately breaking Scotti's jaw so Cap can
take his place as Casey's opponent. During the fight, Casey cheats via choloform & resined gloves, but Cap rallies and defeats him. Months
later, Steve, Betsy and Martha watch Scotti's theater singing performance, Cap having converted the fight receipts into a fund to finance young
artists.

NOTE: Story occurs over at least three months. Killer Casey may be the same man as the identically named Sub-Mariner enemy in MC #20/2,
'41.

TEXT STORY: "Catch a Killer" (2 pages)
CREDITS: Writer unknown
FEATURE CHARACTER: Jug Jordan (Ice Cream Corners clerk)
VILLAIN: "Happy" Sherman ("Houdini of Crime," escaped convict, bts, captured in Westville)
OTHER CHARACTERS: Mr. Bender (Ice Cream Corners owner), Tomasso (circus knife thrower), radio announcer (voice only), Judy (Jug's
girlfriend, mentioned), woman (on soda ad poster)
LOCATIONS/ITEMS: Town inc Ice Cream Corners ("soda and jive emporium"), Ritz theatre & circus (both mentioned), Westville (a couple of
miles from the town, mentioned); Tomasso's knife & wig, banana split
SYNOPSIS: Jug Jordon hears a radio announcement that "Happy" Sherman has escaped prison and may be heading his way. Jug knows that
"Happy" is a knife-wielding, banana split-loving killer, currently in disguise. Jug daydreams about taking his girl out to the movies or the circus
just arrived in town, until a man carrying a knife and wearing a wig enters the ice cream shop and orders a banana split. When the man asks
Jug to stand up against the wall so he can throw knives at him, Jug runs for his life. The customer can't understand Jug's nervousness. After
all when he, Tomasso, "throws the knife in the circus nobody ever get hurt. Not even a flea."
NOTE: Story appears between 2nd & 3rd stories. Followed by "Stamp News" (1/2 page, Kent B. Stiles, writer).

CAPTAIN AMERICA COMICS #68 (September 1948)

"The Enigma of the Death Doll!" (10 pages)

CREDITS: Charles Nicholas (art)
FEATURE CHARACTER: Captain America (also as marionette on splash panel)
SUPPORTING CAST: Golden Girl (also as marionette on splash panel, between MC #87/4-88/4, '48)
VILLAINS: Horatio (dollmaker, dies) & the Dolls (Apache, Axe-Slayer of Nanking, Raffles, 3 little people
impersonating dolls)
OTHER CHARACTERS: Horatio's landlord, Mrs. Waggoner, her butler & her maid, bank guard (dies), audience
members (in splash panel only), police chief, Richards, his son & his victim (prev 4 on cover only)
LOCATIONS/ITEMS: Manhattan inc Horatio's doll shop, clock steeple, bank, Betsy's apartment & Waggoner
home, tenement room (on cover only); dolls inc Apache, Axe-Slayer of Nanking, Raffles, clown & dancing girl,
Mrs. Waggoner's ruby doll house, Apache's rope, Axe-Slayer's axe, Raffles' pistol, Richards & police chief's pistols (both on cover only)
SYNOPSIS: Steve and Betsy meet eccentric dollmaker Horatio, who needs money for back rent. That night, Horatio, seemingly speaking to
his three favorite dolls, plans a crime. Cap and Golden Girl investigate a bank robbery and murder apparently committed by the dolls. Next day,
the two return to the shop, where Horatio now has the rent money. Steve intentionally mentions wealthy Mrs. Waggoner's ruby doll house. That
night, Cap and Golden Girl follow Horatio and his dolls to the Waggoner home and capture the "dolls," actually costumed little people, although
the increasingly insane Horatio seems to think they are his actual dolls. Horatio flees to his shop. Cap and Golden Girl later find him dead, an
apparent suicide, although his body is several feet away from the real Axe-Slayer doll holding a now-bloody axe.
NOTE: Mrs. Waggoner's vault combination is "4-16 right, 8-37-3 to the left."

2ND STORY: (4 pages)
CREDITS: Al Avison (pencils), Charles Nicholas (inks)
FEATURE CHARACTER: Captain America (also in Johnny's dream in splash panel)
OTHER CHARACTERS: Johnny (also in his own dream in splash panel), his mother & his classmates, Miss Sims (Johnny's teacher), Mr.
Simpson (candy store owner), alley cats
LOCATIONS/ITEMS: Manhattan inc Johnny's "shabby" Eastside apartment w/bedroom and kitchen, Miss Sims' apartment, Mr. Simpson's
candy store & school; apple, candy, comic books
SYNOPSIS: Cap visits young Johnny one night. He takes him to see the home lives of his teacher Miss Sims, upon whom he has played
pranks, and candy store owner Simpson, whose window Johnny and friends broke. Johnny sees Miss Simms is much like his mother having
to do tough chores at home and discovers Mr. Simpson might not be able to pay his rent because he must pay for the window. Johnny realizes
that, like children, adults have feelings and problems. The next day, moved by what he thinks was a dream, Johnny brings Miss Sims an apple
and collects money to replace Simpson's window. Cap observes from outside, saying, "Are you sure it was just a dream, Johnny? Are you
sure?"

3RD STORY: "My Son Is a Thief!" (6 pages)
CREDITS: Paul Reinman (art)
FEATURE CHARACTER: Sub-Mariner (Namor McKenzie, Atlantean prince, last in BlonPhan #19/3, '48, next in MC #88/2, '48, SubC #28,
'48, Namora #2/4, '48, HT #33/3, '48, BlonPhan #20/3, '48, SubC #29, '48, MC #89/2, '48, Namora #3/2, '48, BlonPhan #21/3, '49, CapC #70/3,
'49)

SUPPORTING CAST: Namora (Namor's cousin, last in BlonPhan #19/3, '48, next in MC #88/2, '48)

VILLAINS: The Waterfront Gang

OTHER CHARACTERS: Frank Carver (mailman), Harry Carver (Frank's son, undercover Secret Service detective), Mrs. Welton (Houseboat Row resident), John Welton (Mrs. Welton's husband, mentioned, Frank got him a post office job), elderly couple, elderly couple's son Eddie (mentioned, sends them letter after prompted by Frank), mail launch captain, 2 sea captains, policeman (on splash panel only)

LOCATIONS/ITEMS: Houseboat Row inc Mrs. Welton's house, Seamen's Roost & other tavern, Gang's hideout; mail launch, Waterfront Gang's boat & firearms, Frank's mailbag, Harry's badge

SYNOPSIS: Mailman Frank Carver learns his son Harry associates with the Waterfront Gang and fears he will fall into crime. When he expresses his concerns to friends Namor and Namora, they promise to investigate. That night, the Gang hijacks the mail launch, on which Frank is a passenger. When Harry stops one member from shooting Frank, the Gang members turn on him, but Namor and Namora arrive and quickly defeat them. Harry reveals he is an undercover detective who infiltrated the Gang, restoring his father's faith.

4TH STORY: "From the Personal File of Captain America" (7 pages)

CREDITS: Al Avison (pencils), Charles Nicholas (inks)

FEATURE CHARACTER: Captain America (next in MC #88/4, '48)

VILLAINS: Joey Eagen (also as "Mr. Eagen" & "Al Capone," gangster & Capone lookalike, dies), Spud (Toledo gangster leader), Toledo gangsters (some bts, some die, Frankie & Gyp named, Gyp dies), bootlegger (bts, stocks "Eagen's" party) (all in fb early 1930s)

OTHER CHARACTERS: Steve Dorn (Joey's business partner, dies), Joey's mother, Mugsy Brown (boxer, dies), Mrs. Davis (Mugsy's wife), McMillin (Toledo hotel desk clerk, dies), Dayton police inc detective, Toledo police, Indiana police, Toledo hotel bellhop & guests (bts, call to complain about "Eagen's" party), doctor, bartender, barber, apartment dweller, tailor (all in fb), Death (splash only), Al "Scarface" Capone (1899-1947, mentioned)

LOCATIONS/ITEMS: Ohio inc Dayton w/Dorn/Arnold business, Arnold home inc wine cellar and police HQ & Toledo w/police HQ, barber shop, bar, Spud's office, Mrs. Davis' home, Ohio State Hospital, Dixie Park parking lot and hotel inc Room 407, Indiana tailor shop (all in fb); Cap's office, Death's portals & cemetery (in splash panel only); Arnold's gun, gangsters & police firearms (all in fb), electric chair (in splash panel only)

FLASHBACK: Inspired by his resemblance to Al Capone, Joey Arnold turns to crime, starting with the murder of his business partner Steve Dorn. He relocates to Toledo, consorting with gangsters, who recruit him to handle hijacking and illegal gambling. After several murders and other crimes, Arnold flees to Indiana, where, on April 6, 1933, he is finally arrested.

SYNOPSIS: Cap tells Joey Arnold's story, concluding by stating that Joey is executed for his crimes.

TEXT STORY: "Trouble in Grade Five" (2 pages)

CREDITS: Writer unknown

FEATURE CHARACTER: Grandpaw Hicks

OTHER CHARACTERS: General Durkin (Revolutionary War hero, born in 1734) & his horse (dies), George Washington (1732-1799, Continental Army Commander-in-Chief) & his troops (mentioned), Falling Water (American Indian chief, allied w/British, dies), his horse & his Indian band, British Redcoat soldiers, Major Ambrose (dies) & his men (guarding powder train), horses (all in fb in 1775), Lucy Hicks (Grandpaw's granddaughter & teacher) & her 5th grade students, Sugar (Grandpaw's mare), school board (mentioned, coming on General Durkin's Day)

LOCATIONS/ITEMS: New England town inc Grandpaw's house & schoolhouse, powder train battlefield, Washington's headquarters (both in fb); powder kegs, Indian and colonial weapons, Falling Water's tomahawk (all in fb), Grandpaw's envelope, Sugar's tail hair

FLASHBACK: In 1775, Private Durkin, a scout, is traveling to Washington's headquarters with news that the British are paying Chief Falling Water to cut off the colonial powderkeg transport. Discovering the Indians attacking the powder train, Durkin ignites some kegs, scaring the band away, then kills Falling Water in hand-to-hand combat. Washington promotes Durkin to General.

SYNOPSIS: Lucy Hicks worries that her 5th grade class won't recall hometown hero General Durkin's story when the school board comes to question them on General Durkin's Day. She tells Grandpaw who rides his mare Sugar to the school and tells the students Durkin's story, finishing by pulling "Falling Water's scalp" from an envelope. When Lucy comments afterwards that she didn't know Falling Water was scalped, Grandpaw tells her he wasn't. The hair is from Sugar's tail but its impact made sure the kids won't forget Durkin's history.

NOTE: Story appears between 3rd & 4th stories.

CAPTAIN AMERICA COMICS #69 (November 1948)

"Captain America in The Weird Tales of the Wee Males!" (10 pages)

CREDITS: Ken Bald (art), Jean Thompson (editorial consultant), Charles Nicholas (c art)

FEATURE CHARACTER: Captain America (also in fb between CapC #67/3, '48 & CapC #69/2, '48 fb)

VILLAIN: Grinko ("King Grinko," Tiny World prime minister)

OTHER CHARACTERS: The Teeny-Weeny People (race of 6-inch humanoids) inc King Teeny, Princess Petite (Teeny's daughter), doctor & soldiers (in fb only), "Steve's" students (Miss Mason named), giant hand (on cover only)

LOCATIONS/ITEMS: North Pole inc mountain, the Tiny World (Teeny-Weeny People's mountain cavern kingdom) inc royal palace, inn, super market and jail & underground stream (all in fb only), Lee School; Cap's plane (wrecked), Grinko's sword, King Teeny's sceptre, Teeny-Weeny soldiers' bows & arrows (all in fb only), copies of "Gulliver's Travels" (1726 novel by Jonathan Swift, 1667-1745)

FLASHBACK: When Cap's plane crashes near the North Pole, he is rescued by the Teeny-Weeny People, who take him to their Tiny World kingdom. King Teeny's subjects take a great liking to Cap, except for Prime Minister Grinko. Having planned to kill Teeny and take his throne,

Grinko causes a flood and blames it on Cap. Cap easily stops the flood at his source, then returns to find Grinko has imprisoned Teeny and Petite and declared himself king. Grinko orders his soldiers to kill Cap, but their tiny arrows are ineffective, and Cap ends the coup by simply picking up Grinko, who surrenders. After promising Teeny to keep Tiny World's location secret, Cap departs.

SYNOPSIS: Steve recounts the Tiny World adventure, as "told to him" by Cap, to his class. One student, Miss Mason, has apparently deduced that Steve and Cap are one and the same.

NOTE: "Steve" is an English teacher here.

2ND STORY: "Captain America in No Man Is an Island!" (10 pages)

CREDITS: Ken Bald (art)

FEATURE CHARACTER: Captain America (also in fb1 between CapC #69, '48 fb & CapC #70/2, '48 fb, next in HT #33, '48, MC #89/6, '48)

VILLAIN: John Barton (recluse, in fb1 & in fb2 from 30 years before up to fb1, also in his own thoughts, dies)

OTHER CHARACTERS: Anne Johnson (stenographer & Barton's girlfriend, also in Barton's thoughts, dies), Anne's mother (dies), Tom Morley, Anne's landlady, George Green (Tom's friend), Mrs. Morley (Tom's wife), Betty Morley (Tom's daughter), Barton & Anne's imagined daughter (in Barton's thoughts only), Barton's fellow graduates, graduation speaker, Barton's employer, dance attendees, bystanders, brakeman, bartender (all in fb1 only), fish (in fb1 only)

LOCATIONS/ITEMS: The Bahamas (also in fb1 & fb2) inc Nassau w/restaurant (in fb2), Caribbean Sea (in fb1), island inc Barton's shack (in fb1 & fb2), college, Ajax Engineering Corporation, Anne's boarding house, John's home, Anne's mother's home, dance hall, sanitarium (bts, Anne's mother dies there), bar (prev 8 in fb2); Cap's motorboat & fishing pole (in fb1), Morley's sports car (in fb2), island statues

FLASHBACK: Fishing in the Bahamas, Cap seeks shelter from a storm on an island, finding hermit John Barton, near death and consumed by guilt. Barton tells Cap his story (1). Over 30 years ago, Barton, college graduate and successful businessman, becomes engaged to Anne Johnson. One evening, returning early from a business trip, Barton sees Anne with another man, Tom Morley. Insanely jealous, he violently confronts her. Drawing back, she falls down stairs and dies. Barton spends years on the run, working odd jobs and stealing. He becomes a recluse in the Bahamas. One evening, he sees Tom Morley, now a family man, in a restaurant, telling a friend the story of how, years ago, he had driven Anne to her dying mother's bedside, only for Anne to be murdered later that night. Horrified, Barton falls into ill health and mental collapse (2). After telling Cap, Barton, hounded by the supposed voice of his conscience, flees into the storm. Cap finds him dead, a look of peace on his face (1).

SYNOPSIS: Cap tells the story of his encounter with John Barton.

NOTE: Splash panel features refurbished versions of page 3 panel 4, page 5 panel 3, page 6 panel 7 & page 9 panel 3.

3RD STORY: "Let's Play Detective: A Burial for Benny!" (1 page)

CREDITS: Al Bellman (art)

FEATURE CHARACTER: Skip McCoy (next in Crimef #4/4, '48, ComMys #3/2, '48, AllTrue #31/4, '49, Crimef #5/2, '49, SubC #30/3, '49, CapC #71/3, '49)

SUPPORTING CAST: Pepper Burns

VILLAINS: "The Boss" & 2 henchmen, Benny the Bandit (dies)

LOCATIONS/ITEMS: Manhattan inc Boss' building & police HQ; Benny's glasses (broken)

SYNOPSIS: "The Boss" and his men beat up small-timer Benny the Bandit and inadvertently kill him. The criminals plant Benny's body outside, claiming he fell out a window, but McCoy notices that, although Benny's glasses are broken, there are no glass fragments near his body, meaning he died elsewhere. McCoy arrests the criminals.

NOTE: Story followed by "Stamp News" (1 page, Kent B. Stiles, writer).

4TH STORY: "Bargain of Death!" (6 pages)

CREDITS: Unknown

FEATURE CHARACTER: Human Torch (also as "Dan Patcher," next in HT #33, '48, SubC #29/3, '48, MC #89, '48, HT #34, '49, MC #90, '49)

SUPPORTING CAST: Sun Girl (Mary Mitchell, Torch's former personal secretary & new partner, last in SunG #2/4, '48, next in HT #33, '48)

VILLAINS: The Patcher Gang (6 criminals, Pete named), 2 convicts

OTHER CHARACTERS: Dan Patcher (convict), Evelyn Patcher (as "Evelyn Sorrel," Patcher's wife), Bobby Patcher (as "Bobby Sorrel," Dan & Evelyn's son), State Prison warden, Lubin Plant guard, police inc detective, Good Heart Hospital children's ward patients, Western Union employee, switchboard operator, Sorrels' cat, gang's victim (in splash panel only)

LOCATIONS/ITEMS: Good Heart Hospital, State Prison inc warden's office, Evelyn's apartment, Lubin Manufacturing Plant, gang's hideout (across the street from Lubin Plant); gangsters' firearms, guard's gun, makeup-stained towel

SYNOPSIS: Following a performance at Good Heart Hospital's children's ward, Torch bets Sun Girl he can handle their next case without using his powers. Shortly afterward, Patcher, a convict Torch captured years before, requests help. His former associates, seeking the location of years-old loot, have threatened his wife and son. Torch impersonates Patcher, having supposedly escaped prison. Initially "reconciling" with Patcher's gang, Torch refuses to join them in a crime. They thrash him in hope of learning the loot's whereabouts. When his disguise washes off, Torch, adhering to the bet, fights the gang hand-to-hand and is overcome, but the police arrive. Later, Patcher reveals the stolen money's location. Receiving $20,000 of it as reward money, Torch donates it to Good Heart Hospital.

NOTE: Torch originally captured Dan Patcher eight years prior to the story, placing the incident circa MC #13, '40. Although Evelyn is described as "the former Mrs. Dan Patcher," this is attributed to her having taken a new identity. Although the story's events depict Good Heart Hospital and Evelyn Sorrel's apartment as near each other, Torch and Sun Girl have to travel for hours by plane to reach State Prison from Good Heart, meaning Patcher would have had to make a similar trip to reach Evelyn's apartment; Torch's rapid arrival as the supposedly escaped "Patcher" would seem likely to be questioned by both Evelyn and Patcher's gang.

TEXT STORY: "The Cleanup" (2 pages)

CREDITS: Writer unknown
FEATURE CHARACTER: Todd Hunter (diamond cutter)
VILLAINS: Charles Dorchester & his 4 men inc haywagon driver
OTHER CHARACTERS: Hotel chambermaid, police, Mr. Van Dorn (Todd's client), hotel manager (both mentioned)
LOCATIONS/ITEMS: Country road, city hotel inc Room 712; Todd's wristwatch w/hidden compartment, haywagon, police & thieves' guns, Dorchester's knife, hotel chair & ashtray w/cigarette butts, chambermaid's vacuum cleaner
SYNOPSIS: On his way to deliver 5 diamonds to a client, Todd Hunter is waylaid on a country road and taken to head thief Charles Dorchester at a hotel. Todd has his diamonds hidden in his wristwatch but Dorchester deduces that immediately. An insistent chambermaid comes in to clean the room. Todd extinguishes his cigarette, knocking over the ashtray. The chambermaid vacuums the mess up. After she leaves, Dorchester breaks open Todd's watch but doesn't find the diamonds. Todd fights back, throwing a chair out the window, attracting the police. After Dorchester and his men are arrested, Todd reveals that he deftly dropped the diamonds in the ashtray and intentionally toppled it. The chambermaid unknowingly vacuumed them up with the ashes.
NOTE: Story appears between 3rd & 4th stories.

CAPTAIN AMERICA COMICS #70 (January 1949)

"Worlds at War!" (13 pages)

CREDITS: Ken Bald (pencils), Vince Alascia (inks), Jean Thompson (editorial consultant), Al Avison (c pencils), Syd Shores (c inks)
FEATURE CHARACTER: Captain America
SUPPORTING CAST: Golden Girl (next in MC #91/4, '49)
VILLAINS: Oog (War-Lord of Mars), Martian invaders (some die), Martian astronomers (voices only)
OTHER CHARACTERS: "Steve's" students, Betsy's students, Prof. Kendall Kulto (dies), Kulto lecture attendees, Manhattan bystanders, gendarme, 2 French citizens, British bobbie, 2 British citizens, 2 Soviet soldiers, 2 USSR citizens, soldiers/pilots (most bts, many die), London radio dispatcher (voice only), worldwide casualties (die), additional Martians (some die)
LOCATIONS/ITEMS: Manhattan (severely damaged) inc Lee School w/Betsy's classroom and "Steve's" classroom, lecture hall & Kulto's lab, Michigan inc Detroit, (severely damaged), France inc Paris w/Eiffel Tower, England, USSR inc Moscow, Washington DC, Mars inc city, observatory & spaceship facility, outer space; Martian spaceships (some damaged), ray guns & additional equipment, Earth planes & tanks (some destroyed); Kulto's atomic powered planet mover (destroyed)
SYNOPSIS: Believing humanity can only avoid self-destruction by uniting against a common enemy, Prof. Kulto uses his "atomic powered planet mover" to pull the planet Mars to Earth. The warlike Martians have only refrained from invading Earth because their ships cannot travel the necessary distance. Led by Oog, the Martians can now invade Earth, which, though now unified, is unable to defeat them. After learning of Kulto's planet mover, Cap attempts to hijack a Martian spaceship but is rendered unconscious. He revives to learn Oog has designated him emissary to demand surrender from "the rulers of Earth." Cap brings Oog to Kulto's lab, where Kulto has died in the attacks. Pretending to use Kulto's ray machine to summon Earth's leaders, Cap moves Mars back into place. He defeats Oog with a judo throw, slamming him into the machine to destroy it. Cut off from supplies and unable to eat Earth food, the Martians return to space, preferring to die en route to Mars rather than defeated on Earth.
NOTE: Prof. Kulto's first name revealed in OHMU:HC #8, '09. Martians last in MC #3, '40, next in JUW #4, '51.

2ND STORY: "Captain America Meets The Man Who Knew Everything!" (6 pages)
CREDITS: Ken Bald (art)
FEATURE CHARACTER: Captain America (also in fb1 between CapC #69/2, '48 fb & CapC #71/2, '49 fb, next in MC #90/5, '49)
OTHER CHARACTERS: Billy Gleason (theatrical agent), Dora Darling (Ollie's girlfriend), Ollie's landlady, 2 quizmaster MCs, 2 sound men, other "Q&C" employees, Mrs. Hassenffeffer (contestant), 5 chemists & physicists, 4 astronomers, 4 doctors & psychologists, 3 moving men, nightclub dancer, quiz show audiences (all in fb1 only), passerby, bookstore proprietor, man in painting (on bookstore wall) (prev 3 in fb2 only), Ollie Oliphant (in fb1 & fb2 prior to fb1, also in newspaper photo)
LOCATIONS/ITEMS: Manhattan inc "Quiz & Consequences" studio, Ollie's boarding house, Gleason's office, drug store, Palm Grove Night Club, observatory, surgical facility (all in fb1), bookstore (in fb2); Ollie's prizes/merchandise, TV cameras & microphones (all in fb1), pocket-size encyclopedia (in fb1 & fb2)
FLASHBACK: When Cap attends a "Quiz and Consequences" broadcast, he meets Ollie Oliphant, who thinks he can surpass the contestants. With Cap's encouragement, Ollie volunteers and, to everyone's surprise, including his own, answers every question correctly, winning multiple prizes (1). Not long before, Ollie purchases a tiny encyclopedia (2). Ollie tells Cap his sudden knowledge might be attributed to magic from his encyclopedia, which he keeps in his pocket. Ollie appears on more quiz shows becoming nationally famous. Cap's friend, theatrical agent Billy Gleason, signs Ollie up for his own TV show and lecture series. After he starts dating devoted Dora Darling, however, Ollie becomes weary of fame. The couple plans to elope and start a chicken farm so Ollie discards the encyclopedia. Cap quizzes him and finds Ollie's prize-winning knowledge is gone (1).
SYNOPSIS: Cap relates Ollie's story, wondering if Ollie really had a magic encyclopedia or if he lost interest in everything except being with Dora.
NOTE: A newspaper in the story, the Telegram, published in Metropolis, is dated Monday September 6, 1948. Story followed by "Stamp News" (1 page, Kent B. Stiles, writer).

3RD STORY: "Scavengers of the Desert!" (6 pages)

CREDITS: Jimmy Thompson (pencils), Al Gabriele (inks)
FEATURE CHARACTER: Sub-Mariner (also in pfb, next in SubC #30, '49)
SUPPORTING CAST: Namora (also in pfb, last in Namora #3/4, '48, next in SubC #30, '49)
VILLAINS: Squire Bones (pirate, also in pfb) & his Pirate Gang (some in pfb) inc Rogers (in pfb)
OTHER CHARACTERS: Village residents inc chief, sea gulls, donkey, animal skeleton, yacht passengers (bts, robbed by Bones, in pfb only)
LOCATIONS/ITEMS: Sahara Desert (also in pfb) inc aqueduct, underground canal & village w/well, Mediterranean Sea, Bones' airfield (both in pfb); Bones' plane (also in pfb), yacht, Bones' tarps (both in pfb only)
FLASHBACK: In the Mediterranean Sea, Namor and Namora search for Squire Bones' Pirate Gang. They spot Bones' plane robbing a yacht & catch the plane's pontoons just as it takes off, heading for Bones' hidden airfield. Bones' aerial maneuvers fail to dislodge them. He lands the plane, and Namor and Namora defeat his underlings but Bones binds them in tarps, flies them to the Sahara Desert, and drops them (p).
SYNOPSIS: Namor and Namora seek shelter during a sandstorm. They stumble upon a Roman aqueduct, exposed by the storm. Heading underground, they find a water canal and, swimming beneath the Sahara, head for the nearest village, where Bones and company, their plane damaged by the sandstorm, have landed seeking water. At the village's well, Namor and Namora leap to the surface and confront the criminals, who surrender.

TEXT STORY: "Eddie Saves the Dough" (2 pages)
CREDITS: Writer unknown
FEATURE CHARACTER: Eddie (armored car driver)
VILLAINS: Fisher Gang (Shorty Monel & Fisher named, some inc Monel die)
OTHER CHARACTERS: Mr. Waller (armored car company boss), Dan Burr, Brick (both armored car guards), Eddie's wife (mentioned, made Eddie's lunch)
LOCATIONS/ITEMS: City inc armored car company, road to suburban bank; armored car, gang's sedan, Dan's .38, other guns, Gang's Molotov cocktails, Eddie's lunch inc strawberry short cake, a million and a half dollars held in money boxes
SYNOPSIS: Eddie drives an armored car, protected by Dan & Brick, that is carrying a million and a half dollars. Dan and Brick kid Eddie about his wife's cooking but he's looking forward to his lunch, stowed in one of the money boxes, particularly the dessert. The Fisher Gang waylays them, blocking the road and tossing Molotov cocktails. Eddie, Dan, and Brick escape the burning vehicle, then kill or capture the entire Fisher Gang. Eddie rushes back to the blazing armored car and grabs a money box. Dan tells him that the government will replace all lost money. "Yeah, they'd replace the money," Eddie says, pulling his lunch from the box, "but who'd replace this strawberry short cake?"
NOTE: Story appears between 1st & 2nd stories. Typo mistakenly calls Dan "Ran" once here.

CAPTAIN AMERICA COMICS #71 (March 1949)

"Trapped by the Trickster!" (8 pages)

CREDITS: Stan Lee (writer), Al Gabriele (pencils), Al Avison (inks, c pencils), Jean Thompson (editorial consultant), Carl Pfeufer (c inks)
FEATURE CHARACTER: Captain America
SUPPORTING CAST: Bucky (last in CapC #66, '48, chr next in Cap:P #4, '11)
VILLAINS: The Trickster (Milo van Sett, 1st, next in CapC #72/3, '49, see NOTE), Monk (Trickster's henchman, also as cab driver, possibly next in Trickster's gang in CapC #72/3, '49)
OTHER CHARACTERS: "Steve's" students, messenger, doctor, 2 taxi drivers (1 voice only, 1 bts in cab), Golden Girl, 3 criminals (both on cover only)
LOCATIONS/ITEMS: Manhattan inc Lee School w/"Steve's" classroom, City Hospital & Trickster's garage hideout; Monk's car (equipped w/gas dispensers), Trickster's cane, Trickster & Monk's guns, garage's car ramp & gas pump, Cap's match, criminals' safe trap & knife (on cover only)
SYNOPSIS: Steve retrieves Bucky, recovered from his injuries, from City Hospital, but when they hail a cab, they are gassed into unconsciousness by the driver, Trickster's henchman Monk. At his garage hideout, the Trickster reveals he knows Bucky is Cap's crimefighting partner and has abducted him to bait a trap. He releases Steve to inform the media so Cap will find out. Steve instead returns as Cap to find Bucky tied to a car ramp. He moves to untie Bucky, but Trickster elevates the car ramp to shoot them. Cap hurls his shield to disarm Trickster, then knocks out Monk. Bucky grabs a fuel nozzle and dowses Trickster with gasoline. Cap threatens him with a lit match and Trickster surrenders.
NOTE: Per modern continuity, this is the final golden age appearance of Fred Davis as Bucky. Jack Monroe takes up the Bucky identity in YM #24/2, '53. The Trickster holds the distinction of being the first villain confirmed to have realized that Bucky Barnes and Cap's partner Bucky are one and the same, though CapC #8/4, '41 implied that the Black Witch also did so. "Steve" is a physics teacher in this story. Trickster's real name revealed in OHMU:HC #8, '09.

2ND STORY: "Captain America in Terror Is Blind!" (7 pages)
CREDITS: Ken Bald (pencils), Syd Shores (inks)
FEATURE CHARACTER: Captain America (also in fb between CapC #70/2, '48 fb & CapC #67, '48, next in SubC #31/4, '49, MC #91/4, '49)
VILLAIN: Dr. Teague (Astronomy-Physics teacher, in fb only, dies)
OTHER CHARACTERS: Jonathan Presto (Teague's protégé, teacher, also in fb), Helen Bryant (Teague's ward, also in fb), Weston (Astronomy-Physics teacher), Quentin Foss (Teague's financial backer, in fb only), Jonathan's seeing-eye dog
LOCATIONS/ITEMS: Teague's astronomy lab w/telescope & home, hospital (all in fb), Lee School; Teague's electronic binocular (destroyed), filter, Foss' sword-cane (broken) (all in fb only), Jonathan's cane (also in fb)
FLASHBACK: Lee School instructor Dr. Teague and his assistant Jonathan work to create the electronic binocular. Jonathan and Teague's

ward Helen become engaged, but Jonathan spends so much time on Teague's project Helen feels neglected. When Foss, Teague's financial backer, romantically pursues Helen, Jonathan grows jealous. He confronts Foss, but Cap intervenes. When Helen decides to reconcile with Jonathan, Teague becomes concerned Foss will withdraw funds. Allowing Jonathan to take the first look through the electronic binocular, Teague deliberately removes the device's glare-reducing filter, blinding Jonathan so that, in Teague's mind, he will be unable to support Helen. Realizing Teague intentionally blinded him, Jonathan goes from the hospital to the lab. There, he lashes out with his cane, knocking Teague down. Teague falls beneath the binocular which channels enough solar energy to kill him. An anguished Helen later destroys the binocular.
SYNOPSIS: Steve tells the story to Teague's replacement Weston, adding that Foss withdrew funding and the electronic binocular was never repaired. He then introduces Weston to Jonathan, now an Academy for the Blind instructor, and his wife Helen.
NOTE: "Steve" is a history teacher in this story.

3RD STORY: "Let's Play Detective: The Mark of Death!" (1 page)
CREDITS: Al Bellman (art)
FEATURE CHARACTER: Skip McCoy (next in LawLose #7/3, '49, ComMys #5/2, '49, Crimef #7/2, '49, SubC #32/2, '49, ComMys #6/3, '49, CapC #73/2, '49)
VILLAIN: Gambler
OTHER CHARACTERS: Police inc chief, Rick Masters (gambler, dies)
LOCATIONS/ITEMS: Manhattan inc police HQ
SYNOPSIS: After strangling gambler Rick Masters, a man claims Masters tried to mug him, and he killed Masters in self-defense. However, McCoy notices from Masters' wounds that he was strangled from behind, disproving the self-defense claim, and arrests the man, who confesses.
NOTE: Story followed by letter from the editor (1 page), defending comic books from Dr. Fredric Wertham (1895-1981) & his charge that they are a factor in juvenile delinquency.

4TH STORY: "Fate Fixed a Fight!" (7 pages)
CREDITS: Stan Lee (writer), Russ Heath (pencils), Jack Binder (inks)
FEATURE CHARACTER: The Witness (story narrator, unseen by the characters, last in Ideal #4/2, '49, next in AmazMys #32/3, '49)
OTHER CHARACTERS: Dusty "Feet-First" Mangler (boxer, also in photo on tavern wall), Cha-Cha (Dusty's manager), Sid Brophy, Young Hunter & other boxers (some in photos only), Hunter's manager, Sam & fellow bookie, bartender, cab driver, referees, reporters/sports writers, scalpers, bookmakers, boxing match attendees, Slats & other sparring partners, horse (in painting), woman (on poster)
LOCATIONS/ITEMS: Manhattan inc boxing arena w/dressing room & tavern, other boxing arenas (1 w/dressing room), promoters' office, Dusty's apartment, park
SYNOPSIS: Weary of throwing fights for increasingly lower bribes and an equally lowered reputation, 15-year-veteran boxer Dusty Mangler decides to stage a comeback and reach a championship bout. Initially dubious, his manager Cha-Cha becomes convinced of Dusty's chances. As the high-stakes bout approaches, however, Dusty, planning to bet on his opponent and throw the fight, declines to train, to Cha-Cha's dismay. Facing Young Hunter, Dusty plans to take a dive in the fourth round, but Hunter goes down instead and Dusty wins. After the fight, Cha-Cha reveals that he paid Hunter $8,000 to throw the fight. Dusty reveals he bet all of his and Cha-Cha's money on Hunter, ruining them both.

TEXT STORY: "The Whispering Voice" (2 pages)
CREDITS: Writer unknown
FEATURE CHARACTER: Jake Dorgan (ex-con, Blaine's chauffeur, also in fb years before)
OTHER CHARACTERS: Alton Blaine (Psychic Research Society head, also in fb), Annie (Blaine's cook, in fb only), telephone operator (voice only), police, Jake's "pal" (mentioned, gave him gun), haunted house owner & former tenants (mentioned)
LOCATIONS/ITEMS: Lunchroom, haunted house; Jake's guns (1 in fb only), police guns, Blaine's car, telephone
FLASHBACK: Jake Dorgan, Alton Blaine's chauffeur, tries to rob his boss. He shoots and wounds Blaine's cook, Annie but Blaine catches him.
SYNOPSIS: Jake is released from prison. He gets a gun, then visits Blaine, and gets his old job back. When Blaine, in his role as Psychic Research head, decides to investigate a "whispering voice" in a supposedly haunted house at midnight, Jake figures this is the best time to kill him. The two men sit at a table in the dark until Jake pulls his gun but he chooses to postpone the killing in order to torment Blaine. He occasionally hears a ghostly "whispering voice." Suddenly, the police burst in and arrest him, telling Blaine, "the girl called us in a rush." Jake now notices the phone receiver in Blaine's hand and realizes he lifted it off the cradle so the operator, who sounded like a "whispering voice," could eavesdrop and call the police.
NOTE: Appears between 2nd & 3rd stories. Story followed by "Stamp News" (1 page, Kent B. Stiles, writer)

CAPTAIN AMERICA COMICS #72 (May 1949)

"Captain America Meets Murder in the Mind!" (12 pages)

CREDITS: Gene Colan (pencils), Jean Thompson (editorial consultant), Al Avison (c art)
FEATURE CHARACTER: Captain America
SUPPORTING CAST: Golden Girl (between MC #91/4-92/3, '49)
VILLAINS: John Dolan (deformed criminal, also in fb to his childhood), John Dolan's Evil Self (denizen of Dolan's mind)
OTHER CHARACTERS: Dr. Sigmund Adler (criminal psychiatrist), Nancy Lowell (Dolan's girlfriend), police, Dolan's victim, Nerve Center switchboard operator, Acrophobia, Chamber of Nightmares, Claustrophobia, Inferiority Complex, black cat, index finger controller (bts, in contact w/switchboard operator), others (prev 8

enizens of Dolan's mind), Dolan's parents & baby brother (both in fb only) 4 Dolan mind figures (on cover only)

LOCATIONS/ITEMS: Manhattan inc Dolan's apartment, "Steve's" apartment, adjacent alley & Adler's office, Dolan's mind inc nerve center switchboard, memory files, mathematical apparatus, trap door to subconscious & subconscious w/Wit's End (cliff), Dolan's childhood apartment (in fb only); Dolan's pistol, Evil Self's dagger & gun, Adler's light, Dolan's mother's brooch (in fb only)

FLASHBACK: Young Johnny Dolan believes his mother loves his baby brother instead of him. He steals his mother's brooch as a token of her love. When his mother finds out, she slaps him, denouncing him as a thief and future criminal.

SYNOPSIS: Steve and Betsy meet with Dr. Adler. John Dolan, a criminal whose facial paralysis worsens with every crime, robs and pistol-whips a man outside Steve's window. Cap and Golden Girl capture Dolan. Hoping to cure Dolan's criminal tendencies, Adler, via hypnosis, projects himself, Cap and Golden Girl into Dolan's mind. Moving into his subconscious, they encounter Dolan's Evil Self, who hinders their search for a pivotal memory. Cap knocks him aside, and the three observe Dolan's past. Adler realizes Dolan's mother's slap has determined Dolan's actions and resulted in his psychosomatic deformity. After the three return, Dolan, his face no longer paralyzed, expresses remorse and allows himself to be arrested, planning to make a new start upon release.

NOTE: Dr. Sigmund Adler's name is a portmanteau of the names of psychiatrists Sigmund Freud (1856-1939) and Alfred Adler (1870-1937). The version of Dolan's "mind" into which Cap and company travel may be a version of the Mindscape, 1st in Sleep #3, '91. Bottom third of final page features ad for "Amazing Mysteries."

2ND STORY: "The Magnificent Failure!" (4 pages)

CREDITS: Stan Lee (writer)

FEATURE CHARACTER: The Witness (passive observer of crimes, last in AmazMys #32/3, '49, next in MC #92/2, '49; see NOTE)

SUPPORTING CAST: John Sheldon (research chemist, dies)

VILLAINS: Anton & Joseph (Communist agents, both die)

OTHER CHARACTERS: Prof. Jason, Sheldon's science colleagues, award presenters & admirers (in Sheldon's daydream only)

LOCATIONS/ITEMS: Sheldon's lab (in cellar, destroyed), scientist club; Element X (1000 times as powerful as atomic fission), Chemical Y, additional chemicals, Sheldon's equipment, award (in Sheldon's daydream only)

SYNOPSIS: The Witness observes the work of chemist John Sheldon, who has devoted his life to discovering Element X, "the missing link between the animate and the inanimate." Despite limited funding, professional ridicule, and other obstacles, Sheldon spends years on his obsession, finally discovering Element X, which proves to be far more powerful than anticipated. Anton and Joseph, two foreign operatives, offer to buy Element X for their country. When Sheldon declines, they threaten him with death. Realizing how Element X can be abused, Sheldon feigns cooperation but instead combines Element X with "Chemical Y," causing an explosion which kills him, Anton & Joseph. Sheldon's peers presume he died a failure, with only the Witness aware of Sheldon's success and sacrifice.

NOTE: This Witness should not be confused with the Twelve's crimefighting Witness, who debuted in MysC #7, '41. Element X designation next used in Sus #29/5, '53. Story followed by "A Letter to Our Readers and Their Parents!" (1 page) defending comic books, featuring 18th century novel reader.

3RD STORY: "The Tricks of the Trickster!" (7 pages)

CREDITS: Ken Bald (artist)

FEATURE CHARACTER: Captain America (next in MC #92/3, '49)

VILLAINS: The Trickster (last app to date) & his men (Spike named)

OTHER CHARACTERS: Police inc chief & patrol plane pilot (bts, in plane), bank patrons, Manhattan bystanders

LOCATIONS/ITEMS: Manhattan inc First Merchants' Bank, police HQ, Trickster's city hideout, National Bank & underground tunnel, Trickster's hillside hideout; Trickster's truck w/catapult, helicopter/autogyro, blimp w/cloud covering, cane, acetylene torch & steam shovel, police patrol plane (NC4007), police & criminals' firearms, Cap's 2-way radio (on belt), "gold bullion" crate

SYNOPSIS: The Trickster and henchmen rob a bank, then escape by catapulting themselves to a waiting helicopter, which itself docks in a hidden blimp. After Cap meets with police, a newspaper reports a gold shipment's arrival at National Bank. Although recognizing it as a trap, Trickster brazenly targets the bank, using a supposedly out-of-control steam shovel to break in. He and his men abscond with the supposed gold-filled crate, taking it into an underground tunnel. They open the crate and find Cap, who fights them until police, directed to the scene by Cap's two-way radio, arrest Trickster and company.

TEXT STORY: "A Buddy of Mine" (2 pages)

CREDITS: Writer unknown

FEATURE CHARACTER: Dodge Cottrell (last in CapC #63/TEXT, '47, also in fb to chr 1st app during WWII, last app to date)

VILLAIN: Dan (Dodge's army buddy, also in fb, dies)

OTHER CHARACTERS: Helen (Dan's girlfriend), teenage boy & his father (both die), sheriff, bystanders

LOCATIONS/ITEMS: Hospital inc Dan's room, hotel inc dining room, Helen's home inc front porch, levee, boy & father's shack, North Africa, Sicily, European Theater of Operations, town near Berlin (prev 4 in fb only); Dan's .30 caliber carbine & slippers

FLASHBACK: Dodge and army buddy Dan, "the most savage, the most vicious in combat," fight in World War II. Dan is wounded and apparently paralyzed.

SYNOPSIS: Dan writes Dodge for help. As Dodge drives into town, someone takes a shot at him. Dan, apparently confined to a wheelchair, tells Dodge that his girlfriend Helen has gotten threatening notes. Dodge interviews Helen, then hears gunshots as he returns to his hotel. He finds a teenage boy murdered nearby, the only clue being flat footprints in the mud. The boy's father is also murdered. Dodge realizes the footprints came from Dan's slippers. He confronts Dan, telling him he knows he can walk, that his "paralysis" is an alibi allowing him to commit violent crimes, that the boy had previously spotted him sneaking out of the hospital window, and that he invited Dodge to frame him for the boy's murder. Dodge gives Dan the choice of surrendering or taking his own life. Dan chooses suicide.

NOTE: Story appears between 2nd & 3rd stories.

CAPTAIN AMERICA COMICS #73 (July 1949)

"The Outcast of Time!" (12 pages)

CREDITS: Ken Bald (artist), Jean Thompson (editorial consultant), Al Gabriele (c art)
FEATURE CHARACTER: Captain America
VILLAINS: Wolf Turber ("Turber the Traitor," insane android native to AD 3010, also in Alan's television viewer), Turber's AD 3550 armies (bts), Turber's followers in 1649 & 1780 (bts), British soldiers of 1780, Native American raiders of 1649
OTHER CHARACTERS: Alan Tremont, Nanette Tremont (Alan's sister,) policeman (both also in Alan's television viewer), San of AD 2548 (dies), sanitarium guard, Charlie (sanitarium patient), cab driver, 2 bystanders (1 in Alan's television viewer), Nanette's girlfriend (bts, on phone w/Alan), 6 Dutch settlers of 1649, American soldier of 1780, 3 natives of AD 50,000, dinosaur-like creature of AD 50,000, protoplasm creature of AD 2,001,948, native of AD 3550 (bts), George Washington (1732-1799, bts), torch stalactites w/historical figures inc knight, Colonial American, present-day woman, 2 others (on cover only)
LOCATIONS/ITEMS: Manhattan inc Tremont's 5th Ave residence & Central Park, New Jersey inc Turber Sanitarium w/Turber's office, Dutch outpost fort of 1649 (future site of Central Park), Manhattan site of 1780, domed Manhattan of AD 3550 (partially destroyed), Manhattan ruins of AD 50,000, Earth of AD 2,001,948, cavern (cover only); Turber's Time Tower, San's Time Tower, Alan's television receiver, Turber's gunlike weapon, metalite bonds & notes, British muskets, Native Americans' bows & flaming arrows, AD 3550 Manhattan's aircraft & weapons
SYNOPSIS: Cap assists Alan Tremont with an experimental television receiver, which displays a futuristic scene. After Alan's sister Nanette departs, the receiver shows her Central Park abduction. Cap and Alan learn the abductor is Wolf Turber, Nanette's former doctor. A Time Tower arrives, carrying San of the year 2548, to warn them that Turber is a time traveler who briefly conquered San's era before coming to 1948. Consulting Turber's notes, Cap finds conquest plans for 1780, 1649, and 3550. In San's Tower, the three visit 1780, then 1649, but Turber has already failed and departed both eras. They arrive in 3550, where Turber has rallied armies to fight Manhattan's armies. San dies under debris, but Cap and Alan find Turber, still with Nanette. Cap enters Turber's tower. It travels further into the future. Turber imprisons Cap as Earth's civilizations collapse and revert to savagery. Turber stops circa AD 2,001,948, when Earth is lifeless save for protoplasm. Cap escapes and knocks Turber out, discovering he is a robot. Leaving Turber's deactivated form in the future, Cap and Nanette return home, as does Alan in the second Tower.
NOTE: This is the second instance of a Marvel super hero traveling through time, the first being the Blonde Phantom (Louise Grant) in BlonPhan #21, '49.

2ND STORY: "Are You a Detective?: Carnival of Crime!" (2 pages)
CREDITS: Al Bellman (artist)
FEATURE CHARACTER: Skip McCoy (next in Crimef#8/4, '49)
SUPPORTING CAST: Pepper Burns
VILLAIN: Rudolph Blades (circus knife-thrower, also in his story)
OTHER CHARACTERS: Christine Blades (circus knife-thrower, also in Rudolph's story, dies), police chief, circus performers & employees (Smitty named), circus attendees, 2 bystanders, circus animals (black panther, camel seen)
LOCATIONS/ITEMS: Manhattan inc police HQ, circus grounds w/tent; circus trailers & cages, knives & target
SYNOPSIS: After circus knife-throwers Rudolph Blades and his wife Christine, who wants to move on to Broadway, quarrel, Christine is found dead by knife wound. McCoy questions Rudolph, who claims the death was a rehearsal mishap; Christine held out a target that he hit with his first knife but missed with his second, striking Christine in the chest. McCoy notices the target has no tear from a supposed first knife throw and arrests Rudolph, who confesses.
NOTE: Pepper is identified here as McCoy's nephew.

3RD STORY: "The Mystery of the Deadly Dreams!" (10 pages)
CREDITS: Ken Bald (artist)
FEATURE CHARACTER: Captain America (also in pfb)
SUPPORTING CAST: Golden Girl (also in pfb, last in MC #92/3, '49, chr next in Cap:P #4, '11, next in Cap #76, '54)
VILLAINS: The Dream Master (cult leader, also in pfb), Filip & Oris (Dream Master's enforcers, in pfb only)
OTHER CHARACTERS: Principal Bell (also in pfb), Miss Prim (Bell's secretary, also in pfb), Dream Master disciples, sound truck driver (voice only), would-be suicide, retired millionaire, Manhattan bystanders (prev 5 in pfb only), Dream Master's clients & would-be clients (mostly in pfb), imprisoned lunatics (also in pfb), police, Genghis Khan (1162-1227) & his hordes (in Cap & Golden Girl's dreams only), birds (in pfb)
LOCATIONS/ITEMS: Manhattan inc Lee School w/Principal's office (also in pfb), Temple of Silence (777 Hope Rd, also in pfb) w/Room of Peace, auditorium and cellar dungeon, bridge & millionaire's residence (both in pfb only); Dream Master's sound truck (pfb only), dream powder (also in pfb) & knife, lunatics' clubs (also in pfb), disciples' jewels (pfb only), horde's weapons (in Cap & Golden Girl's dreams only)
FLASHBACK: The Dream Master sends disciples to gather the depressed and disabled, to whom he offers contentment. Dozens of people flock to him, including Lee School's Principal Bell. Investigating, Cap and Golden Girl sneak into Dream Master's Temple of Silence and learn the contentment Dream Master offers, for high prices, is seemingly eternal sleep via his dream powder. In a cellar dungeon, they find imprisoned lunatics, driven mad by the powder. They escape into an auditorium full of clients. Cap and Golden Girl outfight hulking aides Filip and Oris, but Dream Master uses dream powder to place them in a shared dream (p).
SYNOPSIS: Before Cap can be killed, either by Dream Master in the real world or by Genghis Khan in his dream, the lunatics swarm Dream Master, who flees. As Cap and Golden Girl revive, the commotion awakens the sleepers and attracts police attention. The lunatics recover from the dream powder's effects, but Dream Master escapes through a secret passage, leaving Cap and Golden Girl to wonder if he will return.

NOTE: This is Betsy's last app as Golden Girl.

TEXT STORY: "The Plainest Clue" (2 pages)
CREDITS: Writer unknown
FEATURE CHARACTER: Peter Snell (Withers' cousin)
OTHER CHARACTERS: Jonathan Withers (family patriarch, dies), Anita (Withers' granddaughter), 2 nephews (Tom Withers named), another cousin, guests, servants, Thomas (butler), police, Police Sergeant Marks
LOCATIONS/ITEMS: Withers' mansion inc third floor study, bath & bedroom; Snell's revolver & silencer, Withers' electric clock
SYNOPSIS: When wealthy Jonathan Withers refuses to allow his ne'er-do-well cousin Peter Snell to marry his granddaughter Anita, Snell murders him with a silenced revolver, missing with his first shot. He returns to the family downstairs at midnight, pretending he put the old man to bed. The butler finds Withers dead and calls the police. Clues point to a burglar and Snell tells them that he left Withers alive at midnight, figuring they cannot pinpoint time of death. However, the police find that the first shot hit an electric clock's plug, interrupting the current and starting it running backwards. They take the mid-point between the clock's time of 10 PM and the current time of 2 AM and come up with midnight as time of death, nailing Snell.
NOTE: Story appears between 2nd and 3rd stories. Followed by "Stamp News" (1 page, Kent B. Stiles, writer) & "A Letter to Our Readers and Their Parents!" (1 page) urging kids to read great literature along with comics.

CAPTAIN AMERICA'S WEIRD TALES #74 (October 1949)

"Captain America in The Red Skull Strikes Again!" (6 pages)

CREDITS: Stan Lee (writer), Jean Thompson (editorial consultant), Martin Nodell (c art)
FEATURE CHARACTER: Captain America (next in Cap:P #4, '11, Cap Ann #6, '82, see NOTE)
VILLAINS: Red Skull (see NOTE), "Master Judge of the Lower Depths," "Messenger of the Powers of Darkness," other demons, Charon (1st but chr last in Conan #250, '91, chr next in Thor #462, '93)
OTHER CHARACTER: Golden Girl (on cover only)
LOCATIONS/ITEMS: "Lower Depths" inc River Styx & "Master Judge's" chamber, Cap's home; Fatal Book ("forbidden book," "Great Volume"), Skull's Grim Reaper scythe
SYNOPSIS: The Red Skull, consigned to "hell," writes 's name in the book of the damned. Reading it, the "Messenger of the Powers of Darkness" retrieves Cap from his home and takes him to the "Lower Depths." Once here, however, the Messenger tells the "Master Judge" that it is a mistake. The Skull appears, admitting the deception, but claiming no one can leave the "Lower Depths" once brought there. The "Master Judge" pits the two in combat. When Cap wins, the "Judge" releases him. Cap finds himself in his armchair, sure it was all a dream, except that he still has a torn piece of the Skull's shirt in his hand.
NOTE: Whether the Skull shown here is the deceased George Maxon, the spirit of Johann Shmidt while in suspended animation, the Skull who apparently dies in CapC #61, '47 or someone else altogether is not specified. The identity of the "Master Judge" and his demons is also not specified. Per modern continuity, this is the final golden age appearance of Jeff Mace as Captain America. Captain America and Bucky next appear in YM #24/2, '53. Cap #155, '72 reveals these are not the originals, but fans who took up their heroes' costumed identities. See CapC #76, '54 NOTE. Splash panel is same as page 4 panel 3.

2ND STORY: "The Legend of...The Frozen Ghost!" (6 pages)
CREDITS: Unknown
FEATURE CHARACTER: Jack Davis (Center City reporter, dies)
VILLAIN: Frozen Ghost (Francis Dillon, killer, also in pfb & as symbolic image)
OTHER CHARACTERS: Bank guard, homeowner, Dillon's 3rd victim, Judge Peter Collins, jury foreman (all die), bystanders (some die, Smitty named), jury (all in pfb)
LOCATIONS/ITEMS: Point Blanc (Canada) inc mountains, Judge Collins' home, grocery store, courtroom, bank, man's home, alley (all in pfb) train station; Dillon's knife (in pfb)
FLASHBACK: Francis Dillon robs the Point Blanc bank, killing the bank guard, then robs and kills others. Caught, he is sentenced to death but escapes. He is found frozen to death after a blinding snow storm. The next time it snows, his frozen ghost appears and kills Judge Collins. Weeks later, with more snow falling, the jury foreman is similarly killed.
SYNOPSIS: Sent by his newspaper to write a feature on the Frozen Ghost, Jack Davis arrives at the train station. He tells a shadowy figure there about his assignment, disbelieving the story. As snow starts to fall, the figure reveals itself as the Frozen Ghost. "Now do you believe?" he asks, as it attacks.
NOTE: Splash panel is same as page 6 panel 2.

3RD STORY: "The Thing in the Swamps!" (6 pages)
CREDITS: Chu Hing (inks)
FEATURE CHARACTER: John Vandiver (descendant of John Vandiver Sr., also as Marsh Monster)
OTHER CHARACTERS: John Vandiver Sr. (current John's ancestor, also as Marsh Monster, dies), John Vandiver Jr. (son, death mentioned), Melanie Vandiver, (wife, dies), Peter Humphries (Vandiver's friend, dies, also as ghost), party guests, bat (all in fb over a hundred years before), Dr. Paul Townslee (psychiatrist), current John's nightmare figures
LOCATIONS/ITEMS: Dr. Townslee's office, Vandiver home (also in fb) inc John's bedroom, marshes on Vandiver property, clock tower (both in fb); Humphries' book
FLASHBACK: More than 100 years ago, the first John Vandiver becomes jealous of his friend Peter Humphries dancing with his wife at his 30th birthday party. He takes Peter out to the nearby marshes and lets him fall in quicksand. While sinking, Peter curses John saying that he

and each subsequent oldest son of the family will become, at age 30, a "horrible monster condemned to dwell for a year in the filthy waters of this marsh going forth only to kill" and becoming incurably insane thereafter. When the clock strikes midnight, John becomes that monster and kills Melanie.

SYNOPSIS: The last John Vandiver tells psychiatrist Paul Townslee of the family curse and that he turns 30 tomorrow. Paul tells him to go home and get some rest. John awakens to find a marshy-smelling book in his room, apparently written by Humphries' ghost and telling the story. At midnight, John becomes the marsh monster. Humphries' ghost appears and watches. Knowing John is the last of his line, he can finally rest.

NOTE: Splash panel is same as page 6 panel 5.

4TH STORY: "The Tomb of Terror!" (6 pages)
CREDITS: Unknown
FEATURE CHARACTERS: Leo Foster, Rae Foster (archeologists)
VILLAIN: Tut-Lak-Omor ("Black Pharoah," bts, possessing Sal-Hammin)
OTHER CHARACTERS: Sal-Hammin (Egyptologist, dies), Egyptian bystanders, sphinx (as statue in tomb, Egyptian figures (as statues in tomb & in hieroglyphs)
LOCATIONS/ITEMS: Egypt inc village, Sal-Hammin's house & pyramid w/Tut-Lak-Omor's tomb; box for Tut-Lak-Omor's heart
SYNOPSIS: Leo & Rae Foster, staying with their colleague Sal-Hammin, seek the tomb of Tut-Lak-Omor, a pharaoh so evil that his people threw his body to wild beasts, leaving only his heart to bury. Sal-Hammin warns the Fosters to avoid the tomb but they sneak out and enter it, finding a box containing Tut's heart. That night, a loud thumping awakens the Fosters. They find the box empty and Sal-Hammin possessed by Tut-Lak-Omor. Sal-Hammin rampages through the village, finally abducting Rae and taking her to the tomb. Leo grabs the box and, confronting Sal-Hammin, pretends to disbelieve that he is possessed, adding that the box was likely always empty. To prove Leo wrong, Tut-Lak-Omor returns his heart to the box, which Leo throws back into the tomb. Sal-Hammin dies from the ordeal and the Fosters know it is their fault.
NOTE: Story takes place in July 1932. Splash panel is same as page 6 panel 7.

TEXT STORY: "For Gold Alone" (2 pages)
CREDITS: Writer unknown
FEATURE CHARACTER: Bob Hammond (Dr. Warwick's assistant)
VILLAINS: Two burglars (1 dies)
OTHER CHARACTERS: Dr. Warwick (art collector, dies), police
LOCATIONS/ITEMS: Dr. Warwick's house w/office & Bob's bedroom; gold cup, Warwick's gun, Egyptian onyx, Bob's tourniquet
SYNOPSIS: Bob is intrigued by Dr. Warwick's inscribed gold cup. Warwick claims every past owner has died violently but that it brings him happiness and peace. That night, a gunshot awakens Bob. He finds Warwick holding a gun on two would-be burglars, one bleeding profusely. The cup, seized by the bleeding burglar, is on the floor. Although Bob applies a tourniquet, the bleeding doesn't stop and the man dies. Months later, Warwick suffers a stroke. Dying, he tells Bob that the gold cup only kills those who possess it for its monetary value, like the burglar who touched it, then bled to death. When Bob says he loves it for its beauty and would never sell it, Warwick gives it to him, and then dies peacefully.
NOTE: Story appears between 2nd & 3rd stories. The cup's inscription reads, "Let him beware who for gold alone should care."

CAPTAIN AMERICA'S WEIRD TALES #75 (February 1950)

"Hoofprints of Doom!" (8 pages)

CREDITS: Gene Colan (pencils, c art), Jean Thompson (editorial consultant)
FEATURE CHARACTER: James Harris (sailor, also in gallows vision, dies following story)
VILLAINS: Invisible creature, fakir (dies)
OTHER CHARACTERS: MacReady ("Mac," Harris' fellow sailor, dies), police (Burke named), reporter, Casbah denizens
LOCATIONS/ITEMS: Algiers inc Casbah, Liverpool (England) inc boarded-up house, prison & gallows, Sahara Desert w/fakir's tent; fakir's flute & knife, plaster, ropes, police billy clubs
SYNOPSIS: On May 10, 1936, sailors Harris and MacReady visit the Casbah, where a fakir promises Harris a personal revelation. Later, he shows them a vision of Harris hanging on a gallows, then attempts to stab him but is killed himself. As Harris and MacReady depart, they see cloven hoofprints in the sand. Two years later, the two linger in Liverpool. On August 12, they take shelter in a boarded-up house, where an invisible creatures kills MacReady. It then attacks Harris, who wounds it, ties it up, covers it with plaster, to render it visible, then calls the police. Disbelieving his account, the police break open the plaster and find nothing. Arrested for MacReady's death, Harris is sentenced to hang. Cloven hoofprints follow him to the gallows.
NOTE: Captain America does not appear in this issue. This is the title's final issue until the publication of Cap #76, '54. Each story features the disclaimer, "All names and places in this true-to-life story are fictitious. Any similarity between actual persons or places and those used in this story are purely coincidental."

2ND STORY: "The Thing in the Chest!" (7 pages)
CREDITS: Unknown
FEATURE CHARACTERS: Ben Jackson (playwright), Nancy Terry (actress)
VILLAINS: The Thing in the Chest (composite entity of the evils within Pandora's Box, also in fb during JIM #74, '61 fb, 1st, next in UT #54/3, '57), Spirits of Fear, Greed, Hate, War (fb only)
OTHER CHARACTERS: Hope (embodiment of hope, also bts in fb, during JIM #74, '61 fb, 1st, next bts in UT #54/3, '57), Pandora (in fb only, during JIM #74, '61 fb, next in JIM #74, '61), town crier, villagers, actor, theatre audience

LOCATIONS/ITEMS: England (in 1426) inc town hall & Ben's dwelling, "the Unknown" ("the Place That Does Not Exist," "the Further Reaches of Space," "the Last Moments of Time," "Where No Light Ever Enters," "the Thing's domain," presumably within Pandora's Box), Pandora's ancient chamber (fb only); Pandora's Box (also in fb during JIM #74, '61 fb, 1st, next in UT #54/3, '57), Ben's script

FLASHBACK: In ancient times, Pandora receives guardianship of a Box but is warned not to open it. Giving into curiosity, she does, and evil spirits escape. From within the Box, Hope promises to forever battle against the evils.

SYNOPSIS: In 1426 England, Ben writes the play "Pandora's Box," with his beloved Nancy in the lead and a box acquired from a gypsy as the central prop. During the performance, Nancy opens the Box, which is the true Box of Pandora, and the Thing emerges to pull her within. After the audience flees, Ben opens the Box to release the Spirit of Hope, who teleports with him to the Thing's domain. While Hope distracts the Thing, Ben runs to Nancy, and Hope teleports them back to the theater. Ben hurls the Box into a fire, and the Thing screams within as the box is seemingly destroyed.

3RD STORY: "The Bat!" (8 pages)

CREDITS: Unknown

FEATURE CHARACTER: Duke Fernando de Toledano (also in fb almost 300 years ago, dies and becomes a vampire, also as bat)

VILLAIN: Countess Dolores Ibanez of Portugal ("Duchess de Toledano," also in fb, a vampire, also as bat)

OTHER CHARACTERS: Count Ramon de la Cruz (dies), Baron Diego Mendoza, Baroness Mendoza, wedding guests, Fernando & Ramon's dueling seconds, Fernando's horse, boar (dies), bats (all in fb), Michael & Grace (vacationing couple), Phillipe (innkeeper)

LOCATIONS/ITEMS: Spain (in 1927 & c 1630s) inc Brihuega w/inn, glen (also in fb), Fernando's ancestral castle, Fernando's Barcelona estate, Mendoza castle (prev 3 in fb only); Ramon & Fernando's swords, Fernando's spear (all in fb)

FLASHBACK: Centuries ago, Fernando de Toledano wounds a boar. He finds it drained of blood and meets Dolores Ibanez, to whom he offers the hospitality of his castle. The two fall in love and marry, but Fernando's friend Ramon warns him Dolores is a vampire. Outraged, Fernando kills him in a duel. When Fernando and Dolores visit Baron Mendoza, Dolores, in batlike form, feeds upon him. Later, Fernando, unaware Dolores has been drinking his blood, falls ill. When Dolores attacks Fernando in bat-form, he stabs her. Reverting to human form, she tells him he too is now a vampire, and they will spend eternity contesting for the blood of any who venture into the glen where they met.

SYNOPSIS: In the summer of 1927, Michael and Grace, touring Spain, stay at an inn in Brihuega. They doze in the vampires' glen but sounds of bloodthirsty winged animals awaken and frighten Grace. The couple return to the inn, where Phillipe tells them of Fernando and Dolores. They remain skeptical until Phillipe points out two giant bats hovering above the glen.

TEXT STORY: "A Cigarette Stamped Death" (2 pages)

CREDITS: Writer unknown

FEATURE CHARACTERS: Police Lieutenant Johnson & 3 police lab technicians ("chemists & physicists")

VILLAINS: FJ "Champ" Maggio, Charlie Danner, their gang (all die) & lawyer

OTHER CHARACTERS: Police, District Attorney, judge, bailiff, jury, Elite Insurance night watchman (mentioned, killed in robbery)

LOCATIONS/ITEMS: Maggio's apartment, police HQ inc cells, DA's office, Elite Insurance Company (mentioned, robbed); technicians' lab equipment, Maggio's pistol (serial # S&W 87559476), suit (labeled "Hart's Clothes for Men") & cigarette butt

SYNOPSIS: Lieutenant Johnson puts Champ Maggio & his men in jail overnight for suspicion of robbing the Elite Insurance Company's safe and killing the night watchmen. While they are held, Johnson brings lab technicians to Maggio's apartment. They do a thorough and scientific search. At the trial, Maggio is sure of acquittal until the DA brings out the lab evidence, proving Maggio's gun did the killing, that the robbed safe contained traces of lint from Maggio's suit, and that Maggio smoked the cigarette stamped out on the Insurance Company's floor. Maggio and his men are convicted and executed.

NOTE: Story appears between 1st & 2nd stories.

CAPTAIN AMERICA #76 (May 1954)

"The Betrayers!" (6 pages)

CREDITS: John Romita (art, co-c art), Carl Burgos (co-c art)

FEATURE CHARACTER: Captain America (William Burnside, last in YM #27/2, '54; see NOTE)

SUPPORTING CAST: Bucky (Jack Monroe, last in YM #27/2, '54; see NOTE), Betsy Ross (last in CapC #73/3, '49, chr last in Cap:P #4, '11)

GUEST STARS: Captain America (Steve Rogers), Bucky (James Buchanan Barnes) (both only in fb between CapC #31/5-32, '43)

VILLAINS: Will Benson (photographer & spy), Connie Blake (editor & spy ring head, dies), 4 spies, safecracker, 9 Communists, 2 muggers, lone spy, Nazi sub crew (fb only)

OTHER CHARACTERS: Top Sgt. Shanty Trucks (1st), US Army soldiers (1st Platoon, "Steve" & "Bucky's" unit, some bts), General, Major, muggers' victim, police, criminals (both on cover only)

LOCATIONS/ITEMS: Manhattan inc 2 Communist meeting places, burglary site & office w/confidential file cabinet, US Army camp inc HQ 101 & Major's office, mountain road, Blake's hideout mansion (destroyed), military plant (on cover only); Blake's film box, enlargements cabinet, microfilm cases & developing photos (all destroyed), Benson's camera w/infra-red lens & photos, Cap's match, "Steve's" rifle, Nazi sub (fb only), police firearms (cover only)

FLASHBACK: The wartime Cap and Bucky battle a Nazi sub crew.

SYNOPSIS: After Steve and Bucky join the army, they learn Betsy Ross has been accused of treason because her Army human interest news stories are invariably followed by security leaks. Betsy's editor Blake, claiming to be Cap's personal friend, promises Cap will investigate. Later, Betsy discovers her photographer Benson is the security leak. Unaware Cap and Bucky are hitching a ride on his car roof, Benson drives her to a mansion where co-conspirator Blake awaits. They try to force Betsy to write a confession and commit suicide, but Cap, who never before met Blake and thus suspected his guilt, sets the mansion ablaze and punches Blake into the fire, leaving him to die. Cap and Bucky capture Benson to clear Betsy.

NOTE: Cover-labeled, "Captain America...Commie Smasher!" Betsy Ross now has red hair and is a reporter. Cap #155, '72 reveals that Captain America and Bucky here are not the originals, but fans William Burnside (name revealed in Cap #602, '10) and Jack Munroe (name revealed in Cap #281, '83) who rediscovered the super soldier formula and elected to become the new Cap and Bucky. Bucky claims Betsy Ross "thinks that Captain America is a great big hero but that Steve Rogers is the all-American flop" even though Betsy should know that "Steve" is Captain America. Per the '72 retcon, this could be because Betsy knows that Burnside, despite his plastic surgery, is not actually Steve Rogers.

2ND STORY: "Captain America Strikes!" (6 pages)
CREDITS: John Romita (art)
FEATURE CHARACTER: Captain America
SUPPORTING CAST: Bucky, Betsy Ross (last chr app)
VILLAINS: Miro & Tomas, neutral nation's Secretary of War, 3 spies
OTHER CHARACTERS: Sgt. Trucks (last app to date), US Army soldiers & officers, 3 MPs, US ambassador, embassy employees & tourists, Communist skeleton (hand only, in symbolic splash panel only)
LOCATIONS/ITEMS: Neutral nation inc US Army camp, US embassy w/pavilion & Secretary of War's home; Miro & Tomas' car, Secretary of War, Tomas & MPs' firearms, gas can
SYNOPSIS: Steve and Bucky are stationed in a neutral nation, where the UN hopes to sufficiently impress the Secretary of War so he will allow US bases to be established there. Communist spies Miro and Tomas try to recruit Steve, whom they perceive as "a typical unhappy victim of Capitalism." Playing along, Steve accepts and meets the spies' leader, the Secretary of War himself. Steve is assigned to start a fire at the US embassy but instead dowses Miro and Tomas with gasoline. More spies break their cover and swarm Steve, who breaks free as Cap to join Bucky in defeating the spies. Meanwhile, the Secretary of War, the US ambassador, and others observe a US military parade. Cap hauls Miro and Tomas before the Secretary, whom they beg for help, blowing his cover. The Secretary takes the ambassador hostage, but Cap easily rescues him.

3RD STORY: "The Human Torch" (5 pages)
CREDITS: Russ Heath (art)
FEATURE CHARACTER: Human Torch (last in Sub #33/3, '54, next in MenAdv #27, '54, HT #37, '54, Sub #34/3, '54, YM #28, '54)
SUPPORTING CAST: Toro, Betty Wilson (both last in Sub #33/3, '54, next in MenAdv #27, '54), Police Chief Wilson (last in Sub #33/3, '54, next in HT #37/2, '54)
VILLAINS: The Vulture (also as illustration on his note to Wilson, last in YM #26, '54, next in YM #28, '54), Metallo (Vulture's "greatest" robot, deactivated), 4 Costene-built robots (short-circuited)
OTHER CHARACTERS: Hotel desk clerk, Seminole chief & villagers (some die prior to story), Prof. Costene (mentioned, kidnapped & killed by Vulture prior to story), sunbathers (on hotel roof), crocodiles
LOCATIONS/ITEMS: Florida inc town w/hotel, airport, Everglades, Seminole village & Vulture's base; Pan Eastern plane, Vulture's gun (on splash panel only) & note
SYNOPSIS: Following Prof. Costene's abduction, Torch and Toro consult Chief Wilson, vacationing in Florida. Wilson receives a note from the Vulture, threatening to kill his daughter Betty unless he leave Florida. Wilson departs, and Torch and Toro, seeking Vulture's lair, check the Everglades, where several Seminoles have been mysteriously killed. Vulture awaits them, accompanied by Costene-built robots that Torch and Toro lure into the water, short-circuiting them. Vulture sets a more powerful robot, Metallo, against them. Unable to burn Metallo, Torch welds its joints together, rendering it immobile. Having previously killed Costene, Vulture escapes, and Torch and Toro depart with Betty.

4TH STORY: "Come to the Commies!" (6 pages)
CREDITS: John Romita (art)
FEATURE CHARACTER: Captain America (next in MenAdv #27/2, '54, YM #28/2, '54)
SUPPORTING CAST: Bucky (next in MenAdv #27/2, '54)
VILLAINS: Indochina Communist officers & soldiers (some bts, shooting at Cap & Bucky)
OTHER CHARACTERS: US Army Colonel, officer & pilot (bts, flies Cap & Bucky into Communist territory), drugged tourists & legation workers, American Eagle (on Great Seal)
LOCATIONS/ITEMS: Vietnam ("Indochina") inc US Army camp w/HQ inc Colonel's office, water and dock behind Communist lines & Communist camp w/radio building and medical supply room; US plane, Communist firearms, broadcast scripts, radio microphone & drugs, water
SYNOPSIS: Assigned to rescue American citizens, who have been inexplicably broadcasting pro-Communist messages, Cap and Bucky fly to Communist territory. Learning Communists have drugged the Americans into cooperating, Cap offers to join the Communist cause and make his own broadcasts, pleasing the Communists. After secretly replacing the latest drug batch with water, Cap broadcasts the truth about the situation, and the prisoners, their drugged state wearing off, join Cap and Bucky in fighting the Communists and escaping.

TEXT STORY: "The Perfect Spy - " (2 pages)
CREDITS: Writer unknown
FEATURE CHARACTER: Johnny Blake (FBI agent)
VILLAINS: Hito (master torturer), Mitsu Haki & the "Japanese underground movement" (bts, planning to attack USA)
OTHER CHARACTERS: FBI agents, Kari Noka (informant, mentioned), Communist soldier (in illustration only)
LOCATIONS/ITEMS: Terrorist hideout, Canadian airstrip w/plane (underground's base, mentioned); Hito's razor-sharp clawed glove, FB

agents' submachine guns

SYNOPSIS: Having captured FBI agent Blake, Japanese terrorists torture him to learn how much he knows about their plans to bomb the UN. Blake reveals that, through an informant, he knows they have a secret Canadian airstrip from which they intend to launch their attack. The terrorists decide to speed up their plans, carelessly mentioning the base's specific location in Montreal. More FBI agents burst in, and Blake reveals his "capture" was arranged to manipulate the villains into revealing this information. After pummeling his torturer, Blake leaves the terrorists to his fellow agents.

NOTE: First page appears between 2nd & 3rd stories, second page between 3rd & 4th stories. Agent Blake may be the adult version of Johnny Blake, a youth who appeared in AllWin #1/TEXT, '41.

CAPTAIN AMERICA #77 (July 1954)

"You Die at Midnight!" (6 pages)

CREDITS: John Romita (art, c art)
FEATURE CHARACTER: Captain America (next in Cap #38, '08 fb)
SUPPORTING CAST: Bucky (last in YM #28/2, '54, chr next in Cap #38, '08 fb)
VILLAINS: 4 Communist spies (Pete named)
OTHER CHARACTERS: Collins (ship designer), Collins' son, Jim (facility guard), 5 Russian ship crew members & their victim, 4 octopi (prev 3 on cover only)
LOCATIONS/ITEMS: Manhattan inc Collins apartment & Ace Shipyards w/government facility inc secret plans room, spies' hideout (in splash panel only); spies' car & firearms, midget atomic engine plans, ship w/octopus hold, Russian firearms & dagger (prev 3 on cover only)

SYNOPSIS: Visiting a troubled blind boy, Cap and Bucky learn Communist spies are extorting his father, ship designer Collins, into stealing secret plans by threatening the boy's life. Leaving Bucky with the boy, Cap follows the spies to the shipyard where Collins is sent into the facility to rob the safe. When Collins refuses to steal the plans, Cap recruits his assistance. "Collins" exits the facility. The spies, intending to kill him, return with him to his apartment building where they have apparently abducted his son. However, "Collins" is Cap concealed by the designer's hat and trenchcoat and the captured boy is Bucky. During the subsequent fight, a bullet grazes the blind boy, somehow restoring his sight. Cap and Bucky defeat the spies and take them to the police.

NOTE: Cover-labeled, "Captain America...Commie Smasher." Both Collins and his son initially believe Cap may be fictitious; this popular belief of the 1950s was first established in YM #24/2, '53.

2ND STORY: "The Man with No Face!" (6 pages)

CREDITS: John Romita (art)
FEATURE CHARACTER: Captain America
SUPPORTING CAST: Bucky (chr last in Cap #38, '08 fb)
VILLAINS: The Man with No Face (Philip Wing, "the Hatchet Man," Communist assassin, 1st but chr last in Cap #43, '08 fb, chr next in Cap #44, '09 fb) & his Communist henchmen (Lu Si named), 3 hoods inc their boss
OTHER CHARACTERS: Lt Howard Wing (Chinatown police), 2 Chinatown detectives (1 in splash panel only), Chinatown residents & tourists, alley cat
LOCATIONS/ITEMS: Manhattan inc Chinatown w/police HQ inc Wing's office (Room 902), businesses w/Chow Mein and Chop Suey restaurants & Man's with No Face's cellar hideout; Man with No Face's hatchet, Communist firearms & clubs, hood boss' hatchet, Wing's revolver

SYNOPSIS: When Communist agents try to extort Chinatown residents' cooperation by threatening their families in China, Cap and Bucky's friend Lt. Wing of the Chinatown police requests their help. Learning a Communist assassin, the Man with No Face, has threatened Wing's own twin brother, Cap and Bucky tail Wing. As expected, the Man with No Face lures Wing into a trap, and Cap and Bucky intervene. The Man flees, with Cap in pursuit. Revealing himself as Wing's twin, the Man jumps to his apparent death, intending the revelation to haunt Wing forever, but Cap vows to never reveal the Man's identity. With the Man's face crushed in the fall, Wing is kept from the truth.

NOTE: The Wing brothers first names revealed in OHMU:HC #4, '08. Although the Man With No Face is confirmed as dead by both Cap and Lieutenant Wing, he faces off against the Winter Soldier in Cap 44, '09 fb.

3RD STORY: "A Human Torch Featurette!" (5 pages)

CREDITS: Dick Ayers (art)
FEATURE CHARACTER: Human Torch (next in MenAdv #28, '54, HT #38, '54, Sub #35/3, '54)
SUPPORTING CAST: Toro (last in YM #28, '54, next in MenAdv #28, '54)
OTHER CHARACTERS: "The Thing" (8-limbed extraterrestrial geneticist from Arc Centauri, also in newspaper photo), fishing village residents inc mob, picnicking family (father, mother & 3 children w/Donny named), news vendor, TV anchorman (on TV)
LOCATIONS/ITEMS: Northern coastal fishing village inc Bait shop & Tackle shop, surrounding countryside w/cliff, lighthouse & sea, Manhattan; Thing's" spaceship, mob's torches & clubs

SYNOPSIS: When fishing village residents sight a strange creature, Torch and Toro investigate. Arriving, they see "the Thing" nearing a child, who falls from a cliff. While Torch rescues the child, Toro keeps the Thing under surveillance but inadvertently flies into a tree. Knocked unconscious, he plummets to his death. The Thing resurrects Toro and telepathically informs the heroes it is a stranded alien scientist. While Torch and Toro help repair its spaceship, an angry mob gathers nearby. The Thing departs, leaving Torch and Toro to regret humanity's unreadiness for alien contact.

NOTE: The Arc Centauri race should not be confused with the Alpha Centaurians from Sub #17, '69, the Centaurans from MysT #15, '53, the Centaurians, from MSH #18, '69, or the Centurii, from Thor #258, '77.

4TH STORY: "Captain America" (6 pages)
CREDITS: John Romita (art)
FEATURE CHARACTER: Captain America (next in MenAdv #28/2, '54)
SUPPORTING CAST: Bucky (next in MenAdv #28/2, '54)
VILLAINS: 2 Communist spies, Communist pilots (bts, within planes, many die), Communist aircraft carrier crew (bts, in craft, die), Communist POWs
OTHER CHARACTERS: US Army soldiers inc Colonel, officer & Sergeant, South Korean POW camp doctor, Communist leader (in photograph, only), Communist claw-like hand (in symbolic splash panel only)
LOCATIONS/ITEMS: Washington DC inc Pentagon, Communist hidden cellar hideout & airport, South Korea inc POW Camp No. 3 UN Command w/dispensary, Atlantic Ocean, England inc refueling site & farmhouse w/windmill, English Channel, Paris (bts, Cap and Bucky are there between panels); 2 US planes (destroyed), Communist aircraft carrier/sub (destroyed), Communist planes (some destroyed), French boat (bts, picks up Cap and Bucky between panels), French transport (bts, takes Cap and Bucky to Paris between panels), airport maintenance vehicle, vial w/medicine, decoy medicine bottle (destroyed bts)
SYNOPSIS: When USA-held communist POWs fall ill, having been poisoned by Communist leaders to discredit the UN, Cap and Bucky ferry medicine to South Korea despite multiple attacks by Communist operatives. Arriving, they oversee the ailing POWs' treatment. The other POWs suspect the medicine is poison and attack, but relent and express gratitude when their fellows recover.

TEXT STORY: "Bait for a Spy" (2 pages)
CREDITS: Writer unknown
FEATURE CHARACTER: Jerry Carter (Secret Service Agent #19, also in pfb)
VILLAIN: Captain Jones (S.S. Algonquin captain, also in pfb)
OTHER CHARACTERS: Sally Carter (Jerry's wife, also in pfb), 2nd Mate Anderson, Dr. Keller (atomic scientist), Monsieur Rodin, Lucien Flandin (French physicist, in pfb only, dies)
LOCATIONS/ITEMS: Atlantic Ocean; S.S. Algonquin w/lifeboat, Jones' gun, Carter's revolver, atomic papers
FLASHBACK: Jerry and Sally Carter are aboard the S.S. Algonquin when physicist Lucien Flandin is murdered. Jerry introduces himself as a detective to Captain Jones and offers his services in the case (p).
SYNOPSIS: Soon after, Jerry convinces Jones to spread a rumor that Flandin entrusted atomic secrets to another passenger, Rodin, whom Jones places under surveillance. However, as Jerry anticipated, the murderer instead targets Flandin's fellow scientist Keller. Jerry intervenes and captures the killer, Jones himself, a Communist agent to whom Flandin had mistakenly given atomic plans for safekeeping.
NOTE: First page appears between 2nd & 3rd stories, second page between 3rd & 4th stories.

CAPTAIN AMERICA #78 (September 1954)

"His Touch Is Death!" (6 pages)

CREDITS: John Romita (art, c art)
FEATURE CHARACTER: Captain America
SUPPORTING CAST: Bucky (last in MenAdv #28/2, '54)
VILLAINS: Electro (Ivan Kronov, Soviet operative, 1st, next in Cap Ann #13, '94), 2 Soviet officers, Soviet soldiers (some on cover only) & pilot (bts, in plane)
OTHER CHARACTERS: Firefighters, marching band, parade participants inc majorette, oilman & WAC driving Cap's float, parade attendees, Communist leader (in photo only)
LOCATIONS/ITEMS: USSR inc military office, Long Island Sound, Long Island inc beach, Manhattan inc Times Square on Broadway & Business Machines Building w/energy display center; fire engines, parade floats, Business Machines' giant typewriter & water-powered dynamo, Electro's asbestos coat & hat
SYNOPSIS: Soviet officials send electrically-mutated Electro to the USA to kill Cap and Bucky. During a parade through Times Square, Electro lures the two to a rooftop battle. They in turn lead him onto an energy display's giant typewriter, pummeling him with typeset keys and roller. Electro short-circuits the device, then downs Bucky with an electrical charge. When Electro reaches for a waterfall-powered dynamo to recharge, Cap, realizing his intent, increases the waterfall's intensity, dousing him with water to short-circuit and seemingly slay Electro.
NOTE: Cover-labeled, "Captain America…Commie Smasher."

2ND STORY: "The Green Dragon!" (6 pages)
CREDITS: John Romita (art)
FEATURE CHARACTER: Captain America
SUPPORTING CAST: Bucky
VILLAINS: Communist spy, Chinese soldiers (some die)
OTHER CHARACTERS: US Army gunners & CO, Chinese defector, Shanghai costumed parade participants & attendees, bystanders, 2 Communist leaders (in photos), Green Dragon (as float/vehicle & on insignia), the God of the Green Dragon (bts, possibly animating the Green Dragon), Buddha (as statue), couple (on Chinese screen)
LOCATIONS/ITEMS: South Korea inc War Records Building & defector's home, China inc Shanghai; Great Wall (Shanghai structure), parade floats, spy's gun, soldiers' firearms, list of reformed Chinese soldiers, "Steve" & "Bucky's" rifles
SYNOPSIS: In South Korea, a Communist spy & member of a "secret organization" worshiping the Green Dragon steals a coded Communist defector list, which Communists can use to locate and kill defectors' families. Cap and Bucky sneak into Shanghai, where the Feast of the Green Dragon, honoring the god who supposedly died to protect China years ago, is underway. Knowing the legend states that the Green Dragon will come to life when China is in danger, Cap and Bucky commandeer a Green Dragon float/vehicle. Cap sends Bucky to man the controls. The Dragon wreaks havoc throughout Shanghai. Cap confronts the spy, who hands over the list, which the Dragon's flames destroy. After telling the

rowd the Green Dragon returned to drive out Communism, Cap congratulates Bucky on a job well done but Bucky reveals that he was knocked nconscious shortly after entering the Dragon. Cap wonders if the legend came true after all.

NOTE: Per modern continuity, the God of the Green Dragon seems connected to the Makluans/Kakaranatharnians, an extraterrestrial dragon-ke race whose ancient Chinese presence was first revealed in ToS #62, '65.

3RD STORY: "Playing with Fire!" (5 pages)
CREDITS: Dick Ayers (art)
FEATURE CHARACTER: Human Torch (in pfb only, chr next in MSH #18/2, '68, next in FF Ann #4, '66)
SUPPORTING CAST: Toro (also in pfb, last in Sub #35/3, '54, next in MSH #18/2, '68)
VILLAINS: North Korean officers ("Comrade Captain" named & "Colonel Tong" designated w/derogatory nickname given by Torch) & soldiers nc "Mao" & "Yam" (derogatory nicknames given by Torch) (all in pfb)
OTHER CHARACTERS: 100 US POWs (most bts), US soldier (all in pfb)
LOCATIONS/ITEMS: North Korea inc Pongtu POW camp, "American zone" (all in pfb); North Korean tanks (some destroyed, #171 designated), irearms, fire extinguisher (destroyed), sword (melted) & flame thrower, Torch & Toro's billy clubs, US soldier's rifle (all in pfb)
FLASHBACK: In North Korea, Torch and Toro, searching for American POWs, battle Communist forces until reaching the POW camp. They ree the POWs, then fight the camp's Communist soldiers to cover their escape (p).
SYNOPSIS: Toro tells the story.

4TH STORY: "The Hour of Doom" (6 pages)
CREDITS: John Romita (art)
FEATURE CHARACTER: Captain America (also on TV, next in Cap Ann #13, '94 fb, Cap Ann #6, '82, CapTW:AF #1, '09, Cap #155, '72, fb, Cap #600/2, '09 fb, MLG #1, '01 fb, Cap #155, '72 fb, Cap #153, '72)
SUPPORTING CAST: Bucky (chr next in Cap Ann #13, '94, next in Cap #153, '72)
VILLAINS: Chuck Blayne (athlete, scholar & Communist agent, also on TV) & his spy leader
OTHER CHARACTERS: Police (2 also on TV), UN officials & diplomats, UN gallery visitors, UN guards, TV anchorman (on TV only), CBC reporter & cameramen, kids across the USA (watching TV), Grand Central Station clerk, fleeing crowds, bystanders
LOCATIONS/ITEMS: Manhattan inc Army Company Dayroom, TV studio (on TV only), spy's office, UN building, Grand Central Station & Brooklyn Bridge, airport (bts, where people try to escape New York), homes across USA (4 shown); UN clock, 2 time bombs, radar equipment, TV sets, policeman's sledgehammer
SYNOPSIS: Beloved idol Chuck Blayne, secretly a Communist spy, visits the UN and, on national TV, threatens to destroy the building to demonstrate the UN's supposed powerlessness and the supposed futility of world cooperation. He announces that he has set a bomb that will explode in an hour. The police arrest Blayne, and Cap and Bucky search the UN building. Finding and disarming a bomb, Cap forces Blayne into the building, making him believe the bomb is still undiscovered. Near the last minute, Blayne cracks, confessing his true allegiance, thus undermining the USA's youths' devotion to him. However, he also states there is a second bomb in a giant clock. While Cap prevents the clock from striking, UN personnel disarm the bomb with seconds to spare.
NOTE: The real Captain America returns in Av #4, '64, the real Bucky returns in Cap #1, '05 as the Winter Soldier. Captain America does not receive his own title again until Cap #100, '68.

TEXT STORY: "Just One Hour" (2 pages)
CREDITS: Writer unknown
FEATURE CHARACTER: Don Forman (FBI agent)
VILLAIN: von Unterdrerd (ex-Nazi spy, as "Reginald Demort," fellow of the Royal Astronomical Society), "remains of the German Nazi movement" (bts, give instructions to von Unterdrerd), SS officials in South America (bts, await instructions from von Unterdrerd)
OTHER CHARACTERS: Agent Wilkes (Forman's FBI superior), foreign officials ("political & scientific bigshots") inc astronomers, photographers, well-wishers, European agent (bts, informs FBI of von Unterdrerd's presence in delegation), 5 policemen, airport bystanders, Skazerrak (mentioned, see NOTE)
LOCATIONS/ITEMS: Manhattan inc Wilkes' FBI office, airport; plane, Forman's pad, pencil & press card
SYNOPSIS: When spy von Unterdrerd is reported to be part of a astronomer delegation, FBI agent Forman investigates. He has only one hour before the delegation flies to South America where von Unterdrerd will meet with other ex-Nazis. Posing as a reporter, Forman questions each scientist. All get annoyed at his question except Reginald Demort who answers civilly. Forman has Demort arrested, telling his boss he deliberately asked about the "meteorites" between Jupiter and Pluto. The true astronomers angrily told him meteors only become meteorites when they enter Earth's atmosphere. The disguised von Unterdrerd did not.
NOTE: First page appears between 2nd & 3rd stories, second page between 3rd & 4th stories. Forman is said to have "cracked the Skazerrak case," about which nothing else is known.

CAPTAIN AMERICA RETURNS! THE AVENGERS AND TALES OF SUSPENSE

Following Captain America Comics #78, Cap took a break from adventuring for nearly a decade, as super hero comics in general took a downturn in favor of crime, war, romance, horror and monsters. But Cap was not forgotten and when Marvel resumed telling tales of costumed adventurers with FF #1, '61, it was only a matter of time before Cap returned. The villainous Acrobat impersonated him in ST #114, '63, and the true Cap was found in ice and revived in Av #4, '64. The revelation that he had been frozen since before the end of the war and Bucky seemingly slain would later cause his post-war adventures to be attributed to others, as noted above. Cap became an Avengers mainstay, and in only a few months resumed his solo adventures in ToS #59, '64, splitting the title with fellow Avenger Iron Man. The Red Skull soon returned too, initially in flashbacks, and then revived from a similar hibernation in ToS #79, '66. Cap's ToS adventures continued until ToS #99, '68, when Iron Man left for his own title, and ToS was retitled Captain America. Cap's ToS adventures are indexed in the Iron Man TPB Index.

CAPTAIN AMERICA #100 (April 1968)

"This Monster Unmasked!" (20 pages)

CREDITS: Stan Lee (writer), Jack Kirby (pencils), Syd Shores (inks), Artie Simek (letters), Stan Goldberg (colors), Sam Rosen (c letters)
FEATURE CHARACTER: Captain America (Steve Rogers, living legend of WWII, also in rfb, last in ToS #99/2, '68, next in Av #51, '68)
GUEST STARS: Black Panther (T'Challa, ruler of Wakanda, last in ToS #99/2, '68, next in Av #51, '68), Col. Nick Fury (Director of SHIELD), Timothy "Dum Dum" Dugan (agent of SHIELD) (both last in IM #1, '68, next in ST #168/2, '68)
SUPPORTING CAST: Sharon Carter (Agent 13 of SHIELD, also as Irma Kruhl, last in ToS #99/2, '68)
VILLAINS: Baron Zemo imposter (Franz Gruber, see NOTE) and his men (all last in ToS #99/2, '68, last app), Destructon (robot, only app)
OTHER CHARACTERS: Avengers: Giant-Man, Iron Man, Thor, Wasp; Sub-Mariner, Eskimos (all in rfb)
LOCATIONS/ITEMS: Wakanda, Zemo's control center, SHIELD base, outer space, North Sea (in rfb); Captain America's shield, Agent 13's gun & document case w/flame-thrower, Zemo's men's guns, orbital solar ray, solar ray control panel & communicator, SHIELD missiles & electric space probe, Wakandan prototype jet, block of ice, submarine (both in rfb)
FLASHBACK: Frozen in ice, Captain America is worshipped by Eskimos until he's found by the Sub-Mariner, who throws him into the North Sea. As Cap thaws he's found and rescued by the Avengers (Av #4, '64).
SYNOPSIS: Captain America wakes up to find himself and Black Panther prisoners of Baron Zemo. Irma Kruhl readies her document case to give Zemo the missile site coordinates for his orbital solar ray, but she destroys the ray's control panel instead. Cap and Black Panther use the confusion to break free and Sharon joins them, removing her disguise. Surrounded by Zemo's men the three escape through an air vent only to be confronted by the Destructon, which Cap quickly defeats. Zemo and his men arrive and attack, but Cap reveals Zemo to be an imposter, formerly Zemo's pilot. Outraged, Zemo's men kill the imposter for deceiving them and Black Panther convinces the men to surrender. Meanwhile with its force field down, Nick Fury destroys the orbital solar ray. With the crisis averted, Cap offers Black Panther membership in the Avengers.
NOTE: Story & series numbering continued from ToS #99, '68, letters column changes its name to "Let's Yap With Cap." Black Panther goes on to join the Avengers in Av #51, '68, but is revealed to have ulterior motives for doing so in BP #8, '99. The Zemo imposter survives his seeming death here and appears next in the Av&Tb novel, '99, where his name is revealed. Solar Ray also called "Death Ray" here. SHIELD stands for Supreme Headquarters International Espionage Law-Enforcement Division. Since Captain America's shield is in virtually every issue, later summaries will only note changes to it.

CAPTAIN AMERICA #101 (May 1968)

"When Wakes the Sleeper!" (20 pages)

CREDITS: Stan Lee (writer), Jack Kirby (pencils), Syd Shores (inks), Artie Simek (letters), Sam Rosen (c letters)
FEATURE CHARACTER: Captain America (next in Av #52, '68)
GUEST STAR: Nick Fury (last in ST #168/2, '68)
SUPPORTING CAST: Sharon Carter
VILLAINS: Red Skull (Johann Shmidt, Nazi, also in fb between ToS #91/2, '67 & Cap:SoL #1, '98 fb; last in ToS #91/2, '67, chr last in Cap:SoL #1, '98 fb), 4th Sleeper (robot, can alter own density & trigger volcanic activity, 1st), Werner Von Krimm (Nazi, Butcher of Lichtengarten, only app), Red Skull's men, Krimm's men
OTHER CHARACTERS: Police, US military, ship crews, pilot, bystanders; Tony Stark (mentioned, designed inflato-suit)
LOCATIONS/ITEMS: New York, Caribbean Sea inc Red Skull's island, US military command center, SHIELD HQ, construction site (destroyed); Krimm & his men's guns, Krimm's car & plane, Fury's gun & homing device, Sleeper's crypt, excavation equipment inc scalding jet-sprays, SHIELD saucer-ship, inflato-suit & X-ray cameras, vibra-gun, Red Skull's men's guns, soni-crystal key, jet, experimental concrete, fleet of ships (both destroyed), XPT-1 (atomic submarine) w/escape capsule (in fb)
FLASHBACK: Red Skull uses an escape capsule as the XPT-1 is destroyed.
SYNOPSIS: Captain America attacks Nazi Werner Von Krimm in the street. Krimm's men fight back until they're interrupted by Nick Fury. Despite Cap's vocal protests Fury lets Krimm go, then explains to Cap that Krimm will lead Cap to a bigger target. Meanwhile, Red Skull oversees his men excavating the 4th Sleeper's crypt. Cap follows Krimm's plane in a SHIELD saucer-ship to an island until it's shot down by a vibra-gun; Cap uses an inflato-suit to land safely on the island only to be overpowered by attacking troops. Krimm greets Red Skull and hands over the soni-crystal key. Skull uses it to wake the 4th Sleeper as Cap is brought in. Unable to control the robot, Red Skull jumps in an escape hatch. Cap follows and grabs the key as the Sleeper destroys the island; the hatch is flooded as it collapses. The Sleeper continues its rampage by igniting volcanic activity as it works its way up the East Coast, destroying a construction site and a fleet of ships. The military tries to cope with the disaster as Fury tells Sharon Carter that Cap died fighting the Sleeper. Meanwhile, Cap surfaces in the Caribbean Sea, still holding the soni-crystal key.
NOTE: It remains unrevealed how Krimm appears relatively youthful in the current day, despite fighting in WWII.

CAPTAIN AMERICA #102 (June 1968)

"The Sleeper Strikes!" (20 pages)

CREDITS: Stan Lee (writer), Jack Kirby (pencils), Syd Shores (inks), Artie Simek (letters), Sam Rosen (c letters)
FEATURE CHARACTER: Captain America
GUEST STAR: Nick Fury (next in Cap #104, '68)
SUPPORTING CAST: Sharon Carter
VILLAINS: Exiles (Red Skull's private Nazi army): Angelo Baldini, Franz Cadavus, Gen. Jun Ching, Eric Gruning, Jurgen "Iron Hand" Hauptmann (Butcher of Bavaria), Ivan Krushki (all 1st in shadows), Gottfried Rothman (only app) (see NOTE); Red Skull, 4th Sleeper (destroyed, chr next in Cap #368/2, '90 fb, next in Cap #354, '89), Red Skull's men inc hover troops, Gottfried's men, killer kelp (1st)
OTHER CHARACTERS: Coast Guard, doctor, nurse, scientists, US military, smelting factory employees; Tony ~ark (mentioned, designed wrist-blaster)
~OCATIONS/ITEMS: US Naval hospital, Caribbean Sea, Isle of Exiles, US government lab, US military command post, Seacoast smelting ~ctory (destroyed); Red Skull's submarine, Gottfried's steel gloves, Red Skull's men's guns, Sharon's gun, Fury's gun, seismograph, SHIELD ~licopter, wrist-blaster & mini-parachute, hover-seats, soni-crystal key, Cadavus' murder chair (in shadows)
~YNOPSIS: Fury meets with Steve at a US Naval hospital; Steve shows Fury the soni-crystal key. Meanwhile, Red Skull retreats to the Isle of ~xiles. Cap suits up to find the 4th Sleeper but is attacked by Gottfried and his men. Cap defeats them with Sharon's help. The Sleeper continues ~ rampage by destroying a smelting factory. Cap and Sharon follow the destruction until they're attacked by Red Skull's hover troops; Cap fights ~em off with a SHIELD wrist-blaster. Cap uses the key to call the Sleeper and attacks, but he is quickly overpowered by the robot. Holding the ~y, Sharon's fear of Cap's death transfers through the key to the Sleeper, causing it to dissipate itself. Watching from afar, Red Skull prepares ~e Exiles to attack.
~OTE: Gruning's surname revealed in Cap #103, '68 Baldini, Cadavus, Ching, Hauptmann & Krushki's surnames revealed in Cap #104, '68. ~adavus, Gruning & Hauptmann's 1st names revealed in MAtlas #1, '07, Baldini, Ching & Krushki's 1st names & Gottfried's surname revealed ~ OHMU HC #4, '08. Though this is the Exiles' 1st confirmed app, they likely previously appear in ToS #41, '63 amongst Carlo Strange's allies. ~ remains unrevealed how the Exiles remain relatively youthful in the current day, despite fighting in WWII.

CAPTAIN AMERICA #103 (July 1968)

"The Weakest Link!" (20 pages)

CREDITS: Stan Lee (writer), Jack Kirby (pencils), Syd Shores (inks), Artie Simek (letters), Sam Rosen (c letters)
FEATURE CHARACTER: Captain America
SUPPORTING CAST: Sharon Carter
VILLAINS: Exiles: Angelo Baldini, Franz Cadavus, Gen. Jun Ching, Eric Gruning, Jurgen "Iron Hand" Hauptmann, Ivan Krushki (all 1st full app); Red Skull & his men (Manfred named), killer kelp (last app)
OTHER CHARACTERS: Diners, restaurant staff, Red Skull's captives, SHIELD pilot; Tony Stark (mentioned, designed oxygen cylinder)
LOCATIONS/ITEMS: Restaurant, Isle of Exiles; Red Skull's nuclear tape, neuro rod, pneumatic sled & jets, Red Skull's men's guns, boat & jeep, SHIELD jet, oxygen cylinder, shock pellets & powdered corrosive, Cadavus' ~urder chair
~YNOPSIS: Steve and Sharon's date is interrupted by the Red Skull's men, who kidnap Sharon. Skull chastises them for not just grabbing ~teve, who is known to be Captain America, but decides to continue with the plan of using her as bait. In the meantime, Skull uses his neuro rod ~ force two of his captives to fight each other as amusement for his Exiles. Looking for Sharon, Cap infiltrates the Isle of Exiles, defeating the ~ler kelp and battling Red Skull's men. Distracted by the Red Skull, Cap is captured and a strip of nuclear tape is placed on Cap's neck. The ~xiles confront Red Skull over leadership of their group as Cap and Sharon escape, but that's all part of Red Skull's plan…
~OTE: Neuro rod named in Cap #104, '68. Gruning misspelled "Grunning" here.

CAPTAIN AMERICA #104 (August 1968)

"Slave of the Skull!" (20 pages)

CREDITS: Stan Lee (writer), Jack Kirby (pencils), Dan Adkins (inks), Artie Simek (letters), Sam Rosen (c letters)
FEATURE CHARACTER: Captain America
GUEST STARS: Nick Fury (next bts in Cap #106, '68, chr next in DD #322, '93 fb, next in NF:AoS #1, '68), Tony Stark (bts, defuses mini H-bomb, between IM #4-5, '68)
SUPPORTING CAST: Sharon Carter (next in Cap #108, '68), Exiles: Angelo Baldini, Franz Cadavus, Gen. Jun Ching, Eric Gruning, Jurgen "Iron Hand" Hauptmann, Ivan Krushki (prev 6 next in Cap #115, '69 fb); Red Skull (chr next in Cap #298, '84 fb, next bts in Cap #108, '68), Red Skull's men
OTHER CHARACTERS: SHIELD agents, doctors & nurse, US military, sharks
~OCATIONS/ITEMS: SHIELD base, Isle of Exiles, Washington DC; LMDs, Red Skull's nuclear tape, neuro rod, mini H-bomb & mini-sub, Red ~kull's men's guns, Cadavus' murder chair (destroyed), Gruning's electro-whip, Hauptmann's iron gloves, Baldini's scarf, Gen. Ching's gun, ~HIELD guns & boats
~YNOPSIS: Captain America trains by fighting a squad of LMDs, then sees a SHIELD doctor about recent headaches. He suddenly reels in

pain as Red Skull activates the neuro rod from afar and gives a radio warning: remove the nuclear tape and it will detonate a mini H-bomb Washington DC. Red Skull demands Captain America's return to the Isle of Exiles, then settles another leadership dispute between the Na group. Cap returns to the Island where Red Skull tortures him while Fury calls Tony Stark to disarm the sophisticated H-bomb. Cap is force to battle the Exiles and when he gains the upper hand, Skull tries to detonate the H-bomb, but to no avail. Just then SHIELD forces attack t island, so Skull and his Exiles retreat to the mini-sub. After the battle is over, Sharon removes the tape from Steve's neck.

NOTE: LMD stands for Life Model Decoy.

CAPTAIN AMERICA #105 (September 1968)

"In the Name of Batroc!" (20 pages)

CREDITS: Stan Lee (writer), Jack Kirby (pencils), Dan Adkins (inks), Sam Rosen (letters)
FEATURE CHARACTER: Captain America (also in film)
VILLAINS: Batroc's Brigade: Batroc the Leaper (Georges Batroc, mercenary & master of savate, last ToS #85/2, '67, next in Cap #130, '70), Living Laser (Arthur Parks, last in Av Ann #1, '67, next in Av #78, '7C Swordsman (Jacques Ducquesne, last in Av Ann #1, '67, next in Av #65, '69); enemy spy (bts, brings seism bomb into city)
OTHER CHARACTERS: Imperial Storage Co. employees (Joe named), studio executives, US Senator, U military, bystanders; Bucky, Allied & Axis troops (both in film)
LOCATIONS/ITEMS: New York, TV studio, Batroc's hideout, military briefing room, Imperial Storage Co. In Swordsman's sword w/force ray, Living Laser's laser gloves, combat robot, spare weapons, seismo-bomb disguised as briefcase w/acid ga self-destruct mechanism
SYNOPSIS: Steve watches newsreel footage of himself and Bucky fighting in WWII with studio executives who want to produce a TV speci with Steve's involvement. Distracted by his thoughts, Steve leaves without giving an answer. Meanwhile, Batroc tells Swordsman and Livir Laser he has a job: find a hidden weapon in the city for a million dollar payment. Meanwhile, Captain America is given an assignment from th military: an enemy spy has brought a seismo-bomb into the city, find and disarm it. Leaping into action Cap finds Batroc's Brigade and battle Swordsman while the others continue their search. A shock wave rocks the city, and Cap moves on to Living Laser, destroying the villain gloves. A second shock waves erupts and Laser tells Cap where Batroc is searching. Cap attacks Batroc and convinces the Leaper to lea after the third shock wave. Finding the seismo-bomb, Cap deactivates it.

CAPTAIN AMERICA #106 (October 1968)

"Cap Goes WILD!" (20 pages)

CREDITS: Stan Lee (writer), Jack Kirby (pencils), Frank Giacoia (inks), Sam Rosen (letters)
FEATURE CHARACTER: Captain America
GUEST STAR: Nick Fury (bts, sends SHIELD agent, chr next in DD #322, '93 fb, next in NF:AoS #1, '68)
VILLAINS: Mao Tse Tung (Chairman of the Communist Party of China, 1st, next in Hulk #108, '68), Captain Americ LMD (only app), Cyril Lucas (treasonous movie director, only app), Chinese agents, army & government officials
OTHER CHARACTERS: Willie Lucas (Cyril's brother, dies), SHIELD agent, police, actors, stagehands
LOCATIONS/ITEMS: New York inc Steve's apartment, China inc LMD factory, Hollywood inc Infinity Production studio; Chinese guns, jet-helicopter w/magnetic grappler, LMD production machine & shipping case, SHIEL LMD file, fake film of Cap, movie props
SYNOPSIS: Captain America battles Chinese agents but fails to stop them stealing a SHIELD LMD file. Approached by a SHIELD agent se by Fury, Steve is shown filmed footage of Cap committing atrocities during WWII. Outraged, Steve immediately makes arrangements to go Hollywood and visit the studio that staged the film. Meanwhile in China, Mao Tse Tung oversees Operation Replica, the creation of a Capta America LMD. Once finished the LMD is shipped to Hollywood. At Infinity Productions, brothers Cyril and Willie Lucas discuss their treasonou deal with China to lure Captain America to Hollywood. They needed money to fund their film, so they could make enough to pay for Willie operation. That night Cap arrives at the studio where he's attacked by the LMD. While the LMD battles Cap it explains that it will take Cap place and convince the world Captain America is evil, ruining America's morals in the name of China. Willie can't stand to see Cap killed so h intervenes but is killed, allowing Cap to take control of the battle. The LMD suddenly overloads and begins to fall apart; the SHIELD agent arrive to explain the LMD file used to create it was untested, and that Cyril was suspected of treason for months. Later, mourning his dead brother, Cy is approached by a Chinese agent with a gun…

NOTE: The faked WWII film is so atrocious it can't even be shown on panel.

CAPTAIN AMERICA #107 (November 1968)

"If the Past Be Not Dead - -" (20 pages)

CREDITS: Stan Lee (writer), Jack Kirby (pencils), Syd Shores (inks), Artie Simek (letters)
FEATURE CHARACTER: Captain America (in Av #56, '68, Av Ann #2, '68)
VILLAINS: Dr. Faustus (Dr. Johann Fennhoff, criminal psychologist, 1st but chr last in MTU #133, '83 fb, next i Cap #161, '73), Ferrett (Dr. Faustus' agent, also as Cap's bellboy & Bucky), Dr. Faustus' actors (some also a Sharon Carter, policeman, Red Skull, Nazis & Zemo's men)
OTHER CHARACTERS: SHIELD agents, bystanders, SHIELD technicians (bts, checks out pills & create mask & gloves); Sharon Carter, astronauts (both in photos); Bucky, Adolf Hitler, Nazis (prev 3 in Cap's nightmare Tony Stark (mentioned, created Plastoid)

LOCATIONS/ITEMS: New York, Steve's apartment w/exercise chamber, Dr. Faustus' office w/hidden stage-rooms, warehouse w/Zemo's English island fortress replica; Dr. Faustus' nightmare pills & aging tablet, copy of "Daily Record", SHIELD Plastoid #427 (robot), Cap's "aged skin" mask & gloves, Zemo's drone-plane replica, motorcycle

SYNOPSIS: Steve Rogers wakes from a nightmare and calls his psychiatrist Dr. Faustus to make an appointment. Dr. Faustus calls in Ferrett, who's posing as Steve's bellboy, and supplies him with more nightmare pills for Rogers. Steve thinks he sees Sharon on the street but it's not her; after he rubs his eyes he sees Red Skull dressed as a policeman. When Steve runs off, the two remove their masks. At Dr. Faustus' office, Steve thinks he's being interrogated on the date of D-Day by Nazis, but he's brought out of it by the psychiatrist. Later, Cap exercises by fighting a SHIELD Plastoid then retires for the night. When Steve wakes up he's aged sixty years and finds Bucky in his apartment. They jump on a motorcycle and find Zemo's drone-plane nearby, but Bucky dies when the plane explodes. With Cap unconscious Ferrett removes his Bucky mask, but Cap suddenly attacks. As he defeats Faustus' men he explains he didn't take the aging tablet but used a mask and gloves to fool Faustus. SHIELD agents arrive to arrest the doctor, and Cap knocks him out with one punch.

CAPTAIN AMERICA #108 (December 1968)

"The Snares of the Trapster!" (20 pages)

CREDITS: Stan Lee (writer), Jack Kirby (pencils), Syd Shores (inks), Artie Simek (letters), Sam Rosen (c letters)
FEATURE CHARACTER: Captain America (next in DD #43, '68, Av #58, '68, Av:EMH #1-2, '07)
GUEST STAR: Nick Fury (bts, sent Sharon on mission, last in NF:AoS #6, '68, next bts in Av #57, '68, chr next in Av:EMH #2, '07, next in NF:AoS #7, '68)
SUPPORTING CAST: Sharon Carter (next in Cap #113, '69)
VILLAINS: Trapster (Peter Petruski, last in DD #36, '68, next in MSH #15, '68), Red Skull (bts, hires Trapster, last in Cap #104, '68, chr last in Cap #298, '84 fb, chr next in Cap #115, '69 fb, next off-panel in Cap #114, '69)
OTHER CHARACTERS: Sharon Carter LMD, SHIELD agent; Tony Stark (mentioned, designed chemical tubes)
LOCATIONS/ITEMS: New York inc SHIELD training facility & Trapster's hideout; SHIELD training missiles & homing device, SHIELD agent's gun, chemical tubes, Trapster's paste-gun & traps inc paste-cannon, coated stairs & bar, trap door, turntable & glass tube, Project Fireball mentioned)
SYNOPSIS: Captain America trains against SHIELD missiles until an agent tells him Sharon Carter has been captured; the agent gives Cap a homing device to find her. Meanwhile, Trapster interrogates Sharon for information on Project Fireball. Cap pinpoints the homing signal to a dilapidated building and is immediately attacked by paste. He destroys the paste-cannon and jumps inside, becoming stuck on a bar. Trapster attacks until Cap falls through a trap door and lands on a paste-covered turntable. Trapster remotely activates the spinning table but his control panel explodes. Cap attacks Trapster but he's trapped in a glass tube which fills with paste. Cap escapes when the paste falls apart. Cap defeats Trapster and saves Sharon only to find she's an LMD; the real Sharon has been hiding the whole time sabotaging the Trapster's traps with chemical tubes. Fury sent her and her LMD to find who Trapster was working for: the Red Skull.

CAPTAIN AMERICA #109 (January 1969)

"The Hero That Was!" (20 pages)

CREDITS: Stan Lee (writer), Jack Kirby (pencils), Syd Shores (inks), Artie Simek (letters)
FEATURE CHARACTER: Captain America (also in fb1 during CapTW:AB #1, '09 fb, in fb2 between Cap:SoL #7/2, '99 fb & CapC #1, '41, also in Cap Ann #10/2, '91 fb, MvPro #4, '10, Cap #176, '74 fb, Cap #255, '81 fb, SR:SSol #1-2, '10 fbs, Cap #25, '07 fb, MSH #3, '90 fb, bts in Cap Ann '00 fb, Cap:Re #2, '09, Cap #215, '77 fb, ToS #63/2, '65, CapC #1, '41, in fb3 between Cap #215, '77 fb & Cap #26, '04 fb, also in Cap:SoL #12, '99 fb, ToS #63/2, '65, CapC #1, '41; next in Av #60, '69, Av:EMH #6-8, '07, see NOTE)
GUEST STAR: Nick Fury (last in NF:AoS #7, '68, chr next in Av #59, '68 fb, next in NF:AoS #8, '69)
SUPPORTING CAST: Bucky (James Buchanan "Bucky" Barnes, Cap's wartime partner, in fb1 between MUni #1, '98 fb & Cap:Re #1, '09, in fb3 between Cap #12, '05 fb & Cap #26, '04 fb, also in Cap:SoL #12, '99 fb, ToS #63/2, '65, CapC #1, '41), Sgt. Mike Duffy (Camp Lehigh drill sergeant, only in fb3 between Cap #50, '09 fb & ToS #63/2, '65)
VILLAINS: Heinz Krueger (Nazi agent, "Frederick Clemson," in fb2 to 1st chr app, also in MvPro #4, '10, CapC #1, '41, ToS #63/2, '65, Av:In Ann #1, '08 fb, dies), Major Albrecht Kerfoot (Krueger's superior, in fb2 to 1st chr app, also in MvPro #4, '10, next in MvPro #5, '10), Kerfoot's handler (1st, next in MvPro #4-5, '10), Agent R (Lt. Cynthia Glass, Nazi spy posing as FBI agent-X, in fb2 between Cap #255, '81 fb & SR:SSol #2, '10 fb), Nazi soldiers, officials (both in fb1), submarine crew & spy (both in fb2)
OTHER CHARACTERS: Prof. Abraham Erskine ("Prof. Reinstein", created Super Soldier Serum, in fb2 between Cap:SoL #7/2, '99 fb & Cap:Re #2, '09, also in Cap #255, '81 fb, Cap #25, '07 fb, MvPro #4, '10, Cap Ann '00 fb, Cap:Re #2, '09, Cap #215, '77 fb, ToS #63/2, '65, CapC #1, '41, Av:In Ann #1/4, '08 fb, dies), Gen. Chester Richard Phillips (recruited Steve into Operation: Rebirth, in fb2 between MvPro #4, '10 & Cap #25, '07 fb, also in Capp Ann #10/2, '91 fb, MvPro #4, '10, Cap #176, '74 fb, Cap #255, '81 fb), US military, volunteers & doctor, Operation: Rebirth & FBI agents, high ranking US government officials (all in fb2), Steve's Camp Lehigh battalion (in fb3)
LOCATIONS/ITEMS: Normandy Beach inc Nazi bunker (fb1), Atlantic Ocean, Army recruitment center, Operation: Rebirth inc fake antique shop front (all in fb2), Camp Lehigh inc Steve's barracks (in fb3), New York inc Steve's apartment; Bucky's circuitry bomb, capsule bombs, Nazi guns & coastal cannons (all in fb1), Nazi submarine, US water mines, Operation: Rebirth equipment inc Vita-Ray device, Krueger's gun (all in fb2)
FLASHBACKS: June, 1944: Captain America and Bucky attack a Nazi bunker on Normandy Beach, sabotaging their defenses and destroying the coastal cannons, paving the way for the D-Day (1) Fall, 1940: Steve Rogers tries to volunteer for military service, but he's declared 4-F again. Gen. Phillips asks Steve if he'd be willing to participate in a secret experiment, and eventually introduces Steve to Prof. Reinstein. Meanwhile,

a Nazi submarine drops off Krueger, who meets with Major Kerfoot in a plan to assassinate Reinstein. Steve is brought to an antique shop, a front for Operation: Rebirth, where Steve prepares to be tested. Later high ranking officials arrive, and after being injected with the Super Soldier Serum Steve is bathed in Vita-Rays. He emerges as a nearly perfect human specimen, but Krueger assassinates Reinstein. Steve accidentally kills the Nazi agent, not yet accustomed to his new strength (2). Spring, 1941: Private Steve Rogers is trained in drills at Camp Lehigh, but his identity is eventually discovered by camp mascot James Barnes. Steve agrees to make him Cap's partner as Bucky (3).

SYNOPSIS: Steve Rogers and Nick Fury reminisce about their time in WWII.

NOTE: Krueger's alias established in MvPro #4, '10, Kerfoot's 1st named revealed in MvPro #5, '10. This issue introduces Vita-Rays to the Super Soldier Serum process, they are later reveled to stave off insanity in Cap #155, '72 fb. The Super Soldier Serum was at least partially recorded by Major Kerfoot in MvPro #4, '10 and found years later by William Burnside in Cap #155, '72 fb. Operation: Rebirth has been revisited and expanded several times, for a full chronology see sidebar. Nick Fury & his Howling Commandos also fought on Normandy Beach on D-Day as seen in SgtF Ann #2, '66.

OPERATION: REBIRTH CHRONOLOGY

FALL, 1940: Steve Rogers is shocked by newsreel footage of the Nazi war machine and decides he has to do something (MSH #3, '90 fb, Cap #25, '07 fb, MvPro #4, '10 fb, Cap #255, '81 fb, Cap #176, '74 fb & Cap:SoL #7/2, '99 fb). Meanwhile, Gen. Phillips approaches Dominic Fortune to be the first Super Soldier, Dr. Erskine and J. Arthur Grover warn him of the dangerous process. Fortune is tested and eventually rejected as a candidate for Project: Rebirth (MSH #3, '90 fb). Steve Rogers tries to volunteer for military duty, but is declared 4-F and rejected several times (Cap #25, '07 fb, MvPro #4, '10 fb, Cap #176, '74 fb & Cap:SoL #7/2, '99 fb). At one rejection he finds himself evading enemy spies (CapC Spec #1, '09 fb). Steve is approached by Gen. Phillips, who offers Steve a chance to serve his country (Cap #109, '69 fb, Cap Ann #10/2, '91 fb, MvPro #4, '10 fb, Cap #176, '74 fb). Steve is introduced to "Dr. Reinstein" and they travel to a curio shop. After passing security they enter the lab, where Steve deduces "Reinstein" is an alias for Abraham Erskine (Cap #109, '69 fb, Cap #176, '74 fb & Cap #255, '81 fb). Extensive testing begins on Steve and other candidates, and Steve meets Lt. Cynthia Glass (Cap #109, '69 fb, Cap #255, '81 fb, SR:SSol #1-2, '10 fbs, NW #4, '90 fb, MvPro #4, '10 fb & Cap #25, '07 fb). During this time Nazi spies attack the secret lab but Steve is saved by Dominic Fortune (MSH #3, '90 fb), and Gen. Saunders grows impatient with Project: Rebirth's timetable. He secretly administers the serum to Private Clinton McIntyre, but when the Private is driven insane, Gen. Phillips arrests Gen. Saunders (Cap Ann '00).

WINTER, 1940: Nazi assassin Heinz Krueger arrives by submarine to kill "Reinstein" (Cap #109, '69 fb), and infiltrates Project: Rebirth (MvPro #4, '10). When Fifth Columnists destroy a munitions factory, President Roosevelt asks about Operation: Rebirth's progress (CapC #1, '41, ToS #63/2, '65 & GSInv #1, '75 fb). Operation: Rebirth prepares as officials arrive (CapC #1, '41, ToS #63/2, '65 & MvPro #4, '10), and Steve asks Erskine about time travel (Cap:Re #2, '09). Entering the lab, Operation: Rebirth begins (Cap #215, '77 fb, ToS #63/2, '65 & Cap #255, '81 fb). Steve is injected with the Super Soldier Serum (CapC #1, '41), drinks the formula (Cap #255, '81 fb & ToS #63/2, '65) and is bombarded with Vita-Rays (Cap #109, '69 fb), changing him into the first Super Soldier (CapC #1, '41, ToS #63/2, '65 & Cap #109, '69 fb). Krueger shoots and kills Erskine, then attacks the other officials (ToS #63/2, '65 & CapC #1, '41). Saving the gathered officials, Steve accidentally kills Krueger (ToS #63/2, '65, CapC #1, '41, Cap #109, '69 fb, Cap:Re #2, '09 & Cap #255, '81 fb). A Nazi spy fails to steal Steve's urine when a Russian spy stops him (Next #9, '06 fb). Steve says goodbye to childhood friend Arnie Roth (Cap #270, '82 fb) and trains his new body (Cap #255, '81 fb & MvPro #5, '10). During this time Gen. Phillips gets the idea of putting Steve into a costume while he and Steve read Steve's ancestor's journal (Cap:SoL #6/3, '99 & Cap:SoL #7, '99).

MARCH, 1941: Gen. Phillips tells Steve of the Red Skull and gives him his uniform (MvPro #5, '10, Cap #255, '81 fb & Cap #2, '05 fb). On his first mission, Captain America saves Col. Henson from Nazi assassins (Cap #255, '81 fb). Cap defeats Nazi saboteurs (MSH #3, '90 fb), stops spies at an aircraft plant (Cap #255, '81 fb), encounters Emil Stein (ToS #1, '95 fb), falls in love with Cynthia Glass (SR:SSol #1, '10 fb), witnesses death on the battlefield (Cap #2, '02 fb) and travels to Wakanda where he trades his shield for Vibranium (BP #30, '01 fb). This will eventually form part of Captain America's indestructible shield (Cap #303, '85 fb & Av Ann '01/2 fb). Biz, a fellow soldier, discovers Steve is Cap but refuses to talk when tortured by spies (Cap Ann #13/2, '94 fb). Donning his suit (MvPro #5, 10), Cap defeats Nazi spies at the Liberty shipyard and meets the Angel (Cap #255, '81 fb, Cap #25, '07 fb & MvPro #5, '10), then defeats saboteurs at Boulder Dam (Cap #255, '81 fb).

SPRING, 1941: Captain America meets President Roosevelt, who gives him a new uniform and indestructible shield (Cap #255, '81, Cap:SoL #7/2, '99, & Cap #303, '85 fb). Gen. Phillips sets Private Steve Rogers up with an identity at Camp Lehigh and Steve meets James "Bucky" Barnes (Cap #12, '05 fb, Cap #215, '77 fb & Cap #109, '69 fb). Steve and Bucky become friends (Cap:SoL #12, '99 fb & ToS #63/2, '65) and Bucky soon discovers that Steve is Captain America (CapC #1, '41 & ToS #63/2, '65). Steve agrees to have Bucky as a partner (CapC #1, '41, ToS #63/2, '65, Cap:SoL #12, '99 fb & Cap #109, '69 fb), gets authorization from the military (Cap #26, '04 fb) and Gen. Phillips makes it official (Cap #14, '06 fb). Still relatively inexperienced, Private Rogers fails to save an Allied recon unit in Europe and almost kills an orphan (Av #213, '81 fb). Cynthia Glass is revealed as a Nazi spy (SR:SSol #2, '10 fb). After months of training, Bucky defeats Nazis on the Maryland coast on his first mission with Cap (Cap:SoL #12, '99 fb & ToS #63/2, '65). Captain America and Bucky meet President Roosevelt and team up with Namor the Sub-Mariner (Cap #423, '94).

CAPTAIN AMERICA #110 (February 1969)

"No Longer Alone!" (20 pages)

CREDITS: Stan Lee (writer), Jim Steranko (pencils, colors, c art), Joe Sinnott (inks), Sam Rosen (letters)
FEATURE CHARACTER: Captain America (also in Cap:Re #4, '10)
GUEST STAR: Hulk (during Hulk #106, '68)
SUPPORTING CAST: Rick Jones (becomes Bucky, last in Hulk #106, '68, also in Cap:Re #4, '10)
VILLAINS: Madame Hydra (Ophelia Sarkissian, leader of New York Hydra branch, 1st but chr last in Gam #6, '99 fb, also in Cap:Re #4, '10), Hydra agents
OTHER CHARACTERS: US military
LOCATIONS/ITEMS: New York, Avengers Mansion, sewers; ionic energy cannon, lamppost, Avenger alarm,

ydra guns, power vest, flame bazookas & water contaminator, Madame Hydra's whip & gun

SYNOPSIS: Steve Rogers wanders into the middle of a battle between the Hulk and the military. He changes into Captain America as the military fires an ionic energy cannon at the Hulk and notices the nearby Rick Jones. Cap tries to calm the Hulk down but he's too angry; the monster accidentally injures Rick and jumps away. Cap takes Rick to Avengers Mansion to recuperate, and when Rick awakens he surprises Cap by donning Bucky's uniform. The Avenger alarm sounds and the two investigate, finding a Hydra army in the sewers. Cap is captured while trying to protect Bucky and Madame Hydra orders his death. Cap battles an agent in a power vest while Bucky evades some agents. Rick returns in time to see a Hydra agent holding Cap's shield, causing him to shout, blowing Cap's cover. No longer disguised as a Hydra agent, Cap attacks and saves Bucky from Madame Hydra's wrath. The heroes foil the terrorist's plan to contaminate the city's water, but the Hydra agents escape.

NOTE: Supreme & Madame Hydra are equal ranks, one title for each gender. Madame Hydra's real name confirmed in OHMU HC #12, '10.

CAPTAIN AMERICA #111 (March 1969)

"Tomorrow You Live, Tonight I Die!" (20 pages)

CREDITS: Stan Lee (writer), Jim Steranko (pencils, colors, c art), Joe Sinnott (inks), Sam Rosen (letters)
FEATURE CHARACTER: Captain America (next in Cap #113, '69)
SUPPORTING CAST: Rick Jones (also as Bucky, next in Hulk #111, '69)
VILLAINS: Madame Hydra (next in Cap #113, '69), Hydra agents (some also as arcade employees), Mankiller (armored Hydra robot, only app)
OTHER CHARACTERS: Police; Bucky (in film), Death (in Rick's hallucination)
LOCATIONS/ITEMS: New York, Penny Arcade, Hydra base, Avengers Mansion inc gym & garage, river; Arcade games inc fortune teller w/card & robotic gunslinger, training film of Cap & Bucky, Madame Hydra's whip & gun, Hydra guns, car, spectro-ray & poison (also as note), Steve's car, police cars, rubber dummy, "Steve Rogers" mask

SYNOPSIS: Thinking he's meeting Nick Fury at the Penny Arcade, Steve Rogers gets a fortune card and is attacked by Hydra agents. He quickly fights them off as Captain America. Meanwhile, Madame Hydra tries a new poison on a Hydra agent that failed her. At Avengers Mansion Steve shows Rick some combat footage of Bucky's fighting style, and begins to train Rick in combat gymnastics. Rick quickly becomes frustrated and Steve decides it's time for a break. Later, Rick receives an urgent note for Captain America, but once he touches it a poisonous gas envelops him, knocking him out. Steve returns to find Hydra agents loading Rick into a car but fails to stop them; he blames his public identity for Rick's capture. Madame Hydra orders Bucky's death, but he wakes up and escapes. Looking at the Penny Arcade for clues, Cap is attacked by the Mankiller. As Cap defeats the robot, both Bucky and Hydra converge on the arcade. Bucky arrives in time to see Hydra gunning down Cap, whose body falls into the river. Police arrive to find Cap's tattered uniform and a "Steve Rogers" mask filled with bullet holes.

NOTE: Steve's fortune reads "Tomorrow You Live, Tonight I Die!" Cap's body revealed to be rubber dummy in Cap #113, '69. Letter column changes its name to "Let's Rap With Cap."

CAPTAIN AMERICA #112 (April 1969)

"Lest We Forget!" (20 pages)

CREDITS: Stan Lee (writer), Jack Kirby (pencils), George Tuska (inks), Artie Simek (letters), Frank Giacoia (c inks)
FEATURE CHARACTER: Captain America (only in rfb & photo)
GUEST STAR: Iron Man (also as Tony Stark, last in Hulk #108, '68)
OTHER CHARACTERS: Red Skull, Bucky, Butterfly, Ringmaster & his Nazi spies, Unholy Legion of Beggars, White Death, Black Toad, Allied & Axis soldiers, Baron Zemo & his men, Sub-Mariner, Eskimos, Nick Fury, Dum Dum Dugan, Sharon Carter, MODOK, AIM agents, bystanders, 4th Sleeper, Batroc, Tumbler, Swordsman, Living Laser, Exiles: Baldini, Cadavus, Gen. Ching, Gruning, "Iron Hand" Hauptmann, Krushki; Tarpster, Dr. Faustus (all in rfb); police
LOCATIONS/ITEMS: New York, river, Avengers Mansion; Captain America's tattered mask, Visa-File
FLASHBACKS: Captain America and Bucky fight Red Skull in his giant drill (CapC #3, '41). Cap fights the Butterfly (CapC #3/4, '41), Ringmaster and his Nazi spy ring (CapC #5, '41), the Unholy Legion of Beggars (CapC #4, '41), White Death (CapC #9, '41), and Black Toad (CapC #7/2, '41). Cap and Bucky fight Nazis (ToS #68/2, '65) and Bucky dies against Baron Zemo and Cap is frozen (Av #4, '64 fb). Namor frees Cap from his ice prison (Av #4, '64). Cap becomes reacquainted with Nick Fury (ST #160, '67), meets Sharon Carter (ToS #76/2, '66), fights MODOK and battles AIM (ToS #94/2, '67), fights the 4th Sleeper (Cap #102, '68), Batroc (ToS #76/2, '66), Tumbler (ToS #83/2, '66), Swordsman and Living Laser (Cap #105, '68), the Exiles (Cap #104, '68), Trapster (Cap #108, '68) and Dr. Faustus (Cap #107, '68).
SYNOPSIS: Police fish Captain America's mask from the river and proclaim him dead. At Avengers Mansion, Iron Man receives a phone call telling him the bad news. He reviews Cap's career on the Visa-File and declares that Cap will be avenged.
NOTE: Black Toad called "Toadman" here.

CAPTAIN AMERICA #113 (May 1969)

"The Strange Death of Captain America" (20 pages)

CREDITS: Stan Lee (writer), Jim Steranko (pencils, colors, c art), Tom Palmer (inks), Artie Simek (letters)
FEATURE CHARACTER: Captain America (also in Av #106-107, '72-73 fb, next in Cap #179, '74 fb)
GUEST STARS: Avengers: Black Panther (last in Av #60, '69, chr last in Av:EMH #8, '07, chr next bts in Av #106, '72 fb, next in Av #61, '69), Hawkeye (last in Av #60, '69, chr last in Av:EMH #8, '07, chr last in Av:EMH #8, '07, chr next in Av #106, '72 fb, next in Av #61, '69), Iron Man (chr next bts in Av #106, '72 fb, next in IM #9, '69), Thor (last in Av #58, '68, chr last in Av:EMH #1, '07, chr next bts in Av #106, '72 fb, next in Thor #160, '69), Vision (last in Av #60, '69, chr last in Av:EMH #8, '07, chr next in Av #106, '72 fb, next in Av #61, '69); Nick Fury (last in Hulk #108, '68, chr next bts in Av #106, '72 fb, next in NF:AoS #9, '69), Gabe Jones (SHIELD agent), Dum Dum Dugan (both last in Hulk #107, '68, next in NF:AoS #9, '69)
SUPPORTING CAST: Rick Jones (also as Bucky, last in Hulk #111, '69, also in Av #106-107, '72-73 fb, also in Av #106-107, '72-73 fb), Sharon Carter (also in fb)
VILLAINS: Madame Hydra (also in fb1 to 1st chr app before W #126, '98 fb, in fb2 between W #126, '98 fb & Gam #6, '99 chr; chr also & next in Av #107, '73 fb, next in Cap #180, '74 as Viper), Space Phantom (bts, during Av #107, '73 fb, see NOTE), Hydra agents (some also as funeral parlor employees, others in fb)
OTHER CHARACTERS: Jasper Sitwell (SHIELD agent, last in IM #8, '68, next in NF:AoS #10, '69), police commissioner, reporters, cameramen; European rioters (in fb)
LOCATIONS/ITEMS: New York, river, Hydra base, Avengers Mansion inc library, Midtown funeral parlor, Drearcliff Cemetery; "Steve Rogers" mask, news cameras, Hydra's Captain America file (burned), newspaper, Captain America's casket, Cap dummy & motorcycle, other caskets, Hydra guns, poison (also as card) & missile launcher w/hunter missiles, hearse, Captain America memorial (on cover)
FLASHBACKS: A young Madame Hydra is orphaned in strife-torn Europe. Her face is permanently scarred; she has to struggle for mere survival, and drifts into a life of crime (1). When Hydra Island is destroyed Madame Hydra simultaneously kills all higher ranking Hydra agents in her sector, advancing her to the rank of Supreme Hydra (2).
SYNOPSIS: Reporters interview police about the fate of Captain America and Madame Hydra burns her Hydra file on Captain America, no longer needing it. At Avengers Mansion, the Avengers try to ask Bucky what happened, but he's still in shock and can't give any answers. Later, the Avengers, Nick Fury, Sharon Carter and other SHIELD agents attend Captain America's funeral where Nick Fury gives a eulogy, Rick Jones doesn't attend. After the ceremony, Fury discovers a Hydra card on Cap's casket. When he touches it, the Avengers are enveloped by poison gas. Rick decides to attend the funeral and arrives to see Hydra agents loading the unconscious heroes inside caskets into a hearse. He follows them to Drearcliff Cemetery and is captured, but is freed when Captain America attacks. Rick grabs a gun and shoots Cap's motorcycle, blowing it up and driving off the Hydra agents. As Cap and Bucky check on the Avengers, Madame Hydra launches hunter missiles at the pair. They dive into an open grave and the missiles hit the next closest target, apparently killing Madame Hydra. Steve explains to Rick that he faked Steve Rogers' death to regain Captain America's secret identity.
NOTE: Hydra Island was destroyed in ST #158, '67. Madame Hydra was revealed to be replaced by a Space Phantom here in Av #107, '73 fb.

CAPTAIN AMERICA #114 (June 1969)

"The Man Behind the Mask!" (20 pages)

CREDITS: Stan Lee (writer), John Romita (pencils, c art), Sal Buscema (inks), Herb Cooper (letters)
FEATURE CHARACTER: Captain America (also in disguise & in his own thoughts)
GUEST STARS: Avengers: Goliath (Clint Barton, also as Hawkeye on symbolic splash page), Wasp (Janet Van Dyne Pym) (both last in Av #65, '69, chr last in Hawk #6, '04 fb, chr next in JA #16, '75 fb, next in Cap #116, '69), Vision (also on symbolic splash page, last in Av #65, '69, chr next in JA #16, '75 fb, next in Cap #116, '69), Black Panther (also on symbolic splash page, last in Av #65, '69, chr last in Hawk #6, '04, chr next in JA #7, '73 fb, next in Av #68, '69), Yellowjacket (Hank Pym, last in Av #65, '69, chr last in Hawk #6, '04 fb, chr next in JA #16, '75 fb), Nick Fury (also on symbolic splash page, last in Sub #14, '69, last voice only in X #65, '70, next in Cap #120, '69)
SUPPORTING CAST: Sharon Carter (also on viewscreen & symbolic splash page), Rick Jones (as Bucky, also on symbolic splash page)
VILLAINS: Red Skull (off-panel, also as Cosmic Cube construct, last bts in Cap #108, '68, chr last in Cap #115, '69 fb), AIM agents
OTHER CHARACTERS: SHIELD barber Sam (last in ST #164, '68, chr last in Av:EMH #2, '07, next in Cap #120, '69) & other SHIELD agents, 5 hotel clerks, restroom bystander; Iron Man, Thor, Madame Hydra (trio on symbolic splash page only)
LOCATIONS/ITEMS: Avengers Mansion, SHIELD barbershop & HQ, Target Area M, restaurant washroom, 5 hotel lobbies, Steve's run-down hotel room; Walking Stiletto (AIM robot w/blast ray), Cosmic Cube (as iteration of itself, last in Av #40, '67, chr last in Cap #115, '69 fb), Sharon's pistol & mini-flame thrower, AIM agents' guns, barbershop window fogger
SYNOPSIS: Determined to keep "Steve Rogers" dead and start a new secret identity, Cap avoids Avengers Mansion, going to SHIELD instead. There he learns that Sharon, believing him dead, has decided to attack AIM at "Target Area M" without reinforcements. When Sharon confronts the AIM agents, one of them activates the Walking Stiletto robot. Soon after, Cap and Rick arrive and help Sharon defeat the agents. Cap decapitates the Walking Stiletto with his shield. Sharon is overjoyed to see Cap alive but cannot accede to his request that she resign from SHIELD. Later, Cap dons a brown wig and nose putty. Disguised, he tries to rent a hotel room but, without luggage or ID, is turned down repeatedly. He finally gets a room in a rundown hotel where the Red Skull suddenly appears, holding the Cosmic Cube.

CAPTAIN AMERICA #115 (July 1969)

"Now Begins the Nightmare!" (20 pages)

CREDITS: Stan Lee (writer), John Buscema (pencils), Sal Buscema (inks), Sam Rosen (letters), Marie Severin (c pencils), Frank Giacoia (c inks)
FEATURE CHARACTER: Captain America (also as Red Skull)
GUEST STAR: Yellowjacket (chr last in JA #16, '75 fb)
SUPPORTING CAST: Rick Jones, Sharon Carter
VILLAINS: Red Skull (also as Captain America & as Cosmic Cube construct, also in fb between bts in Cap #108, '68 & off-panel in Cap #114, '69),Exiles: Jurgen "Iron Hand" Hauptman (only in fb between Cap #104, '68 & Cap #117, '69), Angelo Baldini, Franz Cadavus, Gen. Jun Ching, Eric Gruning, Ivan Krushki (prev 5 only in fb between Cap #104, '68 & Cap #116, '69)
OTHER CHARACTERS: Edwin Jarvis (last in Av #65, '69, chr last in JA #16, '75 fb), Teen Brigade members, SHIELD agent, pedestrians, flying reptile creatures, tentacled monster; Mediterranean fisherman, his wife & villagers (trio only in fb)
LOCATIONS/ITEMS: New York City inc Steve's run-down hotel room, SHIELD HQ & Avengers Mansion, fiery world, rocky planet, a Mediterranean island, fisherman's home, Red Skull's hideout (trio in fb); Cosmic Cube (also in fb between Av #40, '67 & Cap #114, '69 , also as iteration of itself), Avengers communichamber
FLASHBACK: A Mediterranean island fisherman discovers the Cosmic Cube. When he uses it to improve the local villagers' lifestyle, the Red Skull and his Exiles learn of the Cube's location and steal it from the fisherman. The Exiles believe that the Cube belongs to all of them equally, but the Skull uses the Cube to cow the Exiles into accepting his authority.
SYNOPSIS: Red Skull attacks Captain America with the Cosmic Cube. When Cap fights back the "Skull" disappears, only to reveal himself elsewhere in the room and that Cap had been battling a construct. Armed with the Cube, the Skull easily defeats Cap. Drunk with power, the Skull teleports Cap to a world of fire. Meanwhile at SHIELD HQ, Rick confronts Sharon over Cap's disappearance, but when he gets no sympathy from her he tries Avengers Mansion, where Yellowjacket assures him that his partner is probably just taking a few days off. Undeterred, Rick appeals to the Teen Brigade. After teleporting Cap to different planets and shrinking him in a vain effort to drive Cap insane, Red Skull uses the Cube to teleport Sharon to the hotel. Before releasing her from a trance, the Skull uses the Cube to switch appearances with Cap. Now awake, Sharon runs into Red Skull's arms, thinking he is Cap. When Steve tries to convince Sharon that he is really Captain America, she believes that the Skull has gone mad.
NOTE: Cap believes that he and Red Skull have switched bodies, but they have only changed their appearances, revealed in Cap #119, '69.

CAPTAIN AMERICA #116 (August 1969)

"Far Worse Than Death!" (20 pages)

CREDITS: Stan Lee (writer), Gene Colan (pencils), Joe Sinnott (inks), Sam Rosen (letters)
FEATURE CHARACTER: Captain America (as Red Skull)
GUEST STARS: Avengers: Goliath (Clint Barton), Vision, Wasp (all last in Cap #114, '69, chr last in JA #16 '75 fb, next in Av #66, '69), Yellowjacket (next in Av #66, '69)
SUPPORTING CAST: Sharon Carter (next bts in Cap #120, '69, next in Cap #122, '70), Rick Jones (next in Cap #118, '69)
VILLAINS: Red Skull (as Captain America), Exiles: Angelo Baldini, Franz Cadavus, Gen. Jun Ching, Eric Gruning, Ivan Krushki (prev 5 last in Cap #115, '69 fb)
OTHER CHARACTERS: Edwin Jarvis (next in CM #17, '69), Teen Brigade (bts, located "Cap" for Rick), SHIELD (bts, summoned Avengers), police (Harry, Bill & Mac named), government scientists & lab security, mother & daughter, bystanders; Black Panther (cover only)
LOCATIONS/ITEMS: New York City inc Central Park, police precinct & Steve's run-down hotel room, government testing lab, Route 104, Avengers Mansion; Cosmic Cube, police switchboard, barricade, patrol cars & guns, Cap's stolen car, Avengers video sentry system, Sharon's hand blaster
SYNOPSIS: "Captain America" reassures Sharon that "Red Skull" is beaten. Cap realizes he'll never convince Sharon that the Skull has switched bodies with him. The Skull sends Sharon away, uses the Cube to transport Cap to a government lab and causes an explosion. Cap is blamed for the destruction. He escapes from the security guards by stealing a car, but the Skull alerts the police to Cap's location. Cap evades two police roadblocks on his way to seek help from the Avengers, but they've been monitoring the situation from Avengers Mansion. With the Teen Brigade's help Rick locates the Skull in Central Park, but the Skull callously sends Rick away. Stung by "Cap's" rejection, Rick concludes he should never have tried to be Cap's partner. Meanwhile at the Mansion, the Avengers easily defeat Cap, but are summoned by SHIELD and leave Cap behind. The Skull, controlling Sharon, has her enter the Mansion in order to assassinate Cap, but when she fails to pull the trigger Red Skull realizes that not even the Cube can overcome love. Undeterred, he transports Cap to the Isle of Exiles.

CAPTAIN AMERICA #117 (September 1969)

"The Coming of the Falcon!" (20 pages)

CREDITS: Stan Lee (writer), Gene Colan (pencils, co-c pencils), Joe Sinnott (inks), Sam Rosen (letters), John Romita (co-c pencils)
FEATURE CHARACTER: Captain America (as Red Skull)
SUPPORTING CAST: Falcon (Samuel Thomas "Snap" Wilson, social worker & former criminal w/multiple personality disorder, 1st but chr last in Cap #186, '75 fb, also in fb1 during Cap #277/2, '83 fb, see NOTE), Redwing (Sam's falcon, 1st but chr last in Cap #186, '75, see NOTE)
VILLAINS: Red Skull (as Captain America, also in Cap #186, '75 fb), Exiles: Jurgen "Iron Hand" Hauptman (last in Cap #115, '69 fb), Angelo Baldini, Franz Cadavus, Gen. Jun Ching, Eric Gruning, Ivan Krushki; MODOK (former AIM scientist George Tarleton, immense head w/mental powers, last in ToS #94/2, '67, chr last in Cap #119, '69 fb), AIM agents
OTHER CHARACTERS: Carriage riders, cab driver, photographers, Isle of Exiles natives, bystanders, horse; pigeons (in fb1)
LOCATIONS/ITEMS: New York City inc luxury hotel & Central Park, Isle of Exiles, AIM Island inc AIM HQ, Harlem, Rio de Janeiro (both in fb); Cosmic Cube (also in Cap #186, '75 fb), clay, MODOK's Doomsday chair
FLASHBACKS: As a teenager, Sam has the biggest rooftop pigeon coop in Harlem (1). While vacationing in Rio, he is fascinated by falcons and buys Redwing. Sam comes to believe that Redwing is more than just a falcon, and is almost a part of him (see NOTE).
SYNOPSIS: Eager for vengeance against Red Skull, the Exiles attack Captain America. With the help of a falcon, Cap escapes from the Exiles. While in hiding he remembers that the skull he's wearing is just a mask and removes it. Unsure if the Exiles will still recognize him, he uses clay to disguise his facial features. Meanwhile in New York City, the Skull checks into a luxury hotel, reveling in the idol worship that New Yorkers pay to Captain America. At AIM HQ, MODOK is plotting to render the Cosmic Cube powerless. Back on Exile Isle, the bird that helped Cap returns to its master, Sam Wilson, who is enjoying any opportunity to thwart the Exiles' plans. Cap stumbles across Sam in the jungle, who introduces his bird, Redwing. Sam takes Cap to the local village, reveals he's from Harlem, and came to the island when the Exiles hired him and Redwing. When he realized that the Exiles were seeking prisoners rather than employees he quit, and began leading the villagers in fighting back. Cap convinces Sam that he needs a costume and identity, and dubs him...the Falcon!
NOTE: Cap #186, '75 fb reveals Falcon's middle initial, and that his identity as a social worker, his vacation in Rio and reason for being on the Isle of Exiles are fabrications of Red Skull, and the super-normal mental link he shares with Redwing was created by the Cosmic Cube. By Cap #134, '71 Sam does indeed become a social worker. Cap #277/2, '83 reveals Falcon's middle name and that he suffers from multiple personality disorder; the criminal "Snap" is a defense mechanism, but Sam is his true personality. Sam refers to Cap as the "joker in the red jumpsuit," but Cap's jumpsuit is green. Romita redrew Cap's head for this cover. AIM HQ revealed to be on AIM Island in Cap #119, '69. MODOK stands for Mental Organism Designed Only for Killing.

CAPTAIN AMERICA #118 (October 1969)

"The Falcon Fights On!" (20 pages)

CREDITS: Stan Lee (writer), Gene Colan (art, co-c art), Joe Sinnott (inks), Sam Rosen (letters), John Romita (co-c art)
FEATURE CHARACTER: Captain America (as Red Skull, also in photo)
SUPPORTING CAST: Rick Jones (next in CM #17, '69), Falcon, Redwing
VILLAINS: Red Skull (as Captain America, next in CM #17, '69), Exiles: Angelo Baldini, Franz Cadavus (both chr next in AT #4, '71 fb), Gen. Jun Ching, Eric Gruning, Jurgen "Iron Hand" Hauptman, Ivan Krushki (prev 6 next in AT #4, '71); MODOK (bts, commanding AIM scientists), AIM scientists
OTHER CHARACTERS: Isle of Exiles natives, Cap's fans, hotel manager, elevator operator & other staff, bystanders
LOCATIONS/ITEMS: New York City inc Central Park & luxury hotel w/Skull's room & lobby, Isle of Exiles, Avengers Mansion, AIM Island inc AIM HQ; Cosmic Cube (next bts in CM #17, '69), Bunsen burners, catholite block
SYNOPSIS: Using the Cosmic Cube to watch the Exiles from his New York hotel room, Red Skull realizes that Captain America must have evaded the Exiles by removing the Skull mask. On the Isle of Exiles, Sam dons his Falcon costume and Cap trains him in hand-to-hand combat. Back in the states, the Skull evades a crowd of Cap's fans who storm his hotel room, seeking handshakes and autographs. Their disappointment plays into the Skull's plans to ruin Cap's reputation. Meanwhile in his room at Avengers Mansion, Rick makes the fateful decision to take "Cap's" advice and quit as the Avenger's partner. Later at AIM HQ, MODOK's scientists continue their efforts to deactivate the Cube. Back on the Isle of Exiles, Cap and Falcon attack the Exiles and defeat them, but as the Nazis retreat, the Skull exhausts his patience and decides the time has come for the final confrontation.
NOTE: Rick Jones moves on from here to join the supporting cast of yet another series, Captain Marvel, with CM #17, '69. Red Skull mentions Cap's red jumpsuit, but it's still green. Romita retouched this cover, including redrawing Cap's head. "Let's Rap With Cap" includes a letter from Steve Gerber, future writer of Howard the Duck, amongst others.

CAPTAIN AMERICA #119 (November 1969)

"Now Falls the Skull!" (20 pages)

CREDITS: Stan Lee (writer), Gene Colan (pencils), Joe Sinnott (inks), Sam Rosen (letters)
FEATURE CHARACTER: Captain America (also as Red Skull, also in rfb)
SUPPORTING CAST: Falcon, Redwing
VILLAINS: Red Skull (also as Captain America, birdcage, boulder, wall of water & tornado, last in CM #17, '69, next in Cap #128, '70); MODOK (also in fb1 between ToS #94/2, '67 & Cap #117, '69), AIM scientists
OTHER CHARACTER: Sharon Carter (only in rfb)
LOCATIONS/ITEMS: Isle of Exiles, New York City alley, the Skull's Berchtesgaden castle, AIM Island inc AIM HQ, a desert, AIM's underwater base (in rfb); Cosmic Cube (last bts in CM #17, '69, destroyed, next in CM #28, '73), catholite block, MODOK's Doomsday chair (also in rfb), escape sub, sonic beam (both

FLASHBACKS: Cap and Sharon defeat MODOK (ToS #94/2, '67). MODOK escapes from his exploding sub and emits a sonic beam, allowing his agents to find and rescue him (1).

SYNOPSIS: Tiring of the games he's been playing with Captain America, Red Skull uses the Cosmic Cube to return his body to its original appearance, teleports to his Berchtesgaden castle and teleports Cap, Falcon and Redwing to join him. To Falcon's chagrin, the Skull cages Redwing and taunts the Falcon into attempting to wrest the Cube from him. The Skull returns Cap's appearance to normal, and Falcon realizes for the first time that he has been trained by Captain America. While toying with the heroes, the Skull transforms himself into a boulder, a tidal wave and a tornado. Meanwhile from AIM Island, MODOK begins the process to deactivate the Cube. The Skull's tornado transports Cap, Falcon and Redwing to a barren desert where Falcon distracts Red Skull. Cap slings his shield and dislodges the Cube from the Skull's grasp. As the Skull regains the Cube MODOK's process takes effect, and the Cube begins to melt, to everyone's surprise. Red Skull uses the last of the Cube's power to escape, leaving Cap and Falcon to celebrate their victory and begin the walk to civilization.

NOTE: In MODOK's fb Cap refers to Sharon by name, despite not knowing her name at the time.

CAPTAIN AMERICA #120 (December 1969)

"Crack-Up on Campus!" (20 pages)

CREDITS: Stan Lee (writer), Gene Colan (pencils), Joe Sinnott (inks), Sam Rosen (letters)
FEATURE CHARACTER: Captain America (also as "Roger Stevens," also in IM #18, '69, Av #69-71, '69, IM #19, '69, Av #72, '70)
GUEST STARS: Nick Fury (last in Cap #114, '69, also in NF:AoS #12-14, '69, IM #16, '69 fb, IM #16, '69, SMFam #9, '08 fb, bts in SMFam #9, '08, IM #18, '69, NF:AoS #15, '69, Av #72, '70), Dum Dum Dugan (last in Av #67, '69, next in NF:AoS #12, '69)
SUPPORTING CAST: Falcon, Redwing (both next in Cap #126, '70), Sharon Carter (bts, on assignment, also in Captain America's dream, next in Cap #122, '70)
VILLAINS: MODOK (next in Cap #124, '70), AIM agents (R1 aka "Grizzly" & R2 named)
OTHER CHARACTERS: SHIELD Barber Sam (last in Cap #114, '69, next in Cap #124, '70), Mart Baker (college protester), Prof. Paul Fosgrave (top authority on atomic equations), Manning University Dean, administrators & students, riot police, Harlem bystanders
LOCATIONS/ITEMS: Harlem, SHIELD barbershop, Manning university; "Super-Heroes" comic book, SHIELD barber chair, reaction-time tester & slumber seat, newspaper w/Physical Education Teacher advertisement, AIM gun, hypno-beam & portable copter, MODOK's Doomsday chair
SYNOPSIS: Captain America and the Falcon arrive back in Harlem and go their separate ways. Cap heads to the SHIELD barbershop in search of Sharon Carter, but Nick Fury tells Cap she's out on assignment. When Cap falls asleep in Fury's "slumber chair", Fury uses the device to subliminally give Cap an assignment: investigate recent suspicious activity at Manning University. Upon awaking Cap goes to apply for the open Phys Ed position, only to arrive on campus in the midst of widespread unrest as students, led by dissident Mart Baker, protest the university policies. Steve's interview for the job is interrupted when riots break out between the protestors and those who support the university administration. As Captain America he tries to break up the rioting, but two of the protesters are AIM agents who kidnap Prof. Fosgrave, attempting to gain access to his atomic equations. Mart Baker realizes he's been duped into providing cover for their kidnapping and joins Cap in charging the AIM agents on a university rooftop, where Cap rescues the professor. Later, Captain America tells Fury that he just couldn't cut it as a Phys Ed teacher.

CAPTAIN AMERICA #121 (January 1970)

"The Coming of…the Man-Brute!" (20 pages)

CREDITS: Stan Lee (writer), Gene Colan (pencils), Joe Sinnott (inks), Sam Rosen (letters)
FEATURE CHARACTER: Captain America (also in Cap #176, '74 fb)
GUEST STARS: Avengers: Vision, Wasp, Yellowjacket (all between Av #74-75), Black Panther (last in Av #74, chr last DD #69 fb, next in Av #75); Nick Fury (next in Cap #123) (all '70)
VILLAINS: Prof. Silas X Cragg, (mad scientist, only app, dies), Man-Brute (Bart Dietzel, Cragg's super-soldier experiment, 1st, next as Blockbuster in Omega #7, '77)
OTHER CHARACTERS: Edwin Jarvis (between Av #74-75, '70), Robert (Man-Brute's son, next bts in Omega #7, '77), librarian, library patrons, reporters, orphans, nun, bowery residents; Prof. Abraham Erskine, Gen. Phillips, Heinz Krueger, doctor (prev 4 in rfb); Sharon Carter, Rick Jones (both in photos)
LOCATIONS/ITEMS: New York City inc Cragg's mansion and laboratory, library, Avengers Mansion, orphanage & bowery; archived newspapers, Cragg's "ZXX serum", super-soldier testing equipment, & car, Rick Jones & Sharon Carter SHIELD file photographs
FLASHBACKS: Steve Rogers is declared 4-F, is offered a chance to participate in the super-soldier project, is injected with an experimental serum and transforms into a super-soldier. Nazi saboteurs murder Prof. Erskine and Steve becomes Captain America (ToS #63/2, '65).
SYNOPSIS: Prof. Silas X Cragg, a forgotten Captain America WWII foe, is working on his own super-soldier experiment to defeat Captain America. He soon finds a suitable test subject in an ex-convict down on his luck. Cragg empowers the man with his super-soldier experiment, dubbing him "Man-Brute". Cragg soon leaves a message at Avengers Mansion asking Captain America to perform an exhibition show at a local orphanage. When Cap arrives he is attacked by the Man-Brute. As the battle carries them inside, the orphans soon realize the fighting is real. One of the orphans, Robert, attacks the villain, who flees from the child. Later at Cragg's mansion, Man-Brute confronts the scientist, revealing that the orphan who attacked him is his own son, which made him question his attacking Cap. Terrified, Cragg accidentally backs into high-voltage equipment, killing himself. Man-Brute swears never to use his strength again. Later Cap nearly passes the villain on the street, not recognizing the Man-Brute, who has gone back to living in a slum.

NOTE: Man-Brute's real name revealed in NAvF, '06. "Let's Rap With Cap" includes LOC from J.M. De Matteis, future writer of Captain America.

CAPTAIN AMERICA #122 (February 1970)

"The Sting of the Scorpion" (20 pages)

CREDITS: Stan Lee (writer), Gene Colan (pencils), Joe Sinnott (inks), Artie Simek (letters), Sam Rosen (c letters)
FEATURE CHARACTERS: Captain America
SUPPORTING CAST: Sharon Carter (also in Steve's dream, next in Cap #124, '70)
VILLAINS: Scorpion (Mac Gargan, former private investigator, last in ASM #29, '65, chr last in Alias #23, '03, chr next in Cap #151, '72 fb, next in Cap #150, '72), Spy ring operatives (Specs & Smiler named)
OTHER CHARACTERS: SHIELD agents, hotel front desk employee, police, taxi driver, pedestrians; AIM agents (in Steve's dream)
LOCATIONS/ITEMS: New York City inc hotel, "Grove Lane" spy ring house; Steve's suitcase, Scorpion's car with built-in TV monitor, taxi cab, spies' guns, SHIELD guns & car

SYNOPSIS: Captain America retires to the hotel he's currently staying in but has a nightmare about Sharon Carter being in danger. Meanwhile, a group of spies are aware that Agent 13 is on to their spy ring and implement plans to have her killed. Unable to sleep, Captain America vacates the hotel as Steve Rogers. He's attacked by Scorpion, who is testing his combat suit on a civilian before taking a hit job on Sharon Carter; Steve is stunned. The villain flees approaching police, allowing Steve to don his costume. Cap soon finds the Scorpion driving off and follows in a taxi. Scorpion arrives near the spy ring's house to begin tracking down Agent 13, but Sharon has unexpectedly been captured by the spies. Captain America tells the taxi driver to contact SHIELD and battles Scorpion. Defeating Scorpion, Cap then locates the spy ring's house, defeats the villains, but fails to discover Sharon tied up in the basement. Sharon finally frees herself, only to find she just missed Captain America, who's heading back to the city in the taxi.

CAPTAIN AMERICA #123 (March 1970)

"Suprema, the Deadliest of the Species!" (20 pages)

CREDITS: Stan Lee (writer), Gene Colan (pencils), Joe Sinnott (inks), Artie Simek (letters), Sam Rosen (c letters)
FEATURE CHARACTERS: Captain America
GUEST STARS: Tony Stark (last in IM #21, '70, next in Av #76, '70), Nick Fury (last in Cap #121, '70), Dum Dum Dugan (last in Av #72, '70)
VILLAINS: Suprema (Susan Scarbo, hypnotist, 1st, chr next in Cap #15, '06 fb, next bts in Cap #355, '89, next as Mother Night in Cap #356, '89), Scarbo (Melvin "Malachi" Scarbo, Suprema's brother, hypnotist, 1st, next as Minister Blood in Cap #356, '89), Suprema's henchmen, Aces Wilde (gambling crime lord), various crime lords & their henchmen
OTHER CHARACTERS: Jasper Sitwell (last in IM #16, '69), J. Jonah Jameson (between ASM #81-82, '70), police officer, SHIELD agents, bystanders
LOCATIONS/ITEMS: New York, Suprema's base, Aces Wilde's gambling house, SHIELD barber shop, HQ & weapons range, Daily Bugle's news morgue, Stark's laboratory; Suprema's Wolverine jet (truck) w/electro scanner & gas-jets, Suprema's henchmen's face masks & guns, Scarbo's hypnotic disc, Stark's blaster weapons & 321 computer, Daily Bugle's archived newspapers
SYNOPSIS: Suprema and her crime gang begin taking over crime rackets around the state, using Suprema's hypnotic power to make everyone agree to her demands. Meanwhile, Captain America spars with Nick Fury at SHIELD HQ, demonstrating combat moves to Fury's men. Suprema soon seeks to gain control of SHIELD and uses her technology to locate Dum Dum Dugan. Under her control, Dugan leads Suprema to Fury who is conducting weapons testing with Cap and his agents at a firing range. She quickly takes control of Fury and the SHIELD agents, but Cap's shield negates her powers. Cap flees as Suprema's minions attack him. Seeking information on Suprema's identity and the source of her powers, he performs research at the Daily Bugle's archives and on Tony Stark's computer. He soon discovers she and her right hand man Scarbo are ex-performers adept in hypnotism, who have used technology to amplify their powers. He confronts Suprema's forces, using an electrical current to short-circuit her control, freeing Fury and his men. With Suprema captured, Cap scorns the villainess for her power lust.
NOTE: Scarbo's alias "Malachi" revealed in Cap #356, '89, nickname Mel in Av #324, '90, 1st name & Suprema's 1st name in Av #325, '90. Suprema's & Scarbo's last names established in OHMU:ME #2, '91.

CAPTAIN AMERICA #124 (April, 1970)

"Mission: Stop the Cyborg!" (20 pages)

CREDITS: Stan Lee (writer), Gene Colan (pencils), Joe Sinnott (inks), Sam Rosen (letters), Marie Severin (c pencils)
FEATURE CHARACTER: Captain America (next in Av #75-76, '70)
GUEST STARS: Nick Fury, Dum Dum Dugan (both next in Cap #127, '70)
SUPPORTING CAST: Sharon Carter (next in Cap #127, '70)
VILLAINS: MODOK (chr next in Cap #132, '70 fb, next bts in Cap #130, '70, next in Cap #132, '70), Cyborg (AIM agent A-12, only app), AIM agents (A-14 named, dies)
OTHER CHARACTERS: Jasper Sitwell, SHIELD barber Sam (both next in Cap #127, '70), SHIELD agents; bystanders (on cover)
LOCATIONS/ITEMS: New York City inc alley, SHIELD barber shop & HQ, AIM base inc Cyborg creation chamber, Savings bank, AIM trap house; AIM blaster, SHIELD barber chair, window fogger & closed circuit scanner, Cyborg's protective cylinder & micro-wave energizer, AIM trap house's trick stairs, steel bars & water pipe , MODOK's Doomsday chair
SYNOPSIS: Two AIM assassins attack Captain America, but are easily defeated. They retreat to face MODOK, who executes one and offers

the other the chance to be spared, if he will participate in an experiment. The AIM agent is soon transformed into the Cyborg. Meanwhile, Cap heads to SHIELD HQ, where he asks Nick Fury to take Sharon off field duty to keep her out of harm's way. Fury arranges for Sharon to meet Cap, and she agrees to take office duty. SHIELD scanners detect the Cyborg robbing a bank, but the villain flees before they can pursue. Later, Sharon receives a message which she relays to Cap, instructing him to meet Nick Fury at a house. Sharon discovers the message is a trap and rushes off to warn Cap before he can enter the building. Arriving before the Avenger, she is attacked by the Cyborg. Cap arrives and battles the Cyborg, eventually defeating the foe. Sharon embraces Cap, glad that he is safe, but he brushes off her affections, chastising her and Fury for breaking her promise to stay out of danger. He walks away before Sharon can explain she was trying to save him.

NOTE: The AIM trap house is on 211 East Carter Street. "A" stands for Assassin in A-12 & A-14.

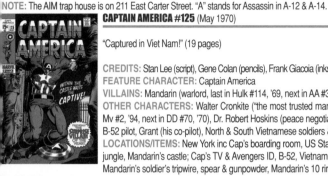

CAPTAIN AMERICA #125 (May 1970)

"Captured in Viet Nam!" (19 pages)

CREDITS: Stan Lee (script), Gene Colan (pencils), Frank Giacoia (inks), Sam Rosen (letters), Marie Severin (c pencils)
FEATURE CHARACTER: Captain America
VILLAINS: Mandarin (warlord, last in Hulk #114, '69, next in AA #3, '70), Mandarin's soldiers
OTHER CHARACTERS: Walter Cronkite ("the most trusted man in America," on television, 1st but chr last in Mv #2, '94, next in DD #70, '70), Dr. Robert Hoskins (peace negotiator, only app), State Department employees, B-52 pilot, Grant (his co-pilot), North & South Vietnamese soldiers & sniper; Sharon Carter (in Cap's thoughts)
LOCATIONS/ITEMS: New York inc Cap's boarding room, US State Department, US Air Force base, Viet Nam jungle, Mandarin's castle; Cap's TV & Avengers ID, B-52, Vietnamese soldier's guns, binoculars & sniper's rifle, Mandarin's soldier's tripwire, spear & gunpowder, Mandarin's 10 rings

SYNOPSIS: When Cap learns that noted peacemaker Dr. Robert Hoskins is missing in Viet Nam, he gets permission from the State Department to gain transport in a B-52 to Southeast Asia. He parachutes into the jungle and is immediately attacked by soldiers and a sniper. He escapes and later allows himself to be captured by soldiers wearing unfamiliar uniforms. The soldiers take Cap to their master, the Mandarin, who reveals that he has captured Hoskins in a plot to further throw Viet Nam into chaos so he can rule in the aftermath. Cap breaks free and searches Mandarin's castle until he finds Hoskins behind a steel door. Using gunpowder to blast through, Cap attempts to escape with Hoskins but they are blocked by Mandarin. Cap knocks Mandarin off the drawbridge into the moat, and after an all-night trek, returns Hoskins to his job of healing the wounded. With both sides realizing they were duped by the Mandarin, they can return to the peace table.

NOTE: Pages 12 & 13 of story are half-pages, resulting in a 19-page story numbered as a 20-page tale; format continues through Cap #140.

CAPTAIN AMERICA #126 (June 1970)

"The Fate of the Falcon!" (19 pages)

CREDITS: Stan Lee (writer), Gene Colan (pencils), Frank Giacoia (inks), Sam Rosen (letters), Jack Kirby (co-c pencils), John Romita (co-c pencils), Bill Everett (c inks)
FEATURE CHARACTER: Captain America
SUPPORTING CAST: Falcon (also as Captain America), Redwing (both last in Cap #120, '69, next in Cap #132, '70)
VILLAINS: Diamond Head ("Rocky the Lynx", Maggia lieutenant & gang leader, only app), Diamond Heads gang
OTHER CHARACTERS: Harlem residents, radio announcer (voice only), radio listeners, diner customer, police, reporter (on television), news photographers, bystanders (also on television), pawnshop owner
LOCATIONS/ITEMS: Harlem inc diner, pawnshop, warehouse, Diamond Heads' hideout & Sam's apartment; radio, Sam's TV, police megaphone, handguns & rifles, Diamond Head's gun, Diamond Heads gangs' guns & rifles

SYNOPSIS: While searching the streets of Harlem, Cap overhears a radio newscast that the police have cordoned off a building where the Falcon is trapped. Investigating, Cap sees Redwing overhead and slips unnoticed into a building in an area surrounded by police, locating the injured Falcon. Sam tells Cap that a Diamond Heads gang member was killed and he's been framed for it. Donning Cap's costume, Sam deceives the police and escapes the dragnet. Meanwhile, Diamond Head sends his gang out to collect protection money from shop owners, assuring them that the Maggia will not interfere. While patrolling past a warehouse Cap sees Rocky the Lynx, a Maggia lieutenant, parked nearby. Just as Cap recognizes a Diamond Head thug standing guard outside the warehouse, other gang members attack him. They take the fight into the warehouse where more gang members shoot at Cap. The Falcon arrives, and together they defeat the gang and unmask Diamond Head, finding Rocky the Lynx under the mask. Rocky reveals that the Maggia was trying to take over Harlem by fomenting racial hatred. His name cleared, the Falcon announces he is staying in Harlem, where he is needed.

NOTE: Romita provided touch-ups for this cover.

CAPTAIN AMERICA #127 (July 1970)

"Who Calls Me Traitor?" (19 pages)

CREDITS: Stan Lee (writer), Gene Colan (pencils), Wally Wood (inks), Artie Simek (letters), Marie Severin (c pencils), Joe Sinnott (c inks), Sam Rosen (c letters)
FEATURE CHARACTER: Captain America (next in Av #78-79, '70, XFac #139, '97 fb)
GUEST STARS: Nick Fury, Dum Dum Dugan (both next in Cap #132, '70), Tony Stark (last in Av #76, '70, chr last in Av #77, '70 fb, next in Av #79, '70)
SUPPORTING CAST: Sharon Carter (next in Cap #132, '70)
VILLAINS: Dr. Ryder (AIM agent posing as SHIELD scientist, only app), Android X-4 (only app, deactivated), AIM agents

OTHER CHARACTERS: Jasper Sitwell (next in Cap #132, '70), SHIELD barber Sam (next in Cap #143, '71), Joe Robertson (Daily Bugle City Editor, between ASM #82-83, '70), SHIELD agents, Stark Industries security guard

LOCATIONS/ITEMS: New York City inc SHIELD HQ, barber shop & weapons range, Steve's boarding room, Fury's apartment, Stark Industries, subway platform; SHIELD protecto-suit, force-bolt blast, barber-shop chair lift, helicopter, handguns, blasters, smoke bomb, walkie-talkies, spinning platform, mini-Geiger counter & gas capsule, AIM's electronic nullifier, Dum Dum's car

SYNOPSIS: At SHIELD HQ Captain America helps Nick Fury test the new Dr. Ryder designed protecto-suit. Cap rejects Fury's suggestion to talk with Sharon and leaves. Later during an outdoor battle test, AIM attacks Fury and his SHIELD agents, having already developed a way to nullify the protecto-suits. After Ryder convinces Fury that Cap is the most likely suspect for betraying SHIELD; an agent calls Cap to warn him he's lost his clearance. Angered, Cap arrives at Fury's house and encounters an exiting Joe Robertson, who tells Cap that he is under suspicion. Fury visits Tony Stark to build X-4, an android that can test Cap, to reassure Fury that the man they've been dealing with is not an imposter. Summoned to SHIELD, Cap arrives eager for answers but is forced to compete with X-4. Successfully calming Fury's fears, Cap is attacked again by X-4 but Fury can't stop it. Hoping to find who's controlling X-4, Sharon traces the radioactivity to Dr. Ryder, revealing him as the traitor. She drops a gas capsule, knocking Ryder out, and deactivates X-4. Fury had suspected Ryder all along, but still stung by his treatment from his friends, Cap rejects their explanations and walks out.

CAPTAIN AMERICA #128 (August 1970)

"Mission: Stamp Out Satan's Angels!" (19 pages)

CREDITS: Stan Lee (writer), Gene Colan (pencils), Wally Wood (inks), Artie Simek (letters), Marie Severin (c art), Joe Sinnott (c inks), Sam Rosen (c letters)

FEATURE CHARACTER: Captain America (also in rfb & on poster)

VILLAINS: Satan's Angels (motorcycle gang inc Whitey, their leader, Red Skull (last in Cap #119, '69)

OTHER CHARACTERS: Dickie (Whitey's younger brother), bystanders (Sammy named), motorcycle dealer, police, rock festival band & attendees; Bucky Barnes, Baron Heinrich Zemo, German soldiers (trio in rfb); W.C. Fields, Clark Gable (both on movie posters)

LOCATIONS/ITEMS: New York City inc Cap's boarding room, car dealership, motorcycle dealership & Holland Tunnel, Coits Neck inc police station w/jail, Steve's motel room, Monroe Park & Satan's Angels' camp; Cap's motorcycle (1st), Satan's Angels' motorcycles & chains, handguns, rock band's bus w/loudspeaker, drums & guitars, Skull's videotronic remoti-scanner, Cap's WWII motorcycle, drone plane (both in rfb)

FLASHBACK: Cap and Bucky attempt to stop Zemo's drone plane but Bucky dies when it explodes (Av #4, '64 fb).

SYNOPSIS: Distraught by overhearing comments by pedestrians that Captain America is a has-been, Steve Rogers buys a motorcycle and leaves town, intending to drive across the country. Entering Coits Neck, he is arrested by a policeman who thinks he's a member of Satan's Angels. Hearing about the arrest of a fellow biker the Angels break Steve out of jail, injuring a policeman. Steve refuses to go with them, opting to help the injured officer, then rents a room in town. That night the Angels terrorize an outdoor music festival by racing their motorcycles through the audience. Captain America arrives on his bike to halt the destruction. Whitey attempts to run down Cap with his cycle, but Cap uses his shield to knock Whitey off. Whitey's runaway motorcycle strikes a young boy in the audience who turns out to be Whitey's younger brother Dickie. Whitey is repentant, but Dickie needs a doctor. Meanwhile, the Red Skull watches this scene on a viewscreen.

NOTE: Coits Neck is "hours away" from NYC. Steve's license plate is 4291. In Cap's flashback both Cap and Bucky are wearing their costumes, but they were wearing army fatigues in Av #4, '64 fb.

Between 1975 and 1982, Hostess ran comic book ads with Marvel (and other) characters promoting their snacks. While thwarting villainy with baked confectionary might seem to suggest these ads are unlikely to be part of regular Marvel (Earth-616) continuity, several antagonists created for the ads reappeared in 616 stories, raising the possibility that events similar to the ones depicted, presumably minus the tasty Hostess cake element, could have taken place in 616. Hence bonus sidebars covering Captain America's Hostess adventures are interspersed through the book; character chronologies are included, identifying when these adventures would have taken place for Cap and his cast, if said events (or similar) actually happened.

"Captain America and the Red Skull" (1 page)

CREDITS: Unknown

FEATURE CHARACTER: Captain America (last in Cap #200, '76, next in CapBiB, '76)

VILLAIN: The Red Skull (Shmidt, last in CB #27, '77, next in SVTU #10, '77)

OTHER CHARACTER: Cosmic Cube (last in CM #33, '74, chr last in Cap Ann #7, '83 fb, next in MTIO #42, '78)

LOCATIONS/ITEMS: Washington Monument; Hostess Twinkies

SYNOPSIS: The Red Skull uses the Cosmic Cube to snatch Captain America from the middle of practicing for his Bicentennial display, but Cap drops a Twinkie next to the Cube, focusing its attention on that rather than the Skull's orders. Without the Cube backing the Skull up, Cap easily pounds him.

NOTE: Appeared in various Marvel titles, July & August 1976. The Cosmic Cube thinks to itself, rendering it an individual and not an item; this is an early indication of the sentience that will later see it turn into Kubik.

CAPTAIN AMERICA #129 (September 1970)

"The Vengeance of the Red Skull" (19 pages)

CREDITS: Stan Lee (writer), Gene Colan (pencils, co-c pencils), Dick Ayers (inks), Artie Simek (letters), Jack Kirby (co-c pencils), Frank Giacoia (c inks), Sam Rosen (c letters)
FEATURE CHARACTER: Captain America
VILLAINS: Red Skull (next in AT #4, '71), Skull's henchmen & field agents
OTHER CHARACTERS: King Hassab (of Irabia, only app), Hassab's driver, spectators, police, jet pilots
LOCATIONS/ITEMS: Red Skull's mountain hideout, Clifton (a town in the Midwest); Cap's motorcycle, Red Skull's videotronic remoti-scanner, Skull's jet-copter w/giant magnet, rocket sled & rocket, Hassab's limo, fighter escort jets, Skull's henchmen's rifles, police guns
SYNOPSIS: From his hideout, Red Skull monitors both Captain America and visiting King Hassab of Irabia. Plotting to kill two birds with one stone the Skull's agents change the road signs, manipulating both parties into arriving in Clifton. Cap arrives in Clifton just as the Skull's henchmen attack Hassab's limo. As Cap fights off the henchmen, the Skull lowers a giant magnet from his hovering helicopter and lifts the limo into the air. Red Skull reveals his plan to Hassab: when Cap attempts to rescue Hassab, the Skull will kill both of them and the world will be plunged into war. Cap tracks the helicopter to the Skull's mountain hideout where he allows himself to be captured. Cap breaks out of his cell and follows the Skull, who is transporting Hassab to a rocket. Inspired by Cap's battles, Hassab fights back, breaking free from the Skull. Cap and Red Skull fight, and the Skull attempts to force Cap into the rocket. Cap flips the Skull into the rocket and leaps off the launching pad just as the rocket takes off, launching the Skull into space.
NOTE: Red Skull face on cover taken from Cap #112, '69's cover by Kirby & Giacoia.

CAPTAIN AMERICA #130 (October 1970)

"Up Against the Wall!" (19 pages)

CREDITS: Stan Lee (writer), Gene Colan (pencils), Dick Ayers (inks), Artie Simek (letters), Marie Severin (c pencils), Joe Sinnott (c inks), Sam Rosen (c letters)
FEATURE CHARACTER: Captain America (also in Cap #132, '70 fb)
GUEST STAR: Peter Parker (last in ASM #85, '70, chr last in Pun:YO #2, '95, next in SS #14, '70)
VILLAINS: The Hood (Baron Strucker robot, 1st, chr next in Cap #132, '70 fb, see NOTE) & his agent (a TV producer, also in Cap #132, '70 fb), MODOK (bts, observing Strucker robot from afar, last in Cap #124, '70, chr during Cap #132, '70 fb), AIM agents (bts, instigating campus riot, last & also in Cap #132, '70 fb), Batroc's Brigade: Batroc (last in Cap #105, '68, next in Cap #132, '70 fb), Porcupine (Alex Gentry, last in X #23, '66, chr last in AFlt Spec #1, '92, next in Cap #132, '70 fb), Whirlwind (David Cannon, last in Av #55, '68, chr last in Av #139, '75 fb, next in Cap #132, '70 fb)
OTHER CHARACTERS: Captain America actor, Hulk actor (both in movie), movie patrons (Joey named), police, student protestors (Sam & Mike named, some chr last in Cap #132, '70 fb), college dean (1st but chr last in Cap #132, '70 fb), WOR-TV crew
LOCATIONS/ITEMS: The Strand movie theatre, mountain (in movie), college administration building w/dean's office, Hood's estate, WOR-TV station, Batroc's hideout; Cap's motorcycle, truncheons, battering ram, escape wire, Batroc's car, curtain
SYNOPSIS: Cap enters a college town on his motorcycle just in time to witness a campus protest turn violent. He breaks up fights between students and police, then rescues the college dean from his office. A television producer witnesses Cap's actions and invites Cap to appear on his show. The producer calls his true boss, the Hood, who is pleased that Cap's appearance will divide the country between the younger and older generations. The next day Cap goes before the cameras, but instead of warning the country against volatile college students he tells the viewers that the students are within their rights to protest peacefully, and that the dean was wrong for locking himself in his office. Under orders from the Hood, the producer contracts the services of Batroc's Brigade, and Batroc and his partners, Whirlwind and Porcupine, storm into the studio to silence Cap. Cap battles the villains, but they retreat when the police arrive. As Cap returns to his cross-country journey the Hood swears vengeance.
NOTE: Whirlwind is shown in his current costume on the cover, but is wearing his Human Top costume from TTA #50, '63 inside. Hood seemingly revealed to be Baron Strucker in Cap #131, '70, but is later identified as a robot built by Machinesmith in Cap #247, '80. MODOK revealed to be observing Strucker robot & AIM agents responsible for campus riot in Cap #132, '70.

CAPTAIN AMERICA #131 (November 1970)

"Bucky Reborn!" (19 pages)

CREDITS: Stan Lee (writer), Gene Colan (pencils), Dick Ayers (inks), Artie Simek (letters), Marie Severin (c art), Joe Sinnott (c inks), Sam Rosen (c letters)
FEATURE CHARACTER: Captain America (also in photos)
VILLAINS: The Hood (Baron Strucker robot, chr last in Cap #132, '70 fb), Bucky robot (1st but chr last in Cap #132, '70 fb), MODOK (bts, influencing Strucker robot, chr last in Cap #132, '70 fb)
OTHER CHARACTERS: Boxers, gymnasts, trainers, waitress, bystanders; radio announcer (voice only); Bucky Barnes, Red Skull & his Exiles: Baldini, Cadavus, Gen. Ching, Krushki; Trapster (prev 7 in photos)
LOCATIONS/ITEMS: Hood's Ocean Bluff Point estate w/lab, San Francisco inc gyms, diner & Golden Gate Bridge, Pacific coast; Cap's motorcycle, gymnasts' rings & parallel bar, radio, Hood's alarm, video monitor, crossbow, cable, mace (destroyed), spear, giant clock & magnetic rings

SYNOPSIS: The Hood scours San Francisco's gyms seeking a young man who resembles Bucky Barnes, finally finding the perfect candidate as Captain America ends his cross-country sojourn. When the Hood discovers the acrobatic youth has amnesia he wonders if this might be the real Bucky. While dining, Steve hears a radio report that Bucky is alive and recovering from amnesia at Ocean Bluff Point. Meanwhile, the Hood hypnotizes the young man into believing he is Bucky. Just as he finishes the procedure an alarm warns him that Cap has arrived. Wandering through the darkened estate Cap is confronted by the unmasked Hood, who stands revealed as Baron Strucker. Cap battles Strucker but is distracted when Bucky rises but fails to join the fight. When Strucker throws a spear at Bucky Cap deflects it with his shield, but Strucker uses the opportunity to knock Cap out. Cap awakens to discover he's pinioned to a giant clock and learns he'll be electrocuted when the clock reaches twelve. Cap calls out to Bucky, encouraging him to fight back. Bucky responds by freeing Cap, who knocks Strucker out. During the battle the young man repeats the same phrase: "I am Bucky Barnes." Cap begins to believe that maybe it is, in fact, Bucky.

NOTE: Cap #132, 70 reveals both that MODOK is secretly influencing the Hood and that Bucky is actually a robot.

CAPTAIN AMERICA #132 (December 1970)

"The Fearful Secret of Bucky Barnes!" (19 pages)

CREDITS: Stan Lee (writer), Gene Colan (pencils), Dick Ayers (inks), Artie Simek (letters), Sam Rosen (c letters)
FEATURE CHARACTER: Captain America (also in rfb, also in fb2 during Cap #130, '70; next in Cap #133, '71 fb, Av #80-82, '70)
GUEST STARS: Nick Fury, Dum Dum Dugan (both last in Cap #127, '70, next in SS #16, '70)
SUPPORTING CAST: Falcon, Redwing (both last in Cap #126, '70), Sharon Carter (last in Cap #127, '70, next in Cap #135, '71)
VILLAINS: MODOK (also in fb1 between Cap #124, '70 & bts in Cap #130, '70, also in fb3 between bts in Cap #130, '70 & bts in Cap #131, '70), Bucky robot (also in fb3 to 1st chr app before Cap #131, '70; destroyed, next bts in Cap #133, '71 fb), the Hood (Baron Strucker robot, also in rfb, also in fb3 between Cap #130-131, '70; destroyed, next in Cap #247, '80), Hood's agent (in fb2 during Cap #130, '70); Batroc's Brigade: Batroc (in fb3, last in Cap #130, '70, next in Cap #149, '72), Porcupine (in fb3, last in Cap #130, '70, next bts in Cap #158, '73, next in Cap #159, '73), Whirlwind (in fb3, last in Cap #130, '70, next in Av #83, '70), Dr. Doom (in fb3 between Sub #20, '69 & FF:WGCM #1, '01), AIM agents (some also in fb1 before & during bts in Cap #130, '70) & scientists
OTHER CHARACTERS: Jasper Sitwell (last in Cap #127, '70, chr next in Web:TS #5, '99, next in IM #23, '70), Walter Cronkite (on television, last in DD #70, '70, last app), college dean (only in fb1 to 1st chr app before Cap #130, '70), college students (only in fb1 before Cap #130, '70), police (others also in rfb), SHIELD agents, news photographers, reporters; WOR-TV staff (in rfb)
LOCATIONS/ITEMS: Sam's Harlem apartment, SHIELD HQ, California highway, AIM Island, Hood's estate (also in fb3 & rfb), college campus (in fb1, 2 & rfb), WOR-TV studio (in rfb), Dr. Doom's Latverian castle (in fb3); Cap's motorcycle, police van, cameras, microphones, Sam's TV & earphones, AIM rifles, blasters, rejection increase control & undersea jet-craft (last only in fb1), MODOK's video monitor (also in fb3) & Doomsday chair, battering ram, curtain (both in rfb), rock
FLASHBACKS: MODOK sends AIM agents to infiltrate a college campus as students and stir discontent (1). Cap breaks up a riot and rescues the dean (Cap #130, '70). MODOK's agent watches Cap accept an offer to appear on television (2). Cap fights off an attack by Batroc and his Brigade (Cap #130, '70). MODOK watches the Hood dismiss Batroc and his henchmen, then contacts Dr. Doom and goads him into creating a robot duplicate of Bucky Barnes (3, between Cap #130-131, '70). MODOK secretly plants the idea in the Hood's brain to locate a Bucky lookalike (Cap #131, '70).
SYNOPSIS: When the news breaks that Cap has teamed up again with his old partner Bucky his friends have mixed reactions. On AIM Island MODOK gloats that his plan is working perfectly, revealing that the young man that Cap believes to be Bucky is actually a robot under MODOK's control. MODOK instructs the Bucky robot to kill Cap, but when the robot refuses, MODOK realizes that the robot was built too well and that it took on some of the real Bucky's characteristics. The disruption in its programming activates the robot's automatic destruct control and the robot collapses. Cap wonders aloud if Bucky didn't reach out from the past to affect the robot's programming.

CAPTAIN AMERICA #133 (January 1971)

"Madness in the Slums!" (19 pages)

CREDITS: Stan Lee (writer), Gene Colan (pencils), Dick Ayers (inks), Sam Rosen (letters), Marie Severin (c pencils), Frank Giacoia (c inks), Morrie Kuramoto (c letters)
FEATURE CHARACTER: Captain America (also in fb2 between Cap #132, '70 & Av #80, '70; next in Cap #25, '07 fb, FF:WGCM #4, '01, bts in FF:WGCM #7, '01, FF:WGCM #8, '01, FF:WGCM #11, '01, bts in FF:WGCM #12, '02, Av #280, '87 fb)
GUEST STAR: Tony Stark (last in SS #17, '70, next in IM #23, '70)
SUPPORTING CAST: Falcon (becomes Cap's partner), Redwing (both chr next in Cap #25, '07 fb)
VILLAINS: MODOK (also in fb1 between MsM #17, '07 fb & Cap Ann #7, '83 fb; chr next in FF:WGCM #4, '01, next in Sub #47, '72), AIM scientists & agents (others also in fb1), Bulldozer (a giant AIM robot, only app, destroyed), AIM Scientist Supreme (George Clinton, 1st, only in fb1 during Cap Ann #7, '83 fb)
OTHER CHARACTERS: Bucky robot (only bts, off-panel, in fb2 after Cap #132, '70; last app), police (Joe named), flight controllers, Harlem residents
LOCATIONS/ITEMS: AIM HQ (also in fb1), Harlem inc Sam's apartment & abandoned church, New Jersey marshlands, Newark Airport, Lincoln Tunnel, Stark's lab; AIM alteration chamber (also in fb1) & jet, police rifles & guns, MODOK's video monitor, truck & Doomsday chair, Stark's portable energy-source detector, Cap's motorcycle (in fb2)

FLASHBACKS: At the Scientist Supreme's instruction, AIM scientists place George Tarleton in the alteration chamber where he is transformed into MODOK. MODOK decides that, rather than serving AIM, he will force AIM to serve him (1). Cap buries the Bucky robot then leaves the burial site on his motorcycle (2).

SYNOPSIS: MODOK instructs AIM scientists to create a giant robot from clay. They dub it Bulldozer and transport it to the marshlands outside Newark, New Jersey. When Bulldozer reaches Harlem it begins to demolish buildings, chanting patronizing slogans which are designed to fool the public into thinking that AIM is operating in Harlem's best interest. Captain America is visiting the Falcon when the building begins shaking. They discover Bulldozer shattering a nearby building, cheered on by local residents. When Cap hears Bulldozer speak he deduces the giant is a robot created by MODOK. Unable to defeat it, Cap contacts Tony Stark who agrees to build a portable detector to analyze Bulldozer's energy source. Meanwhile, MODOK arrives and enters an abandoned church. Redwing delivers Stark's invention to Cap; which confirms that MODOK is controlling Bulldozer. Cap uses the device to jam MODOK's signal, causing Bulldozer to do the opposite of what MODOK wants. Since MODOK wants to remain hidden, Bulldozer heads for the abandoned church, followed by Cap and Falcon. Cap distracts MODOK, preventing him from commanding Bulldozer. Confused, Bulldozer wrecks the church, causing it to collapse around himself and MODOK. Having escaped, Captain America suggests that the Falcon become his partner.

NOTE: Falcon wonders why Captain America would remove his mask in front of him, but Falcon saw Cap without his mask in Cap #126, '70. Scientist Supreme's identity revealed in Cap Ann #7, '83 fb.

CAPTAIN AMERICA #134 (February 1971)

"They Call Him Stone-Face!" (19 pages)

CREDITS: Stan Lee (writer), Gene Colan (pencils), Dick Ayers (inks), Artie Simek (letters), Herb Trimpe (co-c art), Marie Severin (co-c art), John Romita (co-c art), Morrie Kuramoto (c letters)
FEATURE CHARACTERS: Captain America (next in Av #85, '71, Sub #35, '71, Cap:SoL #5-6, '95), Falcon (last in FF:WGCM #4, '01)
SUPPORTING CAST: Sarah Casper (Sam's sister, 1st but chr last in Cap #277/2, '83 fb, next in Cap #272, '82), Redwing (chr last in Cap #25, '07 fb)
VILLAINS: Stone-Face (a gangster, 1st, next in Cap #137, '71) & his gang
OTHER CHARACTERS: Jody Toby Casper (Sarah's son 1st, next in Cap #138, '71), Figaro (Sam's cat, 1st, next in Cap #137, '71), police, store owners, judge, cab driver, bystanders

LOCATIONS/ITEMS: Harlem inc stores, courthouse, Sarah's home, Sam's office & apartment, Stone-Face's lair; Stone-Face's gang's guns, rifles & car

SYNOPSIS: Captain America and the Falcon assist in the arrest of some of Stone-Face's thugs, who are attempting to extort protection money from a shop owner. Meanwhile, Stone-Face sends out several of his men, including Sam's nephew Jody, to run numbers. Jody stops by Sam's office where Sam lectures him about working for Stone-Face. Later, a policeman notices Jody leaving a notorious drop location with money, and arrests him. Cap intercedes at Jody's arraignment and Jody is released, but the boy believes it was Stone-Face who helped get him out of jail. Stone-Face believes that Jody must have ratted on him, and sends two thugs to punish Jody. When Cap and the Falcon discover that Stone-Face's men beat up Jody and shot his mother, they follow the thugs back to Stone-Face's lair. In pitched battle, Cap and the Falcon take down Stone-Face and his gang. Afterward at Sam's office, Jody assures his mother and uncle that he's learned his lesson.

NOTE: Beginning here and continuing through Cap #222, '78 the cover title changes to "Captain America & the Falcon" while the indicia continues to read "Captain America." For this duration the Falcon is treated as a Feature Character. Jody's middle name revealed in Cap #138, '71, Figaro's name revealed in Cap #137, '71. Stone-Face is spelled "Stone Face" on the cover. Severin & Romita provided cover touch-ups.

CAPTAIN AMERICA #135 (March 1971)

"More Monster than Man!" (19 pages)

CREDITS: Stan Lee (writer), Gene Colan (pencils), Tom Palmer (inks), Artie Simek (letters), John Romita (c pencils), Tony Mortellaro (c inks), Sam Rosen (c letters)
FEATURE CHARACTERS: Captain America, Falcon (both also on symbolic splash page)
GUEST STARS: Nick Fury (last in IM #36, '71), Dum Dum Dugan (last in SS #14, '70, chr last in Web:TS #5, '99)
SUPPORTING CAST: Redwing (also on symbolic splash page), Sharon Carter
VILLAIN: Monster Ape (Dr. Erik Gorbo, SHIELD research scientist, 1st, also on symbolic splash page)
OTHER CHARACTERS: Julia (SHIELD agent, 1st, also in Cap #136, '71 fb), other SHIELD agents, dogs (Prince named), Prince's owner, soldiers (Private Adams named), police, television newscaster, ape
LOCATIONS/ITEMS: SHIELD HQ inc combat area & Gorbo's lab, Project Earth Dig, New York City inc bank & zoo's monkey cage, Sam's Harlem apartment; SHIELD barber chair lift, stopwatch & TV, Gorbo's serum, antidote & lab equipment, police guns, army rifles, earth-digging machine, cable

SYNOPSIS: After Cap introduces him to Nick Fury, Falcon spars with Dugan to prove his mettle. Meanwhile, as SHIELD scientist Dr. Gorbo continues his experiments, Agent Julia tells Sharon that Gorbo frightens her. After Falcon defeats Dugan, Cap asks Sharon if she has a moment to talk but she puts him off. Back in his lab Gorbo drinks his experimental ape blood serum, designed to increase his strength, but it unexpectedly turns him into a giant ape; taking the antidote he reverses the effect just before Julia enters with Earth Dig reports. Realizing bitterly that she pities him, he later robs a bank while in his ape form. Cap and Falcon intercept him, but Gorbo use a newfound control over dogs to escape. When Julia later declines a dinner date, opting to watch the Earth Dig on television, an enraged Gorbo shows up at the dig to destroy it, but finds Cap there. During the ensuing fight a cable they are hanging from snaps, plunging them both into the giant Earth Dig hole.

NOTE: The name Monster Ape does not occur in this story, but is taken from George Olshevsky's Marvel Index #8A, '79. Project Earth Dig, also called "Earth-Dig" here, is a deep hole designed to dispose of nuclear waste.

CAPTAIN AMERICA #136 (April 1971)

"The World Below" (19 pages)

CREDITS: Stan Lee (writer), Gene Colan (pencils), Bill Everett (inks), Artie Simek (letters), John Buscema (c pencils), John Verpoorten (c inks), Sam Rosen (c letters)
FEATURE CHARACTERS: Captain America (also in rfb), Falcon
GUEST STARS: Tony Stark (last in Sub #35, '71, next in IM #39, '71), Dum Dum Dugan (next in Cap #139, '71), Nick Fury
SUPPORTING CAST: Sharon Carter, Redwing
VILLAINS: Monster Ape (also in rfb; dies), Mole Man (Harvey Elder, underground ruler, also in rfb; last in Hulk #127, '70), Moloids
OTHER CHARACTERS: Julia (only in fb1 during Cap #135, '71, also in Gorbo's thoughts), soldiers (also in rfb), Project Earth Dig administrators; police, bystander, Mole Man's taunters (trio in rfb)
LOCATIONS/ITEMS: Project Earth Dig, SHIELD HQ, Gorbo's lab (all also in rfb), Subterranea inc Mole Man's weaponry room, Stark's lab; SHIELD TV, Fury's car, Mole Man's anti-gravity beam, tranquilizer mist, cage, elevato-beam & earth-splitting cannon, Stark's jet backpack & car, solidified levi-beam, army rifles, earth digging machine (both also in rfb), Gorbo's serum, police guns, cable (trio in rfb)
FLASHBACKS: Julia wonders if Gorbo is right for her (1). Gorbo takes his serum, robs banks and battles Captain America (Cap #135, '71). Mole Man is taunted by his peers and descends into Subterranea (FF #1, '61).
SYNOPSIS: Arriving at Project Earth Dig, Fury and Sharon find that Falcon is determined to follow Cap into the chasm, but Fury chases him away. Meanwhile, Captain America and Monster Ape are saved by Mole Man's anti-gravity beam, which is laced with a tranquilizer mist. Cap informs Mole Man that Earth Dig's purpose is to safely bury radioactive waste, but Mole Man is appalled. Monster Ape is caged by Moloids and Cap offers a peaceful solution to which Mole Man agrees, warning that if it's a trick he will split the planet in two. Determined to start a war, Gorbo reverts to his human form and "warns" Mole Man that Cap is a spy. At Tony Stark's lab, Tony equips Falcon with a jet backpack. Falcon and Redwing descend into the chasm and locate Cap, who's battling Gorbo. The fight takes them into Mole Man's weaponry room where Mole Man is about to launch his attack. When Gorbo realizes that Julia will be killed in the attack he leaps in front of the firing weapon. As he dies he confesses he lied to Mole Man. Realizing peace can be restored, Mole Man sends Cap and the Falcon back to the surface.

CAPTAIN AMERICA #137 (May 1971)

"To Stalk the Spider-Man" (19 pages)

CREDITS: Stan Lee (writer), Gene Colan (pencils), Bill Everett (inks), Artie Simek (letters), Sal Buscema (c art), Sam Rosen (c letters)
FEATURE CHARACTERS: Captain America, Falcon
GUEST STARS: Spider-Man (Peter Parker, wall-crawling crime fighter, last in Av #85, '71), Nick Fury (next in IM #40, '71)
SUPPORTING CAST: Sharon Carter (next in Cap #139, '71), Redwing
VILLAINS: Stone-Face (last in Cap #134, '71), Stone-Face's thug, muggers, Mole Man (bts, lifting Cap & Falcon to surface, next in FF #127, '72)
OTHER CHARACTERS: Harry Osborn (Peter Parker's roommate, last in ASM #91, '70; chr last in SM:D&D #3, '00), Figaro (last in Cap #134, '71, next in Cap #139, '71), soldiers inc a general, reporters, doctor, police, muggers' victim, bystanders
LOCATIONS/ITEMS: Project Earth Dig, doctor's office, Harlem inc Sam's office, New York City inc Peter & Harry's apartment; Mole Man's solidified levi-beam, Stark's jet backpack, earth digging machine, army rifles, Cap's motorcycle, clothes line, spider tracer, Stone-Face's gun & car
SYNOPSIS: Using Mole Man's levi-beam, Captain America and Falcon return to the surface. Realizing Cap is alive, Sharon faints, and Fury takes her to a doctor's office. Cap and Falcon leave unaware of this, and when Sharon awakes she believes Cap left without bothering to see her. Aggravated at having to fight under Cap's shadow, Falcon later spots Spider-Man being chased by police. Deciding to bring Spider-Man to the police himself, Falcon follows Spidey but is waylaid by a mugging attempt, leaving it up to Redwing to tail the wall-crawler. When Redwing later returns, Falcon follows the bird back to Peter Parker's apartment to find Harry Osborn. Mistaking Harry for Spider-Man, Falcon captures him, but Peter sees Falcon leaving the apartment with Harry and changes into Spider-Man. Tracking Falcon down, Spidey attacks and knocks him out, allowing Harry to escape. Before departing, Spider-Man attaches a spider tracer to Falcon. Led by Redwing, Cap arrives as Falcon recovers, but Sam rejects Cap's offer to help, while Stone-Face covertly watches the strained discussion from his car and vows vengeance on the two heroes.
NOTE: Stone-Face is spelled "Stoneface" and "Stone Face" here.

"It Happens in Harlem!" (19 pages)

CREDITS: Stan Lee (writer), John Romita (pencils, co-inks, c art), Tony Mortellaro (co-inks), Artie Simek (letters)
FEATURE CHARACTERS: Captain America, Falcon (next in Av #88 fb, Av #88, Hulk #140, IM #39, all '71)
GUEST STAR: Spider-Man (next in DD #77, '71)
SUPPORTING CAST: Redwing (next in Av #88, '71 fb)
VILLAINS: Stone-Face (next in Cap #170, '74), Stone-Face's gang (Benny & Chico named)
OTHER CHARACTERS: Jody Casper (last in Cap #134, '71, next in Cap #143, '71), Harry Osborn (next in
ASM #95, '71), police Commissioner Feingold (1st, in shadows), Harrison (governor's representative, only app),
Stone-Face's seamstress, police, bystanders; Sharon Carter (in Steve's thoughts)
LOCATIONS/ITEMS: Harlem inc upper Park Avenue, Stone-Face's warehouse HQ & Steve's apartment, New
York City inc Peter's & Harry's apartment; Cap's motorcycle, Stone-Face's car, guns, rifles, curtain & chair, police cars
SYNOPSIS: After Captain America and Falcon split up Stone-Face and his thugs capture Falcon. Meanwhile at their apartment, Peter
reassures Harry that Falcon won't be coming after him again, changes into Spider-Man, and sets off to find out what Falcon is really up to. Jody
Casper visits Steve, warning him that Stone-Face is back in action. Redwing frantically flies into Steve's apartment, and sensing that Falcon
is in danger, Cap follows. Meanwhile, Spidey uses his spider tracer to track Falcon to Stone-Face's HQ where the gangster is meeting with
Harrison. Stone-Face tells Harrison that if the governor doesn't give him millions of dollars for allowing the state to put a building in Harlem he
will set off riots in the community. While the meeting continues, Spidey rescues Falcon and convinces him that although he is wanted by the
police, Spider-Man is not a villain. Cap arrives with Redwing and is prepared to fight Spidey, but Falcon stops the Avenger. Determining that
Stone-Face is the real villain, the heroes team up to break into the warehouse, rescue Harrison, and defeat Stone-Face and his gang. As Cap
and Falcon turn Stone-Face over to the police a mysterious car pulls up. Offering only a cursory explanation Cap enters the departing vehicle,
leaving Falcon alone on the sidewalk.
NOTE: The man in the mysterious vehicle is the police commissioner, revealed in Cap #139, '71. He's named in Def #39, '76. Stone-Face is
spelled "Stone Face" here.

"The Badge and the Betrayal!" (19 pages)

CREDITS: Stan Lee (story), John Romita (art, co-inks & c art), Tony Mortellaro (co-inks), Artie Simek (letters),
Sam Rosen (c letters)
FEATURE CHARACTERS: Captain America (also in fb between CapC #22/3, '43 & Cap #281, '83 fb; also in
Av #88 fb, Av #88, Hulk #140, IM #39, all '71), Falcon
GUEST STARS: Nick Fury (last in IM #40, '71), Dum Dum Dugan
SUPPORTING CAST: Bucky (in fb between CapC #22/3, '43 & Cap #281, '83 fb), Sgt. Mike Duffy (in fb between
CapC #22/3, '43 & CapC #12, '42), Redwing (last in IM #39, '71), Leila Taylor (radical militant; 1st), Sharon Carter
VILLAINS: Grey Gargoyle (Paul Pierre Duval, living stone villain; last in ToS #96, '67), Cowled Commander (as
Sgt. Brian Muldoon, crime boss & police sergeant, 1st, see NOTE), hoodlums, saboteurs (in fb)
OTHER CHARACTERS: Police Commissioner Feingold (1st full app), Reverend Garcia (1st, also as stone statue), Figaro (last in Cap #137,
'71, next in Cap #157, '73), Harlem residents (Lefty named, Sarah mentioned), SHIELD agents, police, Grey Gargoyle's victims (as stone
statues); Stan Laurel, Oliver Hardy (both mentioned in Falcon's joke)
LOCATIONS/ITEMS: New York City inc police commissioner's office, Harlem inc Sam's office, Steve's apartment, upper Manhattan police
precinct, stonecutter's yard; Falcon's hawk hook (1st), police badges, SHIELD Helicarrier w/magna-beam, Sharon's headphones, police callbox,
trash can lid, saboteurs' dynamite, Steve's rifle (both in fb)
FLASHBACK: In WWII Steve battles saboteurs with Bucky and struggles to keep his identity a secret from Sgt. Duffy.
SYNOPSIS: At the police commissioner's request, Cap agrees to go undercover as a rookie police officer to investigate the recent
disappearances of seven patrolmen and several city officials. The next morning Sam flirts with Leila, a young woman who stops by his office
to tell him Harlem needs heroes, not social workers. Later, while out testing his new hawk hook, a grappling hook which allows him to keep up
with Redwing, a tractor beam hauls Falcon aboard the SHIELD Helicarrier, where Fury has him reassure a moping Sharon that Cap hasn't
forgotten her. Meanwhile at the police precinct, rookie Officer Steve Rogers meets his new boss, Sgt. Muldoon, who reminds him of his WWII
superior, Sgt. Duffy. Out on patrol Officer Rogers fights some hoodlums, but they are chased off by Rev. Garcia. He and Steve wish each other
well and separate, but when Garcia turns the corner, Steve hears a thud; checking, he finds Garcia has vanished without trace. Investigating as
Captain America, he follows a shadowy figure to a stone cutter's yard. When he finds statues of Garcia and the missing policemen, he realizes
the culprit is the Grey Gargoyle!
NOTE: The police commissioner appears to know Cap's secret identity. The magna-beam is named in Cap #141, '71. The Helicarrier is called
"heli-cruiser" here. Leila Taylor's last name is revealed in Cap #188, '75. Romita modeled Sgt. Muldoon after Jack Kirby, revealed in Alter Ego
#35, '04. Muldoon revealed to secretly be Cowled Commander in Cap #159, '73. Falcon's hawk hook appears virtually every time his costume
does, so only changes to it will be noted.

CAPTAIN AMERICA #140 (August 1971)

"In the Grip of Gargoyle!" (19 pages)

CREDITS: Stan Lee (writer), John Romita (pencils & c art), George Roussos (inks), Artie Simek (letters), Sam Rosen (c letters)
FEATURE CHARACTERS: Captain America, Falcon (also as living statue)
GUEST STARS: Dum Dum Dugan (next in Cap #143, '71), Nick Fury
SUPPORTING CAST: Redwing (also as statue), Leila Taylor (both next in Cap #142, '71), Sharon Carter
VILLAINS: Grey Gargoyle (also in rfb), Cowled Commander (as Sgt. Brian Muldoon, next in Cap #143, '71)
OTHER CHARACTERS: Rev. Garcia (also as statue), police Commissioner Feingold (both next in Cap #142, '71), Grey Gargoyle's victims (also as statues), SHIELD agents (some in shadow), pedestrian; Institute director's assistant (rfb); Thor (in Grey Gargoyle's thoughts); Tony Stark (mentioned, built Cap's probe beam, also in Grey Gargoyle's thoughts as Iron Man)
LOCATIONS/ITEMS: New York City, Grey Gargoyle's underground lab, Harlem inc Sam's office & stonecutter's yard, the Roost (SHIELD's mountain stronghold, on monitor); Grey Gargoyle's new chemical solution, Element X (mentioned only), Cap's motorcycle w/high-frequency probe beam, SHIELD Helicarrier w/magna-beam, escort fighters, Roost portals, helicopter (both on monitor), hover-copter lab (in Fury's thoughts)
FLASHBACK: Pierre Duval spills an experimental mixture on his hand and it turns to stone. He quickly learns that anything he touches with that hand turns to stone, including the rest of his body (JIM #107, '64 fb).
SYNOPSIS: Grey Gargoyle attacks Captain America and briefly turns Cap's shield into stone during the battle. When Falcon finally locates Cap and joins the fray, the Gargoyle retreats through a hidden tunnel after hinting at a plan for world domination. While Cap changes back into his police uniform to meet with the commissioner, Falcon & Redwing track the Gargoyle to his underground lab. During the fight, Falcon comes in contact with the Gargoyle's new chemical solution, which changes him into a living statue like the Gargoyle himself. A tranquilizer added to the chemical makes Falcon obedient to the Gargoyle. Later, concerned because he hasn't heard from Falcon, Cap uses his probe beam to signal the SHIELD Helicarrier. Aboard the airship Cap reconciles with Sharon and asks Fury about the Falcon's location. Fury responds that he's more concerned about protecting the Roost where SHIELD scientists are working with Element X, an unstable element that can blow up the world with one drop. When Fury reveals that the only way to safely experiment with Element X is to put a stone lab into orbit, Cap realizes that the Gargoyle plans to steal Element X.
NOTE: Pages 12 & 13 of story are half-pages, resulting in a 19-page story numbered as a 20-page tale, format started in Cap #125, '70 & ends with this issue. Cap calls the Helicarrier a "hover-copter."

CAPTAIN AMERICA #141 (September 1971)

"The Unholy Alliance!" (19 pages)

CREDITS: Stan Lee (writer), John Romita (pencils & c art), Joe Sinnott (inks), Artie Simek (letters)
FEATURE CHARACTERS: Captain America, Falcon (also as living statue)
GUEST STARS: Nick Fury (also as statue)
SUPPORTING CAST: Sharon Carter (also as statue)
VILLAINS: Grey Gargoyle
OTHER CHARACTERS: Construction workers, SHIELD medics (in shadow), Helicarrier crew (as statues), Whistler's mother (mentioned in Fury's joke)
LOCATIONS/ITEMS: Harlem inc construction site & stonecutter's yard, the Roost; SHIELD Helicarrier (destroyed) w/magna-beam, automatic destruct control, escape pods & lifecraft, Cap's motorcycle w/high-frequency probe beam, crane, Roost portals & cannon, Element X, vortex beam (both mentioned only)
SYNOPSIS: After leaving the Helicarrier, Captain America finds Falcon, now a living statue, stumbling through the stonecutter's yard. Obedient to the Gargoyle, Falcon momentarily attacks Cap, but his loyalty to Cap overcomes the Gargoyle's control and he haltingly agrees to accompany Cap aboard the Helicarrier. Sharon has grave concerns about allowing the statuesque Falcon on the carrier, but Cap insists that Falcon isn't dangerous. Sharon's concerns are vindicated when Falcon helps the Gargoyle board the Helicarrier, where he turns the central control crew into stone. While Cap battles Falcon and Fury fights the Gargoyle, Sharon obeys Fury's orders and engages the Helicarrier's self-destruct command. As Cap struggles with Falcon the Gargoyle turns Fury & Sharon into stone. Cap tricks the Gargoyle into stopping the destruct sequence, but the carrier has already reached the Roost. When the Helicarrier doesn't respond to the Roost's hails, the Roost opens fire on the airship. Cap escapes on a lifecraft with Fury, Sharon, and the recovering Falcon, but as the Helicarrier explodes, the Gargoyle soars through the open portals of the Roost where Element X is his for the taking.
NOTE: This issue reveals Sharon has a PhD in metaphysical psychology and heads SHIELD's secret Psyche Squad. The Helicarrier is called "heli-cruiser" and "hover-cruiser" here.

"When It Rains, It Pours" (1 page)
CREDITS: Unknown
FEATURE CHARACTER: Captain America (last in Def #44, '77, next in Cap #204, '77)
VILLAINS: Stormrider ("Satan of the sky", anti-democracy weather manipulator), Cronon (Stormrider's minion)
OTHER CHARACTER: News announcer (on TV)
LOCATIONS/ITEMS: Washington DC inc Capitol Building, radar station, desert, Cap's apartment; Atmospheric ion saturator (generates rain),

television set, Cronon's gun, Hostess Fruit Pies

SYNOPSIS: Stormrider and his minion Cronon plot to disrupt the elections by broadcasting weather altering energies via the nation's radar network, causing widespread flooding. Anticipating Captain America might interfere, the villainous duo catches him off guard at home and captures him. Stormrider leaves Cronon guarding Cap, but Cap convinces Cronon that Stormrider will not share the Hostess Fruit Pies once he takes over. Cronon switches sides, leading Cap to Stormrider before he can activate his weather-manipulating machinery once more.

NOTE: Appeared in various Gold Key titles, January & February 1977. Stormrider apparently is aware of where Cap lives, despite Cap's real identity being a secret at this time.

CAPTAIN AMERICA #142 (October 1971)

"And in the End..." (19 pages)

CREDITS: Gary Friedrich (writer), John Romita (pencils & c art), Joe Sinnott (inks), Sam Rosen (letters), Stan Lee (editor)
FEATURE CHARACTERS: Captain America, Falcon
GUEST STAR: Nick Fury
SUPPORTING CAST: Redwing, Leila Taylor (both last in Cap #140, '71), Sharon Carter
VILLAIN: Grey Gargoyle (next in MTU #13, '73 fb)
OTHER CHARACTERS: Rev. Garcia, police Commissioner Feingold (both last in Cap #140, '71), SHIELD agents (also as statues), nurse; Tony Stark, Steppin Fetchit (both mentioned only)
LOCATIONS/ITEMS: The Roost inc rocket control center, a Harlem hospital; SHIELD lifecraft, tin canister (turned to stone) w/Element X, the Roost's floating turret, ultra-repulsor ray cannon, oxygen cylinder, hover-copter lab, rockets & diaphragm hatch lock
SYNOPSIS: As Fury and Sharon slowly recover from Grey Gargoyle's touch, Redwing joins the four heroes outside the Roost. Inside the complex the Gargoyle fights off SHIELD's defensive efforts and takes control of the Roost. Captain America and Falcon enter the Roost by crashing through a skylight, but not before the Gargoyle finds Element X, stored in a tin canister, which he converts into stone for safekeeping. Meanwhile in the hospital, the police commissioner visits the recuperating Rev. Garcia, but Garcia's complimentary comments about Steve are interrupted by Leila, who accuses Steve of beating Garcia and then covering it up. Leila refuses to listen to Garcia or the commissioner, believing that white people are liars. Back at the Roost, Cap and Falcon locate the Gargoyle. After Redwing swipes the canister from the villain's grasp, he and Falcon carry it into the stone lab. Grey Gargoyle and Cap follow them inside where Cap activates the hatch lock. Cap, Falcon and Redwing slip through the hatch just as it closes. When the Gargoyle instinctively reaches for the hatch, his touch turns it into stone. Fury activates the rockets beneath the lab, sending the structure into orbit with the Gargoyle and Element X aboard.
NOTE: The police commissioner's hair is miscolored red here.

CAPTAIN AMERICA #143 (November 1971)

"Power to the People" (15 pages)
"Chapter Two: Burn, Whitey, Burn!" (11 pages)
"Red Skull in the Morning -- Cap Take Warning!" (8 pages)

CREDITS: Gary Friedrich (writer), John Romita (pencils & c art), Joe Sinnott (inks), Sam Rosen (letters), Stan Lee (editor), Gaspar Saladino (c letters)
FEATURE CHARACTERS: Captain America (also in rfb; next in Cap #600/4, '09 fb, AA #8, '71, Av #93-96, '71-'72, Cap:Re #3, '09, Cap:Re #4, '10 fb, Av #96-97, '72, IM #44, '72), Falcon (also in rfb; next in Cap:SoL #8-9, '99, Cap #176, '74 fb)
GUEST STARS: Nick Fury, Dum Dum Dugan (both next in Av #92, '71)
SUPPORTING CAST: Redwing (also in rfb), Leila Taylor (both chr next in Cap:SoL #8, '99), Sharon Carter (also in rfb)
VILLAINS: Red Skull (also as The Man, People's Militia's leader, last in AT #5, '71, chr last in Cap #298, '84 fb, next bts in Cap #145, '72, next in Cap #147, '72), Skull's henchmen (as The Man's bodyguards), Cowled Commander (as Sgt. Brian Muldoon, last in Cap #140, '71, next in Cap #149, '72)
OTHER CHARACTERS: SHIELD barber Sam (last in Cap #127, '70, next in Cap #149, '72), Jody Casper (last in Cap #138, '71, next in Cap #154, '72), Rev. Garcia (next bts in Cap #278/2, '83), Rafe Michel (black militant, 1st, next in Cap #151, '72), police Commissioner Feingold (next in Cap #157, '73), SHIELD agents (some in rfb as statues), People's Militia members, police; Grey Gargoyle (in rfb); John Lennon (quoted), Uncle Remus (mentioned in People's Militia member's insult)
LOCATIONS/ITEMS: Ellis Island, New York City, SHIELD HQ, Jersey Base Ten & barber shop, Harlem inc Sam's apartment & office, a playground, Garcia's Boys Club, People's Militia headquarters, 125th Street & police precinct, the Roost (in rfb); Statue of Liberty, SHIELD lifecraft, concealed elevator, pneumatic tube & barber shop elevator chair, People Militia's truck, chairs, torches, belt cameras & Molotov cocktail, police walkie-talkie, megaphone & binoculars, Red Skull's descending wall trap, electronic force field, reflaser, escape tunnel & rocket jet, the Roost portals & cannon, SHIELD Helicarrier, escape pods & hover-copter lab (prev 5 in rfb)
FLASHBACK: Cap, Falcon, Fury and Sharon defeat Grey Gargoyle (Cap #142, '71).
SYNOPSIS: Leila invites Sam to a meeting of the People's Militia, a black militant group. As the meeting begins in a local warehouse, Leila's fellow militant Rafe insults Sam. The Man arrives, stirring the crowd into a frenzy. He orders the militia to march on the Boys' Club then burn

Harlem to the ground. Sam jumps onstage to calm the mob, but The Man's bodyguards attack and throw him into the crowd where he is beaten, despite Leila's efforts to protect him. As Steve and Sharon walk by Sam's office the militia dumps Sam on the sidewalk. Cap arrives at the Boys' Club in time to save Rev. Garcia from the People's Militia. When the Falcon recovers, he joins Cap at the Boys' Club, and together they quell the riot. Returning to the warehouse, Cap and Falcon defeat the bodyguards and The Man unmasks, revealing himself as the Red Skull. The Skull traps the heroes in a steel room, but Redwing frees them just as the Skull escapes in a rocket jet. Rafe & Leila, who witnessed The Man's unmasking, tell their fellow militia members that they were duped. Watching from the rooftops above Falcon misunderstands a comment from Cap and leaves in anger. Hoping to explain, Cap follows Falcon to Sam's apartment where he sees Sam & Leila kissing. Thinking he has lost another partner, Cap believes he is destined to be a loner.

NOTE: The Helicarrier is called a "hover-cruiser" here. Rafe's last name revealed in Cap #151, '72.

CAPTAIN AMERICA #144 (December 1971)

"Hydra Over All!" (10 pages)
"Chapter Two: The Falcon Fights Alone!" (10 pages)

CREDITS: Gary Friedrich (writer), John Romita (art pgs 1-10, c art), Gray Morrow (art pgs 11-20), Artie Simek (letters), Stan Lee (editor), Sam Rosen (c letters)
FEATURE CHARACTERS: Captain America (also in rfb; also in Av #98-100, '72, Cap:SoL #8-9, '99, Cap #176, '74 fb, also in dfb), Falcon (only in rfb & dfb) (both also in Cap's thoughts)
GUEST STAR: Nick Fury (last in Av #97, '72, next bts in Av #98, '72)
SUPPORTING CAST: Redwing (only in dfb; chr last in Cap:SoL #9, '99), Leila Taylor (only in rfb & dfb; chr last in Cap:SoL #8, '99, next in Cap #149, '72), la Contessa Valentina Allegro de Fontaine (SHIELD agent & Nick Fury's girlfriend, last in NF:AoS #14, '69), Sharon Carter
VILLAINS: Big Mack & his partner (drug pushers, both in dfb)
OTHER CHARACTERS: SHIELD Femme Force agents (1st, elite all-female squad led by Sharon Carter), SHIELD Aero-Attack Force agents (1st), Richard M. Nixon (U.S. President, last in AT #1, '70, last bts in Sub #44, '71, next bts in Sub #47, '72, next in Thor #187, '71), Spiro T. Agnew (U.S. Vice-President, last in DD #70, '70, next in Hulk #147, '72), Melvin Laird (U.S. Secretary of Defense, only app), Pentagon generals, Presidential staff, SHIELD agents, Ted Clarkson (drug addict), other Harlem citizens (both in dfb), police (in rfb & dfb); People's Militia (in rfb)
LOCATIONS/ITEMS: SHIELD HQ, White House conference room, Steve's apartment, Harlem inc Sam's office & abandoned tenement (both in dfb); SHIELD hand blasters, jet backpacks, gliders & LMDs (as Hydra agents), Falcon's new costume (1st) w/hawk hook, Big Mack's gun, his partner's gun & knife (trio in dfb)
FLASHBACKS: Cap and Falcon stand between police and the People's Militia, Sam later holds Leila (Cap #143, '71). While standing outside Sam's office Captain America overhears an argument between Sam and Leila. When Leila leaves, Cap enters and apologizes for the comments he made the other night. Sam tells Cap that since Cap isn't black he can't understand the situation. Cap agrees, but tries to encourage Sam. Sam changes into a new costume and thanks Cap for training him, but he needs to operate alone and ends their partnership. Alerted to drug pushers that are shooting drugs into a teenager in an abandoned tenement, Falcon rescues the boy and turns the pushers over to the police. A crowd gathers outside the tenement and congratulates Falcon. Cap watches from the rooftops overhead, and although he is glad that Sam has been welcomed by the community, he promises himself he will never take another partner (d).
SYNOPSIS: With Captain America's help SHIELD puts on a display for the White House and the Pentagon, with the Aero-Attack Force and Femme Force wiping out a Hydra rally. After the demonstration, Fury reveals the Hydra agents were actually LMDs. The President assures Fury that his administration will consider Fury's budget requests. Afterwards, Fury tells Sharon to take a vacation, and Sharon asks Cap to join her. He agrees, but tells her he needs a good night's sleep first.

CAPTAIN AMERICA KING-SIZE SPECIAL #1 (January 1971)

"The Origin of Captain America!" (10 pages)

CREDITS: Marie Severin (c pencils), Frank Giacoia (c inks), Sam Rosen (c letters), for other credits see original entries.
NOTE: Reprinted from ToS #63, '65. Original final panel note announcing that succeeding Cap stories will take place in WWII replaced by blurb reading, "More adventures of Cap and Bucky coming right up!" General Wo, from ToS #61, '65, appears on the cover but not in the issue. All stories are recolored.

2ND STORY: "Midnight in Greymoor Castle!" (10 pages)
NOTE: Reprinted from ToS #69, '65. Final panel note replaces "Next Issue" with "Next Chapter." "Greymoor" spelled "Graymoor" on cover.

3RD STORY: "If This Be Treason!" (10 pages)
NOTE: Reprinted from ToS #70, '65. Final panel "Next Issue" blurb replaced with "Continued!"

4TH STORY: "...When You Lie Down With Dogs..!" (10 pages)
NOTE: Reprinted from ToS #71, '65. Followed by pin-up (1 page) of Cap and Steve Rogers (cover shot of ToS #63, '65, Jack Kirby pencils & Vince Colletta inks).

5TH STORY: "30 Minutes to Live!" (10 pages)
NOTE: Reprinted from ToS #75, '66. Final panel changed.

CAPTAIN AMERICA SPECIAL #2 (January 1972)

"The Sleeper Shall Awake!" (10 pages)

CREDITS: Sam Rosen (c letters) for other credits see original entries.
NOTE: Reprinted from ToS #72, '65. Original final panel caption cut here. Cover is redone version of ToS #74, '66 cover. All ToS stories are recolored.

2ND STORY: "Where Walks the Sleeper!" (10 pages)
NOTE: Reprinted from ToS #73, '66. Original final panel caption cut here.

3RD STORY: "The Final Sleep" (10 pages)
NOTE: Reprinted from ToS #74, '66. Original "Next Issue" blurb cut here.

4TH STORY: "The Revengers vs Charlie America!" (7 pages)
NOTE: Reprinted from NBE #5, '67.

CAPTAIN AMERICA #145 (January 1972)

"Skyjacked!" (14 pages)
"Skyjacked! Chapter 2" (7 pages)

CREDITS: Gary Friedrich (writer), Gil Kane (co-pencils), John Romita (co-pencils, inks, c art), Artie Simek (letters), Stan Lee (editor), Sam Rosen (c letters)
FEATURE CHARACTERS: Captain America, Falcon
GUEST STARS: Nick Fury (last bts in Av #98, '72), Dum Dum Dugan (last in Av #92, '71, next in Hulk #148, '72), Eric Koenig (SHIELD agent, last in SgtF Ann #4, '68)
SUPPORTING CAST: Leila Taylor (last in Cap #144, '72 fb, next in Cap #151, '72), Sharon Carter, Contessa Val Fontaine, Redwing
VILLAINS: Supreme Hydra (Richard Fisk, Kingpin's son, last in ASM #85, '70 as Schemer, chr last in LFSM #1, '93 fb), Kingpin (Wilson Fisk, mob leader & Richard's superior, bts, last in ASM #85, '70, chr last in LFSM #1, '93 fb), Red Skull (bts, last in Cap #143, '71, Hydra's true leader) (trio see NOTE), Agent 22 (Hydra infiltrator in Femme Force), Hydra agents
OTHER CHARACTERS: SHIELD Femme Force agents, Ali MacGraw (actress, mentioned in Fury's joke)
LOCATIONS/ITEMS: Las Vegas inc Hydra underground HQ, Steve's apartment, SHIELD HQ inc Sharon's room & war room, skies above U.S. mid-west, Sam's Harlem apartment; Cap's motorcycle, SHIELD Helicarrier, video-map monitor & plane, Hydra intercept saucer w/magne-clamps, attack chute, guns, axe & blaster
SYNOPSIS: From their headquarters Hydra plots to kill Captain America and the Femme Force, opening the door for their takeover of the country. Meanwhile aboard the Helicarrier, Nick Fury summons the Femme Force. Sharon argues with Val, believing that Fury's girlfriend is trying to undermine her authority as leader of the Femme Force, but Fury breaks up the argument when Cap arrives. Fury explains their mission: invade the Hydra stronghold on the Las Vegas strip. On the flight to Las Vegas Val flirts with Cap, making Sharon jealous. Cap is suspicious of Agent 22, and his suspicions are confirmed when she helps Hydra agents board the plane in an assault. While Cap and Femme Force battle Hydra on the plane, Sam Wilson receives a call from Fury who tells him that Cap needs his help. Despite his misgivings, Falcon agrees to meet with Fury. Meanwhile on the plane as the pilot is knocked out, a Hydra agent attempts to shoot Cap but Sharon leaps in the way, taking the blast. Believing Sharon dead, Cap vows to take vengeance against Hydra.
NOTE: Val revealed to be Agent 14 & second in command of Femme Force, Sharon erroneously calls her "Valerie" here. Richard Fisk's rank as Supreme Hydra revealed in Cap #146, '72, identity revealed in Cap #147, '72. Kingpin revealed to be Supreme Hydra's superior in Cap #147, '72. Red Skull revealed to be running Hydra in Cap #148, '72.

CAPTAIN AMERICA #146 (February 1972)

"Mission: Destroy the Femme Force!" (11 pages)
"Chapter Two: Holocaust in the Halls of Hydra!" (10 pages)

CREDITS: Gary Friedrich (writer), Sal Buscema (pencils), John Verpoorten (inks), Sam Rosen (letters), Stan Lee (editor)
FEATURE CHARACTERS: Captain America, Falcon
GUEST STARS: Eric Koenig (next in SgtF #100, '72), Nick Fury
SUPPORTING CAST: Leila Taylor (last in Cap #144, '72 fb, next in Cap #151, '72), Sharon Carter, Contessa Val Fontaine, Redwing
VILLAINS: Supreme Hydra (Richard Fisk), Kingpin (hands only, posing as Harold Howard, see NOTE), Red Skull (bts, true leader of Hydra, also in film), Hydra Agents
OTHER CHARACTERS: SHIELD Femme Force agents, soldiers, EMS personnel, young gambling couple, hotel doorman, nurse, restaurant hostess, casino gamblers, croupier, doctor, bystanders
LOCATIONS/ITEMS: Las Vegas inc Nellis Air Force base, Hydra underground HQ, Harold Howard's hotel w/office, restaurant & hospital, SHIELD HQ; Hydra guns, axe, mace, intercept saucer w/magne-clamps, video monitor, car, ransom note & airship w/vortex beam, ambulance, Cap's motorcycle, Femme Force jetpacks

SYNOPSIS: Enraged, Captain America chokes the Hydra agent who shot Sharon Carter, but Val stops Cap short of killing him. Refocused on the mission, Cap assists Femme Force in stopping Hydra from taking over the SHIELD transport plane, allowing Fury's personal pilot Eric Koenig to safely land at Nellis Air Force Base. Cap brings Sharon to an ambulance as soldiers round up the Hydra agents. A nervous Supreme Hydra reports back to his mysterious benefactor who demands success. At SHIELD HQ, Nick Fury unsuccessfully attempts to convince Falcon to remain Cap's partner. While Steve has dinner with Val, Hydra agents kidnap Sharon from the hospital, leaving a ransom note for Cap. When he receives the note Cap rushes to her aid, racing across the Nevada desert on his motorcycle. A Hydra airship traps him in a vortex beam, lifting him into the ship's belly. Femme Force, secretly trailing Cap with their flying jetpacks, attacks Hydra's underground HQ as the airship docks. As Cap and Femme Force battle the Hydra agents the mysterious benefactor pushes a button, intending to detonate the ship.

NOTE: Cap #147, '72 reveals Kingpin is posing as Harold Howard, America's reclusive richest man. Howard is presumably based on Howard Hughes; the James Bond movie Diamonds are Forever (1971) also features a criminal organization's leader impersonating an imprisoned Hughes stand-in.

CAPTAIN AMERICA #147 (March 1972)

"And Behind the Hordes of Hydra..." (21 pages)

CREDITS: Gary Friedrich (writer), Sal Buscema (pencils), John Verpoorten (inks), Art Simek (letters), Stan Lee (editor), Gil Kane (c pencils), Joe Sinnott (c inks)
FEATURE CHARACTERS: Captain America, Falcon (also in pfb)
GUEST STAR: Nick Fury (also in pfb)
SUPPORTING CAST: Redwing (also in pfb), Sharon Carter, Contessa Val Fontaine
VILLAINS: Supreme Hydra (Richard Fisk, also in fb1 as Schemer between ASM #85, '70 & LFSM #1, '93 fb), Kingpin (also posing as Harold Howard, also in fb1 between ASM #85, '70 & LFSM #1, '93 fb), Red Skull (voice only), Hydra agents (some also in fb1)
OTHER CHARACTERS: Vanessa Fisk (Kingpin's wife, also in fb1 between ASM #85, '70 & Cap #147, '72) SHIELD Femme Force agents (7 & 12 named), SHIELD pilot (voice only), doorman; police, doctors (both in fb1)
LOCATIONS/ITEMS: Las Vegas inc Hydra underground HQ (also in fb1) & Harold Howard's hotel w/office, SHIELD HQ (also in fb1), mental institution (in fb1); Hydra guns, swords, flame thrower & one-man rocket craft, SHIELD guns & jet, Femme Force jetpack, Kingpin's lamp & chair, hyper-shock-treatment equipment (in fb1)
FLASHBACKS: Catatonic after discovering his son Richard was the Schemer, Kingpin is placed in an institution by Richard and Vanessa. Richard then joins Hydra and reorganizes it under his control. As Supreme Hydra he revives Kingpin, all without Kingpin's knowledge (1). Nick Fury hands Falcon orders and sends him to meet Cap in Vegas (p).
SYNOPSIS: Captain America and Femme Force attack Hydra's Nevada desert base as Kingpin watches from Harold Howard's Vegas hotel. Disgusted with the impending loss of the base, Kingpin prepares to destroy it when his wife, Vanessa, intervenes. Losing his fight with Cap the Supreme Hydra electrocutes the comatose Sharon Carter. Cap jumps the Supreme Hydra and removes his mask revealing him to be Richard Fisk, Kingpin's son. When Val tells Cap Sharon is all right, Richard escapes in a rocket. Cap follows Fisk with a Femme Force jetpack to Howard's hotel to discover the Kingpin in Howard's office. Cap fights Kingpin to a standstill until Falcon and Redwing arrive. The struggle ends with a blinding light and a booming voice commanding their attention.
NOTE: Booming voice revealed to be Red Skull in Cap #148, '72.

CAPTAIN AMERICA #148 (April 1972)

"The Big Sleep!" (21 pages)

CREDITS: Gary Friedrich (writer), Sal Buscema (pencils), John Romita (inks, c art), Artie Simek (letters), Stan Lee (editor), Sam Rosen (c letters)
FEATURE CHARACTERS: Captain America (also in Cap #185, '75 fb, next in SgtF #100, '72, Cap #25, '07 fb, Hulk #152, Av #101, Hulk #153, all '72), Falcon
GUEST STAR: Nick Fury (also in rfb; next in Hulk #148, '72)
SUPPORTING CAST: Sharon Carter, Contessa Val Fontaine, Redwing
VILLAINS: Red Skull (also in symbolic image & as hologram, chr next in Cap #185, '75 fb, next in Cap #182, '75), Supreme Hydra (Richard Fisk, next in ASM #163, '76 as Fisk), Kingpin (next bts in DHKF #8/2, '74, next in ASM #154, '76), Kingpin's Lieutenants (Charlie Chicago & Moose Mallard named), 5th Sleeper (giant robot, also in Cap #185, '75 fb, destroyed), Red Skull's men, Lieutenants' gunmen
OTHER CHARACTERS: Harold Howards (bts, released from Kingpin's captivity), SHIELD agents (others in rfb), SHIELD scientists, SHIELD Blue Squadron (fighter jet pilots, Blue leader, Blue Two & Blue Three named), 2 farmers (die), Las Vegas citizens (several die), Harold Howard's employees; Hydra agents (in rfb & symbolic image), Dum Dum Dugan, 1st, 2nd, 3rd & 4th Sleepers (prev 5 in rfb)
LOCATIONS/ITEMS: Las Vegas inc Harold Howard's hotel w/office & lobby, Nevada desert; Femme Force jetpack & guns, SHIELD Helicarrier, fighter jets w/missiles & gas masks, Kingpin's Lieutenant's armored limos & guns, 5th Sleeper's nerve gas, Red Skull's men's guns & spear
FLASHBACKS: Nick Fury and his SHIELD agents fight Hydra (ST #158, '67). Captain America battles the 1st, 2nd, & 3rd Sleepers (ToS #72/2-74/2, '66), then the 4th Sleeper (Cap #101-102 '68).
SYNOPSIS: Appearing as a hologram, Red Skull reveals he's been secretly running Hydra to prepare the world for the Fourth Reich. Kingpin scolds Richard for allying himself with a Nazi and the Skull unveils the 5th and final Sleeper. Aboard the giant robot, Red Skull arises from the Nevada desert and advances on Las Vegas, poisoning all civilians in his path. Kingpin agrees to help stop Red Skull and Cap grabs a Femme Force jet pack to intercept the robot. Falcon contacts Fury who redirects the Helicarrier, as Kingpin sends his criminal associates to intercept the 5th Sleeper. Val and Sharon rally Femme Force to attack the 5th Sleeper with Cap, allowing the Avenger to enter the robot. The 5th Sleeper

he 5th Sleeper. Val and Sharon rally Femme Force to attack the 5th Sleeper with Cap, allowing the Avenger to enter the robot. The 5th Sleeper fights off Femme Force, the Kingpin's men, and a squad of SHIELD fighter jets as Cap fights his way through the 5th Sleeper's body, defeating he Skull's men to confront Red Skull in the control room. Falcon and Redwing join Cap to overpower the Skull, who falls from the Sleeper. Destroying its controls, the heroes cause the robot to explode. Later, Fury debriefs the team at Harold Howard's hotel.

NOTE: Richard Fisk is injured off-panel by the Fifth Sleeper here, revealed in ASM #163 '76. Harold Howard called "Harold Howards" here.

CAPTAIN AMERICA #149 (May 1972)

"All the Colors -- of Evil!" (21 pages)

CREDITS: Gerry Conway (writer), Sal Buscema (pencils), Jim Mooney (inks), Shelly Leferman (letters), Stan Lee (editor), Gil Kane (c pencils), Frank Giacoia (c inks), Morrie Kuramoto (c letters)
FEATURE CHARACTERS: Captain America, Falcon
GUEST STAR: Nick Fury (last in SgtF #100, '72, next in Hulk #152, '72)
SUPPORTING CAST: Leila Taylor (last in Cap #144, '72 fb, next in Cap #151, '72), Sharon Carter, Contessa Val Fontaine, Redwing
VILLAINS: Batroc (last in Cap #132, '70 fb), Jakar (extradimensional being posing as Stranger, 1st but chr last in Cap #150, '72 fb, see NOTE), Batroc's Brigade (hired muscle, 1st), Cowled Commander (as Sgt. Brian Muldoon, last in Cap #143, '71, next in Cap #152, '72), kidnappers
OTHER CHARACTERS: Officer Bob Courtney (Steve's new partner, 1st, next in Cap #152, '72), SHIELD barber Sam (last in Cap #143, '71, next in Cap #161, '73, see NOTE), kidnapped young boys (Paul Santiago named, 1st), Mrs. Santiago (Paul's mother, only app), Ducks (Falcon's toolie), police
LOCATIONS/ITEMS: SHIELD HQ & barber shop, Harlem inc police precinct, Sunset Theater, Sam's apartment, Mrs. Santiago's apartment & 44th St warehouse; kidnapper's minibus & VW Bug, Steve & Bob's squad car, Jakar's stasis chambers
SYNOPSIS: In Harlem, Falcon and Redwing witness a kidnapping but lose the kidnappers when they're fooled by a VW Bug hidden inside a minibus. At SHIELD HQ, Nick Fury offers Captain America a permanent position with SHIELD, but Cap turns him down. Furious, Fury bans Cap from SHIELD. Later, Steve Rogers reports to Sgt. Muldoon for duty, who assigns him a new partner. On patrol Steve spots a disguised Batroc slip into an abandoned theater. Frustrated, Falcon returns to his office and receives a frantic call from Mrs. Santiago. Sam takes the arriving Leila Taylor to Mrs. Santiago where she tells of local boys being kidnapped. Sam returns to his office where Cap invites him to track Batroc, Falcon declines, opting to search for the missing kids. Cap finds Batroc and is attacked by Batroc's Brigade. Falcon tracks the kidnappers to a warehouse and frees a boy. Following the kidnapper's trail to an abandoned theater, Falcon finds Cap a captive of Batroc, and that Batroc is behind the kidnappings. Falcon frees Cap and they attack Batroc, only to be startled by the Stranger's arrival.
NOTE: Cap calls SHIELD barber Sam "Joe" here. Jakar named and revealed not to be the Stranger in Cap #150, '72. Officer Courtney's 1st name revealed in Cap #152, '72, last name in Cap #154, '72. SHIELD barber shop is located near 59th St & Madison Ave.

CAPTAIN AMERICA #150 (June 1972)

"Mirror, Mirror...!" (21 pages)

CREDITS: Gerry Conway (writer), Sal Buscema (pencils), John Verpoorten (inks), Tony Mortellaro (backgrounds inks), Artie Simek (letters), Stan Lee (editor), Gil Kane (c pencils), Frank Giacoia (c inks), John Costanza (c letters)
FEATURE CHARACTERS: Captain America, Falcon
SUPPORTING CAST: Contessa Val Fontaine (next in Cap #152, '72), Sharon Carter, Redwing
VILLAINS: Jakar (also in fb1 to 1st chr app before Cap #149, '72; next in Q #14, '90), Batroc, Batroc's Brigade (both next in MPr #20, '75), Scorpion (last in Cap #122, '70, chr last in Cap #151, '72 fb), Mister Hyde (Calvin Zabo, last in DD #61, '70, chr last in Cap #151, '72 fb)
OTHER CHARACTERS: Kari-Le (Jakar's wife, also in fb1, only app), Jakar's people (in fb1), kidnapped young boys (inc Paul Santiago, last app); commuters; Stranger, Human Torch, Mr. Fantastic, Thing (prev 4 in rfb)
LOCATIONS/ITEMS: Parallel dimension inc Jakar's world (also in fb1), SHIELD HQ inc gym, Harlem inc Sunset Theater & Steve's hotel room, West Side Highway, Hudson shore inc Jakar's hidden base; Jakar's stasis chambers, homing device & inter-dimensional monitor
FLASHBACK: Two millennia ago in another dimension, a cosmic catastrophe destroys all life except Jakar's world. Jakar's ancestors spend two hundred centuries searching the cosmos for other survivors, but even they eventually succumb to the plague. One day Jakar awakes to find his race catatonic, but a dimensional rift opens (1) and Jakar witnesses a meeting between the Stranger and the Fantastic Four (FF #116, 71). Realizing there are other dimensions, Jakar formulates a plan (1).
SYNOPSIS: The Stranger freezes time and removes his disguise, identifying himself as Jakar. After telling his story he reveals the kidnapped children's souls are needed to fill the void in his people's catatonic bodies. Jakar vanishes with the children, restoring time to normal. Intent on clearing his name, Batroc escapes and his Brigade attacks Captain America and Falcon. Batroc, followed by Redwing, uses a homing device to track Jakar to his lair. Meanwhile at SHIELD HQ, Val apologizes to Sharon for her recent advances towards Steve. Cap and Falcon follow Redwing to find a captive Batroc, and are captured themselves. As Jakar locates his home dimension Falcon uses his falcon's claw to escape, then he, Cap, and Batroc battle Jakar until Cap notices Kari-Le on Jakar's monitor. Cap asks what she would think of Jakar's sacrifice of children, causing Jakar to regret his actions, free the children and leave Earth. Cap captures Batroc and returns to his apartment where he meets Sharon. Outside, Mr. Hyde and Scorpion prepare to attack.

CAPTAIN AMERICA #151 (July 1972)

"Panic on Park Avenue" (20 pages)

CREDITS: Gerry Conway (writer), Sal Buscema (pencils, c art), Vince Colletta (inks), Artie Simek (letters), Stan Lee (editor), John Costanza (c letters)
FEATURE CHARACTERS: Captain America (also in Cap's thoughts), Falcon
GUEST STAR: Nick Fury (last in Hulk #152, '72)
SUPPORTING CAST: Leila Taylor (also in Falcon's thoughts, last in Cap #149, '72, next in Cap #153, '72), Sharon Carter (also in Cap's thoughts), Redwing
VILLAINS: Mister Hyde (also in fb between DD #61, '70 & Cap #150, '72), Scorpion (also in fb between Cap #122, '70 & Cap #150, '72), Mister Kline (bts in fb between DD #81-82, '71) (all also in symbolic image)
OTHER CHARACTERS: Rafe Michael (also in Falcon's thoughts, last in Cap #143, '71, next in Cap #153, '72), Harlem residents (Juan named), police, commuter (both in fb), Black Widow, Daredevil (both in rfb), Iron Man, Marianne Rodgers, Mikas, Owl (prev 6 in symbolic image)
LOCATIONS/ITEMS: Harlem inc Sam's apartment, sewers & police station w/Scorpion's cell (in fb), Mister Kline's mansion w/basement (in fb), SHIELD building w/Sharon's dorm, World Trade Center (in rfb); Mister Kline's Glowing Globe, Mr. Hyde's & Scorpion's stasis chambers, stolen car (all in fb), Mr. Hyde & Scorpion androids (both in rfb), lamp post, Fury's car
FLASHBACKS: "Scorpion" dies while fighting Daredevil and Black Widow (DD #82, '71). "Mr. Hyde" stops Daredevil from examining "Scorpion's" body (DD #83, '72). Scorpion is teleported from jail and kept in stasis. He later wakens, freeing himself and the nearby Mr. Hyde. Together they escape the mansion they were held in and steal a car.
SYNOPSIS: Steve Rogers is attacked by Mr. Hyde and Scorpion. After Steve fights them off and escapes, the villains decide to attack their real target Sharon Carter. On his way home, Falcon is given a hard time by Leila and Michael. Cap meets Falcon at his apartment and they decide to figure out why Scorpion and Mr. Hyde aren't dead. Scorpion reminds Hyde that SHIELD are the only ones who could have captured and held them, possibly testing a new jail. Cap and Falcon try to warn Sharon, but they're met by Scorpion and Hyde. While the pairs battle, Sharon comes out to see what the commotion is. She's captured by Hyde and Cap stops Falcon from attacking, admitting defeat. The villains escape as Nick Fury arrives. Fury yells at Cap for disobeying orders, so Cap punches Fury.
NOTE: This issue reveals Mr. Hyde & Scorpion were androids in DD #82-83, '71-72.

CAPTAIN AMERICA #152 (August 1972)

"Terror in the Night!" (20 pages)

CREDITS: Gerry Conway (writer), Sal Buscema (pencils), Frank Giacoia (inks), John Coastanza (letters), Stan Lee (editor), Vince Colletta (c inks), Morrie Kuramoto (c letters)
FEATURE CHARACTERS: Captain America, Falcon (both also in rfb)
GUEST STAR: Nick Fury (also in rfb)
SUPPORTING CAST: Sharon Carter (also in rfb), Contessa Val Fontaine, Redwing
VILLAINS: Mr. Hyde (next in DD #142, '77), Scorpion (next in ASM #145, '75) (both also in rfb), Morgan (Harlem crime boss, 1st, next in Cap #154, '72), Morgan's men (Billie, Reno, Rocky & Smasher Kreel named, Billie next in Cap #154, '72), Commander (as Sgt. Brian Muldoon, last in Cap #149, '72, next in Cap #154, '72)
OTHER CHARACTERS: Bob Courtney (last in Cap #149, '72, chr next in Cap #600/4, '09 fb), SHIELD agents, Joe's Diner patrons (Little Bob named) & waitress, Mrs. Muldoon (Sgt. Muldoon's wife, 1st, next in Cap #154, '72), Weissier (pawnbroker, bts, tells Falcon about chemical truck); Spider-Man (in rfb), J. Jonah Jameson (in Scorpion's thoughts)
LOCATIONS/ITEMS: East River Drive, Harlem (also in fb) inc Joe's Diner, police precienct & SB Co. Storage warehouse w/Mr. Hyde's & Scorpion's hideout, SHIELD dorm building (both in rfb) & HQ, Elmhurst, Queens inc Muldoon home; Rocky & Smasher's stolen Allied Chemical truck w/shipment & guns, Steve & Bob's squad car
FLASHBACKS: Captain America and Falcon battle Mr. Hyde and Scorpion, but the villains escape with Sharon. Upset, Cap punches Nick Fury (Cap #151, '72). Scorpion battles Spider-Man (ASM #20, '65).
SYNOPSIS: Falcon attacks a stolen chemical truck and interrogates the criminals. As Captain America wrestles with his thoughts, Mr. Hyde and Scorpion interrogate Sharon Cater. Nick Fury returns to SHIELD HQ where Val explains that she was only making time with Cap because Fury was spending time with Laura Brown, but Fury will hear nothing of it. Falcon tracks down crime boss Morgan and learns where Hyde and Scorpion are hiding. Steve reports for duty and goes on patrol, but when Falcon contacts him, he slips away, leaving his partner Bob wondering where he went. Cap and Falcon attack and quickly defeat Hyde and Scorpion. Reunited with Sharon, Cap thanks Falcon for his help. Meanwhile in Queens, Sgt. Muldoon tells his wife he's been suspended while on investigation for corruption charges.

CAPTAIN AMERICA #153 (September 1972)

"Captain America - - Hero or Hoax?" (20 pages)

CREDITS: Steve Englehart (writer), Sal Buscema (pencils), Jim Mooney (inks), John Costanza (letters), Roy Thomas (editor), John Verpoorten (c inks), Morrie Kuramoto (c letters)
FEATURE CHARACTERS: Captain America (also in Av #102-104, '72, Cap #600/4, '09 fb), Falcon
GUEST STAR: Nick Fury (next in Av #103, '72)
SUPPORTING CAST: Contessa Val Fontaine (next in Cap #166, '73), Leila Taylor (last in Cap #151, '72), Sharon Carter, Redwing
VILLAINS: Captain America (William "Steve Rogers" Burnside), Bucky (Jack Monroe) (1950's Cap & Bucky, driven insane through improper use of Super Soldier Serum, both last in CapC #78/3, '54, chr last in Cap #155, '72 fb, see NOTE)

OTHER CHARACTERS: Cal Trimble (Steve's hotel manager, 1st, next in Cap #156, '72), Bob Courtney (chr last in Cap #600/4, '09 fb), Rafe Michael (last in Cap #151, '72), police (Daniels named), Fred (restaurateur), Fred's Food patrons (Jack named), airport employee & commuters; SHIELD agent (bts, on phone with Sharon)
LOCATIONS/ITEMS: Harlem inc Steve's hotel room, Fred's Food & Sam's apartment, Brooklyn Bridge, airport; Fury's SHIELD action suit w/steel arm & finger torch, Steve's & Sharon's luggage, Cap's (Burnside) shield
SYNOPSIS: Returning to Steve's hotel room, Captain America, Falcon and Sharon Carter find Nick Fury waiting. Fury challenges Cap and the two fight while Sharon calls for Val. Fury reveals he's jealous of Cap's youth, despite the two technically being the same age, but Cap explains that he didn't gain decades of his life, he lost them. When Val arrives and tells Nick she loves him, Fury calms down and apologizes to Cap. Sharon quits SHIELD, but Fury tells her to take a vacation instead. Later, after Falcon sees Steve and Sharon off at the airport, he returns to Harlem to find Leila spending time with Rafe. Meanwhile, Officer Courtney is told that Sgt. Muldoon's been suspended. Sam Wilson confronts Leila over Rafe, but she yells at him, telling him Captain America has attacking black people in Harlem. Shocked, Falcon investigates and finds Cap beating up an innocent Harlem resident. Attacking, Falcon unmasks Cap to find Steve Rogers underneath. Bucky arrives and the two proclaim themselves to be the real Captain America and Bucky.
NOTE: The Cap & Bucky that appeared in CapC #76-78, '54 were originally intended to be the originals. To make those issues fit with Av #4, #4's revelation that Cap & Bucky "died" in April, 1945, Cap #153-156, '72 retcons those appearances into different characters. The Cap & Bucky appearing in CapC #48-74, '45-49 will be dealt with in WI #4, '77. Burnside's real name revealed in Cap #602, '10, Monroe's in Cap #281, '83. Trimble's name revealed in Cap #158, '73.

CAPTAIN AMERICA #154 (October 1972)

"The Falcon Fights Alone!" (20 pages)

CREDITS: Steve Englehart (writer), Sal Buscema (pencils), John Verpoorten (inks), John Costanza (letters), Roy Thomas (editor), Frank Giacoia (c inks), Sam Rosen (c letters)
FEATURE CHARACTERS: Captain America, Falcon
GUEST STARS: Avengers: Hawkeye, Scarlet Witch (both between Av #104-105, '72), Iron Man (last in Av #104, '72, next in IM #49, '72), Vision (last in Av #104, '72, next in MTU #5)
SUPPORTING CAST: Leila Taylor (next in Cap #157, '73), Sharon Carter, Redwing
VILLAINS: Captain America (Burnside), Bucky (Monroe), Morgan (last in Cap #152, '73, next in Cap #157, '73), Morgan's men inc Billie (last in Cap #152, '72), Bim (1st) (both next in Cap #158, '73), Man-Mountain Quint (1st, next in Cap #157, '73), Cowled Commander (as Sgt. Brian Muldoon, last in Cap #152, '72, next in Cap #156, '72)

OTHER CHARACTERS: Edwin Jarvis (last in Av #102, '72, last bts in Av #103, '72, next in IM #50, '72), Jody Casper (last in Cap #143, '71, next in Cap #272, '82), Bob Courtney (next in Cap #156, '72), Rafe Michael (next in Cap #160, '73), Mrs. Muldoon (last in Cap #152, '72, next in Cap #158, '73), Chunky (Jody's friend, only app), Harlem residents (Wyatt & Jack named), Carribean beach-goers (Arnold named), Falcon's stoolies, saxophonist & guitarist, hotel concierge
LOCATIONS/ITEMS: Harlem inc Tyler's warehouse & Joe's Diner, Elmhurst, Queens inc Muldoon home, New York inc Avengers Mansion w/comm room & living room, Caribbean island; Cap's (Burnside) shield, chair & rope, Billie's gun, Avengers video transceiver
SYNOPSIS: After a pitched fight, Captain America and Bucky defeat Falcon; and take him away to question about the other Cap's whereabouts, unaware their fight was witnessed by Jody Casper. Jody informs other Harlem residents, who decide to help Falcon, despite Rafe's initial protests. Meanwhile, Steve Rogers and Sharon Carter vacation in the Caribbean. Cap and Bucky interrogate the captive Falcon until Rafe and his group attack. During the fight, Falcon escapes, and Cap and Bucky retreat. Falcon hunts the fake Cap, even confronting Morgan, whose warehouse the fake used as a hideout, but to no avail. Meanwhile, Officer Courtney visits Sgt. Muldoon; hearing of Rogers' repeated disappearances, they decide to investigate, as Muldoon is now convinced that Rogers is responsible for his suspension. Failing to reach Steve by phone, Falcon goes to the Avengers to ask them to watch for the fake Cap while he goes to the Bahamas to warn the real one, but having already infiltrated the mansion, the fake overhears him and learns Cap's whereabouts. Discovering this only after the fake has gone, Falcon realizes he must get to Cap first.

CAPTAIN AMERICA #155 (November 1972)

"The Incredible Origin of the OTHER Captain America!" (20 pages)

CREDITS: Steve Englehart (writer), Sal Buscema (pencils), Frank McLaughlin (inks), Jean Izzo (letters), Roy Thomas (editor), John Verpoorten (c inks), Morrie Kuramoto (c letters), John Romita (special thanks)
FEATURE CHARACTERS: Captain America (also in photos), Falcon
SUPPORTING CAST: Sharon Carter, Redwing
VILLAINS: Captain America (Burnside, also in fb1 between Cap #602, '10 fb & CapTW:AF, '09 fb; also in fb3 between CapTW:AF, '09 fb & YM #24/2, '53, also in CapTW:AF, '09 fb, Cap #600/2, '09 fb, Cap #602, '10 fb & Nomad #24, '94 fb; also in fb4 during YM #24/2, '53; also in fb5 between CapTW:AF, '09 & MLG #1, '01 fb; also in fb6 between MLG #1, '01 fb & Cap #153, '72), Bucky (Monroe, also in fb3 between Nomad #23, '94 fb & YM #24/2, '53, also in Nomad #24, '94 fb; also in fb4 during YM #24/2, '53; also in fb5 between Cap Ann #6, '82 & fb6 between MLG #1, '01 fb & Cap #153, '73) (both also in rfb), Major Albrecht Kerfoot (only in fb2 as corpse, last in MvPro #5, '10, last app)
OTHER CHARACTERS: Doctors & nurse (in fb, last in CapTW:AF, '09 fb, also in Cap #602, '10 fb), Lee School students (some also in YM #24/2, '53 & rfb), government officials (in fb3, fb5 & fb6), test monkey (in fb3), bystanders (in fb3 & fb5); Red Skull (Albert Malik), Elektro, Man With No Face, Skull's men (prev 4 in rfb)
LOCATIONS/ITEMS: Bahamas inc Mosca Cay w/Steve & Sharon's rented beach house, Boise, Idaho inc Burnside home, Munchen, Germany inc airport (prev 4 in fb1), Washington DC (in fb3 & fb5), Lee School, "Prof. Roger's" home (both in fb3), UN building (in fb4 & rfb), government lab in southern US (in fb5 & fb6); Cap's (Burnside) shield (also in fb4, fb5 & rfb) & stolen cargo clipper, copy of Daily Bugle, Burnside's Sentinels of Liberty badge, Maj. Kerfoot's journal w/Super Soldier Formula (trio in fb1), copy of Daily Clarion (in fb3), Prof. Rogers' car (in fb4 & rfb) & syringes w/Super Soldier Serum (in fb4), stasis chambers (in fb5 & fb6), copy of Washington Herald (in fb6)
FLASHBACKS: In 1941, 11 year old William Burnside is a member of Captain America's Sentinel of Liberty. He's crushed when the Daily Bugle reports Cap's death in 1945, but graduates summa cum laude in 1952; his thesis is on Captain America. In 1953 he travels to Germany to research another view of Cap. Stumbling across Maj. Kerfoot's journal, he finds the Super Soldier Formula (1). Maj. Kerfoot's body is caught in a bomb blast (2). Burnside brings the formula to Washington and demands that he receive the serum. After a background check reveals no security problems, Burnside changes his name to "Steve Rogers" and has plastic surgery to alter his appearance. The next day, July 27, 1953, a truce is called in the Korean War, ending the need for a new Captain America. Prof. Rogers takes a job at the Lee School where he meets young Jack Monroe, a Cap fan who calls himself Bucky (3). In December 1953, Prof. Rogers and Jack hear of the Red Skull's return on the radio (YM #24/2, '53). The two change into costume and inject the Super Soldier Serum (4). Captain America and Bucky attack the Red Skull at the United Nations building (YM #24/2, '53). The new Cap and Bucky battle communism, Electro and the Man with No Face (CapC #77-78, '54). Eventually, without the stabilizing Vita-Rays the Super Soldier Serum drives the heroes insane. They're captured and put into suspended animation until a cure can be found (5). In the current day, a disgruntled government employee frees Cap and Bucky (6).
SYNOPSIS: Steve Rogers and Sharon Carter spend time in the Bahamas until Steve notices someone who looks like Bucky. He investigates and is ambushed by Cap and Bucky. Cap switches clothes with Steve, but Sharon notices that he's not sunburned like he should be. Cap and Bucky chase Sharon but Falcon arrives just in time to help. However, Cap and Bucky quickly defeat both of them. The heroes wake up captives on a plane. After Falcon goads Cap and Bucky into leaving for the cockpit. Steve frees himself, Sharon and Falcon, and they prepare to attack.
NOTE: Burnside revealed to be from Boise, Idaho in Cap #602, '10.

CAPTAIN AMERICA #156 (December 1972)

"Two Into One Won't Go!" (20 pages)

CREDITS: Steve Englehart (writer), Sal Buscema (pencils), Frank McLaughlin (inks), Sam Rosen (letters), Roy Thomas (editor), Dave Cockrum (c inks)
FEATURE CHARACTERS: Captain America (next in Av #106-108, '72-73, MFeat #10, '73), Falcon
SUPPORTING CAST: Sharon Carter
VILLAINS: Captain America (Burnside, chr next in Cap #281, '83 fb, next in Cap #231, '79 fb as Grand Director) Bucky (Monroe, chr next in Cap #281, '83 fb), Cowled Commander (as Sgt. Brian Muldoon, last in Cap #154, '72)
OTHER CHARACTERS: Bob Courtney (last in Cap #154, '72, next in Cap #158, '73), Cal Trimble (last in Cap #153, '72, next in Cap #158, '73), Miami police (Sgt. JW & Homer named), Coast Guard, bystanders; Vision (mentioned, signed Cap's Avengers ID)
LOCATIONS/ITEMS: Pacific Ocean, Florida inc 5th police precinct, Miami Beach & Torch of Friendship, Harlem inc Steve's hotel room; Cap's (Burnside) shield, stolen cargo clipper & atom-blaster, Coast Guard boat (#471), life boats & raft
SYNOPSIS: As the plane touches down in Miami Beach, Captain America, Falcon and Sharon Carter attack Cap and Bucky. Cap and Bucky shoot their atom-blaster at an arriving Coast Guard boat and escape, demanding a showdown at the Torch of Friendship. Cap, Falcon and Sharon help rescue the stranded Coast Guard. The heroes warn the local police of the fake Cap, and ask for the Torch of Friendship to be cordoned off. Meanwhile, Sgt. Muldoon and Officer Courtney ransack Steve's hotel room but find nothing. Cap, Falcon and Sharon are ambushed by Bucky. Falcon and Sharon stay and fight while Cap continues on to the Torch. Surrounded by onlookers, the two Captain Americas fight. Cap taunts the Avenger, calling him a fake Cap, but Captain America reveals he's the original. Outraged, the insane Cap charges, but is defeated by the true Captain America. Falcon and Sharon arrive with Bucky in tow as the crowd cheers, but Cap asks to be left alone with his thoughts.
NOTE: Torch of Friendship is on Biscayne Boulevard.

CAPTAIN AMERICA #157 (January 1973)

""Veni, Vidi, Vici": Viper!" (21 pages)

CREDITS: Steve Englehart, Steve Gerber (writers), Sal Buscema (pencils), John Verpoorten (inks), Artie Simek (letters), Petra Goldberg (colors), Roy Thomas (editor), Gaspar Saladino (c letters)
FEATURE CHARACTERS: Captain America, Falcon
SUPPORTING CHARACTERS: Leila Taylor (last in Cap #154, '72), Sharon Carter (both next in Cap #159, '72), Redwing
VILLAINS: Viper (Jordon Dixon, ad exec, uses poison darts, 1st, see NOTE), Cowled Commander (as Sgt. Brian Muldoon), Morgan, Man-Mountain Quint (both last in Cap #154, '72), Cowled Commander's men
OTHER CHARACTERS: Figaro (last in Cap #139, '71, next in Cap #183, '75), police Commissioner Feingold (last in Cap #143, '71, next in Cap #159, '72), Mona (Morgan's "friend", 1st), police inc Captain (Carpenter named), firemen
LOCATIONS/ITEMS: Harlem inc 13th (destroyed) & 3rd police precincts, Sam's office & Morgan's brownstone; Cowled Commander's men's brass knuckles & mace, Viper's bomb, venom-tipped darts, fangs & antidote vial
SYNOPSIS: Captain America is attacked by three of the Cowled Commander's men. After defeating them Cap turns the thugs over to the police and continues to the 13th police precinct, where he meets the Commissioner. They discuss Sgt. Muldoon's recent suspension and the mysterious Cowled Commander. The Commissioner leaves to make a call when a bomb goes off, apparently killing Cap. Meanwhile, Leila gives Sam grief in his Harlem office. As Falcon, he heads to Morgan's place where he confronts the crimelord. During their conversation Morgan learns that Cap was killed in a bomb blast. Falcon heads to the 13th precinct where he helps with the rescue. Noticing a reflection on a nearby roof, Falcon investigates and finds Viper, who set the bomb. Falcon attacks, but Viper poisons Falcon with a deadly venom that causes paralysis and death. Cap appears and beats Viper into submission for the antidote, which Viper exchanges for his freedom. Tossing the vial to Cap, Viper poisons the Avenger when he turns his back to retrieve the vial. Viper escapes as Cap succumbs to the poison.
NOTE: Viper's name revealed in Cap #158, '73 & that he's Eel's brother in Cap #159, '73.

CAPTAIN AMERICA #158 (February 1973)

"The Crime Wave Breaks!" (20 pages)

CREDITS: Steve Englehart (writer), Sal Buscema (pencils), John Verpoorten (inks), Artie Simek (letters), Petra Goldberg (colors), Roy Thomas (editor), Gaspar Saladino (c letters)
FEATURE CHARACTERS: Captain America, Falcon
SUPPORTING CAST: Redwing
VILLAINS: Viper, Morgan, Man-Mountain Quint (both next in Cap#165, '73), Bim (last in Cap #154, '72, next in Cap #165, '73), Billie (last in Cap #154, '72, last app), Cowled Commander (as Sgt. Brian Muldoon), Cowled Commander's bank robbers; Eel (Leopold Stryke, last in X #23, '66, chr last in AFlt Spec #1, '92), Plantman (Sam Smithers, last in Sub #3, '68), Porcupine (last in Cap #132, '70 fb), Scarecrow (Ebenezer Laughton, last in X #23, '66) (prev 4 bts responding to Cowled Commander's summons & in symbolic image)
OTHER CHARACTERS: Cal Trimble (last in Cap #156, '72, next in Cap #166, '73), Mrs. Muldoon (last in Cap #154, '72, last app), Mona (last app), Bob Courtney (last in Cap #156, '72), green grocer, pharmacist, police; Scarecrow's raven (in symbolic image)
LOCATIONS/ITEMS: Harlem inc Steve's hotel room & Morgan's Brownstone, Elmhurst, Queens inc Muldoon home, New York inc drug store & Viper's apartment; Viper's antidote vial & poison darts, bank robbers' car (destroyed) & guns, police guns, Muldoon's billy club
SYNOPSIS: Captain America painfully drags himself to the vial and ingests the antidote before administering it to Falcon. Revived, the heroes split up. Cap visits Sgt. Muldoon and they discuss the Cowled Commander. Muldoon believes that Steve Rogers is the mysterious villain. Falcon stops at Morgan's. Trying to get his job back, Billie tries to shoot Falcon but fails. Falcon then confronts Morgan about the Commander. Across town, Cap stops a group of bank robbers but accidentally destroys a car in the process. Falcon tracks Viper to his apartment and captures Viper with Redwing's help. Feeling sick and woozy, Steve returns to his apartment finding it ransacked. He's confronted by Trimble, his landlord, who tries to blackmail Steve for moonlighting. Steve tosses Trimble out and leaves himself, only to be jumped by Muldoon and Officer Courtney. Meanwhile, Viper reveals to Falcon that Eel, Plantman, Porcupine, and Scarecrow work for the Commander, and are about to start a crime wave.
NOTE: Billie was fired by Morgan in Cap #154, '72 for failing to kill Falcon. As a result of Viper's antidote mixing with the Super Soldier Serum Captain America gains super strength here. The extra power will eventually wear off as revealed in Cap #218, '77.

"Captain America and the Sore Sir's Apprentices" (1 page)
CREDITS: Unknown
FEATURE CHARACTER: Captain America (last in Cap Ann #4, '77, next in SVTU #14, '77)
VILLAINS: The Sore Sir (evil wizard, bts), the Sore Sir's Apprentices (duplicating monsters)
LOCATIONS/ITEMS: Sore Sir's lab (bts); Hostess Devil's Food Cake, rope
SYNOPSIS: Captain America tries to subdue monsters released from Sore Sir's lab, but each blow merely creates more of them. As they surround him, Cap distracts them with Hostess Devil's Food Cake, then ties them up while they are busy munching.
NOTE: Appeared in various Marvel titles, May & June 1977.

CAPTAIN AMERICA #159 (March 1972)

"Turning Point!" (20 pages)

CREDITS: Steve Englehart (writer), Sal Buscema (pencils), Joe Sinnott (inks), Ann Scotto (letters), Stan Goldberg (colors), Roy Thomas (editor), George Roussos (c inks), Gaspar Saladino (c letters)
FEATURE CHARACTERS: Captain America (next in FF #133, '73, Av #110-111, '73, Def #15, '74 fb, Av #112, '73), Falcon (both also in symbolic image)
SUPPORTING CAST: Sharon Carter (also in symbolic image), Leila Taylor (both last in Cap #157, '72), Redwing
VILLAINS: Cowled Commander (also as Sgt. Brian Muldoon, next in Cap #232, '79), Viper (both also in symbolic image), Eel (both next in Cap #163, '73), Plantman (next in Def #36, '76), Porcupine (next in Def #37, '76), Scarecrow (next in Cap Ann #6, '82) & his ravens
OTHER CHARACTERS: Police Commissioner Feingold (last in Cap #157, '72, next in Cap #180, '74), Bob Courtney (next in Cap #600/4, '09) (both also in symbolic image), police (Dick named); Nick Fury, Cal Trimble, Mrs. Muldoon (trio in symbolic image only)
LOCATIONS/ITEMS: Harlem inc abandon warehouses & Damon jewelry store; Muldoon's ropes, police cars, stolen jewelry, Plantman's animated plants inc Venus flytrap & gun, Cowled Commander's video monitor, camera & poison gas
SYNOPSIS: Steve awakes from a nightmare to find himself bound to a chair. He's being interrogated by Muldoon and Courtney about being the Cowled Commander. When the pair leaves Steve easily snaps the ropes and changes into Captain America. He follows the police to the jewelry district where he spots Eel, Viper, Plantman, and Porcupine robbing Damon's jewelry store. He engages them in battle and is joined by Falcon and Redwing, but the defeated villains flee before they can be captured. The Commissioner, Muldoon, Courtney, Sharon Carter and Leila all arrive. Redwing locates the crooks, then circles back to alert Falcon. Cap and Falcon follow Redwing to the villain's hideout and attack, but the heroes are subdued by a massive Venus flytrap. Cap and Falcon awake in a chamber where they are taunted and gassed by the Cowled Commander. Tapping into his new-found super strength, Cap rips the steel door off its hinges and they escape. Cap and Falcon quickly defeat the criminals and reveal the Cowled Commander to be Sgt. Muldoon. He explains his plan to weed out weak police officers by running a crime syndicate, and that he planned to frame Steve Rogers for it when he was suspended.
NOTE: John Verpoorten miscredited as inker here. Nick Fury appears in symbolic image without his eyepatch.

CAPTAIN AMERICA #160 (April 1973)

"Enter: Solarr!" (20 pages)

CREDITS: Steve Englehart (writer), Sal Buscema (pencils), Frank McLaughlin (inks), Artie Simek (letters), Petra Goldberg (colors), Roy Thomas (editor), Gil Kane (co-c pencils), Alan Weiss (co-c pencils), Frank Giacoia (c inks), Gaspar Saladino (c letters)
FEATURE CHARACTERS: Captain America, Falcon
SUPPORTING CAST: Sharon Carter, Leila Taylor, Redwing
VILLAINS: Solarr (Silas King, solar-powered heat blaster; 1st but chr last in AFlt Spec, '92; also in fb to 1st chr app before AFlt Spec #1, '92; next in Av #126, '74), Cowled Commander's men (Freddy named)
OTHER CHARACTERS: Rafe Michel (last in Cap #154, '72), stockbrokers, stock exchange guards, police bystanders, nurse (in fb); Charlie the Tuna (animated spokesperson), George Blanda (Oakland Raiders kicker), Cowled Commander, Viper (prev 4 mentioned)
LOCATIONS/ITEMS: Harlem, New York Stock Exchange, Wall Street, office building, SHIELD building w/Sharon's dorm, U.S. Southwest desert, Silas King's hospital room (both in fb); Cowled Commander's men's bazooka, guns & armored car, police guns, building scaffolding, house paint
FLASHBACK: Stranded in the desert Southwest, Silas King wanders under the brutal sun for days until finally reaching civilization. Later, his solar powers manifest in his hospital room.
SYNOPSIS: Captain America uses his new super strength to quickly defeat the Cowled Commander's thugs, leaving the Falcon with little to do. The Falcon confides in Leila, who tries to convince him to break up his partnership with Cap. Later, Solarr robs the New York Stock Exchange, and in the process, kills two guards and several bystanders. Cap arrives and tries to subdue Solarr. The fight takes the combatants into an office building lobby, where Solarr grows weak. Solarr runs into the street where Cap confronts Solarr. Cap's super strength allows him to go toe-to-toe with the rejuvenated villain. Falcon arrives and watches the battle, realizing that once again, he is not needed. Meanwhile, having deduced that the lack of direct sunlight keeps Solarr from recharging, Cap coats the villain with all-weather house paint, which prevents the sun's rays from reaching Solarr. As the police arrest the powerless Solarr, the Falcon and Redwing leave the scene. Cap chases after them, passing Sharon's dorm building on the way. Inside, Sharon moves out of her dorm, leaving behind a note to Cap, asking him not to look for her.
NOTE: Sharon's SHIELD dorm room is #3.

"Cut on the Dotted Line" (1 page)
CREDITS: Unknown
FEATURE CHARACTER: Captain America (last in Thor #271, '78, next in "A Friendly Gesture" Hostess ad, '78)
VILLAIN: Simon Taylor the Tailor (cruel business owner w/magical equipment)
OTHER CHARACTERS: Sewing machine operators inc Operator No.1
LOCATIONS/ITEMS: Taylor's factory; magic tailor's chalk (transforms people into clothing patterns), magic tape measure (binds people), Hostess Fruit Pies, sewing machines

SYNOPSIS: When sewing machine Operator No.1 complains about her work, her evil boss, Simon Taylor the Tailor, turns her into a clothing pattern using his magic tailor's chalk. Witnessing this through a factory window, Captain America intervenes, but Taylor swiftly binds him with a magical tape measure. Another operator distracts Taylor with Hostess Fruit Pies. His attention diverted, Taylor's magic wanes, allowing Cap to break free and turning Operator No.1 human again.

NOTE: Appeared in various Marvel titles, January & February 1978.

CAPTAIN AMERICA #161 (May 1973)

"If He Loseth His Soul!" (20 pages)

CREDITS: Steve Englehart (writer), Sal Buscema (pencils & co-c pencils), John Verpoorten (inks), Artie Simek (letters), Stan Goldberg (colors), Roy Thomas (editor), John Romita (co-c pencils), Gaspar Saladino (c letters)
FEATURE CHARACTERS: Captain America, Falcon
GUEST STAR: Nick Fury (last in AT #20, '73, next in MTU #13, '73)
SUPPORTING CAST: Peggy Carter (Cap's wartime lover, as veiled woman here; last in ToS #77, '66 fb, chr last in Cap #25, '07 fb, see NOTE), Redwing (next in Cap #163, '73), Leila Taylor (next in Cap #165, '73), Sharon Carter
VILLAINS: Dr. Faustus (last in Cap #107, '68), Dr. Johann Wolfgang (psychiatrist; 1st), Rafe Michel (next in Cap #177, '74), Silver Skulls (Rafe's gang; only app), Dr. Faustus' thugs (also as Nazi soldiers)
OTHER CHARACTERS: Amanda Carter, Harrison. Carter (both Sharon Carter's parents; both 1st but chr last in Cap #162, '73 fb), SHIELD barber Sam (last in Cap #149, '72, last app, see NOTE), Ham, Eggs (both SHIELD agents; only app), SHIELD barber Sam's aunt (mentioned)
LOCATIONS/ITEMS: Harlem, Manhattan inc Sharon's SHIELD dorm & SHIELD barber shop; Derby Connecticut inc Lost Souls Asylum & Rest Home; Sharon's note, Cap's motorcycle, Falcon's motorcycle (destroyed), Rafe's knife, Silver Skull's blackjack & guns, Dr. Faustus' thug's rifles & grenade, Dr. Faustus' hidden television cameras & serum
SYNOPSIS: Captain America discovers Sharon has moved out of her dorm. Cap asks Nick Fury for information, but Fury has nothing to offer, except Cap's motorcycle. In Harlem, Cap watches Falcon defeat Rafe Michel and his Silver Skulls gang. Cap appeals to Falcon to restore their partnership. Falcon agrees despite Leila's objections. That night in Derby, Connecticut, Sharon awakens in Lost Souls Asylum. Dr. Wolfgang tells Sharon that she was in a car accident and reunites Sharon with her parents. Meanwhile, in a tower in the rest home, Dr. Faustus waits with a mysterious veiled woman for Cap to arrive. Later, after receiving a tip from a car rental agency, Cap and the Falcon arrive in Derby, and are attacked and captured by Faustus's thugs. At midnight, Sharon escapes from her locked room and finds the veiled woman in a cell. Faustus and Wolfgang knock Sharon out with a serum. Sharon, Cap and Falcon, who's been outfitted as an army soldier, awake together surrounded by Nazis. Faustus and the veiled woman secretly watch from the tower overhead.
NOTE: Peggy is mentioned as Sharon's sister in Cap #162, '73 but revealed to be her aunt in Cap #25, '07. SHIELD barber Sam refers to himself as "Harold" here.

CAPTAIN AMERICA #162 (June 1973)

"This Way Lies Madness!" (20 pages)

CREDITS: Steve Englehart (writer), Sal Buscema (pencils), John Verpoorten (inks), John Costanza (letters), Petra Goldberg (colors), Roy Thomas (editor), Jim Starlin (c pencils), Joe Sinnott (c inks)
FEATURE CHARACTERS: Captain America (also in Sharon's thoughts, next in MTU #9-10, next bts in MTU #11, next in Av #113, MTU #13, Av #114, all '73), Falcon
SUPPORTING CAST: Peggy Carter (also as veiled woman; also in fb between Cap&FT #1, '11 & Cap #25, '07 fb), Sharon Carter (also in Sharon's thoughts, also in fb to 1st chr app before Cap #25, '07 fb)
VILLAINS: Dr. Faustus (chr next in Cap #236, '79 fb, next in Cap #192, '75), Dr. Johann Wolfgang (last app), Dr. Faustus's thugs (also as Nazi soldiers, Red Skull, Baron Heinrich Zemo, Agent Axis & MODOK; Cutler & Sturges named), a monster (called "Godzilla" as illusion)
OTHER CHARACTERS: Amanda Carter, Harrison Carter (both also in fb to 1st chr app before Cap #161, '73), psychologist (in fb), Bucky (as illusion), Douglas Fairbanks (swashbuckling actor; mentioned), Betty Boop (animated flapper, mentioned)
LOCATIONS/ITEMS: Lost Souls Asylum & Rest Home w/ Psycho Pit; Dr. Faustus' thug's rifles, machine guns, flame thrower, rubber masks & handguns, Dr. Faustus' trick mirrors, fear-inducing agent, monitor, hidden television cameras & brain incinerator, Peggy's candlestick holder, Dr. Wolfgang's knife, copy of Daily Bugle (in fb)
FLASHBACK: Following World War II, an amnesiac Peggy Carter is returned to her family. When Captain America "returns" in 1953 Peggy's family decides not to tell Peggy and "Cap" about each other, to protect Peggy's fragile emotional health.
SYNOPSIS: Captain America, Falcon and Sharon battle Faustus's thugs. When the veiled woman sees Cap her memory is restored. Faustus then traps the three heroes in his psycho-pit and retreats to his office, where he unsuccessfully attempts to withdraw information from the veiled woman about her past with Captain America. In the psycho-pit, Cap, Sharon and the Falcon are tortured by images of past foes, but they discover the images are tricks when Falcon breaks through a glass wall. The heroes locate and free Sharon's parents. Sharon explains that she Peggy Carter are related and that when she heard Peggy's amnesia was almost cured, she knew that Cap would discover the truth, and decided to leave him. Cap finds Peggy and frees her, but discovers that Peggy believes they are still fighting in World War II. Faustus fires his brain incinerator at Cap, but is distracted when Peggy throws a candlestick holder. Peggy knocks out Dr. Wolfgang while Cap easily defeats Faustus. Cap and Falcon agree to stay with the Carter family for a while, giving Peggy, who is unaware that Cap is in a relationship with Sharon, a chance to recuperate.
NOTE: "Let's Rap With Cap" contains LOC by Duffy Vohland, future Marvel artist beginning with FOOM #5, '74.

CAPTAIN AMERICA #163 (July 1973)

"Beware of Serpents!" (18 pages)

CREDITS: Steve Englehart (writer), Sal Buscema (pencils), John Verpoorten (co-inks, c inks), Tony Mortellaro (co-inks), Charlotte Jetter (letters), Petra Goldberg (colors), Roy Thomas (editor), John Costanza (c letters)
FEATURE CHARACTERS: Captain America, Falcon
SUPPORTING CAST: Sharon Carter, Peggy Carter (both next in Cap #165, '73), Redwing
VILLAINS: Serpent Squad (1st): Cobra (last in DD #61, '70, next in Cap #180, '75), Eel (next in Cap #180, '75), Viper (also in Cap #170, '74 fb, next in Cap #175, '74); Quentin Harderman (Viper's former advertising partner bts on phone, chr next in Cap #170, '74 fb, next in 1st actual app in Cap #169, '74)
OTHER CHARACTERS: Harrison Carter (next bts in Cap #167, '73, next in Cap #180, '74), Amanda Carter (next bts in Cap #167, '73), Dave Cox (war veteran, 1st, next in Cap #182, '75), Smithers (Carters' butler, 1st, next in Cap #180, '74), prison guards; Dr. Faustus (photo); Richard Nixon (mentioned in Daily Blast)
LOCATIONS/ITEMS: Sing Sing Prison, Caters' Virginia Estate, Serpent Squad's hideout, Dave Cox's cottage; Prison guards' various guns, Daily Blast newspaper, Viper's venom-firer & poison darts, Falcon's pillow, Eel-cannon, Cobra's convulsion pistol
SYNOPSIS: Eel and Viper escape from prison with Cobra's help. They form the Serpent Squad with the intentions of getting revenge on Cap. Meanwhile, Cap and Falcon escort the Carters as Peggy is brought home. There they run into a neighbor, Dave Cox; a war veteran and former POW vowing a life of peace. Viper intends to use his old advertising contacts to ruin Cap's reputation, but the team decides to attack directly upon learning his whereabouts from the newspaper. During the fight, Cap's hands are badly burned by Eel's electrified costume, but the heroes manage to fend them off. The heroes and Peggy search the grounds for the Serpents, who instead find and strike at Cap and Peggy in Dave's cottage. Cap manages to hold them off long enough for Falcon and Redwing to arrive. The heroes defeat the Serpent Squad with Dave's help, who is injured in the process.
NOTE: Falcon calls Viper "Dartagnon" here, parodying the name of a Musketeer.

CAPTAIN AMERICA #164 (August 1973)

"Queen of the Werewolves!" (20 pages)

CREDITS: Steve Englehart (writer), Alan Lee Weiss (art), John Costanza (letters), Jim Starlin (colors), Roy Thomas (editor), John Romita (c art), Gaspar Saladino (c letters)
FEATURE CHARACTERS: Captain America, Falcon (also as Falcon-Wolf, also in pfb)
GUEST STAR: Nick Fury (last in Hulk #165, '73)
SUPPORTING CAST: Redwing (next in Cap #166, '73)
VILLAINS: Nightshade (Tilda Johnson; scientific genius; also bts in pfb allowing Mel to send letter; 1st but chr last in PMIF #53, '78 fb; chr next in Cap #190, '75 fb, next in Cap #189, '75), Yellow Claw (Plan Chu, criminal mastermind; last in YC #4/5, '57, chr last in MLG #3, '00, last bts in ST #161, '67 fb), Grimrock Prison inmates (as werewolves, Sparky named; all die)
OTHER CHARACTERS: Mel Lansing (also as Captain America, Grimrock Prison inmate, former friend of Falcon's; also in pfb, dies), SHIELD agents, Mr. Werner (deli owner; mentioned), New York Yankees (baseball team; mentioned)
LOCATIONS/ITEMS: Maryland's Grimrock Prison, Carter family Virginia estate (in pfb); Cap's motorcycle, Falcon's motorcycle, Nightshade's werewolf serum & gun, SHIELD helicopters & blasters
FLASHBACK: Sam receives a letter from Mel Lansing, asking for help (p).
SYNOPSIS: In Grimrock Prison, Nightshade and the Yellow Claw watch dozens of werewolves kill someone dressed as Captain America. Shortly afterward Captain America, with Falcon & Redwing, arrive at the prison. They split up and Cap is attacked by a horde of werewolves, which he quickly defeats. Nightshade appears, leading Cap to a chamber where Falcon is imprisoned and closes the door, trapping them both. Falcon transforms into a giant werewolf and fights Captain America. Cap escapes by tricking the Falcon-Wolf into breaking down the door. Realizing that their scheme will fail, Nightshade's benefactor, the Yellow Claw, deserts her. Nick Fury and SHIELD arrive, in pursuit of the Claw. Vowing never to be taken alive, Nightshade summons her werewolf servants, and leads them in a suicidal jump off the prison's parapet. Still under Nightshade's control, the Falcon-Wolf attempts to follow, but Cap prevents him from jumping until the serum wears off. Falcon tells Cap that Nightshade revealed that the fake Captain America was Mel, who had refused to submit to Nightshade's serum. Cap is concerned over the apparent return of the Yellow Claw.
NOTE: Yellow Claw is actually an improper translation, the name is closer to "Golden Claw." His real name Plan Chu, which roughly translates to "Master Plan," is revealed in AoAtlas #6, '07 which also reveals him to be a descendant of Genghis Khan.

"A Friendly Gesture" (1 page)
CREDITS: Unknown
FEATURE CHARACTER: Captain America (last in "Cut on the Dotted Line" Hostess ad, '78, next in Cap #217, '78)
OTHER CHARACTER: Unidentified alien
LOCATIONS/ITEMS: Woods; alien's spaceship, Hostess Twinkies
SYNOPSIS: A huge alien attacks Captain America, seemingly just for the thrill of the fight, but Cap makes peace with him by giving him Twinkies.
NOTE: Appeared in various Gold Key titles, February & March 1978.

CAPTAIN AMERICA #165 (September 1973)

"The Yellow Claw Strikes" (19 pages)

CREDITS: Steve Englehart (writer), Sal Buscema (pencils), Frank McLaughlin (inks), Charlotte Jetter (co-letters), Gaspar Saladino (co-letters), George Roussos (colors), Roy Thomas (editor), John Costanza (c letters)
FEATURE CHARACTERS: Captain America, Falcon
GUEST STAR: Nick Fury
SUPPORTING CAST: Leila Taylor (last in Cap #161, '73), Sharon Carter, Peggy Carter
VILLAINS: Yellow Claw and his men, Morgan (last in Cap #158, '73, next bts in Cap #169, '74, next in PM #19, '74) Man-Mountain Quint, Bim (both last in Cap #158, '73, last app), Hop Sung (Yellow Claw's geneticist; bts, creates giant spiders), Commander Fong (Chinese army officer; dies), Chinese soldiers (all die), General Sung (Fong's superior & Yellow Claw's former co-conspirator; mentioned), giant spiders (some die)
OTHER CHARACTERS: Suwan (Yellow Claw's grand-niece; last in YC #4/5, '57, chr last in Cap #166, '73 fb), SHIELD medics, Cliff (construction worker), Alice (Cliff's wife; mentioned), guards (Harv named), bystanders, police, birds
LOCATIONS/ITEMS: Outside Maryland's Grimrock Prison, Carter family Virginia estate, New York City's Chinatown inc wharf & Yellow Claw's hideout; Manhattan inc construction site & Lincoln Tunnel; Harlem inc Leila Taylor's apartment & Morgan's office; sewers beneath New York City inc Yellow Claw's second hideout; Suwan's casket, Chinese rifles, Cap's motorcycle, police callbox & guns, Claw's men's blasters, Claw's sky-writing plane, Tunnel of Fire & giant visi-screen
SYNOPSIS: While SHIELD medics tend to the recovering Falcon, Captain America and Nick Fury argue about the Yellow Claw. The heroes go their separate ways. The next day, the Claw transports a casket holding his grandniece Suwan into his Chinatown hideout, then uses his mind-altering powers to convince a visiting squadron of Chinese soldiers to kill each other. Later, before Cap can depart the Carter mansion, Peggy informs him that a recent flurry of radio commercials has been attacking his reputation. Cap arrives in Manhattan just in time to stop an attack by the Claw's mutated giant spiders, following them into the sewers. Meanwhile, Falcon is resting at Leila's apartment when she informs him that the gangster Morgan wants to meet with him. Morgan offers to give the Falcon super-strength to match Captain America's, but Falcon refuses. In the sewers, Cap follows the spiders' trail to the Yellow Claw's lair, where the Claw confronts him. The battle ends with Cap apparently killing the Claw, but the Claw changes into Fury. The real Yellow Claw appears on a monitor, gloating that Captain America has killed Nick Fury! NOTE: Cap #166, '73 reveals Hop Sung creates Yellow Claw's giant spiders. Although no time has passed between Cap #164, '73 and this story, Fury is wearing a different uniform here.

CAPTAIN AMERICA #166 (October 1973)

"Night of the Lurking Dead!" (19 pages)

CREDITS: Steve Englehart (writer), Sal Buscema (pencils), Frank McLaughlin (inks), Artie Simek (letters), David Hunt (colors), Roy Thomas (editor), Rich Buckler (c pencils), Frank Giacoia (c inks), Morrie Kuramoto (c letters)
FEATURE CHARACTERS: Captain America (also in newspaper photo), Falcon
GUEST STAR: Dum Dum Dugan (last in MTU #13, '73), Nick Fury
SUPPORTING CAST: Redwing (next in Cap #168, '73), Contessa Val Fontaine (last in Cap #153, '72), Leila Taylor (next in Cap #169, '74), Sharon Carter, Peggy Carter
VILLAINS: Yellow Claw (also in rfb, also in fb between YC #4/6, '57 & AoAtlas #1, '06 fb) and his men (Chi Foh named), Hop Sung (1st but last bts in Cap #165, '73), Fan-Le-Tamen (mummified Egyptian princess; spirit merges with Suwan's body), Suwan (body merges with Fan-Le-Tamen's spirit; also in fb between YC #4/6, '57 & Cap #165, '73), giant scorpion (dies), robbers (Frank named), mummies
OTHER CHARACTERS: Cal Trimble (last in Cap #158, '73, last app), SHIELD medics, Scarlett (Corinth Hotel tenant), liquor store manager, bystanders (Barry named), Daily Bugle delivery man, police, museum guard (dies), radio newscaster (voice only), Fritz Voltzmann, FBI agents (both in rfb), Richard Nixon, Osiris, Set (trio mentioned)
LOCATIONS/ITEMS: Yellow Claw's Chinatown & sewer hideouts, SHIELD HQ, Corinth Hotel, Carter family Virginia estate, Harlem inc Sam's apartment building, New York Museum of Natural History w/ Egyptology section; Suwan's casket, Lotus-Vial of Dreamless Sleep (in fb), robbers' guns, museum guard's gun, FBI agent's guns (in rfb), Yellow Claw's man's kris, Falcon's sword
FLASHBACKS: Yellow Claw & Voltzmann fight FBI agents (YC #1, '56). Impatient with Suwan's "treachery," the Claw places her in the Lotus-Vial of Dreamless Sleep.
SYNOPSIS: Detecting that Fury is still alive, Captain America ignores the Yellow Claw's taunts and carries Fury to SHIELD HQ. Later, Steve Rogers stops by his apartment, only to discover he has been evicted, and his belongings sold. He sees a newspaper ad that attacks Cap as a vigilante. Depressed, he calls Sharon from a pay phone. She alerts him that Peggy has disappeared. That night, the Claw takes over the Museum of Modern History in preparation for a deadly ceremony. Meanwhile, Peggy shows up at Sam Wilson's apartment building, looking for Cap. Soon after, Falcon meets with Steve and offers the use of his office, until his partner can find a place to live. They overhear a news report of the Yellow Claw near the museum, and race there to stop the villain. Entering the museum, they are attacked by the Claw's animated mummies, and are unable to prevent the Claw from resurrecting the mummified body of Fan-Le-Tamen. The evil Egyptian princess's body soon crumbles to dust, but her spirit possesses the body of Suwan. The Claw rejoices, claiming that together they will rule the world.

CAPTAIN AMERICA #167 (November 1973)

"Ashes to Ashes" (19 pages)

CREDITS: Steve Englehart (writer), Sal Buscema (pencils & c art), Frank Giacoia (inks), Charlotte Jetter (letters), David Hunt (colors), Roy Thomas (editor), Morrie Kuramoto (c letters)
FEATURE CHARACTERS: Captain America (next in Av #115-116, Def #9, Av #117, Def #10, all '73, Av #157 '77 fb, Av #118, '73, Def #11, '73, Av #119, '74, CM #27-28, '73, bts in CM #29, '73, Def #13, '74 fb), Falcon
GUEST STAR: Nick Fury, Dum Dum Dugan (both next in Av #118, '73)
SUPPORTING CAST: Peggy Carter (next bts in Cap #169, '74, next in Cap #174, '74), Sharon Carter (next in Cap #169, '74), Contessa Val Fontaine (next in Av #118, '73)
VILLAINS: Yellow Claw (chr next in IM #70, '74 fb, next in IM #69, '74), Suwan (body merged with Fan-Le-Tamen's spirit, next in AoAtlas #8, '09 as Jade Claw) (both also as Congress members), Fan-Le-Tamen (spirit merged with Suwan's body, dies), Yellow Claw agents (one as a nurse, dies), mummies
OTHER CHARACTERS: Harrison Carter (bts, worried about Peggy's disappearance; next in Cap #180, '74), Amanda Carter (bts, worried about Peggy's disappearance, last app), Suwan robot (last in ST #167, '68, no more appearances to date), Leila Taylor, SHIELD agents (2 die), U.S. Congress members, doctors; police commissioner (mentioned), Radames (Yellow Claw ally, mentioned)
LOCATIONS/ITEMS: New York Museum of Natural History Egyptology section, Nick Fury's hospital room, Sam Wilson's office & apartment, New Jersey airstrip; sarcophagus, Yellow Claw's steel cables, crossbows & poison-tipped bolts, scoutcraft, blasters, nerve gas & antidote, Yellow Claw's agent's poisoned ring, SHIELD Helicarrier, Cap's & Falcon's jet backpacks
SYNOPSIS: The Yellow Claw and Suwan leave Captain America and the Falcon behind tied to a statue, with poisoned crossbows aimed at their hearts. The heroes escape the death trap by toppling the statue. Later, Cap, Falcon and Sharon go to Sam's apartment, where Peggy is waiting for them. Peggy wants to help Cap fight the Claw, but Cap tries to let her down gently. Meanwhile, during a Congressional tour aboard the SHIELD Helicarrier, the Claw and Suwan release a nerve gas, putting everyone aboard to sleep. Cap and the Falcon visit Nick in the hospital when he suddenly awakens, warning everyone of the Claw's Helicarrier hijacking. Cap, Falcon, Dugan and Val arrive, using jet backpacks, but they're overcome by the nerve gas. As the Claw gloats Suwan shoots him, in retaliation for keeping her in suspended animation. The Claw gives an antidote to the four heroes, hoping they can stop Suwan. While the battle rages with Suwan's henchman, the Claw, who has used a mystical spell to recover from his wounds, recites the incantation that revived Fan-Le-Tamen, turning Suwan to dust. The Yellow Claw escapes.
NOTE: This issue reveals the Suwan appearing in ST #160-167, '67-78 was a robot.

CAPTAIN AMERICA #168 (December 1973)

"And a Phoenix Shall Arise!" (20 pages)

CREDITS: Roy Thomas (co-writer, editor), Tony Isabella (co-writer), Sal Buscema (pencils), John Tartaglione (co-inks), George Roussos (co-inks), Charlotte Jetter (letters), Linda Lessman (colors), John Verpoorten (c inks), Gaspar Saladino (c letters)
FEATURE CHARACTERS: Captain America (also in rfb; also in newspaper photos), Falcon
SUPPORTING CAST: Redwing
VILLAINS: Phoenix (Helmut Zemo; terrorist; 1st but chr last in Tb #-1, '97; also in fbs1 & 2 during Cap:ME #1, '94 fb, also in fb3 between Cap:ME #1, '94 fb & Cap:ME #1, '94; also in pfb, chr next in Tb #54, '01, next in Cap #275, '82 as Baron Zemo), Red Skull (as image in Steve's mind; also in rfb), Baron (Heinrich) Zemo (in rfb, only in fb1 between Cap:ME #1, '94 fb & Tb:Z #3, '07, fb2 between Cap:ME #1, '94 fb & Cap:ME #1, '94)
OTHER CHARACTERS: Baroness (Hilda) Zemo (Helmut's mother, only in fbs1 & 2 during Cap:ME #1, '94 fb), bystanders, Solarr (in rfb), Son of Frankenstein (son of a mad scientist, in movies), Viper, Dr. Faustus (prev 3 mentioned)
LOCATIONS/ITEMS: New York City inc Phoenix's warehouse hideout; Germany's Castle Zemo (in fb); gas-emitting Phoenix robot, SHIELD tracer, Zemo's death-ray & Adhesive X (prev 2 also in rfb)
FLASHBACKS: Red Skull falls from the 5th Sleeper (Cap #148, '72). A rock slide buries Heinrich Zemo (Av #15, '65). Solarr attacks Captain America (Cap #160, '73). Heinrich Zemo plays with his young son Helmut (1). Heinrich Zemo invents a death-ray (SgtF #8, '64). During a battle with Captain America, Heinrich Zemo is doused with Adhesive X (Av #6, '64 fb). With a mask permanently bonded to his face, Heinrich Zemo lashes out at his family (2). Soon after, Helmut Zemo visits his mother's gravesite (3). Reading a newspaper report of Captain America joining the Avengers, Helmut returns to Castle Zemo and develops a new death-ray and Adhesive X (p).
SYNOPSIS: Phoenix attacks Captain America and Falcon while they are on patrol. The Phoenix single-mindedly shoots at Cap, allowing the Falcon to strike the villain from behind, but Phoenix gains the upper hand. When his death-ray gun misfires, Phoenix retreats, leaving Cap and Falcon to ponder why this unknown villain hates Cap with such passion. Not wanting to endanger Falcon, Cap tells him that he doesn't need his help. Scouring New York City, Cap finds a frightened man who claims to be Phoenix's victim. Cap is fooled by a robot which emits a sleep-inducing gas, revealing the "victim" to be Phoenix. Cap awakens later, bound over a vat of Adhesive X. Phoenix reveals that he is Helmut Zemo, son of Baron Heinrich Zemo. When Falcon and Redwing arrive, having placed a tracer on Cap's shield, Cap escapes and stops the brawl between Phoenix and the Falcon. Cap wants to make amends with the Phoenix, but the younger Zemo tries to use Cap's shield to kill him. The shield ricochets back to him, and Phoenix falls into the vat of Adhesive X, apparently drowning.
NOTE: The Falcon calls the Phoenix "Archie" here, a reference to Archie Bunker, a bigoted character on the television series "All in the Family."

CAPTAIN AMERICA #169 (January 1974)

"When a Legend Dies!" (19 pages)

CREDITS: Steve Englehart (plot, script p. 1-9), Mike Friedrich (script p. 10-19), Sal Buscema (pencils), Frank McLaughlin (inks), Charlotte Jetter (letters), Petra Goldberg (colors), Roy Thomas (editor), John Costanza (c letters)

FEATURE CHARACTERS: Captain America (also in video & rfb), Falcon

GUEST STAR: Black Panther (last in Av #119 '74)

SUPPORTING CAST: Peggy Carter (bts, joins SHIELD), Sharon Carter (next in MTIO #4, '74), Contessa Val Fontaine (last in Av #118, '73, next in DD #120, '75), Leila Taylor (last in Cap #166, '73), Redwing

VILLAINS: Moonstone (Lloyd Bloch, lunar rock-powered superhuman, 1st but chr last in Cap #170, '74 fb), Morgan (bts, sends gang to kill Falcon, last in Cap #165, '73, next in PM #19, '74), Tumbler (John Robert Keane, killed acrobat, last in ToS #83/2, '66, dies), Quentin Harderman (also in video, 1st but chr last in Cap #170, '74 fb), Morgan's gang (Slick named), Committee to Regain America's Principles (front group for Secret Empire, created by Harderman, 1st), Secret Empire (subversive organization, bts, orchestrating conspiracy against Cap, last in AA #15, '72, last bts in Av #111, '73, chr last in Cap #174, '74 fb)

OTHER CHARACTERS: Quentin Harderman's receptionist, SHIELD Agent 135, Spirits Shop clerk, charity event attendees, bystanders (Harry named); Dr. Faustus, Red Skull, police (prev 3 only in rfbs); Al Capone (gangster), Avengers, Nick Fury, Henry Pym, Spider-Man, Tony Stark, Viper (prev 7 mentioned)

LOCATIONS/ITEMS: New York inc Quentin Harderman's Madison Ave. advertising agency office, SHIELD HQ, Spirits Shop (liquor store), Sharon Carter's SHIELD dorm, Broadway inc store window; Harlem inc Sam's office, New York Armory inc Exhibit Hall #5, TV station (bts, contacted by Cap); Black Panther's Transatlantic ship, Morgan's gang's car, brass knuckles, clubs & hand guns; storefront TV, SHIELD blaster, Moonstone's laser

FLASHBACKS: Captain America punches the Red Skull (Cap #148, '72). Cap punches Dr. Faustus (Cap #162, '73). Cap pushes past police (Cap #156, '72).

SYNOPSIS: Morgan's gang attacks Falcon; when Captain America joins the fight, the gang flees. The Falcon expresses his feelings of inferiority to Cap, who arranges for the Black Panther to help boost his partner's power. After Falcon and Leila Taylor leave for Wakanda with the Panther, Cap confronts Quentin Harderman, the man behind a TV campaign to discredit him as an unchecked vigilante. Cap agrees to attend a charity event for Harderman to get him off his back; as part of a setup by Harderman, the Tumbler robs a liquor store, fights Cap and escapes. Sharon Carter tells Cap that Peggy has joined SHIELD, but when he goes to SHIELD to convince them to turn Peggy down, Val Fontaine rebuffs him. At the charity event, Harderman introduces Cap to John Robert Keane, whom Cap recognizes as the Tumbler. When Cap attacks Keane, a hidden sniper fires a laser at the Tumbler, making it look like Cap killed the villain.

NOTE: This issue marks the beginning of the seven-issue Secret Empire story arc, which, as noted in the letters page of issue #173, Steve Englehart conceived around Christmas of 1972; the Watergate scandal that unfolded in 1973 influenced both the direction and duration of the story. Harderman's codename is "Station Wagon-1." Moonstone's name is noted as Byron Becton in OHMU #7, '83, but his true name is revealed in Cap #379, '90. The acronym for the Committee to Regain America's Principles is telling.

CAPTAIN AMERICA #170 (February 1974)

"J'Accuse!" (19 pages)

CREDITS: Steve Englehart (plot), Mike Friedrich (script), Sal Buscema (pencils), Vince Colletta (inks), Art Simek (letters), Petra Goldberg (colors), Roy Thomas (editor), Gil Kane, John Romita (c pencils), Gaspar Saladino (c letters)

FEATURE CHARACTERS: Captain America, Falcon

GUEST STAR: Black Panther

SUPPORTING CAST: Leila Taylor

VILLAINS: Quentin Harderman (also in fb between bts in Cap #163, '73 & Cap #169, '74), Moonstone (also in fb to 1st chr app before Cap #169, '74), Stone-Face (last in Cap #138, '71), Tumbler (as corpse, last app), Viper (also in newspaper, only in fb during Cap #163, '73), Stone-Face's men (Jangles named), Committee to Regain America's Principles (bts, implementing campaign against Cap), Sanitation Unit (squad of Secret Empire agents inc Number One, Number Four, Number Seven & Number Eight), Secret Empire (bts, orchestrating conspiracy against Cap)

OTHER CHARACTERS: Tanzika (Wakandan court handmaiden), 2 Wakandan escorts (both die), Wakandan radio operator, New York police (Hank & Lee named), charity event attendees, newspaper reporters & photographers, bystanders, 2 campus policemen (Jack named, only in fb), Wakandan engineers (bts, drew plans), Morgan, Thing (both mentioned), M'Deari (Wakandan woman in escort's thoughts only)

LOCATIONS/ITEMS: New York Armory inc Exhibit Hall #5, New York jail; Lagos, Nigeria, Wakanda inc computer center beneath royal palace, Moonstone's bedroom, Quentin Harderman's Madison Ave. advertising agency office, Midwestern university inc science building (prev 3 in fb only); Falcon's jet-powered glider-wings inc solar-charged power-pack (designed by Black Panther, 1st, see NOTE); Moonstone's rock from Blue Area of the Moon & bag of tools, policemen's guns (prev 3 in fb only), Moonstone's laser, Sanitation Unit's rock-blasters, Stone-Face's men's guns, Stone-Face's car, Wakandan aircraft & spear

FLASHBACK: After gaining his powers while stealing a blue moon rock, Moonstone reports to Quentin Harderman and the Viper, who tell him to lay low. When the Viper is jailed, Harderman tells Moonstone they must begin their campaign to smear and frame Captain America.

SYNOPSIS: Captain America flees the scene of the Tumbler's death, only to be attacked and defeated by the Tumbler's secret murderer, Moonstone. Quentin Harderman and bystanders hail Moonstone as a hero. Cap awakens to find himself jailed in the presence of the press, who interview Moonstone. The Black Panther shows the Falcon Wakandan technology and sends the bored Leila Taylor on an escorted shopping trip to Lagos, Nigeria, where Stone-Face kidnaps her. When Leila's slain escorts fail to report in, Falcon, now sporting jet-powered wings, joins the Black Panther in responding. Meanwhile, a squad of self-proclaimed Cap supporters break into Cap's jail, seeking to free him.

NOTE: The Falcon's wings make their debut; their appearance in subsequent issues is implied. Sanitation Unit agents named in Cap #171, '74. Policemen Hank's and Lee's names are confused from one page to the next.

CAPTAIN AMERICA #171 (March 1974)

"Bust-Out!" (19 pages)

CREDITS: Steve Englehart (plot), Mike Friedrich (script), Sal Buscema (pencils), Vince Colletta (inks), Art Simek (letters), Linda Lessman (colors), Roy Thomas (editor), John Romita (c pencils), Tony Mortellaro (c inks), Gaspar Saladino (c letters)
FEATURE CHARACTERS: Captain America (also in Av #121, '74), Falcon
GUEST STARS: Black Panther (next in Av #121, '74), Iron Man (during Av #120, '74)
SUPPORTING CAST: Leila Taylor (next in Cap #178, '74), Redwing
VILLAINS: Quentin Harderman (also in rfb), Committee to Regain America's Principles (both bts, orchestrating Cap's frame-up), Moonstone (also in rfb), Stone-Face (next in MTU #114, '82), Stone-Face's men (Jangles named), Sanitation Unit (Number One, Number Four, Number Seven & Number Eight named), Secret Empire (bts, orchestrating conspiracy against Cap)
OTHER CHARACTERS: Jail guards (Manny named), Wakandans inc intelligence agent & pilot; Tumbler (as John Robert Keane), bystanders (both only in rfb); Hank Williams (country singer), Morgan (both mentioned)
LOCATIONS/ITEMS: Harlem inc Sam's office, Lagos, Nigeria inc Stone-Face's headquarters & nearby sea cliff, New York jail, Quentin Company HQ; Moonstone's New York hideout; Daily Bugle advertisement (in rfb), Moonstone's laser, Sanitation Unit's rock-blasters & knockout gas, jail guards' nightsticks, Stone-Face's jewels, Stone-Face's men's guns, Wakandan aircraft
FLASHBACK: Quentin Harderman and Moonstone implement their plan to discredit and frame Captain America (Cap #166, '73, Cap #169-170, '74).
SYNOPSIS: When Captain America resists the jailbreak, his apparent supporters, the Sanitation Unit, gas him and take him away. Cap awakens and, realizing his liberators are in league with Quentin Harderman, takes them down. Falcon and Black Panther storm Stone-Face's Lagos headquarters to rescue Leila Taylor, but the Falcon's inexperience with his new wings results in a blunder that knocks out both heroes. Stone-Face's men throw the two off a cliff, but the Falcon masters his wings and saves himself and the Black Panther. The heroes counterattack and defeat Stone-Face. Falcon and Leila return to New York, where Iron Man tells Falcon about Cap's murder charge and jail escape. Despite Iron Man's request for Falcon to arrest Cap, Falcon finds Cap and sides with him. Moonstone arrives and defeats them both after admitting Harderman's plot.
NOTE: This issue includes Marvel Value Stamp #50 – Black Panther. Quentin Co. HQ's address is 1701 Penn St.

CAPTAIN AMERICA #172 (April 1974)

"Believe It or Not: The Banshee!" (19 pages)

CREDITS: Steve Englehart, Mike Friedrich (writers), Sal Buscema (pencils), Vince Colletta (inks), Art Simek (letters), Michelle Brand (colors), Roy Thomas (editor), John Romita, Gil Kane (c pencils), Frank Giacoia (c inks), Gaspar Saladino (c letters)
FEATURE CHARACTERS: Captain America, Falcon
GUEST STARS: X-Men: Cyclops (Scott Summers, mutant w/ optic blasts), Marvel Girl (Jean Grey, telekinetic mutant), Professor X (Charles Francis Xavier, telepathic mutant) (all last in Hulk #172, '74, chr last in Cap #173, '74 fb), Havok (Alex Summers, cosmic-powered mutant), Lorna Dane (mutant mistress of magnetism) (prev 2 bts, captured by Secret Empire, last in Hulk #150, '72); Banshee (Sean Cassidy, mutant w/ ultrasonic scream, last in X #60, '69, last bts in Av #103, '72 fb, next in GSX #1, '75)
SUPPORTING CAST: Redwing
VILLAINS: Quentin Harderman, Moonstone (both next in Cap #174, '74), Committee to Regain America's Principles (bts, implementing conspiracy against Cap), Sanitation Unit (called "Sanitation Squad," Number Twelve, Number Twenty named), Secret Empire (bts, orchestrating conspiracy against Cap)
OTHER CHARACTERS: Trucker, bystanders, Dwight Eisenhower (U.S. president), Douglas MacArthur (U.S. general) (both mentioned by Sanitation Unit only), Bowery Boys (fictional New York street kids, mentioned by Moonstone only), Merle Haggard (country singer, mentioned by Banshee only)
LOCATIONS/ITEMS: Central Park, Quentin Company headquarters, Harlem inc Sam's office; Nashville; produce truck, Professor X's wheelchair, Sanitation Unit's blasters
SYNOPSIS: Quentin Harderman orders Moonstone to take the unconscious Captain America and Falcon to Central Park to be guarded by the Sanitation Unit. While the Sanitation Unit argues, the heroes awaken and quickly escape. Cap and Falcon follow a clue and hitchhike to Nashville. They encounter Banshee, who mistakenly thinks the heroes are after him. Banshee attacks and defeats defeats Cap and Falcon, but when the X-Men's Cyclops shows up, Banshee flees. Professor X appears with Marvel Girl and explains to Cap and Falcon that a mysterious group has been capturing mutants. He notes that he believes it's the same group conspiring against Cap.
NOTE: This issue includes Marvel Value Stamp #43 – Enchantress.

CAPTAIN AMERICA #173 (May 1974)

"The Sins of the Secret Empire!" (19 pages)

CREDITS: Steve Englehart (writer), Sal Buscema (pencils), Vince Colletta (inks), Art Simek (letters), George Roussos (colors), Roy Thomas (editor), John Romita, Gil Kane (c pencils), Frank Giacoia (c inks), Gaspar Saladino (c letters)

FEATURE CHARACTERS: Captain America (also in rfb; also as Roger Stevens), Falcon (also as Willie Samuels) (both also in Mv:Eye #2, '09 fb)

GUEST STARS: X-Men: Cyclops (also in fb2 between Av #111, '73 & Fear #20, '74, in fb3 between Hulk #172, '74 & Cap #172, '74; also in Mv:Eye #2, '09 fb), Marvel Girl (also in fb3 between Hulk #172, '74 & Cap #172, '74; also in Mv:Eye #2, '09 fb), Professor X (also in fb1 during Av #111, '73, fb2 between Av #111, '73 & Shanna #5, '73, & bts in fb3 between Hulk #172, '74 & Cap #172, '74; also in Mv:Eye #2, '09 fb) (all also in rfb), Iceman (only in fb3 between SMFam #8/2, '08 & Cap #174, '74), Havok, Lorna Dane (both bts, captured by Secret Empire); Dum Dum Dugan (last in Av #118, '73, next in Cap #175, '74), Nick Fury (last in Def #11, '73, also in Mv:Eye #2, '09 fb, next bts in MTU #19, '74, next in FF #154, '75), Iron Man (also in rfb, only in fb1 during Av #111, '73)

VILLAINS: Secret Empire, inc: Linda Donaldson (Beast's former girlfriend & Secret Empire's Agent Nine, last in AA #15, '72), Mr. Black (Brand Corporation factory boss & Secret Empire's Number Sixteen), Number Thirteen; Committee to Regain America's Principles (bts, implementing conspiracy against Cap)

OTHER CHARACTERS: Brand Corporation guards (Chuck named), radio announcer, SHIELD agents (some also in Mv:Eye #2, '09 fb), Tennessee State Police; Magneto, Thor (both only in rfb), Beast (in Professor X's thoughts), Quentin Harderman (mentioned by Professor X)

LOCATIONS/ITEMS: Hidden entrance to Secret Empire's Southwestern lair, Number Thirteen's house & boulder-enclosed scout craft shelter, Dallas, Texas inc Prairie View Apartments, Southview Hotel & Brand Corporation plant & research lab; Nashville, Tennessee area inc abandoned mine, Magneto's secret cave headquarters (in rfb), Xavier's School for Gifted Youngsters (in rfb & fb), Havok's & Lorna Dane's Southwestern home (in fb); Brand Corporation's electric eye alarm, sprinkler pipe & guards' pistols; Secret Empire's scout craft & cactus-shaped cover for opening lair entrance; Electron-Gyro (steering device, called "Electro-Gyro") & its case, Linda Donaldson's car & communications unit, Fury's megaphone, Number Thirteen's gun, Professor X's wheelchair, SHIELD blasters, X-Men's jet craft, $5000 cash paid for the Brand Corporation job, Cap's letter

FLASHBACKS: Magneto attacks the X-Men, but the Avengers defeat him (Av #110-111, '73). Iron Man informs Professor X that Angel is missing (1). After Professor X fails to locate the Beast (2), Cyclops, Iceman and Marvel Girl discover Havok and Lorna Dane are missing from their Southwest home (3).

SYNOPSIS: Nick Fury and SHIELD find Captain America, Falcon, Professor X, Cyclops and Marvel Girl. They attempt to arrest Cap, but the heroes flee to an abandoned mine. Professor X explains that the Secret Empire is responsible for the disappearance of several of the X-Men and that Quentin Harderman works for the Secret Empire. Suspecting that the Beast's old girlfriend, Linda Donaldson, may be involved, Professor X sends Cap and the Falcon to Dallas, where they assume disguises and save Donaldson from a staged attack by Cyclops. The Secret Empire takes the bait and hires the disguised duo to steal a device from a Brand Corporation factory. Cap and Falcon steal the Electron-Gyro and leave an explanatory note for the plant's boss, Mr. Black. They resume their disguises and hand the device to the Secret Empire's Number 13, who leads them into the Empire's lair.

NOTE: This issue includes Marvel Value Stamp #61 – Red Ghost. Havok is misspelled "Havoc" here.

CAPTAIN AMERICA #174 (June 1974)

"It's Always Darkest!" (18 pages)

CREDITS: Steve Englehart (writer), Sal Buscema (pencils), Vince Colletta (inks), Charlotte Jetter (letters), George Roussos (colors), Roy Thomas (editor), John Romita, Gil Kane (c pencils), Frank Giacoia (c inks), Gaspar Saladino (c letters)

FEATURE CHARACTERS: Captain America (also as Roger Stevens), Falcon (also as Willie Samuels) (both also in rfb)

GUEST STARS: X-Men: Cyclops, Marvel Girl, Professor X (all also in rfb), Angel (also in fb1 between AA #15, '72 & Av #111, '73 fb, in pfb; last in Av #111, '73 fb), Beast (also in pfb; last in Hulk #161, '73), Havok, Iceman, Lorna Dane; Gabe Jones (as Secret Empire's Number 68, last in SgtF #100, '72)

SUPPORTING CAST: Peggy Carter (as Secret Empire agent)

VILLAINS: Moonstone, Quentin Harderman (both also in rfb), Committee to Regain America's Principles (bts, implementing conspiracy against Cap), Secret Empire (also bts, attacking Angel & Beast in fb1 & fb2 between bts in Av #111, '73 & bts in Cap #169, '74), inc: Linda Donaldson (also as Number Nine, last app), Number One, Number Eight, Number Thirteen (also in rfb), Number Sixteen (Mr. Black), Number Forty-Two; Secret Empire's robot; Blob (Frederick "Fred" J. Dukes, obese mutant able to become immovable), Unus (Gunther Bain/Angelo Unuscione, mutant w/ impenetrable force field) (both last in AA #13, '72, chr last in Tb #33, '99 fb), Mastermind (Jason Wyngarde, mutant illusionist, last in AA #13, '72, chr last in Tb #33, '99 fb), Mesmero (mutant hypnotist, last in Av #103, '72), Magneto (in fb1 between AA #10, '72 & Av #111, '73 fb)

OTHER CHARACTERS: Frank (TV talk show host), Miss Kearney (TV talk show guest), TV cameraman & crew, TV studio audience (applause heard only); Banshee, Tumbler, bystanders (trio in rfb)

LOCATIONS/ITEMS: Nashville, New York Armory's Exhibit Hall #5, New York jail, Quentin Company headquarters, Dallas' Southview Hotel & Brand Corporation plant (all in rfb only), Xavier's School for Gifted Youngsters (in fb1), Brand Corporation's Long Island complex (in fb2), television studio, Secret Empire's Southwestern lair inc air shaft, elevator, Number One's chamber, sleeping quarters & utility duct; Brand Corporation's guards' pistols (in rfb), Electron-Gyro & its case, Professor X's wheelchair (also in rfb), Watergate scandal (mentioned by Number

One & Moonstone), Secret Empire's Atomic Annihilator (ray cannon), alarm, blasters, electrified vent, room lasers & mutant energy siphoning apparatus

FLASHBACKS: Captain America is discredited and framed for murder, jailed by Moonstone, fights the Banshee, works with the X-Men to investigate the Secret Empire and steals the Electron-Gyro (Cap #169-173, '74). Magneto attacks the Angel (1), Angel then falls to the Secret Empire. The Secret Empire captures the Beast (p).

SYNOPSIS: The disguised Captain America and the Falcon meet the Secret Empire's leader, Number One, who explains the conspiracy against Cap. Suspecting danger after being escorted and locked into a sleeping quarters, they change into their costumes and escape a deathtrap. On the run in the Secret Empire's lair, Cap and Falcon fight a deadly robot and rendezvous with Professor X, Cyclops and Marvel Girl, who found another entrance into the facility. Together they discover nine captive mutants and free them from a power-siphoning device but the Secret Empire finds them. A skirmish ensues, and the Secret Empire's Number 68 fires a ray cannon at the heroes, leaving them presumably dead.

NOTE: Professor X attributes Falcon's close bond with Redwing to a paranormal empathic link, which explains the Falcon's ability to faintly perceive telepathic messages from Professor X in this issue; an interpretation of Falcon's ability as a mutant power is reinforced in Falcon #2, '83, but is debunked in Av Ann '01. This issue includes Marvel Value Stamp #48 – Kraven.

CAPTAIN AMERICA #175 (July 1974)

"...Before the Dawn!" (18 pages)

CREDITS: Steve Englehart (writer), Sal Buscema (pencils, c pencils), Vince Colletta (inks), Art Simek (letters), Petra Goldberg (colors), Roy Thomas (editor), John Romita (c pencils), Gaspar Saladino (c letters)
FEATURE CHARACTERS: Captain America (also in AvFo #2, '99 fb, AvFo #1-12, '98-'99, next in Av #125, '74, CM #31-33, '74, Cap Ann #7, '83 fb, GSAv #1, '74 fb, Av #126, '74, GSAv #1, '74, Av #280, '87 fb, MTIO #4-5, '74), Falcon
GUEST STARS: X-Men: Angel, Cyclops, Iceman, Marvel Girl (all next in MTU #23, '74), Havok, Lorna Dane (both next in GSX #1, '75), Beast (next in Cap #183, '75), Professor X (next bts in Hulk #181, '74, chr next in GSX #1, '75, next in Def #15, '74); Gabe Jones (also as Secret Empire's Number 68; also as Number Six in fb2 between TTA #83/2, '66 & ST #149, '66; next in Cap #178, '74), Dum Dum Dugan (next in Cap #181, '75)
SUPPORTING CAST: Peggy Carter (also as Secret Empire agent)
VILLAINS: Secret Empire (also in fb1), inc: Number One (Richard Nixon, last in Hulk #172, '74, last app, see NOTE), Number Two (marshal of Secret Empire's Warrior Squad), former Number Nine (only in fb2), Number Three; Moonstone (chr next in Hulk #229, '78 fb, next in Cap #379, '90 as Nefarius), Viper (last in Cap #163, '73, next in Cap #180, '74), Committee to Regain America's Principles (bts, implementing campaign against Cap), Sanitation Unit (called "Sanitation Squad", bts, planting explosives), Blob, Mastermind, Unus (trio next in Def #15, '74), Mesmero (chr next in CX #17/2, '88, next in X #111, '78), Quentin Harderman
OTHER CHARACTERS: Congressional committee (bts, in conference room), Army soldiers (Harry named), prison guard & 3 prisoners, White House reporters & cameramen, TV viewers; Boomerang (Fred Myers), Hulk, Sub-Mariner, Secret Empire's former Number One (prev 4 in rfb); Marcus Junius Brutus (ancient Roman politician), Julius Caesar (ancient Roman dictator), Nick Fury, SHIELD, Viper (prev 5 mentioned)
LOCATIONS/ITEMS: Secret Empire's Southwestern lair (also in rfb) inc dungeon, Washington, DC inc Congressional office building, Washington Monument, White House w/Oval Office & White House lawn; Watergate scandal (mentioned by Moonstone), Electron-Gyro, TV cameras, Number One's gun, Number Two's mutant-powered helmet, Army tanks, bazooka & guns; Secret Empire's atomic explosives (bts), Atomic Annihilator & saucer craft inc master control room, mutant energy siphoning apparatus, force field, ramp & video screen
FLASHBACKS: Boomerang attacks the Hulk (TTA #82/2, '66). The Secret Empire's old Number One takes control of the Sub-Mariner (TTA #83/2, '66). The old Number One blows himself up (TTA #84/2, '66). The Secret Empire holds a rally (1). Disguised as the Secret Empire's Number Six, Gabe Jones defeats the Empire's old Number Nine (2).
SYNOPSIS: Away from prying eyes in the Secret Empire's dungeon, SHIELD agents Gabe Jones and Peggy Carter tell the revived Captain America that they've infiltrated the Empire and saved him and his companions by pretending to kill them. Gabe and Peggy smuggle Cap, Falcon, Cyclops and Marvel Girl onto the Secret Empire's saucer craft, which is powered by the nine captive mutants. When the craft lands on the White House lawn, Moonstone playacts at fighting the Empire's Number Two and feigns defeat to encourage America to surrender. The heroes counterattack and Cap defeats Moonstone, who exposes Quentin Harderman as a front for the Empire. Cap chases the Empire's leader, Number One, into the White House's Oval Office. Shocked by Number One's identity, Cap fails to prevent him from committing suicide. Emotionally destroyed, Captain America leaves without a word.
NOTE: In the future, Rick Jones and the Kree Supreme Intelligence pluck Captain America from this story to appear in AvFo #1-12, '98-'99. While Number One is heavily implied to be the President here, AvFo #2, '99 states him to be a "highly-placed government official" and Cap:Re #3, '09 verifies that he is indeed the President. This revelation leads Steve Rogers to give up his Captain America identity next issue, but the decision takes a long time to make; Cap has several other adventures between this issue and the next. This issue includes Marvel Value Stamp #77 – Swordsman.

CAPTAIN AMERICA #176 (August 1974)

"Captain America Must Die!" (18 pages)

CREDITS: Steve Englehart (writer), Sal Buscema (pencils), Vince Colletta (inks), Artie Simek (letters), Linda Lessmann (colors), Roy Thomas (editor), John Romita (c art), Gaspar Saladino (c letters)

FEATURE CHARACTERS: Captain America (also in symbolic image & Peggy's thoughts, also in fb1 between Cap #255, '81 fb & Cap:SoL #7/2, '99 fb, fb2 between CapC Spec #1, '09 fb & Cap:SoL #7/2, '99 fb, fb3 between MvPro #4, '10 fb & Cap #109, '69 fb, fb5 during Cap #121, '70, fb6 between Cap:SoL #9, '99 & Cap #144, '71 fb), Falcon (also in Cap's thoughts & rfb, also in fb6 between Cap:SoL #9, '99 & Cap #144, '71 fb)

GUEST STARS: Avengers: Iron Man (last in GSAv #1, '75, chr last in Av #280, '87 fb, next in Av #127, '74), Thor (also in Thor's thoughts, last in GSAv #1, '75, chr last in Av #280, '87 fb, next in MTU #26, '74) (both also in Cap's thoughts), Vision (last in GSAv #1, '75, chr last in Av #280, '87 fb, next in Av #127, '74 fb)

SUPPORTING CAST: Sharon Carter (also in Cap's thoughts, last in MTIO #5, '74), Peggy Carter (next in Cap #178, '74)

VILLAIN: Agent R (in fb4 to 1st chr app before Cap #255, '81 fb)

OTHER CHARACTERS: Edwin Jarvis (last in GSAv #1, '75, chr last in Av #280, '87 fb, next in Av #127, '74), Gen. Phillips (only in fb3 between MvPro #4, '10 fb & Cap #109, '69 fb),Sgt. Stone (in fbs 2 & 3, only app), US Army volunteers, military physician (both in fb2), theater attendees in fb1), children (some in fb4, others in fb5), Hitler (in newsreel only), Captain America (Burnside), Diamondhead & his men, Prof. Erskine, Heinz Krueger, MODOK, Moloids, Nazis, Project: Rebirth scientists, Redwing (prev 11 in rfb), Bucky, Red Skull, Giant-Man, Number One, various Americans (prev 5 in Cap's thoughts), trolls (in Thor's thoughts)

LOCATIONS/ITEMS: Army recruitment center, Curio Shop inc Operation: Rebirth, European battlefield, New York, Harlem, Exile Isle (all in fbs), Avengers Mansion; American flag, swastika (both in symbolic images)

FLASHBACKS: A young Steve Rogers watches newsreels about the Nazis (1). Steve again is declared 4-F (2) and rejected by Sgt. Stone for army service (3). As Agent R prepares (4), Steve is brought to a Curio Shop and undergoes Project: Rebirth. Erskine is killed but Captain America is born (Cap #109, '69 fb). Cap and Thor fight Kang (Av #8, '64). Cap and Thor fight the Mole Man (Av #12, '65). Cap and Iron Man rescue the Wasp's doctor from Moloids in Subterrania (Av #14, '65). Cap battles Nazis (ToS #68, '65). Cap raises money for charity (5). Captain America is jeered at by protesters (Cap #170, '74). Captain America and the Falcon meet for the first time (Cap #117, '69). Cap and Falcon fight Diamond Head (Cap #126, '70), Cap and the Falcon fight MODOK (Cap #133), Cap and the Falcon fight Stone-Face and his henchmen (Cap #134), Cap and Falcon sign autographs (6). Captain America fights the 1950's Captain America (Cap #153, '72).

SYNOPSIS: Feeling that the world has moved beyond his outdated ideals, Steve Rogers debates whether or not to stop being Captain America. At Avengers Mansion, he is confronted by Thor, Iron Man, Vision, Falcon, Peggy Carter and Sharon Carter, each giving him advice against hanging up the uniform, except for Sharon, who says she will stand by Captain America no matter what he decides. Eventually, our hero announces that he will indeed call it quits!

CAPTAIN AMERICA #177 (September 1974)

"Lucifer Be Thy Name" (18 pages)

CREDITS: Steve Englehart (writer), Sal Buscema (pencils), Vince Colletta (inks), Artie Simek (letters), Linda Lessmann (colors), Roy Thomas (editor), Gil Kane, John Romita (c art), Gaspar Saladino (c letters)

FEATURE CHARACTERS: Steve Rogers (also as Captain America in Falcon's dream), Falcon

SUPPORTING CAST: Redwing (last in Cap #173, '74), Sharon Carter

VILLAINS: Lucifer (last in IM #20, '69), Aries (merges w/Lucifer, last in Av #122, '74, last bts in Av #123, '74, chr last in GR #7, '90 fb), Rafe Michel (merges w/Lucifer, last in Cap #161, '73) & his thugs, Morgan (last in PM #20, '74) & his men

OTHER CHARACTERS: Salirann (Nameless Dimension beast, only app), homeless man, police officers, newspaper boy, bystanders; enemy soldiers (in dream only); Charles Gray, Supreme One, X-Men: Beast, Iceman, Marvel Girl (prev 5 in rfb)

LOCATIONS/ITEMS: castle (in dream only), Harlem inc Delicates Groceries, Sam's apartment & office, Nameless Dimension, New York City penitentiary; Brain-Blaster (giant bombshell, in dream only), Casadrax mineral, dimensional transmitter, police cars

FLASHBACKS: Lucifer fights the X-Men (X #9, '64) and the Supreme One banishes Lucifer to the Nameless Dimension (X #21, '66). Lucifer tries to escape the Nameless Dimension by empowering Charlie Gray (IM #20, '69).

SYNOPSIS: Awaking from a nightmare Falcon goes out on patrol, he asks Steve to accompany him. Angered that Falcon isn't taking his "retirement" seriously, Steve reminds Falcon that he's no longer Captain America. Falcon flies off, frustrated. Meanwhile in the Nameless Dimension, Lucifer finalizes powering his dimensional transmitter, enabling his return to Earth. He quickly becomes distracted by a grocery store. Simultaneously, Rafe Michel and his gang attempt to burglarize the grocer, but flee inside when the police arrive. Meeting inside, the villains unite to battle the police. When Lucifer's body begins fading back to the Nameless Dimension, he merges his body with Rafe to anchor him to Earth. Then, to keep Rafe's body from burning out, he breaks into jail and frees Aries, merging half his essence with the Zodiac member to create two Lucifers. Falcon arrives and battles the two Lucifers but is quickly defeated. Steve tries to check on Falcon, but the winged hero rejects Steve's help out of spite. Meanwhile, the two Lucifers are contacted by Morgan, who hires them to kill Falcon.

CAPTAIN AMERICA #178 (October 1974)

"If The Falcon Should Fall!" (18 pages)

CREDITS: Steve Englehart (writer), Sal Buscema (pencils), Vince Colletta (inks), Tom Orzechowski (letters), Phil Rachelson (colors), Roy Thomas (editor), Ron Wilson, John Romita (c pencils), Frank Giacoia (c inks), Gaspar Saladino (c letters)
FEATURE CHARACTERS: Steve Rogers (also as Captain America in photo), Falcon (also in rfb)
GUEST STAR: Gabe Jones (last in Cap #175, '74, next in Cap #181, '75)
SUPPORTING CAST: Roscoe Simons (gym employee, 1st, see NOTE), Leila Taylor (last in Cap #171, '74, next in Cap #183, '75), Sharon Carter, Peggy Carter, Redwing
VILLAINS: Lucifer (last app), Aries (dies, next as corpse in IM Ann '99), Rafe Michel (dies, next bts as corpse in IM Ann '99 fb) (both merged w/Lucifer), Morgan (all also in rfb), Lucifer's Ultra-Robots: Delta, Epsilon & Zeta (trio last in X #21, '66, destroyed, last app), fur store robbers
OTHER CHARACTERS: Bob Russo (baseball player, also as Captain America, only app), Bears team members, kid baseball fans, Mitch (baseball reporter), sports store employee, bystanders
LOCATIONS/ITEMS: Harlem inc Starlin Gym, Sam's apartment & Morgan's office, New York inc Sharon's apartment, fur store & sports store, Bears baseball stadium & locker room, Buchanan's Butte inc Lucifer's hidden lab, Nameless Dimension; electrical wires, private jet, Lucifer's equipment inc gun, Steve's ski mask & garbage can lid
FLASHBACKS: Falcon accosts Morgan after being offered a job by the crimelord (Cap #157, '72). Lucifer merges with Rafe Michael, then merges with Aries (Cap #177, '74).
SYNOPSIS: Falcon feeds Redwing on a rooftop until the two Lucifers attack him from behind. The battle abruptly ends when fallen power lines separate Falcon from the villains. The Lucifers retreat to Morgan, arguing over who is the dominant personality. Falcon visits Leila Taylor, who urges him to get over Cap's quitting. Meanwhile, Steve Rogers enjoys retirement by working out at a gym. Elsewhere, professional baseball player Bob Russo announces to the media that he's quitting sports to become the new Captain America. Steve and Sharon run into Gabe Jones and Peggy at Sharon's apartment; Peggy is worried about the missing Cap. The Lucifers visit their hidden lab and activate their Ultra-Robots. Russo's only outing as Cap ends when he slams into a brick wall, breaking his arm. The next day, Lucifer's Ultra-Robots run rampant through Harlem. Falcon is quickly defeated. Witnessing the conflict, Steve dons a ski mask to battle the foes, destroying the robots. Suddenly the Rafe-Lucifer collapses, Lucifer's energies are too much for the host body, killing him. Linked, Aries dies as well, sending Lucifer back to the Nameless Dimension. Falcon awakens to find he's been rescued again by Steve; in disgust, he demands Steve leave him alone.
NOTE: Roscoe's surname is revealed in Cap #615.1, '11.

CAPTAIN AMERICA #179 (November 1974)

"Slings and Arrows" (18 pages)

CREDITS: Steve Englehart (writer), Sal Buscema (pencils), Vince Colletta (inks), Tom Orzechowski (letters), Petra Goldberg (colors), Roy Thomas (editor), Ron Wilson (c pencils), Frank Giacioa (c inks), Gaspar Saladino (c letters)
FEATURE CHARACTERS: Steve Rogers (also as Captain America in rfb & fb between Cap #113-114, '69), Falcon
GUEST STAR: Hawkeye (also as "Golden Archer," also in Hawkeye's thoughts, also in rfb, also in fb between Av #106, '72 fb and Av #61, '69; last in MTU #22, '74, next in GSAv #2, '74)
SUPPORTING CAST: Peggy Carter (next in Cap #181, '75), Sharon Carter, Redwing, Roscoe Simons
VILLAINS: Morgan (next in Cap #183, '75) & his men, Road Runner gang members
OTHER CHARACTERS: Scar Turpin (motorcycle gang leader, also as Captain America, only app) & his Sickle Cycle gang (Rasputin named), mugging victim; Bob Russo (in newspaper photo); Dr. Strange, Hulk, Rick Jones, Space Phantom, Thor, Valkyrie, Vision (prev 7 in rfb); Daredevil, Quasimodo, Spider-Man (trio in Hawkeye's thoughts)
LOCATIONS/ITEMS: Harlem inc Sam's office, Morgan's office & Starlin Gym, San Rafael, California inc Sickle Cycle club grounds, Avengers Mansion, Dr. Strange's Sanctum Sanctorum (both in rfb); Steve's groceries, Golden Archer's gas arrow, siren arrow & flash arrow
FLASHBACKS: The Space Phantom explains to Captain America that he'll erase the memory that Steve Rogers is Captain America from everyone on Earth (Av #107, '73). Hawkeye leaves the Avengers (Av #109, '73) and joins the Defenders (Def #7, '73). Hawkeye sees Captain America change into Steve Rogers.
SYNOPSIS: Steve Rogers is out shopping with Sharon Carter when they are attacked by the Golden Archer. The Archer seems aware of Steve's identity as Captain America and proclaims that he shall meet Steve Rogers three more times, and kill him on the final meeting. Falcon confronts Morgan, warning the criminal he's out to put him in jail. The Archer attacks Steve again at Starlin Gym and escapes. In San Rafael, California, Scar Turpin of the Sickle Cycle gang declares himself to be the new Captain America. Hiding in the shadows, Steve confronts Peggy Carter as Captain America, telling Peggy that she must move on. The Archer attacks and escapes again. Turpin's only outing as Cap ends when he's overpowered by muggers. Meanwhile, Steve tricks and traps the Golden Archer, only to discover he's actually his fellow Avenger Hawkeye in disguise! Hawkeye merely wished to help Steve remember the excitement of fighting crime, and to remind him that his skills are still needed. Hawkeye gives Steve the idea to become a new kind of hero...
NOTE: "Let's Rap With Cap" contains LOC from Ralph Macchio, future Marvel writer/editor.

CAPTAIN AMERICA #180 (December 1974)

"The Coming of the Nomad!" (18 pages)

CREDITS: Steve Englehart (writer), Sal Buscema (pencils), Vince Colletta (inks), Tom Orzechoswki (letters), Linda Lessmann (colors), Roy Thomas (editor), Gil Kane (c pencils), Frank Giacoia (c inks), Gaspar Saladino (c letters)

FEATURE CHARACTERS: Nomad (Steve Rogers, also as Captain America in rfb & movie), Falcon

SUPPORTING CAST: Sharon Carter, Roscoe Simons

VILLAINS: Serpent Squad: Cobra, Eel (both last in Cap #163, '73), Princess Python (Zelda DuBois, also in pfb, last in DD #118, '75) & her python, Viper (Ophelia Sarkissian, also in rfb & pfb, last in Cap #113, '69 as Madame Hydra, chr last in Cap #181, '75 fb); Viper (Dixon, last in Cap #175, '74, dies); Warlord Krang (last in Sub #33, '71, chr last in Cap #181, '75 fb), Hugh Jones (Roxxon Oil President, 1st but chr last in IM:IA #2, '98)

OTHER CHARACTERS: Harrison Carter (last in Cap #163, '73, last bts in Cap #167, '73, last app), police Commissioner Feingold (last in Cap #159, '72, next in Def #39, '76), Smithers (last in Cap #163, '73), Strand theater employees & patrons, 3 U.S. Marshalls (die), taxi driver, commuters, prison guard; Bucky (Jones), Hawkeye, Hydra troops, Space Phantom (prev 4 in rfb)

LOCATIONS/ITEMS: New York inc Sharon's apartment, Washington DC inc Strand movie theater showing Captain America movie, Virginia inc Virginia State penitentiary, Georgetown warehouse w/Viper's hideout, Carter family estate & shoe store, Sam's office; taxi (license plate # "CA 180"), U.S. Marshall's prison transport, Viper's toxic arrow, Serpent Crown of Lemuria

FLASHBACKS: Hawkeye gives Steve the idea to become a new type of super hero (Cap #179, '74). Cap fights Hydra and Madame Hydra (Cap #113, '69). The Space Phantom hurls Madame Hydra into Limbo (Av #107, '73 fb). The former Madame Hydra recruits Princess Python to join the reformed Serpent Squad (p).

SYNOPSIS: Steve Rogers makes his way across town, now thrilled with the idea of becoming a different kind of super hero. Meanwhile, the former Madame Hydra frees Viper from a prison transport, only to kill him and claim his costume and identity for herself. Her accomplice, Princess Python, frees Cobra and the Eel from prison. At Sharon Carter's apartment, Steve resigns from the police force and tells Sharon his exciting news, but Sharon expresses dismay. The new Viper reforms the Serpent Squad, forcing Cobra to respect her authority. Steve visits the Carter family estate in Virginia. He creates a new uniform, and comes up with the new name, "Nomad". Meanwhile, Falcon runs into Starlin Gym employee Roscoe, who informs the hero that he's going to become the next Captain America. Falcon urges Roscoe to drop the idea. In Washington DC on his first mission, Nomad encounters the Serpent Squad as they kidnap Roxxon Oil Executive Hugh Jones. Nomad is winning the fight until he trips on his own cape, allowing the villains to escape. Later, at the Serpent Society's hideout, Viper reveals she's formed an alliance with Warlord Krang, who possesses the Serpent Crown!

NOTE: Credits contains a "Special Thanks" to Martha 'Duke' Dukeshire, Steve Englehart's girlfriend at the time, for coming up with the name "Nomad". Hugh Jones named in Cap #181, '75.

CAPTAIN AMERICA #181 (January 1975)

"The Mark of Madness!" (17 pages)

CREDITS: Steve Englehart (writer), Sal Buscema (pencils), Vince Colletta (inks), Artie Simek (letters), Linda Lessmann (colors), Roy Thomas (editor), Gil Kane (c pencils), Joe Sinnott (c inks), Gaspar Saladino (c letters)

FEATURE CHARACTERS: Nomad (next in Av #131, '75), Falcon (next in MTU #30, '75)

GUEST STARS: Sub-Mariner (last in GSDef #3, '75, next in GSSVTU #2, '75), Nick Fury (last in FF #154, '75, next in KZ #4, '74), Dum Dum Dugan (last in Cap #175, '74, next in DD #122, '75), Gabe Jones (last in Cap #178, '74)

SUPPORTING CAST: Roscoe Simons (also as Captain America), Redwing (next in MTU #30, '75), Sharon Carter, Peggy Carter (last in Cap #179, '74)

VILLAINS: Serpent Squad: Viper (also in fb between and Cap #180, '74; next bts in Av #131, '75), Eel (next in Def #36, '76), Princess Python (next in PM #24, '75) & her python, Cobra (next bts in Av #131, '75); Warlord Krang (next in SVTU #13, '77, also in fb between Sub #33, '71 and Cap #180, '74), Hugh Jones (next bts in Cap #183, '75, next in Cap #185, '75)

OTHER CHARACTERS: Smithers (next in Cap #184, '75), Roxxon Oil platform workers, Roxxon security guards

LOCATIONS/ITEMS: Washington D.C. inc Lincoln & Washington Memorials, Carter family Virginia estate, Harlem, Krang's base, Pacific Ocean, Roxxon oil platform, SHIELD HQ; Namor's vessel, Serpent Crown of Lemuria, Roxxon helicopter & guns

FLASHBACKS: Krang finds the Serpent Crown on the ocean floor and upon donning it has a vision of Viper, whom he soon contacts, forming an alliance.

SYNOPSIS: Nomad visits the Lincoln Memorial only to be confronted by Namor, who believes that Nomad knows Warlord Krang's location. Namor's short temper leads to battle until Nomad reveals his true identity. Meanwhile, Krang uses the Serpent Crown to force Hugh Jones to broadcast a message instructing Roxxon Oil to follow Krang's demands. Nomad and Namor overhear the broadcast and quickly conclude Krang is after a Roxxon oil platform over the lost continent of Lemuria. Meanwhile, Sharon stops by the Carter family estate looking for Steve. She becomes angry when he's not there. In Harlem, Roscoe confronts Falcon as Captain America. Roscoe tries to show off his skills but it interrupted by Peggy Carter, who mistakes him for the real Cap. Roscoe leaves to avoid confrontation. The Serpent Society attacks the Roxxon oil platform, ordering Jones to reverse the oil flow to cause Lemuria to rise from the depths. Nomad arrives and stops the reversed oil flow and captures Krang, but Viper and the Serpent Squad flee with the Serpent Crown. Nomad punches a Roxxon security guard when they dismiss his role in rescuing Jones.

NOTE: "Let's Rap With Cap" contains LOC from Mark Gruenwald, future editor/writer for Marvel Comics. This issue includes Marvel Value Stamp #46 – Mysterio.

CAPTAIN AMERICA #182 (February 1975)

"Inferno!" (17 pages)

CREDITS: Steve Englehart (writer), Frank Robbins (pencils), Joe Giella (inks), Tom Orzechowski (letters), Bill Mantlo (colors), Len Wein (editor), Ron Wilson, John Romita (c pencils), Frank Giacoia (c inks), Gaspar Saladino (c letters)
FEATURE CHARACTERS: Nomad (next in MTU #84, '72 fb), Falcon (next in Cap #350/2, '89 fb)
GUEST STAR: Gabe Jones
SUPPORTING CAST: Roscoe Simons (as Captain America, chr next in Cap #350/2, '89 fb), Sharon Carter (next in Cap #184, '75), Peggy Carter, Redwing
VILLAINS: Red Skull (last in Cap #148, '72, chr last in Cap #185, '75 fb, chr next in Cap #350/2, '89 fb) & his men, Serpent Squad: Cobra (last bts in Av #131, '75, next in DD #142, '77), Viper (last bts in Av #131, '75, chr next in MTU #84, '79 fb, next bts in MTU #57, '77, next in MTU #83, '79)
OTHER CHARACTERS: Dave Cox (last in Cap #163, '73, next in Cap #184, '75), police (Jim named), paramedics, firefighters (bts off-panel); Mr. Hyde (in Cobra's imagination)
LOCATIONS/ITEMS: The Carters' Virginia estate, New York inc First National Bank, abandoned building; Police guns, handcuffs & tear gas grenade, Cobra & Viper's machine guns, Serpent Crown of Lemuria, Skull's men's laser & suitcases w/counterfeit money, Skull's blaster
SYNOPSIS: Nomad tries to end the standoff between the police and the Serpent Squad, but the police handcuff Nomad for his own protection. Determined to die in a blaze of glory, Viper guns down the police. In Virginia, Sharon, upset with Steve for returning to crimefighting, runs into Dave Cox. Nomad frees himself and breaks into the Squad's fortification as it catches fire from a grenade exploding near a broken gas line. Cobra tries to fight Nomad to escape, but Viper shoots Cobra for insubordination. Nomad is separated from Viper by a fire hose as the building collapses. Cobra is carted off to a hospital while Viper seems lost as the Serpent Crown falls unnoticed into a sewer. Elsewhere, Falcon partners with the new Captain America in order to work on convincing him to quit. Witnessing a bank robbery, the heroes take down the crooks before being ambushed by their leader, the Red Skull.
NOTE: "Let's Rap With Cap" contains LOC from Dean Mullaney, future co-founder/publisher of Eclipse Comics. This issue includes Marvel Value Stamp #36 – Ancient One.

CAPTAIN AMERICA #183 (March 1975)

"Nomad: No More!" (18 pages)

CREDITS: Steve Englehart (writer), Frank Robbins (pencils), Frank Giacoia (inks), Tom Orzechowski (letters), Stan Goldberg (colors), Len Wein (editor) Gil Kane (c pencils), Joe Sinnott (c inks), Gaspar Saladino (c letters)
FEATURE CHARACTERS: Captain America (also as Nomad), Falcon
GUEST STARS: Beast (last in Cap #175, '74, next in Av #137, '75 fb), Gabe Jones
SUPPORTING CAST: Roscoe Simons (as Captain America, chr last in Cap #350/2, '89 fb, corpse only, last app), Leila Taylor (last in Cap #178, '74), Peggy Carter, Redwing
VILLAINS: Red Skull (bts, killed & crucified Roscoe, chr last in Cap #350/2, '89 fb), Gamecock (Carlos Cabrera, chicken-themed villain, 1st, next in Cap #371, '90) & his Harlem Brood Gang (only app), Morgan (last in Cap #179, '74, next in PPSSM #4, '77) & his men, Hugh Jones (bts, ordered attack on Nomad, last in Cap #181, '75, next in Cap #185, '75), Roxxon trooper
OTHER CHARACTERS: Figaro (last in Cap #157, '73, last app), protestors, bank customers, police, bystanders
LOCATIONS/ITEMS: Harlem inc Sam's office, Morgan's office, "Federal" Bank, Luke Cage's theater office & American Savings Bank, Xavier's School for Gifted Youngsters; Roxxon bazooka, protestor's signs
SYNOPSIS: Returning to New York, Nomad battles Gamecock, a villain sent by Morgan to kill Falcon. The fight ends in a stalemate when an unseen assailant fires a bazooka at the combatants. Gamecock flees, leaving Nomad to search for the missing Falcon. Nomad questions Leila Taylor, then encounters protestors praising Viper. Nomad tries to explain her villainous intentions but retreats when the mob attacks. Nomad questions Peggy Carter, Gabe Jones and Morgan to no avail. Nomad encounters chaos at a bank, but calms the crowd by reminding them that their savings are insured, despite being switched with counterfeit bills. After finding Luke Cage's office empty, Nomad calls Xavier's school looking for Falcon, but Beast doesn't know his location. Redwing finds Nomad and takes him to Roscoe's crucified corpse and the nearby Falcon. Falcon tells Nomad the Red Skull is responsible. Nomad realizes that he still has a role to serve as a symbol for his country, even if the country's leaders are corrupt. Overcoming his bitterness, Steve re-dons the Captain America uniform, ready to face the Skull.
NOTE: An editor's note on the last page notes that the date this issue came out is the 34th anniversary of the creation of Captain America by Jack Kirby and Joe Simon. Roxxon revealed to be behind the bazooka attack in Av #141, '75. Gamecock's real name revealed in OHMU #4, '06.

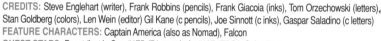

"Captain America vs. the Aliens" (1 page)
CREDITS: Unknown
FEATURE CHARACTER: Captain America (last in Cap #221, '78, next in MTU #71, '78)
VILLAINS: The Masters of the Outer Galaxy (next bts in Thor Meets the Ricochet Monster" Hostess ad, '80) inc commander
OTHER CHARACTERS: Three picnicking kids
LOCATIONS/ITEMS: Picnic fields; alien spaceship, picnic baskets, Hostess Twinkies Snack Cakes
SYNOPSIS: Three teenage picnickers alert Captain America to the arrival of alien invaders in the picnic fields. As Cap cuts a swathe through them, the aliens wonder how an apparently backward species can be beating them, or have cakes as delicious as the Twinkies the picnickers left behind. Watching Cap subduing his men, the alien commander believes their plans defeated, but another alien tells him all is not lost, and whispers something inaudible. The aliens swiftly depart.
NOTE: Appeared in various Gold Key titles, May & September 1978. The aliens' back-up plan appears to have been to send the Ricochet Monster, who Thor battles in a subsequent Hostess strip.

CAPTAIN AMERICA #184 (April 1975)

"Cap's Back!" (18 pages)

CREDITS: Steve Englehart (writer), Herb Trimpe (pencils), Frank Giacoia, Michael Esposito (inks), Tom Orzechowski (letters), George Roussos (colors), Len Wein (editor), Gil Kane (c pencils), John Romita (c inks), Gaspar Saladino (c letters)
FEATURE CHARACTERS: Captain America (also in rfb, also as Nomad in rfb), Falcon
GUEST STAR: Gabe Jones
SUPPORTING CAST: Sharon Carter (last in Cap #182, '75), Leila Taylor (next in Cap #188, '75), Peggy Carter, Redwing
VILLAIN: Red Skull (also in pre-recorded message)
OTHER CHARACTERS: Dave Cox (last in Cap #182, '75), Smithers (last in Cap #181, '75, last app), Herbert Glass (1st member of the Federal Open Market Committee, dies), G. Lawton Sargent (2nd member of the Federal Open Market Committee, dies), SHIELD agents, CBS reporters (Reuters named), Captain America supporters, police, Red Skull's raven; Hawkeye (as Golden Archer), Number One, Cobra, Viper (prev 4 only in rfb)
LOCATIONS/ITEMS: Abandoned warehouse, Sam's Harlem apartment, Washington DC inc Capital building, Carter family estate, Sargent family lighthouse; Glass' limo, Red Skull's jetpack, gun w/Dust of Death & Chopin's "Funeral March" recording
FLASHBACKS: Number One kills himself (Cap #175, '74). Cap clutches his head in grief (Cap #176, '74). Hawkeye, as the Golden Archer, hunts Steve (Cap #179, '74). Nomad fights the Serpent Squad (Cap #180, '74).
SYNOPSIS: Acting on information from Falcon, Captain America searches an abandoned warehouse only to find a prerecorded message left by the Skull. After interviewing with reporters, Cap returns to Falcon, who reveals the Skull warned of an attack in Washington D.C. tomorrow at noon. The next day, Cap and Falcon are greeted by a gathered crowd outside the Capital building as news builds of Captain America's return. Government official Herbert Glass arrives only to be slain by the Skull's Dust of Death. Red Skull taunts that his next victim, fellow bureaucrat G. Lawton Sargent, will be killed at midnight tonight. Cap and Falcon meet with Sharon and Dave Cox, only for Sharon to express her disgust in Steve's return as Captain America. Cap and Falcon arrive at Sargent's home where they encounter Peggy Carter and Gabe Jones, on assignment from SHIELD. After an apology and a moment of understanding between Peggy and Cap, the heroes patrol the grounds, only for the Red Skull to attack Peggy briefly before seemingly retreating. At midnight, the power goes out inside Sargent's home, but when the power is restored, they find Sargent dead at their feet!
NOTE: Red Skull notes this is the 30th anniversary of Hitler's death; this was true at time of publication. "Let's Rap With Cap" contains LOC from Dean Mullaney, future co-founder/publisher of Eclipse Comics.

CAPTAIN AMERICA #185 (May 1975)

"Scream The Scarlet Skull!" (18 pages)

CREDITS: Steve Englehart (writer), Frank Robbins, Sal Buscema (pencils), Frank Giacoia (inks), Tom Orzechowski (letters), Stan Goldberg (colors), Len Wein (editor), Gil Kane (c pencils), Frank Giacoia (c inks), Gaspar Saladino (c letters)
FEATURE CHARACTERS: Captain America (also in fb during Cap #148, '72), Falcon (both also in rfb)
GUEST STARS: Gabe Jones (also in Skull's thoughts)
SUPPORTING CAST: Redwing (next in Cap #189, '75, also in rfb), Peggy Carter (also in Skull's thoughts), Sharon Carter
VILLAINS: Red Skull (also in fb between Cap #148, '72 & Cap #182, '75, also in Cap's & Skull's thoughts) & his henchmen (Henzel & Jordl named, Henzel dies), Hugh Jones (last in Cap #181, '75, last bts in Cap #183, '75)

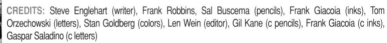

OTHER CHARACTERS: Oscar Brenner (member of the Federal Open Market Committee, dies), Dave Cox, Hugh Jones' driver, Georgetown police, 5th Sleeper (in fb during Cap #148, '72); G. Lawton Sargent, Cobra (both in rfb only); Batroc, Baron Zemo, AIM agent, Nazi soldier, Moonstone, Dr. Faustus, 4th Sleeper robot (prev 7 in nightmare only)
LOCATIONS/ITEMS: Oscar Brenner's Georgetown home, Red Skull's secret base, David Cox's house, Roxxon oil platform (in rfb); Red Skull's acetylene torch & cat o' nine tails, Red Skull's henchmen's jet packs & guns, Brenner's pipe & Red Skull's duplicate pipe w/Dust of Death, Hugh Jones' limo
FLASHBACKS: Captain America lights a candle in the darkened G. Lawton Sargent's home, only to discover Sargent has died from the Dust of Death (Cap #184, '75). Nomad defeats Cobra (Cap #181, '75). Red Skull survives his fall from the 5th Sleeper by grabbing a wire and swinging out of sight.
SYNOPSIS: Captain America awakens from a nightmare while Red Skull celebrates the continued success of his plan. The Skull orders that romantic couple Gabe Jones and Peggy Carter to be captured, and kills his henchman for questioning his orders. Later, Cap, Falcon, Peggy, and Gabe guard Oscar Brenner, the next government official targeted for assassination. When Red Skull's men burst in and kidnap Gabe and Peggy, Cap wonders why they left Oscar Brenner alive. Brenner lights his pipe to find it's been switched with a duplicate covered with the Dust of Death, killing him. In Virginia, Sharon cries on Dave's shoulder as his feelings for her grow deeper. While the Skull tortures Gabe and Peggy, Cap and Falcon are approached by Roxxon CEO Hugh Jones, who wishes to repay Cap for his help in rescuing him from the Serpent Squad. Jones tells Cap where the Red Skull's base is, but leaves before revealing how he knew Cap was Nomad. Cap and Falcon quickly dispatch Red Skull's henchmen. Suddenly, the Skull voices a command and Falcon attacks Captain America.
NOTE: "Let's Rap With Cap" contains LOC from Ralph Macchio, future writer/editor for Marvel Comics.

CAPTAIN AMERICA #186 (June 1975)

"Mind Cage!" (18 pages)

CREDITS: Steve Englehart (plot, script), John Warner (script), Frank Robbins (pencils), Mike Esposito (inks), Dave Hunt (letters), Marv Wolfman (colors), Len Wein (editor), Gaspar Saladino (c letters)
FEATURE CHARACTERS: Captain America (also in rfb, also as Red Skull in rfb), Falcon (also in fb between Cap #277/2, '83 fb & Cap #117, '69 as Snap Wilson, also in rfb)
GUEST STAR: Gabe Jones
SUPPORTING CAST: Redwing (also in rfb, only in fb to 1st chr app before Cap #117, '69), Sharon Carter (also in rfb, next in Cap #202, '76), Peggy Carter
VILLAINS: Red Skull (also in rfb, also as Captain America in rfb, also in fb during Cap #117, '69, next in IM #74, '75 fb) & his henchmen, Jaz (Los Angeles crime lord, 1st, only in fb, next in Cap #191, '75), plane pilot (in fb, dies), Hugh Jones (bts, ordered SHIELD transmission interception, chr next in WoSM Ann #5/6, '89 fb, next in Av #141, '75), Roxxon troops
OTHER CHARACTERS: Dave Cox (next in Cap #293, '84), Dade citizen, Sam's birds, Los Angeles citizens (prev 3 in fb), Sharon's horse; Franz Cadavus, Jurgen "Iron Hand" Hauptmann, Eric Gruning, Yellowjacket, police (prev 6 in rfb only)
LOCATIONS/ITEMS: Red Skull's secret base, Isle of Exiles, Harlem, Dade city limits, Los Angeles, Rio De Janeiro (prev 5 in fb); cosmic cube, Dade citizen's shotgun, Jaz's plane, (prev 3 in fb), Red Skull's Dust of Death
FLASHBACKS: Red Skull assaults Captain America with the Cosmic Cube (Cap #114, '69) and trades appearances with Cap (Cap #115, '69). Cap, as the Skull, tries to convince Sharon Carter of his real identity and evades the authorities (Cap #116, '69). Cap is transported to the Island of Exiles, where he battles the Exiles (Cap #117, '69). Cap talks Sam Wilson into becoming Falcon, and together they battle the Exiles (Cap #118, '69). Cap and Falcon defeat Red Skull (Cap #119, '69). At age 15, Sam Wilson leaves his home in Harlem to travel across the country. He arrives in Los Angeles at age 18 under the name Snap Wilson, where he becomes a gangster working for local crime lord Jaz. Jaz sends Snap on an errand flight to Rio De Janeiro, and while flying back to the States Snap decides to seize control of the plane to keep the crime lord's fortune for himself. The ensuing fight for the cockpit ends with the plane crashing off the Isle of Exiles. As Cap, Red Skull uses the cosmic cube to alter Snap's personality.
SYNOPSIS: Captain America begs Falcon to fight, but Falcon dances like a chicken at Red Skull's command. The Skull explains that Falcon is his puppet. In Virginia Dave Cox tells Sharon he's leaving, to avoid a relationship he knows she doesn't want. Red Skull orders Falcon to kill Captain America. While the partners battle, Peggy and Gabe escape their bonds and radio SHIELD for help, but the call is intercepted by unseen adversaries. As Peggy and Gabe share an intimate moment, Cap overpowers Falcon. Suddenly troops storm the base, attacking the Skull's men. Red Skull unleashes his Dust of Death throughout the base, killing both the attackers and his men. Falcon collapses while the Skull flees. Peggy, Gabe, and Cap ponder what to do with the comatose Falcon.
NOTE: The mysterious troops revealed to be Roxxon employees in Av #141, '75. Cap #277/2, '83 reveals Sam Wilson suffers from multiple personality disorder, the criminal Snap being his defense mechanism, and that Red Skull reverted Snap's personality back into the original Sam personality here.

GIANT-SIZE CAPTAIN AMERICA #1 (1975)

"Captain America" (10 pages)

CREDITS: Gil Kane (c pencils), Mike Esposito (c inks), Gaspar Saladino (c letters), for other credits see original entries
NOTE: Reprinted from ToS #59/2, '64. Final panel's bottom caption blacked out & replaced with "The End."

2ND STORY: "The Army of Assassins Strikes!" (10 pages)
NOTE: Reprinted from ToS #60/2, '64. Last two sentences of final panel caption cut; caption panel resized and relettered. "The End" relettered and re-placed.

3RD STORY: "The Strength of the Sumo!" (10 pages)
NOTE: Reprinted from ToS #61/2, '65. Final panel's bottom caption cut. "The End" relettered and re-placed. Story followed by "A Marvel Masterwork Pin-Up: Captain America" (1 page, John Romita, art).

4TH STORY: "Breakout in Cell Block 10!" (10 pages)
NOTE: Reprinted from ToS #62/2, '65. Final panel's caption replaced with "The End."

5TH STORY: "The Origin of Captain America!" (10 pages)
NOTE: Reprinted from ToS #63/2, '65. Page 10 panel 6 cut and replaced with reprint of Cap #192, '75 cover with caption. "The End" added to page 10 panel 5.

CAPTAIN AMERICA #187 (July 1975)

"The Madness Maze!" (18 pages)

CREDITS: John Warner (writer), Frank Robbins (pencils) Frank Chiaramonte (inks), Charlotte Jetter (letters), George Roussos (colors), Len Wein (editor), Gil Kane (c pencils), John Romita Sr. (c inks), Gaspar Saladino (c letters)
FEATURE CHARACTERS: Captain America, Falcon
GUEST STAR: Gabe Jones
SUPPORTING CAST: Peggy Carter
VILLAINS: Druid (Dredmund Cromwell, last in ST #145, '66, chr last in DF:Av 2.4, '99 fb) & his robed acolytes, Alchemoid (powered by unstable alchemical reactions, 1st)
LOCATIONS/ITEMS: Red Skull's abandoned base, Druid's Madness Maze & Arena of the Ancients; Druid's oblong flying crafts, artificial sulphuric creatures, vat of corrosive liquid, video monitors, flying egg-shaped robots & geometric generators

SYNOPSIS: Captain America, Gabe, and Peggy gather round the comatose Falcon, when Cap is suddenly whisked away by a mysterious flying craft and deposited in a giant maze. A booming voice welcomes Cap to the Madness Maze, telling him that when he reaches the maze's center he'll die. As Cap moves through the maze he is attacked by a trio of artificial creatures that he carves up with his shield. Cap works through the labyrinth and is followed by a shadowy figure. The walls seemingly move on their own, shepherding Cap in a specific direction and almost dropping him in a vat of acid. Nearing the maze's center, Cap is attacked by his pursuer who grabs Cap's wrist, burning his glove, before escaping. Captain America is attacked by flying robots, which he quickly destroys. Cap enters a large laboratory filled with robed acolytes who attack him. Cap is eventually knocked unconscious by an electric jolt. Cap awakens in the Arena of the Ancients, surrounded by large geometric shapes. Druid, surrounded by his acolytes, announces his presence and heralds the arrival of the Alchemoid.

NOTE: "Let's Rap With Cap" contains LOC from Dean Mullaney, future co-founder of Eclipse Comics, and Robert Rodi, future comic writer & novelist.

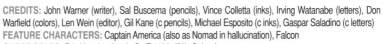

CAPTAIN AMERICA #188 (August 1975)

"Druid-War" (18 pages)

CREDITS: John Warner (writer), Sal Buscema (pencils), Vince Colletta (inks), Irving Watanabe (letters), Don Warfield (colors), Len Wein (editor), Gil Kane (c pencils), Michael Esposito (c inks), Gaspar Saladino (c letters)
FEATURE CHARACTERS: Captain America (also as Nomad in hallucination), Falcon
GUEST STARS: Eric Koening (last in SgtF #100, '72), Gabe Jones
SUPPORTING CAST: Leila Taylor (last in Cap #184, '75, next in Cap #191, '75), Contessa Val Fontaine (last in DD #123, '75), Peggy Carter
VILLAINS: Druid (also on monitor, next in Cap #256, '81) & his robed acolytes, Alchemoid (dies, last app)
OTHER CHARACTERS: Jeff Cochren (SHIELD field operations co-director, 1st), SHIELD agents (Bill & Russ named) & orderly; Red Skull (hallucination)

LOCATIONS/ITEMS: Druid's Arena of the Ancients, SHIELD hospital inc ward 8 w/Falcon's room; SHIELD Helicarrier, tranquilizer gun, jet-packs, blasters & helicopter, Druid's geometric generators, alchemy cylinders, monitors & egg ship

SYNOPSIS: Captain America fights Alchemoid, just barely keeping ahead of his attacks, while Druid and his acolytes watch. Meanwhile, Sam Wilson hallucinates in a SHIELD hospital. Leila Taylor is brought in for SHIELD questioning to Gabe and Peggy's bewilderment. Cap deduces the large geometric shapes surrounding the battleground are powering Alchemoid and destroys enough of them to cause Alchemoid to self-destruct. Meanwhile, Gabe and Peggy approach SHIELD field operations co-director Jeff Cochren over his handling of Falcon as Val Fontaine and Eric Koenig close in on Druid's location. Cap turns his attentions on Druid, angered over Druid's lack of concern for Alchemoid's death. Druid attacks with his alchemy cylinders but Cap plows through Druid and his men. Just as Cap defeats Druid, the villain is whisked away by his ship and escapes. A SHIELD task force arrives and helps Cap corral Druid's acolytes. Angry and tired, Cap's only concern is to get some rest and a ride to Falcon's side.

NOTE: Features a Twinkies ad starring Captain Marvel and Nitro. Normally blonde, Koenig's hair is colored black here.

CAPTAIN AMERICA #189 (September 1975)

"Arena for a Fallen Hero!" (18 pages)

CREDITS: Tony Isabella (writer), Frank Robbins (pencils) Frank Chiaramonte (inks), Karen Mantlo (letters), Dianne Buscema (colors), Len Wein (editor), Gil Kane (c pencils), Michael Esposito (c inks), Gaspar Saladino (c letters)
FEATURE CHARACTERS: Captain America (also in Cap's thoughts), Falcon (also as Red Skull, Yellow Claw's giant spider & Baron Zemo, also in Cap's thoughts)
GUEST STAR: Gabe Jones (bts, investigating Falcon's past, next in Cap #191, '75), Eric Koenig
SUPPORTING CAST: Redwing (last in Cap #185 '75), Peggy Carter (bts, investigating Falcon's past, next in Cap #191, '75), Contessa Val Fontaine
VILLAIN: Nightshade (also as Enchantress, last in Cap #164, '73, chr last in Cap #190, '75, fb)
OTHER CHARACTERS: Jeff Cochren, other SHIELD agents; Druid, Red Skull & his men (prev 3 in Cap's thoughts); Masters of Evil: Black Knight, Hellhorse, Enchantress, Executioner, Melter, Radioactive Man (prev 6 as illusions)
LOCATIONS/ITEMS: SHIELD HQ inc arena w/observation booth; Cochren's gun, SHIELD spotlights & guns

SYNOPSIS: Eric Koenig stops Captain America from visiting Falcon, and Jeff Cochren tells Cap he must fight Falcon to the death to free Falcon from Red Skull's mind control. Cap refuses to fight the zombie-like Falcon, but suddenly Red Skull appears. Cap attacks the Skull, but Falcon falls to the ground in the villain's place. Cap begs Cochren to stop the treatment, but the Yellow Claw's giant spider attacks Cap. When Cap kicks the beast, Falcon falls to the ground in its place. Eric and Val protest Cochren's "therapy" but Cochren pulls rank on them. Cap is attacked by the Masters of Evil and blows up Radioactive Man, but to the SHIELD agents, it looks like Cap is battling thin air. When a woman, who appears to Cap as the Enchantress, enters the arena, Val insists the fight be stopped, but Cochren pulls a gun. "Enchantress" seduces Cap, but when an amnesiac Falcon approaches, Cap attacks, thinking he's Baron Zemo. Eric knocks out Cochren as Falcon directs Redwing to attack Cap. Realizing that Cochren's "therapy" broke Red Skull's control over Falcon, Cap stands still, forcing Falcon to divert Redwing. Cap and Falcon reconcile in time to face off against Nightshade, who has drugged several SHIELD agents to attack Cap and Falcon.

NOTE: Nightshade goes by "Deadly Nightshade" here. "Let's Rap With Cap" contains LoC from future comic critic, historian and OHMU researcher, Peter Sanderson.

CAPTAIN AMERICA #190 (October 1975)

"Nightshade is Deadlier the Second Time Around!" (18 pages)

CREDITS: Tony Isabella (writer), Frank Robbins (pencils), Vincent Colletta (inks), Irving David Hunt (letters), Michele Wolfman (colors), Marv Wolfman (editor), Gil Kane (c pencils), Joe Sinnott (c inks), Gaspar Saladino (c letters)
FEATURE CHARACTERS: Captain America (also in rfb), Falcon (also in rfb as Falcon-Wolf)
GUEST STAR: Eric Koening (next in RH #4/2, '77)
SUPPORTING CAST: Contessa Val Fontaine, Redwing
VILLAIN: Nightshade (also in fb between Cap #164, '73 & Cap #189, '75, also in rfb, chr next in PMIF #53, '78 fb, next in PMIF #51, '78)
OTHER CHARACTERS: Jeff Cochren, other SHIELD agents (others in rfb); Nightshade's werewolves (in fb & rfb, last in Cap #164, '73); Nick Fury (in rfb), Yellow Claw (in Nightshade's thoughts); Tony Stark (mentioned, built "Wild Bill" robot, see NOTE)
LOCATIONS/ITEMS: SHIELD HQ inc documents room & solarium; Maryland inc Grimlock Prison (in fb & rfb); Nightshade's headband (also in fb), SHIELD guns, helicopter (both in rfb), machine pistols, "Wild Bill" (SHIELD security robot, last in ST #142, '66, last app) & flying wedge (multiple-man blaster, last in ST #140, '66)
FLASHBACKS: Fury and his SHIELD agents storm Grimrock prison while Captain America battles Nightshade's werewolves. Sensing defeat at the hands of SHIELD and Cap, Nightshade leads her werewolves in a suicide jump (Cap #164, '73). Nightshade survives the jump by opening a hidden escape route with her remote control headband.
SYNOPSIS: Falcon reacts instinctively to Captain America's commands, allowing the heroes to tumble the Nightshade-controlled SHIELD agents and retreat to regroup. The heroes are attacked by the "Wild Bill" robot, but Redwing is able to distract it long enough for Cap to destroy it. Meanwhile, Contessa heads to the documents room to read up on Nightshade to find a weakness. A SHIELD contingent attack Cap and Falcon with the flying wedge, and when Falcon destroys the weapon his memory is restored of both Sam and Snap Wilson's lives. Contessa has the heroes lead their foes to the solarium where the intense light inside disrupts Nightshade's powers. Nightshade is captured and Cap is relieved to have his partner back, but Falcon worries about paying for his criminal acts.
NOTE: Tony Stark created the SHIELD security robot in ST #142, '66. Features in-house ads to join FOOM and purchase 12 comics. "Let's Rap With Cap" contains LOC from Dean Mullaney, future co-founder of Eclipse Comics.

CAPTAIN AMERICA #191 (November 1975)

"The Trial of the Falcon!" (18 pages)

CREDITS: Tony Isabella (plot), Bill Mantlo (writer), Frank Robbins (pencils), D. Bruce Berry (inks), Karen Mantlo (letters), David Cohen (colors), Marv Wolfman (editor), Sal Buscema (c pencils), Frank Giacoia (c inks), Irving Watanabe (c letters)
FEATURE CHARACTERS: Captain America (also in Av #137, '75), Falcon (next in Cap #25, '07 fb, Av #146, '76, Cap #193, '76) (both also in symbolic splash page)
GUEST STARS: Iron Man (during Av #137, '75), Nick Fury (last in DD #123, '75, next bts in MTU #36, '75, next in CB #15, '76), Gabe Jones (last in Cap #188, '75, last bts in Cap #189, '75, next in Hulk #199, '76),
SUPPORTING CAST: Peggy Carter (last in Cap #188, '75, last bts in Cap #189, '75, next in Cap #231, '79), Leila Taylor (next in Cap #193, '76)
Contessa Val Fontaine (next in MS #31, '76), Redwing (chr next in Cap #25, '07 fb, next in Cap #217, '78), Leila Taylor (next in Cap #193, '76)
VILLAINS: Stilt-Man (last in DD #102, '73, next in BG #4, '76), Trapster (also in rfb, last in GR #13, '75, next in FF #176, '76), Jaz (last in Cap #186, '75 fb, last app) & his men (Brother Raymond named), Hollywood Vine (Jaz's associate)
OTHER CHARACTERS: Jeff Cochren (next bts in SW #13, '79), judge, stenographer (both also in symbolic splash page), prosecutor, bailiff, jury members, reporters (also on TV), SHIELD security, bystanders; Ghost Rider (Johnny Blaze, motorcyclist empowered by demon Zarathos, only in rfb)
LOCATIONS/ITEMS: Los Angeles High Court, SHIELD HQ; Cap's SHIELD priority badge, Trapster's anti-gravity disc & paste bombs, Stilt-Man's hydraulic suit & blaster
FLASHBACK: Ghost Rider battles Trapster, damaging his anti-gravity disc and leaving him stranded in mid-air (GR #13, '75).
SYNOPSIS: Jeff Cochren tries to arrest Falcon for his past crimes despite Gabe Jones and Peggy Carter's protests. Falcon tries to escape but Captain America stops him until Nick Fury arrives to take control of the situation. With Cap and Fury's assurances, Falcon agrees to stand trial in Los Angeles. Afterwards, Fury reinstates Cap's SHIELD security clearance. The media reports on Falcon's upcoming trial and Iron Man makes

a statement on behalf of the Avengers while Snap's former boss Jaz order's Falcon's death. Later, Stilt-Man comes across the still hovering Trapster and takes his weaponry. As Falcon is about to testify against his former associates, Stilt-Man attacks. The heroes eventually manage to topple Stilt-Man and defeat him, despite his advantage of Trapster's weapons. Later, the judge finds Falcon guilty of all charges, but suspends his sentence as long as he reports and proves himself to his parole officer, Nick Fury.

NOTE: Features a Hostess fruit pie ad starring Hulk, Abomination and Wendigo.

CAPTAIN AMERICA #192 (December 1975)

"Mad-Flight!" (18 pages)

CREDITS: Marv Wolfman (writer, editor), Frank Robbins (pencils), D. Bruce Berry (inks), Joe Rosen (letters), Michele Wolfman (colors), John Romita (c pencils), Frank Giacoia (c inks), Gaspar Saladino (c letters)
FEATURE CHARACTER: Captain America (next in Cap #215, '77 fb, Hulk #229, '78 fb, Av #141-144 & 147-149, Cap Ann #3, all '76, also in Cap's thoughts)
VILLAINS: Dr. Faustus (last in Cap #162, '73, chr last in Cap #236, '79 fb, chr next in Cap #224, '78, next in ASM #169, '77) & his men, Dr. Karla Sofen (Dr. Faustus' aide & psychiatrist, 1st but chr last in Tb #1, '97, chr next in Hulk #229, '78 fb, next in Hulk #228, '78 as Moonstone), criminals (Heels named)
OTHER CHARACTERS: Pilot, security guard, ticket agent, flight controllers (Frank named), police, bystanders; Tony Stark (mentioned, created sonic depressors); Falcon (next issue promo only)
LOCATIONS/ITEMS: Los Angeles Airport, New York inc World Trade Center, JFK Airport w/control tower; Cap's SHIELD priority badge, airplane, criminal's various guns, Heels' hollowed shoes & gun, blackjacks, knives, Faustus' sonic depressors, Liberty Bell (next issue promo only)
SYNOPSIS: Steve Rogers is unsure what to do about his partnership with Falcon. He decides to return to New York to clear his head and uses his SHIELD clearance to board a private charter flight. However, he learns the flight is full of criminals at the behest of Dr. Faustus in a bid to pull the ultimate raid on Manhattan. Captain America tries to stop them but is forced into a stalemate. He bides his time until he can strike again, falling victim to the mind-paralyzing sonic depressor weapons Faustus has attained. Cap quickly recovers and one of Faustus' men uses a gun, shattering a window and causing the plane to decompress. Faustus is blown out and Cap uses his shield to plug the hole long enough to land, radioing in a code to the control tower to have police waiting on the tarmac.
NOTE: Karla Sofen's surname and profession revealed in Hulk #228, '78. Cap's emergency code is "9-1-1." This issue includes Marvel Value Stamp #56 – Rawhide Kid. Features a Hostess fruit pie ad starring Hulk, Abomination & Wendigo, and an in-house ad for Marvel Treasury Editions.

CAPTAIN AMERICA ANNUAL #3 (1976)

"The Thing from the Black Hole Star!" (35 pages)

CREDITS: Jack Kirby (writer, pencils, editor), Frank Giacoia (co-inks, c inks), John Verpoorten (co-inks), Gaspar Saladino (letters), Janice Cohen (colors), Marv Wolfman (consulting editor), Irving Watanabe (c letters)
FEATURE CHARACTER: Captain America (next in Cap #25, '07 fb, Av #145-146, '76, CB #15-18, '76, CB #26, '77 fb, CB #20-27, '76-77, Cap #193, '76)
VILLAIN: The Captive ("the Thing from the Black Hole Star," Threkker, Epsiloni parasite, next in Q #14, '90, see NOTE)
OTHER CHARACTERS: Jim Hendricks (farmer, only app, dies), Galactic warship Commander, Troga (second-in-command), spaceship crew, Stalker & Combatron (alien monsters, both die), top-level security committee (John & General named)
LOCATIONS/ITEMS: Jim Hendricks' farm inc house & meadow, Earth orbit, outer space, Epsilon Four, Washington DC inc security committee room; the Captive's spaceship w/shock ray & cannon, Galactic warship w/heat ray, ionic cannon, & light-year sling, Combatron's capsule & pressure arm, Galactic assault vehicle w/Magnoids (alien robots) & their weapons
SYNOPSIS: Having been called by farmer Jim Hendricks to investigate a UFO that landed in his meadow, Cap encounters a monster within. Jim uses an alien shock ray on it then tells Cap he knows the spaceship came from a Black Hole star because the pilot is hiding at his house. In a warship in Earth orbit, Troga, an alien, reports to his Commander that Earthmen killed the Stalker they sent for the UFO's pilot. The Commander orders a Combatron sent. In Jim's house, Cap meets the pilot who calls himself "the Captive." He explains that he escaped from a black hole after a million year effort and that Galactic warships were sent to retrieve him. Soon after, outside, Cap battles the arriving Combatron, holding it off so long that the frustrated Commander ignites its self-destruct with a heat ray, then sends Magnoid robots instead. Seeing another ship landing, Cap sends the others to the Captive's spaceship, then watches as hundreds of Magnoids debark. After briefly battling the robots, Cap retreats to the Captive's ship. There he finds Jim dead, his life force stolen by the Captive. Mutating, the Captive tells of his race that terrorized the galaxy feeding on organic life until inorganic "neo-life" was created that defeated them. Believing himself the last of his species, the Captive plans to feed on all Earth life starting with Cap who, weakened, fends him off with his shield. The Magnoids enter the spaceship but the Captive grows in power and size. Cap knocks him down with his shield and the Magnoids swarm over him and bind him. The Galactic ship slings the Captive and his spaceship into the heart of Epsilon Four just as that star goes nova. Later, Cap reports the incident to a top-level security committee who choose to keep it quiet to prevent any panic.
NOTE: The Captive revealed as an Epsiloni in OHMU #3, '83. His name, Threkker, is revealed in Starb #1, '94. The Commander may also be a King as Troga refers to him as "Sire."

CAPTAIN AMERICA #193 (January 1976)

"The Madbomb Screamer in the Brain!" (18 pages)

CREDITS: Jack Kirby (writer, pencils, editor), Frank Giacoia (inks), John Costanza (letters), Janice Cohen (colors), John Romita (c inks), Gaspar Saladino (c letters)
FEATURE CHARACTERS: Captain America, Falcon
SUPPORTING CAST: Leila Taylor (next in Cap #201, '76)
VILLAINS: Royalist Forces of America inc William Taurey (Royalist Elite leader), General Heshin (mercenaries' leader), Mason Harding (Dynamic Electronics employee, madbomb creator) (all bts) & Madbomb technicians (in photo only)
OTHER CHARACTERS: Henry Kissinger (US Secretary of State, as "Henny" & "Mister Secretary" here, last in Hulk #174, '74, last app), SHIELD agents inc "Panic Course" technician, 4 US Army soldiers, screaming mouth (in symbolic splash only), bystanders (stricken by madbomb)
LOCATIONS/ITEMS: New York inc Leila Taylor's apartment, "Madbomb Control" inc the "Panic Course" & "Henny's" room, Miner's Junction, River City (both on closed circuit monitor only), Royalist headquarters' madbomb assembly room (in photo only); madbombs: "Peanut," "Dumpling" (both on closed circuit monitor only), "Big Daddy" (madbomb model A-B, in photo only) & bomb triggered in New York, "Panic Course's" gas & flying rammers, Leila's knife, Madbomb victims' gun, lead pipe, hammer, & other weapons, soldiers' guns, closed circuit monitor
SYNOPSIS: At Leila Taylor's apartment, Captain America and Falcon are suddenly overcome with madness and hate. They initially fight but come to their senses. While Falcon restrains a similarly maddened Leila, Cap goes outside into a raging mob. He finds a small device wedged between buildings. Although he again succumbs to the madness, he still destroys the device with his shield, ending the riot. Soon after, a SHIELD agent joins Cap and Falcon and calls the shattered device a "madbomb." He takes them to "Madbomb Control," a secret government base, leading them to the "Panic Course," a lethal obstacle course. Successfully emerging, the heroes meet "Henny," the Secretary of State, who has tested them to confirm they are indeed Cap and Falcon. He tells them of two smaller madbombs, dubbed "Peanut" and "Dumpling" that devastated the towns of Miner's Junction and River City. Then he shows them a photo smuggled out by a SHIELD agent, killed in the process, revealing "Big Daddy," a madbomb big enough to destroy the United States which the government thinks is timed to go off for the Bicentennial.
NOTE: "Henny" tells Cap and Falcon that he cannot disclose the reason why they are chosen to fight the madbomb. This reason has never been given. "Let's Rap With Cap" contains LOCs from Dean Mullaney, future publisher of Eclipse Comics, and Steve Rogers! This issue includes Marvel Value Stamp #B01 -- Spider-Man.

CAPTAIN AMERICA #194 (February 1976)

"The Trojan Horde" (18 pages)

CREDITS: Jack Kirby (writer, pencils, editor), Frank Giacoia (inks), Gaspar Saladino (letters), Janice Cohen (colors)
FEATURE CHARACTERS: Captain America, Falcon
VILLAINS: Royalist Forces of America inc William Taurey (Royalist Elite leader), General Heshin (both 1st, both next bts in Cap #195, '76, next in Cap #199, '76), Vickers (Taurey's butler, next in Cap #199, '76), Mason Harding (bts, madbomb creator), mercenary troops, & scientists
OTHER CHARACTERS: SHIELD agents inc doctor & 6 technicians, Labor Zombies (mutated SHIELD agents among others), Sir William Taurey (Taurey's Revolutionary War era British loyalist ancestor), Steven Rogers (Continental Army Captain, Captain America's ancestor) (both in portraits only), madbomb victims (in symbolic image only), Redwing (in front cover logo image only)
LOCATIONS/ITEMS: "Madbomb Control" inc brain-blast room w/power booth & Cap and Falcon's quarters, Taurey's estate (in "exclusive suburb"), South Dakota Badlands inc Royalist Forces headquarters w/Barracks B, Manual Labor Pool, & Treatment Room; SHIELD's brain-blast machine, diffusion helmets, & skimmer, Royalists' camouflage boulders, mind-wave launcher & other weapons, madbomb victims' weapons, "Peanut," "Dumpling," & "Big Daddy" (prev 4 in symbolic image only)
SYNOPSIS: At "Madbomb Control," Captain America and Falcon receive the maximum charge from SHIELD's brain-bolt machine in order to prepare them for their upcoming mission. Meanwhile, William Taurey, who wishes to return the USA to a pre-American Revolution aristocracy, tells the leader of his mercenaries, General Heshin, that he seeks revenge on Steve Rogers whose Continental Army ancestor killed Sir William Taurey in a duel after Taurey tried to warn the British of George Washington's approach. Following an SOS from a missing SHIELD agent, Cap and Falcon, wearing flight suits, fly to the South Dakota Badlands. Landing, they encounter a mutated giant and discover foam rubber boulders concealing the entrance to an underground base. Royalist mercenaries emerge, herd the giant inside, and use a mind-wave launcher on Cap and Falcon who, inured by their brain-bolt treatment, feign unconsciousness. The mercenaries take them to their Manual Labor Pool housing the missing SHIELD agents turned into freakish mutations by Royalist scientists. Removing their flight suits to reveal their costumes underneath, Cap and Falcon prepare for action.
NOTE: Taurey and Heshin are named for the loyalist Tories and German mercenary Hessians of the American Revolution. Taurey's first name incorrectly revealed as Malcolm in Cap #199, '76, revealed as William in Cap #200, '76. Vickers' name revealed in Tb #31, '99. Rogers' ancestor appears as a pin-up in CapBiB, '76, and the story of Taurey's & Rogers' ancestors are told in detail in Cap:SoL #6-7, '99, their 1st actual app. Letters page contains LOC from Fantagraphic Book's Kim Thompson. This issue includes Marvel Value Stamp #B27 -- Dracula.

CAPTAIN AMERICA #195 (March 1976)

"1984!" (17 pages)

CREDITS: Jack Kirby (writer, pencils, editor), D. Bruce Berry (inks, letters), Janice Cohen (colors), Frank Giacoia (c inks), Gaspar Saladino (c & splash page letters)

FEATURE CHARACTERS: Captain America, Falcon

VILLAINS: Royalist Forces of America inc Hesperus Chadwick (Elite member, cardiovascular surgeon, face not shown, 1st, next in Cap #197, '76), Cheer Chadwick (Elite member, Hesperus' daughter, 1st), other Elite (bts, controlling the followers), Tinkerbelle (Kill-Derby captain), mercenary troops, scientists, elevator operator, conditioned followers, 2 workers pushing the "Love Machine," William Taurey (bts, Elite leader), General Heshin (bts, mercenaries' leader), & Mason Harding (bts, madbomb creator)

OTHER CHARACTERS: Gen. Argyle Fist (US Army General, 1st), US military soldiers, jet pilots, & Hound-dog pilot (Blue Leader, Blue Devils named, some voice only), Labor Zombies, SHIELD agent (mutated into "zombie"), composite face (brainwashing the followers), Freedom Freak (hung effigy), Redwing (in front cover logo image only)

LOCATIONS/ITEMS: South Dakota Badlands inc US Army's Base 1 & Royalist Forces Headquarters w/Manual Labor Pool, Treatment Room, elevator, Level Five, & Dr. Chadwick's quarters; US Army's Hound-dog (hovercraft w/ground sonar system), "Love Machine" (gallows w/effigy), Royalist weapons, followers' sticks and clubs, Tinkerbelle's armor w/mirrored light-flash glove

SYNOPSIS: Captain America and Falcon break out of the Labor Pool and fight their way to the Treatment Room. There, Cheer Chadwick, a Royalist Elite member, claims them from the advancing troops, taking them to Level Five. Outside, General Argyle Fist, convinced that the enemy is nearby, orders a ground-sonar sweep. On Level Five, Cap, Falcon, and Cheer observe the brainwashed Royalist followers get whipped into a frenzy by a computer composite face who tells them they cannot rule themselves and need the Elite to do it for them. The mob destroys a hung effigy representing a "Freedom Freak." The computer image rewards them by inviting them to the arena for the games. Cap tries to probe Cheer about the madbomb but Tinkerbelle, a large armored woman, attacks him. Using trickery, she defeats Cap and Falcon, telling Cheer that the heroes won't survive the arena since they "wouldn't understand a sport in which fair play is outlawed." Cheer insists that Tinkerbelle add them to the team. She then contacts her father, telling him Cap asked about the madbomb. Her father replies that the bomb is in place and soon the Elite will wipe out freedom in America.

NOTE: Dr. Hesperus Chadwick named in Tb #31, '99. The Royalist headquarters elevator lists the basement as "Labor Force," Level One as "Military Tactical Troops," Level Two as "Repair and Maintenance Force," and Level Three as "White Collar Force." Cheer Chadwick confirms that the Elite occupy the top floor. This issue includes Marvel Value Stamp #B42 -- Hulk.

CAPTAIN AMERICA #196 (April 1976)

"Kill-Derby" (17 pages)

CREDITS: Jack Kirby (writer, pencils, editor), D. Bruce Berry (inks, letters), Janice Cohen (colors), Marv Wolfman (consulting editor), Frank Giacoia (c inks), Gaspar Saladino (c letters), John Costanza (splash page letters)

FEATURE CHARACTERS: Captain America (also as "Mister Pure"), Falcon

VILLAINS: Royalist Forces of America inc the Elite w/Cheer Chadwick & William Taurey (bts, Elite leader), Tinkerbelle & other Kill-Derby gladiators ("Number Two" named), mercenary troops (bts, capture Hound-dog pilot), conditioned followers, General Heshin (bts, mercenaries' leader), & Mason Harding (bts, madbomb creator)

OTHER CHARACTERS: Gen. Argyle Fist & his soldiers ("Captain" named) inc Hound-dog pilot

LOCATIONS/ITEMS: South Dakota Badlands inc US Army's Base 1, Area B-Three, & Royalist Forces Headquarters w/Kill-Derby arena, & the brig; Kill-Derby team members' electric-powered skateboards, armor, wrist transmitter, flame thrower, heat proof suits, cable-snare rifle, noxious gas tank, whirling blades, staffs, Tinkerbelle's missile fingertips, shield-stealer's electric staff, & the "Stand-In" (explosive mannequin resembling Kill-Derby participant)

SYNOPSIS: Captain America resists joining the Kill-Derby contest until knocked unconscious by gas. One Kill-Derby gladiator takes Cap's shield while two others throw him in the brig with Falcon. As the contest begins, Cheer Chadwick demands that Cap and Falcon compete. At the cell, Tinkerbelle tells Cap that he'll have to fight to regain his shield. The two heroes agree to participate. In the Badlands, the Hound-dog hovercraft reports a "bogie." Cap and Falcon join the Kill-Derby on motorized skateboards. Amid the ensuing mayhem of flame thrower and missile attacks, Falcon takes to the air but is felled by a net shot from a cable-snare rifle. Cap frees him then fights his way through the gladiators until caught in the "Stand-In's" explosion. Outside, General Fist and his men find the wrecked Hound-dog. The pilot is missing. On the Kill-Derby track, Cap recovers and, with Falcon's help, arrives at the man who stole his shield. When the man refuses to give it up, Cap prepares to attack.

NOTE: The Kill-Derby contest pits the "Blues" versus the "Reds." "Let's Rap With Cap" contains LOC from Dean Mullaney, future publisher of Eclipse Comics. The shield-stealer's electric staff becomes a mace next issue.

"Captain America and the Time Warp" (1 page)

CREDITS: Unknown

FEATURE CHARACTER: Captain America (last in MTU #71, '78, next in Cap #222, '78)

GUEST STAR: Nick Fury (last in MTU #71, '78, next in Cap #222, '78)

OTHER CHARACTERS: Gaius Julius Caesar (chr 1st prior to Mm #9, '93), Roman army, picnickers (bts)

LOCATIONS/ITEMS: SHIELD HQ, Central Park; Roman shields, armor & swords, Caesar's wreath, Hostess Twinkie Cakes, picnic baskets

SYNOPSIS: A rip in the space/time continuum drops Caesar and his army in Central Park, their unexpected arrival scaring off the picnickers. Nick Fury sends Captain America to deal with the problem, and finds the new arrivals have raided the abandoned picnic baskets to devour the Twinkies within. With the Romans thus in an amiable mood, Cap negotiates for SHIELD to return them to their own time, with Caesar requesting some more

Twinkies for the trip.

NOTE: Appeared in various Marvel titles, July & August 1978. The Roman leader is only identified as Caesar in the strip; this Index confirms for the first time exactly which Roman emperor he is.

CAPTAIN AMERICA #197 (May 1976)

"The Rocks are Burning!" (17 pages)

CREDITS: Jack Kirby (writer, pencils, editor), Frank Giacoia (inks), John Costanza (letters), Phil Rachelson (colors), Marv Wolfman (exec editor), Gaspar Saladino (c letters)

FEATURE CHARACTERS: Captain America, Falcon

VILLAINS: Royalist Forces of America inc the Elite w/Cheer Chadwick, Hesperus Chadwick (face not shown), (both next in Tb #31, '99) & William Taurey (bts, Elite leader), Tinkerbelle (last app) & other Kill-Derby gladiators inc shield-stealer (dies), mercenary troops (some die), conditioned followers, General Heshin (bts, mercenaries' leader), & Mason Harding (bts, madbomb creator)

OTHER CHARACTERS: Gen. Argyle Fist & his soldiers ("Captain" named) (some die)

LOCATIONS/ITEMS: South Dakota Badlands inc Royalist Forces Headquarters w/Kill-Derby arena & escape tunnel; shield-stealer's electric mace & plastic bomb, military helicopters w/chemical flame throwers, tanks, transports, & weapons, mercenaries' weapons inc high-frequency sound machine, Elite's private pneumatic car, pot of gold

SYNOPSIS: Captain America tackles the shield-stealer who repels him with his electric mace. As the crowd yells "Kill!" the gladiator flings the shield at Cap who dodges. The shield boomerangs and strikes the gladiator who had armed it with a plastic bomb that explodes, killing him. Aboveground, General Fist employs helicopters with flame throwers to ferret out the Royalist entrance and the mercenaries. In the arena, Cap rejects the prize, a pot of gold, turning the crowd against him. However, the army enters the installation, causing the crowd to panic. The mercenaries subject the soldiers to a high-frequency sound machine but Cap destroys it. The Army's strike force takes over the headquarters. However, Cheer, her father, and other Elite members escape. Cheer's father assures her that the madbomb is "safely planted" and ready to go off on Bicentennial day.

NOTE: "Let's Rap With Cap" contains a LOC from future Marvel editor Ralph Macchio. This issue includes Marvel Value Stamp #B78 -- Conan.

CAPTAIN AMERICA #198 (June 1976)

"Captain America's Love Story" (17 pages)

CREDITS: Jack Kirby (writer, pencils, editor), Frank Giacoia (inks), Gaspar Saladino (letters), Michele Wolfman (colors), Marv Wolfman (consulting editor), Irving Watanabe (c letters)

FEATURE CHARACTERS: Captain America (also as "college boy," also in Cap #224, '78), Falcon

VILLAINS: Royalist Forces of America inc Mason Harding (1st) & his personal guards, estate guards, mercenary troops, William Taurey (bts, Elite leader), & General Heshin (bts, mercenaries' leader)

OTHER CHARACTERS: Carol Harding (Mason's daughter, 1st), Gen. Argyle Fist (next in Cap #224, '78) and his soldiers, SHIELD agents (one on walkie-talkie monitor only), Carol's nurse, 4 beach bullies (Piggy named), Kingpin ("finest horse at the local riding academy")

LOCATIONS/ITEMS: South Dakota Badlands inc Royalist Forces Headquarters w/madbomb assembly plant, East Coast seaside estate inc Carol's bedroom, surrounding woods, & sand dunes, beach; Royalist men & SHIELD agents' guns, "Big Daddy" (on specification chart only)

SYNOPSIS: Captain America, Falcon, and General Fist find the madbomb assembly plant at Royalist headquarters but the bomb has been moved elsewhere. Fist tells Cap that SHIELD agents have located electronics genius Mason Harding who vanished two years ago and may be the madbomb creator. Later, at an East Coast estate, Harding visits his daughter Carol who is recovering from a serious operation. Harding's thuggish guards hurry him out. An observing SHIELD agent reports in and is told that two men will take his place. Late that night, Cap infiltrates and comes upon Carol. The two talk and discover a mutual attraction, agreeing to meet the next day on the beach. When Carol arrives, Cap meets her as Steve Rogers, taking her for a horseback ride. Two trailing estate guards prepare to shoot them both but Falcon defeats them. Then, with Cap keeping Carol safe, Falcon and SHIELD raid the estate, capturing nearly all within. As Carol and Steve sit by a beach bonfire, four bullies harass them. Using his great strength, Steve scares them off, making Carol realize he is Captain America.

NOTE: This issue includes Marvel Value Stamp #B91 -- Silver Surfer.

CAPTAIN AMERICA #199 (July 1976)

"The Man Who Sold the United States" (17 pages)

CREDITS: Jack Kirby (writer, pencils, editor), Frank Giacoia (inks), Gaspar Saladino (letters), Phil Rachelson (colors), Marv Wolfman (consulting editor)

FEATURE CHARACTERS: Captain America, Falcon

VILLAINS: Royalist Forces of America inc William Taurey & the Elite, General Heshin, Mason Harding (next in Cap #201, '76) & his 2 personal guards (both die), 3 estate guards, 2 Taurey estate guards, Vickers, & madbomb technicians (2 also on monitor)

OTHER CHARACTERS: Carol Harding (last app), SHIELD agents

LOCATIONS/ITEMS: East Coast seaside estate inc Carol's room & basement, Taurey's estate inc ballroom & transmitting room, Philadelphia inc Madbomb Control at Taurey Towers Building; "Big Daddy" (also in schematic), micro-madbomb, estate guards' guns & sword, personal guards' guns, SHIELD agents' guns, booby-trapped car w/dummies & explosives

SYNOPSIS: Scouring the seaside estate, Captain America and Falcon find and defeat three hidden guards. Soon after, Cap tells Carol about the madbomb and prepares to take her to Morgan Clinic. She tells him her father acted as he did to pay for her care. At Taurey's estate, Harding

demands to go see his daughter but is refused. Harding activates a micro-madbomb driving the guards insane. One kills another. Harding kills the survivor and escapes. Meanwhile, Taurey sends a booby-trapped car to the seaside estate. Cap approaches, thinking it is Harding arriving, but Falcon pulls him away in time to avoid the explosion. Later, as Cap and Falcon bemoan the loss of their only lead, Harding himself arrives, looking for Carol. Breaking with the Elite, he gives Cap and Falcon "Big Daddy's" location as well as a means to block its effects. At his estate, Taurey steps away from his costumed ball to order "Big Daddy's" activation.
NOTE: William Taurey incorrectly called "Malcolm Taurey" here.

CAPTAIN AMERICA #200 (August 1976)

"Dawn's Early Light!" (17 pages)

CREDITS: Jack Kirby (writer, pencils, editor), Frank Giacoia (inks), John Costanza (letters), Don Warfield (colors), Marv Wolfman (consulting editor), Irving Watanabe (c letters)
FEATURE CHARACTERS: Captain America (next in CapBiB, '76), Falcon
VILLAINS: Royalist Forces of America inc William Taurey (chr next in Tb #54, '01 fb, next in Tb #31, '99) & the Elite, General Heshin (last app), mercenary troops (1 on monitor screen), Vickers (next in Tb #31, '99), & madbomb technicians
OTHER CHARACTERS: SHIELD "SWAT" force (Sergeant named) & technicians, "Operation Madbomb" federal troop strike force
LOCATIONS/ITEMS: Taurey estate inc ballroom, mercenary barracks, & grounds, Philadelphia inc Madbomb Control in Taurey Towers Building; "Big Daddy" (destroyed), Taurey estate's sonic wave projector w/activator, SHIELD agents' weapons, smoke grenade, & periscope, mercenary troops' weapons, "Operation Madbomb" helicopters & weapons inc recoilless rifle, Vickers' gun, 2 pistols
SYNOPSIS: Thanks to Mason Harding's information, Captain America and a SHIELD SWAT force infiltrate William Taurey's estate while Falcon and federal troops converge on the Taurey Towers Building in Philadelphia where "Big Daddy" is hidden. There, Falcon dispenses with two sentries, then summons his strike force. Discovered, Falcon and his men attack swiftly. At the estate, Cap enters the ballroom just as William Taurey announces to the Elite that he has ordered "Big Daddy's" activation. As mercenaries and troops fight, Falcon smashes into the Taurey Building's tower, finding the madbomb ten seconds before its activation. Pulling the switch to "Maximum Sonics," Falcon overloads "Big Daddy," fighting its fierce effects. The bomb's unrestrained power destroys the tower. Meanwhile, overhearing Taurey's vow to destroy Steve Rogers, Cap steps forward and offers to fight the duel in Steve's place. With each man taking a pistol, Cap tells Taurey to shoot but Taurey, afraid he will be shot in turn, loses his nerve and can't pull the trigger. In Philadelphia, the madbomb overloads and explodes. Radioing each other, Cap tells Falcon, "the nation stands."
NOTE: Taurey's correct first name revealed here.

MARVEL TREASURY SPECIAL: CAPTAIN AMERICA'S BICENTENNIAL BATTLES (June 1976)

"Chapter One: Mister Buda!!!" (13 pages)
"Chapter Two: The Lost Super-Hero!" (9 pages)
"Chapter Three: My Fellow Americans!" (12 pages)
"Chapter Four: Stop Here for Glory!" (26 pages)
"Chapter Five: The Face of the Future!" (17 pages)

CREDITS: Jack Kirby (writer, pencils, editor), Herb Trimpe, John Romita, Barry Windsor-Smith (inks), John Costanza (letters), Phil Rachelson (colors), Frank Giacoia (c inks), Gaspar Saladino (c letters)
FEATURE CHARACTER: Captain America (1940s era bts, on mission w/Bucky, between Cap:FA #1, '10 fb & Kid #3, '43, current era next in Cap #201, '76)
GUEST STAR: Contemplator (Tath Ki, Elder of the Universe, here as Mister Buda, 1st, next in Cap Ann #6, '82)
SUPPORTING CAST: Bucky (1940s era, between Cap:FA #4, '10 fb & Cap:Who #1, '10 fb)
VILLAINS: Adolf Hitler (last in SgtF #41, '67, next in HT #12/3, '43), Red Skull (last in Cap #5, '05 fb, next in Cap #262, '81 fb), Nazi officers (all 1940s era), mobsters (1930s era, Lefty Larkin named), bounty hunters (1850s era), German pilot (1910s era)
OTHER CHARACTERS: Ben Franklin (a United States founding father) & his print shop employees (John Stacey named), Betsy Ross (seamstress), Philadelphia citizens (Randolph & Hiram named), carriage horses (prev 5 1770s era); John Brown (vehement abolitionist) & his son, escaped slave, bounty hunters' horses (prev 4 1850s era); Chicago citizens inc firemen, fire-carriage horses, Dalmatian, John L. Sullivan (last heavyweight bare-knuckle boxing & first gloved boxing champion), boxing gamblers, police (prev 7 1870s era); Geronimo (Goyathlay, Chiricahua Apache leader, last in Apache #2, '02 fb, last app), his Chiricahua Apache warriors & their horses, US 4th Calvary & their horses (prev 4 1880s era); Kentucky coal miners (Gulik named, 1900s era); US soldiers (1910s era); Jack Kirby (as newspaper boy, 1st chr app, next in FF #10, '63), Officer Clancy, bystanders; Clark Gable, Joan Crawford (both on movie poster), John Dillinger, Franklin D. Roosevelt (both mentioned in newspaper) (prev 7 1930s era); US army (General Halstead & Hogan named), scientists, government officials (prev 3 1940s era); J.B. Shmeltzer (producer), Melvin Grubber (Shmeltzer's son in law), director, cameraman, actors, dancers, choreographer (1950s era); New York citizens, taxi driver, deep-sea research scientist & divers, farmer, student, children, shark; Thing (on t-shirt) (prev 9 current era); Moon combatants (the future)
LOCATIONS/ITEMS: New York inc Contemplator's quarters, Germany, Philadelphia inc Benjamin Franklin's print shop, American Southwest, Kentucky coal mine, Europe, Boston inc boxing ring, Ohio inc John Brown's farm, New Mexico inc Almagordo Bombing and Gunnery Range, Chicago, Pacific Ocean inc deep-sea research station, moon, Hollywood; Contemplator's energy pyramid, psychic-talisman & meditation chair, Red Skull's gun, Nazi's guns, taxi, carriage, mobster's car & guns, Clancy's gun, Chiricahua Apache warrior's guns & lariat, US bi-plane, German bi-plane, bounty hunter's guns, John Brown's son's gun, army jeep & eyeshades, atomic bomb; Chicago fire-carriage, moon combatants' air-jet

vehicle, blasters & space suits, Cap's space suit, farmer's fiddle

SYNOPSIS: Responding to an invitation, Captain America visits Mr. Buda on America's Bicentennial. Mr. Buda offers Cap an opportunity to view America with a universal eye, but Cap isn't interested and leaves. Unable to find his way out, Cap suddenly falls through a trap door and lands in Nazi Germany. Evading some guards he discovers Bucky being tortured by Hitler and Red Skull. Cap frees Bucky and the two escape, but Cap is transported back to Mr. Buda. Angry at first, Cap eventually thanks Mr. Buda for allowing him to see Bucky again. Cap excuses himself to leave, and Mr. Buda tells Cap to broaden his knowledge as he secretly places a Psychic-Talisman on Cap's palm. Taking a taxi, Cap is transported to Philadelphia in the 1770's, where he meets Benjamin Franklin, who designs the American flag after Cap's uniform. Feeling ripped off and disillusioned, Cap runs off but discovers he is now in New York during the Great Depression. After helping a newspaper boy against some gangsters, Cap discovers the Talisman on his palm and is transported to the America Southwest. He's attacked by Apaches, but gains the respect of their leader Geronimo with his wisdom. When they are attacked by the US Calvary, Cap desperately tries to stop the soldiers, but is trampled by their horses and he finds himself in a collapsed mine shaft. He uses his shield to dig a way out, rescuing the miners. After an air-born skirmish in the Great War, Cap is transported back to Mr. Buda, who reminds Cap that history can't be made without turbulence. Cap is suddenly in a boxing match with John L. Sullivan, then freeing a slave from bounty hunters. After Cap departs, John Brown secures the unconscious slavers. Cap appears at Almagordo to witness the first atomic bomb test, and he's terrified of the terrible power. He helps rescue people during the great Chicago fire, and then talks with undersea research scientists. Mr. Buda reminds Cap that experience teaches, not people, and sends the hero to the future. Witnessing a battle on the moon, Cap realizes that people will never stop fighting. Appearing in Hollywood, Cap becomes outraged at the hollow pomp and circumstance, feeling the proceedings are a parody of patriotism. Mr. Buda congratulates Cap for questioning his surroundings, and for thinking for himself. Taking Cap to visit a student, Cap realizes that what makes America great are people who don't complain and just get things done. As Mr. Buda leaves, he reminds Cap that truth is to be shared. Cap finds himself surrounded by children. He tells them that they can grow up to be anything they want.

NOTE: Also includes B&W Table of Contents featuring Captain America & children, w/Cap's shield listing the contents; pin-up featuring "Colonial Captain America" & Red Skull as a "Hessianazi," (this Cap design will later be used for Cap's ancestor in Cap:SoL #6-7, '99, 1st mentioned in Cap #194, '76); pin-up featuring "Western Captain America" & gunfighters (identified as "the Captain from Texas" in MW:OFiles, '06); pin-up featuring Cap on the moon as "Astro-Hero" w/Cap's space suit & shield w/Apollo symbol; B&W pin-up of Steve Rogers revealing his secret identity to readers, w/villains Batroc the Leaper, Dr. Doom, a Hydra agent, mobsters, a Nazi officer & Red Skull voicing their disbelief & a back cover pin-up of Cap wishing Uncle Sam a happy 200th birthday, featuring Statue of Liberty cake & an American Bald Eagle. The Marvel Treasury Specials were printed in an oversized format, 13" X 10".

CAPTAIN AMERICA #201 (September 1976)

"The Night People!" (17 pages)

CREDITS: Jack Kirby (writer, pencils, editor), Frank Giacoia (inks), John Costanza (letters), Phil Rachelson (colors), Archie Goodwin (consulting editor), Gaspar Saladino (c letters)
FEATURE CHARACTERS: Captain America, Falcon (also as "Mister Feathers") (both also as dolls)
SUPPORTING CAST: Leila Taylor (last in Cap #193, '76)
VILLAINS: The Night People (also as "The Night People of Zero Street" & "The Brothers and Sisters of Zero Street"): Brother Wonderful (Dr. Abner Doolittle, nuclear physicist), Brother Inquisitor, Brother Dickens, Brother Peach Pie, Brother Powerful, Brother Searcher, Brother Harmony, Sister Gladiola, & others (asylum inmates, all 1st); Mason Harding (next in Cap #225, '78)
OTHER CHARACTERS: Texas Jack Muldoon (millionaire, 1st), SHIELD agents & guards, police, supermarket guard, theater projectionist, jet pilot & co-pilot, Iron Man (as dolls only), tiger, elephant (both as toys only), dogs, cat (both freed from pet store)
LOCATIONS/ITEMS: New York inc Leila's apartment, toy store, supermarket, pet store, department store, theatrical costume loft, midnight movie theater, police headquarters, & airport, New York Philharmonic & municipal court (both mentioned only), Washington DC inc SHIELD HQ w/Detention Quarters & Steve and Sam's hotel room w/bathroom, Mad Dimension planetoid inc Zero Street w/asylum inc Inquisitor's courtroom; Brother Wonderful's dimension transporter & shock treatment machine, Night People's gas gun, magnetic belt, & mace, Brother Inquisitor's gavel, Texas Jack's jet & lasso, globe, toys, mannequin, grandfather clock, policeman's gun, sonic neutralizer
SYNOPSIS: The grotesque Night People, who crave a super hero, pillage odd objects from Manhattan businesses, appearing and vanishing at will. At the Washington DC SHIELD headquarters, Cap and Falcon visit Mason Harding to thank him for his madbomb information and sonic neutralizers. At their hotel, Falcon calls Leila. Two Night People, Brother Peach Pie and Brother Harmony, eavesdrop. Realizing she knows the Falcon, they abduct her, which Sam overhears. Frantic, Falcon flies high and tries to hitch a ride on a jet. When he loses his grip, a lasso snakes out of the plane and gathers him in. Elsewhere, the Night People take Leila before Brother Inquisitor as bait for the Falcon. Inquisitor confers with Brother Wonderful who, scanning incoming New York flights, finds the Falcon thanking the jet's owner and lassoer, millionaire Texas Jack Muldoon, for rescuing him. Taking off, Falcon flies right into a dimensional portal; the "door to Zero Street" by which the Night People travel. Immediately captured and taken to the "Inquisition," Falcon, with Leila, is subjected to "shock treatment." At SHIELD headquarters, Cap learns that Falcon and Leila are missing and that Falcon was witnessed disappearing into thin air.
NOTE: Among the loot stolen by the Night People is "a shipment of Marvel Comics."

"An Invading Army" (1 page)
CREDITS: Unknown
FEATURE CHARACTER: Captain America (last in Cap #236, '79, next in DrS #35, '79)
VILLAINS: Humanoids (super-strong soldiers)
LOCATIONS/ITEMS: An alley; Hostess Fruit Pies
SYNOPSIS: Attacked by several muscular humanoids, Captain America throws them a couple of Hostess Fruit Pies, then watches them pound each other into unconsciousness fighting over who gets to eat them.
NOTE: Appeared in various Gold Key titles, April 1979.

CAPTAIN AMERICA #202 (October 1976)

"Mad, Mad Dimension!" (17 pages)

CREDITS: Jack Kirby (writer, pencils, editor), Frank Giacoia (inks), John Costanza (letters), George Roussos (colors), Archie Goodwin (consulting editor), Gaspar Saladino (c letters)
FEATURE CHARACTERS: Captain America, Falcon (also as "Brother Super-Hero")
SUPPORTING CAST: Sharon Carter (last in Cap #186, '75, next in Cap #204, '76), Leila Taylor (also as "Sister Sweet")
VILLAINS: The Night People: Brother Wonderful, Brother Inquisitor, & others; 2 planetoid monsters (1 on cover only)
OTHER CHARACTERS: Texas Jack Muldoon & his 3 men, Beamish Beasley (Texas Jack's employee, science & computer expert, only app)
LOCATIONS/ITEMS: New York inc Texas Jack's penthouse, Sharon's apartment, & fused block where Zero Street used to be, Mad Dimension planetoid inc Zero Street w/asylum & muddy pool; Brother Wonderful's dimension transporter & ultra-sonic energizer, Texas Jack's car phone & gun
SYNOPSIS: Cap bulls his way into Texas Jack's penthouse to ask about Falcon's disappearance. Having analyzed the situation, Jack's assistant Beasley has a "fantastic projection." On Zero Street, their minds wiped by the "shock treatment," Falcon and Leila join the Night People as Brother Super-Hero and Sister Sweet. Brother Wonderful sends Falcon out to battle a monster, which has threatened them. Spitting flame and tossing boulders, the monster fells the Falcon. On Earth, Beasley takes Cap and Texas Jack to Zero Street's former site. He tells Cap about Dr. Abner Doolittle, a nuclear physicist who had a nervous breakdown, was committed to the Zero Street asylum, and apparently perfected his dimension machine, swapping the asylum with a patch of an other dimensional planetoid. Cap stakes out the area until the dimensional "fireball" appears. Meanwhile, the Falcon recovers and knocks the monster off the planetoid into "the deep chasm of space." However, fearing further attacks, Brother Wonderful plans to use his machine to send all other monsters to Earth. Testing the machine's components, Brother Wonderful has activated it, creating the "fireball" through which Cap leaps. Texas Jack follows soon after, moments before the portal closes up.
NOTE: "Let's Rap With Cap" contains LOC from Steve Rogers.

CAPTAIN AMERICA #203 (November 1976)

"Alamo II!" (17 pages)

CREDITS: Jack Kirby (writer, pencils, editor), Frank Giacoia (inks), Gaspar Saladino (letters), Hugh Paley (colors), Archie Goodwin (consulting editor)
FEATURE CHARACTERS: Captain America (next in MTU #52, '76, Av #150-153, '76, Av Ann #6, '76, Av #153, '76, SVTU #9, '76, Av #155-156, '77, SVTU #10-12, '77, SW #13, '79 fb, Cap #330, '87 fb, Def #44, '77), Falcon (also as "Brother Falcon," next in MTU #52, '76)
SUPPORTING CAST: Leila Taylor (also as "Sister Sweet," next in MTU #52, '76)
VILLAINS: The Night People: Brother Wonderful (next bts in MTU #52, '76), Brother Inquisitor (next in MTU #52, '76), & others (some next in MTU #52, '76, some apparently die); planetoid monsters (some die, 1 next in MTU #52, '76)
OTHER CHARACTER: Texas Jack Muldoon (next in MTU #52, '76)
LOCATIONS/ITEMS: Mad Dimension planetoid inc Zero Street w/asylum and grounds inc Brother Wonderful's lab; Brother Wonderful's dimension transporter w/sonic homing device & destruct mechanism, Texas Jack's gun
SYNOPSIS: Cap and Texas Jack materialize in Brother Wonderful's lab. Out on the asylum grounds, Cap finds Leila who doesn't remember him. When Cap touches her, Falcon assaults him. Brother Inquisitor breaks up the fight, telling Cap he must submit to the shock treatment or die. Just then the planetoid monsters attack. Cap, Falcon, and Texas Jack fight back but the assault is overwhelming. All retreat into the asylum but the monsters break through. Brother Wonderful uses his dimension transporter's homing device to attract the monsters, planning to send them all to Earth. Cap convinces Brother Wonderful to test his machine by sending Falcon and Leila through. Texas Jack follows. Cap tricks Brother Wonderful into revealing his transporter's destruct mechanism. He grabs it, tosses Brother Inquisitor and Brother Wonderful through the portal, herds the other Night People through and sets the destruct before departing. The destruct goes off, destroying the entire planetoid.
NOTE: "Let's Rap With Cap" contains LOC from Dean Mullaney, future publisher of Eclipse Comics.

CAPTAIN AMERICA #204 (December 1976)

"The Unburied One!" (17 pages)

CREDITS: Jack Kirby (writer, pencils, editor), Frank Giacoia (inks), Gaspar Saladino (letters), Janice Cohen (colors), Archie Goodwin (consulting editor)
FEATURE CHARACTERS: Captain America (also as "Mister Mask"), Falcon (also as "Brother Falcon")
SUPPORTING CAST: Sharon Carter (last in Cap #202, '76, next in Cap #206, '77)
VILLAINS: Agron (energy creature from the future, inhabiting human corpse, 1st but chr last in Cap #205, '77 fb), Brother Wonderful (last bts in MTU #52, '76, next in MTIO #67, '80), Brother Inquisitor (last in MTU #52, '76, next in Cap #410, '92)
OTHER CHARACTERS: Dr. Hartman (SHIELD psychiatrist, 1st), SHIELD psychiatric section's male nurses & security guards

LOCATIONS/ITEMS: New York inc SHIELD psychiatric section w/isolation ward and mortuary & Cap's hotel room 415, suburbs inc woods security guards' rifles, spaceship (on TV only)

SYNOPSIS: At a SHIELD psychiatric facility, Cap and Dr. Hartman try unsuccessfully to get Brother Wonderful and Brother Inquisitor to reveal how to restore Falcon and Leila's memory. Soon after, Hartman shows Cap a strange inmate: a walking corpse without pulse or heartbeat calling himself Agron and claiming to be from the far distant future. Later, having grown larger and more powerful, Agron attacks his attendants and breaks out. Meanwhile, Sharon Carter uses the Falcon's condition to try to get Cap to quit his super-heroing and stalks off when he resists. At the psychiatric facility, Sharon collapses after being repeatedly shot. Hartman has him taken to the mortuary but fears he is not dead but only resting. He contacts Cap, asking for help but Cap, still smarting from Sharon's comments, begs off. Just then, Agron revives, crackling with energy, and crashes through a wall. Desperate, Hartman frees the still amnesiac Falcon, telling him that Agron is threatening his Brothers and Sisters. Falcon attacks but, as Agron continues to transform before him, screams in horror.

NOTE: Agron's future revealed as Earth-76216 in OHMU:HC #4, '09. Steve's hotel room number revealed in Cap #205, '77.

CAPTAIN AMERICA #205 (January 1977)

"Agron Walks the Earth!" (17 pages)

CREDITS: Jack Kirby (writer, pencils, editor), John Verpoorten (inks), Jim Novak (letters), Michele Wolfman (colors), Archie Goodwin (consulting editor), Joe Sinnott (c inks), Gaspar Saladino (c letters)
FEATURE CHARACTERS: Captain America (also as "Mister Red, White, and Blue"), Falcon
VILLAIN: Agron (in human corpse & in energy form, also on TV screen, also in fb to 1st chr app before Cap #204 '76, last app)
OTHER CHARACTERS: Dr. Hartman, SHIELD psychiatric section's security guards, SHIELD SWAT team (some apparently die), SHIELD flash announcer (voice only), Captain Dawson (SHIELD agent, on closed-circuit tele-screen only), car driver, morgue attendant (in fb only), bystanders
LOCATIONS/ITEMS: New York inc Steve's hotel room 415 & SHIELD psychiatric section w/Hartman's office, Earth-76216's future, mortuary (both in fb only); security guards' rifles & grenade, Hartman's closed circuit tele-screen, SHIELD SWAT team's weapons & tube

FLASHBACK: The evolved energy being Agron flees a dying futuristic Earth into the past and inhabits a corpse, walking out of a morgue.
SYNOPSIS: Falcon recoils from Agron's stifling energy that emerges from his eye sockets. A surge of force flings Falcon away. Agron resists the security guards' weapons and breaks out of the psychiatric facility. Captain Dawson informs Hartman that SHIELD is preparing special equipment to contain Agron but are sending their SWAT team in first. SHIELD contacts Cap at his hotel, informing him of the crisis. Cap confronts Agron who throws him into heavy traffic. Falcon, his memory returned after Agron's energy discharge, rescues Cap. SHIELD SWAT members arrive with a metal tube and tell Cap and Falcon to lure Agron's energy form into it. Together the heroes assault Agron's energy-filled eye sockets, prompting him to leave the corpse, chasing after Falcon as pure energy. Falcon flies into the tube, exiting out the other end. Agron enters as well but the SWAT members close both ends, trapping him inside.
NOTE: Sharon Carter incorrectly called "Carol" here.

CAPTAIN AMERICA #206 (February 1977)

"Face to Face with the Swine!" (17 pages)

CREDITS: Jack Kirby (writer, pencils, editor), Frank Giacoia (inks), Jim Novak (letters), Petra Goldberg (colors), Archie Goodwin (consulting editor), Gaspar Saladino (c letters)
FEATURE CHARACTERS: Captain America, Falcon
SUPPORTING CAST: Sharon Carter (last in Cap #204, '76), Leila Taylor (last in MTU #52, '76)
VILLAINS: The Swine (Hector Santiago, Rio De Muerte prison Commandante, 1st), his prison guards, 2 New York agents, & personal waiter
OTHER CHARACTERS: Donna Maria Puentes (Swine's cousin, prison administration worker, 1st), Dr. Hartman (last app), Felix Garcia (New York restaurant waiter, Rio De Muerte escapee, only app), Rio De Muerte prisoners (2 die), SHIELD orderly & pilot, restaurant patrons, bystanders
LOCATIONS/ITEMS: Washington DC inc SHIELD hospital & airport, New York inc restaurant, Sharon's apartment, & Leila's apartment, Central America inc Rio De Muerte prison & surrounding jungle; SHIELD jet, Swine's swagger stick, pistol, food spread, & wine, prison guards' clubs, New York agents' guns & gas-pistol

SYNOPSIS: Leila recovers from the Night People's brainwashing. In Central America, the sadistic Rio De Muerte prison Commandante known as the Swine invites a starving prisoner to eat from a feast-laden table. Meanwhile, Steve, Sam, Sharon, and Leila dine out. Two Swine agents molest their waiter, Felix, a Rio De Muerte escapee, planning to take him back. Sam intervenes. When Steve steps in to help, Felix escapes. At Rio De Muerte, the Swine forces the prisoner to eat until he dies. As the Swine surveys his prison, the brutalized inmates fantasize about killing him. In New York, Steve escorts Sharon home. The Swine's agents follow, knowing they need a prisoner to replace Felix. As Sharon and Steve argue over his continued Cap activities, the agents gas him into unconsciousness and snatch Steve. After ordering a broken-down prisoner to push a piece of fruit ten miles a day with his nose, the Swine confronts his cousin Donna Maria who sunbathes within sight of the guards and inmates. Not intimidated by her cousin, Donna Maria tells him she awaits the day a real man will come and break him as he has broken others.
NOTE: Donna Maria's last name revealed in Q #41, '92. It is the Swine's birthday.

CAPTAIN AMERICA #207 (March 1977)

"The Tiger and the Swine!!" (17 pages)

CREDITS: Jack Kirby (writer, pencils, editor), Frank Giacoia (inks), Jim Novak (letters), George Roussos (colors), Archie Goodwin (consulting editor)
FEATURE CHARACTERS: Captain America, Falcon
SUPPORTING CAST: Sharon Carter (next in Cap #209, '77), Leila Taylor
VILLAINS: The Swine, his prison guards, 2 New York agents & pilot (dies)
OTHER CHARACTERS: Donna Maria Puentes, Nelson (SHIELD regional director, 1st), Rio De Muerte prisoners, 2 sailors (Pete named), dogs
LOCATIONS/ITEMS: Central America inc Rio De Muerte prison w/cell block & surrounding jungle, New York inc Sharon's apartment & SHIELD regional field office, US coastline; Steve's miniature flame device, Swine's gun, prison guards' guns, sleeping gas dispenser, gas masks & stove
SYNOPSIS: Steve awakens in a plane flying over the Rio De Muerte. He breaks free and battles his kidnappers, but the pilot is killed during the melee and the plane crashes in the jungle. Steve emerges from the wreckage and becomes Captain America, only wanting to find a way home. In New York, Sam and Leila find Sharon recovering from the tranquilizer gas in her apartment. Sam fears Cap has been kidnapped. In the jungle, prison guards find Cap but he dispenses with them and finds himself confronting the Swine. Meanwhile, after taking Sharon to the hospital, Sam and Leila check in with SHIELD. The Swine shoots at Cap who deflects the bullet with his shield and hangs the Swine up in a tree. Falcon flies along the coastline searching for Cap who wanders through the jungle until stumbling on a prison work detail. Seeking food, Cap attacks and defeats the guards, discovering that the inmates are so spiritless, they are in an almost zombie state. At the prison, the Swine tortures the prisoners who spoke of his humiliation at Cap's hands. Donna Maria revels in Cap's successes, telling her cousin, "I hope he breaks you, Swine!"

CAPTAIN AMERICA #208 (April 1977)

"The River of Death!" (17 pages)

CREDITS: Jack Kirby (writer, pencils, editor), Frank Giacoia (inks), Jim Novak (letters), George Roussos (colors), Archie Goodwin (consulting editor), Joe Sinnott (c inks), Gaspar Saladino (c letters)
FEATURE CHARACTERS: Captain America, Falcon
SUPPORTING CAST: Leila Taylor
VILLAINS: The Swine (dies) & his prison guards (some die), Arnim Zola ("The Bio-Fanatic," geneticist & biochemist, 1st but chr last in SVTU #16, '79 fb) & his Man-Fish (genetically-engineered creature, only actual app but chr last in Cap #209, '77 fb, arm only)
OTHER CHARACTERS: Donna Maria Puentes, SHIELD Regional Director Nelson & 2 SHIELD agents, "Digger" (man-like termite as large as a horse, mentioned only)
LOCATIONS/ITEMS: Central America inc Rio De Muerte & surrounding jungle w/pit, New York inc SHIELD regional field office, South American badlands inc mountains & giant nest; prison guards' guns & dynamite, Swine's flamethrower, Donna Maria's knife, File 116, Arnim Zola's mental command stimulator & ESP box
SYNOPSIS: As Cap follows the Rio De Muerte searching for a village, a monster emerges from the water and attacks him. Prison guards chase the "Man-Fish" away and capture the now-weakened Cap. At the SHIELD regional office, Nelson tells two agents about File 116, which is cataloguing a spate of monster appearances. He adds that, with the recent appearance of a "Digger," the file is getting ever larger. Meanwhile, the Falcon searches the coastlines all the way to South America. Veering inland, he comes upon a giant bird's nest. In Central America, Cap escapes the guards who throw dynamite at him, steering his flight so that he falls into a pit. As the Swine prepares to roast the trapped Cap with a flame thrower, Donna Maria intervenes. The Swine tosses her into the pit with Cap. Just then, the Man-Fish attacks, killing the Swine and his men. Cap and Donna Maria escape the pit but the Man-Fish attacks them, then suddenly returns to the river after prodded by the mental command device wielded by its master, Arnim Zola.
NOTE: "Let's Rap With Cap" contains LOC by current Marvel Index writer Robert J. Sodaro.

CAPTAIN AMERICA #209 (May 1977)

"Arnim Zola - - The Bio-Fanatic!!" (17 pages)

CREDITS: Jack Kirby (writer, pencils, editor), Frank Giacoia (inks), Jim Novak (letters), George Roussos (colors), Archie Goodwin (consulting editor), Gaspar Saladino (c letters)
FEATURE CHARACTERS: Captain America, Falcon
GUEST STAR: Nick Fury (bts, ordered Sharon's SHIELD reinstatement, last in RH #3/2, '77, next in Def #47, '77 fb)
SUPPORTING CAST: Sharon Carter (last in Cap #207, '77), Leila Taylor (next in MPr #49, '79)
VILLAINS: Arnim Zola (also in original body, also in fb between XFor Ann #3/3, '94, fb & SVTU #17, '80 fb) & his creations Primus, Doughboy, (both 1st) & "Big Bird" (bts, shadow only)
OTHER CHARACTERS: Donna Maria Puentes, SHIELD Regional Director Nelson, Man-Fish (arm only), tiny Zola creation, destructive Zola creation (shadow only, dies) (prev 3 in fb only)
LOCATIONS/ITEMS: Central America inc Rio De Muerte & surrounding jungle, Earth stratosphere, New York inc Sharon's apartment, Switzerland inc Alps w/Castle Zola's inc laboratory (fb only), South American badlands inc mountains & giant nest; File 116, Zola's mental

command stimulator, ESP box (as "transmitter" here), gun, cast iron box & genetics equipment (prev 3 in fb only)

FLASHBACK: During World War II, bio-chemist Arnim Zola uses his cast iron box full of ancient secrets and his modern equipment to create life. He creates a new body with the brain in the torso for better protection, and transfers his consciousness into it.

SYNOPSIS: Arnim Zola summons his creation, Doughboy, who uses his pliable, adhesive body to capture Cap and Donna Maria. Zola joins them and Doughboy levitates them all to the edges of space. Meanwhile, Nelson visits Sharon, who is home from the hospital, and shows her File 116. Telling her, "Someone is playing Frankenstein with the world" by creating monsters, Nelson puts Sharon back on active SHIELD duty. As Doughboy travels through the stratosphere, Cap realizes Zola is the man behind File 116. Cap attacks Zola but Primus, another genetic creation, emerges from Doughboy and retaliates. Elsewhere, the Falcon pursues the resident of the giant bird's nest and flies directly into a boulder avalanche. Meanwhile, Primus defeats Cap and claims Donna Maria as his prize.

CAPTAIN AMERICA #210 (June 1977)

"Showdown Day!" (17 pages)

CREDITS: Jack Kirby (writer, pencils, editor), Mike Royer (inks, letters), George Roussos (colors), Archie Goodwin (consulting editor), Frank Giacoia (c inks), Gaspar Saladino (c letters)
FEATURE CHARACTERS: Captain America, Falcon (next in Cap #213, '77)
SUPPORTING CAST: Sharon Carter (also on Skull's monitor)
VILLAINS: Red Skull (also as Cyrus Fenton, also on viewscreen as Fenton, last in SVTU #12, '77, chr last in SVTU #16, '79 fb), Arnim Zola (also on tele-sight), Primus, Doughboy (both next bts in Cap #212, '77), "Big Bird," organic Chamber Four w/organic shutter, "the Big-Eared Sentry and his Savage Companion" (2 guardian genetic constructs, next in Cap #212, '77), Nazi X (bts, in Chamber Four w/Cap & Donna Maria, chr last in SVTU #17, '80 fb)
OTHER CHARACTERS: Donna Maria Puentes, SHIELD Regional Director Nelson (also on viewscreen, last app to date)
LOCATIONS/ITEMS: Switzerland inc Castle Zola, South American badlands inc mountains, New York inc SHIELD regional field office, Fenton's estate, Zola's ESP box (as "transmitter" here) & mental command stimulator, Sharon's jet-copter, File 116, Doughboy's tele-sight, Red Skull's Cyrus Fenton mask
SYNOPSIS: Cap recovers and takes on Primus, but Zola prods Doughboy to ensnare him and Donna Maria. Primus complains about Zola's intervention, asserting his independence as Doughboy lands at Castle Zola and deposits Cap and Donna Maria into Chamber Four. The two captives realize they are not alone. In South America, Falcon takes shelter from the boulder avalanche, then comes face to face with another Zola creation, a monstrous bird. In New York, Nelson puts Sharon on the File 116 case, instructing her to investigate Cyrus Fenton, an eccentric millionaire, who may be the financial source of the monster-making. At Castle Zola, Primus demands Donna Maria but Zola forces him to merge with Doughboy. Soon after, Zola contacts his benefactor, the Red Skull, to tell him he has captured Cap. Witnessing Sharon Carter's jet-copter landing on his grounds, the Skull dons a mask and greets Sharon at the door as Cyrus Fenton.

CAPTAIN AMERICA #211 (July 1977)

"Nazi "X"!" (17 pages)

CREDITS: Jack Kirby (writer, pencils, editor), Mike Royer (inks, letters), Glynis Wein (colors), Archie Goodwin (consulting editor), Frank Giacoia (c inks), Gaspar Saladino (c letters)
FEATURE CHARACTER: Captain America
SUPPORTING CAST: Sharon Carter
VILLAINS: Red Skull (also as Cyrus Fenton), Arnim Zola, Nazi X (genetic construct w/Adolf Hitler's brain, 1st but last bts in Cap #210, '77, see NOTE), organic Chamber Four & castle pit
OTHER CHARACTERS: Donna Maria Puentes, Adolf Hitler (bts in fb only between SVTU #17, '80 fb & FF #21, '63, off-panel as his brain is removed), Nazi soldiers and scientists (in fb only), demon (as Castle Zola statue only)
LOCATIONS/ITEMS: Switzerland inc Castle Zola w/his lab & underground lab, Fenton's estate, Berlin, Germany inc operating room (in fb only); Zola's ESP box, mental command stimulator, mental possession machine & animated castle weapons, Red Skull's Cyrus Fenton mask, Sharon's electro-pistol
FLASHBACK: Nazi doctors remove Hitler's brain. A Nazi plane spirits it away.
SYNOPSIS: In Chamber Four, Nazi X attacks Cap and Donna Maria. Zola intervenes, commanding Chamber Four to restrain his creation. He opens Nazi X's helmet to reveal "a most valuable human brain." Donna Maria jumps Zola while Cap takes his stimulator. The couple flees but Zola hurries to his lab and connects to a machine that allows his mind to animate the entire castle. He attacks Cap and Donna Maria with curtains, doorknobs, and weapons, forcing them into a dark pit. Meanwhile, Sharon interviews Cyrus Fenton. Thinking him a harmless "old dear," she touches his face and realizes it is a mask. Fenton unmasks as the Red Skull, admitting that he did away with the real Fenton some time before. Sharon uses an electro-pistol to gain the upper hand. The Skull tells her he has captured Cap and agrees to take her to him. Meanwhile, the Castle Zola pit manifests an eye and mouth and goads Cap and Donna Maria to Zola's underground lab. There, Zola reveals that Nazi X houses Adolf Hitler's brain and declares his intention to place it in Captain America's body.
NOTE: Nazi X called "Nazi-X" on cover. YM #24, '53 fb reveals that the Human Torch burns Hitler to death, and SVTU #17, '80 fb reveals that Arnim Zola created a clone brain for Hitler to transfer his consciousness into at that moment. While it is possible that Zola is lying to Cap about Nazi X having Hitler's brain, these issues do not contradict his assertion. The Nazi doctors would be removing Hitler's original brain from his charred body even though Zola previously transferred his consciousness to a clone brain. Nazi X's presence amongst Hitler's cloned bodies in SVTU #17, '80 fb implies that he is a viable option into which Zola could transfer Hitler's consciousness with the brain operating in autonomic mode as Nazi X. Letters page changes its name to "Letters to the Living Legend."

CAPTAIN AMERICA #212 (August 1977)

"The Face of a Hero!" (17 pages)

CREDITS: Jack Kirby (writer, pencils, editor), Mike Royer (inks, letters), Petra Goldberg (colors), Archie Goodwin (consulting editor), Frank Giacoia (c inks), Jim Novak (c letters)
FEATURE CHARACTER: Captain America
SUPPORTING CAST: Sharon Carter (next in Cap #217, '78)
VILLAINS: Red Skull (next in Cap #226, '78), Arnim Zola (next in SVTU #17, '80), Nazi X (last app), "the Big Eared Sentry and his Savage Companion" (both die), Primus, Doughboy (both bts, next in Cap #275, '82)
OTHER CHARACTERS: Donna Maria Puentes (next in Cap #404, '92), SHIELD agents, Adolf Hitler (on viewscreen only)
LOCATIONS/ITEMS: Switzerland inc Alps & Castle Zola (destroyed/dies) w/his underground lab; Red Skull's rocket plane, Zola's lab equipment, Sharon's pistol & homing device, SHIELD weapons & helicopters

SYNOPSIS: As Cap and Zola confront each other in the lab, Donna Maria throws a chemical-filled bottle that starts a fire, engulfing Zola. Grabbing other bottles of chemicals, Cap and Donna Maria flee. Meanwhile, the Red Skull ferries Sharon to the Alps and Castle Zola. The lab re sets off explosions that affect the living castle. It attacks Cap who fights it off with more explosive chemicals. Cap and Donna Maria enter he courtyard where two Zola creations accost them. As Donna Maria sets "the Big Eared Sentry" ablaze, Cap battles his "Murder-Machine" ompanion. The Skull and Sharon arrive. Sharon shoots a chemical vial that explodes and destroys the creature but the explosion and the nonster's assault blind Cap. Soon after, the entire castle explodes. Sharon and Donna Maria escape but the Skull grabs Cap, forcing him to tay. However, a tower falls, separating the combatants. Sharon and Donna Maria pull Cap to safety as SHIELD agents, following Sharon's idden homing device, arrive. They carry the blinded, wounded Cap to a helicopter and lift him, Sharon, and Donna Maria to safety.
NOTE: Cap, referring to Hitler, tells Zola, "You've kept that monster's brain alive since '44" but Hitler's demise takes place in 1945.

CAPTAIN AMERICA #213 (September 1977)

"The Night Flyer!" (17 pages)

CREDITS: Jack Kirby (writer, pencils, editor), Dan Green (inks), Joe Rosen (letters), George Roussos (colors), Archie Goodwin (consulting editor), Frank Giacoia (c inks), Jim Novak (c letters)
FEATURE CHARACTERS: Captain America (also in his own nightmare), Falcon
VILLAINS: Night Flyer (assassin, 1st), The Corporation (criminal organization, last in DHKF #31, '76, last bts in Hulk #212, '77, chr last in NF:AoS #36, '92 fb): Kligger (Eugene Kligger Stivak, Corporation East Coast leader, US Senator, 1st but last bts in DD #127, '75, next bts in DD #131, '76, next in MPr #39, '78), Veda (Lt. Cynthia Glass' daughter, 1st, next in Cap #217, '78), Kurt Jacobi (SHIELD sleeper agent, 1st), Night Flyer's "creator" (bts, voice only, see NOTE)
OTHER CHARACTERS: Red Skull & his Skull-faced men, Nazi soldiers (all in Steve's nightmare only), Defector heavily-bandaged patient, see NOTE), SHIELD agents & orderlies
LOCATIONS/ITEMS: SHIELD medical complex inc Section D w/Steve's room, Corporation office near SHIELD medical complex, Night Flyer's home, Skull's castle w/Door of Death (in Steve's nightmare only); Skull's gun & cannon, Nazi weapons (all in Steve's nightmare only), Night Flyer's hang glider, armor & gun, sleeper agent's steel bar, SHIELD agents' guns, SHIELD patrol planes, Defector dummy
SYNOPSIS: After dreaming that he is fighting the Red Skull, Cap awakens, still blind, in the hospital. The Falcon, whom a SHIELD team escued in South America killing "Big Bird," is by his bedside. Just then, SHIELD orderlies bring in a heavily-bandaged patient whom they call the Defector. That night, a sleeper agent who has infiltrated SHIELD tries to eliminate the Defector but Cap intervenes. Although blind, Cap lefeats the agent, knocking him out the window. Meanwhile, hearing his sleeper agent has failed, Corporation East Coast leader Kligger allows his protégé Veda to call in her assassin, the mystic, perfection-seeking Night Flyer who rides his hang glider to the SHIELD facility. There, he Falcon attacks him. Night Flyer fights off the Falcon, then, leaving his hang glider to circle above, evades a SHIELD assault force, enters Steve's room, and shoots the Defector. The Falcon and SHIELD agents enter and surround him, revealing that the Defector he shot is a dummy, eplacing the real one after the sleeper agent attempt. The Night Flyer surrenders his weapon but announces that he must find and eliminate is target and that "no one here can prevent it."
NOTE: Cap #218, '78 reveals Veda to be Cynthia Glass' daughter. Jacobi named in Cap:AmAv, '11. In Cap #214, '77, Cap speculates that he Defector was never in the medical complex at all but this is not confirmed. Night Flyer communicates over a walkie-talkie device with an associate" who preaches perfection. In Hulk #264, '81, the Corruptor assumes that role telling Night Flyer, "I neither know nor care who it was hat created you" implying that Night Flyer is an artificial being. The shapeshifter Dead Ringer used Night Flyer's ashes to assume his form in Cap #426, '96, implying Night Flyer was biological, but in HfH #5, '06, Orka dismantled several robotic Night Flyers.

"The Deserted City!" (1 page)
CREDITS: Unknown
FEATURE CHARACTER: Captain America (between Cap #241-242, '80)
VILLAIN: The Mad Deserter (mad scientist)
OTHER CHARACTERS: City's inhabitants
LOCATIONS/ITEMS: Unidentified city inc Mad Deserter's lab & town outskirts; Deserter Ray, Hostess Fruit Pies
SYNOPSIS: The Mad Deserter has used his Deserter Ray to turn the city's inhabitants zombie-like, and make them leave their families and homes. When Captain America searches the empty city, the Deserter shoots him too, but Cap shrugs off the effects on the town outskirts to find himself surrounded by the Deserter's other victims. After reviving their free will with Hostess Fruit Pies, Cap captures the Deserter.
NOTE: Appeared in various Gold Key titles, February 1980.

CAPTAIN AMERICA #214 (October 1977)

"Power" (17 pages)

CREDITS: Jack Kirby (writer, pencils, editor), Mike Royer (inks, letters), Sam Kata (colors), Archie Goodwin (consulting editor), Frank Giacoia (c inks), Jim Novak (c letters)
FEATURE CHARACTERS: Captain America, Falcon
VILLAINS: Night Flyer (also on monitor, next in Hulk #263, '81), Kurt Jacobi (next in Cap #217, '78)
OTHER CHARACTERS: SHIELD agents (some die) inc monitor personnel & missile battery five (bts, shoo hang glider down)
LOCATIONS/ITEMS: SHIELD medical complex inc monitor room & Section D w/Steve's room and storage bin; SHIELD agents' guns, Night Flyer's hang glider, armor, electric generator & flame thrower, SHIELD missiles sleeper agent's gun
SYNOPSIS: The Night Flyer uses "the Power," a high-voltage shock forced to repel Cap, Falcon, and the SHIELD agents. He retrieves his gun and fires at Cap whose instincts and reflexes save him. Searching for his target, Night Flyer explores the rest of the complex. Falcon recovers and assaults him but falls to an electric blast. Although still blind, Cap suits up and comes upon the sleeper agent who meets with Night Flyer to lead him to the Defector. Just after the Night Flyer locks Falcon in a storage bin, Cap strikes the sleeper agent with his shield but cannot preven him from grabbing a flame thrower. As the Falcon batters his way out of the bin, SHIELD monitor personnel pinpoint the Night Flyer's hang glide circling overhead. They order it shot down. The hang glider's destruction sends a power surge through Night Flyer, charring and apparently killing him. Soon after, Cap's eyesight returns. He suggests that the Night Flyer's gunshot "jogged the proper nerve into action." Night Flyer and the sleeper agent are taken away. Cap and Falcon decide to call Sharon and Leila to celebrate.
NOTE: Leila Taylor called "Lila" here.

CAPTAIN AMERICA #215 (November 1977)

"The Way it REALLY Was!" (17 pages)

CREDITS: Roy Thomas (writer, editor), George Tuska (pencils), Pablo Marcos (inks), Joe Rosen (letters) George Roussos (colors), Archie Goodwin (consulting editor), Gil Kane (c pencils), Joe Sinnott (c inks), Gaspar Saladino (c letters)
FEATURE CHARACTERS: Captain America (also in fb1 between Cap:Re #2, '09 & ToS #63/2, '65, fb2 between Cap #12, '05 fb & Cap #109, '69 fb, fb3 between Av #4, '64 fb & Cap #220, '78 fb, fb6 between Cap #220, '78 fb & MSaga #1, '85, fb7 between Cap #192, '75 & Hulk #229, '78 fb), Falcon (next in Cap #217, '78) (both also in rfb)
GUEST STARS: Spirit of '76 (William Naslund, becomes Captain America, also in rfb, in fb4 between Cap Ann #13, '94 fb & Twelve #1, '08, in fb5 as corpse during WI #4, '77), Patriot (Jeff Mace, only in fb5 during WI #4, '77)
SUPPORTING CAST: Sgt. Mike Duffy (only in fb2 between ToS #63/2, '65 & Cap:SoL #12, '99 fb)
OTHER CHARACTERS: Avengers: Giant-Man, Iron Man, Scarlet Witch, Thor, Vision; Invaders: Bucky (James Barnes), Human Torch, Spitfire, Sub-Mariner, Toro, Union Jack; Adam-II's android, Bucky (Rick Jones), Bucky (Jack Monroe), Captain America (Burnside), Sharon Carter, Professor Erskine, Hydra agents, Heinz Krueger, Red Skull (Johann Shmidt) & his men, Red Skull (Albert Malik), Redwing, SHIELD doctor, Eskimos, government officials, Nazis, surgeons (all only in rfb); Black Panther, Nick Fury, Adolf Hitler (prev 3 on cover only); Harry S Truman (US President, only in fb4 to 1st chr app before WI #4, '77), Camp Lehigh soldiers (only in fb2); New York citizens & tourists
LOCATIONS/ITEMS: Project: Rebirth, Europe, Camp Lehigh, English Channel, Washington DC inc White House (all in fbs), New York City; Super Soldier Serum, Vita-Rays, Cap's original steel shield, German guns & tanks, Steve's rifle, Zemo's stolen drone plane, Cap's (Naslund) replacement shield, Maj. Kerfoot's journal, Cosmic Cube (all in fbs)
FLASHBACKS: Steve Rogers prepares for Operation: Rebirth (1). Steve drinks Professor Erskine's Super Soldier Serum and is bombarded by Vita-Rays. Heinz Krueger kills Erskine and Steve accidentally kills Krueger (ToS #63/2, '65, Cap #109, '69 fb & CapC #1, '41). Captain America battles spies and Nazis (CapC #1, '41 & ToS #68/2, '65). At Camp Lehigh, Sgt. Duffy gives Pvt. Rogers a hard time (2). Bucky discovers Steve is Captain America (CapC #1, '41) and becomes his partner (ToS #63/2, '65). Cap and Bucky battle the Red Skull (ToS #68/2, '65) and fight with the Invaders (Inv #20, '77). Bucky tries to stop Zemo's stolen drone plane but is caught in the explosion when it detonates. Cap is thrown into the English Channel (Av #4, '64 fb) and begins to drift (3). President Truman calls on the Spirit of '76 to be the new Captain America. Truman says his Bucky is being looked into, and prepares to give the Invaders the news of Captain America's death and replacement (4). As Captain America, Naslund is killed by Adam-II's android (WI #4, '77). The Patriot finds Naslund's corpse and vows to keep Captain America "alive." (5) Steve Rogers lives on, frozen in a block of ice (6). William Burnside finds Maj. Kerfoots journal, undergoes plastic surgery and becomes the new Captain America (Cap #155, '72 fb). He battles the Red Skull (Malik) (YM #24/2, '54) but he and Bucky (Monroe) are placed in suspended animation, having been driven insane through improper use of the Super Soldier Serum (Cap #155, '72 fb). The frozen Steve Rogers is worshipped by Eskimos until he's found by Namor and revived by the Avengers (Av #4, '64). Cap battles Hydra with the new Bucky, Rick Jones (Cap #110, '69), and becomes partners with Falcon while battling the Red Skull (Cap #119, '69). Cap defeats the revived Cap (Burnside) (Cap #156, '72) and fights alongside the Avengers (Av #108, '73). Steve smashes a mirror, ashamed of the youth he feels he doesn't deserve (7). Captain America is blinded during a fight with the Red Skull (Cap #212, '77) and recovers in a SHIELD hospital (Cap #213, '77).
SYNOPSIS: With his sight recently restored, Captain America returns to New York City with Falcon. They're quickly surrounded by admirers who ask for autographs, but Cap declines, lost in thought. When Cap finishes reminiscing he realizes he no longer knows who Steve Rogers is.
NOTE: Issue includes Hostess ad, Spider-Man in "Legal Eagle."

CAPTAIN AMERICA #216 (December 1977)

"The Human Torch Meets…Captain America" (19 pages)

CREDITS: Roy Thomas (page 1 writer), Dave Cockrum (page 1 pencils), Frank Giacoia (page 1 inks), Irving Watanabe (page 1 & c letters), Gil Kane (c pencils), Ernie Chan (c inks) for other credits see original entry
FEATURE CHARACTER: Captain America (next in MSS #1, Av #157-160, all '77, MTE #13, '76, CM #50-51, Av #161-162, IF #12, all '77, Av #169, '78, Av #164-166, X #108, Cap Ann #4, all '77)
OTHER CHARACTERS: Bystanders
NOTE: Reprinted from ST #114, '63. Contains new page 1 showing Cap in Manhattan in current continuity followed by reprinted 18-page story. Adds asterisk and note to title page. Final panel caption is cut w/illustration retouched. Next Issue caption is changed. Story is recolored. Issue includes Hostess ad, Spider-Man in "Legal Eagle."

CAPTAIN AMERICA ANNUAL #4 (1977)

"The Great Mutant Massacre!" (34 pages)

CREDITS: Jack Kirby (writer, pencils, editor), John Tartaglione, John Verpoorten (inks), James Novak (letters), George Roussos (colors), Archie Goodwin (consulting editor), Frank Giacoia (c inks)
FEATURE CHARACTER: Captain America (next in SVTU #14, '77, Av Ann #7, '77, MTIO Ann #2, '77, Av #167-168, '78, Def #58, '78, DD&Cap #1, '08, Av #170-177, '78, Av:KS, '03, CX #20, '88, Thor #271, '78, Cap #217, '78)
VILLAINS: Magneto (last in X #104, '77, chr last in X #76, '98 fb, chr next in CX #12/2, '87, next in SVTU #14, '77) & his Brotherhood of Evil Mutants: Burner (Byron Calley, pyrokinetic), Lifter (Ned Lathrop, telekinetic), Peepers (Peter Quinn, telescopic vision), Shocker (Randall Darby, lobster pincer hands), Slither (Aaron Solomon, snake-like body) (all 1st, next in Def #78, '79)
OTHER CHARACTERS: Mr. One & Mr. Two (mutant with two telepathically connected bodies, both die), Joe Keegan (all only app), SHIELD doctor, scientists & field agents, bird; Professor X (mentioned in Cap's thoughts, unable to be reached)
LOCATIONS/ITEMS: Joe Keegan's house, SHIELD Medical Research Department inc Mr. Two's cell, Magneto's lair inc ready room & escape hatch, park; Joe's newspaper ad & wristwatch for Mr. One, Magneto's Magna-craft, box for Mr. One, candle, monitor & swords, SHIELD medical equipment inc incubator for Mr. One, electric unit, helicopter & guns, miniature spaceship w/self-destruct
SYNOPSIS: Responding to a newspaper ad about mutants, Captain America briefly tussles with Magneto, who is also answering the ad. They're interrupted by Joe Keegan, who tells them that he found a pair of mutants and needs someone with scientific knowledge to care for them. He opens the face of his wristwatch, revealing a tiny man, Mr. One, inside. Magneto levitates the watch away from Joe, only to have his helmet crushed by Mr. Two, the other mutant. Joe takes back his watch, and Mr. Two tosses Magneto through the wall. Later, Steve Rogers checks on the mutants at a local SHIELD medical facility. It seems that Mr. One controls Mr. Two, and Steve has to remind the SHIELD doctor that the two are more than just test subjects when Mr. Two becomes restless. Meanwhile, Magneto inspects a miniature spaceship and convinces his new Brotherhood, Burner, Lifter, Peepers, Shocker and Slither, to abduct Mr. One and Mr. Two. They attack Cap and Mr. Two, who are out for a jog, but the villains are driven off by SHIELD agents. Cap returns to SHIELD only to discover that Magneto kidnapped Mr. One in his absence. Cap theorizes that Mr. One and Mr. Two are one person with two bodies. Meanwhile, Magneto forces Mr. One to do his bidding. Cap and Mr. Two track down Magneto and his minions for a confrontation. Mr. Two is killed by Burner, and, feeling the loss of his other self, Mr. One climbs in the spaceship and sets it to self-destruct. Realizing his cause is lost, Magneto escapes before his base is destroyed.
NOTE: While this Annual was published during Kirby's run on Cap, Magneto's chronology requires this to take place afterward. In addition, Cap #215-216, '77 continue directly from Kirby's last issue, Cap #214, '77, placing this Annual between Cap #216-217, '77-78. Shocker is not to be confused with the Spider-Man villain.

"The Deciding Factor!" (1 page)
CREDITS: Unknown
FEATURE CHARACTER: Captain America (between Cap #246-247, '80)
GUEST STAR: Nick Fury (last in IM #129, '79, next in Cap #247, '80)
VILLAINS: Alien invaders
LOCATIONS/ITEMS: An alley; alien spaceship & breathing apparatus, Hostess Fruit Pies
SYNOPSIS: Finding several four-armed alien invaders getting the upper hand against Captain America, Nick Fury diverts their attention from fighting with Hostess Fruit Pies. The aliens tell one another they should return home to report this tasty find.
NOTE: Appeared in various Whtiman titles, April 1980, and Marvel titles, March 1982.

"Fury Unleashed" (1 page)
CREDITS: Unknown
FEATURE CHARACTER: Captain America (between Cap #252-253, '80-81)
GUEST STAR: Nick Fury (last in MFan #13, '84, next in IM #141, '80)
VILLAINS: The Trapster (last in FF #218, '80, next in ASM #214, '81), Trapster's goon (only app)
LOCATIONS/ITEMS: Trapster's lair; video monitor, Hostess Fruit Pies
SYNOPSIS: In Trapster's lair Captain America find Trapster's giant goon holding Nick Fury by the neck, ready to snap it if Cap makes a wrong move. As the gloating Trapster watches Cap's dilemma from another room, Cap throws his shield loaded with Hostess Fruit Pies towards the goon, who releases Fury in favor of eating the delicious treats.
NOTE: Appeared in various Marvel titles, January 1981.

CAPTAIN AMERICA #217 (January 1978)

"The Search for Steve Rogers!" (17 pages)

CREDITS: Roy Thomas (co-writer, editor), Don Glut (co-writer), John Buscema (pencils), Pablo Marcos (inks), Denise Wohl (letters), Phil Rachelson (colors), Archie Goodwin (consulting editor), Frank Giacoia (c inks), Gaspar Saladino (c letters)

FEATURE CHARACTERS: Captain America, Falcon (joins SHIELD Super-Agents)

GUEST STARS: SHIELD Super-Agents: Marvel Boy (Wendell Elvis Vaughan, powered by Quantum Bands, 1st but chr last in Q #1, '89 fb, see NOTE), Texas Twister (Drew Daniels, able to generate high-power winds, last in FF #192, '78); Nick Fury (last in FF #197, chr last in Q #1, '89 fb), Dum Dum Dugan (last in Godz #15, chr last in Q #1, '89 fb, next in MTU #71, '72)

SUPPORTING CAST: Redwing (last in Cap #191, '75, chr last in Cap #25, '07 fb, next in Cap #220/2, '78), Sharon Carter (last in Cap #212, '77)

VILLAINS: Blue Streak (Don Thomas, wears rocket-powered roller skates), Vamp (Denise Baranger, wears belt to duplicate others' powers) (both SHIELD Super-Agents working for Corporation, 1st, see NOTE), Kurt Jacobi (last in Cap #214, '77, dies), Kligger (last in MPr #40, '78, next in Cap #220, '78), Veda (last in Cap #213, '78), Corporation thugs

OTHER CHARACTERS: 2 SHIELD barbers (only app), barber shop patrons, SHIELD agents, Cap & Falcon fans, bus driver, bank employee, alley cat

LOCATIONS/ITEMS: New York inc SHIELD Barber Shop & HQ, Kligger's office, Steve's apartment & Sharon's apartment; SHIELD batons, guns, interrogation chair, view screen & tracer, Blue Streak's skates, Vamp's belt, Quantum Bands, Kligger's monitor, Corporation thugs' guns

SYNOPSIS: Captain America and Falcon sign autographs until Falcon directs Cap to the SHIELD barber shop HQ entrance. Once below, the heroes are tested by SHIELD agents until Nick Fury & Dum Dum Dugan arrive. Fury introduces them to the SHIELD Super-Agents, Blue Streak, Marvel Boy, Texas Twister, and Vamp, and asks Cap to train them as team leader. Cap turns the offer down so Fury has the team attack Cap to prove their mettle. Cap quickly defeats the Super-Agents and suggests Falcon as team leader. Fury accepts and Cap leaves as he's spied on by Kligger and Veda from afar. After discussing their mole in the SHIELD Super-Agents, Veda leaves to intercept Cap. At his apartment, Steve calls Sharon asking for a break in their relationship while he searches for his past. He goes for a walk where he happens across a staged mugging with Vera as the "victim." She reveals that she knows he's Cap, and that she has information on his past. Veda throws herself at Steve just as Sharon approaches. Steve sees Sharon leave visibly upset, but goes with Vera to learn more.

NOTE: Wendell Vaughan only goes by "Marvel Boy" in this issue, he takes on the code-name "Marvel Man" in Cap #218, '78, and will eventually adopt his more widely known code-name "Quasar" in Hulk #234, '79. His real name is revealed in MTIO #53, '79. Blue Streak's real name revealed in CW:BDR, '07, and that he's a sleeper agent in Cap #229, '79. Vamp's real name revealed in OHMU HC #4, '08, and that she's also a sleeper agent in Cap #230, '79. Bound into the center of the comic is an ad for Marvel's kid's magazine, Pizzazz, featuring Spider-Man, Ms. Marvel, Hulk, Power Man, Stan Lee, and children. Issue includes Hostess ad, Thor in "The Ding-A-Ling Family."

CAPTAIN AMERICA #218 (February 1978)

"One Day in Newfoundland!" (17 pages)

CREDITS: Don Glut (writer), Sal Buscema (pencils), Michael Esposito, John Tartaglione (inks), John Costanza (letters), George Roussos (colors), Joe Sinnot (c inks), Roy Thomas (editor), Gaspar Saladino (c letters)

FEATURE CHARACTERS: Captain America (also in rfb), Falcon (next in Cap #220/2, '78)

GUEST STARS: SHIELD Super-Agents: Marvel Man (Wendell Elvis Vaughan, next in Def #62, '78), Texas Twister (next in Cap #228, '78); Nick Fury (chr next in SW:O #3, '06, next bts in SW #1, '78, next in MTU #71, '78), Iron Man (also in rfb, last in MPr #47, '79, next in IM #113 '78)

SUPPORTING CAST: Sharon Carter (next in Cap #231, '79 fb)

VILLAINS: "General" Lyle Dekker (former Nazi scientist, 1st but chr last in Cap #220, '78 fb), Blue Streak (next in Cap #228, '79), Vamp (next in Cap #222, '78), Veda (next in Cap #220, '78), Corporation thugs, Dekker's men

OTHER CHARACTERS: Edwin Jarvis (last in Av #175, '78, last bts in Av #176, '78, chr last in A #280, '87 fb, next in Cap #220 '78), police, Newfoundland citizens, "Red Lobster Inn" waiter; Avengers: Giant-Man, Thor, Wasp; Agent R (also in photo), Prof. Erskine, Gen. Phillips, Operation: Rebirth scientist (prev 7 in rfb)

LOCATIONS/ITEMS: New York inc SHIELD HQ w/gym & Avengers Mansion w/sub dock, Newfoundland inc Red Lobster Inn, docks & General Dekker's lab w/underground tunnels; Avengers sub (also in rfb) w/ audio tapes & Quinjet, Corporation thugs' guns, Cap's descent bags, stolen cargo, Dekker's men's guns, knife, axe, mace, spear & spiked knuckles, Dekker's Ameridroid (12' tall Captain America robot, 1st) & equipment

FLASHBACKS: Steve Rogers undergoes Operation: Rebirth (Cap #109, '69 fb). The Avengers find Captain America's frozen body floating in the waters off Newfoundland (Av #4, '64).

SYNOPSIS: Corporation thugs attack Captain America and Veda. Cap quickly defeats them and tells the police to turn them over to SHIELD. The pair continue on to Avengers Mansion where Veda shows Cap a photo of Agent R, Veda's mother. As Veda moves closer to Cap Iron Man arrives, who mistakes Veda for Sharon Carter. At SHIELD HQ, Fury directs Sharon to the gym where Falcon is training the SHIELD Super-Agents. She tells Falcon about Cap kissing Veda. Cap and Iron Man go to the sub dock and board the Sub where Cap listens to audio tapes of when the Avengers discovered his frozen body in the water off Newfoundland. Cap then travels to Newfoundland where he hopes to learn more about his past. While walking around a small town, Steve sees uniformed men acting strangely. As Captain America, he chases them through tunnels under the docks, quickly defeating them. Looking around, Cap finds himself in a laboratory, where he's approached by "General" Lyle Dekker, who shows Cap his giant Ameridroid.

NOTE: Bound into the center of the comic is an ad for Marvel's kid's magazine, Pizzazz, featuring Spider-Man, Ms. Marvel, Hulk, Power Man, Stan Lee and children. Issue includes Hostess ad, Thor in "The Ding-A-Ling Family."

CAPTAIN AMERICA #219 (March 1978)

"The Adventures of Captain America!" (17 pages)

CREDITS: Don Glut (writer), John Buscema (pencils), Joe Sinnot (inks), Carolyn Lay (letters), George Roussos (colors), Roy Thomas (editor), Archie Goodwin (consulting editor), Jim Novak (c letters)
FEATURE CHARACTER: Captain America (also as "Grant Gardner," Cap's serial alias, also in fb1 between CapC #35/4-36, '44, in fb2 between CapC #37/4, '44 & Cap #600/2, '09 fb)
SUPPORTING CAST: Bucky (only in fb1 between CapC #35/4-36, '44, in fb2 between CapC #37/4-38, '44), Sgt. Mike Duffy (only in fb1 between CapC #34, '44 & CapC #36, '44)
VILLAINS: "General" Lyle Dekker (also in fb to 1st chr app before Cap #220, '78 fb), Red Skull (only in fb1 between Av/Inv #9, '09 & Cap #220, '78 fb)
OTHER CHARACTERS: Sundown Dawson ("the Singing Cowboy") & his horse Six-Gun (the "smartest horse in the world"), Whit Spencer (director), Glenn Reeper (Captain America stuntman), Adrian (actress playing "Gail Richards"), Democracy Pictures crew (inc choreographer), other actors (some as cowboys), other horses (all only in fb), Franklin D. Roosevelt (bts in fb, sent Cap on mission, between YA #7, '43 & SgtF #51, '68)
LOCATIONS/ITEMS: Fort Lehigh, Democracy Pictures inc backlot, set, Dekker's workshop & warehouse, New York inc movie theater (all in fb), General Dekker's Newfoundland lab; Lehigh potatoes, cargo plane, Cap's & Bucky's parachutes, Democracy Pictures' prop guns, lighting, cameras, helicopter, motorcycle & movie posters inc "Six Gun Shootout" & "Jet-Man vs. Crime Inc." & "Adventures of Captain America," Dekker's special effects equipment, radio, heat ray, gun & truck (all in fb), Dekker's Ameridroid & equipment
FLASHBACKS: Pvt. Steve Rogers and James Barnes are on KP duty at Fort Lehigh when Sgt. Duffy informs them they've been given two week's furlough. By order of the President, they report to Democracy Pictures as Captain America and Bucky to guard the serial "Adventures of Captain America" against Axis sabotage. Parachuting in, the heroes meet movie star Sundown Dawson who introduces them to Lyle Dekker, Democracy's special effects man. Meeting the director, Bucky is chagrined to discover he's not represented in the serial, and that Cap's secret identity is a District Attorney. While filming the fourth chapter, the stuntman is shot, and Cap takes his place for the rest of filming. Later, Dekker reports to Red Skull and rigs a heat ray to kill Captain America. When the ray is fired during filming, Cap destroys the device. Dekker takes Bucky hostage and escapes by truck, so Cap pursues on motorcycle. Cap catches up and overpowers Dekker, forcing the truck off a cliff. Dekker seemingly dies while Cap and Bucky are rescued by Sundown Dawson and Six-Gun (1). Steve and James attend the first chapter showing of the "Adventures of Captain America" serial (2).
SYNOPSIS: In General Dekker's secret lab, Captain America remembers the first time he met Dekker. Dekker electrifies Cap into unconsciousness.
NOTE: The 15 chapter serial "Captain America" was a Republic Pictures production. It was filmed from October 12, 1943 to November 24, 1943 and debuted in theaters on February 5, 1944. Lyle Dekker is named after Republic's in-house special effects team, the Lydecker brothers, Theodore and Howard. Director Whit Spencer is the Marvel Universe stand in for the serial's two directors, Elmer Clifton and John English, stuntman Glenn Reeper is the stand in for Dale Van Sickel, and Adrian is the stand in for actress Lorna Gray. Issue includes Hostess ad, Spider-Man "Spoils a Snatch."

CAPTAIN AMERICA #220 (April 1978)

"The Ameridroid Lives!" (13 pages)

CREDITS: Don Glut (writer), Sal Buscema (pencils), Michael Esposito, John Tartaglione (inks), Carolyn Lay (letters), George Roussos (colors), Roy Thomas (editor), Archie Goodwin (consulting editor), Gil Kane (c pencils), Klaus Janson (c inks), Irving Watanabe (c letters)
FEATURE CHARACTER: Captain America (also in fb2 between Cap:Re #4, '10 & Av #4, '64 fb, in fb3 during Cap #215, '77 fb)
SUPPORTING CAST: Bucky (also in rfb, only in fb2 between Cap:Re #4, '10 & Av #4, '64 fb)
VILLAINS: "General" Lyle Dekker (also in fb1 & fb3 between Cap #219, '78 fb & Cap #218, '78, becomes Ameridroid), Kligger (next bts in Cap #222, '78, next in Cap #223, '78), Veda (next in Cap #222, '78), Red Skull (only in fb1 between Cap #219, '78 fb & Cap #600/2, '09 fb) & his men (in fb1), Dekker's men (others in fb1)
OTHER CHARACTERS: Edwin Jarvis (next in Cap #222, '78), Newfoundland fishermen, bartender & bar patrons (in fb1), Baron Heinrich Zemo & his men (in rfb), fish (in fb1 & fb3)
LOCATIONS/ITEMS: Newfoundland (also in fb1) inc Dekker's lab (also in fb3), English Channel (in rfb, fb2 & fb3), Atlantic Ocean (in fb3), New York inc Avengers Mansion, Kligger's office; Red Skull's sub, fishermen's boat (both in fb1), Zemo's drone plane (also in fb2), Zemo's men's guns, Cap's motorcycle (prev 3 in rfb), Dekker's men's guns (also in fb3), Dekker's sub, nerve gas, heat ray & plane (in fb3), Dekker's Ameridroid & equipment (also in fb3)
FLASHBACKS: Aboard Red Skull's submarine, Red Skull tortures Lyle Dekker for his failure to sabotage the "Captain America" serial. Dekker is jettisoned out a torpedo tube and eventually picked up by fishermen. In Newfoundland, Dekker recruits an army of mercenaries (1). Captain America and Bucky try to stop Baron Zemo's launched drone plane (Av #4, '64 fb). Bucky is caught in the plane's explosion, and Cap is thrown into the English Channel (2). Cap is picked up by Dekker's men and brought onto Dekker's submarine. After his army uniform is removed, he meets Dekker, now calling himself "General" Dekker, as the sub speeds west until it docks in Newfoundland. Dekker brings Cap to his lab and shows Cap his experimental nerve gas and a device designed to transfer Cap's power into Dekker's body. Cap breaks free and retrieves his shield. Out of sight, Cap redresses in his army uniform for a disguise and tries to escape by plane, but Dekker's men shoot it down with a heat ray. Cap is bathed in nerve gas and crashes in the Atlantic Ocean off the coast of Newfoundland (3).
SYNOPSIS: "General" Dekker tells Captain America how he survived their last encounter as he saps Cap's energy with his equipment. Dekker

hooks himself into his equipment and begins the final stages of his plan to steal Cap's power. At Avengers Mansion, Veda checks in with Kligger. In Newfoundland, Dekker's body dies as his mind is transferred into the Ameridroid, now fueled by Captain America's strength.
NOTE: Bucky is also found and retrieved by enemy agents, as revealed in Cap #8, '05 fb & Cap #11, '05 fb.

2ND STORY: "…On a Wing and a Prayer!" (5 pages)
CREDITS: Scott Edelman (writer), Bob Budiansky (pencils), Al Gordon (inks), Jim Novak (letters), George Roussos (colors), Archie Goodwin (editor)
FEATURE CHARACTER: Falcon (also as homeless man, next in MTU #71, '78, Def #62-64, '78, Cap #230, '79)
SUPPORTING CAST: Redwing (next in MTU #71, '78)
VILLAIN: Mortimer Freebish (arrow-themed villain, can't decide to call himself Arrow Ace, Arrowsmith, or something else, only app)
OTHER CHARACTERS: Homeless man, pigeons (one dies)
LOCATIONS/ITEMS: New York inc Washington Square Park, Harlem; Falcon's homeless man disguise, Mortimer's note, glass ball & arrow inc net-arrow, opti-arrow, explosive arrows & pitch-forked arrow
SYNOPSIS: Falcon tries to call for Redwing, but is almost struck by an arrow with an attached ransom note. Falcon responds at Washington Square Park to find Redwing trapped in a glass globe by Mortimer Freebish. Despite the villain's various trick arrows, Falcon quickly knocks him out and frees Redwing.
NOTE: MCIndex #8A, '79 reveals this backup story was needed because the last four pages of the 1st story were lost. Issue includes Hostess ad, Spider-Man "Spoils a Snatch."

CAPTAIN AMERICA #221 (May 1978)

"Cul-de-sac!" (12 pages)

CREDITS: Steve Gerber, David Anthony Kraft (writers), Don Glut (plot, pgs 1-5), Sal Buscema (pencils), Michael Esposito (inks), Irving Watanabe (letters), George Roussos (colors), Archie Goodwin (editor), Gil Kane (c pencils), Tony DeZuniga (c inks), Gaspar Saladino (c letters)
FEATURE CHARACTER: Captain America (next in MTU #71, '78)
VILLAINS: Ameridroid (Lyle Dekker, also as corpse, next in Cap #261, '81), Dekker's men
OTHER CHARACTERS: Newfoundland citizens
LOCATIONS/ITEMS: Newfoundland inc Dekker's lab & a village, New York inc Steve's apartment; Dekker's equipment, Dekker's men's guns, Steve's expired milk
SYNOPSIS: Ameridroid crashes out of his lab into the Newfoundland village to declare his superiority, only to frighten the villagers. Captain America frees himself and attacks, but Ameridroid easily defeats him. Gloating over his victory, Ameridroid quickly realizes that at 12', he can't live a normal life. Enraged, he races back into his lab and beats his old body's lifeless corpse. Cap calms Ameridroid's rage, convincing him he has the chance for a new life. Mollified, Ameridroid heads north, resigned to live a life of solitude. Cap returns to his apartment to find that the power is off and his food has gone bad. Exhausted, he falls asleep in a chair.

2ND STORY: "The Coming of Captain Avenger!" (5 pages)
CREDITS: Scott Edelman (writer), Steve Leialoha (pencils), Al Gordon (inks), Bruce Patterson (letters), Irene Vartanoff (colors), Archie Goodwin (editor)
FEATURE CHARACTER: Captain America (chr last in FF #36, '65, chr next in Av #15, '65)
GUEST STARS: Avengers: Rick Jones (also as "Captain Avenger"), Thor (both chr last in FF #36, chr next in Av #15), Giant-Man, Wasp (both chr between TTA #65-66), Iron Man (chr last in ST #135, chr next in ToS #65) (all '65)
OTHER CHARACTERS: Baron Zemo & his henchmen (in Rick's fantasy), Captain Marvel (in future vision)
LOCATIONS/ITEMS: Avengers Mansion inc conference room; monitor & electrical wires, Zemo's Nullifier, Zemo's men's guns (both in Rick's fantasy)
SYNOPSIS: Rick Jones leaps into the Avengers' conference room during a meeting, trips over some wires, and fall into an electric panel. He stands up as Captain Avenger, only for Baron Zemo and his men to crash into the room. Zemo immobilizes the Avengers with his Nulifier, so Captain Avenger attacks, crushing the gun. Zemo gloats that the Avengers are now forever frozen. Rick swings at Zemo to be stopped by Captain America, realizing that it was all a fantasy. Dejected, Rick leaves thinking he'll never be a super-hero.
NOTE: Rick's Captain Avenger suit consists of Iron Man's pants, Thor's trunks, Captain America's shirt, sleeves, and gloves, and Giant-Man's chest overlay, with no mask. As Rick leaves, an image of Captain Marvel foretells Rick's future. Issue includes Hostess ad "Thor meets a Glutton for Gold."

CAPTAIN AMERICA #222 (June 1978)

"Monumental Menace!" (17 pages)

CREDITS: Steve Gerber (writer), Sal Buscema (pencils), Michael Esposito, John Tartaglione (inks), Annette Kawecki (letters), George Roussos (colors), Jim Shooter (editor), Ernie Chan (c art), Irving Watanabe (c letters)
FEATURE CHARACTER: Captain America (also in photo)
GUEST STARS: Nick Fury (last in MTU #71), Dum Dum Dugan (last in MTU #71, next in Cap #225) (all '78)
VILLAINS: Animus (Denise Baranger, giant-headed telekinetic, last in Cap #218, '78 as Vamp, see NOTE), Veda (also disguised as old woman), Kligger (bts, on phone w/Veda & controlling Animus' power)
OTHER CHARACTERS: Edwin Jarvis (last in Cap #220, '78, next in Av Ann #8, '78), Will Quigley ("Spaly Weekly" editor, only app), Pentagon personnel & MP, "Splay Weekly" secretary; Mike Rogers (in photo); Walter

Elizabeth Rogers (mentioned, Mike's parents)

LOCATIONS/ITEMS: New York inc Steve's apartment, Avengers Mansion, & SHIELD HQ, Washington DC inc Pentagon & Lincoln Monument, Maryland inc "Rogers" family home, "Splay Weekly" newspaper office; remote-controlled VW Beetle, Amtrak metroliner, Steve's military records, rented car, copies of "Splay Weekly," Lincoln statue (destroyed), lamppost, Animus' crystalline club

SYNOPSIS: A Volkswagon Beetle crashes through Captain America's third story window and chases Cap around his apartment. Cap escapes and uses a neighbor's phone to check in with the Avengers and Nick Fury, finding both Veda and Falcon uncharacteristically MIA. After Cap leaves, the neighbor removes her mask revealing Veda underneath, who checks in with Kligger. As Steve Rogers, he travels to the Pentagon to resume his search for his identity, which leads him to an unfamiliar Maryland home. Steve investigates at the local newspaper office, the "Weekly Splay." The paper's editor, Will Quigly, knew the Rogers' and tells Steve his parents died in a plane crash in 1955, their older son Mike died at Pearl Harbor and their younger son Steve hasn't been heard from in years. Retreating to the Lincoln Memorial to think, the Lincoln statue comes to life and attacks. Cap fights back reluctantly, destroying the statue. Animus emerges to kill Cap personally.

NOTE: Beginning in Cap #134, '71 and ending here, the cover title reads "Captain America & the Falcon" while the indicia continues to read "Captain America." As such, Falcon will no longer be treated as a feature character. Animus is revealed to actually be a transformed Vamp controlled by Kligger in Cap #230, '79. Issue includes Hostess ad "Thor meets a Glutton for Gold."

CAPTAIN AMERICA #223 (July 1978)

"Call Me Animus" (17 pages)

CREDITS: Steve Gerber (writer), Sal Buscema (pencils), Mike Esposito, John Tartaglione (inks), Irving Watanabe (letters), Mary Ellen Beveridge (colors), Jim Shooter (editor), Ernie Chan (c art), Gaspar Saladino (c letters)
FEATURE CHARACTER: Captain America (also in dream, next in Cap #225, '78)
GUEST STAR: Nick Fury (next in Cap #225, '78)
VILLAINS: Kligger, Veda (both next in Cap #225, '78), Animus (next in Cap #228, '78 as Vamp)
OTHER CHARACTERS: Taxi driver, hotel employees & guests, waiter, restaurant patrons, Amtrak commuters (many die); psychology professor, faceless students (both in dream)
LOCATIONS/ITEMS: Washington DC inc Lincoln & Washington Monuments, hotel inc Steve's room & restaurant, Kligger's office, classroom (in dream); Lincoln statue (remains), Animus' crystalline club, SHIELD tracer, Corporation tracer, Amtrak metroliner

SYNOPSIS: Captain America fights Animus, savagely beating him until the monstrosity vanishes. Cap tries to make sense of what he's discovered of the Rogers family as he returns to his hotel. Veda tries to invite herself into Cap's room, but Cap declines. Steve discovers tracers in his shield, so he disposes of them and calls Fury to have a background check run on Veda. After a dream about psychology class, Steve realizes that what he's looking for is locked in his mind. Deciding to seek some help for his mental blocks, Cap tells Veda he's returning to New York by train, unknowingly allowing her to give Kligger Cap's whereabouts in lieu of their tracers. Animus attacks Cap's train, and the numerous innocents hurt send Cap into a rage. Discovering Animus can't use his body's strength and telekinesis at the same time, he uses that to his advantage to defeat Animus before he teleports away again.

NOTE: Story continued in Cap #225, '78. Falcon is given billing on the splash page introduction despite his name being removed from the title and not appearing in the issue. Issue includes Hostess ad "Spider-Man meets the Home Wrecker."

CAPTAIN AMERICA #224 (August 1978)

"Saturday Night FUROR!" (17 pages)

CREDITS: Peter Gillis (writer), Michael Zeck (pencils), Mike Esposito, John Tartaglione (inks), Irving Watanabe (letters), Mary Ellen Beveridge (colors), Roger Stern (editor), Bob McLeod (c inks)
FEATURE CHARACTER: Captain America (also in pfb, during Cap #198, '76, see NOTE)
GUEST STARS: Avengers: Wasp, Yellowjacket (both chr last in Av #146, '76, chr next in Av #150, '76), Beast (chr last in Av #146, '76, chr next in X #94, '75), Iron Man (chr last in IM Ann #3, '76, chr next in MTIO #12, '75), Scarlet Witch (chr last in Av #146, '76, chr next in MTU #41, '76), Vision (chr last in Av #146, '76, chr next in IM Ann #3, '76) (all also in pfb), Thor (only in pfb, chr last in Thor #239, '75, chr next in Av #150, '76); Nick Fury (chr last in CB #27, '77, chr next in MS #31, '76)
VILLAINS: Tarantula (Anton Rodriguez, criminal acrobat, wears poison spiked boots, also in pfb, last in ASM #148, '75, next in PPSSM #1, '76), Señor Muerte (Philip Garcia, assassin that wears electro-suit, posing as Señor Suerte, 1st, also in pfb, next in PMIF #63, '80, see NOTE), Dr. Faustus (chr last in Cap #192, '75, chr next in ASM #170, '77 fb), Tarantula's men (also in pfb)
OTHER CHARACTERS: Edwin Jarvis (chr last in Av #149, '76, chr next in MTU #41, '76), Gen. Argyle Fist (last in Cap #198, '76, next bts in Def #135, '84, next in Def #144), Ken Astor (also as "Al Avision," only in pfb, only app, dies), Doug & Ginny Barber (joggers, only app), taxi driver, Statler-Hilton concierge, police, US military; party guests (in pfb, Jenette named)
LOCATIONS/ITEMS: Bronx inc Tarantula's base (in pfb) & Spuyten Dyvel w/Barber home, Avengers Mansion inc gym, bio-chem lab, comm center & conference room, SHIELD HQ, prison, Tarantula's warehouse, Statler-Hilton hotel (also in pfb); taxi, Cap's synthetic skin disguise (also in pfb), Avengers bio-chem equipment, phone records & Quinjet, Tarantula's trucks, Madbomb components

FLASHBACKS: Al Avision covertly meets with Captain America during an Avengers appearance at a Stark International function. Cap and Ken disguise themselves to go undercover to infiltrate a smuggling operation, looking for a shipment of Madbomb components. They are quickly discovered. Cap battles Tarantula, only for Señor Muerte to electrify Cap from behind (p).

SYNOPSIS: Two joggers find Captain America floating unconscious in the water. He comes to in their home and discovers his face is not his own and that he has no memory of recent events. He returns to Avengers Mansion where Iron Man points out that his false face is a synthetic skin disguise. Wasp tells Cap he met Al Avision last night, but Cap knows no one by that name. Following every lead possible, Cap eventually discovers that he's been poisoned. Trying a different tactic, Cap goes through the Avengers phone records and finds his answer. Cap contacts Gen. Fist to tell him that he and Ken were discovered in their mission to stop the Madbomb component smuggling operation, and that Ken must have been tortured and killed. Cap races toward the scheduled Madbomb convoy in time to engage Tarantula and Señor Muerte. Cap quickly defeats the villains and Gen. Fist arrives to secure the Madbomb components.

NOTE: This is an inventory story that takes place during Cap #198, '76. The original Señor Muerte/Señor Suerte, Ramon Garcia, died in L #11, '73, the new Señor Muerte is posing as the original here. PMIF #63-64, '80 reveals Ramon's younger brothers took over his operations Philip as Muerte and Jaimie as Suerte. Issue includes Hostess ad "Spider-Man meets the Home Wrecker."

CAPTAIN AMERICA #225 (September 1978)

"Devastation!" (17 pages)

CREDITS: Steve Gerber (writer), Sal Buscema (pencils), Mike Esposito, John Tartaglione (inks), Irving Watanabe (letters), George Roussos (colors), Jim Shooter (editor), Frank Robbins (c pencils), Terry Austin (c inks), Jim Novak (c letters)
FEATURE CHARACTER: Captain America (also in fb, see NOTE)
GUEST STARS: Nick Fury, Dum Dum Dugan
VILLAINS: Kligger (next in Cap #228, '78), Veda (dies)
OTHER CHARACTERS: Dr. Mason Harding (last in Cap #201, '77, last app), Mrs. Woodshaw (Kligger's secretary, voice only, next voice only in Cap #228, '78), CBS, NBC & ABC reporters & cameramen, firemen medics, Amtrak commuters, Federal penitentiary warden & guards; Elizabeth Rogers, Walter Rogers, Mike Rogers, Gen. Phillips, baseball players, referee, sports fans, art professor, art students, army recruits, Adolf Hitler, Nazis (both in film), reporters (voice only, on radio) (prev 13 in fb, see NOTE); Agent R (in photo)
LOCATIONS/ITEMS: Rogers Maryland home, Statue of Liberty, Empire State University, Greenwich Village café, theater, Army recruitment office, Curio shop façade (all in fb), SHIELD HQ, Federal Penitentiary, Kligger's office, Harding's Connecticut lab; Amtrak metroliner (rubble), SHIELD transport, Kligger's disintegrator, Harding's mind-probe device
FLASHBACK: Steve Rogers was the weaker and more sensitive of two brothers, which disappointed his father severely. Steve attends a school in New York when he learns of his brother's death at Pearl Harbor. Steve is rejected by the Army until approached by a general (see NOTE).
SYNOPSIS: After surveying the Amtrak wreckage, Nick Fury brings Captain America to SHIELD HQ where he argues against Cap's request to have Mason Harding unlock his memories. Dum Dum Dugan shows Cap Veda's file, including a picture of her mother, Agent R. Cap recognizes her from Operation: Rebirth despite her age and scars in the photo. Cap frees Harding from prison when he agrees to help. Meanwhile, the Corporation has deemed Veda a liability, so Kligger kills her. In Connecticut, Harding uses his experimental mind-probe device to unlock Captain America's dormant memories under Nick Fury's supervision. The process is a success, but an unfortunate side-effect renders Captain America's body to its pre-Super Soldier status.
NOTE: Story continued from Cap #223, '78. Cap #247, '80 reveals that all of Cap's memories unlocked in this issue are false memory implants installed by the US government in case Cap was captured and tortured by the Nazis. Walter Rogers worked for the State Department and his two sons, Mike and Grant, were killed at Pearl Harbor. Walter volunteered his family to be the basis for Cap's fictional family life.

CAPTAIN AMERICA #226 (October 1978)

"Am I Still Captain America?" (17 pages)

CREDITS: Roger McKenzie (writer), Sal Buscema (pencils), Mike Esposito, John Tartaglione (inks), Diana Albers (letters), Don Warfield (colors), Roger Stern (editor), Ron Wilson (c pencils), Dan Green (c inks), Jim Novak (c letters)
FEATURE CHARACTER: Captain America
GUEST STARS: Dum Dum Dugan (also as Red Skull), Nick Fury
VILLAIN: Red Skull (last in Cap #212, '77)
OTHER CHARACTERS: SHIELD agents (Jacobs & Crowley named, all also as Red Skull)
LOCATIONS/ITEMS: SHIELD Helicarrier inc training room & control room; Impact 739 (SHIELD training robot destroyed), Impact's staff, SHIELD blasters & rifles, Death's-Head satellite inc modified hate-ray
SYNOPSIS: Desperate to prove he's more than what the Super Soldier serum made him, Captain America faces off against Impact 739, a SHIELD training robot. Before Fury can pull the plug, an agent is suddenly transformed into Red Skull and blasts the controls, deactivating the robot's security protocols. In his weakened form, Cap barely manages to keep ahead of Impact 739. Fury tries to save Cap, but the robot destroys the room's controls from within. In orbit, Red Skull's satellite continues to fire its ray, quickly turning all the SHIELD agents onboard the Helicarrier into Red Skulls. Fury is shocked when Dum Dum becomes a Red Skull, who quickly defeats Fury. Impact 739 overpowers and captures Cap, and as the robot electrocutes him the Super Soldier serum becomes reactivated. Cap defeats the robot, just as an army of Red Skulls enter with an unconscious Nick Fury as their prisoner.
NOTE: Death's-Head satellite named in Cap #227, '78 and that Red Skull received it from Hate-Monger in SVTU #16, '79.

CAPTAIN AMERICA #227 (November 1978)

"This Deadly Gauntlet!" (17 pages)

CREDITS: Roger McKenzie (writer), Sal Buscema (pencils), Mike Esposito, John Tartaglione (inks), Rick Parker (letters), George Roussos (colors), Roger Stern (editor), Jerry Bingham (c art), Jim Novak (c letters)
FEATURE CHARACTER: Captain America (also in pfb & rfb; next in Av Ann #8, '78, MTIO #42-43, '78, Av #201/2, '80, Av #178, '78, Av #179, '79 fb, DD #155-157, '78-'79, Godz #23, '79)
GUEST STARS: Nick Fury (also in pfb; also as Red Skull, next bts in MTIO #42, '78, next in SW #7, '78), Dum Dum Dugan (only in pfb as Red Skull, next in Godz #17, '78)
VILLAIN: Red Skull (also pfb, next in SVTU #16, '79)
OTHER CHARACTERS: SHIELD agents (all as Red Skull); Bucky (in rfb)
LOCATIONS/ITEMS: SHIELD Helicarrier inc control room (also in pfb) & training room; Death's-Head satellite (destroyed) inc modified hate-ray & control unit, SHIELD blasters & rifles, (all also in pfb), Impact 739 (wreckage), Helicarrier's laser defense turrets (both in pfb), Skull's magnifying prism & magnetic barrier, Nick Fury LMD (destroyed), Zemo's drone plane (in rfb)
FLASHBACKS: Cap & Bucky attempt to disarm Zemo's drone plane (Av #4, '64 fb). Captain America tries to free Nick Fury from Red Skull, but Fury betrays Cap and knocks him out. When Cap recovers, the Skull explains from the Helicarrier's control room that he intends to use his mind-bending Death's-Head rays to turn billions of Earth's citizens into an army of Red Skulls. He tells Cap that he can only stop his plan by finding the Death's-Head control unit, then attacks Cap with the Helicarrier's defenses (p).
SYNOPSIS: Captain America runs through the bowels of the Helicarrier, hounded by an army of Red Skulls. In the control room, the true Red Skull gloats. When the sun rises momentarily, its rays will be reflected through a magnifying prism, killing the chained Nick Fury. Soon afterward, Cap defeats a Skull sentry and enters a parlor, where Red Skull awaits. Cap throws his shield, but it's caught in Red Skull's magnetic barrier. Skull alerts Cap that the rising sun is about to kill Fury, and warns Cap that if he attacks or tries to save Fury, he will activate the Death's-Head ray sooner than planned. Recalling Bucky's death, Cap appears frozen with indecision, allowing the rising sun to cook Fury. When Skull taunts Cap, the Avenger lashes out, capturing the control unit and deactivating the Death's-Head satellite, causing it to explode. "Skull" changes back into Nick Fury and collapses. Cap tells Fury that he had tricked Red Skull: noticing that the captured Nick Fury wasn't sweating, he had realized it was actually an LMD.
NOTE: Issue includes Hostess ad "Thor - - in Good Overcomes Evil!"

CAPTAIN AMERICA #228 (December 1978)

"A Serpent Lurks Below" (17 pages)

CREDITS: Roger McKenzie (writer), Sal Buscema (pencils), Mike Esposito, John Tartaglione (inks), Diana Albers (letters), George Roussos (colors), Roger Stern (editor), Ron Wilson (c pencils), Dan Green (c inks), Jim Novak (c letters)
FEATURE CHARACTER: Captain America
GUEST STARS: Avengers: Beast, Hercules (both last in DD #157, '79), Iron Man, Vision (both last in Godz #24, '79, next in Av #179, '78), Scarlet Witch (last in Godz #23, '79, next in Av #179, '78), Thor (last in Godz #24, '79); SHIELD Super-Agents: Texas Twister (last in Cap #218, '78), Marvel Man (last in Def #64, '78); Nick Fury (bts, decides to relocate SHIELD's New York base, last bts in MTIO #42, '78)
VILLAINS: Constrictor (Frank Payne aka Frank Schlichting, costumed assassin, last in Hulk #212, '77), Blue Streak (last in Cap #218, '78), Vamp (last as Animus in Cap #223, '78), Kligger (last in Cap #225, '78, next in Hulk #231, '79), Corporation (last bts in Hulk #230, '78)
OTHER CHARACTERS: Jasper Sitwell (last in IM #113, '78), Mrs. Woodshaw (voice only, last in Cap #225, '78, last app), boys (Ace & Joey named, one as "Marauder"), truck driver, Darlene (Beast's date, bts, waiting for Beast, only app); Korvac, Red Skull (mentioned, recently battled Avengers & Cap), Falcon (mentioned as looking for Jim Wilson), Jim Wilson (mentioned as in trouble), SHIELD ESP Division (mentioned as possible way to find Falcon)
LOCATIONS/ITEMS: New York inc Avengers Mansion & SHIELD HQ w/barbershop front, Washington, DC inc Washington Monument & Kligger's office, SHIELD's Los Angeles HQ; SHIELD viewscreen, defense robot, explosive charges & automatically locking door, Ace delivery truck, Blue Streak's skates, Constrictor's electrically-powered Adamantium-alloy arm cables, Kligger's intercom, Marvel Man's Quantum Bands, trash can lid used as play shield
SYNOPSIS: Captain America broods at Avengers Mansion until Iron Man gives him a pep talk. After saving a boy from being hit by a truck, Cap goes to SHIELD's New York HQ to look for the missing Falcon. He defeats a SHIELD robot and finds the base deserted. Jasper Sitwell radios in and tells Cap that SHIELD has abandoned the base for security reasons and that it's due for destruction in fifteen minutes. Sitwell connects Cap with the SHIELD Super-Agents in Los Angeles, who report that Falcon's been missing for days. Blue Streak explains that Falcon is looking for someone in trouble named Jim. Constrictor, a costumed assassin working for the Corporation, ambushes Cap and reveals the SHIELD Super-Agents have a Corporation mole in their ranks. As they fight, the base starts to come down around them.
NOTE: This issue starts a story arc that crosses over with Hulk #229-232, '78-'79.

CAPTAIN AMERICA #229 (January 1979)

"Traitors All About Me!" (17 pages)

CREDITS: Roger McKenzie (writer), Sal Buscema (pencils), Don Perlin (pencils, inks), Jim Novak (letters), Francoise Mouly (colors), Jim Salicrup (asst editor), Roger Stern (editor), Keith Pollard (c pencils), Bob McLeod (c inks), Jim Novak (c letters)
FEATURE CHARACTERS: Captain America (also in photo)
GUEST STARS: Avengers: Beast (chr next in MTU #90, '80, next in Av #179, '79), Hercules (next in Av #181, '79), Thor (next in Av #179, '79), SHIELD Super-Agents (disbands, last app): Texas Twister (next in Hulk #265, '81), Marvel Man; Nick Fury (bts, waiting for report, next in SW #7, '78)
VILLAINS: Constrictor (next in IM #126, '79), Blue Streak (next in Cap #318, '86), Corporation (next in Hulk #231, '79), Vamp
OTHER CHARACTERS: Edwin Jarvis (last in DD #156, '79, next in MTIO Ann #4, '79), Jasper Sitwell (next bts in Hulk #232, '79, next in Hulk #233, '79), SHIELD agents (Akins named), Billy (boy reading comics on bus), commuters, bus driver, police dispatcher (voice only), Clancy (policeman, bts, receives message from dispatcher), Billy's grandmother (bts, waiting for Billy); Bucky (in photo only), Daredevil (in comic book), Gene Colan (mentioned, comic artist back on Daredevil), Hulk (mentioned, recently fought Constrictor), Jim Wilson (mentioned, Constrictor failed to capture him), Falcon (mentioned, still missing), Black Panther (mentioned, helped Beast decorate his room), Darlene (mentioned, had great time w/Beast last night), Human Torch (mentioned, see NOTE)
LOCATIONS/ITEMS: New York inc Avengers Mansion w/Beast's room, Steve's apartment & SHIELD HQ w/barbershop front & emergency manhole exit, SHIELD Los Angeles HQ, Alcatraz Island Penitentiary (mentioned as where Falcon is); Beast's cold compress, "Little Caesar" film poster & gorilla bank, Blue Streak's skates, Constrictor's cables, Daredevil comic book, Marvel Man's Quantum Bands, Vamp's absorbo-belt, SHIELD flashlights & intruder alert, police call box & phone cable at 59th St. & 10th Av.
SYNOPSIS: SHIELD agents survey the remains of their decommissioned New York HQ. After they leave, Captain America emerges with Constrictor from the wreckage and interrogates the assassin for information about the Corporation, who he believes is responsible for Falcon's disappearance. With his apartment still a mess, Cap stops by Avengers Mansion for some travelling money and takes a bus to SHIELD's new Los Angeles HQ. Cap confronts the SHIELD Super-Agents and fights the team to flush out the traitor in their ranks. Cap's gambit works, and Blue Streak reveals himself as a Corporation spy. Vamp savagely pummels Blue Streak for information, but Cap stops her by removing her absorb-belt. Disgusted, Texas Twister quits the Super-Agents. Blue Streak reveals that the Corporation is holding Falcon at Alcatraz.
NOTE: This issue reveals Texas Twister was trying to recruit the Human Torch for SHIELD in FF #192, '78. Issue includes Hostess ad "Captain Marvel meets the Dreadnought."

CAPTAIN AMERICA #230 (February 1979)

"Assault on Alcatraz!" (17 pages)

CREDITS: Roger McKenzie (plot), Roger Stern (script, editor), Sal Buscema (pencils), Don Perlin (inks), Jim Novak (letters), Nelson Yomtov (colors), Jim Salicrup (asst editor), Ron Wilson (c pencils), Bob Layton (c inks)
FEATURE CHARACTER: Captain America (next in Hulk #232, '79)
GUEST STARS: Hulk (also as Bruce Banner, also in rfb; between Hulk #231-232, '79), Falcon (last in Def #64, '78, next in Hulk #232, '79), Marvel Man (next in Hulk #232, '79)
VILLAINS: Kligger, Moonstone (also as Karla Sofen), Corporation (2 agents disguised as police) (all between Hulk #231-232, '79), Curtiss Jackson (Corporation executive, last in MsM #8, '77, next in Hulk #232, '79), Vamp (also as Animus, next in Hulk #232, '79)
OTHER CHARACTERS: Fred Sloan (Hulk's friend, last in Hulk #231, '79, next in Hulk #233, '79), Jim Wilson (Hulk's friend, also in rfb; between Hulk #231-232, '79), Jim Wilson's dog, tour guide, tourists; Constrictor (only in rfb); Clint Eastwood (actor), Birdman of Alcatraz (Robert Stroud, prison inmate) (both mentioned by tour guide)
LOCATIONS/ITEMS: California freeway, San Francisco Bay, Alcatraz Island Penitentiary inc armored door & stairway, Corporation's West Coast HQ beneath Alcatraz; Corporation computers, electro-sleep harness, intruder alarm, sea gates, transport van, viewscreen & tidewater dynamo w/bypass valves, Vamp's absorbo-belt, Animus' control device & crystalline club, Corporation agents' guns, Fred Sloan's van, Kligger's plane (wreckage), police car, tour boat, Marvel Man's Quantum Bands, SHIELD energy output tracer, Falcon's chains, Jim Wilson's ropes, "The Enforcer" (film, mentioned by tour guide)
FLASHBACK: Hulk defeats the Constrictor (Hulk #212, '77).
SYNOPSIS: Captain America, Marvel Man, and Vamp take a tour guide to Alcatraz. Corporation agents abduct Bruce Banner and his friend, Fred Sloan, and take them to their HQ beneath Alcatraz. Cap, Marvel Man, and Vamp infiltrate the base, but Marvel Man's eagerness gives away their element of surprise. They storm the bunker to find Falcon chained to sea gates. Corporation manager Curtiss Jackson explains that Falcon and Banner are bait for Falcon's nephew, Jim Wilson, a former associate. Kligger, a rival Corporation executive, appears with Moonstone and their captive, Jim Wilson. Kligger proposes a trade of Jim for Cap, and Vamp reveals herself as Kligger's operative. Cap and Marvel Man fight back, and Banner turns into the Hulk and joins the melee. The confused Hulk dispatches Cap and Marvel Man, and Kligger turns Vamp into the monstrous Animus to help Moonstone defeat the Hulk. With the heroes unconscious, Jackson opens the sea gates and water rushes into the chamber.
NOTE: Jim Wilson, a Hulk supporting character, is revealed to be Falcon's nephew here. Story continues in Hulk #232, '79 where Hulk beats Animus with her own club driving her insane, Kligger is killed and the Corporation is defeated. Issue includes Hostess ad "Iron Man in an Irresistible Force!"

CAPTAIN AMERICA #231 (March 1979)

"Aftermath!" (17 pages)

CREDITS: Roger McKenzie (writer), Sal Buscema (pencils), Don Perlin (inks), Tom Orzechowski (letters), Bob Sharen (colors), Jim Salicrup (asst editor), Roger Stern (editor), Keith Pollard (c pencils), Al Milgrom (c inks), Jim Novak (c letters)
FEATURE CHARACTER: Captain America (also in rfb)
GUEST STAR: Falcon (last in Hulk #232, '79, next in Cap #237, '79)
SUPPORTING CAST: Sharon Carter (only in pfb; last in Cap #218, '78), Peggy Carter (last in Cap #191, '75)
VILLAINS: Grand Director (William Burnside, apparent National Force leader, bts controlling his men; also in pfb; last in Cap #156, '72, chr last in Cap #236, '79 fb as Captain America), Dr. Faustus (true leader of the National Force, bts as patron for Grand Director; last in ASM #170, '77, chr last in Cap #236, '79 fb), National Force (1st, so in pfb, some also in newspaper photo), Vamp (also as Animus in rfb; last in Hulk #232, '79, next in Cap #319, '86), Corporation (also in rfb), Captain America's stalker (for the Brotherhood; 1st), stalker's Brotherhood superior (bts, on walkie-talkie with stalker, only app)
OTHER CHARACTERS: Jim Wilson (last in Hulk #232, '79, next in MTU #114, '82), Jasper Sitwell (bts, offers Cap transport; last in Hulk #233, '79, chr next in MSH #10/3, '92, next in MTU #83, '79), Lt. Dwight Stanford (SHIELD Internal Security, 1st, next bts in Cap #237, '79, next in Av #190, '79), other SHIELD agents inc shuttle pilot & medics, bystanders, Karl Janacek (SHIELD agent), police (Williams named), anti-National Force protestors (prev 3 only in pfb); SHIELD Super-Agents: Blue Streak, Marvel Man, Texas Twister; Constrictor, Curtiss Jackson, Kligger, Moonstone (Karla Sofen), Hulk (prev 8 only in rfb)
LOCATIONS/ITEMS: Corporation's West Coast HQ beneath Alcatraz (also in rfb), New York City, Steve Rogers' Yorkville apartment, SHIELD's new Manhattan HQ inc hologram wall & docking bay Alpha; Harlem inc Sam Wilson's office; Central Park (in pfb); SHIELD rifles, Moonbeam III (SHIELD's sub-orbital VTOL shuttle), stalker's walkie-talkie, National Force's blasters, Peggy's car (destroyed), protestor's egg (in pfb), Dr. Faustus' mind-gas (bts in pfb), Animus' crystalline club (in rfb)
FLASHBACKS: Cap fights Constrictor (Cap #228, '78). Cap confronts the SHIELD Super-Agents (Cap #229, '79). Cap fights Moonstone and Hulk fights Animus (Hulk #232, '79). During a National Force rally in Central Park, the Grand Director sways a crowd of protestors, along with SHIELD agents Sharon Carter and Karl Janacek, into a hate-filled mob, causing a riot (p).
SYNOPSIS: Captain America says goodbye to Falcon as SHIELD arrests straggling Corporation agents. Cap rescues the emotionally destroyed Vamp from abuse by SHIELD agents. Upon his return to New York, Cap's efforts to locate Sharon are interrupted by Lt. Stanford, who claims Cap is a security hazard. Cap storms out of SHIELD HQ and returns to his apartment, where he is unknowingly stalked by a member of the mysterious Brotherhood. Cap tries unsuccessfully to sleep. Restless, he stops by Sam's office where he finds Peggy Carter. Peggy tells Cap that Sharon has disappeared after observing a Central Park rally by the political hate group National Force. Cap leaves, determined to investigate Sharon's disappearance. Peggy starts her car, but two National Force agents, worried that she may know too much, fire blasters at the vehicle, destroying it.
NOTE: Grand Director revealed to be the 1950's Captain America and Dr. Faustus revealed to be controlling him in Cap #233, '79. Issue includes Hostess ad "The Incredible Hulk Changes his Mind!" Lt. Stanford's 1st name revealed in Av #190, '79.

CAPTAIN AMERICA #232 (April 1979)

"The Flame and the Fury" (17 pages)

CREDITS: Roger McKenzie (writer), Sal Buscema (pencils), Don Perlin (inks), Elaine Heinl (letters), George Roussos (colors), Jim Salicrup (asst editor), Roger Stern (editor), Keith Pollard (c pencils), Al Milgrom (c inks), Jim Novak (c letters)
FEATURE CHARACTER: Captain America
VILLAINS: Grand Director, Dr. Faustus (in shadows), National Force (some die), Sgt. Brian Muldoon (last in Cap #159, '73 as Cowled Commander, next in Cap #242, '80), Morgan (last in PMIF #52, '78) & his men (Reese named), Pigsticker (Carl Peel, a drug-using informant, only app), Captain America's stalker
SUPPORTING CAST: Peggy Carter (next in Cap #235, '79), Sharon Carter
OTHER CHARACTERS: Commissioner Feingold (last in Def #39, '76, last bts in Av #165, '77, next in Cap #235, '79), police, firefighters, paramedics, cab driver, bystanders, alley cat
LOCATIONS/ITEMS: New York City, Steve Rogers' Yorkville apartment, Harlem inc police headquarters & Morgan's uptown townhouse, Hell's Kitchen, National Force's midtown office tower inc Faustus' office; National Force's flame-belts, guns & torches, Peggy's car (wreckage) & SHIELD communicator, fire hoses, cab, Pigsticker's knife, Morgan's & his men's guns
SYNOPSIS: Peggy Carter leaps from her car just as it explodes. Captain America swoops down to the rescue, capturing the National Force agents and seeing Peggy to an ambulance. Before Cap can question Peggy's attackers, they activate their fire-belts, committing suicide by burning alive. Later, the stalker watches Cap enter his apartment. Believing he can more easily uncover information about the Grand Director as Steve Rogers, Cap dons his police uniform and visits Commissioner Feingold, but the Commissioner tells Cap that he has been instructed by "upstairs" to lay off the National Force. An informant points Cap to Morgan for information, who tells Cap that the National Force is marching on Harlem. Meanwhile at National Force HQ, the Grand Director, reclining on a psychiatrist's couch, is reassured by a mysterious man in shadows that he is doing the right thing. Cap arrives in Harlem to fight the Force's blitzkrieg squads, but he is stopped cold when he is confronted by Sharon, who has apparently joined the National Force. Suddenly, Morgan and his men arrive, and Cap is caught in an imminent crossfire between Morgan and the National Force.
NOTE: Issue includes Hostess ad, Spider-Man "Puts Himself in the Picture!" Letters page contains LOC from Kurt Busiek, future Marvel writer.

CAPTAIN AMERICA #233 (May 1979)

"Crossfire" (17 pages)

CREDITS: Roger McKenzie (writer), Sal Buscema (pencils), Don Perlin (inks), Rick Parker (letters), Nelson Yomtov (colors), Jim Salicrup (asst editor), Roger Stern (editor), Keith Pollard (c pencils), Al Milgrom (c inks), Jim Novak (c letters)
FEATURE CHARACTER: Captain America (also in rfb)
VILLAINS: Grand Director (also as "Dr. Steven Rogers"; also in rfb), Dr. Faustus, National Force (some die, Morgan (next in MTU #88, '79) & his men (Glitterbug named), Captain America's stalker (next in Cap #237, '79)
SUPPORTING CAST: Sharon Carter (also in rfb; chr next in Cap #446, '95 fb, next in Cap #444, '95)
OTHER CHARACTERS: National Guard, firefighters, nurse; Peggy Carter, Karl Janacek, anti-National Force protestors, paramedics (prev 4 only in rfb), Red Skull, MODOK (both holographic projections), Sigmund Freud ("the father of psychoanalysis"; mentioned only)
LOCATIONS/ITEMS: Mt. Sinai Hospital, Steve Roger's Yorkville apartment building inc stalker's apartment, National Force's midtown office tower inc Faustus' office, Harlem (also in rfb) inc Sam Wilson's office, Central Park (both in rfb); Morgan's & his men's guns, National Force's flame belts, guns & blackjack, National Guardsmen's guns, fire trucks & hoses, Cap's Avengers ID card, Dr. Faustus' Sharon Carter robot (destroyed), mind-gas & booby-trapped elevator
FLASHBACKS: In Sam Wilson's office, Peggy asks for Cap's help in finding Sharon (Cap #231, '79). Sharon is brainwashed in a National Force rally, which turns into a riot (Cap #231, '79 fb). Cap watches paramedics treat Peggy (Cap #232, '79).
SYNOPSIS: When gunfire erupts between the National Force and Morgan's gang, Captain America struggles to separate the two factions. The National Guard arrives and arrests the National Force agents, but Morgan's men escape. Cap is shocked when the National Force agents immolate themselves, and he is unable to determine if Sharon was among those committing suicide. As Cap races to Mt. Sinai hospital expecting another attack on Peggy, he passes his apartment building, where the stalker studies a list of Cap's possible secret identities. At the hospital, Cap learns that Peggy has been remanded to the care of Dr. Steven Rogers. Issue includes Hostess ad "Iron Man in Brains over Brawn!" Later, the Grand Director and Dr. Faustus await Cap's arrival, knowing he will follow the clues they've laid for him. Cap enters the National Force's office tower and makes his way through several traps to Faustus' office. Faustus uses his mind-gas to weaken Cap and knocks him out. The Grand Director removes his mask, revealing he is the 1950's Captain America.
NOTE: The stalker's list of possible Captain America secret identities has Dick Yorty, John Michel, Mitch Itkowitz, Caspar Fagin, and Paul McGinley crossed out, leaving only Steve Rogers. Issue includes Hostess ad "Iron Man in Brains over Brawn!"

CAPTAIN AMERICA #234 (June 1979)

"Burn, Cap, Burn!" (17 pages)

CREDITS: Roger McKenzie (writer), Sal Buscema (pencils), Don Perlin (inks), Jim Novak (letters), Nelson Yomtov (colors), Jim Salicrup (asst editor), Roger Stern (editor), Keith Pollard (c pencils), Joe Sinnot (c inks)
FEATURE CHARACTER: Captain America (also in newspaper photo)
GUEST STAR: Daredevil (Matt Murdock, blind hero with super senses, last in DD #157, '79)
VILLAINS: Grand Director, Dr. Faustus, National Force (one agent in newspaper photo)
OTHER CHARACTERS: Franklin "Foggy" Nelson (Matt Murdock's law partner), Becky Blake (Nelson & Murdock's secretary) (both between DD #156-157, '79), brainwashed protestors, police, newsstand dealer; Jester (clown themed villain, mentioned as in prison)
LOCATIONS/ITEMS: Manhattan, National Force's Bismark waterfront warehouse inc soundstage; Matt Murdock's townhouse, 5th Avenue; Daredevil's billy club & TV, Becky Blake's wheelchair, patrol cars, National Force's TV cameras, car & guns, oil barrels
SYNOPSIS: The National Force interrupts local television with a propaganda film. In the broadcast, a brainwashed Captain America defeats a group of brainwashed protestors. He brandishes his shield for the camera, which has been painted with a swastika on flames. Watching incredulously from Matt Murdock's townhouse, Foggy Nelson & Becky Blake turn off the TV in disgust. When his friends leave, Matt changes into Daredevil and scours the streets of Manhattan, believing that Cap is in trouble. After saving an old man during a police chase of a National Force vehicle, Daredevil follows the car to a waterfront warehouse. Alerted by a silent alarm, Dr. Faustus and the Grand Director enter the warehouse with the brainwashed Cap in tow. Convinced that Daredevil is a spy, Cap viciously attacks Daredevil. Realizing that Cap has been brainwashed, Daredevil manipulates Cap into dousing his shield with oil. The oil mixes with the new paint on the shield, sloughing off the swastika. At the sight of his original shield design Cap's memory is restored, but Cap and Daredevil find themselves in the crosshairs of several National Force gunmen.
NOTE: Issue includes Hostess ad, Spider-Man in "Hotshot on the Block."

CAPTAIN AMERICA #235 (July 1979)

"To Stalk the Killer Skies!" (17 pages)

CREDITS: Roger McKenzie (writer), Sal Buscema, Jack Abel (art), John Costanza (letters), Roger Slifer (colors), Roger Stern (editor)
FEATURE CHARACTER: Captain America
GUEST STAR: Daredevil
SUPPORTING CAST: Peggy Carter (last in Cap#232, '79)
VILLAINS: Grand Director (also as Captain America), Dr. Faustus, National Force
OTHER CHARACTERS: Commissioner Feingold (last in Cap#232, '79, next in Hulk Ann #9, '80), firemen, Lakehurst Air Pavillion officer; Sharon Carter (only in rfb)
LOCATIONS/ITEMS: Dr. Faustus' waterfront warehouse, Lakehurst Air Pavillion; National Force's flame belts in rfb) & guns, Daredevil's billy club, Dr. Faustus' mind-gas & escape dirigible, World War I fighter planes
FLASHBACKS: Sharon Carter, manipulated by Dr. Faustus, turns against Captain America. While in Captain America's custody, National Force agents use their self-immolation belts (Cap#233, '79).
SYNOPSIS: As National Force agents set fire to Dr. Faustus' waterfront warehouse with Captain America and Daredevil inside, Dr. Faustus and the Grand Director make their getaway. Cap and Daredevil escape through the flames. Later, they explain the situation to the arriving police Commissioner. The trio find a burned packing crate and Daredevil uses his hyper sense to determine the shipping address. Meanwhile, the Grand Director, disguised as Captain America, and Dr. Faustus arrive at Lakehurst Air Pavillion where the National Force begin loading Faustus' mind-gas into his escape dirigible. Cap and Daredevil arrive to halt Faustus' plans. A brief battle ensues until the Grand Director reveals the captive Peggy Carter, using her as a hostage to escape. Commandeering a nearby WWI fighter plane, Cap and Daredevil pursue the escaping Faustus and Grand Director. Closing in on Faustus' escape dirigible, Cap jumps out of the plane towards the blimp, only to miss when the fighter plane sputters. Cap plunges towards Earth.
NOTE: Frank Miller is credited as "special waterfront consultant" here. Issue includes Hostess ad "The Thing and the Ultimate Weapon!" Letters page features LOCs from future Marvel writers Kurt Busiek & Peter Sanderson.

CAPTAIN AMERICA #236 (August 1979)

"Death Dive!" (17 pages)

CREDITS: Roger McKenzie (plot), Michael Fleisher (script), Sal Buscema (pencils), Don Perlin (inks), Jim Novak (letters), Ben Sean (colors), Roger Stern (editor), Keith Pollard (c pencils), Joe Sinnott (c inks)
FEATURE CHARACTER: Captain America (also in rfb; next in DrS #35, '79)
GUEST STAR: Daredevil (next in PPSSM #26, '79)
SUPPORTING CAST: Peggy Carter (next in Cap #351, '89)
VILLAINS: Grand Director (also as Captain America, also in rfb; also in fbs 1 & 2 between Cap #281, '83 fb & Cap #231, '79 fb; next in Cap #36, '08), Dr. Faustus (also in fb1 between Cap #162, '73 & Cap #192, '75; also in fbs 2 & 3 between ASM #170, '77 & Cap #232, '79; next in MTU #132, '83), National Force (also in rfb), Corporation (providing funding for Faustus bts)
OTHER CHARACTERS: Bucky (Jack Monroe, only in fbs 1 & 2 between Cap #281, '83 fb & Cap #281, '83), dock workers (Wilson named), bystanders, federal agents (both only in fb1); Morgan, Morgan's gang (both only in rfb)
LOCATIONS/ITEMS: New York City, waterfront, New York Harbor, Statue of Liberty; National Force's dirigible, World War I biplane, Daredevil's billy club, Dr. Faustus' mind-gas (also in fb3), Avengers Quinjet, National Force's guns (also in rfb) & flame belts, Morgan's gang's guns (only in rfb)
FLASHBACKS: Captain America defeats the 1950's Cap (Cap #156, '72). Sharon is brainwashed during a National Force rally (Cap #231, '79 fb). Cap is caught in a standoff between the National Force and Morgan's gang (Cap #233, '79). A brainwashed Cap appears in a National Force propaganda film (Cap #234, '79). The 1950's Captain America & Bucky are remanded into the custody of Dr. Faustus for treatment (1). Dr. Faustus brainwashes the 1950's Cap into shooting Bucky (2). Dr. Faustus releases his mind-gas during a National Force rally (3).
SYNOPSIS: As Captain America falls through the air, Daredevil struggles to fly the damaged biplane. Cap tries to maneuver in mid-air toward Faustus' dirigible, but he misses. Flying past Cap, Daredevil tosses his billy club to the Avenger, who uses it to briefly slow his descent by snagging a flagpole. He smashes through an awning and uses his shield to absorb most of the impact of his landing. Daredevil crashes the plane on the docks. Meanwhile aboard the dirigible, Dr. Faustus tells Peggy that he plans to flood New York with his mind-gas. Outside, with Daredevil as the pilot, Cap leaps from an Avengers Quinjet to the blimp and boards through a hatch, quickly finding Dr. Faustus and the Grand Director. When Faustus goads the Director into fighting Cap, the Director responds by activating his flame-belt, setting himself ablaze and starting a fire aboard the airship. As Cap fights through the National Force hoards, Faustus tries to release his mind-gas over the city. Cap stops Faustus by breaking Faustus' wrist with his shield. The dirigible crashes in New York Harbor. Daredevil pulls Peggy into the floating Quinjet. Cap follows with the hapless Faustus in tow.

CAPTAIN AMERICA #237 (September 1979)

"From the Ashes…" (17 pages)

CREDITS: Chris Claremont (plot), Roger McKenzie (script), Sal Buscema (pencils), Don Perlin (inks), Elaine Heini (letters), George Roussos (colors), Jim Salicrup (asst editor), Roger Stern (editor), Keith Pollard (c pencils), Joe Sinnott (c inks)
FEATURE CHARACTER: Captain America (also in photo, also in fb2 between Cap #259, '81 fb & Cap #241 '80 fb)
GUEST STARS: Avengers: Beast (last in Av #180, '79, next in IM #114, '78), Ms. Marvel (last in MTU #77, '79 chr last in MSM #35, '09 fb, next in Av #181, '79) Vision (last in Av #180, '79, next in IM #114, '78), Wasp (last in Av #180, '79, next in IM #115, '78); Falcon (last in Cap #231, '79, next in Av #183, '79), Nick Fury (last in MTIO Ann #4), Peter Parker (last in MTU #89, '80, next in MTU #91, '80)
SUPPORTING CAST: Joshua Cooper (learning disabilities teacher & war veteran), Mike Farrel (firefighter) (both Steve's new neighbors, 1st) Anna Kappelbaum (Steve's new landlady & Diebenwald concentration camp survivor, 1st but chr last in Cap #241, '80 fb, also in fb1 before Cap #245, '80 fb, in fb2 between Cap #245, '80 fb & Cap #241, '80 fb) (all next in Cap #241, '80)
VILLAINS: Dr. Klaus Mendelhaus (Diebenwald physician, 1st, next in Cap #245, '80 fb), Col. Steiger (Diebenwald commandant, only app), Nazi soldiers (Franz named) (all only in fb), Captain America's stalker (last app, see NOTE)
OTHER CHARACTERS: Lt. Dwight Stanford (bts, chewed out by Fury, last in Cap #231, '79, next in Av #190, '79), reporters (Katie Burns named), cameramen (Frank named), bystanders, Anna's family (in fb1), Diebenwald concentration camp prisoners (in fbs 1 & 2), Allied soldiers (in fb2); Sharon Carter, National Force (both in video footage, see NOTE)
LOCATIONS/ITEMS: Steve's former Yorkville apartment, Anna's Brooklyn Heights apartment building inc Steve's & Anna's apartments Avengers Mansion, Fury's apartment, Anna's childhood home (in fb1), Diebenwald concentration camp (in fb2); Nazi guns, clubs & whip, Allied tanks, Cap's motorcycle (all in fb), Steve's new business card
FLASHBACKS: On November 9, 1938, Nazis take Anna Kappelbaum and her family to be interred at Diebenwald concentration camp. Her father is beaten to death and her mother is raped (1). In 1945, as Allied forces advance on Diebenwald, the commandant orders everyone killed to eliminate evidence. Captain America leads the charge to liberate the camp (2).
SYNOPSIS: Captain America holds a press conference to explain his involvement with the National Force, but it doesn't go very well. Afterward a reporter pulls Cap aside to deliver some bad news. Cap views footage of Sharon Carter dying in the mass suicide by the National Force. A week later, Falcon finds Cap's Yorkville apartment empty. At Avengers Mansion, Falcon tells the Avengers that Cap's missing and that Sharon Carter is dead as Steve Rogers arrives to announce his new career as an artist and his new address. Returning to his new home, Steve's neighbor Josh Cooper introduces himself and invites him to dinner. Steve meets their host, Anna, a Jewish woman he freed from a concentration camp in WWII as Captain America. After dinner, Steve retires for the night until Fury calls asking for help.
NOTE: Cap is led to believe that Sharon Carter is dead here, but Cap #446, '95 reveals SHIELD faked her death so she could go on a deep undercover assignment. Apparently, when Captain America moved out of his Yorktown apartment, he inadvertently foiled the Brotherhood's plot to attack his secret identity, as they or his stalker have never been heard from again. Mike's name revealed in Cap #241, '80. Steve's new address is 569 Leaman Place, Brooklyn Heights, NY and his phone number is (212) 555-3592. Anna's Diebenwald identification tattoo number is 3456011.

CAPTAIN AMERICA #238 (October 1979)

"Snowfall Fury!" (17 pages)

CREDITS: Peter Gillis (writer), Fred Kida (pencils), Don Perlin (inks), John Costanza (letters), Bob Sharen (colors), Jim Salicrup (asst editor), Roger Stern (editor), John Byrne (c pencils), Al Milgrom (c inks)
FEATURE CHARACTER: Captain America (also in pfb)
GUEST STAR: Nick Fury (in pfb, next in Micro #12, '79)
VILLAINS: Steven Tuval (the "Mind-Master," last in Sub #43, '71, chr last in Cap #239, '79 fb), Dovecote security; Widowmaker (Dovecote strongman, 1st), Hawk Riders (One & Four named) & their giant hawks, Elite Guard & their giant diatrymas (giant ostrich-like birds), guards
OTHER CHARACTERS: Snowfall (Ginny Snow, telepath & precognitive, in pfb, 1st but chr last in Cap #239, '79 fb), Mentallo (Marvin Flumm, villainous former SHIELD psi-agent, in pfb, also in photo, last in MS #32, '77 fb, chr next in Micro #25, '81 fb, next in Micro #24, '80), SHIELD agents (in photos)
LOCATIONS/ITEMS: Fury's SHIELD office (in pfb), Dovecote(impenetrable mountaintop fortress); Cap's rocket pack & electro-shocker, Dovecote security's laser weapons, hover car & mines, Tuval's equipment, blank metal discs (in pfb), Snowfall's life-support coffin
FLASHBACK: Nick Fury briefs Captain America on the situation: Mentallo and several SHIELD agents have suffered from unexplainable brain hemorrhages. The only link between the "attacks" is blank metal discs found on each victim. When Cap inspects the discs he's telepathically contacted by Snowfall, a telepath who's being held captive at Dovecote begging for Cap's help (p).
SYNOPSIS: Captain America travels to Dovecote, the ultimate safe house, by completing a long treacherous climb up a mountain in high winds. He is attacked by Dovecote security riding giant hawks until one falls victim to the winds. Cap reaches the top and battles the guards, commandeering one of their hover cars to close in on the fortress. The Hawk Riders return, and Cap fends them off with his shield before the car is destroyed by a mine. Dovecote's Elite Guard, riding their large diatrymas, confronts the weaponless Captain America. Cap defeats them by tricking them into the minefield and continues to Dovecote's entrance. Weakened from exhaustion, Cap faces and quickly falls to Widowmaker.
NOTE: Snowfall's real name revealed in Cap #239, '79. Issue includes Hostess ad "The Incredible Hulk and the Ultimate Weapon!"

CAPTAIN AMERICA #239 (November 1979)

"Mind-Stains on the Virgin Snow!" (17 pages)

CREDITS: Peter Gillis (writer), Fred Kida (pencils), Don Perlin (inks), Joe Rosen (letters), Nelson Yomtov (colors), Jim Salicrup (asst editor), Roger Stern (editor), John Byrne (c pencils), Terry Austin (c inks)
FEATURE CHARACTER: Captain America (also in rfb, next in IM #114-115, '78, ASM #187, '78, Av #181-182, '79, BP #14-15, '79, Alias #25, '03 fb, bts in Alias #26, '03 fb, Av #183-185, '79)
VILLAINS: Steven Tuval (also in fb between Sub #43, '71 & Cap #238, '79), Dovecote security: Widowmaker, guards (all also in rfb, last app)
OTHER CHARACTERS: Snowfall (also in rfb, also in fb to 1st chr app before Cap #238, '79 fb, dies), scientists (in fb); Dovecote Security: Hawk Riders & their giant hawks, Elite Guard & their diatrymas (in rfb), Nick Fury (in rfb & illusion); Sub-Mariner, Eskimos, snake (prev 3 in illusion)
LOCATIONS/ITEMS: Dovecote (also in fb), Fury's office, Newfoundland (both in illusion); Cap's concussion packets & mini-plasma torch, Dovecote video monitors, Dovecote security's guns, blank metal discs, Snowfall's life-support coffin, Tuval's equipment (both also in fb)
FLASHBACKS: Snowfall telepathically asks Captain America for help (Cap #238, '79 fb). Invading Dovecote, Cap finds himself up against its numerous forces (Cap #238, '79). Namor the Sub-Mariner defeats Steven Tuval (Sub #43, '71). Tuval kidnaps Snowfall and imprisons her at Dovecote, planning to use her mental powers for his own ends.
SYNOPSIS: Snowfall uses her telepathy to trick her captor, making him think that Widowmaker is befriending Captain America instead of killing him. When the captor tells Widowmaker to stop, Cap takes advantage of the distraction and defeats Widowmaker. Cap makes his way through more Dovecote security and finally enters the fortress. Cap defeats various traps but walks into Nick Fury's office. As Fury begins to brief Cap on the situation, Cap deduces he's stuck in an illusion. Fury's office fades away and Cap is surrounded by ice. He's worshipped by Eskimos until the Sub-Mariner frees him, only to appear in a locked room where a snake attacks him. Cap forces himself to ignore the illusion and he confronts Snowfall's captor: Steven Tuval, the Mind-Master. Tuval admits defeat and reveals Snowfall in her life-support coffin as Widowmaker announces the self-destruction of the fortress. Tuval vanishes and Cap frees Snowfall, learning she is a little girl named Ginny Snow. Cap and Ginny narrowly escape from Dovecote before it explodes. Ginny explains that she can see the future, and that it's beautiful, but she's not in it. She freezes Cap in place and commits suicide.
NOTE: Issue includes Hostess ad "Captain Marvel vs. Professor Sneer." Letters page contains LOC from Kurt Busiek, future Marvel writer.

CAPTAIN AMERICA #240 (December 1979)

"Gang Wars!" (17 pages)

CREDITS: Paul Kupperberg (plot), Alan Kupperberg (writer, pencils), Don Perlin (inks), Joe Rosen (letters), George Roussos (colors), Jim Salicrup (asst editor), Roger Stern (editor)
FEATURE CHARACTER: Captain America (next in FF Ann #14, '79, IM #125, '79, IM/Cap, '06 fb, Av #186-188, '79)
VILLAINS: Coney Island Cruisers (gang, Bernie, Big Thunder, Bobo, Ernie, Georgie & Quiz Kid named), mobsters (Bruno & Mr. Fields named) (all only app, others next in Cap #309, '85)
OTHER CHARACTERS: Jacob Kirsch (only app), Duffy's Bar and Grill bartender, bystanders, police (bts)
LOCATIONS/ITEMS: Coney Island inc boardwalk, parachute jump & penny arcade; Jacob's apartment, Duffy's Bar and Grill; Coney Island Cruisers' knife, handguns, chain, lead pipe, bat & axe, mobster's Tommy gun & shotgun, pinball machines inc Flying Aces, Indy 500, Wild West & Search Party (see NOTE)
SYNOPSIS: Captain America saves Jacob Kirsch from the Coney Island Cruisers gang. He learns the gang is trying to force Jacob from his home. Cap follows the gang to Duffy's Bar and Grill, where he overpowers the gang and forces a Cruiser to take him to their leader, Big Thunder, where Cap is lured into a trap. Surrounded by thugs, Cap meets Big Thunder who reveals the mob wants to use Jacob's home as secret storage. Revealing Jacob as his hostage, Big Thunder demands a "fair" fight to prove his worth to his mob contacts. Cap is able to manipulate the fight to rescue Jacob and defeat Thunder. With the mobsters on the run and police on the way, Cap takes Jacob to help him find a better place to live.
NOTE: Flying Ace & Wild West were real pinball games, Indy 500 would become one in 1995. Next issue caption states writer Roger McKenzie & artist Rich Buckler will return with "Adonis," but this story won't appear until Cap #243, '80. Issue includes Hostess ad "Spider-Man meets June Jitsu!"

CAPTAIN AMERICA #241 (January 1980)

"Fear Grows in Brooklyn!" (17 pages)

CREDITS: Mike W. Barr (writer), Frank Springer (pencils), Pablo Marcos (inks), John Constanza (letters), George Roussos (colors), Jim Salicrup (asst editor), Roger Stern (editor), Frank Miller (c pencils), Bob McLeod (c inks)
FEATURE CHARACTERS: Captain America (also in fb between Cap #237, '79 fb & FallSon:IM, '07 fb)
GUEST STAR: Punisher (Frank Castle, US marine & war veteran turned vigilante, last in ASM #175, '77, chr last in CoH #2, '97, next in ASM #201, '80)
SUPPORTING CAST: Anna Kapplebaum (also in fb between Cap #237, '79 fb & Cap #237, '79), Josh Cooper (both next in Cap #244, '80), Mike Farrel (next in Cap #245, '80) (all last in Cap #237, '79)
VILLAINS: "Shark" Armstrong, "Little John" Giovanni (both mob bosses), 2 hitmen (Joey named), Giovanni's right-hand man, mob courier (dies) (all only app)
OTHER CHARACTERS: Federal agent (undercover as "Shark" Armstrong's bodyguard, only app), Cynthia Maxwell Kramer (Non-Parallel

Publications editor, next in Cap #248, '80), police (Fred & Les named), janitor, valet, bystanders; Maxwell Kramer (Non-Parallel Publications founder, in photo)

LOCATIONS/ITEMS: Arber Rubber Products factory, Anna's Brooklyn Heights apartment building inc Steve's & Anna's apartments, Non-Parallel Publications, Inc. office, "Little John" Giovanni's water tower office; Punisher's guns, combat van (disguised as an "Ace Repairs" van), plastic explosives & detonator, mobster's guns, Federal agent's gun

FLASHBACK: Captain America escorts Anna from the Diebenwald concentration camp.

SYNOPSIS: Captain America stops an assassination attempt, but the intended victim runs away to Cap's confusion. The police explain the assassins are mob hitmen. The victim hides in a room in Anna Kapplebaum's building. Steve Rogers applies for a job at Non-Parallel Publications, where he is hired to illustrate "Ilse: Love-Prisoner of Stalag 18." Returning home, Steve is shocked by Anna's scream. She claims she saw a Nazi in the alley. Later hearing a gunshot, Cap investigates and runs afoul of the Punisher, who is interrogating the man Cap saved earlier, a mob courier. The Punisher shoots the courier, then escapes. As the courier dies, he tells Cap the location of a mob meeting the Punisher will be at. Cap battles the Punisher on the Arber Rubber Products factory roof, stopping the vigilante from blowing up the water tower meeting place. The mobsters rush out to attack, and Punisher decides not to detonate his explosives because Cap would be caught in the blast. One of the mobsters, actually an undercover Federal agent, arrests the Punisher. When he's rounded up with the mobsters the Punisher detonates his explosives and escapes.

NOTE: The Punisher makes his War Journal entries 506 & 510 here. Issue includes Hostess ad "The Human Torch in the Icemaster Cometh."

CAPTAIN AMERICA #242 (February 1980)

"Facades!" (17 pages)

CREDITS: Steve Grant (writer), Don Perlin (pencils), Joe Sinnott (inks), Clem Robins (letters), George Roussos (colors), Jim Salicrup (asst editor), Roger Stern (editor), Al Milgrom (c art)

FEATURE CHARACTER: Captain America (next in MPr #49, Av Ann #9, Av #189, all '79)

VILLAINS: Manipulator (robot, also as boy in fb, last in Av #178, '78, remains next in Cap #247, '80, see NOTE), Sgt. Brian Muldoon (last in Cap #232, '79, last app)

OTHER CHARACTERS: Peggy Carter, Sharon Carter, Dum Dum Dugan, Falcon, Nick Fury, Iron Man, Gabe Jones, Red Skull, Thor Vision (all Manipulator's robot duplicates), Manipulator's hired actors (as army personnel); Manipulator's parents (in fb, see NOTE), Adolf Hitler (in photo)

LOCATIONS/ITEMS: Manipulator's lair; robots' guns, robot Fury's suicide note, Muldoon's gun

FLASHBACK: Manipulator grows up watching his father abused by his mother to the point of suicide, vowing to become better through the study of behavioral science (see NOTE).

SYNOPSIS: Responding to a call for help from Peggy Carter, Captain America finds himself under attack from Nick Fury, Dum Dum Dugan and Gabe Jones. After Cap defeats the SHIELD agents, Peggy draws a gun on Cap. Meanwhile, Manipulator and Sgt. Muldoon watch from afar. Muldoon asks why Cap hasn't been killed yet, despite several opportunities. Manipulator explains that he wants to see what it will take to break the Captain. Cap battles his friends, and some of them are accidentally killed. Cap finds himself worshipped by the Avengers and army personnel. When a soldier in a wheelchair questions Cap's worthiness the Avengers attack, and Cap deduces they're all robots. Cap drops into Red Skull's clutches and finds the villain holds Sharon Carter captive. Cap breaks free and attacks Skull, discovering his own mask beneath Skull's just before Sharon dies in flames again. While Cap grieves, Muldoon tries to kill Cap, but the Avenger was feinting and defeats Muldoon. Manipulator reveals the exercise was actually a test for Muldoon. Muldoon comes to and Cap knocks him out, but a stray shot from Muldoon's gun reveals Manipulator, unknown to himself, was a robot.

NOTE: Cap #249, '80 reveals Machinesmith created the Manipulator robot. As such, the flashback seen here are false memories. Issue includes Hostess ad, Mr. Fantastic in "A Passion for Gold."

CAPTAIN AMERICA #243 (March 1980)

"The Lazarus Conspiracy!" (17 pages)

CREDITS: Roger McKenzie (writer), Rich Buckler (pencils), Don Perlin (inks), Clem Robins, Diana Albers (letters), Roger Slifer (colors), Jim Salicrup (asst editor), Roger Stern (editor), George Perez (c pencils), Joe Sinott (c inks)

FEATURE CHARACTER: Captain America

VILLAINS: Adonis (Eric Cameron, 1st) & his men, Brady Cameron (Adonis' son, 1st)

OTHER CHARACTERS: Brain surgeons, reporters, cameramen, bystanders

LOCATIONS/ITEMS: New York inc Federal Courthouse & Cameron Electronics inc Adonis' lab; SHIELD LMD master matrix, Adonis' men's guns & helicopter, Adonis' equipment inc life support system & security devices inc lasers & flame throwers

SYNOPSIS: At the Federal Courthouse, Captain America fails to stop costumed men from stealing the SHIELD LMD Master Matrix. The LMD Master Matrix is damaged during the robbery, and Cap tails the agents to Cameron Electronics. Inside the complex, Eric Cameron, kept alive through an elaborate life support system, seeks to transfer his mind into an LMD. However, his son Brady wants to sabotage the process to take over his father's empire. Captain America makes his way through the building's security system as Eric's brain is placed in the LMD. Sending the brain surgeons away, Brady sets the machinery to overload just as Cap arrives. Cap tries to shut down the LMD Master Matrix, but Brady distracts the Avenger and the matrix explodes. Eric rises from the matrix wreckage, now a grotesque disfigured monster.

NOTE: Issue includes Hostess ad "Iron Man in the Hungry Battleaxe!" and a house ad for Crazy magazine featuring Batroc the Leaper; this likely occurs between Def #64, '78 & Cap #251, '80.

CAPTAIN AMERICA #244 (April 1980)

"The Way of All Flesh!" (17 pages)

CREDITS: Roger McKenzie (writer), Don Perlin (pencils), Tom Sutton (inks), Mark Rogan (letters), George Roussos (colors), Bob Budianski (asst editor), Jim Salicrup (editor), Frank Miller (c pencils), Al Milgrom (c inks)
FEATURE CHARACTER: Captain America
SUPPORTING CAST: Josh Cooper, Anna Kappelbaum
VILLAINS: Adonis (dies), Brady Cameron (last app), muggers
OTHER CHARACTERS: Ed Plumber (Plumber Publishing publisher, next in Cap #248, '80), Ed's secretary, jogger, police, Hot Cake Diner patrons, bystanders, reporter (voice only), deer
LOCATIONS/ITEMS: Cameron Electronics, Brooklyn Bridge, Anna's apartment building inc Steve's, Josh's & Anna's apartments, Plumber Publishing, Central Park, 59th Street lake, Hot Cake Diner; Adonis' equipment, police guns & helicopter, Steve's art supplies, portfolio & police band radio, mugger's knife, bulldozer, arc light
SYNOPSIS: Adonis attacks his son Brady for sabotaging his transformation but Captain America intervenes. Adonis escapes and leaves a trail of destruction in his wake, but seemingly drowns in a nearby river. The next day, Steve Rogers has breakfast with Josh and Anna, and lands an illustration job by talking about war stories with the interviewing publisher. Meanwhile, Adonis makes his way into the city. After being attacked by muggers and the police, Adonis decides to destroy all things beautiful. Cap hears about Adonis' rampage on his police band radio and investigates, finding Adonis in time to stop him from killing a woman. Cap chases Adonis to the 59th Street lake construction site where Adonis becomes entangled in the controls of a bulldozer. It drives into the lake, hits an arc light, and electrocutes Adonis to death.
NOTE: Issue includes Hostess ad, The Human Torch in "A Hot Time in the Old Town."

CAPTAIN AMERICA #245 (May 1980)

"- -The Calypso Connection!" (17 pages)

CREDITS: Roger McKenzie (writer), Carmine Infantino (pencils), Joe Rubinstein (inks), Jim Novak (letters), Carl Gafford (colors), Bob Budianski (asst editor), Jim Salicrup (editor)
FEATURE CHARACTER: Captain America (next in Av #190-191, '79-80)
GUEST STAR: Jake Lockley (cabbie alter-ego of Moon Knight, last in MTIO#52, '79, chr next in Hulk#11/2, '78, next in MP#21, '80)
SUPPORTING CAST: Anna Kapplebaum (also in fb during Cap #237, '79 fb; next in Cap#254, '81), Mike Farrel (next in Cap #247, '80), Josh Cooper
VILLAINS: Dr. Klaus Mendelhaus (also in fb between Cap #237, '79 fb & this issue, last in Cap #237, '79 fb, dies), Neo-Nazis (Oberlieutenant named, one also as hospital janitor), Diebenwald concentration camp Nazi guards (in fb, General named)
OTHER CHARACTERS: Aaron Heller (Nazi hunter, dies), Marie Heller (Aaron's daughter), Slim (diner owner), Mr. Sams (butcher) (all only app), police (Lieutenant named), paramedics, Slim's Diner patrons, Steve's neighbors, Adonis (corpse), bystanders, Diebenwald concentration camp prisoners (in fb, Marie named); Adolf Hitler (in painting)
LOCATIONS/ITEMS: Central Park, Slim's Diner, Butcher Shop, Brooklyn General Hospital inc Anna's room, Steve's Brooklyn Heights apartment, abandoned waterfront church, Diebenwald concentration camp (in fb); ambulance, Jake Lockley's cab, Nazi guns, Anna's violin (both in fb), Neo-Nazis' guns, tugboat & steamship Calypso (both mentioned), Aaron & Marie Heller's guns
FLASHBACK: In the Diebenwald concentration camp during World War II, Anna is forced to play in a band to entertain the Nazi guards. Anna fights when she's grabbed for Dr. Mendelhaus' pleasure, so Dr. Mendelhaus orders the guards to break Anna's will.
SYNOPSIS: As Captain America returns home following his battle with Adonis, he decides to pay a visit to Slim's Diner, where he befriends cabbie Jake Lockley. Anna Kapplebaum and Josh Cooper visit Mr. Sam's butcher shop where Anna sees Dr. Mendelhaus, the physician at Diebenwald. She faints from the shock. After Steve Rogers and Josh Cooper visit Anna in the hospital, Anna is visited by Nazi hunter Aaron Heller and his daughter Marie. They ask for her help in bringing Dr. Mendelhaus to justice while being secretly observed by a Neo-Nazi janitor. Steve returns home to find that Josh Cooper has thrown him a surprise birthday party. Concerned by Anna's absence, Steve checks her apartment to find it ransacked. Moments later the Hellers arrive, and Aaron shares his suspicions about where Anna has been taken. Meanwhile, Neo-Nazis take the abducted Anna to an abandoned waterfront church where Dr. Mendelhaus is being held prisoner. Cap and the Hellers arrive and attack the Neo-Nazis. During the battle Mendelhaus saves Anna's life. Despite Mendelhaus wishing to escape his past, Anna threatens to shoot the former Nazi. After Aaron Heller dies of a heart attack, Marie Heller kills Dr. Mendelhaus.
NOTE: Dr. Mendelhaus is referred to as "Dr. Menhaus" in this issue's flashback. Issue includes Hostess ad "Thor meets the Ricochet Monster!"

CAPTAIN AMERICA #246 (June 1980)

"The Sins of the Fathers!" (17 pages)

CREDITS: Peter Gillis (writer), Jerry Bingham (pencils), Al Gordon (inks), Jim Novak (letters), Bob Sharen (colors), Bob Budianski (asst editor), Jim Salicrup (editor), George Perez (c pencils), Terry Austin (c inks)
FEATURE CHARACTER: Captain America
SUPPORTING CAST: Josh Cooper (also in pfb)
VILLAIN: Joe Smith (also in pfb, also as "Crimson Bat," last in ASM #38, '66, chr last in Web:TS #3, '99, next in ASM Ann #28/3, '94)
OTHER CHARACTERS: Tommy Tomkins (Joe Smith's agent, last in ASM #38, '66, last app), Joe "Joey" Smith Jr. (Joe Smith's son, only app, dies), Liz Smith (Joe Smith's wife, only app), "Crimson Bat" director, cameramen &

stagehands, moving crew, nurse, learning disabilities children, doctors (all only in pfb), Lt. Kris Keating (Special Powers Task Force head, last in FF Ann #13, '78, next in PPSSM #46, '80), Martin Harris (New York City Board of Education member, dies), Larry Sawyer (Josh's learning disabilities co-teacher, also in pfb, only app), Special Powers Task Force, train engineer, firefighters, paramedics, police, commuters, bystanders (others in pfb)

LOCATIONS/ITEMS: "Crimson Bat" studio, Joe Smith's brownstone, learning disabilities center, hospital (all in pfb), Steve's & Josh's Brooklyn Heights apartments, Chambers Street market, Foley Square Federal Building; Liz's note (in pfb), Steve's art supplies, special powers task force vans, billing machine, train

FLASHBACK: Following his fight with Spider-Man, Joe Smith lands a contract for a TV show starring as the "Crimson Bat." He meets and marries the show's script girl Liz, and the "Crimson Bat" lasts for three seasons. The show is cancelled and Joe is typecast, but Joe's manager wisely invests Joe's money and he buys a brownstone in New York. Joe and Liz have a son, but Joe Jr. is born mentally handicapped. Liz leaves Joe six months later. Despite a tight budget, Joe continues to bring Joey to a learning disability center. Some time later, Josh Cooper works with Joe Jr. until he has a seizure that leads to his death(p).

SYNOPSIS: In an alley, a costumed man beats Martin Harris into a coma. The next day, Josh Cooper tells Steve Rogers about Joey, one of his students that died recently. Days later, Captain America assists the Special Powers Task Force against a villain trashing a social security office. The villain escapes after destroying a billing machine. Cap confers with Lt. Keating, who tells Cap about Martin Harris. Noticing a trend, Steve asks Josh for information on Joey's father and figures out Joe is getting back at those he believes failed to help his son. Cap shadows Josh's co-worker Larry, who worked with Joey directly, until Joe attacks. Knowing Joe feels guilty, Cap reasons with Joe and eventually gets through. As Joe is arrested, Cap acknowledges Joe is as much a victim of circumstance as Joey was.

NOTE: Issue includes Hostess ad, Spider-Man in "The Trap."

CAPTAIN AMERICA #247 (July 1980)

"By the Dawn's Early Light!" (17 pages)

CREDITS: Roger Stern (writer), John Byrne (co-plot, pencils), Josef Rubinstein (inks), Jim Novak (letters), George Roussos (colors), Bob Budiansky (asst editor), Jim Salicrup (editor)
FEATURE CHARACTER: Captain America (also in fb between GSInv #1 '75 & MvPro #8, '10 fb)
GUEST STARS: Nick Fury (last in IM #129, '79), Dum Dum Dugan (last in Shogun #14, '80)
SUPPORTING CAST: Bernadette "Bernie" Rosenthal (Steve's new neighbor, 1st), Josh Cooper, Mike Farrrel
VILLAINS: Machinesmith (Samuel "Starr" Saxon, robot maker, last in MTIO #48, '79, last bts in MSH #2/2, '90), Baron Strucker robot (last in Cap #132, '70, destroyed), Dragon Man (arm only, last in FF #136, '73)
OTHER CHARACTERS: Gen. Phillips (only in fb between Cap #14, '06 fb & Cap:SoL #2, '98 fb), Manipulator (remains, last in Cap #242, '80, last app), Magneto robot (last in X #58, '69, chr last in Cap #368/2, '90 fb, next in Cap #249, '80), Iron Man, Spider-Man, Thing (prev 3 robots, next in Cap #249, '80), Walter Rogers (State Department employee, only app in fb), SHIELD agents, bus driver (see NOTE), bystanders, mailman (bts, delivers letter), H.G. Wells (mentioned, false memory chamber reminded Cap of the writer)

LOCATIONS/ITEMS: Brooklyn Heights inc Brooklyn Bridge & Anna's apartment building, New York inc SHIELD HQ w/Fury's office, Ithaca inc Federal maximum security prison w/"Strucker's" cell, New Jersey inc Ft. Dix storage depot, Machinesmith's lab, Washington DC w/Gen. Phillips' office (in fb); SHIELD hologram wall, Steve's letter, SHIELD agent's gun, Fury's flying Ferrari, extradition papers & guns, "Strucker's" gas grenade & Satan Claw, Cap's WWII footlocker inc original steel shield & war journal, Dum Dum's gun, Machinesmith's robots (as construction workers), false memory chamber (in fb)

FLASHBACK: December, 1941: Reporting to Gen. Phillips, Pvt. Steve Rogers learns that he will be given a false set of memories in case he's captured and tortured by the Germans as Captain America. He meets Walter Rogers of the State Department, whose sons, Mike and Grant, died at Pearl Harbor, and his family will serve as the basis of his fictitious past. Three days later, Captain America finishes the process, believing his father to be a diplomat, his brother Mike to have died at Pearl Harbor, and that his middle name is Grant.

SYNOPSIS: Captain America takes a bus into New York to visit SHIELD HQ, where he demands to see Nick Fury. Meanwhile, Josh Cooper tries to give a recently delivered letter to Steve, but he's not home. Mike Farrel takes Josh to introduce him to their new neighbor. Cap finds Dum Dum Dugan in Fury's office. Cap tells Dugan his memories of his youth are muddled. Dugan reveals that Fury wasn't satisfied with Cap's Maryland history, and looked into Cap's past. Meanwhile, Fury visits the imprisoned Baron Strucker and tells him he's being extradited to Israel for his war crimes. Strucker gasses Fury. Dugan takes Cap to Ft. Dix and reunites the Avenger with his wartime footlocker. Cap is pleased to see his original shield and war journal, which brings a flood of memories. Strucker suddenly attacks, first with Fury's flying Ferrari, then with his Satan Claw. Cap defeats Strucker with Fury's help, but the Nazi explodes! Elsewhere, Machinesmith spies on the proceedings while his robots unearth a large object.

NOTE: Cap #247-249, '80 reveals Machinesmith created robot duplicates used in previous stories: Baron Strucker in Cap #130-132, '70 and Manipulator in Av #178, '78 & Cap #242, '80. OHMU #7, '83 reveals Machinesmith created the Magneto robot in X #50-52 & 58, '68-69. This issue reveals the bus driver mentions his wife's name is Alice, suggesting he may be Ralph Kramden from the TV show "The Honeymooners." This issue reveals that Steve Rogers has no middle name. Bernie named in Cap #248, '80. Issue includes Hostess ad, the Thing in "Sunday Punch!"

CAPTAIN AMERICA #248 (August 1980)

"Dragon Man!" (17 pages)

CREDITS: Roger Stern (writer), John Byrne (co-plot, pencils), Josef Rubinstein (inks), Jim Novak (lettters), Bob Sharen (colors), Bob Budiansky (asst editor), Jim Salicrup (editor)
FEATURE CHARACTER: Captain America
GUEST STARS: Nick Fury (next in MTU #95, '80), Dum Dum Dugan (next in Cap #250, '80)
SUPPORTING CAST: Josh Cooper, Mike Farrel, Bernie Rosenthal
VILLAINS: Machinesmith, Dragon Man
OTHER CHARACTERS: Gaffer (Sydney Levine, SHIELD scientist, last in Hulk #219, '78, next in MGN #18, '85), Baron Strucker robot (remains, last app), Johnny Carson (television host, on TV, last in Av #77, '70 fb, next in WCA #4, '86), Ed McMahon (Carson's sidekick, on TV, last in ASM #50, '67, last bts in Av #77, '70 fb, next in MCP #39/2, '90), Cynthia Maxwell Kramer (last in Cap #241, '80, last app), Carmine (Plumber Publishing art director, 1st, next in Cap #251, '80), Harry & his wife (bystanders), US Army soldiers & medic, commuters, Robin Sagon, Vin (both radio hosts), air tgraffic control, 2 jet pilots (prev 4 voice only)
LOCATIONS/ITEMS: New Jersey inc Fort Dix, Brooklyn Heights inc Steve's apartment, New York inc Harry's apartment, Werschultz, Goodman & Hurtley buildings w/Non-Parallel Publications, Inc. office & Plumber Publishing office; Army jeep, first aid kit & rifles, Gaffer's equipment, Strucker robot's data module, Fury's flying Ferrari, Machinesmith's robots (as construction workers), equipment, gadget-2 (data module) & gadget-12 (ultrasonic control & tracking module), Steve's art portfolio & letters, jet
SYNOPSIS: SHIELD scientist Gaffer studies the Strucker robot until Machinesmith remotely activates its self-destruct. A data module flies away from the wreckage, too swiftly to be stopped or pursued, and returns to Machinesmith, just as his robot minions deliver the inert Dragon Man. After a few hours work, Machinesmith reactivates him, and, controlling him via a flying drone primed with tracking information from the data module, sends him after Captain America. Steve Rogers meanwhile returns home after an unsuccessful day trying to land an art assignment, where his neighbors Josh and Mike introduce him to the building's newest resident, Bernie Rosenthal. Hearing radio reports of strange sightings at the buildings he visited, Steve realizes he is being followed; glancing out a window he spots Dragon Man flying nearby and abruptly excuses himself. Bernie feels insulted, but Josh smoothes things over. When Cap confronts Dragon Man, the drone drives Dragon Man into a frenzy, triggering a running battle that ends when Dragon Man grabs a momentarily distracted Cap and begins to squeeze the life out of him.
NOTE: Carmine named in Cap #251, '80. Issue includes Hostess ad "Hulk vs. the Roller Disco Devils!"

CAPTAIN AMERICA #249 (September 1980)

"Death, Where is Thy Sting?" (17 pages)

CREDITS: Roger Stern (writer), John Byrne (co-plot, pencils), Josef Rubinstein (inks), Jim Novak (letters), Bob Sharen (colors), Bob Budiansky (asst editor), Jim Salicrup (editor)
FEATURE CHARACTER: Captain America(next in Av #192-197, '80)
SUPPORTING CAST: Josh Cooper, Mike Farrel, Bernie Rosenthal
VILLAINS: Machinesmith (also as Mr. Fear in rfb, also in fb as "Starr" Saxon between DD #55, '69 & Cap #368/2, '90 fb, also in Cap #368/2, '90 fb; chr next in Cap #368/2, '90 fb, next bts in Cap #351, '89, next in Cap #354, '89), Dragon Man (next in FF Ann #16, '81)
OTHER CHARACTERS: Magneto, Spider-Man, Thing (all robots, last in Cap #247, '80, next in Cap #354, '89), Air-Walker (robot, only app), firemen, bystanders, Daredevil (in rfb)
LOCATIONS/ITEMS: Brooklyn Heights, New York (also in fb), Machinesmith's lab (also in fb) inc fake barn entrance; fire truck, Machinesmith's gadgets (2 destroyed), 8, 9 & 10 named), robots (others in fb), flying platform (in rfb), equipment & computer bank (both also in fb)
FLASHBACKS: Battling Daredevil as Mr. Fear, Starr Saxon falls to his death (DD #55, '69). Saxon is retrieved by his robots, but he awakens in a robot body as Machinesmith. He eventually creates a new, more human-looking body to inhabit, but finds he's no longer alive, only existing. He attempts suicide, but finds his programming won't allow him to do so.
SYNOPSIS: Captain America frees himself from Dragon Man's grip by throwing his glove into Dragon Man's eye. Retrieving his shield, Cap smashes the drone buzzing round, freeing Dragon Man from its influence, then follows as Dragon Man heads off to confront Machinesmith. Meanwhile, as Josh and Bernie watch Mike's fireman unit put out a fire Dragon Man started, Bernie realizes she is concerned for the absent Steve, and wonders how deep her feelings run for a man she has only just met. Dragon Man destroys a barn to reveal a hidden entrance, and Cap follows Dragon Man inside. Machinesmith attacks and incapacitates Dragon Man. When Cap confronts Machinesmith, his head falls off, revealing him to be a robot, and another Machinesmith taunts Cap as several robots attack simultaneously. Cap fights his way through the onslaught pursuing Machinesmith, who continues to jumps between robot bodies. After explaining how his mind came to reside within a machine, he attacks Cap with a Machinesmith army. Noticing they are guarding a computer bank, Cap destroys it, deactivating the robots. As the damaged computer deactivates, Machinesmith reveals it houses his consciousness, and thanks Cap for helping him end a life no longer worth living.
NOTE: Issue includes Hostess ad, "Captain Marvel Defends the Earth!"

CAPTAIN AMERICA #250 (October 1980)

"Cap for President!" (17 pages)

CREDITS: Roger Stern (writer), John Byrne (co-plot, pencils), Josef Rubinstein (inks), Jim Novak (letters), George Roussos (colors), Bob Budiansky (asst editor), Jim Salicrup (editor), Don Perlin, Roger McKenzie (special thanks)
FEATURE CHARACTER: Captain America (also in photo & on poster, also in fb between ASM #537, '07 fb & Cap:SoL #7/2, '99 fb; next in Av #198-200, '80, MTIO #69, '80, Av #201-205, '80-81, Daz #1, '81, Av #206, '81, Daz #2, '81, FF #220, '80, DD #164, '80, MFan #23, '85)
GUEST STARS: Avengers: Beast, Wasp (both between Av #197-198, '80), Iron Man (also in photo), Vision (both during Av #197, '80); Daredevil (last in DD #159, '79, next in MTIO #69, '80), Dum Dum Dugan (last in Cap #248, '80, next in MPr #56, '80), Nick Fury (last in MTU #95, '80, chr last in Alias #26, '03 fb, next in Av #198, '80), Spider-Man (last in MTU #95, '80, next in ASM Ann #13, '79), Dr. Strange (last in X Ann #4, '80, next in Def #85, '80)
SUPPORTING CAST: Josh Cooper, Mike Farrel (both next in Cap #258, '81), Bernie Rosenthal
VILLAINS: MLA terrorists
OTHER CHARACTERS: Edwin Jarvis (last in Av #197, '80, next in Av #199, '80), J. Jonah Jameson (last in MPr #49, '80, next in PPSSM #40, '80), Joe Robertson (last in MPr #49, next in ASM #201, '80), Charles P. Irwin (CBS reporter, last in Av #190, '79, last app), other reporters (Harv named), cameramen, Samuel T. Underwood (New Populist Party convention chairman), NPP convention staff & hostess, Congressman Gunderson (possible NPP candidate), FBI agent Zimmer, police inc bomb squad, bystanders, Governor Edwards, Senator Gerrar (both possible NPP candidates, only in photo), Mrs. Edna Crosley (Steve's teacher), Steve's classmates (both in fb)
LOCATIONS/ITEMS: New York inc Avengers Mansion, Daily Bugle, condemned school (also in fb) & convention center w/hospitality suite, Brooklyn Heights inc Steve' & Bernie's apartments, Dr. Strange's Sanctum Santorum inc Chamber of Shadows; Steve's letter, copy of Daily Globe, telegrams from both Republican & Democratic parties, Dr. Strange's Eye of Agamotto & Cloak of Levitation, MLA's plastique explosives (mentioned)
FLASHBACK: A young Steve Rogers learns about civics in school.
SYNOPSIS: Captain America stops terrorists from blowing up the New Populist Party's convention and meets Sam Underwood, the convention's chairman. Sam and his staff try to convince Cap to run for President. Cap declines at first, but agrees to think about it when pressed. When Steve returns home, Josh gives him a letter delivered a few days ago, which proves to be an army questionnaire. He and Josh help Bernie move in to her new apartment until Mike arrives with a copy of the Daily Globe, which declares Cap will be running for President. Steve is surprised to find his friends think it's a great idea. Cap arrives at Avengers Mansion to find it besieged by reporters. Inside the mansion, Jarvis gives Cap telegrams from both the Democratic and Republican parties asking Cap to represent them. Beast offers to be his campaign manager, Iron Man warns Cap of the red tape he'll get caught up in, Wasp says he's a candidate the public could trust, and Vision points out that Cap is unqualified. Cap considers his position and calls a press conference. He explains his duty is to uphold the American Dream, but being President of the United States would require him to preserve the reality of the country. Since the two objectives are at odds, Cap must decline the candidacy.
NOTE: Issue includes Hostess ad "The Human Torch Saves the Valley!" Credits & title revealed on page 8 as a Daily Globe front page. Issue closes with a quote from John F. Kennedy's book "Profiles in Courage," from 1955. Arnie Roth may be present yet unidentified in Steve's childhood fb, prior to his Cap #270, '82 fb appearance.

CAPTAIN AMERICA #251 (November 1980)

"The Mercenary and the Madman" (22 pages)

CREDITS: Roger Stern (writer), John Byrne (co-plot, pencils), Josef Rubinstein (inks), Jim Novak (letters), Bob Sharen (colors), Bob Budiansky (asst editor), Jim Salicrup (editor)
FEATURE CHARACTER: Captain America (also in photo, also in Cap #252, '80 fb)
SUPPORTING CAST: Bernie Rosenthal
VILLAINS: Batroc (last in Def #64, '78) & his Brigade, Mr. Hyde (last in PPSSM #46, '80), Monique (Batroc's assistant, 1st)
OTHER CHARACTERS: Blake Tower (New York District Attorney, last in DD #163, '80), Carmine (last in Cap #248, '80, next in Cap #254, '81),Pierce Benedict (Roxxon director of sea-going operations, 1st), Tower's receptionist, Roxxon guards (Pearson named), Ryker's Island guards, commuters; Sub-Mariner, Eskimos, Red Skull, Falcon, Avengers: Giant-Man, Iron Man, Thor, Wasp (prev 8 in rfb), Sharon Carter (in Cap's thoughts & photo), Cobra (mentioned, escaped from prison in PPSSM #46, '80)
LOCATIONS/ITEMS: New York inc Plumber Publishing, Municipal Building w/Tower's office, Roxxon Plaza, Ryker's Island prison inc Cell Block 8 w/Hyde's cell, Brooklyn Heights inc Steve's apartment, New York Harbor inc Verrazano Bridge, Newfoundland, Atlantic Ocean (both in rfb); Batroc's tugboat & barge HQ, Hyde's power sapper, Ryker's Island guards' guns, Batroc Brigade's guns, Queen of Egypt (Roxxon L-N-G super-tanker) w/ liquid natural gas, billion dollar ransom, Cap's knock-out gas & ropes, Hyde's mini-sub, Monique's sign
FLASHBACKS: Sub-Mariner finds Captain America frozen in ice, Cap is later revived by the Avengers (Av #4, '64). Cap battles the Red Skull (ToS #91/2, '67) and fights alongside Falcon (Cap #186, '75).
SYNOPSIS: After using a power sapper to make Ryker's Island prison go dark, armed men storm it and free the drugged Mr. Hyde. Hyde wakes on Batroc's floating barge HQ where Batroc asks for the five million dollars Hyde had promised to whoever freed him. Hyde reveals there is no money yet, and after a brief fight convinces Batroc to partner with him for a much larger prize. The next day, after hearing that some of Hyde's rescuers had French accents Captain America visits District Attorney Blake Tower to share his suspicion Batroc may be involved. Meanwhile, Batroc and Hyde take over the Queen of Egypt, Roxxon's new super-tanker; contacting Roxxon, Hyde demands a billion dollar ransom and Captain America as a prisoner or he'll blow up New York with the super-tanker's volatile cargo. Later, Batroc and Hyde rendezvous with "captive" Cap to retrieve the ransom, but Cap attacks. Cap is quickly defeated and awakes chained to the Queen of Egypt's bow, as it sails directly into New York Harbor.
NOTE: Issue includes LOC from Kurt Busiek, future Marvel writer, and Hostess ad, Mr. Fantastic in "The Power of Gold!"

CAPTAIN AMERICA #252 (December 1980)

"Cold Fire!" (17 pages)

CREDITS: Roger Stern (writer), John Byrne (co-plot, pencils), Josef Rubinstein (inks), John Costanza (letters), Bob Sharen (colors), Bob Budiansky (asst editor), Jim Salicrup (editor)
FEATURE CHARACTER: Captain America (also in fb1 during Cap #251, '80; next in Hulk Ann #11, '82)
SUPPORTING CAST: Bernie Rosenthal
VILLAINS: Batroc (next in Cap #302, '85) & his Brigade (Bob & Terry named), Mr. Hyde (also as Dr. Calvin Zabo in fb2 between Cap #152, '72 & DD #142, '77; next in ASM #231, '82), Monique (last app), Scorpion (only in fb2 between Cap #152, '72 & ASM #145, '75, also in rfb)
OTHER CHARACTERS: Blake Tower (only in fb1, next in PMIF #69, '81), Pierce Benedict (only in fb1, last app), Coast Guard, police, prison inmates, prison guards (prev 3 in fb2), explosion victims (in Cap's thoughts)
LOCATIONS/ITEMS: New York inc Tower's office (in fb1), pharmacy, prison (both in fb2), New York Harbor; Queen of Egypt w/liquid natural gas, Batroc's tugboat & barge HQ, Hyde's mini-sub, billion dollar ransom, Coast Guard's boats, police gun (in fb2)
FLASHBACKS: Captain America confers with Blake Tower and Pierce Benedict. Benedict reveals if the Queen of Egypt explodes, the liquid natural gas will erupt with a force of a small nuclear device (1). Cap defeats Mr. Hyde and ties him up with Scorpion (Cap #152, '72). Mr. Hyde reverts to Dr. Calvin Zabo and escapes. He breaks into a pharmacy to duplicate his Hyde-formula, but he's caught and arrested. Without the funds to hire a good lawyer, Zabo spends six months in prison (2).
SYNOPSIS: Mr. Hyde taunts the chained Captain America as the Queen of Egypt races into New York Harbor. When Hyde leaves, Batroc secretly loosens Cap's chains. As Cap uses the slack to break the chains, he imagines what will happen to New York if the super-tanker explodes. Cap frees himself but falls into the harbor. Batroc learns that Hyde plans to destroy New York, despite already having the billion dollar ransom, and attacks Hyde. As the two battle Cap climbs out of the harbor, retrieves his shield, and attacks Hyde as well. Ripping apart a pipe to use as a weapon, Hyde accidentally freezes himself with liquid natural gas and stumbles overboard. Cap loses Hyde in the harbor, but captures Batroc with the Coast Guard's help.
NOTE: Letters page contains LOC from Kurt Busiek, future Marvel writer. Issue includes Hostess ad "Iron Man vs. the Bank Robbers!" Batroc misspelled "Batrok" on cover.

2ND STORY: "The Life and Times of Captain America!" (2 pages)
"The Apartment of Steve Rogers Esq." (1 page)
"Steve Rogers' Friends and Neighbors" (1 page)
"Captain America's Partners against Crime" (1 page)
CREDITS: Roger Stern (writer), John Byrne (pencils), Josef Rubinstein (inks), John Costanza (letters), Bob Sharen (colors)
FEATURE CHARACTERS: John Byrne (hand only, last in X #121, '79, next in Thing #7/2, '84), Josef Rubinstein (bts, wrote thank you note to John Byrne, only app)
OTHER CHARACTERS: Captain America, Avengers: Beast, Giant-Man, Hawkeye, Iron Man, Quicksilver, Scarlet Witch, Thor, Vision (in shadows), Wasp; Bucky, Falcon, Spider-Man (in shadow), Sharon Carter, Dum Dum Dugan, Nick Fury, Josh Cooper, Mike Farrel, Adolf Hitler, Edwin Jarvis, Anna Kapplebaum, Bernie Rosenthal, Leila Taylor, receptionist, special needs child, Nazis, tourists
STORY: A collection of facts and background information on Captain America, including a brief recap of his history, the floor plan of his apartment, what his neighbors do, and introductions to his partners past and present. However, John Byrne refuses to draw the Avengers in such a small space.
NOTE: Mike Farrel is a graduate of three different colleges and holds six degrees.

CAPTAIN AMERICA #253 (January 1981)

"Should Old Acquaintance be Forgot" (22 pages)

CREDITS: Roger Stern (writer), John Byrne (co-plot, pencils), Josef Rubinstein (inks), Jim Novak (letters), Bob Sharen (colors), Bob Budiansky (asst editor), Jim Salicrup (editor)
FEATURE CHARACTER: Captain America (also in Cap's thoughts)
GUEST STARS: Jacqueline Falsworth, Lady Crichton (retired Spitfire of the Invaders, also in Cap's thoughts), Montgomery, Lord Falsworth (retired Union Jack of WWI) (both last in Inv #41, '79, chr last in CitV #1, '02)
SUPPORTING CAST: Bernie Rosenthal
VILLAINS: Baron Blood (John Falsworth, vampire, also as Dr. Jacob Cromwell, also in pfb; last in Inv #41, '79, chr last in UJack #2, '99 fb), liquor store robbers
OTHER CHARACTERS: Edwin Jarvis (last in Hulk #258, '81, next in MTIO #75, '81), Kenneth Crichton (Spitfire's son, 1st), Joey Chapman (Ken's schoolmate, 1st), Hotchkins (Falsworth's butler, 1st), Jenny ("Cromwell's" patient, 1st), Inspector Sweeney (1st), Scotland Yard constable & coroner, Baron Blood's victim (corpse), "Wine and Spirits" store clerk, stewardess, Heathrow airport inspector, commuters, Charlotte Cromwell (corpse, also in fb), Lily Cromwell (bts in fb, last in UJack #2, '99 fb, next in 1st actual app in UJack #1, '99, see NOTE), townsfolk (in fb), Jackie's cat, Baron Blood's rats; Invaders: Bucky, Human Torch, Sub-Mariner, Toro, Union Jack (Brian Falsworth); Agent Axis, Asbestos Lady, Blue Bullet, the Face, Adolf Hitler, Master Man, Warrior Woman, Nazis (prev 13 in Cap's thoughts)
LOCATIONS/ITEMS: New York inc "Wine and Spirits" store, Brooklyn Heights inc Steve's apartment, Broadway inc theatre, England inc

Heathrow airport, Falsworth Manor, Tower of London w/"Baron Blood's" tomb, New Scotland Yard's coroner's office; robber's shotgun & handgun, "Oklahoma!" poster, coded telegram, Concorde jetliner, "Baron Blood's" coffin, Cap's Avengers ID, garlic & crucifixes

FLASHBACK: Twelve years ago, Dr. Cromwell's house is set on fire during a vampire scare in England (p).

SYNOPSIS: After finding a third slasher victim, an English village constable and Dr. Cromwell inform Lady Crichton, who promises to use her influence to get Scotland Yard involved; however, doubting they can handle the situation, her elderly father prepares to contact someone who can. In Manhattan, after attending a musical together, Steve Rogers and Bernie Rosenthal return to Steve's apartment, but their liaison is interrupted by a phone call from Jarvis, who reads Steve a coded telegram, prompting him to cut the date short, to Bernie's dismay. Traveling to England, Steve reunites with Lady Crichton, formerly his Invaders teammate Spitfire, and learns it was her father, Lord Falsworth, aka WWI's Union Jack, who sent for him, convinced the slasher is their old foe Baron Blood, despite his remains being long interred in the Tower of London. Investigating, Cap discovers a woman's skeleton has been swapped for Blood's; he returns to the Manor to inform Falsworth of this, and meets Jackie's son Ken and his friend Joey. That night, Baron Blood attacks Captain America.

NOTE: This issue reveals WWII Union Jack, Brian Falsworth, died in a car accident in '53. Cap #254, '81 reveals that Dracula's agent, the real Dr. Cromwell, freed Baron Blood, who then killed and replaced him. Cromwell's daughter Charlotte's corpse replaced Blood's in his tomb. UJack #2, '99 reveals Cromwell's 1st name and that his other daughter, Lily, is present bts in the fb. Charlotte's 1st name is revealed in OHMU HC #1, '08. Issue includes Hostess ad "Iron Man vs. the Bank Robbers!"

CAPTAIN AMERICA #254 (February 1981)

"Blood on the Moors" (22 pages)

CREDITS: Roger Stern (writer), John Byrne (co-plot, pencils), Josef Rubinstein (inks), Joe Rosen (letters), Bob Sharen (colors), Bob Budiansky (asst editor), Jim Salicrup (editor), Colin Campbell (special thanks)

FEATURE CHARACTER: Captain America (also in rfb, next in Cap #256, '81)

GUEST STARS: Montgomery, Lord Falsworth (also as Union Jack, also in symbolic image, also in MCP #42/3, '90 fb, dies), Union Jack (Joey Chapman, becomes Union Jack, chr also & next in MCP #42/3, '90 fb, next bts in CoC #1, '82, next in CoC #3, '82), Jacqueline Falsworth, Lady Crichton (chr also & next in MCP #42/3, '90 fb, next in MSH #4/4, '90) (all also in rfb)

SUPPORTING CAST: Anna Kapplebaum (last in Cap #245, '80), Bernie Rosenthal (also in rfb) (both next in Cap #258, '81)

VILLAIN: Baron Blood (also as Dr. Cromwell, also in rfb, next in KoP #10, '93)

OTHER CHARACTERS: Kenneth Falsworth (chr also & next in MCP #42/3, '90 fb, next in MCP #89/3, '91), Carmine (last in Cap #251, '80, last app), Inspector Sweeney, Jenny (both last app), Scotland Yard constables, townspeople, mortician, "Bull and Bush" pub patrons & landlord; Invaders: Human Torch, Sub-Mariner; Lord Falsworth (Montgomery's father, corpse), Dracula, Nazis, Baron Blood's victim (prev 6 in rfb)

LOCATIONS/ITEMS: England inc Falsworth Manor (also in rfb), cave, village, "Bull and Bush" pub, Brooklyn Bridge, Brooklyn Heights in Steve's apartment, Transylvania inc Dracula's castle (in rfb); Union Jack's gun & knife

FLASHBACKS: Scotland Yard discovers another victim. Steve and Bernie's date is cut short. Captain America meets Joey Chapman and Ken Falsworth. Baron Blood attacks Cap (Cap #253, '81). Before WWI, Montgomery Falsworth inherits his late father's title. Traveling Europe, his brother John visits Transylvania, where he tries to enslave Dracula. Overpowered, he becomes the vampire Baron Blood and fights for the Germans in both World Wars (Inv #9, '76 fb). John Falsworth introduces himself to the Invaders, tries to transform Lady Jacqueline and is impaled by the heroes (Inv #7-9, '76). Lady Jacqueline is saved by a blood transfusion from the Human Torch and becomes Spitfire (Inv #11, '76).

SYNOPSIS: Failing to slay Captain America, Baron Blood flees as dawn breaks, returning to the nearby village, where he dons his Dr. Cromwell disguise and meets his first patient of the day, Jenny. As the day progresses a hunt for Blood throughout the surrounding villages draws a blank. Ken and Joey take a break from the search at the pub where Ken's girl Jenny works, but she faints while talking to them, and they find bite marks on her neck. In Brooklyn Heights, Bernie and Anna clean Steve's apartment. Bernie takes a message that Steve lost an art assignment. Lord Falsworth, dressed as Union Jack, insists he will serve as bait to lure Blood, but suffers a heart attack while arguing with Cap and his daughter. They later call family doctor Dr. Cromwell to check on Lord Falsworth. When they leave Cromwell alone with Union Jack, Cromwell reveals himself as Baron Blood and attacks. Union Jack fights back to the Baron's surprise. Captain America joins the battle and is forced to decapitate the vampire. Joey reveals himself as the new Union Jack, and the group later burns Baron Blood's body. During the funeral, Lord Falsworth passes on.

NOTE: Issue includes Hostess ad "Daredevil vs. Johnny Punk!"

CAPTAIN AMERICA #255 (March 1981)

"The Living Legend" (22 pages)

CREDITS: Roger Stern (writer), John Byrne (art pgs 1-21, pencils pg 22), Josef Rubinstein (inks pg 2, c inks), Joe Rosen (letters), Bob Sharen (colors), Bob Budiansky (asst editor), Jim Salicrup (editor), Frank Miller (c pencils)

FEATURE CHARACTER: Captain America (also in symbolic splash page, newspaper & rfb, also in fb1 between MvPro #4, '10 fb & Cap #270, '82 fb, also in MvPro #4, '10 fb, SR:SSol #3, '11 fb, Cap #270, '82 fb, ASM #537, '07 fb, Cap #250, '80 fb, Cap:SoL #7/2, '99 fb & Cap:Re #1, '09; fb2 between MvPro #4, '10 fb & SR:SSol #2, '10 fb, also in Cap #176, '74 fb, Cap:SoL #7/2, '99 fb, Cap #25, '07 fb, MvPro #4, '10 fb, CapC Spec #1, '09 fb, Cap #109, '69 fb & Cap Ann #10/2, '91; fb3 between ToS #63/2, '65 & Next #9, '06 fb, also in CapC #1, '41, ToS #63/2, '65, Cap #109, '69 fb & Cap:Re #2, '09; fb4 between Cap #270, '82 fb & MvPro #5, '10, fb5 between MvPro #5, '10 & Cap:SoL #7/2, '99, also in Cap #2, '05 fb, MSH #3, '90 fb, ToS #1, '95 fb, SR:SSol #1, '10 fb, Cap #2, '02 fb, BP #30, '01 fb, Cap Ann #13/2, '94 fb, MvPro #5, '10 & Cap #25, '07 fb; 1941: during Cap:SoL #7/2, '99; Present: next in Micro #28, Hulk #258, MTIO #75, Av #207-208, FF #230, Cap #258, all '81, see NOTE)

VILLAINS: Heinz Krueger (also as "Special Agent Frederick Clemson," also in rfb, in fb3 to last chr app as corpse after Cap:Re #2, '09, dies), Agent R (also in rfb, in fb2 between Cap #176, '74 fb & Cap #109, '69 fb), Nazis (also in symbolic splash page & newsreel), Axis spies (1 as "Major"), saboteurs (some as maintenance men), bundists (all in fb5)

OTHER CHARACTERS: Franklin Delano Roosevelt (US President, also in rfb, chr last in ToS #63/2, '65, chr next in Cap:SoL #7/2, '99), Sarah Rogers (Steve's mother, 1st, in fb1 during MvPro #4, '10 fb, also in Cap:SoL #7/2, '99 fb, dies), Gen. Phillips (also in rfb, in fb2 between Cap #109, '69 fb & ToS #63/2, '65, also in Cap #109, '69 fb, Cap #25, '07 fb, MvPro #4, '10 fb, Cap Ann '00 fb, CapC #1, '41, MvPro #4, '10, fbs3-4 between ToS #63/2, '65 & bts in Cap:SoL #6/3, '99, fb5 between bts in MvPro #5, '10 & Av Ann '01/2, also in Cap #2, '05 fb), Dr. Anderson (also in rfb, in fb2 to 1st chr app before MSH #3, '90 fb, fb3 between CapC #1, '41 & GSInv #1, '75 fb), Prof. Reinstein (Abraham Erskine, in fb2 between Cap #109, '69 fb & Cap #25, '07 fb, also in Cap #109, '69 fb, fb3 to last chr app after ToS #63/2, '65, also in CapC #1, '41, ToS #63/2, '65, Cap #109, '69 fb, Av:In Ann #1/4, '08 fb & Cap:Re #2, '09, dies, also as corpse), Walter Jameson (in fb5 during Mv #1, '94), G-2 courier, Washington Post editor (bts, waiting in other room), news announcer (voice only), children (in fb1), theater attendees, army doctor, recruiter & draftees, agents L-7 & X-9 (prev 5 in fb2), Under-Secretary Simms (in fb3), Steve's Super-Soldier trainers (in fb4), Col. Henson & his driver, FBI agents (Blazes, McCloskey & O'Brien named), military police, bystanders (prev 5 in fb5), Avengers: Giant-Man, Iron Man, Thor, Wasp; Invaders: Human Torch, Spitfire, Sub-Mariner, Union Jack; Baron Blood, Bucky, Sgt. Mike Duffy, Master Man, Warrior Woman, Baron Zemo (prev 15 in rfb), Adolf Hitler (in symbolic splash page & rfb), Red Skull (in symbolic splash page, photo & rfb)

LOCATIONS/ITEMS: White House inc Oval Office, Camp Lehigh, Brooklyn Heights inc Steve's apartment, New York (also in rfb) inc Lower East Side w/Rogers home (in fb1), movie theater, Army recruitment center (both in fb2), Curio shop (in fb2) w/Project: Rebirth (in fbs2-3 & rfb) & warehouse (in fb5), Maryland countryside, Grumman aircraft plant, Liberty shipyards, Boulder Dam (prev 4 in fb5), Hitler's bunker (in symbolic splash page); Operation: Rebirth dossier, Project: Super-Soldier dossier, Operation: Rebirth equipment (in fbs2-3 & rfb), Super Soldier Serum (both as injection & digestible), Vita-Rays, Krueger's gun (prev 3 in fb3 & rfb), Super Soldier training equipment (in fb4), Cap's original steel shield (also in fb5), new circular shield & motorcycle (in fb5), Nazis' guns, bundists' guns, Jameson's camera, bomb-sight (prev 3 in fb5), Pvt. Rogers' rifle, Zemo's drone plane, Avengers submarine (prev 3 in rfb)

FLASHBACKS: Steve Rogers grows up during the Great Depression, raised by his widowed mother until she dies from pneumonia (1). Steve sees newsreel footage of the Nazi war machine and decides he must do something (2). Steve tries to volunteer for military service but is declared 4-F. Gen. Phillips approaches Steve with an offer (Cap #109, '69 fb). Government agents take Steve to a Curio shop, a front for Operation: Rebirth (2) where Agent R reveals herself (Cap #109, '69 fb). (2) Steve realizes that "Professor Reinstein" is actually an alias for Abraham Erskine and Dr. Anderson explains the ruse is to fool enemy spies. Erskine begins to test Steve (2). Dr. Anderson informs FDR the Super Soldier Serum is ready (GSInv #1, '75 fb). Agent R seats the arriving officials (CapC #1, '41). Erskine prepares to inject Steve with the Super Soldier Serum, and once it's been injected, Erskine hands Steve the compound, which Steve drinks (ToS #63/2, '65). Erskine bombards Steve with Vita-Rays (Cap #109, '69 fb) and Steve begins to grow (ToS #63/2, '65). Steve immediately feels the effects (CapC #1, '41). Steve is astonished, Erskine is proud, and Gen. Phillips orders Dr. Anderson to mass-produce the serum at once (3). Nazi spy Krueger kills Erskine (ToS #63/2, '65 & Cap #109, '69 fb) and Steve attacks Krueger (Cap #109, '69 fb & CapC #1, '41), but accidentally knocks him into the Vita-Ray machine (Cap #109, '69 fb). With the Vita-Ray machine destroyed and both Krueger and Erskine dead, Operation: Rebirth ends (3). Gen. Phillips oversees the training of Steve's new body (4). Gen. Phillips informs Steve of the Red Skull's menace and gives Steve a uniform to be the Red Skull's opposite: Captain America. On his first mission, Captain America saves Col. Henson from Nazis. The next day, Cap breaks up a bund ring in New York, but while chasing one of them down his mask is knocked loose. A reporter almost takes Cap's unmasked picture. Soon after, Cap stops Axis spies from stealing a new bomb-sight from the Grumman aircraft plant, stops saboteurs from destroying the Liberty shipyards, and halts the destruction of Boulder Dam (5). Some time later, Sgt. Duffy gives Pvt. Rogers a hard time until Bucky distracts Duffy (ToS #63/2, '65). Soon after, Bucky discovers that Steve is Cap (CapC #1, '41) and becomes his partner (ToS #63/2, '65). Over the next four years, Cap fights alongside the Invaders against Hitler, Master Man and Warrior Woman (Inv #21, '77) and battles Baron Zemo (Av #6, '64 fb), Baron Blood (Inv #9, '76), Red Skull (ToS #68/2, '65). Near the end of the war Bucky is caught in the explosion of Zemo's drone plane and Cap is frozen (Av #4, '64 fb). Years later, the Avengers find Cap's frozen body and revive him (Av #4, '64).

SYNOPSIS: In 1941: President Roosevelt looks over the dossiers on Operation: Rebirth and Project: Super-Soldier to familiarize himself with Steve Rogers and Captain America. When he's done Captain America is called in. President Roosevelt comments on Cap's modified uniform and gives Cap a new circular shield to replace his triangular one. This new shield is nigh-indestructible, but the metallurgical accident that produced it can't be duplicated. He then tells Cap the army has devised a cover identity for Cap so he can be quickly deployed for special missions. In the Present, Cap returns home after an adventure at Madison Square Garden. He's tired, but has to finish more ad storyboards by morning. He wonders if the double life he leads is worth it, and decides it is.

NOTE: This issue combines the slightly disparate origins shown in CapC #1, '41, ToS #63/2, '65 & Cap #109, '69 into one cohesive origin, explaining discrepancies like Abraham Erskine having two names and there being three versions of the Rebirth process. Steve was watching "Sea Hawk" starring Errol Flynn at the movies when he saw the newsreels to inspire his volunteering for service. The Operation: Rebirth password is "Eagle." Walter Jameson's name revealed in SM:BiBH, '07. Splash page is an homage to CapC #1, '41's cover. The current-day portion of this issue takes place out of publication order; Cap is still in England in both Cap #254, '81 & Cap #256, '81, and he's back in Brooklyn Heights here. Issue includes Hostess ad, Human Torch in "Blown About!"

CAPTAIN AMERICA #256 (April 1981)

"The Ghosts of Greymoor Castle!" (22 pages)

CREDITS: Bill Mantlo (writer), Gene Colan (pencils), Dave Simons, Al Milgrom, Frank Giacoia (inks), Jim Novak (letters), Bob Sharen (colors), Bob Budiansky (asst editor), Jim Salicrup (editor)

FEATURE CHARACTER: Captain America (also in rfb)

VILLAINS: Druid (last in Cap #188, '75, next bts in Cap #402, '92, next in Cap #403, '92), Samhain (embodiment of All Hallows Eve, bts between VSW #1, '82 fb & VSW #1, '82, trapped in druid tome)

OTHER CHARACTERS: Cedric Rawlings (also in painting & rfb, last in ToS #71/2, '65, last app); Bucky, Major Uberhart, soldiers, Nazi spies (prev 4 in rfb); Celia Rawlings (only in painting), Scarlet Witch (mentioned)

LOCATIONS/ITEMS: Geymoor Castle (also in rfb), US Army base (rfb); Cedric's armor, mace, Z-Rays &

equipment (in rfb), Druid's alchemy eggs & battle axe, stone gargoyle, ancient texts, Cap & Bucky figurines (in rfb)

FLASHBACKS: Cap is deployed on a mission, leaving Bucky behind. An explosion at the base leads Bucky to be captured by Nazis. Cedric Rawlings demonstrates his Z-Rays to the Nazis (ToS #69/2, '65).

SYNOPSIS: Memories of past adventures bring Captain America to England's Greymoor Castle. As Cap makes his way through the decrepit castle an armored figure attacks him, sending Cap into the reopened Z-Ray pit. Cap saves himself but lands hard, knocking himself out. The armored figure brings Cap to safety and reveals himself as Cedric Rawlings. Cedric believes ghosts of the past are haunting him in the castle, so Cap investigates some noises. When a stone gargoyle almost crushes him, Cap discovers the Druid is responsible. Druid reveals he is searching the castle for an arcane source of alchemical knowledge, and their battle leads back to the Z-Ray pit. Cedric saves Cap by knocking Druid into the pit, but he almost falls in as well. Cap saves Cedric and discovers the ancient texts Druid was looking for. Cedric tells Cap to take the books, and Cap considers having Scarlet Witch translate them.

NOTE: Issue includes Hostess ad, Spider-Man in "The Rescue!"

CAPTAIN AMERICA #257 (May 1981)

"Deadly Anniversary!" (17 pages)

CREDITS: Mike W. Barr (writer), Jim Shooter (co-plot), Lee Elias (pencils), Many Hands (inks), Joe Rosen (letters), Bob Sharen, Ed Hannigan (colors), Bob Budiansky (asst editor), Jim Salicrup (editor), Al Milgrom (c art)
FEATURE CHARACTER: Captain America (also in rfb, next in Cap #255, '81, see NOTE)
GUEST STAR: Hulk (also as Bruce Banner, also in symbolic image, last in Hulk Ann #11, '82, next in MTIO Ann #5, '80)
VILLAINS: Master of Matrix Eight (leader of extra-legal research agency & weapons supplier, only app), Matrix Eight agents (one as a cabbie)
OTHER CHARACTERS: Derek (pilot), Nancy (flight attendant), commuters; Bucky (rfb); Baron Zemo (mentioned, Master of Matrix Eight's former master)

LOCATIONS/ITEMS: Midwestern hotel, England inc airport & Matrix Eight's lair; Matrix Eight's Gammadroid, gas canister, guns, heat ray, flame thrower & Adhesive X, Zemo's drone plane (in rfb)
FLASHBACK: Cap and Bucky try to stop Zemo's drone plane (Av #4, '64 fb).
SYNOPSIS: In the American Midwest, Bruce Banner is abducted from his hotel room. Sometime later in England, Captain America disembarks a plane and takes a taxi to a remote location. Matrix Eight agents attack Cap and bring him before the Master of Matrix Eight, a former assistant to Baron Zemo. He shows Cap the Gammadroid, a powerful robot based on the captured Hulk's unique metabolism. Hearing enough Cap breaks away and frees Banner, accidentally overexciting him into the Hulk. Cap directs the Hulk's rage to take down their mutual foes. Hulk overcomes Adhesive X and the Gammadroid before he's knocked out by gas. Sabotaging the lair Cap carries the unconscious Banner out, escaping through an underwater tunnel. The Master finds himself trapped as the base explodes. On land, Cap tells Bruce he was visiting the area for the anniversary of Bucky's death.
NOTE: Cap returns to America after this story so he can appear in the current portion of Cap #255, '81. Issue includes Hostess ad, Thing in "Earthly Delights."

2ND STORY: "Charlie America's Family Album!" (3 pages)
CREDITS: For credits see original entries.
NOTE: Reprinted from NBE #12/5, '69. New footnote added to page 1.

3RD STORY: "How to be a Comic Book Artist!" (2 pages)
NOTE: Reprinted from NBE #11, '68. New editor's box & footnote added to page 1.

CAPTAIN AMERICA #258 (June 1981)

"Blockbuster!" (22 pages)

CREDITS: Chris Claremont (plot, script pg 1-12), David Michelinie (script pg 13-22), Mike Zeck (art), Jim Novak (letters), Bob Sharen, Roger Slifer (colors), Bob Budiansky (asst editor), Jim Salicrup (editor)
FEATURE CHARACTER: Captain America (also on TV)
SUPPORTING CAST: Josh Cooper (last in Cap #250, '80, next in Cap #261, '81), Mike Farrel (also on TV, last in Cap #250, '80, next in Cap #269, '82), Anna Kappelbaum (last in Cap #254, '81, next in Cap #269, '82), Bernie Rosenthal (last in Cap #254, '81, next in Cap Ann #5, '81)
VILLAINS: Blockbuster (Frederic Woolrich, arsonist, 1st, next in Q #41, '92, as Heat-Ray), Harry (land developer, only app) (both also in photo)

LOCATIONS/ITEMS: Roseland Ballroom, Brooklyn Heights inc Anna's apartment building w/Steve's, Bernie's & Anna's apartments, 31-47 Culver Street, bar, warehouse; Blockbuster's arson supplies, gun & fire-suit inc flamethrower & force beam, fire trucks, copy of Daily Bugle

SYNOPSIS: Steve Rogers and Bernie Rosenthal enjoy an evening of big band music and carriage rides, until an explosion rocks the building next door. Steve responds as Captain America, saving the building's residents, but is caught by falling debris. A firefighter, Sam Douglas, is killed while rescuing Cap. Later, Blockbuster, the arsonist responsible for the explosion, reports to Harry, a land developer who hired him to torch the building so he could buy the property cheap. Meanwhile, Steve, Josh, Bernie and Anna try to cheer up Mike, who knew Sam. The next night Captain America and the police patrol the neighborhood, looking for the arsonist. Blockbuster suddenly attacks Cap. During their battle Cap manages to disable Blockbuster's fire-suit and strip him of it, but Blockbuster pulls a gun on Cap. Mike's arriving fire squad disables Blockbuster with a fire hose. The police arrest Blockbuster, planning to use the pending murder charge as leverage for his boss' identity. Days later, the Daily Bugle reports on Harry's arrest.

NOTE: Blockbuster's real name revealed in OHMU HC #11, '10. Issue includes Hostess ad, Iron Man in "The Charge of the Rhinos!"

CAPTAIN AMERICA #259 (July 1981)

"Rite of Passage!" (21 pages)

CREDITS: Jim Shooter (plot), David Michelinie (writer), Mike Zeck (pencils), Quickdraw Studios (inks), Jim Novak (letters), Roger Slifer (colors), Bob Budiansky (asst editor), Jim Salicrup (editor)
FEATURE CHARACTER: Captain America (also in fb between SecWs #18, '10 fb & Cap #237, '79 fb; next in MTU #106, '81)
GUEST STAR: Beast (last in FF #230, '81, next in Daz #5, '81)
VILLAIN: Dr. Octopus (Otto Octavius, scientist w/four mechanical arms, last in DD #165, '80, last bts in Thor #304, '81, next in ASM Ann #15, '81)
OTHER CHARACTERS: Edwin Jarvis (between Av #208-209, '81), Ray Coulson (war veteran, also in fb), John Coulson (Ray's son, also in photo), the Huns (biker gang, Soledad & Turk named), bartender, cabbie, commuters, bystanders; Allied & Axis soldiers (in fb)

LOCATIONS/ITEMS: Brooklyn Heights inc Steve's apartment, Avengers Mansion inc gym, Ray's cycle shop & house, Huns' shack (outside Saugerties, New York), European battlefield (in fb); Avengers exercise equipment, Steve's art portfolio, Ray's letter, Huns' motorcycles, ropes & chain, Cap's custom motorcycle (1st), WWII motorcycle, Allied & Axis guns (both in fb)

FLASHBACK: Pinned down by enemy fire, Captain America borrows Cpl. Ray Coulson's motorcycle to attack the Axis soldiers.

SYNOPSIS: Feeling he's being followed, Captain America unsuccessfully tries to find his pursuer. Cap exercises at Avengers Mansion where Jarvis gives Cap a letter from Ray Coulson. After dropping off an art assignment, Cap visits Ray, who asks Cap for help. Ray wants Cap to deliver a message to his son John who ran off to join a biker gang. Cap tracks the gang down and agrees to a test in order to talk to John. After Cap is tied to two motorcycles for the test, Dr. Octopus crashes in and steals Cap's shield. Octopus reveals he's been following Cap, waiting to strike in order to steal his shield and analyze it to make his arms stronger. Cap quickly defeats Octopus, retrieves his shield and delivers Ray's message to John, an apology for not being a better father. John decides to return home and make amends. Days later, John visits Avengers Mansion to give Cap his thanks in the form of a custom-built motorcycle.

NOTE: Letters page contains LOC from future Marvel writer Barry Dutter. Issue includes Hostess ad "Spider-Man vs. the Human Computer!"

CAPTAIN AMERICA #260 (August 1981)

"Prison Reform!" (22 pages)

CREDITS: Al Milgrom (writer, co-inks, c art), Alan Kupperberg (pencils), Quickdraw Studios (co-inks), Jim Novak (letters), George Roussos, Don Warfield (colors), Bob Budiansky (asst editor), Jim Salicrup (editor)
FEATURE CHARACTER: Captain America (also on TV, next in Av Ann #10, '81, IM #148, '81)
VILLAINS: "Thumper" Morgan, Deacon (both last in ToS #62, '65/2, last app), other prison inmates (some also in pfb, Eddie named)
OTHER CHARACTERS: Clark Kent (reporter, last in MTU #79, '79, next in Av #228, '83), Jimmy Olsen (cub reporter, chr last in Mv #1, '94, next in ASM #332, '90), Tony Zack (prison inmate, also in pfb, only app), Warden Michaels, prison guards (some also in pfb), other reporters (Hildy named), bailiff, judge, lawyer, Acme Loan Co. security guard, gang members (prev 5 in pfb), Carlson (mentioned, previous Warden)

LOCATIONS/ITEMS: Prison (also in pfb) inc general population, Warden's office, mess hall & workshop; Bronx inc Acme Loan Co., courtroom (both in pfb); Prison exercise equipment, guards' guns, inmate's knife, Deacon's lock pick, Cap's make-shift shield, Tony's knife, Acme Loan Co. safe w/money, magnetic door (prev 3 in pfb)

FLASHBACK: Tony joins a gang but is caught robbing a safe. A judge sentences him to prison. Later at the prison, an inmate accidentally says "Captain America," which happens to be the sound combination for the security door. The door opens and almost allows a mass escape (p).

SYNOPSIS: Captain America is thrown in prison! After fighting with his new cellmates, Cap meets Tony Zack, a young inmate who didn't join the fight. The next day Cap attends a press conference in the warden's office, announcing that he's been asked to attempt an escape in order to help test the prison's security. Cap lives amongst the prisoners for several days, causing them to get anxious at his presence and start several fights. Tony doesn't get involved, but he's surprised when Cap stands up for the inmates to the guards. Tony's surprised again when Thumper plans to follow Cap to freedom and kill Cap anyway. When Cap finally makes his move, so do the prisoners. Tony warns Cap of Thumper's plan.

Cap uses a make-shift shield to help get him over the wall, with the prisoners unable to follow. The prisoners are rounded up by the guards, and Cap puts in a good word for Tony. Since only Cap manages to escape, the Warden's measures are deemed a success.
NOTE: Issue includes Hostess ad, Fantastic Four in "Wonders of Nature."

CAPTAIN AMERICA #261 (August 1981)

"Celluloid Heroes!" (22 pages)

CREDITS: J.M. DeMatteis (writer), Michael Zeck (pencils, c art), Quickdraw Studios (inks), Jim Novak (letters), Christi Scheele, Dan Warfield (colors), Bob Budiansky (asst editor), Jim Salicrup (editor)
FEATURE CHARACTER: Captain America (also as Nomad in rfb)
GUEST STARS: Avengers: Beast (last in MTIO #78, '81, next in Def #98, '81), Iron Man (also in rfb, last in IM #150, '81, chr last in CW:Conf #1, '07, next in Def #98, '81), Vision (also in rfb, last in Av Ann #10, '81, next in Av #210, '81); Falcon (also in rfb, last in Av #194, '80, next in MTU #114, '82)
SUPPORTING CAST: Josh Cooper (next in Cap #268, '82)
VILLAINS: Red Skull (as "Teacher," also in rfb & pfb, last in SVTU #17, '80, chr last in Cap #350/2, '89 fb),Ameridroid (also in rfb & pfb; last in Cap #221, '78), Nomad (Edward Ferbel, 1st, also on TV & in pfb), Will Brynner (TV reporter on Red Skull's payroll, also on TV, 1st), Nihilist Order agents (Operative M named), muggers (Vince named)
OTHER CHARACTERS: Redwing (last in Av #194, '80, next in MTU #114, '82), Lenny Spellman (Galactic Pictures producer, 1st but chr last in Cap #262, '81 fb), Wally Lombego (Lenny's production assistant, 1st), Jason Staid (actor, 1st), camera men (Morty named), American Airlines stewardess, Wally's chauffeur, police, reporters, bystanders, Suzanne Dimmbulb (actress, in pfb); Bucky, Captain America (Roscoe), Cobra, Eel, Hawkeye (as Golden Archer), Thor, Sharon Carter, Nazi soldier (prev 8 in rfb)
LOCATIONS/ITEMS: Brooklyn Heights inc bar & Steve's apartment, Brooklyn Bridge, Avengers Mansion (also in rfb) inc gym, LA International Airport, Democracy Pictures studio (also in rfb), Galactic Films studios, Beverly Hills inc Suzanne's Dimmbulb's home (destroyed in pfb); mugger's gun, Cap's motorcycle, Galactic Pictures telegram, Nihilist Order jeep, rifle & helicopter, Nomad's gun
FLASHBACKS: Cap quits (Cap #176, '74). Hawkeye convinces Cap to become a hero again (Cap #179, '74). Cap becomes Nomad (Cap #180, '74). Red Skull kills Roscoe (Cap #183, '75). Lyle Dekker fails to sabotage the Captain America movie serial (Cap #219, '78 fb) and is punished by Red Skull (Cap #220, '78 fb). Cap faces Dekker as the Ameridroid (Cap #221, '78). Teacher finds Dekker in Newfoundland. Later, Nomad saves actress Suzanne Dimmbulb from the Nihilist Order (p).
SYNOPSIS: Steve Rogers spends a night on the town with Sam Wilson and Josh Cooper. The trio happens across a mugging, so Josh gets the police. When Josh returns, Steve and Sam have already defeated the muggers, but the police warn them to let the authorities handle it next time. The next day, Captain America and Falcon report to Avengers Mansion. They learn that Galactic Films is filming a new Captain America movie and that a new Nomad is patrolling the streets of Los Angeles. Cap visits Galactic Films as an excuse to investigate Nomad, only to be confronted by the Nihilist Order. Nomad intervenes and upstages Cap. Elsewhere, the mysterious Teacher confers with Ameridroid and prepares for his battle with Cap. At a studio press conference, a reporter reveals herself as a Nihilist Order agent. Cap tries to stop her and her accomplices, but Nomad's upstaging gets in the way. Cap thanks Nomad anyway. Later, Nomad is punished by his secret mentor and employer Teacher for failing to discredit Captain America.
NOTE: Issue includes Hostess ad, Human Torch in "Hot-Tempered Triumph!"

CAPTAIN AMERICA #262 (October 1981)

"Death of a Legend?" (22 pages)

CREDITS: J.M. DeMatteis (writer), Michael Zeck (pencils), Quickdraw Studios (inks), Jim Novak, Rick Parker (letters), Bob Sharen (colors), Bob Budiansky (asst editor), Jim Salicrup (editor), John Beatty (c inks)
FEATURE CHARACTER: Captain America (also on t-shirts, as a blimp, in photos & as Nomad in rfb, also in fb1 between USA #9, '43 & FallSon:IM, '07 fb)
VILLAINS: Red Skull (also as Teacher, also in fb1 between CapBiB, '76 & FallSon:IM, '07 fb), Nomad (also on TV, also in rfb, also in fb2 during Cap #261, '81, dies), Nihilist Order (also in rfb), Will Brynner (also on TV), Ameridroid
OTHER CHARACTERS: Lenny Spellman (also in fb1 to 1st chr app before Cap #261, '81), Wally Lombego, Jason Staid, Mr. Hunkley (reporter), "8 Eyewitness News" stagehand, talk show host, musicians, celebrities (Benny Bernhart, a comedian, named), bystanders, Ted (news anchor, voice only); soldiers (Jeffy named, in fb1); Falcon (also in photo), Iron Man, Thor, Sharon Carter, Viper, police (prev 6 in rfb); Bucky, Human Torch, Sub-Mariner, Redwing, Whizzer, Franklin D. Roosevelt (prev 6 in photos)
LOCATIONS/ITEMS: Galactic Films studios (also in rfb) inc Lenny's office, Democracy Pictures studio inc gym, 8 Eyewitness News stage, Los Angeles International Airport, Avengers Mansion (both in rfb); Lenny's Cap scrapbook, Nihilist Order's guns, bomb, tripwire & hovercrafts, soldier's guns, Cap's WWII motorcycle, Red Skull's hovercraft & death ray (prev 4 in fb1), Nomad's magnet gun (in fb2)
FLASHBACKS: Captain America and Nomad fight the Nihilist Order at LAX, where Nomad crashes a jeep into the police. Cap attends a press conference. Nomad prevents Cap from stopping the Nihilist Order and Cap thanks Nomad for his help (Cap #261, '81). Cap quits (Cap #176, '74). Nomad fights Viper (Cap #182, '75). 1943: Lenny and his unit are trapped behind enemy lines. The Red Skull attacks, killing Lenny's friend with a death ray. Captain America arrives to battle the Skull (1). Nomad uses a magnet to maneuver Cap's shield (2).
SYNOPSIS: The media continues to hype Nomad at Captain America's expense. Lenny shows Cap his scrapbook, and explains that since Cap saved his life once, he wants to make the Cap movie as good as it can be. Meanwhile, Teacher chastises Nomad. Once Nomad leaves, Teacher and Ameridroid discuss Nomad's naiveté. Over the next few days, Cap makes various public appearances until the Nihilist Order strikes during a benefit. Once again Nomad upstages Cap, thanks to a Nihilist Order agent tripping Cap. Later, Nomad worries once the caper is over that he'll be reduced to a nothing again, but Ameridroid assures him otherwise. Later, the Nihilist Order attacks Galactic Films' Captain America Day parade.

Cap is surprised to see Ameridroid, who paralyzes Cap with gas and kills Nomad. When Cap awakens, he reminds Ameridroid that they're friends. Angry, Ameridroid turns on Teacher, only to be knocked out. With his plan near completion, Teacher reveals himself as the Red Skull!
NOTE: Issue includes Hostess ad "The Hulk vs. the Phoomie Goonies."

CAPTAIN AMERICA #263 (November 1981)

"The Last Movie!" (22 pages)

CREDITS: J.M. DeMatteis (writer), Mike Zeck (pencils), Quickdraw Studios (inks), Jim Novak (letters), Bob Sharen (colors), Bob Budiansky (asst editor), Jim Salicrup (editor), John Beatty (c inks)
FEATURE CHARACTER: Captain America (also on TV & in rfb)
VILLAINS: Red Skull (chr next in Cap&Crb #1, '11 fb, next in Cap #290, '84), Nihilist Order (also in rfb), Will Brynner (last app)
OTHER CHARACTERS: Ameridroid (also in rfb, dies), Nomad (corpse, also in rfb), Wally Lombego, Lenny Spellman, Jason Staid (all last app), Lt. Cal Lummbo (only app), reporters (Billie & Joe named), camera man, KMBC employee, paramedics, police, bystanders; brainwashing victims (in Red Skull's thoughts), Beast, Vision(both in rfb)
LOCATIONS/ITEMS: Democracy Pictures studio, Galactic Films studios (also in rfb) inc Lenny's office & president's office, KMBC Burbank studios, Avengers Mansion (in rfb), Los Angeles International Airport (also in rfb); Skull's remote, force field, Red Skull robots & flying video screen, Nihilist Order's clubs & bats, Cap documentary film reel, Cap's lighter, Lenny's car, airplane
FLASHBACKS: Captain America learns about Nomad. Cap and Nomad fight the Nihilist Order. Nomad upstages Cap (Cap #261, '81). Cap is captured and Nomad killed (Cap #262, '81). Cap and Dekker part ways on good terms (Cap #221, '78).
SYNOPSIS: Red Skull uses a remote control to have Ameridroid attack Captain America. During their battle, Cap is able to get through to Dekker's human side, helping him overcome the Skull's control. Dekker attacks Red Skull, but is overpowered by the Skull's force field. Cap follows up the attack, discovering Skull was a robot. Meanwhile, Nomad's body is taken by paramedics and Will Brynner is arrested. The police have proof he's been working with the Nihilist Order. Cap follows the Skull's lead to Democracy Pictures, and battles an army of Nihilist Order agents. Meanwhile, Lenny learns the Cap movie is cancelled, to be replaced with a documentary that will air tonight. Cap eventually finds himself in the Galactic Films' owner's office, where the Skull waits. Red Skull reveals that by discrediting Cap, then exposing his own anti-Cap scheme to the media, he was able to guarantee everyone in the country would watch his pre-made documentary laced with hypnotic suggestions that will induce a violent frenzy. Dekker bursts into the office and attacks the Skull, apparently destroying himself, Skull and Galactic Studios in the process. Cap seizes the documentary before it can air and burns it.
NOTE: Cal Lummbo's name is a parody of TV detective Columbo. Issue includes Hostess ad, Thing in "A Lesson to be Learned!"

CAPTAIN AMERICA #264 (December 1981)

"The American Dreamers!" (21 pages)

CREDITS: J. M. DeMatteis (writer), Mike Zeck (pencils), Quickdraw Studios (inks), Jim Novak (letters), Don Warfield (colors), Bob Budiansky (asst editor), Jim Salicrup (editor), John Beatty (c inks)
FEATURE CHARACTER: Captain America (also as an old man & child, next in Cap Ann #5, '81)
VILLAINS: Morgan MacNeil Hardy (also in rfb & pfb, last in SW #33, '80, dies, next in Av #218, '82 as child), Subject A (latent psychic & racist), Subject C (latent psychic & Nazi supporter) (both die, also in pfb, only app), Dr. August Masters (bts in pfb, funding Hardy's research, 1st chr app before Def #102, '81)
OTHER CHARACTERS: Avengers: Bucky, Giant-Man, Iron Man; X-Men: Angel, Beast, Cyclops, Iceman, Marvel Girl; Falcon, CBS reporters (Bill named), Captain America fans, child carnival patrons, Jewish, black & mutant captives, Ku Klux Klan members, Nazis, police, racist shoeshine patron, robbers, Secret Service agents (Tomlinson named), bystanders, cowboy (on TV), John F. Kennedy (US president, in photo), Ultron, Vision, Brain-Child, Grim Reaper (prev 4 statues) (all in altered reality only); Subject B (Phillip Le Guin, latent psychic child), Subject D (Ursula Richards, latent psychic woman) (both 1st, also in pfb, next in Cap #268, '82), Nomad, Spider-Woman, Turner D. Century, Wally Lombego, Lenny Spellman, Jason Staid, Nihilist Order agent, construction worker (prev 8 in rfb), Dean Martin, Jerry Lewis (both on poster)
LOCATIONS/ITEMS: Avengers Mansion, Wilson Headquarters, carnival (all in altered reality), Waldheim hotel (also in altered reality); American Airlines Flight 776, Nazi Mini-Jet (both in altered reality), Telepathy Augmenter inc Psyche-Graph
FLASHBACKS: As a child, Morgan MacNeil Hardy survives the 1906 San Francisco Fire. Later, Hardy builds his Marin County hills retreat (SW #33, '80 fb). Spider-Woman battles Turner D. Century, and later infiltrates Hardy's retreat (SW #33, '80). Captain America & Nomad battle the Nihilist Order (Cap #261, '81). Wally Lombego, Leonard Spellman and Jason Staid give Cap a ride to the airport (Cap#263, '81). Hardy escapes his retreat's destruction and eventually hires four people with latent psychic abilities (p).
SYNOPSIS: In a remote hotel, four people are hooked into strange machinery. Meanwhile, Captain America finds himself in various confusing scenarios, including working for President John F. Kennedy, Bucky leading the Avengers, Sam Wilson as a shoe-shiner, himself as a child at a carnival, and Nazis parading around captive Jews, blacks, and mutants. Cap attacks the Nazis and finds a message calling him to the Waldheim hotel. Meanwhile, Morgan MacNeil Hardy adjusts his machine, a Telepathy Augmenter, not understanding why the four people hooked into it keep changing reality from what he wants. Cap travels to the hotel, battling as a child through Klu Klux Klan members to find Hardy has hooked himself into the machine to stabilize reality. Cap challenges Hardy, asking whose morals are correct: the racist, the Nazi supporter, or the child who wants to play? In response, Hardy tries to erase Cap from reality. The machine overloads and kills Hardy along with two of the subjects hooked into it.
NOTE: Av #218, '82 reveals SHIELD agents buried Morgan after this issue, under orders from Captain America. Ursula Richards and Phillip Le Guin both named in Cap #268, '82. Masters revealed to be bts in Cap #268, '82. Issue includes Hostess ad "Spider-Man's Dream Girl!"

CAPTAIN AMERICA ANNUAL #5 (1981)

"Deathwatcher!" (38 pages)

CREDITS: David Michelinie (writer), Gene Colan (pencils), Dave Simons (inks), Joe Rosen (letters), Bob Sharen (colors), David Anthony Kraft (editor), Frank Miller (c art)

FEATURE CHARACTER: Captain America (next in Def #98, Av #210-211, Rom #23, all '81, SS #14, '88 fb, MGN #1, '82, SS Ann #6, '93 fb, Av #212-213, '81)

SUPPORTING CAST: Bernie Rosenthal (chr last in Cap #600/3, '09 fb) (last in Cap #258, '81, next in Cap #267, '82)

VILLAINS: Constrictor (last in Hulk #265, '81, next in PMIF #84, '82) & his henchmen (Curtis named, some die bts), Samson Scythe (wealthy recluse & snuff enthusiast, only app, dies, also in fb), Kenneth Hanson (butler & ex-soldier, only app to date, also in fb), Scythe & Hanson's henchmen (Mark, McKay, & Smitty named, one in fb), mugger (in fb, dies)

OTHER CHARACTERS: Carlo Ferrini (mob boss, dies) & his henchmen, Sean Gamble (mob boss) & his 2 bodyguards, Irene Clancy (Concept Inc.'s art director), Ms. Pemberton (Irene's secretary), Fur-Person (Scythe's cat) (all only app), police (Lt. Powell named) inc desk sergeant, U.S. Shore Patrol officers, Arkham Trust patrons & employees, Ferrini's birthday party attendees, Hearth Club waitress, Central Park visitors, 2 barred diners, firefighters, albino mouse (dies), U.S. Army soldiers (one dies), Scythe's nurse & previous butler, socialite, boat passengers (prev 5 in fb); Stillborn (band, mentioned on radio)

LOCATIONS/ITEMS: New York inc New York Bay, Governor's Island, the World Trade Center, Concept, Inc. offices, the Hearth Club, NYPD 11th Precinct w/Powell's office, Gamble's office building, Central Park (also in fb) w/bike trail & Arkham Trust's 79th Street branch, Steve's Brooklyn Heights apartment, Edgewood, N.Y. inc Scythe's estate (also in fb) w/Hanson's room, video surveillance room (also in fb), & sitting room (in fb only), U.S. Army camp, Southeast Asia (both in fb); Scythe's hidden cameras, monitors, wheelchair, intravenous nutritional solution, fake roast turkey booby-trap, elevator booby-trap, modified semi truck, fire extinguisher, security systems inc mechanical guard dogs, gold-dust booby-trap, & vibrational statue weapons, Steve's art supplies & portfolio, Steve & Bernie's bicycles, Hanson & his men's SCUBA gear, cameras, scrambled transceiver, limpet mine (mentioned), van, & guns, Hanson's motorcycle & flamethrower, Coast Guard cutter (#120), NYPD launch (#48557), Cap's soft magnets, Constrictor's men's guns, Shore Patrol's guns, Avengers Quinjet, FDNY fire trucks

FLASHBACK: Born into wealth and privilege, Scythe enters his teens bored with life, having seen and done much by that age. He enlists in the Army in order to alleviate his boredom. While serving in Southeast Asia he develops a fascination with witnessing death. After the war, Scythe becomes a wheelchair-bound recluse interested by virtually nothing. He hires fellow ex-soldier, Hanson, as his butler, and eventually agrees to Hanson's proposal to arrange the murders of criminals and film the killings for Scythe's amusement.

SYNOPSIS: Captain America's attempt to stop Constrictor and his men from attacking New York with a stolen Coast Guard ship is momentarily stymied by an onboard explosion. As Cap hands his adversaries over to Police Lt. Powell, a diver team led by Ken Hanson swims to shore, having caused the explosion and videotaped the resulting deaths for Hanson's employer, Samson Scythe. As Cap returns home, Hanson returns to Scythe's estate and reports on the status of their next "project." Steve Rogers inadvertently fails an ad agency interview by spurning the art director's romantic advances. Later, mob boss Carlo Ferrini is fatally electrocuted by a booby-trapped roast turkey at his birthday party. Cap arrives at the NYPD's 11th precinct at the invitation of Lt. Powell and meets Sean Gamble, Ferrini's chief rival. Fearing himself a potential target, Gamble agrees to let Cap shadow him. Cap later rescues Gamble from a rigged elevator. Watching from afar, Scythe orders Hanson to engineer a robbery at one of his banks. The next day, while cycling with Bernie, Steve overhears a news report on the robbery and ditches her to intervene. Cap defeats the robbers, but Hanson escapes and lures Cap into a forced meeting with Scythe. Coerced by Scythe to come alone to his estate that night, Cap fights his way through Scythe's extensive array of security systems before finally confronting Scythe and Hanson. Hanson's flamethrower accidentally explodes, setting the house ablaze. Scythe is engulfed in the flames and watches himself burn to death on his own monitors. Cap escapes the inferno with Hanson, just as Powell and responding firefighters arrive.

NOTE: The signage on Powell's office door says "Detective Powell," despite his rank as lieutenant. Stillborn was a fictitious band at the time of this issue's publication; a real-life Polish death metal band using that name formed in 1997. Issue includes Hostess ad "The Hulk vs. the Phoomie Goonies."

CAPTAIN AMERICA #265 (January 1982)

"Thunderhead!" (21 pages)

CREDITS: David Anthony Kraft (writer), Mike Zeck (pencils), John Beatty (inks), Jim Novak (letters), Bob Sharen (colors), Bob Budiansky (asst editor), Jim Salicrup (editor)

FEATURE CHARACTER: Captain America

GUEST STARS: Nick Fury (last in MTIO #77, '81, last bts in Av Ann #10, '81), Spider-Man (last in MGN #1, '82)

VILLAINS: SULTAN (Systematic Ultimate Lawless Takeover of All Nations, former SHIELD weapons designer turned cyborg, 1st) & his biotronic constructs (Biotron 3 named), Street Suckers (the "toughest street gang in Manhattan")

OTHER CHARACTERS: J. Jonah Jameson (bts, hosted party, last in DD #180, '82, next in FF #242, '82), SHIELD agents, Sydney E. Levine (mentioned, designed Fury's grappling cable)

LOCATIONS/ITEMS: New York inc SHIELD HQ, Thunderhead Island (SULTAN's floating HQ); Steve's art portfolio, Spider-Man's camera, film & spider-tracer, SHIELD hologram wall & pay phone, SULTAN's molecular transfer unit, biotronic constructs' blasters, Fury's Porsche, cocoon shirt & grappling cable w/force field, Sultan's rocket & steel wall street barricade

SYNOPSIS: As Steve Rogers leaves a party hosted by J. Jonah Jameson, the Street Suckers try to mug him. Leaving the same party, Peter Parker is surprised to see an ordinary citizen defeat the gang. Peter photographs the event, but Steve doesn't want his picture in the paper. His spider-sense tingling, Peter follows Steve as Spider-Man. Spider-Man is able to tag Steve with a spider-tracer when Steve suddenly teleports away while using a pay phone. Spider-Man is grabbed from behind, but his attackers vanish through a wall when he fights back. Elsewhere, robots attack Steve. He quickly changes into Captain America but, is overpowered. Meanwhile, Spider-Man's attackers pull him through the wall. He's greeted by Nick Fury, who enlists Spider-Man's help to track down Cap. SULTAN reveals himself to Cap, explaining that when he was fired from SHIELD he turned himself into a cyborg and began his quest for revenge against America, starting with Washington DC's destruction. Fury and Spider-Man are captured and brought to SULTAN, but launch a counter-offensive with Cap. SULTAN launches a nuclear rocket, so Fury grapples onto it. When Spider-Man and Cap follow they discover SULTAN's base is really a flying island and plummet to their doom.

NOTE: Letters page includes LOC from Rick Jones! Issue includes Hostess ad, Captain Marvel in "Flea Bargaining."

CAPTAIN AMERICA #266 (February 1982)

"Flight from Thunderhead!" (21 pages)

CREDITS: David Anthony Kraft (writer), Mike Zeck (pencils, c art), John Beatty (inks), Janice Chiang (letters), Bob Sharen (colors), Lance Tooks (asst editor), Jim Salicrup (editor)
FEATURE CHARACTER: Captain America (also in rfb)
GUEST STARS: Nick Fury (next in FF #240, '82), Spider-Man (next in FF #242, '82) (both also in rfb)
VILLAINS: SULTAN (dies) & his biotronic constructs (both also in rfb)
OTHER CHARACTERS: SHIELD interceptors (bts, destroying Thunderhead Island)
LOCATIONS/ITEMS: Thunderhead Island (also in rfb, destroyed), District of Columbia; Biotronic constructs' blasters & jetpacks, Fury's grappling cable w/ force field (also in rfb), electronic code-beam & gun, SULTAN's rocket, identity module & blaster

FLASHBACK: Cap is teleported to SULTAN's base, battles SULTAN's biotronic constructs and meets SULTAN. Fury and Spider-Man are captured. Fury latches onto SULTAN's rocket while Spider-Man and Cap plummet to their doom (Cap #265, '82).

SYNOPSIS: Spider-Man snags a web-line to SULTAN's floating island while Captain America wrests a jetpack from an attacking biotronic construct. Meanwhile, Fury works his way into the rocket and tries to disarm it, discovering it to be a decoy. The real bomb is Thunderhead Island. Cap retrieves Spider-Man and together they defeat SULTAN, seemingly killing him. Cap and Spidey escape the island only to learn SULTAN can transfer himself into different bodies. When Thunderhead Island explodes in the distance, Cap viciously defeats Sultan. When SULTAN's mobile identity module tries to escape, Fury shoots and destroys it before it can transfer to another body. Fury tells Cap that the earlier blast was SHIELD destroying Thunderhead Island, and that Washington DC is fine.

NOTE: Issue includes Hostess ad "Daredevil's Longest Fight!"

CAPTAIN AMERICA #267 (March 1982)

"The Man who Made a Difference!" (21 pages)

CREDITS: J.M. DeMatteis (writer), Mike Zeck (pencils, c art), John Beatty (inks), Jim Novak (letters), Bob Sharen (colors), Lance Tooks (asst editor), Jim Salicrup (editor)
FEATURE CHARACTER: Captain America (also on poster, next in Av #214-216, '81-82, IM #30, '00 fb, Av #217-218, '82, MTIO #82, '81, FF #243, '82, FF #244, '82 fb, Cap #600/3, '09 fb)
GUEST STARS: Iron Man, Tigra (both between Av #213-214, '81)
SUPPORTING CAST: Bernie Rosenthal (last in Cap Ann #5, '81, chr next in Cap #600/3, '09 fb)
VILLAINS: Everyman (Larry Ekler, self-styled defender of the common man, 1st, also in pfb & dfb, next in MTU #132, '83), Ira (Everyman follower, only app)
OTHER CHARACTERS: Edwin Jarvis (between Av #213-214, '81), Benjamin Q. Hillson (DeWitt Clinton high school principal), DeWitt Clinton high school students (Karen Berger & Neil Marks named), neighborhood kids (Gilbert, Mike & Pedro named), Maggie (Everyman follower & Ira's sister), other Everyman followers, Milton Josh Ekler (Everyman's father, only in pfb), police (some in dfb, 2 die), reporters, service crew, bystanders
LOCATIONS/ITEMS: DeWitt Clinton high school, Steve's Brooklyn Heights apartment, Hell's Kitchen inc tenements shelter, Avengers Mansion, Liberty Island w/Statue of Liberty; Ira's revolver, Everyman's blaster foil & shield, Cap's motorcycle, police barricades

FLASHBACKS: Everyman's father worked hard and believed in the American dream until he died. Unable to pay for a funeral, Larry created the Everyman identity to reveal the lies in the American dream (p). Everyman holds a press conference, challenging Captain America to a duel at the Statue of Liberty. When the police try to arrest him, Everyman murders them (d).

SYNOPSIS: When Captain America addresses a high school assembly, a student ridicules Cap's "false" American dream and tries to assassinate him. Cap quickly subdues the student, but even a date later with Bernie Rosenthal can't get the confrontation off his mind. In Hell's Kitchen, Everyman preaches to his followers and plots Cap's destruction. Later, while Cap befriends some neighborhood kids Everyman contacts the press. As Cap shows the kids around Avengers Mansion, he's appalled by a news report on Everyman. Meanwhile, Maggie, one of Everyman's followers, asks why violence is a necessary part of his movement. Instead of answering, Everyman talks about his father. That night on Liberty Island, Cap easily defeats Everyman. Everyman desperately takes Maggie hostage and declares he'll kill her, despite having gained the fame he craves by spitting on Cap in front of the press. Cap distracts Everyman, saves Maggie, and defeats Everyman again. Maggie tells Cap that Everyman's view represents despair, but Cap's view represents helping people out of despair. She decides she likes Cap's view better.

NOTE: Everyman's real name is revealed in MTU #132, '83. Everyman's father was named "Milton" in MTU #132, '83, and "Josh" in MTU #133, '83. Issue includes Hostess ad "Daredevil's Longest Fight!"

CAPTAIN AMERICA #268 (April 1982)

"Peace on Earth - - Good Will to Man" (22 pages)

CREDITS: J.M. DeMatteis (writer), Mike Zeck (pencils), John Beatty (inks), Jim Novak (letters), Bob Sharen (colors), Lance Tooks (asst editor), Jim Salicrup (editor)

FEATURE CHARACTER: Captain America (also in rfb, also as a scientist, next in Def #106-107, '82)

GUEST STARS: Defenders: Gargoyle (Isaac Christians), Hellcat (Patsy Walker), Kyle Richmond (also as Nighthawk in rfb), Valkyrie (Brunnhilde) (all last in Def #104, '82, also in dfb, next in Def #106, '82); Dum Dum Dugan (last in FF #241, '82, next in MTIO #89, '82)

SUPPORTING CAST: Arnold "Arnie" Roth (Steve's childhood friend, 1st but chr last in Cap #270, '82 fb, next in Cap #270, '82), Josh Cooper (last in Cap #261, '81), Bernie Rosenthal (chr last in Cap #600/3, '09 fb)

VILLAINS: Dr. August Masters (Secret Empire agent, last in Def #103, '82, also bts in pfb, also in dfb, next in Def #106, '82) & his private army (some in pfb, Ronaldson named), Professor Power (bts, funding August Masters, last bts in Def #102, '81, next in 1st actual app in MTU #117, '82)

OTHER CHARACTERS: Phillip le Guin, Ursula Richards (both last in Cap #264, '81, also in pfb, next in Def #106, '82), Mindy Williams (last in Def #102, '82, next in Def #106, '82), Al Gentle, Theodore Kroeber, Georgia Orr (prev 3 captured psychics, 1st, next in Def #106, '82), Gail Runciter (SHIELD agent, 1st but chr last in Q #1, '89 fb, next in Cap #275, '82), bartender, bystanders; Bucky, Falcon, Giant-Man, Iron Man, Morgan Hardy, CID Agents, Nazis (prev 7 in rfb); Doctor Strange (mentioned)

LOCATIONS/ITEMS: Colorado Rockies inc Mt. Charteris (also in dfb) & Bar & Grill, Steve's Brooklyn Heights apartment, Ursula Richards' apartment; Bernie's Volkswagen, Cap's motorcycle, SHIELD Helicarrier, psychic prober & jetcraft, Master's private army's blasters & psychic equipment, Valkyrie's sword

FLASHBACKS: Nighthawk visits Mindy in a sanitarium where she is placed in a secret telepathy experiment (Def #102, '82). Masters' fellow agents bomb Nighthawk's penthouse with gas (Def #104, '82). Morgan MacNeil Hardy attempts to restructure reality, but dies when the machine overloads (Cap #264, '81). Masters' agents abduct Phillip le Guin and Ursula Richards (p). Masters explains to Richmond that the fictitious group CID is staffed by former government agents, then reveals he also has Mindy Williams captive. Mindy is a powerful but unstable telepath and Masters needs Kyle to keep her calm. If Richmond doesn't cooperate, Masters will kill the other Defenders. When Kyle asks why, Masters responds that he's preparing for World War III (d).

SYNOPSIS: Kyle Richmond awakes to find the Defenders captured by August Masters. Masters warns Richmond not to try anything heroic, reminding him that he's paralyzed during daylight hours, and reveals the CID agency is only a front. Weeks later, Steve and Bernie go on a date where Bernie lets slip that she loves Steve. When Steve tries to change the subject, Bernie ends the date. From across the street, a man recognizes Steve. That night, Steve receives a mental call from Phillip and Ursula. Discovering they've been kidnapped, Captain America gains SHIELD's help to track them down to a small Colorado town. Cap infiltrates Mt. Charteris only to be captured. Sensing Cap's presence, Phillip and Ursula use their powers to revive the Defenders to help. Masters tells Cap his plan to attack the USSR with psychics as the Defenders escape. As Cap and the Defenders attack, Masters threatens to destroy the base, so Cap surrenders. As the heroes are incarcerated, Mindy hears Kyle's thoughts and sends out a telepathic call to Doctor Strange.

NOTE: Story continues in Def #106, '82. Arnie Roth named in Cap #270, '82. Gail Runciter's 1st named revealed in Cap #275, '82. CID called "CIB" in Def #102, '81. Steve & Bernie see the movie "Raiders of the Lost Ark." Issue includes Hostess ad "Daredevil's Longest Fight!"

CAPTAIN AMERICA #269 (May 1982)

"A Mind is a Terrible Thing to WASTE!" (23 pages)

CREDITS: J.M. DeMatteis (writer), Mike Zeck (pencils, co-inks), John Beatty (co-inks, c inks), Josef Rubinstein (co-inks), Jim Novak (letters), Bob Sharen (colors), Lance Tooks (asst editor), Jim Salicrup (editor)

FEATURE CHARACTER: Captain America (next in Av #219-220, '82)

GUEST STARS: Team America (motorcycle stunt team, 1st): Honcho (James McDonald), R. U. Reddy (Winthrop Roan, Jr.), Wolf, Marauder (all chr between TAm #2-3, '82); Nick Fury (last in FF #241, '82, last bts in Def #110, '82, next in MTIO #89, '82)

SUPPORTING CAST: Mike Farrel, Anna Kappelbaum (both last in Cap #258, '81, next in Cap #275, '82), Josh Cooper (next in Cap #275, '82), Bernie Rosenthal

VILLAINS: Mad Thinker (last in Rom #14, '81, chr last in Cap #311, '85 fb, next in MTIO #96, '83), his Intellectual Robots (androids resembling famous thinkers): Sam Clemens, Confucius, Fyodor Dostoyevsky (bts), Albert Einstein, Alfred Knopfler, Abraham Lincoln, Machiavelli, Friedrich Nietzsche, Plato, William Shakespeare, Socrates (all next in MTU #129, '83), Sigmund Freud, Leonardo da Vinci, Virginia Woolf (prev 3 bts, next bts in MTU #129, '83) & Captain America, one giant android

OTHER CHARACTERS: Madison Square Garden security (Security Chief Hinkler named), motorcycle exhibition attendees inc international dignitaries (Nobel Prize winner Alfred Knopfler named), other Nobel Prize winners (bts, captured by Mad Thinker), bystanders

LOCATIONS/ITEMS: Anna's Brooklyn Heights apartment, Madison Square Garden, Mad Thinker's New Hampshire town; Cap's motorcycle, Team America's motorcycles, Mad Thinker's equipment

SYNOPSIS: Steve Rogers eats brunch with his neighbors and talks with Bernie about their relationship. As Captain America, he travels to Madison Square Garden to participate in a motorcycle exhibition and is informed the arena has heightened security for this show. There are Nobel Prize winners in the audience, and other Nobel Prize winners have been kidnapped lately. New motorcycle stunt performers Team America start the show and Cap joins in, but a giant appears from a portal and kidnaps Nobel Prize recipient Alfred Knopfler. Cap and Team America follow, finding themselves in a rural town run by the Mad Thinker, populated by android duplicates of great thinkers throughout history. Mad Thinker reveals he kidnapped the Nobel Prize winners so their duplicates can replace the historic figures, who have no new knowledge to offer. Capturing Team America, Thinker sets his sights on Cap's mind until a black-clad biker crashes in and frees Cap and Team America. Together, they destroy Thinker's androids and call SHIELD for clean up, but there's no trace of the mysterious other biker. NOTE: Nietzsche is spelled without the "s" here. Team America started as an Evel Knievel line of toys from Ideal Toys. The concept was later retooled into Team America and licensed by Marvel who developed the characters.

CAPTAIN AMERICA #270 (June 1982)

"Someone Who Cares" (22 pages)

CREDITS: J.M. DeMatteis (writer), Mike Zeck (pencils), John Beatty (co-inks, c inks), Many Hands (co-inks), Jim Novak (letters), Bob Sharen (colors), Jim Salicrup (editor)
FEATURE CHARACTER: Captain America (also in fb1 between SR:SSoI #3, '11 fb & ASM #537, '07 fb, fb2 between Cap #255, '81 fb & Cap:SoL #7/2, '99 fb, fb3 between Next #9, '06 fb & Cap #255, '81 fb; next in Av Ann #11)
SUPPORTING CAST: Arnie Roth (also in fbs1-3 to 1st chr app before Cap #268, '82, last in Cap #268, '82, next in Cap #275, '82), Bernie Rosenthal
VILLAINS: Baron Zemo (Helmut Zemo, bts, commanding his men & giant mutate, last in Cap #168, '73 as Phoenix, chr last in Tb #54, '01 fb, next bts in Cap #272, '82, next in Cap #275, '82), his giant mutate (1st, next in Cap #275, '82) & his men, Raymond "Little Angel" Curtis (gang member, in shadows, 1st but chr last in Cap #272, '82 fb, next in Cap #272, '82), childhood bullies (in fb1), young hooligans
OTHER CHARACTERS: Jim Wilson (last in MTU #114, '82, next in Cap #272, '82), Michael Bech (Arnie's partner, 1st, next in Cap #275, '82, see NOTE),Olympia (crazy bag lady); Arnie's parents (in fb1), Arnie & Steve's dates (in fb2), Navy officers (in fb3); Merv Griffin (mentioned, Olympia's reason for what's wrong with the world)
LOCATIONS/ITEMS: Brooklyn Heights inc Anna's apartment building w/Steve's & Bernie's apartments, Olympia's tenement, New York's Lower East Side inc Arnie's childhood home (in fb1); Cap's motorcycle, Olympia's knife, childhood bully's clubs & chain (in fb1)
FLASHBACKS: Arnie protects Steve from bullies and Arnie's family becomes Steve's surrogate family (1). Arnie and Steve go on a double date, despite them beginning to grow apart as they get older (2). Arnie meets Steve again after Arnie joined the Navy and Steve went through Operation: Rebirth (3).
SYNOPSIS: As Steve Rogers and Bernie attempt to reconcile their feelings, they're interrupted by Arnie Roth, Steve's childhood friend. Bernie leaves so Steve can catch up with Arnie, who reveals he knows that Steve is Captain America. Meanwhile, Jim Wilson is shot. Arnie asks for Cap's help, because his "roommate" Michael has been kidnapped. Meanwhile, Bernie saves Olympia, a bag lady, from some neighborhood punks and escorts her home. Elsewhere, Arnie reveals he's leading Cap into a trap. When Arnie drunkenly boasted that he's Cap's friend, someone offered to pay Arnie's debts if he delivered Cap. Michael is the collateral. Cap defeats the kidnappers, but has to save Arnie from a giant mutated android. Meanwhile, Olympia threatens to kill Bernie, but Bernie is able to talk Olympia out of it. As Cap battles the grotesque android, Arnie finds Michael's body. When the android sees Arnie, it calls out his name and disintegrates. Michael revives, saying his mind was taken and placed somewhere else. Later, Steve reunites with Bernie.
NOTE: Baron Zemo is revealed to be behind the attack on Cap in Cap #275, '82. Raymond Curtis is named in Cap #272, '82. Strongly hinted at here, Arnie and Michael are confirmed as being lovers in Cap #296, '84 when Cap equates Arnie's love for Michael to his own love for Bernie. Michael's last name revealed in OHMU #2, '07. Letters page contains LOC from Rick Jones!

CAPTAIN AMERICA #271 (July 1982)

"The Mystery of Mr. X" (22 pages)

CREDITS: David Anthony Kraft (writer), Alan Kupperberg (pencils), John Beatty & Co. (inks), Rick Parker (letters), Christie Scheele (colors), Lance Tooks (asst editor), Jim Salicrup (editor)
FEATURE CHARACTER: Captain America (also in recording & rfb, next in Micro #43, '82, Av #221, '82)
SUPPORTING CAST: Bernie Rosenthal (next in Cap #275, '82)
VILLAINS: King Arthur (wrestler & trainer, also on poster, also as Mr. X, only app), steroid dealers
OTHER CHARACTERS: Mr. X (Ray Deacon, wrestler, also in recording & pfb, only app), Jumpin' Jack Flash (wrestler, dies), Marty (wrestling announcer), "Lucky Florist" florist & deliveryman, police (inc a Lieutenant), prostitutes, cameraman, wrestling fans, reckless driver, bystanders; Nazis (in rfb); judge, prosecutor, stenographer (prev 3 in pfb); Midnight Slasher (mentioned, serial killer), Ronald Reagan (US President, on TV Guide), Kid Kong (wrestler, on poster)
LOCATIONS/ITEMS: Brooklyn Heights inc Bernie's apartment, New York inc All-Star Wrestling arena w/King Arthur's office & tape library, police precinct, "Lucky Florist" flower shop & Madison Square Garden; King Arthur's cane & anabolic steroids, Cap's Avengers ID, steroid dealer's gun
FLASHBACKS: Captain America battles Nazis during WWII (ToS #68/2, '65). Years ago, Ray Deacon is sentenced to prison for the Midnight Slasher killings. Five years later, Ray is released from prison when the real Midnight Slasher is caught. Ray drops out of sight soon after (p).
SYNOPSIS: Steve Rogers joins Bernie to watch the newest "All-Star Wrestling" on TV. During the match, Mr. X kills Jumpin' Jack Flash, then escapes. Captain America investigates, only to find the police have no idea where Mr. X is. King Arthur, already at the police precinct, announces that Mr. X contacted him and is willing to wrestle to clear his name. Cap convinces King Arthur to let him be the opponent. That afternoon, Steve saves Bernie from a speeding car. She admits to being depressed over Jumpin' Jack Flash's death. A week later at Madison Square Garden,

Cap defeats and unmasks Mr. X in the ring, revealing him to be Ray Deacon. Still bothered days later by the difference in fighting styles between the Mr. X he fought and the one he saw on TV, Steve investigates the tape library at All-Star Wrestling. Confirming his suspicions, Steve stumbles across King Arthur buying a shipment of steroids. King Arthur reveals that Jumpin' Jack Flash was going to report King Arthur to the police for giving his trainees steroids, so he posed as Mr. X and killed him. Cap defeats Arthur and his associates and sees Mr. X released from jail.

CAPTAIN AMERICA #272 (August 1982)

"Mean Streets" (22 pages)

CREDITS: J.M. DeMatteis (writer), Mike Zeck (pencils), John Beatty (inks), Rick Parker (letters), Bob Sharen (colors), Mike Carlin (asst editor), Mark Gruenwald (editor)
FEATURE CHARACTER: Captain America (next in Av #222-224, '82)
GUEST STARS: Falcon (last in MTU #114, '82, next in Cap #275, '82), Redwing (last in MTU #114, '82, next in Cap #277/2, '82)
VILLAINS: Baron Zemo (bts, instructed Vermin, last bts in Cap #270, '82, next in Cap #275, '82), Vermin (Edward Whelan, mutated into humanoid rodent by Baron Zemo, 1st but chr last in PPSSM #183, '91 fb, next in Cap #275, '82) & his rats, Raymond "Little Angel" Curtis (also in fb to 1st chr app before Cap #270, '82, last in Cap #270, '82, last app) & his fellow gang members (others also in fb)
OTHER CHARACTERS: Jody Casper (last in Cap #154, '72, last app), Sarah Wilson Casper (last in Cap #134, '71, next in Cap #275, '82), Leila Taylor (last in MPr #49, '79, next in Cap #276/2, '82), Jim Wilson (last in Cap #270, '82, next in Hulk #279, '83), Diane Curtis (Raymond's mother, also in fb), Raymond's infant sibling (both only app), Raymond's theft victim (in fb), doctor, terrified woman, taxi drivers (1 as corpse), newstand man, bystanders
LOCATIONS/ITEMS: Roosevelt Hospital (mentioned, where Cap takes injured cabbie), Harlem inc Community Hospital & Curtis apartment, church (in fb); Cap's motorcycle, gang members' handguns, stolen necklace (in fb)
FLASHBACKS: Despite his mother's intentions, actions and prayers, Raymond Curtis falls into a life of crime at a young age.
SYNOPSIS: As Captain America drives through Manhattan late at night in answer to a call from Falcon, a bystander alerts the hero to a taxi driver with a slashed throat. After getting the injured man medical attention, Cap goes to Harlem Community Hospital where Sam and his family are waiting for word on Sam's nephew Jim Wilson, shot while trying to prevent a liquor store robbery. A frustrated Sam storms off angrily, and later, patrolling as the Falcon, rescues a stoned gang member, Raymond Curtis, from some homicidal pursuers. Meanwhile, a robed man attacks Cap, clawing him and sending an army of rats after him. Disrobing to reveal a rat-like visage, the attacker identifies himself as Vermin, and announces his master wants Captain America dead. Following Raymond home, Falcon discovers the boy was Jim's shooter, while Cap beats Vermin unconscious following a particularly savage battle; rage almost drives both heroes over the edge, but they come to their senses in time. The next day, after hearing that Jim will recover, Sam announces that he will take the school board up on their offer to run for congress.

CAPTAIN AMERICA #273 (September 1982)

"Cap and the Howlers…Together Again!" (22 pages)

CREDITS: David Anthony Kraft (writer), Mike Zeck (pencils, c art), John Beatty (inks), Jim Novak (letters), Bob Sharen (colors), Mike Carlin (asst editor), Mark Gruenwald (editor)
FEATURE CHARACTER: Captain America
GUEST STARS: Howling Commandos: Nick Fury, Dum Dum Dugan (both last in MTIO #89, '82), Isadore "Izzy" Cohen, Dino Manelli, Percival "Pinky" Pinkerton, Robert "Reb" Ralston (prev 4 last in SgtF #100, '72), Gabe Jones (last in Micro #29, '81), Eric Koenig (last in RH #4/2, '77)
SUPPORTING CAST: Mike Farrel, Anna Kappelbaum (both last in Cap #258, '81, next in Cap #275, '82), Josh Cooper (next in Cap #275, '82), Bernie Rosenthal
VILLAINS: Baron Strucker LMD (as Supreme Hydra), Hydra agents LMDs, Sam Sawyer LMD (all 1st)
OTHER CHARACTERS: General Samuel "Happy Sam" Sawyer (Howling Commandos' wartime Commanding Officer, last in Thor #234, '75, chr last in MFan #10, '83), Phil Leonard (Gabe's nephew), Phil's mother (both only app), Mrs. Cohen (Izzy's wife, last in SgtF Ann #4, '68, last app), Izzy's son (bts, supplied jeeps only app), Libby (Reb's date), other Howlers' Reunion party attendees, Sawyer's driver, Grand Forks base commander, personnel & military police
LOCATIONS/ITEMS: New York City ballroom, Grand Forks air force base; Hydra helicopter, Sawyer's microfilm, Fury's microfilm scanner & blaster, Sawyer LMD's gun, army jeeps, B-52s & SAC ariel command center, Hydra machine guns, Howlers' guns, Reb's private jet
SYNOPSIS: Captain America attends a Howling Commandos reunion, but spots Hydra kidnapping the arriving General Sawyer. Cap fails to stop the abduction, but retrieves microfilm Sawyer was carrying, which points them to North Dakota's Grand Forks air force base. Though all the Howlers want to take part in rescuing Sawyer, Fury insists that only active SHIELD agents Gabe and Dum Dum can accompany Cap and him. A few hours later, Cap assists Hydra in seizing control of Grand Forks. Cap and the SHIELD agents try to sneak into the base but they're quickly captured. The remaining Howling Commandos suddenly burst in with guns blazing. During the melee Fury discovers Sawyer is an LMD while Cap unmasks the Supreme Hydra, revealing him to be Baron Strucker. Despite Cap's and the Howlers' efforts, Hydra escape with a stolen SAC aerial command center that gives them control over hundreds of nuclear missiles.
NOTE: Cap #274, '82 reveals that the Baron Strucker LMD is a failsafe in case the real Baron Strucker died. It is programmed to believe itself to be the real Strucker, and all of its Hydra agents are LMDs as well. Gen. Sawyer's serial number is 05-292-810.

CAPTAIN AMERICA #274 (October 1982)

"Death of a Hero!" (22 pages)

CREDITS: David Anthony Kraft (writer), Mike Zeck (pencils, c art), John Beatty (inks), Janice Chiang (letters), Bob Sharen (colors), Mike Carlin (asst editor), Mark Gruenwald (editor)
FEATURE CHARACTER: Captain America (also in rfb, next in MFan #5/2, '82, Cap Ann #6, '82)
GUEST STARS: Howling Commandos: Nick Fury (also in rfb), Dum Dum Dugan (both next in Cap #276, '82), Izzy Cohen, Pinky Pinkerton (both next in NF:AoS #44, '93), Gabe Jones (next in Hulk #297, '84), Eric Koenig (next in NFVS #2, '88), Dino Manelli (next in MTU #139, '84), Reb Ralston (next in Cap Ann #9/2, '90) (all also in rfb)
VILLAINS: Baron Strucker LMD (as Supreme Hydra), Hydra agents LMDs (all also in rfb), 2 Sam Sawyer LMDs (all destroyed, last app)
OTHER CHARACTERS: General Sam Sawyer (also in rfb, dies, last app), Grand Forks base officer; Baron Strucker robot (in rfb)
LOCATIONS/ITEMS: Grand Forks air force base, Hydra Island (both also in rfb), cemetery near Arlington, Virginia w/Sawyer's grave; stolen SAC ariel command center (also in rfb), SHIELD jetpack & submarine, Strucker LMD's mind-sap serum, Fury's blaster, Hydra machine guns, Howlers' guns, Sawyer LMD's internal bomb
FLASHBACKS: Hydra abducts Sam Sawyer. Cap and the Howling Commandos raid Grand Forks but are captured by a Sam Sawyer LMD. Cap defeats Strucker's personal guard but is electrocuted by Strucker and Hydra agents escape (Cap #274, '82). Fury is caught in an Alpha-particle Reactor Cube (ST #158, '67). Cap learns the Baron Strucker attacking him was a robot (Cap #247, '80). Hydra Island is destroyed (ST #158, '67).
SYNOPSIS: Captain America and the Howling Commandos try to locate the stolen SAC aerial command center, but Fury finds it hard to believe that Baron Strucker is alive. Meanwhile, Gen. Sawyer suffers a heart attack but disables the SAC's anti-detection device despite it. When the SAC is located, Fury is surprised to see it landing on the previously destroyed and rising Hydra Island. Cap uses a jetpack to infiltrate the island undetected and interrupts Baron Strucker's interrogation of Sawyer. Meanwhile, Col. Fury and his Howling Commandos sneak into the island in a submarine, but they're quickly discovered by Hydra. Sawyer orders Cap to help Fury, which provides the element needed to turn the tide. Sawyer steals a Hydra uniform and slips away. The Howlers are fooled twice by Sawyer LMDs, but the real Sawyer defeats Strucker, revealing him to be an LMD. Sawyer uses his own body to shield the others when the LMD self destructs. Cap and the Howlers escape when Hydra Island sinks back into the ocean. Two days later, Sawyer is buried a hero.
NOTE: Gen. Sawyer's tombstone reveals him to be a four star General and reads March 21, 1910 – June 30, 1982. A footnote erroneously credits Cap #237, '79 instead of Cap #247, '80 here.

CAPTAIN AMERICA ANNUAL #6 (1982)

"The Shadows of the Past!" (39 pages)

CREDITS: J.M. DeMatteis (writer), Ron Wilson (pencils), Vince Colletta (inks), Diana Albers (letters), Don Warfield (colors), Mark Gruenwald (editor), John Beatty (c inks)
FEATURE CHARACTERS: Captain America (Steve Rogers, next in Daz #1, Av #225-226, Cap #275, all '82), Captain America (William Naslund, also as Spirit of '76 in his thoughts, also in rfb, last in WI #4, '77, next in CapC #49, '45), Captain America (Jeff Mace, also as Patriot in his thoughts, also in rfb, last in CapC #74, '49, chr last in Cap:P #4, '11, next in Cap #284, '83), Captain America (William Burnside, last in Cap Ann #13, '94 fb, next in CapTW:AF, '09)
GUEST STARS: Invaders: Miss America, Whizzer (both also in rfb), Human Torch, Toro (all during WI #4, '77), Sub-Mariner (also in rfb, last in WI #4, '77, next in SagaSM #5 '89 fb); Contemplator (last in Cap:BiB, '76, next in #37, '92)
SUPPORTING CAST: Bucky (Fred Davis, last in WI #4, '77, next in CapC #49, '45), Bucky (Jack Monroe, last in Cap Ann #13, '94 fb, next in Cap #155, '72 fb)
VILLAINS: Adam-II & his androids (Special agent Smith named), Bucky (Fred Davis), Human Torch, Miss America, Sub-Mariner, Toro, Whizzer (all of Earth-8206, only app), Scarecrow (last in Cap #159, '73, next in Cap #279, '83) & his crows, Japanese soldiers (1945 era)
OTHER CHARACTERS: Ralph Laughton (Scarecrow's brother, posing as his chauffer "Anthony," 1st, next in Cap #280, '83), Card players (1954 era), bank guards, Earth-8206 citizens, Adam-II, criminals (both in rfb); Elders of the Universe: Champion, Collector, Gardener, Grandmaster, Possessor (prev 5 in Contemplator's thoughts); Golden Girl (mentioned, replaced Bucky as Cap's partner)
LOCATIONS/ITEMS: Pacific Theater of Operations (1945 era), Watts (1954 era) inc warehouse, New York inc First City Bank, Contemplator's chamber, Earth-8206 inc underground bunker & Castle Computronex; Japanese soldier's guns & solar-powered tank prototype (1945 era), Scarecrow's stolen money & car, bank guards' guns, Cap's motorcycle, Contemplator's meditation chair
FLASHBACKS: William Naslund is killed so Jeff Mace takes his place as Captain America to defeat Adam-II (WI #4, '77). As Captain America and Bucky, Jeff Mace and Fred Davis fight crime (CapC #59, '46).
SYNOPSIS: June, 1945: The Invaders battle Japanese soldiers in the Pacific Theater of Operations. Still relatively inexperienced as Captain America, William Naslund is taken off-guard when the Japanese soldiers fire their solar-powered tank prototype at him. As he falls unconscious, Naslund vanishes from the battlefield. July, 1954: Convinced some people playing cards are Communists, William Burnside and Jack Monroe as Captain America and Bucky attack. They quickly overpower the unsuspecting group, but one is able to escape. As Burnside retrieves his errant shield, he vanishes. August, Now: Steve Rogers as Captain America happens upon the bank robbing Scarecrow and attacks. Cap quickly overpowers Scarecrow until he's distracted by Scarecrow's crows. Scarecrow escapes to his waiting car. Cap frees himself and leaps at the vehicle, but vanishes in mid-air. Cap appears in front of Mr. Buda, who reveals himself to be an Elder of the Universe, and that his true

name in the Contemplator. An aged Jeff Mace appears in his Captain America uniform, and tells Rogers he regrets that his career ended in retirement, and that he is now dying of cancer. Mace reveals that by pulling Naslund from the past, an alternate world was created where Adam-II conquered the world. Contemplator says the four Captains can overthrow Adam-II and grant Mace his wish of glory. Rogers is upset at Mace's selfishness and Contemplator's actions, but agrees to help. Arriving on the alternate Earth, Adam-II's androids quickly defeat Naslund through his naiveté. Naslund finds a bunker, but is fooled by a cyborg that manipulates his prejudices. Rogers and Mace are confronted and defeated by their old teammates turned cyborgs. Awaking in Adam-II's Castle Computronex, Rogers and Mace find Naslund and Burnside enslaved by Adam-II. Mace attacks Adam-II, but realizes that his strength is being taken from Rogers, and he must choose between glory and sacrifice. Choosing sacrifice Mace is defeated, but Rogers is able to distract Adam-II long enough for Naslund and Burnside to overcome their enslavement and for Mace to recover. Together, the four Captains defeat Adam-II and are returned to their own times. Back home, Mace tells Rogers he no longer regrets his choices.
NOTE: "Anthony's" real name and relationship to Scarecrow revealed in Cap #280, '83.

CAPTAIN AMERICA #275 (November 1982)

"Yesterday's Shadows!" (22 pages)

CREDITS: J.M. DeMatteis (writer), Mike Zeck (pencils), John Beatty (inks), John Morelli (letters), Don Warfield (colors), Mike Carlin (asst editor), Mark Gruenwald (editor)
FEATURE CHARACTER: Captain America
GUEST STARS: Peter Parker (last in ASM #236, '83, next in MTU #121, '82), Sam Wilson (last in Cap #272, '82, next in Cap #276/2, '82)
SUPPORTING CAST: Josh Cooper, Mike Farrel, Anna Kappelbaum (all last in Cap #269, '82, next in Cap #284, '83), Arnie Roth (last in Cap #270, '82), Bernie Rosenthal
VILLAINS: Baron Zemo (1st full app as Baron Zemo, also in photo as boy) & his giant mutate (also in Michael' thoughts, last in Cap #270, '82), Primus (merged with Doughboy, posing as Arnim Zola, last in Cap #210, '77, last bts in Cap #212, '77),Vermin (last in Cap #272, '82), Neo-Nazis (inc leader Harry Todd)
OTHER CHARACTERS: Sarah Wilson Casper (last in Cap #272, '82), Carol Davis (Sam's campaign manager, 1st) (both next in Cap #276/2, '82), Gail Runciter (last in Cap #268, '82), Michael Bech (last in Cap #270, '82), Arthur Bennett (advertising executive, 1st, next in Cap #277, '83), Sheila Donohue (Bennett's secretary, 1st, next bts in Cap #277, '83), Sammy Bernstein (Jewish Protection Organization leader & Bernie's ex-husband, 1st), other JPO members, Rabbi Kessler (Anna's rabbi), Arthur Grossman (businessman, bts, on his way to Bennett's agency) reporters (inc Channels 2 & 7 news, Williams named), SHIELD agents (Sanderson named) inc psychiatrist, police, Neo-Nazi protestors bystanders; Adolf Hitler, Heinrich Zemo, Hilda Zemo (prev 3 in photo)
LOCATIONS/ITEMS: New York inc SHIELD HQ w/infirmary & Vermin's cell, Beth-Ohr (synagogue) & Bennett Advertising office, Baron Zemo's castle, Harlem Baptist church, Robert Moses State Park; SHIELD containment pod & medical equipment, protestor's garbage inc bottle, protestor nightsticks
SYNOPSIS: Captain America checks in on Arnie and Michael in the SHIELD infirmary while their experts analyze Vermin. Later, Steve, Bernie and Anna discover that Neo-Nazis have painted a swastika on the synagogue Anna attends. Elsewhere, Zemo plots his revenge on Cap while the Neo-Nazis prepare to expand their message. Sam Wilson holds a press conference to announce his candidacy for Congress when a reporter rattles him with questions about his past as "Snap" Wilson. Later, after snubbing his anti-Semitic boss, Steve attends a peaceful protest organized by Bernie's ex-husband Sammy. The event turns violent as the two leaders attack each other. Meanwhile, Zemo remotely reconstitutes his giant mutate and it rampages through SHIELD, freeing Vermin and attacking Arnie and Michael. At the rally Cap breaks up the fight and delivers a calming speech, but Bernie recognizes his manner and speech and realizes that Steve Rogers is Captain America.
NOTE: Harry Todd named in Cap #276, '82. Sheila's surname revealed in Cap #309, '85.

CAPTAIN AMERICA #276 (December 1982)

"Turning Point!" (16 pages)

CREDITS: J.M. DeMatteis (writer), Mike Zeck (pencils), John Beatty (inks), John Morelli (letters), Bob Sharen (colors), Mike Carlin (asst editor), Mark Gruenwald (editor)
FEATURE CHARACTER: Captain America
GUEST STARS: Dum Dum Dugan (last in Cap #274, '82, next in Hulk #279, '83), Nick Fury (last in Cap #274, '82, next in Cap #279, '83)
SUPPORTING CAST: Arnie Roth (also in pfb), Bernie Rosenthal
VILLAINS: Baron Zemo, Primus (merged w/Doughboy, also posing as Arnim Zola, also in pfb), giant mutate (also in pfb), Vermin, Harry Todd (last app)
OTHER CHARACTERS: Sammy Bernstein (next in Cap #284, '83), Gail Runciter (next in Cap #278, '83), Coalition for an Upstanding America (inc Mr. Burns (next in Cap #279, '83), James Wilson MacArthur Sr. (next in Cap #280, '83) & Jimmy McArthur Jr., all 1st), Corrigan (SHIELD agent), Baron Zemo's mutates (1st), police; Michael Bech (bts, present in Zemo's castle, also in pfb)
LOCATIONS/ITEMS: Robert Moses State Park, CUA offices, Anna's Brooklyn Heights apartment building, SHIELD HQ (also in pfb), South Bronx, Mexico inc Castle Zemo; Harry's handgun, SHIELD car & tracer, Zemo's ransom note, ship & stasis tanks
FLASHBACK: Zemo's giant mutate abducts Arnie and Michael (p).

SYNOPSIS: After Harry Todd tries unsuccessfully to shoot Captain America, the police arrest both him and Sammy. Cap meanwhile realizes Bernie has seen through his secret identity. Elsewhere, the Coalition for an Upstanding America decides to use Cap's image in their ad campaign. Later, Steve and Bernie discuss the latest revelation in their relationship until SHIELD agent Runciter arrives. At SHIELD HQ, Cap learns that Arnie and Michael have been kidnapped. Reading the ransom note Cap angrily storms off, unaware he's being followed by SHIELD. Cap meets Primus, who takes Cap to Castle Zemo in Mexico. Inside, Cap fights through dozens of mutates before finding Arnie in a stasis tube. Cap turns around to confront the kidnapper and mastermind, Baron Zemo.

NOTE: Mr. Burns named in Cap #279, '83, James & Jimmy's full names revealed in Cap #280, '83.

2ND STORY: "Snapping! Part 1" (6 pages)

CREDITS: J.M. DeMatteis (writer), Mike Zeck (pencils), John Beatty (inks), Mike Higgins (letters), Bob Sharen (colors)

FEATURE CHARACTER: Sam Wilson (also in rfb as Falcon & "Snap" Wilson, also on campaign posters & in newspaper)

SUPPORTING CAST: Leila Taylor (last in Cap #272, '82), Carol Davis, Sarah Wilson Casper

OTHER CHARACTERS: Bystanders (others in rfb); Captain America, Redwing, Red Skull, judge (prev 4 in rfb)

LOCATIONS/ITEMS: Harlem inc Sam's campaign office, Los Angeles (in rfb); copy of Daily Bugle, garbage can lid, cosmic cube (in rfb)

FLASHBACKS: Red Skull uses Falcon against Cap (Cap #185, '75). "Snap" Wilson walks the streets of Los Angeles (Cap #186, '75 fb). Posing as Cap, the Skull uses the cosmic cube to revert "Snap" Wilson to his original Sam Wilson personality (Cap #186, '75 fb). Falcon and Cap become friends and partners (Cap #117-119, '69). Falcon stands trial for his crimes as "Snap" Wilson (Cap #191, '75).

SYNOPSIS: Sam Wilson is upset by the Daily Bugle's reporting of his criminal past and storms off. Sam's sister Sarah explains to Leila and Carol that Sam has multiple personality disorder. Sam wanders the streets to clear his head and angrily throws a garbage can lid. When he sees it flying towards a woman and her child he stops it, but a man chastises Sam for throwing it in the first place. Sam angrily accosts the commenter and catches himself as he refers to himself as "Snap." Sam runs off, wondering if he's losing his mind.

CAPTAIN AMERICA #277 (January 1983)

"In Thy Image" (16 pages)

CREDITS: J.M. DeMatteis (writer), Mike Zeck (pencils), John M (inks), John Morelli (letters), Bob Sharen (colors), Mike Carlin (asst editor), Mark Gruenwald (editor)

FEATURE CHARACTER: Captain America (also in rfb)

SUPPORTING CAST: Bernie Rosenthal (next in Av #233, '83), Arnie Roth (both also in photo)

VILLAINS: Baron Zemo (also in paintings as boy & in rfb as Phoenix), Primus (merged w/Doughboy, also posing as Arnim Zola & Steve Rogers), Vermin, giant mutates

OTHER CHARACTERS: Arthur Bennett (last in Cap #275, '82), Jimmy McArthur Jr. (both next in Cap #280, '83), Sheila Donohue (bts, in another room, last in Cap #275, '82, next in Cap #309, '85), Michael Bech, Baron Zemo's mutates; Falcon (in rfb & photo); Heinrich Zemo, Hilda Zemo (both in paintings); Josh Cooper, Mike Farrel, Anna Kappelbaum (prev 3 in photo)

LOCATIONS/ITEMS: Mexico inc Castle Zemo, Bennett Advertising offices, Anna's Brooklyn Heights apartment building; Zemo's stasis tanks & rusty chains, Primus' drug, Adhesive-X (in rfb)

FLASHBACK: Cap and Falcon battle Phoenix. Cap's shield knocks Phoenix into a vat of Adhesive-X (Cap #168, '73).

SYNOPSIS: Baron Zemo reveals he is Helmut Zemo, formerly the Phoenix and Heinrich Zemo's son. He desires revenge against Captain America, who he blames for Heinrich's death and for his permanent disfigurement when Cap knocked him into a vat of Adhesive-X. Zemo explains he's been spying on both Captain America and Steve Rogers, and plans to destroy them both. Arnim Zola reveals himself to actually be Primus in disguise using Doughboy's power, and changes his form into Steve. Cap attacks Primus but is quickly overpowered. Meanwhile, Jimmy McArthur of the CUA hires Bennett Advertising for their ad campaign. Cap awakens chained next to Vermin. Zemo sets two giant mutates, powered by Arnie and Michael's minds, against them. Cap frees himself and Vermin, but while battling the giants Vermin kills one. The shock wakes Arnie, but Michael seems to have died. Meanwhile, Primus posing as Steve returns home and meets with Bernie.

2ND STORY: "Snapping - - Part II" (6 pages)

CREDITS: J.M. DeMatteis (writer), Mike Zeck (pencils), Joe Rubinstein (inks), Rick Parker (letters), Bob Sharen (colors)

FEATURE CHARACTER: Sam Wilson (also in fb to 1st chr app before Cap #186, '75 fb, also in Cap #117, '69 fb; also as "Snap" Wilson)

SUPPORTING CAST: Redwing (last in Cap #272, '82), Sarah Wilson Casper (also in fbs1-2 to 1st chr app before Cap #134, '71), Carol Davis, Leila Taylor

VILLAINS: Rival gangs, mugger (in fb)

OTHER CHARACTERS: Reverend Garcia (also as hallucination, only in fb to 1st chr app before Cap #139, '71), Reverend Paul Wilson (Sam's father), Darlene Wilson (Sam's mother) (both in fb, die, only app), Gideon Wilson (Sam's brother, in fb, 1st, chr next in WWHulk:GC #2, '07 fb, next in WWHulk:GC #1, '07 as Mister Gideon), coffee shop patrons

LOCATIONS/ITEMS: Harlem (also in fb) inc Sam's childhood home (in fb) & Coffee shop, Los Angeles (in rfb); gang members' knife & gun (both in fb)

FLASHBACKS: Young Sam Wilson witnesses his father's murder, who was trying to break up a rival gang dispute. Rev. Garcia oversees the funeral. Over time Sam tries to embody what his father stood for by helping in the community, but Sam's mother is killed by a mugger. Sam becomes filled with rage towards the world and snaps, becoming "Snap" Wilson and moving to Los Angeles.

SYNOPSIS: Sarah explains to Leila and Carol that Sam created the "Snap" personality as a defense mechanism to deal with the death of their parents. Meanwhile, Sam sits on a rooftop thinking about his mental state and recent outbursts. As he begins to curse the world and his father, family friend Reverend Garcia comes to talk to Sam. But, Sam reverts to "Snap" and punches him.

NOTE: Gideon's 1st name revealed in WWHulk:GC #2, '07.

CAPTAIN AMERICA #278 (February 1983)

"Oh, Thus be it Ever…" (16 pages)

CREDITS: J.M. DeMatteis (writer), Mike Zeck (pencils), John Beatty (inks), John Morelli (letters), Bob Sharen (colors), Mike Carlin (asst editor), Mark Gruenwald (editor)
FEATURE CHARACTER: Captain America (also in rfb)
SUPPORTING CAST: Arnie Roth (also on screen), Bernie Rosenthal
VILLAINS: Baron Zemo (next in Cap #290, '84), Primus (merged w/Doughboy, also in rfb as Arnim Zola, posing as Steve Rogers), Vermin (next in MTU #128, '83), giant mutates (1 also in rfb, last app)
OTHER CHARACTERS: Gail Runciter (last in Cap #276, '82, next in MTU #128, '83), Baron Zemo's mutates (last app), Michael Bech, SHIELD agents
LOCATIONS/ITEMS: Mexico inc Castle Zemo, Brooklyn diner; Zemo's rifle, equipment & ship (also in rfb), SHIELD blasters
FLASHBACKS: Arnie and Michael are abducted (Cap #275, '82). Primus takes Cap to Baron Zemo (Cap #276, '82). Zemo reveals his disfigurement, Primus takes on Steve Rogers' appearance and Vermin kills the giant mutate with Michael's mind still inside (Cap #277, '83).
SYNOPSIS: Arnie blames Captain America for Michael's death then passes out. Baron Zemo orders his mutates to attack Cap and Vermin as Arnie wakes back up. As Cap battles the mutates, Arnie apologizes for blaming Cap, but tells him the mutates are actually transformed people, and not to blame for their actions. Cap is able to convince the mutates to calm down and that he's not their enemy. Teaming with the mutates, Cap grabs Michael, feeling he may still be alive. Seeing that events are turning against him, Zemo tries to escape but Arnie stops him with one punch. The mutates destroy Zemo's equipment, but SHIELD agents led by Runciter suddenly storm the castle, shooting the mutates. Cap stops the massacre, but Zemo escapes in the confusion. As Zemo flies away in his ship, an angry Vermin attacks from behind. The next day, Steve Rogers and Bernie have lunch until Captain America arrives.

2ND STORY: "Snapping (Part III)" (6 pages)
CREDITS: J.M. DeMatteis (writer), Mike Zeck (pencils), John Beatty (inks), John Morelli (letters), Bob Sharen (colors)
FEATURE CHARACTER: Sam Wilson (also as "Snap" Wilson & Falcon, also in Sam's thoughts, next in CoC #1, '82)
SUPPORTING CAST: Redwing (next in CoC #1, '82), Leila Taylor (next in Cap #284, '83), Sarah Wilson Casper (next in Cap Ann #11/3, '92), Carol Davis (last app)
OTHER CHARACTERS: Rev. Garcia (bts, out of town, last in Cap #143, '71, last app, also as hallucination); Captain America, Red Skull (both in Sam's thoughts)
LOCATIONS/ITEMS: Harlem inc Sam's campaign office; copy of Daily Bugle
SYNOPSIS: Reverend Garcia reasons with Sam, making him realize the "Snap" personality is just a defense mechanism and not his true persona. The words help, and Sam comes back to his senses, finally feeling free. Later, Sam reads his Daily Bugle interview about his past. When he thanks Sarah for putting Garcia on him, she tells him he's been out of town for weeks. Sam wonders if it was all in his mind, or something more.

CAPTAIN AMERICA #279 (March 1983)

"Of Monsters and Men" (22 pages)

CREDITS: J.M. DeMatteis (writer), Mike Zeck (pencils), John Beatty (inks), John Morelli (letters), Bob Sharen (colors), Mike Carlin (asst editor), Mark Gruenwald (editor)
FEATURE CHARACTER: Captain America (next in CoC #1, bts in CoC #2, CoC #3, all '82, Hulk #277-279, '82-83, MTIO #92, '82, FF #250, '82, MTIO Ann #7, '82, MTIO #96, '82, FF #258, '83 fb, VSW #3, '83, ASM Ann #16, '82, Av #227, '83, Hulk #281-284, '83, FF #258, '83)
GUEST STARS: Iron Man (last in IM Ann #5, '82, next in CoC #1, '82), Nick Fury (last in Cap #276, '82, next in Hulk #279, '83)
SUPPORTING CAST: Bernie Rosenthal (next in FF #250, '82), Arnie Roth (next in Cap #284, '83)
VILLAINS: Primus (merged w/Doughboy, also as Steve Rogers & handsome men, Primus next in NW #3, '90, Doughboy next in Cap #383/4, '91), Scarecrow (last in Cap Ann #6, '82) & his crows
OTHER CHARACTERS: Mr. Burns (last in Cap #276, '82, dies), Michael Bech (bts, dies, last app), Mrs. Burns, Burns' maid, Howie & his girlfriend, CUA member's wife (corpse), diner staff, SHIELD (bts)
LOCATIONS/ITEMS: Brooklyn diner, New York inc Central Park, cemetery w/Michael's grave, Avengers Mansion inc lab, Burns mansion, Lakewood, New Jersey inc Camp Arrowhead w/abandoned cabin; Iron Man's equipment, psychometer
SYNOPSIS: Captain America confronts Steve Rogers as Bernie looks on in disbelief. Cap attacks, beating on Steve until he reverts to his true form as Primus. Bernie faints. Primus takes Bernie, changes into Doughboy, and escapes. Later at Avengers Mansion, Iron Man reconfigures a psychometer so Cap can track Primus. Nick Fury calls in and tells Cap Michael died. Elsewhere, CUA member Mr. Burns is found dead in his home, surrounded by crows. At Camp Arrowhead in Lakewood, New Jersey, Primus holds Bernie captive, telling her his plan to save the planet by turning everyone into mutates, and for her to be his friend. Cap bursts in and battles Primus, but ultimately falls to his raw strength. Bernie comes to Cap's aid, making Primus realize he still has much to learn. Primus apologizes and leaves. Days later, Steve and Arnie visit Michael's grave. Steve wallows in self-pity and Arnie chastises him for it, reminding Steve that everything Arnie wanted from life was dead. This is Arnie's time for grief, not Steve's. In Central Park, a woman is found dead, surrounded by crows.
NOTE: The corpse found in Central Park is revealed to be a CUA's member's wife in Cap #280, '83.

CAPTAIN AMERICA #280 (April 1983)

"Sermon of STRAW" (22 pages)

CREDITS: J.M. DeMatteis (writer), Mike Zeck (pencils), John Beatty (inks), John Morelli (letters), Bob Sharen (colors), Mark Gruenwald (editor)
FEATURE CHARACTER: Captain America (next in Av #228-230, '83, MTU #127-128, '83)
VILLAINS: Scarecrow (also as James McArthur Sr., chr next in X23 #3, '05, next in AvS #26, '89), his crows & his men
OTHER CHARACTERS: James Wilson McArthur Sr. (also on TV, last in Cap #276, '82), Jimmy McArthur Jr. (last in Cap #277, '83), Buckly (CUA member, dies), other CUA members (all last app), Arthur Bennett (last in Cap #277, '83, next in Cap #292, '84), Ralph Laughton (also as "Anthony," last in Cap Ann #6, '82, last app), phone operator (bts, on phone w/Cap), Buckley's neighbors, CUA cable network film crew, police, bystanders
LOCATIONS/ITEMS: New York inc Buckley's apartment, CUA office, Bennett Advertsing & CUA cable network, Rhinebeck New York inc Laughton farm, Greenwich Village; copy of Daily Bugle, Steve's art portfolio, Scarecrow's tape recorder, chains & razor
SYNOPSIS: Scarecrow murders yet another CUA member, Mr. Buckly. Later, Captain America confronts the CUA for using his likeness without his permission. Jimmy tries to convince Cap to side with them, but Cap tells the group that he represents all American people, not any one group, and tells them to take the posters down. Cap learns that Scarecrow has been killing their members. Cap decides the best way to keep an eye on them is to accept Arthur Bennett's job offer to work on their campaign. Upstate, Scarecrow watches a press conference where James McArthur calls him a madman, fueling his rage. Later, Cap finds Scarecrow attacking Bennett and intervenes, but Scarecrow uses his crows to cover his escape. The day of the CUA Network's launch, Scarecrow reveals that James Sr. has been using the CUA for personal gain. Cap, quietly takes down Scarecrow's men as he rants before defeating Scarecrow himself. As Scarecrow is taken away, his brother reveals Scarecrow went insane while in prison.
NOTE: Cap's Avengers Priority code is CA1477B.

CAPTAIN AMERICA #281 (May 1983)

"Before the Fall!" (22 pages)

CREDITS: J.M. DeMatteis (writer), Mike Zeck (pencils), John Beatty (inks), Diana Albers (letters), Bob Sharen (colors), Mike Carlin (asst editor), Mark Gruenwald (editor)
FEATURE CHARACTER: Captain America (also in rfb, also in fb1 between Cap #139, '71 fb & Inv #29, '78 fb)
GUEST STAR: Spider-Woman (Jessica Drew, private investigator & spider-themed adventurer, last in CoC #1, '82, last bts in CoC #3, '82 bts)
SUPPORTING CAST: Bucky (Monroe, also in rfb, also in fb2 between Cap #156, '72 & Cap #236, '79 fb; last in Cap #236, '79 fb), Bucky (Barnes, only in fb1 between Cap #139, '71 fb & Inv #29, '78 fb), Bernie Rosenthal (last in MTU #128, '83)
VILLAINS: Viper (also as "Mrs. Smith" & in recording, last in SW #44, '82) her agents (Brian Hendricks named, ies) & giant vipers, Constrictor (last in MTIO #96, '83), Captain America (Burnside, also in rfb, only in fb2 between Cap #156, '72 & Cap #236, '79 fb), Defenders (WWII subversive militarists, only app in fb1)
OTHER CHARACTERS: Gail Runciter (also as Viper agent, last in MTU #128, '83), Franklin Delano Roosevelt (US President, bts in fb1 between Mystic #6/4, '41 & GSInv #1, '75 fb), mailman, movie theater attendees & usher, government officials (in rfb & fb2), Dr. Faustus, Red Skull (Malik) (both in rfb)
LOCATIONS/ITEMS: Brooklyn Heights inc movie theater & Steve's apartment, San Francisco inc abandoned warehouse, Viper's hidden base, Hartsdale Illinois inc "Mrs. Smith's" house, Washington DC inc White House (in fb1), Catskills mental institution (in fb2), government lab, Bahamas (both in rfb); Viper's monitor & gun, Viper agents' helicopter & guns, Constrictor's electrified cables, Defenders' guns (in fb1), government agent's gun (in fb2), Cap & Bucky's stasis tubes, Super Soldier Serum (both in rfb)
FLASHBACKS: November 22, 1941: In Washington DC, Captain America and Bucky battle the Defenders to stop them from killing the President (1). Jack becomes friends with "Prof. Steve Rogers." The two later take the Super Soldier Serum to become the new Cap and Bucky (Cap #155, '72 fb) to battle the Red Skull (YM #24/2, '53). Cap and Bucky go insane and are placed in suspended animation (Cap #155, '72 fb). Burnside fights Rogers (Cap #156, '72). Burnside and Monroe are committed to a mental institution in the Catskills (2), but become pawns of Dr. Faustus (Cap #236, '79 fb).
SYNOPSIS: After a night at the movies, Steve Rogers and Bernie are followed home by Jack Monroe, the 1950's Bucky. In San Francisco, Spider-Woman tracks Viper to an abandoned warehouse only to find a recording of Viper. While Spider-Woman battles two giant vipers, Viper's recording explains she's not Spider-Woman's mother. Spider-Woman surmises that Morgan LeFay tricked both her and Viper. At Steve's apartment, Jack explains he was rehabilitated by SHIELD but he has nowhere to go. Steve offers his apartment and to help him acclimate to the present. Meanwhile, Viper learns that Spider-Woman escaped her trap. Viper kills the agent that told her and feeds his body to her giant vipers. Later, Captain America takes Bucky on patrol until the Constrictor attacks. Constrictor easily defeats Bucky, and Viper's agents surprise Cap from behind. Constrictor and the agents take Cap and go, leaving a distraught Bucky behind.
NOTE: Monroe's hair is colored black here, but reverts to brown next issue. Letters page contains LOC from future Marvel writer Barry Dutter.

CAPTAIN AMERICA #282 (June 1983)

"On Your Belly You Shall Crawl, and Dust You Shall Eat!" (22 pages)

CREDITS: J.M. DeMatteis (writer), Mike Zeck (pencils), John Beatty (inks), Diana Albers (letters), Bob Sharen (colors), Mike Carlin (asst editor), Mark Gruenwald (editor)
FEATURE CHARACTER: Captain America (also as child in hallucination)
GUEST STARS: Spider-Woman (next in SW #47, '82), Dum Dum Dugan (last in Hulk #279, '83), Nick Fury (also as "Poppa," last in DD #187, '82), Sam Wilson (also in pfb, last in Hulk #279, '83, next in Cap #284, '83)
SUPPORTING CAST: Bucky (becomes Nomad), Bernie Rosenthal (next in Cap #284, '83) (both also in Cap's thoughts & pfb)
VILLAINS: Viper (also as "Mrs. Smith"), her agents (some also in Viper's future vision) & giant viper, Constrictor (also in Cap's thoughts)
OTHER CHARACTERS: Gail Runciter (also as Viper agent & "Baby"), Hartsdale residents, Viper's scientists, snakes (prev 3 only in Viper's future vision), Joseph Rogers (Steve's father, only in hallucination)
LOCATIONS/ITEMS: Viper's hidden base, Steve's Brooklyn Heights apartment, Sam's Harlem campaign office & apartment, Hartsdale, Illinois (also in Viper's future vision); SHIELD Helicarrier, jet, parachute & transmitter, Gail's wrist communicator, Viper's bubonic plague (in Viper's future vision), hallucinogen & gas
FLASHBACK: Bucky tells Bernie about Cap's situation. They ask Sam Wilson for help, and he sends them to SHIELD (p).
SYNOPSIS: Gail Runciter, undercover as a Viper agent, spots the captured Captain America and calls SHIELD. When her call is cut off, Fury tells Bucky and Bernie that SHIELD has been tracking Viper's movements, and Bucky volunteers to be sent in. As Cap hallucinates, Viper tells Cap that she plans to unleash the bubonic plague. Overhearing Viper's tirade, Constrictor realizes she's insane. Jack, now as Nomad, and Dum Dum infiltrate Viper's base. Cap appears and helps Nomad, but, as Dum Dum suffers a heart attack, Cap proves to be under Viper's control and her agents overpower Nomad, who signals for Dum Dum's help, but Dugan is unable to respond.
NOTE: Gail's authorization code is "Alpha-Beta 6."

CAPTAIN AMERICA #283 (July 1983)

"America the Cursed!" (22 pages)

CREDITS: J.M. DeMatteis (writer), Mike Zeck (pencils), John Beatty (inks), Diana Albers (letters), Bob Sharen (colors), Mike Carlin (asst editor), Mark Gruenwald (editor)
FEATURE CHARACTER: Captain America (also as child in hallucination)
GUEST STARS: Dum Dum Dugan, Nick Fury
SUPPORTING CAST: Nomad
VILLAINS: Viper (also as "Mrs. Smith," next in NM #5, '83) & her agents, Constrictor (chr next in DP #35, '99 fb, next in Cap #309, '85)
OTHER CHARACTERS: Gail Runciter (next in NFVS #1, '88), Ronald Reagan (US President, bts on phone w/ Fury, last in Hulk #279, '82, next in Av #231, '83), SHIELD agents, Hartsdale residents (Mr. Wise named), reporter (on TV); Josh Cooper, Mike Farrell, Anna Kappelbaum, Joseph Rogers, Sarah Rogers, Bernie Rosenthal, Arnie Roth, Sam Wilson (prev 8 in hallucination)
LOCATIONS/ITEMS: Viper's hidden base, Hartsdale, Illinois inc "Mrs. Smith's" house; SHIELD Helicarrier & transmitter, Dum Dum's heart pills, Viper agents' guns, Viper's gun, hallucinogen & hot air balloons w/bubonic plague
SYNOPSIS: Constrictor tries to revive the hallucinating Captain America, but stops when Viper arrives. She learns that this Nomad is new, and the Nomad that defeated her previously was actually Cap. Constrictor covertly disobeys Viper's order to drug Cap again. Dugan revives and takes his heart medication and signals SHIELD for help, but Viper agents capture him. Only receiving half of Dugan's message, Fury calls the President. Viper sees a news report announcing that Hartsdale is being quarantined due to a "toxic spill," but Viper blocks the broadcast. She holds a parade featuring the brainwashed Cap, Nomad and Gail, which draws the attention of the entire town. Viper reveals she will release the virus through hot air balloons. Cap fights off the leftover effects of the hallucinogen and attacks Viper, aided by Constrictor. Nomad, seeing Cap hanging from a balloon, snaps out of it and runs to help. Grabbing Viper's fallen gun, he waits for Cap and Dugan to get clear before blasting the balloons at the last second.
NOTE: Letters page contains LOC from Steve Rogers!

CAPTAIN AMERICA #284 (August 1983)

"Diverging…" (22 pages)

CREDITS: J.M. DeMatteis (writer), Sal Buscema (pencils), Kim DeMulder (inks), Diana Albers (letters), Bob Sharen (colors), Mike Carlin (asst editor), Mark Gruenwald (editor), Mike Zeck (c pencils), John Beatty (c inks)
FEATURE CHARACTER: Captain America
GUEST STARS: Dum Dum Dugan (next in X Ann #7, '83), Nick Fury (next in Av #231, '83), Jeff Mace (also as Patriot in his thoughts, last in Cap Ann #6, '82 as Captain America),Sam Wilson (next in Falcon #1, '83)
SUPPORTING CAST: Josh Cooper, Mike Farrel (both last in Cap #275, '82), Anna Kappelbaum (last in Cap #275, '82, next in Cap #317, '86), Arnie Roth (last in Cap #279, '83, next in Cap #290, '84), Nomad, Bernie Rosenthal
VILLAIN: Tommy Beehan (angry & unemployed drunk, only app)

OTHER CHARACTERS: Mary Beehan (Tommy's pregnant wife), Susan Beehan, Teddy Beehan, Troy Beehan (Tommy & Mary's children) (all only app), Sammy Bernstein (last in Cap #276, '83, next in Cap #427, '94), Leila Taylor (last in Cap #278/2, '83, next in Cap&Falc #1, '04 1), Diana Nicholls (Josh's date), other party guests (Lenny named), Dr. Hamer (1st) & his nurse, police (Captain DiMarco named), reporter (voice only)

LOCATIONS/ITEMS: New York inc SHIELD HQ w/infirmary, Beehan apartment & East Side luxury apartment building inc Mace's apartment, Brooklyn Heights inc Steve's & Bernie's apartments; Cap's motorcycle, Beehan's gun & bottle, police guns & sniper rifle

SYNOPSIS: Dum Dum Dugan recovers in a SHIELD infirmary. Fury refuses to let Dugan retire and instead promotes him to deputy director. On the way home, Captain America and Nomad run across a man, Tommy Beehan, drunkenly abusing his family. They stop him, but his wife Mary begs for them not to call the police. Cap reluctantly agrees, which confuses Nomad. Later, they attend Bernie's party where Jack and Arnie, both feeling out of place, become friends. Later as Steve and Bernie settle down to watch a movie, they catch a report of Beehan shooting at people. Meanwhile, Jeff Mace is dying and has requested Cap's presence. Cap races to the scene and tries to talk Beehan down, but ends up taking a sniper's bullet for him. Beehan prepares to shoot Cap until his family stops him, and Cap disarms Beehan before he can turn the gun on himself. Later, Steve finally tells Bernie he loves her.

CAPTAIN AMERICA #285 (September 1983)

"Letting Go" (22 pages)

CREDITS: J.M. DeMatteis (writer), Sal Buscema (pencils), Kim DeMulder (inks), Diana Albers (letters), Bob Sharen (colors), Mike Carlin (asst editor), Mark Gruenwald (editor), Mike Zeck (c pencils), John Beatty (c inks)
FEATURE CHARACTER: Captain America (next in Av #231-232, '83, S #2, '00 fb, Av Ann #12, '83, Cap Ann #7, '83)
GUEST STAR: Jeff Mace (as Patriot & Captain America in rfb, dies)
SUPPORTING CAST: Josh Cooper (next in Cap #303, '85), Mike Farrel (next in Cap #316, '86), Bernie Rosenthal (next in Av #233, '83), Nomad
VILLAINS: Porcupine (last in IM #127, '79, chr next in CoH #3, '97, next in Cap #315, '86), Secret Empire's Number 43, robbers

OTHER CHARACTERS: Edwin Jarvis (between Av #230-231, '83), Dr. Hamer (last app), deli clerk & his wife (Esther), bystanders; All-Winners Squad: Bucky (Davis), Captain America (Naslund), Human Torch (Hammond), Miss America, Sub-Mariner, Whizzer; Adam-II, Nazi spies (prev in rfb)
LOCATIONS/ITEMS: New York inc Mace's apartment, abandoned tenement & Avengers Mansion, Porcupine's Brooklyn hideout, Bernie's apartment; muggers' guns, Porcupine's eye-in-the-sky device, quills, Cap mannequins & missile, Cap's bike, Nomad's discs, garbage can
FLASHBACKS: Patriot fights Nazi spies (MC #21, '41). Mace replaces Naslund as Captain America (WI #4, '77). Cap defeats Adam-II. Mace tells Rogers that he's dying of cancer (Cap Ann #6, '82).
SYNOPSIS: Captain America races across town, barely pausing to stop a robbery. As Nomad follows Cap he spots a flying device that's also tailing Cap. Arriving at his destination, Cap learns that Mace is near death, and has requested Cap's presence. Nomad follows the device to its source. Meanwhile, Porcupine reports to the Secret Empire that he's finished his new suit. Porcupine attacks, but Porcupine quickly defeats him. Later, Jarvis forwards a call to Cap from Mace's doctor, telling him it's time. Cap races to Mace, but the Porcupine attacks, dangling Nomad as his hostage. The fight goes on longer than Cap can spare and with Nomad proving ineffectual, Cap fakes being felled to spark Nomad into action. When Nomad finally attacks, Cap defeats the distracted Porcupine. Cap reaches Mace for his final moments, and salutes his passing.
NOTE: The All-Winners Squad are called the Invaders here.

CAPTAIN AMERICA ANNUAL #7 (1983)

"The Last Enchantment!" (38 pages)

CREDITS: Peter B. Gillis (writer), Brian Postman (pencils), Kim DeMulder (inks), Diana Albers (letters), Bob Sharen (colors), Mike Carlin (asst editor), Mark Gruenwald (editor), Joe Sinnott (c inks)
FEATURE CHARACTER: Captain America (also in rfb, also in fb3 between CM #33, '74 & GSAv #1, '74 fb; next in Av #233, FF #256, Av #234, IM #172, Thor #334, Av #235, Hawk #3, Av #236-237, all '83)
GUEST STARS: Aquarian (Wundarr, pacifist Dakkamite, last in MTIO #74, '81, next in Q #4, '89), Shaper of Worlds (cosmic being, also in fb4 to 1st chr app before Hulk #155, '72 as the Skrull Cosmic Cube; also in pfb, last in Hulk #267, '82, next in FF #319, '88)
VILLAINS: MODOC (George Tarleton, Mental Organism Designed Only for Computation, only in fb1 between Cap #133, '71 fb & SVTU #17, '80 fb, fb2 between SVTU #17, '80 fb & ToS #92/2, '67; becomes MODOC), Dr. George Clinton (founding AIM scientist, also in rfb, only in fbs1-3 to 1st chr app before SVTU #17, '80), Bernard Worrell (founding AIM scientist, also as lizard-creature, 1st, also in fbs1-3), AIM agents (ruling committee only in fbs1-2, dies, others also in fbs1-3), Supreme Intelligence (Kree ruler, also in fb5 to 1st chr app before Av #134, '75 fb; also in rfb & pfb, last in MGN #1, '82, next in SS #4, '87), Skrulls (inc Emperor, only in fb4, others in rfb)
OTHER CHARACTERS: Cosmic Cube (gains sentience, also in rfb, also in fb1 to 1st chr app before FF #319, '88 fb, fb3 between CM #33, '74 & MTIO #42, '78; last in MTIO #43, '78, next in Def #150, '85 as Kubik), Dr. Myron Wilburn (Project Pegasus Director, last in MTU Ann #5, '82, chr last in Av Ann #18/2, '89 fb, next in Q #53, '93), Project Pegasus personnel, Cube-created creatures, Kree (some in fb5, others in rfb); Arnim Zola, Captain Marvel (Mar-Vell), Hate Monger, Red Skull, Thanos, Rick Jones (prev 6 only in rfb)
LOCATIONS/ITEMS: Adirondack Mountains inc Project Pegasus, Ohio countryside, AIM subterranean facility (also as Technopolis), distant

galaxy inc Shaper of Worlds' chambers, Tibetan mountains; AIM gunships & blasters, Avengers Quinjet, Cap's shield (turned into a crab-like creature)

FLASHBACKS: Bernard Worrell and his mentor Dr. George Clinton help found AIM, and the two scientists participate in the construction of MODOC. Later, AIM traps a meta-singularity in a series of force-screens, creating the Cosmic Cube (1). Red Skull obtains the Cube (ToS #80/2, '66). Captain America defeats the Red Skull (ToS #81/2, '66). Exposure to the Cube has driven MODOC insane, and he becomes MODOK when he kills AIM's ruling committee. Worrell and Clinton survive MODOK's rampage and hide within AIM as low-level agents (2). MODOK destabilizes the Cube's force-casing, seemingly destroying it (Cap #119, '69). Thanos interrogates Rick Jones for the location of the Cube (CM #27, '73). Using the Cube, Thanos makes himself a god (CM #31, '74). Captain Marvel defeats Thanos (CM #33, '74). Captain America takes the Cube to Project Pegasus. Meanwhile, Clinton and Worrell create an AIM splinter group (3). Red Skull, Hate Monger and Arnim Zola capture Dr. Clinton and attempt to build a second Cosmic Cube. When the project fails, Clinton is killed (SVTU #17, '80). Millennia ago, the Skrulls create a Cosmic Cube. Using the Cube, the Skrull Emperor declares himself a god. The Cube eventually gains sentience, destroys two-thirds of the Skrull galaxy and evolves into the Shaper of Worlds (4). Wanting a Cosmic Cube for themselves, the Kree construct the Supreme Intelligence. However, the Supreme Intelligence refuses to build a Cube for them, opting instead to see if another race is able to build one (5). During the Kree/Skrull War (Av #97, '72) the Supreme Intelligence implants the location of the Earth's Cosmic Cube into Rick Jones (CM #27, '73 fb). The Supreme Intelligence contacts the Shaper of Worlds (p).

SYNOPSIS: The Cosmic Cube begins to glow at Project Pegasus. In space, the Supreme Intelligence tells the Shaper of Worlds of the disturbance. In Ohio, Aquarian notices the disturbance. Homing in on the Cube's frequency, AIM attacks Project Pegasus to steal it. Captain America responds to Pegasus' distress call, arriving in time to stop Aquarian from leaving with the Cube. AIM takes advantage of Cap's misunderstanding of Aquarian's motives and captures the Cube. Cap and Aquarian follow AIM to their facility. As Cap battles AIM agents, Bernard Worrell takes control of the Cube. Cap and Aquarian confront Worrell. Despite Aquarian's warning that Worrell is causing the Cube pain, Worrell uses the Cube to alter reality in multiple attacks against the heroes. Unable to break Captain America's will, Worrell pushes the Cube too far and the Cube fights back by mimicking Worrell's hate and fear. Cap fails at reasoning with the Cube, but the Shaper of Worlds arrives and calms the Cube. He explains the Cube is sentient and evolving. He returns to space with the Cube to oversee its development.

NOTE: This issue reveals that Cosmic Cubes are sentient creatures, and FF #319, '88 further explains they are from the Realm of the Beyonders, sent to our dimension to learn about life in other realms.

CAPTAIN AMERICA #286 (October 1983)

"One Man in Search of…HIMSELF!" (22 pages)

CREDITS: J.M. DeMatteis (writer), Mike Zeck (pencils), John Beatty (inks), Diana Albers (letters), Bob Sharen (colors), Mike Carlin (asst editor), Mark Gruenwald (editor)
FEATURE CHARACTER: Captain America
GUEST STARS: Deathlok the Demolisher (Col. Luther Manning, cyborg from Earth-7484, also in rfb; last in MTIO #34, '77, chr last in Cap #287, '83 fb), Vision (bts in Avengers Mansion, last in Av #236, '83, last bts in MFan #24/2, '86, next bts in Cap #289, '84)
SUPPORTING CAST: Bernie Rosenthal (last in Hawk #3, '83), Nomad
VILLAINS: Cannibalistic street gang (from Earth-7484), Roxxon agents
OTHER CHARACTERS: Luther Manning clone (also in rfb; last in AT #36, '76), Godwulf (resistance leader, also in rfb; last in MS #33, '77), surgeons, US military (both in rfb), cannibal (all from Earth-7484), booth attendant, police, commuters, bystanders
LOCATIONS/ITEMS: New York inc 23rd Street station (also Earth-7484) & Avengers Mansion inc gym, Brand Corporation Long Island plant inc genetic division; Godwulf's time machine (Earth-7484), Col. Manning's rifle (in rfb), Manning clone's gun, tracker & knife; police car & guns, Bernie's car, Deathlok's blaster
FLASHBACKS: Col. Luther Manning participates in war games (AT #27, '74 fb). Transformed into the cyborg Deathlok, who later escapes the military's control (AT #25, '74 fb). Deathlok's cerebral imprints are copied to his clone (AT #35, '76). Godwulf sends Deathlok back in time (AT #36, '76).
SYNOPSIS: Godwulf sends Luther Manning from the dystopian future of 1991 to the past so he can find the lost Deathlok. Unaccustomed to a populated city, Manning inadvertently draws attention to himself, but manages to evade the police. Meanwhile Steve Rogers meets with Bernie and they head to her parents' house to have dinner, but en route Bernie almost runs over Manning, who's making his way to an abandoned Brand facility, and to Bernie's frustration, Steve leaves to investigate. Cap catches up with Manning, who explains his mission. Breaking into the facility, they find it fully operational and staffed by Roxxon agents, who they battle until Deathlok appears, and shoots Manning through the chest.
NOTE: The Brand Corporation was shut down in ASM #236, '83, but as a subsidiary of Roxxon some of their facilities are still in use by Roxxon, such as the one seen here. Its address is revealed to be 410 Gannon Ave, Long Island City in Cap #310, '86.

CAPTAIN AMERICA #287 (November 1983)

"Future Shock!" (22 pages)

CREDITS: J.M. DeMatteis (writer), Mike Zeck (pencils), John Beatty (inks), Diana Albers (letters), Bob Sharen (colors), Mike Carlin (asst editor), Mark Gruenwald (editor)
FEATURE CHARACTER: Captain America (also in rfb)
GUEST STAR: Deathlok (also in rfb; in fb between Dlk #32, '94 fb & Cap #283, '86)
SUPPORTING CAST: Nomad, Bernie Rosenthal
VILLAINS: Sister Pleasure (as "Scarlet" here, 1st but chr last in Cap #298, '84 fb), Mother Superior (bts, sent Sister Pleasure to seduce Nomad, 1st but chr last in Cap #15, '07 fb, next in Cap #290, '84), Brand agents (in fb), Roxxon agents (Joel named), muggers

THER CHARACTERS: Godwulf, Luther Manning clone (dies) (both from Earth-7484, also in rfb), Nancy Rosenthal (Bernie's sister, 1st), **ernie's** parents (1st, next in Cap #317, '86), police (others in rfb), firemen, homeless man; Deathlok robot, Quasar (both in rfb)

OCATIONS/ITEMS: Brand Corporation Long Island inc genetic division (destroyed), Rosenthal home, Manning clone's grave, New York inc 3rd Street station (also Earth-7484 & in rfb); Deathlok's blaster & metal pipe, Manning clone's gun (in rfb), Roxxon agents' guns, muggers' guns, **odwulf's** time machine

LASHBACKS: The Manning clone arrives in the present, is chased by police, meets Captain America and is shot by Deathlok (Cap #286, 3). Col. Manning dies (AT #26, '74 fb) and is turned into Deathlok (AT #25, '74 fb). Deathlok's cerebral imprints are copied to his clone (AT #35, 6). Godwulf sends Deathlok back in time (AT #36, '74). The Deathlok robot self-destructs while battling Quasar (MTIO #54, '79). Brand agents **udy** and improve Deathlok.

YNOPSIS: With the Roxxon agents' aid, Deathlok subdues Cap, but when he turns to finish off Manning, they touch and Deathlok's memories **re** restored as Manning dies. Enraged at Roxxon using him, Deathlok slaughters the agents, and he and Cap escape, with Deathlok destroying **e** facility as they leave, his callous attitude to killing shocking Cap. Elsewhere, Bernie's family isn't pleased that Steve stood them up, while **omad** finds himself smitten after saving a beautiful lady, Scarlet, from muggers. After burying Manning Deathlok tells Cap that his world's **eroes** disappeared in 1983, Cap's present day, so Cap follows Deathlok back to his world to save the future. Arriving in 1991 via Godwulf's time **achine**, Deathlok demands to know why Godwulf sent him back in the first place. Godwulf promises answers.

OTE: Scarlet is revealed to be Sister Pleasure and working under Mother Superior's orders in Cap #296, '84.

CAPTAIN AMERICA #288 (December 1983)

"Mazes!" (22 pages)

CREDITS: J.M. DeMatteis (writer), Mike Zeck (pencils), John Beatty (inks), Diana Albers (letters), Bob Sharen (colors), Mike Carlin (asst editor), Mark Gruenwald (editor)
FEATURE CHARACTER: Captain America (also in Bernie's thoughts)
GUEST STARS: Deathlok (also in rfb; chr next in Dlk #32, '94 fb, next in MFan #1, '96), Avengers (from Earth-7484): She-Hulk, Starfox, Thor, Wasp (prev 4 die, only app)
SUPPORTING CAST: Nomad (next in Cap #290, '84), Bernie Rosenthal
VILLAINS: Hellinger (Harlan Ryker, scientist turned cyborg, also in photo, last in MS #33, '77, dies), Nth Command (Roxxon storm troopers, 1st, only in fb) Alpha Mechs ("walking plutonium bombs," aka Doomsday Mechs & Homo Ascendants, one last in MS #33, '77) (all from Earth-7484), Sister Pleasure (as "Scarlet," next in

ap #294, '84)

THER CHARACTERS: Redeemers: Big Man, Gentle Sam, Iron Butterfly, Sage, Swashbuckler (all 1st, next in Dlk #32, '94 fb), Godwulf (also **fb** to 1st chr app before AT #36, '76; chr next in Dlk #32, '94 fb, next in Dlk #29/2, '93); resistance fighters, Luther Manning clone (in rfb) (all **om** Earth-7484), Nancy Rosenthal

OCATIONS/ITEMS: New York inc resistance central command, Hellinger's upstate New York base w/maze, Washington DC (in fb) (all Earth-484), Central Park, Rosenthal home; Hellinger's blaster probes & Project: Alpha-Mech control systems, resistance's flyers, Swashbuckler's **laster** & sword, Godwulf's bow & arrows, Sage's staff, Deathlok's blaster, Nth projectors, hovercrafts (both in fb) (all Earth-7484), Bernie's car

LASHBACKS: The Manning clone restores Deathlok's memories (Cap #287, '83). As an Nth Commando, Godwulf joins in the attack on **Earth's** super heroes, using Nth Projectors to send them into hostile dimensions for instant death. With no heroes to resist them Roxxon **ttempts** to take over America, but the populace resists. The American government fractures and the world is thrown into chaos.

YNOPSIS: Godwulf explains how the world as it is came to be as he leads Captain America and Deathlok to resistance headquarters. **odwulf** introduces them to the Redeemers, tells Cap of Hellinger's plan to destroy the remaining population with his Alpha Mechs, and explains **hat** he sent Deathlok back in time so Hellinger couldn't find him. Cap helps rally Deathlok and the resistance to attack Hellinger. Back in the **resent**, Bernie is frustrated that Steve didn't come to her family's dinner. Meanwhile, "Scarlet" brainwashes Nomad. Cap and the resistance **aid** Hellinger's base, eventually falling into a deadly maze. The Redeemers are separated one by one until only Cap and Deathlok are left to **ace** Hellinger. Hellinger takes control of Deathlok's internal computer, forcing him to shoot Cap. Deathlok fights back and turns his blaster on **Hellinger** and his systems. With Hellinger dead the Redeemers are freed, and Cap congratulates Deathlok on a job well done.

OTE: This issue says the year is 1993, despite 1991 being used in Cap #286-287, '83.

CAPTAIN AMERICA #289 (January 1984)

"Tomorrow, the World?" (19 pages)

CREDITS: J.M. DeMatteis (writer), Mike Zeck (pencils), John Beatty (inks), Diana Albers (letters), Bob Sharen (colors), Mike Carlin (editor)
FEATURE CHARACTER: Captain America (also in rfb)
GUEST STARS: Nick Fury (last in X Ann #7, '83, chr last in MFan #24/2, '86, next in Def #126, '83), Avengers: She-Hulk (last in X Ann #7, '83, next in Thing #8, '84), Starfox (between Av #237-238, '83), Thor (during Thor #336/2, '83 fb), Vision (bts in Avengers Mansion, last bts in Cap #286, '83), Wasp (last in Av #237, '83); X-Men (bts, attacked by Nth Command): Ariel (Kitty Pryde), Colossus, Nightcrawler, Professor X, Storm (prev 5 last in X Ann #7, '83, next in UXM #175, '83), Cyclops (during UXM #175, '83), Rogue (last in X Ann #7, '83, next bts in

UXM #175, '83, next in UXM #178, '84), Wolverine (last in X Ann #7, '83, chr last in MFan #24/2, '86, next in UXM #175, '83); Fantastic Four (bts, attacked by Nth Command) Human Torch (last in FF #262, '84, next in MK #35, '84), Invisible Girl (last in FF #262, '84, chr last in MFan #43/2, '89, next in MK #35, '84), Mr. Fantastic (last in MTU #133, '83, chr last in MFan #43/2, '89, next in MK #35, '84), Thing (last in FF #262 '84, chr last in MFan #24/2, '86, next in MK #35, '84)

VILLAINS: Albert DeVoor (Nth Project Director & Roxxon employee, last in MTIO #67, '80, next in SH #21, '07), Nth Command (inc Godwulf & Iron Butterfly, see NOTE), Zinneman (Metrobank security guard & Roxxon employee)

OTHER CHARACTERS: Madelyne Pryor (Cyclops' fiancée, during UXM #175, '83), Lockheed (Ariel's pet dragon, last in X Ann #7, '83, next in X&M #1, '84) (both bts, attacked by Nth Command), SHIELD agents, bystanders, telephone operator (voice only); Deathlok, Luther Manning clone, Hellinger, Redeemers: Godwulf, Iron Butterfly (prev 5 from Earth-7484, only in rfb); Defenders, Daredevil, Moon Knight, Power Man, Spider-Man (prev 5 mentioned as tomorrow's Nth Command targets); J.M. DeMatteis, Mike Carlin, Mike Zeck, John Beatty, Danny Fingeroth (prev 5 on cover)

LOCATIONS/ITEMS: New York inc Nth Command base w/Metrobank front, DeVoor's office, & Nth generator complex, 23rd St station, Baxter Building & Avengers Mansion, Xavier's School for Gifted Youngsters, Brand Corporation Long Island (in rfb); Brand Corporation's Nth projectors (also in fantasy), lasers, gas, psi-null field generator, Nth emanation-core generator & psycho-rays, Cap's gas mask, robot guardian (in Cap's hallucination)

FLASHBACKS: Cap meets the Luther Manning clone (Cap #286, '83). Cap and Deathlok escape the Brand Corporation (Cap #287, '83). Cap helps Godwulf and the Redeemers defeat Hellinger (Cap #288, '83).

SYNOPSIS: Albert DeVoor addresses the Nth Command as they prepare for Operation: Purge. Meanwhile, Captain America arrives back in the present and tries to warn the Avengers, but the telephone operator won't accept his emergency code and demands twenty cents. As Nth Commandoes surround the Baxter Building, Cap breaks into Metrobank, a front for Roxxon, and battles through an army of Nth Commandoes. Meanwhile, Nth Commandoes surround Xavier's school for Gifted Youngsters. Cap finds the Nth emanation-core generator but DeVoor floods the room with psycho-rays, causing Cap to hallucinate a giant robot. Cap destroys the Nth emanation-core generator, rendering the Nth projectors useless just as Nth Commandoes attack the Avengers. As SHIELD arrests DeVoor, Cap takes off for his overdue meeting with Bernie's parents.

NOTE: This is Assistant Editor's Month, where the Assistant Editors took over while the editors were at the San Diego International Comic Con. The cover lampoons DC, using a facsimile of the '60s DC logo with "go-go checks." It also reverses the Captain America logo image. By stopping Operation: Purge, Cap creates the divergence point that splits Earth-7484 from Earth-616. This is the only app for the Earth-616 versions of Godwulf & Iron Butterfly. While unseen, presumably Earth-616 versions of Big Man, Gentle Sam, Sage & Swashbuckler are present here too. Earth-616's Harlan Ryker later appears in Dlk #1, '90, and Earth-616's Luther Manning in Dlk #25, '93. Cap's emergency code is "A-S-1A."

2ND STORY: "Bernie America, Sentinel of Liberty" (5 pages)

CREDITS: J.M. DeMatteis (writer), Mike Zeck (art), Diana Albers (letters), Bob Sharen (colors), Mike Carlin (editor)

FEATURE CHARACTER: Bernie Rosenthal (also as Bernie America in dream)

SUPPORTING CAST: Nancy Rosenthal (next bts in Cap #255, '89), Steve Rogers (also in Bernie's dream)

OTHER CHARACTERS: Avengers: Hawkeye, Iron Man, She-Hulk, Thor, Wasp; Mo-Skull (MODOK/Red Skull amalgamation), bystander (voice only) (all in Bernie's dream), Baron Zemo, Primus, Scarecrow, Vermin, Viper (prev 6 in Bernie's thoughts), Mike Carlin (as the Watcher, narrator)

LOCATIONS/ITEMS: Rosenthal home, Avengers Mansion (in Bernie's dream); Bernie America's shield, Mo-Skull's Doomsday chair (both in Bernie's dream)

SYNOPSIS: Bernie dreams about what it would be like if her and Steve's roles were reversed: Bernie America and the Avengers hang out until Mo-Skull crashes in, determined to open a chain of Pizza Huts across the Milky Way. Bernie America easily dispatches the foe. Bernie takes a moment to visit with Steve Rogers, who tells her she's breaking his heart with all her heroics. Another crisis calls Bernie away. Back in reality, Nancy wakes Bernie up to tell her Steve has finally arrived. Bernie races downstairs and embraces her love, preferring reality over fantasy.

NOTE: In Bernie's dream, Hawkeye confuses himself with Hawkeye from the TV show "M*A*S*H" and Bernie suggests there's a Larry-Skull and Curly-Skull to go along with the Mo-Skull seen here.

CAPTAIN AMERICA #290 (February 1984)

"Echoes" (22 pages)

CREDITS: J.M. DeMatteis (writer), Ronald Frenz (pencils), Stephen Leialoha (inks), Diana Albers (letters), Bob Sharen (colors), Mike Carlin (asst editor), Mark Gruenwald (editor), John Byrne (c art)

FEATURE CHARACTER: Captain America (also in Nomad's nightmare & rfb; also in MFan #12/2, '84, Falcon #3-4, '84, Cap #8, '02 fb)

GUEST STARS: Avengers: Vision (bts in Avengers Mansion), Wasp (both next in Av #238, '83); Falcon (also in photo, last in Falcon #4, '84, chr next in CoH #3, '97, next bts in Av #243, '84, next in Cap #296, '94), Redwing (last in Falcon #4, '84, next in PMIF #112, '84)

SUPPORTING CAST: Nomad (also in nightmare), Bernie Rosenthal (both next in Cap #292, '84), Arnie Roth also in nightmare, last in Cap #284, '83, next in Cap #292, '84)

VILLAINS: Red Skull (last in Cap #263, '81, chr last in Cap #15, '07 fb, chr next in 1985 #1 '08, next in Cap #293, '84), Mother Superior (Synthea Shmidt, Red Skull's daughter, 1st but last bts in Cap #287, '83, next in Cap #293, '84), Baron Zemo (last in Cap #278, '83, chr next in 1985 #6, '08, next in Cap #293, '84), Black Crow (Jesse Black Crow, Navajo & avatar of pre-colonial America, only as crow here, 1st but chr last in Cap #292, '84 fb, next in Cap #292, '84)

OTHER CHARACTERS: Juvenile delinquent, bystanders, Michael Bech (as zombie in Arnie's nightmare), Nth Commandoes (in rfb)

LOCATIONS/ITEMS: New York inc Avengers Mansion, Steve's & Arnie's Brooklyn Heights apartments, Sam's Harlem campaign office, Skull-House; Steve's art portfolio, "Wilson for Congress" signs

FLASHBACK: Cap battles the Nth Commandoes (Cap #289, '84).

SYNOPSIS: Captain America and Bernie spend time together at Avengers Mansion, where Bernie mistakes the Wasp for a mosquito. Meanwhile, Jack Monroe has a nightmare of Cap aging and withering away. Steve arrives and they leave to visit Sam Wilson. Baron Zemo spies on the pair until Mother Superior recruits him for a sinister purpose. Cap and Nomad catch up with Falcon, who tells the pair he lost his Congressional bid. Nomad becomes distracted while Cap gives a juvenile delinquent a pep talk. Arnie Roth wakes from a nightmare of Michael as a zombie to see Mother Superior and Zemo. Mother Superior puts Arnie back to sleep, and when he wakes again, Cap, Nomad and Falcon greet him. Mother Superior takes Zemo to Skull-House and introduces him to her father, the Red Skull. After the heroes leave Arnie spots Zemo's footprints. Meanwhile, a giant crow mysteriously attacks Cap and Nomad.

NOTE: Mother Superior's real name revealed in Cap #15, '06. Black Crow named in Cap #292, '84.

CAPTAIN AMERICA SPECIAL EDITION #1 (February 1984)

"No Longer Alone!" (20 pages)

CREDITS: Ken Feduniewicz, George Roussos, Christie Scheele (colors), Jim Salicrup (reprint editor) for other credits see original entries.
NOTE: Reprinted from Cap #110, '69. Front cover taken from Cap #110, '69, back cover from Cap #111, '69. Issue box & CCA stamp removed for front cover. Also includes introduction page by Jim Salicrup. All stories are recolored.

2ND STORY: "Tomorrow You Live, Tonight I Die!" (20 pages)
NOTE: Reprinted from Cap #111, '69.

3RD STORY: "At the Stroke of Midnight!" (7 pages)
NOTE: Reprinted from Tower #1, '69.

CAPTAIN AMERICA SPECIAL EDITION #2 (March 1984)

"The Strange Death of Captain America" (20 pages)

CREDITS: Ken Feduniewicz, George Roussos (colors), Jim Salicrup (reprint editor) for other credits see original entries.
NOTE: Reprinted from Cap #113, '69. Front cover taken from Cap #113, '69, back cover from ST #159, '67. Issue box & logo replaced with table of contents for back cover. Also includes introduction page by Jim Salicrup. All stories are recolored.

2ND STORY: "Dark Moon Rise, Hell Heck Hound Kill! Hurt*" (7 pages)
NOTE: Reprinted from NBE #11/4, '68.

3RD STORY: "My Heart Broke in Hollywood!" (7 pages)
NOTE: Reprinted from My Love Story #5, '56.

4TH STORY: "Spy School" (12 pages)
NOTE: Reprinted from ST #159, '67.

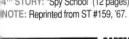

CAPTAIN AMERICA #291 (March 1984)

"To Tame a Tumbler!" (22 pages)

CREDITS: Bill Mantlo (writer), Herb Trimpe (pencils), Jack Abel (inks), Diana Albers (letters), Andy Yanchus (colors), Mike Carlin (asst editor), Mark Gruenwald (editor), John Byrne (c art)
FEATURE CHARACTER: Captain America
GUEST STAR: Tumbler (Lt. Michael Kenneth Keane, ex-Green Beret, costumed acrobat & original Tumbler's brother, also in fb, only app)
VILLAINS: Matthews (Guardian Life Insurance Company executive, also in fb, only app), GLIC security guards
OTHER CHARACTERS: Mrs. Keane (John & Michael's mother, only app in fb, dies), police, bystanders
LOCATIONS/ITEMS: New York inc GLIC offices w/Matthews' office (in fb), records storage room & elevators

& Manhattan Bridge, cemetery w/John Keane's & Mrs. Keane's graves (in fb), Tumbler's Brooklyn apartment (also in fb); Cap's motorcycle. Tumbler's bag w/John Keane's insurance policy, GLIC guards' guns

FLASHBACK: Following John Keane's funeral, his brother Michael attempts to cash in John's $1 million life insurance policy to provide for his elderly mother, but GLIC executive Matthews refuses to honor the policy due to John's criminal activities as the Tumbler. Despite being a decorated Green Beret, Michael is unable to secure work in the private sector due to his brother's reputation. Following his mother's death, Michael extensively trains himself in acrobatics and assumes his brother's mantle as the Tumbler to seek vengeance against GLIC.

SYNOPSIS: Captain America stops the new Tumbler from robbing the GLIC offices. The acrobat's skills allow him to escape, but he forgets his loot, a life insurance policy for the original Tumbler. Tumbler returns home to find Cap waiting for him. After a skirmish Cap convinces Tumbler of their shared interest in investigating GLIC and offers to help. The two return to the GLIC offices to find Matthews and his security guards relocating their policy records in response to the break-in. Cap and Tumbler sneak into the building and discover that GLIC has policies on several costumed criminals as part of an elaborate fraud scheme. Though Matthews and his men catch them in the act, Cap and Tumbler are able to overcome the daunting odds and subdue their opponents. Cap and Tumbler turn the GLIC personnel over to the police and Cap accepts Tumbler's offer of breakfast. Tumbler tells Cap that with his goals accomplished, he's retiring as the Tumbler.

NOTE: GLIC was founded in 1884; their offices' street number is #437. Cap found policy files in Guardian Life's records for Jonathan Powers (Jester), Otto Octavius (Dr. Octopus), Calvin Zabo (Mister Hyde), Klaus Voorhees (Cobra), Silas King (Solarr) and Sam Smithers (Plantman).

CAPTAIN AMERICA #292 (April 1984)

"An American Christmas!" (23 pages)

CREDITS: J.M. DeMatteis (writer), Paul Neary (pencils), Ed Baretto (inks), Diana Albers (letters), Bob Sharen (colors), Mike Carlin (asst editor), Mark Gruenwald (editor), Ed Hannigan (c pencils), Klaus Janson (c inks)
FEATURE CHARACTER: Captain America (also in Black Crow's visions & pfb; also in Cap #600/3, '09 fb, PPSSM #89, '84, Av #241-242, '84, next in SecWars #1-2, '84, Thor #383, '87 fb, SecWars #3-12, '84-'85, Av #243, '84, ASM #252, '84, IM #182, '84, CoH #3, '97, 1985 #6, '08, Av #244-245, '84, AFlt #10, '84, Av Ann #13, '84, MGN #17, '85, WM #1, '86)
GUEST STARS: Avengers: Hawkeye, Thor, Wasp (all last & also in Av #242, '84, next in SecWars #1, '84), Captain Marvel (Monica Rambeau), She-Hulk (both last in Av #238, '83, also in Av #240-242, '84, next in SecWars #1, '84), Mockingbird, Vision (both during & also in Av #242, '84), Scarlet Witch, Starfox (both last in Av #238, '84, also in Av #240-242, '84, next in Av #242, '84)
SUPPORTING CAST: Nomad (also in pfb), Bernie Rosenthal (next in AFlt #10, '84) (both also in Cap #600/3, '09 fb), Arnie Roth (next in Cap #295, '84)
VILLAIN: Black Crow (1st full app, also in crow, mist & lightning forms, also in pfb & fb to 1st chr app before Cap #290, '84; last in Cap #290, '84, next in Cap #299, '84)
OTHER CHARACTERS: ISAAC (Titan's sentient computer, bts in contact w/Vision, bts during & also in Av #242, '84), Arthur Bennett (last in Cap #280, '83, next in Cap #309, '85), Ann Brennan (Bernie's friend, 1st, next in Cap #307, '85), receptionist, bystanders, Black Crow's great-grandfather, construction workers (both in fb), Native Americans, US Cavalry, teachers, students (prev 4 in Black Crow's vision)
LOCATIONS/ITEMS: Steve's Brooklyn Heights apartment, Black Crow's Queens apartment, Bennett Advertising, Brooklyn Bridge, Central Park, Navajo reservation, construction site, hospital (prev 3 in fb); Black Crow's wheelchair, Steve's "Kwikkee Burger" art samples, Beyonder's gateway
FLASHBACKS: A giant crow attacks Captain America and Nomad for the second time, then escapes (p). As a boy, Jesse Black Crow listens to his great-grandfather's teachings. As an adult, Jesse works as a construction worker until he's paralyzed by a 20-story fall. As he recovers in a hospital, Jesse finds he can release his spirit self into the world.
SYNOPSIS: Steve Rogers and Bernie share a romantic moment until Jack Monroe blunders in. Meanwhile Jesse Black Crow has another vision, reminding him that as the spirit of old America, he must kill Captain America, the spirit of new America, to balance the scales. Three weeks later, Steve and Bernie leave Bennett Advertising. Black Crow attacks Steve, steals a lock of his hair, and vanishes. In the weeks that follow, Cap attends Avengers meetings, Jack interviews for jobs, and Steve shops with Bernie and works on art assignments. On Christmas Eve, Steve and Bernie throw a holiday party until a crow flies in and scratches Steve. Cap and Nomad investigate and Bernie follows. Black Crow attacks the heroes, quickly defeating them at the Brooklyn Bridge. As Black Crow prepares to kill Cap, the Avenger kneels in respect. Laughing, Black Crow announces that the Earth Spirit is pleased and departs in peace. Elated that Cap survived, Bernie proposes marriage. Days later in Central Park, the Avengers vanish in a flash of light.
NOTE: The last page mirrors the last pages of Av #242, '84, story continued in SecWars #1, '84. Cap #296, '84 reveals that Nomad is unwittingly poisoning Cap here.

CAPTAIN AMERICA #293 (May 1984)

"Field of Vision!" (22 pages)

CREDITS: J.M. DeMatteis (writer), Paul Neary (pencils), Ed Barreto (inks), Diana Albers (letters), Bob Sharen (colors), Mike Carlin (asst editor), Mark Gruenwald (editor), Josef Rubinstein (c inks)
FEATURE CHARACTER: Captain America (also in thoughts & rfb)
SUPPORTING CAST: Nomad
VILLAINS: Red Skull, Baron Zemo (both chr last in 1985 #6, '08), Mother Superior (both also in Slayer's thoughts & as monsters in hallucination) (all last in Cap #290, '84), robber
OTHER CHARACTERS: Jesus Christ, John F. Kennedy, John Lennon, Abraham Lincoln, assassin (hand only), cavemen, Mayan warriors, priest & sacrifice, Roman Centurions, African slaves, slave trader, Knights of the

crusades, WWI Allied Powers soldier, WWI Central Powers soldier (all as images in Mother Superior's psionic simulation), Peggy Carter, Serpent Squad: Cobra, Eel, Viper (prev 4 in rfb); Sharon Carter (in Cap's thoughts); Dave Cox (as the Slayer, last in Cap #186, '75, also in Cap's thoughts & rfb), Julie Morgan (Dave's wife), Cody Richard Cox-Morgan (Dave's son) (both 1st), Meat-O-Rama owner, police, bystanders
LOCATIONS/ITEMS: Skull-House w/laboratory & gym; Cox Virginia home & surrounding woods, New York inc Meat-O-Rama; Mother Superior's psionic simulator & brainwashing equipment, Avengers quinjet, Red Skull's cane, robber's gun, Cobra's blaster (in rfb), Slayer's shadow cloak & mace (see NOTE)
FLASHBACK: Cap and Peggy Carter meet Dave Cox. The Serpent Squad attacks Dave, who refuses to fight back (Cap #163, '73).
SYNOPSIS: Mother Superior shows Baron Zemo a simulation of mankind's bloody history to prepare him for her father's schemes. In Virginia, Captain America visits old friend Dave Cox and his family. Meanwhile, Red Skull interrupts a sparring session between Zemo and Mother Superior, and then assaults Zemo for questioning him. Dave dissuades Cap's fears that marrying Bernie would disrespect Sharon Carter's memory. Once Cap departs, Mother Superior abducts Dave and brainwashes him into rejecting his pacifistic ideals. The next night, Cap and Nomad discuss Cap's experiences on Battleworld, Bernie's proposal and Dave's pacifism, the latter of which Nomad dismisses as cowardice. The pair intervene in an armed robbery, but Cap angrily and publicly admonishes Nomad for using excessive force. Nomad storms off, and Cap follows only to find Nomad barely conscious on a nearby fire escape. A costumed and bloodthirsty Dave Cox, calling himself the Slayer, attacks Cap. Though the heroes initially fend him off, the Slayer knocks Cap out with his mace, leaving Nomad to face the Slayer alone.
NOTE: Dave Cox's Slayer costume is revealed in Cap #294, '84 to be the same used by Eric Payne as Devil-Slayer. Letters page changes its name to "American Graffiti."

CAPTAIN AMERICA #294 (June 1984)

"The Measure of a Man!" (22 pages)

CREDITS: J.M. DeMatteis (writer), Paul Neary (pencils), Josef Rubinstein (inks), Diana Albers (letters), Bob Sharen (colors), Mike Carlin (asst editor), Mark Gruenwald (editor)
FEATURE CHARACTER: Captain America (also in rfb)
SUPPORTING CAST: Bernie Rosenthal (last in AFlt #10, '84), Nomad (both also in rfb)
VILLAINS: Red Skull, Baron (Helmut) Zemo (also as Phoenix in rfb), Mother Superior (also in rfb) & her Sisters of Sin: Sister Agony, Sister Death, Sister Dream (prev 3 1st but chr last in Cap #298, '84 fb), Sister Pleasure (last in Cap #288, '83), Horst Lederer (last in ToS #79/2, '66)
OTHER CHARACTERS: Dave Cox (as the Slayer, also in rfb), Cody Cox-Morgan (next in Cap #300, '84), Julie Morgan, delivery man, police (bts, discovered that Slayer's costume belonged to the Devil-Slayer); Falcon, Baron (Heinrich) Zemo, Bucky, Arnie Roth, Michael, robber (prev 6 in rfb); Milton Berle (comedian, mentioned by Nomad)
LOCATIONS/ITEMS: New York inc St. Vincent's Hospital, Bernie's Brooklyn Heights apartment, Cox's Virginia home (in rfb), Project: Pegasus (mentioned); Skull-House inc Mother Superior's church, Skull's bedchamber & laboratory (in rfb); Slayer's shadow cloak, mace, blaster, bolas, & scythe, Mother Superior's forcefield, Red Skull's video monitor, cane & miniature mask
FLASHBACKS: Cap meets with Dave Cox, who is captured and tortured by Mother Superior and Baron Zemo. Later as the Slayer, Dave attacks Cap and Nomad, knocking Cap unconscious (Cap #293, '84). Cap and Bucky attempt to stop Heinrich Zemo's drone plane (Av #4, '64 b). Cap and Falcon battle the Phoenix, Helmut Zemo, and inadvertently disfigure his face (Cap #168, '73). Zemo schemes to destroy Cap's private life, resulting in the death of Arnie Roth's boyfriend Michael (Cap #276-279, '83-'84).
SYNOPSIS: As Nomad battles the Slayer, Captain America awakens to find himself trapped inside Mother Superior's forcefield. The Slayer defeats Nomad, but Dave Cox's true personality re-emerges and prevents him from delivering a fatal blow. Mother Superior psionically attacks Dave for his disobedience, rendering him unconscious, and then escapes. Later at a nearby hospital, Dave's wife Julie tearfully tells the two heroes that Dave may have suffered fatal nerve damage. At Skull-House Mother Superior introduces Zemo to her disciples, the Sisters of Sin, unaware that Red Skull watches them via a video linkup in his bedchamber. Steve Rogers tells Bernie that he can't marry her, fearing that his enemies may attack him through her. Bernie refuses to accept that or the idea that super heroes have the monopoly on risk. Bernie's words and a few persistent kisses convince Steve to say yes, but their elation is horrifically cut short by the arrival of a package containing a miniature of the Red Skull's mask.
NOTE: Bernie sings the Eurythmics' "Love is a Stranger" while listening to the song.

CAPTAIN AMERICA #295 (July 1984)

"The Centre Cannot Hold!" (22 pages)

CREDITS: J.M. DeMatteis (writer), Paul Neary (pencils), Brett Breeding (inks), Diana Albers (letters), Bob Sharen (colors), Mike Carlin (asst editor), Mark Gruenwald (editor), Joe Sinnott (c inks)
FEATURE CHARACTER: Captain America (also in illusion)
GUEST STARS: Starfox (last in Thor #351, last bts in Thor #353), Wasp (last in Av #249, last bts in Thor #353, '85)
SUPPORTING CAST: Arnie Roth (last in Cap#292, '84), Bernie Rosenthal (also in illusion), Nomad
VILLAINS: Red Skull, Baron Zemo, Mother Superior & her Sisters of Sin: Sister Agony, Sister Death, Sister Dream, Sister Pleasure
OTHER CHARACTERS: Dave Cox (last in Cap #294, '84 as Slayer), Julie Morgan (also in illusion) (both next in Cap#299, '84), Horst Lederer (as corpse), movie patrons
LOCATIONS/ITEMS: New York inc St. Vincent's Hospital & movie theater, Steve's & Arnie's Brooklyn Heights apartments, Skull-House; Arnie

Roth robots (one as Baron Zemo, one destroyed), Red Skull's cane

SYNOPSIS: As Captain America visits Dave Cox at the hospital, Baron Zemo and Mother Superior kidnap Arnie Roth. Later, Steve meets Bernie and Jack Monroe after a movie, where Bernie notices that Steve looks older. Steve receives a distressed call from Arnie Roth. Rushing to Arnie's apartment, they find a skull burned into the wall and a robot Arnie. The robot announces that Arnie is Red Skull's captive. Red Skull examines the recently deceased Horst as Cap and Nomad enter Skull-House. The Sisters of Sin attack Cap and Nomad, but the heroes are able to outmaneuver the villains. Spying Baron Zemo from afar, Cap savagely attacks only to discover he's actually a disguised Arnie. Horrified, Cap doesn't realize that the walls are closing in until it is too late. Meanwhile, Starfox and Wasp ring Bernie's doorbell, unaware that Mother Superior is kidnapping her on the other side of the door.

NOTE: Arnie as Zemo is revealed to be another robot in Cap #296, '84.

CAPTAIN AMERICA #296 (August 1984)

"Things Fall Apart!" (22 pages)

CREDITS: J.M. DeMatteis (writer), Paul Neary (pencils), Sam DeLarosa (inks), Diana Albers (letters), Bob Sharen (colors), Mike Carlin (asst editor), Mark Gruenwald (editor), Bob Budiansky (c pencils), Tom Mandrake (c inks)
FEATURE CHARACTER: Captain America (also in rfb; next in Cap #350/2, '89 fb)
GUEST STARS: Falcon (last in Falcon #4, '84, chr last in CoH #3, '97, last bts in Av #243, '84), Avengers: Starfox, Wasp (both next in Cap #299, '84)
SUPPORTING CAST: Nomad (also in rfb), Bernie Rosenthal, Arnie Roth
VILLAINS: Red Skull, Baron Zemo (also as Heinrich Zemo), Mother Superior (all chr next in Cap #350/2, '89 fb) & her Sisters of Sin: Sister Pleasure (also in rfb as "Scarlet"), Sister Agony, Sister Death, Sister Dream (prev 4 next in Cap #299, '84)
OTHER CHARACTERS: Horst Lederer (as corpse, last app), Bucky (in Cap's thoughts)
LOCATIONS/ITEMS: Harlem, Bernie's Brooklyn Heights apartment, Skull-House inc Red Skull's bedchamber, Rothkeller Cabaret replica room; Arnie Roth robots (one as Baron Zemo), Red Skull's cane & video monitor, Mother Superior's forcefields, grenade, & poisoned dart, Sister Agony's poisoned claws
FLASHBACKS: Nomad dreams of Cap aging and withering away (Cap #290, '84). "Scarlet" brainwashes Nomad (Cap #288, '83). Jack Monroe unwittingly poisons Steve Rogers' coffee (Cap #292, '84).
SYNOPSIS: The Sisters of Sin attack and capture Falcon atop a Harlem rooftop. Meanwhile, Starfox and Wasp find Bernie's apartment empty and a skull insignia burned into a wall. At Skull-House, Captain America and Nomad are shocked to find the Arnie Roth they had mistaken for Zemo to be yet another robot. A door opens, leading the pair to Horst's body, but as they examine it, a mirror reveals to Cap that he has physically aged decades. Cap and Nomad enter a room decorated like a 1940's-era cabaret, filled with more Arnie robots and Sister Pleasure as a hostess. Nomad blames Sister Pleasure for brainwashing him into drugging Cap with a chemical that rapidly aged the Avenger. Nomad vanishes, and the real Arnie appears on stage. Brainwashed into denouncing his sexuality, Arnie collapses from the strain of fighting his brainwashing. Mother Superior appears, reveals herself to be responsible for Cap's aging and torture and attacks Cap. As they fight Cap tries to reason with her, but she poisons Cap anyway.

NOTE: Cap #350/2, '89 fb reveals that Arnim Zola is present though unseen during this story arc.

CAPTAIN AMERICA #297 (September 1984)

"All My Sins Remembered!" (22 pages)

CREDITS: J.M. DeMatteis (writer), Paul Neary (pencils, c art), Roy Richardson (inks), Diana Albers (letters), Bob Sharen (colors), Mark Gruenwald (editor)
FEATURE CHARACTER: Captain America (also in rfb)
GUEST STAR: Falcon (also in rfb)
SUPPORTING CAST: Nomad (also as Bucky), Bernie Rosenthal, Arnie Roth
VILLAINS: Red Skull, Baron Zemo (Helmut) (also as Heinrich Zemo & in rfb as Phoenix), Mother Superior (all chr last in Cap #350/2, '89 fb)
OTHER CHARACTERS: Baron Zemo (Heinrich), Hilda Zemo, Humanoid (all in rfb)
LOCATIONS/ITEMS: Skull House inc laboratory & dungeon, Allied air base (in simulation); Red Skull's cane & "deus machina" illusion-casting equipment, Adhesive X, Phoenix's gun (both in rfb); Heinrich Zemo's blaster & drone-plane, motorcycle (prev 3 in simulation)
FLASHBACKS: Heinrich Zemo spends time with his family and works in his lab (Cap #168, '73 fb). Captain America shatters a tank of Adhesive X, permanently affixing Heinrich Zemo's mask to his face (Av #6, '73 fb). Helmut cries for his scarred father as his mother holds him back (Cap #168, '73 fb). Cap and Falcon battle the Phoenix, Helmut Zemo, causing him to fall into a vat of Adhesive X (Cap #168, '73).
SYNOPSIS: Mother Superior attacks Baron Zemo for intruding on her defeat of Captain America, but Red Skull interrupts them both and berates his daughter for using cheap deception to best Cap. Meanwhile, as Cap finds himself alongside Bucky, battling Baron Zemo at an Allied air base in 1945, the captive Bernie, Falcon and catatonic Arnie seek to escape Skull-House's dungeon. Mother Superior and Red Skull watch Cap re-experience the worst day of his life, but Zemo and Mother Superior are shocked when Cap prevents "Bucky's" death. Zemo, who was controlling the reenactment via the Skull's "deus machina" device, blames Mother Superior for Cap's victory, but the Skull reveals Cap's will wrested control from Zemo, allowing him the chance to change the past, and is pleased that he can face Cap in their final battle with the hero's heart free of the guilt of his greatest tragedy. Unmasking, Cap demands the Skull reveal his plan, and the Skull unmasks in turn, revealing himself to be just as physically aged as Cap.

CAPTAIN AMERICA #298 (October 1984)

"Sturm und Drang: The Life and Times of the Red Skull!" (23 pages)

CREDITS: J.M. DeMatteis (writer), Paul Neary (pencils, c art), Roy Richardson (inks), Diana Albers (letters), Bob Sharen (colors), Mark Gruenwald (editor)
FEATURE CHARACTER: Captain America (also in rfb)
GUEST STAR: Falcon (also in rfb)
SUPPORTING CAST: Nomad, Bernie Rosenthal, Arnie Roth
VILLAINS: Red Skull (also in fb1 to 1st chr app before & during ToS #66/2, '65 fb, fb2 between ToS #72/2, '65 fb & ToS #79/2, '66 fb, fb3 between #104, '68 & bts in Cap #108, '68, fb4 between AT #5/2, '71 & Cap #143, '71, also in Cap #15, '06 fb, fb5 between SVTU #17, '80 & Cap #350/2, '89 fb, fb6 during Cap #15, '06 fb), Baron Zemo (also in photo), Mother Superior (also in fb4-5 to 1st chr app before Cap #350/2, '89 fb, also in Cap #15, '06 fb; in fb6 during & also in Cap #15, '06 fb) & her Sisters of Sin: Sister Agony, Sister Death, Sister Dream (prev 3 only in fb6 to 1st chr app before Cap #294, '84), Sister Pleasure (only in fb6 to 1st chr app before Cap #287, '83)
OTHER CHARACTERS: Herman and Martha Shmidt (Red Skull's parents, both die, only app), Esther (shopkeeper's daughter, also in rfb; in fb1 after ToS #66/2, '65 fb, dies), doctor (one in fb1, another in fb4), orphans (in fb1), maid (in fb3-4, dies); Adolf Hitler (also in photo), Exiles: Angelo Baldini, Franz Cadavus, Jun Ching, Eric Gruning, Jurgen Hauptmann, Ivan Krushki; 5th Sleeper, Redwing, German citizens, German police, Gestapo chief, Nazis, street thugs, Jewish shopkeeper (prev 15 in rfb)
LOCATIONS/ITEMS: Skull House (also in fb5-6) inc lab, Mother Superior's church (both also in fb6), Rothkeller Cabaret replica room, dungeon & graveyard, Germany inc Shmidt home, orphanage (both in fb1), jail cell (in rfb), barn (in fb1 & rfb), hotel w/Nazi military HQ & Berlin bunker (both in rfb), Sargasso Sea inc Isle of Exiles w/study & bedroom (in fb3); Red Skull's deus machina (also in fb6), cane & video monitors, water basin, bedsheet rope, shovel (prev 3 in fb1), Nazis' guns, manacle, Cosmic Cube (prev 3 in rfb)
FLASHBACKS: 1899: Martha Shmidt dies while giving birth to her son Johann. In a rage, Herman Shmidt tries to kill the child, but the doctor stops him. Herman commits suicide and Johann grows up in various orphanages (1). At age 7, Johann lives a life of petty crime (ToS #66/2, '65 fb) and vagrancy (1). Often in jail, Johann works various menial labor jobs (ToS #66/2, '65 fb). He first experiences a taste for death when he kills a shopkeeper's daughter for spurning his affections (1). Johann Shmidt meets Adolf Hitler while working as a hotel bellboy. Hitler takes Shmidt under his wing, transforming him into the Red Skull (ToS #66/2, '65 fb). Red Skull meets Captain America (ToS #66/2, '65), and is buried alive near WWII's end (ToS #72/2, '65 fb). After spending decades in suspended animation (2), the Skull menaces Cap with the Cosmic Cube (ToS #80, '66), battles Cap with the Exiles (Cap #104, '68), is defeated by Cap and Falcon (Cap #119, '69), unleashes the Fifth Sleeper on Cap (Cap #148, '72) and attacks a blinded Cap (Cap #212, '77). On the Isle of Exiles, Red Skull conceives an heir with a maid (3). Months later, the maid dies in child birth. The Skull almost kills his daughter, disappointed that she isn't a boy, but changes his mind (4). Red Skull fills his daughter with hatred (5). The Skull artificially ages his daughter to adulthood, and teams her with the Sisters of Sin, four also artificially aged orphans. With the gas that maintained his youth wearing off, the Skull considers Zemo as a possible successor (6).
SYNOPSIS: Red Skull sends Mother Superior and Baron Zemo away, ordering them to deposit Nomad in the dungeon with the rest of Captain America's captive friends. Finally alone, Red Skull tells Cap his life story. When Nomad is thrown into the dungeon, he and Falcon quickly engineer their escape. Mother Superior and Zemo separately watch in shock from afar as the Skull denounces them both as unworthy successors. The Skull is surprised in turn that Cap, who has remained silent since the Skull unmasked, pities rather than despises him upon hearing his life story.
NOTE: The rfbs of ToS #80, '66, Cap #104, '68, Cap #119, '69, Cap #148, '72 & Cap #212, '77 comprise a montage of those issues' covers. Herman Shmidt's name is misspelled as "Hermann" once.

CAPTAIN AMERICA #299 (November 1984)

"The Bunker" (23 pages)

CREDITS: J.M. DeMatteis (writer), Paul Neary (pencils, c art), Roy Richardson (inks), Diana Albers (letters), Julianna Ferriter (colors), Mark Gruenwald (editor)
FEATURE CHARACTER: Captain America (also in Black Crow's vision)
GUEST STARS: Avengers: Scarlet Witch (last in Thor #353, '85), Vision (last in WCA #4, '84), Starfox, Wasp (both last in Cap #296, '84) (all next bts in Av #275, '87 fb, next in Cap #301, '85); Jesse Black Crow (last in Cap #292, '84), Falcon
SUPPORTING CAST: Nomad (as Bucky), Bernie Rosenthal
VILLAINS: Red Skull (also in painting & in Black Crow's vision), Baron (Helmut) Zemo (chr next in Av #275, '87 fb, next in SecWar2 #7, '86), Mother Superior (also in video image, next in Cap #301, '85) & her Sisters of Sin: Sister Agony, Sister Death, Sister Dream, Sister Pleasure (prev 4 last in Cap #296, '84, next in Cap #301, '85); Adolf Hitler (trapped in faulty Cosmic Cube, also in photo; last in SVTU #17, '80, chr next in Cap #446, '95 fb, next bts in Cap #445, '95), Immortus (bts, manipulating Vision, last bts in WCA #4, '84, next bts in Cap #301, '85)
OTHER CHARACTERS: Dave Cox, Julie Morgan (both last in Cap #295, '84), ISAAC (bts in contact w/Vision, last bts in WCA #4, '84, next bts in Cap #301, '84), Baron (Heinrich) Zemo (in Helmut Zemo's thoughts), Bing Crosby & Bob Hope (actors, mentioned by Nomad)
LOCATIONS/ITEMS: Skull House inc tunnels, torture chamber, underground bunker & Mother Superior's church, New York inc St. Vincent's Hospital w/Dave Cox's room & Avengers Mansion w/meeting room, Black Crow's Queens apartment; faulty Cosmic Cube, Red Skull's cane & miniature mask, Black Crow's wheelchair

SYNOPSIS: Falcon, Nomad, Bernie, and Arnie search for a way out of Skull-House as Captain America searches for them. Cap passes Red Skull's quarters, not noticing a faulty Cosmic Cube with Hitler trapped inside. Cap locates a subterranean bunker but is sealed inside with Red Skull. Goading Cap into a final battle, the Skull reveals that he injected both of them with a poison that will kill them both within hours. Mother Superior, incensed by her father's denouncement of her, takes her rage out on Baron Zemo. Meanwhile, Julie Morgan watches over Dave Cox, Jesse Black Crow has a vision of Cap and Red Skull and the Avengers mobilize to rescue Cap. The Sisters of Sin attack Cap's friends, but the fight is interrupted by Mother Superior and Baron Zemo's battle. Mother Superior fells Zemo with a psionic attack, then vows to wrest her father's mantle of evil by force. In order to irrevocably push Cap over the edge, the Skull triggers an explosion that seemingly destroys Skull-House and everyone inside. Enraged, Cap attacks the Skull, determined to end his reign of terror.

CAPTAIN AMERICA #300 (December 1984)

"Das Ende!" (22 pages)

CREDITS: J.M. DeMatteis (plot), Michael Ellis (script), Paul Neary (pencils, c inks), Dennis Janke (inks), Diana Albers (letters), Bob Sharen (colors), Howard Mackie (asst editor), Mark Gruenwald (editor), Mike Zeck (c pencils)
FEATURE CHARACTER: Captain America (also in rfb)
GUEST STARS: Falcon (also in rfb & in Cap's thoughts), Black Crow (also in crow form, next in DD #225, '85)
SUPPORTING CAST: Nomad, Arnie Roth (both also in rfb), Bernie Rosenthal (all also in Cap's thoughts)
VILLAIN: Red Skull (also in rfb, dies)
OTHER CHARACTERS: Dave Cox (also in rfb as the Slayer; next bts in Cap #302, '85, next in Cap #49, '09), Cody Cox-Morgan (last in Cap #294, '84, next in Cap #49, '09), Julie Morgan (last app to date); Baron Zemo, Mother Superior & her Sisters of Sin: Sister Agony, Sister Death, Sister Dream, Sister Pleasure (prev 6 in rfb), Native Americans, US Cavalry, Allied soldiers, anti-war protestors (prev 4 in Cap's thoughts)
LOCATIONS/ITEMS: Black Crow's Queens apartment, St. Vincent's Hospital w/Dave Cox's room; Skull-House (also in rfb) inc underground bunker, dungeon, & nearby cemetery, Steve's Brooklyn Heights apartment (in rfb); Black Crow's wheelchair, medicine pouch, & spear, Red Skull's cane, Slayer's shadow cloak & blaster, Arnie Roth robot (as Baron Zemo), Zemo's drone plane (prev 4 in rfb); Liberty Bell (in Cap's thoughts)
FLASHBACKS: Mother Superior recruits Baron Zemo (Cap #290, '84). Jack Monroe poisons Steve Rogers' coffee (Cap #292, '84). Cap and Nomad battle the Slayer (Cap #294, '84). Cap and Nomad are fooled by an Arnie Roth robot, (Cap #295, '84) the real Arnie later collapses (Cap #296, '84). Cap rescues Nomad from a re-enactment of Bucky's death (Cap #297, '84). Red Skull tells Cap his life story (Cap #298, '84). Falcon and Nomad battle the Sisters of Sin, Mother Superior psionically attacks Zemo and Red Skull destroys Skull-House (Cap #299, '84).
SYNOPSIS: Jesse Black Crow has a vision of Captain America's recent troubles and assumes his mystic crow form to fly to his aid. Meanwhile, as Red Skull and a grief-maddened Cap viciously battle one another in the Skull's bunker, Dave Cox's condition worsens as Julie and Cody watch helplessly. Even though the Skull reveals the poison in both of them has no antidote, Cap stops himself from delivering the killing strike, angering the Skull. He begs Cap to kill him, but the Nazi's pleas are silenced as he finally succumbs to the poison's effects and dies in Cap's arms. At that instant, Dave Cox regains consciousness and embraces his thankful family as Black Crow watches from the window. Cap carries the Skull's body above ground and finds that Skull House's destruction was yet another illusion, just as the poison overtakes him. As Black Crow arrives and revives Cap with his mystic abilities, Bernie, Falcon, Nomad, and Arnie escape from Skull-House. Nomad re-enters Skull-House alone and finds Cap still alive. The aged Avenger carries the Skull's corpse outside, remarking that the time to bury the past has finally come.
NOTE: "American Graffiti" features a pin-up of Captain America and Red Skull by Paul Neary.

CAPTAIN AMERICA #301 (January 1985)

"All Good Things..." (22 pages)

CREDITS: Mike Carlin (writer), Paul Neary (pencils, c art), Dennis Janke (inks), Diana Albers (letters), Bob Sharen (colors), Howard Mackie (asst editor), Mark Gruenwald (editor)
FEATURE CHARACTER: Captain America (also in rfb, in fb between Av #145, '76 fb & Av #25, '66; next in Av #251, '85, UXM #190-191, '85, MFan #18, '85, MFan #29/2, '86)
GUEST STARS: Avengers: Captain Marvel, Hercules (both last in Thor #353, '85, last bts in Av #275, '87 fb), Hawkeye (also in rfb & in fb between Av #145, '76 fb & Av #25, '66; last in WCA #4, '84), Wasp (also in rfb), Scarlet Witch, Starfox, Vision (prev 4 last in Cap #299, '84, last bts in Av #275, '87 fb) (all next in Av #250, '84); Falcon (next in PMIF #112, '84), Dr. Hank Pym (also in rfb as Giant-Man; last in Av Ann #13, '84, next in IM #194, '85)
SUPPORTING CAST: Nomad (also as Bucky, next in MTU #146, '84), Bernie Rosenthal (both also in rfb), Arnie Roth
VILLAINS: Red Skull (as corpse, also in Bernie's thoughts; chr next in Cap #350/2, '89, next bts in Cap #326, '87, next in Cap #346, '88), Mother Superior & her Sisters of Sin: Sister Agony (next as Slash in Cap #355, '89), Sister Death (next as Torso in Cap #356, '89), Sister Dream (next as Hoodwink in Cap #356, '89), Sister Pleasure (next as Raunch in Cap #355, '89) (prev 5 last in Cap #299, '84) (all also in rfb); Immortus (bts, manipulating Vision, next bts in Av #250, '84)
OTHER CHARACTERS: Edwin Jarvis (last in Thor #345, '84, next in MTU #148, '84), ISAAC (bts in contact w/Vision, next bts in Av #250, '84); Iron Man, Sub-Mariner, Thor, Dr. Abraham Erskine, Eskimos, Nazis (prev 6 in rfb), Baron Zemo, Primus (both in Bernie's thoughts)
LOCATIONS/ITEMS: Avengers Mansion inc gym (in fb & rfb) & Medical Facility, Skull-House; Avengers Quinjet, Dr. Pym's equipment, Red Skull's deus machina, Super-Soldier Serum (in rfb)
FLASHBACKS: Captain America and Nomad battle the Sisters of Sin and Bernie notices Steve's rapid aging (Cap #295, '84). Cap fights Red Skull to the death (Cap #300, '84). Cap trains Sam Wilson to fight (Cap #117, '69). Dr. Erskine injects Steve Rogers with the Super-Soldier Serum (CapC #1, '41). Cap fights Nazis (Cap #259, '81 fb). Sub-Mariner finds and frees the frozen Cap. Cap is found by and joins the Avengers

(Av #4, '64). Steve meets Bernie (Cap #248, '80). Cap shows off for Bernie (Cap #290, '84). Steve and Bernie go holiday shopping (Cap #292, '84). Cap trains Hawkeye to fight.

SYNOPSIS: Captain America gives Red Skull's body to Mother Superior, commenting that he belongs with family. Leaving Skull-House, Cap and Nomad are reunited with Falcon, Bernie and Arnie as the Avengers arrive. Returning to Avengers Mansion, the Avengers look into methods to rejuvenate the aged Captain. Meanwhile, Mother Superior and her Sisters of Sin give the Red Skull a hate filled funeral pyre. As Dr. Pym takes medical readings of Cap, Hercules and Starfox arrive with the Skull's deus machina device. Vision assembles the machinery and starts the process, but the radiation treatment is interrupted when Mother Superior and her Sisters of Sin attack. Despite Cap's attempts at reason a savage battle ensues. The Avengers can only watch; if they intervene it could disrupt the de-aging process. When the Vision announces the procedure is over, Bernie opens the door to find the Sisters of Sin reverted to children and Captain America hearty and whole.

CAPTAIN AMERICA #302 (February 1985)

"...And Other Strangers!" (22 pages)

CREDITS: Mike Carlin (writer), Paul Neary (pencils, c art), Dennis Janke (inks), Diana Albers (letters), Ken Feduniewicz (colors), Howard Mackie (asst editor), Mark Gruenwald (editor)
FEATURE CHARACTER: Captain America (also in rfb & off-panel in pfb)
SUPPORTING CAST: Nomad (also in Cap's thoughts, last in MTU #146, '84), Arnie Roth (bts, recovering from shock, next in Cap #306, '85), Bernie Rosenthal (also in pfb)
VILLAINS: Batroc (last in Cap #252, '80, chr last in 1985 #6, '08) & his Brigade: Machete (Ferdinand Lopez, bladed weapons master, 1st), Zaran (Maximillian Zaran, weapons master, also in rfb; last in MKF #109, '82) (both also in Cap #304, '85 fb); Mother Superior (bts, in custody of juvenile authorities, next as Sin in Cap #355, '89), Obadiah Stane (bts, ordered Cap's shield stolen, last in IM #190, '85), Richard Arons (bts, hired Batroc, 1st)
OTHER CHARACTERS: Dave Cox (bts, due for release from hospital, next in Cap #49, '09), Richie, Tony & "Woim" (3 service station attendants, 1st, next in Cap #325, '87); Red Skull, Shang-Chi (both in rfb), San Diablo revolutionaries (in Machete's thoughts)
LOCATIONS/ITEMS: Brooklyn Heights inc Steve's apartment, service station & wharf, Batroc's warehouse HQ, Brooklyn Bridge; Cap's motorcycle & makeshift shield-painting setup, Machete's knives, machetes, magnetic gauntlets & pocketed flak jacket & boots, Zaran's sais & bo staff/spear/blow gun
FLASHBACKS: Red Skull dies in Cap's arms (Cap #300, '84). Cap regains his youth (Cap #301, '85). Shang-Chi defeats Zaran (MKF #109, '82). Bernie admires her new engagement ring (p).
SYNOPSIS: Captain America picks up his motorcycle from storage. Machete, a South American master of bladed weapons, attacks Captain America to test his mettle. Realizing he's no match for Cap, Machete creates a distraction and retreats. Later at his apartment, Steve chats with Bernie before heading out on patrol with Nomad. Meanwhile Machete reports to Batroc, who sends Machete back out with Zaran, another weapons master, to find the hero. While on patrol, Cap and Nomad encounter Machete and Zaran. In the ensuing skirmish, Zaran separates Cap from his shield. Machete grabs Nomad and threatens to kill him, forcing Cap to let the villains go. While Nomad wastes time apologizing, Cap realizes that the villains took his shield.

CAPTAIN AMERICA #303 (March 1985)

"Double Dare!" (22 pages)

CREDITS: Mike Carlin (writer), Paul Neary (pencils, c art), Dennis Janke (inks), Diana Albers (letters), Ken Feduniewicz (colors), Howard Mackie (asst editor), Mark Gruenwald (editor)
FEATURE CHARACTER: Captain America (also in rfb; also in fb between Cap:SoL #7/2, '99 & Cap #12, '05 fb)
SUPPORTING CAST: Josh Cooper (last in Cap #285, '83, next in Cap #317, '86), Bernie Rosenthal (next in Cap #305, '85), Nomad (also in rfb)
VILLAINS: Batroc (next in AvS #3, '88) & his Brigade: Machete (next in AvS #3, '88), Zaran (also in rfb; next in WCA #11, '86) (all also as "Mark's Oldtime Pizza" deliverymen); Obadiah Stane (malicious head of Stane International), Richard Arons (Stane International employee, 1st actual app)
OTHER CHARACTERS: Gen. Phillips (only in fb between Av Ann '01/2 fb & Cap #12, '05 fb), Dr. Myron MacLean (scientist/metallurgist, also in fb to 1st chr app before Cap #21, '99 fb & between Av Ann '01/2 fb & W #-1, '97; last in Av #68, '69), McClain's wife & son (bts, being held hostage by Arons), US military officer, US government official (both only in fb), bartender, bar patrons, alley cat
LOCATIONS/ITEMS: Brooklyn Heights inc Steve's & Bernie's Brooklyn Heights apartments, Stane International Long Island facility inc Lab 16 & parking lot; US government lab (only in fb), Long Island City bar; Captain America's original steel shield, Vibranium, crucible (both in fb), Batroc's car, Steve's portfolio; Stane International electron microscope, lab laser, laser door & video monitor
FLASHBACKS: Captain America and Nomad fight Zaran (Cap #302, '85). Working to create a super-strong tank metal for the U.S. government during World War II, Dr. MacLain successfully bonds Vibranium to a steel alloy and pours the metal into a disc-shaped mold, but he is unable to replicate the process. He soon discovers that the government has given the disc to Captain America to use as a shield.
SYNOPSIS: Captain America and Nomad return home to tell Bernie that Cap's shield has been stolen. The next day, disguised as pizza deliverymen, Batroc's Brigade sells Captain America's shield to Stane International, where Richard Arons is coercing Dr. Myron MacLain, the shield's creator, into trying to replicate the indestructible material the shield is made from. To celebrate their victory Batroc's Brigade gets drunk, and Machete and Zaran taunt Batroc over his inability to defeat Cap solo. Seeking to prove himself, Batroc finds and challenges Cap. As he pummels the inebriated Batroc, Cap is surprised to see Machete and Zaran laughing at their leader. Anxious to retrieve his shield, Cap offers Batroc a free shot at him in exchange for information about the shield's location. Batroc takes it, sending the hero flying, but to the mercenaries' surprise, Cap weathers the blow and wins anyway. Machete and Zaran flee, and Cap resolves to get his shield from Stane.
NOTE: Arons' 1st name revealed in AvA #1, '10.

CAPTAIN AMERICA #304 (April 1985)

"Undercover of the Night" (22 pages)

CREDITS: Mike Carlin (writer), Paul Neary (pencils, c art), Dennis Janke (inks), Diana Albers (letters), Ken Feduniewicz (colors), Howard Mackie (asst editor), Mark Gruenwald (editor)
FEATURE CHARACTER: Captain America (also as Australian Munitions representative "Anthony Schwarz" & in rfb; next in Av #252-255, '85, Rom #65-66, '85)
GUEST STAR: Nick Fury (last in PMIF #113, '85, chr next in W/NF:SC, '89, next in Cap #309, '85)
SUPPORTING CAST: Nomad
VILLAINS: Obadiah Stane (next in IM #194, '85), Richard Arons (last app), Machete, Zaran (both only in fb during Cap #302, '85)
OTHER CHARACTERS: Myron MacLain (next in AWC #89, '92), Miss Rudolph (Obadiah Stane's secretary, only app), SHIELD security force, Stane International employees & security guards; Batroc (in rfb)
LOCATIONS/ITEMS: SHIELD's New York HQ inc hologram wall entrance, Stane International's Long Island facility inc elevator, front gates, Lab 16 & Obadiah Stane's office, Myron MacLain's home; alloy created by MacLain, ersatz shields, Arons' gun, Cap's motorcycle, security guards' flashlight, guns, nightstick & radiophone, Stane Industries alarms, crucible, girders, instrument panel, intercom, suit of armor & video monitor, SHIELD firearms, monitor screen & surveillance devices
FLASHBACKS: Cap stands over the defeated Batroc (Cap #303, '85). Machete and Zaran flee with Captain America's shield.
SYNOPSIS: Captain America consults with Nick Fury, hoping the SHIELD director will arrange for Dr. MacLain to make him a temporary shield, but they discover that MacLain is missing, his home ransacked. After studying Cap's shield at Stane International, MacLain produces an alloy approximating it. He tries to kill his captor, Arons, with the molten alloy, but Arons protects himself with the shield. In disguise, Cap meets Obadiah Stane and learns that Stane is working on an impervious metal in one of his labs. Infiltrating Stane International, Nomad creates a diversion as Cap raids the lab. Arons dons an armor covered with MacLain's new alloy to fight Cap. MacLain tosses Cap his shield and the Avenger uses it to defeat Arons. Cap and Nomad flee Stane International with the freed MacLain.
NOTE: "American Graffiti" includes LOC from future fiction writer Adam-Troy Castro.

CAPTAIN AMERICA #305 (May 1985)

"Walk upon England!" (22 pages)

CREDITS: Mike Carlin (writer), Paul Neary (pencils, c art), Dennis Janke (inks), Diana Albers (letters), Ken Feduniewicz (colors), Howard Mackie (asst editor), Mark Gruenwald (editor)
FEATURE CHARACTER: Captain America
GUEST STAR: Captain Britain (Brian Braddock, British adventurer, also in pfb; last in Rom #65, '85, last bts in Rom #66, '85)
SUPPORTING CAST: Bernie Rosenthal (also in photo), Nomad
VILLAINS: Modred the Mystic (6th-century English mage, also as Captain Britain; also in pfb; last in VSW #4, '83), 3 thieves
OTHER CHARACTERS: Janitor, train driver, commuters, deli owner; Captain Clean, plague pixies (both in ad)
LOCATIONS/ITEMS: Steve's Brooklyn Heights apartment, Brooklyn inc deli; Heathrow Airport inc restroom, London inc Big Ben's Clocktower, Post Office Tower, St. Paul's Cathedral, Tower Bridge, River Thames & dungeon, abandoned Cumbrian castle (in pfb); British Airways plane, tube train, radar dish, Steve's portfolio, ad & note, shackles
FLASHBACK: Modred the Mystic returns to England, regains his powers and memory, attacks Captain Britain, and retrieves the hero's mystic body armor after Captain Britain sends it to Steve Rogers for safekeeping (p).
SYNOPSIS: As Steve Rogers works on an overdue advertising assignment, a costume adorned with a British flag momentarily appears on him. Intrigued, Steve drops everything and leaves for England. Meanwhile, Nomad foils a robbery, but is chagrined to be mistaken for Captain America. Arriving in London, Captain America begins searching the city, only to be attacked and eventually overpowered by Captain Britain, wearing the costume that brought Steve to the UK. Cap awakens chained in a dungeon alongside an underwear-clad man, the real Captain Britain; Cap's attacker reveals himself to be Modred, and announces his intention to summon and dispose of the wizard Merlin.
NOTE: This is the 1st US comics app of Captain Britain's red, white and blue suit, which he has worn in UK comics since MSH #377, '81. Cap jumps on a Victoria Line train at Heathrow; however, only the Piccadilly Line services Heathrow.

CAPTAIN AMERICA #306 (June 1985)

"The Summoning!" (22 pages)

CREDITS: Mike Carlin (writer), Paul Neary (pencils, c art), Dennis Janke (inks), Diana Albers (letters), Ken Feduniewicz (colors), Howard Mackie (asst editor), Mark Gruenwald (editor)
FEATURE CHARACTER: Captain America
GUEST STAR: Captain Britain
SUPPORTING CAST: Arnie Roth (last in Cap #301, '85, last bts in Cap #302, '85, next in Cap #431, '94), Nomad, Bernie Rosenthal
VILLAINS: Modred the Mystic (next in Q #11, '90), jewel thief, reanimated Tower of London corpses
OTHER CHARACTERS: Merlin (as psychic projection, chr last in DDs #2, '83, chr next in DDs #9, '83, next in Ex:P, '91), London citizens, Wayne (Arnie's uncle in Florida, mentioned only, Arnie will move in with him)

LOCATIONS/ITEMS: Brooklyn Heights inc video store & "Jewel Box" jewelry store; London inc St. Paul's Cathedral, Tower Bridge, subterranean corridors, Tower of London & its cemetery, Tower of the Darkhold (in rfb), Bernie's Greenwich Village "Glass Managerie" shop; Darkhold (book of dark magic, in rfb), medieval weapons, Modred's shackles & wall stone, corpses' shields, swords & maces

FLASHBACKS: In the age of Camelot, Modred, suspicious of Merlin, refuses to become the wizard's apprentice, is overwhelmed by the book of the Darkhold and spends centuries in a death-like trance (MChil #1, '75). Modred is used as a pawn of the demon Chthon (Av #185, '79).

SYNOPSIS: Modred unsuccessfully tries to coax Merlin from Otherworld by laying siege to London. In Greenwich Village, Arnie visits Bernie's shop to say he's moving in with his uncle Wayne in Florida. In London, Captains America and Britain escape their dungeon prison. In Brooklyn Heights, Nomad's confidence builds as he stops another robbery. Meanwhile, Captain Britain tells Modred that only he can summon Merlin and that he needs his body armor to do so. Modred returns the armor to Captain Britain, who fails to summon Merlin. Feeling deceived, Modred animates corpses from the Tower of London cemetery to battle the two heroes. The Captains defeat the corpses and knock Modred unconscious by turning his power back on himself. Merlin appears in a ghostly form and transports Modred to Otherworld, saying he will attempt to reeducate Modred.

NOTE: Hulk #210, '77 revealed Modred's misplaced distrust of Merlin stems from the evil Maha Yogi's impersonation of the Arthurian wizard.

CAPTAIN AMERICA #307 (July 1985)

"Stop Making Sense" (22 pages)

CREDITS: Mark Gruenwald (writer), Paul Neary (pencils, c art), Dennis Janke (inks), Diana Albers (letters), Ken Feduniewicz (colors), Michael Higgins (asst editor), Mike Carlin (editor)
FEATURE CHARACTER: Captain America (next in SecWar2 #1, '85)
GUEST STAR: Captain Britain (chr next in DDs #5, '83, next in CB #7, '85)
SUPPORTING CAST: Nomad (next in Cap #309, '85), Bernie Rosenthal
VILLAINS: Madcap (regenerating anarchist, 1st but chr last in Cap #309, '85 fb, next in Cap #309, '85), Anaconda (Blanche Sitznski, extendable arms, chr last in IML #8, '11), Black Mamba (Tanya Sealy, manipulates darkforce), Death Adder (Roland Burroughs, poison claws) (prev 3 former Serpent Squad members, last in IM #160, '82)
OTHER CHARACTERS: Anne Brennan (last in Cap #292, '84, next in Cap #310, '85), Mr. Menzies (grocery store manager), grocery store staff (Carmela & Jim named), Raoul (Carmela's boyfriend), airplane crew & commuters, costume shop owner, police, bystanders, dog, Invaders: Bucky, Human Torch, Sub-Mariner, Toro (prev 4 in Cap's thoughts)
LOCATIONS/ITEMS: Heathrow Airport, Steve's Brooklyn Heights apartment, New York inc Ace Costume Shop, Glass Menagerie, grocery store, Roosevelt hospital, subway, Sidewinder's apartment; Madcap's bubble gun, Cap's Avengers ID, Iron Man & Hulk masks
SYNOPSIS: Captain Britain gives Captain America a lift to Heathrow, where Cap catches a flight home. In Brooklyn, Bernie admonishes Nomad to find a job. Elsewhere, a man with a bubble gun breaks into a costume shop and drives the owner crazy, then selects an outfit. Jack goes to a grocery store and obtains a job as a bagboy. At the Glass Menagerie, Bernie learns that with her lease up, her rent will increase by three hundred percent, effectively putting her out of business. Madcap drives people in the streets crazy. Jack works at the grocery store until Madcap's riot reaches the store. Jack abandons his job to fight Madcap as Nomad, but the impervious-to-pain Madcap drives Nomad crazy. Later when Madcap's effect wears off, Jack returns to work only to be fired and to discover a girl he likes already has a boyfriend. Elsewhere, Anaconda, Death Adder and Black Mamba break into their ex-employer, Sidewinder's apartment looking for a confrontation.

CAPTAIN AMERICA #308 (August 1985)

"The Body in Question" (22 pages)

CREDITS: Mark Gruenwald (writer), Paul Neary (pencils), Dennis Janke (inks), Diana Albers (letters), Ken Feduniewicz (colors), Michael Higgins (asst editor), Mike Carlin (editor), John Byrne (c pencils)
FEATURE CHARACTER: Captain America
GUEST STARS: Avengers: Hawkeye, Mockingbird (both last in IM #195, '85, next in IM #200, '85), Wonder Man (bts, preparing for his movie's premiere, last in Av #255, '85, chr next in MGN:ED, '87, next in WCA #1, '85)
SUPPORTING CAST: Bernie Rosenthal
VILLAINS: Armadillo (Antonio Rodriguez, mutated into humanoid armadillo by Dr. Malus, 1st, also in pfb, also in SenSH #30, '91, next in Cap #316, '86), Dr. Karl Malus (criminal scientist, also in pfb, last in IM Ann #7, '84, chr next in Cap #328, '87 fb, next in Thing #35, '86), Goliath (last in IM Ann #7, '84, next in WCA #1, '85), Sidewinder (Seth Voelker, teleporter, former Serpent Squad leader, last in MTIO #66, '80, chr last in IML #8, '11), Black Mamba (next in Cap #310, '85), Anaconda, Death Adder
OTHER CHARACTERS: Beyonder (extradimensional entity, last in NM #30, '85, next in UXM #196, '85), Bonita Rodriguez (Armadillo's wife, 1st, next in Cap #316, '86), bystanders (Amy named), doctors (in pfb), Asp (see note), Cobra, Constrictor, Princess Python (prev 4 as photographs)
LOCATIONS/ITEMS: Avengers Compound inc gas, stun gun & cage w/net traps, Steve's Brooklyn Heights apartment, Eagle Warehouse, Sidewinder's apartment, Dr. Malus' lab (also in pfb), Rodriguez home (in pfb); Hawkeye's bow & arrows inc bola arrow, Avengers Quinjet, Dr. Malus' shrinking capsule, Bonita's life support container (also in pfb)
FLASHBACK: Antonio Rodriguez returns home from a short prison sentence to find his wife inexplicably paralyzed. Desperate to help her, he makes a deal with Dr. Malus to become a test subject, transformed via gene splicing into the Armadillo. Malus sends the Armadillo to break Goliath out of the Avengers Compound (p).
SYNOPSIS: Captain America visits the Avengers Compound in Los Angeles, easily dodging the security systems. Hawkeye gives Cap a tour of the grounds then leaves with Mockingbird to attend the opening of Wonder Man's new movie. The Armadillo breaks into the Compound. Cap confronts him, eventually trapping him in a security net. Hearing Armadillo's story, Cap lets him loose and takes him to Goliath. Armadillo

had hoped to shrink him down for transport, but Dr. Malus' shrinking capsule was broken during the fight. Cap lets Armadillo return to Malus but secretly follows him. Bernie checks Steve's apartment to find Jack Monroe has moved out. Cap confronts Dr. Malus, but Malus threatens to kill Bonita if Cap comes near him. Cap outfoxes Malus and breaks his arm, and tells Armadillo to hold Malus until the police arrive. Having secretly observed the day's events and impressed by Cap's actions, the Beyonder adopts a body based on Cap's form. At Sidewinder's apartment, the ex-Serpent Squad members confront Sidewinder. He pays them for their previous job, explains he's been looking into new opportunities, and promises that their next operation will be much bigger.

NOTE: Asp appears as a photo here, making her 1st actual app in Cap #310, '85. Armadillo's first name revealed in OHMU:DE #1, '85.

CAPTAIN AMERICA #309 (September 1985)

"Nomad Madcap Cap..." (22 pages)

CREDITS: Mark Gruenwald (writer), Paul Neary (pencils), Dennis Janke (inks), Diana Albers (letters), Ken Feduniewicz (colors), Michael Higgins (asst editor), Mike Carlin (editor)
FEATURE CHARACTER: Captain America (next in MGN:ED, '87, Av #256-258, '85, ASM #270, '85)
GUEST STARS: Nick Fury (last in Cap #304, '85, chr last in W/NF:SC, '89, next in MGN #18, '85), Sam Wilson (last in PMIF #113, '85, next in PMIF#121, '86), Wasp (bts in fb2, lets Nomad use Avengers computers, between Av #255, '85 & MGN:ED, '87)
SUPPORTING CAST: Nomad (also in rfb & fb2, chr next in Cap #325, '87 fb, next in Cap #324, '86), Bernie Rosenthal (also in rfb)
VILLAINS: Madcap (also in fb1 to 1ˢᵗ chr app before Cap #307, '85; last in Cap #307, '85, next in DD #234, '86), Coney Island Cruisers (George, Lou, Murray & Tony, others last in Cap #240, '79, last app), AIM agents (in fb1, Agent 17 named), Cobra (last in PPSSM #88, '84, chr last in IML #8, '11), Princess Python (last in Hulk #292, '84), Constrictor (last in MTIO #96, '83), Anaconda, Death Adder, Sidewinder
OTHER CHARACTERS: Edwin Jarvis (also in fb2, last in Thor #356, '85, chr next in MGN:ED, '87, next in PP #15, '85), Arthur Bennett (last in Cap #292, '84, next in Cap #317, '86), Shelia Donohue (last in Cap #275, '82, last bts in Cap #277, '83, last app), Ma's Diner waitress, Katy (Madcap's sister), Madcap's parents, church group (prev 3 in fb1, die), doctors, nurses (both in fb1)
LOCATIONS/ITEMS: Coney Island, Avengers Mansion (also in fb2) inc gym, Steve's Brooklyn Heights apartment, Bennett Advertising Agency, Ryker's Island, Shamrock Bar, Ma's Diner, hospital (in fb1), costume shop (in rfb); Madcap's bubble gun, Cap's motorcycle, Murray's blackjack, Lou's knife
FLASHBACKS: Bernie has a tense meeting with Jack (Cap #307, '85). A church group traveling by bus is struck by a truck carrying experimental chemicals made by AIM. Only one man survives but he's driven insane from the ordeal; he tries to kill himself, but finds the chemicals have left him able to instantly regenerate any injury. He gets a costume and becomes Madcap (Cap #307, '85). Nomad visits Avengers Mansion to ask for help finding Madcap; Jarvis suggests looking for him in an amusement park (2).
SYNOPSIS: Madcap encounters the Coney Island Cruisers at Coney Island and drives them insane. Entering his hideout, he finds Nomad waiting for him. Steve returns to his apartment where Bernie catches him up on current events. At Coney Island, Nomad claims to sympathize with Madcap and learns his origin. Meanwhile, Sidewinder teleports into Ryker's Island and releases Cobra, Death Adder finds Princess Python in Oshkosh, Wisconsin and Anaconda recruits Constrictor at a Pittsburgh bar. The next day, Steve goes to Bennett's office and amicably terminates his freelance career. After finding no leads from Nick Fury and Falcon on Nomad's whereabouts, Cap gets a tip from Jarvis. Nomad follows as Madcap expresses his philosophy of no inhibitions and uses his powers on locals. Nomad tries to stop Madcap by stealing his bubble gun, only to find Madcap's madness power is innate, the gun merely a prop. Cap arrives on the scene but hangs back to let Nomad win. Nomad realizes Madcap can only affect people through eye contact and defeats him. Nomad suggests to the arriving Cap that he work solo from now on, grateful to Cap for his help but ready to be on his own.
NOTE: Coney Island Cruisers members are named for Marvel Index pioneers George Olshevsky, Lou Mougin, Murray Ward and Tony Frutti.

CAPTAIN AMERICA #310 (October 1985)

"Serpents of the World Unite!" (22 pages)

CREDITS: Mark Gruenwald (writer), Paul Neary (pencils), Dennis Janke (inks), Diana Albers (letters), Ken Feduniewicz (colors), Michael Higgins (asst editor), Mike Carlin (editor)
FEATURE CHARACTER: Captain America (also on comic book cover & in dfb)
GUEST STARS: Starfox (last in Av #258, '85, next in VSW #1, '85), Black Knight (last in Av #258, '85, chr last in MWoM #13, '84, next in Av #259, '85)
SUPPORTING CAST: Bernie Rosenthal
VILLAINS: Serpent Society (1ˢᵗ): Sidewinder (leader), Diamondback (Rachel Leighton, uses throwing diamonds), Rattler (Gustav Krueger, has bionic sonic tail) (both 1st but chr last in IML #8, '11), Asp (Cleopatra Nefertiti, has venom-blast powers, 1st), Bushmaster (Quincy McIver, has snake-like cyborg body, 1st but chr last in Cap Ann #10/2, '91 fb), Cottonmouth (Burchell Clemens, has bionic jaw, 1st but chr last in CoH #3, '97), Anaconda (also in dfb), Black Mamba (last in Cap #308, '85), Cobra, Death Adder, Princess Python; Constrictor
OTHER CHARACTERS: Edwin Jarvis (last in Av #258, '85, chr last in IM #202, '86 fb, next in Av #259, '85), Anne Brennan (last in Cap #307, '85, last app), Armand (Anne's boyfriend), Wilburn (Sidewinder's butler, 1ˢᵗ, next in Cap #315, '86), Joe ("Mc And S" Bar bartender), "Mc And S" Bar patrons, police (in dfb), newsstand vendor, reporter, commuters, bystanders, Thor (on comic book cover)
LOCATIONS/ITEMS: Avengers Mansion inc gym, Glass Menagerie, hotel, Steve's Brooklyn Heights apartment, Brand Corporation Long Island plant, "Mc And S" Bar; Cap's motorcycle, Serpent Society van, Brand equipment, Constrictor's coils, Cobra's wrist-shooters, Rattler's bionic tail, copies of Captain America, Thor & Avengers comic books

FLASHBACK: Anaconda is taken into police custody (d).

SYNOPSIS: Captain America defeats Starfox and Black Knight in a training exercise. Steve overhears two boys talking about comics on the subway and wonders if he could draw comic books. Steve helps Bernie and Anne pack up the out of business Glass Menagerie. At a hotel, Sidewinder convenes a meeting with all the serpent-themed villains he's gathered and proposes the Serpent Society, a profit-sharing criminal organization with benefits. The Constrictor opts out but spies on the hotel, alerting the Avengers to the team's location so that the Serpents don't compete with him. When the Serpents start leaving the hotel, Constrictor tails them. Steve practices his art and arranges an interview at Marvel Comics. Cap responds to Constrictor's alert and arrives at a Brand Corporation plant at Long Island, battling Cobra, Rattler and Anaconda as they steal equipment. Cap defeats Anaconda but the others escape, reporting the incident to Sidewinder. Later, a freed Anaconda gets revenge on Constrictor by luring him into an alleyway and pummeling him, telling him not to cross the Serpent Society.

NOTE: Asp's first name revealed in Cap #369, '90, last name in Cap #385/2, '91. Bushmaster's real name revealed in Cap Ann #10/2, '91. Cottonmouth's real name revealed in OHMU #10, '09. Diamondback's real name revealed in OHMU:DE #3, '86. Rattler's real name revealed in OHMU:DE #10, '86.

CAPTAIN AMERICA #311 (November 1985)

"Working..." (22 pages)

CREDITS: Mark Gruenwald (writer), Paul Neary (pencils), Dennis Janke (inks), Diana Albers (letters), Ken Feduniewicz (colors), Michael Higgins (asst editor), Mike Carlin (editor), Joe Rubinstein (c inks)
FEATURE CHARACTER: Captain America (next in Av #259-260, Av Ann #14, FF Ann #19, Av #261, SecWar2 #4-5, all '85)
SUPPORTING CAST: Bernie Rosenthal
VILLAINS: Serpent Society: Sidewinder (leader), Anaconda (both also in rfb), Asp, Black Mamba, Cobra, Cottonmouth, Death Adder, Princess Python, Rattler (all next in Cap #313, '86), Bushmaster, Diamondback; Scourge (super villain serial killer, disguised as "nurse Emmett," last in MA Ann #1, '85, next in WCA #3, '85), Constrictor (also in rfb, next in FF #333, '89), Awesome Android (also in rfb & fb, last in Rom #14, '81, next in Av #286, '87), Mad Thinker (only in fb between Rom #14, '81 & Cap #269, '82; also in rfb), Kingpin (also in photo, last in SecWar2 #3, '85, next in ASM Ann #18, '85) & his men, AIM's inner council (five agents, one other in photo)
OTHER CHARACTERS: Mike Carlin (Marvel editor), Michael Higgins (Marvel assistant editor) (both 1st, next in Cap #314, '86), Bobby Hutchinson (child, 1st, next in Av #286, '87), Mr. Hutchinson (Bobby's father), doctor, police, Rom (on comic book cover & in rfb), MODOK, Hydra, Maggia, Secret Empire, Zodiac (prev 5 in photo), Thing (on poster), Spider-Man (on Marvel logo)
LOCATIONS/ITEMS: Marvel Comics Manhattan office, St. Vincent's Hospital, Serpent Society HQ, Steve's Brooklyn Heights apartment, Kingpin's office, AIM base, a barn near Dayton, Ohio; Scourge's gun, Scourge's nurse disguise, Avengers Quinjet, Bushmaster's wheelchair
FLASHBACKS: Constrictor declines the Serpent Society's offer and gives the Avengers an anonymous tip. Cap fights Anaconda, who later beats up Constrictor (Cap #310, '85). Rom reprogrammed the Awesome Android, turning him against the Mad Thinker (Rom #14, '81). The Mad Thinker sent the Android away, telling him to keep out of his sight (after Rom #14, '81).
SYNOPSIS: Captain America visits Constrictor in the hospital, but the villain refuses to identify his assailant. A nurse shoots Constrictor; Cap deflects her aim so Constrictor is only wounded but the nurse escapes. Steve visits Marvel Comics where editor Mike Carlin offers him the art duties on the Captain America comic. While there, Steve obtains a letter asking for Cap's help. The Serpent Society gather at their new base and Sidewinder orders them to spread the word about their organization to other criminal enterprises. Cap investigates the letter and journeys to Dayton, Ohio, where he meets young Bobby Hutchinson. Bobby directs him to a deserted barn. Inside, Cap finds the Awesome Android, but no evidence of the robot's master. Asp and Cottonmouth leave their business card with the Kingpin. After an inconclusive battle, Cap realizes that the Awesome Android is on standby, guarding the barn until he receives new orders. Cap tells Bobby to keep an eye on the barn in case the situation changes. Diamondback and Bushmaster meet with AIM and receive an assignment: murder MODOK!

CAPTAIN AMERICA #312 (December 1985)

"Deface the Nation" (22 pages)

CREDITS: Mark Gruenwald (writer), Paul Neary (pencils), Dennis Janke (inks), Diana Albers (letters), Ken Feduniewicz (colors), Michael Higgins (asst editor), Mike Carlin (editor), Bob Layton (c inks)
FEATURE CHARACTER: Captain America (next in Av #262, '85)
SUPPORTING CAST: Bernie Rosenthal
VILLAINS: Flag-Smasher (Karl Morgenthau, anti-nationalist, 1st, also in pfb, next in Cap #321, '86), Diamondback, Bushmaster
OTHER CHARACTERS: Michele March (reporter, 1st, next in Cap #317, '86), Ms. Steckley (telecommunications consultant), UN security guards (Jake named), Ambassador Morgenthau (Flag-Smasher's father, in photo & pfb), Flag-Smasher's childhood classmates & martial arts trainer, protestors (prev 3 in pfb), mailman, banker, public relations specialists, IBM employees, renovators, various reporters, cameramen, police SWAT team, bystanders
LOCATIONS/ITEMS: UN Building, Stars & Stripes office, Steve's Brooklyn Heights apartment, deserted AIM base near Maine, Acme Flag Company warehouse, Flag-Smasher's Park Avenue penthouse, Municipal Convention Center; Flag-Smasher's jetcycle, mace, incendiary bomb & flame thrower, Diamondback's trick diamonds (1st) & time bomb, Stars & Stripes computers, Steve's back pay check
FLASHBACKS: Karl Morgenthau spent his childhood traveling around the world with his father, a Swiss ambassador. After his father died during a "peaceful" protest outside the Latverian Embassy, Karl became anti-nationalist (p).
SYNOPSIS: Flag-Smasher attacks the UN at night, destroying their flagpoles and burning the flags. The next day, Steve receives almost a

million dollars in back pay from the Army. Steve doesn't think he's earned the money but his encounter with Bobby Hutchinson makes him decide to use it to fund a national hotline so that in the future he can be reached easily by people across the USA. Steve and Bernie get to work to prepare for the enterprise. Diamondback and Bushmaster look for MODOK in one of his old bases; they destroy the base without finding him. Flag-Smasher breaks into a flag manufacturing storehouse and burns all of the flags. Captain America's Stars & Stripes hotline is ready to launch and Flag-Smasher hears about it on the news. At Cap's press conference for the Stars & Stripes, Flag-Smasher crashes the event and tries to air his views while holding his gun on the crowd, but the onlookers dislike his philosophy. When a SWAT team arrives, Flag-Smasher is distracted long enough for Cap to attack and ultimately best him in combat.

NOTE: Flag-Smasher's real name revealed in revealed in OMHU #12, '10. The army questionnaire Steve filled out in Cap #250, '80, resulted in the back pay Steve receives here. Diamondback's trick diamonds appear virtually every time she does, and only changes to them will be noted.

CAPTAIN AMERICA #313 (January 1986)

"Mission: Murder MODOK!" (23 pages)

CREDITS: Mark Gruenwald (writer), Paul Neary (pencils), Al Williamson (inks), Diana Albers (letters), Ken Feduniewicz (colors), Michael Higgins (asst editor), Mike Carlin (editor), John Byrne (c pencils)
FEATURE CHARACTER: Captain America (also on poster, next in SecWar2 #6, '85, VSW #6, '86, Av #263, '86, FF #286, '86)
SUPPORTING CAST: Bernie Rosenthal
VILLAINS: Serpent Society: Sidewinder (leader), Anaconda, Asp, Black Mamba, Cobra, Cottonmouth, Death Adder, Princess Python, Rattler (all last in Cap #311, '85), Bushmaster, Diamondback (all next in Cap #315, '86); MODOK (last in Hulk #290, '83, chr last in 1985 #6, '08, dies, next in Cap #315, '86 as corpse)
OTHER CHARACTERS: Hiram "Ram" Riddley (computer hacker), Holly Riddley (Hiram's mother) (both 1st, next in Cap #321, '86), Toyland staff (Nathan named), Mr. Friedman (mall security chief), mall shoppers, bystanders
LOCATIONS/ITEMS: Atlantic Ocean, Stars & Stripes office, truck stop, New Jersey shopping mall inc Toyland, Riddley home; AIM submarine, Bushmaster's flashlight, MODOK's Doomsday chair & feeding station, Toyland truck, Serpent Saucers, Stars & Stripes computers, Cap's motorcycle, Hiram's computer
SYNOPSIS: Diamondback and Bushmaster invade a sunken AIM submarine where they find and attack MODOK. MODOK escapes, blasting Bushmaster's arms off in the process. Cap visits the Stars & Stripes office, where Bernie suggests he hire a full-time staffer. Cap discovers that someone is hacking his computers. MODOK boards a truck bound for Toyland, unaware the Serpent Society are following. Cap traces the hacker, teenager Hiram Riddley, to Montclair, New Jersey. Hiram apologizes and shows how his computer can keyword search data. Cap notices a bulletin about MODOK. Arriving at the scene Cap catches the fleeing terrified Princess Python, but lets her go when she reveals her team's name and mission. Cap catches up to the Society at Toyland and fights Asp, Black Mamba and Diamondback; at one point, Diamondback has a chance to kill him, but flinches when she considers how handsome he is. Defeating the three Serpents, Cap reaches MODOK to find him being killed by Cottonmouth and Death Adder. Although Cap beats the Serpents, MODOK dies. Cap returns to Hiram's home and offers to make him an assistant to help organize information on the Stars & Stripes hotline.

CAPTAIN AMERICA #314 (February 1986)

"Asylum" (22 pages)

CREDITS: Mark Gruenwald (writer), Paul Neary (pencils, c art), Dennis Janke (inks), Diana Albers (letters), Ken Feduniewicz (colors), Michael Higgins (asst editor), Mike Carlin (editor)
FEATURE CHARACTER: Captain America (also in rfb)
GUEST STARS: Avengers: Black Knight, Captain Marvel, Wasp (all last in Av #263, last bts in FF #286, next in Av #264), Hercules (Invisible Woman (both last in FF #286, next in Av #264), Mr. Fantastic (last in XFac #1, next in Av #264), Nighthawk (Kyle Richmond, Earth-S hero, also in rfb, between SqS #6-7) (all '86)
SUPPORTING CAST: Bernie Rosenthal (next in Cap #316, '86)
VILLAINS: Mink, Pinball, Remnant (all Earth-S super criminals, between SqS #6-7, '86)
OTHER CHARACTERS: Edwin Jarvis (last in FF #286, '86, next in Av #264, '86), Professor Imam (Wizard Supreme of Earth-S, 1st but chr last in WoSM Ann #5/6, '89 fb, next in SqS:DoU, '89), Mike Carlin, Michael Higgins (both last in Cap #311, '85, last app), Reggie (teenage Stars & Stripes volunteer), "Magic Carpet" nightclub employees & patrons, bystanders; Avengers: Beast, Goliath, Hellcat, Iron Man, Quicksilver, Scarlet Witch, Vision; Squadron Supreme: Arcanna, Blue Eagle, Dr. Spectrum, Golden Archer, Hyperion, Lady Lark, Princess Power, Tom Thumb, Whizzer; Ape X, Foxfire, Lamprey, Master Menace, Quagmire, Shape, Earth-S criminal (prev 23 in rfb)
LOCATIONS/ITEMS: Earth-S inc Temple of Contemplation, Avengers Mansion, Steve's Brooklyn Heights apartment, "Magic Carpet" nightclub, Industrial Display Company, Marvel Comics Manhattan office; Cap's motorcycle & hotline briefcase, Nighthawk's rope line, Mink's claws, Remnant's carpet
FLASHBACKS: The Squadron Supreme once fought the Avengers by mistake (Av #85, '71) and were mind-controlled by the Serpent Crown in another instance (Av #147-149, '76). Attempting to rebuild after Earth-S was conquered by the Over-Mind, the Squadron assumed political power and Nighthawk opted out; the Squadron began shipping food, eradicating guns, altering criminals' minds and brainwashing their enemies (SqS #1-6, '85-86). Master Menace sent Mink, Remnant and Pinball to Earth-616 to escape the Squadron (SqS #6, '86).
SYNOPSIS: On Earth-S, Professor Imam transports Nighthawk to the Avengers' world in the hope that they will help against the Squadron Supreme. Appearing in Avengers Mansion, Nighthawk explains his world's problems to Captain America. The Avengers and Fantastic Four debate the issue but decide they can't involve themselves in another world's politics. While Nighthawk looks for other allies, Cap receives a distress call about a criminal on a flying carpet. Nighthawk recognizes that as a description of his foe Remnant and joins Cap in investigating. Nighthawk finds a clue that another foe of his, Mink, is also on this world and begins an investigation. After dropping off work with Marvel, Steve

goes home to learn Bernie has passed her LSAT. She wants to celebrate, but Caps leave to follow a lead on Nighthawk, leaving Bernie alone with her second thoughts on their relationship. Nighthawk finds and fights Mink, Remnant and Pinball; Cap helps him defeat the trio and they learn how they escaped Earth-S. Nighthawk recruits his former enemies as the first of his Redeemers, and they return to Earth-S.

CAPTAIN AMERICA #315 (March 1986)

"The Hard Sell" (22 pages)

CREDITS: Mark Gruenwald (writer), Paul Neary (pencils), Dennis Janke (inks), Diana Albers (letters), Ken Feduniewicz (colors), Michael Higgins (asst editor), Mike Carlin (editor), Dan Green (c inks)
FEATURE CHARACTER: Captain America (also in Av #264, next in SecWar2 #8, Av #265, SecWar2 #9, Av #266, VSW #7, MFan #26/2, NM #40, Av #267-270, bts in Et #8, Et #12, Hulk #320-323, PMIF #125, all '86)
VILLAINS: Serpent Society: Sidewinder (leader), Asp, Black Mamba, Bushmaster, Cottonmouth, Cobra, Diamondback, Rattler (all next in Cap #319, '86), Death Adder, Princess Python (both next in Cap #318, '86), Anaconda (next bts in Cap #318, '86) (all last in Cap #313, '86); AIM agents (71X named)
OTHER CHARACTERS: Porcupine (last in MA Ann #1, '85, dies), MODOK (corpse, next in IM #205, '86), Wilburn (last in Cap #310, '85, last app), Lt. Burns (police detective), coroner, Joe (coroner's assistant), police officer; Ant-Man, Count Nefaria, Cyclops, Dr. Strange, Eel, Iceman, Iron Man, Nighthawk, Nomad, Plant Man, Power Man, Red Guardian, Scarecrow, Unicorn (prev 14 in rfb)
LOCATIONS/ITEMS: Monmouth County Morgue, Avengers Mansion, Cadence Industries AIM base, Serpent Society HQ, Porcupine's hotel room, Steve's Brooklyn Heights apartment, construction site; Cap's motorcycle, Serpent Society van, Porcupine's battlesuit, Bushmaster's wheelchair, Stars & Stripes briefcase
FLASHBACKS: The Porcupine faced many setbacks in his career, starting with Ant-Man (TTA #48, '63); working with Count Nefaria was a highlight (X #22-23, '66), but his recent attempts to sell the suit led to his defeat by Cap and Nomad (Cap #285, '83).
SYNOPSIS: The Serpent Society steal MODOK's corpse, deliver it to AIM and collect their fee. While at AIM's base Cobra meets Alexander Gentry, formerly the Porcupine, who's trying to sell his Porcupine suit; Cobra gives Gentry the Society's business card. Sidewinder tortures Princess Python for betraying them. When Gentry phones Sidewinder to try and sell him the suit, Sidewinder hangs up on him. Desperate, Gentry calls Captain America's hotline and Cap visits him, ironing out an agreement to buy the suit from him in return for leading him to the Serpent Society. Sidewinder arranges to ransom Princess Python back to the Circus of Crime. Porcupine calls Sidewinder and claims to have defeated Cap; Cottonmouth, Death Adder, Diamondback & Rattler answer the call and find Cap tied up, but Cap's bonds are faked and he attacks the Serpents. Porcupine tries to run, but dies accidentally during the melee. With the three male Serpents defeated, Cap stays with Porcupine in his final moments. Cap subsequently learns that Sidewinder is teleporting the Serpents out of jail when they're arrested. Later, Porcupine's battlesuit is put on display at Avengers Mansion, honoring him as a fallen foe.
NOTE: At the time of publication, Cadence Industries were the corporate owners of Marvel Comics.

CAPTAIN AMERICA #316 (April 1986)

"Creatures of Love" (22 pages)

CREDITS: Mark Gruenwald (writer), Paul Neary (pencils, c art), Dennis Janke (inks), Diana Albers (letters), Ken Feduniewicz (colors), Michael Higgins (asst editor), Mike Carlin (editor)
FEATURE CHARACTER: Captain America
GUEST STARS: Hawkeye (last in PMIF #125, '86), Mockingbird (last in Hulk #323, '86)
SUPPORTING CAST: Josh Cooper (last in Cap #303, '85), Mike Farrell (last in Cap #285, '83), Bernie Rosenthal (last in Cap #314, '86)
VILLAIN: Armadillo (also on flier, last in Cap #308, '85, next in Cap #340, '88)
OTHER CHARACTERS: Doc Sawbones (UCWF wrestler, also on flier, 1st, next in Cap #328, '87), Bonita Rodriguez (last in Cap #308, '85, last app), Ramon (Armadillo's staffer & Bonita's lover, only app), Lennie J. Feitler (Armadillo's agent, only app), Armadillo's entourage, hotel employees, UCWF fans, Madison Square Garden security, waiter, police, SWAT team, bystanders
LOCATIONS/ITEMS: Brooklyn Heights inc Steve's apartment, riverside promenade & diner, New York inc Madison Square Garden, Empire State Building & hotel w/Armadillo's 31st floor executive suite; Hawkeye's skycycle, bow & trick arrows, SWAT gear inc riot shields, truncheons & gas guns
SYNOPSIS: As Hawkeye and Mockingbird make their way into the city, Bernie and Steve have a heart-to-heart. Bernie will attend law school at University of Wisconsin at Madison; she made the decision without Steve because of his absences. Bernie is convinced that this separation will only make their love stronger. The duo are interrupted by Hawkeye & Mockingbird's arrival. Elsewhere, the Armadillo has become an Unlimited Class Wrestler; Steve hears about his match with Doc Sawbones and decides to attend. After the match, Captain America visits Armadillo and happens to catch Armadillo's wife with one of his staffers. Cap is pleased to see Armadillo has reformed, but the next day Armadillo goes on a rampage in Manhattan, finally climbing the Empire State Building while Cap tries to stop him. Armadillo is distraught that his wife cheated on him and tries jumping to his death, only to survive the fall.

CAPTAIN AMERICA #317 (May 1986)

"Death-Throws" (23 pages)

CREDITS: Mark Gruenwald (writer), Paul Neary (pencils), Dennis Janke (inks), Diana Albers (letters), Ken Feduniewicz (colors), Michael Higgins (asst editor), Mike Carlin (editor), Jackson Guice (c inks)
FEATURE CHARACTER: Captain America
GUEST STARS: Hawkeye, Mockingbird (both next in WCA #11, '86), Sam Wilson (last in PMIF #125, '86 fb)
SUPPORTING CAST: Anna Kappelbaum (last in Cap #284, '83, next in Cap #380, '90), Josh Cooper, Mike Farrell (both next in Cap #380, '90), Bernie Rosenthal (also in Steve's thoughts, next in Cap #327, '87)
VILLAINS: Death-Throws (juggling mercenaries, 1st): Ringleader (Charles Last), Knickknack (Nick Grossman), Tenpin (Alvin Healey) (all 1st, next in AvS #23, '89), Bombshell (Wendy Conrad), Oddball (Elton Healey) (both last in Hawk #4, '83, next in AvS #23, '89); Crossfire (William Cross, Hawkeye's arch-foe, last in Hawk #4, '83, chr last in AWC #100/2 fb, '93, next bts in AvS #22, '89, next in AvS #24, '89)
OTHER CHARACTERS: Michele March (last in Cap #312, '85, last app), Arthur Bennett (last in Cap #309, '85, next bts in Cap #324, '87), Mr. Rosenthal (Bernie's father, last in Cap #287, '83, next bts in Cap #255, '89), Jeannie Rosenthal (Bernie's youngest sister, only app), movers (Ralphie named), party-goers (Omar & Renee named), police (Guido named), reporters, cameramen
LOCATIONS/ITEMS: Anna's Brooklyn Heights building inc Steve's & Bernie's apartments, New York County Courthouse, World Trade Center, abandoned 158th St. railroad terminal; Ringleader's throwing rings, Oddball's trick balls, Tenpin's throwing pins, Bombshell's bombs, Hawkeye's skycycle, bow & trick arrows, police guns, Cap's Stars & Stripes hotline briefcase, Bernie's note
FLASHBACK: Crossfire hires Bombshell & Oddball to aid him against Hawkeye and Mockingbird, but they are defeated (Hawk #3-4, '83).
SYNOPSIS: The Death-Throws liberate Crossfire as he's being led to court. Hawkeye and Mockingbird arrive to testify at the trial and learn of the escape. Steve helps Bernie move out while Mrs. Kappelbaum is disappointed to see them separate; Bernie's father, however, is glad to see them part. Josh reveals that he's throwing a party for them tonight. The Death-Throws interrogate Crossfire for the money he owes them, but his funds are tied up by the law. They decide to ransom him to Hawkeye instead. Clint and Bobbi arrive at Steve and Bernie's party to let Steve know about the Death-Throws' ransom demand; Steve leaves the party to join Hawkeye. As they head into an abandoned railroad terminal to meet the Death-Throws, Captain America gives Hawkeye his shield for protection; Hawkeye gives Cap his bow and some arrows. The Death-Throws attack and the heroes switch weapons again, finally beating the villains with Mockingbird's help. They discover the Death-Throws' plan was to capture Hawkeye and ransom him to the Avengers. Steve returns to the apartment to find Bernie gone, leaving behind a farewell letter for him.
NOTE: Ringleader, Tenpin & Knickknack's real names revealed in OHMU #3, '86.

CAPTAIN AMERICA #318 (June 1986)

"Justice is Served!" (22 pages)

CREDITS: Mark Gruenwald (writer), Paul Neary (pencils, c art), Dennis Janke (inks), Diana Albers (letters), Ken Feduniewicz (colors), Bobbie Chase (asst editor), Mike Carlin (editor)
FEATURE CHARACTER: Captain America
GUEST STARS: Avengers: Hercules, Sub-Mariner (both last in PMIF #125, '86 fb, next in Av #270, '86), Wasp (last in PMIF #125, '86 fb, next in Av #271, '86); Black Panther (bts, provides Cap's new van, last in MTU Ann #7/2, '84, next in WCA Ann #1, '86), Falcon (bts, questioned Cap's plan to travel the country, next in WCA Ann #1, '86)
VILLAINS: Scourge (disguised as taxi driver & truck driver, last in ASM #276, '86), Blue Streak (last in Cap #229, '79, dies, next in Pun #5, '09), Death Adder (last in Cap #315, '86, dies), Firebrand (Gary Gilbert, last in IM #172, '83, chr last in Cap #320, '86 fb), Princess Python (last in Cap #315, '86, next in SenSH #1, '89), Anaconda (bts, didn't accompany Death Adder so she could go on a date, last in Cap #315, '86)
OTHER CHARACTERS: Edwin Jarvis (last in Hulk #321, '86, next in PP #22, '86), Kobaru (Wakandan Design Group, only app), Charlie (BW/NN security guard), Bart (BW/NN bartender), bystanders; Enforcer, Fly, Melter, Miracle Man, Titania, Wraith (prev 6 in newspaper clippings, killed by Scourge)
LOCATIONS/ITEMS: South Bronx, Bar With No Name, Avengers Mansion; Serpent Saucer (destroyed), Cap's van, motorcycle & crash helmet, Blue Streak's rocket skates, energy gauntlets & tacks, Scourge's taxi, semi truck & gun
SYNOPSIS: Death Adder is ferrying Princess Python to the Circus of Crime when something damages his Serpent Saucer, forcing him to crash. He commandeers a cab, but the cab driver shoots him with an explosive bullet, killing him. The Sub-Mariner and Hercules help Captain America move into Avengers Mansion and the Wakanda Design Group delivers Cap's new van, which can transport his motorcycle and has various features including changeable colors. At the Bar With No Name, Firebrand tries to convince Blue Streak that as a super-criminal he's in danger from the serial killer targeting them, but Blue Streak brushes off his warnings. Testing out his van on the highway, Cap runs into Blue Streak and fights him, but Blue Streak manages to trick Cap into thinking he fell off a cliff. Hitchhiking, he gets a lift from a trucker, but the trucker shoots him with an explosive bullet.
NOTE: "American Graffiti" includes LOC from future comics artist & writer Norman Breyfogle.

CAPTAIN AMERICA #319 (July 1986)

"Overkill" (22 pages)

CREDITS: Mark Gruenwald (writer), Paul Neary (pencils), Dennis Janke (inks), Diana Albers (letters), Ken Feduniewicz (colors), Bobbie Chase (asst editor), Mike Carlin (editor), Joe Sinnott (c inks)

FEATURE CHARACTER: Captain America

VILLAINS: Hijacker, Mirage, Shellshock (all last in MTIO #96, '83), Turner D. Century (last in MTU #120, '82), Cheetah (last in CM #49, '77), Cyclone (last in PPSSM #23, '78), Grappler (last in SavSH #18, '81, chr last in SH #3, '06 fb), Hellrazor (last in MTU #87, '79), Jaguar (last in DD #123, '75), Commander Kraken (last in IM #94, '77), Letha (last in Thing #33, '86), Mind-Wave (last in DD #133, '76), Rapier (last in PPSSM Ann #2, '80), Ringer (last in PPSSM #58, '81, chr last in CoH #3, '97, dies), Steeplejack (last in MsM #14, '78), Vamp (last in Cap #231, '79), Firebrand (all die); Serpent Society: Sidewinder (leader, last in Cap #315, '86, next in Cap #338, '88), Asp, Bushmaster, Cottonmouth, Rattler (prev 4 last in Cap #315, '86, next in Cap #341/3, '88), Diamondback (also in fb between Cap #400/3, '92 fb & Cap #403/2, '92 fb; last in Cap #315, '86), Black Mamba (last in Cap #315, '86, next bts in Av #273, '86, next in Av #274, '86), Anaconda (next in Cap #341/3, '88), Cobra (last in Cap #315, '86); Blacklash (last in PPSSM #101, '85, chr next in MSH #12/3, '93, next in IM #223, '87), Clown, Ringmaster (both last in Hulk #292, '84, next in SenSH #1, '89), Trapster (only in fb between ASM #215, '81 & FF #265, '84), Tinkerer (bts, provided weapons detector, last in PPSSM #53, '81, next in Cap #324, '86), AIM agents, two of the Kingpin's men, Scourge (disguised as bartender "Jake")

OTHER CHARACTERS: Death Adder (corpse, next in Pun #5, '09), Greg Salinger (formerly Foolkiller, last in ASM #226, '82, next in Fool #1, '90), Ricky Leighton (only in fb, Diamondback's brother, 1st but chr last in Cap #400/3, '92 fb, dies, last app), Mr. & Mrs. Burroughs (Death Adder's parents, only app), police (Max named, others in fb), shop owner (in fb), Nurse Upham, orderly, a farmer; Enforcer, Miracle Man (both in newspaper clippings, killed by Scourge)

LOCATIONS/ITEMS: Bar With No Name, Serpent Society HQ, Cadence Industries AIM base, Indiana inc mental hospital & cornfield; Cap's van, helmet, motorcycle & Stars & Stripes briefcase, Bushmaster's wheelchair, Serpent Saucer, Firebrand's weapons detector, Scourge's guns, Blacklash's whip, Clown's cane, farmer's shotgun

FLASHBACK: Teenager Rachel Leighton commits crimes with her brother Danny. When Danny is killed by a policeman she vows revenge and eventually obtains trick throwing diamonds from the Trapster, taking the codename Diamondback.

SYNOPSIS: Captain America foils an attempted jewelry store robbery by Blacklash. Learning that Blacklash is afraid of being killed by the super-villain assassin, Cap begins an investigation. Sidewinder returns Death Adder's corpse to the Society's base and sends the team out to find their comrade's killer; they interrogate various criminals and inform Death Adder's parents of his death. At the Bar With No Name, Firebrand meets with Jaguar, Ringer and Letha to share information on the killer. Cap visits a mental hospital to see if Greg Salinger, formerly Foolkiller, could be involved, but Salinger is hopelessly insane. Cap meets Diamondback following the same lead and they agree to share information. At the Bar, Firebrand prepares for his summit. Diamondback makes a pass at Cap; he rebuffs her and ends their brief partnership. Cap exits the Saucer into a farmer's field with Diamondback in pursuit, but a frightened farmer shoots her, grazing her arm. At the Bar, eighteen criminals gather and begin to discuss how to deal with the killer, but the bartender suddenly pulls out a gun and shoots them, declaring "justice is served."

CAPTAIN AMERICA #320 (August 1986)

"The Little Bang Theory" (23 pages)

CREDITS: Mark Gruenwald (writer), Paul Neary (pencils), Dennis Janke (inks), Diana Albers (letters), Ken Feduniewicz (colors), Bobbie Chase (asst editor), Mike Carlin (editor)

FEATURE CHARACTER: Captain America (also as Mirage, next in DD #233, '86, MFan #31-32, '87, Cap Ann #8, '86)

VILLAINS: Scourge (dies, also in rfb & fb, see NOTE, next in Herc #129, '09 as spirit), Scourge (successor, last in ASM #278, '86, next in Cap #351, '89), Domino (Dominic Dunsinane, Scourge's information specialist, last in RH #8/2, '78, chr last in USAgent #4, '93 fb, next in USAgent #1, '93), Diamondback, Cobra (both next in Cap #341/3, '88), Water Wizard (also in fb1 & pfb; last in GR #62, '81, next in FF #336, '90), Kraven (bts, being moved from LA to New York for deportation, last in SecWars2 #7, '86, next in WoSM #31, '87), Puppet Master (bts, in Omaha heading East by train, last in Thing #34, '86, next in FF #300, '87)

OTHER CHARACTERS: Bird-Man, Letha, Mind-Wave (all also in pfb), Turner D. Century, Cheetah, Cyclone, Hijacker, Mirage (all corpses, next in Pun #5, '09), Grappler, Hellrazor, Jaguar, Commander Kraken, Rapier, Shellshock, Steeplejack, Vamp (prev 8 corpses, last app), Firebrand (corpse, also in fb1 between IM #172, '83 & Cap #318, '86, also in pfb; next in Pun #5, '09), Ringer (corpse, also in pfb; next in LFSM #3, '93 as Strikeback), Katy Karins (reporter), Brett (news anchor), police, paramedics, coroners; Enforcer (in rfb), "Coot" Collier, Delazny Studio actors (prev 3 in fb, see NOTE), Blue Streak, Fly, Melter, Titania, Wraith (prev 5 in Scourge's thoughts)

LOCATIONS/ITEMS: Bar With No Name, Lake Erie, County police station w/morgue, sherriff's cabin, Delazny Studios (in fb, see NOTE); Cap's van & motorcycle, Scourge's van, gun & infrared goggles, Serpent Saucer, ambulances, Water Wizard's car (also in pfb)

FLASHBACKS: At the Bar With No Name, Firebrand tells Water Wizard about Scourge's killings (1). On his way to the summit Water Wizard's car gets a flat; arriving late, he discovers the rest of the attendees' bodies (p). The son of a famous Hollywood director, Scourge is disgusted when he discovers his brother is the Enforcer, and hates him for disgracing the family's name. He murders the Enforcer (IM #194, '85), and decides to use the family fortune to finance his war against all costumed criminals (see NOTE).

SYNOPSIS: At Lake Erie, Water Wizard attacks Captain America. Satisfied he's the genuine Cap, Water Wizard brings him to the Bar and shows him the bodies of Scourge's victims. Cap moves Water Wizard to a safe location and brings in the police. Scourge is contacted by his ally Domino, who gives him the location of Diamondback's hospital bed. Scourge tries to kill Diamondback, but she escapes the hospital with Cobra aboard a Serpent Saucer. Cap arranges with the authorities to report that Mirage survived the barroom massacre and is in protective custody. Hoping to draw the killer out, Cap poses as Mirage and is sent to a secluded cabin. When Scourge attempts to kill him, Cap exposes his real identity and battles Scourge in the woods, finally disarming him. Scourge relates his motivation to Cap until suddenly, an explosive bullet strikes him in the chest and kills him. Somewhere in the woods a voice says "justice is served."

NOTE: There are holes in Scourge's story. USAgent #4, '93 fb reveals the Golden Age hero Angel, Thomas Halloway, funds the Scourge of the Underworld program, with his partner Domino providing recruits to be the various Scourges. This Scourge claims to be the only Scourge and to be funding the entire operation, which isn't true. Further, Scourge claims to be Enforcer's brother, but Enforcer was the son of Charles Delazny, a producer. At one point Enforcer was thought to be the son of "Coot" Collier, the director seen in this flashback, but that proved to be false. Further still, when future Scourges are caught they will claim to be out for vengeance against relatives gone bad, just like this Scourge.

CAPTAIN AMERICA ANNUAL #8 (1986)

"Tess-One" (40 pages)

CREDITS: Mark Gruenwald (writer), Mike Zeck (pencils), John Beatty (inks, pages 1-31 & c inks), Joe Rubinstein (inks, pages 32-40), Jim Novak (letters), Glynis Oliver (colors), Mike Carlin (editor)
FEATURE CHARACTERS: Captain America (also on poster & in rfb; next in Av #270-272, AFlt #39, Av Ann #15, WCA Ann #1, Cap #321, all '86)
GUEST STAR: Wolverine (last in SecWar2 #9, '86, next in UXM #205, '86)
VILLAINS: Overrider (Richard Rennselaer, mutant that controls machines & former SHIELD agent, 1st, next in NF:AoS #33, '92 fb), TESS-One (super-soldier hunting robot, 1st, next in Av #288, '88)
OTHER CHARACTERS: Robert Frank Jr. (son of Whizzer & Miss America, mutant that discharges nuclear energy, last in VSW #2, '82, next in Av #311, '89), Franklin Delano Roosevelt (only in fb between HT #3/3, '40 & CapC #1, '41), Prof. Erskine (also in rfb as corpse), Gen. Phillips (both in fb between MvPro #3, '10 & MSH #3, '90 fb), Dr. Anderson (also in rfb; in fb to 1st chr app before Cap #255, '81 fb), Johnny Rennselaer (catatonic son of Overrider, only app), Prof. Daniel Schumann (TESS-One robot creator, only app in fb), Gary Naslund (gas station employee), Abel Baker (both Stars & Stripes hotline helpers, only app), police (Gannon named), Richie's Bar patrons (Arnie named) & bartender, Kwikkie Burger customers (Mr. McNulty named) & employee, bystanders (Henry named), paramedics, doctors, nurses, Offut Air Force Base soldiers (inc Gen. Landon, Commanding Officer) & personnel, Reggie (truck driver), Adametco security & employees, Vollman Center kids, Heinz Krueger (in rfb as corpse)
LOCATIONS/ITEMS: Richie's Bar, Kwikkie Burger w/hidden underground bunker, hospital, Washington DC inc Library of Congress, X-Men's Mansion, Nebraska gas station, Adametco Metallurgy company, Offut Air Force Base, West Virginia inc Vollman Center for Disturbed Children; Cap's van, motorcycle & Stars & Stripes briefcase, hidden bunker's gun mounts, steel spikes & Phosgene gas, Overrider's Hovercraft, Cerebro, Adametco's Adamantium, nuclear missile terminals
FLASHBACKS: Professor Daniel Schumann proposes to President Roosevelt and his Project: Super-Soldier staff a failsafe against the upcoming Super-Soldier Project: the TESS robots that can hunt down any Super-Soldiers that may rebel. The project is cancelled when Prof. Erskine is killed (Cap #255, '81 fb).
SYNOPSIS: After witnessing a barroom brawl, Wolverine follows the winner, Bob Frank, only to see him attacked by a giant robot. When Wolverine attempts to intervene, the robot, TESS-One, flees at the command of a nearby hovering figure. Captain America investigates a hole in a nearby Kwikkie Burger's parking lot, discovering a WW2 era underground bunker. After rescuing two people who fell in, he determines that a robot has recently escaped and learns the bunker's former owner was Prof. Schumann. Override and TESS-One hijack a truck. Meanwhile, Wolverine takes Bob Frank to a hospital. He tracks the robot and learns it recently emptied a truck destined for Adametco. Override and TESS-One attack Adametco and force the employees to coat TESS-One in Adamantium. Cap is alerted to the attack through his hotline, and both he and Wolverine arrive at the plant. Overrider and TESS-One escape, and Cap and Wolverine agree to investigate individually. Overrider visits his catatonic son, who's terrified of nuclear war. Cap learns that Schumann created TESS-One as a failsafe against Super-Soldiers while Wolverine learns that Overrider is Richard Rennselaer, a former SHIELD agent that can control machines. Overrider and TESS-One assault the Offut Air Force Base. Cap and Wolverine arrive, barely defeating the robot before tracking Overrider into the control room. The mutant plans to disarm America by launching all of the country's nuclear missiles into the ocean, thus "healing" his son of his nuclear psychosis. When Cap knocks Overrider off his hoverboard, Wolverine decides not to impale the villain, but instead lets him fall. The two heroes part ways in disgust with each other's methods.
NOTE: TESS stands for Total Elimination of Super-Soldiers.

CAPTAIN AMERICA #321 (September 1986)

"Ultimatum!" (22 pages)

CREDITS: Mark Gruenwald (writer), Paul Neary (pencils), John Beatty (inks), Diana Albers (letters), Ken Feduniewicz (colors), Bobbie Chase (asst editor), Mike Carlin (editor), Mike Zeck (c art)
FEATURE CHARACTER: Captain America (also as ULTIMATUM agent & on poster)
VILLAINS: Flag-Smasher (last in Cap #312, '85), ULTIMATUM agents (Flag-Smasher's terrorist network, 1st, Krantz, Hatari, Rivvik, Luft, Dimitri named), Vladimir Korda (ULTIMATUM agent, dies), Red Skull (bts, funding ULTIMATUM, last in Cap #301, '85, chr last in Cap #368/2, '90 fb, next bts in Cap #326, '87)
OTHER CHARACTERS: Hiram Riddley (last in Cap #313, '86, next in Cap #332, '87), Holly Riddley (next bts in Cap #332, '87), Captain Walker (pilot), O'Reilly (co-pilot), flight attendants, 110 airline passengers (inc a physician, 4 die), SHIELD (bts, provided Cap ULTIMATUM's location)
LOCATIONS/ITEMS: Riddley home, Hydra base, sentry station, monastery; Avengers Quinjet & Skycycle, ULTIMATUM flying skis, uzis & grappling hooks, TWA jet (flight M32), Stars & Stripes baseball jacket, Cap's van, broadcast equipment

SYNOPSIS: Flag-Smasher leads ULTIMATUM in skyjacking an airplane. Captain America goes to the Riddleys and presents Hiram with a jacket. Cap stays for dinner and Holly makes romantic overtures when she sees Cap unmasked. Hiram interrupts, showing Cap news of the skyjacking. Flag-Smasher demands that Captain America come alone to arrange the release of his hostages, intending to prove that his viewpoint is superior to Cap's. Cap uses SHIELD intelligence to determine the location where the hostages are held and manages to best a pair of sentries, taking an ULTIMATUM uniform and weapon to disguise himself. Cap finds the monastery where the hostages are being held but is outnumbered. While trying to defeat the terrorists one at a time, one of them opens fire on the hostages; Cap is forced to shoot the terrorist to save the hostages. Cap is horrified by his own actions; after transport for the hostages is secured, Cap brings the dead terrorist's body with him, intending to avenge his death.

NOTE: ULTIMATUM stands for Underground Liberated Totally Integrated Mobile Army To Unite Mankind; Red Skull is revealed to be funding them in Cap #349, '89. Korda's name revealed in Cap #326, '87.

CAPTAIN AMERICA #322 (October 1986)

"The Chasm" (22 pages)

CREDITS: Mark Gruenwald (writer), Paul Neary (pencils), John Beatty (inks), Diana Albers (letters), Ken Fedunewicz (colors), Bobbie Chase (asst editor), Mike Carlin (editor), Joe Rubinstein (c inks)
FEATURE CHARACTER: Captain America (also in rfb)
VILLAINS: Flag-Smasher, ULTIMATUM (also in rfb) (both next in Cap #348, '88)
OTHER CHARACTERS: Jerry Hunt (SHIELD agent, last in SW #16, '79, next in Alias #20, '03), other SHIELD agents (Felker, Wohl, Riley, Dave named)
LOCATIONS/ITEMS: Hydra base; SHIELD firearms, helicopter, ULTIMATUM uzis, knife, helicopters, Flag-Smasher's Luger
FLASHBACK: ULTIMATUM hijacks a plane and battles Captain America, forcing the Avenger to kill an agent Cap #321, '86).

SYNOPSIS: Captain America joins SHIELD agents in raiding the ex-Hydra base where ULTIMATUM is located, still grappling with having taken a terrorist's life. Cap manages to catch Flag-Smasher as he escapes in a helicopter, but as they fight aboard the craft it crashes into a mountain. They both survive and continue their battle in the snow, but Flag-Smasher falls off a cliff when Cap sidesteps his attack. Cap finds Flag-Smasher and keeps his unconscious foe alive, providing shelter through the evening's storm. With Flag-Smasher's right leg broken Cap transports him through the snow, debating Flag-Smasher's anti-nationalist views with him along the way. An ULTIMATUM helicopter finds the pair thanks to a homing signal in Flag-Smasher's costume; Cap defeats the craft's crew, but Flag-Smasher retrieves a gun. Rather than shoot Cap he surrenders, doubting he could beat him, but determined to find an opportunity another day. Cap turns Flag-Smasher over to SHIELD and Flag-Smasher declares that Cap will regret letting him live.

CAPTAIN AMERICA #323 (November 1986)

"Super-Patriot is Here" (22 pages)

CREDITS: Mark Gruenwald (writer), Paul Neary (pencils), John Beatty (inks), Diana Albers (letters), Ken Feduniewicz (colors), David Wohl (asst editor), Don Daley (editor), Mike Zeck (c pencils), Joe Rubinstein (c inks), John Romita (c frame art)
FEATURE CHARACTER: Captain America (also in rfb & in photos; next bts in Av #273, '86)
GUEST STARS: Avengers: Black Knight (as Dane Whitman), Hercules (both last in PP #28, '87, next in Av #273, '86)
SUPPORTING CAST: Super-Patriot (John Walker, publicity-seeking patriotic hero, also in photos, 1st but chr last & also in Cap #381/2, '91 fb, next in Cap #327, '87), Bernie Rosenthal (last in Cap #317, '86, next in Cap #327, '87)
VILLAINS: Bold Urban Commandos ("BUCkies," Super-Patriot's super-strong subordinates): Lemar Hoskins, Jerome Johnson, Hector Lennox (all 1st but chr last in Cap #381/2, '91 fb, next in Cap #327, '87)
OTHER CHARACTERS: Ethan Thurm (Super-Patriot's agent, last in Thing #30, '85, chr last & also in Cap #381/2, '91 fb), Candy (Super-Patriot's chauffeur, 1st), Paul (Bernie's classmate, 1st) (all next in Cap #327, '87), Edwin Jarvis (last in PP #28, '87, next in Av #273, '86), Jasper Sitwell (last in Thor #337, '83, next in NFVS #1, '88), Michele March (last in Cap #312, '85, last app), SHIELD agents, Hercules' party guests, Super-Patriot's rally attendees, actors (as police), reporters, cameramen, police, waiter, bystanders; Flag-Smasher (in photo), Angel, Ant-Man, Beast, Captain Marvel, Colossus, Cyclops, Daredevil, Dr. Strange, Hawkeye, Hulk, Human Torch, Iceman, Invisible Woman, Iron Man, Marvel Girl, Mr. Fantastic, Nightcrawler, Phoenix, Power Man, Puck, Rogue, Scarlet Witch, Shadowcat, She-Hulk, Spider-Man, Storm, Sub-Mariner, Thing, Thor, Vision, Wasp, Wolverine (prev 32 on cover)
LOCATIONS/ITEMS: Statue of Liberty, Avengers Mansion, SHIELD base, Central Park, University of Wisconsin at Madison inc Bernie's dorm, restaurant; Avengers Skycycle, Porcupine's battle suit, SHIELD jetcrafts, Bold Urban Commandos' guns, Super-Patriot's fireworks & fiery sword, Daily Bugle
FLASHBACK: Cap fights ULTIMATUM and kills an agent (Cap #321, '86).
SYNOPSIS: Super-Patriot announces his arrival at the Statue of Liberty with a fireworks display. SHIELD agents intercept Captain America and escort him to Jasper Sitwell, who states that Switzerland wants to extradite Cap. Sitwell offers to protect Cap by making him a SHIELD agent, but Cap is reluctant to accept. Cap returns to Avengers Mansion to find Hercules and Black Knight throwing a toga party. Bernie has trouble studying after reading about Cap in the newspaper; she still has feelings for him. In Central Park, Steve happens across Super-Patriot holding a rally. Super-Patriot mocks Cap's old fashioned ways and declares that he should replace Cap as the USA's hero. The Bold Urban Commandos "attack" Super-Patriot, claiming to be Captain America's allies, but Super-Patriot quickly defeats them. Steve

realizes the show is a sham and later confronts Super-Patriot and his agent. Super-Patriot proposes a public fight to see who's superior, but Steve refuses and leaves. Super-Patriot sends the "BUCkies" to attack Steve, but he defeats them. Cap holds a press conference and admits to killing the ULTIMATUM agent, taking full responsibility even if it means extradition. Super-Patriot watches the televised speech and remains determined to replace the hero.

NOTE: Most titles published in November 1986, including this issue, have a unified cover design celebrating 25 years of Marvel Comics. Super-Patriot's last name revealed in Cap #333, '87. Lemar's first name revealed in Cap #333, '87, surname in Cap #334, '87. Jerome's first name revealed in Cap #334, '87, surname in Cap #347, '88. Hector's first name revealed in Cap #327, '87, surname in Cap #347, '88.

CAPTAIN AMERICA #324 (December 1986)

"Speed Trap" (22 pages)

CREDITS: Mark Gruenwald (writer), Paul Neary (pencils), Vince Colletta (inks), Diana Albers (letters), Ken Feduniewicz (colors), David Wohl (asst editor), Don Daley (editor), Mike Zeck (c pencils), John Beatty (c inks)
FEATURE CHARACTER: Captain America (next in Av #274-277, '86-87)
SUPPORTING CAST: Nomad (last in Cap #309, '85, chr last in Cap #325, '87 fb)
VILLAINS: Whirlwind (also posing as Nomad in message, last in PMIF #106, '84, last bts in Av #273, '86, next in WCA #16, '87), Trapster (last in FF #265, '84, chr last in 1985 #5, '08, next in PPSSM #158, '89), Tinkerer (last in PPSSM #53, '81, last bts in Cap #319, '86, next in ASM #310, '88), Slug (Ulysses X. Lugman, obese crime lord, 1st), Nicol Ortega (Slug's enforcer), Mr. Rickert (manager of Milky Way Club), Slug's staff, five drug dealers (Paco named), Baron Zemo (bts, hired Whirlwind to attack Cap, during Av #273, '86)
OTHER CHARACTERS: Arthur Bennett (bts, talks w/Steve on phone, last in Cap #317, '86, last app), Teenagers (Robbie named), I-72 truckstop patrons & staff, Nowhere Fast staff, Slug's party guests
LOCATIONS/ITEMS: Tinkerer's laboratory, Milky Way Club, Melonville, North Carolina inc I-72 truckstop; Whirlwind's modified costume, Trapster's modified costume, Lubricant Z & projectors, Cap's van, motorcycle & Stars & Stripes briefcase, Nowhere Fast yacht, teenagers' water guns, Tinkerer's robot, Nomad's modified costume & stun discs
FLASHBACK: Cap kills the ULTIMATUM terrorist (Cap #321, '86).
SYNOPSIS: Captain America confronts a group of teenagers with guns in a warehouse, only to find them using water guns; the teens are terrified of Cap's new "killer" reputation. Whirlwind goes to the Tinkerer for help upgrading his equipment and receives light armor for protection and buzzsaws he can fire from his wrists. Trapster is also upgrading his equipment, having added Lubricant Z to his arsenal. Upset that Baron Zemo only ordered him to distract Cap, Whirlwind proposes an alliance with Trapster to actually defeat Cap. In Miami, Nomad roughs up drug dealers working for the Slug. Cap decides to hire a PR agent. Nomad goes to work at the Milky Way Club as a bartender to get a lead on the drug lord. Responding to a message from "Nomad," Cap battles Whirlwind at a truckstop. Whirlwind leads Cap into Trapster's ambush, but Cap quickly defeats the villains. Nomad finally gains enough respect at the Milky Way Club that they take him to Nowhere Fast, the Slug's yacht. Nomad plans to kill the Slug.

CAPTAIN AMERICA #325 (January 1987)

"Slugfest" (22 pages)

CREDITS: Mark Gruenwald (writer), Paul Neary (pencils), John Beatty (inks), Diana Albers (letters), Ken Feduniewicz (colors), David Wohl (asst editor), Don Daley (editor), Mike Zeck (c pencils)
FEATURE CHARACTER: Captain America
GUEST STAR: Nomad (also in fb between Cap #309, '85 & Cap #324, '86; next in Cap #336, '87)
VILLAINS: Slug (next in WoSM Ann #4, '88), Slug's men (Larry named), inc Phil Lyons (Priscilla's brother), Mitch Schiffman (Slug's aide), drug dealers (Julio named)
OTHER CHARACTERS: Richie, Worm, Tony (all last in Cap #302, '85, last app), Priscilla Lyons (Nomad's girlfriend, 1st but chr last in USAgent #2, '93 fb, also in fb; next in Cap #336, '87), Don Daley (Marvel Comics editor), Dave Wohl (Daley's assistant) (both only app), police, Nowhere Fast staff (Henri named), Slug's party guests, bystanders, slugs; Mr. Rickert (in rfb)
LOCATIONS/ITEMS: Richie's garage, Marvel Comics offices, Milky Way Club (in rfb); Cap's van, motorcycle, Stars & Stripes briefcase & rented motorboat, Nowhere Fast yacht, Slug's wheelchair, hypodermic w/heroin, ferryboat, Nomad's motorcycle (in fb) & stun discs
FLASHBACK: While travelling through Kentucky, Nomad meets Priscilla and learns that her brother Phil is working for the Slug; Nomad offers to bring Phil home. Nomad gets a job at the Milky Way Club (Cap #324, '87).
SYNOPSIS: Captain America breaks up a drug deal in Brooklyn, only to discover he ruined a sting operation. Nomad watches the Slug discipline a follower by dunking him in a pool of slugs. Nomad finds Phil and gives him Priscilla's message of reconciliation, but Phil refuses to leave the Slug. Meanwhile, Priscilla grows impatient waiting for Nomad and calls Cap's hotline, and Steve drops his latest assignment off at the Marvel offices. That night Phil drugs Nomad and two of Slug's men throw Nomad overboard. Renting a motorboat, Cap finds Nomad floating in the ocean. They return to Nowhere Fast, where Nomad starts a fire in the galley to distract Slug's men. Cap evacuates the yacht while Nomad viciously attacks Slug; Cap halts Nomad's attack and tries to get Slug to safety. Nomad escapes moments before the fire destroys the yacht, leaving unconscious members of Slug's gang to die. Cap loses sight of the Slug when the yacht goes down and swims to shore with Nomad. Slug soon floats to the ocean's surface, his buoyant body saving him.

NOTE: Priscilla's phone number is (305) 555-6907.

CAPTAIN AMERICA #326 (February 1987)

"The Haunting of Skull-House" (24 pages)

CREDITS: Mark Gruenwald (writer), Paul Neary (pencils), John Beatty, Keith Williams (inks), Diana Albers (letters), Ken Feduniewicz (colors), Daryl Edelman (asst editor), Don Daley (editor), Mike Zeck (c pencils), Bob McLeod (c inks)

FEATURE CHARACTER: Captain America (also in fb)

VILLAINS: Dr. Faustus (last in MTU #133, '83, next bts in Nomad #18, '93 fb, next in Cap #420, '93), Red Skull (also in painting, rfb & as hologram, bts controlling Faustus' holograms, last bts in Cap #321, '86, next bts in Cap #328, '87)

OTHER CHARACTERS: Bucky, MODOK, Porcupine, Scourge, Sharon Carter, Vladimir Korda, Joseph Rogers, Sarah Rogers (all as holograms), Falcon, Nomad, Mother Superior, Sister Agony, Sister Death, Bernie Rosenthal, Arnie Roth (prev 7 in rfb)

LOCATIONS/ITEMS: Skull-House inc holographic control room; Cap's flashlight, Dr. Faustus' wheelchair & hallucinogens

FLASHBACKS: Red Skull captures Cap and his friends in an attempt for a final momentous battle with Cap (Cap #295-300, '84).

SYNOPSIS: Responding to a tip from his Stars & Stripes hotline that the lights are on at Skull-House, Captain America investigates. Entering the building, Cap is faced by the Red Skull's "ghost," who introduces Cap to the "ghosts" of Vladimir Korda, the terrorist Cap killed, Porcupine, MODOK and Scourge. Cap battles and defeats his deceased foes. Dr. Faustus watches from his control room. Frustrated that his plan to break Cap with hallucinogens and images of dead foes has failed, he tries to break him with images of dead family and friends. Bucky, Sharon and Cap's parents try to convince Cap to commit suicide to atone for murdering Korda, but Cap refuses to take the coward's way out. As Faustus prepares to flee, the Red Skull's "ghost" appears and strangles him for trying to usurp his role as Cap's arch-nemesis. Cap finds Faustus unconscious and removes him from Skull House.

NOTE: Half of page 24 is the last panel of the story, and half "America Graffiti."

CAPTAIN AMERICA #327 (March 1987)

"Clashing Symbols" (22 pages)

CREDITS: Mark Gruenwald (writer), Paul Neary (pencils), John Beatty (inks), Diana Albers (letters), Ken Feduniewicz (colors), Daryl Edelman (asst editor), Don Daley (editor), Mike Zeck (c pencils), Bob McLeod (c inks)

FEATURE CHARACTER: Captain America (next in Av #278-279 & 281-285, '87, ASM #502, '04 fb, MVs #4, '87, Thor #381, '87, XvA #1-4, '87)

SUPPORTING CAST: Super-Patriot (last in Cap #323, '86, next in Cap #332, '87), Bernie Rosenthal (last in Cap #323, '86, next bts in Cap #332, '87, next in Cap #336, '87)

VILLAINS: Bold Urban Commandos: Lemar Hoskins, Jerome Johnson, Hector Lennox (all last in Cap #323, '86, next in Cap #333, '87)

OTHER CHARACTERS: Ethan Thurm (last in Cap #323, '86, next in Cap #332, '87), Paul (last in Cap #323, '86, next in Cap #332, '87), Candy (last in Cap #323, '86, last app), Hutchinson (government bureaucrat, 1st), Suzanne (Bernie's classmate), University of Wisconsin students (inc International House residents), AmericAid '86 performers (inc Bob Dylan, Michael Jackson, Joan Jett, Willie Nelson, Prince & Tina Turner), security guards, police

LOCATIONS/ITEMS: Capitol Building, University of Wisconsin at Madison inc International House & Bernie's dorm, Milwaukee Stadium; Cap's van & motorcycle, Super-Patriot's throwing stars & fiery sword

SYNOPSIS: The Bold Urban Commandos attack foreign exchange students at the University of Wisconsin; Super-Patriot later congratulates them for threatening "terrorists." Steve comes to town to visit Bernie and investigate the Commandos' activities. Captain America tries to investigate the attacks, but the police won't cooperate with him and, disturbingly, some students agree with the Commandos and think Cap endorses them. The next day, Steve and Bernie attend the AmericAid '86 concert where Super-Patriot is making an appearance alongside various popular music acts. Cap confronts Super-Patriot backstage and threatens to expose Super-Patriot's ties to the Commandos. Super-Patriot attacks Cap to see who's better. Their battle lasts twenty-seven minutes, but despite Cap's best effort, the fight ends in a draw. Steve meets up with Bernie afterward, upset that he couldn't best Super-Patriot. In Washington, a bureaucrat investigates Steve's million dollar tax return and deduces that he's Captain America.

NOTE: Jerome called "Jake" here. Hutchinson's name revealed in Cap #328, '87.

CAPTAIN AMERICA #328 (April 1987)

"The Hard Way!" (22 pages)

CREDITS: Mark Gruenwald (writer), Paul Neary (pencils), Vince Colletta (inks), Diana Albers (letters), Ken Feduniewicz (colors), Daryl Edelman (asst editor), Don Daley (editor), Mike Zeck (c art)

FEATURE CHARACTER: Captain America (also as "Mr. Stevens" & in his own thoughts)

SUPPORTING CAST: Dennis "Demolition" Dunphy (super-strong UCWF wrestler, becomes Demolition Man, also in fb to 1st chr app before Thing #28, '85; last in Thing #36, '86)

VILLAINS: Power Broker (Curtiss Jackson, also bts in fb between Hulk #237 '79 & bts in Cap #381/2, '91 fb; voice only, last in Thing #35, '86, last bts in Thing #36, '86), Dr. Karl Malus' (Power Broker's chief scientist, also in fb between Cap #308, '85 & bts in Cap #381/2, '91 fb; last in Thing #35, '86), Mangler (Lucius O'Neil, last in Thing #36, '86), Bludgeon (Anthony Manning, 1st) (pair of erudite Power Broker enforcers, both next in Cap #363/2, '89), Lt. Michael Lynch (Power Broker's military aide, last in Thing #36, '86, chr last in Cap #331, '87 fb, next in Cap #331, '87), Nurse Lawlor

(Malus' assistant, only app), Power Broker's talent scout (other in fb) & doorman, Douglas Rockwell (Commission on Superhuman Activities commissioner, voice only, 1st, see NOTE), Red Skull (bts, last bts in Cap #326, '87, see NOTE)
OTHER CHARACTERS: Doc Sawbones (last in Cap #316, '86), Jersey Devil (UCWF wrestler, last in Thing #29, '85) (both last app), Red Zepplin (UCWF wrestler, 1st, next in Cap #375/2, '90), other UCWF wrestlers (Icepick & Steamroller named, others in rfb), Edward Garner (UCWF owner & operator, bts in other room, last in Thing #28, '85, last app) & his secretary (bts, told Cap where to look for Garner), Hutchinson (last app), Killough (Hutchinson's associate, only app), 2 FBI agents, boxers, bystanders, Demolition Man's classmates, football players & coach, Power Broker's pharmacist (prev 4 in fb); Bold Urban Commandos, Ms. Marvel (Sharon Ventura), Thing, Super-Patriot & his rally attendees (prev 5 in rfb)
LOCATIONS/ITEMS: Los Angeles inc UCWF headquarters, Rahman's Chinese Theater, diner & Power Broker lab w/ice cream parlor front, Washington DC inc Capitol Building; Malus' augmentation equipment, Power Broker's dummy (both also in fb), stabilizing drugs (in fb) & infra-scanner, Cap's van
FLASHBACKS: Dennis Dunphy is a college football player who can't make it as a professional. He's contacted by the Power Broker who grants him strength augmentation, but the process makes him so strong he can't play football. He becomes a UCWF wrestler instead (1). Thing helps expose Power Broker's use of addictive stabilizing drugs to keep his augments in line and helps Dennis beat his addiction (Thing #35, '86). Cap fights the Bold Urban Commandos (Cap #323, '86) and Super-Patriot (Cap #327, '87).
SYNOPSIS: Captain America visits the UCWF Headquarters, but the wrestlers mistake him for a new athlete and attack him as an initiation. Demolition Dunphy intervenes on Cap's behalf and offers to help Cap in his quest to find the Power Broker, who's possibly responsible for Super-Patriot's enhanced strength. In Washington, Hutchinson relays his findings on Cap's identity to the FBI. Dunphy dons a costume and assumes the identity Demolition Man; he and Cap locate one of Power Broker's fronts after days of searching. Cap enters undercover as "Mr. Stevens," an applicant for power augmentation. When Steve fails the interview, Mangler and Bludgeon attack. Steve evades them, but Lt. Lynch shoots Steve from behind. Dr. Malus begins to augment Steve, just to see what happens when the process is applied to someone already augmented. He theorizes his muscles will explode. D-Man breaks in, rescues Steve and captures Malus. Meanwhile, the FBI relays Cap's information to the Commission.
NOTE: The Commission on Superhuman Activities (CSA) is a US government agency that regulates activity and legislation of paranormal and costumed individuals. The group is not evil, but Douglas Rockwell is revealed to be working under someone who is manipulating the group to undermine Captain America and his legacy in Cap #346, '88; that someone is revealed to be the Red Skull in Cap #350, '89. Rockwell's first name revealed in Cap #344, '88, his surname in Cap #346, '88. Demolition Man often goes by "D-Man" for short; his costume is a combination of Daredevil's original suit and Wolverine's mask. Power Broker revealed to be Curtiss Jackson, formerly of the Corporation, in Cap #330, '87. Bludgeon's real name is revealed in OHMU HC12, '10. Mangler's real name is revealed in OHMU HC3, '08.

CAPTAIN AMERICA #329 (May 1987)

"Movers and Monsters" (22 pages)

CREDITS: Mark Gruenwald (writer), Paul Neary (pencils), Vince Colletta (inks), Diana Albers (letters), Ken Feduniewicz (colors), Daryl Edelman (asst editor), Don Daley (editor), Mike Zeck (c art)
FEATURE CHARACTER: Captain America (also in rfb)
GUEST STAR: Captain Marvel (last in XvA #4, '87, next in WCA Ann #2, '87)
SUPPORTING CAST: Demolition Man (also in rfb)
VILLAINS: Sweat Shop (Power Broker's super-strong "movers," 1st, Earl, Flaherty, Floyd, Joe, Moranis, O'Hara & Ramis named, one next in Cap #350, '89), Power Broker, Dr. Karl Malus, Malus' failed augmentation patients (1st, see NOTE), Red Skull (bts, funding Sweat Shop, next bts in Cap #335, '87)
OTHER CHARACTERS: Jake Farber, Elwood McNulty (both FBI agents, 1st, next in Cap #331, '87); Super-Patriot, Power Broker's doorman (both in rfb)
LOCATIONS/ITEMS: Los Angeles inc Power Broker lab (also in rfb) w/ice cream parlor front (in rfb), sewers & Power Broker's office, Avengers Mansion; Malus' augmentation equipment (in rfb), Avengers security tendrils, Sweat Shop's truck & tools, Power Broker's machinery, McNulty's Avengers key-card & ID
FLASHBACKS: Cap battles Super-Patriot (Cap #327, '87) and joins forces with D-Man to find the source of superhuman augments (Cap #328, '87).
SYNOPSIS: Captain America interrogates Dr. Malus while D-Man goes for food, but the Sweat Shop arrives to secure the Power Broker's equipment from the compromised lab. Cap attacks. Meanwhile, FBI agents Jake and Elwood look for Captain America at Avengers Mansion. D-Man returns and attacks by driving one of the Sweat Shop's trucks into the front of the building. The Sweat Shop seal Cap inside the building's boiler room and eventually overpower D-Man; they load up the Broker's machines and take D-Man as a prisoner. Cap finds a passage out of the boiler room into the sewers, dragging Malus along. After being captured by Avengers Mansion's security, Jake and Elwood leave their card with Captain Marvel. The Sweat Shop brings D-Man to the Power Broker, who recognizes him and orders him sent to his research facility as an expendable test subject. In the sewers, Malus' failed augmentation patients attack Cap and Malus escapes.
NOTE: Red Skull is revealed to be funding the Sweat Shop in Cap #350, '89. AWC #76, '91 reveals that Night Shift recruited one of Malus' failed augmentation patients, Misfit, into their ranks following Cap #331, '87; he is presumably present but unseen in Cap #329-331, '87. Jake & Elwood, as their first names suggest, strongly resemble the Blues Brothers.

CAPTAIN AMERICA #330 (June 1987)

"Night Shift" (22 pages)

CREDITS: Mark Gruenwald (writer), Tom Morgan (pencils), Sam DeLaRosa (inks), Diana Albers (letters), Ken Feduniewicz (colors), Daryl Edelman (asst editor), Don Daley (editor), Mike Zeck (c pencils), Bob McLeod (c inks)
FEATURE CHARACTER: Captain America (also in fb between SVTU #12, '77 & Def #44, '77)
SUPPORTING CAST: Demolition Man
GUEST STARS: Night Shift (Shroud's criminal group that secretly fights for justice, 1st): Shroud (Maximillian Coleridge, blind hero able to manipulate Darkforce, also in fb between SVTU #12, '77 & SW #15, '79 fb; last in Av #276, '87), Dansen Macabre (priestess of Shiva), Ticktock (precognitive) (both last in SW #50, '83), Brothers Grimm (Barton & Percy Grimes, magically armed twins, last in IM #188, '84), Digger (Roderick Krupp, macabre raconteur, last in SW #47, '82), Gypsy Moth (Sybil Dvorak, mutant, last in SW #50, '83, chr last in Av #240, '84 fb), Needle (Josef Saint, paralyzing gaze, last in SW #50, '83), Tatterdemalion (Michael Wyatt, disheveled villain, last in Daz #36, '85), Werewolf (Jack Russell, werewolf by night, last in IM #209, '86); Ms. Marvel (Sharon Ventura, super-strong former UCWF wrestler, last in WCA #10, '86, chr last in Cap #331, '87 fb)
VILLAINS: Power Broker & his augmented thugs, Dr. Karl Malus, Malus' failed augmentation patients
OTHER CHARACTERS: Power Broker's gate guard & scientists: Maggie, Mr. Jackson & Dr. Lund, (prev 3 1st)
LOCATIONS/ITEMS: Los Angeles sewers, Power Broker's San Fernando Valley mansion w/underground lab, hospital (in fb); Needle's needles, Digger's shovel, Grimm's eggs, Night Shift's hearses, Power Broker's hover car & augmentation equipment
FLASHBACK: Cap visits Shroud in the hospital as he recovers from Red Skull's nerve gas.
SYNOPSIS: Captain America battles Dr. Malus' failed augmentation patients but is overpowered. Night Shift saves Cap and captures Malus, but then turns on the Avenger. Shroud takes Cap off to the side and convinces Cap to play along with his ruse over the group, and protects him from Dansen Macabre's abilities to fake Cap being mind-controlled into working with them. Malus, under Dansen's thrall, leads them to Power Broker's mansion, where they launch a full-frontal assault. As Night Shift holds Power Broker's augmented guards at bay, Cap confronts Power Broker: Curtiss Jackson. Jackson takes Cap to his underground lab where D-Man and Ms. Marvel are being held captive. When Cap frees D-Man, one of Jackson's scientists injects him with a stimulant. D-Man, now augmented further, goes into a blind rampage and attacks Cap. His body unable to handle the strain of double augmentation, D-Man has a heart attack and collapses.
NOTE: Dr. Lund named in Cap #331, '87.

CAPTAIN AMERICA #331 (July 1987)

"Soldier, Soldier" (22 pages)

CREDITS: Mark Gruenwald (writer), Paul Neary (pencils), Vince Colletta (inks), Diana Albers (letters), Bob Sharen (colors), Daryl Edelman (asst editor), Don Daley (editor), Mike Zeck (c pencils), Bob McLeod (c inks)
FEATURE CHARACTER: Captain America (also in rfb; next in FF #306, WCA Ann #2, Av Ann #16, all '87)
GUEST STARS: Night Shift: Shroud, Brothers Grimm, Dansen Macabre, Digger, Needle (all also in rfb), Gypsy Moth, Tatterdemalion, Ticktock, Werewolf (all next in SAv #3/2, '88); Ms. Marvel (also in rfb & in fb between WCA #10, '86 & Cap #330, '87; next in FF #306, '87)
SUPPORTING CAST: Demolition Man (also in rfb)
VILLAINS: Power Broker (also in rfb; chr next in USAgent #2, '93 fb, next in Cap #358/2, '89) & his augmented thugs (some in fb & rfb), Dr. Karl Malus (also in rfb; next in Cap #363/2, '89), Lt. Michael Lynch (also in rfb & in fb between Thing #36, '86 & Cap #328, '87; last in Cap #328, '87, last app) & Special Task Force 17 (only app), G.I. Max (augmented Special Task Force 17 soldier, dies, only app), Malus' failed augmentation patients (bts, brought to Power Broker's mansion, also in rfb; last app), Douglas Rockwell (1st full app, last voice only in Cap #328, '87)
OTHER CHARACTERS: CSA: Orville Sanderson (next in Cap #335, '87), George Mathers, Adrian Sammish (all 1st), Gen. Lewis Hayworth (last in DD #233, '86); Jake Farber, Elwood McNulty (both last in Cap #329, '87), Power Broker's scientists: Maggie, Mr. Jackson, Dr. Lund (prev last app); Thing (both in rfb)
LOCATIONS/ITEMS: Power Broker's San Fernando mansion w/underground lab, Washington DC inc CSA building, UCWF headquarters, Power Broker's lab (both in rfb); Power Broker's augmentation equipment (also in rfb), Malus' augmentation equipment (in rfb), Ticktock & Lt. Lynch's guns, army helicopter, G.I. Max & other soldiers' rifles
FLASHBACKS: Cap meets Demolition Man, who rescues Cap from Dr. Malus' augmentation machine (Cap #328, '87). Entering the sewers, Cap battles Malus' failed augments (Cap #329, '87). Cap meets Night Shift. They breaks into Power Broker's mansion, but D-Man suffers heart failure after fighting Cap (Cap #330, '87). Lt. Lynch helps Ms. Marvel & Thing escape from Power Broker's thugs (Thing #35-36, '86). While Lynch watches, Power Broker's thugs capture Ms. Marvel.
SYNOPSIS: Captain America successfully performs CPR on D-Man. When Ms. Marvel is released she tries to flee in a panic. Cap calms her by reassuring her she's safe now; she elects to stay with Cap. Cap has Dr. Malus de-augment D-Man. Meanwhile, Jake and Elwood report to the Commission that they haven't been able to find Cap yet. D-Man emerges from the de-augmentation process in stable condition. Shroud and the Night Shift leave while Power Broker gloats that Cap can't pin anything on him. Lt. Lynch and his Special Task Force 17 arrive, assuring Cap he's here to arrest Power Broker. Ms. Marvel recognizes Lynch as Power Broker's partner and attacks. Cap breaks up the fight, but recognizing that Cap knows too much, Lynch instructs GI Max to neutralize Cap. During the fight Lynch panics and accidentally shoots GI Max, killing him. Epilogue: Lynch is reassigned to desk work, Power Broker is released on one million dollar bail and remains in the augmentation business, D-Man is admitted to the hospital, Cap takes Ms. Marvel to the East Coast, and Shroud brings Malus' failed augmentation patients to Power Broker's mansion for treatment.
NOTE: Power Broker's mansion is on Tupelo Drive. Mathers' name is revealed in Cap #333, '87, Sammish's name is revealed in Cap #335, '87.

CAPTAIN AMERICA #332 (August 1987)

"The Choice" (23 pages)

CREDITS: Mark Gruenwald (writer), Tom Morgan (pencils), Bob McLeod (inks), Diana Albers (letters), Ken Feduniewicz (colors), Daryl Edelman (asst editor), Don Daley (editor), Mike Zeck (c pencils), Klaus Janson (c inks)
FEATURE CHARACTER: Captain America (also in rfb, photos & his own thoughts as Nomad, retires as Captain America, next in Cap #336, '87)
GUEST STARS: Captain Marvel (also in Cap's thoughts, last in Av Ann #16, next in Av #285), Sam Wilson (last in ASM #288, next in Cap #336), Nick Fury (bts, out of the country, last in Com #5, next bts in WCA #26, next in WCA #27), Hawkeye (bts, out saving the world, between WCA #25-26) (all '87)
SUPPORTING CAST: Demolition Man (next in Cap #336, '87), Super-Patriot (last in Cap #327, '87), Bernie Rosenthal (bts, in class, last in Cap #327, '87, next in Cap #336, '87 fb)
VILLAINS: Warhead (William Musico, war activist, dies, only app), AIM (bts, created Warhead's bomb), Douglas Rockwell
OTHER CHARACTERS: CSA: Gen. Lewis Hayworth, George Mathers, Adrian Sammish, James Adams (Director of FBI), William Casey (Director of CIA), Gen. Brandon Halstan (prev 3 only app), Henry Peter Gyrich (bts, last in WCA Ann #1, '86, chr last in UXM #228, '88 fb), Dr. Valerie Cooper (bts, last in IM #214, '87, chr last in AWC #84, '92 fb) (both involved yet unseen in CSA meeting); Hiram Riddley (also in Cap's thoughts, last in Cap #321, '86, next in Cap #443, '93), Holly Riddly (bts, on phone w/Cap, last in Cap #321, '86, last app), Ethan Thurm (last in Cap #327, '87), Paul (last in Cap #327, '87, last app), Jake Farber, Elwood McNulty, Gen. Wexler (Commander in Chief of Human Resources Research, only app), Inger Sullivan (Avengers' lawyer, only app), Warhead's mom (bts, packed Warhead's lunch), police (Red, Unit 54 & Mobile 717 named), CBS reporters (inc news anchor), SHIELD receptionist, news vendor, taxi driver, Pentagon security, bystanders (Lance named, others in Cap's thoughts); Freedom Force: Avalanche, Blob, Pyro; Iron Man (also in Cap's thoughts as Tony Stark), Wasp (prev 5 in rfb); Hawkeye (voice on answering machine), Mockingbird, Quicksilver, Scarlet Witch (prev 4 in photo); Black Knight, She-Hulk, Thor, Contrast's replacement Captain America (prev 5 in Cap's thoughts)
LOCATIONS/ITEMS: Washington DC inc Washington Monument, Pentagon w/General Wexler's office & CSA's meeting room, Super-Patriot's hotel room, Cap's hotel room, Bernie's dorm, Sam's office, SHIELD HQ, Demolition Man's hospital room, Hawkeye's apartment, Avengers Mansion; Warhead's uzi, grenades, platform, bullhorn & nuclear bomb, police helicopter & bullhorn, cameras, Cap's contract, Patriot's grapple claws & throwing stars
FLASHBACK: The Avengers fight Freedom Force (Av Ann #15, '86).
SYNOPSIS: Warhead parachutes onto the Washington Monument and prepares his nuclear bomb. Gen. Wexler brushes aside Captain America's citizen's complaint about Lt. Lynch's actions. Wexler hands Cap over to Jake and Elwood, who bring Cap before the CSA. Warhead demands the USA start more wars. The CSA inform Cap since he hasn't been operating officially for the government since his return, he can either do so now or forfeit his identity and the million dollars he was paid. Cap takes 24 hours to consider it. Super-Patriot hears about Warhead on the news. Steve spends the day in a hotel room calling friends and thinking over his situation. Super-Patriot slips past police and into the Washington Monument, captures Warhead's bomb and knocks him off the Monument. Warhead kills himself with a grenade before he can land. Steve returns to the CSA and informs them that his duty is to uphold the American Dream, but being a government employee would require him to preserve the reality of the country; he can't risk compromising his or the Nation's ideals. Steve Rogers returns the uniform and retires as Captain America.
NOTE: Cap's Avengers ID number is 39-55-819A. Cap's wartime file listed his middle initial as "G" in Cap #328, '87, which is consistent with Cap's #247, '80's revelation that he had no middle name but "Grant" was listed to fool enemy spies; this issue erroneously lists the initial as "M."

CAPTAIN AMERICA #333 (September 1987)

"The Replacement" (22 pages)

CREDITS: Mark Gruenwald (writer), Tom Morgan (pencils), Dave Hunt (inks), Ken Lopez, Bill Oakley (letters), Ken Feduniewicz (colors), Daryl Edelman (asst editor), Don Daley (editor), Mike Zeck (c pencils), Bob McLeod (c inks)
FEATURE CHARACTER: Captain America (John Walker, also as Super-Patriot & in photo, becomes Captain America, also in fb1 during Cap #380/2, '90 fb, in fb2 between Cap #372/2, '90 fb & Cap #381/2, '91 fb & in fb3-4 during Cap #381/2, '91 fb)
GUEST STARS: Freedom Force (CSA's super-team): Avalanche, Blob, Pyro (all last in XFac #10, '86), Demolition Man (only in fb4 as "Demolition" Dunphy between Thing #29, '85 & Thing #33, '86)
SUPPORTING CAST: Bold Urban Commandos: Lemar Hoskins (also in fb3 during Cap #381/2, '91 fb), Jerome Johnson, Hector Lennox (all last in Cap #327, '87); Ethan Thurm (also in fb4 during Cap #381/2, '91 fb)
VILLAIN: Douglas Rockwell
OTHER CHARACTERS: CSA: Henry Gyrich, George Mathers, Adrian Sammish (all next in Cap #335, '87), Dr. Valerie Cooper, Gen. Lewis Hayworth; Jake Farber, Elwood McNulty (both next in XFac Ann #4, '89), Mr. X (in fb4 after Cap #271, '82, last app), Caleb & Emily Walker (John's parents), Kate Walker (John's sister) (prev 3 1st, only in fb1 during Cap #380/2, '90 fb), Mike Walker(John's brother, bts in coffin in fb1, only app) (prev 4 also in John's thoughts), priest, soldiers (both in fb1), Power Broker's secretary (in fb3), Capt. Lou Albano (in fb4), Katy ("AM Washington" host), "AM Washington" production assistant & film crew; Warhead, police, reporters, bystanders (prev 4 in rfb), G.I. Max, Nuke (both in Gen. Hayworth's thoughts), Falcon, Nomad, Nick Fury (prev 3 in photos & on cover), Thing (as Blackbeard), Beast, Dr. Octopus, Punisher, Tony Stark, Wyatt Wingfoot, Dawn Geiger (Marvel designer), Laura Hitchcock (Star Comics asst editor), Not Irving Forbush, Still Not Irving Forbush, Jack Kirby, Stan Lee (prev 12 on cover)

LOCATIONS/ITEMS: Washington DC inc CSA's Pentagon meeting room, "AM Washington" studio, Dr. Cooper's office, Walker's hotel room, Lincoln Memorial & Washington Monument (rfb); copy of Washington Post, News 6 cameras

FLASHBACKS: Super-Patriot stops Warhead's protest on top of the Washington Monument (Cap #332, '87). John Walker and his family attend his brother's funeral (1). John joins the army (2). John signs up for Power Broker's treatment (3). Ethan turns John into Super-Patriot (4).

SYNOPSIS: The CSA discusses who could replace Captain America until Dr. Cooper suggests Super-Patriot. After Super-Patriot completes an interview with "AM Washington," Jake and Elwood escort him into Dr. Cooper's office. She interviews him and says he's being considered to replace Cap. He jumps at the chance, but continues to wonder why Cap quit. Walker decides to call Cap's hotline to arrange a meeting, but instead of Cap he's "ambushed" by the Bold Urban Commandos. Walker promises to take them all with him in his career move. Later, Walker is given Cap's uniform and is told to train with Freedom Force, but they take the opportunity to beat him up. Val is forced to end the session when Blob strangles Cap; she orders Cap to study footage of the original Cap in combat. Later, Cap is told only one of his friends passed the FBI's background check and he'll have to drop Ethan as his manager. Cap accepts the ruling.

NOTE: "American Graffiti" features a front cover character key.

CAPTAIN AMERICA #334 (October 1987)

"Basic Training" (22 pages)

CREDITS: Mark Gruenwald (writer), Tom Morgan (pencils), Dave Hunt (inks), Ken Lopez (letters), Ken Feduniewicz (colors), Daryl Edelman (asst editor), Don Daley (editor), Mike Zeck (c pencils), Bob McLeod (c inks)
FEATURE CHARACTER: Captain America (also as Guardsman XL5)
GUEST STARS: Freedom Force: Avalanche, Blob, Pyro (all next in UXM #223, '87), Destiny, Mystique (both last in XFac #10, '86, chr next in XFac Ann #6/3, '91 fb, next in UXM #223, '87); Taskmaster (can duplicate any fighting style he sees, last in Thing #26, '85, chr last in Cap Ann #11/3, '92 fb, next bts in Cap #346, '88)
SUPPORTING CAST: Bucky (Lemar Hoskins, becomes Bucky, also as Guardsman), Jerome Johnson, Hector Lennox (both next in Cap #341/2, '88), Ethan Thurm (next in Cap #347, '88)
VILLAIN: Douglas Rockwell

OTHER CHARACTERS: CSA: Dr. Valerie Cooper (next in UXM #223, '87), Gen. Lewis Hayworth; Sgt. Don Simmons (Cap's drill sergeant, 1st), Dr. Cooper's secretary (voice only, only app), Guardsmen (armored sentries), cook, soldiers, Sand Bar patrons & bartender, bystanders; Captain America (Rogers) Red Skull, Nazis (prev 3 in archival video footage)
LOCATIONS/ITEMS: Fort George G. Meade inc video room, Val's office, gym & cafeteria; Sand Bar; training equipment inc dummies & guns, Guardsmen armors, Taskmaster's cape & shield
SYNOPSIS: Captain America studies archival footage of Steve Rogers as Cap in combat and learns that his friend Lemar has been brought in as his partner, Bucky. Cap's training isn't doing much good to improve his fighting skills and he continues to be ridiculed by Freedom Force. Cap and Bucky fail miserably in a sparring session against some Guardsmen; they later meet with Ethan, who blackmails John and Lemar for one million dollars or he'll tell the public they're replacements. Cap trains with Taskmaster, who's photogenic reflexes allow him to train Cap in Rogers' fighting style. Posing as Guardsmen Cap and Bucky attack Ethan, Jerome and Hector, telling Ethan he'll be arrested for treason if he goes public. Dr. Cooper later confronts Cap about the incident, and Cap admits to stealing the suits and wrecking the tavern.
NOTE: Sgt. Simmons' name is revealed in OHMU HC12, '10.

CAPTAIN AMERICA #335 (November 1987)

"Baptism of Fire" (22 pages)

CREDITS: Mark Gruenwald (writer), Tom Morgan (pencils), Dave Hunt (inks), Jack Morelli (letters), Bob Sharen (colors), Marc Siry (asst editor), Ralph Macchio (editor), Joe Sinnott (c inks)
FEATURE CHARACTER: Captain America (also as Watchdog)
SUPPORTING CAST: Bucky (also as "Looker Magazine" talent scout, next in Cap #338, '88)
VILLAINS: Watchdogs (fanatics against indecency, 1st, Watchdog Prime, Harold Simmons, Willie Gordon & Monty named, next in Cap #345, '88), Douglas Rockwell (next bts in Cap #341/2, '88, next in Cap #344, '88), Red Skull (bts, funding Watchdogs, last in Cap #329, '87, next bts in Cap #343, '88)
OTHER CHARACTERS: CSA: Dr. Valerie Cooper (between UXM #223-224, '87), Henry Gyrich (last in Cap #333, '87, next in NFVS #2, '88), Gen. Lewis Hayworth (next in Cap #344, '88), George Mathers (last in Cap #333, '87, next in Cap #344, '88), Orville Sanderson (last in Cap #331, '87, next in Cap #345, '88), Adrian Sammish (last in Cap #333, '87, next in Cap #339, '88), Martin Farrow, Wesley Werner, Henry Yates (prev 3 1st, next in Cap #347, '88); Kate Tollifson (John's sister, bts, invites John over for dinner, last in Cap #333, '87 fb, chr last in Cap #381/2, '91 fb, next bts in Cap #353, '89), Sgt. Don Simmons (last app), "Adult Books and Toys" store owner (dies), potential models (Mary-Lynn Norfolk, Jobeth Tucker, Tammy named), firemen, police, bystanders
LOCATIONS/ITEMS: Fort George G. Meade inc gym, locker room & Sammish's office; Custer's Grove, GA inc barber shop, hotel, police station, men's club basement & library, "Adult Books and Toys" store (destroyed); training equipment inc spiked balls, training robots, mallet & rods, Watchdogs' guns, firebomb, torches & noose
SYNOPSIS: With his training completed, the CSA swears Captain America into service. Meanwhile, the Watchdogs blow up a porn shop and kill the owner. The CSA sends Cap and Bucky to investigate Cap's hometown, Custer's Grove, a Watchdog hotspot. Lemar poses as a "Looker Magazine" talent scout and John "breaks up" the auditions to infiltrate the Watchdogs. They're both arrested; John is set free and joins the Watchdogs, but Lemar is going to be hung by the group. Cap leaves Lemar to take care of himself while he saves a library that refused to remove the books the Watchdogs found offensive. Cap races back to find Lemar managed to free himself and stop his executioners. Cap figures the CSA had key people placed in the Watchdogs in order to test him; a realization that angers him and leads him to wonder if that was why Steve quit.
NOTE: Kate's married name is revealed in Cap #353, '89. Douglas Rockwell is called "Miles" here.

CAPTAIN AMERICA #336 (December 1987)

"Natural Calling!" (22 pages)

CREDITS: Mark Gruenwald (writer), Tom Morgan (pencils), Dave Hunt (inks), Jack Morelli (letters), Bob Sharen (colors), Marc Siry (asst editor), Ralph Macchio (editor), Mike Zeck (c art)
FEATURE CHARACTER: Captain America (only in fb1, next in Cap #338, '88)
GUEST STARS: Demolition Man, Falcon (both last in Cap #332, '87), Nomad (last in Cap #325, '86) (all also in fb2), Redwing (last in ASM #287, '87)
SUPPORTING CAST: Steve Rogers (also in rfb as Captain America, also in fb1, last in Cap #332, '87)
VILLAINS: Brother Nature (Mark Diering, controls plants & animals, 1st, also in photo & pfb; next in Tb:BP, '08) Watchdogs (only in fb1, next in Cap #345, '88)
OTHER CHARACTERS: Vagabond (last in Cap #325, '86 as Priscilla Lyons), Bernie Rosenthal (only in fb2, last in Cap #327, '86, next voice only in Cap #355, '89), loggers (others in pfb), news anchor, bartender, deer, owl, grizzly bear, police, firemen, reporters (prev 3 in fb1), judge, lawyers (both in pfb); CSA: Douglas Rockwell, Gen. Lewis Haywerth, George Mathers, Adrian Sammish (all in rfb), Bucky (Hoskins, only on cover logo image)
LOCATIONS/ITEMS: Kleppel Health Clinic in Harristown, Alabama (in fb1), Steve's hotel room, Bernie's dorm (both in fb2), CSA's Pentagon meeting room (in rfb), Washington State inc bar & forest, D-Man's Santa Monica home; Steve's van & motorcycle, Nomad's motorcycle, D-Man's Stars & Stripes briefcase
FLASHBACKS: Captain America stops the Watchdogs from attacking a health clinic (1). Steve Rogers is ordered to work for the CSA, but ultimately decides to retire as Cap (Cap #332, '87). Bernie tries to talk Steve into fighting the CSA legally, Falcon suggests a protest, Nomad suggests blowing the whistle on the CSA's tactics, and D-Man offers his support (2). As a park ranger, Brother Nature tries to fight the logging industry legally, but is laughed out of court. He takes matters into his own hands, but is seemingly killed by loggers (p).
SYNOPSIS: As the news reports on Captain America and logging industry saboteur Brother Nature, Steve Rogers stops loggers from going on a murderous rampage against Brother Nature. As Steve drives across Washington State his van suddenly falls into a chasm in the road. Meanwhile D-Man, now in charge of the Stars & Stripes hotline, calls Nomad and Falcon to his home to propose they search for Steve. Steve meets Brother Nature, who caused the chasm. When Steve confronts Brother Nature over his actions the activist attacks with wind, animals and earthquakes, eventually causing them both to fall into a chasm. Steve tends to Brother Nature's wounds, to the activist's surprise. When Steve carries them out of the pit Brother Nature realizes he's caused the damage he sought to prevent. Steve realizes he could also cause damage if he goes to war with the government, and decides not to.
NOTE: Brother Nature's real name revealed in CW:BDR #1, '07.

CAPTAIN AMERICA #337 (January 1988)

"The Long Road Back" (22 pages)

CREDITS: Mark Gruenwald (writer), Tom Morgan (pencils), Dave Hunt (inks), Joe Rosen (letters), Gregory Wright (colors), Marc Siry (asst editor), Ralph Macchio (editor), Michael Zeck (c pencils), Bob McLeod (c inks)
FEATURE CHARACTER: Captain America (only on cover logo image)
GUEST STARS: Redwing (next in Cap #339, '88), Demolition Man, Falcon, Nomad
SUPPORTING CAST: Steve Rogers (also as Nomad in Nomad's thoughts, also in rfb, becomes the Captain)
VILLAINS: Serpent Squad: Black Racer (Ariana Saddiqi, super fast), Copperhead (Davis Lawfers, fires electric discharge), Fer-de-Lance (Teresa Vasquez, has long blades in gloves) (all 1st), Puff Adder (Gordon Fraley, swells in size & strength, sprays venom & gas, 1st but chr last in IML #8, '11), Viper (bts, leading Serpent Squad, last in NM #54, '87, next in Cap #341/3, '88)
OTHER CHARACTERS: Vagabond, Gold Obelisk Casino patrons (inc Sean Connery), guards (some die) & employees, police, bystanders, fish; Brother Nature (only in rfb), Bucky (Hoskins, only on cover logo image)
LOCATIONS/ITEMS: Washington State, Las Vegas inc Gold Obelisk Casino; Steve's red, white & black uniform (1st), van & motorcycle, Nomad's motorcycle, D-Man's Stars & Stripes briefcase, motorcycle & rented limo, casino guard's guns, police guns
FLASHBACK: Steve battles Brother Nature (Cap #336, '87).
SYNOPSIS: Searching for Steve Rogers in Washington State, Falcon, Demolition Man, Nomad and Vagabond happen upon Steve's van, which is still wedged in a crevice in the road. Despite his heart condition, D-Man lifts the van out. In Las Vegas, Black Racer, Copperhead, Fer-de-Lance and Puff Adder sneak into the Gold Obelisk Casino and force their way to the vault. Steve returns to his van and reunites with his friends, announcing that he's returning to crime-fighting but he won't challenge the government over the Captain America name. D-Man gives Steve a "basic black" version of his uniform, and Steve decides on the name "the Captain." The Serpent Squad hole up in the casino's penthouse with hostages; their main concern is that the police spell their names right. Hearing of the hostage situation, the Captain and his team travel to Vegas and offer their help, but the police don't recognize any of them and refuse their help. They sneak in anyway and quickly defeat the villains.
NOTE: The cover pays homage to Av #4, '64's cover. Black Racer's real name is revealed in OHMU HC10, '09, Copperhead's in OHMU:ME #6, '91, Fer-de-Lance's in OHMU:ME #13, '91 and Puff Adder's in OHMU:ME #12, '91.

CAPTAIN AMERICA #338 (February 1988)

"Power Struggle" (22 pages)

CREDITS: Mark Gruenwald (writer), Kieron Dwyer (pencils), Tom Morgan (inks), Jack Morelli (letters), Gregory Wright (colors), Marc Siry (asst editor), Ralph Macchio (editor), Ron Frenz (c pencils), Joe Sinnott (c inks)
FEATURE CHARACTER: Captain America
GUEST STARS: Demolition Man, Falcon, Nomad
SUPPORTING CAST: Bucky (last in Cap #335, '87), the Captain
VILLAINS: Serpent Squad: Black Racer, Copperhead, Fer-de-Lance, Puff Adder (all also in rfb, next in Cap #341/3, '88); Sidewinder (last in Cap #319, '86, next in Cap #341/3, '88), Professor Power (also in rfb & bts in pfb, last in Def #130, '84, dies, next in AWC Ann #7, '92, see NOTE), his scientists (Mercater & Zevon named, one also in rfb), Roman guards & robot centurions, Leviathan (Edward Cobert, immense size & strength, last in Def #128, '84, next in AvS #28/2, '90 as Gargantua)
OTHER CHARACTERS: Vagabond (bts, waiting for Nomad to be released from jail), SHIELD agent (in pfb), Sidewinder's chauffeur, police, bystanders; Defenders: Angel, Beast, Iceman, Valkyrie; Moondragon, Secret Empire, Gold Obelisk Casino employees (all in rfb)
LOCATIONS/ITEMS: Power's castle inc lab, Las Vegas jail; Power's psychometer, rocket (both in rfb), equipment & jet-car, Roman guards' uzis, police guns, Sidewinder's limo
FLASHBACKS: The Captain and his allies defeat the serpent-themed villains (Cap #337, '88). Presidential advisor Anthony Power tends to his mentally ill son (MTU #118, '82). Power transfers his mind into his son's body (MTU #124, '82), and reorganizes the Secret Empire (Def #127, '84 fb). The Defenders battle Power and Moondragon drives Power insane (Def #130, '84). Power escapes SHIELD custody (pfb).
SYNOPSIS: Captain America and Bucky raid Professor Power's castle and overpower his Roman guards, but fall to Power's robot centurions. Meanwhile in Las Vegas, the Captain and his friends are in jail for obstruction of justice alongside the Serpent Squad. Cap and Bucky rally to defeat the robots and find Power being worked on in his lab, but they're grabbed by a giant man. Sidewinder teleports into the Las Vegas jail and offers the Serpent Squad a spot in his Serpent Society. Cap and Bucky defeat Leviathan. The Captain and his friends break free to stop Sidewinder from freeing the villains. Cap and Bucky prevent Power's men from fleeing with Power. The Captain surrenders when Sidewinder threatens to kill Fer-de-Lance. Power groggily tries to fend off Cap; Cap retaliates by beating Power to death, which he later regrets.
NOTE: AWC Ann #7, '92 reveals that Power's mind is restored to his original body when his son's body dies here; PPSSM #198, '93 reveals that his son's body will also be revived.

CAPTAIN AMERICA #339 (March 1988)

"America the Scorched!" (22 pages)

CREDITS: Mark Gruenwald (writer), Kieron Dwyer (pencils), Tony DeZunga (inks), Jack Morelli (letters), Gregory Wright (colors), Marc Siry (asst editor), Ralph Macchio (editor), Ron Frenz (c pencils), Bob McLeod (c inks)
FEATURE CHARACTER: Captain America (next in Cap #341/2, '88)
GUEST STARS: Freedom Force: Avalanche (last in UXM #226, '88, last bts in UXM #227, '88, next in NM #65, '88), Blob, Pyro (both last in UXM #227, '88, next in NM #65, '88); Tony Stark (last & also in IM #227, '88, also in IM #228, '88 fb, chr next in Thor #390, '88, fb, next in IM #228, '88), Redwing (last in Cap #337, '88), D-Man, Falcon, Nomad
SUPPORTING CAST: Bucky (next in Cap #341/2, '88 as Battlestar), the Captain (also bts in IM #228, '88 fb, IM #227, '88 & IM #228, '88 fb, chr next in Thor #390, '88 fb, next in IM #228, '88)
VILLAINS: Famine (Autumn Rolfson, Apocalypse's Horseman, can cause extreme hunger & disintegrate organic matter), Apocalypse (bts, teleports Famine away) (both between XFac #25-26, '88)
OTHER CHARACTERS: Vagabond, US military (Redfox One & Redfox Two named) & officers, farmer (dies), pilot, soldiers, cows (some die); government bureaucrats, Ronald Reagan (both in dream)
LOCATIONS/ITEMS: Kansas cornfield, Fort George G. Meade inc barracks #17, Stark Enterprises LA; Famine's robot horse, D-Man's rented plane, US military helicopters & plane, the Captain's, D-Man's & Nomad's parachutes, the Captain's make-shift shield, new Adamantium shield (1st) & target dummies
SYNOPSIS: Famine ravages Kansas farmland, destroying any source of food she sees. Steve Rogers wakes from a dream of fighting government bureaucrats on a plane rented by D-Man and hears reports of Famine's rampage. Meanwhile, Captain America and Bucky are ordered to deal with Famine. Famine battles military helicopters until the Captain's team parachutes in to stop her; Falcon is quickly removed from the fight when Famine starves him. D-Man battle's Famine's robot horse and Nomad is starved; the Captain uses a tractor grille as a make-shift and defeats Famine. Famine and her steed are suddenly teleported away. Later, Cap and Bucky arrive to find no suspects in sight. Two weeks later, Steve visits Tony Stark to see if Tony Stark has made him a new shield. Stark has, but with the hope it will keep Steve away from his secret agenda.
NOTE: Cover-labeled "Fall of the Mutants Tie-In." Fort George G. Meade is mistakenly called Fort George M. Meade. The last two pages are mirrored and expanded on in IM #227, '88 & IM #228, '88 fb. Story continues in IM #228, '88, erroneously listed here as IM #238, '89.

CAPTAIN AMERICA #340 (April 1988)

"Breakout" (22 pages)

CREDITS: Mark Gruenwald (writer), Kieron Dwyer (pencils), Al Milgrom (inks), Jack Morelli (letters), Bob Sharen (colors), Marc Siry (asst editor), Ralph Macchio (editor), Ron Frenz (c art)
FEATURE CHARACTER: Captain America (only on cover logo image)
GUEST STARS: Demolition Man, Nomad (both next in Cap #342, '88), Falcon, Redwing (both next in SAv #6/2, '88), Iron Man (also in rfb; during IM #228, '88)
SUPPORTING CAST: The Captain (also in rfb & as Captain America in rfb; last & also in IM #228, '88, next in Av #290, '88)
VILLAINS: Armadillo (last in Cap #316, '86, next in AvS #26, '89), Griffin (Johnny Horton, part lion & eagle mutate, last in WCA #10, '86, next in AvS #26, '89), Mr. Hyde (also in rfb; last in IM #228, '88, next in AvS #26, '89), Titania (Mary MacPherran, super strong, last in IM #228, '88, next in SAv #14/2, '88), Vibro (Dr. Alton Vibereaux, controls seismic vibrations, last in IM #192, '85, next in AWC #58, '90)
OTHER CHARACTERS: Vagabond (next in Cap #342, '88), James Rhodes (during IM #228, '88), Guardsmen (some also in rfb), Vault personnel (Adams, Cucola, Galvin, Grau, Hargrave, Kostmeier & Terry named); Edwin Jarvis, cook (both in rfb), Bucky (Hoskins, only on cover logo image)
LOCATIONS/ITEMS: The Vault & surrounding mountain highway, Avengers Mansion, diner (both in rfb); the Captain's rebreather, van & motorcycle (destroyed), Iron Man's negator pack, D-Man's & Nomad's motorcycles (destroyed), Vault personnel's laser guns, Hyde's stolen truck
FLASHBACKS: Steve gets a new shield from Tony Stark (Cap #339, '88). Steve tries to talk Stark out of his crusade, but ends up fighting him at the Vault (IM #238, '88). Mr. Hyde pummels Jarvis (Av #274, '86).
SYNOPSIS: At the Vault, Iron Man paralyzes the Captain and destroys the last of the Guardsman armor and escapes. While the Captain regroups with his friends, Mr. Hyde, Titania, Armadillo, Griffen and Vibro take advantage of the Vault's power loss to make an escape. Hearing an explosion caused by Vibro, the Captain and his friends investigate; Falcon battles Griffin and Cap angrily takes on Mr. Hyde, remembering how he mercilessly beat Jarvis. Titania throws D-Man off the mountain. While fighting Nomad, Vibro accidentally causes an avalanche and falls off the mountain. Falcon catches D-Man, who knocks out Griffin. The Captain viciously defeats Hyde, but stops short of killing him. D-Man secretly lets Titania escape, scared that she might throw him off the mountain again. Vagabond pulls up in the van with Armadillo in tow, having talked him into giving himself up.
NOTE: The first two pages mirror the last pages of IM #228, '88. Vagabond is listening to the song "Bad" by Michael Jackson.

CAPTAIN AMERICA #341 (May 1988)

"Break-in" (8 pages)

CREDITS: Mark Gruenwald (writer), Kieron Dwyer (pencils), Al Milgrom (inks), Jack Morelli (letters), Bob Sharen (colors), Marc Siry (asst editor), Ralph Macchio (editor), Ron Frenz (c pencils)
FEATURE CHARACTER: The Captain (last in Thor #390, '88, last bts in WCA #31, '88)
GUEST STAR: Iron Man (between IM #229-230, '88)
OTHER CHARACTERS: Dawn Lovett (Tony's date, only app), Louis (Stark's driver, bts on phone)
LOCATIONS/ITEMS: Tony Stark's mansion; the Captain's Adamantium shield (last app)
SYNOPSIS: Tony Stark returns home to find the Captain waiting for him. The Captain returns his Adamantium shield, tells Stark that his actions at the Vault resulted in two villains escaping, and that he's taking Stark to the authorities. Tony quickly armors up and the two fight. Iron Man paralyzes the Captain with his high-density beam and promises they'll talk when he finishes destroying his stolen technology. Steve realizes he needs to focus on his own responsibilities rather than track Iron Man down, and hopes that Stark keeps his word when it's over.

2ND STORY: "Free Speech" (8 pages)
CREDITS: Mark Gruenwald (writer), Kieron Dwyer (pencils), Al Milgrom (inks), Jack Morelli (letters), Bob Sharen (colors), Marc Siry (asst editor), Ralph Macchio (editor)
FEATURE CHARACTER: Captain America (next in PPSSM #137-138, '88, Cap #343, '88)
SUPPORTING CAST: Battlestar (Lemar Hoskins, 1st as Battlestar, also in pfb as Bucky; last in Cap #339, '88 as Bucky, next in Cap #343, '88)
VILLAINS: Left-Winger (Hector Lennox, 1st as Left-Winger), Right-Winger (Jerome Johnson, 1st as Right-Winger) (both last in Cap #334, '87, next in Cap #347, '88), Douglas Rockwell (bts, approved Lemar's name change, last in Cap #335, '87, next in Cap #344, '88)
OTHER CHARACTERS: Guardsman (in pfb), press conference announcer & attendees (inc politicians & reporters), Secret Service, helicopter pilot; Bucky (Barnes, in Guardsman's thoughts)
LOCATIONS/ITEMS: Fort George G. Meade, Washington Monument; Battlestar's shield (1st), Right-Winger's fiery sword & helicopter, secret service's guns
FLASHBACK: A Vault Guardsman tells Bucky that "Buck" is a racist term in some parts of the country, and that "Bucky" isn't a fitting name for a black man who's just as strong as Cap, despite being his partner (p).
SYNOPSIS: Battlestar shows Captain America his new identity and uniform. The two hold a press conference, where Cap reveals he's not the original and introduces his partner Battlestar. The proceedings are interrupted when Left-Winger and Right-Winger, Cap's former Bold Urban Commandos buddies from his time as Super-Patriot, crash the stage and reveal Cap's identity, John Walker, to the world. The Wingers are

oset that John and Lemar left them behind to become "sell-outs." Cap and Battlestar fight and eventually subdue the pair, allowing the Secret Service to arrest them. Cap and Battlestar may have won, but the damage has already been done.
NOTE: Fort George G. Meade erroneously called Fort George M. Meade here.

3RD STORY: "In Our Midst!" (7 pages)
CREDITS: Mark Gruenwald (writer), Kieron Dwyer (pencils), Al Milgrom (inks), Jack Morelli (letters), Bob Sharen (colors), Marc Siry (asst editor), Ralph Macchio (editor)
FEATURE CHARACTER: Sidewinder (last in Cap #338, '88)
SUPPORTING CAST: Serpent Society: Anaconda, Asp, Bushmaster, Cottonmouth, Rattler (all last in Cap #319, '86), Cobra, Diamondback (both last in Cap #320, '86), Black Mamba (Tanya Sealy, last in Av #274, '86)
VILLAINS: Serpent Squad: Viper (also as Tanya Sealy, last bts in Cap #337, '88), Black Racer, Copperhead, Fer-De-Lance, Puff Adder (prev last in Cap #338, '88), Boomslang (Marc Reimer, throws "serpent-rangs," 1st), Coachwhip (Beatrix Keener, uses whips, 1st), Rock Python (M'Gula, rock hard body, 1st)
LOCATIONS/ITEMS: Serpent Society HQ inc meeting room, communications room, Black Mamba's, Sidewinder's, Diamondback's & rooms; Fer-de-Lance's signal beacon, Viper's teleportation ring, gun & poison, anti-venom
SYNOPSIS: Sidewinder welcomes Black Racer, Copperhead, Fer-de-lance and Puff Adder to the Serpent Society before outlining the success they've experienced as a group. After adjourning, Fer-de-Lance uses her signal beacon to allow Viper to teleport in. Viper knocks out Black Mamba, disguises herself in Tanya's maid costume and arrives for Tanya's liaison with Sidewinder. Viper poisons Sidewinder, but he manages to teleport away into Diamondback's room. Giving him anti-venom, Diamondback teleports them to the communications room as Viper's Serpent Squad storms the headquarters. Realizing there's only one person she can trust for help, Diamondback calls Captain America's Stars & Stripes hotline.
NOTE: Boomslang, Coachwhip and Rock Python are named in Cap #342, '88. Boomslang's real name is revealed in OHMU HC10, '09 and Rock Python's in OHMU:ME #2, '91. Coachwhip's first name is revealed in OHMU:T, '05, her surname is revealed in OHMU HC5, '08.

CAPTAIN AMERICA #342 (June 1988)

"The Snake Pit" (22 pages)

CREDITS: Mark Gruenwald (writer), Kieron Dwyer (pencils), Al Milgrom (inks), Jack Morelli (letters), Bob Sharen (colors), Marc Siry (asst editor), Ralph Macchio (editor), Ron Frenz (c pencils)
FEATURE CHARACTER: Captain America (only on cover logo image)
GUEST STARS: Demolition Man, Nomad (both last in Cap #340, '88), Falcon, Redwing (both last in SAv #6/2, '88), Black Panther (via satellite, last in FF #313, '88 fb, next in BP #1, '88)
SUPPORTING CAST: The Captain
VILLAINS: Viper & her Serpent Squad: Cottonmouth (next in X Ann #13, '89), Anaconda, Cobra, Rattler (prev 4 join Viper's Serpent Squad), Coachwhip, Puff Adder (both next in Cap #355, '89), Black Racer, Fer-De-Lance (both next in X Ann #13, '89), Slither (last in Def #130, '84), Boomslang, Copperhead, Rock Python; Serpent Society: Sidewinder (next in Cap #345, '88), Asp, Black Mamba, Bushmaster (prev 3 next in X Ann #13, '89), Diamondback
OTHER CHARACTERS: Vagabond (last in Cap #340, '88, next in Cap #345, '88), M'Daka (Wakandan mechanic, 1st, next bts in Av#300, '89, next in Cap#370, '90), K'Bali (Wakandan scientist), Bill (Fred's Lube & Pump employee), paramedic, snakes, Battlestar (only on cover logo image)
LOCATIONS/ITEMS: D-Man's Santa Monica home, Serpent Society HQ, Fred's Lube & Pump gas station; the Captain's Vibranium shield (1st), Stars & Stripes briefcase, Wakandan aircraft, Viper's gun, poison & mutagenic chemical canisters
SYNOPSIS: Demolition Man shows Vagabond some fighting moves until Nomad stops them. They swear nothing untoward is happening, but Nomad tries to start a fight with D-Man anyway. A Wakandan aircraft arrives, the Captain enters, and is given a new Vibranium shield compliments of Black Panther. Falcon tells the Captain that Diamondback has called the Stars & Stripes hotline. Meanwhile, Diamondback escapes from Viper's attacking Serpent Squad with Sidewinder. The Captain receives another message and meets Diamondback at a gas station. Vagabond sees Sidewinder to the hospital. As Viper poisons the Serpent Society members that won't join her, the Captain and his friends storm the headquarters. Viper escapes with some of her Squad, and the Captain sees to administering antivenom to the loyal Serpent Society members. Vagabond stops Black Racer from attacking Sidewinder's ambulance. The Captain is pleased that so many Serpents have been captured, but is worried about what Viper's plan is.

CAPTAIN AMERICA #343 (July 1988)

"Slippery People" (22 pages)

CREDITS: Mark Gruenwald (writer), Kieron Dwyer (pencils), Al Milgrom (inks), Jack Morelli (letters), Bob Sharen (colors), Marc Siry (asst editor), Ralph Macchio (editor), Ron Frenz (c pencils), John Romita (c inks)
FEATURE CHARACTER: Captain America
GUEST STARS: Dr. Druid (bts on phone w/Falcon, last in Av #294, '88), Falcon, Redwing (both next in Cap #345, '88), Demolition Man, Nomad
SUPPORTING CAST: Battlestar (last in Cap #341/2, '88), the Captain
VILLAINS: Resistants (mutant rights activists, 1st): Crucible (Byron Calley), Meteorite (Ned Lanthrop), Paralyzer (Randall Darby) (all last in Def #130, '84, next in Cap #346, '88), Occult (Peter Quinn, last in Def #87, '80, next in Cap #346, '88); Viper & her Serpent Squad: Anaconda, Rattler (both next in X Ann #13, '89), Rock Python (next

in Cap #355, '89), Boomslang, Cobra, Copperhead, Slither; Red Skull (bts, funding the Resistants, last bts in Cap #335, '87), Diamondback

OTHER CHARACTERS: Quill (mutant teen, 1st, next in Cap #346, '88), Ronald Reagan (US President, voice only, last in UXM #201, '86, last bts in PPSSM #127, '87), Nancy Reagan (voice only, last in Av #246, '84), water purification plant employees (Dan named), pilot (dies), bystanders

LOCATIONS/ITEMS: Washington, DC inc water purification plant & White House, Cleveland, OH, Serpent Society HQ; helicopter, Serpen Saucers, Viper's teleportation ring, gun & mutagenic chemical

SYNOPSIS: In Cleveland Captain America and Battlestar arrest Quill, a teenage mutant, for being an unregistered mutant. Battlestar is uneasy; he feels the Mutant Registration Act is just a way to oppress the mutant minority. Meanwhile, the Captain latches onto the escaping Viper's Serpent Saucer. Diamondback and the Captain's friends follow in a second Serpent Saucer. The Resistants attack Cap and Battlestar's helicopter in mid-air, quickly defeating the heroes and liberate Quill. In Washington, DC, Copperhead and Cobra poison the capital's water supply. Meanwhile, Nomad and Diamondback fire on Viper's Serpent Saucer, against D-Man's advice. Viper teleports out before it crashes, but the Captain is forced to land on his new Vibranium shield; it absorbs the impact of his landing. The Captain quickly defeats Viper as Falcon tells the Avengers of Viper's poisoning Washington's water. Cap and Battlestar find their pilot dead and Cap swears vengeance against the Resistants. That night, the President enjoys a refreshing glass of water…

NOTE: Red Skull is revealed to be funding the Resistants in Cap #350, '89. Quill is named in Cap #346, '88.

CAPTAIN AMERICA #344 (August 1988)

"Don't Tread On Me!" (39 pages)

CREDITS: Mark Gruenwald (writer), Kieron Dwyer (pencils), Al Milgrom (inks), Joe Rosen (letters), Bob Sharen (colors), Marc Siry (asst editor), Ralph Macchio (editor), Ron Frenz (c pencils)

FEATURE CHARACTER: Captain America (also in photo)

GUEST STARS: Dr. Druid (bts on phone w/Sikorsky, next in NFVS #2, '89), Mr. Fantastic (bts, called in to analyze Viper's poison, last in PP #36, '88, next bts in ASM #300, '88, chr next in MCP #13/3, '89 fb, next in C&D #2, '88), Dr. Hank Pym (bts, called in to analyze Viper's poison, last in WCA #37, '88, next in WoSM #46, '89), Demolition Man, Nomad

SUPPORTING CAST: Battlestar (also in photo), the Captain (also in rfb as Captain America; chr next in Cap #345, '88 fb, next in MCP #2/4, '88)

VILLAINS: Viper & her Serpent Squad: Boomslang, Cobra, Copperhead (prev 3 next in X Ann #13, '89), Slither (next in Cap #419, '93); Red Skull (bts, listening to Rockwell on phone), Douglas Rockwell (last bts in Cap #341, '88), Diamondback

OTHER CHARACTERS: CSA: Gen. Lewis Hayworth, George Mathers (both last in Cap #335, '87), Raymond Sikorski (last in Av Ann #15, '86, last bts in Av #278, '87), Dr. Valerie Cooper (last in UXM #224); Ronald Reagan (also in photo & as snake man, next in Cap #348, '88), Nancy Reagan (also as snake woman, next in MCP #40/2, '90), Adrian Sammish's secretary (bts on phone w/Cap, only app), Washington, DC residents (many turned into snake people), Secret Service, police, firefighters, paramedics, reporters, birds; Franklin D. Roosevelt (rfb), George Washington (as statue & bust), Freedom Force: Avalanche, Blob, Crimson Commando, Destiny, Pyro, Mystique, Stonewall, Super Sabre (prev 8 in photos)

LOCATIONS/ITEMS: Washington, DC inc CSA building w/Rockwell's office & White House w/oval office (also in rfb), master bedroom & press room, Fort George G. Meade inc holding cells; Serpent Saucers, Serpent Society micro-communicator, Red Skull's listening device, Viper's guns & mutagenic chemical, Secret Service guns, police guns

FLASHBACK: President Roosevelt gives Captain America his circular shield (Cap #255, '81).

SYNOPSIS: Washington, DC erupts in riots as Viper's poison transform people into snake men. Viper's remaining Serpent Squad return to their Serpent Saucer to find the Captain and Diamondback waiting for them. Cobra escapes to another nearby Serpent Saucer, but D-Man and Nomad are inside guarding Viper and Slither. Cobra tries to kill Viper, but Nomad inadvertently helps her escape. Nomad chases Cobra while Viper poisons D-Man. CSA Commissioner Rockwell calls Captain America and Battlestar to Washington; Battlestar becomes even more frustrated with the CSA. Finding the poisoned D-Man, Diamondback administers anti-venom while the Captain searches for Viper. Nomad is overpowered by snake men as Viper enters the White House. Cap and Battlestar find the Serpent Saucers and capture Diamondback and D-Man without bothering to hear their story. The Captain tracks Viper to the White House where he battles the President, now fully a snake man. Viper kills the arriving Secret Service and escapes and physical exertion causes the President's body to burn away Viper's mutagenic chemical, returning him to normal. The Captain chases Viper, but she's already been subdued by Cobra. Later, Rockwell demands that Steve Rogers be arrested for invading the White House.

CAPTAIN AMERICA #345 (September 1988)

"Surrender" (23 pages)

CREDITS: Mark Gruenwald (writer), Kieron Dwyer (pencils), Al Milgrom (inks), Jack Morelli (letters), Bob Sharen (colors), Marc Siry (asst editor), Ralph Macchio (editor), Ron Frenz (c pencils)

FEATURE CHARACTER: Captain America (also in rfb as Super Patriot & in photo, also in fb2 to 1st chr app before Cap #380/2, '90 fb)

GUEST STARS: Falcon (last in Cap #343, '88, next in Av Ann #17, '88), Redwing (last in Cap #343, '88, next in Cap #355, '89), Nomad (next in MCP #14/4, '89), Demolition Man

SUPPORTING CAST: The Captain (also in rfb as Captain America & photos, in fb1 between Cap #344, '88 & MCP #2/4, '88; last in MCP #2/4, '88, next in Cap #347, '88), Battlestar

VILLAINS: Watchdogs (last in Cap #335, '87, next in Cap #350, '89, nine die), Sidewinder (last in Cap #342,

8, next in X Ann #13, '89), Diamondback (next in X Ann #13, '89),Viper (also in rfb; in fb1, next in ASM Ann #23, '89), Red Skull (bts, has Watchdogs kidnap Cap's parents), Douglas Rockwell

OTHER CHARACTERS: CSA: Gen. Lewis Haywerth, George Mathers (both next in Cap #347, '88), Orville Sanderson (last in Cap #335, '87, next in Cap #347, '88), Adrian Sammish (last in Cap #339, '88), Dr. Valerie Cooper, Raymond Sikorski; Vagabond (last in Cap #342, '88), Caleb Walker (also in fb2 to 1st chr app before Cap #380/2, '90 fb), Emily Walker (both last in Cap #333, '87 fb, chr last in Cap #380/2, '90 fb, die, last op), police (in fb1), Michael O's Saloon patrons & employees, CNN reporter, Pentagon security guard, National Guard, US military pilot, WOHL reporters & cameramen, bystanders; Ronald Reagan (as snake man in rfb), Guardsmen (on cover)

LOCATIONS/ITEMS: Fort George G. Meade inc video room & holding cells, Washington, DC inc Pentagon w/CSA meeting room, Lincoln & Washington Memorials, police station (in fb1) & Oval Office (in rfb), Custer's Grove, GA inc Walker home (also in fb2) & Simon's Road House, Bethesda inc Michael O's Saloon; Watchdog's shotguns, noose & pitchfork, the Captain's Stars & Stripes briefcase, National Guard jeep, military helicopter

FLASHBACKS: Viper turns the President into a snake man, who battles the Captain (Cap #344, '88). Super-Patriot fights Captain America Cap #327, '85). The Captain hands Viper over to the police (1). Young John Walker plays on his father's lap (2).

SYNOPSIS: Douglas Rockwell orders Captain America and Battlestar to arrest Steve Rogers. Meanwhile, Falcon returns to New York while the Captain stays in Washington, DC to look for his missing friends. In Georgia, the Watchdogs kidnap Cap's parents. Learning of his parents' abduction Cap asks for time off but is denied; he goes AWOL to rescue them. Sidewinder teleports into the holding cells with Vagabond for Diamondback. Diamondback convinces him to free Nomad and D-Man too, but only Nomad is willing to go. While searching at his parents' house, Captain America is contacted by the Watchdogs. Nomad contacts Steve through the Stars & Stripes hotline to meet. After hearing Steve plans to surrender and barter for his friends' release, a drunk Nomad storms off. Captain America surrenders himself to the Watchdogs as the Captain does the same to the CSA. The Watchdogs ready a noose for Captain America, but when Cap tries to escape the Watchdogs gun down his parents. Cap flies into a murderous rage, kills all the Watchdogs, and has a conversation with his dead parents.

NOTE: Simon's Road House has King Kirby beer on tap.

CAPTAIN AMERICA #346 (October 1988)

"Ambush!" (23 pages)

CREDITS: Mark Gruenwald (writer), Kieron Dwyer (pencils), Al Milgrom (inks), Jack Morelli (letters), Bob Sharen (colors), Marc Siry (asst editor), Ralph Macchio (editor), Ron Frenz (c pencils)

FEATURE CHARACTER: Captain America (also in rfb & in photo)

GUEST STARS: Freedom Force: Mystique (also as Quicksilver, last in XFac #33, '88, next in XFac #40, '89), Blob (also as a judge), Spiral (also as a jury member) (both last in XFac #33, '88, next in DD #269, '89), Crimson Commando, Destiny (both also in photo & as jury members, last in XFac #33, '88, next in NM #78, '89), Stonewall (also as a lawyer), Super Sabre (also as a jury member) (both also in photo, last in XFac #31, '88, both next in NM #78, '89), Avalanche (also in photo & as jury member, last in XFac #33, '88, chr next in MCP #41/4, '90, next in NM #78, '89), Pyro (also as a lawyer, last in Cap #339, '88, next in DD #269, '89); Demolition Man (next in Cap #349, '89)

SUPPORTING CAST: Battlestar (also as a Guardsman)

VILLAINS: Resistants: Crucible (last in Cap #343, '88, next in Cap #350, '89), Mentallo (also as Think-Tank, joins Resistants, last in Av#287, '88, next in Av:Vault, '91), Meteorite (also in photo, last in Cap #343, '88, next in Cap #368, '90), Mist Mistress (acidic mist-manipulator, 1st, in Cap #368, '90), Occult (last in Cap #343, '88, next in Cap #426, '94), Paralyzer (last in Cap #343, next in Cap #368, '90), Quill (last in Cap #343, '88, next in FF #335, '89), a dozen others; Red Skull (in shadows, 1st as "John Smith"), Taskmaster (bts, released from detention, last in Cap #334, '87, next in ASM #308, '88), Douglas Rockwell

OTHER CHARACTERS: CSA: Dr. Valerie Cooper, Adrian Sammish, Raymond Sikorski; Vagabond (bts, interrogated by Rockwell, chr next in USAgent #2, '93 fb, next in Cap #358/2, '89), Georgia police (Sheriff Oakley named), US military personnel (inc a Lieutenant & military police), Vault Guardsmen, mock trial attendees; Watchdogs, Caleb Walker, Emily Walker (prev 3 in rfb), Ronald Reagan (in photo)

LOCATIONS/ITEMS: Carson City inc County Courthouse, Simon Shoe Repair & Kirby Katering, Colorado Rocky Mountains, CSA building inc Rockwell's office & meeting room, Ft. George G. Meade inc D-Man's holding cell, Georgia jail, Resistants' stronghold, Vault armored transport, Mentallo's restraints, Watchdogs' shotguns & noose (both in rfb)

FLASHBACK: The Watchdogs abduct Caleb and Emily Walker and kill them; Captain America kills the Watchdogs in retaliation (Cap #345, '88).

SYNOPSIS: Battlestar and Adrian Sammish get Captain America released from jail into the CSA's custody. Meanwhile, Douglas Rockwell interrogates D-Man. In Colorado, the Resistants liberate Mentallo from a Vault prison transport. Douglas Rockwell suspends John Walker as Captain America and reports to his mysterious superior, who tells him to keep Walker on as Cap and to arrange for the Taskmaster to escape from detention. Battlestar attends a Freedom Force briefing session where he is ordered to participate in a mock trial of Quicksilver, actually Mystique in disguise, in an effort to lure the Resistants into a trap. Rockwell tells John Walker that his suspension is lifted, but he must be backup for Freedom Force for a while. The Resistants accept Mentallo under the new name Think-Tank into their group. Days later, the Resistants attack Freedom Force's mock trial and Captain America savagely defeats the mutants. Pyro yells at Cap; they were supposed to let some of the Resistants escape so they could be followed. Cap tells Battlestar he missed his parents' funeral for this operation.

NOTE: Red Skull's "John Smith" alias is revealed in Cap #350, '89.

CAPTAIN AMERICA #347 (November 1988)

"Vengeance" (22 pages)

CREDITS: Mark Gruenwald (writer), Kieron Dwyer (pencils), Al Milgrom (inks), Jack Morelli (letters), Gregory Wright (colors), Marc Siry (asst editor), Ralph Macchio (editor), Ron Frenz (c pencils)
FEATURE CHARACTER: Captain America
SUPPORTING CAST: Ethan Thurm (last in Cap #334, '87, next in Cap #373/2, '90), Battlestar, the Captain
VILLAINS: Left-Winger, Right-Winger (both also in rfb, last in Cap #341/2, '88, next bts in Cap #350, '89), Red Skull (Malik, last in SAv #6, '88, dies), Scourge (rogue Scourge, as helicopter pilot, 1st, next in Cap #350, '89) & his mercenaries (all die), Red Skull (Schmidt, as "John Smith"), Douglas Rockwell
OTHER CHARACTERS: CSA: Gen. Lewis Hayworth, George Mathers (both last in Cap #345, '88), Martin Farrow, Wesley Werner (both 1st), Henry Gyrich (last in NFVS #2, '88), Orville Sanderson (last in Cap #345, '88), Dr. Valerie Cooper, Adrian Sammish, Raymond Sikorski; Jack Johnson (Right-Winger's father), Mrs. Johnson & her kids (Right-Winger's mother & siblings), Mrs. Lennox (Left-Winger's mother), Alphie (Mrs. Lennox's dog), Vanna White (on TV), Battlestar's teacher & classmates; "Air Train" commuters, Algerian prison guards, construction workers (Bob named), Watchdogs, press; conference attendees (prev 4 in rfb), bystanders; Caleb Walker, Emily Walker, Watchdogs, press; Spider-Man (on Battlestar's t-shirt)
LOCATIONS/ITEMS: Park Ridge, IL inc Lennox home, Las Vegas, NV inc Gleason's gym, CSA building inc staff room, the Captain's For George G. Meade holding cell, Philadelphia, PA inc Mrs. Johnson's' apartment, Alexandria, VA inc Battlestar's classroom, Algerian prison construction site outside Dallas, TX; Algerian prison guards' guns, Scourge's mercenaries' guns, Scourge's gun & helicopter, Left-Winger's & Right-Winger's fiery swords, pipe, oil drum & tanker truck
FLASHBACKS: Left-Winger and Right-Winger expose Cap's identity (Cap #341, '88). Cap's parents are killed (Cap #345, '88).
SYNOPSIS: In Park Ridge, Captain America tells Mrs. Lennox that the next time he sees her son Left-Winger, he's a dead man. She calls Hector and the Wingers decide to teach Cap a lesson. In Washington, DC, the CSA discusses Walker's fate as Captain America while Douglas Rockwell interrogates Steve Rogers; Steve wonders if the CSA is acting without official sanction. In Philadelphia, Cap tells Right-Winger's mother her son is a dead man, but she doesn't care. In Algeria, mercenaries liberate Albert Malik from prison. When Malik dons his Red Skull mask, Scourge kills him. At a construction site outside Dallas, the Wingers find Cap telling Right-Winger's father that his son is a dead man and attack. Cap brutally beats them. Tying them up, Cap gives them one of their fiery swords to free themselves before the other fiery sword ignites an oil tank. Cap walks away as the tank explodes and briefly smiles.
NOTE: Farrow and Werner are named in OHMU #2, '89. Malik's prison ID is A3415B. Mrs. Lennox is watching "Wheel of Fortune," the phrase is "Simon and Kirby."

CAPTAIN AMERICA #348 (December 1988)

"Out of Commission" (22 pages)

CREDITS: Mark Gruenwald (writer), Kieron Dwyer (pencils), Al Milgrom (inks), Jack Morelli (letters), Gregory Wright (colors), Marc Siry (asst editor), Ralph Macchio (editor), Ron Frenz (c pencils)
FEATURE CHARACTER: Captain America
SUPPORTING CAST: The Captain (also in rfb, next in Av #298, '88), Battlestar
VILLAINS: Flag-Smasher, ULTIMATUM (Vladimir Krantz named, dies with one other) (both last in Cap #322, '86), Red Skull (as "John Smith"), Douglas Rockwell (both next in Cap #350, '89)
OTHER CHARACTERS: CSA: Dr. Valerie Cooper, Martin Farrow, Henry Gyrich, Gen. Lewis Hayworth, George Mathers, Adrian Sammish, Orville Sanderson, Raymond Sikorski, Wesley Werner (all next in Cap #350, '89), Ronald Reagan (last in Cap #344, '88, next in Cap #352, '89), Guardsman (bts, waiting outside CSA meeting room), Ice Station Able scientists; ULTIMATUM's hostages (in rfb), Rockwell's wife (in photo)
LOCATIONS/ITEMS: North Pole inc Ice Station Able, CSA's Pentagon meeting room, CSA building inc Rockwell's office, Fort George G. Meade inc holding cells; ULTIMATUM air-skis, laser blasters & armor, Flag-Smasher's energy-absorbing exoskeleton, mace & luger, Air Force jet, Cap's parachute, CSA's tracer, the Captain's Stars & Stripes briefcase
FLASHBACKS: Cap is forced to use a gun to free Ultimatum's hostages (Cap #321, '86). Cap captures Flag-Smasher in the Alps (Cap #322, '86).
SYNOPSIS: At the North Pole, Flag-Smasher evades the attacking ULTIMATUM and makes his way to a nearby scientific outpost. In Washington, DC, the CSA fires Captain America and places him under arrest, but President Reagan unexpectedly drops by during the proceedings and commends Cap; Reagan also tells them to free Steve Rogers when he learns the Captain is being held for questioning. Flag-Smasher occupies Ice Station Able and demands Captain America's presence. Rockwell informs his mysterious superior of Reagan's orders and mobilizes Cap to deal with Flag-Smasher. Meanwhile, the power goes out in Steve's prison and he's able to walk right out, finding his shield waiting for him with a secret tracer planted on it. Cap invades Ice Station Able, but Flag-Smasher realizes he's not the original and is able to defeat him out by absorbing his strength through his exoskeleton. Flag-Smasher tells the arriving Battlestar to bring the original Cap or the world will be plunged into chaos.
NOTE: Story continues in Av #298, '88. Fort George G. Meade called Fort George M. Meade here.

CAPTAIN AMERICA #349 (January 1989)

"Icecap" (23 pages)

CREDITS: Mark Gruenwald (writer), Kieron Dwyer (pencils), Al Milgrom (inks), Jack Morelli (letters), Gregory Wright (colors), Marc Siry (asst editor), Ralph Macchio (editor), Ron Frenz (c pencils)

FEATURE CHARACTER: Captain America (also in rfb)

GUEST STARS: Avengers (reserve): Beast (next in XFac #35), Falcon (next in Cap #355, '89), Yellowjacket (Rita DeMara, next in Cap #389, '91) (all bts, flying in Quinjet from Hydro-Base, last in Av Ann #17, '88); Demolition Man (joins Avengers, seemingly dies, last in Cap #346, '88, next in Cap #384, '91)

SUPPORTING CAST: Battlestar (also in rfb), the Captain (also in rfb, last in Av Ann #17, '88, next in Av #299, '89)

VILLAINS: Flag-Smasher (also in rfb, next in MSMK #8, '89), ULTIMATUM

OTHER CHARACTERS: Ice Station Able scientists, Bucky (in rfb)

LOCATIONS/ITEMS: North Pole inc Ice Station Able & ULTIMATUM's base, Hydro-Base; US military helicopter, Quinjet, ULTIMATUM air-skis, laser guns, armor, bombs & doomsday device, Flag-Smasher's energy-absorbing exoskeleton, mace, luger & machine gun

FLASHBACKS: Flag-Smasher defeats Cap (Walker) and tells Battlestar to find the real Cap (Cap #348, '88). Cap (Rogers) and Bucky try to stop Zemo's drone-plane before it explodes (Av #4, '64 fb).

SYNOPSIS: The Captain arrives at Hydro-Base with the intention of reforming the Avengers but D-Man, who's been looking for the Captain, is the only one there. The Captain recruits D-Man into the Avengers just as Battlestar arrives; Battlestar fills the Captain in on Flag-Smasher and asks for his help. At Ice Station Able, Flag-Smasher tortures Captain America by half-suspending him in ice water. The heroes arrive by Quinjet to find ULTIMATUM attacking the station. Plowing through ULTIMATUM's forces, the Captain finds Flag-Smasher, who tells him ULTIMATUM thinks he's a traitor; he discovered the Red Skull was funding his operations and tried to dismantle ULTIMATUM's doomsday device. Battlestar frees Cap while the Captain and Flag-Smasher rendezvous with D-Man to find ULTIMATUM's doomsday device. With no time to disarm the device, the Captain tells D-Man to crash the Quinjet into the building to destroy it. D-Man does, but ULTIMATUM sabotages the Quinjet and D-Man is caught in the explosion. The Captain searches for D-Man but finds no trace of him.

NOTE: Story continues from Av Ann #17, '88, erroneously listed as Av Ann #18, '89 here. The cover pays homage to Cap #193, '76's cover.

CAPTAIN AMERICA #350 (February 1989)

"Seeing Red" (40 pages)

CREDITS: Mark Gruenwald (writer), Kieron Dwyer (pencils), Al Milgrom (inks), Jack Morelli (letters), Gregory Wright (colors), Marc Siry (asst editor), Ralph Macchio (editor)

FEATURE CHARACTERS: Captain America (Rogers, also as the Captain, resumes his role as Captain America, also in rfb; last in Av #300, '89), Captain America (Walker, also in rfb as Super-Patriot, next in Cap #382/2, '91 fb)

SUPPORTING CAST: Battlestar (also in rfb)

VILLAINS: Red Skull (also in rfb & as "John Smith," revealed as Red Skull, last in Cap #348, '88, next bts in ASM #320, '89, next in ASM #325, '89), Douglas Rockwell (last in Cap #348, '88, dies), Taskmaster (bts, provided Red Skull's sparring partners, last in ASM #308, '88, next in IM #254, '90), Scourge (rogue Scourge, last in Cap #347, '88, next in Cap #394 '91), Crucible (last in Cap #346, '88, next in Cap #368, '90), Watchdogs (others in rfb), Sweat Shop (both one member, next in ASM #325, '89), ULTIMATUM (one member, next in ASM #322, '89)

OTHER CHARACTERS: CSA: Martin Farrow, Henry Gyrich, George Mathers, Adrian Sammish, Orville Sanderson, Wesley Werner (all last in Cap #348, '88, next in Cap #352, '89), Dr. Valerie Cooper, Raymond Sikorski (both last in Cap #348, '88), Gen. Lewis Haywerth (last in Cap #348, '88, chr next in Cap #382/2, '91 fb); Left-Winger, Right-Winger (both bts, taken off hospital's critical list but have burns on 90% of their bodies, last in Cap #347, '88, see NOTE); Elron ("John Smith's" assistant, only app), Red Skull's 5 sparring partners (dressed as Captain America, die), doctors (Mannheim named), Smith Building doorman, secretary, elevator operator & security guards, paramedics, police, bystanders (Mikey named); Professor Power, Super-Patriot's rally attendees (both in rfb)

LOCATIONS/ITEMS: Washington, DC inc Smith Building w/Red Skull's office, gym & meeting room, CSA Building w/meeting room & Rockwell's office, CSA's Pentagon meeting room & Smith Building, New York City, Fort George G. Meade inc med center; Red Skull's cigarette w/Dust of Death, spray capsule in Rockwell's phone & spike wall, copies of Daily Bugle & Captain America comic #350, Scourge's, ULTIMATUM agent's & Watchdog's guns

FLASHBACKS: An aged Red Skull dies in Captain America's arms (Cap #300, '84). Super-Patriot holds a rally (Cap #323, '86), fights Cap (Cap #327, '87), trains as Captain America with Battlestar (Cap #334, '87), kills Professor Power (Cap #338, '88), the Watchdogs (Cap #345, '88), and Left-Winger and Right-Winger (Cap #347, '88).

SYNOPSIS: John Smith battles and kills five men dressed as Captain America and calls Douglas Rockwell for an update on the search for Steve Rogers. In New York, the Captain saves a baby from being run over by a truck. At Fort Meade, Rockwell admonishes John Walker for failing against Flag-Smasher; Walker then chides Battlestar for recruiting the Captain. Smith calls Walker, telling him his missing shield is at the Smith Building. After a CSA meeting Rockwell calls John Smith, but he's interrupted by the Captain who's returning Captain America's missing shield. When Rockwell's phone rings he's gassed and dies, his face turned into a Red Skull. At the Smith Building, Captain America finds a gathering between Scourge and members of the Resistants, Sweat Shop, ULTIMATUM and Watchdogs. John Smith reveals he's behind all the groups, and claims to be Steve Rogers. When Smith leaves Cap brutally battles the villains. The Captain arrives but doesn't believe Smith when he claims to be the Red Skull. Wondering who else could have orchestrated his resignation as Cap, the Captain walks in on a crazed Captain America. Meanwhile, Cooper and Sikorsky find Rockwell's body. Captain America savagely attacks the Captain; the Captain is eventually able to defeat his irrational replacement. Smith arrives and gloats that he can't be stopped but Captain America throws his shield, causing Smith to inhale his cigarette's Dust of Death and turning his face into an actual Red Skull. Shortly, the CSA says they will decommission Walker as Captain America, but the Captain refuses to resume the role until Walker convinces him that if he doesn't, the CSA will just get someone else. Convinced, Steve Rogers returns as Captain America.

NOTE: Issue dedicated to Joe Simon and Jack Kirby. Cap #383/3, '91 reveals that Left-Winger and Right-Winger both commit suicide shortly after this issue. They possibly appear next in AWC #61, '90, but those may be Immortus' Space Phantoms. Left-Winger's corpse is next in Cap #383/3, '91. The Smith Building is on Pennsylvania Ave. Story is followed by three 2-page pin-ups: "Captain America's Partners!" by John Buscema & Al Milgrom featuring Captain America, Falcon, Jack Flag, Nomad, Bucky Barnes & Demolition Man, "The Women in Captain America's Life" by Ron Frenz & Joe Sinnott featuring Sharon Carter, Peggy Carter, Bernadette Rosenthal, Donna Maria Puentes, Gail Runciter, Holly Riddley, Rachel Leighton & the Viper, and "The Six Captain America!" by Tom Morgan featuring Steve Rogers (I), William Naslund, the Spirit of '76 (II), Jeff Mace, the Patriot (III), Grand Director (IV), Roscoe (V) & Super-Patriot (VI).

2ND STORY: "Resurrection" (10 pages)
CREDITS: Mark Gruenwald (writer), John Byrne (pencils), José Marzan Jr. (inks), Joe Rosen (letters), Gregory Wright (colors), Marc Siry (asst editor), Ralph Macchio (editor)
FEATURE CHARACTER: Red Skull (also in rfb, in fb1 between Cap #298, '84 fb & Cap #261, '81 fb, in fb2 between Cap #182, '75 & bts in Cap #183, '75, in fb3 between Cap #296-297, '84; chr last in Cap #301, '85, chr next in Cap #383/4, '91)
GUEST STARS: Captain America (in rfb, in fb3 between Cap #296-297, '84), Falcon (also in rfb, in fb2 between Cap #182-183, '75), Roscoe Simons (in fb2 as Captain America between Cap #182-183, '75)
SUPPORTING CAST: Mother Superior (in fb1 between Cap #298, '84 fb & Cap #15, '06 fb, in fb3 between Cap #296-297, '84), Mother Night (Susan Scarbo, in fb1 during Cap #15, '06 fb)
VILLAINS: Arnim Zola (also in rfb & in fb3; last in Av Ann #13, '84, chr next in Cap #383/4, '91, next in MCP #24/3, '89), Baron Helmut Zemo (in fb3 between Cap #296-297, '84)
OTHER CHARACTERS: Exiles: Angelo Baldini, Franz Cadavus, Gen. Jun Ching, Eric Gruning, Jurgen "Iron Hand" Hauptman, Ivan Krushki; Ameridroid, Bucky robot, Dr. Doom, Kingpin, Nomad, Redwing, 4th & 5th Sleepers, "the Big Eared Sentry and his Savage Companion," Nick Fury, Adolf Hitler (also as Hate-Monger), Herbert Glass, Wolfgang Brenner, Horst Lederer, Donna Maria Puentes, Bernie Rosenthal, Arnie Roth, Esther, Gestapo chief, a doctor, a maid (all in rfb); Sharon Carter, King Hassab of Irabia (both mentioned in rfb)
LOCATIONS/ITEMS: Arnim Zola's Swiss Alps lab, Isle of Exiles (in rfb & fb1), Skull-House (in rfb & fb3); Arnim Zola's equipment inc Red Skull's stasis tube, Red Skull's "dues machina" (in fb3) & mask, Cosmic Cube (in rfb)
FLASHBACKS: Hermann Shmidt tries to kill his newborn son Johann, but the doctor stops him; Johann grows up a vagrant and kills his boss's daughter (Cap #298, '84 fb). Johann meets Hitler while working as a bellboy; Hitler transforms him into the Red Skull (ToS #66/2, '65 fb). Red Skull meets Captain America (ToS #66/2, '65), and is buried alive near WWII's end (ToS #72/2, '65 fb). Red Skull is found and revived in the current day (ToS #79/2, '66 fb), battles Cap with the Cosmic Cube (ToS #81, '66), traps Cap in plastic bubbles (ToS #88/2, '67), torments Cap with a Bucky robot (ToS #89/2, '67), battles Cap with the 4th Sleeper (Cap #101, '68) and abducts Sharon Carter (Cap #104, '68). Red Skull conceives an heir with a maid but will almost kill it when she's born a girl (Cap #298, '84 fb), but instead will have Mother Night raise her (1). After the conception, Red Skull uses the Cosmic Cube to assume Cap's form (Cap #115, '69), brainwashes Sam Wilson (Cap #186, '75 fb), uses the Exiles to fight Cap and Falcon (Cap #118, '69), but loses when the Cube is destroyed (Cap #119, '69). Red Skull attempts to overthrow both King Hassab (Cap #129, '70) and Dr. Doom (AT #4/2-5/2, '71). After his daughter's birth, Red Skull incites riots in Harlem (Cap #143, '71) and battles the Kingpin over the leadership of Hydra with the 5th Sleeper (Cap #148, '72). Red Skull murders a Captain America impersonator (2) and a politician (Cap #184, '75), and reveals the Falcon's origin to Cap (Cap #186, '75). Red Skull battles Dr. Doom on the moon (SVTU #12, '77) and is introduced to Arnim Zola by the Hate-Monger (SVTU #16, '78). Red Skull fights Cap with Zola's genetic monstrosities (Cap #212, '77) and overtakes the SHIELD Helicarrier with his Death's-Head satellite (Cap #227, '78). While molding his daughter in his image, Red Skull attacks Cap with the Ameridroid (Cap #263, '81). Red Skull artificially ages his daughter into adulthood (Cap #298, '84 fb) and as Mother Superior, she kidnaps Cap's girlfriend (Cap #295, '84) and friends (Cap #296, '84). As Red Skull's cohorts place Cap into the "dues machina," Zola takes a genetic sample of the Super-Soldier (3). Red Skull tells Cap that he's poisoned them both (Cap #299, '84) and dies in Cap's arms (Cap #300, '84).
SYNOPSIS: Arnim Zola revives the Red Skull; he's transferred the Nazi's consciousness from his recently deceased body and placed it in a clone of Steve Rogers. Pleased with his new Aryan body the Red Skull decides not to wear his mask; he has more subtle plans to destroy the decadent heart of corporate America from within...

CAPTAIN AMERICA #351 (March 1989)

"Changing of the Guard" (23 pages)

CREDITS: Mark Gruenwald (writer), Kieron Dwyer (pencils), Al Milgrom (inks), Jack Morelli (letters), Bob Sharen (colors), Marc Siry (asst editor), Ralph Macchio (editor)
FEATURE CHARACTERS: Captain America (Rogers, next in Thor #402, IM #238, Av #301-303, Av Ann #18/2, all '89), Captain America (Walker, also in dfb1, next in Cap #382/2, '91 fb, next in Cap #354, '89 as USAgent)
GUEST STARS: Nick Fury (in dfb2, last in NFvS #6, '88, chr next in BW:ColdW, '90, next in NF:AoS #1, '89), Dum Dum Dugan (last in NFvS #6, '88, next in NF:AoS #1, '89), Gabe Jones (last in NFvS #6, '88, next in NF:AoS #8, '90)
SUPPORTING CAST: Battlestar (also in dfb1), Peggy Carter (last in Cap #236, '79, next in Av #302, '89)
VILLAINS: Machinesmith (bts, controlling SHIELD machinery, last in Cap #249, '80, chr last in Cap #368/2, '90 fb, next in Cap #354, '89), Scourge (successor, last in Cap #320, '86, next in Cap #358/2, '89)

CAPTAIN AMERICA #352 (April 1989)

"Refuge" (22 pages)

CAPTAIN AMERICA #353 (May 1989)

"The Great Bear" (22 pages)

CREDITS: Mark Gruenwald (writer), Kieron Dwyer (pencils), Al Milgrom (inks), Jack Morelli (letters), Gregory Wright (colors), Marc Siry (asst editor), Ralph Macchio (editor), Tom DeFalco (editor-in-chief)
FEATURE CHARACTER: Captain America
GUEST STARS: Soviet Super-Soldiers: Darkstar (chr next in SSS #1, '92, next in MCP #70/4, '91), Ursa Major (next in SSS #1, '92), Vanguard (chr next in SSS #1, '92, next in Q #28, '91 fb) (all also as Darkforce bear-beast construct & in fb during Cap #352, '89); Supreme Soviets: Red Guardian (leader), Perun, Sputnik (prev 3 chr next in SSS #1, '92, next in Av #319, '90), Fantasia (chr next in SSS #1, '92 as Fantasma, next in Av #319, '90); Crimson Dynamo (next in IM Ann #10/2, '89); Lemar Hoskins
SUPPORTING CAST: Avengers Crew: Dr. Keith Kincaid (chr next bts in MCP #44, '90, next in Av #311, '89), Michael O'Brien (also in fb during Cap #352, '89)
OTHER CHARACTERS: Mikhail Gorbachev (General Secretary of the Soviet Communist Party, 1st but chr last in CrimD #5, '04 bts, last bts in BW:ColdW, '90, next in MK:Div, '92), Boris Prokofiev (Russian foreign relations consulate), Mr. Krysenko (Special Powers Committee director) (both only app), Kate Tollifson (bts, moved away w/out a word to her neighbors, last bts in Cap #335, '87, next in Cap #378/2, '90), Moscow citizens & children (Stanya & Vladimir named), Avengers security guards (in fb), 2 Soviet fighter pilots, Russian government officials & soldiers, Kate's neighbor; Vladimir Lenin (in photo)
LOCATIONS/ITEMS: Avengers Island inc training facility (in fb) & infirmary, Moscow inc airfield, Cap's hotel, Lenin's Tomb, Cathedral of St Basil, market district, Special Powers Directorate building w/Krysenko's office, & Kremlin, Custer's Grove, GA inc Kate Tollifson's home, New York; Avengers security guards' guns (in fb), 2 Soviet fighter jets, Avengers Quinjet ("QJ2"), Russian soldiers' guns, Red Guardian's shield, Perun's axe, Crimson Dynamo's armor
FLASHBACK: Michael O'Brien and his security team find the Soviet Super-Soldiers near death in the training facility.
SYNOPSIS: As the Soviet Super-Soldiers apparently die, Captain America arrives in Moscow to an auspicious welcome by the Russian government. That night Cap encounters a gigantic black bear-like creature on a destructive rampage. The beast shrugs off Cap's efforts to stop it and vanishes. Meanwhile, Lemar Hoskins investigates John Walker's body's disappearance and learns Walker's sister and her family disappeared days ago. Cap is provided Red Guardian as his escort. As they tour Moscow the beast reappears; it absorbs Red Guardian but leaves Cap alone, and vanishes. Cap fends off Mr. Krysenko's suspicions and the beast reappears, attacking the Kremlin. The Supreme Soviets attack the beast but are also absorbed. Cap dives into the beast's substance and finds the Soviet Super-Soldiers' spirits inside preparing to drain the Supreme Soviets' life force to restore their own, an act that will kill them. Cap persuades them against doing so, and the beast vanishes, leaving the Soviets unconscious but alive. Cap returns to Avengers Island to find the Super-Soldiers awake and alive, albeit still bed-ridden.
NOTE: SSS #1, '92 reveals the Soviet Super-Soldiers fall into a coma after this issue. Kate's home is located on Orchard St.

CAPTAIN AMERICA #354 (June 1989)

"Reawakening" (22 pages)

CREDITS: Mark Gruenwald (writer), Kieron Dwyer (pencils), Al Milgrom (inks), Jack Morelli (letters), Bob Sharen (colors), Marc Siry (asst editor), Ralph Macchio (editor)
FEATURE CHARACTERS: Captain America (also in rfb, next bts in MCP #21/3, '89 fb, next in Av #304, '89)
GUEST STARS: USAgent (John Walker, 1st as USAgent, last in Cap #351, '89, chr last in Cap #382/2, '91 fb as Captain America, next in WCA #44, '89), Battlestar
SUPPORTING CAST: Avengers Crew: Fabian Stankowicz (joins Avengers Crew, last in Cap #352, '89, next in Cap #358, '89), Michael O'Brien (next in Av Ann #18/3, '89), Peggy Carter (voice only, last in Cap #352, '89)
VILLAIN: Machinesmith (also as 4th Sleeper, last bts in Cap #351, '89, next bts in Cap #367, '90)
OTHER CHARACTERS: CSA: Martin Farrow, George Mathers, Adrian Sammish, Orville Sanderson, Wesley Werner (all next in Pun:NE, '90), Henry Gyrich (next in FF #335, '89), Gen. Lewis Hayworth (next in Cap #358/2, '89), Raymond Sikorsky (next in WCA #44, '89), Dr. Valerie Cooper (all last in Cap #352, '89); Gregory Smoot (Guardsman, as Iron Monger, only app), 4th Sleeper (also in rfb, last in Cap #102, '68, chr last in Cap #368/2, '90 fb, chr next in Av Ann #19/3, '90 fb, next in Cap #367, '90), Awesome Android (last in Av #389 '88, last bts in Av #290, '88, chr next in Av Ann #19/3, '90 fb, next in AvS #27/2, '89), Sentry #459 (last in Av #289, '88, last bts in Av #290, '88 next in Av Ann #19/3, '90 fb), Super-Adaptoid (last in Av #290, '88, chr next in Av Ann #19/3, '90 fb, next in FF #336, '89), TESS-One (last in Av #289, '88, last bts in Av #290, '88, chr next in Av Ann #19/3, '90 fb, next in PPSSM #160, '90), Magneto robot (last in Cap #249, '80, next in Cap #368, '90), Spider-Man, Thing (both robot remains, last in Cap #249, '80, last app), Machinesmith robots (remains), Mr. Gladstone (Stane International employee), Avengers crewmen, Georgetown citizens, paramedics; Sharon Carter (in rfb)
LOCATIONS/ITEMS: Machinesmith's Morris County, NJ lab inc fake barn entrance, Avengers Island inc Hangar 3, Waltham, MA, Georgetown morgue, Stane International, Fort George G. Meade inc containment facility; Avengers Quinjet & stasis field generator, Machinesmith's computer bank, Cap's communicator watch, Fabian's equipment, Watchdog uniform, Iron Monger armor, USAgent's shield
FLASHBACK: Captain America and Sharon Carter defeat the 4th Sleeper (Cap #102, '68).
SYNOPSIS: Captain America searches Machinesmith's old lab in vain; he takes a Machinesmith head as a souvenir. Returning to Avengers Island, Cap greets Fabian Stankowicz and the two investigate a robot sighting in Massachusetts: the 4th Sleeper. They take the inert robot back to Avengers Island to put it in storage, but it awakens and attacks. Machinesmith reveals he's controlling the robot and Cap defeats him by placing the Sleeper into a stasis field. Meanwhile, Battlestar discovers that the Watchdog who killed John Walker was wearing a fake uniform; he calls Dr. Cooper and updates her on his investigation. Elsewhere, Gen. Hayworth buys the Iron Monger armor; he later calls the CSA and reveals his new operative: the USAgent. USAgent demonstrates his fighting ability by sparring with a Guardsman piloting the Iron Monger

rmor while Gen. Haywerth explains that USAgent is actually John Walker. Gen. Hayerth orchestrated Walker's "death" to give him a new ecret identity.

OTE: Both stories this issue are presented simultaneously, all pages are split in half horizontally. Gregory Smoot's name revealed in IManual, 8. USAgent's shield was previously Captain America's vibranium shield, made by Black Panther in Cap #342, '88; as a part of USAgent's ostume it appears virtually every time he does and only changes to it will be noted. Gen. Hayerth's surname is misspelled "Hayworth" and George Mathers is miscolored white here.

CAPTAIN AMERICA #355 (July 1989)

"Missing Persons" (22 pages)

CREDITS: Mark Gruenwald (writer), Rich Buckler (pencils), Al Milgrom (inks), Jack Morelli (letters), Bob Sharen (colors), Marc Siry (asst editor), Ralph Macchio (editor), Ron Frenz (c pencils)
FEATURE CHARACTER: Captain America (also in rfb & as teenager "Roger Grant")
GUEST STARS: Battlestar (next in Cap #372/2, '90), Falcon (last bts in Cap #349, '88, chr next in MSH #12/2, '93 fb, next in MCP #23/3, '89), Redwing (last in Cap #345, '88, next in MCP #23/3, '89), Sersi (also in photo, last in SS Ann #1, '88, next in Cap #357, '89)
SUPPORTING CAST: Peggy Carter (next in Av Ann #18/3, '89), Bernie Rosenthal (voice only, also in photo & rfb, last in Cap #336, '87 fb, next in Cap #357, '89)
VILLAINS: Coachwhip, Puff Adder (both last in Cap #342, '88, next in X Ann #13, '89), Rock Python (last in Cap 343, '88, next in X Ann #13, '89) (prev 3 see NOTE), Mother Night (bts, sent for new runaway recruits, last in Cap #350/2, '89 fb, chr last in ap #15, '06 fb), Sin (also in rfb, last bts as Mother Superior in Cap #302, '85) & her Sisters: Raunch (last as Sister Pleasure in Cap #301, '85), lash (last as Sister Agony in Cap #301, '85) (prev 3 also in Cap's thoughts)
THER CHARACTERS: CSA: Dr. Valerie Cooper (next in UXM #254, '89), Raymond Sikorski (last in WCA #44, '89, chr next in SSS #1, '92, ext in Pun:NE, '90); Nancy Rosenthal (bts, ran away from home, last in Cap #289/2, '84, next bts in Cap #357, '89), Guardsmen, teenage inaways, YMCA clerk, hot dog vendor, bus driver, bystanders; Sister Death, Sister Dream (both in Cap's thoughts); Soviet Super-Soldiers: arkstar, Ursa Major, Vanguard; Black Knight, Flag-Smasher, Machinesmith, Red Skull, Scourge, Sidewinder, Starfox (prev 10 in photo)
OCATIONS/ITEMS: Avengers Island inc Cap's executive office, Fort George G. Meade inc Val's office, Sersi's Manhattan penthouse, Sam Wilson's office, Port Authority bus terminal, YMCA, Brooklyn Bridge, Bernie's apartment, Steve's apartment (prev 3 in rfb); Cap's computer, uardsmen's armors & guns, Sin's marijuana, Mother Night's bus, Battlestar's car, Rock Python's coil eggs, Coachwhip's whips
LASHBACKS: Steve meets Bernie (Cap #248, '80). Steve and Bernie kiss (Cap #270, '82). Bernie discovers Cap's identity (Cap #275, '82). Bernie proposes marriage to Cap (Cap #292, '84). Mother Superior captures Bernie (Cap #295, '84). Bernie tells Steve she's leaving to attend aw school (Cap #317, '86).
YNOPSIS: While getting caught up on paperwork Raymond Sikorski tells Captain America that John Walker is alive, and asks if Walker can se Cap's "the Captain" uniform as the USAgent; Cap agrees. Bernie calls and asks if Cap can look in to her sister Nancy's disappearance. Meanwhile, Battlestar invades Fort Meade and confronts Dr. Cooper over John Walker's "death," she confirms that Walker is alive and poologizes for not telling Battlestar sooner, but she's restricted from saying where Walker is now. Cap visits Sersi and has her transform him to a teenager so he can investigate a recent rash of missing runaways undercover. Battlestar goes to Falcon for help finding Walker, only interrupt Coachwhip, Puff Adder and Rock Python attacking him. Teaming up, Battlestar and Falcon eventually defeat the villains. Outside he Port Authority bus terminal, two teen girls pick Steve up on a street corner. Bringing him to a nearby YMCA, the girls try to seduce Steve ith drugs and Steve passes out. Hours later, Steve wakes up on a bus with other kids, realizing the girls who found him are members of the isters of Sin.
NOTE: Battlestar posits that Coachwhip, Puff Adder and Rock Python were sent to steal Falcon's wings as an initiation test to join the Serpent Society; Cap #364, '89's "American Graffiti" confirms the theory. Even though they fail, they're members of the group in X Ann #13, '89, their ext app. Cover pays homage to TTA #43, '63's cover.

CAPTAIN AMERICA #356 (August 1989)

"Camptown Rages" (22 pages)

CREDITS: Mark Gruenwald (writer), Al Milgrom (art), Jack Morelli (letters), Jack Fury (colors), Marc Siry (asst editor), Ralph Macchio (editor), Ron Frenz (c pencils)
FEATURE CHARACTER: Captain America (as teenager "Roger Grant")
VILLAINS: Mother Night & her teenage recruits, Minister Blood (Melvin Scarbo, last in Cap #123, '70), Sin & her Sisters: Hoodwink (last as Sister Dream in Cap #301, '85), Torso (last as Sister Death in Cap #301, '85), Raunch, Slash; a Watchdog (dies)
OTHER CHARACTERS: Teenage runaways (Jennifer named)
LOCATIONS/ITEMS: Mother Night's Camp of Hate inc arena & office; Mother Superior's holding cells & truth serum, Sin's, Hoodwink's, Raunch's & Torso's bo staffs, Hoodwink's flashlight
YNOPSIS: The Sisters of Sin corral Steve and the other teenage runaways out of the bus and into Mother Night's Camp of Hate. Rebellious eens are beaten into submission and everyone is locked into outhouse-sized cells for the night. Steve manages to escape, and finds Mother light preaching to her brainwashed teenage recruits, leading them into a hate-filled frenzy. Minister Blood leads a Watchdog member into the Ritual of Hate. Mother Night's mob kills the Watchdog, throwing him into a bonfire. In his teenage body Steve is powerless to stop them. Steve rees a girl, Jennifer, and the two find an office where Steve looks through the files for information on Bernie's sister. Sin discovers the pair and uickly overpowers Steve, finding his Captain America uniform under his clothes. Mother Night and Minister Blood interrogate Steve and the Sisters of Sin decide to have some fun. They kill Jennifer and beat Steve to a pulp.

NOTE: Minister Blood is called "Malachi" here. The title is a play on the song title "Camptown Races," otherwise known as "Camptown Ladies," by Stephen Foster from 1850.

CAPTAIN AMERICA #357 (Early September 1989)

"Night of Sin" (12 pages)

CREDITS: Mark Gruenwald (writer), Al Milgrom (art), Jack Morelli (letters), J. Shmoe (colors), Marc Siry (asst editor), Ralph Macchio (editor), Kieron Dwyer (c art)
FEATURE CHARACTER: Captain America (also as teenager "Roger Stevens," next in Av #305-310, '89, FF #333, '89, AWC #47-49, '89, bts in SenSH #8, '89, MCP #44/2-45/2, '90, Av Ann #18/3, '89, AWC #56/2, '90, Av Ann #18, '89, AWC Ann #4, '89, Thor Ann #14, '89, FF Ann #22, '89, bts in Thor #410, '89, ASM #323-325, '89, MCP #34/4, '89)
GUEST STAR: Sersi (last in Cap #355, '89, next in Av #308, '89)
SUPPORTING CAST: Bernie Rosenthal (last voice only in Cap #355, '89, next in Cap #380, '90)
VILLAINS: Mother Night (next in Cap #369, '90) & her teenage recruits (Bill named), Minister Blood (next in Av #324/2, '90), Sin (next in Cap #394, '91) & her Sisters: Hoodwink, Raunch, Slash, Torso (prev 4 next in I♥M:OL, '06)
OTHER CHARACTERS: Nancy Rosenthal (bts, at Grateful Dead concert, last bts in Cap #355, '89, last app), teenage runaways (inc Jennifer) Sersi's musicians, police
LOCATIONS/ITEMS: Mother Night's Camp of Hate, Sersi's Manhattan penthouse; Minister Blood's spiked knuckles, Mother Night's buses & blindfold
SYNOPSIS: Sin stops Torso from killing Steve, demanding to kill him herself. When they all attack in unison, Steve reverts to Captain America and quickly defeats them. Mother Night leaves with the Sisters of Sin as Cap battles and defeats Minister Blood. With Hoodwink gone, Cap learns that Jennifer isn't dead; it was only an illusion. Wading through brainwashed teenagers, Cap finds Mother Night and knocks her out. Cap later turns a blindfolded Mother Night and Minister Blood over to the police, warning them of her hypnotic abilities. Cap phones Bernie to learn that Nancy didn't run away after all, she's following the Grateful Dead's concert tour and forgot to tell anyone. That night, Cap joins a flirty Sersi for dinner.
NOTE: Cover labeled "The Blood Stone Hunt: Part 1 of 6." The title goes bi-weekly with this issue.

2ᴺᴰ STORY: "The Blood Stone Hunt: Prolog" (10 pages)
CREDITS: Mark Gruenwald (writer), Kieron Dwyer (pencils), Al Milgrom (inks), Jack Morelli (letters), Greg Wright (colors), Marc Siry (asst editor), Ralph Macchio (editor)
FEATURE CHARACTER: Diamondback (last in X Ann #13, '89)
VILLAINS: Baron Zemo (last in Av #277, '87), Batroc & his Brigade: Machete, Zaran (prev 3 last in SAv #3, '88); Tristram Micawber (psychic detective, 1ˢᵗ, next in Cap #359, '89)
OTHER CHARACTERS: Ulysses Bloodstone (skeletal remains, also in rfb, fb1 to 1ˢᵗ chr app before MPres #1, '75 fb, & fb2 between RH #8/2, '78 fb & CapSoL #6/3, '99 fb; last in RH #8/2, '78), American Museum of Natural History guard, wooly mammoth (in fb1), winged creature (in fb2); Ulluxy'l Kwan Tae Syn, Exo-Mind, Creature from the Sea, Dr. Judas Bardham (prev 4 in rfb)
LOCATIONS/ITEMS: American Museum of Natural History, Silverman Funeral Home; MacRay Rentals truck, museum guard's gun, Machete's & Zaran's weapons, Zemo's neck brace, Bloodstone's spear (in fb1 & rfb) & shotgun (in rfb), Bloodstone (one-fifth, also complete in rfb)
FLASHBACKS: Approximately 8250 BC: The man who would become Ulysses Bloodstone fights a wooly mammoth (1). He sees a meteorite fall from the sky. Investigating, he finds the alien Ulluxy'l Kwan Tae Syn, who has a large gemstone (MPres #1, '75 fb). He shatters the Bloodstone, embedding a fragment into his chest, making him immortal (MPres #2, '75 fb). In Puritan times, Ulysses Bloodstone battles a winged creature (2). In the current era, Ulysses Bloodstone fights the Creature from the Sea. (MPres#1, '75). Dr. Judas Bardham removes the Bloodstone fragment from Ulysses' chest and uses it to recreate the Exo-Mind; Ulysses dies when the Exo-Mind explodes (RH #8/2, '78).
SYNOPSIS: Batroc's Brigade breaks into the American Museum of Natural History and steals a crate; Batroc has to stop Machete and Zaran from killing the guard. As Diamondback follows unseen, the mercenaries meet with Baron Zemo. They open the crate to find the skeletal remains of Ulysses Bloodstone. Psychic detective Tristram Micawber tells Zemo they can use Ulysses' Bloodstone to find the other four fragments. Zaran notices Diamondback spying on them and attacks; Batroc's Brigade quickly defeats her. Zemo removes Ulysses' sternum, along with the embedded Bloodstone, to use as a divining rod. They toss Diamondback into the crate and later throw it into a pit.
NOTE: Zemo hopes to use the Bloodstone to reanimate his dead father Heinrich, as revealed in Cap #362, '89.

CAPTAIN AMERICA #358 (Late September 1989)

"Bones of Contention" (17 pages)

CREDITS: Mark Gruenwald (writer), Kieron Dwyer (co-plot, pencils), Danny Bulanadi (inks), Jack Morelli (letters), Marc Siry (colors, asst editor), Ralph Macchio (editor), Al Milgrom (c inks)
FEATURE CHARACTER: Captain America
SUPPORTING CAST: Avengers Crew: Col. John Jameson (last in Av Ann #18, '89), Michael O'Brien (last in Av Ann #18/3, '89, next in Cap #363, '89), Fabian Stankowicz (last in Cap #354, '89, next in Av #311, '89), Diamondback (also in rfb)
VILLAINS: Baron Zemo, Batroc & his Brigade: Machete, Zaran (prev 3 also in rfb); Incans
OTHER CHARACTERS: Conspiracy: Centurius (next in NAv #1, '05, see NOTE), Atlan, Dr. Juden Bardham,

Kaballa, Bubbles O'Day (all corpses, last in RH #8/2, '78), Ulysses Bloodstone (skeletal remains, also in photo), Moloids (corpses), Avengers crewmen, Wakadan Design Group (bts, provided modified Quinjet)

LOCATIONS/ITEMS: Bedrock caverns beneath Central Park inc Lair of Conspiracy, Avengers Island inc Cap's office & airstrip, Amazon inc Incan temple; Cap's modified Quinjet (1st), transmitter & spelunking equipment, radiometer (attached to Ulysses' skull), Diamondback's beacon, Zemo's neck brace, Incan idol, Wheel of Death, spears & curare blowdarts, Bloodstone (one-fifth)

FLASHBACK: Diamondback investigates Batroc's Brigade's heist (Cap #357/2, '89).

SYNOPSIS: Captain America follows a tracking signal into underground caverns and through various death-traps, finding Moloid corpses and strange bodies along the way. He lowers himself into a pit to find the thankful Diamondback; Cap takes Ulysses Bloodstone's skull when they leave. Cap and Diamondback return to Avengers Island, where Cap researches Bloodstone and Fabian Stankowicz attaches a radiometer to Ulysses' skull, creating a makeshift Bloodstone-Detector. Diamondback demands to accompany Cap and the two leave with Cap's new pilot, Col. John Jameson, in Cap's new modified Quinjet for South America. Searching the Amazon, Cap and Diamondback are soon captured by Incans and taken to a temple, where the pair find Baron Zemo and Batroc's Brigade already captive and tied to the Incans' Wheel of Death. Before they can take action, Cap and Diamondback are drugged by Incan darts.

NOTE: Cover labeled "The Blood Stone Hunt: Part 2 of 6." Despite being a corpse here Centurius is next in NAv #1, '05 alive and well; his revival remains unrevealed.

2ND STORY: "The Night of the Scourge! Part One: Siege" (5 pages)

CREDITS: Mark Gruenwald (writer), Mark Bright (pencils), Don Hudson (inks), Jack Morelli (letters), Marc Siry (colors, asst editor), Ralph Macchio (editor)

FEATURE CHARACTER: USAgent (last in AWC #47, '89)

SUPPORTING CAST: Gen. Lewis Hayworth (last in Cap #354, '89, next in Cap #380/2, '90)

VILLAINS: Scourge (also as a Power Broker augmented thug, last in Cap #351, '89), Power Broker (last in Cap #331, '87, chr last in USAgent #2, '93 fb) & his augmented thugs (Kalousek & Scanlon named, all die)

OTHER CHARACTERS: Priscilla Lyons (last bts in Cap #346, '88, chr last in USAgent #2, '93 fb), Avengers West crewman

LOCATIONS/ITEMS: Power Broker's San Fernando Valley estate; USAgent's skycycle, Scourge's guns

SYNOPSIS: The Scourge of the Underworld storms the Power Broker's estate, killing all of his augmented guards. He disguises himself as one and cuts the building's power. Inside, the Power Broker is about to tell Priscilla Lyons, the sometimes vigilante Vagabond, about his augmentation process when the lights go out. Power Broker phones Gen. Hayworth, who sends USAgent to investigate.

CAPTAIN AMERICA #359 (Early October 1989)

"The Bloodstone Hunt Part 3: Wheel of Death" (17 pages)

CREDITS: Mark Gruenwald (writer), Kieron Dwyer (co-plot, pencils), Danny Bulanadi (inks), Jack Morelli (letters), Bob Sharen (colors), Marc Siry (asst editor), Ralph Macchio (editor), Al Milgrom (c inks)

FEATURE CHARACTER: Captain America

SUPPORTING CAST: Diamondback, Col. John Jameson

VILLAINS: Baron Zemo, Batroc & his Brigade: Machete, Zaran; Crossbones (in shadows, 1st but chr last in Cap #383/4, '91), Red Skull (bts, sent Crossbones to steal the Bloodstone, last in ASM #325, '89, chr last in X-23 #3, '05, next in Cap #364, '89), Tristram Micawber (last in Cap #357/2, '89), Incans

OTHER CHARACTERS: Ulysses Bloodstone (skeletal remains), Mr. Druer & Tinky (both sailors, 1st), other sailors, fish, sharks (one dies)

LOCATIONS/ITEMS: Amazon inc Incan temple, Bermuda; Incan Wheel of Death, curare blowdarts, spears, machine guns, bows & arrows, Cap's modified Quinjet & radiometer, Zemo's neck brace & aircraft, Cap's, Diamondback's & Batroc's Brigade's scuba gear, sunken Pan Am airliner, Bloodstone (two-fifths)

SYNOPSIS: Captain America and Diamondback are strapped to the Incans' Wheel of Death and lowered into position, where Incan soldiers hurl spears at the captives. Freeing himself and saving Baron Zemo from near-death, Cap battles the Incans and returns to free Diamondback, discovering that Zemo and Batroc's Brigade have escaped with the Incan ruler's Bloodstone fragment. A shadowy figure watches Cap and Diamondback return to the Quinjet. The trio follows Zemo to the Bermuda Triangle. Cap scuba dives to find the Bloodstone fragment while Diamondback searches various yachts to find Zemo. Finding a sunken Pan Am airliner, Cap battles Batroc's Brigade over the Bloodstone fragment. During the fight Batroc kills a shark; the blood attracts a school of sharks, which closes in on Cap and Batroc's Brigade.

NOTE: Cover labeled "The Blood Stone Hunt: Part 3 of 6." Red Skull is revealed to be bts here in Cap #364, '89. Mr. Durer is named in Cap #360, '89.

2ND STORY: "Night of the Scourge Part 2: Death Calling" (5 pages)

CREDITS: Mark Gruenwald (writer), Mark Bright (pencils), Don Hudson (inks), Jack Morelli (letters), Bob Sharen (colors), Marc Siry (asst editor), Ralph Macchio (editor)

FEATURE CHARACTER: USAgent

VILLAINS: Scourge (also as a Power Broker augmented thug), Power Broker

OTHER CHARACTERS: Priscilla Lyons, Power Broker's augmented thugs (corpses)

LOCATIONS/ITEMS: Power Broker's San Fernando Valley estate; USAgent's skycycle, Scourge's guns

SYNOPSIS: USAgent arrives at Power Broker's estate while Scourge hunts Power Broker. Scourge narrowly misses Power Broker and Priscilla as they take the Broker's elevator bed to his underground lab. USAgent finds the elevator shaft pried open; when he jumps down Scourge fires at him.

CAPTAIN AMERICA #360 (Late October 1989)

"The Bloodstone Hunt Part 4: Blood in the Sea" (17 pages)

CREDITS: Mark Gruenwald (writer), Kieron Dwyer (co-plot, pencils, c art), Danny Bulanadi (inks), Jack Morelli (letters), Bob Sharen (colors), Mike Rockwitz (asst editor), Ralph Macchio (editor)
FEATURE CHARACTER: Captain America
SUPPORTING CAST: Diamondback, Col. John Jameson
VILLAINS: Baron Zemo, Batroc & his Brigade: Machete, Zaran; Crossbones (Brock Rumlow, Red Skull's mercenary, 1st full app), Tristram Micawber
OTHER CHARACTERS: Ulysses Bloodstone (skull), Mr. Durer, Tinky (both last app), Pan Am airline passengers (corpses), fish, sharks, birds, snakes
LOCATIONS/ITEMS: Bermuda, Egypt inc pyramids, Sphinx & tomb; Mr. Durer's sailboat; Zemo's yacht, luger & neck brace, Cap's modified Quinjet & radiometer, Micawber's uzi, Cap's, Diamondback's & Batroc's Brigade's scuba gear, Diamondback's sling, Crossbones' binoculars, sunken Pan Am airliner, Bloodstone (three-fifths)
SYNOPSIS: As Captain America and Batroc's Brigade battle sharks, Diamondback locates Zemo's yacht and and quickly overpowers Zemo. Tristram Micawber surprises Diamondback from behind. Deciding that death by shark is an unfitting end for Captain America, Batroc saves Cap and his Brigade retreats. Diamondback knocks out Micawber and holds Zemo hostage when Batroc's Brigade arrives, forcing them to hand over the Bloodstone fragment. Diamondback escapes, but Zaran wounds her and she falls in the water. The villains leave and Zemo realizes Diamondback stole the other two Bloodstone fragments. Cap rescues Diamondback and returns to his Quinjet; Crossbones watches them from afar. Arriving in Egypt, Cap and Diamondback enter an ancient tomb where they trigger a trapdoor that drops them into a snake pit.
NOTE: Cover labeled "The Blood Stone Hunt: Part 4 of 6." Crossbones is named in Cap #362, '89 and his real name is revealed in Cap #400/3, '92.

2ND STORY: "Night of the Scourge Part 3!: Conflagration" (5 pages)
CREDITS: Mark Gruenwald (writer), Mark Bright (pencils), Don Hudson (inks), Jack Morelli (letters), Bob Sharen (colors), Mike Rockwitz (asst editor), Ralph Macchio (editor)
FEATURE CHARACTER: USAgent
VILLAINS: Scourge, Power Broker
OTHER CHARACTER: Priscilla Lyons
LOCATIONS/ITEMS: Power Broker's San Fernando Valley estate inc lab; Scourge's guns & bomb
SYNOPSIS: USAgent disarms Scourge by throwing his shield, but the killer escapes. Meanwhile, Power Broker locks himself and Priscilla in his lab. Scourge ambushes USAgent and traps him under debris. Scourge blows Power Broker's door off its hinges.

CAPTAIN AMERICA #361 (Early November 1989)

"Bloodstone Part Five: Lair of the Living Mummy" (17 pages)

CREDITS: Mark Gruenwald (writer), Kieron Dwyer (co-plot, pencils, c art), Danny Bulanadi (inks), Jack Morelli (letters), Bob Sharen, Greg Wright (colors), Mike Rockwitz (asst editor), Ralph Macchio (editor)
FEATURE CHARACTER: Captain America
GUEST STAR: Living Mummy (N'Kantu, last in MTIO #95, '83, next in Q #45, '93)
SUPPORTING CAST: Col. John Jameson (also as Man-Wolf in own thoughts), Diamondback
VILLAINS: Baron Zemo, Batroc & his Brigade: Machete, Zaran; Crossbones, Tristram Micawber
OTHER CHARACTERS: Ulysses Bloodstone (skull), snakes; Asp (mentioned, taught Diamondback how to speak Egyptian)
LOCATIONS/ITEMS: Egypt inc tomb; Zemo's aircraft & neck brace, Cap's modified Quinjet & radiometer, Living Mummy's herbs & torches, Diamondback's sling, Bloodstone (four-fifths)
SYNOPSIS: Captain America and Diamondback land in the snake pit, and Cap tosses Diamondback back out. When Cap leaps for Diamondback's hand, his weight dislocates her shoulder. He resets it and she passes out. Cap turns his back and Diamondback disappears. Zemo and Batroc's Brigade arrive, planning to ambush Cap when he finds the fourth Bloodstone fragment. Cap eventually finds Diamondback, but in the Living Mummy's possession. Cap battles the Living Mummy until Diamondback wakes up; she stops the fight and explains the mummy was tending to her wounds. Able to speak Egyptian, she translates that N'Kantu has a Bloodstone fragment, hoping it would restore his humanity. N'Kantu lets Cap borrow the Bloodstone. Meanwhile, Micawber tells Zemo someone else wants the Bloodstone while Crossbones spies on Col. Jameson. When Cap and Diamondback exit the tomb, Batroc's Brigade ambushes them. Col. Jameson picks up Cap and Diamondback, but Zemo ambushes them in his airship.
NOTE: Cover labeled "The Bloodstone Hunt Part 5 of 6."

2ND STORY: "Night of the Scourge Part 4: Augmentation!!" (5 pages)
CREDITS: Mark Gruenwald (writer), Mark Bright (pencils), Don Hudson (inks), Jack Morelli (letters), Bob Sharen (colors), Mike Rockwitz (asst editor), Ralph Macchio (editor)
FEATURE CHARACTER: USAgent
VILLAINS: Scourge, Power Broker
OTHER CHARACTER: Priscilla Lyons
LOCATIONS/ITEMS: Power Broker's San Fernando Valley estate inc; Power Broker's augmentation equipment, Scourge's guns & bomb
SYNOPSIS: Scourge taunts Power Broker. Feeling he has to fight Scourge, Power Broker straps himself into his augmentation equipment and

ells Priscilla to work the controls. USAgent struggles to free himself from the rubble. Priscilla begins the augmentation process and distracts Scourge by taking off her clothes. Confused, Scourge continues to hunt Power Broker, finding him hiding under a table.

CAPTAIN AMERICA #362 (Mid November 1989)

"The Bloodstone Hunt Part 6: Necromancing the Stone!" (18 pages)

CREDITS: Mark Gruenwald (writer), Kieron Dwyer (co-plot, pencils), Danny Bulanadi (inks), Jack Morelli (letters), Bob Sharen (colors), Mike Rockwitz (asst editor), Ralph Macchio (editor)
FEATURE CHARACTER: Captain America
SUPPORTING CAST: Diamondback, Col. John Jameson
VILLAINS: Baron Helmut Zemo (chr next in PPSSM #196, '93 fb, next in PPSSM #195, '92), Batroc (next in MCP #97/4, '92) & his Brigade: Machete, Zaran (both next in Cap #411, '93); Exo-Mind (extra-dimensional energy life form powered by the Hellfire Helix, last in RH #8/2, '78, last app), Tristram Micawber (next in Cap #370, '90), Crossbones
OTHER CHARACTERS: Baron Heinrich Zemo (corpse, last in GSAv #3, '75, next in Av #353, '92), Ulysses Bloodstone (skull, last app), Boss Lao (corpse), old man (dies), waiters, busboys, Tokyo citizens
LOCATIONS/ITEMS: Tokyo inc restaurant, an inactive volcano; Cap's modified Quinjet & radiometer, Zemo's aircraft, neck brace, communicator & detonator, Heinrich Zemo's coffin, Crossbones' crossbow, waiters' knives, Bloodstone (complete)
SYNOPSIS: Col. Jameson evades Zemo's airship, but Captain America realizes he dropped the Bloodstone fragment while Crossbones hides in the Quinjet. Zemo sends Batroc's Brigade into a Tokyo restaurant where they find people attempting to revive a dead man with the final Bloodstone fragment. After retrieving the fragment, Batroc's Brigade find Cap waiting for them in the street. While Batroc gives Cap Zemo's communicator, Diamondback stows away on Zemo's aircraft. Later at a volcano, Cap meets Zemo, who threatens to blow up a downtown Tokyo city block to gain Cap's Bloodstone fragments. Cap returns to his Quinjet to find Col. Jameson unconscious and the Bloodstone fragments missing. Zemo's aircraft suddenly explodes; the Exo-Mind emerges, possessing Heinrich Zemo's corpse and powered by the Hellfire Helix, and activates the volcano. Upset that the Bloodstone reassembled itself, Crossbones knocks out Diamondback. Zemo doesn't understand that the Exo-Mind is not his father, and stops Cap from attacking his father's reanimated corpse. Crossbones shoots and shatters the Bloodstone; dissipating the Exo-Mind. Zemo jumps in the volcano to follow his father's corpse.
NOTE: Cover labeled "The Blood Stone Hunt Part 6 of 6." "American Graffiti" contains LOC from Myron Gruenwald, the writer's father.

2ND STORY: "The Night of the Scourge Part 5: Won't Get Scourged Again" (5 pages)
CREDITS: Mark Gruenwald (writer), Mark Bright (pencils), Don Hudson (inks), Jack Morelli (letters), Bob Sharen (colors), Mike Rockwitz (asst editor), Ralph Macchio (editor)
FEATURE CHARACTER: USAgent (next bts in Cap #364/2, '89)
VILLAINS: Scourge (dies, last app), Scourge (successor, 1st, off-panel, next in USAgent #1, '93), Power Broker
OTHER CHARACTERS: Priscilla Lyons, Power Broker's augmented thugs (corpses)
LOCATIONS/ITEMS: Power Broker's San Fernando Valley estate inc lab, USAgent's skycycle, Scourge's gun
SYNOPSIS: USAgent finally frees himself as Scourge shoots Power Broker. USAgent confronts Scourge, who holds Priscilla hostage; she kicks Scourge in the crotch. USAgent secures the killer and finds Power Broker, who has become so augmented he can no longer move. Scourge tells USAgent he wanted to kill Power Broker because the Broker turned Scourge's brother Jake into a monster, but the killer is killed from afar. USAgent spends an hour looking for the shooter before taking Scourge's body to a hospital.
NOTE: Scourge claims to be out for vengeance for a relative before being killed by his successor; a similar story was given by the first Scourge in Cap #320, '86 before he was killed by his successor.

CAPTAIN AMERICA #363 (Late November 1989)

"Moon Over Madripoor" (17 pages)

CREDITS: Mark Gruenwald (writer), Kieron Dwyer (pencils, c art), Danny Bulandi (inks), Jack Morelli (letters), Bob Sharen (colors), Mike Rockwitz (asst editor), Ralph Macchio (editor)
FEATURE CHARACTER: Captain America (also in rfb; also in DC2 #1, '89)
GUEST STAR: Wolverine (last in UXM #246, '89, next in W #19, '89)
SUPPORTING CAST: Avengers Crew: Peggy Carter (last in Av Ann #18/3, '89, also in AvS #26, '89, next in Av #311, '90), Col. John Jameson (next in Cap #365, '90), Michael O'Brien (last in Cap #358, '89, next in Av #311, '90); Diamondback (also in rfb)
VILLAINS: Crossbones (also in rfb), Mr. Phun (brothel bodyguard, 1st), Madam Xiona & her prostitutes (Lia named), Crossbones' stooge
OTHER CHARACTERS: Avengers crewmen, Bronze Monkey bartender & patrons, Madripoor citizens, fishermen; Tristram Micawber (in rfb)
LOCATIONS/ITEMS: Avengers Island inc Cap's room & executive office, Madripoor inc Madam Xiona's brothel & Bronze Monkey bar, volcano; Cap's modified Quinjet, Crossbones' crossbow, handcuffs & bear trap
FLASHBACKS: Crossbones knocks out Diamondback (Cap #362, '89). Diamondback is ordered to kill Cap (Cap #315, '86). Cap and Diamondback hunt Scourge (Cap #319, '86).
SYNOPSIS: Crossbones watches Captain America leave the volcano and steals a fishing boat while carrying the unconscious Diamondback. Cap returns to Avengers Island. As Crossbones rows to Madripoor, Diamondback begins to recognize his voice. To his surprise, Cap can't get Diamondback off his mind. Crossbones secures Diamondback in a brothel and contacts Cap, telling him to meet in Madripoor. As Diamondback escapes, Crossbones unknowingly passes Wolverine in the street. Cap arrives in Madripoor as Diamondback makes her way past Mr. Phun

and the prostitutes trying to stop her. Cap meets with Crossbones only to get his foot caught in a bear trap.

2ND STORY: "Malus Aforethought" (5 pages)

CREDITS: Mark Gruenwald (writer), Mark Bright (pencils), Don Hudson (inks), Jack Morelli (letters), Gregory Wright (colors), Mike Rockwitz (asst editor), Ralph Macchio (editor)

FEATURE CHARACTER: Vagabond (Priscilla Lyons)

VILLAINS: Dr. Karl Malus (last in Cap #331, '87), Bludgeon, Mangler (both last in Cap #328, '87), Malus' other augmented enforcers, Power Broker

OTHER CHARACTERS: Doc's Diner waiter, orderly, hospital patrons, police

LOCATIONS/ITEMS: Doc's Diner, Los Angeles County Hospital; Malus' limo, epidermold & exploding tracker bracelet

SYNOPSIS: Bludgeon and Mangler find Priscilla Lyons at Doc's Diner and escort her to Dr. Malus' limo. Malus orders Priscilla to obtain Power Broker's fingerprints by using his epidermold, so Malus can continue to run Power Broker, Incorporated. Otherwise, he'll have her killed. An hour later with an explosive bracelet on her wrist, Priscilla visits Power Broker at the hospital.

CAPTAIN AMERICA #364 (December 1989)

"Man Trap" (17 pages)

CREDITS: Mark Gruenwald (writer), Kieron Dwyer (pencils, c art), Danny Bulandi (inks), Jack Morelli (letters), Bob Sharen, Gregory Wright (colors), Mike Rockwitz (asst editor), Ralph Macchio (editor)

FEATURE CHARACTER: Captain America

SUPPORTING CAST: Diamondback

VILLAINS: Red Skull (last bts in Cap #359, '89), Crossbones, Mr. Phun (dies, last app) & his men

OTHER CHARACTERS: Madripoor citizens (Eddie named), Bronze Monkey patrons

LOCATIONS/ITEMS: Madripoor inc Bronze Monkey bar, abandoned building & toy factory, Red Skull's office; Crossbones' knife gauntlet, bear trap, pressure-plate & bomb, Mr. Phun's wire, Wolverine toys

SYNOPSIS: Captain America fights Crossbones until Cap gets the upper hand; Cap removes the bear trap and demands Crossbones take him to Diamondback. Meanwhile, Diamondback evades Mr. Phun and his men while searching for the Crossbones' rendezvous point with Cap. Crossbones leads Cap to an abandoned building, tricking him onto a pressure-plate connected to a bomb. Mr. Phun chases Diamondback into a toy factory, where he drowns in a vat of molten plastic. Crossbones calls his boss, Red Skull, and reports that he's captured Cap. Red Skull is outraged that Crossbones directly confronted Cap and orders him back to the States. Using his shield as a buffer, Cap is able to set off the bomb without being hurt. The explosion gets Diamondback's attention; she races over and finds Cap.

2ND STORY: "Wristy Business" (5 pages)

CREDITS: Mark Gruenwald (writer), Mark Bright (pencils), Don Hudson (inks), Jack Morelli (letters), Gregory Wright (colors), Mike Rockwitz (asst editor), Ralph Macchio (editor)

FEATURE CHARACTER: Vagabond (chr next in USAgent #2, '93 fb, next in USAgent #1, '93)

GUEST STAR: USAgent (bts on phone, last in Cap #362/2, '89, next in AWC #50, '89)

VILLAINS: Dr. Karl Malus (chr next in USAgent #2, '93 fb, next in AvS #29, '90), Bludgeon (voice only, next in Cap #419, '93), Mangler (next in Cap #395, '91), Power Broker (next bts in Cap #373/2, '90)

OTHER CHARACTERS: Police, nurse, orderly

LOCATIONS/ITEMS: Los Angeles County Hospital inc Power Broker's room; Malus' limo, epidermold, exploding tracker bracelet & hypodermic

SYNOPSIS: Priscilla gets Power Broker's fingerprints, but demands Dr. Malus retrieve them in person. Malus removes the explosive bracelet and tries to inject Priscilla with a hypodermic, but she knocks Malus out, puts the bracelet on him and flushes the key. Once outside, she reports the incident to USAgent over the phone.

CAPTAIN AMERICA #365 (Mid December 1989)

"Submission" (17 pages)

CREDITS: Mark Gruenwald (writer), Kieron Dwyer (pencils, c art), Danny Bulanadi (inks), Jack Morelli (letters), Bob Sharen (colors), Mike Rockwitz (asst editor), Ralph Macchio (editor)

FEATURE CHARACTER: Captain America (also in FF #334, '89, Q #5, '89, Av Ann #19/3, '90 fb)

GUEST STARS: Sub-Mariner (last in MCP #33/4, '89), Quasar (last in Av #311, '89, next in Q #5, '89), Stingray (last in Thor #390, '88, chr last in MCP #56/3, '90, next in Q #5, '89) (both bts, salvaging the sunken Avengers Island)

SUPPORTING CAST: Diamondback, Avengers Crew: Peggy Carter (last in Av #311, '89, next in Q #6, '90), Col. John Jameson (last in Cap #363, '89, next in Cap #368, '90), Edwin Jarvis (last in Av #311, '89, next in DC2 #7, '89), Michael O'Brien (last in Av #311, '89, next in Q #5, '89), Fabian Stankowicz (last in Av #311, '89)

VILLAINS: Loki (last in Av #311, '89, also in Q #5, '89, AvS #27, '89, AvS #28/2, '90, AWC #53, '89) & his Prime Movers: Dr. Doom, Wizard (both last in PPSSM #159, '89), Magneto (last in AWC #53, '89), Mandarin (last in Av #311, '89) (both off-panel), Kingpin (last in ASM #327, '89), Red Skull (joins Prime Movers) (all chr next in Av Ann #19/3, '90 fb); Controller (last in IM #225, '87, last bts in IM #226, '87), Crossbones

OTHER CHARACTERS: Dr. Doom's robots (in rfb), fish

LOCATIONS/ITEMS: New York inc Avengers Mansion basement, Empire State Building, World Trade Center & Staten Island w/Statue of Liberty, Atlantic Ocean inc Avengers Island (sunk, also in rfb), Red Skull's office, Isle of Silence; Cap's modified Quinjet & skycycle, 4 Avengers Quinjets, Red Skull's booby traps, pistol & aircraft, Crossbones' pistol, Controller's control discs

FLASHBACK: Dr. Doom's robots sink Avengers Island (Av #311, '89).

SYNOPSIS: Red Skull chastens Crossbones for confronting Captain America and sends him to the Vault; there was a recent breakout and the Skull wants some new villainous recruits. Loki appears, easily evades the Skull's booby-traps and offers Red Skull a place in his new cabal; he leaves a magic doorway in case the Skull decides to join him. Meanwhile, Cap and Diamondback return from Madripoor to find Avengers Island has been sunk. In the Atlantic Ocean, Loki approaches Namor with an offer to join his cabal, but Namor refuses and decides to tell the Avengers. Later, Crossbones captures the recently escaped Controller and convinces him to work for the Skull. Meanwhile, Jarvis suggests the Avengers use the Avengers Mansion basement as their temporary base. Namor finds the sunken Avengers Island, where Controller ambushes him and affixes a control disc to his neck. Cap finds Sub-Mariner at the Statue of Liberty but Namor attacks; Cap notices the control disc and smashes it, which knocks Namor out. Elsewhere, the Skull joins Loki's alliance.

NOTE: Cover labeled "Acts of Vengeance!" signaling this issue is part of the crossover in which major villains form a cabal to arrange for villains to fight heroes other than their traditional opponents. Cap calls his skycycle a "skymobile" here.

2ND STORY: "Hyde - - And Seek!" (5 pages)

CREDITS: Mark Gruenwald (writer), Mark Bright (pencils), Don Hudson (inks), Jack Morelli (letters), Nel Yomtov (colors), Mike Rockwitz (asst editor), Ralph Macchio (editor)

FEATURE CHARACTER: Cobra (also in his own thoughts, last in X Ann #13, '89)

SUPPORTING CAST: Serpent Society: Anaconda, Asp, Black Mamba, Black Racer, Boomslang, Bushmaster, Coachwhip, Cottonmouth, Fer-de-Lance, Puff Adder, Rock Python (all last in X Ann #13, '89), Rattler (last in DC2 #1, '89) (all next in Cap #367/2, '90)

VILLAINS: Mr. Hyde (also as Calvin Zabo, in photo & Cobra's thoughts, last in AvS #26, '89, chr last in Av Ann #19/3, '90 fb), Loki (last in AvS #26, '89, chr last in Av Ann #19/3, '90 fb, next in PPSSM #158, '89)

OTHER CHARACTERS: Howard G. Hardman (Vault Warden, bts, warned citizens of Vault breakout), news anchor

LOCATIONS/ITEMS: Serpent Society HQ inc Cobra's office, private quarters & meeting room, Mr. Hyde's hideouts (all but one destroyed); Serpent Saucer, Cobra's explosives

SYNOPSIS: Cobra hears that Mr. Hyde has escaped from the Vault and worries that Hyde will try to kill him again. Loki appears and offers Cobra a spot in his cabal; Cobra declines, explaining that the Serpent Society is motivated by profit and has no arch-nemesis. Cobra orders the Society to find out what they can about Loki and starts destroying Hyde's various hideouts. He waits in the remaining hideout until Hyde arrives.

CAPTAIN AMERICA #366 (January 1990)

"Remote Control" (18 pages)

CREDITS: Mark Gruenwald (writer), Ron Lim (pencils), Danny Bulanadi (inks), Jack Morelli (letters), Nel Yomtov (colors), Mike Rockwitz (asst editor), Ralph Macchio (editor)

FEATURE CHARACTER: Captain America (next in NW #1, '90, bts in Av Ann #19/3, '90 fb, C&D #9, '89, Av #312, '89)

GUEST STARS: Dr. Hank Pym (last in AWC #53, '89, chr last in AWC Ann #5/5, '90, next in Av #312, '89), Thor (during Thor #411, '89), Sub-Mariner

SUPPORTING CAST: Diamondback (next in Cap #368, '90), Fabian Stankowicz

VILLAINS: Loki (also in Thor #411-412, '89, XFac #49, '89, XFac #50/2, '90, next bts in ASM #328, '90, next in PPSSM #160, '90) & his Prime Movers: Dr. Doom, Kingpin (both next in Pun #28, '89), Magneto, Red Skull (both next in W #19, '89), Mandarin, Wizard (both next bts in ASM #328, '90, next in WoSM #61, '90) (all chr last in Av Ann #19/3, '90 fb); Voice Jason Cragg, commands others with his voice, last in WCA #37, '88, next in Cap #369, '90), Juggernaut (during Thor #411, '89), Controller, Crossbones

OTHER CHARACTERS: Avengers crewmen, police, bystanders

LOCATIONS/ITEMS: New York inc Avengers Mansion basement & Central Park, Washington DC inc Red Skull's office & White House, Isle of Silence; Controller's Control Discs, Cap's skycycle & armored neck plate, Crossbones' aircraft & crossbow, police gun

SYNOPSIS: Dr. Pym examines the comatose Sub-Mariner's control disc, deciding not to remove it to avoid causing Namor possible neurological damage. Captain America has Fabian trace the disc's broadcast to find the Controller. Elsewhere, Loki's group adjourns and Magneto asks Loki if that's the original Red Skull. The Skull returns to his office and orders Crossbones to locate the Controller; he finds him watching a battle between Thor and the Juggernaut, wanting to sap Thor's strength. Controller refuses to return to the Skull's service, so Crossbones has the Voice command Controller to do it anyway. Cap finds Controller and ambushes Crossbones' aircraft, where he battles Controller; Controller falls out of the aircraft and Cap jumps out after him. Controller attaches a control disc to Cap and escapes; Cap removes the disc from the armored plate on his neck. Red Skull has Controller try to place a control disc on Loki, but the Asgardian easily removes it, commenting on how untrustworthy the Skull is.

NOTE: Cover labeled "Acts of Vengeance!" signaling this issue is part of the crossover in which major villains form a cabal to arrange for villains to fight heroes other than their traditional opponents. Title returns to monthly status here.

2ND STORY: "Nowhere to Hyde!" (5 pages)

CREDITS: Mark Gruenwald (writer), Mark Bagley (pencils), Don Hudson (inks), Jack Morelli (letters), Nel Yomtov (colors), Mike Rockwitz (asst editor), Ralph Macchio (editor)

FEATURE CHARACTER: Cobra

VILLAIN: Mr. Hyde

LOCATIONS/ITEMS: Hyde's hideout; Cobra's "venom"

SYNOPSIS: Mr. Hyde savagely attacks the terrified Cobra for destroying his hideouts. Cobra narrowly avoids continued attacks until Hyde catches him by the throat. Cobra spits in Hyde's mouth, telling him it's poison and he'll be dead in a minute.

CAPTAIN AMERICA #367 (February 1990)

"Magnetic Repulsion" (17 pages)

CREDITS: Mark Gruenwald (writer), Kieron Dwyer (pencils, c art), Danny Bulanadi (inks), Jack Morelli (letters), Steve Buccellato (colors), Mike Rockwitz (asst editor), Ralph Macchio (editor)
FEATURE CHARACTER: Captain America (next in Pun #29, '90, DC2 #2, '89, AWC #54, '90)
GUEST STARS: Sub-Mariner (next in Pun #29, '90), Dr. Hank Pym (last in Av #312, '89, next in AWC #54, '90)
SUPPORTING CAST: Fabian Stankowicz
VILLAINS: Red Skull (last in Av #312, '89, next in Cap #369/2, '90) & his men, Controller (next in Av:Vault, '91), Machinesmith (bts, controlling 4th Sleeper, last in Cap #354, '89), Magneto (last in Av #312, '89, next in AWC #54, '90), Crossbones
OTHER CHARACTERS: 4th Sleeper (last in Cap #354, '89, chr last in Av Ann #19/3, '90 fb), Ilsa Schultz (Red Skull's secretary, 1st, next voice only in Cap #376, '90), fish
LOCATIONS/ITEMS: Washington DC inc Smith Building w/Red Skull's office & underground tunnels, Avengers Mansion basement, Atlantic Ocean, Magneto's underground fallout shelter; Cap's modified Quinjet, Red Skull's guns, force field & escape car (destroyed), Red Skull's men's guns, Controller's Control Disc, Avengers communicator, Red Skull robots (destroyed)
SYNOPSIS: Dr. Pym resuscitates Sub-Mariner, who tells Captain America he'll pretend to accept Loki's previous offer. In the Smith Building, Magneto attacks Red Skull. The Skull momentarily traps Magneto in a force field and escapes; Controller tries to attach a control disc to Magneto. Cap happens by as Controller is thrown out of the Smith Building. Magneto defeats the 4th Sleeper as Cap defeats Controller by putting one of his own discs on him, causing a feedback loop. Magneto destroys an army of Red Skull robots and catches up to the Skull himself. Namor finds Loki's door is no longer there as Cap only finds the aftermath of Magneto's attack. Later, Red Skull wakes up; Magneto tells him he's in a fallout shelter with no way out as he leaves him trapped in solitary confinement for his war crimes during WWII.
NOTE: Cover labeled "Acts of Vengeance!", signaling this issue is part of the crossover in which major villains form a cabal to arrange for villains to fight heroes other than their traditional opponents. Ilsa's surname is revealed in Cap #393, '91.

2ND STORY: "The Way of the Snake" (5 pages)
CREDITS: Mark Gruenwald (writer), Mark Bagley (pencils), Don Hudson (inks), Jack Morelli (letters), Nel Yomtov (colors), Mike Rockwitz (asst editor), Ralph Macchio (editor)
FEATURE CHARACTER: Cobra (becomes King Cobra)
SUPPORTING CAST: Serpent Society: Cottonmouth, Fer-de-Lance, Puff Adder, Rattler, Rock Python (all next in Cap #380, '90), Anaconda (next in Cap #371, '90), Asp (next in AFlt #79, '89), Black Racer (next in Q #17, '90), Boomslang (next in Cap #372, '90), Coachwhip (next in MSMK #10, '90), Black Mamba (all last in Cap #365/2, '89)
VILLAIN: Mr. Hyde (next in Hulk #368, '90)
LOCATIONS/ITEMS: Hyde's hideout, Serpent Society HQ; Cobra's "antidote," Serpent Saucer
SYNOPSIS: Cobra tells Mr. Hyde to let him go, or he won't give him the antidote; when Hyde does, Cobra asks for reassurance that Hyde will stop trying to kill him. Hyde falls to his knees and begs Cobra. Cobra gives Hyde a sedative and after Hyde passes out, Cobra tells him there was no venom, only spit. Cobra returns to the Serpent Society feeling renewed, and tells them his name is now King Cobra.

CAPTAIN AMERICA #368 (March 1990)

"Red Twilight" (17 pages)

CREDITS: Mark Gruenwald (writer), Ron Lim (pencils), Danny Bulanadi (inks), Jack Morelli (letters), Steve Bucellato (colors), Mike Rockwitz (asst editor), Ralph Macchio (editor)
FEATURE CHARACTERS: Captain America (also in video footage, next in Av #313, AWC #55, Av Ann #19/3 fb, AvS #29/2, DC2 #3-4, Av Ann #19/3, all '90)
GUEST STAR: Scarlet Witch (last in Av #313, '90, next in AWC #55, '90)
SUPPORTING CAST: Avengers Crew: Peggy Carter (last in Q #7, '90, next in Cap #370, '90), Col. John Jameson (last in Cap #365, '89, next in Cap #370, '90), Edwin Jarvis (last in DC2 #2, '89, next in Av #313, '90), Fabian Stankowicz (next in DC2 #3, '90); Diamondback (last in Cap #366, '90)
VILLAINS: Serpent Society: King Cobra (voice only, next in Q #8, '90), Asp (last in AFlt #80, '90), Black Mamba (next in Cap #371, '90); Resistants: Crucible (last in Cap #350, '89, next in Cap #394, '91), Meteorite (last in Cap #346, '88, next in Cap #426, '94), Mist Mistress (last in Cap #346, '88, last app), Paralyzer (last in Cap #346, '88, next in MSUn #3, '93), Quill (last in FF #335, '89, next in AvS #29/2, '90), a dozen others; Red Skull robot (1st, next in Av #312, '90), Machinesmith (also as Magneto, next in Cap #368/2, '90), Magneto (last in Av #313, '90, next in AWC #55, '90), Magneto robot (also in video footage, last in Cap #354, '89, destroyed, last app), Selene (Hellfire Club's Black Queen & energy vampire, last in NM #75, '89, chr last in MCP #78/4, '91), Crossbones, Red Skull's men
OTHER CHARACTERS: 4th Sleeper (next in Cap #368/2, '90), Ilsa (last app), landscapers, construction workers, bartender, bar patrons, news anchor, police; Ant-Man, Hulk, Vision, Wasp (prev 4 statues), Colossus, Spider-Man, Thing, Wonder Man (prev 4 robots), Iron Man, Namor, Thor (prev 3 statues & robots)
LOCATIONS/ITEMS: Washington DC inc White House & Smith Building w/Red Skull's office, Machinesmith's lab & underground tunnels, Avengers Mansion basement, Selene's Hellfire Club office; Red Skull's escape car (wreckage), Red Skull robots (remains), Cap's modified Quinjet & skycycle, Avengers security tentacles
SYNOPSIS: Surveying the aftermath of Magneto's attack, Crossbones and Machinesmith find no trace of Red Skull. Crossbones tells Machinesmith that no one can know that Red Skull is missing. Captain America returns to the Avengers' temporary base and researches

Magneto. Crossbones meets the Red Skull robot, a contingency plan in case the Skull goes missing. Crossbones and Machinesmith hatch a plan to draw Magneto out into the open so they can interrogate him as to Red Skull's whereabouts. Diamondback meets with Asp and Black Mamba for drinks until they're called away by King Cobra; Red Skull has put a $100,000 bounty on Magneto. Diamondback tells them that Magneto is a member of the Hellfire Club. Responding to reports of Magneto attacking a Resistants protest at the White House, Cap quickly discovers that Magneto is a robot and destroys it. Later, the Hellfire Club's Black Queen sees the Cap and "Magneto" battle on the news and wonders what Magneto could be up to. Elsewhere, the real Magneto approaches his daughter, the Scarlet Witch…
NOTE: The Magneto/Scarlet Witch story is continued in AWC #55, '90.

2ND STORY: "A Clockwork Origin" (5 pages)
CREDITS: Mark Gruenwald (writer), Mark Bagley (pencils), Don Hudson (inks), Jack Morelli (letters), Nel Yomtov (colors), Mike Rockwitz (asst editor), Ralph Macchio (editor)
FEATURE CHARACTER: Machinesmith (also as Mr. Fear in rfb; in fb1 as Samuel Saxon to 1st chr app before bts in X #49, '68, fb2 as Starr Saxon during Cap #249, '80 fb, fb3 between Cap #249, '80 fb & MTIO #47, '79, fb4 between Cap #249, '80 & bts in Cap #351, '89)
VILLAINS: Red Skull (as John Smith, in fb4 between Cap #383/4, '91 & bts in Cap #321, '86), Tinkerer (Phineas Mason, criminal inventor, bts in fb1 between ASM #2/2, '63 & bts in ASM #159, '76)
OTHER CHARACTERS: 4th Sleeper (also in fb4 between Cap #102, '68 & Cap #354, '89), Magneto robot (in fb3 between X #58, '69 & Cap #247, '80), Colossus, Thor, Wonder Man (prev 3 robots), Dr. Doom's Servobot (remains, in fb1), Captain America, Daredevil, Dragon Man, Jack of Hearts, Thing, Machinesmith's robot assassin (prev 6 in fb3), & robots (in fb3); Machinesmith's mother (mentioned in fb1)
LOCATIONS/ITEMS: Machinesmith's Smith Building lab & his father's garage, subway tunnel (both in fb1); Machinesmith's equipment, 1st robot creation (in fb1), hover-platform & computer bank (both in rfb)
FLASHBACKS: At age fourteen Samuel Saxon finds a discarded Dr. Doom Servobot in a subway tunnel. He studies it for months in his father's garage, but when his mother disapproves she dies in a "lab accident" involving his first robot creation. Over the next five years he's mentored by the Tinkerer (1). Daredevil fights one of Saxon's robots (DD #49, '69), and is forced to let Saxon go (DD #52, '69). Saxon assumes the guise of Mr. Fear (DD #54, '69), but falls to his death in battle against Daredevil (DD #55, '69). Saxon is retrieved by his robots (Cap #249, '80 fb), who download his consciousness into a robot body (2). Saxon awakes as Machinesmith (Cap #249, '80 fb). Machinesmith perfects his robot simulations of various superhumans (3), battles the Thing (MTIO #47, '79) and Jack of Hearts (MTIO #48, '79). Recruiting Dragon Man (Cap #248, '80), Machinesmith battles Cap and tricks him into destroying the computer bank holding his consciousness in a suicide attempt (Cap #249, '80). Machinesmith wakes up in another body moments later and realizes machine life has more possibilities than organic life. He's later recruited by John Smith and repairs the 4th Sleeper's tangibility circuits (4).
SYNOPSIS: As Machinesmith repairs the 4th Sleeper he relates his life story. When he's finished, Machinesmith kisses the 4th Sleeper.

CAPTAIN AMERICA #369 (April 1990)

"The Skeleton Crew" (18 pages)

CREDITS: Mark Gruenwald (writer), Ron Lim (pencils), Danny Bulanadi (inks), Jack Morelli (letters), Steve Buccellato (colors), Mike Rockwitz (asst editor), Ralph Macchio (editor)
FEATURE CHARACTER: Captain America
SUPPORTING CAST: Michael O'Brien (bts, told Cap where to find Asp, last in Q #5, '89, chr last in Av Ann #19/3, 90 fb, next in Cap #371, '90), Diamondback
VILLAINS: Skeleton Crew (Red Skull's agents, 1st as group): Mother Night (last in Cap #357, '89), Voice (last in Cap #366, '90), Crossbones, Machinesmith, 4th Sleeper; Asp (also in photos, next in Cap #371, '90), Selene (next in MCP #89/3, '91), Hellfire Club soldiers
OTHER CHARACTERS: Tinkerer (last in AFlt #79, '89, next bts in Cap #385/2, '91), b ystanders
LOCATIONS/ITEMS: New York inc Pink Flamingo Lounge w/Asp's dressing room, Tinkerer's workshop, Hellfire Club & sewer tunnels; Tinkerer's workshop items inc Dr. Octopus' tentacles, Mysterio's helmet, Stiltman's helmet & Stingray's wings, Crossbones' crossbow, Skeleton Crew's Con Ed utility truck, Hellfire Club soldier's guns
SYNOPSIS: Captain America confronts Asp at her side job as a dancer at the Pink Flamingo lounge, in an attempt to contact Diamondback. Soon after, Diamondback leaves a message with Cap's hotline to meet. Meanwhile, Crossbones and the Skeleton Crew are looking for the missing Red Skull, thinking Magneto may be holding him at the Hellfire Club. When they enter the sewers they draw Diamondback's attention. The Skeleton Crew enters the Hellfire Club through a secret entrance and Voice stops the attacking Hellfire Club soldiers. Machinesmith hacks into the security system to discover the Skull isn't there. Investigating, Diamondback finds Selene attacking the Skeleton Crew; Selene damages Voice's larynx so he can't control her. Cap's arrival provides enough distraction for the Skeleton Crew to escape. Selene causes the ceiling to collapse, trapping Cap and Diamondback in the rubble.

2ND STORY: "Out Of His Skull" (5 pages)
CREDITS: Mark Gruenwald (writer), Mark Bagley (pencils), Don Hudson (inks), Jack Morelli (letters), Mike Rockwitz (asst editor), Ralph Macchio (editor)
FEATURE CHARACTER: Red Skull (last in Cap #367, '90)
OTHER CHARACTERS: Captain America, Adolf Hitler, Arnim Zola, Hermann Shmidt, Synthia Shmidt (all in hallucination)
LOCATIONS/ITEMS: Red Skull's Bergen County, NJ fallout shelter prison; Synthia's glass shard (in hallucination)
SYNOPSIS: Still trapped in his prison, Red Skull hallucinates his father, Hitler and his daughter telling him to commit suicide. Arnim Zola reasons that when the Skull dies, he will just awake in a new body. Captain America urges the Skull to hold out hope for rescue. Despising the sympathy Cap offers, the Skull's hatred keeps him from succumbing to despair.

CAPTAIN AMERICA #370 (May 1990)

"House Calls" (22 pages)

CREDITS: Mark Gruenwald (writer), Ron Lim (pencils), Danny Bulanadi (inks), Jack Morelli (letters), Steve Buccellato (colors), Mike Rockwitz (asst editor), Ralph Macchio (editor)
FEATURE CHARACTER: Captain America
GUEST STAR: Eric Masterson (between Thor #413 & 414, '90)
SUPPORTING CAST: Avengers Crew: Peggy Carter, Col. John Jameson (both last in Cap #368, '90), Edwin Jarvis (last in Av #313, '90, chr last in Av Ann #19/3, '90), M'Daka (last in Av #311, '89, last app), Fabian Stankowicz (last in DC2 #3, '90)
VILLAINS: Red Skull (also in holograms, next bts in Cap #372, '90, next in Cap #376, '90) & his Skeleton Crew: Crossbones (also as a doctor, next in Q #9, '90), Machinesmith (next bts in Av #323/2, '90, next in Av #324, '90), Mother Night (also as a nurse, chr next in Av #324/2, '90 fb, next bts in Av #319/2, '90, next in Av #323/2, '90), 4th Sleeper (next in Cap #387/2, '91), Voice (last app); Tristram Micawber (last in Cap #362, '89, dies, last app), Red Skull's men (Rankin named)
OTHER CHARACTERS: Mrs. Devereau (Micawber's customer), firemen, police, paramedics; Exiles: Angelo Baldini, Franz Cadavus, Gen. Jun Ching, Eric Gruning, Jurgen "Iron Hand" Hauptmann, Ivan Krushki; Adolf Hitler (prev 7 in photo)
LOCATIONS/ITEMS: New York inc Avengers HQ, Washington DC inc Smith Building, Bergen County, NJ inc fallout shelter, Skull-House, Micawber's office; Cap's modified Quinjet, Skeleton Crew's helicopter & jet, Red Skull's replicas: Ameridroid, Bucky robot, Death's-Head satellite, 1st, 2nd, 3rd, 4th & 5th Sleepers, Skull-House staircase boobytrap
SYNOPSIS: Captain America and Diamondback free themselves from the rubble. Meanwhile, the Skeleton Crew returns to the Smith Building and review their attempts to find Red Skull. Cap takes Diamondback to the Avengers temporary headquarters. The Skeleton Crew hires Tristram Micawber, who leads them to Red Skull's prison and suffers a heart attack. Crossbones retrieves the Skull, who asks to be taken home to die. Meanwhile, Diamondback plays cards with the Avengers Crew. At Skull-House, Red Skull asks to see Captain America. Cap finishes a meeting with Eric Masterson to discuss reconstruction of Avengers Mansion and Peggy tells Cap that lights are on at Skull-House. When Cap and Diamondback arrive they fight past booby traps and replicas of Red Skull's past schemes. Eventually arriving at the Skull's bedside, Cap renews Red Skull's hatred and will to live. Captain America leaves, finally accepting that the Red Skull still lives.

CAPTAIN AMERICA #371 (June 1990)

"Cap's Night Out" (17 pages)

CREDITS: Mark Gruenwald (writer), Ron Lim (pencils), Danny Bulanadi (inks), Jack Morelli (letters), Steve Buccellato (colors), Mike Rockwitz (asst editor), Ralph Macchio (editor)
FEATURE CHARACTER: Captain America (also in rfb, next in FF #337, NF:AoS #10, BK #1, all '90, SSS #1, '92, Av #314-318, '90, Av:Vault, '91, MCP #47/3, ASM #335, Av #319-325, MSH #3, Cap Ann #9, all '90)
SUPPORTING CAST: Avengers Crew: Col. John Jameson, Edwin Jarvis (both next in Av #314, '90), Peggy Carter (next in Av #316, '90), Michael O'Brien (last bts in Cap #369, '90, next in Av #316, '90), Fabian Stankowicz (chr next bts in Av #324/2, '90 fb, next in Av #319/2, '90); Diamondback (next in Cap #371/2, '90)
VILLAINS: Serpent Society: Anaconda (last in Cap #367/2, '90, next in Cap #380, '90), Asp (last in Cap #369, '90, next bts in Cap #379/2, '90), Black Mamba (last in Cap #368, '90, next in Cap #371/2, '90); Gamecock (last in Cap #183, '75, next bts in Cap #394, '91), Jackhammer (uses wrist-mounted vibrational hammers, last in DD #123, '75, next in Cap #373/2, '90), Poundcakes (Marian Pouncy, UCWF wrestler, last in Thing #36, '86, next in Cap #389, '91), Trump (Carlton Sanders, criminal stage magician, last in DD #203, '84, next in Cap #411, '93)
OTHER CHARACTERS: Charlotte (Gamecock's girlfriend, only app), Panchito's employees & patrons, Mostly Magic stage magician & patrons, taxi drivers, police, bystanders, Eugene (Black Mamba's personal hairdresser, bts, does Diamondback's hair); Bernie Rosenthal (in rfb)
LOCATIONS/ITEMS: New York inc Upper West Side, Rachel's apartment, beauty salon, Avengers HQ w/Cap's quarters, Greenwich Village w/closed Italian restaurant, Panchito's, Village Cigars & Mostly Magic, Lower East Side w/Steve's boyhood apartment building & tenement building; police guns, Gamecock's talons, Jackhammer's wrist-hammers
FLASHBACK: Bernie proposes marriage to Steve (Cap #292, '84).
SYNOPSIS: Diamondback asks Captain America out on a date and insists that the evening involve no costumed heroics. Tanya Sealy treats Diamondback to a makeover and Jarvis takes Steve out shopping for new clothes. Steve picks up Rachel at her apartment and they head to a favorite restaurant of Steve's, unaware that Black Mamba, Asp and Anaconda are following them. The trip is momentarily stalled by a police standoff with Gamecock; Asp defeats Gamecock for the police. Steve and Rachel find the restaurant is closed down, and opt for the Mexican restaurant next door. After dinner, the two go to a magic show nearby, which is interrupted by the grandstanding Trump. Black Mamba mesmerizes Trump into leaving, leaving Steve and Rachel none the wiser. Steve and Rachel show each other their childhood homes, but a nearby lover's quarrel between Jackhammer and Poundcakes prompts Steve to intervene, much to Rachel's chagrin. Before Steve can reach them, Rachel's Serpent friends subdue the unhappy couple and drive off. Steve walks Rachel home, and Rachel ends the night with a kiss.
NOTE: The closed Greenwich Village Italian restaurant is on Bleecker St. & Thompson St.; Mostly Magic is on Carmine St.

2ND STORY: "Girl Talk" (5 pages)
CREDITS: Mark Gruenwald (writer), Mark Bagley (pencils), Don Hudson (inks), Jack Morelli (letters), Nel Yomtov (colors), Mike Rockwitz (assy editor), Ralph Macchio (editor)
FEATURE CHARACTER: Diamondback (next in Av #325, '90)
SUPPORTING CAST: Black Mamba (next bts in Cap #379/2, '90)
OTHER CHARACTER: Maggie (Sidewinder's sister, runs Collette's Fashion Boutique, mentioned only)

LOCATIONS/ITEMS: Rachel's New York apartment; Rachel's throwing diamonds

SYNOPSIS: Rachel finds Tanya waiting for her in her apartment and the two dish about her date. When Rachel mentions going straight, Tanya asks her if her new beau is worth sacrificing her career. Tanya sees Rachel's growing discomfort and leaves. After spending the night soul-searching, Rachel calls Tanya to ask if Sidewinder's sister still runs a fashion boutique, intending to ask her for a sales job.

NOTE: Rachel is employed at Collette's Fashion Boutique as of Cap #374, '90.

CAPTAIN AMERICA ANNUAL #9 (1990)

"The Terminus Factor Part I: You ARE What You Eat" (23 pages)

CREDITS: Roy & Dann Thomas (writers), Jim Valentino (pencils, c art), Sam DeLaRosa (inks), Jean Simek (letters), Michael Heisler (asst editor), Ralph Macchio (editor)

FEATURE CHARACTER: Captain America (next in AWC Ann #5, Av Ann #19, 19/4-19/5, Cap Ann #9/2, all '90)

GUEST STAR: Iron Man (last in Av #318, '90, chr last in Av:Vault, '92, last bts in Av #320/2, '90, next in IM Ann #11/3, '90)

VILLAIN: Termini (Stage 1, Terminex creations designed to evolve into Terminus in five stages, 1st but chr last in Thor Ann #15, '90 fb, Stage 2 next in IM Ann #11, '90)

OTHER CHARACTERS: Dr. Ramona Napier (volcanologist, 1st, next in IM #5, '98), Leonard (Stark Enterprises chief engineer), Stark Enterprises employees, Georgville citizens (inc Mayor), Walakima Native-American tribe (Bob Twelvetrees named), bear (next in IM Ann #11, '90), trout, deer

LOCATIONS/ITEMS: Washington State inc Mt. Saint Cloud, Georgeville & Cascade Mountains; Termini containment pod (destroyed), Persephone-1 (volcanic exploration capsule), Whirlybird-3 (helicopter), Twelvetrees' shotgun & fishing net, power lines, bucket of ice

SYNOPSIS: Captain America and Dr. Ramona Napier take Persephone-1 into active volcano Mt. Saint Cloud, unaware the volcano's heat has also hatched a swarm of microscopic Termini, which surround Persephone-1 and incapacitate it before shooting out the volcano and landing in a nearby river. When the Stark Enterprises crew notices the trouble, Tony Stark slips away to become Iron Man, and drags Persephone-1 out of the volcano. The Termini infect some fish, which are netted by some locals. Later, Cap, Iron Man and Ramona attend Georgeville's annual Trout Fest, but everyone who eats the fish, including Iron Man, suddenly goes berserk. While trying to restore order Cap notices that an infected child returns to normal after being put in a bucket of ice. Cap and Ramona try to retreat in a helicopter, but Iron Man shoots it down. Cap gets Iron Man's attention, and he pursues Cap up a nearby mountain, with the townspeople following, drawn by the energy within Iron Man's armor. As the two fight, Iron Man slowly regains his senses, as do the townspeople; Cap explains the cold counteracted whatever was making people go crazy. Meanwhile, an infected bear kills a deer.

NOTE: Cover labeled "The Terminus Factor Part One of Five." Includes "Terminus Factor Stage One" contents page (1 page) featuring Terminus Stages 1-5. Part 1 of the "Terminus Factor" crossover event running through Marvel's 1990 Avengers-related Annuals, continuing in IM Ann #11, Thor Ann #15, AWC Ann #5 & Av Ann #19, all '90. Colors are not credited for this story.

2ND STORY: "A Soldier's Story" (22 pages)

CREDITS: Randall Frenz (writer), Mark Bagley (pencils), Mike DeCarlo (inks), Diana Albers (letters), Evelyn Stein (colors), Michael Heisler (asst editor), Ralph Macchio (editor)

FEATURE CHARACTER: Captain America (also in fb between CapC #40/4, '44 & Cap Spec, '06 fb; next in MCP #60/4, SS #36, PPSSM #168-170, SS Ann #3, all '90, NF:AoS #24, '91, Thor #420-421, '90, Cap #372, '90)

GUEST STARS: Sgt. Fury & his Howling Commandos: Izzy Cohen, Dum Dum Dugan, Gabe Jones (all only in fb between NF:AoS #11, '90 fb & Cap Spec, '06 fb), Dino Manelli, Pinky Pinkerton (both only in fb between SgtF #81 '70 & Cap Spec, '06 fb), Senator Reb Ralston (also in fb between NF:AoS #11, '90 fb & Cap Spec, '06 fb; last in Cap #274, '82, last in Hulk #434, '95)

SUPPORTING CAST: Bucky (only in fb between CapC #40/4, '44 & Cap Spec, '06 fb)

VILLAINS: Red Skull (only in fb between CapC #37/4, '44 & Cap Spec, '06 fb) & his enforcer, German soldiers (Heinz named) (all only in fb), anti-Communist assassin

OTHER CHARACTERS: Howard Stark (industrialist & Iron Man's father, only in fb to 1st chr app before SHIELD #1, '10 fb), Maria Stark (Iron Man's mother, only in fb to 1st chr app before IM #285, '92 fb), reporters (Mr. Donaldson named), cameraman, doctor, nurses

LOCATIONS/ITEMS: Washington, DC pressroom, Reb's hospital room, Germany inc Red Skull's mountain stronghold (in fb); Howling Commandos' guns, parachutes, ropes & explosives, German soldiers' guns & spotlights, Red Skull's swastika branding iron, Gabe's bugle, Pinky's umbrella, Bucky's lockpick, Allied plane, Nazi plane (all in fb), assassin's gun

FLASHBACK: April, 1944: Red Skull has captured Howard Stark and his wife, so Sgt. Fury and his Howling Commandos parachute into Germany to rescue them. Nazi soldiers ambush them and Reb freezes in fear, but Captain America and Bucky arrive to assist, defeating the Germans. Meanwhile, Red Skull tortures Howard and Maria Stark. As Cap and the Howlers climb the mountain towards Red Skull's stronghold, Reb falls and Cap saves him again. Finding an exposed grate, Cap suggests Bucky and Reb slide through to rescue the Starks while he and the other Howlers create a diversion elsewhere in the castle stronghold; Sgt. Fury reluctantly agrees. The double-pronged attack works and the heroes narrowly escape in a stolen Nazi plane.

SYNOPSIS: Captain America attends Senator Reb Ralston's speech, but an anti-Communist shoots Reb. Cap consoles Reb until paramedics arrive. Cap is present when Reb awakes in his hospital room.

NOTE: Gabe Jones is erroneously colored white here.

3RD STORY: "Walking the Line" (10 pages)

CREDITS: Fabian Nicieza (writer), Don Hudson (pencils), Tom Morgan (inks), Pat Brosseau (letters), Ed Lazellari (colors), Michael Heisler (asst editor), Ralph Macchio (editor)

FEATURE CHARACTER: Nomad (last in MCP #14/4, '89, next in Nomad #1, '90)

VILLAINS: Umberto Safilios (drug dealer & pimp) & his men (Martinson named) (all only app)
OTHER CHARACTERS: Patty Joplin (mentioned, Nomad's friend), Patty's parents & daughter, funeral attendees, priest, airport commuters, Joplin Estate security (Hennison named) (all only app)
LOCATIONS/ITEMS: Savannah, GA inc cemetery, airport & Joplin Estate, Nomad's Miami motel room; Nomad's new costume, car & shotgun
SYNOPSIS: Nomad attends Patty Joplin's funeral from afar, but is upset to Patty's former pimp Safilios there. He follows Safilios to the airport and confronts him over it, but Safilios laughs in his face. Nomad goes to the Joplin Estate, fights his way through security and is surprised to see Patty's father playing with Patty's young daughter. Mr. Joplin reveals that Safilios is the father and he knew that Safilios was Patty's pimp. Nomad leaves in silence, and later decides he needs to change the way he does things.
NOTE: Story continues in Nomad #1, '90.

CAPTAIN AMERICA #372 (Early July 1990)

"Sold on Ice!" (17 pages)

CREDITS: Mark Gruenwald (writer), Ron Lim (pencils, c inks), Danny Bulanadi (inks), Joe Rosen (letters), Steve Buccellato (colors), Michael Heisler (asst editor), Ralph Macchio (editor)
FEATURE CHARACTER: Captain America (also as homeless man & the Punisher)
SUPPORTING CAST: Avengers Crew: Col. John Jameson (also as "James" & the Punisher), Michael O'Brien (next in Cap #374, '90), Fabian Stankowicz (all last in Av #325, '90); Diamondback (last in Av #325, '90, see NOTE)
VILLAINS: Boomslang (last in Cap #367/2, '90, next in Cap #379/2, '90), Bullseye (Lester, pinpoint accuracy with thrown weapons, last in DD #200, '83, chr last in 1985 #4, '08); Red Skull (bts, last in Cap #370, '90, next in Cap #376, '90, see NOTE) & his ice dealers: Ground Chuck, Lowlife (Gregory Laslo, both 1st), Jailbait, Kid Gloves, Moosemeat, Tone Def (prev 4 only app to date), Napalm (dies), gang-bangers (one dies)
OTHER CHARACTERS: Willie & Warren (prison guards, both die)
LOCATIONS: New York inc Diamondback's apartment building, Roosevelt Hospital, Avengers HQ w/Fabian's workshop & drug supply warehouse (destroyed), upstate New York inc prison w/Bullseye's cell; Cap's sky-cycle & van, Boomslang's binoculars and boomerang, gangsters' guns, Chuck and Lowlife's guns, Bullseye's teeth, guards' guns, Kid Gloves' gun, Napalm's detonator
SYNOPSIS: On his way to Diamondback's apartment, Captain America spots Boomslang surveilling it. Boomslang runs from Cap but is shot by a group of teenage gangsters. Cap defeats the gangsters and waits with Boomslang for an ambulance and the police. Cap returns to Avengers Headquarters and discovers Fabian Stankowicz has been using crystal methamphetamine, or "ice." He suspends Fabian from his position and promises to get him into a rehab program. Lowlife and Ground Chuck, a pair of drug dealers, inspect the alley where Boomslang was shot, but are warned away by Diamondback. Upstate, Bullseye uses a self-inflicted injury to escape from prison. Cap devotes himself towards ending the ice gang that got Fabian hooked and, with John Jameson's help, rounds up a number of their crew in order to learn the location of their supply house. Once there, a gang member, Napalm, blows the place up with himself and Cap inside.
NOTE: Cover labeled "Streets of Poison." Red Skull is revealed as behind the ice operation in Cap #376, '90. Lowlife's real name is revealed in Cap #377, '90. The woman who confronts Lowlife and Ground Chuck is never identified; it is presumably Diamondback, based on her silhouette and Diamondback's involvement elsewhere in the story. Boomslang sings Young MC's "Bust a Move" and Kid Gloves sings Technotronic's "This Beat is Technotronic."

2ND STORY: "Agent Provocateur" (5 pages)
CREDITS: Mark Gruenwald (writer), Mark Bagley (pencils), Don Hudson (inks), Chris Eliopoulos (letters), Nel Yomtov (colors), Michael Heisler (asst editor), Ralph Macchio (editor)
FEATURE CHARACTER: Battlestar (also in fb between Cap #380/2, '90 fb & Cap #381/2, '91 fb, also as a Bold Urban Commando & Bucky in rfb; last in Cap #355, '89)
GUEST STAR: USAgent (also in fb between USAgent #1, '01 fb & Cap #381/2, '90 fb, also as Super-Patriot & Captain America in rfb; last in Q #11, '90)
LOCATIONS/ITEMS: West Coast Avengers Palos Verdes, CA Compound; Fort Bragg, NJ inc barracks (in fb); Battlestar's supplies inc rifle, binoculars, & "El Supremo Nacho Bites" USAgent's shield & sky-cycle, Super-Patriot's fiery sword (in rfb)
FLASHBACKS: John Walker and Lemar Hoskins play cards at Fort Bragg (1). John and Lemar debut as Super-Patriot and a "BUCky" (Cap #323, '86). John and Lemar train as the new Cap and Bucky (Cap #334, '87). John, as Cap, is "assassinated" (Cap #351, '89).
SYNOPSIS: After staking out the Avengers' West Coast compound for days, Battlestar spots USAgent leaving on a sky-cycle. He fires an explosive round to draw USAgent's attention. USAgent denies that he is John Walker, even as Battlestar recounts their shared history. When Battlestar mentions that USAgent's parents are dead, USAgent angrily backhands him, claiming they're alive. Battlestar decides he needs to beat some sense into USAgent.
NOTE: Cap #380/2, '90 reveals that Gen. Haywerth is responsible for USAgent's altered memories.

CAPTAIN AMERICA #373 (Late July 1990)

"After Blow" (17 pages)

CREDITS: Mark Gruenwald (writer), Ron Lim (pencils, c inks), Danny Bulanadi (inks), Joe Rosen (letters), Steve Buccellato (colors), Michael Heisler (asst editor), Ralph Macchio (editor)
FEATURE CHARACTER: Captain America (also as "High Eagle," also in rfb & pfb)
GUEST STAR: Black Widow (Natalia "Natasha" Romanova, Avenger & former Soviet spy, last in MCP #53/4, '90)
SUPPORTING CAST: Avengers Crew: Peggy Carter (last in Thor #420, '90), Fabian Stankowicz (bts, admitted into the Tuscon House for drug rehab), Col. John Jameson (also as "Carwolf"); Diamondback
VILLAINS: Kingpin (last in DFSM #4, '91), Typhoid Mary (Mary Mezinis, schizophrenic pyrokinetic assassin, last in C&D #9, '89), Red Skull's ice dealers: Kid Gloves, Moosemeat (both bts, released by Jameson), Ground Chuck

(next in Cap #375, '90), Lowlife, suicide bomber (dies); Kingpin's drug dealers (bts, 6 injured & 2 die), Bullseye
OTHER CHARACTERS: Kingpin's secretary, firefighters, paramedics, onlookers, loiterer; Napalm (in rfb)
LOCATIONS/ITEMS: New York inc drug supply warehouse's ruins (also in rfb & pfb), Avengers HQ w/communications center & mess hall, Diamondback's apartment, Fisk Building w/Kingpin's office, 164th St. crackhouse (destroyed) & Hudson River; Napalm's detonator (in rfb), Typhoid's machetes, garbage truck wired w/explosives, Black Widow's infrared binoculars & widow's line, Cap's sky-cycle & van, Bullseye's false teeth, flashlight & shovel
FLASHBACK: Napalm blows up the warehouse (Cap #372, '90) and Cap leaps out a window (p).
SYNOPSIS: John Jameson notifies Peggy Carter of the explosion; Peggy signals Black Widow for backup and calls Diamondback. Worried, Diamondback meets with John just as Captain America emerges from the burning warehouse and surprises Diamondback with a kiss. Returning to Avengers Headquarters, John and Rachel notice Cap behaving strangely. Bullseye arrives at the Kingpin's office wanting his old job as Kingpin's assassin back. Meanwhile, someone drives a truck filled with explosives into a crackhouse. Fisk sends Bullseye to investigate the bombing as Cap, Diamondback and John do the same. When John reports sighting Bullseye, Cap abandons Diamondback mid-air from his sky-cycle, forgetting Diamondback is unfamiliar with the cycle's controls. Black Widow boards the cycle as Diamondback struggles to control it. Mistaking each other for villains, the two women trade blows and crash into the Hudson River as Bullseye ambushes Cap.
NOTE: Cover labeled "Streets of Poison." The warehouse is located on 18th St. and 11th Ave.; John calls the explosion into Peggy as "Priority Blue." Kingpin refers to Bullseye as his frequent alias of Benjamin Poindexter, which is misspelled here as "Pondexter." The loiterer sings Technotronic's "Pump Up the Jam."

2ND STORY: "Fists of Truth" (5 pages)
CREDITS: Mark Gruenwald (writer), Mark Bagley (pencils), Don Hudson (inks), Janice Chiang (letters), Nel Yomtov (colors), Michael Heisler (asst editor), Ralph Macchio (editor)
FEATURE CHARACTER: Battlestar
GUEST STARS: Avengers West Coast: Iron Man (last in ImpSVS #1/6, '90, next in AWC Ann #5/4, '90), Wonder Man (last in Q #12, '90, next in AWC Ann #5/4, '90), USAgent
SUPPORTING CAST: Ethan Thurm (last in Cap #347, '88)
VILLAINS: Power Tools (all in shadows, see NOTE): Buzz-Saw (wields wrist-mounted circular saws, 1st), Drill (wields wrist-mounted drills, 1st), Jackhammer (last in Cap #371, '90), Dr. Karl Malus (bts, sent Power Tools, last in AvS #29, '90), Power Broker (bts, working w/Malus, last in Cap #364/2, '89) (both next in Cap #375/2, '90)
OTHER CHARACTER: Leon Hoskins (Battlestar's brother, only app)
LOCATIONS/ITEMS: West Coast Avengers Palos Verdes, CA Compound, Pacific Coast Highway, Ethan's Los Angeles, CA motel room; Wonder-Man's jet-belt, Battle Star's car (1st), Buzz-Saw's wrist-saws, Drill's wrist-drills, Jackhammer's wrist-jackhammers
SYNOPSIS: Battlestar and USAgent fight as USAgent continues to deny his true identity and his parents' deaths . When Iron Man and Wonder Man arrive Battlestar surrenders, acknowledging his friend doesn't want to be reminded of his past. On the drive home Battlestar phones his brother, who tells him he received a call from Ethan Thurm requesting Battlestar's presence. Battlestar reluctantly meets Ethan, unaware he's walking into an ambush.
NOTE: A previous Power Tools team consisting of different members appeared in AvS #29, '90; they also worked for Malus. Buzz-Saw and Drill's names are revealed in Cap #374/2, '90. Cap #375/2, '90 reveals Power Broker is working w/Malus again.

CAPTAIN AMERICA #374 (Early August 1990)

"Falling Out" (17 pages)

CREDITS: Mark Gruenwald (writer), Ron Lim (pencils), Danny Bulanadi (inks), Joe Rosen (letters), Steve Buccellato (colors), Michael Heisler (asst editor), Ralph Macchio (editor)
FEATURE CHARACTER: Captain America (also in DD #283, '90)
GUEST STARS: Black Widow (next in Cap #376, '90), Daredevil (last in DD #283, '90)
SUPPORTING CAST: Avengers Crew: Michael O'Brien (last in Cap #372, '90), Fabian Stankowicz (bts, responding well to drug rehab) (both next in Cap #380, '90), Peggy Carter (next bts in Cap #376, '90), Col. John Jameson; Diamondback
VILLAINS: Kingpin & his crack dealers (3, all die), Bullseye, Typhoid Mary, Red Skull's ice dealers: Hotwire, Potshot, Rubout (prev 3 only app), Lowlife (bts, sent others to kill Kingpin's crack dealers)
OTHER CHARACTERS: Fabian's Tuscon House counselor (bts, on phone w/Peggy), Julio (ice addict) & his friend, crack buyer (dies), prostitutes, bystanders; Ritzo (mentioned, Julio's ice dealer)
LOCATIONS/ITEMS: New York inc warehouse ruins, Hudson River, Fisk Building w/Kingpin's office, Avengers HQ w/communications center & lounge, Diamondback's apartment, video arcade, Collette's Fashion Boutique; Bullseye's flashlight, shovel, throwing knives, shuriken, throwing spikes & sai, drug dealers' guns, Cap's sky-cycle, Diamondback's undercover costume & wig (both 1st); Daredevil's billy club
SYNOPSIS: Captain America battles Bullseye as Diamondback emerges from the Hudson. She flies Cap's sky-cycle back to the warehouse; when Bullseye spot her he runs off. Meanwhile, a number of Kingpin's drug dealers are killed in drive-by shootings. Later, Typhoid Mary tells Kingpin she thinks a gang war is brewing. At Avengers Headquarters, Cap uncharacteristically scolds Peggy for summoning Black Widow without his consent, orders Diamondback out, offended by her concerns over his behavior, and threatens to fire John and Michael for talking back to him. At a video arcade, Bullseye interrogates an addict over where he buys his ice. Later, Daredevil muses on a recent encounter with the erratic Cap. Meanwhile, Cap violently stops a drug deal and threatens the buyer instead of chasing the dealer. John meets with Diamondback, who suspects that Cap's behavior resulted from inhaling a massive dose of ice in the warehouse explosion. She shields John with her body when they're suddenly gunned down in a drive-by shooting.
NOTE: Cover labeled "Streets of Poison." Concurrent with DD #283, '90, wherein Daredevil encounters the drug-addled Cap.

2ND STORY: "Power Tools" (5 pages)

CREDITS: Mark Gruenwald (writer), Mark Bagley (pencils), Dan Panosian (inks), Chris Eliopoulos (letters), Nel Yomtov (colors), Michael Heisler (asst editor), Ralph Macchio (editor)

FEATURE CHARACTER: Battle Star

GUEST STAR: USAgent (bts, following Battlestar)

SUPPORTING CAST: Ethan Thurm

VILLAINS: Power Tools: Buzz-Saw, Drill, Jackhammer (all next in Cap #376/2, '90)

OTHER CHARACTERS: Motel guests

LOCATIONS/ITEMS: Los Angeles, CA inc warehouse & motel w/Ethan's room; Buzz-Saw's wrist-saws, Drill's wrist-drills, Jackhammer's knuckle guards, Power Tools' truck & handcuffs, elevator gas chamber

SYNOPSIS: The Power Tools ambush Battlestar and Ethan flees into the bathroom. Battlestar surrenders when the Power Tools capture and hold Ethan hostage. The Power Tools take Ethan and Battlestar to a warehouse and shove Battlestar into an elevator, which floods with gas.

NOTE: Cap #378/2, '90 reveals that USAgent is following Battlestar and Ethan is being held captive here.

CAPTAIN AMERICA #375 (Late August 1990)

"The Devil You Know" (17 pages)

CREDITS: Mark Gruenwald (writer), Ron Lim (pencils), Danny Bulanadi (inks), Joe Rosen (letters), Steve Buccellato (colors), Michael Heisler (asst editor), Ralph Macchio (editor)

FEATURE CHARACTER: Captain America

GUEST STAR: Daredevil

SUPPORTING CAST: Diamondback, Col. John Jameson

VILLAINS: Kingpin & his men, Bullseye (also as homeless man), Typhoid Mary, Crossbones (last in Q #9, '90), Red Skull's ice dealers: Ground Chuck, Joyride, Lowlife (prev 3 apparently die, last app), Harly (bts, on phone w/ Lowlife), 2 others

OTHER CHARACTERS: Jerry "Jerkweed" Weiderman (Rhythm Room owner), Rhythm Room patrons, waiter

LOCATIONS/ITEMS: New York inc Rhythm Room & Diamondback's apartment, Little Italy inc Italian restaurant & playground, Brooklyn inc Lowlife's apartment; Cap's sky-cycle, drug dealers' guns, Jerkweed's gun, Ground Chuck's gun, Daredevil's billy club, copy of Daily Bugle

SYNOPSIS: John Jameson awakens to find Diamondback barely conscious but alive, saved by her armored costume. Uptown, Captain America abducts a nightclub owner with ties to the Kingpin and coerces information from him by dangling him from his sky-cycle. Ground Chuck and members of Lowlife's crew return home after a series of drive-by shootings and are attacked by Bullseye, who forces information about the ice operation from Chuck at gunpoint. Cap interrupts Kingpin's and Typhoid Mary's dinner at a restaurant; Cap questions Fisk about the brewing gang war. When Cap leaves Daredevil happens by. Diamondback regains consciousness in her apartment, John having been brought her there. Meanwhile, Bullseye confronts Lowlife. Daredevil's concerns for Cap's mental state fall on deaf ears and the two come to blows. Cap viciously beats Daredevil and walks away, leaving the barely conscious hero to be found by the arriving Crossbones.

NOTE: Cover labeled "Streets of Poison."

2ND STORY: "The Steel Balloon" (5 pages)

CREDITS: Mark Gruenwald (writer), Mark Bagley (pencils), Dan Panosian (inks), Phil Felix (letters), Nel Yomtov (colors), Michael Heisler (asst editor), Ralph Macchio (editor)

FEATURE CHARACTER: Battlestar (also as "De-Augmentation Test 19A")

GUEST STAR: USAgent (bts, following Battlestar)

SUPPORTING CAST: Ethan Thurm (bts, being held captive)

VILLAINS: Dr. Karl Malus, Power Broker (both last in Cap #373/2, '90), Lynch & Frost (both Power Broker's augmented thugs, 1st)

OTHER CHARACTERS: Red Zeppelin (last in Cap #328, '87), Power Broker's captives

LOCATIONS/ITEMS: Power Broker's Los Angeles, CA underground complex w/captives' restraint room & Malus' lab; Adamantium restraint armatures, Power Broker's exoskeleton, Malus' wheelchair, sleeping gas dispenser & de-augmentation equipment

SYNOPSIS: Battlestar awakens in a room with several other men who underwent the Power Broker's augmentation process, all also shackled into Adamantium harnesses. Red Zeppelin is taken away by two henchmen. Soon, Battlestar is taken and brought into a lab where Dr. Karl Malus and Power Broker wait. Battlestar is strapped to a table and Malus begins the process to remove Battlestar's superhuman strength.

NOTE: Battlestar is Malus' 19th attempt at testing his de-augmentation equipment. Frost & Lynch's names are revealed in Cap #376/2, '90.

CAPTAIN AMERICA #376 (Early September 1990)

"Cross Purposes" (17 pages)

CREDITS: Mark Gruenwald (writer), Ron Lim (pencils), Danny Bulanadi (co-inks, c inks), Bob Downs (co-inks), Joe Rosen (letters), Steve Buccellato (colors), Michael Heisler (asst editor), Ralph Macchio (editor)

FEATURE CHARACTER: Captain America

GUEST STARS: Black Widow (last in Cap # 374, '90), Daredevil (next in DD #284, '90), Falcon (bts, hasn't heard from Cap, last in Av Ann #19/5, '90, chr next in Hulk #388, '91 fb, next in Cap #383, '91)

SUPPORTING CAST: Avengers Crew: Peggy Carter (bts, on phone w/ John, last in Cap #374, '90), Col. John Jameson (also as "Carwolf"); Diamondback (both also in Cap's hallucination)

VILLAINS: Red Skull (also as "Death's Head" & in Cap's hallucination, last bts in Cap #372, '90), Crossbones (also as "Jolly Roger"), Machinesmith (bts, built Red Skull robot, last in Av #325, '90, next in Cap #378, '90),

Kingpin & his men (2 die), Bullseye, Typhoid Mary

OTHER CHARACTERS: Red Skull robot R-19 (1st), Ilsa Schultz (voice only, last in Cap #367, '90, next bts in Cap #393, '91), restaurant employees (Donald named, all die), teenagers; Fabian Stankowicz, Douglas Rockwell (both in Cap's hallucination)

LOCATIONS/ITEMS: New York inc Diamondback's apartment, Battery Park & Red Skull's hotel suite, Little Italy inc playground & restaurant; Crossbones' throwing knives, speargun & video communicator, Kingpin's men's gun, Cap's van, Daredevil's billy club, Black Widow's widow's bite, Bullseye's sai & shotgun

SYNOPSIS: Daredevil feigns unconsciousness as Crossbones toys with the battered hero. After looking under Daredevil's mask, Crossbones bursts into the restaurant where Kingpin and Typhoid Mary are dining and attempts to kill the Kingpin. A partially recovered Daredevil arrives and attacks Crossbones, allowing Kingpin and Typhoid to escape. Captain America wanders the streets, descending deeper into drug-induced madness. Black Widow meets with Diamondback and John Jameson, and the two women apologize for their earlier misunderstanding. As Kingpin vows to discover who tried to assassinate him, Crossbones reports his failure to Red Skull. John, Diamondback, and Black Widow find Cap assaulting a pair of teenagers; since Cap won't come peacefully Black Widow is forced to shoot Cap in the face point blank with her widow's bite. The next morning, Red Skull demands details of Crossbones' failure to kill Fisk, unaware that Bullseye lurks outside the window.

NOTE: Cover labeled "Streets of Poison." Cap #379's "American Graffiti" credits Bob Downs for co-inks here. Cap #377, '90 reveals that the Red Skull Crossbones meets with here is a Machinesmith-created robot.

2ND STORY: "Stronghold of the Weak" (5 pages)

CREDITS: Mark Gruenwald (writer), Mark Bagley (pencils), Dan Panosian (inks), Phil Felix (letters), Nel Yomtov (colors), Michael Heisler (asst editor), Ralph Macchio (editor)

FEATURE CHARACTER: Battlestar

GUEST STAR: USAgent

SUPPORTING CAST: Ethan Thurm (bts, being held captive)

VILLAINS: Power Tools: Buzz-Saw, Drill, Jackhammer (all last in Cap #374/2, '90); Power Broker & his augmented thugs (inc Frost & Lynch), Dr. Karl Malus

OTHER CHARACTERS: Red Zeppelin, Power Broker's captives (all next in Cap #378/2, '90)

LOCATIONS/ITEMS: Power Broker's Los Angeles, CA underground complex w/Malus' lab & "recovery room" dungeon; Malus' wheelchair & de-augmentation equipment, Power Broker's exoskeleton, Buzz-Saw's wrist-saws, Drill's wrist-drills, Jackhammer's wrist-jackhammers

SYNOPSIS: Malus successfully de-augments Battlestar, reverting him to his natural physique. Despite Power Broker's demands, Malus refuses to de-augment Power Broker until Battlestar's results can be examined further. The heavily weakened Battlestar is deposited in the "recovery room" with the other de-augmented captives, all of whom, including Red Zeppelin, were horribly disfigured by the process. Nevertheless, Battlestar staggers to the door just as Malus and his assistants enter and grabs Malus as a hostage, but finds himself surrounded by the Power Tools and more of Malus' henchmen. Suddenly, USAgent smashes through the ceiling.

NOTE: No credits given for this story; they are supplied in Cap #379's "American Graffiti."

CAPTAIN AMERICA #377 (Late September 1990)

"The 100% Solution" (17 pages)

CREDITS: Mark Gruenwald (writer), Ron Lim (pencils), Danny Bulanadi (co-inks, c inks), Romeo Tanghal (co-inks), Joe Rosen (letters), Steve Buccellato (colors), Michael Heisler (asst editor), Ralph Macchio (editor)

FEATURE CHARACTER: Captain America (also in his own dream)

GUEST STARS: Black Widow (next in Nam Ann #1/4, '91), Dr. Hank Pym (last in AWC #63, '90)

SUPPORTING CAST: Avengers Crew: Peggy Carter (next in Cap #379, '90), Dr. Keith Kincaid (last in Av #311, '89, last bts in Q #11, '90, next in Cap #384, '91), Col. John Jameson; Diamondback

VILLAINS: Red Skull (also in Cap's dream), Crossbones, Kingpin & his men (Martino named), Bullseye (next in DD #284, '90), Typhoid Mary (next in DD #292, '91)

OTHER CHARACTERS: Red Skull robot R-19 (destroyed, last app), Miss Conrad (Red Skull's accountant, dies), ice drug manufacturers, Boston Red Sox, New York Yankees, baseball spectators, Dr. Abraham Erskine (in Cap's dream)

LOCATIONS/ITEMS: New York inc Red Skull's hotel suite, Avengers HQ w/infirmary, lab, monitor room, & Cap's quarters & Fisk Building w/Kingpin's office, Newark inc Hangar 13 (Red Skull's ice factory), the Bronx inc Yankee Stadium w/Kingpin's private box; Cap's sky-cycle, Bullseye's sai, knife, shotgun, shuriken, false tooth & cable-gun, Red Skull's private jet, walking stick w/Dust of Death dispenser & helicopter

SYNOPSIS: After Red Skull admonishes Crossbones, Bullseye bursts through the window and shoots the Skull. Crossbones attacks Bullseye, who narrowly escapes by spitting a fake tooth in Crossbones' eye and stabbing him in the arm. Crossbones discovers the "Skull" was merely a robot. At Avengers Headquarters, Dr. Keith Kincaid places Captain America under heavy sedation. Bullseye reports his success to Kingpin, but the crimelord is unconvinced. Aboard his private jet, the real Skull orders Crossbones to meet him at Hangar 13. Cap wakes from a nightmare and wrecks the infirmary, refusing to believe that Captain America is defined by a physique-altering drug. After killing his accountant on a whim, Red Skull orders Crossbones to arrange a meeting with Kingpin. Hank Pym determines the only treatment for Cap is a complete blood transfusion, which will rob him of the Super-Soldier serum. The next day despite doctor's orders, Cap gears up to prove to himself he can be Captain America without the serum. Meanwhile, Red Skull and Kingpin meet at Yankee Stadium.

NOTE: Cover labeled "Streets of Poison." Cap #379's "American Graffiti" credits Romeo Tanghal for co-inks here. The Red Sox defeat the Yankees 26-2.

2ND STORY: "Going for Broke" (5 pages)

CREDITS: Mark Gruenwald (writer), Mark Bagley (pencils), Dan Panosian (inks), Clem Robins (letters), Nel Yomtov (colors), Michael Heisler (asst editor), Ralph Macchio (editor)

FEATURE CHARACTER: Battlestar
GUEST STAR: USAgent
SUPPORTING CAST: Ethan Thurm (bts, being held captive)
VILLAINS: Power Tools: Buzz-Saw, Drill, Jackhammer; Power Broker & his augmented thugs (inc Frost & Lynch), Dr. Karl Malus
LOCATIONS/ITEMS: Power Broker's Los Angeles, CA underground complex w/Malus' lab; Buzz-Saw's wrist-saws, Drill's wrist-drills, Jackhammer's wrist-hammers, Malus' wheelchair & de-augmentation equipment, Power Broker's exoskeleton, fire extinguisher
SYNOPSIS: As USAgent tears into the Power Broker's thugs, Battlestar forces Malus back into his lab, but Power Broker surprises and grabs him. Battlestar frees himself and despite being injured when he falls, holds the Broker at bay by threatening to smash Malus' equipment with a fire extinguisher. A bloodied USAgent enters the lab to ensure that Malus restores Battle Star's strength.
NOTE: "American Graffiti" contains LOC from future comics creator Matthew Spatola.

CAPTAIN AMERICA #378 (October 1990)

"Grand Stand Play!" (17 pages)

CREDITS: Mark Gruenwald (writer), Ron Lim (pencils), Danny Bulanadi (inks), Joe Rosen (co-letters), Michael Heisler (co-letters, asst editor), Steve Buccellato (colors), Ralph Macchio (editor)
FEATURE CHARACTER: Captain America (next in AWC #64, '90, Nomad #1, '90, Nomad #3-4, '91, Thor #427/2, '90, Nam #10, Nam #12, Nam Ann #1/4, all '91, Av #326-328, '90-91, AvS #40, '91)
GUEST STAR: Dr. Pym (next in AWC #65, '91)
SUPPORTING CAST: Diamondback (next in Av #328, '91), Col. John Jameson
VILLAINS: Red Skull (next in NF:AoS #20, '91) & his men, Machinesmith (last bts in Cap #376, '90, next in Cap #387/2, '91), Crossbones (next in Cap #387/2, '91), Kingpin (next in DD #287, '90) & his men
LOCATIONS/ITEMS: New York inc Avengers HQ, the Bronx inc Yankee Stadium; Cap's sky-cycle, Kingpin's men's guns, Red Skull's men's guns, Red Skull's activator, helicopter & plastidome, Crossbones' "Ginsu knife"
SYNOPSIS: As Captain America soars over the city, Red Skull challenges Fisk to a one-on-one unarmed fight; the winner will retain control of the ice operation. Cap notices the lights are still on at Yankee Stadium and investigates. Red Skull activates an impenetrable dome around the two of them and the battle begins. Meanwhile, Diamondback notices that Cap is missing. Crossbones, noticing Cap's arrival, intercepts Cap in the bleachers. Cap eventually defeats Crossbones, just as Kingpin pins the Skull under his considerable body mass and threatens to gouge out the Skull's eyes. Admitting defeat, Red Skull drops the dome and is airlifted by helicopter. Cap returns to Avengers Headquarters, where Hank Pym says that he was able to filter the ice out of Cap's original blood supply and offers to re-transfuse his blood. Cap graciously declines Pym's offer, satisfied that he no longer needs the serum to be Captain America.
NOTE: Cover labeled "Streets of Poison." Title returns to monthly status. Cap #379's "American Graffiti" credits Michael Heisler for co-letters here.

2ND STORY: "Grave Concerns" (5 pages)
CREDITS: Mark Gruenwald (writer), Mark Bagley (pencils), Dan Panosian (inks), Clem Robins (letters), Nel Yomtov (colors), Michael Heisler (asst editor), Ralph Macchio (editor)
FEATURE CHARACTER: Battlestar (next in Q #28, '91 fb)
GUEST STAR: USAgent (next in Cap #380/2, '90)
SUPPORTING CAST: Ethan Thurm (last app)
VILLAINS: Power Tools: Buzz-Saw (last app), Drill (next in Cap #411, '93), Jackhammer (next in GotG #28, '92); Power Broker (next in Cap #394, '91) & his augmented thugs (inc Frost & Lynch, both last app), Dr. Karl Malus (next in Cap Ann #12, '93)
OTHER CHARACTERS: Red Zeppelin (last app), Power Broker's captives (all last in Cap #378/2, '90), Kate Tollifson (last bts in Cap #353, '89, last app) & her child
LOCATIONS/ITEMS: Power Broker's Los Angeles, CA underground complex inc Malus' lab, Custer's Grove, GA inc Tollifson home & Forest Estates cemetery w/Caleb & Emily Walker's grave; Power Broker's exoskeleton, Malus' wheelchair & de-augmentation equipment, Battlestar's car
SYNOPSIS: Malus restores Battlestar's superhuman physique, who demands that Malus re-augment Power Broker's captives before Power Broker receives the treatment. Once all of the Broker's captives are restored USAgent "accidentally" destroys Malus' equipment, robbing the Broker of his salvation. Later, USAgent finally admits his true identity to Battlestar and asks him why he said his parents were dead. Battlestar drives USAgent to Custer's Grove and shows him his parents' grave. Battlestar comforts his devastated friend, and the two part ways.
NOTE: Caleb Walker was born on June 3, '30 and Emily Walker on August 22, '36; they died on May 3. USAgent claims he regularly exchanged letters w/his parents and spoke to his mother on the phone once, all presumably arranged by Gen. Hayworth to perpetuate the illusion that USAgent's parents were still alive. Battlestar will go on to join Silver Sable's Wild Pack in SSWP #3, '92.

CAPTAIN AMERICA #379 (November 1990)

"Moonstruck" (18 pages)

CREDITS: Mark Gruenwald (writer), Chris Marrinan (pencils), Robert Hedden (inks), Joe Rosen (letters), Nel Yomtov (colors), Michael Heisler (asst editor), Ralph Macchio (editor), Ron Lim (c art)
FEATURE CHARACTER: Captain America
GUEST STAR: Quasar (last in Q #17, '90, last bts in AvS #40, '91, next in Q #18, '91)
SUPPORTING CAST: Avengers Crew: Peggy Carter (last in Cap #377, '90), Col. John Jameson
VILLAINS: Nefarius (Lloyd Bloch, 1st as Nefarius, also in pfb as Moonstone, last in Hulk #229, '78 fb as Moonstone, next in Cap #443, '95), Moonstone (Dr. Karla Sofen, last in FF Ann #23/2, '90 fb, next in Cap #388, '91)
OTHER CHARACTERS: Police (inc a Lieutenant), bystanders, scientist (in fb)

LOCATIONS/ITEMS: New York inc Central Park, church & courthouse, lab (in fb); Cap's & Quasar's Avengers ID cards, Cap's art portfolio, Karla's energy dampner bracelets & ankle cuffs, police guns, Project N (in fb)

FLASHBACKS: Lloyd Bloch gives the moonstone gem to Karla Sofen, turning her into the new Moonstone (Hulk #229, '78 fb). Bloch undergoes the Project N process to become Nefarius (p).

SYNOPSIS: Captain America, Quasar, and John Jameson jog through Central Park when they're notified of a super-villain attack at a local courthouse. Cap and Quasar investigate, where Nefarius escapes with the shackled Moonstone, Dr. Karla Sofen. As the heroes follow, Cap recognizes Nefarious as Lloyd Bloch, the original Moonstone. Nefarius stops in a church and reveals he wants revenge against Sofen for "stealing" his moonstone and causing him to be institutionalized. Karla delays Lloyd's wrath by playing to his lustful desires. Cap and Quasar soon locate the villains and attack. As Quasar deals with Nefarious, Cap is forced to knock Sofen out when she tries to escape. Nefarius defeats Quasar and tries to escape with Karla, but she defeats Nefarius by blasting him in his ears. Pinned under Nefarius' body, Moonstone realizes she can't beat Cap and surrenders. Quasar takes the Moonstones to the Vault.

NOTE: Chris Marrinan is misspelled "Chris Marinnan." Robert Hedden is credited as "D. Hedd."

2ND STORY: "The Warning" (4 pages)

CREDITS: Mark Gruenwald (writer), Mark Bagley (pencils), Dan Panosian (inks), Joe Rosen (letters), Nel Yomtov (colors), Michael Heisler (asst editor), Ralph Macchio (editor)

FEATURE CHARACTER: Diamondback (last in Av #328, '91)

SUPPORTING CAST: Asp (last in Cap #371, '90), Black Mamba (also as voice on answering machine, last in Cap #371/2, '90) (both bts, sent warning note to Diamondback)

VILLAINS: Serpent Society: King Cobra (bts, ordered Diamondback captured, last in Q #9, '90), Black Racer (as Ariana Saddiqi & "street walker," last in Q #17, '90), Boomslang (in shadows, last in Cap #372, '90, next in Cap #411, '93)

OTHER CHARACTERS: Maggie (Collette's Fashion Boutique manager, only app), Peggy Carter, gym patrons, bystanders

LOCATIONS/ITEMS: New York inc Collette's Fashion Boutique, Avengers HQ's communication room, gym w/locker room; Diamondback's warning note, Serpent Society limo

SYNOPSIS: While at her day job at Collette's Fashion Boutique, Diamondback receives a note warning her that her life is in danger. She takes an early lunch to figure out who sent the note, but unable to reach Black Mamba or Cap she comes up empty. Unaware she's being followed, Diamondback stops by Avengers HQ to wait for Captain America, but before she can ring the doorbell the Serpent Society ambushes her.

NOTE: This story occurs simultaneously with the 1st story; Peggy notes Cap is at the courthouse when Diamondback calls.

CAPTAIN AMERICA #380 (December 1990)

"With Friends Like These..." (17 pages)

CREDITS: Mark Gruenwald (writer), Ron Lim (pencils), Danny Bulanadi (inks), Joe Rosen (letters), Christie Scheele, Steve Buccellato (colors), Michael Heisler (asst editor), Ralph Macchio (editor)

FEATURE CHARACTER: Captain America (also as the Captain in rfb)

SUPPORTING CAST: Avengers Crew: Edwin Jarvis (last in AvS #40, '91, next voice only in Cap #382, '91), Michael O'Brien (last in Cap #374, '90, next in Cap #383, '91), Fabian Stankowicz (last bts in Cap #374, '90, next bts in Cap #382, '91), Peggy Carter, Col. John Jameson; Josh Cooper (last in Cap #285, '83, next in Cap #600/3, '09), Mike Farrel (last in Cap #317, '86, next in Cap #382, '91), Anna Kapplebaum (last in Cap #317, '86, last app), Bernie Rosenthal (last in Cap #357, '89, next in Cap #382, '91), Diamondback (also in rfb)

VILLAINS: Serpent Society: King Cobra (leader), Bushmaster, Coachwhip, Cottonmouth, Fer-de-Lance, Puff Adder, Rattler, Rock Python (prev 7 last in Cap #367/2, '89), Anaconda (last in Cap #371, '90), Asp, Black Mamba, Black Racer; Sidewinder (last in X Ann #13, '89)

OTHER CHARACTERS: Party guests; Mr. Hyde, Viper (both in photo)

LOCATIONS/ITEMS: Serpent Society HQ inc holding cell, meeting area, Cobra's office & Black Mamba's quarters; Avengers HQ inc gym, Anna's apartment building, Brooklyn Bridge; Diamondback's manacles, King Cobra's venom

FLASHBACKS: Diamondback receives a warning note and goes to Avengers HQ (Cap #379/2, '90). Diamondback teams up with Captain America (Cap #313, '86). Diamondback calls the Captain for help (Cap #342, all '88). Cap rescues Diamondback and she joins him in the Bloodstone hunt (Cap #358, '89).

SYNOPSIS: Diamondback awakens in a cell and finds the Serpent Society is putting her on trial for treason because of her relationship with Captain America. Meanwhile, Cap welcomes Fabian Stankowicz back to active duty with the Avengers Crew. As her defense council, Black Mamba preps Diamondback for the trial. In Brooklyn Heights, Steve attends a welcome back party for Bernie, who's graduated from law school. As Diamondback's trial proceeds, Steve and Bernie catch up. In a seven-to-four vote, the Serpent Society finds Diamondback guilty. King Cobra's sentence is death by lethal injection unless Diamondback gives the Society information about Cap. Black Mamba and Asp threaten to quit if Diamondback is killed, but Cobra is unrelenting. Black Mamba calls Sidewinder for help. At the deadline, Diamondback refuses to betray Cap. Sidewinder teleports in and rescues Diamondback. King Cobra declares war on the Serpent Society's former leader.

NOTE: Asp, Black Mamba, Bushmaster and Rock Python vote innocent, eve ryone else votes guilty except King Cobra, who doesn't bother.

2ND STORY: "The Unremembered Past" (5 pages)

CREDITS: Mark Gruenwald (writer), Mark Bagley (pencils), Dan Panosian (inks), Joe Rosen (letters), Nel Yomtov (colors), Michael Heisler (asst editor), Ralph Macchio (editor)

FEATURE CHARACTER: USAgent (also in fb1 between Cap #345, '88 fb & Cap #333, '87 fb, fb2 between Cap #333, '87 fb & USAgent #1, '01 fb; last in Cap #378/2, '90)

SUPPORTING CAST: Gen. Lewis Haywerth (last in Cap #358/2, '89), Lemar Hoskins (only in fb2 to 1st chr app before Cap #372/2, '90 fb)

OTHER CHARACTERS: Caleb Walker (only in fb1 between Cap #345, '88 fb & Cap #333, '87 fb, fb2 between Cap #333, '87 fb & Cap #345, '88), Emily Walker (only in fb1 to 1st chr app before Cap #333, '87 fb, fb2 between Cap #333, '87 fb & Cap #345, '88), Kate Walker (only in fb1 to 1st chr app before Cap #333, '87 fb, fb2 between Cap #333, '87 fb & bts in Cap #335, '87), Fort George G. Meade scientist (1st) & guards

LOCATIONS/ITEMS: Fort George G. Meade inc Gen. Hayworth's office & psych lab, Walker farm (in fbs1-2), Fort Bragg, NJ inc barracks (both in fb2); memory altering equipment

FLASHBACKS: Caleb and Emily Walker tell their children John and Kate that their brother Mike was killed in action (1). John's family sees him off when he enlists in the army. At boot camp, John meets and befriends Lemar Hoskins (2).

SYNOPSIS: USAgent storms into Gen. Hayworth's office, demands to know why his memories were altered and demands they be restored. Hayworth says it was for USAgent's own good, but agrees to restore them. USAgent begins to relive his memories.

CAPTAIN AMERICA #381 (January 1991)

"This Gun's For Hire" (17 pages)

CREDITS: Mark Gruenwald (writer), Ron Lim (pencils), Danny Bulanadi (inks), Joe Rosen (letters), Christie Scheele (colors), Michael Heisler (asst editor), Ralph Macchio (editor)
FEATURE CHARACTER: Captain America (also as "Spangler")
GUEST STAR: Paladin ("Paul Denning", mercenary, last in Pun:NE, '90)
SUPPORTING CAST: Avengers Crew: Col. John Jameson (also as "Carwolf"), Peggy Carter; Diamondback
VILLAINS: Serpent Society: King Cobra, Anaconda, Asp, Black Mamba, Black Racer, Bushmaster, Coachwhip, Cottonmouth, Fer-de-Lance, Puff Adder, Rattler, Rock Python; Sidewinder (next in Cap Ann #10/4, '91)
OTHER CHARACTERS: Kenny (Serpent Society front guard, only app), restaurant employee, bartender
LOCATIONS/ITEMS: New York inc Sidewinder's town house, Serpent Society HQ w/meeting area, Black Mamba's quarters & gym, New York Public Library, restaurant, bar, Diamondback's apartment & Stuyvesant Arms hotel; Cap's Avengers ID card & van, Paladin's business card & gun, Rock Python's snake-wire, Serpent Saucer, Cobra's venom sting
SYNOPSIS: Knowing Cobra will come after him for rescuing Diamondback, Sidewinder prepares to abandon his home; King Cobra sends the Serpent Society to find both him and Diamondback. Diamondback calls Captain America for help, but when he's unable to promise that Asp and Black Mamba will escape prosecution she leaves in a huff. Meanwhile, King Cobra overpowers Asp and Black Mamba. Cap finds Anaconda, Puff Adder and Rock Python at Diamondback's apartment as Diamondback hires Paladin to rescue her friends. As Cap is overpowered, Diamondback and Paladin infiltrate Serpent Society HQ. They capture Bushmaster, who leads them to the captured Asp and Black Mamba. Cobra gets the drop on them and during the fight Cobra hits Diamondback with a venom sting. Paladin surrenders for the antidote.
NOTE: Christie Scheele is credited as "Max Scheele" here.

2ND STORY: "Ask Not What Your Country Can Do For You…" (5 pages)
CREDITS: Mark Gruenwald (writer), Mark Bagley (pencils), Dan Panosian (inks), Clem Robins (letters), Nel Yomtov (colors), Michael Heisler (asst editor), Ralph Macchio (editor)
FEATURE CHARACTER: USAgent (also in rfb as Super-Patriot; also in fb1 between Cap #333, '87 fb & Cap #323, '86, also in Cap #333, '87 fb; fb2 during Cap #323, '86)
SUPPORTING CAST: Lemar Hoskins (only in fb1 between Cap #372/2, '90 fb & Cap #323, '86, also in Cap #333, '87 fb), Jerome Johnson, Hector Lennox (both only in fb1 to 1st chr app before Cap #323, '86) (all also in rfb as Bold Urban Commandos), Ethan Thurm (only in fb1 between Thing #30, '85 & Cap #323, '86, also in Cap #333, '87 fb; fb2 during Cap #323, '86), Gen. Lewis Hayworth (off panel)
OTHER CHARACTERS: Dr. Karl Malus (only bts in fb1 between Cap #328, '86 fb & Thing #35, '86), Power Broker (only bts in fb1 between bts in Cap #328, '86 fb & Thing #35, '85), his agent & secretary, UCWF wrestlers (prev 3 only in fb1); Captain America, Dr. Valerie Cooper, Warhead, "AM Washington" host, Super-Patriot rally attendees, waiter (prev 6 in rfb), Fort George G. Meade scientist (off panel)
LOCATIONS/ITEMS: Maryland bar, Los Angeles, CA inc Power Broker's lab & UCWF headquarters (all in fb1), Central Park, Washington Monument, Val's office (prev 3 in rfb), Fort George G. Meade psych lab; Power Broker's business card (in fb1), Super-Patriot's fiery sword, Warhead's bomb (both in rfb)
FLASHBACKS: Power Broker's agent approaches John, Lemar, Hector and Jerome to offer them the Power Broker's treatment. They sign up for the augmentation process and gain super-strength. While auditioning for the UCWF they're recruited by Ethan Thurm, who turns them into Super-Patriot and the BUCkies (1). Super-Patriot holds a rally (Cap #323, '86), where Ethan convinces him to stage a fight with the Buckies (2). Cap lectures Super-Patriot about using theatrics (Cap #323, '86). Super-Patriot fights Cap (prev 4 in Cap #327, '87). Super-Patriot stops Warhead's protest on top of the Washington Monument (Cap #332, '87). Val Cooper offers John the chance to be Captain America (Cap #333, '87).
SYNOPSIS: USAgent continues to relive his memories.

CAPTAIN AMERICA #382 (February 1991)

"Why Does it Always Have to be Snakes?" (17 pages)

CREDITS: Mark Gruenwald (writer), Ron Lim (pencils), Danny Bulanadi (inks), Joe Rosen (letters), Christie Scheele (colors), Michael Heisler (asst editor), Ralph Macchio (editor)
FEATURE CHARACTER: Captain America
GUEST STAR: Paladin (next in Ex #36, '91)
SUPPORTING CAST: Avengers Crew: Peggy Carter (bts, on phone w/John), Edwin Jarvis (voice only, last in Cap #380, '90), Fabian Stankowicz (bts, provided translocator, last in Cap #380, '90), Col. John Jameson; Mike Farrel, Bernie Rosenthal (both last in Cap #380, '90, next in Cap #385, '91), Diamondback (next in Cap #385/2, '91)
VILLAINS: Serpent Society: King Cobra, Black Racer, Bushmaster, Coachwhip, Cottonmouth, Fer-de-Lance,

Puff Adder, Rattler (all next bts in Cap #385/2, '91), Anaconda, Rock Python (both next in Cap #385/2, '91), Asp, Black Mamba (both leave Serpent Society, next in Cap #385/2, '91)

OTHER CHARACTERS: Hallsy (Serpent Society mechanic), Keener (Serpent Society communications) (both only app), Vault Guardsmen

LOCATIONS/ITEMS: Diamondback's apartment, Serpent Society HQ inc communications room, gym, hangar & med lab, Mike's apartment, Avengers HQ inc Cap's quarters; Serpent Saucer, Serpent Society communicator, Cap's van, translocator & sky-cycle, antitoxin

SYNOPSIS: Rock Python drops Captain America off the roof of Diamondback's apartment just as King Cobra orders them to return. Having used his shield to take the brunt of the impact, Cap calls John for a pick up and uses his translocator to trace the Society's communication signal. King Cobra gloats while Cap secretly infiltrates the Society's headquarters. Meanwhile, Bernie contemplates how to win Cap back. Cap fights his way to the gym where he's able to free the captives. Black Mamba takes Diamondback to the medlab for the antitoxin as Cap battles the remaining Serpent Society. Diamondback saves herself and Black Mamba from Coachwhip. Soon, Cap hands the Society over to Vault Guardsmen except Diamondback, Black Mamba and Asp. Diamondback tries to make Cap jealous by purposely flaunting going on a date with Paladin. Later, Bernie pays Cap a surprise visit.

2ND STORY: "Thanks for the Memories" (5 pages)

CREDITS: Mark Gruenwald (writer), Mark Bagley (pencils), Dan Panosian (inks), Clem Robins (letters), Nel Yomtov (colors), Michael Heisler (asst editor), Ralph Macchio (editor)

FEATURE CHARACTER: USAgent (also as Captain America in rfb; also in fb1 between Cap #350-351, '89, fb2 between Cap #351, '89 fb & Cap #354, '89)

SUPPORTING CAST: Gen. Lewis Haywerth (also in fb1 between Cap #350, '89 & bts in Cap #351, '89, fb2 between bts in Cap #351, '89 & Cap #352, '89; next bts in AvS #31/2, '90, next in Pun:NE, '90)

OTHER CHARACTERS: Battlestar, the Captain, Left-Winger, Right-Winger, Red Skull, Caleb Walker, Emily Walker, Watchdogs, Secret Service, bystanders (all in rfb); Fort George G. Meade scientist (last app)

LOCATIONS/ITEMS: Washington Monument, Custer's Grove, GA, Texas construction site (all in rfb), Fort George G. Meade (in fb1) inc psych lab (also in fb2); memory altering equipment (also in fb2), Left-Winger's fiery sword (in rfb)

FLASHBACKS: Left-Winger and Right-Winger publicly expose Cap's identity as John Walker (Cap #341/2, '88). The Watchdogs murder Cap's parents; Cap kills the Watchdogs in retaliation and has a psychotic breakdown (Cap #345, '88). Cap tries to kill the Wingers by blowing them up (Cap #347, '88). Haywerth threatens to suspend Cap (Cap #348, '88). Captain America and the Captain fight Red Skull and John convinces Steve to become Cap again (Cap #350, '89). Haywerth sets up John's fake assassination in order to re-establish his secret identity (1). John Walker is "assassinated" (Cap #351, '89). Haywerth has John's memories altered while setting up John's "Jack Daniels" identity (2).

SYNOPSIS: While USAgent relives his memories, Haywerth has the scientist alter them so USAgent thinks he asked for the memory of his parents' deaths to be removed. USAgent wakes up and apologizes for accusing Haywerth of messing with his mind without permission.

CAPTAIN AMERICA #383 (March 1991)

"I am Legend" (26 pages)

CREDITS: Mark Gruenwald (writer), Ron Lim (pencils), Danny Bulanadi (inks), Joe Rosen (letters), Christie Scheele (colors), Dan Slott (asst editor), Ralph Macchio (editor), Jim Lee (c inks)

FEATURE CHARACTER: Captain America

GUEST STARS: Avengers: Sersi (last in AvS #40, '91, next in Av #329, '91), Vision (last in AvS #40, '91, next in Av #329, '91), She-Hulk (between SenSH #25-26, '91), Thor (last in MHol/7, '91); Avengers: West Coast: Hawkeye (also as Father Time, last in AvS #36, '90, next in Av #329, '91), Dr. Pym (last in Nam Ann #1/4, '91, next in Av #329, '91), Iron Man (last in Av #328, '91, chr last in AWC #89, '92 fb, next in Av #329, '91), Wasp (last in AvS #30, '90, next in Av #329, '91), Wonder Man (last in MSH #4/3, '90, next in Av #329, '91); Black Widow (last in MCP #70/4, '91, next in Av #329, '91), Falcon (last bts in Cap #376, '90, chr last in Hulk #388, '91 fb, next in Av #329, '91), Quasar (last in Q #18, '91, next in Av #329, '91), Father Time (Elder of the Universe, commemorates significant events, only app)

SUPPORTING CAST: Avengers Crew: Edwin Jarvis, Fabian Stankowicz (both next in Av #329, '91), Michael O'Brien (last in Cap #380, '90, next in Av #329, '91), Peggy Carter, Col. John Jameson

OTHER CHARACTERS: Johnny Appleseed, Pecos Bill, Widow-Maker (Pecos Bill's horse), John Henry, Paul Bunyan, Babe (Paul Bunyan's ox, bts, waiting for dinner), Uncle Sam (also as "the Old Man of the Mountain Top"), (all only app), homeless man, bald eagle

LOCATIONS/ITEMS: New York inc Avengers Mansion, Father Time's Land of Legends; Father Time's doorway & scythe, John Henry's hammer, Paul Bunyan's axe, Cap's anniversary cake

SYNOPSIS: Responding to a Stars and Stripes report, Captain America chases Father Time down an alley and falls through a doorway into a forest. Cap meets Johnny Appleseed; when Cap asks about Father Time, Johnny directs him to the Old Man of the Mountain Top. As Cap makes his way to the mountain he meets Pecos Bill, John Henry and Paul Bunyan. On the mountain top Cap meets Uncle Sam, who explains they're in the Land of Legends and that Cap is on the verge of becoming legendary. However, Cap must stay and retire. Cap refuses, saying he still has work to do. Father Time appears and Cap attacks. Father Time explains he's an Elder of the Universe who commemorates significant events, but Cap continually refuses to retire, even when Father Time rapidly ages him. The Elder concedes and returns Cap to the alley he came from. Cap attacks Father Time again, but learns it's actually Hawkeye in disguise. Cap returns to Avengers Mansion where the Avengers throw a surprise anniversary party for Cap.

NOTE: Issue celebrates 50th anniversary of CapC #1, published March 1941.

2ND STORY: "Fighting Side-by-Side with… Sgt. Fury and his Howling Commandos!" (9 pages)

CREDITS: Tom DeFalco (writer), Ron Frenz (co-plot, pencils), Bob Petrecca (inks), Michael Heisler (letters), Paul Becton (colors), Dan Slott (asst editor), Ralph Macchio (editor)

FEATURE CHARACTER: Captain America (also as prisoner, during & also in SgtF #13, '64, also in DF:Av #2.4, '99 & DF:Av #3.6, '00)
GUEST STARS: Sgt. Fury & his Howling Commandos: Reb Ralston (both also as prisoners, during & also in SgtF #13, '64, also in DF:Av #2.4, '99 & DF:Av #3.6, '00), Izzy Cohen, Dum Dum Dugan, Gabe Jones, Dino Manelli, Pinky Pinkerton (prev 5 during & also in SgtF #13, '64)
SUPPORTING CAST: Bucky (also as Hitler Youth, during & also in SgtF #13, '64, also in DF:Av #2.4, '99 & DF:Av #3.6, '00)
VILLAINS: Nazi soldiers (inc a Commandant, some also in SgtF #13, '64)
OTHER CHARACTERS: Nazi slave laborers (some also in SgtF #13, '64)
LOCATIONS/ITEMS: France, English Channel; Nazi guns, Howitzer, jeep, motorcycle & prisoner train, Howling Commandos' guns, Gabe's bugle, Pinky's umbrella, Operation: Einfall plans, Allied submarine
SYNOPSIS: Captain America and Bucky ambush a Nazi convoy carrying slave laborers. They free the laborers, Bucky steals a Hitler Youth uniform and Cap poses as Bucky's prisoner. Meanwhile, Sgt. Fury and his Howling Commandos defeat a Nazi outpost when Dum Dum and Dino commandeer a Howitzer; they continue on to rendezvous with Cap. While Steve is loaded into a labor train Bucky discovers what the labor is for; building an underwater tunnel to Britain. The Howlers arrive and jump in the labor train, where Sgt. Fury tries to give Steve a gun. Steve turns it down and the laborers are put to work. Cap and Bucky create a diversion, allowing the Howlers to evacuate the laborers while they blow up the tunnel. The Howlers make it to the surface before the explosion and Cap and Bucky surface afterwards. With Operation: Einfall defeated Cap and Bucky swim to their pick-up submarine.
NOTE: Retells and expands SgtF #13, '64 from Cap and Bucky's perspective.

3RD STORY: "Man of Straw" (10 pages)
CREDITS: Mark Gruenwald (writer), Mark Bagley (pencils), Dan Panosian (inks), Joe Rosen (letters), Nel Yomtov (colors), Dan Slott (asst editor), Ralph Macchio (editor)
FEATURE CHARACTER: USAgent (also in rfb as Captain America, also in fb between AWC #62, '90 & Q #11, '90, next in AvS #31/2, '90)
SUPPORTING CAST: Hector Lennox (corpse, also in photo & rfb as Left-Winger, last bts in Cap #350, '89, chr last in USAgent #3, '93 fb, last app)
OTHER CHARACTERS: Right-Winger (also in photo), Battlestar, West Coast Avengers: Dr. Pym, Iron Man, Wonder Man; Legion of the Unliving: Grim Reaper, Iron Man 2020, Toro; Caleb & Emily Walker, Secret Service (all in rfb), Dr. Oratz (burn ward physician, in fb, only app)
LOCATIONS/ITEMS: Illinois cemetery inc Hector's grave, cornfield, Avengers West compound, hospital inc Dr. Oratz's office (both in fb); Left-Winger's fiery sword (in rfb), Avengers datanet (in fb), scarecrow, broken lighter
FLASHBACKS: Left-Winger and Right-Winger publicly reveal Captain America's secret identity as John Walker (Cap #341/2, '88). John Walker's parents are killed (Cap #345, '88). John Walker sets Left-Winger and Right-Winger on fire (Cap #347, '88). While the West Coast Avengers fight the Legion of the Unliving, USAgent watches Left-Winger and Right-Winger impale each other (AWC #61, '90). Not believing Left-Winger and Right-Winger are dead, USAgent uses the Avengers datanet to learn what hospital they were in. He interrogates their doctor who reveals they both committed suicide. Having faked his own death once, USAgent still doesn't believe they're dead.
SYNOPSIS: Using his shield, USAgent digs up Hector Lennox's grave and is dismayed to find Hector's corpse. Horrified at the confirmation of his friend's death, USAgent runs until he stops at a scarecrow. He screams for a sign and finds a lighter. Feeling he should set himself on fire like he set Hector on fire, he becomes upset when the lighter doesn't work. In a moment of clarity, USAgent realizes he has to move past his grief and become a better person.

4TH STORY: "Bad to the Bone!" (10 pages)
CREDITS: Mark Gruenwald (writer), Ron Wilson (pencils), Fred Fredrickson (inks), Clem Robbins (letters), Nel Yomtov (colors), Dan Slott (asst editor), Ralph Macchio (editor)
FEATURE CHARACTER: Red Skull (Shmidt, last in Cap #350/2, '89, next in Cap #368/2, '90 fb)
SUPPORTING CAST: Crossbones (becomes Crossbones, last in Cap&Crb #1, '11 fb, next in Cap #359, '89), Arnim Zola (last in Cap #350/2, '89, next in MCP #24/3, '89)
VILLAINS: Red Skull (Malik, bts, sent mercenaries, last in Cap Ann #13, '94 fb, next in SAv #6, '88), mercenaries (Ballard, "Kimby" Kimbale, Milano & Pogue named, all die)
OTHER CHARACTER: Doughboy (last in Cap #279, '83, next in Cap #393, '91)
LOCATIONS/ITEMS: Swiss Alps inc Zola's castle; castle guns, Red Skull's mask & gun, Crossbone's bow, arrows & knife
SYNOPSIS: Mercenaries storm Arnim Zola's Swiss Alps castle, but the castle guns and Doughboy kill all but two. Red Skull interrogates the survivors; when they say they were sent by the Red Skull he kills one and spars with the other. Impressed by the survivor's fighting skills, Red Skull decides to hire him, naming him Crossbones.

CAPTAIN AMERICA #384 (April 1991)

"Lair of the Ice Worm" (22 pages)

CREDITS: Mark Gruenwald (writer), Ron Lim (pencils), Danny Bulanadi (inks), Joe Rosen (letters), Steve Buccellato (colors), Dan Slott (asst editor), Ralph Macchio (editor)
FEATURE CHARACTER: Captain America (also in rfb as the Captain; next in Av #329-331, '91, AWC #69, '91)
GUEST STARS: Jack Frost (ice generating WWII hero, also in photo, last in Inv #38, '79, last app), Thor (next in Av #329, '91)
SUPPORTING CAST: Avengers Crew: Peggy Carter, Col. John Jameson (both next in Av #329, '91), Dr. Keith Kincaid (last in Cap #377, '90, next in Q #29, '91); Demolition Man (also in rfb; last in Cap #349, '89, next in Cap #400/2, '92)
VILLAIN: Ice Worm (giant snake-like ice creature, only app)
OTHER CHARACTERS: Eskimos (also in photo) inc shaman; Bucky, Giant-Man, Iron Man, Thor, Wasp, ULTIMATUM agent (prev 6 in rfb), Grim Reaper, Statue of Liberty (both in Cap's dream), Elvis Presley (in photo)

LOCATIONS/ITEMS: New York inc World Trade Center & Avengers Mansion w/reflex room, North pole inc ULTIMATUM base; Cap's modified quinjet, Dr. Kincaid's medical testing equipment inc treadmill & weights, copy of National Tattler, Zemo's drone plane, Quinjet (both in rfb)

FLASHBACKS: Bucky tries to stop Baron Zemo's stolen drone plane but is caught in the explosion when it detonates. Cap is thrown into the English Channel (Av #4, '64 fb). The Avengers find Captain America (Av #4, '64). While battling ULTIMATUM at the North Pole, Demolition Man seemingly dies. The Captain searches the frigid waters for him, to no avail (Cap #349, '89).

SYNOPSIS: Dr. Kincaid performs tests on Captain America to determine why Cap's body still remains at his peak without the Super-Soldier serum; it's determined that the Super-Soldier serum must be self-replicating in Cap's body. Peggy tells Cap about a frozen man at the North pole and Cap races off to investigate, thinking it may be Demolition Man. Cap finds a group of Eskimos worshiping a man frozen in ice. When Cap tries to break the ice a giant ice worm attacks and swallows him. Inside, Cap meets Jack Frost, the man in the ice who's been trapped there for years. When the two are unable to defeat the beast, Jack Frost sacrifices himself to make the ice worm dormant again. Thor arrives too late to help and Cap leaves unaware that Demolition Man is nearby, frozen in ice...

NOTE: Thor wonders if an Asgardian legend where a Frost Giant's son who was banished to Midgard for being born too small is actually Jack Frost. Cap notes he had his tonsils taken out when he was seven, and as a child he had mumps, measles, and chicken pox.

CAPTAIN AMERICA #385 (May 1991)

"Going to the Dogs" (17 pages)

CREDITS: Mark Gruenwald (writer), Ron Lim (pencils), Danny Bulanadi (inks), Joe Rosen (letters), Christie Scheele (colors), Michael Heisler (asst editor), Ralph Macchio (editor)
FEATURE CHARACTER: Captain America
GUEST STARS: Reserve Avengers: Rage (Elvin Halliday, youth in powerful adult body, between Av #331-332, '91), Sandman (William Baker, made of sand & former villain, last in Av #330, '91, next in Av #332, '91)
SUPPORTING CAST: Avengers Crew: Peggy Carter (between Av #331-332, '91), Edwin Jarvis (voice only, last in Av #331, '91), Col. John Jameson (bts, plays racquetball w/Cap, last in Av #331, '91); Mike Farrel (joins Watchdogs, see NOTE), Bernie Rosenthal (both last in Cap #382, '91)
VILLAINS: Watchdogs (inc Stu Bartlett (1st), Bukowski, Goetzke, Kearny, May, Mick, Mitchell & Omar, group last in ASM #325, '89)
OTHER CHARACTERS: Enrique Parcair (artist, 1st), Hobart (Enrique's agent), art exhibition employees; janitor (dies), police, bystanders; Diamondback (in photo), USAgent (in next issue box)
LOCATIONS/ITEMS: New York inc Rabid Records offices & Avengers Mansion w/training room & Cap's quarters, Mike's Brooklyn Heights apartment, SoHo art exhibition; Cap's sky-cycle & Avengers ID, Watchdogs' guns, explosives & vans, Enrique's art
SYNOPSIS: The Watchdogs set fire to Rabid Records' offices, but recent recruit Mike Farrel is upset when a janitor is left inside the building before it explodes. Bernie visits Cap at Avengers Mansion and offers to help him furnish his room. Later, Bernie visits Mike, who confesses that he's joined the Watchdogs and committed arson last night. He makes her promise not to tell the police, but the eavesdropping Watchdogs are upset Mike told anyone. Bernie interrupts Cap training the Reserve Avengers to tell him Mike is in trouble; when he investigates he finds Watchdogs in Mike's apartment wanting to kill Mike for treason. Meanwhile, Mike warns the Watchdogs' next target, artist Enrique Parcair, to no avail. The Watchdogs take Bernie hostage to fend off Cap, leaving behind a bomb which he defuses. Mike returns home and sees the police outside and thinks Bernie's betrayed him.
NOTE: Cap #600/3, '09 reveals that Mike is suffering from a brain tumor that makes him act irrationally, explaining why a fireman would join the Watchdogs and commit arson. The art exhibition is south of Houston St. Mike is watching "In Living Color." Christie Scheele is credited as "Max Scheele" here.

2ND STORY: "Loose Ends" (5 pages)
CREDITS: Mark Gruenwald (writer), Mark Bagley (pencils), Dan Panosian (inks), Clem Robins (letters), Nel Yomtov (colors), Michael Heisler (asst editor), Ralph Macchio (editor)
FEATURE CHARACTER: Diamondback (also in photo, forms BAD Girls, Inc, last in Cap #382, '91)
SUPPORTING CAST: Asp, Black Mamba (both also in photo, forms BAD Girls, Inc w/Diamondback, last in Cap #382, '91)
VILLAINS: Serpent Society: King Cobra (also in photo, next in Cap Ann #10/4, '91), Black Racer (next in Cap #30, '04), Bushmaster (next in Cap Ann #10/3, '91), Coachwhip, Cottonmouth, Fer-de-Lance, Rattler (prev 4 next in Cap #434, '94) (all bts, being held w/out bail), Puff Adder (bts, driving Serpent Saucer), Anaconda, Rock Python (prev 3 also in photo) (all last in Cap #382, '91)
OTHER CHARACTERS: Tinkerer (bts, provides traps to Diamondback, last in Cap #369, '90, next in DFSM #1, '91), news anchor
LOCATIONS/ITEMS: Paladin's Trump Plaza apartment, Diamondback's apartment; Serpent Saucer, Asp's & Black Mamba's new costumes
SYNOPSIS: At Paladin's apartment, Diamondback, Asp & Black Mamba learn from the news that Anaconda, Puff Adder and Rock Python have escaped arrest. They decide to stay together as BAD Girls, Inc and return to Diamondback's apartment, where a Serpent Saucer crashes into the apartment and the fugitive Serpent Society members attack.
NOTE: BAD Girls, Inc stands for Black Mamba, Asp, Diamondback Girls, Inc. Diamondback's apartment is on West End Ave.

CAPTAIN AMERICA #386 (June 1991)

"For Righteousness's Sake" (19 pages)

CREDITS: Mark Gruenwald (writer), Ron Lim (pencils), Danny Bulanadi (inks), Joe Rosen (letters), Christie Scheele (colors), Michael Heisler (asst editor), Ralph Macchio (editor)
FEATURE CHARACTER: Captain America (next in XFac Ann #6, '91, XFac #66, '91, NF:AoS #26, '91, Cap Ann #10/2, '91)
GUEST STAR: USAgent (last in AWC #69, '91, next in AWC #71, '91)
SUPPORTING CAST: Avengers Crew: Edwin Jarvis (next in Av Ann #20/4, '91), Fabian Stankowicz (between Av #331-332, '91), Col. John Jameson (next in Av #332, '91); Mike Farrel (next in Cap #425, '94), Bernie Rosenthal (next in Cap #393, '91)
VILLAINS: Watchdogs (inc Watchdog Prime ("Top Dog," leader, 1st, next in Cap #394, '91) & Stu Bartlett (last app), Darla (receptionist) named)
OTHER CHARACTERS: Enrique Parcair (last app), Watchdog's abductees & patrol dogs; mother, children, baseball player (prev 3 in photos)
LOCATIONS/ITEMS: New York inc Watchdog local division HQ & Avengers Mansion w/training room & lounge, Mike's Brooklyn Heights apartment, Stu's Queens apartment, SoHo art exhibition, Watchdog Lodge (Vermont ski lodge); Watchdogs' handcuffs, vans, guns & "Dog collars" (electric shock devices), Cap's van & sky-cycle, Avengers training equipment, USAgent's tracer, Mike's razor, scarecrow (in rfb)
FLASHBACK: USAgent decides he needs to be a better person (Cap #383/3, '91).
SYNOPSIS: The Watchdogs take the captive Bernie to their Lodge. At Avengers Mansion, USAgent offers his help against the Watchdogs but Captain America refuses, knowing Agent's violent history with the group. Mike shaves off his mustache so he won't be recognized. In Vermont, Bernie is secured at the Lodge. Mike goes to Stu for help, not realizing the Watchdogs consider him a traitor; Stu turns him over to the Lodge. Thanks to information from Fabian, Cap tries to warn Enrique he's in danger but ends up using him as bait when Enrique doesn't listen. The Watchdogs kidnap Enrique and Cap follows; infiltrating the Lodge and discovering it's a brainwashing facility. Cap finds Mike inside when USAgent suddenly breaks in; USAgent quickly subdues the Watchdogs. Mike tells Cap he joined the Watchdogs and asks to be arrested.

2ND STORY: "Snake Heist" (4 pages)
CREDITS: Mark Gruenwald (writer), Dan Panosian (art), Clem Robins (letters), Nel Yomtov (colors), Michael Heisler (asst editor), Ralph Macchio (editor)
FEATURE CHARACTER: Diamondback (also in BAD Girls, Inc)
SUPPORTING CAST: BAD Girls, Inc: Asp, Black Mamba
VILLAINS: MODAM (Olinka Barankova, Mobile Organism Designed for Aggressive Maneuvers, last in Q #9, '90), Superia (bts, sent MODAM to recruit BAD Girls, Inc, chr last in Cap #391, '91 fb), Serpent Society: Anaconda, Puff Adder, Rock Python
LOCATIONS/ITEMS: Diamondback's apartment; Serpent Saucer, Rock Python's ether eggs, MODAM's flight harness
SYNOPSIS: Anaconda, Puff Adder and Rock Python capture the BAD Girls and bring them aboard their Serpent Saucer. Suddenly, MODAM attacks the ship and throws out Puff Adder and Rock Python, stating she's on a rescue mission for Diamondback.

CAPTAIN AMERICA ANNUAL #10 (1991)

"The Origin of Captain America" (2 pages)

CREDITS: D.G. Chichester (writer), Mike Manley (art), Ralph Macchio (editor), Mike Mignola (c art)
FEATURE CHARACTERS: Captain America (also in symbolic iamge)
GUEST STARS: Avengers: Giant-Man, Iron Man, Thor, Wasp
VILLAINS: Red Skull (also in symbolic image), Heinz Krueger, Nazis (also in newsreel)
OTHER CHARACTERS: Gen. Phillips, Abraham Erskine, theater attendees, army doctor & draftees, Steve's trainers; Baron Zemo, Crossbones, Flag-Smasher, Mother Night, Viper (prev 5 in symbolic image)
LOCATIONS/ITEMS: Movie theater, army recruitment center, Project: Rebirth, Atlantic Ocean; Operation: Rebirth equipment, Krueger's gun, Steve's training equipment, drone plane, Avengers submarine
SYNOPSIS: Steve Rogers is appalled at newsreel footage of Nazis in Europe and tries to volunteer for military service, but is declared 4-F; Gen. Phillips offers Steve a chance to serve in another way. Steve becomes America's first and only Super Soldier when he undergoes the Operation: Rebirth process and scientist Abraham Erskine is killed by a Nazi spy. Steve trains his new body for months, is given his Captain America uniform and fights the Red Skull. At the end of the war Cap falls into the Atlantic Ocean and freezes, to be found in the current day by the Avengers.
NOTE: Cover labeled "The Von Strucker Gambit Part 3." Includes contents page (1 page) featuring Captain America. This is an abbreviated retelling of Cap #255, '81's combination of Cap's previously disparate origins. Letters & colors are not credited for this story. Followed by "Cap and Company" pin-up (1 page) by Ron Lim & Danny Bulanadi, featuring Cap, Diamondback, Nick Fury, Falcon, Redwing, Nomad, Demolition Man, Col. John Jameson, Peggy Carter, Edwin Jarvis, Michael O'Brien, Fabian Stankowicz & Bernie Rosenthal.

2ND STORY: "The Von Strucker Gambit (Part 3)" (25 pages)
CREDITS: D.G. Chichester (writer), Mike Manley (art), Rick Parker (letters), Ed Lazelarri (colors), Ralph Macchio (editor)
FEATURE CHARACTER: Captain America (also in photo, rfb & fb between Cap #109, '69 fb & MvPro #4, '10 fb; next in Cap Ann #10/4, av #332-333, AFlt #98-100, all '91, Pun/Cap:B&G #1-3, '92, Nam #13, Nam #15 fb, Av Ann #20, AWC Ann #6, ASM #348, WoSM #75-76, Av #334-339, all '91, S #4-5, '00-01 fbs, Thor #433-434, MCP #80/2-81/2, Av #340, IM #273, Dhawk #6, all '91)
GUEST STAR: Nick Fury (last in Pun Ann #4, '91, next in NF:AoS #27, '91)
VILLAINS: Baron Strucker (last in Pun Ann #4, '91, next in NF:AoS #27, '91), Cassandra Romulus (Hydra super-agent, also in photo, last in DD Ann #7, '91, next in NF:AoS #27, '91), Dakini (Hydra elite bounty hunter, last in Pun Ann #4, '91, dies, last app), Hydra agents
OTHER CHARACTERS: Gen. Phillips (only in fb between Cap #109, '69 fb & MvPro #4, '10 fb), Dr. Jonathan Fishman (Double Helix scientist, only app), Double Helix facility security (Charlie named, many die), 2 corpses (Double Helix genetic experiments), paramedics, motel manager, Dr. Fishman's cat; Abraham Erskine (in rfb), Daredevil, Punisher, Guillotine, Sathan, Ron Takimoto (prev 5 in photo)
LOCATIONS/ITEMS: New York inc Double Helix facility w/lab, Dr. Fishman's apartment, motel & Hydra base, Project: Rebirth (in rfb); Cap's motorcycle, Dakini's rifle, grappling hook & knives, Fury's flying motorcycle & needle gun, Dr. Fishman's genetic solution
FLASHBACKS: Gen. Phillips asks Steve if he's sure of the decision he's making (1). Steve enters Project: Rebirth (Cap #215, '77 fb).
SYNOPSIS: Cassandra Romulus breaks into the Double Helix facilities. Responding to an Avengers alert, Captain America arrives and fights her off, but he lets her go so he can tend to a wounded guard. Romulus steals some body parts and escapes. Nick Fury meets with Cap and they decide to research Romulus using a genetic sample Cap gained during the fight. Meanwhile, Dakini briefs herself on Romulus' activities and prepares to find her. Cap and Fury meet with Dr. Fishman who determines Romulus' genetic structure has been altered and augmented. As Romulus listens from outside, Fishman explains the genetic solution Double Helix has been working on could revert her to normal, and that must be why she broke into the facility. Dakini shoots Romulus, who falls through Fishman's window. Cap chases Dakini as Romulus obtains the genetic solution. Cap defeats Dakini as Romulus escapes from Fury; she then kills Dakini in front of Cap. Sympathetic because of her history of being genetically experimented on, Cap lets Romulus go to use the genetic solution, angering Fury. Romulus returns to Baron Strucker, who destroys the genetic solution.
NOTE: Story continued from DD Ann #7, '91 & Pun Ann #4, '91.

3RD STORY: "Brothers" (7 pages)
CREDITS: Mark Gruenwald (writer), Don Heck (art), Rick Parker (letters), Many Hands (colors), Ralph Macchio (editor)
FEATURE CHARACTER: Bushmaster (Quincy McIver, also in fb to 1st chr app before Cap #310, '85; last bts in Cap #385/2, '91, next in Cap #435, '95)
GUEST STAR: Seth Voelker (Roxxon executive & future Sidewinder, only in fb to 1st chr app before MTIO #64, '80)
SUPPORTING CAST: John McIver (Quincy's brother, also as "John Bushmaster" & as original Bushmaster in Quincy's thoughts, only in fb to 1st chr app before IF #15, '77)
OTHER CHARACTERS: Herve Argosy (John's drug lord boss, only app), his men & ladies, shop keeper, cocaine smugglers, police, doctors, nurse, Roxxon scientists, bystanders (all only in fb), Mr. Senescu (Bushmaster's lawyer, only app)
LOCATIONS/ITEMS: Caribbean island, Argosy Estate, docks, hospital, Roxxon lab (all in fb), John McIver 's grave (in Quincy's thoughts), Bushmaster Vault cell; cocaine, police helicopters, boat, Roxxon lab equipment (all in fb)
FLASHBACK: Quincy and John McIver lead a life of crime as young men, until police catch Quincy smuggling cocaine. He tries to escape but a boat propeller chops off his arms and legs. John visits Quincy in the hospital to tell him he's now going by "John Bushmaster" and is moving to Europe to oversee his boss' drug operations. Later, Seth Voelker offers Quincy a chance to regain his limbs, courtesy of Roxxon. Quincy agrees and undergoes the process, but is shocked when he awakes to find he has a snake tail instead of legs. Quincy takes the name Bushmaster to honor his now dead brother.
SYNOPSIS: In his Vault prison cell, Bushmaster reminisces on his life until his lawyer tells him he's being released because of insufficient

evidence of wrongdoing. Bushmaster wonders what a freak like himself will do in the outside world and decides he'll commit a stupid crime and get thrown back in prison.

4ᵀᴴ STORY: "Forgive us our Trespasses" (7 pages)
CREDITS: Mark Gruenwald (writer), James Brock (pencils), Don Hudson (inks), Rick Parker (letters), Nel Yomtov (colors), Ralph Macchio (editor)
FEATURE CHARACTER: Sidewinder (also in rfb & fb between Cap #345, '88 & X Ann #13, '89; last in Cap #381, '91, next in Cap #424, '94)
GUEST STAR: Captain America (on live viewscreen, last in Cap Ann #10/2, '91, next in Av #332, '91)
VILLAINS: King Cobra (also in photo, rfb & fb between Cap #344, '88 & X Ann #13, '89; last bts in Cap #385/2, '91, next in FF #358, '91), Halflife (Banca Rech, extraterrestrial, last in Q #10, '90, last app)
OTHER CHARACTERS: Katy Fong (news anchor, only app), Vault Guardsmen (one also in photo), judge, bystanders, horses, rabbit; Serpent Society: Anaconda, Black Racer, Copperhead, Cottonmouth, Puff Adder, Rattler; Diamondback, Viper (prev 8 in rfb)
LOCATIONS/ITEMS: Sidewinder's Central Park West apartment, American towns, Colorado inc Vault w/teleconference court room; Guardsmen armors, hover cars & guns, Halflife's energy sphere cell, King Cobra's restraints
FLASHBACKS: Sidewinder rescues Diamondback from being executed by the Serpent Society (Cap #380, '90). Viper takes over the Society (Cap #342, '88). Sidewinder hands over the Society leadership to Cobra in exchange for twenty-five percent of the group's earnings.
SYNOPSIS: Sidewinder realizes that even though King Cobra is in prison, Cobra will eventually come after him in retribution for his saving Diamondback. Sidewinder decides to settle the score and teleports across the country in fifty mile leaps until he arrives at the Vault. Sidewinder teleports inside, interrupts Cobra's trial, and teleports him out. Vault Guardsmen injure Sidewinder's shoulder during the escape, forcing Sidewinder to leave Cobra to fend for himself. Unable to escape, Cobra surrenders and swears vengeance against Sidewinder.

5ᵀᴴ STORY: "Worth Fighting For" (10 pages)
CREDITS: Fabian Nicieza (writer), Larry Alexander (pencils), Tim Dzon (inks), Brad K. Joyce (letters), Nel Yomtov (colors), Ralph Macchio (editor)
FEATURE CHARACTER: Nomad (last in Nomad #4, '91, next in Nomad #1, '92)
SUPPORTING CAST: Bucky (infant girl, last in Nomad #4, '91, next in Nomad #1, '92)
OTHER CHARACTERS: Billy & his mom, wolves; Mickey Mouse (on Bucky's baby harness)
LOCATIONS/ITEMS: Canada, Billy's mom's cabin; Billy's mom's shotgun, Billy's gun, bandages
SYNOPSIS: In Canada, Nomad comes across a wolf pack that almost kills him. A stranger rescues Nomad and takes him back to her cabin, where she and her son discover Nomad is carrying an infant. Nomad wakes up with a shotgun pointed at his face. The woman explains she killed her husband in self-defense and says she can't trust Nomad to care for a child or not to tell authorities where she is. When Nomad notes he could say the same about her, she points out she has the gun; however, he snatches it from her, then promises to leave her be if she will let Bucky and him go on their way.
NOTE: Story continues in Nomad #1, '92. Followed by "The Serpent Society" pin-up (2 pages) by Mark Bagley, featuring King Cobra, Anaconda, Black Racer, Fer-de-Lance, Rock Python, Rattler, Black Mamba, Asp, Bushmaster, Coachwhip, Cottonmouth, Boomslang, Puff Adder, Copperhead, Sidewinder, Diamondback, Death Adder, Princess Python, Constrictor & Viper. Followed by "The Skeleton Crew" pin-up (1 page) by Kieron Dwyer & Al Williamson, featuring Red Skull, Machinesmith, Crossbones, the 4ᵗʰ Sleeper, Mother Night & Minister Blood.

CAPTAIN AMERICA #387 (Early July 1991)

"Maiden Voyage" (17 pages)

CREDITS: Mark Gruenwald (writer), Rik Levins (pencils), Danny Bulanadi (inks), Joe Rosen (letters), Christie Scheele (colors), Michael Heisler (asst editor), Ralph Macchio (editor), Ron Lim (c pencils)
FEATURE CHARACTER: Captain America
GUEST STARS: Paladin (last in Ex #36, '91), Wasp (voice only on phone, last in Av #340, '91, next bts in InfG #2, '91, next in AWC Ann #6/3, '91), BAD Girls, Inc: Asp, Black Mamba
SUPPORTING CAST: Avengers Crew: Peggy Carter (last in Thor #433, '91), Edwin Jarvis (last in Av #340, '91, next in Cap #393, '91), Col. John Jameson (last in Av #332, '91, last bts in Av #333, '91); Diamondback (also in BAD Girls, Inc)
VILLAINS: Superia (bts, overseeing operations on S.S. Superia), her lieutenants: Dr. Nightshade (in shadows, last in PMIF #110, '84 as Nightshade, see NOTE), Blackbird (bts, Heather O'Gara, 1ˢᵗ as Blackbird, last in Hulk #284, '83 as Jackdaw), Iron Maiden (bts, Melina Vostokovna, last in MFan #12, '84), Moonstone (bts, last in Cap #379, '90), Snapdragon (bts, Sheoke Sanada, last in MFan #13, '84); her Femizons (all but MODAM bts): MODAM, Bloodlust (Beatta Dubiel), Knockout (Elizabeth Rawson), Mindblast (Danielle Forte), Whiplash (Leeann Foreman) (prev 4 last in ASM #343, '91 as Femme Fatales), Dansen Macabre, Gypsy Moth (both last in WCA #40, '89), Frenzy (Joanna Cargill), Vapor (Ann Darnell) (both last in Av:Vault, '91), Golddigger (Angela Golden), Chimera, Ice Princess, Impala, Mysteria (Winters) (prev 5 1ˢᵗ), Arclight (Philippa Sontag, last in UXM #240, '89), Battleaxe (Anita Ehren, last in Thing #33, '86), Black Lotus (last in MFan #12, '84), Bombshell (last in AvS #25, '89), Dragoness (Tamara Kurtz, last in NM #94, '90), Dragonfly (Veronica Dultry, last in Q #20, '91), Ferocia (last in PMIF #100, '83 as Fera), Gladiatrix (last in Cap #352, '89), Ion (Voletta Todd, last in MacM #15, '80), Karisma (Mary Brown, last in FF #266, '84), Pink Pearl (Pearl Gross, last in AFlt #22, '85), Poundcakes (last in Cap #371, '90), Princess Python (last in SenSH #1, '89), Quicksand (last in Thor #403, '89), Screaming Mimi (Melissa Gold, last in AvS #29, '90), Steel Wind (Ruriko Tsumura, last in GR #75, '82), Titania (last in WoSM #65, '90), Vertigo (last in UXM #241, '89), Water Witch (last in Rom #28, '82), Whiteout (last in UXM #274, '91), Wrangler (last in MFan #13, '84 as Larralee), Yellowjacket (last bts in Cap #349, '89); & her Femizon enforcers (in shadows); Serpent Society: Puff Adder (next in GotG #28, '92), Rock Python (next in Cap #411, '93), Anaconda; Super-Adaptoid (as "Alessandro Brannex," A.I.M. chairman of the board, last in Q #9, '90, next bts in Cap #411, '93, see NOTE), A.I.M. agents (one also in photo, Aldo named)
OTHER CHARACTERS: Superia's female recruits (see NOTE), police (Lt. Peltino named), paramedics, bystanders; Avengers: Giant-Man, Hulk, Iron Man, Thor, Wasp (prev 5 as statues)

LOCATIONS/ITEMS: Diamondback's apartment, Avengers Mansion, Brooklyn inc Bay Ridge, Atlantic Ocean, Boca Caliente inc A.I.M. HQ; Cap's modified Quinjet & Avengers ID card, Diamondback's electronic case & homing beacon, Paladin's limo & guns, MODAM's flight harness, Serpent Saucer, Superia's invitations, S.S. Superia (luxury liner)

SYNOPSIS: Captain America investigates the ruins of Diamondback's apartment, but doesn't find any leads to her whereabouts. Getting his phone number from Wasp, Cap contacts Paladin, who offers to help Cap in his search. Peggy tells Cap that Puff Adder and Rock Python have been found unconscious in Bay Ridge, Brooklyn; they tell Cap of MODAM's attack. Meanwhile, MODAM takes BAD Girls, Inc and Anaconda to the S.S. Superia, giving them each an invitation and one hundred thousand dollars. Leary, Diamondback activates her homing beacon. Cap and Paladin visit Boca Caliente and talk with A.I.M.'s new chairman but learn nothing. Picking up Diamondback's signal, Cap investigates. MODAM intercepts them, putting Col. Jameson into a trance and crashing Cap's modified Quinjet. As they parachute out, MODAM attacks.

NOTE: Cover-labeled "The Superia Stratagem Part One of Six." Cap #413, '93 reveals Alessandro Brannex to be an Adaptoid, and Cap #441, '95 reveals him to be the Super-Adaptoid. Cap #391, '91 reveals Superia's female recruits total 10,572 women. Paladin's answering service phone number is 555-7170. Diamondback's homing beacon broadcasts on frequency 11.7. The title goes bi-weekly with this issue.

2ND STORY: "The Masque Club" (5 pages)

CREDITS: Mark Gruenwald (writer), Dan Panosian (art), Clem Robins (letters), Nel Yomtov (colors), Michael Heisler (asst editor), Ralph Macchio (editor)

FEATURE CHARACTER: Red Skull (last in NF:AoS #26, '91)

GUEST STARS: Schutz Heiligruppe (German super team): Hauptmann Deutschland (Markus Ettlinger, stores & redirects kinetic energy, as Masque Club patron, 1st), Blitzkrieger (Franz Mittelstaedt, manipulates electricity, 1st as Blitzkrieger, bts, raided Zola's castle, last in Rom #65, '85, last bts in Rom #66, '85 as Blitzkrieg) (see NOTE)

SUPPORTING CAST: Skeleton Crew: Crossbones, Machinesmith (both last in Cap #378, '90, next in Cap #389/2, '91), Mother Night (last in Av #325, '86), 4th Sleeper (last in Cap #370, '90) (both next in Cap #389/2, '91); Arnim Zola (last in MCP #24/3, '89, next in Cap #393, '91)

VILLAINS: Baron (Wolfgang von) Strucker (Supreme Hydra, last in NF:AoS #27, '91, last bts in DD #293, '91, next in Cap #394, '91), Zeitgeist (Larry Ekler, bts, raided Zola's castle, last in AFlt #78, '89, next in Cap #390/2, '91, Schutz Heiligruppe infiltrator, see NOTE)

OTHER CHARACTERS: Crossbones' date, Witold (Masque Club waiter), Masque Club patrons

LOCATIONS/ITEMS: Smith Building inc Masque Club & meeting room; phone, Skull's luger

SYNOPSIS: At his newly opened Masque Club, Red Skull entertains Baron Strucker until he receives a phone call. He excuses himself and gathers his Skeleton Crew, and Arnim Zola reveals that his resurrection apparatus and the Skull's spare clone bodies have been destroyed. The Skull tasks his Skeleton Crew to discover who's responsible and returns to the Club, where a masked man spies on him.

NOTE: Schutz Heiligruppe translates literally as "Group of Protecting Saints", or figuratively "League of Guardian Angels," Hauptmann Deutschland means "Captain Germany," Blitzkrieger "Lightning Warrior," and Zeitgeist "Spirit of the Times." The group's name is revealed in Cap #390, '91, Hauptmann Deutschland's codename in Cap #389/2, '91 and real name in MAtlas #1, '08. Zeitgeist appeared previously as Everyman in Cap #267, '82; Cap #442, 95 reveals Zeitgeist and Everyman are the same person, and that issue's "Let's Rap With Cap" reveals Dr. Faustus gave him the Zeitgeist identity and arranged for him to join Schutz Heiligruppe to murder them. In Germany, Schutz Heiligruppe is renamed Helden-Liga, "Heroes League," Hauptmann Deutschland is Freiheitskämpfer, "Freedom Fighter," and Blitzkrieger is Generator.

CAPTAIN AMERICA #388 (Late July 1991)

"Deep Sixed" (17 pages)

CREDITS: Mark Gruenwald (writer), Rik Levins (pencils), Danny Bulanadi (inks), Joe Rosen (letters), Christie Scheele (colors), Michael Heisler (asst editor), Ralph Macchio (editor), Ron Lim (c pencils)

FEATURE CHARACTER: Captain America

GUEST STARS: BAD Girls, Inc: Asp, Black Mamba; Paladin

SUPPORTING CAST: Avengers Crew: Peggy Carter (next in Cap #392, '91), Col. John Jameson; Diamondback (also in BAD Girls, Inc)

VILLAINS: Superia (bts, overseeing operations on S.S. Superia), her lieutenants: Blackbird, Iron Maiden, Snapdragon, Moonstone, Dr. Nightshade (bts); & her Femizons: Arclight, Battleaxe, Black Lotus, Bloodlust, Bombshell, Chimera, Dansen Macabre, Dragoness, Ferocia, Frenzy, Gladiatrix, Golddigger, Gypsy Moth, Ice Princess, Ion, Karisma, Knockout, Mindblast, Mysteria, Pink Pearl, Poundcakes, Princess Python, Screaming Mimi, Steel Wind, Titania, Vapor, Vertigo, Water Witch, Whiplash, Whiteout, Wrangler, Yellowjacket (prev 32 bts), Anaconda (joins Femizons), Impala (1st full app), MODAM (next in Cap #391, '91), Dragonfly, Quicksand

OTHER CHARACTERS: Superia's female recruits inc waitress; Quasar (mentioned, see NOTE)

LOCATIONS/ITEMS: Atlantic Ocean; S.S. Superia, MODAM's flight harness, Paladin's guns, rubber raft

SYNOPSIS: Cap evades MODAM's attack and rescues the unconscious Col. Jameson as Paladin drives MODAM off. Meanwhile on the S.S. Superia, BAD Girls, Inc relaxes with other super powered women and meets Impala, who invites them to tonight's Power Pageant. Their conversation is interrupted when Anaconda picks a fight with Quicksand. Diamondback is chloroformed from behind and taken away. Cap tries to get Quasar to pick them up, but Blackbird and Moonstone attack; tying Paladin up and knocking Cap out. Diamondback wakes up to learn her old academy classmate Snapdragon attacked her. Snapdragon knocks Diamondback out and throws her overboard into the ocean.

NOTE: Cover-labeled "The Superia Stratagem Part Two of Six." Events in Q #25-26, '91 prevent Quasar responding to Peggy's distress call.

2ND STORY: "The Red Skull Slaughterhouse" (5 pages)

CREDITS: Mark Gruenwald (writer), Larry Alexander (pencils), Dan Panosian (inks), Clem Robins (letters), Nel Yomtov (colors), Michael Heisler (asst editor), Ralph Macchio (editor)

FEATURE CHARACTER: Red Skull

GUEST STARS: Schutz Heiligruppe: Hauptmann Deutschland (as Larry "Dutch" Conrad & Captain America), Blitzkrieger (bts, teleports Red Skull & Hauptmann Deutschland away)
VILLAIN: Taskmaster (bts, provided Red Skull's sparring partners, last in DD #293, '91, chr last in Dp #68, '02 fb, next in Cap #394, '91)
OTHER CHARACTERS: Buzz, Dan, Lenny & Marlon (Red Skull's sparring partners, dressed as Captain America, all die), Red Skull's security (Mr. Brice & Elron named)
LOCATIONS/ITEMS: Smith Building inc locker room & gym; surveillance equipment
SYNOPSIS: Red Skull battles five men dressed as Captain America and kills four; when he attacks the last they both suddenly disappear, much to the surprise of the Skull's security.

CAPTAIN AMERICA #389 (Early August 1991)

"Pageant of Power" (17 pages)

CREDITS: Mark Gruenwald (writer), Rik Levins (pencils), Danny Bulanadi (inks), Joe Rosen (letters), Christie Scheele (colors), Len Kaminski (asst editor), Ralph Macchio (editor), Ron Lim (c pencils), Art Thibert (c inks)
FEATURE CHARACTER: Captain America
GUEST STARS: Vision (last in Av #389, '91, next in Cap #392, '91), Paladin, BAD Girls, Inc: Asp, Black Mamba
SUPPORTING CAST: Diamondback (leaves BAD Girls, Inc), Col. John Jameson (next in Cap#392, '91)
VILLAINS: Superia (bts, overseeing operations of S.S. Superia), her lieutenants: Blackbird, Moonstone (both next in Cap #411, '93), Iron Maiden, Dr. Nightshade, Snapdragon; & her Femizons: Golddigger (see NOTE), Chimera, Ice Princess, Mysteria (prev 4 1st full app), Anaconda, Arclight, Battleaxe, Black Lotus, Bloodlust, Bombshell, Dansen Macabre, Dragoness, Dragonfly, Ferocia, Frenzy, Gladiatrix, Gypsy Moth, Impala, Ion, Karisma, Knockout, Mindblast, Pink Pearl, Poundcakes, Princess Python, Quicksand, Screaming Mimi, Steel Wind, Titania, Vapor, Vertigo, Water Witch, Whiplash, Whiteout, Wrangler, Yellowjacket
OTHER CHARACTERS: Superia's female recruits inc doctors & assistants
LOCATIONS/ITEMS: Atlantic Ocean; S.S. Superia inc infirmary, Avengers Quinjet & Neuronic-Disruptor Cuffs, Cap's sky-cycle, Paladin's guns, suction climbers
SYNOPSIS: Paladin unties himself and shoots Moonstone. Blackbird swoops down to check on Moonstone, but the recovered Captain America grabs Blackbird's foot. Blackbird tries to escape, but can't shake Cap off. Meanwhile, Quicksand has defeated Anaconda and Diamondback's absence is noticed. Dr. Nightshade sends Ion out to find her. Diamondback is returned to the S. S. Superia where Asp and Black Mamba are determined to learn what happened. Cap defeats Blackbird, and Vision arrives in a Quinjet. Vision takes Blackbird and Moonstone away while Cap and Paladin take a sky-cycle to the S. S. Superia. Diamondback recovers, but badly shaken by her experience, swears off her life of adventure. Cap and Paladin infiltrate the S. S. Superia during the Power Pageant, where the various super powered women demonstrate their powers for each other. The men are noticed and the army of women attack.
NOTE: Cover-labeled "The Superia Stratagem Part Three of Six." While this is Golddigger's 1st app, her likeness has appeared before in Thing #33, '86 when Scourge impersonated her to kill Titania. Cap #402/2, '92 reveals Diamondback is clinically dead for two minutes here.

2ND STORY: "Kidnaped" (5 pages)
CREDITS: Mark Gruenwald (writer), Larry Alexander (pencils), Bud La Rosa (inks), Michael Higgins (letters), Kevin Tinsley (colors), Len Kaminski (asst editor), Ralph Macchio (editor)
FEATURE CHARACTER: Red Skull
GUEST STARS: Schutz Heiligruppe: Hauptmann Deutschland, Blitzkrieger
SUPPORTING CAST: Skeleton Crew: Crossbones, Machinesmith, Mother Night, 4th Sleeper (all last in Cap #387/2, '91)
LOCATIONS/ITEMS: Airspace over Switzerland; Hauptmann Deutschland's airship, Skeleton Crew's aircraft, Red Skull's homing transmitter
SYNOPSIS: Red Skull awakens shackled in an airship. Hauptmann Deutschland reveals he infiltrated Taskmaster's organization so he could capture the Skull, who will be put on trial and executed for war crimes during WWII. Meanwhile, the Skeleton Crew pick up the Skull's homing transmitter signal and follow it. Blitzkrieger tells Hauptmann Deutschland he senses the signal, who is pleased they will be able to capture the Skull's flunkies as well.

CAPTAIN AMERICA #390 (Late August 1991)

"When Women Wage War!" (17 pages)

CREDITS: Mark Gruenwald (writer), Rik Levins (pencils), Danny Bulanadi (inks), Joe Rosen (letters), Christie Scheele (colors), Len Kaminski (asst editor), Ralph Macchio (editor), Ron Lim (c art)
FEATURE CHARACTER: Captain America
GUEST STARS: BAD Girls, Inc: Asp, Black Mamba; Paladin
SUPPORTING CAST: Rachel Leighton
VILLAINS: Superia (Dr. Deidre Wentworth, strength-augmented feminist, 1st full app), her lieutenants: Iron Maiden, Dr. Nightshade, Snapdragon; her Femizons: Anaconda, Arclight, Battleaxe, Black Lotus, Bloodlust, Bombshell, Chimera, Dansen Macabre, Dragoness, Dragonfly, Ferocia, Frenzy, Gladiatrix, Golddigger, Gypsy Moth, Ice Princess, Impala, Ion, Karisma, Knockout, Mindblast, Mysteria, Pink Pearl, Poundcakes, Princess Python, Quicksand, Screaming Mimi, Steel Wind, Titania, Vapor, Vertigo, Water Witch, Whiplash, Whiteout, Wrangler, Yellowjacket; & her Femizon enforcers
OTHER CHARACTERS: Superia's female recruits
LOCATIONS/ITEMS: Atlantic Ocean, Femizona Island inc command center; S.S. Superia inc infirmary, Paladin's guns, Superia's hover-platform

SYNOPSIS: Cap and Paladin face off against the super powered women army while Black Mamba and Asp visit Diamondback in the infirmary. Cap and Paladin are soon defeated by sheer numbers and Diamondback, Black Mamba and Asp witness their capture before Diamondback frees Snapdragon and ducks away. Dansen Macabre binds Cap and Paladin to her will and Dr. Nightshade interrogates them, but Cap manages to reveal nothing. Paladin reveals they're looking for Diamondback and the Avengers may be on their way. Cap and Paladin are taken to Superia, who plans to transform Cap and Paladin into women.

NOTE: Cover-labeled "The Superia Stratagem Part Four of Six." Superia's real name revealed in Cap #431, '94.

2ND STORY: "Sneak Attack" (6 pages)

CREDITS: Mark Gruenwald (writer), Larry Alexander (pencils), Dan Panosian (inks), Rick Parker (letters), Dan Slott (colors), Len Kaminski (asst editor), Ralph Macchio (editor)

FEATURE CHARACTERS: Skeleton Crew: Crossbones, Machinesmith, Mother Night, 4th Sleeper

GUEST STARS: Schutz Heiligruppe (1st full app): Hauptmann Deutschland, Blitzkrieger

SUPPORTING CAST: Red Skull (bts, held captive by Schutz Heiligruppe)

VILLAIN: Zeitgeist (also in Schutz Heiligruppe, last bts in Cap #387/2, '91, next in Cap #393, '91)

OTHER CHARACTERS: German war crimes trial guards

LOCATIONS/ITEMS: Converted German airplane hangar; Skeleton Crew's flight harnesses & Skull-Tracker, 4th Sleeper's neuronic disruptors, Mother Night's gun, guards' guns

SYNOPSIS: The Skeleton Crew attempt to rescue the captive Red Skull, but the Schutz Heiligruppe quickly defeat them.

CAPTAIN AMERICA #391 (Early September 1991)

"No Man's Land" (17 pages)

CREDITS: Mark Gruenwald (writer), Rik Levins (pencils), Danny Bulanadi (inks), Joe Rosen (letters), Marie Javins (colors), Len Kaminski (asst editor), Ralph Macchio (editor), Ron Lim (c pencils)

FEATURE CHARACTER: Captain America (also as Black Mamba)

GUEST STARS: Paladin (also as Asp), BAD Girls, Inc: Asp, Black Mamba (both also as Femizon enforcers)

SUPPORTING CAST: Rachel Leighton (bts, being held captive by Femizons)

VILLAINS: Superia (also in fb to 1st chr app before bts in Cap #386/2, '91), her lieutenants: Iron Maiden, Dr. Nightshade, Snapdragon; her Femizons: MODAM (last in Cap #388, '91), Anaconda, Arclight, Battleaxe, Black Lotus, Bloodlust, Bombshell, Chimera, Dansen Macabre, Dragoness, Dragonfly, Ferocia, Frenzy, Gladiatrix, Golddigger, Gypsy Moth, Ice Princess, Impala, Ion, Karisma, Knockout, Mindblast, Mysteria, Pink Pearl, Poundcakes, Princess Python, Quicksand, Screaming Mimi, Steel Wind, Titania, Vapor, Vertigo, Water Witch, Whiplash, Whiteout, Wrangler, Yellowjacket; & her Femizon enforcers

OTHER CHARACTERS: Superia's female recruits inc store clerk & assistants; Thundra (in holographic image)

LOCATIONS/ITEMS: Femizonia Island inc lab, command center & Great Mall; Superia's Time-Probe (in fb), Feminization Treatment equipment, hover-platform & Sterility Seed rockets, MODAM's flight harness

FLASHBACK: Superia creates her Time-Probe.

SYNOPSIS: Now on Femizon Island, Superia checks on the progress of turning Captain America and Paladin into women. Gathering all the super powered women together, Superia explains she learned that in the future, most of North America will be called Femizona and women will be the rulers, led by Thundra. Superia believes she is an ancestor to Thundra, and will cause the event that leads to this future. Not liking the way this future sounds, Asp and Black Mamba find Cap and Paladin and help free them from Superia's Feminization Treatment. Donning Black Mamba and Asp's costumes respectively to disguise themselves as women, Cap and Paladin infiltrate command center and confront Superia. After a brief fight, Superia reveals her plan to sterilize all the women on Earth except for the 10,572 women on Femizonia Island, and that she's already launched her Sterility Seed rockets.

NOTE: Cover-labeled "The Superia Stratagem Part Five of Six." Ralph Macchio is mis-spelled "Ralf Macchio" here.

2ND STORY: "The Skeleton Key" (5 pages)

CREDITS: Mark Gruenwald (writer), Larry Alexander (pencils), Dan Panosian (inks), Joe Rosen (letters), Kevin Tinsley (colors), Len Kaminski (asst editor), Ralph Macchio (editor)

FEATURE CHARACTERS: Skeleton Crew: Crossbones, Machinesmith, Mother Night, 4th Sleeper (all next in Cap #393, '91)

GUEST STARS: Schutz Heiligruppe: Hauptmann Deutschland, Blitzkrieger (both next in Cap #393, '91)

SUPPORTING CAST: Red Skull (next in Cap #393, '91)

OTHER CHARACTERS: Mr. Buehller (defense attorney), Mr. Leiberthal (prosecuting attorney), German war crime trial judge (all 1st, next in Cap #393, '91), jury, witnesses, guards & set-up crew

LOCATIONS/ITEMS: Converted German airplane hangar; Red Skull's & Skeleton Crew's restraint chairs, guards' guns

SYNOPSIS: Hauptmann Deutschland introduces Red Skull to his appointed lawyer, Mr. Buehller, but the Skull refuses to recognize the war crime trial's authority or legality. Meanwhile, Machinesmith's consciousness is trapped in an electric lock, until he beams himself back into his body. When the trial begins Machinesmith springs to action.

NOTE: Mr. Leiberthal is named in Cap #393, '91. Cap #400, '92's "American Graffiti" reveals the war crime trial is not officially sanctioned by the German government.

CAPTAIN AMERICA #392 (Late September 1991)

"Superia Unbound" (22 pages)

CREDITS: Mark Gruenwald (writer), Rik Levins (pencils), Danny Bulanadi (inks), Joe Rosen (letters), Mari Javins, Steve Buccellato (colors), Ralph Macchio (editor), Ron Lim (c pencils)
FEATURE CHARACTER: Captain America (also as Black Mamba & Superia)
GUEST STARS: BAD Girls, Inc: Asp (also as Ice Princess), Black Mamba (both also as Femizon enforcers), Paladin (also as Asp & Whiteout), Quasar (bts, transports Sterility Seed Rockets to Uranus, during Q #26, '91); Vision (last in Cap #389, '91, next in Dlk #4, '91)
SUPPORTING CAST: Avengers Crew: Peggy Carter (last in Cap #388, '91), Col. John Jameson (last in Cap #389, '91, next in Cap #395, '91); Rachel Leighton (also as Iron Maiden)
VILLAINS: Superia (next bts in Cap #394/2, '91), her lieutenants: Dr. Nightshade (bts, next in Cap #402, '92), Snapdragon (bts, next in Cap #411, '93), Iron Maiden (next in Cap #411, '93); & her Femizons: Anaconda, Frenzy, Gladiatrix, Knockout, Poundcakes, Screaming Mimi, Vertigo (prev 7 bts, next in Cap #411, '93), Bloodlust, Mindblast (both bts, next in MKSM #6, '04), Dansen Macabre, Gypsy Moth (both bts, next in AWC #76, '91), Black Lotus, Chimera, Karisma (prev 3 bts) Mysteria (prev 4 last app), Ice Princess, Wrangler (both next in FearIt:HF #1, '11), Arclight (next in XMan #13, '96), Battleaxe (bts, next in Cap #394/2, '91), Bombshell (next in PPSSM Ann #12, '92), Dragoness (bts, next in Cable #1, '92), Dragonfly (bts, next in IM Ann #12/4, '91), Ferocia (next in Cap #402, '92), Golddigger (bts, next in Cap #394, '91), Impala (bts, next in Cap #395, '91), Ion (bts, next in Q #52, '93), MODAM (bts, next bts in Cap #411, '93), Pink Pearl (bts, next in AFlt #105, '92), Princess Python (bts, next in MCP #97/4, '92), Quicksand (bts, next in WoSM #107, '93), Steel Wind (bts, next bts in Cap #394, '91), Titania (bts, next in Thor #436, '91), Vapor (bts, next in Dhawk #6, '91), Water Witch (bts, next in IM Ann #12, '91), Whiplash (bs, next in HFH #4, '97), Whiteout (next in XMU #6, '94), Yellowjacket (bts, next in GotG #28, '92); & her Femizon Enforcers
OTHER CHARACTERS: Superia's female recruits inc assistants
LOCATIONS/ITEMS: Femizonia Island inc command center & infirmary, Atlantic Ocean; Superia's hover-platform & Sterility Seed rockets, Feminzonia Island's force field, Mysteria's Mist-Sticks, boat, Avengers Quinjet
SYNOPSIS: With her Sterility Seed rockets launching into orbit, Superia leaves Captain America to deal with four of her Femizons: Arclight, Bombshell, Mysteria and Wrangler. As Cap fights them off, Asp and Paladin find Diamondback; as they escape, four more Femizons: Ferocia, Ice Princess, Iron Maiden and Whiteout fail at defeating them. Emerging victorious, Cap has Black Mamba use her power in a new way to disguise him as Superia. He infiltrates the command center and gets a message out to Peggy Carter. Superia discovers Cap's deceit and Cap quickly takes their battle outside. Cap provokes Superia into firing an energy blast that disrupts Femizonia's protective barrier; Superia retreats to deactivate her Sterility Rockets. Shortly, Cap meets with Black Mamba, Asp, Paladin and Diamondback and the group commandeers one of Superia's boats to escape, and Vision picks them up in an Avengers Quinjet. Cap learns that Quasar has harmlessly hauled the Sterility Seed rockets to Uranus.
NOTE: Cover-labeled "The Superia Stratagem Part Six of Six."

CAPTAIN AMERICA #393 (October 1991)

"Prolog: The Skeleton Crew" (7 pages)
"Skullbound" (15 pages)

CREDITS: Mark Gruenwald (writer), Larry Alexander (pencils pages 1-7), Rik Levins (pencils pages 8-22), Bud LaRosa (inks pages 1-7), Danny Bulanadi (inks pages 8-22, c inks), Joe Rosen (letters), Renee Witterstaetter (colors), Len Kaminski (asst editor), Ralph Macchio (editor), Ron Lim (c pencils)
FEATURE CHARACTER: Captain America
GUEST STARS: Schutz Heiligruppe: Hauptmann Deutschland (last in Cap #391/2, '91), Blitzkrieger (last in Cap #391/2, '91, next in Cap #442, '95); Paladin (next in MCP #86/4, '91), BAD Girls, Inc: Asp, Black Mamba
SUPPORTING CAST: Avengers Crew: Fabian Stankowicz (last in Av #332, '91, last bts in Av #333, '91, next in Cap #408/2, '92), Peggy Carter (next in Av #341, '91), Edwin Jarvis (last in Cap #387, '91); Bernie Rosenthal (last in Cap #386, '91), Rachel Leighton
VILLAINS: Red Skull (last in Cap#391/2, '91) & his Skeleton Crew: Crossbones, Machinesmith, Mother Night (prev 3 last in Cap #391/2, '91), 4th Sleeper (last in Cap #391/2, '91, next in Cap #409, '93); Arnim Zola (last in Cap #387/2, '91) & his bioplastoids: Secondus (also as Thor), Tertius (also as Iron Man), Quatrus (also as Captain America & Red Skull corpse) (prev 3 1st); Doughboy (also as an Avengers Quinjet, last in Cap #383/4, '91, next in Cap #395, '91); Zeitgeist (also in Schutz Heiligruppe, last in Cap #390/2, '91, next in Cap #442, '95)
OTHER CHARACTERS: Mr. Buehller, Mr. Leiberthal, German war crime trial judge (all last in Cap #391/2, '91, last app), jury, witnesses & crew; Ilsa Schultz (bts, on phone w/Red Skull, last voice only in Cap #376, '90, next in Cap #395, '91), Paladin's chauffeur
LOCATIONS/ITEMS: German airplane hangar, Avengers Mansion, Washington DC inc White House & Smith Building w/Skull's office, Skeleton Crew's ship (destroyed), Avengers Quinjet, Paladin's limo, Red Skull's luger, Cap's Avengers ID, sky-cycle & decoder key, Hauptmann Deutschland's weapons harness w/ball bearings grenade & cable-gun
SYNOPSIS: Machinesmith frees Red Skull and the Skeleton Crew. Red Skull denies that he's the original Skull and declares the trial a travesty of justice. Suddenly, the Avengers crash through the ceiling and demand that the Skull be handed over to their custody. When they leave, Arnim Zola reveals the Avengers to be his bioplastoids and their Quinjet to be Doughboy. Machinesmith remote detonates their ship, still in the Schutz Heiligruppe's hands. Meanwhile, Paladin leaves Avengers Mansion with BAD Girls, Inc and Captain America notices that Col. Jameson is missing. Jarvis deflects a visit from Bernie as Diamondback tells Cap that she's retiring from adventuring. Hauptmann Deutschland calls Cap to verify the Skull is in his custody, but Cap has no idea what he's talking about. Meanwhile, Red Skull evacuates the Smith Building. That night

Cap looks for Red Skull at the Smith Building, but the arriving Hauptmann Deutschland assumes Cap is the same imposter he met earlier and attacks. The battle takes the pair inside the Smith Building, where they find Red Skull's corpse.
NOTE: Title returns to monthly status. Red Skull's corpse is revealed to be a bioplastoid in Cap #395, '91.

CAPTAIN AMERICA #394 (November 1991)

"The Crimson Crusade" (18 pages)

CREDITS: Mark Gruenwald (writer), Rik Levins (pencils), Bud LaRosa (inks), Joe Rosen (letters), Renee Witterstaetter, Marie Javins (colors), Len Kaminski (asst editor), Ralph Macchio (editor)
FEATURE CHARACTER: Captain America (also in WI #28, InfG #1-3, SS #52, SS #54, InfG #4, SS #57, InfG #6, DC #4, Av #341-342, Thor #436, Av #343, WM #5, Av #344, all '91, next in Cap Ann #11/2, '92)
GUEST STARS: Avengers: Quasar (last in InfG #6, '91, next in Q #28, '91), Sersi (last in Av #344, '91, next in Thor #437, '91); Hauptmann Deutschland (also in rfb, next in Cap #442, '95 as Vormund)
SUPPORTING CAST: Rachel Leighton (chr next in Cap Ann #11/2, '92, next in Cap #394/2, '91), Edwin Jarvis (also in Av #343-344, '91, next in Cap #397, '91), Bernie Rosenthal
VILLAINS: Red Skull (also in rfb), his Division Chiefs: Baron Strucker (last in Cap #387/2, '91, next in DD #298, '91), Crucible (last in Cap #368, '90, next in Cap #426, '94), Minister Blood (last in Av #325, '90, last app), Number Seven of the Secret Empire (last in MSMK #24, '91, next in ASM #353, '91), Power Broker (last in Cap #378/2, '90, chr next in USAgent #3, '01 fb, next bts in USAgent #1, '01, next in USAgent #2, '01), Scourge (rogue, also in pfb, last in Cap #350, '89, dies, last app), Sin (last in Cap #357, '89, chr next in Cap #15, '06 fb, next in Cap #9, '05), Taskmaster (last bts in Cap #388/2, '91, next in Cap #396, '92), Watchdog Prime (last in Cap #386, '91, last app), Arnim Zola; & his Skeleton Crew: Crossbones (fired from the Skeleton Crew), Machinesmith (next in Cap #396, '92), Mother Night; Viper (last in Av Ann #18, '89), Zola's bioplastoids: Secondus (as Crossbones corpse, also as Thor in rfb), Tertius (as Mother Night corpse, also as Iron Man in rfb) (both also in pfb), Quatrus (as Red Skull corpse, also as Captain America in rfb) (prev 3 last app), Gamecock (last in Cap #371, '90, next in W #167, '01), Shocker (last in DFSM #3, '91, chr last in SMFam:AF, '06, next in MCP #97/4, '92), Steel Wind (last bts in Cap #392, '91, next in Cap #394/2, '91) (prev 3 bts, eluded Scourge), Sweat Shop (Bongert, LaGraves, Leaman, Pucci & "Mophandle 9" named)
OTHER CHARACTERS: Black Abbott (last in MTU #148, '84), Lionfang (Alejandro Cortez, last in LC #13, '73), Wrench (Kurt Klemmer, last in Omega #6, '77) (all bts, killed by Scourge, last app), Derek Freeman (FBI agent, last in Av #286, '87), other FBI agents, paramedics, police, Federal penitentiary guards; Blitzkrieger, Mr. Leiberthal (both in rfb)
LOCATIONS/ITEMS: Washington DC inc Smith Building, White House & Washington Monument, Avengers Mansion inc Diamondback's room & gym, Red Skull's Rocky Mountains hideaway inc Red Skull's office, meeting room & Crossbones' room, Virginia Federal penitentiary inc Viper's cell, Red Skull's gas chamber, Cap's sky-cycle, Sweat Shop's airship & jet-packs, Federal penitentiary guards' guns
FLASHBACKS: "The Avengers" bringing the Red Skull into their custody (Cap #393, '91). Scourge "kills" Crossbones and Mother Night (p).
SYNOPSIS: Captain America finds the apparent bodies of Crossbones and Mother Night. Hauptmann Deutschland and Cap tell Derek Freeman what they know while the bodies are taken to the morgue. Meanwhile at his Rocky Mountain hideaway, Red Skull gloats at his subterfuge. The Skull holds a meeting with his Division Chiefs, who update him on their recent activities. Red Skull kills his Scourge for failing to kill Gamecock, Shocker and Steel Wind. Cap returns to Avengers Mansion where Rachel asks to join the Avengers Staff, possibly as Cap's executive secretary. Red Skull orders his Skeleton Crew to break Viper from federal custody; when Crossbones questions him the Skull fires Crossbones. Later, Cap works out with Sersi and Quasar before Bernie Rosenthal arrives to tell Cap she got a job as a lawyer. Cap introduces Bernie to Rachel. The Sweat Shop breaks Viper out of prison and presents her to Red Skull.

2ND STORY: "The Face of Fear" (5 pages)
CREDITS: Mark Gruenwald (writer), Larry Alexander (pencils), Dan Panosian (inks), Dave Sharpe (letters), Renee Witterstaetter, Marie Javins (colors), Len Kaminski (asst editor), Ralph Macchio (editor)
FEATURE CHARACTERS: BAD Girls, Inc: Asp, Black Mamba (both also in Cap #395, '91, also & next in Cap #395/2, '91)
GUEST STAR: Impala (off-panel, last bts in Cap #392, '91, also & next in Cap #395, '91 & Cap #395/2, '91)
SUPPORTING CAST: Rachel Leighton (last in Cap #394, '91, chr last in Cap Ann #11/2, '92)
VILLAINS: Superia (bts, put bounty on BAD Girls, Inc, last in Cap #392, '91, next in Cap #411, '93), Battleaxe, Golddigger (both last bts in Cap #392, '91), Steel Wind (last bts in Cap #394, '91) (all also in Cap #395, '91, also & next in Cap #395/2, '91), Crossbones (last & also in Cap #395, '91, also & next in Cap #395/2, '91), Wrecking Crew: Wrecker (last in FF #355, '91, next in AFlt #118, '93), Thunderball (last in FF #355, '91, next in ASM #353, '91), Bulldozer, Piledriver (both last in Thor #430, '91, next in AFlt #118, '93), Blacklash (last in Hulk Ann #17/5, '91, next in MCP #97/4, '92), Princess Python (last bts in Cap #392, '91, next in MCP #97/4, '92)
OTHER CHARACTERS: Michael O'Brien (last in Q #28, '91, next in NW #22, '92), Roscoe (bartender, 1st, also in Cap #395, '91, also & next in Cap #395/2, '91), Snapdragon (in Black Mamba's illusion), taxi driver, Bar patrons, bystanders; Hulk, Iron Man, Thor (prev 3 statues)
LOCATIONS/ITEMS: Avengers Mansion, the Bar; Black Mamba's Bar passcard
SYNOPSIS: BAD Girls, Inc stops by Avengers Mansion to pick up their replacement costumes and visit Rachel Leighton. Rachel reminds them she's given up a life of adventure, but Black Mamba tricks Rachel into revealing that Snapdragon's attack caused her retirement. Outraged that her friends would trick her, Rachel has O'Brien escort them out. BAD Girls, Inc go to the Bar looking for a lead on Snapdragon's whereabouts, but Battleaxe, Golddigger and Steel Wind stop them; they're looking to collect the ten thousand dollar bounty Superia put on BAD Girls, Inc.
NOTE: Story overlaps with Cap #395, '91 & Cap #395/2, '91. Roscoe's name is revealed in Cap #395, '91. The Bar is on Varick and 10th.

CAPTAIN AMERICA #395 (December 1991)

"Rogues in the House" (17 pages)

CREDITS: Mark Gruenwald (writer), Rik Levins (pencils), Danny Bulanadi (inks), Joe Rosen (letters), Marie Javins (colors), Len Kaminski (asst editor), Ralph Macchio (editor)

FEATURE CHARACTER: Captain America (also in Q #28-29, '91)

GUEST STARS: Avengers: Hercules (during Q #28, '91), Quasar (also in photo, also voice only recorded between Thor #437, '91 & Q #28, '91; during Q #28, '91), Rage (voice only, recorded between Av #342, '91 & NW #22, '92), Sersi (also in photo, voice only, recorded between Et #1, '91 & Av #344, '91), Thor (Eric Masterson, also in photo, last in Thor #430, '91, also in Q #28, '91), Vision (voice only, recorded between Av #344, '91 & Cap #396/2, '91); BAD Girls, Inc: Asp (off-panel), Black Mamba (both last & also in Cap #394/2, '91, also & next in Cap #395/2, '91), Impala (last & also off-panel in Cap #394/2, '91, also & next in Cap #395/2, '91)

SUPPORTING CAST: Avengers Crew: Peggy Carter (last in Av #341, '91), Col. John Jameson (last in Cap #392, '91); Bernie Rosenthal (next in Cap #404, '92), Rachel Leighton

VILLAINS: Red Skull (last in NF:AoS #26, '91), Crossbones (also off-panel in Cap #394/2, '91, also in next in Cap #395/2, '91), Battleaxe Golddigger Steel Wind (off-panel) (prev 3 last & also in Cap #394/2, '91, also & next in Cap #395/2, '91), 8-Ball (Jeff Hagees, engineer specializing in propulsion systems, last in Sleep #2, '91, next in Sleep #19, '92), Oddball (Elton Healy, juggler, last in AvS #25, '89, next in Hawk #1, '98), Cutthroat (Daniel Leighton, assassin, last in MTU #89, '80, see NOTE), Deathstroke (Tani Uiruson, assassin, last in SW #39, '81, dies last app), Mangler (last in Cap #364/2, '89, dies, last app), Doughboy (last in Cap #393, '91), Mother Night, Viper, Arnim Zola

OTHER CHARACTERS: Derek Freeman (next in CM #1, '95), Ilsa Schultz (last bts in Cap #393, '91, last app), Roscoe (last & also in Cap #394/2, '91, also & next in Cap #395/2, '91), Dr. Miles Lipton (bts, performing synaptic analysis, last in AvS #40, '91, next in Av #348, '92), taxi driver, Bar patrons, bystanders; Jerry Cooney, Ken Norton (both boxers, on poster)

LOCATIONS/ITEMS: New York inc the Bar & Avengers Mansion w/gym, Cap's office & library, Skull-House, Red Skull's Rocky Mountain hideaway inc spa & training room; Cap's sky-cycle, Col. Jameson's car

FLASHBACK: Quasar, Rage, Sersi and Vision each record separate debrief logs.

SYNOPSIS: Captain America works out with Rachel, gets caught up on paperwork and learns from agent Freeman that the Red Skull corpse's fingerprints match Cap's, and just may be the real thing. At his Rocky Mountain chalet, Viper joins Red Skull in the hot tub to brainstorm new ideas of anarchy, which upsets Mother Night. Crossbones goes to the Bar for a drink, but leaves when a fight breaks out. At Avengers Mansion, Rachel is surprised when Col. Jameson arrives; she explains she's trying out for an Avengers Staff position and he makes a pass at her. Cap debriefs Thor, Hercules and Quasar on their recent adventures. Cutthroat, Deathstroke and Mangler apply for Crossbones' position in Red Skull's Skeleton Crew. Mother Night instructs them to fight to the death. Cap and Thor look for Red Skull at Skull-House, but are quickly captured by Doughboy. Arnim Zola tells them the Skull is dead. As Cutthroat emerges as the only survivor, Col. Jameson drives Rachel to class. Crossbones spies on them from afar.

NOTE: Cap #406/2, '92 reveals Cutthroat as Diamondback's brother. Story overlaps with Cap #394/2, '91 & Cap #395/2, '91. When Cap gets caught up on paperwork, he listens to Avengers debrief logs; Sersi reports on the events of Et #1, '91, Quasar on the events of Thor #437, '91, Rage on the Martinez beating seen in Av #341-342, '91, and Vision on assisting Dr. Miles Lipton in synaptic analysis first seen in AvS #40, '91.

2ND STORY: "The Big Brawl" (5 pages)

CREDITS: Mark Gruenwald (writer), Larry Alexander (art), Dave Sharpe (letters), Greg Wright (colors)

FEATURE CHARACTERS: BAD Girls, Inc: Impala (joins BAD Girls, Inc), Asp, Black Mamba (all last & also in Cap #394/2, '91, also in Cap #395, '91)

VILLAINS: Battleaxe (next in Cap #411, '93), Golddigger (next in Cap #428, '94), Steel Wind (next in SoV #7, '93) (all last & also in Cap #394/2, '91, also in Cap #395, '91), Crossbones (during & also in Cap #395, '91, also in Cap #394/2, '91)

OTHER CHARACTERS: Roscoe (last & also in Cap #394/2, '91, also in Cap #395, '91, last app), Bar patrons

LOCATIONS/ITEMS: The Bar; Battleaxe's axes

SYNOPSIS: Battleaxe, Golddigger and Steel Wind attack BAD Girls, Inc. Impala joins the fight and allows BAD Girls, Inc to escape. Impala follows them out, explains she helped because the odds were unfair, and joins BAD Girls, Inc.

NOTE: Story overlaps with Cap #394/2, '91 & Cap #395, '91.

CAPTAIN AMERICA #396 (January 1992)

"Trick or Treat" (17 pages)

CREDITS: Mark Gruenwald (writer), Rik Levins (pencils), Danny Bulanadi (inks), Joe Rosen (letters), Christie Scheele (colors), Len Kaminski (asst editor), Ralph Macchio (editor)

FEATURE CHARACTER: Captain America

GUEST STAR: Thor

SUPPORTING CAST: Avengers Crew: Peggy Carter (bts, relaying messages between Cap & Thor, next in Cap #396/2, '92), Col. John Jameson; Rachel Leighton

VILLAINS: Red Skull & his Skeleton Crew: Cutthroat (joins Skeleton Crew), Machinesmith (next in Cap #398/2, '92), Mother Night, Blackwing (Joseph Manfredi, controls bats, last in DD #123, '75), Jack O' Lantern (Steven Mark Levins, causes hallucinations, also in Cap's hallucination, 1st), Taskmaster (last in Cap #394, '91, next in Cap Ann #11/3, '92), Arnim Zola (next in Cap #437, '95), Doughboy (next in W #139, '99), Crossbones, Viper

OTHER CHARACTERS: Red Skull's waiter, taxi driver, bystanders, Blackwing's bats

LOCATIONS/ITEMS: Skull-House inc basement & Devil's Lake, Haltech Building, Red Skull's Rocky Mountain hideaway inc training room & tavern; Cutthroat's knives, Col. Jameson's car, Cap's Avengers ID, Jack O' Lantern's pogo platform & hallucinogen bomb, Blackwing's glider throwing stars

SYNOPSIS: Arnim Zola orders Doughboy to drown Captain America and Thor in Devil's Lake. Meanwhile, Taskmaster trains Cutthroat to replace Crossbones. Thor breaks free from Doughboy and Cap returns to Skull-House to find it gone. Elsewhere, Col. Jameson drops Rachel off at class and kisses her. Rachel tells him not to pick her up after class. Cap looks around Skull-House's basement only to find Blackwing and Jack O' Lantern already there, looking to loot the place. Cap attacks. Zola reports to the Skull that he's shrunken Skull-House, and Red Skull tells him to bring it to his chalet. Jack O' Lantern hits Cap with an hallucinogen bomb. Rachel leaves her class, only for Crossbones to kidnap her.

NOTE: Jack O' Lantern's real name is revealed in NAvF, '06.

2ND STORY: "Where to Begin" (5 pages)

CREDITS: Mark Gruenwald (writer), Larry Alexander (pencils), Dan Panosian (inks), Steve Dutro (letters), Dan Slott (colors), Len Kaminski (asst editor), Ralph Macchio (editor)

FEATURE CHARACTERS: BAD Girls, Inc.: Asp, Black Mamba, Impala (all also as snakes)

GUEST STARS: Avengers: Crystal (between Av #344-345, '91), Vision (last voice only in Cap #395, '91, chr next in Slap #4, '93, next in Av #345, '91) (both bts, on the moon), Sersi (last in Thor #437, '91)

OTHER CHARACTER: Peggy Carter (last bts in Cap #396, '92)

LOCATIONS/ITEMS: South Bronx inc abandoned Serpent Society HQ; Serpent Saucer, Impala's staffs (also as flowers), Sersi's Avengers ID

SYNOPSIS: BAD Girls, Inc break into the former Serpent Society HQ hoping to find information on Snapdragon, but their activity sets off an alarm at Avengers Mansion. Peggy Carter sends Sersi to investigate. Upset the power is out and they can't find a lead on Snapdragon, BAD Girls, Inc decide to take a Serpent Saucer. Sersi arrives, upset that she's missing a party. Not knowing who Sersi is, BAD Girls, Inc attacks, and Sersi turns them into snakes. Peggy suggests Sersi find out why they were there in the first place, Sersi turns Black Mamba back to normal to interrogate her.

CAPTAIN AMERICA #397 (February 1992)

"Shot in the Dark" (17 pages)

CREDITS: Mark Gruenwald (writer), Rik Levins (pencils), Danny Bulanadi (inks), Steve Dutro (letters), Christie Scheele (colors), Lan Kaminski (asst editor), Ralph Macchio (editor)

FEATURE CHARACTER: Captain America (next in ASM #354, '91, Thor #444, '92, MHol/5, '91, Slap #4, '93, Av Ann #21/2, '92, DHII #4, '93)

GUEST STAR: Thor (next in Thor #438, '91)

SUPPORTING CAST: Avengers Crew: Edwin Jarvis (last in Cap #394, '91, next bts in FF #359, '91, next in Q #34, '92), Col. John Jameson; Rachel Leighton (next in Cap #399/2, '92)

VILLAINS: Red Skull & his Skeleton Crew: Mother Night (also as Scourge), Cutthroat; Jack O' Lantern (also in Cap's hallucination), Blackwing, Viper (also as snake woman in Mother Night's hallucination) (all next in Cap #398/2, '92), Crossbones (next in Cap #399/2, '92)

OTHER CHARACTERS: Blackwing's bats; giant bat, pumpkin monsters, skeletons (prev 3 in Cap's hallucination)

LOCATIONS/ITEMS: Skull-House inc basement and sewers, Red Skull's Rocky Mountain hideaway inc living quarters, Cutthroat's quarters & torture room; Avengers Mansion inc John's quarters, abandoned 91st Street subway station; Jack O' Lantern's pogo platform & bombs, Blackwing's glider, Red Skull's communications card, plastic force bubble & wheel of sorrow (recreational torture device), Cutthroat's knives, Cap's Avengers ID, Crossbones' knife

SYNOPSIS: As Cap hallucinates, Jack O' Lantern and Blackwing try to kill him. Red Skull watches the fight from his chalet and orders Mother Night to recruit them; she gets Cutthroat and leaves. Cap fights off Jack O' Lantern and Blackwing through his hallucinations. When Blackwing tries to escape he finds they're trapped by a plastic force bubble; he and Jack head for the sewers to find another way out. Col. Jameson returns to Avengers Mansion, not knowing why he kissed Cap's girlfriend. Cap finally shakes off the hallucinogen's effects and looks for Blackwing and Jack O' Lantern. Red Skull uses his personal torture devices to flirt with Viper. Cap defeats Blackwing and Jack and calls Thor for a pick-up, but the villains are suddenly shot by Scourge. Cap attacks with Jack's hallucinogen bomb and learns Scourge is actually Mother Night. Jack and Blackwing escape, their death only an illusion. Cap is satisfied that he now knows the Skull is not dead. In an abandoned subway station, Crossbones begins to torture Rachel.

2ND STORY: "Snake-Off" (5 pages)

CREDITS: Mark Gruenwald (writer), Larry Alexander (pencils), Dan Panosian (inks), Steve Dutro (letters), Marie Javins (colors), Len Kaminski (asst editor), Ralph Macchio (editor)

FEATURE CHARACTERS: BAD Girls, Inc: Asp, Impala (both also as snakes, next in Cap #411, '93), Black Mamba (next in NW #33, '93)

GUEST STAR: Sersi (next bts in Av #340, '91, next in Av #344, '92)

OTHER CHARACTERS: Peggy Carter (bts, verifies Mamba's ID for Sersi, chr next in Slap #4, '93, next in NW #22, '92); Telemachus (in Black Mamba's illusion)

LOCATIONS/ITEMS: Abandoned Serpent Society HQ, Atlantic Ocean; Sersi's Avengers ID, Serpent Saucer

SYNOPSIS: Black Mamba points out that Sersi never identified herself as an Avenger. With Peggy Carter's help Sersi quickly verifies BAD Girls, Inc's identities and tells them to leave. Sersi threatens to turn them into something worse than snakes when Black Mamba asks to take the Serpent Saucer; Black Mamba says if Sersi just lets them have what they want she can return to her party. Sersi obliges, and BAD Girls, Inc leave for Europe to get some mercenary work and look for leads on Snapdragon.

CAPTAIN AMERICA #398 (March 1992)

"Operation: Galactic Storm Part 1: It Came From Outer Space" (18 pages)

CREDITS: Mark Gruenwald (writer), Rik Levins (pencils), Danny Bulanadi (inks), Joe Rosen (letters), Christie Scheele (colors), Len Kaminski (asst editor), Ralph Macchio (editor)
FEATURE CHARACTER: Captain America (also in Rick's dream as Supreme Intelligence & in Delphi's image, next in AWC #80, Q #32, WM #7, Av #345, IM #278, all '92)
GUEST STARS: Rick Jones (also as Bucky in Delphi's image, last in Hulk #392, '92, next in AWC #80, '92), Hulk (voice only, between Hulk #392-393, '92), Delphi (precog, last in Hulk #386, '91, next in Cage #9, '92), Imperial Guard: Warstar (B'nee & C'cll, mechanoid symbiote unit, last in UXM #275, '91), Oracle (voice only, last in UXM #277, '91), Tempest (voice only, last in UXM #275, '91) (prev 3 next in AWC #80, '92)
SUPPORTING CAST: Avengers Crew: Peggy Carter (last in NW #22, '92, next in Q #32, '92), Col. John Jameson (next bts in Cap #402, '92 as Man-Wolf)
VILLAINS: Supreme Intelligence (last in SS #31, next in WM #7, '92), Supremor (physical manifestation of Supreme Intelligence, 1st)
OTHER CHARACTERS: Kree (in Rick's dream), diner staff & patrons
LOCATIONS/ITEMS: Hala (also in Rick's dream) inc Harfax (industrial city-state) w/Hecnic Vault (precious metals salvaging center), Pantheon inc Rick's room, Avengers Mansion inc communications center, Benson, AZ diner; Nega Bomb (in Rick's dream), Cap's modified Quinjet, sky cycle & Avengers ID, Imperial Guard ship
SYNOPSIS: Rick Jones wakes from a dream where the Kree are destroyed and Captain America turns into the Supreme Intelligence. After talking with the Pantheon's precog Delphi, he decides to warn Cap. Cap and John leave to meet with Rick, but John is antagonistic during the flight to Cap's surprise. During the meeting, Warstar of the Imperial Guard attacks Rick. While Cap battles Warstar, Rick escapes, only to be captured by two other Imperial Guard members; they plan to use him against the Supreme Intelligence. Meanwhile, Supreme Intelligence creates Supremor, a robotic surrogate for himself. He plans to form the Kree Starforce to further his plans for the Kree Empire.
NOTE: Start of the "Operation: Galactic Storm" crossover running through the Avengers-related titles. Continued into AWC #80, '92. Rick's dream is a prophecy; a Nega-Bomb destroys the Kree in Av #347, '92, and the Supreme Intelligence nearly absorbs Cap in Cap #400, '92.

2ND STORY: "Silence of the Night" (5 pages)
CREDITS: Mark Gruenwald (writer), Larry Alexander (pencils), Dan Panosian (inks), Steve Dutro (letters), Renee Witterstaetter (colors), Len Kaminski (asst editor), Ralph Macchio (editor)
FEATURE CHARACTERS: Skeleton Crew: Mother Night, Cutthroat (both next in Cap #402/2, '92), Machinesmith (last in Cap #396, '92, next in Cap #409, '92), Batwing, Jack O' Lantern (both join Skeleton Crew, next in Cap #405/2, '92)
VILLAINS: Red Skull (next bts in Cap #402/2, '92), Viper (next in ASM #366, '92)
OTHER CHARACTERS: Batwing's bats, police
LOCATIONS/ITEMS: Upstate New York inc police station, Red Skull's Rocky Mountain chalet inc helipad & lounge; Cutthroat's knives, Skeleton Crew's ship
SYNOPSIS: Cutthroat, Batwing and Jack O' Lantern prepare to break Mother Night out of jail, but she's released on bail before they can. They return to Red Skull where the Skull punishes Mother Night for being seen by Captain America. She begs to be killed for failing him, but Red Skull leaves her alive for future punishments.

CAPTAIN AMERICA #399 (April 1992)

"Operation: Galactic Storm Part 8: Twenty Million Light Years From Earth" (18 pages)

CREDITS: Mark Gruenwald (writer), Rik Levins (pencils), Danny Bulanadi (inks), Joe Rosen (letters), Christie Scheele (colors), Pat Garrahy (asst editor), Ralph Macchio (editor), Don Hudson (c inks)
FEATURE CHARACTER: Captain America (also in photo & as Kree Accuser, next in Av #346, '92, IM #279, '92)
GUEST STARS: Avengers: Black Knight, Crystal, Hercules, Sersi (all last in IM #278, '92, next in Av #346, '92), Goliath (Barton), Iron Man (both between IM #278-279, '92)
VILLAINS: Ronan the Accuser (last in SS #25, '89), Korath the Pursuer (last in Q #32, '92), Ultimus (last in WM #7, '92), Supremor (all next in Av #346, '92), Shatterax (last in IM #278, '92, next in Q #33, '92), Kree Accusers & soldiers
OTHER CHARACTERS: Kree
LOCATIONS/ITEMS: Hala inc subterranean power station, landing dock & rest room; Avengers Quinjet, Cap's Avengers ID, Ronan's Universal Weapon, Korath's Beta-Batons & boot jets, Kree sky-cycles, guns & flying billboard
SYNOPSIS: On Hala, Shatterax hands the captive Avengers over to Ronan the Accuser. Following Captain America's cue, Sersi disguises the Avengers as Kree Accusers in a flash of light and claim the Avengers escaped. The Avengers retreat to a rest room and Iron Man demands to be returned to his original state. Without explaining that his armor is also his life support, he breaks from the group to fly reconnaissance solo, but Goliath insists on going with him. Meanwhile, Supremor meets with Shatterax, Korath and Ultimus with a plan to restore the Supreme Intelligence as leader of the Kree. Iron Man tells the Avengers to meet him at the government building, so they commandeer a flying billboard to get there. Korath spots them and attacks, but Cap quickly defeats him.
NOTE: Part of "Operation: Galactic Storm", continued from Thor #445, '92 and into AWC #81, '92.

2ND STORY: "Cross to Bear" (5 pages)
CREDITS: Mark Gruenwald (writer), Larry Alexander (pencils), Dan Panosian (inks), Steve Dutro (letters), Ed Lazellari (colors), Pat Garrahy

asst editor), Ralph Macchio (editor)
FEATURE CHARACTER: Diamondback (as Rachel Leighton, last in Cap #397, '92)
VILLAINS: Crossbones (last in Cap #397, '92), punk kids (Rob, Mug & Rip named, all die)
LOCATIONS/ITEMS: Subway station; handcuffs, Rob's & Mug's knives, Rip's pipes, Crossbones' crossbow & knife
SYNOPSIS: Crossbones leaves Rachel alone in the subway station to get some food. A group of punks happen by and start to attack the handcuffed Rachel, but Crossbones returns and kills them. Crossbones starts to interrogate Rachel about Captain America as he eats.

CAPTAIN AMERICA #400 (May 1992)

"Operation: Galactic Storm Part 15: Murder by Decree!" (20 pages)

CREDITS: Mark Gruenwald (writer), Rik Levins (pencils), Danny Bulanadi (inks), Joe Rosen (letters), Christie Scheele (colors), Pat Garrahy (asst editor), Ralph Macchio (editor), Dan Panosian (c inks)
FEATURE CHARACTER: Captain America (also in pfb, next in Av #347, '92)
GUEST STARS: Avengers: Black Knight, Crystal, Goliath (Barton), Hercules, Iron Man (all last in IM #279, '92, next in WM #9, '92)
VILLAINS: Supreme Intelligence (also in pfb, last in IM #279, '92, next in Av #347, '92), 2 Kree Accusers (in pfb)
OTHER CHARACTERS: Batroc, Crossbones, Flag-Smasher, King Cobra, Red Skull, Viper (all Supreme Intelligence's constructs), Kree corpses (also in pfb)
LOCATIONS/ITEMS: Hala inc Citadel of Judgment (rubble), outer space; Quinjet, Nega-Bomb, Shi'ar starship
FLASHBACK: Kree Accusers escort Captain America through the Citadel of Judgment to Supreme Intelligence, who prepares to assimilate Captain America into his gestalt consciousness (p).
SYNOPSIS: Captain America narrowly avoids an explosion that collapses the Citadel of Judgment, but he's trapped in the resulting rubble. Meanwhile, Iron Man reassures the Avengers they made the right decision to abandon Cap; because they had no time to save both Cap and the Kree Galaxy from the Nega-Bomb. Several of Cap's foes attack him, but he soon realizes they're not real when he asks Batroc to remove his mask; never having seen his real face, Batroc's face is a blank. The Supreme Intelligence reveals he constructed Cap's attackers, but curses Cap's innate desire for freedom. Meanwhile, the Nega-Bomb continues its path to the Kree Empire.
NOTE: Part of the "Operation: Galactic Storm" crossover running through the Avengers-related titles. Continued from Thor #446, '92, continued into AWC #82, '92. Front cover interior gatefold includes cover reproductions of Cap #100, 111, 132, 143, 188, 200, 228 & 241. Back cover interior gatefold includes cover reproductions of Cap #248, 254, 286, 300, 321, 332, 278 & 383.

2ND STORY: "Out in the Cold" (18 pages)
CREDITS: Mark Gruenwald (writer), Larry Alexander (pencils), Kathryn Bolinger (inks), Steve Dutro (letters), Marie Javins (colors), Pat Garrahy (asst editor), Ralph Macchio (editor)
FEATURE CHARACTERS: Falcon (last in AWC #81, '92), USAgent (last in AWC #82, '92)
GUEST STARS: Avengers ("Earth Force" during Galactic Storm): Mockingbird, Dr. Pym, Wasp (all between AWC #82-83, '92), Gilgamesh, She-Hulk (both last in AWC #81, '92), Spider-Woman (last in AWC #82, '92); D-Man (also in rfb, last in Cap #384, '91)
VILLAINS: Flag-Smasher (last in GR #6, '90, next bts in GR #50/2, '94, next in Cap #438, '95), ULTIMATUM (one also in rfb, Garrey, Strauss & Wilkins named)
OTHER CHARACTERS: Peggy Carter (last in Q #32, '92), Inuits, fish
LOCATIONS/ITEMS: Arctic Circle inc North Pole w/ULTIMATUM base, Project: Pegasus; Avengers Quinjet, ULTIMATUM's guns & doomsday device, Flag-Smasher's mace & gun, Pym Particles
FLASHBACK: While fighting ULTIMATUM, D-Man tries to destroy their doomsday device, but is caught in an explosion (Cap #349, '89).
SYNOPSIS: An aircraft flies over some Inuits fishing with Demolition Man. The mute D-Man leaves to follow the craft, and finds an ULTIMATUM base three days later, where Flag-Smasher recognizes him. Soon, Peggy Carter informs the Avengers that Flag-Smasher has D-Man and demands Captain America's presence. With Cap in space, Falcon and USAgent leave to handle it. Flag-Smasher is upset that the "imposter" Cap has been sent and orders him killed. USAgent uses Pym Particles to re-enlarge his shield and defeat his attackers while Falcon searches for D-Man. Meanwhile, Flag-Smasher inspects the ULTIMATUM doomsday device, determined not to repair or use it. Falcon rescues D-Man while USAgent attacks Flag-Smasher; their battle takes them outside where USAgent stops Flag-Smasher from falling over a cliff. Flag-Smasher refuses to be rescued by an imposter and causes an avalanche, but Falcon catches the falling USAgent on the roof of their Quinjet.

3RD STORY: "Crossing Back" (11 pages)
CREDITS: Mark Gruenwald (writer), Rik Levins (pencils), Dan Panosian (inks), Steve Dutro (letters), Gina Going (colors), Pat Garahy (asst editor), Ralph Macchio (editor)
FEATURE CHARACTER: Diamondback (as Rachel Leighton, also in fb to 1st chr app before Cap #319, '86 fb)
VILLAINS: Crossbones (also in fb as Brock Rumlow between Cap&Crb #1, '11 fb & Cap #403/2, '92 fb), Savage Crims (Brock's gang, in fb)
OTHER CHARACTERS: Daniel Leighton (in fb to 1st chr app before Cap #408/2, '92 fb), Ricky Leighton (in fb to 1st chr app before Cap #319, '86 fb), Willy Leighton (all Rachel's brothers), Mrs. Leighton (Rachels' mother) (both only app in fb), Crims' girlfriends, police (both in fb), rat; "Buttface" Buckley (mentioned, taught Rachel lock picking), Yancy Street Gang (mentioned, Savage Crims rivals)
LOCATIONS/ITEMS: New York inc Leighton home, Savage Crim's hangout (both in fb), subway station; Willy's wheelchair & rifle, Brock's knife, Rachel's lock pick (all in fb), Rachel's chains & cinderblock
FLASHBACK: The Leightons eat dinner, but Danny and Ricky leave to hang out with a gang despite their war veteran brother Willy's protests. Danny mouths off at the gang's leader, Brock Rumlow. Rachel accidentally saves Danny when she makes a racket spying on the gang. Rachel impresses Brock when she punches him and he tells her to leave. She later tries to break into the Crims hangout, but Brock is already there. He agrees to let her into the gang if she'll be his girlfriend for a few hours. Ricky and Danny later see that Rachel has a black eye and confront

Brock. When Brock refuses knowledge, Ricky and Willy try to kill Brock. Brock kills Willy, Danny runs away to never be heard from again, and Ricky goes wild, and is later killed while robbing a grocery store.
SYNOPSIS: Crossbones sleeps in the subway as the handcuffed Rachel picks up a cinderblock to crush his head. She decides not to kill Crossbones, because Captain America wouldn't understand.

4TH STORY: "Captain America Joins… the Avengers!" (23 pages)
CREDITS: Mike Rockwitz (colors) for other credits see original entry.
NOTE: Reprinted from Av #4, '64. Numbering removed from pages 2-16 and pages 6-7 are in reverse order.

CAPTAIN AMERICA #401 (June 1992)

"After the Storm" (22 pages)

CREDITS: Mark Gruenwald (writer), Rik Levins (pencils), Danny Bulanadi (inks), Joe Rosen (letters), Christie Scheele, Gina Going (colors), Pat Garrahy (asst editor), Ralph Macchio (editor)
FEATURE CHARACTER: Captain America (also in rfb as the Captain & Kree Accuser, also in Q #35, '92, next in NW #26, '92)
GUEST STARS: Avengers: Crystal, Hercules (also in rfb) (both next in NW #26), Hawkeye (also as Goliath), Wonder Man (both also in rfb, next in Cage #6), Living Lightning, Scarlet Witch (both next bts in Cage #8, next in InfW #1), Black Knight (also in rfb, next in KoP #2), Captain Marvel (next in Cap #408/3), Iron Man (also in rfb, next in KoP #1), Quasar (next in Q #35), Sersi (also in rfb, next in Av #350/2), Starfox (next in SS Ann #5/3), Thor (Masterson, also in rfb, next in FF #367), Vision (also in rfb, next bts in Cage #8, next in NW #26) (all last in Av #347), Dr. Pym (last in AWC #83, next in InfW #1), Mockingbird (last in AWC #83, next in InfW #2), Spider-Woman (last in AWC #82, next in InfW #1), Wasp (last in AWC #83, next in FF #367), Black Widow (last in Av #345), Falcon (next in Cap Ann #11/3), She-Hulk (next in SenSH #38), USAgent (next in MCP #104/4) (all '92), Gilgamesh (next in FFU #10, '95)
SUPPORTING CAST: Avengers Crew: Edwin Jarvis (last in Q #34, '92, next in Cap #403, '92), Peggy Carter; Dennis Dunphy, Rachel Leighton
VILLAIN: Crossbones
OTHER CHARACTERS: Laughing Morse Bar patrons (inc Avengers: Emma Peel & John Steed; Gomez Addams, Morticia Addams, Lurch, Humphrey Bogart, James Bond, Dagwood Bumstead, Albert Einstein, Minnesota Fats, Reid Fleming, Groucho Marx, Popeye the Sailor, Elvis Presley, Rod Serling, Dick Tracy & the Yellow Kid) & staff, gas station attendant; Avengers: Giant-Man, Hulk, Iron Man, Thor, Wasp (prev 5 statues), Shatterax, Kree, Vault Guardsman (prev 3 in rfb)
LOCATIONS/ITEMS: New York inc Laughing Morse Bar & Avengers Mansion inc Cap's room & office, meeting room, kitchen, communications center & lecture hall, New Jersey inc gas station & Magneto's fallout shelter, Hala (in rfb); Crossbones' stolen car, Black Widow's sky-cycle
FLASHBACKS: The Captain fails to stop Iron Man from deactivating the Vault Guardsmen armors (IM #228, '88). Captain America and Iron Man smooth over their professional lives, but not personal (IM #238, '89). Iron Man surrenders the Avengers to the Kree without consulting Cap (IM #279, '92). After Sersi disguises the Avengers, Iron Man goes solo without explaining his armor is also his life support (Cap #399, '92). Iron Man leads the Avengers to execute the Supreme Intelligence against Cap's wishes (Av #347, '92).
SYNOPSIS: Captain America offers to step down as Avengers chairman, but despite the majority of the group not agreeing with Cap's stance against the Supreme Intelligence's execution, no one votes for his proposal. After the meeting Quasar resigns from the Avengers and Peggy tells Cap that John Jameson has gone missing. That night, Cap holds an ethics seminar, but only Black Widow, Hawkeye and Scarlet Witch attend. Cap leaves and Thor arrives late. Hawkeye takes Cap out for a night on the town in an attempt to cheer him up. Meanwhile, Crossbones has Diamondback call the Avengers to tell Cap not to look for her. Tony Stark meets with Steve and Clint in a belated attempt to explain his actions during Galactic Storm. Black Widow investigates Diamondback's phone call but finds nothing while Crossbones imprisons Diamondback in Magneto's fallout shelter. Returning to Avengers Mansion, Steve is greeted by Falcon and USAgent, accompanied by Demolition Man. Steve is overjoyed at D-Man's return.
NOTE: Epilogue to the "Operation: Galactic Storm" crossover running through the Avengers-related titles. Continued from Av #347, '92.

CAPTAIN AMERICA #402 (Early July 1992)

"The Prowling" (17 pages)

CREDITS: Mark Gruenwald (writer), Rik Levins (pencils), Danny Bulanadi (inks), Joe Rosen (letters), Gina Going (colors), Pat Garrahy (asst editor), Ralph Macchio (editor)
FEATURE CHARACTER: Captain America
GUEST STARS: Black Widow (next in Av #350/2, '92), Dr. Druid (last in DrS #36, '91), Wolverine (last in MCP #116, '92), Wong (bts, spoke w/Peggy, between DrS #40-41, '92), Werewolf (last in MCP #113/4, '92), Wolfsbane (last in AFlt #107, '92, chr last in Cap #406, '92 fb) (both bts, Moonhunter's captives, see NOTE)
SUPPORTING CAST: Avengers Crew: Peggy Carter (next bts in Q #44, '93, next in Q #45, '93), Man-Wolf (bts, Moonhunter's captive, also in photo as John Jameson & in rfb, last in Cap #398, '92, see NOTE), Dennis Dunphy
VILLAINS: Druid (in shadows, last in Cap #256, '81), Dr. Nightshade (in shadows, last bts in Cap #392, '92), Ferocia (last in Cap #392, '91)

OTHER CHARACTERS: Moonhunter (Zachary Moonhunter, armored adventurer, 1st but chr last in Cap #406, '92 fb), J. Jonah Jameson (last in PPSSM #187, '92, next in ASM #362, '92), Dr. Mifune (Dr. Curt Conners' former ESU co-worker, only app), Starkesboro werewolves, werewolf victim (dies), reporter, paramedics, bystanders; Dr. Curt Connors (in photo & rfb), Spider-Man (in rfb); Dr. Strange (mentioned, unavailable for the indefinite future)

LOCATIONS/ITEMS: Starkesboro inc surrounding woods & Druid's lair w/Wolf Pit, New York inc Avengers Mansion w/gym & communications center, Daily Bugle w/JJJ's office & ESU science center (also in rfb), Dr. Druid's Boston suburb townhouse; Avengers exercise equipment, Moonhunter's whip & sky-cycle, Cap's sky-cycle, moonstone (rfb)

FLASHBACK: Spider-Man defeats Man-Wolf, who reverts to John Jameson when the Moonstone disintegrates (PPSSM Ann #3, '81).

SYNOPSIS: A werewolf kills a man and Wolverine investigates. Dennis is still unable to talk after his ordeal, which convinces Captain America to find the missing John Jameson and Diamondback. Cap hands the Avengers chairmanship over to Black Widow and takes a leave of absence from the Avengers. Peggy shows Cap a report on recent werewolf-related killings, giving Cap a lead on John, the former Man-Wolf. Cap learns the Man-Wolf's moonstone is missing from ESU, and that his father, J. Jonah Jameson, hasn't seen John in almost two years. Meanwhile, Moonhunter disciplines captured werewolves. With Dr. Strange unavailable, Cap recruits Dr. Druid. The two investigate the site of the latest murder where Ferocia attacks them. Suddenly, Moonhunter appears and snags Ferocia around the neck with his whip.

NOTE: Cover-labeled "Man and Wolf Part 1 of 6." Title goes bi-weekly with this issue. Werewolf is revealed to be bts in Cap #403, '92 and Man-Wolf and Wolfsbane in Cap #406, '92. Druid revealed to be in shadows in Cap #405, '92 and Nightshade in Cap #403, '92.

2ND STORY: "The Pit and the Pitiful" (5 pages)

CREDITS: Mark Gruenwald (writer), Larry Alexander (pencils), Ariane Lenshoek (inks, colors), Steve Dutro (letters), Pat Garrahy (asst editor), Ralph Macchio (editor)

FEATURE CHARACTER: Diamondback (as Rachel Leighton, also in rfb)

VILLAINS: Cutthroat (next in Cap #405/2, '92), Mother Night (next in Cap #407/2, '92), Red Skull (bts, abused Mother Night, next bts in DD #307, '92, next in ASM #366, '92) (all last in Cap #398/2, '92), Crossbones

OTHER CHARACTERS: Snapdragon (in rfb); Captain America (in Rachels's thoughts)

LOCATIONS/ITEMS: Magneto's fallout shelter, Red Skull's Rocky Mountain chalet inc Cutthroat's room; Crossbones' stolen car, Mother Night's sunglasses

FLASHBACK: Snapdragon almost kills Diamondback (Cap #390, '91).

SYNOPSIS: Crossbones begins to physically and mentally condition Rachel through torture; planing to use her to get back into Red Skull's good graces. Meanwhile, Cutthroat finds Mother Night bruised from "discipline" by the Skull and begins to romance her.

NOTE: Crossbones' torture includes constant exercise, starvation and claustrophobia; Cap #408/2, '92 implies he also uses rape.

CAPTAIN AMERICA #403 (Late July 1992)

"City of Wolves" (17 pages)

CREDITS: Mark Gruenwald (writer), Rik Levins (pencils), Danny Bulanadi (inks), Joe Rosen (letters), Gina Going (colors), Pat Garrahy (asst editor), Ralph Macchio (editor)

FEATURE CHARACTER: Captain America

GUEST STARS: Dr. Druid, Wolverine, Werewolf, Wolfsbane (bts, Moonhunter's captive)

SUPPORTING CAST: Avengers Crew: Dr. Keith Kincaid (last in Q #34, '92, next in Av #351, '92), Edwin Jarvis (last in Cap #401, '92), Man-Wolf (bts, Moonhunter's captive); Dennis Dunphy

VILLAINS: Druid (in shadows), Dr. Nightshade, Ferocia

OTHER CHARACTERS: Moonhunter, Starkesboro werewolves

LOCATIONS/ITEMS: Starkesboro inc surrounding woods, Druid's lair w/Nightshade's lab, Avengers Mansion medlab; Moonhunter's whip, sky-cycle, tranq darts, gun & shotgun, Cap's sky-cycle, Nightshade's wolf serum, moonstone

SYNOPSIS: Captain America battles Moonhunter, but fails to rescue Ferocia. Hiding, Wolverine watches Moonhunter bring Fercoia to Dr. Nightshade, who's creating a wolf serum from the Werewolf, Jack Russel. Meanwhile, Dr. Kincaid gives Dennis another check-up and tells Jarvis Dennis is suffering from selective amnesia. Cap returns to Dr. Druid and they continue the search for John. Nightshade reports to Druid, who reveals he has the reconstituted moonstone. He deduces the moonstone may be drawing werewolves to Starkesboro. Wolverine battles werewolf townsfolk until Moonhunter takes him down with three shotgun blasts. Cap and Dr. Druid arrive in Starkesboro only to be surrounded by werewolves.

NOTE: Cover-labeled "Man and Wolf Part 2 of 6."

2ND STORY: "Taken to Task" (5 pages)

CREDITS: Mark Gruenwald (writer), Larry Alexander (pencils), Ariane Lenshoek (inks, colors), Steve Dutro (letters), Pat Garrahy (asst editor), Ralph Macchio (editor)

FEATURE CHARACTER: Diamondback (as Rachel Leighton, also in fb between Cap #319, '86 fb & IM:L #7, '10)

VILLAINS: Crossbones (also in fb as "Mr. Brock" between Cap #400/3, '92 fb & Cap&Crb #1, '11 fb), Anaconda (in fb as Blanche Sitznski to 1st chr app before MTIO #64, '80), Snapdragon (in fb as Shoeke Sanada to 1st chr app before MFan #12, '84), Taskmaster (in fb between SW:O #3, '06 & bts in Av #194, '80) & his students (in fb)

LOCATIONS/ITEMS: Taskmaster's Academy of Criminal Arts and Sciences (in fb), Magneto's fallout shelter; Crossbones' rope

FLASHBACK: With her family gone, Rachel joins Taskmaster's school to learn self-defense. She quickly discovers one of the instructors is Brock Rumlow and tries to leave, but another instructor, Blanche, stops her and starts a scuffle. Rachel proves she can fight and Blanche allows her into the locker room. Rachel cuts her hair to disguise herself.

SYNOPSIS: Crossbones continues to mentally condition Rachel.

CAPTAIN AMERICA #404 (Early August 1992)

"Children of the Night" (18 pages)

CREDITS: Mark Gruenwald (writer), Rik Levins (pencils), Danny Bulanadi (co-inks, c inks), Donald Hudson, Raymond Kryssing (co-inks), Joe Rosen (letters), Gina Going (colors), Pat Garrahy (asst editor), Ralph Macchio (editor)
FEATURE CHARACTER: Captain America
GUEST STARS: Dr. Druid, Wolverine, Werewolf, Wolfsbane (both bts, Moonhunter's captives)
SUPPORTING CAST: Avengers Crew: Donna Maria Puentes (receptionist, last in Cap #212, '77), Man-Wolf (bts, Moonhunter's captive), Edwin Jarvis; Bernie Rosenthal (last in Cap #395, '91), Dennis Dunphy
VILLAINS: Druid (in shadows), Dr. Nightshade, Ferocia (bts, Moonhunter's captive)
OTHER CHARACTERS: Moonhunter, Starkesboro werewolves (some also as humans, Dougie named)
LOCATIONS/ITEMS: Starkesboro inc Druid's lair w/Nightshade's lab, Avengers Mansion; Nightshade's wolf serum, Moonhunter's sky-cycle & tranq darts, moonstone
SYNOPSIS: Captain America fends off the Starkesboro werewolves while Dr. Druid casts an invisibility spell, then teleports Cap away. Meanwhile, Dr. Nightshade tries to inject Wolverine with her wolf serum, but his healing factor quickly counteracts it so Druid mesmerizes him. Moonhunter looks for Cap, and Dr. Druid makes him and Cap invisible to Moonhunter. Bernie arrives at Avengers Mansion looking for Cap, but ends up accompanying Jarvis on his daily walk with Dennis. As the sun rises, the Starkesboro werewolves return to human form. Cap and Dr. Druid continue to search for John, but Wolverine and Nightshade attack them. Wolverine fights Cap long enough for Moonhunter to tranquilize Cap. Cap wakes up in Nightshade's lab to find Nightshade administering her wolf serum to him.
NOTE: Cover-labeled "Man and Wolf Part 3 of 6."

2ND STORY: "Real World" (5 pages)
CREDITS: Mark Gruenwald (writer), Larry Alexander (pencils), Ray Kryssing (inks), Steve Dutro (letters), John Kalisz (colors), Pat Garrahy (asst editor), Ralph Macchio (editor)
FEATURE CHARACTER: Diamondback (resumes Diamondback identity)
VILLAINS: Crossbones, Tinkerer (bts, provided throwing diamonds, last in DFSM #1, '91, last bts in WoSM #79, '91, next in ASM #369, '92)
OTHER CHARACTERS: Avengers Crew: Donna Maria Puentes (last bts in Cap #405, '92), Michael O' Brien (last in NW #22, '92)
LOCATIONS/ITEMS: Magneto's fallout shelter, Avengers Mansion inc med-lab; Crossbones' stolen car, Cap's blood, Diamondback's throwing diamonds
SYNOPSIS: Convinced that her "training" is complete, Crossbones gives Rachel a new Diamondback costume and takes her out of the fallout shelter. To prove her loyalty Crossbones orders her to steal the bags of Cap's blood kept in storage at Avengers Mansion. Diamondback enters claiming to go to her quarters, but is spotted on camera in the med-lab.

CAPTAIN AMERICA #405 (Late August 1992)

"Dances with Werewolves" (18 pages)

CREDITS: Mark Gruenwald (writer), Rik Levins (pencils), Steve Alexandrov (inks), Joe Rosen (letters), Gina Going (colors), Pat Garrahy (asst editor), Ralph Macchio (editor), Danny Bulanadi (c inks)
FEATURE CHARACTER: Captain America (also as Capwolf)
GUEST STARS: Dr. Druid, Wolverine, Werewolf, Wolfsbane (both bts, Moonhunter's captives)
SUPPORTING CAST: Avengers Crew: Edwin Jarvis (next in Av #350/2, '92), Donna Maria Puentes (bts, on phone, next in Cap #404/2, '92), Man-Wolf (bts, Moonhunter's captive); Dennis Dunphy (next in Cap #408, '92), Bernie Rosenthal
VILLAINS: Druid, Dr. Nightshade, Ferocia (bts, Moonhunter's captive), purse snatcher
OTHER CHARACTERS: Moonhunter, Starkesboro werewolves (some as humans), bystanders
LOCATIONS/ITEMS: Starkesboro inc Druid's lair w/Nightshade's lab, Central Park; Nightshade's wolf serum, Moonhunter's sky-cycle & lasso, Bernie's purse, moonstone
SYNOPSIS: Captain America turns into a werewolf, but his super soldier serum enhanced physiology allows him to shake off Druid's hypnosis. Druid uses his power to transform some townspeople into wolves to pursue Cap. Meanwhile, Jarvis heads back to Avengers Mansion while Bernie stays with Dennis in Central Park. A mugger suddenly snatches Bernie's purse and she chases him, leaving Dennis alone. Dr. Druid investigates Starkesboro, finding a church filled with druid artifacts including the moonstone. Druid confronts Dr. Druid and they enter a magic battle of wills. Capwolf tries to reason with the werewolves chasing him, but ends up fighting Wolverine, having to blind Wolverine to get away. Bernie discovers that Dennis has wandered off. While Dr. Druid loses to Druid, Moonhunter chases Capwolf towards Nightshade; she calms Capwolf down with her pheromones.
NOTE: Cover-labeled "Man and Wolf Part 4 of 6."

2ND STORY: "Cross Country" (5 pages)
CREDITS: Mark Gruenwald (writer), Larry Alexander (pencils), Ariane Lenshoek (inks, colors), Steve Dutro (letters), Pat Garrahy (asst editor), Ralph Macchio (editor)
FEATURE CHARACTER: Diamondback
VILLAINS: Skeleton Crew: Blackwing, Jack O' Lantern (both last in Cap #398/2, '92), Cutthroat (last in Cap #402/2, '92); Crossbones
OTHER CHARACTERS: Avengers Crew: Donna Maria Puentes (next in Cap #409, '92), Michael O'Brien (next in IM #297, '93), Blackwing's

oats, bystanders
LOCATIONS/ITEMS: Avengers Mansion inc med-lab, Colorado Rockies; Cap's blood, Diamondback's throwing diamonds, Crossbones' stolen car & climbing gear, Blackwing's glider, Jack O' Lantern's pogo platform, Cutthroat's sword & hover platform
SYNOPSIS: Diamondback convinces O'Brien she needs Cap's blood for a mission and is allowed to leave with them. Crossbones takes the blood and Diamondback to the Colorado Rockies to meet with Red Skull, but while climbing the mountain the Skeleton Crew attacks, prepared to execute any trespassers.
NOTE: "American Graffiti" includes photo of Rik Levins as the Wolfman.

CAPTAIN AMERICA #406 (Early September 1992)

"Leader of the Pack" (18 pages)

CREDITS: Mark Gruenwald (writer), Rik Levins (pencils), Danny Bulanadi (inks), Joe Rosen (letters), Gina Going (colors), Pat Garrahy (asst editor), Ralph Macchio (editor)
FEATURE CHARACTER: Captain America (as Capwolf)
GUEST STARS: X-Force (mutant combat unit): Cable (Nathan Summers), Feral (Maria Callasantos, bts, responding to Dr. Nightshade's werewolf call) (both last in XFor #5, '91), Shatterstar (Mojoworld warrior, last in W #54, '92, next in XFor #6, '92); Wolfsbane (Rahne Sinclair, also in fb between AFlt #107, '92 & bts in Cap #402, '92), Dr. Druid, Wolverine, Werewolf
SUPPORTING CAST: Bernie Rosenthal (next in Cap #426, '94), Man-Wolf
VILLAINS: Druid, Dr. Nightshade, Ferocia
OTHER CHARACTERS: Moonhunter (also in fb to 1st chr app before Cap #402, '92), Starkesboro werewolves (some also in fb), hotdog vendor, police, bystanders
LOCATIONS/ITEMS: Starkesboro inc surrounding woods (in fb), Druid's lair w/Nightshade's lab & Wolf Pit (also in fb), X-Force HQ, Central Park; Cable's guns, Moonhunter's whip (in fb), Druid's knife, moonstone
FLASHBACK: Moonhunter captures Wolfsbane and later disciplines other captured werewolves.
SYNOPSIS: Dr. Nightshade leads Capwolf into the Wolf Pit where he finally finds John Jameson, but as Man-Wolf. The two fight for dominance; when Cap wins, he gains the other werewolves' respect. Meanwhile, Druid prepares the captive Dr. Druid for a ceremony. Wolfsbane, lured to Starkesboro by the moonstone, teaches Capwolf to talk in his new form. Elsewhere, Shatterstar tells Cable that Feral has gone missing. Capwolf rallies the werewolves and they escape through teamwork. Meanwhile, Bernie continues to search for Dennis. Passing a captive Wolverine, Capwolf and the werewolves run into Moonhunter and Nightshade, capturing them both. Nightshade tells Capwolf that Druid is performing a ceremony to solidify his power, but Capwolf arrives too late to stop Druid from slashing Dr. Druid's throat onto the moonstone. Druid places the blood soaked moonstone on his own throat, empowering himself.
NOTE: Cover-labeled "Man and Wolf Part 5 of 6."

2ND STORY: "Fight on Skull Mountain!" (5 pages)
CREDITS: Mark Gruenwald (writer), Larry Alexander (pencils), Ariane Lenshoek (inks, colors), Steve Dutro (letters), Pat Garrahy (asst editor), Ralph Macchio (editor)
FEATURE CHARACTER: Diamondback
VILLAINS: Skeleton Crew: Blackwing, Cutthroat, Jack O' Lantern; Crossbones, Red Skull's men (Sevelin named)
OTHER CHARACTERS: Blackwing's bats
LOCATIONS/ITEMS: Colorado Rockies inc Red Skull's chalet; Cap's blood, Crossbones' crossbow & climbing gear, Diamondback's venom diamond, Blackwing's glider, Jack O' Lantern's pogo platform, Cutthroat's sword & hover platform, Red Skull's men's guns
SYNOPSIS: Diamondback and Crossbones battle and eventually overpower the Skeleton Crew. The Crew takes them to Red Skull's chalet, where Red Skull's men capture Diamondback and Crossbones. As Crossbones and Diamondback are taken inside, Cutthroat recognizes Diamondback as his sister.

CAPTAIN AMERICA #407 (Late September 1992)

"Lord of the Wolves!" (18 pages)

CREDITS: Mark Gruenwald (writer), Rik Levins (pencils) , Danny Bulanadi (inks), Joe Rosen (letters), Gina Going (colors), Pat Garrahy (asst editor), Ralph Macchio (editor)
FEATURE CHARACTER: Captain America (as Capwolf)
GUEST STARS: X-Force: Cable, Feral (both next in XFor #6, '92); Wolverine (next in DrS #41, '92), Dr. Druid, Werewolf, Wolfsbane
SUPPORTING CAST: Man-Wolf
VILLAINS: Druid (also as Starwolf), Dr. Nightshade, Ferocia (last app)
OTHER CHARACTERS: Moonhunter, Starkesboro werewolves
LOCATIONS/ITEMS: Starkesboro inc Druid's lair w/Nightshade's lab & Wolf Pit; Cable's guns, Nightshade's wolf serum, Moonhunter's grapple claws, moonstone
SYNOPSIS: Druid turns into Starwolf, a cosmically-powered werewolf, and orders the Starkesboro werewolves to attack Capwolf. Capwolf's werewolf allies arrive and fight the Starkesboro werewolves while Capwolf frees the chained Dr. Druid. Cable finds Feral outside Starkesboro and tranquilizes her. Cable investigates, finding the fracas in progress between Starwolf, Capwolf, and the werewolves. Capwolf stops Cable from slaughtering all the innocent wolves, inadvertently allowing Starwolf to capture them both. Man-Wolf takes the unconscious Dr. Druid to Dr. Nightshade's lab and turns Nightshade into a werewolf to force her to find an antidote. Moonhunter frees himself and Wolverine; when they

enter Nightshade's lab, a partially healed Dr. Druid wakes up and removes Druid's hypnosis over them. Joining the fight, they allow Capwolf to get close enough to Starwolf to rip the moonstone from his throat. Cable crushes the moonstone, reverting Druid to normal.
NOTE: Cover-labeled "Man and Wolf Part 6 of 6."

2ND STORY: "Uncut Diamonds" (5 pages)
CREDITS: Mark Gruenwald (writer), Kevin Kobasic (pencils), Rodney Ramos (inks), Steve Dutro (letters), Scott Marshall (colors), Pat Garrahy (asst editor), Ralph Macchio (editor)
FEATURE CHARACTER: Diamondback
VILLAINS: Red Skull (last in ASM #367, '92, next in Cap #409, '92), Skeleton Crew: Mother Night (last in Cap #402/2, '92), Blackwing, Cutthroat, Jack O' Lantern; Crossbones, Skull's guards
LOCATIONS/ITEMS: Rocky Mountains inc Skull-House & Red Skull's chalet w/Skull's office, Mother Night's quarters & Diamondback's cell; Cap's blood, Red Skull's gun, Red Skull's men's guns
SYNOPSIS: Crossbones lobbies to get his old job back by handing over Cap's blood and explaining that he brainwashed Diamondback; Red Skull says he'll think about it. Meanwhile, Jack roughly locks up Diamondback and Cutthroat threatens him for it. Later, he sneaks into Diamondback's cell and reveals that he's her long-thought-dead brother, Danny.
NOTE: "American Graffiti" features a pin-up of Cap by Frank Miller & Bob Wiacek.

CAPTAIN AMERICA #408 (October 1992)

"Dark Dawn" (10 pages)

CREDITS: Mark Gruenwald (writer), Rik Levins (pencils), Danny Bulanadi (inks), Joe Rosen (letters), Greg Roussos (colors), Barry Dutter (asst editor), Mike Rockwitz (editor), Ralph Macchio (group editor), Don Hudson (c inks)
FEATURE CHARACTER: Captain America (also as Capwolf, next in Nam #26, Av #350/2, InfW #1-2, AFlt #110, FF #367, WM #13, MSMK #41, FF #368, InfW #3, NW #27, Q #38, Wlk&IW #8, FF #369, AFlt #111, InfW #4, WM #14, Q #39, InfW #5, WM #15, InfW #6, FF #370, GR/Cap, Cap Ann #11 fb, Thor Ann #17 fb, Cap Ann #11, all '92)
GUEST STARS: Dr. Druid (next in WM #13, '92), Werewolf (next in MSMK #50, '93), Wolf (last in Thing #28, '85, last app), Wolfsbane (next in XFac Ann #7, '92)
SUPPORTING CAST: Col. John Jameson (also as Man-Wolf, next in ASM #375/3, '93), Dennis Dunphy (last in Cap #405, '92, also in Cap #409, '92 fb)
VILLAINS: Druid (last app), Dr. Nightshade (next in MFan #1, '96), Captain America doppelganger (dies, only app, see NOTE), Demolition Man doppelganger (1st, also in Cap #409, '92 fb)
OTHER CHARACTERS: Moonhunter, Starkesboro werewolves (also as humans, inc mayor), Guardsmen
LOCATIONS/ITEMS: Starkesboro inc Nightshade's lab, Central Park Lagoon; Nightshade's antidote, Cap doppelganger's shield, Guardsmen armors & van, Cap's & Moonhunter's sky-cycles
SYNOPSIS: Dr. Nightshade uses the antidote on herself and John, but before she can administer it to Capwolf, an evil Captain America doppelganger teleports in and attacks. Stabbed with the syringe in the confusion, Capwolf begins reverting to human form during the fight. Dr. Druid senses the double isn't really alive, so the now human Captain America impales the double on its own bladed shield. Later, as Guardsmen cart away the villains, John tells Cap he has to quit due to feelings of inadequacy when surrounded by heroes. Moonhunter, now free from Druid's influence, offers Cap and Druid a ride home. Meanwhile, a Demolition Man doppelganger attacks Dennis, but only the double emerges from the fight.
NOTE: Cover-labeled "An Infinity War Crossover." Title returns to monthly status. Other Cap doppelgangers appear in InfW #1 & 5, '92.

2ND STORY: "Night of the Knife" (7 pages)
CREDITS: Mark Gruenwald (writer), Larry Alexander (pencils), Don Hudson (inks), Susan Crespi (letters), John Kalisz (colors), Barry Dutter (asst editor), Mike Rockwitz (group editor)
FEATURE CHARACTER: Diamondback
VILLAINS: Crossbones (also in rfb as Brock Rumlow), Skeleton Crew: Cutthroat (also in rfb as Danny Leighton & in fb between Cap #400/3, '92 fb & MTU #89, '80), Blackwing, Jack O' Lantern, Mother Night
OTHER CHARACTERS: Deathstroke, Mangler, Nightcrawler, Spider-Man, Willie Leighton (all in rfb), Cutthroat's victim (in fb)
LOCATIONS/ITEMS: Red Skull's Rocky Mountain chalet inc Diamondback's cell, Mother Night's quarters & Crossbones' room; Cutthroat's knives (also in rfb & fb), gun (in rfb) & sword
FLASHBACKS: Brock Rumlow kills Willie Leighton (Cap #400/3, '92 fb). Daniel becomes Cutthroat (1). Cutthroat fights Spider-Man and Nightcrawler (MTU #89, '80). Cutthroat battles Mangler & Deathstroke for a chance to work for Red Skull (Cap #395, '91).
SYNOPSIS: Cutthroat explains he's sorry for letting Diamondback think he was dead and promises to make up for all the lost time. To ensure he's not replaced in the Skeleton Crew, Cutthroat plans to kill Crossbones. Cutthroat angrily finds Crossbones catching up with Mother Night and that night, he tries to kill Crossbones in his sleep. Crossbones cuts Cutthroat's throat.

3RD STORY: "Joyride" (5 pages)
CREDITS: Mark Gruenwald (writer), Rik Levins (pencils), Don Hudson (inks), Dave Sharpe (letters), Ariane Lenshoek (colors), Barry Dutter (asst editor), Mike Rockwitz (editor), Ralph Macchio (group editor)
FEATURE CHARACTER: Falcon (last in Cap Ann #11/3, '92)
GUEST STARS: Avengers: Black Widow (chairman, last in Pun/BW, '92, next in Av #348, '92), Captain America (last in AWC #88, '92);

Reserve Avengers: Captain Marvel (last in Cap #401, '92, next in Q #41, '92), Dr. Druid (last in Av Ann #21, '92), Quicksilver (last in InfW #4, '92, next in Av #350, '92), She-Hulk (last in InfW #6, '92, next in MTW #1, '93)

SUPPORTING CAST: Captain America (last in AWC #88, '92)

OTHER CHARACTERS: Avengers Crew: Fabian Stankowicz (last in Cap #393, '91, next in Cap #422, '93), Moonhunter (joins Avengers Crew); Ant-Man, Hulk, Iron Man, Thor, Wasp (prev 5 statues)

LOCATIONS/ITEMS: New York inc Avengers Mansion; Moonhunter's sky-cycle

SYNOPSIS: Falcon spots Moonhunter joyriding on an Avengers sky-cycle. The two return to Avengers Mansion where Falcon learns that Moonhunter applied to be Captain America's new pilot. Later, after a debriefing of reserve members, Cap tells Falcon about his search for Diamondback and, with some spare time on his hands, offers to help.

CAPTAIN AMERICA ANNUAL #11 (1992)

"Citizen Kang! Part 1 of 4: An Epic Adventure" (25 pages)

CREDITS: Roy Thomas (writer), Larry Alexander (pencils), Kathryn Bolinger (inks), Christie Scheele, John Kalisz (colors), Pat Garrahy (asst editor), Ralph Macchio (editor), Dan Panosian (c art)

FEATURE CHARACTER: Captain America (also in fb1 between GR/Cap, '92 & Thor Ann #17, '92 fb; next in Thor Ann #17, '92, bts in Hulk #400, '92 fb, NF:AoS #43-44, '93, IM #284 fb, Thor #447, ASM #366, AWC #88, Cap #408/3, Cap #409, all '92)

GUEST STARS: Dr. Druid (last in FF #370, '92, next in Thor Ann #17, '92), Vision (also in fb1, last in InfW #6, '92, next in Av Ann #21, '92), Gilgamesh (as King of Uruk circa 3,000 BC, also in fb2 to 1st chr app, next in Thor Ann #21, '92), Sersi (as child circa 3,000 BC, 1st chr app before Et #3, '76), Ikaris (in fb3 to 1st chr app before Et #1, '91 fb)

VILLAINS: Kang the Conqueror (last in InfW #5, '92, chr last in Thor Ann #17, '92 fb, next bts in Thor Ann #17, '92, next in FF Ann #25, '92), Ravonna ("Ravonna Lexus Renslayer," as Nebula here, last in AvS #37, '90, next in Thor Ann #17, '92, see NOTE), Kronans (rock-like aliens, 1st chr app before JiM #83, '62)

OTHER CHARACTERS: Utnapishtim (wise man of Shurrupak, also bts in fb3, only app), Urshanabi (Utnapishtim's boatman, only app), Enkidu (beast-man & Gilgamesh's friend, only app in fb2), Deviants (in fb3), Mesopotamian guard, giant (both in fb2), sea serpent (all circa 3,000 BC), Timely residents (Butch & Lyle named) & police

LOCATIONS/ITEMS: Timely, WI (1st inc Timely Industries, Avengers Mansion (in fb1), Mesopotamia (also in fb2), Dr. Druid's Boston suburbs townhouse, Lemuria (in fb3), Chronopolis; Avengers Quinjet, Kronans guns & starship, Enkidu's spear (in fb2), Utnapishtim's ark (in fb3), plant of immortality, Kang's robots

FLASHBACKS: Vision tells Captain America that he's just discovered some of his parts were manufactured in Timely, Wisconsin. This information makes no sense to him, so Vision leaves to investigate Timely (1). Gilgamesh meets, fights, and befriends the beast-man Enkidu; together, they have adventures until Enkidu dies, and Gilgamesh realizes he will also die one day (2). Lemuria is destroyed in a flood, and Ikaris, mistaken for a bird, leads Utnapishtim's ark to a mountaintop (3).

SYNOPSIS: Captain America arrives in Timely, Wisconsin, but quickly discovers things are too picturesque to be real. Searching inside Timely Industries for the missing Vision, Cap opens a door to find himself intervening in a fight between a man and some rock-like aliens. When the aliens escape, he recognizes the man as Gilgamesh, and deduces he's been sent back in time by five thousand years. Cap accompanies Gilgamesh in his quest and they receive a boat ride from Urshanabi. In the current day, Nebula tries to warn Dr. Druid of impending danger, but Dr. Druid ignores her. Urshanabi takes Cap and Gilgamesh to Utnapishtim, who offers Gilgamesh eternal life if Gilgamesh can retrieve the plant of immortality from the river. When Gilgamesh dives in, a giant sea serpent attacks him. Cap helps Gilgamesh against the serpent and Gilgamesh, but they lose the plant. Cap and Gilgamesh part ways as friends and Cap meets the child Sersi, who shows Cap the way to the nearby Chronopolis. Meanwhile, inside Chronopolis, Kang taunts his captive, Vision.

NOTE: Cover-labeled "Citizen Kang Part 1." Story continued into Thor Ann #17, '92. Contains Content Page featuring Captain America by Mark Pacella (pencils) & Dan Panosian (inks). Nebula revealed as Ravonna in Av Ann #21, '92. Christie Scheele credited as "Max Scheele" here.

2ND STORY: "Captain America's Top 10 Villains" (3 pages)

CREDITS: George Caragonne (writer), Larry Alexander (art), Jon Babcock (letters), Renee Witterstaetter (colors), Pat Garrahy (asst editor), Ralph Macchio (editor)

FEATURE CHARACTER: Steve Rogers (between Cap #394-395, '91)

SUPPORTING CAST: Rachel Leighton (also in Steve's thoughts as Diamondback, last in Cap #394, '91, next in Cap #394/2, '91)

OTHER CHARACTERS: Batroc & his Brigade: Machete, Zaran; Red Skull & his Skeleton Crew: Crossbones, Machinesmith, Minister Blood, Mother Night, 4th Sleeper; Serpent Society: Sidewinder, Anaconda, Asp, Black Mamba, Black Racer, Bushmaster, Cobra, Cottonmouth, Fer-de-Lance, Puff Adder, Rattler, Rock Python; Baron Heinrich Zemo, Baron Helmut Zemo, Doughboy, Dr. Faustus, Flag-Smasher, Viper, ULTIMATUM, Sharon Carter, Arnim Zola, Steve Rogers clone (all in Steve's thoughts)

LOCATIONS/ITEMS: McCann's Bar on West 46th street

SYNOPSIS: Despite being retired from adventuring, Rachel still wants to know about Steve's life as Captain America and asks who his top ten enemies are. In descending order, Steve says, the Serpent Society, Flag-Smasher and ULTIMATUM, Dr. Faustus, Viper, Batroc, Arnim Zola, the Zemo family, the Skeleton Crew, Crossbones, and Red Skull.

NOTE: Followed by one-page schematic "Captain America's Shield" and two-page schematic "Captain America's Jet," both by Eliot R. Brown.

3RD STORY: "Test Flight" (14 pages)

CREDITS: Mark Gruenwald (writer), James Brock (co-plot, pencils), Charles Barnett (inks), Dave Sharpe (letters), Christie Scheele (colors),

Pat Garrahy (asst editor), Ralph Macchio (editor)

FEATURE CHARACTER: Falcon (last in Cap #401, '92, next in Cap #408/3, '92)

SUPPORTING CAST: Redwing (last in Av Ann #19/5, '90, next in MFan #1, '96), Sarah Wilson Casper (last in Cap #278/2, '83, last app)

VILLAINS: Taskmaster (also in fb between Thing #26, '85 & Cap #334, '87; last in Cap #396, '92, next in ASM #366, '92), his agents (Benetton, Griff & Kenner named) & his students (in fb)

OTHER CHARACTERS: Tyrone McQuaid (former Taskmaster student), Desmond "Dez" Burrell (Stark Enterprises employee) (both only app), Harlem residents (Dwayne named, also in dfb), Social Service employees, police

LOCATIONS/ITEMS: Harlem inc Sam's Social Services office & apartment (in dfb), Sarah's apartment, Stark Enterprises, Taskmaster's Academy of Criminal Arts and Sciences (in fb); Taskmaster's shield & sword, his agents' guns, Tyrone's gun, Falcon's new suit (1st) inc wings, infrared lenses & hawk hook

FLASHBACKS: Dwayne spots Taskmaster's men at Sam's apartment (d). Tyrone trains at Taskmaster's Academy but drops out, upsetting Taskmaster.

SYNOPSIS: Wielding a gun, Tyrone McQuaid demands to see Sam Wilson, publicly known as Falcon. Sam arrives and disarms Tyrone, but recognizes Tyrone and takes him in his office. Tyrone explains the Taskmaster is after him and Sam offers to take Tyrone to his apartment. Informed that his apartment is being watched, Sam takes Tyrone to his sister's apartment instead. Sam calls his friend Dez at Stark Enterprises, who sends Sam's new Falcon suit over. That night, Falcon and Redwing attack Taskmaster's agents stationed at his apartment. With his men defeated, Taskmaster attacks Falcon. Tyrone appears, threatening to kill Taskmaster. Taskmaster attacks Tyrone and escapes when Falcon saves Tyrone instead of chasing the villain. Falcon tries to reassure Tyrone that Taskmaster will leave him alone, but Tyrone is upset that Taskmaster is still alive.

NOTE: Falcon's new suit & equipment are considered part of his costume, so only changes to them will be noted. Christie Scheele credited as "Max Scheele" here.

4TH STORY: "Birth of a Warlord" (10 pages)

CREDITS: Peter Sanderson (writer), Rich Yanizeski (pencils), Fred Fredericks (inks), Dave Sharpe (letters), Christie Scheele (colors), Pat Garrahy (asst editor), Ralph Macchio (editor)

FEATURE CHARACTER: Kang the Conqueror (also in fb1 as Nathaniel Richards between YAv #2, '05 fb & FF #19 '63 fb, fb2 to 1st chr app as Scarlet Centurion between FF Ann #2/3, '64 & Av Ann #2, '68 fb; last in Av #292, '88, chr last in Av Ann #21/4, '92 fb, next in Thor Ann #17/4, '92)

OTHER CHARACTERS: Avengers: Captain America, Black Panther, Goliath, Hawkeye, Iron Man, Tigra, Wasp, Wonder Man; Earth-689 Avengers: Giant-Man, Iron Man, Hulk, Thor, Wasp; Fantastic Four: Human Torch, Invisible Girl, Mr. Fantastic, Thing; Dr. Doom, Dr. Strange, Lady Lark, Tom Thumb, Rick Jones, Other-Earth bystanders, Earth-616 Egyptians & bystanders (all in rfb); Quicksilver (in photo), Scarlet Witch, Vision (both in hologram), Divergent Scarlet Centurion (in fb3 to chr 1st app before SqS #9, '86 fb)

LOCATIONS/ITEMS: Earth-616 inc Egypt & Washington, DC, Earth-689 (all in rfb), Other-Earth (Earth-6311, in fb1 & rfb), Chronopolis; Kang's Time-Sphere, Sphinx, robots & guns (all in rfb)

FLASHBACKS: In the future on Other-Earth, the man who will be Kang is bored with utopian society (1). He re-lives the adventures of Earth-616's heroes, and eventually discovers his ancestor's citadel and plans for a time machine inside. He builds a time machine disguised in a Sphinx and travels to Earth-616 circa 2950 BC, but is blinded when he crash-lands. He subjugates the natives and becomes Pharaoh Rama-Tut (FF #19, '63 fb). Called by the Egyptian god Khonshu, the time-travelling Fantastic Four and West Coast Avengers drive Rama-Tut from Egypt (FF #19, '63, DrS #53, '82 & WCA #20-22, '87). Escaping in his Time-Sphere (Av #269, '86 fb), Rama-Tut finds Dr. Doom floating in space and rescues him, convincing Doom that they're the same man at different points in time (FF Ann #2/3, '64). Adopting the new identity Scarlet Centurion (2), he battles the Avengers and loses (Av Ann #2, '68), which creates a divergent Scarlet Centurion (3). Resuming his role as Rama-Tut, he travels to his own future and conquers it (Av #8, '64 fb) and assumes his Kang identity (Av #269, '86 fb). Kang attacks Earth-616's modern age of heroes, but the Avengers force him to flee (Av #8, '64).

SYNOPSIS: Kang begins recording a chronicle of his life.

NOTE: Continued into Thor Ann #17/4, '92. Christie Scheele credited as "Max Scheele" here.

CAPTAIN AMERICA #409 (November 1992)

"Blood and Diamonds" (22 pages)

CREDITS: Mark Gruenwald (writer), Rik Levins (pencils), Danny Bulanadi (inks), Joe Rosen (letters), George Roussos (colors), Barry Dutter (asst editor), Mike Rockwitz (editor), Ralph Macchio (group editor)

FEATURE CHARACTER: Captain America

GUEST STARS: Dr. Druid (next in Q #45, '93), Falcon

SUPPORTING CAST: Diamondback (also in Dr. Druid's conjuration), Dennis Dunphy (also in fb during Cap #408, '92), Avengers Crew: Edwin Jarvis (last in Thor #447, '92, next in Av #350, '92), Donna Maria Puentes (last in Cap #405/2, '92, next in Q #41, '92), Moonhunter

VILLAINS: Red Skull (last in Cap #407/2, '92) & his Skeleton Crew: Crossbones (also in Dr. Druid's conjuration, rejoins Skeleton Crew), Cutthroat (as "corpse," next in NAv #1, '05, see NOTE), Machinesmith (last in Cap #398/2, '92, next in Cap #420, '93), 4th Sleeper (last in Cap #393, '91), Blackwing, Jack O'Lantern, Mother Night; Demolition Man Doppelganger (only in fb during Cap #408, '92), Dr. Benway (Skull's doctor), Renard (Skull's jet-copter pilot, (both 1st))

OTHER CHARACTERS: Federal Aeronautics Administration agent (voice only), National Park Service agent (bts, talks w/Cap)

LOCATIONS/ITEMS: New York inc Central Park Lagoon (in fb), World Trade Center, underground cavern & Avengers Mansion w/ kitchen & reception area; Rocky Mountains inc Dr. Benway's medical barracks & Red Skull's chalet w/ conference room, helipad, Diamondback's cell, Crossbones' quarters & Machinesmith's lab; Cap's blood, jet w/ scanner, Red Skull robot, Machinesmith robot duplicates, Skull's jet-copter, Blackwing's glider, Cutthroat's sword, Jack O'Lantern's pogo platform & pumpkin grenade, Mother Night's communications card, Crossbones'

crossbow & spring-loaded stiletto

FLASHBACK: Dennis Dunphy battles his doppelganger in Central Park Lagoon. Left for dead, Dennis later awakens in a cavern.

SYNOPSIS: With Dr. Druid's help, Captain America and Falcon determine that Diamondback is held captive by Crossbones in the Rocky Mountains . At Red Skull's chalet, Diamondback struggles to escape her cell while Red Skull confronts Crossbones over Cutthroat's demise. Mother Night admits to Machinesmith that she had been cheating on Skull with Cutthroat. Later, Skull explains his plans for Diamondback to the Skeleton Crew. When Mother Night attempts to fetch Diamondback from her cell, Rachel defeats the villainess and dons her costume. Taking Blackwing by surprise, Diamondback confiscates his glider and escapes. Crossbones and Jack O'Lantern quickly recapture Diamondback, but not before Cap and Falcon pick up her distress signal. Meanwhile, Dennis finds an underground city. Twenty miles from the Skull's chalet, Dr. Benway prepares Diamondback for a transfusion of Cap's super-soldier serum blood. Suddenly, Cap and Falcon attack.

NOTE: While Jack O' Lantern disposes of Cutthroat's body here, Cutthroat survives and is recovered by S.H.I.E.L.D. Renard & Dr. Benway's names are revealed in Cap #410, '92.

CAPTAIN AMERICA #410 (December 1992)

"Diamonds Are For Vengeance" (22 pages)

CREDITS: Mark Gruenwald (writer), Rik Levins (pencils), Danny Bulanadi (inks), Joe Rosen (letters), John Cebollero (colors), Barry Dutter (asst editor), Mike Rockwitz (editor), Ralph Macchio (group editor)
FEATURE CHARACTER: Captain America (next in MTW #1-4, '93, Ex #59-60, '92-'93, Thor #458, '93)
GUEST STAR: Falcon (next in MSH #12/2, '93)
SUPPORTING CAST: Diamondback (also as Mother Night), Moonhunter, Dennis Dunphy
VILLAINS: Red Skull (bts, evacuating his chalet, next in Hulk #402, '93) & his Skeleton Crew: Crossbones (next in MCP #129/2, '93), Blackwing (next in Tb #24, '99), Jack O' Lantern (next in AFlt #121, '93), Mother Night (next in Cap #3, '05), 4th Sleeper; Dr. Benway, Renard (prev 3 last app)
OTHER CHARACTERS: Brother Wonderful (last in Cap #204, '76 as Brother Inquisitor), Jikjak (child, 1st, next in Cap #418, '93), Brother Reeko (only app), other Night People
LOCATIONS/ITEMS: Rocky Mountains inc Dr. Benway's medical barracks (destroyed); Zerotown (Night People's camp); Cap's blood jet & Avengers ID, Skull's jet-copter (destroyed), Blackwing's glider, Jack O'Lantern's pogo platform, ghost grabbers & pumpkin magnesium flare bombs, Crossbones' crossbow, knife, shuriken & spring-loaded stiletto, Dr. Benway's gun
SYNOPSIS: Captain America battles Crossbones while Falcon chases Jack O' Lantern. Dr. Benway calls for reinforcements and Blackwing and Mother Night respond from their approaching jet-copter. Meanwhile, beneath the Central Park lagoon, Dennis enters Zerotown, where he is taken to Brother Wonderful. Angered at not receiving answers to his questions, Wonderful threatens the mute Dennis. The 4th Sleeper attacks Moonhunter in Cap's jet, and Blackwing aids Crossbones against Cap. Diamondback escapes from the barracks and tries to help Cap, but Mother Night interferes. Enraged, Diamondback knocks out Mother Night and attempts to strangle Crossbones. Before Cap can break them up, Blackwing knocks Cap off the ledge. Returning with the defeated Jack O' Lantern, Falcon rescues Cap. Moonhunter dislodges the Sleeper by swiping the jet-copter, sending the copter crashing into the barracks. Shrapnel from the explosion injures Crossbones, ending the fight. As the Skeleton Crew is taken into custody, Cap and Rachel are finally reunited.

NOTE: Jikjak is named in Cap #418, '93.

CAPTAIN AMERICA #411 (January 1993)

"The Arena" (22 pages)

CREDITS: Mark Gruenwald (writer), Rik Levins (pencils), Danny Bulanadi (inks), Joe Rosen (letters), George Roussos (colors), Barry Dutter (asst editor), Mike Rockwitz (editor), Ralph Macchio (group editor)
FEATURE CHARACTER: Captain America (also as Crossbones)
GUEST STARS: Falcon (also as Jack O' Lantern, last in MSH #12/2, '93), Nick Fury (last in Pun/BW, '92, next in Cap #414, '93), Sersi (bts, transforms Cap, Falcon & Diamondback into Crossbones, Jack O'Lantern & Mother Night, last in MTW #2, '93, next in Av #358, '93), BAD Girls, Inc: Asp, Impala (both last in Cap #397/2, '92), Black Mamba (last in NW #34, '93)
SUPPORTING CAST: Avengers Crew: Peggy Carter (voice only, last in Q #45, '93, next bts in Cap #414, '93), Dr. Keith Kincaid (bts, tested Diamondback's blood, last in Av #351, '92, last bts in Av #357, '92, next bts in Dhold #3, '92 fb, next in Cap #425, '94), Moonhunter (bts, piloting Cap's jet, next in Cap #414, '93); Dennis Dunphy (next in Cap #418, '93), Diamondback (also as Mother Night)
VILLAINS: Batroc (last in Pun #70, '92) & his Brigade: Machete, Zaran (both last in Cap #362, '89); Superia (last bts in Cap #394/2, '91) & her Femizons: Blackbird (last in Cap #389, '91), Iron Maiden (last in Cap #392, '91), Snapdragon (also in photo, last bts in Cap #392, '91); Wrecking Crew: Piledriver, Wrecker (both bts, last in AFlt #119, '93); Absorbing Man, Jackhammer (both bts), Oddball, Puff Adder, Shocker, Titania (prev 6 last in GotG #29, '92), Frenzy, Knockout, MODAM (bts), Poundcakes, Screaming Mimi, Vertigo (prev 6 last bts in Cap #392, '91), Bombshell, Hydroman, Stiletto (prev 3 last in NW Ann #2, '92), Knickknack, Razor-Fist (bts), Trickshot (prev 3 last in AvS #25, '89), Anaconda, Gladiatrix (both last in Cap #392, '91), Angar, Mad Dog (both last in NF:AoS #35, '92), Beetle, Speed Demon (both last in Sleep #20, '93), Blizzard, Spymaster (both last in IM #286, '92), Flying Tiger, Ringer (Keith Kraft) (both last in MYiR, '92), Hammerhead, Tombstone (both last in PWJ #47, '92), Ringmaster, Stilt-Man (both last in MCP #97/4, '92), Super-Adaptoid (as "Alessandro Brannex," bts, organizing A.I.M. Weapons Expo, last in Cap #387, '91), Aqueduct (last in NW #30, '92 fb), Battleaxe (last in Cap #395/2, '91), Black Talon (last in SenSH #35, '92), Blacklash (bts, last in IM #286, '92), Boomerang (last in WoSM Ann #8, '92), Boomslang (last in DD #379, '90), Bullet (last in DD #291, '91), Coachwhip (bts, last bts in Cap #385/2, '91), Constrictor (bts, last in MCP #120/2, '92), Dragonfly (last in IM Ann #12/5, '91), Drill (last in Cap #378/2, '90), Eel (last in AvS #29/2, '90), Electro (last in ASM #369, '92), Firebrand (Russ Broxtel, last in NW #30, '92 fb), Grey Gargoyle (bts, last in SenSH #27,

'91), Killer Shrike (last in WoSM #91, '92), Klaw (bts, last in FF Ann #24/2, '91), Lady Deathstrike (last in UXM #281, '91), Man-Ape (last in FF #336, '90), Man-Bull (last in Hulk #341, '88), Mentallo (bts, last in Hulk #404, '93), Mesmero (last in Ex #34, '91), Moonstone (last in Cap #389, '91), Ramrod (last in FF #335, '89), Resistants (2 members, group last in Cap #368, '90), Rhino (last in Cage #10, '93), Rock Python (last in Cap #387, '91), Scorpion (last in ASM #370, '92), Shockwave (last in WCA #11, '86), Slyde (bts, last in WoSM #23, '87), Sunstroke (last in WCA #24, '87), Tarantula (last in Pun #70, '92), Thermo (last in Q #21, '91), Triple-Iron (last in MPr #18, '74), Trump (last in Cap #371, '90), Whirlwind (last in AFlt #102, '91), Wildfire (last in PM #32, '76), Gen. Wo (last in ToS #61, '65), A.I.M. agents

OTHER CHARACTERS: Brother Wonderful, other Night People (all next in Cap #418, '93), Boca Caliente air traffic controller (voice only) & hotel staff

LOCATIONS/ITEMS: Avengers Mansion inc gym & Cap's quarters, Zerotown, Boca Caliente inc airport, arena & luxury hotel; Cap's computer, jet & shuttle, A.I.M. biometric scanner

SYNOPSIS: Captain America tells Diamondback that Dr. Kincaid has given her a clean bill of health, and she admits that she wants to bring Snapdragon to justice. Fury suggests that Snapdragon might be attending the A.I.M. Weapons Expo on Boca Caliente. In Zerotown, Brother Wonderful is frustrated when the mute Dennis doesn't answer his questions, and orders the Night People to attack him. When Dennis fights back, Wonderful is impressed with his strength. Later, Cap, Falcon and Diamondback disguised by Sersi as Crossbones, Jack O' Lantern & Mother Night, arrive at Boca Caliente. Bluffing their way through A.I.M.'s security checks, "Crossbones" runs into Batroc, who reminds him of an old wager that Crossbones could defeat any five men in unarmed combat. Cap accepts the challenge to avoid suspicion and in front of an audience filled with super-villains, first defeats Mad Dog. As Cap battles Ramrod, Diamondback finds Snapdragon with Superia and her Femizons. Cap defeats Ramrod and meets his next opponent, General Wo.

CAPTAIN AMERICA #412 (February 1993)

"Disguise the Limit" (22 pages)

CREDITS: Mark Gruenwald (writer), Rik Levins (pencils), Danny Bulanadi (inks), Joe Rosen (letters), George Roussos (colors), Barry Dutter (asst editor), Mike Rockwitz (editor), Ralph Macchio (group editor)
FEATURE CHARACTER: Captain America (also as Crossbones)
GUEST STARS: Shang-Chi (Master of Kung-Fu, last in MK Spec, '92), Falcon (also as Jack O' Lantern), BAD Girls, Inc: Asp, Black Mamba, Impala (prev 3 bts)
SUPPORTING CAST: Diamondback (also in rfb & as Mother Night)
VILLAINS: Batroc & his Brigade: Machete (bts), Zaran; Superia & her Femizons: Snapdragon (also in rfb), Blackbird, Iron Maiden; Wrecking Crew: Wrecker, Piledriver (bts); Super-Adaptoid (as "Alessandro Brannex"), Absorbing Man, Beetle, Black Talon, Blizzard, Boomerang, Boomslang, Coachwhip, Constrictor, Dragonfly, Drill, Eel, Electro, Flying Tiger, Frenzy, Grey Gargoyle, Hydroman, Killer Shrike, Klaw, Man-Bull, Mentallo, MODAM, Moonstone, Oddball, Razor-Fist, Rhino, Ringer, Rock Python, Scorpion, Shocker, Shockwave, Slyde, Speed Demon, Stiletto, Stilt-Man, Sunstroke, Triple-Iron, Trump, Whirlwind, Gen. Wo, Anaconda, Angar, Aqueduct, Battleaxe, Blacklash, Bombshell, Bullet, Firebrand, Gladiatrix, Hammerhead, Jackhammer, Knickknack, Knockout, Lady Deathstrike, Mad Dog, Man-Ape, Mesmero, Poundcakes, Puff Adder, Ramrod, Resistants, Ringmaster, Screaming Mimi, Spymaster, Tarantula, Thermo, Titania, Tombstone, Trickshot, Vertigo, Wildfire (prev 31 bts), A.I.M. agents (inc Brannex's secretary & dock worker)

LOCATIONS/ITEMS: Boca Caliente inc dock, arena & Brannex's office; forklift, crate, Superia's comlink, S.S. Superia (in rfb)

FLASHBACK: Snapdragon tries to drown Diamondback (Cap #388, '91).

SYNOPSIS: While Captain America, disguised as Crossbones, battles General Wo, Superia offers Diamondback, disguised as Mother Night, a position in her Femizons. As Cap defeats Wo and faces off against Razorfist, Falcon, disguised as Jack O' Lantern, searches for Diamondback. Meanwhile, Shang-Chi breaks out of a crate on a mission to dismantle any business relationships A.I.M. had with his late father, Fu Manchu. Cap defeats Razorfist only to be confronted by the final opponent Batroc, who recognizes Cap through his fighting style. When Cap refuses to let Batroc defeat him, "Crossbones" is revealed to the audience as Captain America. Meanwhile, in a bid to take over A.I.M., Superia assassinates Alessandro Brannex. When MODAM attacks Superia in retaliation, Blackbird and Iron Maiden fly to Superia's aid. "Mother Night" confronts Snapdragon, revealing herself as Diamondback. Falcon drops his Jack O' Lantern disguise to search for Diamondback, but Shang Chi attacks him, thinking he's an A.I.M. agent. In the arena, Cap faces off against a horde of super villains.

CAPTAIN AMERICA #413 (February 1993)

"Hostile Takeover" (22 pages)

CREDITS: Mark Gruenwald (writer), Rik Levins (pencils), Danny Bulanadi (inks), Joe Rosen (letters), George Roussos (colors), Barry Dutter (asst editor), Mike Rockwitz (editor), Ralph Macchio (group editor)
FEATURE CHARACTER: Captain America
GUEST STARS: Falcon, Shang-Chi, BAD Girls, Inc: Asp, Black Mamba, Impala (prev 3 bts)
SUPPORTING CAST: Diamondback
VILLAINS: Batroc & his Brigade: Machete, Zaran; Superia & her Femizons: Snapdragon (dies, last app), Blackbird, Iron Maiden; Wrecking Crew: Pildriver, Wrecker; Super-Adaptoid (as "Allesandro Brannex", next in IM #296, '93), Beetle, Blizzard, Boomerang, Boomslang, Dragonfly, Drill, Eel, Electro, Firebrand, Flying Tiger,

Frenzy, Jackhammer, Killer Shrike, Knickknack, Knockout, Man-Ape, Man-Bull, MODAM, Oddball, Poundcakes, Puff Adder, Rhino, Ringer, Rock Python, Scorpion, Shocker, Shockwave, Speed Demon, Spymaster, Stiletto, Stilt-Man, Sunstroke, Tarantula, Thermo, Titania, Tombstone, Triple-Iron, Trump, Whirlwind, Absorbing Man, Anaconda, Angar, Aqueduct, Battleaxe, Black Talon, Blacklash, Bombshell, Bullet, Coachwhip, Constrictor, Gladiatrix, Grey Gargoyle, Hammerhead, Hydroman, Klaw, Lady Deathstrike, Mad Dog, Mentallo, Mesmero, Moonstone, Ramrod, Razor-Fist, Resistants, Ringmaster, Screaming Mimi, Slyde, Trickshot, Vertigo, Wildfire, Gen. Wo (prev 31 bts)

LOCATIONS/ITEMS: Boca Caliente island inc arena, Atlantic Ocean; A.I.M. hover platforms & forcefield, Falcon's Avengers ID, Cap's emergency blinker, Superia's shackles

SYNOPSIS: As Captain America battles a horde of super-villains, Diamondback challenges Snapdragon to a rematch. Superia asks MODAM to join her in using A.I.M.'s money to fund her schemes, but MODAM is loyal to A.I.M.. Shang-Chi and Falcon discover neither are villains and team-up to rescue Cap. MODAM captures Superia and Allesandro Brannex, still alive, stands up and reveals that he's a Super-Adaptoid. Falcon retrieves Cap from the melee; he and Shang-Chi holds off the villains while Cap searches for Diamondback. Overcome with a thirst for vengeance, Diamondback drwons Snapdragon in a water fountain. Cap spies MODAM carrying Superia away from the island. Mistaking Superia for Diamondback, Cap attacks MODAM, causing her to drop Superia into the Atlantic Ocean. Realizing she's Superia, Cap dives in after her.

CAPTAIN AMERICA #414 (March 1993)

"Escape from A.I.M. Isle" (22 pages)

CREDITS: Mark Gruenwald (writer), Rik Levins, M.C. Wyman (pencils), Danny Bulanadi & his friends (inks), Rick Parker (letters), George Roussos (colors), Barry Dutter (asst editor), Mike Rockwitz (editor), Ralph Macchio (group editor)

FEATURE CHARACTER: Captain America

GUEST STARS: Black Panther (last in Dlk #25, '93), Nick Fury (last in Cap #411, '93, next in IM #292, '93), Ka-Zar (last in C:Gene #4, '93), Shang-Chi (next in DD Ann #10, '94), Falcon, BAD Girls, Inc: Asp (next in Cap #30, '04), Black Mamba (next in Dlk #7, '00), Impala (last app) (prev 3 bts)

SUPPORTING CAST: Avengers Crew: Moonhunter (last bts in Cap #411, '93), Peggy Carter (bts, forwarded Black Panther's message, last voice only in Cap #411, '93, next in Starb #1, '94); Diamondback (also in rfb)

VILLAINS: Batroc (next in MCP #139/4, '93) & his Brigade: Machete (bts, next bts in Cap #442, '95), Zaran (bts, next in Nomad #18, '93); Superia (next in Cap #431, '94) & her Femizons: Blackbird (bts, last app), Iron Maiden (bts, next in Tb #105, '06); Wrecking Crew: Wrecker (bts, next in Tstrike:MDF #13/2, '94),Piledriver (bts); Angar, Screaming Mimi (both bts) (prev 3 next in AvUnp #4, '96), Beetle, Constrictor, Grey Gargoyle, Ringmaster, Stilt-Man (prev 5 bts), Rhino (prev 7 next in AFlt #121, '93), Anaconda, Coachwhip, Rock Python (prev 3 bts),Puff Adder (prev 5 next in Cap #434, '94), Ringer, Whirlwind (both bts), Blacklash, Blizzard, Spymaster (prev 5 next in SenSH #59, '94), Boomslang, Drill, Triple-Iron, Wildfire, Gen. Wo (prev 5 bts, last app), Aqueduct, Man-Bull (both bts, next in NW #36, '93), Black Talon, Man-Ape (bts) (both next in WM #24, '93), Bullet, Razor-Fist (both bts, next in Elektra #5, '97), Firebrand, Jackhammer (both bts, next in UJack #2, '06), Oddball, Trickshot (both bts, next in Hawk #1, '98), Absorbing Man (bts, next in InfC #3, '93), Battleaxe (bts, next in MsM #18, '07), Boomerang (bts, next in UJack #1, '06), Boomslang (bts, next in LFSM #1, '93), Dragonfly (bts, next in Tb #24, '00), Eel (next in WoSM #98, '93), Electro (bts, next in SM #38, '93), Flying Tiger (bts, next in Tb #3, '97), Frenzy (next in UXM #298, '93), Gladiatrix (bts, next in CW:FL #4, '06), Hammerhead (bts, next in PPSSM #204, '93), Hydroman (bts, next in SMU #6, '94), Killer Shrike (next in NW #35, '93), Klaw (bts, next in FFu #1, '93), Knickknack (bts, chr next in Av:In #27, '09 fb, next in Tb #53, '01), Knockout (bts, next in MKSM #6, '04), Lady Deathstrike (bts, next in W #76, '93), Mad Dog (bts, next in SirenInf, '95), Mentallo (next in WoSM #100, '93), Mesmero (bts, next in X #21, '93), MODAM (next in IM #296, '93), Moonstone (bts, next in AvUnp #1, '95), Poundcakes (bts, next bts in USAgent #1, '01, next in USAgent #2, '01), Ramrod (bts, next in ASM #562, '08), Resistants (bts, group next in Cap #326, '94), Scorpion (next in SMU #1/2, '93), Shocker (bts, next in WoSM #109, '93), Shockwave (bts, next in SM #81, '97), Slyde (bts, next in SMU #6/2, '94), Speed Demon (bts, next in SM:PoT #1, '95), Stiletto (bts, next in BP #16, '00), Sunstroke (bts, chr next in Tb #25, '99 fb, next in Tb #24, '99), Tarantula (bts, next in MCP #124/4, '93), Thermo (bts, next in WWHulk:FL #3/2, '07), Titania (bts, next in SenSH #52, '93), Tombstone (bts, next in MSMK #48, '93), Trump (bts, next in Starb #1, '94), Vertigo (bts, next in XMan #13, '96), Saur-Lords (anthropomorphized dinosaurs, all 1st): Styro (styracosaurus), Bront (brontosaurus), 3 others (allosaurus, pteranodon, & ankylosaurus); A.I.M. agents

OTHER CHARACTERS: Wakandans, Danno (of the Savage Land Fall People, bts, told Ka-Zar of A.I.M.'s mining operation, only app)

LOCATIONS/ITEMS: Boca Caliente, Atlantic Ocean, Savage Land inc mining site & Saur-Lords' hut, Wakanda inc airfield & royal stateroom; Superia's shackles (destroyed), Falcon's & Diamondback's Avengers IDs, A.I.M. hover platforms, guns, automated drilling machine & aquatic androids (all destroyed), Cap's sky-cycle, emergency kit w/cable-shooter & jet w/EMP bombs, Fury's aircraft, Antarctic Vibranium

FLASHBACK: Diamondback nearly drowns (Cap #388, '91).

SYNOPSIS: Captain America rescues an ungrateful Superia from MODAM. Moonhunter picks Cap up, and Cap takes a sky-cycle back to Boca Caliente where Falcon and Shang-Chi are still battling a horde of super-villains. In the Savage Land, Ka-Zar discovers A.I.M. drilling for Vibranium. Cap picks up his allies, but aquatic A.I.M. androids stop them from escaping, sending them plunging into the Atlantic. Falcon and Cap battle the A.I.M. androids until Moonhunter picks them up. Nick Fury arrives and destroys the androids. Moonhunter tells Cap that he's been invited to Black Panther's wedding. Cap and his allies arrive in Wakanda but learn the wedding has been called off due to a recent crisis. Wakanda's economy is in chaos becasue the country's monopoly on Vibranium trade is in jeopardy due to an unknown competing source. Black Panther plans to investigate the Savage Land, the only other known source of Vibranium, and Cap offers his aid. A.I.M. captures Ka-Zar and brings him to the waiting Saur-Lords.

NOTE: Bront's name is revealed in Cap #416, '93. Letters page changes its name back to "Let's Rap with Cap."

CAPTAIN AMERICA #415 (May 1993)

"Savage Landings!" (22 pages)

CREDITS: Mark Gruenwald (writer), Rik Levins (pencils), Danny Bulanadi (inks), Joe Rosen (letters), George Roussos (colors), Joe Andreani (asst editor), Mike Rockwitz (editor), Ralph Macchio (group editor)
FEATURE CHARACTER: Captain America
GUEST STARS: Black Panther, Falcon, Ka-Zar
SUPPORTING CAST: Moonhunter (bts, piloting Cap's jet, next bts in Cap #417, '93), Diamondback
VILLAINS: High Technician (geneticist mentored by the High Evolutionary, 1st), Lorelei (Lani Ubana, Savage Land Mutate that enthralls men, last in MFan #4, '82), Saur-Lords: pteranodon & ankylosaurus; AIM agents
OTHER CHARACTERS: Zabu (last in C:Gene #4, '93), Zebra People inc Maza (1st) & chieftain, dinosaurs, Snapdragon (in Diamondback's hallucination)
LOCATIONS/ITEMS: Savage Land inc Ka-Zar's treehouse, High Technician's citadel & Zebra People's village; Cap's sky-cycle & Avengers ID, Black Panther's sky-cycle, Falcon's Avengers ID, invisible container, automated digger, AIM guns & hovercraft, Antarctic Vibranium
SYNOPSIS: Captain America, Diamondback, Falcon and Black Panther arrive in the Savage Land and split up. Cap and Diamondback search for Ka-Zar but find Zabu instead, who leads them to Ka-Zar. Falcon locates an advanced citadel and enters, but finds himself trapped in a containment device. The Panther asks directions to the mining operation from the Zebra People, who assign her a girl named Maza as a guide, secretly hoping that the Panther takes her as a wife. Maza leads Panther to the mining operation, where a crazed Ka-Zar attacks the Panther. Cap and Zabu encounter two of the Saur-Lords; as they fight Diamondback hallucinates Snapdragon and crashes the sky-cycle. Black Panther determines that Ka-Zar has been brainwashed, but they both become stuck in a tar pit. Cap and Zabu's fight with the Saur-Lords ends when armed AIM agents surround them. Falcon's captor, the High Technician, orders Lorelei to enthrall Falcon with her powers.
NOTE: "Let's Rap With Cap" contains LOC from future comics writer B. Clay Moore.

CAPTAIN AMERICA #416 (June 1993)

"Escape from A.I.M. Isle" (22 pages)

CREDITS: Mark Gruenwald (writer), Rik Levins (pencils), Danny Bulanadi (inks), Joe Rosen (letters), George Roussos (colors), Joe Andreani (asst editor), Mike Rockwitz (editor), Ralph Macchio (group editor)
FEATURE CHARACTER: Captain America
GUEST STARS: Black Panther, Falcon, Ka-Zar
SUPPORTING CAST: Diamondback (also in pfb & as AIM agent)
VILLAINS: High Technician, Lorelei; Saur-Lords: Bront, Styro, allosaurus (prev 3 last in Cap #414, '93), ankylosaurus, pteranodon; AIM agent Macross (as Terminus, 1st, see NOTE), other AIM agents (inc teams Unit K & Unit R, Unit R leader Magnusen named, some also in pfb)
OTHER CHARACTERS: Zabu (next in TMU #1, '97), Maza (last app), dinosaurs, Snapdragon (in Rachel's hallucination)
LOCATIONS/ITEMS: Savage Land inc High Technician's citadel; AIM agents' guns & radios, Black Panther's sky-cycle & Avengers ID, High Technician's electrical shackles
FLASHBACK: Diamondback subdues and impersonates an AIM agent, and opens fire on the other AIM agents (p).
SYNOPSIS: An AIM agent's wild gunfire allows Captain America and Zabu to overpower their captors. Diamondback reveals herself and defeats the Saur-Lords. Black Panther frees himself from the tar pit and leaves a vine for the brainwashed Ka-Zar. As the Panther reunites with Maza, the High Technician explains to Falcon that he has exchanged Vibranium mining rights to AIM for the energy needed for his experiments, then sends Falcon out to summon Cap and the others. Falcon contacts Cap and the Panther and requests a rendezvous, just as the Saur-Lords' pteranodon abducts Maza. AIM Unit K calls for backup, but AIM Unit R is busy investigating a metallic artifact. The heroes meet at the citadel, where Falcon reveals that, protected from Lorelei's power by his lenses, he faked being brainwashed. After freeing Maza, Panther joins the heroes to defeat the remaining Saur-Lords. Suddenly, Terminus arrives and begins to uproot the citadel from its foundation.
NOTE: AIM agent Macross is named & revealed to be piloting the Terminus armor in Cap #417, '93. "Macross" is also the name of an anime series beginning in 1982 featuring humans piloting giant robots. Terminus himself is last in Av Ann #19, '90, next in FF #3, '98.

CAPTAIN AMERICA #417 (July 1993)

"Termination Day" (22 pages)

CREDITS: Mark Gruenwald (writer), Rik Levins (pencils), Danny Bulanadi (inks), Joe Rosen (letters), George Roussos (colors), Joe Andreani (asst editor), Mike Rockwitz (editor), Ralph Macchio (group editor)
FEATURE CHARACTER: Captain America
GUEST STARS: Black Panther (next in MCP #148/3, '94), Ka-Zar (chr next in XMU #1, '93 fb, next in TMU #1, '97), Falcon
SUPPORTING CAST: Moonhunter (bts, piloting Cap's jet, last bts in Cap #415, '93), Diamondback
VILLAINS: High Technician, Saur-Lords: Bront, allosaurus, ankylosaurus (prev 3 bts, inside High Technician's citadel), Styro, pteranodon (all last app), Lorelei (next in Cable&Dp #49, '08), AIM agent Macross (as Terminus, last app), other AIM agents
OTHER CHARACTERS: Dinosaurs, Snapdragon (in Diamondback's hallucination)
LOCATIONS/ITEMS: Savage Land inc the High Technician's citadel & AIM's Vibranium mine; Cap's sky-cycle (destroyed) & Avengers ID, AIM agents' guns, hovercraft & hard-plastic mining barge, Antarctic Vibranium

SYNOPSIS: The sight of Terminus' footprint enrages Ka-Zar enough to free him from Lorelei's control. Captain America, Diamondback and Black Panther leap onto Terminus as he shakes the citadel. Diamondback falls off, but Falcon catches her. Terminus grabs the High Technician and walks away. Diamondback attacks Terminus with Cap's sky-cycle, but she hallucinates Snapdragon again and crashes against Terminus' face; Cap barely gets his shield in front of her before the sky-cycle explodes. Cap leaps off Terminus and catches her as she falls into the jungle. The Panther enters Terminus' head and finds an AIM agent inside, who traps Black Panther. Cap summons Moonhunter to retrieve the injured Diamondback. Falcon waits with Rachel and lends Cap his wings so Cap can return to Terminus. Cap finds Ka-Zar on Terminus' leg, and they ride on Terminus to AIM's mine. Cap and Ka-Zar trick Terminus into grabbing a cache of Antarctic Vibranium, which causes Terminus to fall apart. Black Panther offers Cap the use of Wakanda's medical facilities for Diamondback, then announces his intent to stay behind and drive away the Savage Land's invaders.

CAPTAIN AMERICA #418 (August 1993)

"To Have and to Have Not" (22 pages)

CREDITS: Mark Gruenwald (writer), Rik Levins (pencils), Danny Bulanadi (inks), Joe Rosen (letters), George Roussos (colors), Joe Andreani (asst editor), Mike Rockwitz (editor), Ralph Macchio (group editor)
FEATURE CHARACTER: Captain America (next in SSol #5, Av #360-366, AvCol, Hulk #406, PPSSM #202, WoSM #103, ASM #380, SM #37, PPSSM #203, IM #292, SenSH #55, SecDef #6-8, SSWP #15 all '93, Plas #3-4, '94)
GUEST STAR: Falcon (next in MCP #147/3, '94)
SUPPORTING CAST: Diamondback (next bts in Cap #420, '93), Moonhunter (next in Cap #422, '93), Dennis Dunphy (also as "Brother D" & in rfb, last in Cap #411, '93, next in Cap #422, '93)
VILLAIN: Brother Have-Not (Night People's strength-sapping leader, only app)
OTHER CHARACTERS: Brother Wonderful (last in Cap #411, '93, last app), Jikjak (also in rfb, last in Cap #410, '92, last app), other Night People (Brother Broomstick, Brother Glove, Brother Post, Brother Redeye, Brother Waycool & Sister Sweet named); Wakandans (Dr. Uburu named), police; Demolition Man doppelganger, Brother Reeko, Bernie Rosenthal (prev 3 in rfb)
LOCATIONS/ITEMS: Zerotown (also in rfb); New York inc Central Park Lagoon (in rfb), bodega & Avengers Mansion w/hangar; Wakanda inc airfield & hospital w/Diamondback's hospital room; electric chair, Dennis' cage, police guns & shotgun
FLASHBACKS: Dennis and Bernie walk through Central Park (Cap #405, '92). Dennis is attacked and nearly drowned by an evil doppelganger (Cap #409, '92). Dennis awakens in Zerotown (Cap #410, '92).
SYNOPSIS: In Zerotown, Brother Wonderful tortures Dennis Dunphy until Brother Have-Not commands that Dennis be released, since he cannot speak if he dies. Dennis is caged and Have-Not drains Dennis' strength. At a Wakandan hospital, Captain America holds vigil over the stabilized but still comatose Diamondback. The young Jikjak wakes Dennis and asks him to free Zerotown from Have-Not's insane leadership. Have-Not stops Dennis and Jikjak from escaping Zerotown. Dennis stops Have-Not from punishing Jikjak with a beating, and says "Don't," the first word Dennis has spoken in months. Falcon convinces Cap to return to the States. Impressed with Dennis' fighting spirit, Have-Not invites Dennis on a foraging mission aboveground. Dennis protests when he realizes "foraging" actually means stealing, but Have-Not easily beats Dennis by stealing his power. Dennis sends Jikjak to Avengers Mansion for Cap. Dennis fights Have-Not by throwing things from a distance, out of Have-Not's power's range. Cap arrives in time to save the intervening police and Dennis defeats Have-Not. Cap greets Dennis, who says he has found a new purpose.

CAPTAIN AMERICA #419 (September 1993)

"Television Blind" (22 pages)

CREDITS: Mark Gruenwald (writer), Rik Levins (pencils), Danny Bulanadi (inks), Joe Rosen (letters), George Roussos (colors), Joe Andreani (asst editor), Mike Rockwitz (editor), Ralph Macchio (group editor)
FEATURE CHARACTER: Captain America (next in InfC #1, Thor #464, MSMK #57, InfC #2, WoSM #104, DrS #55, Wlk&IW #19, InfC #3, WoSM #106, InfC #4-6, Av:TO #1-4, Cap Ann #12/2, all '93)
GUEST STARS: Silver Sable & her Wild Pack: Battlestar, Amy Chen, Doug Powell, Raul Quentino (all between SSWP #15-16, '93)
VILLAINS: Red Skull (last in NF:AoS #45, '93, last bts in SSWP #15, '93), Iron Monger (Christoph Pfeifer, Red Skull's agent, dies only app), Viper (also in photo, last in SSWP #15, '93, next in Hawk #1, '94) & her Fangs: Bludgeon (last voice only in Cap #364/2, '89), Heat-Ray (last in Q #41, '92), Razorblade (last in Av #130, '74) (prev 3 last apps), Slither (last in Cap #344, '88, next in NW #6, '00); Viper's men
LOCATIONS/ITEMS: Bronx, Red Skull's lair, American Southwest desert inc Viper's broadcast base; Viper's antenna tower, restraints & muzzle, Silver Sable's gun, chais grappling hook, jet & micro-infinity bugs, Battlestar's knockout gas, Red Skull's monitor, Fangs' helicopter
SYNOPSIS: Captain America stops Silver Sable from killing the captive Viper. Cap tells Sable that it was Red Skull who hired the Wild Pack to capture Viper, and Sable agrees to use Viper as bait to lure out the Skull. They leave Viper at the contractually agreed upon drop site in the America Southwest, but with micro-infinity bugs under Viper's skin. Iron Monger arrives with a monitor through which Red Skull interrogates Viper about her plan. When Viper doesn't answer, Iron Monger breaks one of her legs. Viper's Fangs arrive, free Viper and kill Iron Monger. Cap, Sable, and Battlestar follow the Fangs back to the Viper's base, a broadcast station set to emit a television signal that will blind everyone watching television in America, and defeat Viper's Fangs. Cap destroys the antenna tower, and Viper realizes her plan is foiled when the power cuts out.
NOTE: Story continued from SSWP #15, '93. Pfeifer's name is revealed in IManual, '08.

"Blood of a Fighter" (16 pages)

CREDITS: Mark Gruenwald, David Wohl (writers), M.C. Wyman (pencils), Charles Barnett III (inks), Rick Parker (letters), John Kalisz (colors), Barry Dutter (asst editor), Mike Rockwitz (editor), Ralph Macchio (group editor)
FEATURE CHARACTER: Bantam (Roberto Velasquez, augmented boxer w/healing powers, 1st)
VILLAINS: Armando Aviles (businessman, 1st) & his augmented men (inc Hammerhand (Rico Lazar, boxer, 1st), some die), Dr. Karl Malus (last in Cap #378/2, '90)
OTHER CHARACTERS: Manuel Torres (boxer, 1st), Trini (boxing trainer, 1st), Emilio Garzon (boxer, dies), chicken fighters, boxing announcer, referee & fans, paramedics, police, chickens, alligator
LOCATIONS/ITEMS: San Juan, Puerto Rico inc Trini's gym, Miami, FL inc Malus' lab, boxing arena, Aviles' apartment & sporting goods store; Malus' augmentation equipment, Aviles' gun, augmented men's guns
SYNOPSIS: In Puerto Rico, Armando Aviles approaches promising young boxer Roberto Velasquez with an offer: come with him to Miami and he can make Roberto the best fighter who ever lived. Roberto soon undergoes Dr. Malus' augmentation treatment, but doesn't notice a difference. When Roberto begins to lose his first boxing match, he finds himself in a berserker rage and accidentally kills his opponent Emilio Garzon. Roberto confronts Aviles and leaves. Needing a new boxer, Aviles recruits Roberto's friend Manuel Torres, who's later gravely injured in the ring against Rico "Hammerhand" Lazar. Roberto returns to confront Aviles over Manuel's injury and Aviles shoots Roberto, leaving him for dead. Roberto wakes up to find he's not injured, robs Aviles' sporting goods store for a costume and returns as Bantam. Aviles' men are killed in the ensuing shootout and Bantam escapes.
NOTE: All of Marvel's 1993 Annuals were bagged with trading cards featuring a new character introduced in each issue. This issue's card, #2 in the series, featured Bantam with pencils by Ron Lim, inks by Michael Kraiger and colors by Paul Mounts. Also includes Contents Page featuring Captain America and Falcon by Andy Smith.

2ND STORY: "...And in This Corner... the Battling Bantam!" (19 pages)
CREDITS: Mark Gruenwald, David Wohl (writers), M.C. Wyman (pencils), Charles Barnett III (inks), Rick Parker (letters), John Kalisz (colors), Barry Dutter (asst editor), Mike Rockwitz (editor), Ralph Macchio (group editor)
FEATURE CHARACTER: Captain America (also as "Mr. Stevens," next in Cap #420, '93)
GUEST STAR: Bantam
VILLAINS: Armando Aviles & his augmented men (inc Hammerhand) (all last app), Dr. Karl Malus (next in Cage #13, '93)
OTHER CHARACTERS: Manuel Torres (dies), Mr. Cruz (boxing promoter), Rollo (augmented boxer), other boxers, hospital staff & patients, Miami bystanders
LOCATIONS/ITEMS: Miami, FL inc hospital w/Manuel's room, gym w/Aviles' office, Malu's lab & docks; Cap's motorcycle, Malus' augmentation equipment, Aviles' gun & boat
SYNOPSIS: Captain America arrives in Miami to investigate a report of augmented boxers. Cap interviews Manuel Torres in his hospital room, but Manuel refuses to talk. When Cap leaves, Hammerhand kills Manuel. As "Mr. Stevens," Cap auditions to be one of Armando Aviles' boxers, and easily defeats his sparring opponent Rollo. Suspicious, Aviles and his men interrogate Cap, who claims to be a mutant. Meanwhile, Bantam learns that Manuel is dead. Cap is brought to Dr. Malus' lab, but Bantam bursts through the door and attacks Aviles' men in a berserker rage. Aviles escapes while Cap subdues Malus and calms down Bantam. Cap captures the fleeing Aviles while Bantam defeats Hammerhand. Cap and Bantam depart as friends.

3RD STORY: "The Bantam Returns" (11 pages)
CREDITS: Barry Dutter (writer, asst editor), Grant Miehm (art), Diana Albers (letters), Dave Sampson (colors), Mike Rockwitz (editor), Ralph Macchio (group editor)
FEATURE CHARACTER: Bantam (also in rfb as Roberto Velasquez, chr next bts in CW:BDR, '07, next in CW:FL #3, '06)
OTHER CHARACTERS: 2 street gangs (Hector named, some become boxers), Trini (last app); Captain America (in rfb & Bantam's thoughts), Emilio Garzon (in rfb)
LOCATIONS/ITEMS: San Juan, Puerto Rico inc Trini's gym; boxing equipment, Hector's gun
FLASHBACKS: Roberto accidentally kills Emilio Garzon (Cap Ann #12, '93) and as Bantam, meets Captain America (Cap Ann #12/2, '93).
SYNOPSIS: Upset that his boxing career is over, Bantam exercises in Trini's gym. Trini offers him a job as a trainer and Bantam says he'll think about it. Outside, Bantam comes across two fighting gangs. He questions their toughness and challenges their best fighter, Hector, to a fight. Hector shoots Bantam, who doesn't die. Bantam makes his point that guns and killing are no way to live, and they should think about taking up boxing to settle their differences. Later, Bantam trains some of the gang members in boxing.
NOTE: Followed by five pin-ups: Falcon (2 pages) by Don Hudson, Crossbones (1 page) by Andy Smith, Captain America and Falcon (1 page, same image as Contents Page) by Andy Smith, Diamondback (2 pages) by Don Hudson and a Bantam origin recap (2 pages) by M.C. Wyman, pencils and Charles Barnett III, inks.

CAPTAIN AMERICA #420 (October 1993)

"Skull Sessions" (22 pages)

CREDITS: Mark Gruenwald (writer), Richard Levins (pencils, c art), Danny Bulanadi (inks), Joe Rosen (letters), George Roussos (colors), Joe Andreani (asst editor), Mike Rockwitz (editor), Ralph Macchio (group editor)
FEATURE CHARACTER: Captain America (next in Cap #421, '93 fb, Nomad #18, '93)
GUEST STARS: Blazing Skull (Jim Scully, occult investigator w/glowing skeleton, also in rfb, last in Q #50, '93, next in Hawk #1, '94), Dr. Druid (bts, vouches for Blazing Skull, last in Q #51, '93 fb, next in SecDef #15, '94), Nomad (last in Nomad #17, '93, chr last in Nomad #18, '93 fb, next in Nomad #18, '93), Quasar (between Q #52-53, '93), Nick Fury (last in SSol #7, '93, next in W/NF:SR '94), Gabe Jones (last in NF:AoS #47, '93, next in Hulk #434, '95)
SUPPORTING CAST: Peggy Carter (voice only, last bts in Cap #414, '93, next in Starb #1, '94), Diamondback (bts, in coma, last in Cap #418, '93, next in Cap #422, '93)
VILLAINS: Nightshift: Brothers Grimm (next in AvUnp #4, '96), Digger (next bts in Tb #111, '07, next in MZ4 #2, '09), Misfit (last app), Needle (next in Av:In Ann #1/2, '08) (all last in AWC #79, '93); Red Skull (next in DCut #3, '94) & his men, Machinesmith (last in Cap #409, '92, chr next in Cap #451, '96 fb, next in IM #320, '95), Dr. Faustus (last in Cap #326, '87, last bts in Nomad #18, '93 fb, chr next in Cap #421, '93 fb, next in Nomad #18, '93)
OTHER CHARACTERS: Alexander Pierce (last in SSWP #17, '93, next bts in SSWP #25, '94, next in SecWs #12, '10), Clay Quartermain (last in SSWP #17, '93, next in SSWP #25, '94), Gail Runciter (last in NF:AoS #43, '93, next bts in NAvF, '06), Jimmy Woo (last in SSWP #17, '93, next in DD Ann #10, '94), other SHIELD agents, Giscard Epurer (Favor Banker, between Nomad #17-18, '93), Dr. Ugani (Wakandan doctor, only app); dinosaur (in rfb)
LOCATIONS/ITEMS: Red Skull's Rocky Mountain chalet & backup hideout, Dr. Faustus's psychiatric ward; Red Skull's robots, booby trapped mannequin & satellite, Red Skull's men's guns, Brothers Grimm's flying crescent moons, meat cleavers & buzz saws, Digger's shovel, Needle's needlegun, SHIELD jet packs, guns & plasma cannons
FLASHBACK: Jim Scully fights a dinosaur (MTIO #35, '78).
SYNOPSIS: Captain America, Nick Fury and SHIELD storm Red Skull's Rocky Mountain chalet, but quickly discover the Skull has already fled. As Quasar and SHIELD clean up, Fury gives Cap a possible lead on where the Skull may be. In Los Angeles, Blazing Skull battles Digger and begins to interrogate him, but Cap arrives and interrupts. Cap accuses Blazing Skull as having ties with Red Skull, Blazing Skull accuses Cap of being a villain in disguise, and the two fight. The Night Shift arrive to assist Digger, so Cap and Blazing Skull team up to defeat them. Meanwhile, Red Skull laments to Machinesmith to having to abandon yet another base. Later, Cap receives a message from Giscard Epurer that Dr. Faustus is holding Nomad prisoner.
NOTE: Continued in Nomad #18, '93, erroneously listed as Nomad #19, '93.

CAPTAIN AMERICA #421 (November 1993)

"Gauntlet" (22 pages)

CREDITS: Mark Gruenwald (writer), Rik Levins (pencils), Dan Day (inks, c inks), Brian Garvey, Danny Bulanadi (inks), Joe Rosen (letters), George Roussos (colors), Joe Andreani (asst editor), Mike Rockwitz (editor), Ralph Macchio (group editor)
FEATURE CHARACTER: Captain America (also in rfb & in fb between Cap #420, '93 & Nomad #18, '93; next in Nomad #19, Dhawk #33, Av #367, AWC #100, Av #368, X #26, AWC #101, UXM #307, Av #369, AWC #102, all '93, Dhawk #37, Q #58 & 60, Wlk&IW #26-28, Av #370-371, Tstrike #4, all '94, Cap/NF:BT, '95)
GUEST STAR: Nomad (also in rfb as Jack Monroe; between Nomad #18-19, '93)
VILLAINS: Dr. Faustus (only in fb between Cap #420, '93 & Nomad #18, '93), his 3 hitmen (Li, Mr. Pinkus & Mr. Waxman, 1ˢᵗ, only in fb, see NOTE) & his Wanderers: Billy, Chisel, Flintlock (prev 3 between Nomad #18-19, '93), Outback (last in Nomad #18, '93, last app); Slug (last in Nomad #18, '93, next in SM #43, '94) & his Cannibal Catch: Folio, Hardhat, Transom (prev 3 last in Nomad #18, '93, last app)
OTHER CHARACTERS: Ed Monroe (Nomad's father), Giscard Epurer (both in rfb); Adolf Hitler (in painting)
LOCATIONS/ITEMS: Dr. Faustus' psychiatric ward (also in fb), Miami, FL inc Slug's estate; Cap's jet pack & motorcycle (both in fb), Nomad's shotgun, Slug's mobile platform, Faustus' hitmen's guns, Wanderer's guns
FLASHBACKS: Giscard Epurer tells Cap that Dr. Faustus is holding Nomad prisoner (Cap #420, '93). When young Jack Monroe discovers his father is a Nazi spy, he's given a beating (Nomad #19, '93 fb). Captain America breaks into Dr. Faustus' psychiatric ward, confronting Faustus and defeating his men. Faustus admits he's sent Nomad to kill Slug.
SYNOPSIS: Captain America battles Nomad, stopping from killing Slug, who slips away during the fight. Nomad insists that Dr. Faustus revealed the truth to him; that he's a Nazi like his father was. Cap gets Nomad to realize that his father's sins are not his own, snapping Nomad out of his delusion. Seeing that Slug has escaped, Cap races outside in time to see Faustus' Wanderers shoot down the escaping Slug's flying platform. As Slug crashes in the ocean, Cap quickly defeats both the Wanderers and Slug's Cannibal Catch. Cap doubles back to check on Nomad but discovers his old is partner gone, and concludes Nomad has left to confront Dr. Faustus.
NOTE: Continued from Nomad #18, '93, continued in Nomad #19, '93. Mr. Pinkus is named in Cap #422, '93.

CAPTAIN AMERICA #422 (December 1993)

"Going Ballistic" (22 pages)

CREDITS: Mark Gruenwald (writer), Rik Levins (pencils), Danny Bulanadi (inks), Joe Rosen (letters), George Roussos (colors), Joe Andreani (asst editor), Mike Rockwitz (editor), Ralph Macchio (group editor)
FEATURE CHARACTER: Captain America (next in Cap #424, '94)
GUEST STARS: Avengers: Black Widow (last in Av #370, '94 fb, next in Cap #424, '94), Vision (bts, looking for hitmen, last in Av #370, '94 fb, next in Cap #425, '94)
SUPPORTING CAST: Avengers Crew: Peggy Carter (last in Starb #1, '94, last bts in Q #60, '94, next bts in MCP #147/3, '94, next voice only in Cap #424, '94), Moonhunter (last in Cap #418, '93, next in Cap #427, '94), Michael O'Brien (last in IM #300, '94, next in Av Ann '99 fb), Fabian Stankowicz (last in Cap #408/3, '92, next in Cap #424, '94, leaves Avengers Crew); Diamondback (also in photo, last bts in Cap #420, '93, next in Cap #424, '94), Dennis Dunphy (last in Cap #418, '93, next in Cap #440, '95)
VILLAINS: Blistik (Victor Lillian, crazed vigilante, only app), Dr. Faustus' 2 hitmen (Mr. Pinkus & Mr. Waxman, both last app)
OTHER CHARACTERS: Luna Maximoff (last in Av #369, '93, next in Av #372, '94), Marilla (Luna's nanny, last in Av #368, '93, next in Av #373, '94), Wakandan doctor & nurse, taxi driver, police, firemen, paramedics, noise polluters, bystanders; Avengers: Captain America (destroyed), Hawkeye, Hulk, Iron Man, Thor, Wasp (prev 6 statues)
LOCATIONS/ITEMS: New York inc Avengers Mansion w/Fabian's workshop, hotel & Central Park, Brooklyn Bridge, Wakandan General hospital; Fabian's robot & note, Blistik's staff, hit-men's sniper rifles & van, Cap's sky-cycle & Avengers ID, Stars & Stripes office
SYNOPSIS: Dr. Faustus' hitmen send a message by destroying the Captain America statue outside Avengers Mansion; Cap cuts his visit with Dennis short to investigate. Meanwhile, Blistik attacks some teens with loud boomboxes for the crime of noise pollution. The hitmen shoot at Cap and drive off, but Blistik blows up their van for running a red light. Unable to find Blistik, Cap returns to Avengers Mansion where Black Widow tells Cap it may be time to fire Fabian; he's only productive when Cap is around. Cap says he'll think about it. In Wakanda, Diamondback comes out of her coma. Unable to sleep, Cap looks for Fabian but only finds his goodbye note. Searching, Cap finds Fabian atop the Brooklyn Bridge with Blistik goading him to jump. Blistik attacks Cap for interfering in his mission, but loses control when Cap fights back and falls into the water below. Cap tells Fabian he has no intention of firing him, and reveals it's time for Captain America to take a break from the Avengers.
NOTE: Blistik's real name is revealed in CW:BDR, '07.

CAPTAIN AMERICA #423 (January 1994)

"War Zones" (22 pages)

CREDITS: Roy Thomas (writer), M.C. Wyman (pencils), Charles Barnett III (inks), Diana Albers (letters), Ovi Hondru (colors), Joe Andreani (asst editor), Mike Rockwitz (editor), Ralph Macchio (group editor), Danny Bulanadi (c inks), Walt Weffelf ("Technical Advisor")
FEATURE CHARACTER: Captain America (also on splash page, last in ToS #63/2, '65, next in CapC #1/2, '41)
GUEST STARS: Human Torch (Jim Hammond, last in HT #3/3, '41, next in MC #14, '41), Sub-Mariner (last in HT #3/3, '41, next in MC #15/2, '41)
SUPPORTING CAST: Bucky (also on splash page, last in ToS #63/2, '65, next in CapC #1/2, '41)
VILLAINS: Nazi saboteurs, German Navy (inc a Captain)
OTHER CHARACTERS: Franklin D. Roosevelt (US President, last in Cap:SoL #7/2, '99, next in CapC #4, '41), Life Magazine representative, US Navy (Charlie & Sam named) & Army, reporters, police, bystanders; British, Italian, Japanese & Russian soldiers (on splash page)
LOCATIONS/ITEMS: Manhattan, Atlantic inc island, Washington DC inc Capitol, White House & Potomac River; munitions train, saboteurs' explosives, Atlantean ship, US guns, planes & Destroyers, German U-boat, scuba gear & luger, Allied & Axis tanks & guns (on splash page)
SYNOPSIS: Captain America and Bucky stop Nazis from sabotaging a munitions train. Meanwhile, Namor the Sub-Mariner escapes following another battle with the Human Torch. Overhearing Navy men arguing about America not being involved in the war in Europe yet, Namor decides he's been warring against the surface world in the wrong way. At a presidential press conference Cap introduces his new partner Bucky to the press but Namor attacks and kidnaps Roosevelt; Cap pursues while Bucky deals with the press. Taking Roosevelt to a small island, Namor radios his ransom demands to the US, but a U-boat intercepts the transmission. Arriving at the island Cap fights Namor until the Germans arrive and capture Roosevelt. Cap and Namor team-up to defeat the Germans and rescue the President. Impressed with Cap's and Roosevelt's bravery, Namor departs in peace, thinking that maybe not all surface dwellers are bad.

CAPTAIN AMERICA #424 (February 1994)

"The Last Operation" (22 pages)

CREDITS: Mark Gruenwald (writer), Phil Gosier (pencils), Romeo Tanghal (inks), Joe Rosen (letters), George Roussos (colors), Joe Andreani (asst editor), Mike Rockwitz (editor), Ralph Macchio (group editor), Danny Bulanadi (c inks)
FEATURE CHARACTER: Captain America (next in CM #1, '94)
GUEST STAR: Black Widow (last in Cap #422, '93)
SUPPORTING CAST: Diamondback (last in Cap #422, '93), Peggy Carter (voice only, last in Cap #422, '93, last bts in MCP #147/3, '94), Fabian Stankowicz (last in Cap #422, '93, next in Cap #426, '94)
VILLAINS: Sidewinder (last in Cap Ann #10/4, '91, next in NTb #7, '05), drug dealers (Mariano, Morgan, Mr. Dinsdale & Mr. Henshaw named)
OTHER CHARACTERS: Amelia Voelker (Sidewinder's daughter), Mrs. Voelker (Sidewinder's ex-wife), Dr.

Clendening (Amelia's doctor) (all only app), Vault personnel, police; Snapdragon (in Diamondback's hallucination)

LOCATIONS/ITEMS: New York inc Avengers Mansion w/Steve's room & Fabian's workshop, hospital w/Amelia's room & corner of 37th St & 7th Ave, Lower Manhattan drug dealer's hideout, South Bronx drug dealer's hideout; Sidewinder's smoke bombs & emergency beeper, Cap's Avengers ID & video communicator suitcase, drug dealers' guns & knives, Vault van

SYNOPSIS: Captain America is reunited with Diamondback. Meanwhile at a nearby hospital, Sidewinder visits his daughter Amelia, who needs a costly brain operation. As Steve, Fabian and Rachel pack up their belongings, Sidewinder contacts Captain America. The two meet and Sidewinder asks Cap for money to pay for his daughter's operation, stating he's retired from crime. When Cap is hesitant to help, Sidewinder furiously leaves and later robs some drug dealers. As Diamondback confronts Sidewinder Cap interviews his ex-wife, learning Sidewinder was telling the truth. Later, Sidewinder runs into trouble trying to rob other drug dealers and Cap and Diamondback come to his rescue. Cap agrees to help Amelia if Sidewinder turns himself in; Sidewinder accepts. Diamondback later admits to Cap that she killed Snapdragon. Cap says they'll have to verify Snapdragon's death, and that he'll stand by her if it goes to court.

CAPTAIN AMERICA #425 (March 1994)

"Fighting Chance Part One: Super Patriot Games" (31 pages)

CREDITS: Mark Gruenwald (writer), Dave Hoover (pencils, c art), Danny Bulanadi (inks), Joe Rosen (letters), George Roussos (colors), Joe Andreani (asst editor), Mike Rockwitz (editor), Ralph Macchio (group editor)
FEATURE CHARACTER: Captain America (next in DD #326-329, '94)
GUEST STARS: Avengers: Black Knight (last in Av #371, '94, next in DD #327, '94), Black Widow (also in dfb, next in DD Ann #10/2, '94), Vision (also as statue, last bts in Cap #422, '93, next in DD #327, '94)
SUPPORTING CAST: Avengers Crew: Dr. Keith Kincaid (last in Av #351, '92, last bts in Dhold #3, '92 fb, next in Cap #431, '94), Peggy Carter; Diamondback (next in Cap #427, '94)
VILLAINS: Super-Patriot (Mike Farrel, also as Captain America, last in Cap #386, '91, chr last in Cap #439, '95 fb), Dead Ringer (Lou Dexter, mimics appearance & powers of deceased, also as Porcupine, Mirage & Purple Man, 1st but chr last in Cap #439, '95 fb, also in dfb, see NOTE), Tinkerer (last in SenSH #59, '94, next in SM:DMH, '97)

OTHER CHARACTERS: Rudolph & Constance Bradley (mayoral candidate & wife), restaurant patrons (Barney named), bar patrons (Bruzo, Lenny & Tony named), bartender, Super-Patriot's date, comic shop owner & shoplifter, Plaza hotel doorman, staff & guests, cameramen, reporters, bystanders; Masters of Evil: Baron Zemo, Black Knight, Executioner, Melter (prev 4 holograms); Hulk, Quicksilver (both statues)

LOCATIONS/ITEMS: Tinkerer's workshop, Cap's Brooklyn HQ inc Rokatanski's costume shop, Lower East Side bar, Plaza hotel restaurant, Columbus Ave. café, Avengers HQ inc Avengers Park, security room & training room; Avengers training robots, Tinkerer's equipment inc Goblin Glider, Stilt-Man's legs, pumpkin bomb, Gladiator's buzz-saw, MODOK's Doomsday Chair, Dr. Octopus' arms, Titanium Man armor & Guardsman pants, Super-Patriot's shield, Porcupine's quills, comic books, Cap's Avengers ID, Black Knight's energy sword, masks of Beast, Conan, Guy Fawkes, Howard the Duck, Hulk, Magneto, a mummy, Night Thrasher, Spider-Man & Thor

FLASHBACK: Mirage turns into Purple Man and commands Black Widow to release him (d).

SYNOPSIS: Super-Patriot obtains a Captain America shield replica from the Tinkerer. Elsewhere, Dr. Kincaid tells Cap that the Super Soldier serum has broken down in his system, and that if he doesn't slow down he could be paralyzed within a year. Meanwhile, a faux Cap goes to a dive bar and gets into a minor fracas with a tough guy. Steve tells Rachel about his predicament and they go on a date to take his mind off things. The faux Cap attends Mayoral candidate Rudolph Bradley's fundraiser and gets into a fight with Porcupine, injuring bystanders in the process. Steve's date is interrupted when Peggy calls to report the Cap battle. The next day Cap holds a press conference to publicly declare someone is impersonating him, but the original Masters of Evil attack. Super-Patriot arrives to reveal the Masters are an illusion, and defeats the villain casting them, Mirage. Diamondback chases the fleeing Super-Patriot but loses him. When Cap learns that Black Widow released the captured villain, he becomes determined to get to the bottom of the latest smear campaign, despite his health problems.

NOTE: Cover-labeled "Fighting Chance Book 1." Features a diagram of Cap's Brooklyn Heights HQ (2 pages) by Elliot R. Brown & reveals it's located near the Atlantic and Flatbush Ave intersection. Also includes pin-up of Cap, Diamondback, Red Skull & his men (1 page) by Dave Hoover, pin-up of Cap, Diamondback & thugs (1 page) by Dave Hoover, pin-up of Diamondback (1 page) by Rik Levins & Danny Bulandi, and pin-up of Cap (1 page) by Mal. Cap #439, '94 reveals Super-Patriot to be Mike Farrel. Dead Ringer is named in Cap #427, '94, his first name is revealed in Cap #426, '94, and his surname in Cap #428, '94. Porcupine died in Cap #315, '86, Mirage in Cap #319, '86, and Purple Man was believed dead in MGN:ED, '87, seen in his grave in AFlt #62, '88, but XMan #34, '98 revealed he never actually died. Cap #439, '94 fb reveals Dead Ringer steals dead tissue from those he mimics, explaining how he could copy someone still alive.

CAPTAIN AMERICA #426 (April 1994)

"Graven Images" (22 pages)

CREDITS: Mark Gruenwald (writer), Dave Hoover (pencils, c art), Danny Bulanadi (inks), Joe Rosen (letters), George Roussos (colors), Joe Andreani (asst editor), Mike Rockwitz (editor), Ralph Macchio (group editor)
FEATURE CHARACTER: Captain America (next in IM #302-304, Hulk #417-418, Hulk Ann #20/4, all '94)
GUEST STAR: Falcon (last in MCP #147/3, '94, next in FW #10/2, '95)
SUPPORTING CAST: Peggy Carter (bts, contacts Cap, next bts in Cap #429, '94), Bernie Rosenthal (last in Cap #406, '92), Fabian Stankowicz (last in Cap #424, '94)
VILLAINS: Resistants: Crucible (last in Cap #394, '91), Meteorite (last in Cap #368, '90), Occult (last in Cap #346, '88) (all next in NW #6, '00); Super-Patriot (also as Captain America), Dead Ringer (also as Death Adder & Night Flyer, see NOTE)

OTHER CHARACTERS: Code: Blue (special division of New York Police Department for paranormal threats): Daniel "Fireworks" Fielstein, Andrew "Jock" Jackson, Julius "Mad Dog" Rassitanio, Margarita "Rigger" Ruiz (all last in SSWP #27, '94, next in Tstrike #5, '94), Lt. Marcus

Stone (last in SSWP #27, '94, next in Cap #428, '94), Death Adder (corpse, off panel, last in Cap #319, '86, next in Pun #5, '09), Sam Wilson's secretary, Nadine (waitress), armored car guards, workmen, diner patrons

LOCATIONS/ITEMS: Cemetery inc Death Adder's grave, Cap's Brooklyn HQ inc gym & Rokatanski's costume shop, Super-Patriot's Bay Ridge apartment, Harlem inc diner & Sam's office, Major Deegan Expressway; Super-Patriot's shield, guards' guns, Dead Ringer's gun, Code: Blue helicopter, Cap's motorcycle & Avengers ID

SYNOPSIS: Super-Patriot and Dead Ringer dig up Death Adder so Dead Ringer can copy him. At Captain America's HQ, Diamondback and Cap exercise. Needing money to pay Tinkerer for his shield, Super-Patriot, as Captain America, and Dead Ringer, as Night Flyer, continue their smear campaign against Cap by plotting to commit crimes in his name. Meanwhile, Steve visits Falcon to recruit him in looking for the Cap imposter. "Cap" and "Night Flyer" rob an armored car, but the Resistants happen by during their escape. Thinking he's the real Cap, the Resistants attack and "Cap" is forced to battle them in order to preserve his identity's integrity. Bernie stops by Cap's HQ looking for Steve and ends up setting an appointment for counsel with Diamondback. Peggy tells Steve about the robbery. The Resistants are defeated as Code: Blue arrives on the scene; "Cap" bluffs his way out of questioning. Cap and Falcon arrive too late to catch the imposter.

NOTE: Cover-labeled "Fighting Chance Book 2." Night Flyer died in Cap #214, '77; a robot duplicate previously appeared in Hulk #263-264, '81 and others will later appear in HFH #5, '07. Death Adder was killed by Scourge in Cap #318, '86, and will later be resurrected by the Hood in Pun #5, '09.

CAPTAIN AMERICA #427 (May 1994)

"Enemy Fire" (23 pages)

CREDITS: Mark Gruenwald (writer), Dave Hoover (pencils, c art), Danny Bulanadi (inks), Joe Rosen (letters), George Roussos (colors), Joe Andreani (asst editor), Mike Rockwitz (editor), Ralph Macchio (group editor)
FEATURE CHARACTER: Captain America (next in SS #93, Av #372-375, PWJ #65-66, all '94)
GUEST STAR: Quicksilver (last in Hulk Ann #20/4, '94, next in Av #372, '94)
SUPPORTING CAST: Diamondback (also in rfb, last in Cap #425, '94), Moonhunter (last in Cap #422, '93), Bernie Rosenthal (next in Cap #431, '94), Fabian Stankowicz
VILLAINS: Super-Patriot (last in Cap #425, '94, next in Cap #438, '95), Dead Ringer (also as Solarr, Cheetah, Blue Streak & Blackout, see NOTE) (both also in photo & pfb)
OTHER CHARACTERS: Sammy Bernstein (last in Cap #284, '83, last app), fast food restaurant patrons (Timmy named) & staff; Snapdragon (in rfb)
LOCATIONS/ITEMS: New York inc Sullivan and Krakower law offices, Cap's Brooklyn HQ inc meeting room & Cap's office, Pennsylvania fast food restaurant, Super-Patriot's Bay Ridge apartment; Super-Patriot's shield & gun, Cap's motorcycle
FLASHBACKS: Super-Patriot, as Captain America, battles Dead Ringer, as Solarr (p). Diamondback battles Snapdragon (Cap #412, '93).
SYNOPSIS: Captain America suspects that Super-Patriot is impersonating him to ruin his reputation. Meanwhile, "Cap" battles "Cheetah" in a fast food restaurant until an employee douses Cheetah with boiling water. Diamondback meets Bernie to seek legal advice regarding Snapdragon murder, but Bernie's ex-husband Sammy interrupts, storming in demanding Bernie take him back. Cap enlists Quicksilver's help to capture Super-Patriot. Diamondback walks Bernie home, but Dead Ringer captures them using Blackout's Darkforce powers. Super-Patriot calls Cap to ransom Bernie. Quicksilver arrives only for Dead Ringer to change into Blue Streak, tricking Quicksilver into chasing him. Super-Patriot knocks out Diamondback to "rescue" Bernie as Cap arrives. During their battle the building catches on fire. Cap's failing health stops him from rescuing Super-Patriot from the collapsing building. Quicksilver rescues Cap and captures Dead Ringer.
NOTE: Cover-labeled "Fighting Chance Book 3." Solarr died in PMIF #123, '86. Blue Streak (in Cap #318, '86) and Cheetah (in Cap #319, '86) were both killed by Scourge and both will later be resurrected by the Hood in Pun #5, '09. Blackout was thought dead in Av #277, '87, but NTb #18, '06 reveals his body was brain-dead but still alive while his mind retreated into the Darkforce Dimension.

CAPTAIN AMERICA #428 (June 1994)

"Policing the Nation" (22 pages)

CREDITS: Mark Gruenwald (writer), Dave Hoover (pencils, c art), Danny Bulanadi (inks), Joe Rosen (letters), George Roussos (colors), Joe Andreani (asst editor), Mike Rockwitz (editor), Ralph Macchio (group editor)
FEATURE CHARACTER: Captain America
SUPPORTING CAST: Arnie Roth (last in Cap #306, '85, next in Cap #431, '94), Fabian Stankowicz (next in Cap #431, '94), Diamondback, Moonhunter
VILLAINS: Americop (Bart Gallows, ultra-violent vigilante, 1st but chr last in Cap #430, '94 fb), Dead Ringer (also as Snapdragon, next in Cap #439, '94, see NOTE), Golddigger (last in Cap #395/2, '91), Kono Sanada (Snapdragon's brother, last in MFan #12, '84), 2 car thieves (both die), 3 robbers, gun smugglers (most die)
OTHER CHARACTERS: Lt. Marcus Stone (last in Cap #426, '94, next in Tstrike #5, '94), diner patrons & staff, firemen inc Mr. Morgan, St. Elmo's Firehouse staff (inc bartender Mortie), Bamaville police, bystanders
LOCATIONS/ITEMS: Maryland, New York police station, Kentucky inc diner, Brooklyn Heights, Cap's Brooklyn HQ inc Rokatanski's costume shop, New Orleans inc French Quarter, St. Elmo's Firehouse & Damon Dran's Estate, Bamaville, VA; Americop's jeep, guns, armors & billy club, Cap's sky-cycle, car thieves', robbers' & smugglers' guns, Golddigger's limo, gas mask & knockout gas, Spider-Man mask
SYNOPSIS: In Maryland, Americop murders two car thieves. Captain America and Diamondback watch Lt. Stone interrogate Dead Ringer. When Dead Ringer demonstrates his abilities by changing into Snapdragon, Diamondback demands to know where he found Snapdragon's body. In a Kentucky diner, Americop continues his violent justice by killing a group of robbers while looking for missing children. Meeting Arnie Roth at his HQ, Cap learns of Americop's spree and leaves to investigate. Diamondback and Moonhunter search for Snapdragon in New Orleans. Cap finds Americop in Virginia, but his flagging health causes him to fail in stopping Americop from killing a group of gunrunners. Diamondback and Moonhunter meet with Golddigger, who claims to know where Snapdragon is. She gasses the pair in her limo and takes

hem to her boss's mansion. Meanwhile, Americop escapes as the police arrive.

NOTE: Cover-labeled "Fighting Chance Book 4." Americop's real name is revealed in Cap #430, '94. Snapdragon was killed in Cap #413, '93.

CAPTAIN AMERICA #429 (July 1994)

"The Beaten Path" (22 pages)

CREDITS: Mark Gruenwald (writer), Dave Hoover (pencils, c art), Danny Bulanadi (inks), Joe Rosen (letters), George Roussos (colors), Joe Andreani (asst editor), Mike Rockwitz (editor), Ralph Macchio (group editor)
FEATURE CHARACTER: Captain America
SUPPORTING CAST: Diamondback (also in rfb & as "Rachel Rosencrantz" & "Nancy"), Moonhunter (also as "Zack Guildenstern" & "Sluggo"), Peggy Carter (bts, on phone, last bts in Cap #426, '94, next in Cap #431, '94)
VILLAINS: Damon Dran (indestructible businessman, last in MFan #13, '84) & his men (Maynard named), Kono Sanada, Golddigger, Americop, homophobic bullies
OTHER CHARACTERS: Bill Clinton (US President, bts on phone w/Sherriff, last in X #25, '93, next bts in Nova #9, '94, next in Cap #444, '95), Bamaville Sheriff & deputies (Marley named), gay couple; Snapdragon, gun smugglers (both in rfb)
LOCATIONS/ITEMS: Virginia inc Bamaville Sheriff's office & video rental store, Damon Dran's New Orleans estate inc cage, bedroom & spa; Cap's Avengers ID & sky-cycle, Americop's jeep w/oil slick, armor & gun, Kono's cane sword
FLASHBACKS: Gun smugglers lie dead in the street (Cap #428, '94). Diamondback drowns Snapdragon (Cap #413, '93).
SYNOPSIS: Captain America tries to convince the authorities to let him go, eventually going free when the President vouches for him over the phone. Meanwhile, Americop cripples some homophobic bullies, and evades the police. In New Orleans, Kono Sanada and Golddigger interrogate Diamondback and Moonhunter as to why they're looking for Snapdragon. Diamondback and Moonhunter knock out Golddigger and call for help. Peggy relays the message to Cap, and he abandons his search for Americop. Searching for Snapdragon, Diamondback and Moonhunter meet Damon Dran and learn that Kono is Snapdragon's brother, who confirms Snapdragon's death. Cap arrives and finds Golddigger imprisoned. He unknowingly releases her and she sucker punches him. Diamondback battles Kono and almost drowns him; when she changes her mind Dran's men capture her and Moonhunter. Cap escapes from Golddigger just as Americop crashes his jeep through the wall; his search for the missing children has led him to Damon Dran. Dran arrives with Diamondback and Moonhunter as his prisoners.
NOTE: Cover-labeled "Fighting Chance Book 5."

CAPTAIN AMERICA #430 (August 1994)

"Cop Out" (22 pages)

CREDITS: Mark Gruenwald (writer), Dave Hoover (pencils, c art), Danny Bulanadi (inks), Joe Rosen (letters), George Roussos (colors), Joe Andreani (asst editor), Mike Rockwitz (editor), Ralph Macchio (group editor)
FEATURE CHARACTER: Captain America (next in WarM #1, IM #306, bts in FW #2, Av Ann #23, all '94, SKK #2-3, '95, Cap Ann #13, '94)
GUEST STAR: Black Widow (last in Av #375/2, '94, next in FW #1, '94)
SUPPORTING CAST: Diamondback, Moonhunter
VILLAINS: Golddigger, Kono Sanada, Damon Dran (all last app) & his men (Maynard, Hernandez, Jake, LaGraves & Reinhold named, all die), Americop (also in fb to 1st chr app before Cap #428, '94, next in Tb:DM, '07)
OTHER CHARACTERS: Police captain, criminals, victim (all in fb), Dran's guard dogs
LOCATIONS/ITEMS: Damon Dran's New Orleans estate; Americop's jeep, armor & guns, Dran's men's gas grenades & tasers, Cap's sky-cycle w/communicator, Dran's helicopter
FLASHBACK: Disillusioned with the justice system, Houston cop Bart Gallows resigns, deciding to ensure the guilty stay punished, his way.
SYNOPSIS: Americop refuses to yield to Dran, forcing Captain America to attack Americop before Dran's men break Diamondback's and Moonhunter's spines. Diamondback slips out and finds Cap's sky-cycle; she uses the communicator to call for backup. Dran admits that he's selling the missing children Americop is looking for to a foreign client. Dran's men torture Cap and Americop. Afterwards, Americop breaks free, finds an arsenal of weapons and starts killing Dran's men. Meanwhile, Cap fails to convince Golddigger to release him. Black Widow arrives and finds Diamondback; together they rescue Cap and Moonhunter. Racing outside, Cap fails to stop Americop from destroying Dran's helicopter when his flagging health causes his shield to fall short. Dran survives and Americop escapes.
NOTE: Cover-labeled "Fighting Chance Book 6." Features a Cap vs. Red Skull pin-up by Dante Bastianoni (pencils) & Ralph Cabrera (inks) advertising the upcoming Streets of Poison TPB.

CAPTAIN AMERICA ANNUAL #13 (1994)

"Part I: Heritage of Hatred" (8 pages)
"Part II: A Funeral for Berlin" (11 pages)
"Part III: RED is the Color…" (11 pages)
"Part IV: Eyes on the Prize" (10 pages)

CREDITS: Roy Thomas (writer), Arvell Malcolm Jones (pencils), David Day, Dan Day (inks), Diana Albers (letters), Ovi Hondru, Dave Sampson (colors), Joe Andreani (asst editor), Mike Rockwitz (editor), Ralph Macchio (group editor), Brian Kong (c art)
FEATURE CHARACTERS: Captain America (Rogers, also in rfb; in fb1 between Twelve #1, '10 & Cap:MoT #1, '11, also in ToS #72/2, '65 fb & ToS #79/2, '66 fb), Captain America (Burnside, also in rfb; in fb4 between CapC

GUEST STARS: Spirit of '76 (William Naslund, in fb1 between Cap #4, '05 fb & Cap #215, '77 fb), Patriot (Jeff Mace, in fb1 between MC #74/4 '46 & WI #4, '77), Red Guardian (Aleksey Lebedev, Soviet agent, in fbs1-2 between Nam Ann #1/3, '91 fb & Nam Ann #1/3, '91)
SUPPORTING CAST: Bucky (Monroe, also in rfb; in fb4 between CapC #78/3, '54 & Cap Ann #6, '82)
VILLAINS: Red Skull (Shmidt, also in fb1 between Twelve #1, '10 & ToS #72/2, '65 fb; last in DCut #4, '94, chr next in Cap #447, '96, next in Cap #437, '95) & his men (Raoul named), Red Skull (Malik, also in rfb; in fb3 between YM #24/2, '53 fb & YM #24/2, '53, fb4 between YM #27/2, '54 & ASM Ann #5, '68 fb, fb5 between ASM Ann #5, '68 fb & ASM Ann #5, '68, bts in fb6 between SAv #6, '88 & Cap #347, '88), Adolf Hitler (also in photo, as child, in fb1 between Fury #1, '94 & SM:FI, '92 fb), Joseph Stalin (also in photo, in fb2 between HT #14/5, '43 & Nam Ann #1/3, '91, as corpse in fb3 between Nam Ann #1/3, '91 & AWC #98, '93), Electro (Ivan Kronov, also in rfb; in fb4 after CapC #78, '54, last app), Nazi soldiers (in fb1 & rfb)
OTHER CHARACTERS: Nikita Khrushchev (First Secretary of the Party, in fb3 to 1st chr app before ToS #41, '63), Georgi Malenkov (Chairman of the Council of Ministers), Nikolai Bulganin (First Vice-Chairman) (both in fb3, only app), morgue guard, United Nations guard (both in fb4, die), former Nazi (in fb5); UN delegates, Red Skull's (Malik) men (both in rfb); Klara Hitler (Adolf's mother, in photo), Vladimir Lenin (photo), Bucky (Barnes, only on cover), Dr. Klaus Fuchs (Soviet spy, 1st, bts in fb1, alerts Stalin to Allied mission, next in Cap:P #2, '10)
LOCATIONS/ITEMS: Berlin inc Hitler's bunker w/surrounding underground tunnels (fb1), Moscow inc Stalin's office (fb3), New York inc city morgue (fb4) & United Nations building (fb4 & rfb) w/vault, Paris, France (fb5), Malik's estate, West Germany inc castle w/crypt & Red Skull's sanctuary; Allied bombers & parachutes, Nazi soldiers' guns (both in fb1), Red Skull's (Malik) car, EMS paddles (both in fb4), fake Hitler's strongbox w/plaque (fb4), Malik's journal (also in fbs), Red Skull's guns & helicopter, Red Skull's men's armor & guns, Avengers Quinjet, castle's booby traps, Hitler's strongbox (see NOTE) w/Hitler's personal effects
FLASHBACKS: April, 1945: Hitler gives Red Skull his other strongbox to safeguard as Captain America, Spirit of '76 and Patriot parachute into Berlin. They meet Red Guardian and Cap reminds Spirit of '76 and Patriot that they're working with the Russians to defeat the Germans Together they storm Hitler's bunker and Cap chases Red Skull while the others battle the Nazi soldiers (1). Cap battles Red Skull until the Skull is trapped by an explosion. As Allied bombers attack Berlin, Red Skull tells Cap about Der Tag and the Sleepers and is buried in rubble (ToS #72/2, '65 fb). Cap reunites with Spirit of '76 and Patriot and says goodbye to Red Guardian (1). Red Skull falls into suspended animation (Cap #298, '84 fb). Joseph Stalin scolds Red Guardian for failing to retrieve Hitler's strongbox (2). When Stalin dies in 1953, Albert Malik is appointed the new Red Skull (3). Captain America (Burnside) and Bucky (Monroe) battle the new Red Skull (YM #24/2, '53) and Electro (CapC #78, '54) Red Skull (Malik) revives Electro. They storm the United Nation and find Hitler's strongbox. Captain America (Burnside) and Bucky (Monroe) confront the villains and defeat Electro, but Red Skull escapes only to discover the strongbox is a fake (4). In Paris, Malik contacts the former Nazi holding the true strongbox (5). In prison, Malik writes in his journal that he's learned the true strongbox is in a West German castle (p).
SYNOPSIS: Red Skull searches Albert Malik's Estate until Captain America crashes in. Red Skull's men overpower Cap and the Skull obtains Malik's journal. Red Skull escapes and later summons Cap to a castle in West Germany. Cap makes his way through booby traps and confronts the Skull, who opens the vault using Malik's journal as the key and gains Hitler's strongbox. Cap attacks, but the Skull steals Cap's Quinjet to escape. Red Skull is dismayed to learn there is no master plan of destruction in the strongbox but rather Hitler's personal effects; he wanted to be remembered as an artist, a thinker and a war hero. Cap resumes his attack and easily defeats the Skull.
NOTE: Includes Contents Page featuring Captain America & Red Skull. This is the 2nd Hitler's strongbox; a previous was seen in ToS #72/2, '65.

2ND STORY: "Symbols" (10 pages)
CREDITS: Ron Marz (writer), Rik Levins (pencils), Ricardo Villagren (inks), Rick Parker (letters), Ovi Hondru (colors), Joe Andreani (asst editor), Mike Rockwitz (editor), Ralph Macchio (group editor)
FEATURE CHARACTER: Captain America (also in own thoughts & in fb between BP #30, '01 fb & MvPro #5, '10; next in Cap #431, '94)
VILLAINS: Foreign operatives (in fb)
OTHER CHARACTERS: Clarence "Biz" Duckett (corpse inside coffin, also in fb, only app), priest, 3 bigots, Army soldiers (in fb)
LOCATIONS/ITEMS: Fort LeHigh inc barracks (in fb), cemetery inc Biz's grave; Cap's steel shield & gun (in fb), Biz's casket
FLASHBACK: African American soldier Clarence "Biz" Duckett finds the segregated US army only trusts him with doing Fort LeHigh's laundry Finding Steve Rogers' Captain America uniform, he swears to keep Steve's secret. Soon after, foreign agents with intelligence that Cap operates out of Fort LeHigh torture Biz for information. Even facing death, Biz refuses to talk; luckily Cap arrives in time to save him.
SYNOPSIS: Steve Rogers is the only person to attend Clarence Duckett's funeral. When he turns to leave he overhears three bigots planning to throw Clarence's casket into the woods. Steve confronts them over their bigotry and makes the point that Clarence will be buried here, through force if necessary. The bigots leave in fear.
NOTE: Followed by three pin-ups: Captain America, Bantam, Flacon, Black Panther & Diamondback (2 pages) by M.C. Wyman (pencils), Matt Banning (inks) & Nel Yomtov (colors), Captain America (1 page) by John Herbert (pencils), Jim Amash (inks) & Ovi Hondru (colors), and Captain America (1 page) by Brian Kong (pencils), Mike DeCarlo (inks) & Ovi Hondru (colors).

CAPTAIN AMERICA #431 (September 1994)

"The Next Generation" (23 pages)

CREDITS: Mark Gruenwald (writer), Dave Hoover (pencils, c art), Danny Bulanadi (inks), Joe Rosen (letters), George Roussos (colors), Joe Andreani (asst editor), Mike Rockwitz (editor), Ralph Macchio (group editor)
FEATURE CHARACTER: Captain America (also in DD #331-332, Hulk #421, '94, Av #378, '94, FW #5, '94, Justice #3, '94 fb, Av #380 & 382, all '94, Nam #57-58, '94-95, ToS #1, MHol 1994/2, FW #8, FanFor #4, FW #10/2, Av/UF #1, UF/Av #1, FF #400/2, CPU #1, all '95)
GUEST STARS: Avengers: Crystal (last in Av Ann #23, '94), Quicksilver (last in Av #377, '94), Vision (bts, searching for missing children, last in Av Ann #23/2,'94) (all next in Av #378, '94), Black Widow (last in Tstrike #10, '94, next in DD #332, '94)

SUPPORTING CAST: Free Spirit (Cathy Webster, 1st), Moonhunter (next in Cap #435, '95), Arnie Roth, Fabian Stankowicz (both last in Cap #428, '94, next in Cap #438, '95), Peggy Carter (last bts in Cap #429, '94, next in Tstrike #13, '94), Dr. Keith Kincaid (last in Cap #425, '94, next in Cap #434, '94), Bernie Rosenthal (last in Cap #427, '94, next in Cap #438, '94), Diamondback

VILLAINS: Baron (Helmut) Zemo (last in PPSSM #196, '94), Baroness Zemo (Heike Zemo, Helmut's wife, last in SM:FI, '92), Superia (as Dr. Deidre Wentworth, last in Cap #414, '93), Zemo's Plastoids

OTHER CHARACTERS: Jennifer (Cathy's roommate), Joe (Jennifer's boyfriend), Mary Ellen (resident assistant), Prof. Suzanne Prolukort (Cathy's teacher), other Hayden College students (Lindquist named) & staff, the Kinder (Zemo's 25 children, 1st)

LOCATIONS/ITEMS: Avengers Mansion inc gym & communications room, Hayden College inc classroom, Cathy's dorm room & frat house, Arnie's office, Glasser Institute, Cap's Brooklyn HQ inc Rokatanski's costume shop, Zemo's Mexican castle; Avengers' exercise & medical equipment, Superia's subliminal helmet, Cap's jet, hang gliders & battle vest (1st) w/thermal scanner, Zemo's mask, Kinder's guns, Iron Man, Spider-Man & Thor masks

SYNOPSIS: Dr. Kincaid tells Captain America that his condition is worsening. Meanwhile, Bernie advises Diamondback not to turn herself in to the Boca Caliente authorities as they will likely execute her. At Hayden College, Dr. Wentworth recruits Cathy Webster to be part of a subliminal enhancement experiment. Cap finds Arnie Roth at his Brooklyn HQ, who offers to run the costume shop front. Fabian gives Cap a new battle vest filled with equipment to compensate for Cap's physical shortcomings. Meanwhile, Cathy is physically stronger and faster thanks to Wentworth's process. Adopting the guise of Free Spirit, she goes to a toga party where she attacks the frat boys. Confused by her actions she runs away. Cap and Diamondback discover the children were taken by Zemo and travel to his Mexican castle. Free Spirit discovers Wentworth's process programmed her to be a man-hater. She vows to hunt the missing Wentworth down. Captured by Plastoids, Cap learns that Zemo has brainwashed the missing children into hating Cap.

NOTE: Cover-labeled "Fighting Chance Book 7."

CAPTAIN AMERICA #432 (October 1994)

"Baron Ground" (22 pages)

CREDITS: Mark Gruenwald (writer), Dario Carrasco (pencils), Danny Bulanadi (inks), Joe Rosen (letters), George Roussos (colors), Joe Andreani (asst editor), Mike Rockwitz (editor), Ralph Macchio (group editor), Dave Hoover (c art)

FEATURE CHARACTER: Captain America

SUPPORTING CAST: Free Spirit (also in pfb), Diamondback

VILLAINS: Baron Zemo, Baroness Zemo (also in rfb) (both also in photo), Superia (as Dr. Deidre Wentworth, also in pfb), Zemo's Plastoids (Franz named)

OTHER CHARACTERS: The Kinder (Courtney, Joseph & Lisa named), Frau Reinhold (the Kinder's teacher), truck driver, airline staff (in pfb); Silver Sable, Spider-Man (both in rfb); luggage handlers, bystanders (all in pfb)

LOCATIONS/ITEMS: Mexico inc Malpaso & Zemo's castle w/throne room, surveillance room, pit, study & classroom; Kinder's guns, Cap's battle vest w/smoke capsules, capture cables, grappling hook & explosives, Zemo's mask, Adhesive-X

FLASHBACK: Cathy sees Wentworth buy a flight to Malpaso, Mexico (p). The Baroness fights Silver Sable and Spider-Man (SM:FI, '92).

SYNOPSIS: Captain America throws Diamondback out of the room as the Kinder shoot them. Cap learns the Kinder's guns only have blank ammunition and is dropped down a trap door while a Plastoid captures Diamondback. Meanwhile, Free Spirit hitchhikes to Malpaso, Mexico. As Zemo sends his Plastoids after Cap, Baroness Zemo meets with Dr. Wentworth, who tells her about the physical enhancement process. A Plastoid captures Cap. Free Spirit breaks into the castle looking for Wentworth, and comes across Diamondback, freeing her from the Plastoid. Zemo overhears his wife consider killing him in exchange for Wentworth's process. Zemo condemns Cap to a death in Adhesive-X while he tearfully tells his children their "mother" will be going away. Diamondback and Free Spirit find the two women. Cap manages to free himself and tries to escape, but the exertion causes his body to begin to cramp up.

NOTE: Cover-labeled "Fighting Chance Book 8."

CAPTAIN AMERICA #433 (November 1994)

"Diamonds Aren't Forever!" (23 pages)

CREDITS: Mark Gruenwald (writer), Dave Hoover (pencils, c art), Danny Bulanadi (inks), Joe Rosen (letters), George Roussos (colors), Joe Andreani (asst editor), Mike Rockwitz (editor), Ralph Macchio (group editor)

FEATURE CHARACTER: Captain America

SUPPORTING CAST: Diamondback, Free Spirit

VILLAINS: Superia (next in Cap #439, '95), Baron Zemo, Baroness Zemo, Zemo's Plastoids (Wolfgang named)

OTHER CHARACTERS: The Kinder

LOCATIONS/ITEMS: Zemo's Mexican castle inc dungeon & vat room; Cap's battle vest w/grappling gun, explosives & tripwire, Adhesive-X, Zemo's masks, Baroness' gun

SYNOPSIS: Captain America escapes from the Plastoid. Baron Zemo captures his wife and Superia. Diamondback and Free Spirit split up to search for the women, but Free Spirit finds Cap instead. Together they defeat a Plastoid. The Baroness convinces her husband her betrayal was a ruse and Zemo frees her. Diamondback finds Superia who tells her she must finish Snapdragon's mercenary contract as restitution. If Diamondback agrees, Superia will provide an antidote for Cap's condition. Meanwhile, a Plastoid captures Cap and Free Spirit. Cap manages to release Free Spirit, but he's brought to Zemo. Free Spirit finds Superia. Cap avoids being dumped in Adhesive-X, but Zemo's mask is doused with the Adhesive. He removes his mask only to terrify his Kinder. Diamondback knocks Free Spirit out from behind and agrees to Superia's deal. Zemo trips and Cap catches him, but his body fails and Zemo is dropped into Adhesive-X. The Baroness dives in after him.

NOTE: Cover-labeled "Fighting Chance Book 9."

CAPTAIN AMERICA #434 (December 1994)

"Snake Bites" (22 pages)

CREDITS: Mark Gruenwald (writer), Dave Hoover (pencils, c art), Danny Bulanadi (inks), Joe Rosen (letters), George Roussos (colors), Joe Andreani (asst editor), Mike Rockwitz (editor), Ralph Macchio (group editor)
FEATURE CHARACTER: Captain America
GUEST STARS: Avengers: Black Widow (last in UF/Av #1, '95, next in IM #315, '95), Crystal (last in FF #400/2, '95, next in Vision #2, '94), Giant-Man (last in Bwulf #6, '94), Hercules (last in FW #10/2, '95, next in SM:PoT #3, '95), Quicksilver (last in FF #400/2, '95, next in Av #384, '95), Vision (last in UF/Av #1, '95, next in Vision #1, '94)
SUPPORTING CAST: Jack Flag (Jack Harrison, 1st, also in pfb), Diamondback (bts, left note, next in Cap #439, '95), Dr. Keith Kincaid (last in Cap #431, '94), Free Spirit
VILLAINS: Baron Zemo (chr next in Tb Ann '97 fb, next in Tb #1, '97 as Citizen V), Baroness Zemo (last app, see NOTE), Zemo's Plastoids, Mr. Hyde (last in GR #55, '94), Serpent Society: King Cobra (also bts in pfb, last in AFlt #121, '93), Anaconda, Coachwhip, Rock Python (prev 3 last bts in Cap #414, '93), Cottonmouth, Fer-de-Lance, Rattler (prev 3 last bts in Cap #385/2, '91), Puff Adder (last in Cap #414, '93)
OTHER CHARACTERS: Drake Harrison (Jack's brother), Jack's parents, property inspector, muggers, drug dealers, movers (all in pfb), the Kinder (last app)
LOCATIONS/ITEMS: Zemo's Mexican castle inc dungeon & escape hatch, Arizona inc town & Sandhaven Community Center, Avengers Mansion lab, Reno, NV inc Hyde's home; Cap's battle vest w/handcuffs, Diamondback's note, Jack Flag's boom box, Avengers Quinjet & medical equipment, Serpent Society helicopter, Rock Python's coil bombs, Fer-De-Lance's UZI, Hyde's painting
FLASHBACK: Stars & Stripes members Jack and Drake fight criminals until Drake is paralyzed. Jack's parents use all their money to move but are forced to sell at a loss when told their dream home is built on a toxic waste dump. Discovering the Serpent Society is responsible, Jack becomes Jack Flag to get evidence against them (p).
SYNOPSIS: Captain America catches the Zemos trying to flee through an escape hatch. In Arizona, Jack Flag stops a Serpent Society robbery. He feigns interest in joining them, and Puff Adder knocks him out. As the Avengers round up Zemo's Plastoids and Kinder, Cap discovers Diamondback's good bye note. Free Spirit asks Cap to give her some pointers in fighting. Jack Flag insists he wants to join the Serpent Society, so King Cobra sends him to steal a painting for initiation. Cobra calls Mr. Hyde to warn him of Jack's arrival. Meanwhile, Dr Kincaid calls Giant-Man for a second opinion. After being doused with chemicals, Jack escapes from Mr. Hyde. Feeling woozy, he reports the Serpent Society to Cap's Stars & Stripes hotline. Hyde attacks, but this time Jack easily defeats him. After sparring for hours with Free Spirit, Cap's body gives out. Jack arrives at the Society's resort with Hyde's painting.
NOTE: Cover-labeled "Fighting Chance Book 10." Tb Ann '97 suggests that Baroness Zemo dies in prison after this appearance. Jack Flag's Stars & Stripes member number is AZ-1260. Puff Adder is called "Willard" here.

CAPTAIN AMERICA #435 (January 1995)

"Snake, Battle and Toll" (22 pages)

CREDITS: Mark Gruenwald (writer), Dave Hoover (pencils, c art), Danny Bulanadi (inks), Joe Rosen (letters), George Roussos (colors), Joe Andreani (asst editor), Mike Rockwitz (editor), Ralph Macchio (group editor)
FEATURE CHARACTER: Captain America
GUEST STAR: Giant-Man
SUPPORTING CAST: Moonhunter (next in Cap #438, '95), Free Spirit (also as Coachwhip), Jack Flag (also as Cobra), Dr. Keith Kincaid
VILLAINS: Mr. Hyde, Serpent Society: King Cobra, Anaconda, Coachwhip, Cottonmouth, Fer-de-Lance, Puff Adder, Rattler, Rock Python, Bushmaster (last in Cap Ann #10/3, '91)
OTHER CHARACTER: Diamondback (Cap's thoughts)
LOCATIONS/ITEMS: Sandhaven Community Center, Zemo's Mexican Castle, Avengers Mansion med lab; Cap's battle vest, jet, Stars & Stripes laptop
SYNOPSIS: Jack Flag auditions for the Cobra identity by battling the Serpent Society. Moonhunter picks up Captain America and Free Spirit and Cap receives Jack's Stars & Stripes hotline warning about the Society. Meanwhile, Giant-Man confirms Dr. Kincaid's fears, declaring Cap must stop all activity at once. Mr. Hyde storms Sandhaven to confront King Cobra about Jack Flag's attack. Moonhunter drops Cap off at Sandahven where he meets Jack Flag dressed as Cobra. Jack convinces Cap to let him beat him to foil the Serpents. Moonhunter receives Giant-Man's distress call, and he drops Free Spirit off to find Cap. As Jack and the Serpents bring Cap to Cobra, Free Spirit defeats and disguises herself as Coachwhip. Hyde and Cobra interrogate Cap by dunking him in a swimming pool until Free Spirit arrives. Cobra flushes Cap down an escape hatch in the pool and he and Hyde follow, as the Serpent Society surround Free Spirit and Jack Flag.
NOTE: Cover-labeled "Fighting Chance Book 11."

CAPTAIN AMERICA #436 (February 1995)

"Everybody Hurts Sometime" (22 pages)

CREDITS: Mark Gruenwald (writer), Dave Hoover (pencils, c art), Danny Bulanadi (inks), Joe Rosen (letters), George Roussos (colors), Joe Andreani (asst editor), Mike Rockwitz (editor), Ralph Macchio (group editor)
FEATURE CHARACTER: Captain America
GUEST STAR: Giant-Man
SUPPORTING CAST: Dr. Keith Kincaid (next in Thor #5, '98), Free Spirit (also as Coachwhip), Jack Flag (also as Cobra)
VILLAINS: Mr. Hyde, Serpent Society: King Cobra, Anaconda, Bushmaster, Cottonmouth, Fer-de-Lance, Puff Adder, Rattler, Rock Python, Coachwhip (bts, unconscious)
OTHER CHARACTERS: Bucky, Death, Lady Liberty (all in Cap's hallucination), rattlesnake
LOCATIONS/ITEMS: Sandhaven Community Center, Arizona desert; Cap's battle vest w/handcuffs, metal foil restraint & airbags, Avengers Quinjet, Rattler's rattling gun
SYNOPSIS: Captain America is dumped into the desert; King Cobra and Mr. Hyde follow behind. Cap struggles to fight them both. Jack Flag and Free Spirit escape from the Serpent Society and see an Avengers Quinjet approaching. Cap handcuffs Cobra, only for Hyde to pummel him. Hyde frees Cobra and Cap's body freezes up. The Serpents find and attack Free Spirit and Jack Flag, and Giant-Man comes to their rescue. Cap's battle vest gadgets subdue both Cobra and Hyde, but he still can't move. Cap hallucinates until Giant-Man finds him unconscious and suffering from cardiac arrest.
NOTE: Cover-labeled "Fighting Chance No More!"

CAPTAIN AMERICA #437 (March 1995)

"If I Should Die Before I Wake..." (22 pages)

CREDITS: Mark Gruenwald (writer, group editor), Dave Hoover (pencils, c art), Danny Bulanadi (inks), Joe Rosen (letters), George Roussos (colors), Joe Andreani (asst editor), Mike Rockwitz (editor)
FEATURE CHARACTER: Captain America (also in dream, next in IM #314, '95)
GUEST STARS: Giant-Man (next in IM #314, '95), Force Works: Century, Spider-Woman, USAgent (prev 3 between FW #10/2-11, '95) Iron Man (also in Cap's dream, last in FF #400/2, '95, next in IM #314, '95), Scarlet Witch (last in FW #10/2, '95, chr next in FW #11, '95 fb, next in WarM #14, '95)
SUPPORTING CAST: Free Spirit, Jack Flag
VILLAINS: Serpent Society: King Cobra (bts, in Force Works custody, next in Cap #15, '99 as Cobra), Bushmaster, Coachwhip, Fer-de-Lance, Rattler, Rock Python (prev 5 next in Cap #30, '04), Anaconda (next in W #167, '01), Cottonmouth (next in BP #16, '00), Puff Adder (next in Dlk #7, '00); Mr. Hyde (bts, in Force Works custody, next in AvUnp #4, '96), Red Skull (also in Cap's dream, last in Cap Ann #13, '94, chr last in Cap #446, '95 fb, next in Av #385, '95), Arnim Zola (last in Cap #396, '92, next bts in Tb #1, '97, next in Tb #4, '97), Agent 88 (Red Skull's agent, Stark Enterprises spy, voice only)
OTHER CHARACTERS: Batroc, Black Panther, Diamondback, Falcon, Hawkeye, MODOK, Sub-Mariner, Swordsman, Thor, Nick Fury, Irma Kruhl, Gen. Wo, AIM agent (all on cover), Bucky, Lady Liberty, Red Skull's men (prev 3 in Cap's dream); Stark Enterprises doctors
LOCATIONS/ITEMS: Red Skull's hideout, Stark Enterprises inc med lab; Avengers Quinjet, Force Works Hex Ship, Iron Man's cybernetic helmet, Cosmic Cube (in Cap's hallucination)
SYNOPSIS: As Captain America dreams of past battles with Red Skull, Giant-Man and Iron Man frantically work to save Cap's life. Feeling he should be doing more to help, Iron Man sends Force Works to assist Jack Flag and Free Spirit in defeating the Serpent Society. Iron Man uses a cybernetic helmet to communicate with Cap by entering his mind. As Cap contemplates dying, Iron Man arrives and awakens Cap. Iron Man and Giant-Man tell Cap his body is ninety-five percent paralyzed. Elsewhere, Red Skull learns of Cap's paralysis. Arnim Zola tells the Skull he's studied the Super-Soldier Serum in Red Skull's cloned Cap body, and it caused Cap's paralysis. The Skull commands Zola to find a cure.
NOTE: Cover-labeled "Fighting Chance Epilogue: While I Lie Dying…" Cap's hallucinations reflect past battles, including Cap & Bucky vs. the Red Skull (CapC #1, '41), Cap vs. Cosmic Cube-wielding Red Skull (ToS #80, '66) and a poisoned Cap vs. aged Red Skull (Cap #300, '84).

CAPTAIN AMERICA #438 (April 1995)

"The Bombs Bursting in Air" (22 pages)

CREDITS: Mark Gruenwald (writer, group editor), Dave Hoover (pencils, c art), Danny Bulanadi, Scott Koblish (inks), Joe Rosen (letters), Ashley Posella (colors), Matt Idelson (asst editor), Ralph Macchio (editor)
FEATURE CHARACTER: Captain America (next in PPSSM Spec #1, '95)
GUEST STARS: Giant-Man (last in IM #314, '95, next in Vision #1, '94), Iron Man (between IM #314-315, '95)
SUPPORTING CAST: Bernie Rosenthal, Arnie Roth, Fabian Stankowicz (all last in Cap #431, '94), Moonhunter (last in Cap #435, '95, next in Cap #440, '95), Free Spirit, Jack Flag
VILLAINS: Flag-Smasher (last in Cap #400/2, '92, last bts in GR #50/2, '94, next in MTU #3, '97), ULTIMATUM (inc Alpha Unit & Beta Unit, Johnson, Rice & Schoepke named), Super-Patriot (hand only, last in Cap #427, '94)
OTHER CHARACTERS: Gavin (Stars & Stripes hacker, only app), bystanders
LOCATIONS/ITEMS: Stark Enterprises training facility, Washington DC inc Washington Monument, Potomac River & White House, Sandhaven, AZ, Super-Patriot's Bay Ridge apartment, Cap's Brooklyn HQ; Cap's jet & mobility armor (1st, see NOTE) w/mylex shrouds, electromagnetic homing gauntlet, anti-missile missiles & telescopic lenses, Avengers Quinjet, ULTIMATUM ski-jets, guns, attachable rockets & missiles, Flag-Smasher's gun & bomb

SYNOPSIS: Giant-Man and Iron Man help Captain America test his new mobility armor. In Washington, DC, Flag-Smasher holds one of Cap's Stars & Stripes hackers hostage to get Cap's attention. In Arizona, Moonhunter collects Free Spirit and Jack Flag; they pick up Flag-Smasher's message. Giant-Man gives Cap a ride to the East Coast. In Bay Ridge, Super-Patriot kidnaps Bernie. Moonhunter arrives in DC, only for ULTIMATUM to shoot him down. Cap arrives and quickly defeats ULTIMATUM as Jack pulls Moonhunter out of the Potomac River. Cap finds Flag-Smasher, but when Cap bests him he seemingly blows himself up. Cap narrowly escapes with Gavin. Later, Cap tells his crew that the Super-Soldier Serum is killing him. Afterwards, Arnie tells Cap he has bone cancer.

NOTE: Iron Man gave Cap a biochip to make the armor move in IM #314, '95.

CAPTAIN AMERICA #439 (May 1995)

"O'er the Ramparts We Watched" (22 pages)

CREDITS: Mark Gruenwald (writer, group editor), Dave Hoover (pencils, c art), Dany Bulanadi, Scott Koblish (inks), Joe Rosen (letters), Ashley Posella (colors), Matt Idelson (asst editor), Ralph Macchio (editor)
FEATURE CHARACTER: Captain America (also in rfb; next in Av #386, '95)
GUEST STAR: Falcon (last in FW #10/2, '95)
SUPPORTING CAST: Diamondback (last bts in Cap #434, '95, next as Snapdragon), Peggy Carter (last in Tstrike #16, '95, next in Cap #443, '95), Bernie Rosenthal (next in Cap #443, '95), Fabian Stankowicz (also as Mechanaut), Free Spirit, Jack Flag, Arnie Roth
VILLAINS: Dead Ringer (also as Nighthawk, Basilisk & Death-Stalker, also as his father in fb2 to 1st chr app before Cap #425, '94; last in Cap #428, '94, last app, see NOTE), Super-Patriot (also as Watchdog in rfb, also in fb1 between Cap #386, '91 & Cap #425, '94, dies, next in Cap #600/3, '09 as ashen remains), Superia (last in Cap #433, '94)
OTHER CHARACTERS: Contessa Val Fontaine (last in SSWP #24, '94, next in FoS #1, '95), doctor, nurse, Dead Ringer's father (corpse), random corpse, funeral attendees, police (prev 4 in fb2), USAgent, Watchdogs (both in rfb)
LOCATIONS/ITEMS: New York, Cap's Brooklyn HQ, Super-Patriot's Bay Ridge apartment, Brooklyn Bridge, Superia's lab, Harlem, hospital, Cap's exercise equipment & mobility armor w/mylex shroud, audio amplifiers & compressed air cannon, Superia's medical equipment & cure, Dead Ringer's cigar box (see NOTE), Mechanaut armor, Super-Patriot's shield
FLASHBACKS: Mike Farrel joins the Watchdogs (Cap #385, '91) and turns himself in to Cap (Cap #386, '91). When he's released from prison, Mike blames Cap for his downfall and becomes Super-Patriot (1). Lou Dexter discovers he can copy the appearance of corpses when he finds his father's body. When he tries to dig up a superhuman corpse he's arrested for grave robbing (2).
SYNOPSIS: Falcon sees Nighthawk flying over Harlem. Falcon tries to get his attention, but Nighthawk escapes. At Cap's Brooklyn HQ, Cap plans an attack on AIM with Contessa Val Fontaine. Meanwhile, Mike Farrel tells Bernie how he came to be Super-Patriot. They're joined by Dead Ringer, who becomes angry when Mike voices concern with their plan against Cap. Cap meets Falcon and tells him about his physical condition. Meanwhile, Superia tests her cure on Diamondback, since she has Cap's Super-Soldier serum in her system. At Cap's HQ, Arnie collapses. Cap hears Bernie with his armor's audio amplifiers and crashes into Mike's apartment. Dead Ringer attacks as Death-Stalker, but when Mike learns Dead Ringer only joined him against Cap to kill and replace Cap, he attacks Dead Ringer. Dead Ringer accidentally kills Mike; Cap takes advantage of the confusion and knocks out Dead Ringer. As Arnie is admitted to the hospital, Superia discovers her cure for the Super-Soldier Serum deterioration works.
NOTE: Death-Stalker died in DD #158, '79. Basilisk was killed by Scourge in FF #289, '86 and will later be resurrected by the Hood in Pun #5, '09. Nighthawk was thought dead in Def #106, but Nhawk #1, '98 reveals he was only in a coma. Dead Ringer's cigar box contains severed fingers of several people he's copied, but not all.

CAPTAIN AMERICA #440 (June 1995)

"Dawn's Early Light" (22 pages)

CREDITS: Mark Gruenwald (writer, group editor), Dave Hoover (pencils, c art), Marie Severin, Danny Bulanadi, Don Hudson (inks), Joe Rosen (letters), Ashley Posella (colors), Matt Idelson (asst editor), Ralph Macchio (editor)
FEATURE CHARACTER: Captain America (next in Av #387, '95)
GUEST STARS: Avengers: Black Widow, Crystal, Hercules, Quicksilver (all between Av #386-387, '95), Giant-Man (last in Av #384, '95, next in Av #387, '95); Falcon (next in Av #387, '95), Nick Fury (during FoS #2, '95)
SUPPORTING CAST: Free Spirit, Jack Flag (both also as AIM agents, next in Av #387, '95), Dennis Dunphy (last in Cap #422, '93, next in Av #1, '98 as Demolition Man), Arnie Roth (next in Cap #442, '95), Snapdragon (last as Diamondback), Moonhunter, Fabian Stankowicz
VILLAINS: Super-Adaptoid (as "Allessandro Brannex," last in FanFor #4, '95, next in Av #387, '95), MODOK (last in IM #205, '86, next in Av #387, '95), MODAM (last in IM #297, '93, next in Cap #3, '98), AIM Adaptoids (3 as Rhino, Knockout & Killer Shrike) & agents (CN-232, TH-662 & NF-678 named), Red Skull (between Av #386-387, '95), Superia
OTHER CHARACTERS: Jesse Black Crow (last in PPSSM Ann #13/3, '93, next in Cap #443, '95), Night People, youths, Boca Calientians
LOCATIONS/ITEMS: Zerotown, Brooklyn basketball court, Tisch hospital, Boca Caliente inc AIM mountain base w/control room, Avengers Mansion; Cap's mobility armor & jet w/floating platform, Fury's HAWK (High Altitude Wing Kite) harness, Superia's boat & cure, respirator treated w/Pym Particles, AIM guns, Red Skull's battlesuit, Fabian's robots, new Cosmic Cube (bts, being created)
SYNOPSIS: Captain America fails to recruit Dennis Dunphy for his attack on AIM. Meanwhile, Falcon learns that Jesse Black Crow can't hear Cap. Later, Cap's group meets with Nick Fury, who briefs them on AIM and the new Cosmic Cube they're making. On Boca Caliente, energy flares shoot into the sky as MODAM tries to repair the Cosmic Cube's containment vessel. Superia and Snapdragon near the island while Cap's group sneaks in. Meanwhile, the Avengers belatedly realize that Cap's warnings about AIM were accurate and leave for Boca Caliente. Cap's

roup splits up and Jack Flag and Free Spirit discover Red Skull entering the AIM base, but AIM Adaptoids attack them before they can follow ne Skull. Cap is enveloped in an energy flare, which shorts out his armor. As the Avengers near Boca Caliente, an Adaptoid attacks Falcon. uperia finds the immobilized Cap and injects him with a "free sample" of her cure.
NOTE: Cover-labeled "Taking AIM Part 1 of 4." Story continued from Av #386, '95 and into Av #387, '95.

CAPTAIN AMERICA #441 (July 1995)

"Through the Perilous Fight" (23 pages)

CREDITS: Mark Gruenwald (writer, group editor), Dave Hoover (pencils, co-inks, c art), Danny Bulanadi, Rick Hoover, Don Hudson, Keith Williams (co-inks), Moyer, Scum (art assist), Joe Rosen (letters), Ashley Posella (colors), Matt Idelson (asst editor), Ralph Macchio (editor)
FEATURE CHARACTER: Captain America (next in Av #388, '95)
GUEST STARS: Falcon, Avengers: Black Widow, Hercules (all between Av #387-388, '95)
SUPPORTING CAST: Free Spirit, Jack Flag (both between Av #387-388, '95), Snapdragon, Fabian Stankowicz (both next in Av #388, '95), Moonhunter (next in Cap #443, '95)
VILLAINS: MODOK, Red Skull (both between Av #387-388, '95), Superia (next in Av #388, '95), Super-Adaptoid (also as "Alessandro Brannex," last in Av #387, '95, chr next in HFH #10, '98 fb, next in HFH #7, '98), AIM daptoids (U31 & L77 named, also as Free Spirit & Jack Flag, others as Beetle, Blacklash & Dragonfly)
OTHER CHARACTERS: Bucky, Red Guardian, Taylor Madison (all Cosmic Cube constructs)
LOCATIONS/ITEMS: Boca Caliente inc AIM mountain base; Cap's mobility armor & jet, Superia's dampening discs, Red Skull's battlesuit, ree Spirit's blaster, Jack Flag's baton, new Cosmic Cube (bts, creating constructs)
SYNOPSIS: MODOK destroys the Bucky construct and Falcon saves Captain America from MODOK. Alessandro Brannex orders AIM daptoids to eliminate Free Spirit and Jack Flag. Investigating the Cosmic Cube's energy flares, MODOK determines there's only one hour before ne Cube destructs and destroys the world. Hercules and Widow face Cube-constructed ghosts of their pasts. Red Skull attacks Brannex, who veals himself as the Super-Adaptoid. Superia's serum wears off and Cap is paralyzed again. Jack and Free Spirit escape and happen across ed Skull and the Super-Adaptoid just as the AIM base begins to fall apart. Falcon flies Cap outside and meets with Jack and Free Spirit. Jack elps Falcon fight attacking Adaptoids while Snapdragon overpowers Free Spirit. Cap recognizes Snapdragon as Diamondback just as more nergy flares separate them. Cap wishes for his armor and the Cube returns it, and he leaves to assist MODOK save the world.
NOTE: Cover-labeled "Taking AIM Part 3 of 4." Story continued from Av #387, '95 and into Av #388, '95.

CAPTAIN AMERICA #442 (August 1995)

"Broad Stripes and White Stars" (23 pages)

CREDITS: Mark Gruenwald (writer, group editor), Dave Hoover (co-pencils, c art), Sandu Florea (co-pencils), Danny Bulanadi (inks), Joe Rosen (letters), Ashley Posella (colors), Matt Idelson (asst editor), Ralph Macchio (editor)
FEATURE CHARACTER: Captain America (also in photo, next in Tstrike #23-24, '95, Tstrike #1/2, '11 fb)
GUEST STARS: Schutz Heiliggruppe: Vormund (last as Hauptmann Deutschland in Cap #394, '91), Blitzkrieger (also in photo, last in Cap #393, '91, dies) (both last app), Jerry Carstairs (Thunderer, also as bust, last in Mv #1, '94, last app), Simon Halloway (fill-in Angel, last in Hulk #432, '95, dies, last app), Dan Kane (Captain Terror, last in USA #4/5, '42, chr last in Twelve #1, '08, last app), Dan Lyons (Black Marvel, last in Mv #1, '94, chr last in Twelve #1, '08, chr next in Sling #11, '01, fb, next in Sling #1, '00), other retired '40s heroes
SUPPORTING CAST: Free Spirit, Jack Flag, Fabian Stankowicz (all last in Av #388, '95), Arnie Roth (last in Cap 440, '95)
VILLAINS: Zeitgeist (also as Vormund, Everyman & waiter, last in Cap #393, '91, dies), Thomas Halloway (former '40s hero Angel, now funds courge program, also as statue, bts, sent invitations, last in USAgent #4, '93) (both last app), Madcap (last in GR #33, '93, chr next in Tb Ann 7 fb, next in HFH #10, '98)
OTHER CHARACTERS: Machete (bts, last bts in Cap #414, '93, last app), Captain Forza, Defensor, El Condor, La Bandera, Ojo Macabra, ona Rosa (all in photos, killed by Zeitgeist), Thin Man, Spider-Queen (both statues), Whizzer (bust), Halloway's waitresses, bystanders
LOCATIONS/ITEMS: Buenos Aires inc Schutz Heiliggruppe base, IRT subway line, Cap's Brooklyn HQ inc Rokatanski's costume shop, Tisch ospital, Central Park, Halloway's Palos Verdes estate; Zeitgeist's future camera, foil & hologram projector belt, Cap's mobility armor w/mylex hroud & Pym Particles, Halloway's invitation, Madcap's bomb, Schutz Heiliggruppe plane
SYNOPSIS: Zeitgeist murders Blitzkrieger; Vormund later finds the body. Zeitgeist, as Everyman, continues his murder spree by killing Simon alloway, the sometimes '40s hero Angel. Cap learns of Simon's death and receives an invitation to Thomas Halloway's, the original Angel, arty celebrating the end of WWII. Jack Flag and Free Spirit find Madcap threatening suicide by bomb in Central Park. Cap crashes Thomas' arty and finds Vormund there. They determine they're both looking for the same killer when Cap is stabbed in the back. Jack grabs Madcap to top him, but Madcap activates his bomb. Both Madcap and Jack survive. The retired '40s heroes blame Vormund for attacking Cap. Vormund scapes their wrath in time to assist Cap in confronting Everyman. When Everyman stabs Vormund, Vormund's power redirects the attack back n Everyman and he dies. Cap reveals Pym Particles in his armor shrunk Everyman's foil as it stabbed him.
NOTE: "Let's Rap With Cap" features editorial detailing how Everyman became Zeitgeist. Thomas Halloway's address is 2500 Heavenview states, Palos Verdes, CA.

CAPTAIN AMERICA #443 (September 1995)

"Twilight's Last Gleaming" (22 pages)

CREDITS: Mark Gruenwald (writer, group editor), Dave Hoover (pencils, c art), Danny Bulanadi (inks), Joe Rosen, Michael Higgins (letters), Ashley Posella (colors), Matt Idelson (asst editor), Ralph Macchio (editor)
FEATURE CHARACTER: Captain America (also in photo, next in Cap #445, '95 fb, Cap #451, '96 fb)
GUEST STARS: Avengers: Giant-Man, Hercules (both last in Av #390, '95, chr last in Tstrike #1/2, '11 fb, next in AvUnp #1, '95), Black Widow (last in Av #389, '95, next in AvUnp #1, '95), Crystal (last in Av #390, '95, chr last in Tstrike #1/2, '11 fb), Quicksilver (last in Av #390, '95); Black Crow (also as crow, last in Cap #440, '95, next in CW #6, '07), Sam Wilson (last in Av #388, '95, next in MFan #1, '96)
SUPPORTING CAST: Peggy Carter (last in Cap #439, '95, next in StarM #2, '95), Edwin Jarvis (last in IM #319, '95, next in Av:C, '95); Jack Flag (chr next in Tb #111, '07 fb, next in Tb #110, '07), Bernie Rosenthal (last in Cap #439, '95, next in Cap #600/3, '09), Fabian Stankowicz (next in Av Ann '99 fb), Free Spirit, Moonhunter, Arnie Roth (dies) (prev 3 last app)
VILLAINS: Batroc (last in MCP #139/4, '93, next in Cap #4, '98), Crossbones (last in Sleep #20, '93, next in Cap #24, '99), Nefarius (last in Cap #379, '90, next in AvUnp #1, '95) (both also in Cap's thoughts)
OTHER CHARACTERS: Hiram Riddley (last in Cap #332, '87), Holly Riddley (bts, in a coma, last bts in Cap #332, '87) (both last app), prison guards; Diamondback, Red Skull, Superia (prev 3 in Cap's thoughts); Sharon Carter (in photo & Cap's thoughts), Bucky (photo), Namor (bust)
LOCATIONS/ITEMS: Cap's Brooklyn HQ inc Rokatanski's costume shop & Cap's quarters, prison, courthouse, Sam's office, Tisch hospital, Riddley home, Avengers Mansion inc study & Cap's quarters; Cap's mobility armor w/rockets, prison guards' guns, Avengers' security cables
SYNOPSIS: Black Crow tells Captain America he has only a day to live. Deciding to make the most of his time, Cap tells his close colleagues and requests they continue running the Stars & Stripes hotline. Wanting to see if he made any inspiration on his foes, Cap visits Crossbones and expectedly discovers no humanity within him. Cap briefly checks in on Bernie and Falcon before visiting Arnie to say goodbye. Arnie dies after Cap leaves. Cap visits Ram, who tells Cap his mother was shot and is in a coma. Cap goes to Avengers Mansion where he finds Batroc who's upset that Zeitgeist killed his friend Machete. Noticing that Cap is depressed, Batroc insists on mourning with Cap. Batroc leaves hours later and Cap goes to rest. Later, the Avengers discover Cap's empty armor with Cap nowhere to be seen.
NOTE: "Let's Rap With Cap" features a farewell letter from Mark Gruenwald.

CAPTAIN AMERICA #444 (October 1995)

"Hope and Glory" (22 pages)

CREDITS: Mark Waid (writer), Ron Garney (pencils), Mike Sellers (inks), John Costanza (letters), John Kalisz (colors), Matt Idelson (asst editor), Ralph Macchio (editor), Mark Gruenwald (group editor)
FEATURE CHARACTER: Captain America (also in rfb & Quicksilver's thoughts)
GUEST STARS: Avengers: Giant-Man, Hercules (both last in AvUnp #2, '95), Black Widow (last in StarM #2, '95), Quicksilver (also in thoughts), Crystal; Deathcry (last in AvUnp #2, '95) (all also in rfb, next in Hulk #434, '95)
SUPPORTING CAST: Sharon Carter (in shadows, last in Cap #233, '79, chr last in Cap #451, '96 fb)
VILLAINS: Red Skull (shadowed, last in Av #388, '95, chr last in Cap #451, '96 fb) & his men (some as terrorists)
OTHER CHARACTERS: Bill Clinton (last in X #25, '93, last bts in Nova #9, '94, next in Hulk #434, '95), James McElroy (FBI agent, 1st, next in Cap #3, '98), other FBI agents, police (one also as Captain America), Secret Service, reporters; Iron Man, Thor, Wasp, Red Skull (prev 4 in rfb), Hawkeye, Scarlet Witch, Dr. Doom (prev 3 in Quicksilver's thoughts)
LOCATIONS/ITEMS: Washington, DC inc Jefferson Memorial, Red Skull's base, Avengers Mansion (rfb); Red Skull's men's terrorist armor & guns, block of ice, Cap's mobility armor, Cosmic Cube (both in rfb)
FLASHBACKS: The Avengers find Cap's empty armor (Cap #443, '95). The Avengers revive Captain America (Av #4, '64).
SYNOPSIS: At the Jefferson Monument, armored terrorists hold the President hostage and threaten to blow him up unless Captain America arrives. FBI agent McElroy wonders aloud what makes Cap so special, which angers the Avengers. Giant-Man explains that Cap believes there's always a way and can survive anything. Quicksilver explains that Cap inspires everyone around him, including himself. Deathcry stops a police officer from posing as Cap, saving his life. The terrorists bump up their deadline because of the ruse. To make McElroy understand, Hercules explains that the Olympians measure wisdom against Athena, speed against Hermes and power against Zeus, but they measure courage against Captain America. Inspired, Agent McElroy helps the Avengers defeat the terrorists and save the President. Black Widow tells the press that Cap has died. Meanwhile, Cap lies in a block of ice…
NOTE: Letters page rechanges its name back to "American Graffiti."

CAPTAIN AMERICA #445 (November 1995)

"Operation: Rebirth Chapter One: Old Soldiers Never Die" (22 pages)

CREDITS: Mark Waid (writer), Ron Garney (pencils), Scott Koblish (inks), John Costanza (letters), John Kalisz, Paul Becton & Malibu (colors), Matt Idelson (asst editor), Ralph Macchio (editor), Mark Gruenwald (group editor)
FEATURE CHARACTER: Captain America (also in rfb & fb between Cap #443, '95 & Cap #451, '96 fb)
GUEST STARS: Avengers: Black Widow (also in rfb, last in Hulk #434, '95, next bts in DCvM #1, '96, next in DCvM #3, '96), Quicksilver (last in Hulk #434, '95, next in DCvM #1, '96); Thing (last in FFUnp #1, '95, next in DCvM #1, '96), Cyclops (last in W #91, '95, next in DCvM #1, '96), Rick Jones (last in Hulk #427, '95, next bts in DCvM #1, '96, next in DCvM #2, '96)
SUPPORTING CAST: Sharon Carter (also in photo & fb between Cap #446, '95 fb & Cap #451, '96 fb)

VILLAINS: Red Skull (also bts in fb between Av #388, '95 & Cap #451, '96 fb) & his men (also in fb), Adolf Hitler (bts in faulty Cosmic Cube, last in Cap #299, '84, last bts in Cap #446, '95 fb), Kubekult agents

OTHER CHARACTERS: Bill Clinton (last in Hulk #434, '95, next in Hulk #439, '96), Gen. Ulysses R. Chapman (1st), US military, funeral attendees, news reporter (voice only); Bucky (rfb), Sarah Rogers (photo)

LOCATIONS/ITEMS: Arlington cemetery inc Cap's grave, Red Skull's base, Cap's Avengers Mansion quarters (fb), Kubekult compound (also as fortress); faulty Cosmic Cube (last in Cap #446, '95 fb), block of ice (also in fb), Cap's empty casket, blood transfusion equipment, Skull's men's cryogenics guns (fb) & clubs, Kubekult agents' guns, Sharon's ultrasonic cannon, Zemo's drone plane (rfb)

FLASHBACKS: Black Widow announces that Captain America is dead (Cap #444, '95). Cap fails to save Bucky (Av #4, '64 fb). Sharon Carter and Red Skull's men freeze and abduct Cap, then give him a blood transfusion.

SYNOPSIS: As a funeral is held in his honor, Captain America breaks free from his block of ice. Cap makes his way through the deserted base until he's reunited with a bitter Sharon Carter. At first overjoyed, Cap becomes suspicious when Sharon unleashes agents to test him in battle. The agents quickly defeat Cap, who's still weak from the blood transfusion. Sharon gives him no time to recuperate, telling Cap the world is at stake before teleporting them to an enemy compound. Cap begins to feel like his old self as they defeat attacking men. Cap is disgusted when he realizes the blood transfusion came from the arriving Red Skull. The Skull easily defeats the weak Cap, who demands answers from Sharon. Their conversation is interrupted when a flash of light transforms the compound into a fortress.

NOTE: Gen. Chapman's surname is revealed in Cap #446, '95, his first name is revealed in Cap #8, '98.

CAPTAIN AMERICA #446 (December 1995)

"Operation: Rebirth Chapter Two: The Devil You Know" (24 pages)

CREDITS: Mark Waid (writer), Ron Garney (pencils), Denis Rodier (inks), John Costanza (letters), John Kalisz & Malibu (colors), Matt Idelson (asst editor), Ralph Macchio (editor), Mark Gruenwald (group editor)
FEATURE CHARACTER: Captain America
SUPPORTING CAST: Sharon Carter (also in fb2 between Cap #233, '79 & Cap #451, '96 fb, also in Cap #12, '98 fb)
VILLAINS: Red Skull (also in rfb & fbs1-2 between Cap Ann #13, '94 & Cap #437, '95), Adolf Hitler (also in photo, as Hate-Monger in rfb & bts in fb1 between Cap #299, '84 & Cap #445, '95; bts in faulty Cosmic Cube), Kubekult agents (disguised as AIM agents in fb)
OTHER CHARACTERS: Gen. Chapman (next in Cap #450, '96), US military (also as Kubekult agents), soldiers of fortune (fb2)

LOCATIONS/ITEMS: Kubekult compound, government alternative energy research installation, Red Skull's base (fb2); faulty Cosmic Cube (also in fb1 between Cap #299, '84 & Cap #445, '95), original Cosmic Cube (rfb), Kubekult agent's guns, grenade & jet, Skull's jet, US military guns, power generator, tanks & armor

FLASHBACKS: Red Skull and Hate-Monger oversee the creation of a new Cosmic Cube, but the Skull traps Hate-Monger inside it (SVTU #17, '80). When Hitler seemingly vanishes from the Cube, the Kubekult poses as AIM and steals the Cube from the Skull (1). Cap battles the Cosmic Cube wielding Skull (ToS #81, '66). Sharon Carter is on an undercover mission for SHIELD until she's suddenly cut loose. She survives by becoming a soldier of fortune, and eventually spies on the Kubekult. She teams up with Red Skull to defeat them (2).

SYNOPSIS: Red Skull tells Captain America the Kubekult has a Cosmic Cube with Hitler trapped inside, and they plan to alter reality to fit Hitler's vision. Cap is skeptical that the Skull wants to stop Hitler's vision from coming to life. Red Skull explains that he trapped Hitler in the Cube, and will take vengeance on him if he's freed. Besides, the Fourth Reich will be no good to the Skull unless he's in charge. Cap attacks the Kubekult agents, but the Skull tries to grab the Cube. Cap stops him, allowing the Kubekult agents to escape. Sharon interrogates an agent, and the three leave for the Kubekult's destination: a government alternative energy research installation that can bring the Cosmic Cube to full power. Cap has to fight his way through the installation's guards, who have orders to let no one inside. Cap is forced to strike Gen. Chapman to gain entry. When a wave of energy transforms the installations guards into Kubekult agents, Cap notices that Sharon has vanished.

CAPTAIN AMERICA #447 (January 1996)

"Operation: Rebirth Chapter Three: Triumph of the Will" (22 pages)

CREDITS: Mark Waid (writer), Ron Garney (pencils), Mike Manley (inks), John Costanza (letters), John Kalisz & Malibu (colors), Matt Idelson (asst editor), Ralph Macchio (editor), Mark Gruenwald (group editor)
FEATURE CHARACTER: Captain America
SUPPORTING CAST: Sharon Carter
VILLAINS: Red Skull, Adolf Hitler (bts in faulty Cosmic Cube)
OTHER CHARACTERS: US military (as Kubekult agents), Bucky (Cube illusion)
LOCATIONS/ITEMS: Government alternative energy research installation; US military power generator, guns, tanks & armor, faulty Cosmic Cube

SYNOPSIS: Captain America and Red Skull fight through the Kubekult agents, actually transformed American troops. When armored Kubekult agents arrive as reinforcements, Red Skull abandons Cap to search for the Cosmic Cube. The Skull quickly runs into more Kubekult agents, who overpower him. Cap arrives as the agents open fire on Red Skull, saving his life as repayment for the Skull saving his. Cap finds Sharon, who has the Cosmic Cube. She plans to override Hitler's influence on it with her own values, but gives the Cube to Cap instead. As Cap orders the Cube to self-destruct, Kubekult agents attack and make him drop it. Red Skull catches the Cosmic Cube and traps Cap inside it, making him think he's partnered with Bucky again.

CAPTAIN AMERICA #448 (February 1996)

"Operation: Rebirth Conclusion: American Dream" (37 pages)

CREDITS: Mark Waid (writer), Ron Garney (pencils), Denis Rodier (inks), John Costanza (letters), John Kalisz & Malibu (colors), Matt Idelson (asst editor), Ralph Macchio (editor), Mark Gruenwald (group editor)
FEATURE CHARACTER: Captain America (next in DCvM #1-4, Prime/Cap, Av:Ts, IM #325, Av #395, AI:RIM, SMTU #4, all '96, Tb #111, '07 fb)
SUPPORTING CAST: Sharon Carter
VILLAINS: Red Skull (next in Cap #1, '98), Adolf Hitler (bts in faulty Cosmic Cube, next in Cap #25, '00)
OTHER CHARACTERS: Invaders: Bucky, Human Torch (Hammond), Sub-Mariner; Sgt. Fury & his Howling Commandos: Izzy Cohen, Dum Dum Dugan, Reb Ralston; Dr. Anderson, Dr. Erskine, Heinz Krueger, Gen. Phillips, Sarah Rogers, Baron (Heinrich) Zemo, Agent R, US military, Rebirth witnesses, Nazis, police, reporters, bystanders (all in Cube illusion); US military (also as Kubekult agents)
LOCATIONS/ITEMS: Project: Rebirth, New York inc Empire State building, Germany inc Hitler's bunker (all in Cube illusion), government alternative energy research installation; faulty Cosmic Cube (destroyed, last app), Zemo's drone plane, Nazi airship & guns, Howling Commandos guns, Cap's motorcycle (all in Cube illusion), US military jeep & guns, nitrating glycerin
SYNOPSIS: Steve Rogers becomes America's first Super-Soldier, saves Dr. Erskine from a Nazi assassin and is joined by his partner Bucky. Red Skull gloats over trapping Captain America inside the Cosmic Cube. He hopes Cap will defeat Hitler inside the Cube, allowing the Skull to access the Cube's power. In the Cube, Cap is reunited with his mother. As he waits, the Skull fights off attacking Kubekult agents. Cap and Bucky battle Nazis, who tell them that Hitler is in his bunker in Germany. Cap and Bucky steal a Nazi airship, only for Baron Zemo to capture Bucky and strap him to a drone plane. Cap saves Bucky and sets a course for Germany. Cap joins the Howling Commandos and the Invaders, who hold off the Nazis as Cap makes his way to Hitler's bunker. Cap is confused when Bucky tells Cap not to go after Hitler. Bucky explains that defeating Hitler is a trap; if Cap succeeds, then Red Skull wins. Bucky fades away and Cap crashes through the bunker's door back into reality. The Skull goes after the Cube, but Cap destroys it with his shield. The blast atomizes Red Skull, leaving only his shadow burned into the wall.
NOTE: Includes title page (1 page).

CAPTAIN AMERICA #449 (March 1996)

"First Sign Chapter One: I'll Take Manhattan" (22 pages)

CREDITS: Mark Waid (writer), Ron Garney (co-pencils), Sandu Florea (co-pencils, co-inks), Denis Rodier (co-inks), Scott Koblish (co-inks, c inks), Michael Higgins (letters), John Kalisz & Malibu (colors), Matt Idelson (asst editor), Ralph Macchio (editor), Mark Gruenwald (exec editor), Carlos Pacheco (c pencils)
FEATURE CHARACTER: Captain America (next in Thor #496, IM #326, Av #396, Hulk #440, all '96)
GUEST STAR: Thor (between Thor #495-496, '96)
SUPPORTING CAST: Edwin Jarvis (last in Thor #495, '96, next in IM #326, '96), Sharon Carter
VILLAINS: Libra (leader of the "First Sign" Zodiac, bts controlling the Zodiac agents, 1st, next bts in Thor #496, '96, next in Av #396, '96), Zodiac agents, Enchantress (between Thor #495-496, '96)
OTHER CHARACTERS: Contessa Val Fontaine (last in Pun #1, '95, next in Pun #7, '96), other SHIELD agents, paramedics, coast guard, bystanders; Nick Fury (mentioned, see NOTE)
LOCATIONS/ITEMS: Brooklyn Bridge, Manhattan, Avengers Mansion, Enchantress's apartment; SHIELD jets, helicopter & Helicarrier w/ tractor beam, Zodiac force field, guns & knives, Cap's Avengers ID
SYNOPSIS: Captain America stops Sharon Carter from randomly harassing SHIELD agents about why she was cut loose. They go to find Nick Fury, but Contessa tells them Fury's dead. Contessa threatens to arrest Sharon for going AWOL, but Cap calms everyone down and Contessa releases them. A force field suddenly separates Cap and Sharon, and Cap realizes all power has been lost inside the field. He directs paramedics to the nearest hospital and saves a crashed helicopter crew from drowning before battling Zodiac agents on his way to Avengers Mansion. The Avengers are gone so Jarvis tells him where to find Thor. Cap evades Zodiac agents until he crashes into Thor's apartment. Cap asks Thor to zap the attacking Zodiac with Mjolnir, but Thor tells him he's no longer magically empowered.
NOTE: Story continued in Thor #496, IM #326 & Av #396, all '96. Fury was thought killed by Punisher in DE:Ω, '95, but Fury/13 #1-2, '98 reveals it was only an advanced LMD.

CAPTAIN AMERICA #450 (April 1996)

"Man Without a Country Chapter One: Executive Action" (22 pages)

CREDITS: Mark Waid (writer), Ron Garney (pencils, c art), Scott Loblish (inks), John Costanza (letters), John Kalisz & Malibu (colors), Matt Idelson (asst editor), Ralph Macchio (editor), Mark Gruenwald (exec editor)
FEATURE CHARACTER: Captain America (also in rfb & photo)
SUPPORTING CAST: Sharon Carter (also in rfb)
VILLAIN: Machinesmith (also in holographic image, bts in pfb, fired Argus anti-aircraft cannon, last in IM #325, '96)
OTHER CHARACTERS: Bill Clinton (last in Hulk #439, '96, next bts in Cap #452, '96), Gen. Chapman (also in rfb, last in Cap #446, '95, next in Cap #8, '98), Criminal Investigation Department agents (Nyland named), military police, London authorities & bystanders; Red Skull & his men, US military (prev 3 in

fb), Bernie Rosenthal, Rachel Leighton & her horse (prev 3 in photo)

LOCATIONS/ITEMS: Brooklyn inc Cap's HQ (see NOTE), Washington, DC inc Washington Monument & White House w/Oval Office, London inc Heathrow Airport, Moldavia (pfb); CID's guns & handcuffs, Cap's exiles paperwork, Air Force One, Sharon's pogo-plane, Argus anti-aircraft canon (photo & off-panel in pfb), 2 US jets (destroyed in pfb), faulty Cosmic Cube (rfb)

FLASHBACKS: Cap, Sharon and Red Skull fight the US military and Cap strikes Gen. Chapman (Cap #446, '95). Cap fights the Skull over the Cosmic Cube (Cap #447, '96). Two US jets are destroyed by the Argus anti-aircraft cannon (p).

SYNOPSIS: Sharon Carter rummages through Steve Roger's apartment until CID agents break down the door. She fights them off and escapes. Steve returns home only to be arrested for treason. Later, the President and Gen. Chapman question Cap about his working with Red Skull before telling him that Machinesmith, based out of Moldavia, has built the Argus anti-aircraft cannon and used it to shoot down US jets. This has brought the US dangerously close to declaring war on Moldavia. Machinesmith is a known associate of the Skull, and Cap is the only possible leak of information about the schematics for the Argus, so the President asks Cap if he traded State secrets to Red Skull for his miraculous revival. After considering the circumstances, the President tells Cap he can't jail him without trial. However, the nation couldn't stand to see Cap on trial, so he's exiling Cap instead. Steve Rogers is flown to London as Sharon follows.

NOTE: Cap's HQ is now just his apartment; Rokatanski's costume shop is closed and the space is for rent.

CAPTAIN AMERICA #451 (May 1996)

"Man Without a Country Chapter Two: Plan "A"" (22 pages)

CREDITS: Mark Waid (writer), Ron Garney (pencils, c art), Scott Koblish (inks), John Costanza (letters), John Kalisz & Malibu (colors), Matt Idelson (asst editor), Ralph Macchio (editor)
FEATURE CHARACTER: Steve Rogers (also as "Nathan Hale" & in fb between Cap #445, '95 fb & Cap #444, '95)
SUPPORTING CAST: Sharon Carter (also in fb between Cap #445, '95 fb & Cap #444, '95)
VILLAINS: Machinesmith (also in fb between Cap #420, '93 & IM #320, '95) & his drones, Red Skull (only in fb between bts in Cap #445, '95 fb & Cap #444, '95), Moldavian military
OTHER CHARACTERS: London bystanders, US military, birds
LOCATIONS/ITEMS: London inc hotel, Machinesmith's Moldavian base, European countryside inc US Air Force base, Red Skull's base (in fb); Cap energy shield (prototype, 1st), Sharon's guns & taser, Machinesmith's gold coin, Machinesmith's drone's guns, US military guns & jets, Argus anti-aircraft cannon, block of ice (in fb)
FLASHBACK: As Red Skull and Sharon Carter watch, Machinesmith enters the frozen Cap's mind.
SYNOPSIS: Sharon gives Steve a new costume, similar to his Captain America suit but without the stars and stripes, and an energy shield prototype. They take a train to Moldavia, where Sharon taunts Steve with her fake passport name "Nathan Hale" before Machinesmith's drones attack. Cap and Sharon easily evade the drones. They run to a nearby US Air Force base where they fight past the troops and steal a jet. Cap flies over Moldavian airspace to draw the Argus anti-aircraft cannon's fire to learn where it is. The Argus destroys the jet.
NOTE: Includes recap page (1 page) w/image reproductions from Av #4, '64, Cap #113, '69, Cap #247, '80, Cap #287, '83 & MFan #18, '85.

CAPTAIN AMERICA #452 (June 1996)

"Man Without a Country Chapter Three: Plan "B"" (22 pages)

CREDITS: Mark Waid (writer), Ron Garney (pencils, c art), Scott Koblish (inks), John Costanza (letters), John Kalisz & Malibu (colors), Polly Watson (asst editor), Bobbie Chase (editor)
FEATURE CHARACTER: Steve Rogers (also as a Moldavian soldier & Captain America in Sharon's fantasy)
GUEST STAR: Dum Dum Dugan (bts, in SHIELD Helicarrier, last in Av #396, '96)
SUPPORTING CAST: Sharon Carter (also as Moldavian soldier & in fantasy)
VILLAINS: Machinesmith & his drones, Moldavian military
OTHER CHARACTERS: Bill Clinton (bts, meeting w/Moldavians, last in Cap #450, '96), SHIELD agents, Secret Service, Moldavian delegates, CNN reporter, birds; Hydra, Guerilla fighters (both in Sharon's fantasy)
LOCATIONS/ITEMS: Moldavia inc cave & Machinesmith's base, Mt. Hood, Camp David; Cap's energy shield, Sharon's ejector seat w/parachute, Moldavian jeep, guns & gas bomb, Argus anti-aircraft cannon (destroyed), Machinesmith's gold coin, SHIELD Helicarrier
SYNOPSIS: Having abandoned his own parachute, Cap falls to earth as he gets the rhythm of Sharon's spinning ejector seat. He finally catches it and uses his energy shield to force the seat's parachute open. Once on ground, Cap finds a cave to get some rest, but Sharon refuses to sleep next to him for warmth conservation. Sharon awakens surrounded by Moldavian troops. She fights them off and Cap picks her up in a jeep. They disguise themselves as Moldavian soldiers and cause a distraction at the entrance to Machinesmith's base. As Sharon fights the Moldavian troops Cap destroys the Argus cannon, but the Moldavian troops gas them. They wake up in Machinesmith's base, where Machinesmith reveals he has a gold coin encoded with every shred of knowledge from Cap's mind. He demonstrates by taking control of a SHIELD Helicarrier and steering it to crash into Mt. Hood. Machinesmith transfers his mind to a drone disguised as a Moldavian delegate meeting with the President, forcing Cap to choose which crisis to deal with.

CAPTAIN AMERICA #453 (July 1996)

"Man Without a Country Chapter Four: Executive Action" (22 pages)

CREDITS: Mark Waid (writer), Ron Garney (pencils p10-22, c art), Pino Rinaldi (pencils p1-9), Scott Koblish (inks), John Costanza (letters), John Kalisz & Malibu (colors), Polly Watson (asst editor), Bobbie Chase (editor)
FEATURE CHARACTER: Captain America
GUEST STAR: Dum Dum Dugan (next in XFor #55, '96)
SUPPORTING CAST: Sharon Carter
VILLAINS: Machinesmith (next bts in IM/Cap Ann '98 fb, next in Tb #64, '02) & his drones (some as Secret Service), Dr. Doom (last in FF #409, '96, next in Doom2099 #40, '96)
OTHER CHARACTERS: Bill Clinton (next bts in SS #123, '96, next in Hulk #462, '98), SHIELD agents, Latverians, Moldavian delegates, Secret Service, US military
LOCATIONS/ITEMS: Moldavia inc Machinesmith's base, Latveria inc Doomstadt, Camp David, White House inc Oval Office; SHIELD Helicarrier & jets, Machinesmith's computer terminal & gold coin, Cap's Avengers ID, Latverian security cameras, Doombots, US military guns & helicopters, Doom's replacement Cap suit & shield, the "football"
SYNOPSIS: Sharon Carter uses Machinesmith's gold coin to hack into the SHIELD Helicarrier's command codes to stop it from crashing into Mt. Hood. Meanwhile, Cap uses his Avengers ID to prove who he is to nearby Latveria. Doombots picks him up and deposit him in Dr. Doom's presence. Cap convinces Dr. Doom to quickly get him to America, or else war between the USA and Moldavia would have an ill effect on Latveria. Doom agrees because it suits his fancy. At Camp David, Moldavian delegates meet with the President until Machinesmith's drones attack the Secret Service. Machinesmith steals the "football", the President's nuclear briefcase, and enters the President's mind to learn the activation codes, his ultimate plan all along. Captain America appears and quickly fights through Machinesmith's drones. Cap deduces Machinesmith has transferred himself into the football, so Cap destroys it. Later, the President reinstates Cap's citizenship and apologizes.

CAPTAIN AMERICA #454 (August 1996)

"Sanctuary" (22 pages)

CREDITS: Mark Waid (writer), Ron Garney (pencils, c art), Scott Koblish (inks), John Costanza (letters), John Kalisz & Malibu (colors), Polly Watson (asst editor), Bobbie Chase (editor)
FEATURE CHARACTER: Captain America (next in MFan #1, Av #399-400, Ons:XM, UXM #335, Av #401, X #55, bts in Thor #502, Hulk #445, Av #402, X #56, Ons:MU fb, Cap #1, all '96)
SUPPORTING CAST: Sharon Carter (chr next in Cap #49, '09 fb, next in Cap #1, '98)
VILLAINS: X12 (Tap-Kwai ruler, only app), Tap-Kwai military (Hong Fan named) inc prison guards
OTHER CHARACTERS: Tap-Kwai prisoners, SHIELD pilot (voice only)
LOCATIONS/ITEMS: Tap-Kwai inc Yankeetown & surrounding countryside w/prison camp; Machinesmith's gold coin & Sharon's replica, X12's taser, Tap-Kwai military guns, jeeps & helicopters, Cap's motorcycle & Jet Ski, SHIELD jet & Helicarrier w/tractor beam
SYNOPSIS: In Tap-Kwai, Sharon Carter tries to barter Machinesmith's gold coin for sanctuary. X12, Tap-Kwai's leader, agrees to the deal but orders the military to kill her anyway. Captain America suddenly crashes in and rescues Sharon. Cap evades the Tap-Kwai military, but doesn't understand why Sharon is upset with him. She says she wasn't going to actually sell the gold coin and takes Cap to a nearby prison camp. She reveals she spent eight months in a cell after SHIELD cut her loose, and says she returned to Tap-Kwai because it's the only stable place she's had since her SHIELD days. Cap says the only sanctuary she'll ever need is in her mind. Against Sharon's protests, Cap sets the prisoners free. She sees the prisoners to the arriving SHIELD Helicarrier while Cap holds off the Tap-Kwai military. Sharon refuses to leave with SHIELD, but gives Cap the gold coin while revealing she bartered with a replica. Cap salutes Sharon as the SHIELD tractor beam pulls him up.
NOTE: Story continued in the Onslaught crossover, where the heroes are "killed" and sent to a pocket universe by Franklin Richards. "American Graffiti" includes farewell letters from Mark Waid & Ron Garney. Series continued in Cap #1, '96.

CAPTAIN AMERICA: THE LEGEND #1 (September 1996)

CREDITS: Paul Becton (spot recoloring), Comicraft (design), Jason Franzone, Mark Gruenwald (research), Mark Powers Lending Library (thanks), Polly Watson (assoc editor), Bobbie Chase (exec editor), Ron Garney (c art), Suzanne Gaffney (c design), Todd Klein (c letters), John Kalisz (c colors)
NOTE: Tribute issue containing features on Captain America. Contains inside front cover pin-up reproducing the Cap figure from the cover, using mirror image of same figure on inside back cover; table of contents (1 page) & indicia page (1 page) featuring Cap; "Fighting Skills of the Foes I Fought!" (4 pages) ranking Cap's opponents in skill categories of "Off the Chart," "Augmented Strength Highly Skilled," "Augmented Strength Limited Skills," "Peak Human Strength Highly Skilled," "Peak Human Strength Moderately Skilled" & "Average Human Strength Limited Skills" featuring Cap, Terminus, Super-Adaptoid, Thanos, Jakar, MODOK, MODAM, Dragon Man, Ameridroid, USAgent, Wolverine, Cable, Grand Director, Deathlok, Americop, Primus, Nomad, Armadillo, Vormund, Man-Brute, Power Man (Josten), Animus, Vermin, Baron Blood, Grey Gargoyle, Mr. Hyde, Nefarious, Batroc, Crossbones, Black Panther, Nick Fury, Punisher, Tumbler, Razorfist, Viper, Gen. Wo, Red Skull, King Cobra, Zaran, Machete, Mother Night, Swordsman (Ducquesne), Bullseye, Flag-Smasher, Mad Dog, Constrictor, Dr. Faustus, Eel, Machinesmith, Asp, Baron (Helmut) Zemo, Zeitgeist, Scourge, Whirlwind, Everyman, Madcap, Sidewinder, Arnim Zola, Black Mamba & Trapster

Mark Gruenwald, writer); Pin-up featuring Cap by John Romita Jr.; "The Loved and the Lost" (4 pages) featuring Peggy Carter, Sharon Carter, Bernie Rosenthal, Diamondback, Rick Jones, Bucky Barnes, Falcon, Nomad, Demolition Man, Fabian Stankowicz, Col. John Jameson & Moonhunter (Mark Gruenwald, writer); "Brooklyn Heights HQ" (2 pages) schematics by Eliot Brown, design by Hyperdesign; "Captain America, This is your Life!" (4 pages) featuring Joseph & Sarah Rogers, Arnie Roth, Gen. Phillips, Dr. Erskine, Dr. Myron McLean, Sgt. Mike Duffy, Sub-Mariner, Human Torch (Hammond), Toro, Edwin Jarvis, Col. Nick Fury, Hawkeye, Quicksilver, Scarlet Witch, Black Panther, Dave Cox, Donna Maria Puentes, Josh Cooper, Anna Kappelbaum, Mike Farrel, Free Spirit & Jack Flag (Mark Gruenwald, writer); "Test Your Strength" (2 pages) quiz featuring Cap & Nazis (Mark Gruenwald, writer); "Captain America's Lamest Foes" (2 pages) featuring Ameridroid, Animus, Blistik, Brother Nature, Everyman, Gamecock, Mr. X & Peeper (Mark Gruenwald, writer); "Captain America's Top Ten Greatest Foes" (2 pages) featuring Dr. Faustus, Flag-Smasher, Viper, Baron (Heinrich) Zemo, Arnim Zola, Crossbones, Batroc, MODOK, Red Skull & Machinesmith (Mark Gruenwald, writer); "Outnumbered!" (2 pages) featuring Serpent Society, AIM, Skeleton Crew & Watchdogs (Mark Gruenwald, writer); "Cap Creators Speak Out" (2 pages) w/quotes from Ron Garney, Mark Gruenwald, Mark Waid, Paul Neary, Ralph Macchio & Stan Lee (Matt Idelson, writer, Jimmy D., photos); "He Looks Good in Tights, but Can He Hold a Job?" (2 pages) featuring Steve Rogers as a soldier, teacher, policeman, commercial artist & costume shop owner (Mark Gruenwald, writer); "Top Ten Most Embarrassing Moments" (4 pages) pointing to Cap #391, '91, 148, '72, 163, '73, 182, '75; ToS #92/2, '67; Cap #389, '91, 438, '95; Cap #307, '85's cover; Cap #355, '89 & 405, '92 (A. Guillory, writer); "Captain America, Fashionable Guy!" (2 pages) featuring the original Nomad, the Captain, armor, ex-patriot & traditional uniforms (Mark Gruenwald, writer); "Mega-Milestone Issues" (8 pages) reproducing covers to CapC #1, '41 & 75, '50; YM #24, '53; CapC #76, '54; Av #4, '64 & 16, '65; ToS #58, '64, 66, '65, 75, '66, 94, '67 & 97, '68; Cap #100, '68, 183, '75, 193, '76, 200, '76, 209, '77, 223, '78, 231, '79, 237, '79, 247-248 & 250, '80, 275, '82, 281-282, '83; Cap Ann #8, '86; Cap #300, '84, 309-310 & 312, '85; 317, 320, 322, all '86; 328, 332, 333, all '87; 350, 354, 360, all '89, 368, '90, 372, '90, 383, '91, 400, '92'; 425, 431, 434, all '94; 438, 443, 445, all '95; 450, 452 & 454, all '96 (Mark Gruenwald, writer).

"Scenes We Never Saw" (3 pages)

CREDITS: Mark Waid (writer), Dan Jurgens (pencils), Jerry Ordway (inks), Jim Novak (letters), John Kalisz (colors)

FEATURE CHARACTER: Captain America (during Av #5, '64)

VILLAINS: Muggers

OTHER CHARACTERS: Jack Kirby (last in FF #10, '63, next in FF Ann #3, '65), Joe Simon (voice only, only app), Department of Motor Vehicles employee & customers, taxi driver, police, news anchor (on TV)

LOCATIONS/ITEMS: New York inc DMV & Steve's old neighborhood; Steve's birth records, mugger's knife

SYNOPSIS: Steve Rogers is unable to get a driver's license when the DMV employee notices he was born in 1922 and doesn't believe him. Steve takes a taxi to his old neighborhood but finds a store where his apartment building used to be. He's mugged, so he changes into Cap and captures the muggers. Jack Kirby congratulates Cap on capturing the muggers and welcomes him back, telling him the world needs him now more than ever.

NOTE: Story followed by "The Last Word: What We All Love about Captain America" (2 pages) showing Marvel staffers favorite Cap characters featuring Glenn Greenburg (Cap), Chris Fagan (Cap), Polly Watson (Armadillo), Tom Brevoort (Batroc), Andy Ball (Blistik), Ben Raab (Falcon), Ralph Macchio (Cap-Wolf), Matt Idelson (Ron Garney).

CAPTAIN AMERICA #1 [#455] (November 1996)

"Courage" (50 pages)

CREDITS: Jeph Loeb (writer), Rob Liefeld (plot, pencils, editor), Chuck Dixon (co-plot), Jon Sibal (inks), Richard Starkings, Comicraft's Dave Lanphear (letters), Brian Haberlin & Extreme Color (colors)

FEATURE CHARACTER: Captain America (last in Ons:MU, '96 fb)

SUPPORTING CAST: Rikki Barnes (ballerina, 1st but chr last in HR #1/2, '96)

VILLAINS: Nick Fury LMD (see NOTE), Red Skull (World Party leader, voice only), Master Man (Alexander, Red Skull's super-powered agent), Hauptman (Master Man's assistant), World Party (racist group, inc Team Alpha) & rally attendees inc John Barnes (Rikki's brother, chr last in HR #1/2, '96) & Gus (Johns' friend, next in Cap #4, '97) (all 1st, see NOTE)

OTHER CHARACTERS: Sharon Carter, Dum Dum Dugan (next in Cap #3, '97), Special Agent Hunt (all SHIELD agents), Peggy Rogers, Rick Rogers (both SHIELD LMDs posing as Steve's family), Abraham Wilson (Caps' shield keeper, dies, only app), Nathan (SHIELD agent undercover as Steve's co-worker) (all 1st, see NOTE), Steve's other co-workers, cafeteria employee, reporter (on TV); Nazi soldiers (in Steve's dream)

LOCATIONS/ITEMS: Philadelphia inc Rogers home, Steve's workplace w/cafeteria, Barnes home, Wilson home & World Party HQ; Nazi planes & tanks (in Steve's dream), Cap's shield, Team Alpha's guns & armor, SHIELD Helicarrier & jet, World Party nuclear missiles

SYNOPSIS: After a night dreaming about Captain America, Steve Rogers says goodbye to his family and leaves for work. When he tells his co-workers about his dream one of them makes a phone call, informing the person on the other end they have a problem. The next day, Rikki Barnes fails to talk her brother John out of attending that night's World Party rally. At the rally, SHIELD agent Hunt finds nuclear missiles, but is captured. Meanwhile, Abraham Wilson finds Steve in the street and convinces Steve to accompany him home, where Abraham gives Steve Captain America's shield. Before Steve can question Abraham regarding the gift, the World Party's Team Alpha attacks Abraham's home; Steve easily fights them off, but Abraham dies. On SHIELD's Helicarrier, Nick Fury learns that Cap has returned.

NOTE: The bracketed issue number above is retroactive, stemming from the return to the original numbering with Cap #600, '09, and is not seen on the issue itself. Dual numbering officially begins with Cap #42, '01. HR:R #1, '97 reveals that with the exception of Cap, the cast are not the Earth-616 originals, but pocket universe counterparts created by Franklin Richards. The Nick Fury herein is revealed as an evil LMD leading the Sons of the Serpent in Cap #11, '97, where the pocket universe's real Nick Fury 1st appears. Steve's address is 85 Chestnut St.

CAPTAIN AMERICA #2 [#456] (December 1996)

"Secrets" (22 pages)

CREDITS: Jeph Loeb (writer), Rob Liefeld (plot, pencils, editor), Jon Sibal (inks), Richard Starkings & Comicraft (letters), Extreme Color (colors), Andrew Troy (c colors)
FEATURE CHARACTER: Captain America
SUPPORTING CAST: Sam Wilson (last in Ons:MU, '96 fb as Falcon), Rikki Barnes (next in Cap #4, '97)
VILLAINS: Nick Fury LMD, Red Skull (1st full app), John Barnes (next in Cap #4, '97), Master Man, Hauptman
OTHER CHARACTERS: Peggy Rogers LMD, Rick Rogers LMD, Special Agent Hunt (last app), Andy (US Air Force); Abraham Wilson (in Falcon's thoughts)
LOCATIONS/ITEMS: Philadelphia inc Rogers home, Barnes home & World Party HQ; Fury's LMD remote control, restraining table, SHIELD dispatch letter, US Air Force jets, US Navy aircraft carrier
SYNOPSIS: Steve races home to check on his family, but they're frozen like statues. Nick Fury introduces himself as head of SHIELD and reveals Steve's family as LMDs. Meanwhile, Rikki wakes up to find her brother stealing from her. He says he's joining the World Party and leaves. Elsewhere, Lt. Sam Wilson learns that his father Abraham has died. At the World Party HQ, Red Skull tortures SHIELD agent Hunt.
NOTE: Issue is dedicated to Mark Gruenwald.

CAPTAIN AMERICA #3 [#457] (January 1997)

"Patriotism" (22 pages)

CREDITS: Jeph Loeb (writer), Rob Liefeld (plot, pencils, editor), Jon Sibal (co-inks, c inks), Larry Stucker (co-inks), Richard Starkings & Comicraft (letters), Andy Troy & Extreme Color (colors)
FEATURE CHARACTER: Captain America (also in fb, also in Av #1-3, '96-'97, FF #3, '97, see NOTE)
SUPPORTING CAST: Sam Wilson
VILLAINS: Nick Fury LMD (next in Av #1, '96), Crossbones (silent World Party soldier, 1st), Hauptman (next in Cap #5, '97), Red Skull, Master Man, Team Alpha
OTHER CHARACTERS: Peggy Rogers LMD, Rick Rogers LMD (both last app), Sharon Carter (last in Cap #1, '96, next in Cap #5, '97), Dum Dum Dugan (last in Cap #1, '96, next in FF #2, '96), other SHIELD agents, Harry S. Truman (US President), Nick Fury, Gen. Ross, military personnel (prev 4 in fb, see NOTE)
LOCATIONS/ITEMS: Philadelphia inc Rogers home, Arlington National cemetery inc Abraham Wilson's grave, White House inc Oval Office (in fb, see NOTE); SHIELD Helicarrier, Team Alpha's guns & armor
FLASHBACKS: Captain America opposes President Truman's use of nuclear weapons (see NOTE).
SYNOPSIS: Nick Fury tells Steve Rogers that after Cap opposed President Truman's use of nuclear weapons, the US government put Cap into "Operation Sleeper" and moved him around the country since WWII. Fury offers to put Steve back to sleep, or he can work for SHIELD as Captain America. Steve agrees, resumes his role as Cap, and Fury tells him about the Avengers. Later, Red Skull introduces Crossbones to Master Man. Cap meets Lt. Sam Wilson in Arlington National cemetery at Abraham Wilson's grave, where Sam blames Cap for his father's death. Sam punches Cap, but they're interrupted when Crossbones attacks and knocks Cap out.
NOTE: Crossbones is an inhabitant of the pocket universe. HR:R #3, '97 reveals the pocket universe is less than a year old which would normally make the flashback seen here a false memory, but Cap #12, '97 reveals that the Fury LMD is lying about those false memories.

CAPTAIN AMERICA #4 [#458] (February 1997)

"Fire" (22 pages)

CREDITS: Jeph Loeb (writer), Rob Liefeld (plot, pencils), Jon Sibal (co-inks, c inks), Lary Stucker (co-inks), Richard Starkings & Comicraft's Albert Deschesne (letters), Andy Troy & Extreme Color (colors), Eric Stephenson (editor)
FEATURE CHARACTER: Captain America
SUPPORTING CAST: Rikki Barnes (last in Cap #2, '96), Sam Wilson
VILLAINS: Red Skull, Master Man, Crossbones (last app), John Barnes (last in Cap #2, '96), Gus (last in Cap #1, '96) (both join World Party), World Party agents
LOCATIONS/ITEMS: World Party HQ; World Party agents' guns & armor, John's gun, World Party's nuclear missiles
SYNOPSIS: Rikki Barnes tracks her brother John to the World Party HQ and learns he's already joined the group when he ambushes her, holding her at gunpoint. Rikki escapes, only for Red Skull to stop her. Held captive several floors below, Cap tries to make amends with Sam Wilson. Red Skull arrives holding Cap's shield, which angers Cap. The Skull tries to recruit Cap into the World Party, but Cap breaks free from his chains, defeats Crossbones, retrieves his shield and frees Sam. Master Man arrives and his agents shoot Sam. Meanwhile, Rikki awakens to find herself strapped to a nuclear missile.
NOTE: Includes a pin-up (1 page) of Bucky (Rikki Barnes) by Pop Mhan.

CAPTAIN AMERICA #5 [#459] (March 1997)

"Victory" (23 pages)

CREDITS: Jeph Loeb (writer), Rob Liefeld (plot, pencils), Jonathan Sibal (co-inks, c inks), Larry Strucker (co-inks, variant c inks), Richard Starkings, Comicraft's Kolja Fuchs (letters), Andy Troy (colors, variant c colors), Extreme Color (separations), Drew (enhancement), Eric Stephenson (editor)
FEATURE CHARACTER: Captain America (also in photo, next in HR #1/2, '96)
GUEST STARS: Sam Wilson (next in Cap #10, '97 as Falcon)
SUPPORTING CAST: Rikki Barnes (next in HR #1/2, '96 as Bucky)
VILLAINS: Nick Fury LMD (last in FF #3, '97, next bts in IM #3, '97, next in Av #5, '97), Master Man (next in HR:Rebel, '00), Red Skull, Hauptman, John Barnes, Gus, World Party inc Team Alpha (prev 5 last app)
OTHER CHARACTERS: Sharon Carter (last app), other SHIELD agents
LOCATIONS/ITEMS: World Party HQ; WP's nuclear missiles, remote missile controller, Fury's armor & gun, SHIELD guns & Helicarrier
SYNOPSIS: As SHIELD nears the World Party HQ, Captain America quickly defeats Master Man and his agents, but Red Skull escapes. Hoping the Super-Soldier Serum in his blood will heal the dying Sam Wilson, Cap uses his shield to cut himself and bleeds into Sam's mouth. Meanwhile, Rikki tries to talk John into cutting her free from the nuclear missile she's strapped to until Master Man arrives with the remote missile controller. Cap arrives, frees Rikki and battles Master Man while Rikki fights her brother. Sam arrives, healed and now super-strong, and defeats Master Man with Cap. Fury arrives with SHIELD agents, and Rikki hands over the missile controller.
NOTE: Cap's blood is green here.

CAPTAIN AMERICA #6 [#460] (April 1997)

"Soldiers" (20 pages)

CREDITS: Jeph Loeb (writer), Rob Liefeld (plot, pencils), Jon Sibal (co-inks, c inks), Larry Stucker (co-inks), Richard Starkings & Comicraft (letters), Andy Troy & Extreme Color, Don Skinner (colors), Brian Murray (3-D shield imaging), Eric Stephenson (editor)
FEATURE CHARACTER: Captain America (next in Av #4-6, '97, IM #6, '97)
GUEST STAR: Cable (between Cable #42-43, '97)
SUPPORTING CAST: Bucky (Rikki Barnes, next in Cap #8, '97)
VILLAINS: Baron Zemo (Heinrich Zemo, World Party ally), MODOK (both next in Av #8, '97), AIM agents (all 1st)
OTHER CHARACTERS: Dum Dum Dugan (last in FF #2, '96, next in FF #12, '97), other SHIELD agent
LOCATIONS/ITEMS: SHIELD Helicarrier; Cable's gun, AIM guns
SYNOPSIS: Suddenly, Cable finds himself in the middle of a battle with AIM, MODOK and Baron Zemo alongside Captain America on the SHIELD Helicarrier. Cable asks Cap why he's not dead, but Cap has no idea what he's talking about. The two are joined by Bucky as they fight the AIM agents. Cable defeats MODOK as Cap defeats Baron Zemo. As SHIELD arrests the AIM agents, Cap commends Cable on his fighting skills, but Cable suddenly vanishes. Now that he knows Cap is alive, Cable vows not to rest until he finds the other missing heroes.
NOTE: Baron Zemo and MODOK are inhabitants of the pocket universe.

2ND STORY: "Industrial Revolution Epilogue" (3 pages)
CREDITS: Jeph Loeb (writer), Rob Liefeld (plot, pencils pg 1), Ian Churchill (pencils pgs 2-3), Larry Stucker (inks), Andy Troy & Extreme Color, Don Skinner (colors), Comicraft's Dave Lanphear (letters), Eric Stephenson (editor)
FEATURE CHARACTER: Captain America (next in Av #7-8, '97)
GUEST STARS: Iron Man (last in IM #6, '97, next in Hulk #450/2, '97), Thor (last in IM #6, '97, next in Av #7, '97)
VILLAIN: Nick Fury LMD (last in IM #6, '97, next in Av #7, '97)
OTHER CHARACTER: SHIELD agent
LOCATIONS/ITEMS: SHIELD Helicarrier inc Fury's quarters
SYNOPSIS: Cap, Iron Man and Thor tell Nick Fury the Avengers will no longer be run by SHIELD.
NOTE: Thor is an inhabitant of the pocket universe. The real Thor will later appear in Av #9, '97.

CAPTAIN AMERICA #7 [#461] (May 1997)

"Crossroads" (22 pages)

CREDITS: James Robinson (writer), Ryan Benjamin, Mat Broome, Travis Charest, Joe Phillips, Tom Raney, Scott Williams (pencils), Homage Studios (inks), Richard Starkings & Comicraft (letters), Wildstorm FX (colors), Michael Heisler (asst editor), Mike Rockwitz (editor), Jim Lee (c pencils), Richard Bennett (c inks)
FEATURE CHARACTER: Captain America (also in Clinton's thoughts & fb, next in Av #9-11, '97, see NOTE)
VILLAIN: Nick Fury LMD (between Av #8-9, '97)
OTHER CHARACTERS: Col. von Wagner, Iron Valkyrie, Nazi soldiers & officer, Super-Soldier volunteers, US soldiers, bystanders (all in fb, see NOTE), Red Skull (in fb & in rfb, see NOTE), Avengers: Iron Man, Thor; Baron Zemo, Cable, MODOK (prev 5 in rfb); Bill Clinton (US President, last bts in FF #3, '97, last app), la Contessa Valentina de Fontaine (last in FF #2, '96, next in FF #12, '97)

LOCATIONS/ITEMS: White House's Oval Office; Cap's eagle emblem

FLASHBACKS: Alongside others, Steve Rogers volunteers as a test subject for the Super-Soldier Serum, and is the only successful recipient. He becomes Captain America, fights in WWII and battles villains including Red Skull, Col. von Wagner and Iron Valkyrie. After being put into Operation Sleeper, Cap is revived to fight in the Korean War as "Capt. John Battle" and in the Vietnam Conflict as "Capt. Jack Strike;" in the latter Steve goes mad at the sight of tortured American soldiers (see NOTE). Cap reawakens in the modern day (Cap #1, '96), joins the Avengers (Av #1, '96), battles Red Skull (Cap #4-5, '97), and alongside Cable, fights Baron Zemo and MODOK (Cap #6, '97).

SYNOPSIS: The President demands to know everything there is to know about Captain America so Nick Fury tells him, but warns him that when Nixon learned everything about Cap he was forced to resign. Fury explains that when Cap protested Truman's use of nuclear weapons Cap was put into the Sleeper Program, but was occasionally brought out to fight in wars. Recently, SHIELD tried to put Cap into a civilian environment with LMDs posing as his family. Cap enters the room and announces that he is leaving SHIELD's "protection" to rediscover America. Cap tears the eagle emblem from his mask and leaves with the President's blessing.

NOTE: Joe Phillips drew the main story; the other pencilers, collectively credited as "Homage Studios," drew the flashbacks. Cap #12, '97 reveals the Fury LMD is lying about the flashbacks. President Clinton is an inhabitant of the pocket universe.

CAPTAIN AMERICA #8 [#462] (June 1997)

"Serpents & Eagles Part 1: A First Small Hisssss" (22 pages)

CREDITS: James Robinson (writer), Joe Bennett (co-pencils), Alvaro Rio (co-pencils, co-inks), Sandra Hope (co-inks), Richard Starkings & Comicraft (letters), WildStorm FX (colors), Michael Heisler (asst editor), Mike Rockwitz (editor), Jim Lee (c pencils), Richard Bennett (c inks)
FEATURE CHARACTER: Captain America (also in pfb)
SUPPORTING CAST: Bucky (in pfb, last in Cap #6, '97, next in Cap #10, '97)
VILLAINS: Sons of the Serpent (racist militant organization, 1st)
OTHER CHARACTERS: SHIELD agents (in pfb), Mexia police (Sheriff Jake Wang named), TWTV reporter & cameraman, Dori's diner patrons (Grover Williams named), FBI agents, paramedics, bystanders, eagle, snake
LOCATIONS/ITEMS: Mexia, TX inc Dori's Diner & Sons of the Serpent compound; SHIELD Helicarrier, sky-cycle & jets (all in pfb), Steve's motorcycle, Sons of the Serpent's guns & ships

FLASHBACK: Captain America tells Bucky he's taking a hiatus to find the spirit of America (p).

SYNOPSIS: Steve Rogers arrives in Mexia, Texas, where he discovers that the racist Sons of the Serpent have set up a compound. While talking with the sheriff, he learns of a hostage situation at a nearby diner involving the Sons of the Serpent. Captain America busts into the diner and quickly defeats the Sons of the Serpent. Sheriff Wang takes Cap to the Sons of the Serpent's compound, which is surrounded by police and FBI agents. Cap fails to negotiate the Sons to surrender and inadvertently causes them to attack. Cap is able to defeat the Sons of the Serpent's fleet of airships and vows to take down the nationwide Sons of the Serpent operation.

CAPTAIN AMERICA #9 [#463] (July 1997)

"Serpents & Eagles Part 2: Horror for Hollywood" (22 pages)

CREDITS: James Robinson (writer), Joe Bennett (pencils), Sandra Hope & Homage Studios (inks), Richard Starkings, Comicraft's Kolja Fuchs (letters), Wildstorm FX (colors), Michael Heisler (asst editor), Mike Rockwitz (editor), Tom Raney (c art)
FEATURE CHARACTER: Captain America (also in dfb)
VILLAINS: Nick Fury LMD (in pfb as Serpent King, last in Av #11, '97), Sons of the Serpent (one in pfb)
OTHER CHARACTERS: Los Angeles police (Det. O'Brian named, one dies in pfb), filmmakers (Barry named), news anchor (on TV), Hollywood pimp, prostitute, vagrant (prev 3 in pfb) & bystanders (some in pfb), dog
LOCATIONS/ITEMS: Pacific Coast Highway (in pfb), Los Angeles, CA (also in pfb) inc Mann's Chinese Theater (in pfb), Sons of the Serpent's lair & arms base, La Brea Tar Pits, police station, Griffith Park w/Mt. Lee & the Hollywood sign; Cap's motorcycle (also in pfb), Sons of the Serpents' guns, tanks, chemical weapons, aircraft, powered exoskeletons, computer terminal & explosives

FLASHBACK: Steve tours Hollywood but is depressed by the state of the area (d). A Son of the Serpent kills a policeman and the Serpent King threatens to kill half the American populace (p).

SYNOPSIS: Steve Rogers arrives on the Pacific Coast. Later, Captain America storms a Sons of the Serpent lair, defeating everyone inside. While transferring custody to the LAPD, Cap trades notes on the Serpents with detective O'Brian. Cap interrogates one of the captured Serpents by dunking him in the La Brea Tar Pits and raids a nearby Serpent weapons cache. Cap is furious to learn that the Serpents' weapons are supplied by the government. After notifying O'Brian of the arsenal, Cap travels to Griffith Park, where the Serpents have tied several local Jewish filmmakers to the Hollywood Sign with timed explosives. Cap arrives, defeats the Serpents, and rescues the hostages. While conferring with O'Brian, Caps sees on the news that the Serpents have bombed mosques and synagogues in seventeen states and murdered 57 policemen. Cap leaves for Washington, DC.

NOTE: Steve remembers visiting Hollywood in 1938 at the age of 19; this may be a genuine memory from Cap's Earth-616 life.

CAPTAIN AMERICA #10 [#464] (August 1997)

"Serpents & Eagles Part 3: Capital Punishment" (22 pages)

CREDITS: James Robinson (writer), Joe Bennett (pencils), Sandra Hope (co-inks, c inks), Mark Irwin (co-inks), Richard Starkings, Comicraft's Kolja Fuchs (letters), Wildstorm FX (colors), Michael Heisler (asst editor), Mike Rockwitz (editor)
FEATURE CHARACTER: Captain America (also in pfb)
SUPPORTING CAST: Bucky (last in Cap #8, '97), Falcon (last in Cap #5, '97 as Sam Wilson) (both also in pfb)
VILLAINS: Nick Fury LMD (also as Serpent King), Sons of the Serpent (some die)
OTHER CHARACTERS: Stealth Flight Gamma (armored SHIELD agents, 1st, Joseph Litvak & Benjamin Shalboub named, Shalboub dies), other SHIELD agents (some in pfb)
LOCATIONS/ITEMS: Washington, DC (also in pfb) inc Lincoln Memorial & Washington Memorial, Sons of the Serpents' lair (destroyed), & Fury's mansion (Sons of the Serpent HQ); SHIELD helicarrier (also in pfb), hovercraft, sky-cycles, guns & Stealth Flight Gamma exoskeletons, Sons of the Serpent's guns & grenade, Fury's flying car
FLASHBACKS: Bucky tells Cap that she senses something strange within SHIELD. Cap tells her to trust her instincts and investigate it. Later, Cap asks Sam Wilson, now a super-hero going by his old callsign Falcon, to find the Serpents' lair (p).
SYNOPSIS: Captain America meets Nick Fury at the Lincoln Memorial. Fury tells Cap that SHIELD has found the Sons of the Serpent's local HQ and has assigned a team to attack it. Cap offers his aid and leaves with the team. Meanwhile, Bucky searches the SHIELD Helicarrier and Falcon battles the Sons of the Serpent. Cap and SHIELD's Stealth Flight Gamma arrive at the Serpent lair, but Cap is leery when they find it empty. Cap notices that Stealth Flight Gamma is comprised of ethnic, racial and religious minorities just as the Sons of the Serpent ambush them. Cap seemingly vanishes during the battle, and the SHIELD team tells the arriving Fury that Cap was killed. Fury leaves, unaware Cap is hiding in the trunk of his flying car. Cap follows Fury and is shocked to see that Fury is the Serpent King and is holding Falcon hostage.
NOTE: Cover-labeled "The World's Greatest Comics!" Includes recap page (2 pages) featuring Cap, Falcon, Bucky, and Nick Fury.

CAPTAIN AMERICA #11 [#465] (September 1997)

"Serpents & Eagles Part 4: Into the Snake Pit" (22 pages)

CREDITS: James Robinson (writer), Joe Bennett (pencils), Sandra Hope (inks), Richard Starkings, Comicraft's Kolja Fuchs (letters), Nathan Lumm & Wildstorm FX (colors), Michael Heisler (asst editor), Mike Rockwitz (editor), Edgar Tadeo (c colors)
FEATURE CHARACTER: Captain America (next in FF #12, '97, Av #12, '97, IM #12, '97)
GUEST STAR: Nick Fury (1st, next in FF #12, '97)
SUPPORTING CAST: Falcon (next in HR:R #3, '97), Bucky
VILLAINS: Nick Fury LMD (also as Serpent King, destroyed), Sons of the Serpent (some as SHIELD agents) (both last app), Galactus (between FF #11-12, both '97)
OTHER CHARACTERS: Stealth Flight Gamma (last app), SHIELD agent (bts, warns Fury of Galactus)
LOCATIONS/ITEMS: Fury's mansion; SHIELD Helicarrier w/Fury's cell & ventilation shaft, Sons of the Serpent's guns, Fury LMD's gun, Fury's gun, Stealth Flight Gamma exoskeletons & guns, Galactus' ship
SYNOPSIS: Captain America watches Fury order the Sons of the Serpent to attack Washington, DC. On the Helicarrier, Bucky finds a high-security cell and knocks out the guards, but is shocked to see who is in the cell. Cap challenges Fury to one-on-one combat, with Fury canceling the attack if he loses, but mid-fight Fury reneges and has the Sons attack Cap en masse. Cap frees Falcon and the two battle the Serpent army. Fury prepares to shoot Cap, but his head suddenly explodes, revealing the real Nick Fury behind him. As SHIELD agents arrest the Serpents, Fury reveals that he ordered Cap's re-assimilation into society with no intent to reactivate him, but was drugged and replaced with the LMD by parties unknown. A SHIELD agent notifies Fury of Galactus' approach.
NOTE: Cover-labeled "The World's Greatest Comics!" Includes recap page (2 pages) featuring Cap, Falcon, Bucky, and Nick Fury. Galactus and Nick Fury are inhabitants of the pocket universe. It remains unrevealed who replaced Fury with an LMD.

CAPTAIN AMERICA #12 [#466] (October 1997)

"Let it Be" (40 pages)

CREDITS: Jeph Loeb (writer), Ed Benes, Joe Bennett (pencils), Homage Studios (inks), Richard Starkings, Comicraft's Albert Deschesne (letters), Nathan Lumm & Wildstorm FX (colors), Michael Heisler (asst editor), Mike Rockwitz (editor)
FEATURE CHARACTER: Captain America (next in IM #13, '97)
GUEST STARS: Avengers: Hawkeye, Scarlet Witch, Thor, Vision (all last in IM #12, '97, next in FF #13, '97), Ant-Man (last in IM #12, '97, next in FF #13, '97 as Giant-Man), Iron Man (last in IM #12, '97, next in X #65, '97), Swordsman (last in Av #7, '97, next in FF #13, '97), Wasp (last in IM #12, '97, next in HR:R #4, '97); Fantastic Four: Invisible Woman, Mr. Fantastic, Thing (prev 3 last in IM #12, '97, next in FF #13, '97), Human Torch (last in

IM #12, '97); Hulkbusters: Doc Samson (last in IM #12, '97, last app), She-Hulk (last in IM #12, '97, next in HR:R #4, '97), Hulk (also as Bruce Banner, last in IM #12, '97); Dr. Doom (last in IM #12, '97, next in FF #13, '97), Nick Fury (last in IM #12, '97, last app), Uatu the Watcher (last in IM #11, '97, next in FF #7, '98)

SUPPORTING CAST: Bucky (next in HR:R #3, '97)

VILLAINS: Galactus & his heralds: Air-Walker, Firelord, Plasma, Silver Surfer, Terrax (all last in IM #12, '97, last app)

OTHER CHARACTERS: Richard Barnes, Peggy Carter-Barnes (Bucky's grandparents, both 1st, next in HR:YA #1, '00); Falcon (only on recap page)

LOCATIONS/ITEMS: Philadelphia, PA inc Barnes home, outer space, New York inc Baxter Building, Avengers Mansion w/assembly room, kitchen, & courtyard, Central Park w/Jacqueline Kennedy Onassis reservoir, Arlington National cemetery inc Abraham Wilson's grave; Dr. Doom's Power Siphon (destroyed) & chronometer, Firelord's lance, Terrax's axe, Galactus' ship & energy converter, Rebel's armor (gloves destroyed), Ultimate Nullifier (destroyed), Cap's sky-cycle & motorcycle

SYNOPSIS: Dr. Doom attacks Rikki Barnes, believing Rikki, designated a chronal anomaly by SHIELD, should not exist and thus may be the key to defeating Galactus before he consumes the world in less than a day. Captain America arrives and Doom asks for his help. In New York, the Avengers and Fantastic Four battle Galactus' heralds until Doom defeats them with his Power Siphon. After Doom explains his previous failures to defeat Galactus, Banner suggests feeding Galactus to bursting. Surfer arrives and beseeches Bucky to convince the heroes to evacuate Earth, but she demands the Surfer help her and grabs his board when he flies off. When Galactus strikes Bucky with his eyebeams, the Surfer, shaken by Galactus' callousness, offers his aid to the heroes, who fit him with their Ultimate Nullifier, a combination of Doom's Power Siphon and Rebel's armor. Attacking, the Surfer overloads Galactus, killing them both. Later, Cap meets Bucky's grandparents, Richard and Peggy Barnes, at Abraham Wilson's grave, who tell him Bucky is recovering. Fury arrives to tell Cap that his LMD was lying about Cap's past.

NOTE: Cover-labeled "Heroes Reunited Part 4 of 4" & "The World's Greatest Comics!" The covers for FF #12, Av #12, IM #12 & Cap #12, all '97, join to form one large image. Includes recap page (2 pages) featuring Cap, Bucky, Falcon & Nick Fury. Doc Samson, She-Hulk, Swordsman, Galactus & his heralds are all pocket universe inhabitants. The Thor appearing here is the Earth-616 version, not the pocket universe inhabitant that appeared in Cap #6/2, '97. Issue dedicated to Mark Gruenwald.

CAPTAIN AMERICA #13 [#467] (November 1997)

"World War 3 Part 4: War Without End..." (23 pages)

CREDITS: James Robinson (witer), Ron Lim (pencils), Danny Bulanadi (inks), Richard Starkings, Comicraft's Miranda Emerson & Kolja Fuchs (letters), Nathan Lumm & WildStorm FX (colors), Michael Heisler (asst editor), Mike Rockwitz (editor), Tom Raney (c pencils), Richard Bennett(c inks)

FEATURE CHARACTER: Captain America (next in HR:R #3-4, '97, Cap #1, '98)

GUEST STARS: Avengers: Scarlet Witch (last in IM #13, '97, next in HR:R #4, '97), Spartan (Hadrian-7, android, last in IM #13, '97, chr next in WildCATS #30, '96), Thor (last in IM #13, '97, next in HR:R #1, '97); Fantastic Four: Invisible Woman, Mr. Fantastic, Thing (prev 3 last in IM #13, '97, next in HR:R #1, '97), Maul (Jeremy Stone, super-strong human-alien hybrid, last in IM #13, '97, chr next in WildCATS #30, '96); Stormwatch: Battalion (Jackson King, Stormwatch training officer), Jenny Sparks ("spirit of the 20th century"), Winter (Nikolas Kamarov, ex-Spetznaz energy manipulator) (prev 3 last in IM #13, '97, chr next in Stormwatch #37, '96); WildCATS: Giant-Man, Gorgon (both last in IM #13, '97, next in HR:R #4, '97), Grifter (Cole Cash, mercenary), Void (Adrianna Tereshkova, ex-cosmonaut), Zealot (Lady Zannah, ex-Majestrix of the Coda Sisterhood) (prev 3 last in IM #13, '97, chr next in WildCATS #30, '96), Warblade (human-alien hybrid that can form his hands into blades, last in Av #13, '97, chr next in WildCATS #30, '96); Deathblow (Michael Cray, mercenary, last in IM #13, '97, chr next in Deathblow #26, '96), Majestic (Lord Majestros, super-strong alien, last in IM #13, '97, chr next in WildCATS #30, '96), Triton (last in IM #13, '97, next in HR:R #4, '97), Grunge (Percival Edmund "Eddie" Chang, last in FF #13, '97, chr next in Gen13 #12, '96), Rick Jones (last in FF #13, '97, last app)

VILLAINS: Dr. Doom (last in IM #13, '97, next in HR: R #3, '97), Helspont (last in IM #13, '97, chr next in WildCATS #30, '96), Skrull High-Emissary (also as Invisible Woman, last in IM #13, '97, dies, last app), Elementrons: Hulk, Human Torch (both next in HR:R #1, '97), Sub-Mariner (last in IM #13, '97, next in HR:R, #4, '97), Rainmaker (Sarah Rainmaker, "Gen-Active" weather manipulator, chr between Gen13 #11-12, '96); Skrulls, Daemonites

OTHER CHARACTERS: American soldiers

LOCATIONS/ITEMS: Latveria, Negative Zone; American planes & parachutes, Doom's land mines, Doombots, Negative Zone gateway & Dimensional Lock, Skrull High-Emissary's gun, Rick's grenade

SYNOPSIS: As the American invasion force flies to Latveria, Captain America speaks with Rick Jones while the heroes prepare themselves for war. While Cap's group attacks Latveria, Mr. Fantastic's group battles Dr. Doom and his Skrull/Daemonite army in the Negative Zone. Fearing defeat, Helspont and the Skrull High-Emissary release the Elementrons. Rainmaker kills Gorgon, Sub-Mariner and Thing kill each other, Hulk kills Warblade, Grunge kills Rainmaker, Invisible Woman kills Human Torch and Maul dies from a heart attack, having grown too large. Battalion dies, Doom kills Winter and Spartan sacrifices himself to close the Negative Zone gateway. Deathblow forces Helspont into the Negative Zone to give Cap time to close it from his end, but the Skrull High-Emissary, posing as Invisible Woman, shoots Cap. Cap kills the Skrull, and Rick Jones destroys the Dimensional Lock with a grenade. The world fades to white as the universes are separated.

NOTE: Cover-labeled "World War 3 Part 4 of 4" & "The World's Greatest Comics!" FF #13, Av #13, IM #13 & Cap #13's covers form one large image. Includes 2 page recap featuring Cap, Falcon, Bucky & Fury. The pocket and Wildstorm universes merged in FF #13, '97 to create a joint reality that the characters all consider their true past. Continues in HR:R #1-4, '97, where the heroes return to Earth. Series continues in Cap #1, '98.

CAPTAIN AMERICA #1 [#468] (January 1998)

"The Return of Steve Rogers" (34 pages)

CREDITS: Mark Waid (writer), Ron Garney (pencils, c art), Bob Wiacek (inks), Joe Rosas & Digital Chameleon (colors), John Costanza (letters), Paul Tutrone (asst editor), Matt Idelson (editor)

FEATURE CHARACTER: Captain America (also in photos, toys & statue, next in Tb #10, '98 fb, SM/King, '97, Av Ann '01/2 fb, Av #1-3, '98, Av Ann '01/2 fb, Tb #11-12, '98, SS/Thor Ann '98, SenSM #28, '98)

GUEST STARS: Fantastic Four: Mr. Fantastic, Human Torch, Invisible Woman, Thing (all last in HR:R #4, '97, also in X #71, '98 fb & Tb #10, '98 fb, next in FF #1, '98)

SUPPORTING CAST: Sharon Carter (last in Cap #454, '96, chr last in Cap #49, '09 fb, next in Cap #3, '98)

VILLAINS: Lady Deathstrike (last in W #114, '97, next in X Ann '00), Michael Korvac (cosmic powered cyborg, disguised as Kang the Conqueror, last in GotG Ann #1, '91, next in Cap #10, '98), Red Skull (as living shadow, last in Cap #448, '96, next in Cap #4, '98), Strikeforce Ukiyoe (extreme Japanese nationalists, Osamu Akutagawa & Tetsuo named)

OTHER CHARACTERS: Uncle Sammy's patrons & staff, Tokyo police (Shusaku named), reporters & bystanders, Istanbul bar patrons, actors portraying Captain America, Nuke, Red Skull & Sub-Mariner (prev 4 in movie); Popeye the Sailor, Bluto (both in photo), Bucky, Iron Man, Wasp, Dr. Anderson, Prof. Erskine, Nazi soldiers, Operation: Rebirth witnesses (prev 7 in Cap's thoughts)

LOCATIONS/ITEMS: Tokyo, Japan inc "Uncle Sammy's," movie theater & Lady Deathstrike's home, Instanbul bar, government alternative energy research installation; Strikeforce Ukiyoe's guns & bomb w/remote detonator, bar patron's lead pipe, Korvac's ship

SYNOPSIS: The Strikeforce Ukiyoe protest the Americanization of Japan by holding the patrons and staff of Uncle Sammy's hostage. Captain America appears and chases the Strikeforce off, but Tokyo citizens and police prevent him from capturing the leader Osamu by swarming and asking for autographs. Cap sees a news report of the Fantastic Four stating they've returned from the Onslaught battle, the last thing Cap remembers. Later, Osamu asks Lady Deathstrike to help his cause; she agrees only if Osamu sacrifices himself. Cap surmises that the Strikeforce will attack the premiere of a movie based on his life and heads for the movie theater, where he battles and defeats Lady Deathstrike as Osamu and his men rig a bomb. Cap confronts Osamu, who is unable to kill himself. As Osamu is arrested Cap realizes his popularity has spread past America and across the globe in his absence. Meanwhile, Sharon Carter hears of Cap's return and Red Skull's atomic shadow reanimates as Kang the Conqueror watches from afar.

NOTE: Cover-labeled "Heroes Return." Includes recap page (2 pages) featuring Captain America, title page (1 page) & "Behind the Scenes with Ron Garney" (2 pages) detailing the cover's creation. American Graffiti features a welcome back letter from the editors. The Fantastic Four scene is mirrored in X #71, '98 & Tb #10, '98. Cap #17, '99 reveals Kang is actually a disguised Korvac.

CAPTAIN AMERICA #2 [#469] (February 1998)

"To Serve and Protect" (22 pages)

CREDITS: Mark Waid (writer), Ron Garney (pencils, c art), Bob Wiacek (inks), John Costanza (letters), Joe Rosas & Digital Chameleon (colors), Paul Tutrone (asst editor), Matt Idelson (editor)

FEATURE CHARACTERS: Captain America

VILLAINS: Hydra agents (Teams Alpha & Beta named, Team Beta dies), Sensational Hydra (bts, orders Hydra mission), Supreme Intelligence (bts, last in IG #3, '97, see NOTE)

OTHER CHARACTERS: US admiral, naval scientist, submarine crew (Jack & Commanding Officer Lt. Cmdr. Rebecca Houston named), seagulls

LOCATIONS/ITEMS: Atlantic Ocean inc East Coast US naval base; Cap's shield (see NOTE), Babel Virus (Russian computer virus), USS McKenzie (US submarine) inc torpedo tube, control panel & communications core, US helicopter, 3 bombers, 2 torpedoes, 2 breathing masks & 3 life rafts, Hydra poison, knife, guns & Adamantium-jacketed bullet

SYNOPSIS: Captain America easily defeats a squad of Hydra agents at a US naval base. He learns that another Hydra squad has stolen a captured Russian code that can cripple the entire naval fleet and leave it vulnerable to a Hydra nuclear strike, and uploaded it into the communications core of a seized US submarine. With only minutes before the Navy destroys the sub, Cap infiltrates the vessel. Battling Hydra agents aboard the sub wastes precious time, forcing Cap to evacuate the crew and, with the help of Lt. Cmdr. Rebecca Houston, rig the vessel's torpedoes to detonate. Cap and Houston escape out a torpedo tube, propelled by the force of the resulting explosion and protected from the blast by Cap's shield. The shield sinks to the bottom of the ocean and Cap is forced to abandon it to bring the unconscious Houston to life boats on the surface. Cap laments the loss of the shield.

NOTE: Cover-labeled "Heroes Return." Includes recap page (2 pages) featuring Captain America & title page (1 page). "American Graffiti" features an essay on Captain America by the editors. Av #7, '98 reveals the Supreme Intelligence is manipulating the Sensational Hydra. With Cap's shield lost, it will only be noted when it reappears.

CAPTAIN AMERICA #3 [#470] (March 1998)

"Museum Piece" (22 pages)

CREDITS: Mark Waid (writer), Ron Garney (pencils, c art), Bob Wiacek (inks), John Costanza (letters), Joe Rosas & Digital Chameleon (colors), Paul Tutrone (asst editor), Matt Idelson (editor)
FEATURE CHARACTER: Captain America (also as statue & in museum display; next in Av #4, '98, MTU #9-10, '98, bts in MTU #11, '98)
GUEST STARS: Avengers: Black Panther, Machine Man (X-51, alias Aaron Stack), Quasar, Spider-Woman (Carpenter), Tigra (Greer Nelson) (all between Av #3-4, '98), Hawkeye, Thor (both last in SS/Thor Ann '98, next in Av #4, '98), Wasp, Tony Stark (both last in SenSM #28, '98, next in Av #4, '98), Black Widow (last in Av #3, '98, chr last in Av Ann '01/2, next bts in Av #4, '98, next in DD #375, '98), Giant-Man (Pym, last in Tb #12, '98, next in Av #4, '98), Hercules (last in HFH #13, '98, next in Av #4, '98), Sub-Mariner (also in museum display; last in Av #3, '98, last bts in HFH #12, '98, next in MTU #8, '98); Dum Dum Dugan (last in KZ #11, '98, next in Cap #5, '98)
SUPPORTING CAST: Sharon Carter (last in Cap #1, '98)
VILLAINS: Sensational Hydra (Skrull posing as new Supreme Hydra, 1st), MODAM (corpse, last in Cap #440, '95, last app), Supreme Intelligence (bts), Hydra agents
OTHER CHARACTERS: James McElroy (last in Cap #444, '95, last app), SHIELD agents inc "barber," police (inc a detective), Smithsonian Institution official, 2 schoolboys, reporters, bystanders (Joolie named), Mrs. Dacrone (schoolteacher, bts, leads museum field trip); Human Torch (Hammond), Nazi soldiers (both in museum display), Bucky (on cover)
LOCATIONS/ITEMS: Washington, DC inc Smithsonian Castle, Hydra HQ, Manhattan inc SHIELD New York HQ w/barber shop front & Avengers Mansion w/living room; Cap's replacement shield (designed by Stark), Cap's original steel shield replica, Baron Strucker's sword, Hydra booby traps & guns
SYNOPSIS: At Avengers Mansion, Captain America tests out a replacement shield designed by Tony Stark as Namor reports that his search for Cap's original shield has been fruitless. Cap learns that Hydra has raided the Smithsonian and heads to Washington. At Hydra HQ, a new, flamboyant Supreme Hydra crawls from MODAM's corpse and names himself the Sensational Hydra. Inside the museum, Cap encounters two visiting school kids and protects them from a series of Hydra booby traps and Hydra agents. Cap discovers the unfamiliar replacement shield is useless in battle and is shot in the shoulder. He grabs a replica of his original triangular shield from an exhibit and uses it to defeat the agents. The Smithsonian donates the steel shield to Cap as a gift, and Cap makes a televised announcement that he's declaring war on Hydra. The Sensational Hydra is mysteriously pleased with the outcome.
NOTE: Cover-labeled "Heroes Return." Includes recap page (2 pages) featuring Captain America, the Avengers, Hydra, Agent McElroy & Sharon Carter & title page (1 page). Cap #4, '98 provides the missing word balloons on the last four panels of page 12. Sensational Hydra is revealed as a Skrull in Cap #5, '98. One museum display features a mannequin dressed almost identically to Superman and a reproduction of the cover of the pulp magazine, War Birds #66, '33, published by Dell.

CAPTAIN AMERICA #4 [#471] (April 1998)

"Capmania" (22 pages)

CREDITS: Mark Waid (writer), Ron Garney (pencils, c art), Bob Wiacek (inks), John Costanza (letters), Joe Rosas & Digital Chameleon (colors), Paul Tutrone (asst editor), Matt Idelson (editor), Atomic Paintbrush (c colors)
FEATURE CHARACTER: Captain America (also in ads, on jackets, hats, foam hand & "Capcorn" bag, as toy & mannequin; next in W #124, '98)
GUEST STAR: Hawkeye (last in Av #4, '98, next in Cap #6, '98)
SUPPORTING CAST: Sharon Carter (next in Fury/13 #1, '98)
VILLAINS: Batroc (last in Cap #443, '95, next in Hawk #1, '98), Red Skull (as living shadow, last in Cap #1, '98, next in Cap #10, '98) & 2 of his men (both die), Sensational Hydra, Supreme Intelligence (bts), Hydra agents
OTHER CHARACTERS: Andrew Bolt (New York councilman & Congressional candidate, 1st, next in Cap #6, '98), TV reporter & cameraman, hot dog vendor, bystanders; Nick Fury (in photo)
LOCATIONS/ITEMS: Caribbean Sea inc Skull Island, Manhattan inc gift shop & Avengers Mansion, SHIELD's New York HQ, Rockefeller Center w/skating rink; Batroc's whip-cane, Cap's original steel shield replica, Hawkeye's blunt, rope & net arrows, Hydra nerve gas canister, Sharon's laptop
SYNOPSIS: Captain America and Hawkeye save New York from a Hydra agent's nerve gas attack. After Cap is beset by adoring fans, he and Hawkeye change into civilian clothes and wander Manhattan, where they are surrounded by Cap-inspired ads and merchandise. Cap answers a challenge by Batroc. Disappointed that Batroc hasn't reformed, Cap refuses to engage in a pointless grudge match. At Skull Island, Red Skull's atomic shadow kills two of his men. Hawkeye attacks Batroc, and Cap joins the battle to help his friend. Batroc tells Cap that Hydra hired him to take a fall in a staged public skirmish with the hero. After forcing Batroc to retreat, Cap realizes that his victory has inspired the public. The Sensational Hydra tells an agent that he intends to make the world worship Cap as part of his master plan.
NOTE: Includes recap page (2 pages) featuring Captain America, Hawkeye, Batroc, Sharon Carter & Sensational Hydra.

CAPTAIN AMERICA #5 [#472] (May 1998)

"Power and Glory Chapter One: Credibility Gap" (22 pages)

CREDITS: Mark Waid (writer), Ron Garney (pencils, c art), John Beatty, Andy Smith (inks), John Costanza (letters), Joe Rosas (colors), Paul Tutrone (asst editor), Matt Idelson (editor)
FEATURE CHARACTERS: Captain America
GUEST STARS: Avengers: Iron Man (last in IM #5, '98), Scarlet Witch (last in Qsilv #6, '98), Thor (last in Av #4, '98); Dum Dum Dugan (last in Cap #3, '98, next in JIM #519, '98)
VILLAINS: Sensational Hydra (also as Captain America, SHIELD agent & "American Exclusive" reporter Gordon Winchester) & his 2 Skrull lackeys (inc Strzya; both also as hostages), Supreme Intelligence (bts), Hydra agents (some die)
OTHER CHARACTERS: News reporters (Bob McKnight of WNYX, Roger Ramos of WCBS & Sue Harvey named), SHIELD agents, police, waitress, bystanders
LOCATIONS/ITEMS: London inc Tower of London, Tower Bridge & Hydra base beneath River Thames, Hydra's Paris compound, Brooklyn inc diner, Manhattan inc Empire State Building w/observation deck, stairwell & utility room; "Skrull handcuffs" (shape-shifting restraint), Cap's original steel shield replica, Hydra guns & SHIELD guns & hand restraints, Sensational Hydra's camera & parachute
SYNOPSIS: As their fellow Avengers raid Hydra's Paris compound, Captain America and Thor storm Hydra's London base with SHIELD and learn that the Sensational Hydra is the leader of a Hydra splinter group, not the entire organization. After the heroes leave, Sensational Hydra sheds his SHIELD agent disguise, kills the Hydra informant and flees. Later, Cap chats with Thor about hero worship until they hear the Sensational Hydra has taken hostages at the Empire State Building. Cap infiltrates the building, accompanied by a persistent reporter. The reporter ambushes Cap, revealing himself as the Hydra leader and a Skrull. The hostages, also Skrulls, kill the Hydra agents present and take Cap prisoner using Skrull handcuffs. Motivated by revenge for the suffering Earth inhabitants have caused his race, Sensational Hydra assumes the Avenger's likeness and basks in the adulation of a public who believes he is the real Cap.
NOTE: Includes recap page (2 pages) featuring Captain America, Sensational Hydra, Thor & the Avengers. Strzya is named in Cap #6, '98.

CAPTAIN AMERICA #6 [#473] (June 1998)

"Power and Glory Chapter Two: Exposé" (22 pages)

CREDITS: Mark Waid (writer), Dale Eaglesham (pencils), Scott Koblish (inks), John Costanza (letters), Joe Rosas & Digital Chameleon (colors), Paul Tutrone (asst editor), Matt Idelson (editor), Ron Garney (c art)
FEATURE CHARACTERS: Captain America (also in rfb)
GUEST STARS: Avengers: Hawkeye (last in Cap #4, '98), Iron Man, Scarlet Witch, Thor
VILLAINS: Sensational Hydra (also as Captain America, TV cameraman & pterosaur; also in rfb) & his 2 Skrull lackeys (inc Strzya; both also as terrorists, congressman & reporter, TV camera & TV, table & garment rack; both also in rfb; both die), Supreme Intelligence (bts), Hydra agents
OTHER CHARACTERS: Andrew Bolt (last in Cap #4, '98, next in Cap #8, '98), Bill Clinton (last in Hulk #462, '98, next in Hulk #465, '98), Edwin Jarvis (between Av #4-5, '98), WLNY employees & reporters (John named), Secret Service agents, bystanders (inc mob & victims)
LOCATIONS/ITEMS: Manhattan inc WLNY studios w/Studio A, dressing room, hallway & stage; Avengers Mansion w/Cap's quarters & communications room; Empire State Building w/utility room & elevator shaft, laundromat, residential living room; Cap's original steel shield replica, "Skrull handcuffs" (both also in rfb), Secret Service agents' guns, "terrorists' guns," high voltage electrical panel, welding torch
FLASHBACK: Sensational Hydra assumes Captain America's identity (Cap #5).
SYNOPSIS: As Sensational Hydra takes delight in posing as Captain America, the real Cap tries to escape his Skrull handcuffs. With his two Skrull lackeys' help, Sensational Hydra stages and thwarts a terrorist attack on the President at a Manhattan TV studio, and endorses Congressional candidate Andrew Bolt on a lark. Meanwhile, Cap escapes. To foment a public panic, the Sensational Hydra announces that Skrulls have infiltrated America and exposes his surprised associates to prove his claim. As the crowd kills the two betrayed Skrulls, Sensational Hydra uses Cap's reputation to stoke the fires of suspicion and paranoia by telling a national television audience that anyone who is perceived as different is a Skrull. Cap rushes to the studio and attacks Sensational Hydra, who turns into a pterosaur and flies away. A horrified Cap looks out on a mob scene instigated by the public's blind allegiance to him.
NOTE: Includes recap page (2 pages) featuring Captain America, Sensational Hydra, Andrew Bolt & the Avengers.

CAPTAIN AMERICA #7 [#474] (July 1998)

"Power and Glory Chapter Three: Hoaxed" (22 pages)

CREDITS: Mark Waid (writer), Dale Eaglesham (pencils pgs 1-11), Andy Kubert (pencils pgs 12-22, c pencils), Scott Koblish (inks pgs 1-11), Jesse Delperdang (inks pgs 12-22, c inks), John Costanza (pgs 1-11), Todd Klein (pgs 12-22) (letters), Joe Rosas (pgs 1-11), Jason Wright (pgs 12-22) & Digital Chameleon (colors), Paul Tutrone (asst editor), Matt Idelson (editor)
FEATURE CHARACTER: Captain America (next in SM:Made, Ex #125, Thor #1-2, Av #5-6, all '98)
GUEST STARS: Avengers: Hawkeye, Scarlet Witch, Thor (all next in Thor #1, '98); Iron Man (next in Hulk #465, '98); Fantastic Four: Mr. Fantastic (last in FF #4, '98, next in Hulk #465, '98), Thing (last in SS #138, '98, next in ASM Ann '98); Quicksilver (between Qsilv #9-10, '98)

VILLAINS: Sensational Hydra (also as Captain America & dragon; last app), Supreme Intelligence (bts, next in IM #7, '98)
OTHER CHARACTERS: 3 TV news reporters (Jenny named), other reporters, cameramen, bystanders (inc Hindu family, African-American schoolteacher & his students, mother & her teenage son, looters, mobs & victims)
LOCATIONS/ITEMS: Montgomery, AL home, Los Angeles, CA, Denver, CO classroom, Manhattan inc US Armed Forces recruiting office, World Trade Center, WLNY studios w/stage, New York Harbor inc Liberty Island w/Statue of Liberty, Mr. Fantastic's Pier 4 lab; Stark's & Richards' Skrull reversion ray, Cap's original steel shield replica & Avengers ID, Hawkeye's gas arrow, Stark's communicator, Richards' equipment
SYNOPSIS: Frenzied mobs across America attack their neighbors and families, convinced that anyone other are disguised Skrulls. Fearing that a public appearance may feed the xenophobic panic, Captain America lies low and waits for his imposter to resurface while the Avengers attempt to quell the violent hysteria. When Sensational Hydra appears on TV as Cap to rally the public and incite further chaos, Cap zaps him with a ray created by Tony Stark and Reed Richards to revert the alien shape-shifter to his true form. Joined by Mr. Fantastic, Thing and the Avengers, Cap defeats the Skrull and exposes his plot in a press conference. Cap expresses his feelings of culpability for his status as an icon and his regret that it allowed the Skrull to perpetrate his deadly hoax. In an inspiring speech, Cap reaffirms his role as a man of the people, dedicated to fighting injustice, cynicism and intolerance in pursuit of the American dream.
NOTE: Includes recap page (2 pages) featuring Captain America, the Avengers, Tony Stark, Mr. Fantastic, Sensational Hydra & Thing. "American Graffiti" includes LoC from Chaos Magazine writer/editor Joel Grineau.

CAPTAIN AMERICA #8 [#475] (August 1998)

"Live Kree or Die! Chapter Two: Stuck in the Middle" (22 pages)

CREDITS: Mark Waid (writer), Andy Kubert (pencils), Jesse Delperdang (inks), Todd Klein (letters), Jason Wright & Digital Chameleon (colors), Paul Tutrone (asst editor), Matt Idelson (editor)
FEATURE CHARACTER: Captain America (also in photo; next bts in Qsilv #10, '98, next in Av #7, '98, Av Ann '98)
GUEST STAR: Warbird (Carol Danvers, last in IM #7, '98, next in Qsilv #10, '98)
VILLAINS: Lunatic Legion (Kree Imperial Fleet members): Galen-Kor, Kona-Lor, Dylon-Cir, Talla-Ron, (all last in IM #7, '98, next in Qsilv #10, '98), Ept-Rass, Sig-Rass (both last in IM #7, '98, next in Av #7, '98), Bron-Char (last in AvStrike #1, '94, last app), Nightmare ("Edvard Haberdash," demonic Dream Dimension ruler, bts, manipulates Gen. Chapman, last in Ex #120, '98), 2 thieving arsonists (Augie named), Kree soldiers
OTHER CHARACTERS: Andrew Bolt (last in Cap #6, '98, next in Cap #11, '98), Gen. Chapman (last in Cap #450, '96, next in Cap #10, '98), Bill Clinton (bts, briefed on Moldavia mission, last in Hulk #465, '98, next in BP #6, '99), Barry (TV interviewer, see NOTE), Nazi concentration camp prisoners (only in fb), White House staff (voices only), Lunatic Legion's prisoners & victims, military police, firefighters, bystanders
LOCATIONS/ITEMS: Nazi concentration camp inc gas chamber (in fb), White House, Los Angeles TV studio, abandoned missile silo near Cape Canaveral, Brooklyn inc hardware store & Andrew Bolt's campaign HQ; Cap's original steel shield replica (destroyed, see NOTE), Warbird's shackles, Cap's & Warbird's Avengers IDs, Kree Cyclo-Generator (experimental power source) & genetic experimentation apparatus, Lunatic Legion's blasters, rocket & Stasinet, Terrigen Mist (mutagenic vapor), arsonists' gun, copy of Daily Bugle
FLASHBACK: Nazi concentration camp prisoners are herded into a gas chamber.
SYNOPSIS: Captain America defeats arsonists at Andrew Bolt's campaign HQ and learns that Bolt is humiliated now that the public knows a Skrull endorsed him. Cap receives an emergency call from Warbird, who is fighting the Lunatic Legion. The Legion overpowers Warbird and uses her unique human/Kree physiology as a catalyst in a genetic experiment, gassing human prisoners with Terrigen Mist in the hope to evolve humans into a Kree slave corps. Meanwhile, Gen. Chapman inexplicably divulges military secrets in a TV interview. Cap arrives in time to save the test subjects and free Warbird, who says the Kree are preparing to transport a stolen experimental generator it to their lunar base via rocket. The two Avengers battle a squad of Kree soldiers including the brutish Bron-Char, who crushes Cap's replica shield. After vanquishing the squad, Cap is too occupied with the evacuation of prisoners to stop the Legion. He reprimands Warbird for not alerting other Avengers in her misguided effort to impress him. Seeking to prove herself, Warbird attacks the Legion, but they capture her and escape aboard their rocket.
NOTE: Cover-labeled "Live Kree or Die! 2 of 4." Story continues from IM #7, into Qsilv #10 and concludes in Av #7, all '98. Av Ann '98 reveals the shield destroyed here is replaced by another replica, which debuts in Av #7, '98. Barry resembles real life TV interviewer Larry King.

CAPTAIN AMERICA #9 [#476] (September 1998)

"American Nightmare Chapter 1: The Bite of Madness" (22 pages)

CREDITS: Mark Waid (writer), Andy Kubert (pencils), Jesse Delperdang (inks), Todd Klein (letters), Chris Sotomayor (colors), Paul Tutrone (asst editor), Matt Idelson (editor), Eliot Brown (special thanks)
FEATURE CHARACTER: Captain America (also in rfb)
SUPPORTING CAST: Sharon Carter (last in Fury/13 #2, '98)
VILLAINS: Rhino (last in SenSM #31, '98), Nightmare (bts influencing Patterson & Ranier)
OTHER CHARACTERS: Luiz Ramirez (homeless unemployed construction worker), Alma Ramirez (Luiz' wife), Javier Ramirez, Marta Ramirez, Rosa Ramirez (prev 3 Luiz & Rosa's children), Mike Ranier (housing developer), Mr. Genuardi (grocery owner, next in Cap #13, '99) (all 1st), Jack Patterson (baseball player) & his fans, police (inc a lieutenant), Ranier Properties' construction foreman & workers (Billy named), Lightman (shuttle astronaut, bts, destroys museum display), bystanders; Gen. Chapman (in photo), Warbird, Lethal Legion (both in rfb)
LOCATIONS/ITEMS: Yankee Stadium (also in pfb), Brooklyn inc Steve' apartment & Ranier Properties' construction site (demolished); baseball bat, police taser & truncheons (all in pfb), Cap's photonic shield (built into glove, 1st, see NOTE) & original steel shield replica (remains), copy of Daily Bugle, rivet gun, crane

FLASHBACK: Cap & Warbird battle the Lunatic Legion (Av #7, '98).

SYNOPSIS: Baseball star Jack Patterson attacks his fans with his bat and police taser him at Yankee Stadium; Sharon wonders if there's a connection with Gen. Chapman's recent behavior. Meanwhile, Steve returns home to find an unemployed and apologetic construction worker, Luiz Ramirez, and his family occupying the apartment. Later, Sharon stops by to see Steve entertaining the Ramirez children. Privately, she gives Steve a new photonic shield and asks for help investigating recent instances of prominent Americans acting irrationally. Captain America agrees, but first they stop at a nearby construction site, where Cap asks the developer, Mike Ranier, to provide a home for Luiz in return for labor. Ranier says he would sooner destroy his construction site, just as Rhino attacks. While Sharon evacuates the workers Cap learns that Ranier hired Rhino to demolish the site. As Cap and Sharon rush to save a worker, Rhino collapses the building on top of them.

NOTE: Includes recap page (2 pages) featuring Captain America, Sharon Carter, Gen. Chapman & Andrew Bolt. Cap's new photonic shield is an upgraded version of the prototype previously seen in Cap #450-453, '96.

CAPTAIN AMERICA #10 [#477] (October 1998)

"American Nightmare Chapter 2: The Growing Darkness" (22 pages)

CREDITS: Mark Waid (writer), Andy Kubert (pencils), Jesse Delperdang (inks), Todd Klein (letters), Chris Sotomayor (colors), Paul Tutrone (asst editor), Matt Idelson (editor)
FEATURE CHARACTER: Captain America (also in Nightmare's realm)
GUEST STARS: USAgent (last in Av #3, '98), Dum Dum Dugan (last in JIM #519, '98)
SUPPORTING CAST: Sharon Carter
VILLAINS: Korvac (disguised as Kang, last in Cap #1, '98, next in Cap #14, '99), Red Skull (as living shadow, last in Cap #4, '98, next in Cap #14, '99), Rhino (next in Tb #26, '99), Nightmare (also as Captain America) & his lizard-demons (see NOTE)
OTHER CHARACTERS: Dream-Stalker (Nightmare's horse, last in DrS #79, '95, next in BP #21, '00), Gen. Chapman (last in Cap #8, '98), Edwin Jarvis (last in Hawk #1, '98, next in Av #8, '98), Mike Ranier (arrested bts, last app), boys, greedy man (both in Nightmare's realm, 1st, next in Cap #12, '98), Luiz, Alma, Javier, Marta & Rosa Ramirez; construction worker, rescue workers, judge, defendant, Nobel Prize-winning author (bts, setting fire, also in photo), speaker, inner-city teen (prev 5 in pfb), SHIELD technicians, soldiers, birds
LOCATIONS/ITEMS: Brooklyn inc Steve's apartment & Ranier Properties' construction site remains, Skull Island, Avengers Mansion w/ monitor room, Cincinnati courtroom, Miami, Los Angeles (prev 3 in pfb), upstate New York Air Force base, SHIELD HQ, Nightmare's realm; Cap's photonic shield, rivet gun, judge's gun, teen's heroin syringe (both in pfb), jet, soldiers' guns
FLASHBACKS: A judge shoots a defendant in traffic court, an author orchestrates a book-burning and an award-winning inner-city teen attempts suicide (p).

SYNOPSIS: Captain America uses his shield to brace the collapsed building and Sharon blasts a hole in the floor with a rivet gun, allowing them to escape to the basement. Rhino finds them and attacks, only for Cap to defeat him. Just before they run out of air, rescue workers find them. Later, Steve tells the Ramirez family they can stay at his place for a while and notices a law textbook in Javier's backpack. While walking with Sharon, Steve experiences an unexplained attack of bitterness over American politics and has an epiphany. On Skull Island, Kang promises Red Skull they can conquer the future. At Avengers Mansion, Cap explains to Sharon that all the victims of madness have achieved the American dream. Alerted by Jarvis that USAgent is attempting to steal a military jet, Cap and Sharon race to the base and defeat USAgent. At SHIELD HQ, Cap convinces Dugan to insert him into the victim's shared dreams. Inside the dreamscape, Cap encounters Nightmare. Meanwhile, a possessed Cap attacks Dugan.

NOTE: Includes recap page (2 pages) featuring Captain America, Sharon Carter, Rhino, Ramirez family & Gen. Chapman. Cap #12, '98 reveals Nightmare's lizard-demons are disguised as his victims' greatest desires.

CAPTAIN AMERICA #11 [#478] (November 1998)

"American Nightmare Chapter 3: Finger on the Pulse" (22 pages)

CREDITS: Mark Waid (writer), Andy Kubert (pencils), Jesse Delperdang (inks), Todd Klein (letters), Chris Sotomayor (colors), Paul Tutrone (asst editor), Matt Idelson (editor)
FEATURE CHARACTER: Captain America (also in Nightmare's realm)
GUEST STARS: USAgent (next in W #134, '99), Dum Dum Dugan (both off-panel)
SUPPORTING CAST: Sharon Carter (also in Nightmare's realm)
VILLAINS: Nightmare (also as Cap, Luiz Ramirez, Andrew Bolt & Sharon Carter), his lizard demons
OTHER CHARACTERS: Luiz, Alma, Javier, Marta & Rosa Ramirez (all next in Cap #13, '99), Andrew Bolt (last in Cap #8, '98, next in Cap #13, '99), Gen. Chapman (next bts in FF #506, '04), Mary (Bolt's campaign manager), Bolt's political supporters, soldiers, SHIELD agents (Tyler named), hanger crewman (voice only) & technicians, fat man, rock star, White House staffer & father (prev 4 in Nightmare's realm), Dream-Stalker (on cover)
LOCATIONS/ITEMS: SHIELD HQ w/aircraft hanger, Nightmare's realm, Steve's Brooklyn apartment, auditorium, Fort Carstairs missile silo; Cap's photonic shield & Avengers ID SHIELD J-49 pocket rockets w/ejector seat, Nightmare's bubble cage, heat-seeking missiles, parachutes, hammer, Sharon's gun, soldier's rifle

SYNOPSIS: Possessed by Nightmare, Captain America runs amok through SHIELD HQ. Sharon pursues Cap when he confiscates a pocket rocket. In Nightmare's realm, Nightmare taunts the trapped Cap, explaining that he is infiltrating the dreams of successful Americans, twisting their idea of the American dream. Nightmare plans to use Cap to unleash a nuclear winter, leading to perpetual night that will fuel his power. Sharon realizes that Cap's destination is a missile silo and shoots Cap down. Cap ejects and escapes. In Brooklyn, a possessed Luiz barricades his family in Steve's apartment. Elsewhere, the possessed Andrew Bolt anticipates crushing his enemies after the election. In Nightmare's realm, Cap breaks free, but Nightmare demonstrates that in his realm he is supreme. Cap infiltrates the silo and Sharon follows, warning Cap to stop or she'll kill him. Cap calls her bluff, and when she can't bring herself to kill Cap she collapses. Sharon appears in Nightmare's realm as Nightmare possesses Sharon.

NOTE: Includes recap page (1 page) featuring Captain America, Sharon Carter, Ramirez family, Gen. Chapman & Nightmare.

CAPTAIN AMERICA #12 [#479] (December 1998)

"American Nightmare Finale: Nuclear Dawn" (29 pages)

CREDITS: Mark Waid (writer), Andy Kubert (pencils), Jesse Delperdang (inks), Todd Klein (letters), Chris Sotomayor (colors), Paul Tutrone (asst editor), Matt Idelson (editor)
FEATURE CHARACTER: Captain America (also in Nightmare's realm, next in FF #9, Av #8-9, IM #10, XMan #46, Hulk #470, AvFo #1, SS #146, Av #10-11, all '98, IM/ Cap Ann, '98, ASM #1, '99, Thor #6, '98, Cap/CitV Ann '98)
GUEST STAR: Dum Dum Dugan (also in Nightmare's realm, next in Cap #20, '99)
SUPPORTING CAST: Sharon Carter (also in Nightmare's realm, also in fb during Cap #446, '95 fb)
VILLAINS: Nightmare (also as Captain America, Sharon Carter & Dum Dum Dugan, next in BP #21, '00), his lizard demons & winged demons
OTHER CHARACTERS: SHIELD agents & medical personnel, soldiers, missile silo technicians (Bill named), boy & greedy man (both last in Cap #10, '98, last app), rock star, fat man & other Nightmare victims (prev 5 in Nightmare's realm)
LOCATIONS/ITEMS: Streets of a "top secret hot spot," prison cell (both in fb), Nightmare's realm, Fort Carstairs missile silo w/launch room, SHIELD HQ w/medical facility; Cap's photonic shield, soldiers' guns
FLASHBACK: Cut loose from SHIELD, Sharon lives in the streets and is later held in prison.
SYNOPSIS: Captain America and Sharon Carter escape from Nightmare's imprisonment. They find Dum Dum Dugan in Nightmare's realm and realize he's fallen prey to Nightmare's temptations. They try to convince Nightmare's other victims to stop deluding themselves, but Nightmare sends a band of winged demons to recapture Cap. Meanwhile, the possessed Cap and Sharon gain control of the missile silos launch room. Cap realizes that if Nightmare can draw psychic power from the American dream, then so can he. Cap punches Nightmare. As Cap pummels Nightmare, the other victim's temptations revert to their lizard-demon forms. Sharon rallies the other victims into an army that marches on Nightmare's castle. Cap draws on the psychic energy of Nightmare's victims to defeat the demon, releasing everyone from Nightmare's realm. Cap is too late to stop the nuclear missile from launching, but he seals the titanium doors covering the silo. The missile crashes into the doors and explodes, but Cap is protected by his photonic shield.
NOTE: Includes recap page (1 page) featuring Captain America, Sharon Carter, Nightmare, Dum Dum Dugan & SHIELD. Followed by "The Skull is Dead. Long Live the Skull," (9 pages) written by Jim Krueger & designed by Johnny Greene. A saga-style recap of the Red Skull's career, it includes panels reprinted from Cap #298, '84 fb, Cap #350/2, '89 fb, ToS #66/2, '65 fb, OHMU #13, '84, ToS #79/2, '66 fb, Av #4, '64, ToS #81/2, '66, Cap #115, '69 fb, Cap #300, '84, Cap #350/2, '89, Cap #444, '95 & Cap #1, '98.

CAPTAIN AMERICA/CITIZEN V ANNUAL 1998 (1998)

"For Victory … Again!" (39 pages)

CREDITS: Kurt Busiek (writer), Karl Kesel (co-plot, c inks), Barbara Kesel (co-script), Mark Bagley (pencils), Greg Adams, Scott Hanna (inks), Richard Starkings & Comicraft's Miranda Emerson (letters), Joe Rosas (colors), Tom Brevoort (editor)
FEATURE CHARACTERS: Captain America (also in rfb & fb2 between CapC Spec #1, '09 & CapC #21, '42; next in DD #8, W Ann '99/2, Tb #0, Av #12, Cap Ann '99, Cap #13, all '99), Citizen V (Lt. John Watkins, WWII hero, in fb2 between Comedy #9/6, '42 & CitV #1, '01 fb), Citizen V (Paulette Brazee, Lt. Watkins' wife/widow, 1ˢᵗ, also as She-Wolf in fb2, in fb3 before CitV #1, '02), Citizen V (John Watkins, Jr., son of Lt. Watkins & Brazee, 1ˢᵗ, as infant in fb3 before CitV #2, '02), Citizen V (John Watkins III, mentioned, son of Watkins Jr. & grandson of Lt. Watkins & Brazee), Citizen V (Dallas Riordan, granddaughter of Brazee & Riordan & half-cousin to Watkins III, last in Tb #17, '98, next in Tb #21, '98)
SUPPORTING CAST: Bucky (in rfb & fb2 between CapC Spec #1, '09 & CapC #21, '42)
VILLAINS: Baron (Helmut) Zemo (also in rfb & fb1 between Tb #17, '98 & Tb #20, '98; last in Tb #20, '98, next in Tb #0, '99) & his mercenaries, Baron (Heinrich) Zemo (in rfb, fb2 between Cap #168, '73 fb & Cap:ME, '94, & bts in fb3 between Tb #-1, '97 & FallSon:IM, '07 fb) & his Nazis (in fbs2-3), Techno (also in rfb & fb1 between Tb #17, '98 & Tb #20, '98; last in Tb #20, '98, next in Tb #33, '99)
OTHER CHARACTERS: Davos (only app), Eamonn, Piers (all bts, Citizen V's (Riordan) support team, 1ˢᵗ, prev 2 next bts in Tb #24, '99, next in Tb #27, '99), Riordan (Brazee's new lover & Dallas Riordan's grandfather, only app in fb3), Citizen V's V-Battalion (in fb3, all die), US Army Company C (in fb2), Amazon Rainforest natives (inc Zemo's slaves & Citizen V's resistance); Thunderbolts: Atlas, Jolt, Moonstone (prev 3 in rfb)
LOCATIONS/ITEMS: Amazon Rainforest inc Temple Zemo, Helmut Zemo's Mexican castle (in rfb), mine, stronghold & Citizen V's (Riordan) hidden HQ, Germany inc Castle Zemo w/moat & sewer tunnels (in fb2); Cap's photonic shield, Citizen V's (Riordan) equipment inc sword & mag-clamp, Helmut Zemo's Particle X (also in fb2) w/rocket (in fb2) & missile, sword & luger, Zemo's men's guns & grenades, native's guns, Nazi's guns, Citizen V's (Watkins) gun, Paulette's gun, Heinrich Zemo's gun (prev 4 in rfb) & drone plane (in rfb)
FLASHBACKS: The Thunderbolts, save Techno, abandon Baron (Helmut) Zemo (Tb #12, '98). Citizen V (Riordan) destroys Helmut Zemo's Mexican castle (Tb #17, '98). Helmut Zemo rescues Techno from the castle's rubble (1). As Baron (Heinrich) Zemo prepares to jam Britain's

radio operations with his new Particle X, Captain America and Bucky meet with Citizen V. The trio sneaks into Zemo's castle and meet Paulette Brazee, Citizen V's wife posing as Baron Zemo's She-Wolf. She leads them in an assault on Zemo from within as US Army Company C attacks from outside. Cap destroys Zemo's Particle X rocket but Zemo escapes (2). Heinrich Zemo kills Citizen V (Watkins) (Tb #-1, '97). Heinrich Zemo's Nazis slaughter the V-Battalion but Brazee escapes. She later gives birth to her son John Watkins, Jr., works for the OSS during the rest of WWII, and eventually finds a new lover in a fellow soldier (3). Cap fails to save Bucky (Av #4, '64 fb).

SYNOPSIS: In the Amazon Rainforest, Baron (Helmut) Zemo uses natives for slave labor to look for his father's Particle X until Techno finds it. Meanwhile, Citizen V heads a resistance against Zemo. Searching for Zemo, Captain America arrives and attacks Citizen V, believing him to still be Zemo. Cap is surprised when the natives protect Citizen V, and he learns it's not Zemo but a new hero. Cap quickly realizes that Citizen V is a woman wearing padding to disguise herself as a man. Two days later, Cap and the natives storm Temple Zemo as Citizen V sneaks inside, where Techno easily subdues her. Cap realizes Zemo has retreated inside his temple and follows, where he finds Citizen V strapped to Zemo's Particle X missile. Cap frees Citizen V and battles Techno, but the missile launches. Citizen V latches onto the missile and reprograms it while Cap defeats Techno. Cap escapes before the missile destroys Temple Zemo. Later, Zemo watches from his new stronghold as Cap, Citizen V and the natives celebrate their victory.

NOTE: Includes recap page (1 page) featuring Captain America, Baron (Heinrich) Zemo, Baron (Helmut) Zemo, Citizen V (Watkins), Citizen V (Riordan), Bucky & Techno. 1998 has two Captain America Annuals, this and IM/Cap Ann, '98; for the latter see the Iron Man Index TPB. Issue dedicated to Ben Thompson, creator of the original Citizen V.

CAPTAIN AMERICA #13 [#480] (January 1999)

"Plausible Deniability" (21 pages)

CREDITS: Mark Waid (writer), Dougie Braithwaite (pencils), Robin Riggs (inks), Todd Klein (letters), Shannon Blanchard, Kevin Tinsley (colors), Paul Tutrone (asst editor), Matt Idelson (editor)
FEATURE CHARACTER: Captain America (also in photo, next in Dp #23-25, '98-'99, Av #14-15, '99, Cable #66-68, '99, MagR #1, '99, Cap #15, '99)
GUEST STAR: Jim Rhodes (Rhodes Recovery CEO, former War Machine, last in IM #12, '99, next in IM #14, '99)
SUPPORTING CAST: Sharon Carter (last in Cap #12, '98, next in Cap #15, '99)
VILLAIN: Mr. Rilker (also as "Mr. Reynolds," AIM engineer & lobbyist, only app)
OTHER CHARACTERS: Alma Ramirez, Javier Ramirez, Luiz Ramirez (all last in Cap #11, '98, next in Cap #15, '99), Marta Ramirez, Rosa Ramirez (both last in Cap #11, '98, last app), Andrew Bolt (also in photo, last in Cap #11, '98), Mr. Genuardi (last in Cap #9, '98) (both last app), Phil Oxnard (Bolt's political opponent, also in photos, only app), neighborhood family (Danny, Bobby & Katie named), Bolt campaign supporters, Rhodes Recovery employees, waiter, Oxnard's family (in photo)
LOCATIONS/ITEMS: Brooklyn inc Steve's apartment, Bolt's campaign HQ & neighborhood home, Georgetown inc restaurant & Rilker's apartment (#365), Washington DC inc Oxnard's office & Washington Monument, Atlantic Ocean; Cap's shield (breaks) & photonic shield, copies of Daily Bugle, AIM AD-45 Riotbots (destroyed), Rhodes Recovery ship & diving equipment
SYNOPSIS: Steve talks with Sharon about his reluctance to involve Captain America in partisan politics. As Sharon looks into Javier Ramirez's hidden proclivity for law books, Cap visits Andrew Bolt, who says his political opponent Phil Oxnard is taking suspicious campaign contributions. Cap finds Oxnard dining with Rilker, an AIM lobbyist. Cap confronts Rilker, who attacks with AIM AD-45 riotbots. Meanwhile, Rhodes Recovery finds Cap's missing shield in the Atlantic, but it shatters when dropped. Cap defeats the riotbots and learns that Oxnard knows its AIM giving him contributions. Instead of going public with the information, Cap confronts Oxnard and asks if he's still proud of his political career. Oxnard resigns and Cap begins campaigning for Bolt as Steve Rogers.
NOTE: Includes recap page (1 page) featuring Captain America, Sharon Carter, Andrew Bolt, Ramirez family & AIM.

CAPTAIN AMERICA #14 [#481] (February 1999)

"Turnabout" (21 pages)

CREDITS: Andy Kubert (pencils), Jesse Delperdang (inks), Todd Klein (letters), Chris Sotomayor (colors), Paul Tutrone (asst editor), Matt Idelson (editor)
FEATURE CHARACTER: Captain America (in Red Skull's thoughts)
VILLAINS: Red Skull (also as living shadow & in his own thoughts), Korvac (disguised as Kang) (both last in Cap #10, '98)
OTHER CHARACTERS: Adolf Hitler, Eve (Skull's love interest) & her family, Skull's slaves & captives, Skull's Hotel Berlin boss, American soldiers, Hotel Berlin guests, Nazi soldiers, visiting delegates, bystanders (all in Skull's thoughts)
LOCATIONS/ITEMS: Berlin, Germany inc Hotel Berlin, Eve's home (all in Skull's thoughts); Skull's luger & flowers, Cosmic Cube (all in Skull's thoughts), Korvac's ship
SYNOPSIS: Red Skull relives his angry, spite-filled life. He despises that other cultures have infested his homeland, and would rather live in filth and garbage than to be associated with the stink of non-Aryan races. When Hitler trains him he's born anew, but repeatedly fails in battle against Captain America. Working as a busboy, the Skull is attracted to Eve, but brutally murders her and her family when he realizes she can never see the world the way he does. Emboldened, the Skull returns to the Hotel Berlin and kills the visiting Captain America. Kang watches as Red Skull's shadow reforms itself, horrified at the evil wrath in the Skull's mind. Red Skull has internalized the Cosmic Cube's power.
NOTE: Includes recap page (2 pages) featuring Red Skull & title page (1 page). Mark Waid is credited on the cover, but his name is removed from the interior credits.

CAPTAIN AMERICA #15 [#482] (March 1999)

"First Gleaming" (23 pages)

CREDITS: Mark Waid (writer), Andy Kubert (pencils), Jesse Delperdang (inks), Todd Klein (letters), Chris Sotomayor (colors), Paul Tutrone (asst editor), Matt Idelson (editor)
FEATURE CHARACTER: Captain America (also in rfb)
GUEST STAR: Iron Man (also in "Watcher's" vision, last in MagR #3, '99)
SUPPORTING CAST: Sharon Carter (also in "Watcher's" vision & rfb, last in Cap #13, '99), Connie Ferrari (lawyer, 1st, next in Cap #20, '99)
VILLAINS: Red Skull (also as statue in "Watcher's" vision & in rfb), Korvac (disguised as Kang & Uatu the Watcher), King Cobra (last in Cap #436, '95, last bts in Cap #437, '95, next in Cap #50/6, '02), Mr. Hyde (last in ASM #433, '98, next in IM #43, '01)
OTHER CHARACTERS: Javier Ramirez (last in Cap #13, '99, next in Cap #20, '99), Alma Ramirez, Luiz Ramirez (both last in Cap #13, '99, last app), Connie's co-workers, police, bystanders, birds; Gen. Chapman, Thor, Wasp, Red Skull's soldiers & slaves, dinosaurs (prev 6 in "Watcher's" vision)
LOCATIONS/ITEMS: Brooklyn inc Steve's apartment, Connie's office & Brooklyn Bridge, New York, Skull Island; Cap's shield fragments & photonic shield (upgraded), faulty Cosmic Cube (in rfb)
FLASHBACKS: Cap destroys the Cosmic Cube, seemingly atomizing Red Skull in the process (Cap #448, '96). Kang promises the Skull they can conquer the future (Cap #10, '98), but is terrified by the hate in Red Skull's mind (Cap #14, '99).
SYNOPSIS: Iron Man interrupts Captain America's battle with Cobra and Mr. Hyde to show Cap the fragments of his shield. Meanwhile, Kang tells Red Skull that he's been merged with the Cosmic Cube and offers him a way to quickly master his newfound power. In Brooklyn, Sharon Carter gives Cap an upgraded photonic shield that can take new shapes. The two visit Javier Ramirez at his job at Connie Ferrari's law office. Sharon is jealous when Steve and Connie hit it off. Steve and Sharon return to Steve's apartment where the Watcher is waiting for them. Red Skull attacks, reveals he's internalized the Cosmic Cube, and leaves. The Watcher shows Cap that by tomorrow, the Skull will enslave the world and Cap is responsible.
NOTE: Cap #17, '99 reveals the Watcher is actually Korvac in disguise.

CAPTAIN AMERICA #16 [#483] (April 1999)

"Red Glare" (18 pages)

CREDITS: Mark Waid (writer), Andy Kubert (pencils), Jesse Delperdang (co-inks, c inks), Joe Kubert (co-inks), Todd Klein (letters), Chris Sotomayor, Jean Segarra (colors), Paul Tutrone (asst editor), Matt Idelson (editor)
FEATURE CHARACTER: Captain America
GUEST STARS: Avengers: Justice (last in MagR #3, '99, next in Av #16, '99), Scarlet Witch (last in MagR #3, '99, next in Tb #25, '99), Thor (also in "Watcher's" visions, last in Cable #68, '99, next in Tb #25, '99), Tony Stark (also as Iron Man in Watcher's visions, next in IM #16, '99) (both also in rfb)
SUPPORTING CAST: Sharon Carter (also in "Watcher's" visions)
VILLAINS: Red Skull (also as statue in "Watcher's" vision & in hologram), Korvac (disguised as Uatu the Watcher & as Kang in rfb)
OTHER CHARACTERS: Agent Chen (SHIELD scientist), Red Skull's victims & soldiers; Moondragon, Captain Marvel (both in rfb)
LOCATIONS/ITEMS: Washington DC inc Lincoln Memorial (in "Watcher's" vision) & Capitol building, New York inc Avengers Mansion & SHIELD HQ w/lab, Oxford, MI, Los Angeles; Galactus' starship, Ultimate Nullifier, Sharon's gun, Cap's shield fragments & photonic shield
FLASHBACKS: Kang teams with Red Skull (Cap #15, '99). Korvac battles the Avengers (Av #168, '78).
SYNOPSIS: The Watcher takes Captain America and Sharon Carter to Galactus' arriving starship. Meanwhile, Red Skull enslaves the Avengers. The Watcher tells Cap that the Skull will download the information contained in the starship, enabling him to fully understand how to use the Cosmic Cube's power and making him unstoppable. Claiming the only way to stop the Skull is to kill him before he reaches the starship, the Watcher offers Cap his choice of Galactus' weapons. Cap refuses to kill the Skull, but Sharon secretly grabs a gun. At SHIELD HQ, Tony Stark discovers why Cap's shield shattered. Cap attacks Red Skull, who taunts Cap by starving New York, flooding Oxford, Mississippi and freezing Los Angeles. To taunt him further, Red Skull reverts Cap to his powerless pre-Super-Soldier self.
NOTE: Followed by "A Peek into the Future of… Captain America (4 pages) featuring previews of Cap #17-19, Cap:SoL #8-10 & 12, all '99.

CAPTAIN AMERICA #17 [#484] (May 1999)

"Extreme Prejudice" (18 pages)

CREDITS: Mark Waid (writer), Andy Kubert (pencils), Jesse Delperdang (inks), Todd Klein (letters), Christie Scheele (colors), Paul Tutrone (asst editor), Matt Idelson (editor)
FEATURE CHARACTER: Captain America
SUPPORTING CAST: Sharon Carter (also in "Watcher's" vision, next in Cap #19, '99)
VILLAINS: Red Skull (next in Cap #19, '99), Korvac (also diguised as Uatu the Watcher & Kang)
OTHER CHARACTERS: Red Skull's soldiers & victims, dinosaurs; Iron Man, Thor (both in "Watcher's" vision)
LOCATIONS/ITEMS: New York, Washington, DC inc White House & Washington Monument; Galactus' original starship w/databeam, Cap's photonic shield, Sharon's gun

SYNOPSIS: As Galactus' starship nears Earth, the powerless Captain America and Sharon Carter weigh their options in defeating Red Skull. Cap confronts the Skull and is quickly defeated. Unsatisfied with his victory, Red Skull reverts Cap to his true self, then defeats Cap again. Sharon shoots the Skull in the back, but he diverts the blast back to Sharon. Galactus' ship arrives, and with Red Skull distracted in gaining its information, Cap sees no other option and stabs the Skull with his photonic sword, killing him. The Cosmic Cube energy flows from the Skull's body into the Watcher, who reveals himself first as Kang, then as Korvac. Now that he has infinite power, Korvac leaves to conquer the future. As Korvac teleports away, Cap follows him into the future.

NOTE: Followed by "½ Man, ½ Desk: The Life and Times of Korvac" (4 pages). A saga-style recap of Korvac's career, it includes panels reprinted from Av #172-177, '78.

CAPTAIN AMERICA #18 [#485] (June 1999)

"Man Out of Time" (31 pages)

CREDITS: Mark Waid (writer), Lee Weeks (pencils), Robert Campanella, Jesse Delperdang, Bob McLeod, Al Milgrom, Tom Palmer (inks), Todd Klein (letters), Christie Scheele, Greg Wright (colors), Paul Tutrone (asst editor), Matt Idelson (editor), Andy Kubert (c art)
FEATURE CHARACTER: Captain America (also in rfb2)
VILLAIN: Korvac (also in rfb)
OTHER CHARACTERS: Primax (Jaromel, Korvac's adjutant, also as Captain America, only app), Terrasphere citizens inc rebels, Valerons (inc an Ambassador), cargo crew Badoon (die) (all in alternate futures (see NOTE) of 3007); Sharon Carter (in rfb)
LOCATIONS/ITEMS: Terrasphere inc Korvac's citadel & rebel base w/Statue of Liberty (all in alternate future of 3007), Washington, DC (in rfb); Korvac's gifts from across the galaxy, Valerons' guns & starships, Zenn-La transporter & gun, cargo ship (all in alternate future of 3007), Cap's photonic shield
FLASHBACKS: Korvac gains god-like powers (Av #175, '78 fb). After Captain America kills Red Skull, Korvac reveals himself, steals the Skull's power and Cap follows him into the future (Cap #17, '99).
SYNOPSIS: In the future of 3007 Korvac rules the world like a machine with the aid of his adjutant Primax. Captain America leads a rebel group against Korvac, inspiring many of Korvac's slaves to similarly rebel. Korvac eradicates Cap then resets time to erase the rebellion. Primax notes this is the seventy-second time Korvac has had to reset. Korvac attacks Cap's rebellion as it forms, slaughters the rebels, and tells Cap he too will now remember when time is reset. Months later, Cap and his rebellion attack by hiding in gifts from across the galaxy. With Korvac distracted, Cap fails to gain Primax's help. In 3052, Cap attacks with the aid of the Valerons, who have amassed a galactic strikeforce against Korvac. In 3014, Cap attacks Korvac with the aid of Zenn-La. In 3023, Cap inspires a rebellion in galactic trade lines, crippling galactic government. In 3017, Cap inspires sabotage throughout Earth. Korvac moves in to kill Cap, but Primax stabs Korvac using Cap's photonic shield. Korvac realizes he must reboot time to when he gained his infinite power and then kill Cap. After Korvac and Cap leave, Primax continues Captain America's legacy in the future.
NOTE: Followed by "The Life Story of Cap's Shield (or everything you wanted to know to enjoy issue 20)" (6 pages) written by Mark D. Beazley & designed by Dave Sharpe. A saga-style recap of Cap's missing shield, it reprints panels from Cap #2, 3, 8, 9, 13, 15 & 16, all '98-99. Korvac's reboots generate several timelines. The initial one seen is Reality-69972; the ones Primax mentions preceded it are 69901-69971. Korvac destroys the rebellion as it forms in 69973; Cap hid in Korvac's gifts in 69974; the Valerons aided him in 69975; Zenn-La assists Cap in 69977; Cap targets trade lines in 69976; Primax turned against Korvac in 69978; Jaromel becomes Captain America in Reality-69979.

CAPTAIN AMERICA #19 [#486] (July 1999)

"Triumph of the Will" (22 pages)

CREDITS: Mark Waid (writer), Andy Kubert (pencils), Jesse Delperdang (inks), Todd Klein (letters), Greg Wright (colors), Brian Smith (asst editor), Matt Idelson, Bobbie Chase (editors)
FEATURE CHARACTER: Captain America (also in rfb, next in Nova #2, CoC2 #1 & 4-5, BP #8 fb, BP #9, Av #16-18, Av #0, Av #20-22, all '99, Av Ann, '01 fb)
SUPPORTING CAST: Sharon Carter (also in rfb, last in Cap #17, '99)
VILLAINS: Red Skull (also as Cosmic Cube & in rfb, last in Cap#17, '99, chr next in X Ann, '99 fb, next bts in UXM #371, '99, next in X #91, '99), Korvac (also disguised as Uatu the Watcher, also in rfb, next in AvAc #11, '11)
LOCATIONS/ITEMS: Washington, DC, New York; Cap's photonic shield, Galactus' original starship w/databeam & antimatter engine core
FLASHBACK: Cap battles Korvac in the future (Cap #18, '99).
SYNOPSIS: Korvac resets time. Galactus' ship arrives, and with Red Skull distracted in gaining its information, Cap sees no other option and smacks the Skull with his photonic baton. Red Skull fights back, but the Watcher protects Cap. Cap reveals he remembers his time in the future and Korvac retreats with Cap and Sharon to Galactus' starship. Korvac wants to flee the galaxy, but Cap has a different plan. As Cap finds

a specific spot, Red Skull senses them on Galactus' ship and spreads Korvac's molecules across six dimensions. The Skull takes control of Sharon and attacks Cap with her. Cap shakes loose Red Skull's control over Sharon by telling her he loves her. Sharon is momentarily shocked and Cap knocks her out. Cap begs Red Skull not to enter the databeam to finish learning the starship's knowledge. Red Skull enters the beam anyway, but learns it's actually the ship's antimatter engine core and disintegrates. As the Skull's body whittles down to the Cosmic Cube, Cap briefly touches it and teleports himself and Sharon back to Earth. Cap begins to explain his feelings to Sharon, but she's already gone.

CAPTAIN AMERICA #20 [#487] (August 1999)

"Danger in the Air!" (16 pages)

CREDITS: Mark Waid (writer), Andy Kubert (pencils), Jesse Delperdang (inks), Todd Klein (letters), Gregory Wright (colors), Brian Smith (asst editor), Bobbie Chase (editor)
FEATURE CHARACTER: Captain America (also in rfb)
GUEST STARS: USAgent (last in Tb #32, '99, next in Cap #33, '00), Dum Dum Dugan (last in Cap #12, '98, next in W #144, '99), Tony Stark (bts, voice only, last in Av #22, '99)
SUPPORTING CAST: Sharon Carter (also in rfb), Connie Ferrari (last in Cap #15, '99)
VILLAINS: AIM agents
OTHER CHARACTERS: Javier Ramirez (last in Cap #15, '99), David Ferrari (Connie's brother, see NOTE) & Connie's other family members (all in photos), SHIELD agents (Murphy named) inc Mandroids, US military (inc a Sgt.), Turkish bar patrons (Steve named), bystanders
LOCATIONS/ITEMS: Ft. Colan Army base, CO, Brooklyn inc Connie's apartment, New York inc SHIELD HQ w/reactor containment chamber, Turkish bar; Cap's photonic shield & Avengers ID, USAgent's new Vibranium shield (destroyed, only app), AIM agents' guns & photon cannon, SHIELD Mandroid armors (destroyed), guns & radiation suits
FLASHBACK: Cap tells Sharon that he loves her (Cap #19, '99).
SYNOPSIS: AIM agents raid Ft. Colan looking for Nanomite Bombs. USAgent stops them, but his new Vibranium shield suddenly explodes. Steve Rogers has dinner with Connie Ferrari, but when conversation turns to Connie's dead brother David, Steve can't help but think of Sharon Carter. Steve excuses himself, but promises to call Connie later. In Turkey, an angry Sharon beats up a man for being named Steve. Hoping to find Sharon Cap checks at SHIELD HQ, but Dum Dum doesn't know where she is. Suddenly, the SHIELD Mandroid armors start exploding. Cap helps the Mandroid pilots until the HQ's power reactor starts losing parts. Cap dons a radiation suit, saves an agent stuck inside the reactor core and narrowly avoids a nuclear meltdown. Tony Stark calls Cap and tells him that the entire country may have just become one giant bomb.
NOTE: David Ferrari is believed to have died in a military hazing accident involving his homosexuality, but Cap #36, '00 reveals that to be a SHIELD cover story & he 1st appears in Cap #41, '01.

2ND STORY: "Bloodline" (6 pages)
CREDITS: Bill Rosemann (writer), Vince Evans (art, colors), Todd Klein (letters), Brian Smith (asst editor), Bobbie Chase (editor)
FEATURE CHARACTER: Sgt. Nick Fury (last in SgtF #92, '71)
SUPPORTING CAST: Howling Commandos: Izzy Cohen, Dum Dum Dugan, Gabe Jones (all bts, held in other room, also in pfb), Reb Ralston (voice only, also in pfb) (all last in SgtF #92, '71)
VILLAINS: Baron Blood (also bts in pfb; last in Nam Ann #2/2, '92), Nazi soldiers (in pfb, some as corpses)
OTHER CHARACTER: Col. William Poprycz (of the 5th Infantry, voice only, 1st)
LOCATIONS/ITEMS: European countryside inc Nazi bunker w/Fury's cell; Howling Commandos rifles, Nazi gas
FLASHBACK: Sgt. Fury and his Howling Commandos battle Nazi soldiers until they're gassed and pass out (p).
SYNOPSIS: Sgt. Fury wakes up bound to a chair. He calls out for the Howlers and Reb responds, telling him they're tied up in a cell. Col. William Poprycz tells Fury his unit was captured and bled dry by the Nazis. Baron Blood appears and offers Sgt. Fury the gift of vampirism.

CAPTAIN AMERICA #21 [#488] (September 1999)

"Soundquake!" (16 pages)

CREDITS: Mark Waid (writer), Andy Kubert (pencils), Jesse Delperdang (inks), Todd Klein (letters), Gregory Wright (colors), Brian Smith (asst editor), Bobbie Chase (editor), Christopher Sotomayor (c colors)
FEATURE CHARACTER: Captain America (also in rfb)
GUEST STARS: Avengers: Giant-Man (Pym), Wasp (both between Av #22-23, '99); Tony Stark
SUPPORTING CAST: Sharon Carter (chr next in Cap #30, '00 fb, next in Cap #25, '00), Connie Ferrari (next in Cap #23, '99)
VILLAINS: Klaw (Ulysses Klaw, master of sound, last in Tb #25, '99), Warden Mosley (bts, sends 2 goons to intimidate Connie Ferrari, next in Cap #23, '99) & his 2 goons
OTHER CHARACTERS: Tom Brevoort, Kurt Busiek, Peter David, Adam Kubert, Andy Kubert, George Pérez, John Romita, Jr., Mark Waid (all comic professionals), Alanya (Turkish intelligence agent) (all only app), Kanu Chakara (US immigrant, 1st, in Cap #23, '99), Madan Chakara (Kanu's brother, bts, imprisoned in detention center, next in Cap #23, '99), Barney (dinosaur posing as Turkish intelligence operations director Mehmet Kemel, 1st but chr during Cap #30, '00 fb, next in Cap #25, '99, see NOTE), Dr. Myron MacLain (only in fb2 during Cap #303, '85 fb), Javier Ramirez (next in Cap #28, '00), American Foundation for AIDS Research representative (bts, on phone w/ Javier Ramirez), 2 US soldiers (Arnie named), Turkish bar patrons (inc Steve), taxi driver & passengers
LOCATIONS/ITEMS: Wakanda (in fb1), Myron MacLain's lab (only in fb2), Fort Avison, ME inc Klaw's cell, Connie's Brooklyn office, Stark's

Manhattan lab, Turkey inc bar, Avengers Mansion inc med lab & Hawkeye's subbasement workshop, Central Park baseball diamond; Vibranium meteorite (in fb1), Cap's shield fragments & photonic shield, Avengers Quinjet, cases of Vibranium, Stark's equipment

FLASHBACKS: Millennia ago, a meteorite containing Vibranium strikes Wakanda (1). Myron McLean works on what will become Captain America's shield (2). Cap's shield is destroyed and Cap reconstructs it through force of will, but one of the shield's Vibranium molecules is unknowingly out of alignment (SecWars #11-12, '85).

SYNOPSIS: In Central Park, Captain America rescues Giant-Man from his crashing Quinjet. In Turkey, an intelligence officer shows Sharon Carter that an operations director has changed into a reptilian creature. In Brooklyn, Kanu Chakara asks Connie Ferrari to help his brother, whom he feels is unjustly imprisoned by the US government. At Avengers Mansion, Cap shields the spontaneous explosion of a stash of Vibranium. In Maine, Klaw escapes from prison when his Vibranium cell explodes. Tony Stark tells Cap that his shield broke into pieces because of a progressive dissonant energy that spread throughout its Vibranium molecules. The destructive power of the "Vibranium cancer" is traveling through the air and is destabilizing other items made of Vibranium. The molecular plague must be stopped before it reaches Wakanda's Vibranium Mound and causes a cataclysmic explosion. Stark explains that he can build something to nullify the vibration but it will require him to destroy what remains of Cap's shield.

NOTE: Cap #30, '00 reveals the dinosaur Sharon meets is not a human turned into a dinosaur, but rather a dinosaur given human intelligence; he's named in Cap #25, '00. MacLain is misspelled "McLean" here.

2ND STORY: "Bloodline Part Two" (6 pages)

CREDITS: Bill Rosemann(writer), Vince Evans (art, colors), Todd Klein (letters), Brian Smith (asst editor), Bobbie Chase (editor)

FEATURE CHARACTER: Sgt. Nick Fury (next in SgtF Ann #4, '68 fb)

SUPPORTING CAST: Howling Commandos: Izzy Cohen, Dum Dum Dugan, Gabe Jones, Reb Ralston (all next in SgtF Ann #4, '68 fb)

VILLAINS: Baron Blood (next in Inv #2, '10 fb), Nazi soldiers (all die)

OTHER CHARACTER: Col. William Poprycz (voice only, also as corpse, last app)

LOCATIONS/ITEMS: Nazi bunker w/the Howlers' cell; Howling Commandos' rifles, Col. Poprycz's dog tags, Nazi pistol & radio

SYNOPSIS: Nick Fury defies Baron Blood, who proceeds to bite a willing Colonel Poprycz, whom Fury thinks has turned traitor. Fury frees himself and his fellow Howling Commandos and discovers that his Nazi captors have been drained of blood, not by Baron Blood, who was called away, but by the vampiric Poprycz, who committed suicide by exposing himself to sunlight. Fury realizes that Poprycz deliberately sacrificed himself to defeat the Nazis.

NOTE: Poprycz's dog tags misspell his name as "Popryzc."

CAPTAIN AMERICA #22 [#489] (October 1999)

"Sacrifice Play" (22 pages)

CREDITS: Mark Waid (writer), Andy Kubert (pencils), Jesse Delperdang (inks), Todd Klein (letters), Gregory Wright (colors), Brian Smith (asst editor), Bobbie Chase (editor), Chris Sotomayor (c colors)

FEATURE CHARACTER: Captain America (also in pfb; next in BP #12, '99, FF #23, '99, Cap Ann '99)

GUEST STAR: Tony Stark (also in pfb, voice only, next in Hulk #3, '99)

VILLAIN: Klaw (next in BP #26, '01)

OTHER CHARACTERS: Wakandans

LOCATIONS/ITEMS: Wakanda inc Vibranium Mound; Avengers Quinjet, Stark's transformer, Wakandan battle armor, Cap's shield (reconstituted) & photonic shield

FLASHBACK: Tony tells Cap that his shield is needed to help Stark's transformer find the counter-vibration needed to cure the Vibranium cancer, but the shield will be destroyed (p).

SYNOPSIS: Captain America speeds to the Wakandan Vibranium Mound and sets up Stark's transformer, lamenting over the fate of his shield and their time together. Suddenly, Klaw attacks and the transformer is destroyed. Klaw then absorbs the sonic wave coming for the mountain, becoming the loudest sound on Earth. He plans to shatter the Vibranium and become unstoppable. When Klaw destroys Cap's photonic shield, Cap instinctively grabs his damaged round shield and uses it to repel Klaw's advance. Klaw is filtered through the shield's Vibranium, resulting in the shield emerging repaired. Cap throws his shield through Klaw, shattering him into billions of echoes scattered on the wind. The world is saved, and Cap's oldest partner is back in action.

CAPTAIN AMERICA ANNUAL 1999 (1999)

"Full Court Press" (38 pages)

CREDITS: Joe Casey (writer), Pablo Raimondi (pencils), Walden Wong (inks), Paul Tutrone & Sharpefont (letters), Matt Hicks, Marie Javins (colors), Bobbie Chase (editor)

FEATURE CHARACTER: Captain America (also in Davis' thoughts, next in Cap:SoL #11, '99, Galact #1-6, '99-00, DF:Av #1.2, 2.4 & 3.6, '99-00, DF:FF #4.7, '00, DF:Av #4.8, '00, FF #24, '99, GenX #59, '00, Cap #23, '99)

GUST STAR: Scarlet Witch (last in FF #23, '99, next in Galact #1, '99)

VILLAINS: Flag-Smasher (also in rfb, last in MTU #3, '97, next in CitV #2, '02), Roxxon thieves (Kenneth Bradley (also in dfb) named, all die), Calvin Haldeman (Roxxon president), Dr. Bob (Roxxon scientist) (both only app), Don Kaminski (new Roxxon president, in photo, bts, replaces Halderman, next in MCP #6/2, '07), prisoners (1 dies)

OTHER CHARACTERS: Betty Brant (last in PPSM #8, '99, next in PPSM #11, '99), Kate Cushing (last in PPSSM #215, '94, last bts in PPSSM #225, '95, last app), J. Jonah Jameson (also on billboard, last in ASM #8, '99, next in Galact #3, '99), Edwin Jarvis (last in IM Ann '99, next in Wlk #5, '00), Joe Robertson (last in PPSM #8, '99, next in ASM #11, '99), Sam Dunne (Daily Bugle national editor), Sid Frankin, Dan Davis

(both Daily Bugle reporters) (prev 3 only app), Kevin Stein (Brand employee, bts on phone), Mr. Carroll (Bradley's lawyer), Roxxon security guard, SHIELD agents, Daily Bugle staff, police, prison guards, reporters (Debra & Ted Chin named), UN security guards (Victor named, 1 dies), Spider-Man (photo)

LOCATIONS/ITEMS: New York inc United Nations, Sid's apartment, Daily Bugle w/Jonah's office, conference room, Robbie's office & parking garage; courthouse, Avengers Mansion w/training room & dining room, diner, Roxxon Corporation inc Haldeman's office & lab, jailhouse; SHIELD Helicarrier, Flag-Smasher's maces, spray paint & jetpack (destroyed), Roxxon chemical syringes, guard's gun, Avengers training robots, copies of Daily Bugle

FLASHBACKS: Flag-Smasher attacks the Chunnel (MTU #3, '97). Bradley body is found in prison (d).

SYNOPSIS: Three men working for Roxxon break into the United Nations looking for information on Trebekistan's oil resources. The mission turns bad when Flag-Smasher, under Roxxon's control through chemical injections, kills a guard. Ken Bradley is arrested while the others escape. Daily Bugle reporters Franken and Davis are assigned the story; when it's printed Captain America stops by the Daily Bugle to look at Franken's and Davis' notes, concerned that Flag-Smasher has returned. Unhappy that the Daily Bugle has tied Roxxon to the UN break-in, Haldeman has Flag-Smasher kill Bradley's co-workers. Later, Flag-Smasher tries to kill Ken Bradley. Cap intervenes and saves Ken, but Flag-Smasher escapes. The next day, Cap visits Franken and inspires him to press on with his story. Halderman denies any Roxxon involvement, but Ken Bradley fully confesses. The Daily Bugle runs the story, inciting lawsuit threats from Roxxon and resulting in Ken being killed in prison. Certain Flag-Smasher will come after them, Cap convinces the reporters to act as bait. Flag-Smasher attacks and Cap defeats him. The Daily Bugle runs a story connecting Flag-Smasher to Roxxon, but Halderman escapes prosecution by resigning.

CAPTAIN AMERICA #23 [#490] (November 1999)

"Land of the Free" (22 pages)

CREDITS: Mark Waid (plot), Jay Faerber (script), Frederick Zircher (pencils), Denis Rodier (inks), Todd Klein (letters), Gregory Wright (colors), Brian Smith (asst editor), Bobbie Chase (editor), Andy Kubert (c pencils), Tim Townsend (c inks), Chris Sotomayor (c colors)
FEATURE CHARACTER: Captain America (also as "Buck Jones" & in dfb, next in IM #25, '00)
SUPPORTING CAST: Connie Ferrari (next in Cap #28, '00)
VILLAINS: Warden Mosley (1st but last bts in Cap #21, '99, last app) & his prison guards
OTHER CHARACTERS: Kanu Chakara (last in Cap #21, '99), Madan Chakara (1st but last bts in Cap #21, '99) (both last app), hot dog vendor, justice representative, Immigration and Naturalization Services agents (Vogler named), prisoners, swing band & dancers, bystanders

LOCATIONS/ITEMS: Mosley's New Jersey prison, Manhattan inc swing club & INS Manhattan Division; SHIELD digital camera shades, Mosley's DVD, prison guards' nightsticks & Uzis, prisoners' Molotov cocktail

FLASHBACK: Cap shows his evidence to the Department of Justice (d).

SYNOPSIS: Connie tells Steve about her latest case; a man's brother imprisoned for coming to America unknowingly on false documents. Due to prison overcrowding, INS locked Madan in a corrupt private facility. Captain America joins the ongoing FBI/INS investigation into the prison and takes their agent's place as an undercover guard. Using camera glasses, Steve observes the inhuman conditions and regular torture the prisoners undergo, as well as the measures Warden Mosley takes to pass Federal inspections. When Cap attempts to help Madan after he's been beaten, the guards inadvertently expose his costume and blow his cover. Cap confronts Mosley just as a riot breaks out. Cap keeps Mosley alive to stand trial while defending the prisoners from the guards. The prisoners eventually see Cap is on their side. Cap follows Mosley to a CD containing the evidence Cap needs to shut Mosley down. Using the evidence, Cap gets Madan processed swiftly and reunited with his brother.
NOTE: This issue contains the 8-page Spider-Man story "Fast Lane, part 1 of 4;" it is indexed as Av #22/2 in the Avengers Index, '11.

CAPTAIN AMERICA #24 [#491] (December 1999)

"The Difference!" (22 pages)

CREDITS: Tom DeFalco (writer), Ron Frenz (co-plot, pencils), Jesse Delperdang (inks), Todd Klein (letters), Marie Javins (colors), Brian Smith (asst editor), Bobbie Chase (editor)
FEATURE CHARACTER: Captain America (next in Av #23, '99, Hulk #11 fb, FF #26-28, Av #24-25, Av #26 fb, all '00)
GUST STAR: Dum Dum Dugan (last in Hulk #8, '99)
VILLAINS: Absorbing Man (Carl "Crusher" Creel, last in FF #22, '00, next in Thor #25, '00), Crossbones (last in Cap #443, '95, next in Gam #18, '00), Hydra agents
OTHER CHARACTERS: SHIELD agents (Whedon named), International Peace Initiative delegates (bts, preparing for conference), bystanders

LOCATIONS/ITEMS: New York inc embassy row & warehouse; Cap's motorcycle, Hydra agents' guns, vibro-shock gloves & bomb, Crossbones' crossbow & gas arrows, Absorbing Man's ball & chain

SYNOPSIS: Captain America rescues Agent Whedon from Hydra and learns the terrorists plan to bomb the visiting delegates staying in embassy row. Cap investigates only for Crossbones and Absorbing Man to attack. Crossbones escapes as Cap battles Absorbing Man. When Crusher turns into electricity, Cap dumps a water tower on him and tricks Creel into touching his shoulder. When he reverts to human form, Cap knocks him out with one punch. Cap finds Crossbones setting the bomb and attacks, but Crossbones escapes. Absorbing Man returns and attacks, but Cap tells Creel he's been tricked and thousands of people will die. Inspired by Cap's passion, Carl absorbs Cap's shield and uses his body to shield the bomb's explosion. Crusher thanks Cap for cluing him in and leaves to make Hydra and Crossbones pay for using him.
NOTE: Issue dedicated to Stan Lee & Jack Kirby.

CAPTAIN AMERICA #25 [#492] (January 2000)

"Twisted Tomorrows Part 1 of 3" (38 pages)

CREDITS: Dan Jurgens (writer), Andy Kubert (pencils), Dan Green (inks), Todd Klein (letters), Gregory Wright (colors), Brian Smith (asst editor), Bobbie Chase (editor), Chris Sotomayor (c colors)

FEATURE CHARACTER: Captain America (also in own thoughts & rfb)

GUEST STARS: Falcon (last in BP #17, '00), Nick Fury (last in FF #27, '00), Dum Dum Dugan (next in Cap #27, '00)

SUPPORTING CAST: Sharon Carter (last in Cap #21, '99, chr last in Cap #30, '00 fb)

VILLAINS: Hate-Monger (last in Cap #299, '84, last bts in Cap #448, '96), Branson (white supremacist, 1st), other white supremacists, Clete Billups (SHIELD double agent for AIM, 1st), Protocide (bts in government crate, chr last in Cap Ann '00 fb), Turkish mercenaries (Ahkim named), terrorists

OTHER CHARACTER: Barney (last in Cap #21, '99, chr last in Cap #30, '00 fb), Stanley Klein (WWII veteran, 1st but chr last in Cap #32, '00 fb), Shriley Klein (Stanley's wife, 1st) (both next in Cap #32, '00), Corbin, Pyle (both SHIELD agents, 1st) other SHIELD agents, Gen. McAllister Groves (bts on ID card, captured by Hate-Monger), police (Detective O'Neil named, inc SWAT), bystanders, supremacists' giant panthers; Gen. Phillips, Prof. Erskine, Heinz Krueger, US soldiers (prev 4 in Cap's thoughts)

LOCATIONS/ITEMS: Idaho wilderness, new York inc Chez Louise restaurant & SHIELD HQ w/barber shop front, Virginian government warehouse, Turkey airfield; Cap's motorcycle, SHIELD global positioning device, Turkish mercenaries' guns, SHIELD agents' guns, supremacists' helicopters, guns & gas missile, government crates

FLASHBACK: Steve Rogers undergoes Operation: Rebirth, but Prof. Erskine is killed (CapC #1, '41).

SYNOPSIS: In Idaho, Branson eventually captures Nick Fury. In New York, Captain America helps police stop a hostage situation at Chez Louise restaurant, afterwards meeting Stanley Klein and his wife; Cap recalls Stanley as a private during WWII. After, three SHIELD agents try to arrest Cap until Dum Dum Dugan radios, asking for Cap's help. Meeting Dugan at SHIELD HQ, Cap and Falcon are briefed on the disappearances of Gen. Groves, a Soviet warehouse full of anthrax, and Nick Fury when he investigated the situation. SHIELD believes white supremacists are responsible and Cap agrees to help. In Turkey, Sharon and Barney escape hostiles in a stolen airplane. In Virginia, the three SHIELD agents are out on inventory duty as punishment for trying to arrest Cap. Later in Idaho, Cap and Falcon pose as fishermen until the supremacists attack. Cap and Falcon beat them back, but succumb to a gas attack. As Cap and Falcon pass out Hate-Monger makes his presence known.

NOTE: Includes Spider-Man story "Fast Lane Part 2 of 4: Feel the Rush!" (8 pages); it is indexed as ASM #13/2, '00 in Index #11, '10.

CAPTAIN AMERICA #26 [#493] (February 2000)

"Twisted Tomorrows Part 2 of 3" (23 pages)

CREDITS: Dan Jurgens (writer), Andy Kubert (pencils), Dan Green (inks), Todd Klein (letters), Gregory Wright (colors), Brian Smith (asst editor), Bobbie Chase (editor), Tim Townsend (c inks) Chris Sotomayor (c colors)

FEATURE CHARACTER: Captain America (also in rfb)

GUEST STARS: Falcon, Nick Fury

SUPPORTING CAST: Sharon Carter

VILLAINS: Hate-Monger (also in photo as Adolf Hitler & rfb), Branson, white supremacists, Clete Billups, Protocide (off-panel)

OTHER CHARACTERS: Corbin, Pyle (both die, last app), Gen. McAllister Groves (1st but last bts in Cap #25, '00), Barney; FF: Human Torch, Invisible Girl, Mr. Fantastic, Thing; Hate-Monger's men (prev 5 in rfb)

LOCATIONS/ITEMS: Hate-Monger's stronghold, government warehouse, Antarctica; Supremacists' rifles & anthrax rocket launcher, government crates inc Capone's tommy gun, Pyle's gun

FLASHBACK: Nick Fury and the Fantastic Four face Hate-Monger, discovering he's Adolf Hitler (FF #21, '63).

SYNOPSIS: Hate-Monger reveals his plans to cleanse the world with anthrax to the captive Captain America and Falcon. Cap breaks free and attacks Hate-Monger, but Bronson threatens to kill Falcon if Cap continues. To taunt Cap, Hate-Monger paints a swastika on Cap's shield and throws Cap into a pit. Cap is reunited with Fury, but the pit begins to fill with water. In Virginia, the SHIELD agents discover something astonishing in a crate. Billups kills the other two agents and plans to bring the crate's contents to his masters. In Antarctica, Sharon is caught in a blizzard and crashes her plane. Cap and Fury escape the pit and go after Hate-Monger. Outside, Falcon and Gen. Groves are strapped to two anthrax rockets. Cap and Fury arrive too late to stop Hate-Monger from launching the rockets.

CAPTAIN AMERICA #27 [#494] (March 2000)

"Twisted Tomorrows Part 3 of 3" (20 pages)

CREDITS: Dan Jurgens (writer), Andy Kubert (pencils, c art), Dan Green (inks), Todd Klein (letters), Gregory Wright (colors), Brian Smith (asst editor), Bobbie Chase (editor), Chris Sotomayor (c colors)

FEATURE CHARACTER: Captain America (also in fb between MSH #3/3, '90 fb & MvPro #4, '10 fb)

GUEST STARS: Falcon (next in Av #27, '00), Nick Fury (also in fb between MHol '93/2 fb & FoS #4, '95 fb), Dum Dum Dugan (last in Cap #25, '00, next in Cap #33, '00)

SUPPORTING CAST: Sharon Carter

VILLAINS: Hate-Monger (next in Cap #45, '01 as Adam Hauser), Branson (last app), other white supremacists, AIM Director (Chet Madden, 1st), Clete Billups, other AIM agents, Protocide (off-panel)

OTHER CHARACTERS: Barney (chr next in Cap #30, '00 fb, next in Cap #29, '00), Gen. McAllister Groves (last app), SHIELD agents; Midnight Racer & Chauffeur (radio serial characters, in young Steve's & Nick's thoughts)

LOCATIONS/ITEMS: Hate-Monger's stronghold, Savage Land, New York inc Fury's apartment, AIM base; SHIELD agents' guns & aircraft, supremacists' guns, 2 anthrax missiles w/Falcon & Groves' restraints, government crate, "Midnight Racer" CD

FLASHBACK: As children, Steve Rogers and Nick Fury listen to "The Midnight Racer" radio show.

SYNOPSIS: Captain America fights through the Hate-Monger's supremacists as the anthrax missiles, with Falcon and Gen. Groves strapped to them, launch. Cap reaches the Hate-Monger, retrieves his shield and burns off the swastika in the rocket's blast. Cap throws his shield after the missiles and frees Falcon from his restraints. Falcon secures the anthrax and frees Groves from the other missile. As Nick Fury battles the supremacists Cap captures Bronson but Hate-Monger escapes. SHIELD agents later arrest the supremacists. In the Savage Land, Sharon Carter and Barney are caught in a net trap. Elsewhere, Billups shows his AIM cohorts his amazing discovery. Steve arrives at Fury's apartment, where Fury apologizes for faking his death and treats him to a recorded broadcast of "The Midnight Racer," a radio serial both men enjoyed as children.

NOTE: Followed by a pin-up of Captain America (1 page) by Dan Jurgens. Chet Madden 1st appears in his civilian identity in Cap #35, '00; he's revealed to be the AIM Director in Cap #39, '01.

CAPTAIN AMERICA #28 [#495] (April 2000)

"Grotesqueries" (21 pages)

CREDITS: Dan Jurgens (writer), Andy Kubert (pencils), Dan Green, Joe Kubert (inks), Todd Klein (letters), Gregory Wright (colors), Brian Smith (asst editor), Bobbie Chase (editor), Tim Townsend (c inks), Chris Sotomayor (c colors)

FEATURE CHARACTER: Captain America (also in Av #27, '00, bts in CM #1, '00)

GUEST STARS: Thor (last in Dp #37, '00, next in Av #27, '00), Nick Fury (next in Cap #30, '00)

SUPPORTING CAST: Connie Ferrari (last in Cap #23, '99, next in Cap #30, '00), Sharon Carter

VILLAINS: Count Nefaria (as "Stox", last in IM Ann '99, chr last in Cap #29, '00 fb) & his dino-mutates, AIM Director, Clete Billups, other AIM agents, Protocide (Pvt. Clinton McIntyre, Super-Soldier Serum recipient, 1st but last off-panel in Cap #27, '00)

OTHER CHARACTERS: Edwin Jarvis (last in Av #28, '00, next in Cap #32, '00), Javier Ramirez (last in Cap #21, '99, last app), Matthew Plunder (Adam Plunder bio-replicant, 1st, see NOTE), Cunningham (Connie's client, voice only); David Ferrari (in photo)

LOCATIONS/ITEMS: Antarctica inc Savage Land w/Nefaria's camp, Connie's Brooklyn office, Avengers Mansion inc training & meeting rooms, AIM base outside Washington, DC; Fury's flying car, Protocide's containment tank & shield, dinosaurs' swords, spears, & axes, Matthew's armor & axes

SYNOPSIS: Sharon Carter awakens inside a cage, surrounded by intelligent dinosaurs commanded by a masked man named Stox. At Avengers Mansion, Thor uses Mjolnir to test Captain America's shield's resilience. Later, Steve arrives at Connie Ferrari's office to ask her out for Valentine's Day. Annoyed by Steve's multiple stand-ups, Connie insists on an extravagant date of dinner and dancing. Nick Fury interrupts to speak with Steve, noting the picture of Connie's deceased brother on her desk. Outside, Fury informs Steve of Sharon's situation and gives him his flying car as transport to Antarctica. Meanwhile, Billups shows the AIM Director his discovery, an Operation: Rebirth test subject predating Cap. Cap arrives in Antarctica and finds Sharon's wrecked plane. While searching it, the plane loosens from the mountain and falls, taking Cap with it. Cap finds himself in the Savage Land just as Stox's dinosaurs swarm him. A young man in Stone Age armor rescues Cap and introduces himself as Matthew Plunder, Ka-Zar's son.

NOTE: Includes Spider-Man story "Fast Lane Part 3 of 4: On the Edge" (8 pages); it is indexed as ASM #15/2, '00 in Index #11, '10. Protocide is named in Cap #29, '00 & his real name is revealed in Cap Ann '00. Adam Plunder is Ka-Zar's son, whose full name is Adam Kyle Matthew Plunder. Cap #31, '00 reveals the Adam Plunder appearing here, who goes by Matthew, is an age-accelerated bio-replicant of Adam.

CAPTAIN AMERICA #29 [#496] (May 2000)

"The Savage Man" (22 pages)

CREDITS: Dan Jurgens (writer), Brent Anderson (pencils), Dan Green (inks), Todd Klein (letters), Gregory Wright (colors), Brian Smith (asst editor), Bobbie Chase (editor), Andy Kubert (c pencils), Scott Hanna (c inks)

FEATURE CHARACTER: Captain America

GUEST STARS: Ka-Zar (in fb between Cap #30, '00 fb & Cap #31, '00), Shanna the She-Devil (in fb between KZ #20, '98 & Cap #31, '00)

SUPPORTING CAST: Sharon Carter

VILLAINS: Count Nefaria (also as "Stox" & in fb between IM Ann '99 & Cap #28, '00, also in Cap #30, '00 fb) & his dino-mutates (some as captive Savage Landers in fb), Dr. Manning (geneticist, Arnim Zola student, 1st but chr last in Cap #30, '00 fb, also in fb to 1st chr app before & during Cap #30, '00 fb), AIM Director, Clete Billups (next in Cap #35, '01), other AIM agents, Protocide

OTHER CHARACTERS: Zabu (last in KZ #20, '98, next in Cap #31, '00), Ka-Zar bio-replicant (dies), Shanna bio-replicant (both only app), Adam Plunder (in fb between KZ #20, '98 & Cap #31, '00), Matthew Plunder bio-replicant, Barney (last in Cap #27, '00, chr last in Cap #30, '00 fb), captive Savage Landers (in fb)

LOCATIONS/ITEMS: Savage Land inc Ka-Zar & Shanna's treehouse & Stox's stronghold w/lab (also in fb), AIM base w/medical lab; Matthew's sword, dino-mutates' axes, spears, guns, swords, & shields, AIM medical equipment, Protocide's shield

FLASHBACK: Stox and his personal army and Dr. Manning arrive in the Savage Land. Stox and Manning later genetically alter Savage Landers into dinosaurs as the captive Ka-Zar and Shanna watch.

SYNOPSIS: Captain America is stunned to see Matthew at his age knowing he should still be an infant. When more of Stox's dino-mutates arrive, Cap and Matthew fight off their attackers with Zabu's help long enough to escape on pterodactyls. Matthew takes Cap to his parents' treehouse where an elderly Ka-Zar and Shanna explain what Stox did to the Savage Land peoples and of Sharon Carter's capture. Ka-Zar dies from a heart attack. In Stox's stronghold, Sharon tries to free Barney but is laid low by an energy blast from Stox's eyes. Cap, Matthew, and Zabu breach the stronghold but are also subdued by Stox's eyeblasts. Cap recognizes Stox's voice and power signature, so Stox dispenses with his disguise and reveals himself as Count Nefaria. Meanwhile, AIM revives the dormant super-soldier and names him Protocide.

NOTE: Includes Spider-Man story "Fast Lane Part 4 of 4: Back on Target" (8 pages); it is indexed as ASM Ann, '00/2 in Index #11, '10.

CAPTAIN AMERICA #30 [#497] (June 2000)

"Waste of Dreams" (22 pages)

CREDITS: Dan Jurgens (writer), Andy Kubert (pencils), Dan Green (inks), Todd Klein (letters), Gregory Wright (colors), Brian Smith (asst editor), Bobbie Chase (editor), Matt Banning (c inks), Chris Sotomayor (c colors)
FEATURE CHARACTER: Captain America (also in photo)
GUEST STARS: Nick Fury (last in Cap #28, '00), Ka-Zar (in fb between KZ #20, '98 & Cap #29, '00 fb)
SUPPORTING CAST: Sharon Carter (also in fb between Cap #21, '99 & Cap #25, '00), Connie Ferrari (last in Cap #28)
VILLAINS: Count Nefaria (also as Stox in fb1 during Cap #29, '00 fb & fb3 between Cap #28-29, '00), his henchmen (in fb1) & dino-mutates (1 also in fb1), Dr. Manning (also in fb1 during Cap #29, '00 fb & fb3 between Cap #29, '00 fb & Cap #29, '00, last app), AIM Director & agents, Protocide
OTHER CHARACTERS: Barney (also in fb1 to 1st chr app in fb1 before Cap #21, '00, fb2 between Cap #21, '99 & Cap #25, '00 & fb3 between Cap #27, '00 & Cap #29, '00, last app), Mehmet Kemel (Turkish intelligence operations director, only app in fb1), Matthew Plunder bio-replicant, prehistoric python; David Ferrari (in photo)
LOCATIONS/ITEMS: Savage Land (also in fb1) inc Nefaria's stronghold w/lab (also in fb1), Turkish warehouse (in fb2), Connie's Brooklyn apartment (#717), AIM biomechanics lab; Nefaria's cybernetic earpiece link & flyer (destroyed), Nefaria's henchmen's spears & snares (in fb1), Manning's lab equipment inc ion infusion device (also in fb1)
FLASHBACKS: Stox invades the Savage Land and defeats Ka-Zar. As part of Stox's quest to create living sources of ion power, Dr. Manning transfers Turkish intelligence director Mehmet Kemel's intelligence into a dinosaur. The dinosaur shows no immediate change and is freed, but afterwards attains Kemel's memories, intelligence and ability to speak. He travels to Turkey for help (1). Passing himself off as Kemel, the dinosaur meets Sharon Carter (2). Stox and Dr. Manning experiment on the recaptured dinosaur (3).
SYNOPSIS: Count Nefaria tells the captive Captain America he's conducting experiments in the Savage Land to find living sources of ion power. As Cap and Sharon argue over their relationship, Nefaria and Dr. Manning bombard Barney with ion energy. Cap escapes and chases Nefaria over a rope bridge, where Nefaria commands his personal flyer to fire on the bridge, severing it in two. While both cling to the fallen bridge, Cap reaches Nefaria and removes his cybernetic link to the flyer before he can summon it, inadvertently causing him to fall into the chasm. Matthew, intent on making Nefaria answer for his crimes, swings along a vine into the chasm and catches him. In New York, Connie Ferrari returns home and muses over her brother's photo, unaware that Nick Fury is watching her. Meanwhile, AIM tells Protocide that Cap is his greatest enemy.

CAPTAIN AMERICA #31 [#498] (July 2000)

"Hidden Paths" (22 pages)

CREDITS: Dan Jurgens (writer), Andy Kubert (pencils, c art), Dan Green (inks), Todd Klein (letters), Gregory Wright (colors), Brian Smith (asst editor), Bobbie Chase (editor), Chris Sotomayor (c colors)
FEATURE CHARACTER: Captain America (also in rfb; next in Av Ann '00, SW #15, '00)
GUEST STARS: Nick Fury (also bts in Blade #1, '99, also in Blade #2, '00 & BW #1-3, '01, next in Hulk #16, '00), Ka-Zar (last in KZ #20, '98, chr last in Cap #29, '00 fb, next in Alias #24, '03), Shanna the She-Devil (last in KZ #20, '98, chr last in Cap #29, '98 fb, next in XMU #48, '03)
SUPPORTING CAST: Sharon Carter (becomes acting SHIELD Director, also in rfb; chr next in SM/M, '01 fb, next in Av #32, '00), Connie Ferrari (next in Cap #33, '00)
VILLAINS: Count Nefaria (chr next in Av #33, '00 fb, next bts in Tb #42, '00, next in Av #32, '00) & his dino-mutates, AIM Director (next in Cap #35, '00) & agents, Protocide (next in Cap #33, '00)
OTHER CHARACTERS: Zabu (next in UXM #457, '05), Adam Plunder (last in KZ #20, '98, chr last in Cap #29, '00 fb, last app to date), Matthew Plunder bio-replicant (dies, last app), Savage Landers inc Nefaria's guard, Pastorini's waiters, patrons & 6-piece band, carriage driver, 2 passengers & horse
LOCATIONS/ITEMS: Savage Land inc Nefaria's stronghold w/prison, cavern & Ka-Zar & Shanna's treehouse, New York inc Pastorini's restaurant, AIM base; dino-mutates' spears, shields, guns, & swords; Sharon's plastique packs, det cord & guns, Matthew's armor & axes, Nefaria's guard's spear, Fury's flying car, Protocide's shield, AIM battle droids
FLASHBACK: Cap tells Sharon that he loves her (Cap #19, '99).
SYNOPSIS: Captain America, Matthew Plunder, and Sharon Carter fight their way through Nefaria's mutates in order to find the means to restore the mutates' humanity, even as Cap and Sharon continue to bicker. Matthew suddenly dies of old age. Cap and Sharon soon find the Savage Land's entire human population, including the real Plunders, asleep in containment chambers. Once freed, Ka-Zar reveals that the Savage Land peoples were not actually mutated by Nefaria, but simply used as DNA sources to create the mutates, including the aged Plunder replicants. Cap agrees to let Ka-Zar retain custody of Nefaria. Cap and Sharon depart, begin arguing again and almost kiss, but are interrupted when Nick Fury arrives. Later, Steve arrives for his date with Connie. Outside, Fury confirms that Sharon will take the acting SHIELD Directorship while he ties up some loose ends. Elsewhere, AIM tests Protocide against battle droids.
NOTE: Cap:SoL #1, '98 featured a story set in the future where Sharon Carter was SHIELD's Director, a prediction now fulfilled.

CAPTAIN AMERICA #32 [#499] (August 2000)

"Heart" (22 pages)

CREDITS: Dan Jurgens (writer), Jerry Ordway (art), Todd Klein (letters), Gregory Wright (colors), Brian Smith (asst editor), Bobbie Chase (editor), Andy Kubert (c art), Richard Isanove (c colors)
FEATURE CHARACTER: Captain America (also in fb2 between USA #15, '45 & WS:WK #1, '07 fb; next in Tb #44, '00 Av #34, '00, IF/W #2-4, '00-01, Cap:SoL #1, '99)
GUEST STARS: Nick Fury (also in fb during SgtF Ann #4, '68 fb; last in MKn #4, '00, next in Hulk #19, '00) & his Howling Commandos: Dum Dum Dugan, Gabe Jones, Pinky Pinkerton, Reb Ralston (prev 4 in fb during SgtF Ann #4, '68 fb)
SUPPORTING CAST: Bucky (in fb between USA #15, '45 & WS:WK #1, '07 fb)
VILLAINS: German soldiers (in fb)
OTHER CHARACTERS: Edwin Jarvis (last in Cap #28, '00, next in BP #22, '00), Stanley Klein (also in pfb & fb to 1st chr app before Cap #25, '00), Shirley Klein (also in photo & pfb) (both last in Cap #25, '00, last app), Cameron Klein (SHIELD agent & Stanley's grandson, also in pfb, 1st, next in Cap #37, '01), Klein family (also in pfb), US Army 106th Infantry (Teddy Doyle, Hauser & Charlie named, prev 2 die), field medics (both in fb), doctor, nurses
LOCATIONS/ITEMS: Belgium inc Ardennes Mountains (in fb), Klein household (in pfb), Avengers Mansion, Queensboro Bridge, veteran's hospital; 106th Infantry guns & grenades, German guns, grenades & tanks (all in fb), Klein's SHIELD ID & gun, SHIELD hovercar, Stan's purple heart
FLASHBACKS: Stanley Klein regales his family with yet another retelling of his meeting Captain America in WWII, before suffering a heart attack (p). During the Battle of the Bulge, Stanley's infantry is hit by a German surprise attack. As his division is dwindled down, Stanley tries to save a wounded comrade, the only other survivor, until Captain America and the Howling Commandos arrive and defeat the Germans. Afterwards, Cap returns Stanley's lost picture of Shirley.
SYNOPSIS: SHIELD Agent Cameron Klein comes to Avengers Mansion looking for Cap, supposedly under orders from Fury. Cap goes along with it, feeling something is amiss since Klein, a technician, shouldn't have access to a hovercar or gun. Cap attempts to arrest Klein when Fury appears on screen and calls him off. Cameron brings Cap to the veteran's hospital where they and Fury see Stanley one last time. Stanley shows Cap his purple heart for saving lives during the war, and thanks him for giving him fifty years of life before he dies.

CAPTAIN AMERICA #33 [#500] (September 2000)

"Impending Rage!" (22 pages)

CREDITS: Dan Jurgens (writer, pencils), Art Thibert (inks), Todd Klein (letters), Gregory Wright (colors), Brian Smith (asst editor), Bobbie Chase (editor)
FEATURE CHARACTER: Captain America
GUEST STARS: Falcon (last in Av #27, '00), USAgent (last in Cap #20, '99), Dum Dum Dugan (last in Cap #27, '00), Nick Fury (last in Hulk #20, '00)
SUPPORTING CAST: Sharon Carter (last in IF/W #3, '00, last bts in IF/W #4, '01, chr last in Cap:SoL #1, '98)
VILLAINS: Protocide (last in Cap #31, '00), Cache (sentient Artificial Intelligence altered by AIM, 1st), AIM Director (last in Cap #31, '00) & agents (Spelling named)
OTHER CHARACTERS: Berger (SHIELD trainer), Josh Howard (computer programmer), Dawn Ridgeway (Josh's girlfriend) (all 1st), garbage man, security guard, SHIELD trainees
LOCATIONS/ITEMS: New York inc Parliamech building, SHIELD HQ, AIM base & warehouse, SHIELD Saudi Arabian training facility; SHIELD training equipment, Cache's gas & battle drones, USAgent's new shield (destroyed), Protocide's shield
SYNOPSIS: While AIM gives Protocide a test run, Captain America and Falcon stop Josh Howard and his girlfriend Dawn from breaking into the Parliamech building. Josh tells Cap about Parliamech using its new ISP to steal information from subscribers' hard drives. They're initially dismissed as conspiracy nuts until Josh reveals he founded Parliamech. Meanwhile, Sharon Carter and Dum Dum investigate AIM while Nick Fury investigates David Ferrari's history at a Saudi Arabian SHIELD training facility. At Parliamech, Cap and Falcon intend to pay a visit to the CEO, but walk into a trap as the elevator falls and douses them with gas. Cap and Falcon battle drones before succumbing to the effects of the gas and passing out. Meanwhile, USAgent invades an AIM warehouse. Protocide destroys USAgent's shield and stabs him in the chest.

CAPTAIN AMERICA #34 [#501] (October 2000)

"Cache is King!" (22 pages)

CREDITS: Dan Jurgens (writer, pencils), Art Thibert (inks), Todd Klein (letters), Gregory Wright (colors), Brian Smith (asst editor), Bobbie Chase (editor)
FEATURE CHARACTER: Captain America (also in photo)
GUEST STARS: Falcon (next in Cap #47, '01), Jake Olson (Thor's mortal identity, also as Thor in own thoughts, last in Av #27, '00, next in Thor #28, '00), USAgent, Dum Dum Dugan, Nick Fury
SUPPORTING CAST: Sharon Carter
VILLAINS: Enchantress (as Christine Collins, last in Thor #27, '00, next in Thor #29, '00), Cache (next in Cap Ann, '00), Protocide, AIM Director & agents

OTHER CHARACTERS: Josh Howard, Dawn Ridgeway (both last app), Berger, other SHIELD agents, Sammy (warehouse employee), police; ice giants, ice pterodactyls (both holograms)

LOCATIONS/ITEMS: New York inc Parliamech building w/holographic studio, AIM base & warehouse, Saudi Arabia SHIELD clean up site; EMT equipment inc defibrillator, SHIELD transport & guns, Falcon's & Cache's manacles

SYNOPSIS: Captain America wakes up in an ice cave with rivers of lava and attacking ice creatures. Meanwhile, Jake Olson and his partner Christine tend to USAgent's wounds until SHIELD takes USAgent into their custody. Falcon, Josh and Dawn find themselves in a swamp. Cap deduces he's trapped in a virtual reality game and damages the system controlling it, revealing himself to be trapped in a holographic studio at Parliamech. Cache, the now sentient Artificial Intelligence program Josh had created to eliminate the need for employees in Parliamech's data storage services, reveals himself as the mastermind. Cap is able to use Cache's quest for knowledge by distracting him with the question, who is Captain America under the mask? Cap defeats Cache. As police take Cache away, Cap tells Josh he needs to return Cache's stolen information to its original owners. In Saudi Arabia, Fury and Berger continue investigating David Ferrari. Elsewhere, AIM prepares Protocide for his next target, Captain America.

CAPTAIN AMERICA #35 [#502] (November 2000)

"When Strikes Protocide!" (22 pages)

CREDITS: Dan Jurgens (writer, pencils), Walden Wong (inks), Todd Klein (letters), Gregory Wright (colors), Brian Smith (asst editor), Bobbie Chase (editor)
FEATURE CHARACTER: Captain America (also in photo, next in Cap Ann, '00)
GUEST STARS: Dum Dum Dugan (next in Cap Ann 2000), USAgent (next in MaxS #1, '00) , Nick Fury
SUPPORTING CAST: Sharon Carter (next in Cap Ann 2000), Connie Ferrari (last in Cap #31, '00)
VILLAINS: Protocide, AIM Director (also as Chet Madden) (both next in Cap Ann, '00), Clete Billups (last in Cap #29, '00, next in Cap Ann, '00), other AIM agents, burglars
OTHER CHARACTERS: Jasper Sitwell (last in Av #34, '00, next in IM #36, '01 fb), Berger, other SHIELD agents, New York Mets (bts, playing at Shea Stadium), doctor, police, bystanders

LOCATIONS/ITEMS: New York inc AIM base, jewelry store & airport, Shea Stadium, Saudi Arabia SHIELD clean up site, SHIELD Colorado hospital; USAgent's exo-skeleton, burglars' guns, Minute Max (SHIELD ship), SHIELD gyro-plane & guns, Omega Compound, Protocide's shield

SYNOPSIS: AIM tells Protocide that SHIELD are fascists and Captain America is the man who ruined Protocide's life. Meanwhile, Cap stops a robbery before meeting Connie at Shea for a Mets game. They meet Connie's client Chet Madden, who gave them the tickets, but Steve doesn't trust Chet. Elsewhere, Jasper Sitwell explains to Nick Fury how SHIELD agent David Ferrari led a team to destroy an AIM lab. With himself wounded and his team dead, Ferrari was forced to use two drops of the Omega Compound, a very volatile chemical weapon, to complete the mission. Ferrari's body was never recovered. In Colorado, USAgent is fitted with an exoskeleton to help him recover from Protocide's attack. Cap ends his date with Connie to help SHIELD move the Omega Compound from its holding facility in New York. Protocide attacks the transport and battles Cap, beating him into near unconsciousness. Protocide escapes without the Omega Compound and Cap collapses.
NOTE: Story continued in Cap Ann, '00.

CAPTAIN AMERICA ANNUAL 2000 (2001)

"Who is… Protocide?!" (30 pages)

CREDITS: Dan Jurgens (writer), Greg Scott (pencils), Dan Green (inks), Jon Babcock (letters), Marie Javins (colors), Bobbie Chase (editor), Art Thibert (c inks), Chris Sotomayor (c colors)
FEATURE CHARACTER: Captain America (also bts in fb between MSH #3, '90 fb & Cap:Re #2, '09; next in Av:I #1, '00, Cap #36, '00)
GUEST STAR: Dum Dum Dugan (last in Cap #35, '00, next in Cap Ann '00/2)
SUPPORTING CAST: Sharon Carter (last in Cap #35, '00, next in X #106, '00)
VILLAINS: Protocide (also in photo, Cap's thoughts & fb as Pvt. Clinton McIntyre to 1st chr app before bts in Cap #25, '00; last in Cap #35, '00, next in Cap #37, '01), Cache (also in Cap's thoughts & as Captain America, last in Cap #35, '00, next in Cap #38, '01), Chet Madden (last in Cap #35, '00, next in Cap #37, '01), Clete Billups (last in Cap #35, '00, next in Cap #38, '01), other AIM agents (Skip named), Agent R (in fb between SR:SSol #2, '10 fb & CapC #1, '41)
OTHER CHARACTERS: Clay Quartermain (last in Cable #62, '98, next in Alias #5, '02), other SHIELD agents (inc prison guards), Gen. Phillips (in fb between MvPro #4, '10 fb & CapC #1, '41), Dr. Erskine (in fb between MvPro #4, '10 fb & Cap:Re #2, '09 fb), Gen. Maxfield Saunders (only app in fb) (all also in photo), other US Generals, Operation: Rebirth technician, military police, Army guard, bystanders (prev 5 in fb), airport employees

LOCATIONS/ITEMS: New York (also in fb), inc Operation: Rebirth w/curio shop front (in fb), AIM base, airport & SHIELD prison w/Cache's cell; Super-Soldier serum (in fb), SHIELD Omega Compound, gyro-plane, stasis carrier, particle cannon & guns, AIM vehicle, Protocide's shield, Cap's motorcycle

FLASHBACK: As Steve Rogers prepares for Project: Rebirth, Gen. Saunders grows impatient. He believes Rogers is an unsuitable candidate for the Super-Soldier Serum, and secretly brings in his own subject: Pvt. Clinton McIntyre, who's awaiting the death penalty for killing his commanding officer. Saunders administers the oral serum to McIntyre, but without the injection compound or Vita-Rays, McIntyre is immediately driven insane, and rampages through the streets until his heart gives out. Gen. Phillips arrests Saunders.
SYNOPSIS: Protocide assaults a SHIELD facility, easily defeating the SHIELD agents stationed there. AIM is pleased with Protocide's prowess. Meanwhile, Sharon Carter wakes up Captain America. Despite his injuries, Cap immediately begins an investigation into who Protocide is. Cap

questions Cache at a SHIELD prison. At first Cache is reluctant to help, but when Cap questions his abilities he tells Cap what he knows about Protocide. When Cap leaves Cache contacts the AIM Director, who tells Cache he's done his job. Cache invades the SHIELD prison's security system, frees himself and walks out disguised as Cap.
NOTE: Story continued in Cap #36, '00.

2ND STORY: "The Test" (7 pages)
CREDITS: Bill Rosemann (writer), Scot Eaton (pencils), Bud LaRosa (inks), Jon Babcock (letters), Paul Tutrone (colors), Bobbie Chase (editor)
FEATURE CHARACTERS: Elite Agents of SHIELD: the Kid (E.B. Farrell), M-80 (Sayuri Kyoto), Nails (Joan Eaton), Silicon (Gerald Simms), Skul (John Skulinowski) (all 1st, next in Tb #69, '02)
SUPPORTING CAST: Sharon Carter (last in X #106, '00, next in Tb #48, '01), Dum Dum Dugan (last in Cap Ann '00, next in MBoy #2, '00)
VILLAINS: Hydra agents, arms dealers
OTHER CHARACTER: Captain America (in rfb)
LOCATIONS/ITEMS: SHIELD HQ, Gobi Desert inc black market bazaar; SHIELD aircraft & guns, stolen technology inc planes & exo-skeleton
FLASHBACK: Sharon Carter and Captain America almost kiss (Cap #31, '00).
SYNOPSIS: The Elite Agents of SHIELD break up a Hydra black market bazaar. Sharon Carter and Dum Dum Dugan discuss the new team's success, points of concern and possible upcoming assignments.
NOTE: Followed by pin-up (1 page) of Captain America by Sean Chen (pencils) & Tim Townsend (inks).

CAPTAIN AMERICA #36 [#503] (December 2000)

"Maelstrom Within" (22 pages)

CREDITS: Dan Jurgens (writer, pencils), Art Thibert (inks), Todd Klein (letters), Gregory Wright (colors), Brian Smith (asst editor), Bobbie Chase (editor), Chris Sotomayor (c colors)
FEATURE CHARACTER: Captain America (next in MaxS #1, Av #35, MaxS #3, all '00, Av #36-37, BP #27, S #5, S/FF, S/Hulk, S/SM, S/X, S/Void, all '01, Hcat #3, '00)
GUST STAR: Nick Fury (next in XFor #111, '01)
SUPPORTING CAST: Connie Ferrari
VILLAINS: Mercurio (Gramosian, manipulates psionic energy, also as Karl Sarron, last in Q #16, '90, apparently dies, last app), Hydra agents
OTHER CHARACTERS: David Ferrari (in photo), imprisoned aliens, bystander
LOCATIONS/ITEMS: Brooklyn inc Steve's apartment, Kazakhstan inc Hydra base, New York inc Avengers Mansion & Liberty Island w/Statue of Liberty; Cap's motorcycle, Mercurio's Dimensional Oscillator, Fury's hang glider, computer, grenade & gun
SYNOPSIS: Captain America saves Connie from aliens in the street. She insists on going to Steve Rogers' apartment, so he escorts her there, quickly changes, then makes an excuse and sneaks out as Cap. In Kazakhstan, Nick Fury invades a Hydra base where he uses their database to verify that David Ferrari is still alive. At Avengers Mansion, Karl Sarron helps Cap fight off some aliens. Sarron tells Cap his Dimensional Oscillator can lift the barrier keeping the imprisoned aliens on Earth, allowing them to leave, but he needs Cap's shield to make it work. Cap joins him atop the Statue of Liberty and puts his shield in the device. Sarron reveals himself as Mercurio, and that the device will only enable his own escape from Earth. Cap disables the device and the resulting feedback causes Mercurio to overload and explode. Regretting the outcome, Cap puts it behind him as he rejoins the battle to save Earth.
NOTE: Cover-labeled "Maximum Security," a crossover in which the Galactic Council turns Earth into a prison planet.

CAPTAIN AMERICA #37 [#504] (January 2001)

"Brothers" (22 pages)

CREDITS: Dan Jurgens (writer, pencils), Art Thibert (inks), Todd Klein (letters), Gregory Wright (colors), Brian Smith (asst editor), Bobbie Chase (editor)
FEATURE CHARACTER: Captain America (also in rfb)
GUEST STARS: Dum Dum Dugan (last in MBoy #6, '01), Nick Fury (last in XFor #112, '01, chr next in Cap #1, '02 fb, next in W #163, '01)
SUPPORTING CAST: Sharon Carter (last in Tb #49, '01), Connie Ferrari (next in Cap #39, '01)
VILLAINS: AIM Director (as Chet Madden), Protocide (also in rfb & pfb) (both last in Cap Ann '00), Hydra agents (others in pfb)
OTHER CHARACTERS: Cameron Klein (last in Cap #32, '00), other SHIELD agents; Prof. Erskine, Gen. Phillips (both in rfb), David Ferrari (in photo)
LOCATIONS/ITEMS: SHIELD HQ, Connie's Brooklyn apartment, Hydra base; Protocide's shield, Hydra agents' neural shock guns & energy core
FLASHBACKS: Steve Rogers (ToS #63/2, '65) and Pvt. McIntyre take the Super-Soldier serum (Cap Ann '00). Protocide attacks Hydra (p).
SYNOPSIS: While SHIELD searches for Protocide, Nick Fury tells Captain America that Connie's brother David Ferrari is a SHIELD agent who has gone rogue. That night, Steve starts to ask Connie about David until his SHIELD pager goes off. As Steve begins to leave, Chet Madden arrives at Connie's apartment to work on his case. When Steve leaves, Chet makes a call to dig up information on Steve. Cap finds Protocide fighting Hydra agents and attacks. Realizing that neither Cap nor Protocide are paying attention to them, the Hydra agents take the opportunity and attack them both. The two are forced to team-up against Hydra. Protocide is knocked into Hydra's energy core and Cap saves him, trying to convince him to reject AIM and be a hero. Protocide knocks Cap into the energy core instead.

CAPTAIN AMERICA #38 [#505] (February 2001)

"Across the Rubicon" (23 pages)

CREDITS: Dan Jurgens (writer, pencils), Art Thibert (inks), Todd Klein (letters), Gregory Wright (colors), Brian Smith (asst editor), Bobbie Chase (editor)
FEATURE CHARACTER: Captain America (also in Protocide's thoughts & rfb)
GUST STAR: Dum Dum Dugan
SUPPORTING CAST: Sharon Carter (next in SM/M, '01)
VILLAINS: Protocide (also in rfb & false memory, last app), Cache (last in Cap Ann, '00), AIM Director, Clete Billups (last in Cap Ann, '00, next in Cap #40, '01), other AIM agents
OTHER CHARACTERS: Cameron Klein, other SHIELD agents (McCluskey named), truck driver (bts), Hydra agents (as corpses), truck driver (voice only); Prof. Erskine, German soldier (both in Protocide's thoughts)
LOCATIONS/ITEMS: AIM base, Hydra base, SHIELD HQ; Hydra energy core, AIM memory inducer & helicopter, SHIELD tracking device, laser drill & personal assault vehicle, Omega Compound
FLASHBACK: Cap saves Protocide, but Protocide tries to kill Cap in return (Cap #37, '01).
SYNOPSIS: Protocide questions his AIM superiors about Captain America's character and his own history. Cache attaches a memory inducer on Protocide to reinforce the idea that Cap ruined his life, but Protocide can't forget that Cap saved his life. At the Hydra base, SHIELD discovers Cap is inside the energy core, still using his shield to keep from being incinerated. They help Cap escape, who refuses medical attention, takes Sharon's tracker and an assault vehicle to find and finish Protocide. As Cap attacks an AIM base, Klein notices that Cap took the Omega Compound. Cap plows through the AIM agents and confronts Protocide. During the battle Cap downs the AIM Director and Cache's helicopter, causing a chain reaction of explosions. A moment of clarity hits Protocide and he saves Cap as the base explodes. Later, a disguised Protocide hitches a ride from a truck driver.

CAPTAIN AMERICA #39 [#506] (March 2001)

"A Gulf so Wide" (22 pages)

CREDITS: Dan Jurgens (writer, pencils), Bob Layton (inks), Todd Klein (letters), Digital Chameleon (colors), Brian Smith (asst editor), Bobbie Chase (editor)
FEATURE CHARACTER: Captain America (also in pfb, next in Cap #1, '02 fb, ASM #36, '01, Cap #1, '02 fb, X #111, '01 fb, Av #38-40, '01, USAgent #2-3, '01, BP #30, '01)
GUEST STAR: Dum Dum Dugan (also in pfb, next in W #163, '01)
SUPPORTING CAST: Sharon Carter (also in pfb, last in SM/M, '01, next in X #111, '01 fb), Connie Ferrari (also in pfb)
VILLAINS: AIM Director (also as Chet Madden & in pfb), Red Skull (bts, sold Mandroid plans to AIM, last in FF #27, '00, next in Cap #41, '01), Cache, AIM agents
OTHER CHARACTERS: Cameron Klein (also in pfb), 2 Federal agents; Mephisto & his demons (both in Cache's illusions), Bucky, German soldiers (both in Steve's thoughts)
LOCATIONS/ITEMS: Arlington National Cemetery inc David Ferrari's grave, Chet Madden's Iowa factory office (both in pfb), Mephisto's realm in Cache's illusion), AIM's Iowa base; AIM guns, Mandroid armor & robot sentries, SHIELD guns & data capture device, Federal helicopter
FLASHBACK: Steve Rogers and Connie Ferrari visit David Ferrari's grave at Arlington National Cemetary. Sharon Carter and Cameron Klein interrupt to report that AIM's leader escaped and that they've tracked a supply of genetic biomechanical material being shipped to him. Chet Madden calls Connie for legal help when Federal agents issue an arrest warrant for him (p).
SYNOPSIS: Acting on a lead, Captain America, Sharon Carter, Dum Dum Dugan and Cameron Klein raid an Iowa AIM base to stop the high-tech crime syndicate from cloning another super-soldier. After battling AIM robot sentries, they find themselves facing Mephisto in his hellish realm. Cap realizes that their surroundings are illusions cast by Cache, and as the villain tries to escape, Klein captures him in a data storage device. The AIM Director appears in Mandroid armor and attempts to fly away, but Cap brings him down and opens the armor to discover Chet Madden inside. Connie arrives, tells Cap and the SHIELD agents to stand down, and asserts her client's innocence.

CAPTAIN AMERICA #40 [#507] (March 2001)

"Fighting Back" (22 pages)

CREDITS: Dan Jurgens (writer, pencils), Bob Layton (inks), Todd Klein (letters), Digital Chameleon (colors), Andrew Lis (asst editor), Bobbie Chase (editor)
FEATURE CHARACTER: Captain America (also as AIM agent)
GUEST STAR: Dum Dum Dugan (last in USAgent #3, '01)
SUPPORTING CAST: Sharon Carter (also as AIM agent, last in W #164, '01), Connie Ferrari
VILLAINS: Clete Billups (last in Cap #38, '01), Cache (bts, incarcerated) (both last app), Chet Madden, AIM agents
OTHER CHARACTERS: Cameron Klein (last app), other SHIELD agents, municipal judge, prosecuting

attorney, TV news reporters & cameramen, bystanders
LOCATIONS/ITEMS: Far Point (Midwest AIM base) inc communications tracking room, AIM's Iowa base, Manhattan inc municipal court building, SHIELD's Pennsylvania maximum security facility inc Billups' cell; AIM aircraft, blasters, electronic personnel files, knife & communications console w/purge button, Avengers Quinjet, Cap's data disk, SHIELD aircraft & guns
SYNOPSIS: Steve Rogers and Connie Ferrari argue about Chet Madden's right to due process. Connie presents her pretrial statement in court, and Steve is surprised that the judge is inclined to dismiss the case. When Sharon Carter tells Steve that SHIELD has been unable to find evidence of any wrongdoing by Madden, he heads back as Captain America to AIM's Iowa base with Cameron Klein to find some, but the search proves fruitless. Later, Cap and Sharon, disguised as AIM agents, break Clete Billups out of a SHIELD maximum security facility and trick him into taking them to the AIM base Far Point. Once inside, Billups' rescuers reveal their true identities and send a signal to Dum Dum Dugan and Klein. As SHIELD aircraft assault Far Point, Cap reaches the AIM communications records stored there before they can be purged. Cap takes incriminating evidence against Madden to court, and the judge rules that Madden's trial proceed.

CAPTAIN AMERICA #41 [#508] (May 2001)

"Duel" (22 pages)

CREDITS: Dan Jurgens (writer, pencils), Bob Layton (inks), Todd Klein (letters), Digital Chameleon (colors), Andrew Lis (asst editor), Bobbie Chase (editor)
FEATURE CHARACTER: Captain America
GUEST STARS: Nick Fury (last in W #166, '01), Dum Dum Dugan (next in Tb #52, '01)
SUPPORTING CAST: Sharon Carter, Connie Ferrari
VILLAINS: Red Skull (last in FF #27, '00, next bts in Cap #45, '01 fb), Answer (David Ferrari, Connie Ferrari's brother & former SHIELD agent, 1st full app) & his guard, Batroc (also in photo, last in W #164, '01, next in Cap #50/6, '02) & his Brigade, Chet Madden (bts, convicted, last app)
OTHER CHARACTERS: Billy Blanks (Tae Bo instructor, on TV), US Army Major & 2 soldiers
LOCATIONS/ITEMS: Khamiskan, New York inc East Coast beach & Federal facility, Connie's Brooklyn apartment; Batroc's neural shock boots & stolen data disc, Batroc's Brigade's guns, Answer's gun, Answer's guard's gun, SHIELD flying car, Red Skull's stolen Helicarrier
SYNOPSIS: Batroc's Brigade distracts Captain America long enough for Batroc to steal battle plans for an upcoming SHIELD offensive maneuver. Later, Steve Rogers apologizes to Connie Ferrari for not respecting her role as the convicted Chet Madden's attorney, but their conversation is interrupted when Sharon Carter and Dum Dum Dugan call him away. The SHIELD agents tell Cap that Batroc's heist points to a plot to seize the stolen Helicarrier from the Red Skull. Eager to flush out Batroc's employer, Cap tracks down and battles Batroc, intercepting the savateur's delivery of SHIELD data to Red Skull. The Skull escapes aboard his stolen Helicarrier. After handing Batroc and the data disk over to SHIELD, Rogers returns to Connie. Meanwhile, Nick Fury arrives in Khamiskan and finds David Ferrari alive and well. David shoots Fury.
NOTE: David Ferrari's codename, the Answer, is revealed in Cap #42, '01.

CAPTAIN AMERICA #42 [#509] (June 2001)

"Fractured" (22 pages)

CREDITS: Dan Jurgens (writer, pencils), Bob Layton (inks), Todd Klein (letters), Avalon Studios' Bart (colors), Andrew Lis (asst editor), Bobbie Chase (editor)
FEATURE CHARACTER: Captain America (also in pfb)
GUEST STAR: Nick Fury
SUPPORTING CAST: Sharon Carter (only in pfb, next bts in IM #36, '01 fb, next in Tb #51, '01), Connie Ferrari (also in pfb)
VILLAINS: Answer (bts, sends Crimson Dynamo and Nick Fury to attack Captain America), Crimson Dynamo (Answer's armored agent, 1st), Khamiskan soldiers
OTHER CHARACTERS: Khamiskan family (father, mother & sons Anton & Dimitri, 1st), SHIELD agents, US President (mentioned, see NOTE); Burke Lincoln, Ronnie Warren (both actors, as Midnight Racer & the Chauffeur, on movie poster)
LOCATIONS/ITEMS: Steve's Brooklyn apartment (in pfb), Khamiskan; Fury's locater implant, SHIELD mind-control drugs, Crimson Dynamo's armor w/lasers & extinguishers, fire pit, Khamiskan soldiers' guns, Cap's medical kit w/penicillin, SHIELD aircraft & reflector suit w/cooling system
FLASHBACK: Connie Ferrari gives Steve Rogers a "Midnight Racer" movie poster as a gift, but when Connie leaves, Sharon Carter calls asking Steve to rescue Nick Fury, who has gone missing in Khamiskan, a former Soviet republic where someone calling himself the Answer has been stirring up trouble (p).
SYNOPSIS: Captain America arrives in politically unstable Khamiskan, where he gives medical assistance to the mother of a homeless family. Suddenly, a new Crimson Dynamo attacks Cap. No sooner does Cap vanquish the armored Russian than he is assaulted by a masked man he assumes is David Ferrari, aka the Answer. Crimson Dynamo recovers and grabs Cap, and the masked assailant reveals himself as Nick Fury.
NOTE: 1st issue to feature dual numbering; one for the current volume, another if the series hadn't been rebooted. This continues until Cap #50, '02. The President ordered Fury to get a SHIELD locator implant shortly after Cap #27, '00; this was Bill Clinton at the time and likely happened between FF #27, '00 & IF/W #3, '01.

CAPTAIN AMERICA #43 [#510] (July 2001)

"Candor" (22 pages)

CREDITS: Dan Jurgens (writer), Dave Ross (pencils), Bob Layton (inks), Todd Klein (letters), Avalon Studios' Bart (colors), Andrew Lis (asst editor), Bobbie Chase (editor)
FEATURE CHARACTER: Captain America
GUEST STAR: Nick Fury (next in IM #36, '01)
SUPPORTING CAST: Connie Ferrari
VILLAINS: Answer, Crimson Dynamo (both last app), Khamiskan soldiers
OTHER CHARACTERS: Khamiskan family (father, mother, Anton & Dimitri, last app), New York policeman
LOCATIONS/ITEMS: Khamiskan, New York police station; SHIELD mind-control drugs & antidote, Crimson Dynamo's armor w/ lasers & targeting device, Khamiskan father's bow & arrow, Khamiskan soldiers' guns, nuclear missile & launch control, Answer's manacles
SYNOPSIS: Answer outlines his plan for world domination in the aftermath of the fall of the Soviet Union as Captain America is bound between two tractors. Answer injects Nick Fury with an antidote to the mind-control drugs he administered so Fury can watch in torment as Cap is pulled apart by the tractors. The father of the Khamiskan family Cap helped fires an arrow that severs one of the ropes binding Cap. One of the tractors drags Cap, but he breaks free. Liberated from mind control, Fury joins Cap in fighting Crimson Dynamo, Answer and the Khamiskan soldiers with whom they are allied. Cap prevents Answer from launching a nuclear missile at America and arrests the deranged ex-SHIELD operative. In custody in a New York police station, David Ferrari is reunited with his sister, Connie, who refuses to believe his involvement in conspiracy, terrorism, murder and treason. She lashes out at Cap, and when Cap tries to get Connie to trust him, she realizes that he is Steve Rogers.

CAPTAIN AMERICA #44 [#511] (August 2001)

"Conclusions" (22 pages)

CREDITS: Dan Jurgens (writer, pencils), Bob Layton (inks), Todd Klein (letters), Avalon Studios' Bart (colors), Andrew Lis (asst editor), Bobbie Chase (editor)
FEATURE CHARACTER: Captain America (next IM #39, '01 fb, Tb #50, '01, Def #1, '01, InfA #1, '02, Tb #51-52, '01, Av #41-44, '01, IM #42, '01, Tigra #1, '02, IM Ann, '01, Av:UI #1, '01)
SUPPORTING CAST: Connie Ferrari
VILLAINS: Taskmaster (last in W #168, '01, next in Task #1, '02) & 3 of his men (disguised as police)
OTHER CHARACTERS: New York police (Hal named), Homer (fine payer)
LOCATIONS/ITEMS: New York inc Brooklyn Bridge, East River & police station, Steve's Brooklyn apartment; Cap's photonic shield, Connie's "Dear John" letter, Taskmaster's airship w/cables, bow w/concussion & shock arrows, bomb, neural dart pistol & shield, Taskmaster's men's guns
SYNOPSIS: Shocked and upset about her boyfriend's true identity, a brokenhearted Connie Ferrari questions Captain America's honesty and doubts she can have a meaningful relationship with a living legend who harbors secrets. Suddenly, three police officers attack Cap and Connie, and an airship blasts open the side of the police station. Cables from the craft grab Cap and Connie, and Cap uses his shield to free his girlfriend but she is whisked away before he can retrieve it. Connie picks up the shield and realizes that she can't be a burden to a man whose destiny denies him a normal life. Cap's abductor reveals himself as Taskmaster, who aims to defeat the Avengers by overcoming them one by one, starting with Cap. On the Brooklyn Bridge, Taskmaster uses his arsenal of weapons against Cap, who surprises his foe by using his old photonic shield to defend himself. Taskmaster escapes when they plunge into the East River. Steve Rogers returns to his apartment, where he finds his shield and a "Dear John" letter from Connie.

CAPTAIN AMERICA #45 [#512] (September 2001)

"America Lost Part I of IV" (22 pages)

CREDITS: Dan Jurgens (writer, pencils), Bob Layton (inks), Todd Klein (letters), Avalon Studios' Bart (colors), Andrew Lis (asst editor), Bobbie Chase (editor)
FEATURE CHARACTER: Captain America (only in fb, also in symbolic image)
GUEST STARS: Iron Man (only in fb, last in Av:UI #1, '01), Nick Fury (resumes SHIELD Directorship, also in fb, last in IM #36, '01, chr last in Cap #48, '01 fb), Dum Dum Dugan (last in Tb #52, '01, chr last in Tb #58, '02 fb)
SUPPORTING CAST: Sharon Carter (only in fb, last in Tb #51, '01), Connie Ferrari (bts in fb, moved away, next in Cap #49, '02)
VILLAINS: Hate-Monger (also as Adam Hauser, only in fb, last in Cap #27, '00), Red Skull (bts in fb, sends

Hauser to foment hatred, last in Cap #41, '01)

OTHER CHARACTERS: Edwin Jarvis (only in fb, last in Av:UI #1, '01, next in Tb #55, '01), "Trident Construction employees" (also as lynch mob, Duke, Norm & Stevie named, see NOTE), CNN reporter, Mexican schoolteachers

LOCATIONS/ITEMS: Louisiana coastal town inc motel & Trident Construction building (see NOTE), Avengers Mansion inc computer room & training room (all in fb), North Sea island, SHIELD base inc elevator; Avengers training robots, lynch mob's hatchet & masks, Adam Hauser's note (all in fb), flag-draped casket, SHIELD hovercar

FLASHBACK: In Louisiana, labor union representative Adam Hauser incites a group of striking workers to target illegal aliens hired to take their places by their employer. At Avengers Mansion, Nick Fury tells Captain America that Connie Ferrari has moved away. Sharon Carter arrives, upset that Fury has resumed his position as SHIELD Director, and the three turn their attention to finding the Helicarrier stolen by Red Skull. That night, Hauser works the construction laborers into a hate-fueled frenzy and they brutally murder numerous Mexicans in a Louisiana motel. After Iron Man discovers that the Helicarrier is underwater in the Gulf of Mexico, he, Cap, Carter, and Fury watch a news report about the Louisiana hate crime. They learn that the victims were actually visiting Mexican teachers and that the attackers are from various professions who inexplicably believe themselves to be union employees of the non-existent Trident Construction firm. Hauser sheds his disguise and reports to Red Skull, who intends to destabilize and destroy America from within through racial hatred.

SYNOPSIS: Fury and Dugan are the first to arrive at a funeral on an island in the North Sea.

NOTE: Cover-labeled "America Lost Part 1 of 4." Trident Construction is a false company that existed only in the minds of those brainwashed to think they were its employees.

CAPTAIN AMERICA #46 [#513] (October 2001)

"America Lost Part II of IV" (22 pages)

CREDITS: Dan Jurgens (writer, pencils), Bob Layton (inks), Todd Klein (letters), Avalon Studios' Bart (colors), Andrew Lis (asst editor), Bobbie Chase (editor)
FEATURE CHARACTER: Captain America (only in fb, also in symbolic image)
GUEST STARS: Avengers: Scarlet Witch (off-panel), Thor, Vision, Wasp (all last in Av:UI #1, '01), Jack of Hearts (off-panel), Triathlon (Delroy Garrett, Jr., enhanced athlete), Quicksilver (prev 3 last in Av #44, '01), Iron Man (also in fb, last in Av:UI #1, '01, chr last in Cap #47, '01 fb), Warbird (last in IM Ann, '01); Nick Fury (also in fb), Dum Dum Dugan
SUPPORTING CAST: Sharon Carter (also in fb, last in Tb #51, '01, chr last in Cap #48, '01 fb)
VILLAINS: Hate-Monger (as Adam Hauser), Red Skull & his men (all in fb)

OTHER CHARACTERS: Stonewater residents (also as lynch mob, Buzzie named); American citizens (in Red Skull's thoughts)
LOCATIONS/ITEMS: Avengers Mansion computer room, Gulf of Mexico, Stonewater, LA inc burning building (all in fb), North Sea island, Cap's scuba gear, Red Skull's stolen Helicarrier inc Red Skull's office, Red Skull's men's knives & scuba gear, SHIELD hovercar & force shield, lynch mob's board, brick, hatchet & pipe (all in fb), Avengers Quinjet, flag-draped casket

FLASHBACK: Guided by Iron Man at Avengers Mansion and monitored by Sharon Carter in a nearby SHIELD hovercar, Captain America locates and approaches the stolen Helicarrier, now adapted to underwater operations, beneath the surface of the Gulf of Mexico. After fighting off two of Red Skull's men, Cap boards the vessel. While investigating a Louisiana town that has fallen prey to more hate-fueled violence, Nick Fury finds himself in the middle of a racial conflict in which white men are goaded into attacking their black neighbors. Joined by Adam Hauser, the white men assault Fury. Inside the Helicarrier, Cap battles more of the Skull's men and reaches his arch-nemesis, who outlines his plan to destroy America before ejecting Cap from the now airborne craft.

SYNOPSIS: Sharon Carter and the Avengers join Fury and Dugan at the funeral.

NOTE: Cover-labeled "America Lost Part 2 of 4."

CAPTAIN AMERICA #47 [#514] (November 2001)

"America Lost Part III of IV" (22 pages)

CREDITS: Dan Jurgens (writer, pencils), Bob Layton (inks), Todd Klein (letters), Digital Chameleon (colors), Andrew Lis (asst editor), Bobbie Chase (editor)
FEATURE CHARACTER: Captain America (only in fb, also in symbolic image)
GUEST STARS: Avengers: Iron Man (also in fb before Cap #46, '01), Jack of Hearts, Quicksilver, Scarlet Witch, Thor, Triathlon, Vision, Warbird, Wasp; Falcon (last in Cap #34, '00), Sub-Mariner (also in fb, last in Def #7, '01, chr last in Cap #48, '01 fb), Nick Fury (also in fb), Dum Dum Dugan
SUPPORTING CAST: Sharon Carter (also in fb)
VILLAINS: Hate-Monger (also as Adam Hauser), Red Skull & his men (all in fb)
OTHER CHARACTERS: Louisiana residents

LOCATIONS/ITEMS: Gulf of Mexico, Louisiana (all in fb), North Sea island; Red Skull's stolen Helicarrier inc blaster & cannons, Red Skull's men's blasters, SHIELD hovercar, SHIELD hovercraft (all in fb), flag-draped casket

FLASHBACK: Sharon Carter attempts to save the plummeting Captain America with her SHIELD hovercar, but Red Skull uses the Helicarrier's cannons to blast the two into the Gulf of Mexico. Summoned to the scene by Iron Man, Namor the Sub-Mariner rescues Cap and Carter, and Cap convinces Namor to join them in stopping the Skull. Meanwhile, Adam Hauser assumes a variety of forms to spread his message of hate to hundreds of Louisianans of all races. He has them board the Helicarrier, where Red Skull forces the captive Nick Fury to watch his evil scheme unfold. Cap, Sharon, and Namor raid the Helicarrier, and as they fight Red Skull's men, Hauser stands revealed as the Hate-Monger.

SYNOPSIS: Joined by Falcon and Sub-Mariner, attendees of the funeral discuss Cap's mission against Hate-Monger and Red Skull.
NOTE: Cover-labeled "America Lost Part 3 of 4." Secondary issue number erroneously listed as #515 on cover.

CAPTAIN AMERICA #48 [#515] (December 2001)

"America Lost Part IV of IV" (22 pages)

CREDITS: Dan Jurgens (writer, pencils), Bob Layton (inks), Todd Klein (letters), Avalon Studios (colors), Andrew Lis (asst editor), Bobbie Chase (editor)
FEATURE CHARACTER: Captain America (also in symbolic image & fb, next in Tb #53-54, '01, Tb #57, '01, bts in Tb #58, '02, Cap Ann, '01)
GUEST STARS: Avengers: Jack of Hearts, Quicksilver, Thor, Triathlon, Vision, Warbird, Wasp (all next in Tb #57, '01), Iron Man (next in IM #46, '01), Scarlet Witch (next in Tb #55, '01); Sub-Mariner (also in fb before Cap #47, '01, next in Tb #57, '01), Nick Fury (also in fb before Cap #45, '01, next in PPSM #40, '02), Dum Dum Dugan (next in Tb #61, '02), Falcon
SUPPORTING CAST: Sharon Carter (also in fb between Cap #47, '01 fb & Cap #46, '01)
VILLAINS: Hate-Monger (only in fb, dissipates, last app), Red Skull (also in Cap's thoughts, also in fb, bts, in SHIELD custody, next in Cap #50/6, '02) & his men (only in fb)
OTHER CHARACTERS: Alicia Masters (blind sculptress, bts, creates Bucky statue, last in Def #5, '01, next in FF #509, '04), Rebecca Proctor (Bucky Barnes' sister, last in MHol '91/5, last app), Louisiana residents (in fb); Crossbones, Machinesmith, Baron (Heinrich) Zemo, American citizens (prev 4 in Cap's thoughts), Bucky Barnes (statue)
LOCATIONS/ITEMS: North Sea island; Red Skull's men's blasters, Red Skull's stolen Helicarrier inc helicopter, hovercraft, psi-phones, psionic antennae & restrictor beam w/power source (all in fb), SHIELD transport, casket, flag
FLASHBACK: The immobilized Captain America, Sharon Carter, Nick Fury and Namor learn that Red Skull used the Cosmic Cube to revive Hate-Monger as a living manifestation of Red Skull's sinister emotions. The Skull explains that he intends to wire the hate-filled Louisianans aboard the Helicarrier to SHIELD's psionic equipment to broadcast a contagion of enmity throughout America. When Hate-Monger fails to gain mental control over Cap, he possesses Namor and orders him to attack the star-spangled Avenger. As Cap tries to snap Sub-Mariner out of his enforced rage, Fury and Carter are freed from the Helicarrier's restrictor beam and fight Red Skull's men. Wearing psi-phones, the Louisianans surround Cap, who frees them from Hate-Monger's influence with a stirring speech about diversity and freedom. The resulting mental feedback destroys Hate-Monger and Cap defeats the Skull.
SYNOPSIS: Captain America arrives at the funeral with Rebecca Proctor, Bucky Barnes's sister. Cap officiates a funeral for Bucky and unveils a statue of his former partner, which everyone present salutes.
NOTE: Cover-labeled "America Lost Part 4 of 4." Cap #11, '05 reveals Bucky Barnes is still alive.

CAPTAIN AMERICA ANNUAL 2001 (2001)

"Denial" (39 pages)

CREDITS: Dan Jurgens (writer), Lee Molder (pencils pgs 1-4, 17, 27 & 38-39), Darryl Banks (pgs 5-16), Ignacio Calero (pencils pgs 18-26 & 28-37), Walden Wong (inks pgs 1-4, 17, 27 & 38-39), Sandu Florea (inks pgs 5-16), Joe Weems, Marco Galli, Pierre-Andre Dery (inks pgs 18-26 & 28-37), Chris Eliopoulos (letters), Chris Sotomayor (colors), Andrew Lis (asst editor), Bobbie Chase (exec editor)
FEATURE CHARACTER: Captain America (also in own thoughts & fb between Cap:Re #2, '09 & ToS #75/2, '66 fb; next in Cap #49, '01)
GUEST STARS: Invaders: Human Torch (Jim Hammond), Toro (both in fb between AWC #65/2, '90 fb & Cap #25, '07 fb), Sub-Mariner (in fb between Order #7, '08 fb & Cap #3, '05 fb)
SUPPORTING CAST: Bucky (in fb between CapC #42/4, '44 & Cap #25, '07 fb)
VILLAINS: Red Skull (in fb between Cap:Re #2, '09 & Cap #37, '08 fb), Warrior Woman (Julia Lohmer, super-Nazi, in fb between BP #21, '06 fb & Inv #2, '10 fb), Nazi sailors (Oscar & Victor named) & soldiers (Bruno, Hans & Otto named), Japanese Navy (all in fb)
OTHER CHARACTERS: George W. Bush (US President, 1st, next in Av #49, '02), George Bush (bts in fb to 1st chr app before MK:Div, '92), Franklin Delano Roosevelt (in fb between CapC #40/3, '44 & Cap:Re #2, '09), Karrina Rose (Russian prisoner, also in fb), Sergei (Russian prisoner), Chelwid (Atlantean), 2 US Generals, Allied pilots & Admiral (prev 5 in fb), Secret Service (Saunders named), Dr. Erskine (in Cap's thoughts), Adolf Hitler (in Red Skull's thoughts)
LOCATIONS/ITEMS: White House inc Oval Office (also in fb), Pacific Ocean inc underwater cave w/Cap's & Karrina's cells (in fb), Karrina's Idaho farm; Allied planes & aircraft carrier, Japanese destroyer & guns, Nazi guns, cameras & sub w/electro-cables, Warrior Woman's whip, Atlantean ship, Cap's lock pick (all in fb), Cap's motorcycle
FLASHBACK: August 2, 1944: The Invaders battle the Japanese Navy in the Pacific until Sub-Mariner is electrocuted by Red Skull's submarine. Cap rescues Namor, but is captured himself. As Warrior Woman begins to torture Cap for the location of Atlantis, the Invaders worry that Cap has drowned. Cap awakes in a cavern, where Red Skull plans to film Cap's death and release the footage as propaganda. Warrior Woman begins beating Cap, but when he doesn't make a sound the Skull decides to wait until Cap gives a better show for the cameras. Red Skull's men throw Cap into a cell, where he witnesses Nazis murder Sergei, a Russian prisoner. Cap befriends Karrina Rose, a fellow prisoner and Sergei's wife. At the White House, in case of Captain America's death, two US Generals detail a plan to deny Cap's demise. President Roosevelt realizes that if Cap died, the German's war effort would be revived and the tide could turn against the Allies. The Invaders learn of the Skull's sub's location. Cap and Karrina free themselves and battle their captors. Karrina is captured and Cap surrenders, but the Invaders arrive and drive Red Skull off. Cap offers Karrina a life in America.

SYNOPSIS: Captain America meets with President George Bush, who thanks Cap for his service, and for saving his father's life; if the Invaders hadn't been active in the Pacific in August, 1944, his father wouldn't have been rescued after being shot down. Cap requests the President send a thank you letter to Karrina Rose, which he does.

NOTE: President Truman later denied Cap's death, as seen in WI #4, '77.

CAPTAIN AMERICA #49 [#516] (January 2002)

"Closure" (22 pages)

CREDITS: Dan Jurgens (writer), Juan Bobilio (pencils), Marcelo Sosa (inks), Todd Klein (letters), Avalon Studios' Edgar Tadeo (colors), Andrew Lis (asst editor), Bobbie Chase (editor)
FEATURE CHARACTER: Captain America
GUEST STAR: Sam Wilson
SUPPORTING CAST: Sharon Carter (last in Tb #53, '01), Connie Ferrari (last bts in Cap #45, '01, last app)
VILLAINS: Sumo warriors
OTHER CHARACTERS: Tango Leader (SHIELD agent, voice only), birds, fish
LOCATIONS/ITEMS: Idaho lake, Connie's new Ohio home, New York inc Sumo warriors' base; Avengers Quinjet, Sumo warriors' katanas & laptop w/computer virus, Sharon's explosives, night vision goggles, stealth suit & transceiver, SHIELD aircraft
SYNOPSIS: While fishing on an Idaho lake, Sam Wilson convinces Steve Rogers that he should seek out and resolve matters with Connie Ferrari. Steve finds Connie at her new home in Ohio and they discuss his secret identity as Captain America and what it means for his personal goals and relationships. Realizing who he is and what he really wants, Steve leaves Connie and returns to New York, where as Captain America he finds Sharon Carter in the middle of a covert SHIELD mission to deactivate a computer virus. Cap professes his love and he and Sharon resume their romance.

CAPTAIN AMERICA #50 [#517] (February 2002)

"Silent Night, Silent Morning" (22 pages)

CREDITS: Dan Jurgens (writer, pencils), Bob Layton (inks), Todd Klein (letters), Avalon Studios (colors), Andrew Lis (editor), Gene Ha (c art)
FEATURE CHARACTER: Captain America
VILLAINS: Absorbing Man (last in W #164, '01), Titania (also in photo, last in Thor #27, '00, next in Thor #55, '02)
OTHER CHARACTERS: Lloyd Grunnell (laid off Lennco employee), his wife, son & daughter (prev 3 also in Lloyd's thoughts) (all also in photo), John Sullivan (U-Bank president) (all only app), bell-ringer Santa, Lennco employees, cameraman, holiday shoppers, police, bystanders
LOCATIONS/ITEMS: Lennco offices, Grunnell home, Titania's flophouse, toy store, U-Bank; copy of Daily Bugle, Grunnell family Christmas tree, Titania's necklace w/Creel's note, Lloyd's U-Bank reward check for $20,000
SYNOPSIS: Lennco employee Lloyd Grunnell is laid off from his job on Christmas Eve. He puts on a cheerful face for his children, but privately worries with his wife over how they will pay the bills. With the last of his money he heads to a toy store to buy presents, but a battle erupts between Captain America and Absorbing Man in a bank next door, which spills into the toy store. Lloyd helps Cap by distracting Absorbing Man. The news broadcasts Lloyd's involvement in the fight. As Absorbing Man is arrested, the villain explains he was stealing to get Titania a present. The bank gives Lloyd a reward check for twenty thousand dollars, which Lloyd uses to buy presents for his family. On Christmas morning, Cap leaves a present with a note from Absorbing Man for Titania.
NOTE: Secondary issue number erroneously listed as #518 on cover. This issue is part of 'Nuff Said month, a line-wide stunt where most of Marvel's books were published without dialogue of any kind. Followed by an excerpt of Dan Jurgens' script (4 pages), and the rest was available at the time on Marvel.com.

2ND STORY: "Keep in Mind" (8 pages)
CREDITS: Kathryn Kuder (writer), Stuart Immonen (art, colors), Todd Klein (letters), Andrew Lis (editor)
FEATURE CHARACTER: Steve Rogers (also as Captain America in photo & own thoughts)
VILLAINS: German soldiers (in fb)
OTHER CHARACTERS: Mr. Scott (WWII US Reconnaissance plane co-pilot, also in photo & fb, only app), Mrs. Watt (school teacher) & her students, French Resistance fighter (in fb), US soldiers (in photo & fb), French airport personnel, tourists
LOCATIONS/ITEMS: East Park public school, France inc airport, Normandy beach, cemetery, rural house inc cellar (in fb), turrets (also in fb); US reconnaissance plane (destroyed in fb), German tanks (in fb)
FLASHBACK: October 9, 1944: A US Reconnaissance plane is shot down over France; Scott is the only one to parachute to safety. When he spots German tanks advancing he flees in the opposite direction and hides in a rural farmhouse's cellar. A week later, a French Resistance fighter finds him after the battle has ended.
SYNOPSIS: Steve Rogers travels to France to pay his respects at Normany beach and a local cemetery. Meanwhile, WWII veteran Mr. Scott tells Mrs. Watt's classroom what his experience was during the war.

3RD STORY: "To The Core" (14 pages)
CREDITS: Dan Jurgens (writer, pencils pgs 1-3, 5, 7, 9, 11 & 13-14), John Romita (pencils pg 4), Ron Frenz (pencils pg 6), Rick Veitch (pencils pg 8), Mike Zeck (pencils pg 12), Bob Layton (inks pgs 1-3, 5, 7, 9, 11 & 13-14), Bruce Timm (inks pgs 4 & 6), Tom Palmer (inks pg 8), Al Gordon

inks pg 12), Sal Buscema (art pg 10), Todd Klein (letters), Avalon Studios' Edgar Tadeo (colors), Andrew Lis, Bobbie Chase (editors)

FEATURE CHARACTER: Captain America (also in hologram & as Nomad, next in SM:SweetC, '02)

SUPPORTING CAST: Sharon Carter (also in hologram)

OTHER CHARACTERS: Bucky, Cobra, Diamondback, Dragon Man, Eel, Falcon, Red Skull, Redwing, Super-Adaptoid, Viper, Warlord Krang, Roscoe (as Captain America), Peggy Carter, Connie Ferrari, Bernie Rosenthal (all in holograms)

LOCATIONS/ITEMS: Maine inc SHIELD holographic facility

SYNOPSIS: Captain America meets with Sharon Carter at a SHIELD holographic facility and uses the holograms to illustrate his love for her. Sharon says she's hesitant to commit to a relationship and asks Steve to give her time to think things over. They share a kiss for old time's sake.

4TH STORY: "Relics" (15 pages)

CREDITS: Brian David-Marshall (writer), Igor Kordey (art), Todd Klein (letters), Avalon Studios (colors), Andrew Lis (editor)

FEATURE CHARACTER: Captain America (next in Av #45-46, '01, Av #48, 50 & 52-54, Cap:DMR #1-3, Av #55, all '02, JLA/Av #1-4, '03-04, Av #56 fb, Order #2-3 & 5-6, BP #41-42, Tigra #4 fb, all '02, Alias #1 & 5, '01-02, CitV #3, Tigra #4, Dp #69, all '02, Av #56-61, '02-03, XX #11, 13 fb & 18, '02, Cap:WPG #1-4, MDS #2/2, ASM #50, all '03, Cap #2, '02, Cap #1, '02)

GUEST STAR: Nick Fury (last in PPSM #41, '02)

SUPPORTING CAST: Sharon Carter (voice only)

VILLAINS: Red Skull cultists (defected Nazi scientists, also in pfb, all die)

OTHER CHARACTERS: SHIELD agents, Saturday Night Live actors (on TV as Captain America, Ghost Rider, Punisher & Wolverine), US soldiers (in fb), Steve's cat (only app)

LOCATIONS/ITEMS: Steve's Brooklyn apartment, Chancey, NJ inc condemned buildings & church; Cap's autographed Iron Man helmet, Stars & Stripes briefcase & motorcycle, SHIELD helicopter, nuclear bomb

FLASHBACKS: Following WWII's end, a group of Nazi scientists are allowed to defect and secretly move to America in exchange for information on a nuclear bomb Hitler was developing. Years later the American government forces the defectors and their families from the town to make way for a planned dam that never materialized. Disenchanted with America, the scientists hold secret meetings, planning to strike out against America. They eventually obtain a nuclear device (p).

SYNOPSIS: Steve receives a phone call from Sharon asking for time alone. Disheartened, Steve is prepared to call it a night but he receives a message on his old Stars & Stripes hotline that warns him of a nuclear bomb in New Jersey. He races to the given address only for a group of elderly Nazis to ambush and trap him. They plan to nuke New Jersey in a suicide bombing for retaliation against how the American government treated them. Cap frees himself and separates the nuclear components from the bomb. The bomb goes off, destroying the town but not unleashing the full nuclear payload. Nick Fury and SHIELD later perform clean up, but Captain America is nowhere to be found.

5TH STORY: "A Moment of Silence" (8 pages)

CREDITS: Jennifer Van Meter (writer), Brian Hurtt (pencils), Jim Mahfood (inks), Todd Klein (letters), Avalon Studios (colors), Andrew Lis (editor)

FEATURE CHARACTER: Captain America (in photos & as toy)

OTHER CHARACTERS: Ranji (immigrant schoolboy & Captain America fan, only app), his classmates (Brendan, George, Kim, Lisa, Luis, Mark, Missy, Scott, Shawna & Smita named) & mother, Principal Harris, teachers, reporter (voice only); Spider-Man (in photo)

LOCATIONS/ITEMS: School inc playground, Ranji's home; Ranji's Captain America newspaper clippings

SYNOPSIS: Schoolchildren play heroes and villains at recess. Ranji wants to play as Captain America, but usually ends up as a villain. After recess it's announced that Cap has died. The other children blame and attack Ranji for being different. A devastated Ranji goes home where his room is covered with Cap images, including a news clipping showing Cap rescuing Ranji.

6TH STORY: "Stars and Stripes Forever" (8 pages)

CREDITS: Evan Dorkin (writer), Kevin Maguire (art), Todd Klein (letters), Avalon Studios (colors), Andrew Lis (editor)

FEATURE CHARACTER: Captain America (in photos & as toys & statues)

GUEST STARS: Avengers: Iron Man, Jack of Hearts, Quicksilver, Scarlet Witch, Wasp (as Janet Van Dyne), Yellowjacket (as Hank Pym) (all last in Tb #57, '01, last bts in Tb #58, '02, next in Av #45, '01), Black Knight, Hercules, Stingray (prev 3 last in Tb #57, '01, last bts in Tb #58, '02, next in Av #46, '01), Thor (last in SM:SweetC, '02, next in Av #45, '01), Vision (last in Tb #57, '01, last bts in SM:SweetC, '02, next in Av #45, '01); Defenders: Dr. Strange, Hulk, Silver Surfer, Sub-Mariner (prev 4 between Def #11-12, '02), Hellcat, Nighthawk, Valkyrie (prev 3 last in Def #11, '02, next in Def #12/2, '02); Fantastic Four: Human Torch, Mr. Fantastic, Thing (prev 3 last in SM:SweetC, '02, chr next in Venom #11, '04, next in Av #51, '02 fb), Invisible Woman (last in Def #10, '01, chr next in Venom #11, '04, next bts in Av #52, '02, next in DD #34, '02); X-Men: Beast (last in G&B #1, '01, chr next in W #174, '02 fb, next bts in W #173, '02, next in XX #1, '01), Cyclops (as Scott Summers, last in UXM #394, '01, next in XFor #116, '01), Nightcrawler (last in G&B #1, '01, next in W #173, '02), Storm (last in XMU #30/2, '01, chr last in XX #2, '01 fb, next in XX #1, '01), Wolverine (last in Dp #61, '02, last bts in SM:SweetC, '02, chr next in W #175/3, '02, next in W #170, '02); Black Panther (last in Dp #61, '02, next in JLA/Av #2, '03), Black Widow (last in Tb #57, '01, last bts in Tb #58, '02, next in MKn #1, '02), Daredevil (last in PPSM #41, '02, next in SM/DD #1, '02), Doc Samson (last in Tb #58, '02, next in Hulk:G #1, '03), Hawkeye (last in SM:SweetC, '02, next in Tb #65, '02), Nomad (last in Tb #50, '01, next in Inv #2, '04 fb), She-Hulk (last in Thing/SH, '02, next in Av #46, '01), Spider-Man (last in PPSM #43, '02, next in SM/DD #1, '02), Union Jack (last in Tb #57, '01, next in Av #82, '04), USAgent (last in Tb #57, '01, last bts in Tb #58, '02, next in Av #56, '02), Dum Dum Dugan (last in Tb #61, '02, next in Elektra #2, '01), Nick Fury (chr next in Venom #12, '04, next in Elektra #1, '01), Rick Jones (last in InfA #6, '02, next in CM #32, '02), Sam Wilson (next as Falcon in Av #57, '02)

SUPPORTING CAST: Sharon Carter (next bts in Elektra #2, '01, next in W/Cap #1, '04),

VILLAINS: Absorbing Man (next in Thor #55, '02), Batroc (last in Cap #41, '01, next in Dline #2, '02), Dr. Doom (last in FF #54, '02, next in JLA/Av #1, '03), King Cobra (as Klaus Vorhees, last in Cap #15, '99, next in SM:GetK #1, '02), Mad Thinker (last in FF #23, '99, next in Cap #31, '04) & his Awesome Android (last in FF #44, '01, next in SH #2, '04), Mr. Hyde (last in TWoS #13, '02, next in DD #35, '02), MODOK (last in Def #10, '01, next in SH #1, '04), Red Skull (last bts in Cap #48, '01, next in Av #61, '02), Whirlwind (as David Cannon, last in TWoS #13, '02, next in TWoS #19, '02), Arnim Zola (last in W #139, '99, next in Cap #31, '04) & his genetic creations, AIM agents, Hydra agents, prison inmates

OTHER CHARACTERS: G.W. Bridge (last in Tb #56, '02, next in Dp #69, '02), Henry Gyrich (last in Cable #95, '01, next in BP #41, '02), J. Jonah Jameson (last in SM:SweetC, '02, next in DD #34, '02), Edwin Jarvis (last in Tb #57, '01, next in Av #45, '01), Jasper Sitwell (last in IM #36, '01 fb, next in SecWar #1, '04), SHIELD agents, Whirlwind's friend, bar patrons, Cap memorabilia collector, funeral attendees, homeless man, police officer, US Military veterans, UK citizens, youth

LOCATIONS/ITEMS: Absorbing Man's flophouse, AIM base, Arlington National Cemetery, Atlantis, Avengers Mansion, Batroc's apartment, Daily Bugle, Hydra base, Latveria, Mad Thinker's lab, Red Skull's prison cell, Stark Enterprises, Pier 4, Wakanda, Washington, DC inc. Washington Monument, Zola's lab, bar, prison labor camp; Cap's flag-draped casket

SYNOPSIS: Heroes, villains and people from the across the globe share their thoughts on Captain America's death. Later at Cap's funeral, Falcon delivers a speech mourning the loss of his friend, with many of Earth's heroes in attendance.

NOTE: Followed by pin-up (1 page) of Captain America by Daniel Zezelj & a preview of Cap:DMR #1, '02 (4 pages). Series is replaced for three month with Cap:DMR #1-3, '02, and series continues in Cap #1, '02. Cap shows up injured but alive in Av #45, '01.

CAPTAIN AMERICA #1 [#518] (June 2002)

"Enemy, Chapter One: Dust" (36 pages)

CREDITS: John Ney Rieber (writer), John Cassaday (art), Wes Abbott, Richard Starkings & Comicraft's Wes Abbott (letters), Dave Stewart (colors), Kelly Lamy (assoc editor), Nanci Dakesian (managing editor), Stuart Moore (editor)

FEATURE CHARACTER: Captain America (also in fb1 between ASM #36, '01 & X #111, '01 fb, in fb2 between Cap #39, '01 & ASM #36, '01)

GUEST STAR: Nick Fury (also in fb1 between Cap #37, '01 & W #163, '01; last in Call #4, chr last in Cap #2, '02, next in Cap #4, '02)

VILLAINS: Faysal al-Tariq (terrorist, bts, laced Centerville w/landmines, chr last in Cap #2, '02 fb), al-Qaeda (inc Osama bin Laden, in fb1)

OTHER CHARACTERS: American Airlines Flight 11 passengers, 9/11 relief workers & victims (corpses), Samir (bodega owner), Jenny's (mentioned) grieving father & his friends (all in fb1), bystanders (in fb2), Jack (Centerville convenience owner), Johnny (Jack's son) (both die), Sam (convenience store customer), SHIELD helicopter crewman

LOCATIONS/ITEMS: al-Qaeda camp, New York (also in fb2) inc Ground Zero, Sneaky Pete's (bar), & Jordun Market (all in fb1); Centerville (largely destroyed) inc Jack's convenience store; American Airlines Flight 11, al-Qaeda box-cutter & rifles, stretchers, grieving father's pocketknife (all in fb1), al-Tariq's plane & parachute-equipped landmines, SHIELD helicopter, CATtag (Casualty Awareness Tracking tags)

FLASHBACKS: 9/11: Terrorists overtake American Airlines Flight 11. Twenty minutes later, al-Qaeda celebrates. Soon after, Steve Rogers aids relief workers in searching the rubble of the Twin Towers for survivors. He finds a corpse and helps a relief worker load the body onto a stretcher. Nick Fury arrives to recruit Steve for a mission, but Steve angrily refuses. On his way home, Steve, as Captain America, saves a Middle Eastern bodega owner from a man whose daughter was killed in the attacks. Cap persuades the attacker to save his anger for the enemy, not a scapegoat (1). 9/10: Steve jogs contentedly through New York (2).

SYNOPSIS: Centerville is laced with parachuted landmines, killing a boy and his father. Fury flies Cap to Centerville, giving him a device that will notify Fury if Cap is killed and signal Delta Force deployment. Cap leaves the device behind and drops into Centerville from the SHIELD helicopter. Cap surveys the destroyed town before charging in.

NOTE: Includes credits page (1 page) & dedication page (1 page) featuring dedications by John Ney Rieber & John Cassaday. John Cassaday donated all proceeds from the sale of original art from this issue to the families of NYC firefighters lost responding on 9/11 from Engine 40/Ladder 35. 1st issue published in the Marvel Knights imprint. John Cassaday's style of rendering the scale-mail portion of Cap's uniform that debuts this issue has since become the design standard.

CAPTAIN AMERICA #2 [#519] (July 2002)

"Enemy, Chapter Two: One Nation" (23 pages)

CREDITS: John Ney Rieber (writer), John Cassaday (art), Richard Starkings & Comicraft's Wes Abbott (letters), Dave Stewart (colors), Kelly Lamy (assoc editor), Nanci Dakesian (managing editor), Stuart Moore (editor)

FEATURE CHARACTER: Captain America (also in fb2 between SR:SSol #1, '10 fb & BP #30, '01 fb; also in Cap #1, '02)

GUEST STAR: Nick Fury (last in Call #4, '03, chr next in Cap #1, '02, next in Cap #4, '02)

VILLAINS: Faysal al-Tariq (1st, voice only, also in fb1 between Cap #6, '02 fb & bts in Cap #1, '02) & his men (some also in fb1) inc al-Tariq's 4 "shepherds" (children suicide bombers)

OTHER CHARACTERS: Jessica Seldon (TV reporter, 1st, also in fb1), Centerville citizens (in fb1, inc minister), civilians (corpses), Allied soldiers (both in fb2), Jessica's cameraman & sound engineer, 5 TV home viewers

LOCATIONS/ITEMS: Jessica's house (in fb1), Centerville inc church (in fb1) & cemetery, London (in fb2); Cap's original steel shield (in fb2), tripwire bombs (also in fb1, some destroyed), parachute-equipped landmines, terrorists' guns (both also in fb1) inc shotgun w/attached garrote & box-cutter (in fb1), SHIELD helicopter, shepherds' hatchets & bombs

FLASHBACKS: A masked assailant abducts TV reporter Jessica Seldon from her home while al-Tariq and his men take hostages in a Centerville church (1). WWII: Cap finds the bodies of a civilian couple in London. A soldier tells Cap to get used to the sight of death (2).

SYNOPSIS: En route, Fury briefs Captain America on Centerville, telling Cap that the mines will self-destruct in two hours and that al-Tariq has demanded Cap's presence. Jessica Seldon is forced at gunpoint to deliver a TV broadcast on behalf of the terrorists. Cap moves through the town, evading mines and subduing a platoon of terrorists. As the nation watches Jessica's broadcast, she notices the sound of gunfire and

reports Cap's arrival. Cap continues fighting his way through the terrorists and deactivating as many mines as he can. When Cap enters a cemetery, a quartet of hooded, armed children ambush him. They're each wearing a speaker through which al-Tariq taunts him.
NOTE: Story overlaps with Cap #1, '02.

2ND STORY: "The Call of Duty" (5 pages)
NOTE: Part 2 of a 5-part preview of CallD:B #1, '02, each part of which was printed in five of Marvel's July 2002 releases. Four pages of the issue were condensed into two pages for the preview. Also printed in MKnDS #2, MManga #2, Order #4, and XX #13, all '02.

CAPTAIN AMERICA #3 [#520] (August 2002)

"Enemy, Chapter Three: Soft Targets" (22 pages)

CREDITS: John Ney Rieber (writer), John Cassaday (art), Richard Starkings & Comicraft's Wes Abbott (letters), Dave Stewart (colors), Kelly Lamy (assoc editor), Nanci Dakesian (managing editor), Stuart Moore (editor)
FEATURE CHARACTER: Captain America (also bts in rfb)
VILLAINS: Faysal al-Tariq (seemingly dies, next bts in Cap #5, '02, see NOTE) & his men inc 4 "shepherds" (3 die)
OTHER CHARACTERS: Jessica Seldon, Centerville citizens (inc minister, 3 as corpses)
LOCATIONS/ITEMS: Centerville (also in rfb) inc church & cemetery; terrorists' guns & rocket launchers, tripwire bombs, shepherds' hatchets, knives, grenades, prosthetic limbs & CATtags, al-Tariq's gun, detonator & CATtag
FLASHBACK: Cap surveys the destroyed Centerville (Cap #2, '02).
SYNOPSIS: Al-Tariq tells his prisoners that he has targeted them because many of them work for an explosives manufacturer outside town. Captain America fights off al-Tariq's "shepherds," and discovers that all of them wear prosthetic limbs to replace those lost in landmine explosions. Cap saves one of the four when another blows himself and the other two up in a suicide run to kill Cap. Cap finds a CATtag like the one Fury tried to give him on one of the other boys. As Jessica continues her gunpoint broadcast, Cap confronts al-Tariq, whom he is forced to kill before he can detonate the bombs. Cap spots another CATtag on al-Tariq's neck. After announcing the danger has passed, Cap speaks to her camera, saying he has had enough of nations being blamed for the actions of an individual. Taking off his mask, Cap reveals his face to the nation and takes personal responsibility for killing al-Tariq.
NOTE: Cap #6, '02 reveals CATtags transfer consciousness from one body to another; al-Tariq uses this to survive his death.

CAPTAIN AMERICA #4 [#521] (September 2002)

(22 pages)

CREDITS: John Ney Rieber (writer), John Cassaday (art), Richard Starkings & Comicraft's Wes Abbott (letters), Dave Stewart (colors), Kelly Lamy (assoc editor), Nanci Dakesian (managing editor), Stuart Moore, Joe Quesada (editors)
FEATURE CHARACTER: Captain America (also in pfb)
GUEST STAR: Nick Fury (last in Cap #1, '02)
VILLAINS: Faysal al-Tariq's men (disguised as soldiers)
OTHER CHARACTERS: Jessica Seldon (last app), Jessica's cameraman & sound engineer (all off-panel in pfb), Secretary Dahl, 6 government officials, security troops (inc a lieutenant, Simic named); fireworks spectators (Cat, Joel & their father named); Sharon Carter & her 2 sons (both in Cap's daydream)
LOCATIONS/ITEMS: Virginia inc underground bunker & Great Falls Park, Aqueduct Dam suburban house (in Cap's daydream); security troops' guns, al-Tariq's CATtag, Cap's motorcycle (destroyed), terrorists' guns & grenade launchers
FLASHBACK: Broadcasting from Centerville, an unmasked Cap reveals his real name and accepts full responsibility for al-Tariq's death (p).
SYNOPSIS: Nick Fury and a room full of government officials watch Captain America's televised divulging of his dual identity. Secretary Dahl, one of the officials, thinks this has compromised Cap's usefulness, but Fury dismisses his concerns. Cap arrives, and Fury lets him in despite Dahl ordering him to keep Cap out. Cap demands to know how al-Tariq's men had CATtags. Fury gives him an address despite Dahl's national security protests. Cap leaves for Dresden, Germany. As Cap rides past a crowd watching a fireworks display near the Potomac, he muses about a life with Sharon Carter. Suddenly, soldiers attack Cap and blow up his bike with a grenade launcher. Cap dives over the side of the dam, attempting to use an American flag to break his fall, but one of the soldiers fires on Cap on the way down, causing him to plummet into the river.
NOTE: Includes recap/title page (1 page). The soldiers who attack Cap are revealed as al-Tariq's men in Cap #5, '02.

CAPTAIN AMERICA #5 [#522] (October 2002)

"Warlords Part 2: Above the Law" (22 pages)

CREDITS: John Ney Rieber (writer), John Cassaday (art), Richard Starkings & Comicraft's Wes Abbott (letters), Dave Stewart (colors), Kelly Lamy (assoc editor), Nanci Dakesian (managing editor), Stuart Moore, Joe Quesada (editors)
FEATURE CHARACTER: Captain America (also in rfb)
GUEST STAR: Nick Fury (next in Cap #9, '03)
VILLAINS: Faysal al-Tariq (bts, set bomb, last in Cap #3, '02) & his men (disguised as soldiers, all die)
OTHER CHARACTERS: SHIELD agents, fireworks spectators, airline passengers, policeman, relief workers (in rfb), Dresden civilians (in fb, some as corpses, all die)

LOCATIONS/ITEMS: Potomac Great Falls w/Riverside Park, Dresden, Germany (also in fb) inc CATtag lab (destroyed); SHIELD helicopter & guns, Fury's CATtag, terrorists' guns & CATtags, al-Tariq's timed bombs
FLASHBACKS: Steve helps search for survivors at Ground Zero (Cap #1, '02). February 13-14, 1945: Allied forces fire-bomb Dresden.
SYNOPSIS: Spectators see Captain America being fired on and, en masse, begin contacting police on their cell phones. Cap emerges from the Potomac and quickly subdues the disguised terrorists save one, who accidentally shoots two of his own men. The last terrorist suddenly falls over dead as the other terrorists also die. Fury arrives with a SHIELD team. Suspecting the CATtags killed the terrorists, Cap demands to know the CATtags' full capabilities and if they can be used to kill soldiers to prevent interrogation. The next day, Steve takes a commercial airliner to Dresden and is recognized by a female passenger in the seat next to him, who mentions Steve broke her great-grandfather's jaw during the war. In Dresden, Steve arrives at the CATtag laboratory and finds it abandoned. Timed explosives detonate and the building collapses on top of Steve.
NOTE: Includes recap/title page (1 page).

CAPTAIN AMERICA #6 [#523] (December 2002)

(22 pages)

CREDITS: John Ney Rieber (writer), John Cassaday (art), Richard Starkings & Comicraft's Wes Abbott (letters), Dave Stewart (colors), Kelly Lamy (assoc editor), Nanci Dakesian (managing editor), Stuart Moore, Joe Quesada (editors)
FEATURE CHARACTER: Captain America (next in DD #65, '04 fb, bts in Hood #4, '02)
VILLAINS: Faysal al-Tariq (also in fb to 1st chr ap before Cap #2, '02 fb, last app) & his men (disguised as police)
OTHER CHARACTERS: Faysal al-Tariq's parents (both die), guerrilla soldiers (all in fb), Centerville citizens (in rfb)
LOCATIONS/ITEMS: Dresden, Germany inc CATtag lab (remains), al-Tariq's childhood home (in fb, destroyed), Centerville inc church (in rfb); Guerrilla soldier's guns (in fb), al-Tariq's CATtag, grenade & knife, al-Tariq's men's guns
FLASHBACKS: Faysal al-Tariq attacks Centerville (Cap #1, '02) and takes the citizens hostage (Cap #2, '02 fb). Guerrilla soldiers kill Faysal al-Tariq's parents and burn down his house.
SYNOPSIS: Steve Rogers braces the falling rubble with his shield. He changes into Captain America and starts digging himself out. Waiting for Cap above, a man drops a grenade at Cap. When Cap emerges, he learns the man is a revived al-Tariq. Capp attacks as al-Tariq's men surround them. Cap confronts al-Tariq over what the CATtags do, and al-Tariq sends his men away before confessing that he can transfer his consciousness into other bodies who wear the CATtags. Cap battles al-Tariq, who taunts Cap with America's history of funding the wrong sides of wars for profit. Cap defeats al-Tariq and tosses his CATtag into the building's rubble, removing al-Tariq's ability to revive himself should he die again.
NOTE: Includes recap/title page (1 page). Followed by preview for UXM #416, '02 (3 pages).

CAPTAIN AMERICA #7 [#524] (February 2003)

"The Extremists: Part 1 of 5 "Barricade"" (23 pages)

CREDITS: John Ney Reiber (writer), Trevor Hairsine (pencils), Danny Miki (inks), Richard Starkings, Comicraft's Wes Abbott (letters), Dave Stewart (colors), Nick Lowe (asst editor), Joe Quesada (editor), John Cassaday (c art)
FEATURE CHARACTER: Captain America (also in own dream & in Cap #8, '03)
VILLAINS: Inali Redpath (Sioux, Interrogator's agent & former SHIELD agent, in pfb, 1st but chr last in Cap #11, '03 fb), Haokah (Sioux god of thunder, bts, joined w/Redpath, bts in pfb, chr last off-panel in Cap #11, '03 fb), Barricade (Interrogator's agent & rogue SHIELD agent, 1st, during Cap #8, '03) & his men (see NOTE), Samantha Twotrees (Interrogator's agent & rogue SHIELD agent, 1st), Interrogator (bts, posing as Nick Fury on phone w/ Steve, chr next in Cap #14, '03 fb, next in Cap #12, '03), Red Skull (bts, last in MDS #2/2, '03, chr next in Inv #7, '05 fb, next in Av #64, '03, see NOTE), gang members (inc Bone Disciples & Hook Redz, Tony named)
OTHER CHARACTERS: Redpath clone (corpse), Dom (Brooklyn boy), concentration camp detainees (in Cap's dream)
LOCATIONS/ITEMS: Brooklyn inc Steve's Red Hook apartment & Navy Yards, Florida inc Smokehouse (Human Engineering facility, destroyed); gang members' guns, SHIELD helicopter, Cap's motorcycle, Barricade's guns, Barricade's men's guns & armor
FLASHBACK: Inali Redpath commands a tornado to destroy the Smokehouse (p).
SYNOPSIS: Gunfire wakes Steve Rogers from a dream of concentration camps, atomic bombs and being frozen in ice. He leaps out his window and breaks up a gang fight. The next day, Steve works at the Brooklyn Navy Yards and talks two street gangs into calling a truce. Nick Fury calls Steve to tell him Inali Redpath has died, so Steve travels to Florida as Captain America to investigate. SHIELD agent Samantha Twotrees who shows him Redpath's corpse, but Cap realizes the body is a clone. Twotrees takes Cap to the nearby Smokehouse, a cloning facility that was destroyed by Redpath. Cap leaves only to run into a wall of fire. Barricade introduces himself, and he and his men attack Cap.
NOTE: Cover-labeled "The Extremists Part 1 of 4." Includes recap/title page (1 page). Cap #8, '03 overlaps with this issue & reveals Twotrees is working w/Barricade. Cap #9, '03 reveals Redpath is working w/Barricade's men, that Steve's Brooklyn apartment is in Red Hook and names Haokah. Cap #10, '03 reveals Barricade's men are clones of Cap and Bucky, Cap #11, '03 that Barricade & Twotrees are rogue SHIELD agents, Cap #12, '03 that Interrogator is behind the cloning facilities, and Cap #16, '03 that Red Skull sent Interrogator to brainwash Cap.

CAPTAIN AMERICA #8 [#525] (March 2003)

(23 pages)

CREDITS: John Ney Reiber, Chuck Austen (writers), Trevor Hairsine (pencils), Danny Miki (inks), Dave Sharpe (letters), Dave Stewart (colors), Nick Lowe (asst editor), Kelly Lamy (assoc editor), Joe Quesada (editor), John Cassaday (c art)

FEATURE CHARACTER: Captain America (also as UN refugee responder in fb between Falcon #4, '84 & Cap #290, '84; also in Cap #7, '03)

VILLAINS: Inali Redpath (also as UN refugee responder in fb to 1st chr app before Cap #11, '03 fb), Haokah (bts), Barricade (also in Cap #7, '03, dies) & his men, Samantha Twotrees (last app), Balkan prison camp guards (in fb)

OTHER CHARACTERS: Balkan prison camp detainees (in fb), school children, bystanders

LOCATIONS/ITEMS: Washington DC inc Lincoln Memorial, Florida, Balkan prison camp (in fb); Cap's motorcycle, Barricade's guns, manacles & road flare, Barricade's men's guns & armor, school bus, Redpath's gun, Balkan prison guards' guns (both in fb)

FLASHBACKS: Five years ago on a SHIELD mission, Steve Rogers and Inali Redpath liberate a Balkan prison camp.

SYNOPSIS: As Captain America leaves, Inali Redpath calls Samantha Twotrees and tells her the body she found is a clone. Redpath calls Barricade and tells him not to kill Cap, but because he thinks he killed Redpath, Barricade doesn't believe it's him and sets fire to the surrounding forest. Redpath proves who he is by sending a hurricane after Barricade, but Redpath is too far away for it to be effective. Cap arrives into a wall of fire. Barricade introduces himself, and he and his men attack Cap. Cap quickly defeats Barricade and his men, but Barricade takes a school bus full of children hostage and demands Cap don a set of manacles. When Cap does, Carricade prepares to kill the children anyway. Suddenly, a hurricane appears, Barricade dies and Redpath greets Cap.

NOTE: Cover-labeled "The Extremists Part 2 of 4." Includes recap/title page (1 page). The Cap meeting Barricade scene is mirrored from Cap #7, '03.

CAPTAIN AMERICA #9 [#526] (April 2003)

(22 pages)

CREDITS: John Ney Reiber, Chuck Austen (writers), Trevor Hairsine (pencils), Dany Miki, Allen Martinez (inks), Dave Sharpe (letters), David Stewart (colors), Nick Lowe (asst editor), Kelly Lamy (assoc editor), Joe Quesada (editor), John Cassaday (c art)

FEATURE CHARACTER: Captain America

GUEST STAR: Nick Fury (voice only, last in Cap #5, '02)

VILLAINS: Inali Redpath, Barricade's men, Haokah (bts)

OTHER CHARACTERS: Barricade (corpse, last app), clone soldiers, pilots, schoolchildren, bystanders; Batroc, Red Skull, Ultron, Baron (Heinrich) Zemo (all in Cap's hallucination), George Washington, crime victim, homeless man (all in Redpath's thoughts)

LOCATIONS/ITEMS: Florida inc Miami; Redpath's bitters & helicopters, Cap's parachute, school bus, Barricade's men's guns & armor

SYNOPSIS: Inali Redpath takes control of Barricade's men and tells Captain America he plans to take back America from those who stole it from his ancestors. Disgusted by Redpath's murder of Barricade, Cap attacks Redpath. Redpath easily subdues Cap with his power over the weather. Hoping to convince the hero to see the righteousness of his cause, Redpath forces Cap to drink bitters. Redpath escapes by helicopter and Cap follows. Fury calls Redpath but fails to stop him. Redpath flies out of the helicopter and starts a hurricane over Miami. Cap is unable to stop Redpath because the bitters finally take effect and send him into a hallucinatory vision quest.

NOTE: Cover-labeled "The Extremists Part 3 of 5." Includes recap/title page (1 page).

CAPTAIN AMERICA #10 [#527] (May 2003)

(22 pages)

CREDITS: Chuck Austen (writer), Jae Lee (art), Dave Sharpe (letters), Jose Villarrubia (colors), Nick Lowe (asst editor), Kelly Lamy (assoc editor), Joe Quesada (editor), John Cassaday (c art)

FEATURE CHARACTER: Captain America

GUEST STARS: Sub-Mariner (bts, last in SM:GetK #2, 02, next in Cap #16, '03, see NOTE), Dum Dum Dugan (last in Call #4, '03), Nick Fury

VILLAINS: Inali Redpath, Barricade's men, Haokah (bts)

OTHER CHARACTERS: Hana (Atlantean Ambassador to Lemuria, 1st), Captain America & Bucky clones, beachgoers; Baron Blood, Baron Strucker, Baron (Heinrich) Zemo, Bucky, MODOK, Red Skull, Viper, Sharon Carter, Hydra agent, scientists (prev 10 in Cap's hallucination)

LOCATIONS/ITEMS: Florida inc Miami, Atlantic Ocean; Vengeance (SHIELD Sky-Destroyer, 1st), helicopter & jets

SYNOPSIS: Hallucinating, Captain America unknowingly attacks two beachgoers, sees himself and Bucky in a cloning facility and falls into the ocean. The mysterious Atlantean Hana happens by and saves Cap. Meanwhile, Inali Redpath continues his rampage through Miami. Awakening still under the bitters' influence, Cap kisses Hana thinking she is Sharon Carter. Nick Fury arrives and picks up Cap and Hana. Fury is suspicious of Hana and reveals he never sent Cap to Florida in the first place. Fury takes Cap to the SHIELD Sky-Destroyer and reveals that Redpath is using clones of Cap and Bucky as his personal soldiers.

NOTE: Cover-labeled "The Extremists Part 4 of 5." Includes recap/title page (1 page). Cap #14, '03 reveals Hana to be the Atlantean Ambassador to Lemuria & Cap #16, '03 reveals Sub-Mariner sent Hana to aid Cap. Vengeance is named in Cap #11, '03.

CAPTAIN AMERICA #11 [#528] (May 2003)

(21 pages)

CREDITS: Chuck Austen (writer), Jae Lee (art), Dave Sharpe (letters), José Villarrubia (colors), Nick Lowe (asst editor), Kelly Lamy (assoc editor), Joe Quesada (editor), John Cassaday (c art)
FEATURE CHARACTER: Captain America
GUEST STARS: Nick Fury (next in Cap #23, '04), Dum Dum Dugan (next in Tb #69, '02), Thor (between Thor #55-56, '02-'03)
VILLAINS: Inali Redpath (also in fb between Cap #8, '03 fb & Cap #7, '03 fb, seemingly dies), Haokah (1st actual app, also off-panel in fb to 1st chr app before bts in Cap #7, '03 fb) (both last app)
OTHER CHARACTERS: Hana (chr next in Cap #14, '03 fb, next in Cap #13, '03), Redpath's grandfather (also bts in fb, only app), SHIELD agents (Eddings named), scientist (only in fb), Redpath clones, bystanders
LOCATIONS/ITEMS: Florida Human Engineering facility (only in fb), Red Cloud (Lakota Sioux reservation, North Dakota) inc clone facility w/ containment chamber (destroyed), Washington, DC inc Capitol building; Vengeance inc pri-fly (Primary Flight Control command center) & gym, SHIELD jets & guns
FLASHBACK: SHIELD agent Inali Redpath is mortally wounded while investigating a cloning facility. When he calls on the spirit of his ancestors to save him, Redpath's grandfather bonds him to Haokah, the Sioux god of thunder.
SYNOPSIS: Captain America summons Thor to counter Inali Redpath's power. Nick Fury briefs them and Hana on Redpath's death and rebirth and Cap realizes Redpath coordinated everything from Washington, DC, so the SHIELD Sky-Destroyer Vengeance takes them there as Cap works out with Hana. When they arrive, Thor challenges Redpath, forcing him to release Haokah to battle the Norse thunder god. Cap attacks the now powerless Redpath and denounces him for his extremism. Cap tells Redpath that he knows that his anti-American grandfather is responsible for his bonding with Haokah and the movement of his consciousness from one clone body to another. As Redpath's latest clone body fades away, Fury and SHIELD raid his grandfather's facility on a North Dakota reservation and destroy the clone bodies stored there. Disheartened, Cap reflects on noble causes, reprehensible actions and national pride.
NOTE: Cover-labeled "The Extremists Part 5 of 5." Includes recap/title page (1 page). Captain America and Thor quote lines from the play, "Richard III," by William Shakespeare.

CAPTAIN AMERICA #12 [#529] (June 2003)

(23 pages)

CREDITS: John Ney Rieber, Chuck Austen (writers), Jae Lee (art), Dave Sharpe (letters), José Villarrubia (colors), Nick Lowe (asst editor), Kelly Lamy (assoc editor), Joe Quesada (editor), John Cassaday (c art)
FEATURE CHARACTER: Captain America (also in fb, see NOTE)
VILLAINS: Interrogator ("Severs," scientist w/Lemurian hand, 1st but chr last in Cap #14, '03 fb, also in fb, see NOTE) & his daughter (Lemurian Assassins Guild member, 1st but chr last in Cap #14, '03 fb)
OTHER CHARACTERS: Sub-Mariner, Lemurian (corpse), Severs' colleagues, Severs' girlfriend (in photo) (all in fb, see NOTE), scientist (in faked film, see NOTE), Martin (Brooklyn boy), deliveryman
LOCATIONS/ITEMS: Lemuria (undersea kingdom in Atlantic Ocean) inc Interrogator's chamber, scientific outpost (inc monitor room) at ancient Atlantean arctic burial ground (in fb, see NOTE), Red Hook, Brooklyn inc Steve's apartment; block of ice, lab equipment, land mines, self-destruct mechanism, tank (all in fb, see NOTE), hoist (in faked film), Interrogator's probes, crate w/film projector & faked film
FLASHBACK: After freeing Captain America from a block of ice, Sub-Mariner raids a covert, arctic US research outpost in which Severs, a scientist, amputates the bio-technological hand of a dead Lemurian exhumed from an ancient burial ground. The infuriated Namor cuts off Severs' hand and the Lemurian hand merges with Severs. As Cap and Namor fight, Severs destroys the outpost and sends the two heroes into the ocean (see NOTE).
SYNOPSIS: Captain America receives a crate from the Army. Meanwhile, the Interrogator tells his "origin" to his daughter and orders her to bring Cap to him. In the crate, Cap finds a film showing him being lowered into an iceberg.
NOTE: Cover-labeled "Ice Part 1 of 5." Includes recap/title page (1 page). Interrogator's story is hinted to be false in Cap #13, '03, revealed to be questionable in Cap #16, '03 and confirmed as fake in Cap #6, '05.

CAPTAIN AMERICA #13 [#530] (July 2003)

(22 pages)

CREDITS: Chuck Austen (writer), Jae Lee (art), Dave Sharpe (letters), José Villarrubia (colors), Nick Lowe (asst editor), Kelly Lamy (assoc editor), Joe Quesada (editor), John Cassaday (c art)
FEATURE CHARACTER: Captain America (also in fb between Av:EMH #1, '05 & Av #4, '64, during Av #4, '64 & during MAv #20, '09 fb)
GUEST STARS: Avengers: Giant-Man (Henry Pym, in fb between AoH #4/2, '10 fb & Av:EMH #1, '05, between Av:EMH #1, '05 & Av #4, '64 & during Av #4, '64), Iron Man (in fb between AoH #4/2, '10 fb & Av:EMH #1, '05, during Av:EMH #1, '05 & during Av #4, '64), Thor (in fb between JIM #100, '64 & Av:EMH #1, '05, between Av:EMH #1, '05 & Av #4, '64 & during Av #4, '64), Wasp (in fb between TTA #53/2, '64 & Av:EMH #1, '05, between Av:EMH #1, '05 & Av #4, '64 & during MAv #20, '09 fb)
VILLAINS: Lemurian Assassins Guild (3 female warriors 1st but chr last in Cap #14, '03 fb, inc Interrogator's daughter)

OTHER CHARACTERS: Hana (last in Cap #11, '03, chr last in Cap #14, '03 fb), Japanese citizens (in Cap's thoughts), US soldiers (in faked film)
LOCATIONS/ITEMS: Hiroshima, Nagasaki (both in Cap's thoughts), Arctic (in faked film), Atlantic Ocean (in fb), Steve's Brooklyn apartment; hoist (in faked film), Avengers submarine, block of ice (both in fb), film projector, Hana's lock pick & pistol, faked documents, film & photographs
FLASHBACK: The Avengers rescue Captain America from the thawing ice block in which he was encased for years.
SYNOPSIS: Hana breaks into Steve's apartment to find a depressed Captain America amid the photos, film and documents that show the US government purposefully put him on ice. Hana tries to comfort Cap, but he ponders the extent of his government's deceit. Suddenly, three warriors attack. Cap quickly subdues them and Hana reveals they're members of the Lemurian Assassins Guild.
NOTE: Cover-labeled "Ice Part 2 of 5." Includes recap/title page (1 page). The documents say Hiroshima was bombed on June 11, '45. This should have clued Cap in that they were faked, as Hiroshima was bombed on August 6, '45.

CAPTAIN AMERICA #14 [#531] (August 2003)

(22 pages)

CREDITS: Chuck Austen (writer), Jae Lee (art), Dave Sharpe (letters), José Villarrubia (colors), Nick Lowe (asst editor), Kelly Lamy (assoc editor), Joe Quesada (editor), John Cassaday (c art)
FEATURE CHARACTER: Captain America (also in photo, rfb & fb, see NOTE)
VILLAINS: Interrogator (also in fb1 between bts in Cap #7, '03 & Cap #12, '03), Lemurian Assassins Guild (inc Interrogator's daughter, all also in fb1 to 1st chr app, last app), Gen. Phillips imposter (dies, only app, see NOTE)
OTHER CHARACTERS: Hana (also in rfb & fb1 between Cap #11, '03 & Cap #13, '03), Rolanda (Nelson Veterans' Hospital employee), Franklin D. Roosevelt & his Cabinet, Prof. Erskine, Army doctor & recruits (prev 5 in fb, see NOTE)
LOCATIONS/ITEMS: Army recruitment center, Operation: Rebirth, White House Oval Office (all in fb, see NOTE), Interrogator's Lemurian chamber (in fb1), Vengeance gym (in rfb), Steve's Brooklyn apartment, Kentucky's Nelson Veterans Hospital inc "Gen. Phillips'" room; Interrogator's probes, Assassins Guild's nunchucks
FLASHBACKS: Interrogator asks Hana to bring Captain America to Lemuria, but she resists. The Lemurian Assassins Guild attack her and she escapes (1). Hana falls in love with Cap as they work out together (Cap #11, '03). Impressed with frail Steve Rogers' fervent patriotism, Gen. Phillips recommends the boy for Prof. Abraham Erskine's experiments. Later Prof. Erskine dies. In 1945, Phillips recommends Cap's removal from duty because the hero's moral code runs counter to the military's impending plans to bomb Japan (see NOTE).
SYNOPSIS: Hana reveals she loves Captain America, but he can't reciprocate. Meanwhile, Interrogator watches from afar. Seeking answers to his questions about the government's possible involvement in his suspended animation at the end of WWII, Cap travels with Hana to a Kentucky veterans' hospital where he visits his wartime military liaison, Gen. Phillips. Before any questions can be answered, the Assassins Guild suddenly attack, slit Phillips' throat, and retreat with Cap's shield, forcing him to follow them to Lemuria.
NOTE: Cover-labeled "Ice Part 3 of 5." Includes recap/title page (1 page). Cap learned where "Gen. Phillips" lives from the faked documents. He's called "Albert" in Cap #15, '03 despite his name being Richard, and his story seen here is refuted in Cap #6, '05. It's not stated directly, but he's likely an agent of Interrogator.

CAPTAIN AMERICA #15 [#532] (September 2003)

(21 pages)

CREDITS: Chuck Austen (writer), Jae Lee (art), Rus Wooton (letters), José Villarrubia (colors), Nick Lowe (asst editor), Kelly Lamy (assoc editor), Joe Quesada (editor), John Cassaday (c art)
FEATURE CHARACTER: Captain America (also in own thoughts & dream)
VILLAINS: Interrogator, Lemurian soldiers (all also in Cap's dream)
OTHER CHARACTERS: Hana (also in Cap's dream), Bucky (in Cap's thoughts)
LOCATIONS/ITEMS: Atlantic Ocean inc Lemuria w/Interrogator's chamber (all also in Cap's dream), island (only in Cap's dream); Cap's replacement shield & plane, Interrogator's probes, Lemurian soldiers' spears (also in Cap's dream)
SYNOPSIS: Armed with a replacement shield, Captain America travels with Hana to Lemuria, where they meet Interrogator. The villain expresses his desire to understand Cap's moral code and worldview. He commands Lemurian soldiers to attack and Cap easily defeats them. Interrogator injects Cap with his probes and Hana severs them. Cap retreats with Hana to a deserted island. Cap's physical attraction to Hana leads him to agree that in seclusion, making love with her would not be wrong. Suddenly, Hana is slain by a spear, and as Lemurian soldiers surround the couple, Interrogator wonders if Cap's opposition to killing is as malleable as his moral precepts about sex, especially if he were faced with the killer of someone he desired.
NOTE: Cover-labeled "Ice Part 4 of 5." Includes recap/title page (1 page). Cap #16, '03 reveals that all events after the Interrogator injects Cap with his probes are part of a dream forced on Cap.

CAPTAIN AMERICA #16 [#533] (October 2003)

(22 pages)

CREDITS: Chuck Austen (writer), Jae Lee (art), Virtual Calligraphy's Rus Wooton (letters), José Villarrubia (colors), Nick Lowe (asst editor), Kely Lamy (assoc editor), Joe Quesada (editor)
FEATURE CHARACTER: Captain America (next in Cap #21, '04)
GUEST STAR: Sub-Mariner (last bts in Cap #10, '03, next in Alias #28, '04)
VILLAINS: Interrogator (also in Cap's dream, dies, last app), Lemurian soldiers (1 also in Cap's dream)
OTHER CHARACTERS: Baron Blood, Sharon Carter, Nick Fury, SHIELD medics (all in Cap's dream), Hana (last app)
LOCATIONS/ITEMS: Atlantic Ocean island, SHIELD base inc Sharon Carter's office, graveyard, restaurant (all in Cap's dream), Interrogator's Lemurian chamber; Cap's replacement shield, Interrogator's probes, Lemurian soldiers' spear & knife
SYNOPSIS: Captain America subdues Interrogator and brings Hana's corpse to SHIELD. Encounters with Sharon Carter and Baron Blood challenge Cap's belief that all life is sacred and killing is wrong. When Interrogator kills Sharon and pushes Cap to the breaking point, the hero realizes that he's experiencing a dream. He frees himself from Interrogator's control to find that he's still in the villain's Lemurian chamber, standing with Hana and the newly arrived Sub-Mariner. Namor explains that he sent Hana to investigate Interrogator when he heard that an unknown party hired the villain to brainwash Cap into a killer. Cap rips the Lemurian hand from Interrogator's arm, inadvertently killing him. The still living Lemurian hand reveals that Secretary of Defense Dell Rusk is behind the plot to brainwash Cap and mocks the hero for killing Interrogator.
NOTE: Cover-labeled "Ice Part 5 of 5." Includes recap/title page (1 page). Interrogator reveals he was hired by Dell Rusk; the name is an anagram for "Red Skull," and the character, introduced in Av #61, '03, is an alias of the Skull, as revealed in Av #68, '03. Sub-Mariner does not corroborate Interrogator's story from Cap #12, '03, revealing it to be questionable.

CAPTAIN AMERICA #17 [#534] (November 2003)

(22 pages)

CREDITS: Dave Gibbons (writer), Lee Weeks (pencils), Tom Palmer (inks), Virtual Calligraphy's Rus Wooton (letters), Dave Stewart (colors), Nick Lowe (asst editor), Kelly Lamy (assoc editor), Nancy Dakesian (managing editor), Joe Quesada (editor), Gene Ha (c art)
FEATURE CHARACTER: Captain America (also in fb)
GUEST STAR: Sub-Mariner (in fb)
SUPPORTING CAST: Bucky (in Cap's thoughts & fb)
VILLAINS: Red Skull, Nazi sailors inc captain & lieutenant, Nazi doctors, SS officer & soldiers
OTHER CHARACTERS: Franklin D. Roosevelt, Nazi soldiers, US military men (all in Cap's thoughts), Adolf Hitler (in photo), Nazi prisoners (in fb), servants, bystanders
LOCATIONS/ITEMS: New Berlin (formerly New York) inc Albert Speer Dome, Josef Goebbels Communication Tower, Hermann Goering International Airport, Times Square, Brooklyn factories & labor camps & Reichstag Building (formerly Empire State Building) inc Red Skull's penthouse office, Atlantic Ocean (also in fb), Detroit (in fb); bomb, drone plane, motorcycle, Nazi warplanes & warships, V-3 atomic missile (all in fb), dirigibles, guns, submarine & military vehicles, block of ice, Excelsior Movie-News reel
FLASHBACKS: In 1944, Captain America is helpless to save Bucky from an exploding drone plane. With Cap gone, the Nazis win WWII by overtaking Europe, North Africa and the US, and start to purge the non-Aryan races of conquered lands.
SYNOPSIS: March, 1964: Nazi sailors find Captain America frozen in a block of ice in the Atlantic Ocean. The Nazis take Cap prisoner and transport him to New Berlin, the Nazi-occupied city once called New York. Cap is brought before Red Skull, the leader of the Nazi horde that won WWII and has taken control of the world. The Skull tries to convince Cap to swear allegiance to him, but Cap refuses and jumps through a window of the villain's penthouse office atop the former Empire State Building amid a hail of bullets.
NOTE: Cover-labeled "Cap Lives Part 1." Includes recap/title page (3 pages) reproducing images from ToS #94, '67 and the covers of Av #4, '64, Cap #1, '02, ToS #76, '66, ToS #84, '66, Av #6, '64, ToS #80, '66, Av #18, '65 & Cap #15, '03, by John Cassaday, Jack Kirby and John Romita, Sr. This 4-issue story occurs on Earth-31117, not Earth-616 (the "mainstream" Marvel Universe); thus, no chronology is listed for this arc's characters.

CAPTAIN AMERICA #18 [#535] (November 2003)

"Captain America Lives Again Chapter Two" (22 pages)

CREDITS: Dave Gibbons (writer), Lee Weeks (pencils), Tom Palmer (inks), Virtual Calligraphy's Rus Wooton (letters), Dave Stewart (colors), Nick Lowe (asst editor), Kelly Lamy (assoc editor), Nanci Dakesian (managing editor), Joe Quesada (editor), Gene Ha (c art)
FEATURE CHARACTER: Captain America
GUEST STARS: Underground States of America: Peter Parker (bts, captured by Nazis), Ben Grimm, Reed Richards, Tony Stark, Johnny Storm, Sue Storm
VILLAINS: Red Skull, Viktor von Doom, Baron Strucker, Nazi Iron Men, Nazi scientists, SS colonel & soldiers
OTHER CHARACTERS: Dinner guests, dinosaur (corpse), bystanders
LOCATIONS/ITEMS: New Berlin inc Axel's pub, Broadway & Lafayette St., Delancey St. & 2nd Ave. subway

stations, Reichstag Building inc Red Skull's penthouse office, Baxter Building, subway tunnels, Yancy Street, Rommel Square & Times Square, Stark Industries inc Project Overlord HQ; Nazi dirigible & tracking device, Johnny's gasoline canister w/hose & matches, Ben Grimm's, Baron Von Strucker's & SS colonel's guns, Reed Richards' prototype Exo-frame, Doom's Space-Time Transporter inc temporal transducer & spatial re-integrator

SYNOPSIS: Captain America lands on a dirigible and hops into the Baxter Building, where Reed Richards and Sue Storm, secret members of an underground resistance group, tell him to flee to Yancy Street to meet a friend. Unbeknownst to Cap, he is wearing a tracking device that Nazi Iron Men use to pursue him through the city. Cap eludes the armored troops and meets Ben Grimm. Ben destroys Cap's tracking device and he and Johnny Storm hold off another squad of Iron Men as they get Cap to safety. Red Skull attends a dinner held by Tony Stark at Stark Industries, home of the restricted HQ of Project Overlord. There, the Nazi leader checks on Viktor von Doom's progress with a time machine, which is tested by Baron Strucker. With the device, the Skull plans to conquer the world for all eternity.

NOTE: Cover-labeled "Cap Lives Part 2." Includes recap/title page (1 page). The Underground States of America is named in Cap #19, '03.

CAPTAIN AMERICA #19 [#536] (December 2003)

"Captain America Lives Again Chapter Three" (22 pages)

CREDITS: Dave Gibbons (writer), Lee Weeks (pencils), Tom Palmer (inks), Virtual Calligraphy's Rus Wooten (letters), Dave Stewart (colors), Nick Lowe (asst editor), Kelly Lamy (assoc editor), Nanci Dakesian (managing editor), Joe Quesada (editor), Gene Ha (c art)
FEATURE CHARACTER: Captain America
GUEST STARS: Underground States of America: Ben Grimm, Peter Parker, Tony Stark, Johnny Storm (all die), Bruce Banner, James Barnes, Don Blake, Luke Cage, Frank Castle, Sgt. Nick Fury, Edwin Jarvis, Rick Jones, Matt Murdock, Henry Pym, Reed Richards, Sue Storm, Steven Strange, Janet Van Dyne
VILLAINS: Red Skull, Viktor von Doom, SS officer & soldiers inc oberleutenant
OTHER CHARACTERS: Ben Parker, May Parker, unnamed resistance members, bystanders

LOCATIONS/ITEMS: New Berlin inc Keppel Café, Times Square & Underground States of America's subterranean HQ, Stark Industries inc utility housing & Cap's cell; explosives w/remote control, Fantasti-car, gallows w/noose, Stark's Iron Men deactivator, Nazi military vehicles, SS soldiers' guns, Underground's buses, cars, trucks & guns

SYNOPSIS: Captain America meets the members of the underground resistance, including their leader, James Barnes. Don Blake reports that fellow patriot Peter Parker is scheduled to be hung by the Nazis in Times Square the next morning. The resistance stages a daring rescue, during which Cap rallies the oppressed bystanders with a rousing speech. Red Skull turns the tables on the heroes when he captures Cap and detonates explosives strapped to the freed Parker, killing him, Ben Grimm, and Johnny Storm. The rest of the resistance return to their base, where Blake delivers photos of the Nazis' time machine that were smuggled out of Stark Industries by an inside source. As the patriots raid Stark Industries, Tony Stark, a spy for the resistance, frees Cap from his cell and gives him a device to take to Henry Pym. Stark sacrifices himself in a firefight with Nazi soldiers to give Cap time to escape.

NOTE: Cover-labeled "Cap Lives Part 3." Includes recap/title page (1 page).

CAPTAIN AMERICA #20 [#537] (January 2004)

"Captain America Lives Again Chapter Four" (22 pages)

CREDITS: Dave Gibbons (writer), Lee Weeks (pencils), Tom Palmer (inks), Virtual Calligraphy's Randy Gentile (letters), Dave Stewart (colors), Nick Lowe (assist editor), Kelly Lamy (assoc editor), Nanci Dakesian (managing editor), Joe Quesada (editor), Gene Ha (c art)
FEATURE CHARACTER: Captain America
GUEST STARS: Underground States of America: Henry Pym (dies), Bruce Banner, James Barnes, Don Blake, Luke Cage, Frank Castle, Dum Dum Dugan, Sgt. Nick Fury, Rick Jones, Reed Richards, Sue Storm, Steven Strange, Janet Van Dyne; Avengers: Giant-Man (Hank Pym), Iron Man, Thor, Wasp
VILLAINS: Red Skull, Viktor von Doom, Baron Strucker & his Elite Squad, Nazi Iron Men, Nazi soldiers
OTHER CHARACTERS: Unnamed resistance members

LOCATIONS/ITEMS: Stark Industries inc Project Overlord HQ, Hollywood, CA, New Orleans, LA, Cleveland, OH, Texas; Stark's Iron Men deactivator, Doom's Space-Time Transporter, resistance guns, Nazi guns, Avengers Sub

SYNOPSIS: Captain America and the resistance storm Stark Industries. Using Stark's device, Henry Pym deactivates the Iron Men, clearing the way for the rebels. As cities across America overthrow their Nazi overlords, Red Skull pressures Doom into finalizing Project Overlord so he can travel back in time and kill every member of the resistance. Cap and the patriots fight their way to Doom's Space-Time Transporter and confront the Skull. After Pym is killed, Bruce Banner angrily smashes the time machine controls, unleashing temporal energy that severely burns Viktor von Doom's face. Red Skull takes James Barnes hostage, but James frees himself and Cap attacks. Both Cap and the Skull fall into the Space-Time Transporter and disappear. March, 1964: A frozen Captain America floats in the Atlantic Ocean. The Avengers find and rescue the thawing man, discovering to their shock that he is Captain America, missing since WWII…

NOTE: Cover-labeled "Cap Lives Part 4." Includes recap/title page (1 page).

CAPTAIN AMERICA #21 [#538] (February 2004)

"Homeland Part One" (21 pages)

CREDITS: Robert Morales (writer), Chris Bachalo (pencils, colors), Tim Townsend (inks), Virtual Calligraphy's Randy Gentile (letters), Warren Simmons, Jennifer Lee (asst editors), Axel Alonso (editor), Dave Johnson (c art)
FEATURE CHARACTER: Captain America
VILLAINS: Slave traffickers (Danny named), assassins
OTHER CHARACTERS: Damian Spinrad (FBI agent, last in Truth #6, '03, last app), George W. Bush (bts, orders that Hedayat be tried, last in XX #11, '02, next bts in Av #68, '03, next in XStat #15, '03), Rebecca Quan (commercial artist, 1st), Phil (Steve's diner co-owner, 1st, next in Cap #27, '04), Gen. Linc Barron (US Army officer, 1st), Fernand Hedayat (Iranian-born historian, bts, taken to Guantanamo Bay for trial, also in photo), Agent Harry Bender, Agent Helper (both Dept. of Homeland Security agents), Hal Tolliver (US Dept. of Justice regional director), Anna (US Dept. of Justice employee, voice only) (prev 4 only app), Broward County Sheriff's deputies, FBI agents, diner patrons & waitress, abductees, bystanders
LOCATIONS/ITEMS: Broward County, FL, Statue of Liberty, US Dept. of Justice's Manhattan HQ in Federal Plaza inc Tolliver's office, Brooklyn Bridge, Red Hook, Brooklyn inc Steve's diner & waterfront; assassins' assault rifle, Agent Bender's gun, slave traffickers' guns & knives
SYNOPSIS: Captain America helps law enforcement officials break up a slave trafficking ring in Florida. Later in Brooklyn, Steve Rogers eats at his new diner and meets commercial artist Rebecca Quan. Two Homeland Security agents arrive to escort Rogers to a meeting with General Linc Barron and Department of Justice regional director Hal Tolliver. On the way there, the three are ambushed by assassins on the Brooklyn Bridge. Barron and Tolliver brief Rogers on Fernand Hedayat, an Iranian-born historian whose US citizenship has been revoked and who has been taken to Guantanamo Bay to be tried for treason. Because Hedayat's case is a cause célèbre, they ask Rogers to serve on the secret military tribunal at his trial to reassure the public that the Iranian is being treated fairly.
NOTE: Includes title page (1 page) w/Captain America frontispiece by Chris Bachalo & Tim Townsend. Cap #25, '04 reveals that Gen. Barron sent the assassins.

CAPTAIN AMERICA #22 [#539] (March 2004)

"Homeland Part Two" (21 pages)

CREDITS: Robert Morales (writer), Chris Bachalo (pencils, colors), Tim Townsend (inks), Virtual Calligraphy's Randy Gentile (letters), Jennifer Lee (asst editor), Axel Alonso (editor), Dave Johnson (c art)
FEATURE CHARACTER: Captain America
VILLAINS: Khalid El-Gamal (Islamic jihadist, also in photos), Al-Qaeda members (militant Islamic activists) (both bts, assault Gen. Oliver & escape Camp Hasmat, 1st), Camp Hasmat inmates
OTHER CHARACTERS: Col. John D. Boyle (Camp Hasmat commanding officer, 1st), Fernand Hedayat (1st but last bts in Cap #21, '04), Gen. Anthony "Tony" MacPherson (US Army officer, 1st), Gen. Martin "Marty" Oliver (US Army officer, 1st, dies), Sen. Lester Paley (US legislator, 1st), Rebecca Quan (next in Cap #25, '04), Paige Rand (artist, only app), Gen. Barron's dog (1st), Rebecca Quan's cat (only app), Gen. Linc Barron, art patrons, US Army soldiers inc corporal
LOCATIONS/ITEMS: Rebecca's apartment, Camp Hasmat, Guantanamo Bay inc mess hall & watchtower, New York inc Grant Austen Galleries; US military helicopter & rifles, Paige Rand's "Ultimate Trademarks" art show inc Captain America, Dr. Doom, Iron Man & Namor exhibits
SYNOPSIS: Steve Rogers attends an opening at a New York art gallery with Rebecca Quan before heading to Camp Hasmat at Guantanamo Bay. Captain America meets the other members of the military tribunal and clashes with commanding officer Colonel Boyle over the treatment of prisoners at the camp. Cap encounters Fernand Hedayat's self-appointed defense counsel, Senator Paley, who tells the hero that tribunal member General Oliver warned him to remove himself from the trial. The camp is breached and a tortured and slain Oliver is found strung up with barbed wire.
NOTE: Includes title page (1 page) w/Captain America frontispiece featuring Captain America by Chris Bachalo & Tim Townsend.

CAPTAIN AMERICA #23 [#540] (April 2004)

"Homeland Part Three" (21 pages)

CREDITS: Robert Morales (writer), Chris Bachalo (pencils, colors), Tim Townsend (inks pgs 1-13), Aaron Sowd (inks pgs 14-15 & 17), Al Vey (inks pgs 16 & 18-21), Virtual Calligraphy's Randy Gentile (letters), Jennifer Lee (asst editor), Axel Alonso (editor), Dave Johnson (c art)
FEATURE CHARACTER: Captain America
GUEST STAR: Nick Fury (last in Cap #11, '03)
VILLAINS: Khalid El-Gamal, Al-Qaeda members (both bts, on the run from Camp Hasmat)
OTHER CHARACTERS: Gen. Linc Barron, Gen. Anthony MacPherson, Sen. Lester Paley (all next in Cap #25, '04), Arturo Gutierrez, Luisa Prohias (both Cuban soldiers, 1st), Col. John D. Boyle (next bts in Cap #25, '04), Fidel

Castro (Cuban leader, 1st), Fernand Hedayat (bts, escapes Camp Hasmat), Gen. Martin Oliver (corpse, last app), Cuban soldiers (some killed bts by escapees), Gen. Barron's dog (next in Cap #25, '04), SHIELD agent, US Army medics & soldiers

LOCATIONS/ITEMS: Camp Hasmat, Guantanamo Bay inc Col. Boyle's office, Fernand Hedayat's cell & watchtower; SHIELD hovercraft, video transmitter & Sky-Destroyer inc cloaking device, US military helicopter, bag of GPS tracking devices, medical equipment, US & Cuban soldiers' rifles

SYNOPSIS: The military officers at Camp Hasmat discover that Fernand Hedayat has escaped with a band of Islamic terrorists led by Khalid El-Gamal. Although the brass believes this confirms Hedayat's guilt, Senator Paley insists that the historian must have been taken against his will. Captain America calls in Nick Fury, who tells Cap and the officers that the escapees are likely headed for Havana to assault Cuba with a stash of bio-weapons, an act they hope will be blamed on the United States. Cap sets out alone to stop the terrorists and is attacked by Cuban soldiers on a beach. Suddenly, Fury appears with a surprise ally, Cuban leader Fidel Castro.

NOTE: Includes title page (1 page) w/frontispiece featuring Captain America by Chris Bachalo & Tim Townsend.

CAPTAIN AMERICA #24 [#541] (May 2004)

"Homeland Part Four" (21 pages)

CREDITS: Robert Morales (writer), Chris Bachalo (pencils, colors), Tim Townsend (inks pgs 1-15 & 17-21), Wayne Faucher (inks pg 16), Virtual Calligraphy's Randy Gentile (letters), Jennifer Lee (asst editor), Axel Alonso (editor), Dave Johnson (c art)

FEATURE CHARACTER: Captain America

GUEST STAR: Nick Fury

VILLAINS: Khalid El-Gamal, Al-Qaeda members (all die, last app)

OTHER CHARACTERS: Uwe Kael (SHIELD Sky-Destroyer commander, only app), Fidel Castro, Arturo Gutierrez, Fernand Hedayat, Luisa Prohias, SHIELD agents

LOCATIONS/ITEMS: Cuba inc Cienfuegos, Marianao & Playa Baracona, Havana inc Habana Veija, Paseo de Marti, Plaza de la Revoluci n, Museo de la Revoluci n, Havana Bay docks & warehouse; Al-Qaeda knives & rifles, bio-weapons, Cuban soldiers' rifles, detonation device, missile, SHIELD hovercraft, signal transmitter & Sky-Destroyer inc mess hall & anti-missile gun

SYNOPSIS: Allied with Fidel Castro for political reasons, SHIELD tracks the Al-Qaeda escapees to Havana, where the terrorists intend to detonate bio-weapons. Castro insists that two Cuban soldiers, Arturo Gutierrez and Luisa Prohias, accompany Captain America in his mission to stop the deadly plot. The three raid the Havana Bay warehouse where the bio-weapons are stored. Fernand Hedayat is injured and the Al-Qaeda members are killed in the ensuing firefight. When Prohias claims the bio-weapons for Castro, Cap signals Nick Fury to microwave the warehouse from the overhead SHIELD Sky-Destroyer.

NOTE: Includes recap/title page (1 page) w/frontispiece featuring Captain America by Chris Bachalo & Tim Townsend.

CAPTAIN AMERICA #25 [#542] (June 2004)

"Homeland Part Five" (21 pages)

CREDITS: Robert Morales (writer), Chris Bachalo (pencils, colors), Tim Townsend, Aaron Sowd, Al Vey (inks), Virtual Calligraphy's Randy Gentile (letters), Jennifer Lee (asst editor), Axel Alonso (editor), Dave Johnson (c art)

FEATURE CHARACTER: Captain America (next in BP #59, '03, IM #64, '03, Av #63, '03, CapTW:TSO #1, '09 fb, W/Cap #1-4, '04, Av #65-70, '03, SM:BBRead #1, '06, Av #72-76, '03-'04, IM #73, '03, IM #75, '04, IM #79, '04, CapTW:TSO #1, '09 fb, SecWar #2, '04 fb)

GUEST STAR: Nick Fury (on phone, next in IM #65, '03)

OTHER CHARACTERS: Gen. Linc Barron, Gen. Anthony MacPherson (both last in Cap #23, '04), Col. John D. Boyle (bts, reassigned by Army, last in Cap #23, '04), Fidel Castro, Arturo Gutierrez, Fernand Hedayat, Luisa Prohias, Gen. Barron's dog (all last app), Rosaura Gutierrez (Arturo's mother), Guillermo Prohias (Luisa's husband) (both only app), Rebecca Quan (last in Cap #22, '04, next in Cap #27, '04), Sen. Lester Paley (last in Cap #23, '04), Celia Cruz (salsa singer, on TV), Havana citizens inc children, Cuban soldier, hospital nurse, birds

LOCATIONS/ITEMS: Camp Hasmat inc Gen. MacPherson's office, Havana inc Havana Bay warehouse, hotel inc Steve's room, Plaza de la Revoluci n & Hospital de Comandante Manuel Fajardo inc Fernand Hedayat's room; Cuban soldiers' rifles, SHIELD signal transmitter

SYNOPSIS: Captain America convinces Luisa Prohias to allow SHIELD to neutralize the bio-weapons with radiation and fool Fidel Castro by turning the worthless viruses over to him. Cap visits the hospitalized Fernand Hedayat, who decides to decline the political asylum Castro offers him so he can continue his international defense fund for Arabs, an activity that originally made him a target of the US government. Seeing a conspiracy, Cap accuses Gen. Barron of sending the assassins who tried to prevent him from serving on Hedayat's tribunal, and Barron doesn't deny it. Cap decides to stay in Havana for New Year's and invites Rebecca Quan, Luisa, Ferdinand and their families to a party at his hotel room. There, Senator Paley announces his intention to run for President to call public attention to civil liberties issues. He asks Cap to be his running mate, but the Avenger declines.

NOTE: Includes recap/title page (1 page) w/frontispiece featuring Captain America by Chris Bachalo & Tim Townsend.

CAPTAIN AMERICA #26 [#543] (July 2004)

"The Bucky Issue" (21 pages)

CREDITS: Robert Morales (writer), Chris Bachalo (pencils), Tim Townsend, Al Vey (inks), Virtual Calligraphy's Randy Gentile (letters), Brain Reber (colors), Jennifer Lee (asst editor), Axel Alonso (editor), Dave Johnson (c art)
FEATURE CHARACTER: Captain America (also in rfb & fb3 between Cap #109, '69 fb & Cap #14, '06 fb, fb2 between Cap:DMR #2, '02 fb & IM #73, '03 fb, fb1 between AvCl #5/2, '07 fb & AllSel #7, '45, fb4 between Cap:MoT #1, '11 & Cap:SoL #12, '99, & pfb; next in SecWar #2, '04 fb, SecWar #5, '05 fb, Av/Tb #1, '04 fb, MHol '04, Alias #24, '03, Alias #28, '04, SH #1, '04)
SUPPORTING CAST: Bucky (in symbolic image, rfb & fb3 between Cap #109, '69 fb & Cap #14, '06 fb, fb2 between Cap:Re #1, '09 & CapC #43, '44, fb1 between AvCl #5/2, '07 fb & AllSel #7, '45, fb4 between Cap:MoT #1, '11 & Cap:SoL #12, '99)
OTHER CHARACTERS: Col. Walker Price (US Army officer, in fb3 to 1st chr app before Truth #2, '03), Lester Paley & his campaign workers, Harry Camus (Sen. Paley's campaign strategist, only app), Matt Drudge (political commentator, bts, phones Sen. Paley, only app), US soldiers (in fbs 1, 3), nun, schoolchildren (both in fb2), pilot, co-pilot, police, bystanders (prev 4 in pfb), Nazi soldiers (in rfb)
LOCATIONS/ITEMS: Washington, DC inc Lincoln Memorial, Reflecting Pool & Washington Monument (all in pfb) & Sen. Paley's campaign office; European city (in fb2), US Army base inc Col. Price's office (in fb3), English Allied hangar (in fb4), Baron Zemo's English Channel island base (in rfb); US fighter jets, airplanes (both in pfb), missiles, US military planes, soldiers' rifles (prev 3 in fb1), bomb, drone plane, motorcycle, Nazi soldiers' rifles (prev 4 in rfb)
FLASHBACKS: Steve Rogers crash lands a plane in the Lincoln Memorial Reflecting Pool (p). Captain America and Bucky escort US soldiers aboard a plane under fire (1). Bucky encourages European schoolchildren in a city under enemy fire (2). Col. Price agrees to use Bucky as a propaganda figure against Hitler Youth (3). Cap and Bucky guard an Allied hangar (4). Cap fails to save Bucky (Av #4, '64 fb).
SYNOPSIS: Steve Rogers reports to Senator Paley's Washington, DC campaign office, where Paley and his advisor address issues involving Captain America that may affect the campaign. After speculating about the crash of his plane, Rogers responds to a charge of child endangerment on the matter of his partnership with young Bucky Barnes during WWII, stating that Bucky died not because he was a kid but because he was a hero.
NOTE: Includes recap/title page (1 page) w/frontispiece featuring Captain America by Chris Bachalo & Tim Townsend. Henry Camus erroneously refers to Bucky as Michael Barnes instead of James Buchanan Barnes.

CAPTAIN AMERICA #27 [#544] (August 2004)

"Requiem Part 1 of 2" (22 pages)

CREDITS: Robert Morales (writer), Eddie Campbell, Stewart McKenny (art), Virtual Calligraphy's Randy Dentile (letters), Brian Reiber (colors), Jennifer Lee (assist editor), Axel Alonso (editor), Dave Johnson (c art)
FEATURE CHARACTERS: Captain America (also in photos)
GUEST STARS: Iron Man (last in SH #1, '04, chr last in IM:Hyper #2, '07 fb, next in IM #84, '04)
VILLAIN: Becky Barnes (insane daughter of Earth-40727 Isaiah Bradley, 1st but chr last in Cap #28, '04 fb, dies, last chr app)
OTHER CHARACTERS: Rebecca Quan (also in own dream, last in Cap #25, '04), Phil (last in Cap #21, '04, last app), Lester Paley (last app), Steve's diner patrons & employees, firemen, paramedics, US military, bystanders (some also as corpses); Adolf Hitler, Bucky, Thor (prev 3 in photos)
LOCATIONS/ITEMS: Red Hook, Brooklyn inc Steve's diner& Steve's apartment, Cleveland, OH inc daycare center, World Trade Center (in Rebecca's dream); Avengers Quinjet, Scarabs (Earth-40727 self-cleaning nanotech toys), Cap's original steel shield replica, Cap's mobility armor, Rebecca's knife
FLASHBACK: A Cleveland daycare center is destroyed in an explosion (p).
SYNOPSIS: In his diner, Steve Rogers' breakfast with Rebecca Quan is interrupted by a phone call telling him Lester Paley has been killed in an explosion at the Cleveland daycare center he was visiting. Investigating, Cap and Iron Man are attacked by hundreds of mechanical scarabs, which Iron Man disables with an electromagnetic pulse. Suddenly, the explosion reverses itself, restoring the daycare center and resurrecting the people killed, including Lester. Examining the scarabs, Iron Man finds they are toys from the future and not weapons. Meanwhile, when Rebecca enters Steve's apartment, she is attacked by a woman demanding to know where her father, Captain America, is. Seeing a picture of Steve in costume, the woman becomes confused, identifying her father to be Isaiah Bradley. Fighting back, Rebecca fatally stabs the woman in self-defense. As she dies, the women tells Rebecca her name is Becky Barnes, then she disappears.

CAPTAIN AMERICA #28 [#545] (August 2004)

"Requiem Part Two of Two" (22 pages)

CREDITS: Robert Morales (writer), Eddie Campbell, Stewart McKenny (art), Virtual Calligraphy's Randy Gentile (letters), Brian Reber (colors), Jennifer Lee (assist editor), Axel Alonso (editor), Dave Johnson (c art)
FEATURE CHARACTERS: Captain America (also in photos & stamps, also in Av/Tb #1, '04, next in Run #17, '04, Av/Tb #2-6, '04, Hawk:BS #3, '11 fb, XX #46, XStat #21-22, XStat #25, XStat #26 fb, all '04, CapTW:AB #1, '09, GLA #1, '05 fb, Av #77-79, Av #81-84, Inv #0, Hawk #7 fb, all '04, WM #5, '07 fb, MK4 #1, '04, Thor #80-81, '04, SMU #6, '05 fb, DD #61, '04, MKSM #1-2, '04, Cap #1, '05 fb, Run #18 fb, Cap&Falc #1 fb, Cap&Falc #2-8, all '04), Isaiah Bradley (also in Omega Con sign, Earth-40727 US president & former Captain America, only app)
GUEST STARS: Bucky Barnes (in fb2), Howard the Duck (both of Earth-40727, only app)
VILLAINS: Becky Barnes (of Earth-40727, in fb1 to 1st chr app before Cap #27, '04), Becky Barnes (of Earth-40828, only app), Krimson Klansman (of Earth-40727, in fb2, only app)
OTHER CHARACTERS: Rebecca Quan (last app), Earth-40727 & Earth-40828 San Diego Omega Con patrons & vendors (inc patrons dressed as Cyclops, Daredevil, Doop, Elektra, Gambit, Punisher, Rogue, Spider-Man, Sub-Mariner, Thor, U-Go Girl, Uatu the Watcher & Wolverine, some in fb1), post office employee & patron, bystanders; Thing (on Earth-40828 Omega Con sign), Captain America (Burnside), Bucky, Dwight Eisenhower, Adolf Hitler (prev 4 in photos), Giant-Man, Hulk, Iron Man, Thor, Wasp (prev 5 on stamps)
LOCATIONS/ITEMS: San Diego Omega Con inc Toys & Stuff booth (of Earth-40727 & Earth-40828), Red Hook, Brooklyn inc Steve's apartment & promenade; Becky Barnes' mini-copter (of Earth-40727 & Earth-40828), Earth-40727 & Earth-40828 comic books (inc Wow Comics, X-Treme, Crash, Cops, Action, Crikey, Gogo), Scarabs (Earth-40727 & Earth-40828 nanotech toys), KreeToyz Infinihedron (Earth-40727 reality-altering toy), Just Add Villains (Earth-40828 villainous homunculi, inc Galactus, Dormammu, AIM agents, Sentinel, Krimson Klansman, Mole Man, Dr. Octopus, Dr. Doom, Viper, Loki, Moloids), Sky-Destroyer Steranko (Earth-40727 Intrepid Air Museum exhibit, in fb2), Cap's original steel shield replica, Cap's mobility armor
FLASHBACKS: At the San Diego Omega Con, Becky Barnes buys a KreeToyz Infinihedron, Scarabs and Just Add Villains (1). Bucky defeats the Krimson Klansman, but they both fall off the Sky-Destroyer Steranko and die (2).
SYNOPSIS: Steve Rogers and Rebecca Quan are cleaning up Steve's apartment when Isaiah Bradley materializes, looking for his daughter Becky. Isaiah explains he's from a parallel future where he's retired as Captain America and served as the US president from 2005-2013, and that his insane daughter blames him for the death of her surrogate father, Bucky Barnes. Isaiah recruits Cap and Rebecca and they travel to Isaiah's timeline, where they find Becky at the San Diego Omega Con buying an Infinihedron. They stop her from escaping into the past, erasing the daycare center explosion and creating a new timeline where Rebecca does not kill Becky. Isaiah sends Cap and Rebecca to their own time and stops Becky from killing herself. Weeks later, Steve runs into Rebecca at the post office. Despite breaking up, they're still friends.
NOTE: Includes recap/title page (1 page) featuring Captain America. Last issue published in the Marvel Knights imprint.

CAPTAIN AMERICA #29 [#546] (September 2004)

"Super Patriot Part 1" (22 pages)

CREDITS: Robert Kirkman (writer), Scot Eaton (pencils), Drew Geraci (inks), Virtual Calligraphy's Randy Gentile (letters), Rob Schwager (colors), Andy Schmidt, Nicole Wiley (asst editors), Tom Brevoort (editor), Dave Johnson (c art)
FEATURE CHARACTER: Captain America (also in photo, next in Av #500-503, '04)
GUEST STARS: Moon Knight (last in Tb #57, '01, last bts in Hawk #8, '04), Spider-Man (last in Arana #4, '04, next in Av #501, '04)
VILLAINS: Red Skull (last in Av #70, '03), Diamondback LMD (Unit Four, 1st, see NOTE), Mr. Hyde (last in SM:GetK #1, '02, chr last in SM:BBRead, '06, last bts in Alias #26, '03, next bts in NAv #1, '05, next in NAv #2, '05), Hydra agents, Cpl. Mark Nolan (rogue SHIELD agent, 1st, also disguised as Nick Fury) & his rogue SHIELD agents
OTHER CHARACTERS: Richard Winslow (US senator), "Video Zone" employee, construction workers, police, bystanders; Diamondback, Cutthroat (both in photo)
LOCATIONS/ITEMS: New York, Brooklyn inc Video Zone & Steve's apartment, HYDRA's Florida Keys base w/break room & Winslow's cell, Diamondback's apartment; Cap's Avengers ID, SHIELD subcarrier & jetpacks, Nolan's holo-disguise, Hydra agents' guns, Red Skull's new armor (1st)
SYNOPSIS: Captain America defeats Mr. Hyde and turns him over to the police. After renting a DVD, Cap returns home to find Diamondback waiting for him. Before they can watch the movie, Nick Fury arrives and requests Cap's aid. Diamondback tags along, and Fury briefs Cap on Robert Winslow, a US senator captured by Hydra. "Fury" delivers Cap and Diamondback to the Hydra base then drops his holographic disguise to report his progress to Red Skull. Cap and Diamondback assault the Hydra base and rescue Winslow. While Cap and Diamondback sleep aboard the subcarrier En route to New York, Winslow settles up with Nolan, who rigged the abduction as a means of boosting Winslow's reelection chances. "Fury" returns Cap and Diamondback to Steve's apartment, only for Cap to immediately respond to an Avengers Code White alert. Diamondback returns home and reports to Red Skull that she has succeeded in rekindling Cap's interest in her.
NOTE: Cover labeled "Disassembled," an event running through Avengers-related titles. The Code White alert to which Cap responds involves a crippling assault on Avengers Mansion, as seen in Av #500, '04. Cap #32, '04 reveals that the Diamondback appearing here is an LMD. Cap #30, '04's recap page reveals Nolan's name. Cap #30, '04 reveals that the Skull's armor was designed and provided by Nolan's rogue SHIELD faction.

CAPTAIN AMERICA #30 [#547] (October 2004)

"Super Patriot Part Two" (22 pages)

CREDITS: Robert Kirkman (writer), Scot Eaton (pencils), Drew Geraci (inks), Virtual Calligraphy's Randy Gentile (letters), Rob Schwager (colors), Andy Schmidt, Nicole Wiley (asst editors), Tom Brevoort (editor), Dave Johnson (c art)
FEATURE CHARACTER: Captain America
GUEST STARS: BAD Girls, Inc.: Asp (last in Cap #411, '93, last bts in Cap #414, '93), Black Mamba (last in Tb #69, '02), Diamondback (bts, last in CitV #1, '01, see NOTE); Nick Fury (last in Av #503, '04)
VILLAINS: Red Skull, Diamondback LMD, Batroc (last in Dline #2, '02, next in NTb #8) & his Brigade (2 disguised as a mascot and a concession vendor),Serpent Society: King Cobra (last in SM:GetK #1, '02), Bushmaster, Coachwhip, Fer-de-Lance, Rock Python (prev 4 last in Cap #437, '95), Anaconda (last in W #167, '01), Black Racer (last in Cap #382, '91), Puff Adder (last in Dlk #7, '00), Rattler (last in Cap #436, '95, last bts in Cap #437, '95); Mark Nolan & his rogue SHIELD agents
OTHER CHARACTERS: SHIELD agents, New York Yankees & fans, opposing team, Video Zone employees, cafe staff & patrons, police
LOCATIONS/ITEMS: New York inc Yankee Stadium, Brooklyn inc Steve's apartment, Video Zone & outdoor cafe, Diamondback's apartment, Serpent Society's subterranean lair; Cap's Avengers ID, Batroc's "detonator," SHIELD subcarrier, Skull's armor w/force field "helmet," SHIELD agents' guns, Diamondback LMD's poison
SYNOPSIS: Rachel Leighton and Steve Rogers' date at a Yankees game ends prematurely when a group of robbers threaten to blow up the stadium unless the crowd hands over their valuables. Captain America and Rachel subdue the robbers only for Batroc to attack Cap. The ill-tempered Cap makes short work of Batroc, whose bomb threat was only a ruse. Meanwhile, Red Skull ends his business relationship with Nolan. After spending the night together, Rachel and Steve part ways, agreeing to get together again that night. As Steve reflects on recent events, Red Skull provides Rachel with poison for Steve. Nick Fury contacts Nolan and orders him to investigate the Hydra base Cap attacked, creating worry that Fury suspects Nolan's plans to overthrow SHIELD. Rachel and Steve's next date is interrupted when Bushmaster, Asp, and Puff Adder burst through his skylight and capture Steve and Rachel. The pair awaken shackled and in costume, as the triumphant Serpent Society gloats over their capture.
NOTE: Cover labeled "Disassembled." Includes recap/title page (1 page). ANOH #3, '06, reveals the real Diamondback learned of her LMD doppelganger and asked Asp and Black Mamba to hire the Serpent Society to hunt the LMD under the pretense that the LMD was the real Diamondback.

CAPTAIN AMERICA #31 [#548] (November 2004)

"Super Patriot Part Three" (22 pages)

CREDITS: Robert Kirkman (writer), Scot Eaton (pencils), Drew Geraci (inks), Virtual Calligraphy's Randy Gentile (letters), Rob Schwager (colors), Andy Schmidt, Nicole Wiley, Molly Lazer (asst editors), Tom Brevoort (editor), Dave Johnson (c art)
FEATURE CHARACTER: Captain America
GUEST STARS: BAD Girls, Inc.: Asp, Black Mamba (both next in Cable&Dp #20, '05); Spider-Man (last in Av #503, '04, next in Gravity #3, '05), Paladin (bts, goes on mission w/Cap, last in GenX #54, '99, next in NX:H #2, '05), Dum Dum Dugan (last in Av #503, '04), Nick Fury
SUPPORTING CAST: Sharon Carter (last in SecWar #1, '04 fb)
VILLAINS: Red Skull, Diamondback LMD, Baron Blood (last in KoP #11, '93, last bts in Alias #26, '03, next in AF #17/2, '06), Baron Strucker (last in CitV #3, '01, next in NTb #1, '05), Dragon Man (last in SH #6, '04, next in Herc #3, '05), Mad Thinker (last in Cap #50/6, '02, chr next in NW #5, '05 fb, next in FF:Foes #1, '05), MODOK (between Cap&Falc #8-9, '04-05), Viper (last in DD #64, '04, next in UXM #448, '04) & her henchman, Arnim Zola (last in Cap #50/6, '02, next in MHol, '06), Serpent Society: King Cobra (next in SecWar #3, '04), Coachwhip, Fer-de-Lance, Puff Adder, Rock Python (prev 4 next in ASM #562, '08), Bushmaster, Rattler (both next in Tb #104, '06), Anaconda (next in Cable&Dp #7, '04), Black Racer (last app), Sidewinder (Gregory Bryan, 1st, next in Nova #19, '09); Mark Nolan & his rogue SHIELD agents
OTHER CHARACTERS: Agnes (Steve's landlady); SHIELD agents (one as voice only), New Yorkers, construction contractor (bts, on phone with Cap)
LOCATIONS/ITEMS: New York, Society's subterranean lair inc Sector 7G, Cap & Diamondback LMD's cell & auction hall, Steve's Brooklyn apartment, Diamondback's apartment; Cap's Avengers ID, Coachwhip's whips, Fer-de-Lance's claws, Viper's henchman's sword, SHIELD subcarrier, SHIELD agents' guns, Red Skull's armor
SYNOPSIS: King Cobra tells Captain America he intends to auction Cap off to the highest bidder and leaves Cap and Diamondback to stew for sixteen hours. Cap worries he'll get late fees for his rented DVD. Cobra, Puff Adder and Anaconda arrive to collect Cap for the auction. Cap overpowers his captors, frees Diamondback and defeats the rest of the Serpent Society as they arrive. Cap calls SHIELD for prisoner transport as a group of villains continue to wait for the auction to start. Meanwhile, Nick Fury arrests Mark Nolan. Spider-Man drops by Cap's wrecked apartment to see him, but leaves when he doesn't find him. Diamondback invites Cap to stay at her place until his is repaired. As Cap arranges repairs, his landlady tells him Paladin visited and requested his aid. Later, Diamondback tells Red Skull she refuses to kill Cap. The Skull snaps her neck just as Steve Rogers knocks on her door.
NOTE: Cover labeled "Disassembled." Includes recap/title page (1 page). Sidewinder's real name is revealed in OHMU #10, '09.

CAPTAIN AMERICA #32 [#549] (December 2004)

"Super Patriot Part Four" (23 pages)

CREDITS: Robert Kirkman (writer), Scot Eaton (pencils), Drew Geraci (inks), Virtual Calligraphy's Randy Gentile (letters), Rob Schwager (colors), Andy Schmidt, Nicole Wiley, Molly Lazer (asst editors), Tom Brevoort (editor), Dave Johnson (c art)
FEATURE CHARACTER: Captain America (next in Cap&Falc #9-14, '05, CapTW:TSO #1, '09 fb, MKSM #11-12, '05, SpSM #15-20, '04, SWar:FNF, '05, Cap #1, '05 fb, SH #12, '05, AvFin, '05, YAv Spec #1, '06 fb, Herc #1, '05 fb, MTU #6, '05, Cap #1, '05 fb, MK4 #13, '05, Cap #1, '05)
GUEST STARS: Diamondback (last bts in Cap #30, '04, next in NX:H #2, '05), Dum Dum Dugan (next in Cable&Dp #7, '04), Nick Fury (next in Cap&Falc #9, '05)
SUPPORTING CAST: Sharon Carter (next in Cap #1, '05)
VILLAINS: Red Skull (next in Cap #1, '05), Diamondback LMD (next in MTU #6, '05), Mark Nolan (last app) & his rogue SHIELD agents
OTHER CHARACTERS: SHIELD agents, paramedics, bystanders, birds
LOCATIONS/ITEMS: New York, Diamondback's apartment; Red Skull's armor (destroyed), SHIELD Helicarrier, transport cylinders, LMD containment tank, & hover-ambulance, SHIELD agents' guns
SYNOPSIS: Red Skull attacks Captain America. Cap becomes enraged when he finds Rachel's body, but in his anger is unable to muster a defense against the Skull, who mercilessly beats him and smashes him through the apartment building's walls. Before Red Skull can finish Cap, structural damage collapses the building around them. The Skull pulls Cap out of the rubble to continue the fight, but Diamondback emerges from the wreckage, fixes her broken neck and viciously attacks Red Skull. She uses newfound computer interface abilities to deactivate the Skull's armor. Before Diamondback can kill Red Skull, Nick Fury arrives and freezes her in place. Fury explains that she is actually an advanced LMD of the real Diamondback, and that Mark Nolan used the LMD and the Skull as pawns in his attempt to usurp SHIELD. As SHIELD places the frantic LMD in containment and takes the Skull into custody, Steve and the real Diamondback reunite.
NOTE: Cover labeled "Disassembled." Includes recap/title page (1 page). Series continued in Cap #1, '05. Nolan's prisoner number is #125578.

CAPTAIN AMERICA #1 [#550] (January 2005)

"Out of Time Part One" (28 pages)

CREDITS: Ed Brubaker (writer), Steve Epting (art), Virtual Calligraphy's Randy Gentile (letters), Frank D'Armata (colors), Nicole Wiley, Molly Lazer (asst editors), Andy Schmidt (assoc editor), Tom Brevoort (editor)
FEATURE CHARACTER: Captain America (also in rfb & fb2 between MKSM #2, '04 & Run #18, '04 fb, fb3 between SWar:FNF, '05 & SH #12, '05, fb4 between MTU #6, '05 & MK4 #13, '05)
GUEST STARS: Hawkeye (in fb2 between MKSM #2, '04 & Av #500, '04), Red Guardian (only app in fb1, dies), Nick Fury (bts, provided Cap's new home, last in MTU #6, '05)
SUPPORTING CAST: Sharon Carter (last in Cap #32, '04)
VILLAINS: Winter Soldier (James Buchanan Barnes, Soviet Assassin, also as Bucky in Cap's dream, in rfb & fb1, last as Bucky in Av #4, '64 fb, chr last in Cap #11, '06 fb, next in Cap #3, '05, see NOTE), Red Skull (also disguised as bystander, also in fb1 between X Ann, '99 & FF #23, '99; last in Cap #32, '04), Aleksander Lukin (Russian General & Kronas Corporation head, 1st in fb1 but chr last in Cap #5, '05 fb; bts, on phone w/Red Skull, next in Cap #4, '05) & his men (in fb1), terrorists (in fb4, 2 die), thieves
OTHER CHARACTERS: Boris Yeltsin (Russian president, bts in fb1, gave executive order for Lukin's arrest), train engineer (corpse, in fb4), bystanders (others in rfb), pigeons (in fb4), Allied soldiers (in Cap's dream & rfb)
LOCATIONS/ITEMS: Russia inc Lukin's inherited storage facility (in fb1), New York inc Red Skull's penthouse, cemetery inc Hawkeye's grave (in fb3), Brooklyn inc Cap's home w/holo-wall; Winter Soldier's stasis tube, Negative Zone portal gun (both in fb1), train, terrorists' helicopter, Uzis & C-4 w/chemical waste (prev 4 in fb4), Red Skull's bystander mask, new Cosmic Cube (1st) w/receiver
FLASHBACKS: In Russia, Gen. Aleksander Lukin kills the Red Guardian when the Guardian tries to arrest him for desertion. Lukin escorts Red Skull into his storage facility, where the Skull is shocked to see a particular man held in stasis. Lukin offers to trade him for the Cosmic Cube, but the Skull doesn't have the Cube yet (1). During WWII, Cap and Bucky fight in Europe (ToS #68/2, '65). Cap trains with Hawkeye (2). Cap visits Hawkeye's grave (3). Cap uses excessive force when defeating terrorists who have hijacked the B train and rigged it with a dirty bomb (4).
SYNOPSIS: Armed with a new Cosmic Cube, Red Skull plans his attack on Manhattan, London and Paris. Sharon Carter, Captain America's new SHIELD liaison, confronts Steve Rogers over his harsh temperament since Hawkeye's death and Red Skull's recent escape. They spend the afternoon catching up before Sharon leaves. Steve doesn't notice a disguised Red Skull spying on him. That night while on the phone with Gen. Lukin, Red Skull is killed. The assassin retrieves the Cosmic Cube.
NOTE: Cover labeled "Out of Time Part 1." Winter Soldier is named in Cap #5, '05 & revealed to be Bucky in Cap #8, '05. Cap #14, '06 reveals the Cosmic Cube transferred Red Skull's mind into Lukin's body here.

CAPTAIN AMERICA #2 [#551] (February 2005)

"Out of Time Part 2" (21 pages)

CREDITS: Ed Brubaker (writer), Steve Epting (art pgs 1-2, 6-10 & 12-21, c art), Michael Lark (art pgs 3-5 & 11), Virtual Calligraphy's Randy Gentile (letters), Frank D'Armata (colors), Nicole Wiley, Molly Lazer (asst editors), Andy Schmidt (assoc editor), Tom Brevoort (editor)
FEATURE CHARACTER: Captain America (also in own dream & fb during Cap #255, '81 fb)
GUEST STAR: Nick Fury
SUPPORTING CAST: Sharon Carter
VILLAINS: Crossbones (last in Gam #19, '00, last bts in Alias #26, '03, next in Cap #4, '05), AID agents (Advanced Ideas in Destruction, AIM splinter, Larry named, 1st)
OTHER CHARACTERS: Red Skull (corpse, also in photo, next bts in Cap #4, '05), Gen. Phillips (in fb during Cap #255, '81 fb), SHIELD agents & doctor; Adolf Hitler, Nazis (both in photo), Invaders: Bucky, Human Torch (Hammond), Toro; Allied & German soldiers (prev 5 in Cap's dream)
LOCATIONS/ITEMS: Manhattan inc Red Skull's penthouse & sewers, Steve's Brooklyn home, Paris, France (in Cap's dream); Cap's SHIELD video communicator, SHIELD Helicarrier inc morgue, AID guns & bomb, Red Skull's bystander mask, new Cosmic Cube (in thermal scan) w/receiver
FLASHBACK: Gen. Phillips briefs the recently trained Steve Rogers on Red Skull.
SYNOPSIS: Crossbones and AID agents wait for Red Skull's call. Steve wakes from a dream when Sharon calls. Captain America meets her and Nick Fury on the SHIELD Helicarrier where Red Skull's corpse is being autopsied. Cap's DNA is taken for comparison to verify if this is the real Skull, whose body is a clone of Cap's. They go to the Skull's penthouse, where Cap finds and recognizes Red Skull's mask and starts to believe the Skull may genuinely be dead. A SHIELD agent finds the Cosmic Cube's receiver and traces its signal. Cap and Sharon investigate in the sewers where they find AID agents waiting for Red Skull's orders. They defeat the AID agents and stop them from setting off a fire-bomb, but miss the hiding Crossbones, who overhears Cap and Sharon report to Fury. After the heroes leave, Crossbones calls other AID cells to set their explosives despite Red Skull's death.
NOTE: Includes recap/title page (1 page). "American Graffiti" changes its name to "Freedom of Speech," which features LOC from comics writer Kurt Busiek.

CAPTAIN AMERICA #3 [#552] (March 2005)

"Out of Time Part 3" (21 pages)

CREDITS: Ed Brubaker (writer), Steve Epting (art pgs 1-4, 6-16 & 20-21, c art), Michael Lark (art pgs 5 & 17-19), Virtual Calligraphy's Randy Gentile (letters), Frank D'Armata (colors), Nicole Wiley, Molly Lazer (asst editors), Andy Schmidt (assoc editor), Tom Brevoort (editor)
FEATURE CHARACTER: Captain America (also in photo & fb between ToS #77/2, '66 fb & Cap:DMR #2, '02 fb, also in Cap #25, '07 fb, ToS #77/2, '66 fb, see NOTE)
GUEST STARS: Invaders: Human Torch (Hammond, in fb between Cap #25, '07 fb & WX #14, '03 fb), Sub-Mariner (in fb between Cap Ann., '01 fb & WX #14, '03 fb), Toro (in fb between Cap #25, '07 fb & YA Spec #1, '09 fb); Union Jack (Chapman, also in dfb, between Inv #3-4, '04-05), Jack Monroe (last in Inv #2, '04 fb, chr last & also in Cap #7, '05 fb, dies, chr also & next in Cap #7, '05, next in Cap #6, '05 as corpse), Nick Fury
SUPPORTING CAST: Sharon Carter
VILLAINS: Winter Soldier (in shadows, also in fb as Bucky between Cap #25, '07 fb & Cap #37, '08 fb; last in Cap #1, '05, chr next bts in Cap #7, '05, see NOTE), Mother Night (last in Cap #410, '92, also off-panel in dfb, dies, last app), AID agents (many die, also in dfb), AIM agents, Kronas soldiers (bts, kill Mother Night & her AID cell), Nazis & German soldiers (both in fb)
OTHER CHARACTERS: Jacques Chirac (French president, bts, thanks Cap, only app), SHIELD agents (some also in dfb, Heinberg named), Maquis (WWII French Resistance), French citizens (both in fb), Curtis (Stop-n-Drink bartender, 1st but chr last in Cap #7, '05 fb), Stop-n-Drink patrons; Baron (Heinrich) Zemo & his Nazis (in fb, see NOTE)
LOCATIONS/ITEMS: London Underground, Paris, France (also in fb) inc Eiffel Tower, Pittsburg, PA inc "Stop-n-Drink" bar; SHIELD Sub-Carrier, Sharon's hovercar & gun, Cap's flash-bomb, AIM hover-jet, Winter Soldier's gun, Bucky's gun, German guns & tank (prev 3 in fb)
FLASHBACKS: Baron Zemo shoots Cap and captures Bucky (see NOTE). Union Jack and SHIELD agents find Mother Night's AID cell dead in the London Underground (d). Cap and the Invaders help liberate Paris.
SYNOPSIS: In London, Mother Night learns of Red Skull's death. She hears gunfire before she can set her AID cell's bomb. As Captain America and SHIELD head towards Paris, Union Jack calls with news of Mother Night's death. Arriving in Paris, Cap quickly finds and defeats the local AIM cell. Cap and Sharon report to Fury that AIM was reclaiming a bomb AID stole from them. Pleased, Fury gives them the night off. At the Stop-n-Drink in Pittsburg, Jack Monroe becomes angry when the bartender doesn't believe he used to be Cap's partner. He goes outside to get his Nomad uniform to be shot dead by a shadowed figure with a robot arm.
NOTE: Includes recap/title page (1 page). Cap #6, '05 reveals the Cosmic Cube is prompting Steve to cut through his faulty memories of Bucky's death. Cap #7, '05 expands Jack Monroe's death. "Freedom of Speech" features LOCs from comics writers Robert Kirkman & Joe Casey.

CAPTAIN AMERICA #4 [#553] (April 2005)

"Out of Time Part 4" (21 pages)

CREDITS: Ed Brubaker (writer), Steve Epting (current day art, c art), Michael Lark (flashback art), Virtual Calligraphy's Randy Gentile (letters), Frank D'Armata (colors), Nicole Wiley, Molly Lazer (asst editors), Andy Schmidt (assoc editor), Tom Brevoort (editor)

FEATURE CHARACTER: Captain America (also in photo & fb3 between Av #56, '68 & Cap:SoL #12, '99)

GUEST STARS: Spirit of '76 (in fb1 between Inv #15, '77 & Cap Ann #13, '94 fb), Patriot (in fb2 between MC #28/4, '42 & MPr #29, '76) (both also as Captain America in rfb), Tony Stark (bts, provides jet, last in FF/IM:Big #4, '06, next in Cap #13, '06), Nick Fury

SUPPORTING CAST: Sharon Carter (next in Cap #6, '05)

VILLAINS: Winter Soldier (arm only, also in fb3 as Bucky between Av #56, '68 & Cap:SoL #12, '99; chr last bts in Cap #7, '05, next in Cap #6, '05), Aleksander Lukin (last bts in Cap #1, '05, next in Cap #6, '05), Red Skull (bts, last in Cap #2, '05, next in Cap #6, '05), Crossbones (last in Cap #2, '05, next in Cap #9, '05), Baron (Heinrich) Zemo (in fb3 between Av #56, '68 & Cap:SoL #12, '99) & his Nazis (in fb3), German soldiers (in fb1), Nazi spies (in fb2)

OTHER CHARACTERS: Leon (Lukin's assistant, 1st, next in Cap #6, '05), Lt. Keller (Arlington official, only app), Allied soldiers (in fb1), SHIELD agents, Arlington guards, reporters, police, bystanders; Falcon, Nomad (both in photo), Adam-II, Bucky (Davis), Human Torch (Hammond), Red Raven, Sub-Mariner, Toro, John F. Kennedy, politicians (prev 8 in rfb)

LOCATIONS/ITEMS: New York's financial district inc Roxxon HQ, Steve's Brooklyn home, Arlington National Cemetery inc William Naslund's & Jeffrey Mace's graves & JFK Memorial, Baron Zemo's base (in fb3); Cap's SHIELD communicator & motorcycle, SHIELD Helicarrier & jets, Crossbones' guns, Sharon's guns

FLASHBACKS: Spirit of '76 meets the Invaders (Inv #14-15, '77) and fights with the Allied forces in Europe (1). Patriot fights Nazi spies in the US (2), holds a press conference with Bucky (MPr #29, '76) and celebrates with the Invaders (MPr #30, '76). As Captain America, Naslund dies in 1946 saving Congressional candidate John F. Kennedy from the android Adam-II. Mace becomes Captain America and destroys Adam-II (WI #4, '77). In his secret English Channel base, Baron Zemo tortures the captive Captain America and Bucky (3).

SYNOPSIS: Alexander Lukin prepares to buy Roxxon with his Kronas Corporation. Fury calls Steve, telling him to go to Arlington National Cemetery. While Tony Stark provides Steve with a ride, Fury informs Sharon Carter that Jack Monroe's fingerprints were on the recently discovered murder weapon used to kill the Red Skull, and sends Sharon to find Monroe. At Arlington, Captain America inspects the destroyed headstones of William Naslund and Jeffrey Mace, both former Captain Americas. Cap is pleased to learn people have to walk past their graves to get to the JFK memorial. As Cap leaves he suddenly remembers being tortured by Baron Zemo, just as Crossbones attacks. Crossbones is disgusted when he easily defeats the distracted Cap. He tells Cap a Russian sent him and leaves. That night, Lukin's assassin overpowers Sharon Carter.

NOTE: Includes recap/title page (1 page). Cap #6, '05 reveals the Cosmic Cube is unlocking Cap's memories here.

CAPTAIN AMERICA #5 [#554] (May 2005)

"Out of Time Part 5" (21 pages)

CREDITS: Ed Brubaker (writer), Steve Epting (art pgs 1-2 & 20-21, c art), Michael Lark (art pgs 3-19), Virtual Calligraphy's Randy Gentile (letters), Frank D'Armata (colors), Stephanie Moore, Molly Lazer (asst editors), Andy Schmidt (assoc editor), Tom Brevoort (editor)

FEATURE CHARACTER: Captain America (also as callsign "Eagle" in fb between bts in Truth #6, '03 & Cap #50, '09 fb)

GUEST STARS: Invaders: Human Torch (Hammond, in fb between Cap #46, '09 fb & Cap #50, '09 fb), Sub-Mariner (in fb between SubC #8/2, '42 & Cap #616/6, '11), Toro (in fb between AllWin #4, '42 & Cap #50, '09 fb); Nick Fury

SUPPORTING CAST: Bucky (also as callsign "Bluejay," only in fb between Cap #46, '09 fb & Cap #50, '09 fb)

VILLAINS: Red Skull (in fb between YA #4, '42 & CapBiB, '76), Master Man (in fb between Inv #41, '79 & Cap:ME, '94), German soldiers (in fb)

OTHER CHARACTERS: Col. Vasily Karpov (1st, in fb before Cap #8, '05 fb), Aleksander Lukin (also in photo, as child in fb to 1st chr app before Cap #1, '05 fb), Kronas villagers (inc Lukin's mother, all die), Russian soldiers (both in fb), Teresa (Fury's secretary)

LOCATIONS/ITEMS: Russia inc Kronas (in fb); German tank, grenade & guns, Russian guns, Bucky's knife, grenade & gun, Nazi super-weapon, Atlantean sir ship (all in fb), SHIELD Helicarrier inc Fury's office, classified Winter Soldier file

FLASHBACK: November, 1942: Working with Russian soldiers, the Invaders battle German soldiers outside Stalingrad. Learning that Red Skull has a new super-weapon in the small village Kronas, they attack. As the Invaders battle Master Man, Cap and Bucky find Red Skull with the super-weapon. The Skull destroys Kronas to cover his escape. After the Invaders leave Karpov finds young Aleksander Lukin, the only Kronas survivor, and takes him under his wing.

SYNOPSIS: Nick Fury tells Captain America that Mother Night was killed by ex-Soviet soldiers who disappeared at the same time Aleksander Lukin did, but Lukin reappeared three years ago as the Kronas Corporation CEO. Fury tells Cap that Karpov died twenty years ago. Fury debates whether to tell Cap who the Winter Soldier is.

NOTE: Includes recap/title page (1 page).

CAPTAIN AMERICA #6 [#555] (June 2005)

"Out of Time Part 6" (21 pages)

CREDITS: Ed Brubaker (writer), Steve Epting (art), Virtual Calligraphy's Randy Gentile (letters), Frank D'Armata (colors), Stephanie Moore, Molly Lazer (asst editors), Andy Schmidt (assoc editor), Tom Brevoort (editor)

FEATURE CHARACTER: Captain America (also in rfb & fb between Cap:SoL #12, '99 & Cap:MoT #1, '11, also in Cap:Re #4, '10, Cap: MoT #1, '11, Cap:SoL #12, '99, Av #4, '64 fb; next in Cap #8, '05)

GUEST STAR: Nick Fury (next in Cap #8, '05)

SUPPORTING CAST: Sharon Carter (last in Cap #4, '05, next in Cap #8, '05)

VILLAINS: Winter Soldier (also as Bucky in photo, rfb & fb between Cap:SoL #12, '99 & Cap:MoT #1, '11, also in Cap:Re #4, '10, Cap:MoT #1, '11, Cap:SoL #12, '99, Av #4, '64 fb; last in Cap #4, '05, next in Cap #8, '05 fb), Aleksander Lukin (last in Cap #4, '05, next in Cap #9, '05) & Kronas soldiers (1st full app), Red Skull (bts, last bts in Cap #4, '05, next bts in Cap #9, '05)

OTHER CHARACTERS: Jack Monroe (corpse, last in Cap #3, '05, chr last in Cap #7, '05, last app), Leon (last in Cap #4, '05, next in Cap #9, '05), Neal Tapper (SHIELD agent & Sharon's ex, dies, only app), other SHIELD agents; Baron (Heinrich) Zemo & his Nazis (both in Cap's hallucination & rfb)

LOCATIONS/ITEMS: English Channel inc Zemo's island base (also in fb), Philadelphia, New York; SHIELD jets, hovercars & Helicarrier inc Fury's office, Zemo's drone plane (in rfb & fb), Nazi guns (in fb), Cap's parachute, Winter Soldier's gun & bomb w/remote control, Lukin's jet, new Cosmic Cube w/receiver

FLASHBACKS: Baron Zemo tortures Cap and Bucky (Cap #4, '05 fb). Cap falls off Zemo's drone plane, but Bucky is stuck and can't let go. The plane explodes.

SYNOPSIS: Winter Soldier sets a bomb in Philadelphia, positions Jack Monroe's corpse to take the blame, and grabs the captive Sharon Carter. Meanwhile, Nick Fury sends Neal Tapper to look for the missing Sharon. Escorted by SHIELD, Captain America revisits Zemo's island base in the English Channel. He relives the last time he saw Bucky. Cap suspects the Cosmic Cube is unlocking his memories but is satisfied that his memories are real. As he prepares to leave the Cosmic Cube sends an image of the captive Sharon, and SHIELD takes him to Philadelphia. Cap rescues Sharon just as Winter Soldier sets off his bomb. The resulting chaos charges the Cosmic Cube, much to Lukin's pleasure.

NOTE: Includes recap/title page (1 page). Story continued in Cap #8, '05.

CAPTAIN AMERICA #7 [#556] (July 2005)

"Interlude: The Lonesome Death of Jack Monroe" (22 pages)

CREDITS: Ed Brubaker (writer), John Paul Leon (art), Steve Epting (c art), Virtual Calligraphy's Randy Gentile (letters), Frank D'Armata (colors), Andy Schmidt, Stephanie Moore, Molly Lazer (asst editors), Tom Brevoort (editor)

FEATURE CHARACTER: Captain America (only in photo & rfb)

GUEST STAR: Nomad (corpse, also in own thoughts & as Bucky & Scourge in rfb, in fb between Inv #2, '04 fb & Cap #3, '05, also in Cap #3, '05; last in Cap #3, '05, next in Cap #6, '05)

VILLAIN: Winter Soldier (also in Nomad's hallucination as Bucky, also in rfb, bts, driving car, last & also in Cap #3, '05, next in Cap #4, '05)

OTHER CHARACTERS: Dr. Jane Foster (in fb between Thor #41, '01 & Thor #60, '03), Julia Winter (in fb, last in Nomad #25, '94 as Bucky, last app) & her adopted mother (in fb), "Stop-n-Drink" patrons (in fb) inc Gunnar (ice cream delivery man) & Joey (both also in fb), Curtis (in fb to 1st chr app before Cap #3, '05), prostitute, news anchor (both in fb), bystanders (in fb, some as criminals in Nomad's hallucination); Captain America (Burnside, in Nomad's thoughts & rfb), Falcon, Bernie Rosenthal, criminals, government officials (prev 4 in rfb), Avengers: Beast, Iron Man, Ms. Marvel (prev 3 in photo), Human Torch (Hammond), Sub-Mariner (both in Nomad's dream)

LOCATIONS/ITEMS: New York inc Greendale Medical Research Clinic w/Dr. Foster's office, Washington, DC inc Nomad's hotel room & Capitol, Philadelphia, Pittsburg inc Winter home (all fb), "Stop-n-Drink" bar (also fb), Lee School, government facility (both rfb); classified file on Bucky (fb), Cap & Bucky's stasis tubes (rfb), Winter Soldier's gun & car (also fb), Gunnar's ice cream truck

FLASHBACKS: Jack Monroe meets Prof. Steve Rogers at the Lee School and they become Captain America and Bucky (YM #24/2, '54). They're driven insane by improper use of the Super-Soldier Serum and put into stasis (Cap #155, '72 fb). Revived, they fight Cap and Falcon (Cap #156, '72). Cured, Jack meets Steve Rogers (Cap #281, '83) and becomes his partner Nomad (Cap #284, '83). Nomad strikes out on his own (Nomad #1, '90), but is tricked into becoming Scourge (Tb #49, '01 fb). Dr. Jane Foster tells Jack Monroe that his body is deteriorating, and that he can expect mental instability before he dies. He eventually runs out of medicine and forgets large chunks of time, but learns where his adopted daughter Bucky, now Julia Winter, is living. He visits her in Pittsburg and overhears at the nearby Stop-n-Drink bar that Gunnar is making a lot of money in front of Julia's elementary school, so he begins searching for the drug dealer responsible. As Nomad he beats up various innocent bystanders, but his hallucinations make him think they're criminals. Later at the Stop-n-Drink, he hears about the Avengers disbanding. After defeating more "criminals," Jack has some beers at the Stop-n-Drink (1). Outside the Stop-n-Drink, Winter Soldier kills Jack and loads him into his trunk (Cap #3, '05).

SYNOPSIS: Winter Soldier drives away as Gunnar parks his ice cream truck and gets a drink.

NOTE: This issue takes place out of publication order, expanding the end of Cap #3, '05.

CAPTAIN AMERICA #8 [#557] (September 2005)

"The Winter Soldier Part 1" (21 pages)

CREDITS: Ed Brubaker (writer), Steve Epting (pencils, co-inks, c art), Mike Perkins (co-inks), Chris Eliopoulos (letters), Frank D'Armata (colors), Molly Lazer, Aubrey Sitterson (asst editors), Andy Schmidt (assoc editor), Tom Brevoort (editor)
FEATURE CHARACTER: Captain America (also in pfb)
GUEST STAR: Nick Fury (last in Cap #6, '05)
SUPPORTING CAST: Sharon Carter (also voice only in pfb, last in Cap #6, '05)
VILLAINS: Winter Soldier (in pfb, also in photos & as Bucky in fb between Cap #50, '09 fb & Cap #11, '05 fb; last in Cap #6, '05, next in Cap #13, '06), AIM agents, MODOC squad (Military Operatives Designed Only for Combat, hive mind, 1st) (both in pfb), Col. Vasily Karpov (in fb between Cap #5, '05 fb & Cap #11, '05 fb), Russian sub crew (in fb, Captain Smislov named)
OTHER CHARACTERS: SHIELD agents, bystanders (in pfb, some die); MI-6 head, Wakandan Vice-Chancellor, Gen. Keller (prev 3 alleged Winter Soldier victims, in photo)
LOCATIONS/ITEMS: Philadelphia (also in pfb), English Channel (in fb); AIM aircraft, guns & scanners, MODOC squad's guns & knives, Winter Soldier's gun (all in fb), SHIELD helicopters & Helicarrier inc Fury's office, Winter Soldier file
FLASHBACKS: With Philadelphia in flames, Captain America saves trapped people while AIM agents murder witnesses. Cap finds and defeats the AIM agents, but the MODOC squad arrives as reinforcements. Cap defeats the MODOC squad, but is surprised to see Winter Soldier at the scene. Cap recognizes him as Bucky before he disappears (p). April, 1945: Col. Karpov, in an experimental Soviet spy-submarine, finds Bucky's frozen body in the English Channel.
SYNOPSIS: Nick Fury tells Captain America that Cold War myth Winter Soldier is actually a revived Bucky Barnes, but Cap refuses to believe it. Fury shows him photos and evidence, which only angers Cap more. Fury suspects Kronas CEO Aleksander Lukin of being responsible for the Philadelphia attack and offers a plan to grab him. When Cap leaves, Fury tells Sharon that her ex Neal Tapper died in Philadelphia.
NOTE: Cover labeled "The Winter Soldier Part 1." Includes recap/title page (1 page).

CAPTAIN AMERICA #9 [#558] (October 2005)

"The Winter Soldier Part 2" (21 pages)

CREDITS: Ed Brubaker (writer), Michael Lark (art), Virtual Calligraphy's Randy Gentile (letters), Frank D'Armata (colors), Molly Lazer, Aubrey Sitterson (asst editors), Andy Schmidt (assoc editor), Tom Brevoort (editor), Steve Epting (c art)
FEATURE CHARACTER: Captain America (also in pfb, next in Cap #11, '05)
GUEST STAR: Nick Fury (also in pfb, next voice only in Cap #11, '05)
SUPPORTING CAST: Sharon Carter (also in pfb, next in Cap #12, '05)
VILLAINS: Aleksander Lukin (last in Cap #6, '05, next in Cap #11, '06), Red Skull (bts, last bts in Cap #6, '05, next voice only in Cap #11, '05), Crossbones (last in Cap #4, '05, next in Cap #15, '06), Sin (as Erica Holstein, last in Cap #394, '91, chr last in Cap #15, '06 fb, next in Cap #15, '06)
OTHER CHARACTERS: Leon (last in Cap #6, '05, next in Cap #12, '05), Chief of Staff to the vice president of the US, Assistant to the Secretary General of the UN (both only app), SHIELD agents (Kirkman named), re-education guards (Ronnie & Murphy named, all die), Kronas Corporation guards, bystanders (in pfb)
LOCATIONS/ITEMS: Brooklyn inc Steve's home w/holo-wall, New York inc subway (both in pfb), Nevada government re-education facility, Mongolia inc Altai Mountains & Kronas Corporation building w/Lukin's office & meeting room; SHIELD helicopters, SHIELD agents' guns, Fury's needle gun, Crossbone's knife, Kronas guards' guns, Lukin's Winter Soldier file, new Cosmic Cube
FLASHBACK: Nick Fury tells Steve Rogers that Jack Monroe is the prime suspect in Red Skull's murder and the recent disaster in Philadelphia. Despite not getting clearance for the Kronas mission, Fury is going ahead with the plan anyway. The next day, Sharon confronts Steve over taking her off the Kronas mission, telling him she's going anyway (p).
SYNOPSIS: Crossbones kidnaps Red Skull's daughter from a government re-education facility. In Mongolia, Captain America, Nick Fury and SHIELD raid the Kronas Corporation building looking for Lukin's assassin. Cap attacks Lukin during a meeting with various corporate heads, including the Chief of Staff to the Vice President and the Assistant to the Secretary General of the UN. Fury is reprimanded for attacking a friend of the US, and he calls off the mission. Cap is upset as they leave. Meanwhile, Crossbones leaves the government facility with the terrified Red Skull's daughter.
NOTE: Includes recap/title page (1 page). Story continues in Cap #11, '05.

CAPTAIN AMERICA #10 [#559] (October 2005)

"House of M" (22 pages)

CREDITS: Ed Brubaker (writer), Lee Weeks (pencils, co-inks pgs 1-11, c art), Jesse Delperdang (co-inks pgs 1-11), Mike Perkins (inks pgs 12-22), Frank D'Armata (c colors), Virtual Calligraphy's Randy Gentile (letters), Avalon Studio's Matt Milla (colors), Aubrey Sitterson, Molly Lazer (asst editors), Andy Schmidt (assoc editor), Tom Brevoort (editor)
FEATURE CHARACTER: Captain America (also in fb, last in HoM #2, '05, next in HoM #5, '05, see NOTE)
GUEST STARS: Sapien Resistance: Luke Cage, Emma Frost, Cloak, Spider-Man, Wolverine (all during HoM #5, '05); Dum Dum Dugan (also in fb, last in NTb #11, '05, next in W #36, '06, see NOTE)
OTHER CHARACTERS: Invaders: Bucky, Human Torch, Sub-Mariner, Toro; Magneto (also in photo), Master Man, Sgt. Nick Fury, Peggy Carter, Heinrich Zemo & his Nazis, Adolf Hitler, Senator Joseph McCarthy, Edward R. Murrow, US President Harry Truman, Watts (Moon landing reporter), Allied & German soldiers, other Senators, secret service, reporters, police, mutants, bystanders (all in fb, see NOTE), Kamar (Namor's son, 1st, next in Sub #1, '07), Cap's anniversary attendees
LOCATIONS/ITEMS: English Channel inc Zemo's base, Berlin, Germany inc Hitler's bunker, White House inc Oval Office, Moon, Steve & Peggy's home, New York inc bar (all in fb) & Veterans Hall; Zemo's drone plane, Astro-5, Sentinels (all in fb)
FLASHBACK: Bucky pulls Captain America onto Zemo's drone plane, and the two turn it around and defeat Zemo. Edward R. Murrow reports as Cap and the Invaders raid Berlin and haul Hitler from his bunker. Cap retires in 1946, later marries Peggy Carter, reveals his secret identity during Joseph McCarthy's Senate Hearings on Mutant Activity in 1951 in protest and becomes the first man to walk on the Moon in 1955, declaring it to be one small step for man, one giant leap for peace between man and mutant-kind. Steve and Peggy's home life begins to fall apart and Bucky begins working for SHIELD in 1957. Magneto begins to rise in power, and despite Steve publicly speaking for equality between man and mutant, he decries Magneto as the new Hitler. In the late '70s Bucky dies on a SHIELD mission, Peggy and Steve divorce and Captain America fades into obscurity as Magneto gains even more political power (see NOTE).
SYNOPSIS: The retired and elderly Captain America attends an anniversary celebration held in his honor. Afterward, he's upset when young mutant hooligans harass him. The Sapien Resistance watch him walk home, but decide not to recruit him.
NOTE: Cover labeled "House of M," an event caused by the mentally unstable Scarlet Witch, who in HoM #1-2, '05 transforms Earth-616 into Earth-58163, where her father Magneto rules and mutants are the majority, lording over the second-class "sapien" minority. In this altered reality everyone has been given false memories to conform them to the new status quo. As such, Steve does not remember his Earth-616 past here. This issue takes place out of publication order, between Cap #15-16, '06. Followed by NFHC #1, '05 preview (4 pages).

CAPTAIN AMERICA #11 [#560] (November 2005)

"The Winter Soldier Part 4" (21 pages)

CREDITS: Ed Brubaker (writer), Steve Epting (pencils, co-inks, c art), Mike Perkins (co-inks), Virtual Calligraphy's Randy Gentile (letters), Frank D'Armata (colors), Molly Lazer, Aubrey Sitterson (asst editors), Andy Schmidt (assoc editor), Tom Brevoort (editor)
FEATURE CHARACTER: Captain America (also in newsreel & fb3 between Inv #41, '79 & CapC #17, '42)
GUEST STAR: Nick Fury (voice only, last in Cap #9, '05)
VILLAINS: Winter Soldier (also as Bucky in rfb, becomes Winter Soldier, only in fb3 between Inv #39, '79 & CapC #17, '42, in fb4 & Av/Inv #12, '09 fb, fb2 between Cap #8, '05 fb & Cap #1, '05 fb, also in Cap #14, '06 fb, W #40, '06 fb, W #38, '06 fb, Cap #27, '07 fb, BW:DO #2, '10 fb, Cap #44-46, '09 fbs, Cap #616/2, '11 fb, Av/Inv #12, '09 fb), Red Skull (voice only, last bts in Cap #9, '05), Aleksander Lukin (last in Cap #9, '05), Col. Vasily Karpov (in photo, rfb & fb2 after Cap #8, '05 fb, also in Cap #14, '06 fb, Cap #27, '07 fb, Cap #44, '09 fb, last app)
OTHER CHARACTERS: James Keller (NATO General), Dalton Graines (British Ambassador) & his guests, Jacques Dupuy (French Defense Minister), Col. Jefferson Hart, Senator Harry Baxter, United Nations Diplomatic Negotiation Team, Algerian Peace Conference Envoy (all die), Parsifal (Russian double agent in MI-6, bts, provides robot arm), Russian government agents (some as police), Department X science team & doctors, American, Russian & UK soldiers (three die), nightclub patrons, staff & singer, bystanders (all in fb2), theater patrons (in fb3), German soldiers (in rfb), Allied soldiers (in newsreel); Valeri (Lukin's secretary), SHIELD agent (both voice only)
LOCATIONS/ITEMS: Russian medical facility, West Berlin, Cairo, Madripoor, Algeria, Paris, Mexico City, Middle East, Karpov's storage facility, Sen. Baxtor's home, Dallas, TX, Chicago, IL (all fb2), movie theater (fb3), Kronas (rfb), Kronas Mongolian building, Steve's Brooklyn home; Bucky's Russian stasis tube, Russian medical equipment, guns & knives, Winter Soldier's rifle, bazooka, machine gun & stasis tube (all fb2), Zemo's drone plane (fb1), Lukin's Winter Soldier file
FLASHBACKS: Cap, Bucky and Karpov battle German soldiers in Kronas (Cap #5, '05 fb). Bucky is blasted loose from Zemo's drone plane, but loses an arm (1). May, 1945: The frozen Bucky is unpackaged in a medical facility where doctors warm him up to discover he's still alive. He has amnesia but keeps fighting his handlers. After two weeks of tests, doctors find he has no Super-Soldier serum in his system and he's put back into stasis. June, 1954: Russian doctors give Bucky a robot arm and mentally condition him to be their operative. November 5, 1954: Bucky goes on a test mission to West Berlin, where he kills three soldiers and escapes. Now the Winter Soldier, he kills several targets between 1955-1957, but the longer he's active the more he questions orders. He's mentally conditioned again and put back into stasis after each mission. March 12, 1973: After killing an American Senator, Winter Soldier disappears in America for two weeks; he's found by Russian agents in New York and can't explain his actions. September 1983: Major Karpov takes Winter Soldier to the Middle East to wreak havoc. August 4, 1988: When Karpov dies, Winter Soldier is put into permanent stasis (2). On furlough, Steve and Bucky relax at the movie theater (3).
SYNOPSIS: In Mongolia, Lukin can't find his Winter Soldier file. A voice taunts him that he misplaced it. Meanwhile, Steve Rogers finds a Winter Soldier file in his home. After reading it he calls Nick Fury, then breaks down.
NOTE: Cover labeled "The Winter Soldier Part 3." Includes recap/title page (1 page).

CAPTAIN AMERICA #12 [#561] (December 2005)

"The Winter Soldier Part 4" (21 pages)

CREDITS: Ed Brubaker (writer), Steve Epting (pencils & co-inks pgs 1-4, 7-13, 16-17 & 20-21, c art), Mike Perkins (co-inks pgs 1-4, 7-13, 16-17 & 20-21), Michael Lark (art pgs 5-6, 14-15 & 18-19), Virtual Calligraphy's Joe Caramagna (letters), Frank D'Armata (colors), Molly Lazer, Aubrey Sitterson (asst editors), Andy Schmidt (assoc editor), Tom Brevoort (editor)
FEATURE CHARACTER: Captain America (also in fb1 between Cap #303, '85 fb & Cap #215, '77 fb, fb2 between AllWin #14/2, '44 & Cap #15, '06 fb)
GUEST STARS: Falcon (last in AvFin #1, '05), Nick Fury (next in W #20, '04)
SUPPORTING CAST: Sharon Carter (last in Cap #9, '05)
VILLAINS: Winter Soldier (also in photo & as Bucky in fb1 between MvPro #7, '10 fb & Cap #109, '69 fb, fb2 between Cap #26, '04 fb & Cap #15, '06 fb), Red Skull (bts, also bts in fb2 between Cap #37, '08 fb & Cap #15, '06 fb), Aleksander Lukin, German soldiers (in fb2), Bartok (Kronas soldier), mugger
OTHER CHARACTERS: Redwing (last in Cap&Falc #14, '05), Leon (last in Cap #9, '05), Gen. Phillips (in fb1 between Cap #303, '85 fb & Cap #14, '06 fb), mugging victim, 8 corporate representatives (Philip Hockney of Chemax named), Bucky's trainers (in fb1), Allied soldiers (in fb2, some as zombies), pigeons
LOCATIONS/ITEMS: Camp Lehigh (fb1), Arnhem, Netherlands (fb2), New York inc Kronas Corporate HQ (formerly Roxxon) w/Lukin's office & meeting room, Brooklyn inc Steve's home; Allied soldiers' guns, German bomb (both in fb2), Winter Soldier file, Sharon's hovercar, new Cosmic Cube
FLASHBACKS: Gen. Phillips shows Steve Rogers the training Bucky, who the military is considering to make Captain America's partner (1). September, 1944: In Arnhem, Captain America, Bucky and Allied soldiers fight German forces. Bucky is disgusted when the Germans send out zombies of fallen Allied soldiers (2).
SYNOPSIS: As the Roxxon logo is replaced with the Kronas logo, Lukin holds an auction with various corporate representatives for the Cosmic Cube. Steve Rogers shows Nick Fury and Sharon Carter the Winter Soldier file and grudgingly agrees that Winter Soldier is a revived Bucky. Sharon fails to convince Cap that they may need to kill him. Hockney of Chemax interrupts the Cosmic Cube auction and demands a demonstration to prove the Cube is real. Lukin forces the representatives to sign over their corporations to Kronas, making them all subsidiaries. Hockney thanks Lukin for the demonstration. When Lukin's assistant Leon tries to pick up the Cube, Lukin smashes his head with a table. That night, Captain America wrestles with his thoughts until Falcon joins him.
NOTE: Cover labeled "The Winter Soldier Part 4." Includes recap/title page (1 page). Falcon's new wings 1st appeared in Cap&Falc #1, '04.

CAPTAIN AMERICA #13 [#562] (January 2006)

"The Winter Soldier Part 5" (21 pages)

CREDITS: Ed Brubaker (writer), Steve Epting (pencils, co-inks, c art), Mike Perkins (co-inks), Virtual Calligraphy's Joe Caramagna (letters), Frank D'Armata (colors), Molly Lazer, Aubrey Sitterson (asst editors), Andy Schmidt (assoc editor), Tom Brevoort (editor)
FEATURE CHARACTER: Captain America
GUEST STAR: Iron Man (last bts in Cap #4, '05, next in W #22, '05), Falcon
SUPPORTING CAST: Sharon Carter
VILLAINS: Winter Soldier (last in Cap #8, '05 fb), Red Skull (voice only), Aleksander Lukin, AID agents (Freidman named)
OTHER CHARACTERS: Redwing (bts), Leon (last app), Kronas doctor
LOCATIONS/ITEMS: New York inc Stark Enterprises w/Stark's office, Kronas Corporation HQ w/medical clinic & Lukin's office & SHIELD HQ w/Sharon's office, Steve's Brooklyn home, West Virginia inc Allegheny Mountains w/Nextgen research facility w/nuclear-safe vault; AID agents' battlesuit & guns, Kronas jet, Winter Soldier's rifle, new Cosmic Cube w/container
SYNOPSIS: Lukin checks on Leon, who may lose an eye from the beating Lukin gave him. At Steve's place, Captain America fills Falcon in on the Winter Soldier. Falcon asks what Cap wants to do. When Cap answers that he wants to save him, Falcon offers his help. Lukin orders Winter Soldier to bury the Cosmic Cube. A voice tells Lukin that getting rid of the Cube is a mistake. The next day, Cap, Falcon and Iron Man raid an AID facility and learn how to track a Cosmic Cube. When they learn the Cube is headed to a recently acquired Kronas facility, Tony Stark has to bow out of the mission; his company narrowly avoided a Kronas buy-out and his participation could be viewed as corporate warfare. Cap and Falcon arrive at the Nextgen facility in Virginia. When Winter Soldier sees them approach, he takes aim and fires.
NOTE: Cover labeled "The Winter Soldier Part 5." Includes recap/title page (1 page).

CAPTAIN AMERICA #14 [#563] (April 2006)

"The Winter Soldier Conclusion" (22 pages)

CREDITS: Ed Brubaker (writer), Steve Epting (art), Virtual Calligraphy's Joe Caramagna (letters), Frank D'Armata (colors), Molly Lazer, Aubrey Sitterson (asst editors), Andy Schmidt (assoc editor), Tom Brevoort (editor)
FEATURE CHARACTER: Captain America (also in rfb, dfb & fb3 between Cap #26, '04 fb & Av #213, '81 fb; next in NTb #6, Inv #7-9, W #23 & 25, NX #13, YAv #1-6, all '05, SecWar #3 fb, voice only in SecWar #3/2, SecWar #2-3, all '04, Pulse #6, SecWar #4, SecWar #5 fb, all '05, MAv #12, '08 fb, Herc #1, NAv #1-2, SM:Break #1, NAv #3, all '05, NAv #42, '08, NAv #4-6, '05, NAv #41, '08 fb, NAv #8 fb, SM:Break #2, bts in SM:Break #4, SM:Break #5, MTU #10, all '05, MTU #20, '06 fb, NAv #7-8 & 10, '05, GSAv #1/5, '08, Herc #4-5, '05, YAv #7-9 & 11-12, '05-06, ASM #519-521, 523 & 524, 'fb, MKSM #13-14 & 18, HoM #1, all '05, NAv #42, '08, HoM #2, Cap

#10, HoM #5 & 8, all '05, Run #9-12, '05-06, NAv #11, '05 fb, NAv #27, '07 fb, NAv #11-15, '05-06, AF #13, '05, NTb #12, '05, MTU #14, '06, CW:Choos #1/6, '06, SM&FF #2, '07, SH #1, '05, MsM #1, '06, S #1-2, '05, W #36-38, '06, W:O #3-4, '06)

GUEST STAR: Falcon (also in dfb, next in W #23, '05)

SUPPORTING CAST: Sharon Carter (next in SecWar #1, '04)

VILLAINS: Winter Soldier (also in rfb as Bucky, dfb & fb1 to 1st chr app before MvPro #7, '10 fb, fb3 between Cap #26, '04 fb & Cap:SoL #12, '99 fb, fb2 during Cap #11, '05 fb; next in W #38, '06), Red Skull (also in rfb), Aleksander Lukin (both next in Cap Spec, '06), Vasily Karpov (in fb2 between Cap #11, '05 fb & Cap #27, '07 fb), Kronas soldiers

OTHER CHARACTERS: Redwing (next in Cap #30, '07), Gen. Phillips (in fb3 between Cap #12, '05 fb & Cap #247, '80 fb), George Barnes (Bucky's father, only app in fb1), SHIELD agents, birds (also in dfb); Baron (Heinrich) Zemo, Master Man, Allied soldiers (prev 3 in rfb)

LOCATIONS/ITEMS: Camp Lehigh (also fb1 & fb3), West Virginia inc Allegheny Mountains w/Nextgen research facility w/nuclear-safe vault & underground tunnels, Kronas Corporate HQ inc Lukin's office; Zemo's drone plane (rfb), Winter Soldier's rifle, knife, gun & flare gun, Kronas jet, Kronas soldiers' guns, SHIELD jet, new Cosmic Cube (destroyed) w/container

FLASHBACKS: Birds spot Winter Soldier and warn Falcon (d). Young Bucky and his father arrive at Camp Lehigh (1). Cap and Bucky fight in Paris (Cap #3, '05 fb), battle Red Skull and Master Man (Cap #5, '05 fb), and fail to stop Zemo's drone plane (Av #4, '64 fb). Bucky loses an arm and becomes the Winter Soldier (Cap #11, '05 fb). Karpov toasts to America's demise with the newly activated Winter Soldier (2). Gen. Phillips officially introduces Captain America to his new partner, Bucky (3).

SYNOPSIS: Winter Soldier fires at Falcon but misses. He retreats as Captain America and Falcon attack the Kronas soldiers. As she approaches Virginia by jet, Sharon calls to warn Cap that if Winter Soldier makes it to the tunnels underneath the Nextgen facility they won't be able to catch him. Cap battles Winter Soldier as Falcon and SHIELD defeat the Kronas soldiers. Cap tries to get Winter Soldier to remember who he is but fails, so he leaves himself open for Winter Soldier to shoot him. Winter Soldier fires. Cap dodges the bullet and knocks the Cosmic Cube from Winter Soldier with his shield. Cap grabs the Cube and uses it to make Winter Soldier remember. Disgusted by what he's done as the Winter Soldier, Bucky destroys the Cosmic Cube and is seemingly vaporized. Bucky reappears at the dilapidated Camp Lehigh. Meanwhile from within Lukin's mind, Red Skull chastises Lukin for losing the Cosmic Cube.

NOTE: Includes recap/title page (1 page). Story continues in Cap #16, '06. "Freedom of Speech" features LOC from actor Bill Mumy.

CAPTAIN AMERICA #15 [#564] (April 2006)

"Red is the Darkest Color" (22 pages)

CREDITS: Ed Brubaker (writer), Mike Perkins (art), Steve Epting (c art), Virtual Calligraphy's Joe Caramagna (letters), Frank D'Armata (colors), Molly Lazer, Aubrey Sitterson (asst editors), Andy Schmidt (assoc editor), Tom Brevoort (editor)

FEATURE CHARACTER: Captain America (also on poster & in rfb, only in fb1 between Cap #12, '06 fb & CapTW:PoD #1, '10)

SUPPORTING CAST: Bucky (in fb1 between Cap #12, '06 fb & IM #73, '03 fb)

VILLAINS: Crossbones (last in Cap #9, '05, next in NAv #1, '05), Synthia Shmidt (also in rfb, also in fb2 as infant during Cap #298, '84 fb, fb4 between Cap #350/2, '89 fb & Cap #298, '84 fb, fb5 during Cap #298, '84 fb, fb6 between Cap #298, '84 fb & bts in Cap #287, '83, fb3 as Sin during Cap #394, '91 & Cap #9, '05; last in Cap #9, '05, resumes Sin identity), Mother Night (in fb2 as Susan Scarbo between Cap #123, '70 & Cap #350/2, '89 fb, in fb4 between Cap #350/2, '89 fb & bts in Cap #355, '89), Red Skull (also in rfb, in fb1 between bts in Cap #12, '05 fb & Cap/NF:OthW, '01, fb2 during Cap #298, '84 fb, in fb4 between Cap&Crb #1, '11 fb & Cap #298, '84 fb, fb6 between Cap #298, '84 fb & Cap #290, '84), his Nazis (in fb1) & scientists (in fb5)

OTHER CHARACTERS: SHIELD agent & doctor (both in fb3), American soldiers (in fb1) & sailors (both on poster), Red Skull's men (only in Synthia's thoughts), Synthia's victim (in fb4), night watchman (dies)

LOCATIONS/ITEMS: Europe (in fb1), Isle of Exiles (in fb2), Skull-House (in fb4), Crossbones' safe house inc his bedroom & Synthia's cell; Bucky's rifle, Nazi & US Army rifles, Red Skull's grenade & pistol (all in fb1), syringe, Taser (both in fb3), Red Skull's deus machina & his scientists' lab suits (both in fb5), Crossbones' gun & throwing knives

FLASHBACKS: During WWII, Captain America, Bucky and American soldiers fight Red Skull and his Nazis (1). Angry that his newborn child is a girl, Red Skull prepares to kill her, but Susan Scarbo convinces him to spare her and promises to raise her to be his hateful heir (2). SHIELD begins reprogramming Synthia (3). Red Skull and Mother Night watch Synthia brutally beat a man, and Red Skull discovers he's dying (4). Synthia is artificially aged to adulthood and indoctrinated in Red Skull's world vision (5). The fully-grown Synthia aims to carry on the Skull's legacy (6). Synthia overhears Red Skull tell Cap about his disappointment in her (Cap #298, '84).

SYNOPSIS: Crossbones physically and mentally conditions Synthia Shmidt through torture to break her of SHIELD's reprogramming and become a worthy heir to Red Skull. Synthia eventually remembers her past and joins Crossbones in bed.

NOTE: The poster depicted on the cover and in the story carries the slogan, "Together We Win," made popular on labor posters during World Wars I and II.

CAPTAIN AMERICA #16 [#565] (May 2006)

"Collision Courses Part 1 of 2" (22 pages)

CREDITS: Ed Brubaker (writer), Mike Perkins (art), Virtual Calligraphy's Joe Caramagna (letters), FrankD'Armata (colors), Molly Lazer, Aubrey Sitterson (asst editors), Andy Schmidt (assoc editor), Tom Brevoort (editor), Steve Epting (c art)
FEATURE CHARACTER: Captain America (also in own dream)
GUEST STAR: Nick Fury (bts, last in NAv #14, '06, next in Cable&Dp #24, '06, see NOTE)
SUPPORTING CAST: Winter Soldier (also in photo & as Bucky in Cap's dream, only in pfb, last in W #40, '06, next in Cap #18, '06), Sharon Carter (also in Cap's dream, last in MsM #1, '06)
VILLAINS: Crossbones (last in NAv #3, '05), Sin (also in dfb), AIM agents
OTHER CHARACTERS: "Terry's Tavern" bartender & patrons (Carl Jackston, also in pfb, named), police (inc a deputy), SHIELD pilot, innkeeper, bystanders (others in pfb); Gretchen Zeller (in photo & Cap's dream), Ed Brubaker (on wanted poster), Red Skull & his Nazis (both in Cap's dream), Maria Hill (mentioned, see NOTE)
LOCATIONS/ITEMS: Lawrence, KS; Pilsburg, IA (also in pfb) inc Sheriff's office, inn & "Terry's Tavern,"; Crossbones' & Sin's guns, AIM spider-robot (in pfb) & guns, SHIELD jet & hover car
FLASHBACK: Carl watches as Winter Soldier destroys an AIM spider-robot (p). Sin drives to Iowa (d).
SYNOPSIS: Crossbones and Sin go on a rampage in Kansas. One of the bystanders Sin kills has an AIM outfit in his trunk, much to their pleasure. A week later, Captain America and Sharon search for the pair in Pilsburg, Iowa, which happens to be the site of a recent Winter Soldier sighting. Checking into a local hotel, Steve spots the former owner's photo, finding the woman in it naggingly familiar. They find the town eerily serene, with no one wanting to talk about a recent "car accident." Eventually they meet Carl Jackston, an outsider uncaring about keeping the town's secrets, who relays his story. Overjoyed to hear Bucky is alive, Steve kisses Sharon, resparking their relationship. Later, in bed with Sharon, Steve wakes up having dreamt of the war, suddenly remembering who the woman in the photo was. AIM agents storm the room but Steve and Sharon easily overpower them, only to learn the agents are seeking Cap's help.
NOTE: Nick Fury went underground after SecWar #5, '05; Maria Hill replaced him as SHIELD Director. Cap #17, '06 reveals Fury sent Winter Soldier to Pilsburg.

CAPTAIN AMERICA #17 [#566] (June 2006)

"Collision Courses Part 2 of 2" (22 pages)

CREDITS: Ed Brubaker (writer), Mike Perkins (art), Virtual Calligraphy's Joe Caramagna (letters), FrankD'Armata (colors), Molly Lazer, Aubrey Sitterson (asst editors), Andy Schmidt (assoc editor), Tom Brevoort (editor), Steve Epting (c art)
FEATURE CHARACTER: Captain America (next in Cap Spec, '06)
SUPPORTING CAST: Sharon Carter (next in Cap Spec, '06)
VILLAINS: Crossbones, Sin (both also in pfb), AIM agents (others in pfb) MODOC squad
OTHER CHARACTERS: Betty Tolin (Gretchen Zeller's daughter, only app), SHIELD agents (Cotton & Morgan named, latter dies); Pilsburg mayor, bystanders (both in pfb); Gretchen Zeller, Winter Soldier (both in photo), RAID (mentioned, see NOTE)
LOCATIONS/ITEMS: Pilsburg, IA (also in pfb) inc mayor's office (in pfb), AIM facility (also in pfb) & Tolin home, Crossbones' safehouse; Crossbones' & Sin's guns, AIM weapons (in pfb) & agent's guns (others in pfb), MODOC squad's guns & knives, SHIELD guns, hovercraft, hover car & Helicarrier
FLASHBACK: Pilsburg is built on top of an AIM research cell. AIM keeps politicians in their pocket while their research benefits the town. Crossbones and Sin take over the AIM facility and break into their advanced weapons vault (p).
SYNOPSIS: The AIM agent tells Steve and Sharon that Crossbones and Sin have taken over their facility. Captain America and Sharon follow him, and he tells them that an agent was tailing the villains hoping for a lead on the new AIM splinter RAID. Cap and Sharon's SHIELD team infiltrate the facility, but Crossbones and Sin are waiting for them. Cap and SHIELD defeat AIM and the MODOC squad only to lose Crossbones and Sin. Confusingly, nothing was taken from the AIM vault but a SHIELD agent was abducted. Later, Steve and Sharon visit Betty Tolin, the daughter of Gretchen Zeller, a woman Bucky loved during the war. They learn he wanted to know where her mother was buried to pay his last respects. Cap realizes that Nick Fury has been helping Bucky, and Bucky plans a suicide attack against Lukin. Elsewhere, Crossbones interrogates and kills the SHIELD agent, learning that Lukin killed Red Skull.
NOTE: Red Skull's AID has changed its name to RAID: Radically Advanced Ideas in Destruction.

CAPTAIN AMERICA 65TH ANNIVERSARY SPECIAL (May 2006)

"Secrets of Iron & Fire" (7 pages)
"Part 2: The Resistance" (5 pages)
"Part 3: Recon" (6 pages)
"Part 4: History Lesson" (4 pages)
"Part 5: A Two-Pronged Attack" (7 pages)
"Part 6: The Sleeper Awakens" (7 pages)
"Epilogue" (2 pages)

CREDITS: Ed Brubaker (writer), Javier Pulido (art Parts 1, 4 & 5), Marcos Martin (art Parts 2, 3 & 6), Mike Perkins (art Epilogue), Dave Lanphear (letters), Javier Rodriguez (colors Parts 1-6), Frank D'Armata (colors Epilogue), Molly Lazer, Aubrey Sitterson (asst editors), Andy Schmidt (assoc editor), Tom Brevoort (editor), Eric Wright (c art)

FEATURE CHARACTER: Captain America (also in fb1 between Cap Ann #9/2, '90 fb & CapC #41, '44; next in Cable&Dp #24, '06, Pulse #12-13, '06, NTb #13-14, '05 fbs, YAvP #1, '08 fb, MHol, '05/2, Cap #616/5, '11, NAv #21, '06 fb, FNSM #1, '05, MKSM #19, '05, FNSM #3, MKSM #21, ASM #527, MKSM #22, Cable&Dp #25, FF Spec, SMU #12/2, BP #16, Cap #18, all '06)

GUEST STARS: Sgt. Fury & his Howling Commandos: Izzy Cohen, Dum Dum Dugan, Gabe Jones, Dino Manelli, Pinky Pinkerton, Reb Ralston (all in fb1 between Cap Ann #9/2, '90 fb & SgtF #65, '69)

SUPPORTING CAST: Bucky (in fb1 between Cap Ann #9/2, '90 fb & CapC #41, '44), Sharon Carter (last in Cap #17, '06, next in Cap #19, '06)

VILLAINS: Red Skull (also in fb1-2 between Cap Ann #9/2, '90 fb & MUni #1, '98; last in Cap #14, '06, next in Cap #18, '06) & his Nazi soldiers (in fb1-2, many die), Sleeper Prototype (in fb1, also in historic drawings, only app), Dr. Doom (bts in fb1 as Baron of Iron, also in historic drawings, see NOTE), Aleksander Lukin (last in Cap #14, '06, next in Cap #18, '06)

OTHER CHARACTERS: Gretchen Zeller (resistance fighter), Dr. Richard Zeller (Gretchen's father) (both in fb1), Hermann Dexx (German scientist, in fb1-2) (all only app), Allied pilot (bts in fb, flying plane), birds (in fb1), SHIELD agent, Kronas employee

LOCATIONS/ITEMS: Germany inc Eisendorf (also in fb2) w/library, Zeller home (all in fb1) & Castle Eisen (as ruins, also in historic drawings & destroyed in fb1); Nazis' guns & excavation equipment, Bucky's grenade & gun, Gretchen's radio & gun, Allied plane, Howlers' guns, Fury's & Dum Dum's knives (all in fb1), SHIELD Helicarrier

FLASHBACKS: April 1944: Captain America, Bucky, Sgt. Fury and his Howling Commandos parachute behind enemy lines but are quickly spotted by Nazis. The enemy is killed but Bucky is wounded, so Cap runs him ahead to the rendezvous in Eisendorf while the Howlers recon Red Skull's activities. While Dr. Zeller tends to Bucky, Cap learns from Gretchen that she and her father are all of the local resistance. Cap meets with the Howlers and that night, he and Fury obtain documents pertaining to the Skull's excavation activities. Meanwhile, Bucky and Gretchen search the library and learn the Skull is searching for an ancient giant robot under Castle Eisen, built centuries ago by the Baron of Iron. Soon, the Howlers storm the Nazi camp while Bucky and Gretchen rescue Hermann Dexx. Cap infiltrates Castle Eisen where Red Skull has found and activated a giant robot. Cap destroys the robot's exposed power source, an organic heart, and the Skull escapes. The robot explodes and destroys Castle Eisen. Bucky kisses Gretchen goodbye, promising to find her after the war (1). Red Skull and his Nazis arrive in Eisendorf with Hermann Dexx in tow (2).

SYNOPSIS: Aboard the Helicarrier, Cap tells Sharon that Bucky never even sent Gretchen a secret wire for fear of exposing her to the Nazis. Meanwhile, Lukin begins excavating the ruins of his newly purchased Castle Eisen.

NOTE: Cap #23, '06 reveals Doom has yet to experience his time as the Baron of Iron 500 years ago.

CAPTAIN AMERICA #18 [#567] (July 2006)

"Twenty-First Century Blitz Part One of Four" (22 pages)

CREDITS: Ed Brubaker (writer), Steve Epting (art), Virtual Calligraphy's Joe Caramagna (letters), Frank D'Armata (colors), Molly Lazer, Aubrey Sitterson (asst editors), Tom Brevoort (editor)

FEATURE CHARACTER: Captain America

GUEST STARS: Spitfire, Union Jack (both last in Inv #9, '05)

SUPPORTING CAST: James Barnes (last in Cap #16, '06)

VILLAINS: Red Skull, Aleksander Lukin (also in photo) (both also in pfb, last in Cap Spec, '06), Crossbones, Sin (both next in Cap #20, '06), Master Man (Max Lohmer, great-nephew of Wilhelm Lohmer, 1st, also in pfb) & his Master Race (1st, also as skinheads in pfb), purse snatcher

OTHER CHARACTERS: Mr. Clarkson (Roxxon VP), Kristy (Clarkson's secretary) (both die), Kronas employees & security force, news vendor, bystanders

LOCATIONS/ITEMS: Hamburg, Germany (pfb), London inc Heathrow airport, Manor House & shipyards, Roxxon's private Dallas, TX airfield; Red Skull mask, Roxxon jet, Crossbone's guns, Sin's guns, Kronas freightliner

FLASHBACK: Two months ago, Red Skull recruits Max Lohmer to be the new Master Man (p).

SYNOPSIS: Steve Rogers arrives in London and reunites with Spitfire and Union Jack. He fills them in on Lukin's activities and Bucky's return. Elsewhere in London, James Barnes stops a purse snatcher. The next night, Captain America, Union Jack and Spitfire investigate a suspicious Kronas shipment. Spitfire follows the offloaded crates while Cap and Jack sneak aboard. In Texas, Crossbones and Sin steal a Roxxon corporate jet. Searching the ship's log, Cap discovers the shipment came from Germany. Suddenly, Master Man and his Master Race attack Cap and Union Jack.

NOTE: Cover labeled "Twenty-First Century Blitz Part One."

CAPTAIN AMERICA #19 [#568] (August 2006)

"Twenty-First Century Blitz Part Two of Four" (22 pages)

CREDITS: Ed Brubaker (writer), Steve Epting (pencils, co-inks, c art), Mike Perkins (co-inks), Virtual Calligraphy's Joe Caramagna (letters), Frank D'Armata (colors), Molly Lazer, Aubrey Sitterson (asst editors), Tom Brevoort (editor)

FEATURE CHARACTER: Captain America (also in pfb)

GUEST STARS: Union Jack (also in pfb), Spitfire

SUPPORTING CAST: Sharon Carter (last in Cap Spec, '06), Winter Soldier

VILLAINS: Red Skull, Aleksander Lukin, Master Man (also in pfb) & his Master Race (one also in pfb, one as corpse), Gerry (arms dealer) & his men

OTHER CHARACTERS: Tony Blair (British Prime Minister, bts, authorized Sharon, 1st, next in NEx #22, '07) Philip Gavin (asst. director of MI-5, 1st, next in UJack #1, '06 fb), reporter (on TV), RAID agents (corpses), Kronas employees & security force

LOCATIONS/ITEMS: London inc Thames House, Gerry's Oddities, sewers & Kronas Corporate HQ w/Lukin's office, shipyards; Red Skull mask, Kronas freightliner & bomb, Union Jack's gun, Bucky's guns

FLASHBACK: Cap and Union Jack battle Master Man (p).

SYNOPSIS: Lukin observes from afar as Captain America and Union Jack fight Master Man and sets explosives to destroy the freighter. Union Jack discovers the bomb and calls Spitfire to evacuate them. Elsewhere, James Barnes plans his attack against Lukin. MI-5's Phillip Gavin chews out Cap and Union Jack until Sharon arrives with orders from Downing Street, authorizing Union Jack to work for her for the next week. Later, Union Jack and Sharon investigate Kronas while Cap and Spitfire look for Winter Soldier by interrogating local arms dealers. MI-5 sends word that the Master Race have been spotted. The four investigate and discover dead a Master Race member and RAID agents, and plans for an air attack on London. Elsewhere, Master Man throws a tantrum over his defeat. Red Skull assures him that everything is going according to plan.

CAPTAIN AMERICA #20 [#569] (September 2006)

"Twenty-First Century Blitz Part Three of Four" (22 pages)

CREDITS: Ed Brubaker (writer), Steve Epting (art), Virtual Calligraphy's Joe Caramagna (letters), FrankD'Armata (colors), Molly Lazer, Aubrey Sitterson (asst. editor), Tom Brevoort (editor)
FEATURE CHARACTER: Captain America
GUEST STARS: Spitfire, Union Jack
SUPPORTING CAST: Winter Soldier, Sharon Carter
VILLAINS: Red Skull, Aleksander Lukin, Crossbones, Sin (both last in Cap #18, '06), Master Man & his Master Race, 6th Sleeper (1st)
OTHER CHARACTERS: Kronas party guests, Zeppelin crew, airfield crew (corpses)
LOCATIONS/ITEMS: Small English airfield, London inc Kronas Corporate HQ, Manor House, River Thames & sewers; SHIELD hovercar, Lukin's vintage aircraft, Zeppelin & explosives, Crossbones' stolen Cessna & gun, Union Jack's gun, Winter Soldier's rifle, Sleeper remote

SYNOPSIS: Outside London, Crossbones and Sin load a Cessna with explosives to use on Kronas Corporate HQ. Meanwhile, Winter Soldier discovers Lukin's secret plan and ups his timetable. The next night, Captain America and Sharon head to Kronas' corporate gala, which was the date for the air attack plans on London. Spotting a Zeppelin amongst the celebratory vintage aircraft circling the Kronas Corporate HQ, Cap and Sharon attack and find Master Man and his Master Race inside. The ensuing battle causes the Zeppelin to catch fire. Cap attempts to steer it towards the Thames, which distracts Winter Soldier from assassinating Lukin. Lukin notices Crossbones' stolen Cessna heading towards him, and at Red Skull's insistence, activates the buried Sleeper. It destroys the Cessna as Cap and Winter Soldier separately look on in terror.

NOTE: Cover labeled "Twenty-First Century Blitz Part Three."

CAPTAIN AMERICA #21 [#570] (October 2006)

"Twenty-First Century Blitz Conclusion" (22 pages)

CREDITS: Ed Brubaker (writer), Steve Epting (art), Virtual Calligraphy's Joe Caramagna (letters), FrankD'Armata (colors), Molly Lazer, Aubrey Sitterson (asst editors), Tom Brevoort (editor)
FEATURE CHARACTER: Captain America (also in dfb; next in DD #81, I♥M:Web #1, X #186, Thing #8 fb, NAv#17-20, NAv Ann #1, MTU #22-23 & 25, SH #7, Thing #8, IM #7-8 & 10-12, all '06, CapTW:TSO #1, '09, CW #1, '06, W #42, '06, Av:In #8, '08 fb, NAv #21, bts in BP #17, NAv #22, MSM #5, MsM #6 fb, CW #2, CW #3 fb, ASM #533, CW:YAv&Run #1, MK #7-8, all '06, BW:DO #4, '10 fb, BP #18, '06, Tb #104-105, '06)
GUEST STARS: Spitfire (also in dfb; next in FallSon:IM, '07), Union Jack (also in dfb; next in UJack #1, '06), Nick Fury (bts, on phone w/Winter Soldier, last in Cable&Dp #25, '06, chr last in CW:Conf #1, '07 fb, next bts in NAv #21, '06, next in Cap #23, '06)
SUPPORTING CAST: Winter Soldier (next in Cap #23, '06), Sharon Carter (next in NAv #18, '06)
VILLAINS: Red Skull, Aleksander Lukin (both also in dfb), Crossbones, Sin (both next in Cap #25, '07), Master Man (also in dfb, next in Inv #2, 10) & Master Race, 6th Sleeper (destroyed, last app)
OTHER CHARACTERS: Kronas party guests, businessmen (corpses), police (in dfb), reporter (on TV), driver, bystanders
LOCATIONS/ITEMS: London inc Kronas Corporate HQ, Manor House, River Thames, Lukin's penthouse, office building & train station; Red Skull mask (dfb), SHIELD hover car, Crossbones' gun, Sin's knife & gun, Union Jack's gun, police guns, Cap's concussion charge

FLASHBACK: Red Skull publicly announces his return. As police arrest Master Man, Lukin admonishes vigilante justice and publicly endorses America's rumored Registration Act (d).

SYNOPSIS: While the Sleeper blitzes London, Sharon rams Master Man with her hovercar. She ricochets into an office building, and dazed, finds herself at Crossbones' and Sin's mercy. Captain America sends Spitfire and Union Jack after Master Man and helps Winter Soldier attack the Sleeper. Meanwhile, Red Skull stops Crossbones from killing Sharon. Cap leads the Sleeper into position while Spitfire makes Master Man so angry that he lunges wildly through the Sleeper's head. Cap distracts the Sleeper and Winter Soldier tosses a concussion charge inside the damaged head, destroying it. Winter Soldier loses his robotic arm in the process and vanishes. The next day, Steve and Sharon bid farewell to Spitfire and Union Jack and James Barnes uses a payphone to contact Nick Fury. At Kronas, Red Skull introduces Lukin to Sin and Crossbones.

NOTE: Cover labeled "Twenty-First Century Blitz Part Four."

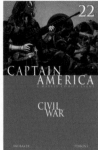

CAPTAIN AMERICA #22 [#571] (November 2006)

"The Drums of War Part One of Three" (22 pages)

CREDITS: Ed Brubaker (writer), Mike Perkins (art), Virtual Calligraphy's Joe Caramagna (letters), Frank D'Armata (colors), Molly Lazer, Aubrey Sitterson (asst editors), Tom Brevoort (editor), Steve Epting (c art)
FEATURE CHARACTERS: Captain America (in symbolic image, rfb & pfb, next in NAv #23, Cable&Dp #30-31, CW #3, ASM #534 fb, CW:FL #6/4, NAv #24 fb, CW:FL #6, CW:X #2, all '06, IM/Cap #1, '07, HFH #2-3, FF #539, ASM #534, CW:Choos #1/2, CW:FL #8-9, all, '06, bts in Cap #28, '07, CW #5, '06, PWJ #1-2, '07, SenSM #34, '06, Cap #24, '06)
GUEST STARS: Maria Hill (SHIELD Director, in pfb, last in CW #1, also in NAv #21, CW #2, NAv #22-23, CW:YAv&Run #2, bts in CW:YAv&Run #3, CW:YAv&Run #4, next in W #47, all '06), Dum Dum Dugan (in rfb & pfb, last in NAv #21, '06, next in AoAtlas #1, '06)
SUPPORTING CAST: Sharon Carter (also in photo & pfb, last in NAv #20, '06)
VILLAINS: Dr. Faustus (also as SHIELD psychiatrist Dr. Benjamin, last in Nomad #19, '93, next in Cap #25, '07), Red Skull, Aleksander Lukin
OTHER CHARACTERS: SHIELD agents (in rfb) inc Cape-Killers (in pfb & rfb), Falcon (in rfb), Iron Man (in symbolic image)
LOCATIONS/ITEMS: New York inc Sharon's safe-room, decoy address (all pfb), cemetery & SHIELD Administrative Affairs Building w/ psychiatrist's office; SHIELD Helicarrier (pfb & rfb) inc med lab (pfb), Sharon's dead drop container, note & signal (prev 3 pfb), SHIELD guns & Cape-Killer armor w/lasers (pfb & rfb), War-Hawk One (SHIELD plane, rfb), Dr. Faustus' illusion caster, Red Skull mask
FLASHBACKS: Captain America fights SHIELD agents tasked with arresting him, and escapes (CW #1, '06). Cap and Falcon battle Dum Dum's SHIELD Cape-Killers (NAv #21, '06). Aboard the Helicarrier, Sharon Carter confronts SHIELD Director Maria Hill over not taking her advice in how to handle Cap's reaction to the Registration Act. Hill orders Sharon to help SHIELD bring Cap into custody. Sharon checks in on the injured and regretful Dum Dum Dugan. Later, Sharon rendezvouses with Cap and takes him to her safe-room, where they make love and debate the Registration Act. Sharon points out that Cap is already registered as a government agent. Cap rebuts that he accepts his responsibility as Captain America, but the role has cost him a normal life; the Registration Act robs others of the choice he had. Sharon says the Act is law, and Cap responds that America was founded on breaking the law, because the law was wrong. Despite her orders, Sharon signals SHIELD Cape-Killer squad to the wrong address (p).
SYNOPSIS: A SHIELD psychiatrist gives Sharon Carter a psychiatric evaluation for disobeying orders. The psychiatrist, a disguised Dr. Faustus whose machinations have caused Carter to fall in love with Cap, later reports to Red Skull.
NOTE: Cover labeled "Civil War." Dr. Faustus' alias is revealed in Cap #30, '07. Cap and Sharon quote from statesman Benjamin Franklin and propagandist Thomas Paine.

CAPTAIN AMERICA #23 [#572] (December 2006)

"The Drums of War Part Two of Three" (22 pages)

CREDITS: Ed Brubaker (writer), Mike Perkins (art), Virtual Calligraphy's Joe Caramagna (letters), Frank D'Armata (colors), Molly Lazer, Aubrey Sitterson (asst editors), Tom Brevoort (editor), Steve Epting (c art)
FEATURE CHARACTERS: Captain America (only in rfb)
GUEST STAR: Nick Fury (last in Cable&Dp #25, '06, chr last in CW:Conf #1, '07 fb, last bts in CW #3, '06, next in WS:WK #1, '07)
SUPPORTING CAST: Winter Soldier (last in Cap #21, '06, next in WS:WK #1, '07), Sharon Carter (bts, tips Fury off)
VILLAINS: Red Skull (also bts in pfb), Aleksander Lukin (also in pfb), Dr. Doom (last in BP #19, '06, next in FF #543, '07 fb)
OTHER CHARACTERS: Nick Fury LMD (see NOTE), SHIELD agents inc Cape-Killer squad (Cleery & Sarge named), Latverian Embassy guard (in pfb), Dr. Doom's archaeologists (bts, digging in Eisendorf, Germany), Demolition Man (hologram decoy), Goliath (Bill Foster), Iron Man, Spider-Man, Thing, Yellowjacket (Skrull) (prev 5 in rfb)
LOCATIONS/ITEMS: New York inc Geffen-Meyer petrochemical plant (in rfb), Latverian Embassy (in pfb), Chase Manhattan Bank & SHIELD monitoring station, Latveria inc Doomstadt; SHIELD Cape-Killer armor & guns, Dr. Doom's chronal device, Red Skull mask, Fury's nano-trojan, Winter Soldier's anti-security device, holographic communicator & power surge device
FLASHBACKS: Captain America and his allies fight pro-registration heroes (CW #3, '06). Aleksander Lukin visits the Latverian Embassy (p).
SYNOPSIS: Acting on a tip from Sharon Carter, the underground Nick Fury sends Winter Soldier on a covert mission to a SHIELD monitoring station. There, Winter Soldier subdues a Fury LMD and injects him with a nano-trojan that will allow the real Fury to spy on SHIELD. As Fury downloads data from the LMD, Winter Soldier watches a video recording of a super-hero battle and ponders the insanity of the heroes' Civil War and the part his Philadelphia bombing played in the passing of the Superhuman Registration Act. After learning that Aleksander Lukin recently visited the Latverian Embassy, Winter Soldier leaves the SHIELD facility and fights and defeats a Cape-Killer squad. In Latveria, Red Skull provides information to Dr. Doom about his future in return for a chronal device, which the Skull plans to use against Cap.
NOTE: Cover labeled "Civil War." NAv:I #1, '06 and this issue reveal and SH #17, '07 explains that SHIELD has been using various Nick Fury LMDs to conceal Fury's absence after he went underground. This issue reveals that the first LMDs were developed to protect VIPs because of Winter Soldier's murder of a UN official in 1959.

CAPTAIN AMERICA #24 [#573] (January 2007)

"The Drums of War Part Three of Three" (23 pages)

CREDITS: Ed Brubaker (writer), Mike Perkins (art), Virtual Calligraphy's Joe Caramagna (letters), Frank D'Armata (colors), Molly Lazer, Aubrey Sitterson (asst editors), Tom Brevoort (editor), Steve Epting (c art)
FEATURE CHARACTERS: Captain America (also as Hydra agent, next in IM #14, '07, Tb #107-108, '06, PWJ #2, '07, CW:WC #1, '07, BP #23-24, '07, CW #6, '06, ASM #537, '07, PWJ #3, '07, BP #25, '07, CW #7, '07, MsM #14, '07 fb, ASM #538, '07, CM #1, '08 fb, CW:FL #11, '07 fb, Cap #600/4, '09 fb, CW #7, '07 fb, CW:FL #11, '07)
GUEST STARS: Nick Fury (voice only, last in WS:WK #1, '07, last bts in HFH #2, '06, chr next in Cap #601, '09), Maria Hill (last in CW #5, '06, next in IM #14, '07)
SUPPORTING CAST: Sharon Carter
VILLAINS: Arnim Zola (last in MHol, '06, next in Cap #26, '07), Red Skull, Aleksander Lukin, Hydra agents
OTHER CHARACTERS: George W. Bush (mentioned, see NOTE), Nick Fury LMD (next in Cap #27, '07), SHIELD agents & cape-killers; Falcon, Hercules, Patriot, Vision, Luke Cage (prev 5 on cover only)
LOCATIONS/ITEMS: New York inc AIM base w/lab & security station, Kronas Corporation w/lab & Brooklyn Bridge; SHIELD Helicarrier & hovercar, SHIELD Cape-Killer armor & guns, Hydra agents' bomb & guns, Fury LMD's retinal scanner, Fury's EMP device, Red Skull mask
SYNOPSIS: Sharon Carter is deemed fit for duty, and after Maria Hill assigns her to hunt down Nick Fury, she has a clandestine meeting with the Fury LMD aboard the Helicarrier. Speaking through the LMD, the real Fury sends Sharon to rescue Cap at an AIM facility where Cap is following a lead on Red Skull. Cap finds the AIM base abandoned and raided by Hydra. Cap battles the Hydra agents and survives a suicide bombing that kills his adversaries. Dazed from the blast, a SHIELD Cape-Killer squad attacks Cap but Sharon disables them with an EMP pulse and Cap and Carter depart in her SHIELD hovercar. Sharon tells Cap she's no longer conflicted about the Civil War since pro-registration forces killed Goliath. In a Kronas lab, Red Skull conspires against Cap with Arnim Zola.
NOTE: Cover labeled "Civil War." Includes recap/title page, where the story is called "Drums of War Part 3." A SHIELD Cape-Killer orders Cap to surrender under the authority of the president; this standing executive order would have been issued to have Cap arrested for treason between CW #1-2, '06.

CAPTAIN AMERICA #25 [#574] (April 2007)

"The Death of the Dream Part One" (33 pages)

CREDITS: Ed Brubaker (writer), Steve Epting (art), Virtual Calligraphy's Joe Caramagna (letters), Frank D'Armata (colors), Molly Lazer, Aubrey Sitterson (asst editors), Tom Brevoort (editor), John Cassaday, Bryan Hitch (variant c art), Ed McGuinness (variant c pencils), Dexter Vines (variant c inks)
FEATURE CHARACTER: Captain America (also in film, TV news illustration, rfb, dfb & fb1 between MvPro #4, '10 fb & MSH #3, '90 fb, fb2 during MSH #3, '90 fb, fb3 between Cap #255, '81 fb & MvPro #4, '10 fb, fb4 between SR:SSol #1, '10 fb & MvPro #4, '10 fb, fb10 between MvPro #5, '10 & Cap #255, '81 fb, fb11 between ToS #71/2, '65 & Cap&Crb #1, '11 fb, fb5 between ToS #75/2, '66 fb & ToS #77/2 '66 fb, fb7 between Cap #3, '05 fb & Cap #49, '09 fb, fb8 during ToS #75/2, '66, fb12 between Cap #133, '71 & FF:WGCM #4, '01, fb9 between SgtF #100, '72 & Hulk #152, '72, fb13 between Cap Ann #3, '76 & Av #145, '76; also in Cap&Crb #1, '11 fb, Cap:Re #1, '09 fb, Cap #600/2, '09 fb, next as corpse in CW:Conf #1, Cap #26 fb, FallSon:W, all '07)
GUEST STARS: Invaders: Human Torch (Jim Hammond), Toro (both in fb5 between Cap Ann, '01 fb & Cap #3, '05 fb); Falcon (also in fb12 between Cap #133, '71 & FF:WGCM #4, '01, fb13 between Cap #191, '75 & Av #146, '76; last in CW #7, '07, next in FallSon:IM, '07), Nick Fury (voice only, chr last in Cap #601, '09)
SUPPORTING CAST: Winter Soldier (also as Bucky in fb5 between Cap Ann '01 fb & Cap #3, '05 fb, fb11 between Cap #616/3, '11 fb & Hulk #284, '83; last in WS:WK #1, '07, chr last in Cap #601, '09, next in FallSon:W, '07), Sharon Carter (also in fb6 between Cap #162, '73 fb & ToS #75/2, '66, also in Cap #49, '09 fb; fb8 during ToS #75/2, '66, fb9 between Cap #148-149, '72; also in dfb, Cap:Re #1, '09 fb, Cap #600/2, '09 fb, chr next in Cap #26, '07 fb, next in FallSon:IM, '07), Peggy Carter (in fb7 between ToS #77/2, '66 fb & Cap #49, '09 fb, fb6 between Cap #162, '73 fb & Cap #161, '73, also in Cap #49, '09 fb; see NOTE)
VILLAINS: Red Skull (voice only), Aleksander Lukin, Crossbones (last in Cap #21, '06, also in Cap&Crb #1, '11 fb, next in FallSon:W, '07) & his pilot, Sin (also as nurse, last in Cap #21, '06), Dr. Faustus (last in Cap #22, '06), Batroc (in fb8 during ToS #75, '66), Nazi soldiers (in fb7 & fb11, also in newsreel footage) & spies (in fb10), criminals (in fb11)
OTHER CHARACTERS: Gen. Phillips (in fb4 between Cap #109, '69 fb & MvPro #4, '10 fb, also in rfb), Redwing (in fb12 between Cap #133-134, '71, in fb13 between Cap #191, '75 & Cap #217, '78), Prof. Reinstein (Abraham Erskine, in fb4 between Cap #255, '81 fb & MvPro, '10 fb, also in rfb), Julie Traylor (News 10 TV correspondent), Vicki (News 10 TV anchor) (both only app), European villagers (in fb11), French Resistance fighter (in fb7), theater attendees (in fb2), army draftees (in fb3), US soldiers (in fb5, fb11 & film in fb6, one in rfb), Operation: Rebirth witnesses (in rfb), police (one also in dfb), SHIELD agents inc Cape-Killers, news reporters & photographers, News 10 TV cameraman, paramedics, US marshals, bystanders (also in fb1, fb8 & dfb); Heinz Kruger (in rfb), Luke Cage, Ms. Marvel, Spider-Man, Spider-Woman (Skrull) (prev 4 in TV news illustration), Iron Man (in rfb2, billboard & TV news illustrations), Adolf Hitler (in newsreel footage), Jack Kirby (on billboard, see NOTE)

LOCATIONS/ITEMS: European villages (in fb5 & fb11), Operation: Rebirth scientific facility (in fb4 & rfb), Carter family's Virginia Estate (in fb6), New York inc Lower East Side (in fb1), movie theater (in fb2), Army recruitment center (in fb3), New York Harbor (in fb10), Kronas Corporation HQ w/Lukin's office, Manhattan federal courthouse & Mercy Hospital w/ladies' room & waiting room; Bucky's & soldiers' guns (both in fb5 & fb11), Heinz Kruger's gun, Super-Soldier Serum (both in rfb), Timely March of News film reel (in fb2), cannon (in fb5), Peggy Carter's gun (in fb7), Operation: Rebirth equipment (in fb4 & rfb) inc Vita-Ray machine (in rfb), Statue of Liberty (in fb10), helicopters (inc one labeled WNYK), Sharon's chronal pistol (also in dfb, see NOTE), Cape-Killers' armor & guns, Crossbones' rifle, Sin's wig, Winter Soldier's pistols, Red Skull mask

FLASHBACKS: During the Great Depression, Steve Rogers lives in New York (1) and sees newsreel footage of the Nazi war machine (2). Rogers is declared 4F again (3) and is prepared for Operation: Rebirth (4). Steve becomes the only Super-Soldier when Erskine dies (CapC #1, '41, ToS #63/2, '65 & Cap #109, '69 fb). Cap, the Invaders and Allied soldiers liberate Paris (5). Cap fights Iron Man during the super-hero Civil War (CW #7, '07). Peggy and young Sharon Carter watch WWII footage of Cap (6). Cap, Peggy and the French Resistance fight Nazis in France (7). Sharon watches Cap fight Batroc (8). Cap and Sharon share a romantic moment (9). Cap fights Nazi spies at the Liberty shipyard (10). Cap and Bucky rout Nazi soldiers from a European village during WWII (11). Cap and Falcon bust criminals (12). Cap bids Falcon and Redwing farewell (13). Sharon shoots Cap (d).

SYNOPSIS: The press and throngs of picketers show up at the Manhattan courthouse as US Marshals escort Captain America to his scheduled arraignment following his voluntary arrest during the super-hero Civil War. Sharon Carter and James Barnes are stationed among the crowd, following orders from Nick Fury. A sniper shoots Cap. As Sharon reaches the wounded hero, another gun blasts Cap at point-blank range. Winter Soldier rushes to the sniper's nest, only to find it deserted. Falcon arrives and thinking Barnes shot Cap, attacks; they quickly resolve the misunderstanding. Fury spots the sniper fleeing in a helicopter and dispatches Winter Soldier to pursue him. Falcon flies Barnes to the chopper and Winter Soldier forces the sniper, Crossbones, to evacuate. After defeating Crossbones, Winter Soldier flees as Cape-Killers arrive to arrest the villain. An ambulance rushes Cap and Carter to the hospital, where Cap is pronounced dead. Posing as a nurse, Sin relays a message from Dr. Faustus to Sharon that causes her to remember that she was the one who shot Cap at close range under Faustus' influence.

NOTE: Cover labeled "Civil War Epilogue." Includes recap page (1 page). Peggy Carter, previously Sharon's sister, is retconned to be her aunt here, as it is no longer feasible for 30-something Sharon to have a sister who fought in WW II. Cap:Re #1, '09 reveals that Sharon shoots Cap with an adapted version of Dr. Doom's chronal device given to Red Skull in Cap #23, '07, freezing him in time and space. In one flashback, a billboard shows the cover to FOOM #11, '75, featuring Jack Kirby.

FALLEN SON: THE DEATH OF CAPTAIN AMERICA - WOLVERINE (June 2007)

"The Death of Captain America Chapter 1: Denial" (23 pages)

CREDITS: Jeph Loeb (writer), Leinil Yu (art, c pencils), Dave McCaig (colors), Richard Starkings & Comicraft (letters), Alejandro Arbona (asst editor), Bill Rosemann (editor), Tom Brevoort (exec editor), Michael Turner (variant c pencils), Peter Steigerwald (c inks, variant c inks)

FEATURE CHARACTERS: Captain America (corpse, also in rfb; next bts in FallSon:IM, '07), Wolverine (last in W #51, '07, next in FallSon:Av, '07)

GUEST STARS: Daredevil (last in DD #93, '07, next bts in NAv #29, '07 fb, next in DD #93, '07), Dr. Strange (last in CW #7, '07, next in FallSon:Av, '07), Iron Man (last in PWJ #8 fb, last bts in PWJ #10, chr last in MAv #2 fb, also in FallSon:Av, next in FallSon:Cap, all '07), Maria Hill (last in PWJ #8, '07 fb, next in MsM #13, '07)

SUPPORTING CAST: Winter Soldier (also as Bucky in rfb, between Cap #25-26, '07)

VILLAINS: Crossbones (last in Cap #25, '07, next in Cap #28, '07), Criti Noll (Skrull, as Yellowjacket, last in CW #7, '07, next in FallSon:IM, '07, see NOTE)

OTHER CHARACTERS: SHIELD agents, birds

LOCATIONS/ITEMS: New York inc Hell's Kitchen & former SHIELD Lower East Side base w/Sam's Barbershop front; Zemo's drone plane (rfb), Daredevil's billy club, Cap's flag-draped casket, SHIELD agent's gun, SHIELD jets & Helicarrier inc Crossbones' cell

FLASHBACK: Captain America and Bucky pursue Zemo's drone plane (Av #4, '64 fb).

SYNOPSIS: Believing Captain America's death to be a SHIELD deception, Wolverine asks Winter Soldier to join him in raiding the SHIELD Helicarrier to identify Cap's body, but Barnes declines. Wolverine enlists Daredevil and the two steal aboard the Helicarrier, cloaked by Dr. Strange's enchantment. They take a detour to Crossbones' cell, where Wolverine questions the villain about the assassination. Daredevil stops Logan's abusive interrogation when he detects that Crossbones knows nothing. Daredevil departs and Wolverine finds and verifies Cap's corpse. Iron Man detects Wolverine's presence when Strange's spell wears off and he confronts the mutant. Yellowjacket tries to prevent Logan from escaping, but Stark allows Wolverine to leave to tell others that Cap is indeed dead. Logan tells Iron Man that he'll kill him if he finds out he had anything to do with Cap's death.

NOTE: Includes recap page (2 pages) where the indicia names this "Fallen Son: The Death of Captain America #1." The Fallen Son mini series is based on an idea by J. Michael Straczynski. The chapter titles are named after the five stages of grief identified by Elisabeth Kübler-Ross in her 1969 book, "On Death and Dying." MAv #17, '08 reveals that due to Yellowjacket's high intelligence and emotional instability, several Skrulls impersonated him in succession; Pym's personality overwhelmed them and when they became erratic or rebellious they were terminated and replaced. At least two, this one and his replacement, are referred to as "Criti Noll;" it remains unrevealed if this is a proper name or a title.

FALLEN SON: THE DEATH OF CAPTAIN AMERICA - AVENGERS (June 2007)

"The Death of Captain America Chapter 2: Anger" (23 pages)

CREDITS: Jeph Loeb (writer), Ed McGuinness (pencils), Dexter Vines (inks), Richard Starkings & Comicraft (letters), Jason Keith (colors), Alejandro Arbona (asst editor), Bill Rosemann (editor), Tom Brevoort (exec editor), Michael Turner (variant c pencils), Peter Steigerwald (variant c inks)

FEATURE CHARACTERS: Captain America (only on recap page), Iron Man (during FallSon:W, '07) & his Avengers: Ares (Greek god of war, last in MAv #1, '07 fb, chr next in Herc #113, '08 fb, next in NAv #28, '07), Black Widow (last in MAv #2, '07 fb, chr next in Av:In #8, '08 fb, next in NAv #28 '07 fb), Ms. Marvel (Carol Danvers, last in MAv #2, '07 fb, next in FallSon:IM, '07), Sentry (Robert Reynolds, mentally unstable powerhouse, last in MAv #2, '07 fb, chr next in Av:In #8, '08 fb, next in NAv #28 '07 fb), Wasp (last in MAv #2, '07 fb, next in FallSon:IM, '07), Wonder Man (last in MAv #2, '07 fb, next in Cap #26, '07); Luke Cage (last in IF #13, '08) & his Avengers: Iron Fist (Daniel Thomas Rand-K'ai, last in IF #14, '08) (both next in FallSon:IM, '07), Spider-Man (last in CW #7, '07), Wolverine (last in FallSon:W, '07) (both next in FallSon:SM, '07)

GUEST STARS: Dr. Strange (last in FallSon:W, '07, next in FallSon:IM, '07), Sub-Mariner (last in CW #7, '07, next in FallSon:IM, '07), Thing (last in CW:FL #11, '07, next in FallSon:IM, '07)

VILLAINS: Tiger Shark (Todd Arliss, insane amphibian renegade, last in NW #1, '05, chr last in NAv #35, '07 fb, next in PWJ #13, '08), Veranke (Skrull, as Spider-Woman, last in CW:In #1, '07 fb, next in FallSon:IM, '07, see NOTE)

OTHER CHARACTERS: Wong (Dr. Strange's servant, last in MHol, '06/2, next in NAv #28, '07 fb), sea monsters

LOCATIONS/ITEMS: Dr. Strange's Greenwich Village home, Maine coast inc lighthouse; Horn of Gabriel (see NOTE), Ares' battleaxe, Avengers Quinjet, Black Widow's gun, Thing's Pabst Blue Ribbon beer, Starbucks banner

SYNOPSIS: Iron Man's Avengers head to the Maine coast to stop Tiger Shark, who summons sea monsters with the Horn of Gabriel. Iron Man sends a transmission to the heroes noting that Wolverine popped up on the Helicarrier's sensors. Meanwhile, Thing arrives at Dr. Strange's Greenwich Village home, where Strange is unconscious while his astral self is elsewhere. As Thing plays poker with Luke Cage and his Avengers, Wolverine returns from the Helicarrier and confirms that he saw Captain America's corpse. He gets into a fight with Spider-Man, who refuses to believe that Cap is dead. In Maine, the Avengers battle the sea monsters and defeat Tiger Shark. Namor appears and admonishes them for taking their anger about Cap's death out on the marine creatures. After threatening to retaliate if missiles housed nearby are pointed at Atlantis, Namor takes Tiger Shark into custody and leaves with the horn and the monsters.

NOTE: Includes recap page (2 pages) where the indicia names this "Fallen Son: The Death of Captain America #2." Iron Man's appearance here overlaps with last issue. The Horn of Gabriel may be another name for the Proteus Horn, the instrument that controls sea monsters introduced in FF #4, '62, or it may be a similar relic. NAv #40, '08 reveals the Spider-Woman appearing here is the Skrull queen Veranke.

FALLEN SON: THE DEATH OF CAPTAIN AMERICA – CAPTAIN AMERICA (July 2007)

"The Death of Captain America Chapter 3: Bargaining" (24 pages)

CREDITS: Jeph Loeb (writer), John Romita Jr. (pencils), Klaus Janson (inks), Richard Starkings & Comicraft (letters), Morry Hollowell (colors), Alejandro Arbona (asst editor), Bill Rosemann (editor), Tom Brevoort (exec editor), Michael Turner (variant c pencils), Peter Steigerwald (variant c inks)

FEATURE CHARACTERS: Captain America (also as statue, only in fb between Av #25, '66 & Hawk:BS #2, '11 fb), Clint Barton (also as Hawkeye in fb between Av #25, '66 & Hawk:BS #2, '11 fb, also as Captain America, last in NAv #26, '07, chr last in SH #20, '07 fb, chr next in NAv #30, '07 fb, next in NAv #27, '07 as Ronin)

GUEST STARS: Young Avengers: Hawkeye (Kate Bishop, archer), Patriot (Elijah "Eli" Bradley, grandson of black "Captain America" Isaiah Bradley) (both last in CW #7, '07, next in FallSon:IM, '07); Avengers: Quicksilver, Scarlet Witch (both in fb between Av #25, '66 & ToS #72/2, '65); Iron Man (also as statue, last in FallSon:W, '07, next in FallSon:IM, '07)

VILLAIN: Firebrand (Russ Broxtel, last in UJack #2, '06, next in Av:In #13, '08)

OTHER CHARACTERS: Avengers: Giant-Man, Hulk, Thor, Wasp (all as statues); Dr. Coleite (SHIELD scientist, only app); Black Panther (mentioned, gave Kate Bishop EMP arrow)

LOCATIONS/ITEMS: New York inc 9th Ave Roxxon gas station & Avengers Mansion ruins; Cap's shield, Patriot's shield, Barton's bow & signal arrow, Kate Bishop's bow & arrows inc EMP & foam arrows, Iron Man's bio-scanner, SHIELD Helicarrier inc containment chamber

FLASHBACK: Hawkeye challenges Captain America's leadership during his early days with the Avengers.

SYNOPSIS: The recently resurrected Clint Barton summons Iron Man to the ruins of Avengers Mansion. Iron Man subdues Clint and takes him aboard the Helicarrier where he confirms his identity. Iron Man offers Clint Captain America's shield and the chance to be the new Cap. Clint dons a Cap costume and accompanies Iron Man on a call to a Manhattan gas station, where Patriot and the new Hawkeye defeat Firebrand. Iron Man moves to arrest the young heroes for violation of the Registration Act, but Hawkeye fends him off with an EMP arrow she received from Black Panther. As they move to escape, Patriot and Hawkeye encounter "Cap." They give him a lecture about how wrong it is to assume Cap's identity and use his shield. When Iron Man returns, Clint lets the two

Young Avengers go, hands Stark the shield and criticizes the Superhuman Registration Act. Iron Man warns Clint not to join Luke Cage's Avengers.
NOTE: Includes recap page (2 pages) where the indicia names this "Fallen Son: The Death of Captain America #3." Clint Barton uses Avengers priority code 1-9-1, username "Trickshot" and password "Purple Man" to identify himself.

FALLEN SON: THE DEATH OF CAPTAIN AMERICA – SPIDER-MAN (July 2007)

"The Death of Captain America Chapter 4: Depression" (23 pages)

CREDITS: Jeph Loeb (writer), David Finch (pencils), Danny Miki (inks), Richard Starkings & Comicraft (letters), Frank D'Armata (colors), Alejandro Arbona (asst editor), Bill Rosemann (editor), Tom Brevoort (exec editor), Michael Turner (variant c pencils), Peter Steigerwald (variant c inks)
FEATURE CHARACTERS: Captain America (only in fb between JIM #105, '64 & TTA #58, '64), Spider-Man (also in fb between SMFam #3, '07 & UToS #16, '96, last in FallSon:Av, '07, next in FallSon:IM, '07)
GUEST STARS: Hulk (in fb between ASM #14, '64 & TTA #59, '64), Wolverine (last in FallSon:Av, '07, next in FallSon:IM, '07)
VILLAIN: Rhino (last in PWJ #4, '07, next in NW #2, '07 fb)
OTHER CHARACTERS: Green Goblin, Gwen Stacy (both in rfb)
LOCATIONS/ITEMS: New York (also in fb) inc Brooklyn Bridge (also in rfb) & Flushing Cemetery; gravestones of Ben, Richard & Mary Parker & Miriam Sytsevich
FLASHBACKS: Green Goblin knocks Gwen Stacy off the Brooklyn Bridge (ASM #121, '73). Spider-Man and Captain America fight Hulk.
SYNOPSIS: Spider-Man visits the graves of his parents and uncle to mourn the loss of Captain America. Nearby, Rhino visits his mother's grave. Mistaking Rhino's presence as an attack, Spider-Man battles Rhino, accidentally destroying Rhino's mother's headstone. Rhino is enraged, but Spider-Man defeats him. Wolverine appears, but Spider-Man leaves the cemetery, wanting to be left alone. Logan follows him to Brooklyn Bridge where he tries to boost Spider-Man's spirits. The two heroes talk about death and grief.
NOTE: Includes recap page (2 pages) where the indicia names this "Fallen Son: The Death of Captain America #4."

FALLEN SON: THE DEATH OF CAPTAIN AMERICA – IRON MAN (August 2007)

"The Death of Captain America Chapter 5: Acceptance" (24 pages)

CREDITS: Jeph Loeb (writer), John Cassaday (art), Richard Starkings & Comicraft (letters), Laura Martin (colors), Alejandro Arbona (asst editor), Bill Rosemann (editor), Tom Brevoort (exec editor), Michael Turner (variant c art)
FEATURE CHARACTERS: Captain America (also as statue, in Iron Man's thoughts, rfb & in fb2 between Cap #262, '81 fb & CapC #29, '43, fb1 between Cap #241, '80 fb & Inv #7, '04 fb, fb3 between Av #4, '64 & Cap:Re #3, '09; bts, in casket in Arctic, next in Cap:Re #1, '09 fb, bts in Cap #42, '08), Iron Man (also in own thoughts, last in FallSon:Cap, '07, also in Cap #26, '07 fb, MsM #13, '07, Av:In #8, '08 fb, CW:FL #11, '07, WI:CW #1, '07, MsM #14, '07 fb, next in FF #544 '07 fb)

GUEST STARS: Fantastic Four: Reed Richards, Sue Richards (both last in CW #7, '07, chr next in Av:In #8, '08 fb, next in FF #543, '07), Johnny Storm (last in ASM #538, '07, next in FF #543, '07), Thing (last in FallSon:Av, '07, next in Cap #26, '07); Invaders: Human Torch (Jim Hammond, in fb2 between Cap:FA #1, '10 fb & Cap #616/3, '11 fb), Sub-Mariner (also in fb2 between Nam Ann #2/2, '92 & Cap #616/3, '11 fb, in fb3 between Av #4, '64 & Cap: Re #3, '09 fb, last in FallSon:Av, '07, next in Hulk #107, '07), Spitfire (also in fb2 between MCP #89/3, '91 fb & Av/Inv #1, '08, last in Cap #21, '06, next in CB&MI13 #1, '08), Toro (in fb2 between Cap:FA #4, '10 fb & Av/Inv #1, '08), Union Jack (Brian Falsworth, in fb2 between Inv #41, '79 & Av/Inv #1, '08), Iron Man's Avengers: Ms. Marvel (last in FallSon:Av, '07, next in Cap #26, '07), Wasp (also in Iron Man's thoughts, last in FallSon:Av, '07, also bts in Cap #26, '07 fb, also in Av:In #8, '08 fb, next in NAv #28, '07 fb); Luke Cage & his Avengers: Iron

Fist, Spider-Man (prev 3 last in FallSon:Av, '07, next in Cap #26, '07), Wolverine (last in FallSon:SM, '07, next in X #200, '07); V-Battalion: Roger Aubrey (last in Inv #9, '05), Elizabeth Barstow (last in Inv #2, '04), Fred Davis (last in CitV #4, '02) Irene Martinez (last in CitV #2, '01) (prev 4 last app); Young Avengers: Hawkeye (Kate Bishop), Patriot (both last in FallSon:Cap, '07, next in Cap #26, '07), Hulkling (Dorrek, aka Teddy Altman, Skrull shapeshifter), Wiccan (Billy Kaplan, spell caster) (both in CW #7, '07, next in SH #21, '07), Speed (Thomas Shepherd, speedster, last in CW #5, '06, next in YAvP #3, '08), Vision (Jonas, last in CW #7, '07, chr next in YAvP #4, '08 fb, next in FF #556, '08); Black Panther, Storm (both last in BP #26, '07, chr last in MCP #7/2, '08, chr next in FF #544, '07 fb, next in BP #26, '07), Angel (Thomas Halloway, in fb2 between SubC #8/4, '42 & DD #66, '04 fb), Dr. Strange (last in FallSon:Av, '07, next in NX #41, '07), Justice (last in ASM #538, '07, chr next in Av:In #8, '08 fb, next in Av:In #1, '07), Namora (last in AoAtlas #6, '07, next in Hulk #107, '07), She-Hulk (last in SH #17, '07 fb, next in AntM #8, '07), Union Jack (Joey Chapman, last in Blade #9, '07, next in CB&MI13 #5, '08), Isaiah Bradley (last in BP #18, '06, next in Cap #600/2, '09), Rick Jones (last in Run #6, '05, next in Cap #26, '07), James Rhodes (last in XPx:W #2, '06, chr next in WarM #7, '09 fb, next in Av:In #1, '07), Sam Wilson (also as Falcon in rfb, between Cap #25-26, '07)
SUPPORTING CAST: Bucky (in fb2 between USA #9, '43 & CapC #29, '43), Sharon Carter (between Cap #25-26, '07)

VILLAINS: Criti Noll (Skrull, as Yellowjacket, last in FallSon:W, '07, next bts in Cap #26, '07), Dum Dum Dugan (Skrull, 1st but chr last in SecInvDC #1, '08, next in Cap #26, '07), Edwin Jarvis (Skrull, last in CW:In #1, '07, next in MAv #4, '07) (all see NOTE), Veranke (Skrull, as Spider-Woman, last in FallSon:Av, '07, next in Cap #26, '07), Red Skull (in fb2 between Cap #262, '81 fb & Cap #616/3, '11 fb), Heinrich, Baron Zemo (in fb2 between bts in Cap Ann, '98 fb & Cap #600/2, '09 fb)

OTHER CHARACTERS: Alicia Masters (blind sculptor, bts, designs Captain America Memorial, last in Thing #8, '06, next in MCP #1/5, '07), Captain America LMD (bts, in casket at Arlington, only app), concentration camp victims, US & Nazi soldiers (prev 3 in fb1), Eskimos (in fb3 during Av #4, '64), US Marines, funeral attendees inc SHIELD agents & WWII veterans & victims, horse; Avengers: Giant-Man, Hawkeye (Barton), Hulk, Quicksilver, Scarlet Witch, Thor (prev 6 in Iron Man's thoughts); Redwing, Exiles: Angelo Baldini, Franz Cadavus, Eric Gruning, "Iron Hand" Hauptman (prev 5 in rfb)

LOCATIONS/ITEMS: Isle of Exiles (rfb), Nazi concentration camp (fb1), Arctic, Dr. Strange's Greenwich Village home, Washington, DC inc Capitol, Arlington National Cemetery inc Captain America Memorial; Nazi soldiers' guns (fb1-2), US Army tank & guns (both in fb1), Avengers Quinjet, Cap's flag-draped casket & Arctic casket, horse-drawn funeral wagon, SHIELD Helicarrier

FLASHBACKS: Cap and Falcon fight the Exiles (Cap #118, '69). Cap and the US Army raid a Nazi concentration camp (1). The Invaders and Angel fight Baron Zemo and Red Skull (2). Namor finds the frozen Cap (3).

SYNOPSIS: Thousands gather at Arlington National Cemetery for Captain America's funeral. Thing, Rick Jones, Black Panther, Tony Stark, Sam Wilson and Ms. Marvel serve as pall bearers, and Stark tries to speak to the crowd but is at a loss for words. Wilson takes the podium and delivers an inspiring eulogy as the fugitive Avengers watch live TV coverage of the ceremony. Sometime later, Iron Man, Yellowjacket and Wasp deliver Cap's real body to the arctic. They meet with Namor, who notes the current tensions between Atlantis and the surface world. Together they drop Cap's casket into the ocean.

NOTE: Includes recap page (2 pages) where the indicia names this "Fallen Son - The Death of Captain America #5." SecInvDC #1, '08 reveals the Dum Dum appearing here is a Skrull. SecInv #1, '08 reveals the Edwin Jarvis and Yellowjacket appearing here are Skrulls. DBCW, '07 reveals Falcon had to register with the government to attend Cap's funeral.

CAPTAIN AMERICA #26 [#575] (May 2007)

"The Death of the Dream Part Two"
"Sharon and the Contessa" (5 pages)
"The Wake" (5 pages)
"The Other Side" (3 pages)
"The Secret Wake" (3 pages)
"How it Begins" (6 pages)

CREDITS: Ed Brubaker (writer), Steve Epting (art pgs 6-10 & 17-22, c art), Mike Perkins (art pgs 1-5 & 11-16), Frank D'Armata (colors), Molly Lazer (asst editor), Tom Brevoort (editor)

FEATURE CHARACTER: Captain America (only as corpse in fb1 between CW:Conf #1, '07 & FallSon:W, '07)

GUEST STARS: Luke Cage (last in FallSon:IM, '07, chr next in NAv #28, '07 fb, next in NAv #27, '07) & his Avengers: Iron Fist (last in FallSon:IM, '07, next in NAv #27, '07), Spider-Man (last in FallSon:IM, '07, next in NX #41, '07); Tony Stark (in fb2 between CW:Conf #1, '07 & CW:In #1, '07, fb2 during FallSon:IM, '07) & his Avengers: Carol Danvers (last in FallSon:IM, '07, chr next in Av:In #8, '08 fb, next in MsM #13, '07), Janet Van Dyne (bts, at wake, last in FallSon:IM, '07, chr next in Av:In #8, '08 fb, next in FallSon:IM, '07), Simon Williams (last in FallSon:Av, '07, chr next in Av:In #8, '08 fb, next in MsM #13, '07); Young Avengers: Hawkeye (Bishop), Patriot (both last in FallSon:IM, '07, next in FF #556, '08); Falcon (last in FallSon:IM, '07), Night Nurse (last in IF #2, '07, next in NAv #34, '07), Thing (last in FallSon:IM, '07, chr next in FF #544, '07 fb, next in FF #543, '07), Jessica Jones (last in BP #18, '06, next in NAv #28, '07 fb), Rick Jones (last in FallSon:IM, '07, next in WWHulk #2, '07), Nick Fury (bts, pages Falcon)

SUPPORTING CAST: James Barnes (last in FallSon:W, '07, next in PWJ #11, '07), Sharon Carter (also in fb1 between Cap #25, '07 & FallSon:IM, '07; last in FallSon:IM, '07)

VILLAINS: Dum Dum Dugan (Skrull, last in FallSon:IM, '07, chr next in MAv #17, '08, next in IM:DoS #15, '07), la Contessa Valentina Allegra de Fontaine (Skrull, last in UJack #4, '07, chr last in SecInvDC #1, '08, next in PWJ #14, '08, see NOTE), Criti Noll (Skrull, as Hank Pym, bts, at wake, last in FallSon:IM, '07, chr next in Av:In #8, '08 fb, next in MAv #17, '08, see NOTE), Veranke (Skrull, as Spider-Woman, last in FallSon:IM, '07, chr next in NAv #28, '07 fb, next in NAv #27, '07), Red Skull, Aleksander Lukin (both next in Cap #29, '07), Sin, Dr. Faustus (both next in Cap #28, '07), Arnim Zola (last in Cap #24, '07, next in X #200/2, '07)

OTHER CHARACTERS: Danielle Cage (Luke & Jessica's baby, last in BP #18, '06, chr last in FF #534, '07 fb, next in NAv #28, '07 fb), priest, reporter (both on TV), Central Park vigil holders (others on TV), wake attendees, 2 bartenders, bar patrons, bystanders

LOCATIONS/ITEMS: New York inc SHIELD HQ (in fb1), 2 taverns & Kronas Corporate HQ w/Lukin's penthouse & Zola's lab, Dr. Strange's Greenwich Village home; Dr. Doom's chronal device, Falcon's pager, Red Skull mask, Ronin costume

FLASHBACKS: SHIELD Director Tony Stark shows Sharon Carter Cap's now shriveled body. Tony theorizes the Super-Soldier Serum went inert upon his death. When Tony tries to defend his part in the Super Hero Civil War and Cap's death, Sharon slaps him (1). Tony Stark fails to make a speech at Captain America's funeral (2).

SYNOPSIS: Sharon tells the Contessa that she resigned from SHIELD and attends Cap's wake. She tries to tell Sam Wilson that she killed Steve, but Faustus' programming won't let her. As a candlelight vigil is held in Central Park, Red Skull sends Sin on a new task and checks on Zola's progress analyzing Dr. Doom's chronal device. Falcon leaves the wake to mourn with Luke Cage and his outlaw Avengers. His visit is cut short when his pager goes off. Elsewhere, James Barnes starts a bar fight when someone calls Cap a traitor. When Falcon arrives Barnes has already knocked everyone out. James compliments Falcon's eulogy and pays his bar tab, but sees Tony Stark on TV and decides to kill him.

NOTE: Cover labeled "The Initiative." Includes recap/title page (1 page). Credits are only given on cover. SecInvDC #1, '08 reveals the Contessa appearing here is a Skrull. This Criti Noll dies in MAv #17, '08; another Criti Noll takes his place there to appear next in MAv #3, '07. Tony Stark was awarded the SHIELD Directorship in CW #7, '07.

CAPTAIN AMERICA #27 [#576] (August 2007)

"The Death of the Dream Part Three"
"White Lies" (4 pages)
"Falling off the Grid" (4 pages)
"Compromised Assets" (3 pages)
"Old Friends" (8 pages)
"Buried in the Past" (4 pages)

CREDITS: Ed Brubaker (writer), Steve Epting (art pgs 1-4 & 11-18, c art), Mike Perkins (art pgs 5-10 & 19-22), Virtual Calligraphy's Joe Caramagna (letters), FrankD'Armata (colors), Molly Lazer (asst editor), Tom Brevoort (editor)
FEATURE CHARACTER: Captain America (only in photo & as statue)
GUEST STARS: Black Widow (also in photo & fb2 during BW:DO #2, '10 fb; last in MAv #11, '08, next in SilW #5, '07), Tony Stark (also as Iron Man in photo & fb1 during MAv #7, '08; last in MAv #11, '08, chr next in WWHulk:FL #3/3, '07, next in IM:DoS #15, '07), Nick Fury (bts, informs Falcon, chr next in MAv #13, '08), Falcon
SUPPORTING CAST: Winter Soldier (also in photo as Bucky & in fb2 between Cap #11, '05 fb & BW:DO #2, '10 fb, also in Cap #11, '05 fb; last in PWJ #11, '07, next in W:O #20, '08), Sharon Carter
VILLAINS: Vasily Karpov (in fb2 between Cap #14, '06 fb & Cap #11, '05 fb) & his agents (in fb2)
OTHER CHARACTERS: Geroge W. Bush (last in CW #7, '07, next in Av:In #2, '07), United Nations Secretary-General (both bts, in meeting w/Stark), Nick Fury LMD (last in Cap #24, '06, deactivated, last app), SHIELD agents (some bts), reporters (off-panel in fb1, 1 voice only), Captain America Memorial patrons & guards, police, firefighters, bystanders, birds; Human Torch (Hammond), Toro, Iron Man's Avengers: Ares, Ms. Marvel, Sentry, Wonder Man (prev 6 in photo), Dr. Faustus (in Sharon's hallucination), Redwing (on cover)
LOCATIONS/ITEMS: Washington, DC inc Washington Memorial & Smithsonian Institution National Museum of American History Behring Center w/Captain America Memorial, New York inc Sharon's apartment & SHIELD HQ w/lab, Natasha's quarters, Red Room, Department X storage room (prev 3 in fb2); Captain America memorabilia, Sharon's gun, SHIELD hovercar & armored cars, Bucky's guns, Cap's shield
FLASHBACKS: Stark gives a press conference, announcing the role of Captain America is retired (1). A young Black Widow and Winter Soldier have a secret rendezvous; he's disciplined when they're discovered. Later, Natasha finds Winter Soldier frozen in stasis (2).
SYNOPSIS: James Barnes visits the Captain America exhibit planning to steal the shield, but discovers replicas on display instead. Elsewhere, overcome with grief, Sharon tries to kill herself but Faustus' programming won't let her. Falcon arrives and says Nick Fury has a job for them: stop Barnes from killing Tony Stark. Meanwhile, Fury's LMD within SHIELD is compromised, forcing Stark to transfer Cap's shield to a different location. Winter Soldier attacks the transport and discovers Black Widow with the shield. Both recognize each other as former lovers, but reluctantly fight anyway. Winter Soldier gains the upper hand and takes the shield. Later, Stark debriefs Widow who tells Stark she believes Winter Soldier plans to kill him.
NOTE: Cover labeled "The Initiative." Includes recap/title page (1 page). Cap Memorial includes posters of CapC #30, '43 and Chapter 10 of the 1944 Captain America Republic serial, and a statue of Av #4, '64's cover.

CAPTAIN AMERICA #28 [#577] (September 2007)

"The Death of the Dream Part Four"
"Silencers" (3 pages)
"Out of Mind" (2 pages)
"Anarchy in the US" (4 pages)
"Underground" (1 page)
"A New Plan" (3 pages)
"The Doctor Is In" (1 page)
"Dead Letter Office" (3 pages)
"Counter-Surveillance" (3 pages)
"Rescue Mission" (2 pages)

CREDITS: Ed Brubaker (writer), Steve Epting (art pgs 1-5, 11-13 & 15-17, c art), Mike Perkins (art pgs 6-10, 14 & 18-22), Virtual Calligraphy's Joe Caramagna (letters), FrankD'Armata (colors), Molly Lazer (asst editor), Tom Brevoort (editor)
FEATURE CHARACTER: Captain America (bts, wrote letter between CW:FL #9, '06 & CW #5, '06)
GUEST STARS: Nick Fury (chr last in MAv #13, '08, next in MAv #18, '08), Tony Stark (last in ASM #544, '07), Charles Xavier (last in WWHulk: X #3, '07, next in GSAX #1, '08), Falcon
SUPPORTING CAST: Winter Soldier (last in W:O #25, '08, also in YAvP #1, '08), Sharon Carter
VILLAINS: Sin (last in Cap #26, '07) & her Serpent Squad: Cobra (Piet Vorhees, last in WTig #6, '07), Eel (Edward Lavell, last in PWJ #4, '07), Viper (1st) (all also as SHIELD agents); Crossbones (last in FallSon:W, '07), Dr. Faustus (also as Dr. Benjamin, last in Cap #26, '07, next in Cap #30, '07), AIM agents
OTHER CHARACTERS: SHIELD agents (Hermann named, inc Patrick Stansfield, most die), Maurice Greely (Cap's lawyer), Anna (Stark's secretary, 1st, next in Cap #30, '07), Violet (Dr. Benjamin's secretary), Merv (innkeeper) & his friend, financial center guards, stockbrokers (both die), birds; Matt Murdock (mentioned, once vouched for Greely)
LOCATIONS/ITEMS: New York inc hotel, financial center, Daily Bugle, SHIELD HQ w/Benjamin's & Stark's offices, Fury's safe house, AIM listening-post, SHIELD monitoring station; SHIELD Helicarrier, financial center guards' guns, Sin's guns, Serpent Squad's image inducers, Steve's letter

SYNOPSIS: James Barnes ponders how to get to Tony Stark. On the SHIELD Helicarrier, Charles Xavier mentally interrogates Crossbones, but discovers his memory has been erased. Meanwhile, Sin and her new Serpent Squad crash the Chinese stock market. Elsewhere, Falcon tells Nick Fury he hasn't been able to find Barnes. Deciding not to partner with SHIELD, Falcon and Sharon start looking for Red Skull, hoping that will lead them to Barnes. At SHIELD, Faustus programs an agent, while Cap's lawyer meets with Stark, giving him a letter from Steve Rogers. Winter Soldier infiltrates an AIM base, learning that Sin has been investigating SHIELD monitoring stations. That night, Sin and her Serpent Squad kills a squad of SHIELD agents and steals their uniforms in order to rescue Crossbones.

NOTE: Cover labeled "The Initiative." Includes recap/title page (1 page). Issue dedicated to Doris Lee. Stansfield named in Cap #29, '07.

CAPTAIN AMERICA #29 [#578] (October 2007)

"The Death of the Dream Part Five"
"One Step Behind" (5 pages)
"Spy Versus Spy" (3 pages)
"The Prodigal Son" (3 pages)
"Altered Egos" (2 pages)
"Proactive" (6 pages)
"Reactive" (3 page)

CREDITS: Ed Brubaker (writer), Steve Epting (art pgs 1-5, 9-11 & 19-22, c art), Mike Perkins (art pgs 6-8 & 12-18), Virtual Calligraphy's Joe Caramagna (letters), Frank D'Armata (colors), Molly Lazer (asst editor), Tom Brevoort (editor)

FEATURE CHARACTER: Captain America (only in photo & rfb)

GUEST STARS: Black Widow (last in NAv #38, '08), Falcon, Tony Stark

SUPPORTING CAST: Winter Soldier (also in pfb), Sharon Carter (also in rfb)

VILLAINS: Red Skull, Aleksander Lukin (both last in Cap #26, '07), Sin (also in pfb) & her Serpent Squad: Cobra, Eel, Viper (prev 3 in pfb, next in Cap #35, '08); Crossbones (also in photo), Kronas soldier, AIM agents

OTHER CHARACTERS: SHIELD agents (others die in pfb), Gergen (ex-con), reporter (on TV in pfb), bartender (in fb), bar patrons (others in pfb); bystanders (in rfb), Patrick Stansfield (in photo), Vladimir Lenin (statue in Lukin's mind)

LOCATIONS/ITEMS: New York inc SHIELD HQ, AIM base & Kronas Corporation HQ w/Lukin's penthouse; SHIELD Subcarrier (in pfb), Sin's guns, SHIELD agents' guns, AIM agents' guns & flamethrower, Sharon's gun, Crossbones' gun

FLASHBACKS: Sharon shoots Cap (Cap #25, '07). The Serpent Squad frees Crossbones. Barnes hears about Crossbones' escape (p).

SYNOPSIS: Tony Stark learns of Crossbones' rescue, and that agent Patrick Stansfield inexplicably just let them in and Crossbones' security detail is missing. Meanwhile, Black Widow tries to track down Winter Soldier. Winter Soldier storms Kronas Corporate HQ looking for Red Skull. Inside Lukin's mind, the Skull and Lukin battle for dominance. Falcon and Sharon raid an AIM base. Sharon corners one of the agents, but she suddenly vomits. As they leave Black Widow spots them, realizing they're on the same trail. At Kronas, Winter Soldier confronts Lukin, demanding to know where the Skull is. Winter Soldier realizes too late that Lukin is the Skull when Crossbones and Sin arrive.

NOTE: Cover labeled "The Initiative." Includes recap/title page (1 page).

CAPTAIN AMERICA #30 [#579] (November 2007)

"The Death of the Dream Part Six" (22 pages)

CREDITS: Ed Brubaker (writer), Steve Epting (art pgs 3-8, 14-16 & 19-22, c art), Mike Perkins (art pgs 1-2, 9-13 & 17-18), Virtual Calligraphy's Joe Caramagna (letters), Frank D'Armata (colors), Molly Lazer (asst editor), Tom Brevoort (editor)

FEATURE CHARACTER: Captain America (only in photo & rfb)

GUEST STARS: Black Widow, Falcon, Iron Man

SUPPORTING CAST: Winter Soldier (also as Bucky in photo), Sharon Carter (also in rfb)

VILLAINS: Red Skull, Aleksander Lukin, Crossbones (next in Cap #36, '08), Sin (next in Cap #35, '08), Dr. Faustus (also in Sharon's hallucination, last in Cap #28, '07)

OTHER CHARACTERS: Redwing (last in Cap #14, '06, next in Cap #32, '08), Anna (last in Cap #28, '07, last app), SHIELD agents (Agent 32 named, some in photo), Dr. Benjamin (corpse); bystanders (in rfb), Nick Fury, Dum Dum Dugan (both in photo), Kronas soldiers (on cover)

LOCATIONS/ITEMS: New York inc Sharon's apartment, RAID base & Kronas Corporation HQ w/Lukin's penthouse, Falcon's Harlem apartment, Dr. Benjamin's home; Stark's SHIELD Helicarrier office, Sin's knife, Falcon's Hawk Hook, Steve's letter, Sharon's pregnancy test & stun gun, Red Skull mask

FLASHBACK: Sharon shoots Cap, and she stays with him until he dies (Cap #25, '07).

SYNOPSIS: Realizing that SHIELD psychologist Dr. Benjamin is the common link between the missing SHIELD agents, Tony Stark sends a team to Benjamin's home. They find his body. At Kronas, Winter Soldier easily defeats Sin and almost kills Crossbones, until Red Skull's taunts make him stop. Winter Soldier attacks the Skull, who uses a Soviet shutdown code to stop him. Later, Black Widow approaches Falcon with the offer to work together, while Sharon discovers she's pregnant. Elsewhere, Stark mulls over Steve's letter, which begs Stark not to let the Captain America legacy die. Meanwhile, Dr. Faustus begins to brainwash Winter Soldier. Stark realizes that Sharon was also seeing Dr. Benjamin. Falcon and Black Widow meet Sharon at her apartment. Stark tries too late to warn Black Widow of Faustus' control over Sharon, and Sharon shoots Falcon and Black Widow.

NOTE: Cover labeled "The Initiative." Includes recap/title page (1 page). Winter Soldier's one-time shutdown code is "Sputnik."

CAPTAIN AMERICA #31 [#580] (December 2007)

"The Death of the Dream: Act 2, the Burden of Dreams: Part One" (22 pages)

CREDITS: Ed Brubaker (writer), Steve Epting (art), Virtual Calligraphy's Joe Caramagna (letters), FrankD'Armata (colors), Molly Lazer (asst editor), Tom Brevoort (editor)
FEATURE CHARACTER: Captain America (only in Winter Soldier's hallucination)
GUEST STARS: Black Widow, Falcon, Tony Stark
SUPPORTING CAST: Winter Soldier (also as Bucky in hallucination), Sharon Carter (also as nurse)
VILLAINS: Red Skull (also in Winter Soldier's hallucination), Aleksander Lukin, Dr. Faustus, Kronas soldiers
OTHER CHARACTERS: Human Torch (Hammond), Sub-Mariner, Vasily Karpov, Russian doctors & soldiers, American soldiers, Nazi soldiers (all in Winter Soldier's hallucination), bystanders
LOCATIONS/ITEMS: New York inc RAID base & SHIELD HQ w/medlab, Kronas camp; Dr. Faustus' drugs & gun, Red Skull mask

SYNOPSIS: Sharon Carter fails to shake off Dr. Faustus' programming. Later, Faustus continues his attempts to brainwash Winter Soldier. Falcon wakes up in a SHIELD medlab where Stark tells him about Sharon's brainwashing. Meanwhile, Red Skull marshals the Kronas soldiers together in preparation for his plans. Dr. Faustus continues his attempts to brainwash Winter Soldier. Eventually, Winter Soldier succumbs and Faustus frees him. To prove his loyalty, Faustus orders Winter Soldier to shoot his nurse, Sharon Carter.
NOTE: Includes recap/title page (1 page).

CAPTAIN AMERICA #32 [#581] (January 2008)

"The Death of Captain America Act 2, the Burden of Dreams: Part Two" (22 pages)

CREDITS: Ed Brubaker (writer), Steve Epting (pencils, c art), Butch Guice (inks), Virtual Calligraphy's Joe Caramagna (letters), FrankD'Armata (colors), Molly Lazer (asst editor), Tom Brevoort (editor)
FEATURE CHARACTER: Captain America (only on cover)
GUEST STARS: Black Widow, Falcon, Tony Stark (also as Iron Man on cover)
SUPPORTING CAST: Winter Soldier, Sharon Carter (also in photo)
VILLAINS: Red Skull, Aleksander Lukin, Dr. Faustus, RAID agents
OTHER CHARACTERS: Redwing (last in Cap #30, '07), SHIELD doctor, SHIELD agents (bts in helicopters)
LOCATIONS/ITEMS: New York inc RAID base & abandoned building; SHIELD Helicarrier & helicopters, Dr. Faustus' gun, Winter Soldier's Adamantium mesh harness, RAID agents' guns & ship, Sharon's stun gun, Red Skull mask

SYNOPSIS: Winter Soldier fires on Dr. Faustus, but the gun was filled with blanks. Faustus subdues Winter Soldier and begins to brainwash him again. Meanwhile, Redwing leads Falcon and Black Widow into the sewers, where they find the entrance to a RAID base. On the SHIELD Helicarrier, Tony Stark confirms the results of Sharon's pregnancy test and has all records of it destroyed. Red Skull reminds Faustus of his timetable as Falcon and Black Widow storm the facility. Winter Soldier uses the distraction to escape. Faustus sends Sharon after Winter Soldier, and she takes him captive. Falcon pursues the escaping Faustus, and Sharon dumps Winter Soldier out of the hatch over the city to get Falcon off their tail. Falcon catches Winter Soldier, but they crash into an abandoned building. Faustus questions Sharon's loyalty as Black Widow arrests Winter Soldier.
NOTE: Includes recap/title page (1 page).

CAPTAIN AMERICA #33 [#582] (February 2008)

"The Death of Captain America Act 2, the Burden of Dreams: Part Three" (23 pages)

CREDITS: Ed Brubaker (writer), Steve Epting (pencils, c art), Butch Guice (inks), Virtual Calligraphy's Joe Caramagna (letters), FrankD'Armata (colors), Molly Lazer (asst editor), Tom Brevoort (editor)
FEATURE CHARACTER: None
GUEST STARS: Black Widow (chr next in BW:DO #4, '10 fb), Iron Man (next in NW #12, '08), Falcon (next in Cap #35, '08)
SUPPORTING CAST: Winter Soldier (chr next in BW:DO #4, '10 fb), Sharon Carter (bts, imprisoned, next in Cap #35, '08)
VILLAINS: Red Skull, Aleksander Lukin (also in photo), Dr. Faustus (chr next in Cap #35, '08 fb), Kronas soldiers
OTHER CHARACTERS: Redwing (next in Cap #35, '08), SHIELD technicians (Milton & Creighton named), SHIELD agents, reporter (voice only), rescue crew (both in dfb)
LOCATIONS/ITEMS: New York inc Kronas Corporation HQ, Atlantic Ocean (on TV); Kronas jet, rescue equipment (both in dfb), SHIELD Helicarrier inc lab & Stark's office, SHIELD agents' guns, SHIELD mind-probe equipment, Steve's letter, Red Skull mask
FLASHBACK: Rescue crews search for survivors in Lukin's downed corporate jet (d).

SYNOPSIS: Red Skull chastises Dr. Faustus for losing Winter Soldier and moves up his timeline because Winter Soldier knows who Red Skull is. On the SHIELD Helicarrier, technicians examine Winter Soldier's arm until it activates and fights its way out of the lab. As Falcon searches for Sharon, the power cuts out on the Helicarrier and Winter Soldier escapes. Winter Soldier attacks Iron Man and the two soon end up in a stalemate. Stark reasons with Winter Soldier long enough to show him Steve's letter. Winter Soldier tells Stark Red Skull is inside Lukin, but Stark reveals that Lukin "died" today. Stark asks Winter Soldier to become the new Captain America, who agrees on two conditions: SHIELD must verify there's no more Soviet programming in his brain, and he must act on his own with no government oversight. Stark agrees.

NOTE: Includes recap/title page (1 page).

CAPTAIN AMERICA #34 [#583] (March 2008)

"The Death of Captain America Act 2, the Burden of Dreams: Part Four" (22 pages)

CREDITS: Ed Brubaker (writer), Steve Epting (pencils, c art), Butch Guice (inks), Virtual Calligraphy's Joe Caramagna (letters), Frank D'Armata (colors), Molly Laser (assoc editor), Tom Brevoort (editor), Alex Ross, Dynamic Forces (variant c art)
FEATURE CHARACTER: Captain America (James Buchanan Barnes, 1st as Captain America, also as Winter Soldier)
GUEST STARS: Black Widow (chr last in BW:DO #4, '10 fb), Tony Stark (last in NW #13, '08, last bts in NW #16, '08 fb)
VILLAINS: Red Skull, Aleksander Lukin (also on TV as Vladmir Morovin, fictional new Kronas Corporation CEO), Dr. Faustus (chr last in Cap #35, '08 fb), Arnim Zola (last in Tb:II, '08), AIM agents, RAID agents
OTHER CHARACTERS: Senator Gordon Wright (chairman of Defense Appropriations Committee, 1st), Matthew Fritchman (CNN analyst, on TV), Molly (TV news reporter), Toni (CNN reporter, on TV), US Secretary of the Treasury, SHIELD agents, TV cameraman, police, protesters
LOCATIONS/ITEMS: Chicago, Cable News Network (CNN) studio (both on TV), RAID upstate New York base inc Zola's lab, Manhattan inc Brooklyn Bridge & Wall Street, Washington, DC inc Sen. Wright's office & White House; Cap's shield, handgun (see NOTE) & explosive disc, AIM/RAID rifles & Turbo-Walkers, Kronas helicopter, SHIELD agents' guns, SHIELD Helicarrier & aircraft, Red Skull mask
SYNOPSIS: As TV news programs report on the disastrous effects Lukin's death is having on the world economy, James Barnes dons a new Captain America uniform and with Black Widow, thwarts an AIM/RAID attack on Wall Street's gold reserves. Stark tells the Secretary of the Treasury that Lukin is not dead and that the crisis is an orchestrated attack by Kronas and Red Skull on the US, and he accuses the Secretary of being in their pocket. At Arnim Zola's upstate New York lab, he and Red Skull plot their next moves. In four US cities, mobs of picketers protest against the Kronas Corporation's foreclosure on thousands of American mortgages. Stark discovers that the missing SHIELD agents are handling crowd control in Washington, but before he can act, Dr. Faustus orders the agents to fire on the protesters.
NOTE: Includes recap/title page (1 page). Alex Ross designed James Barnes' Captain America uniform; Cap:Who #1, '10 reveals it's based on a design by Janet Van Dyne. Barnes continues to use Steve Rogers' shield and also uses a handgun; both weapons are assumed as appearing in future issues. Plot reflects the real-life sub-prime lending scandals and mortgage crisis of 2008.

CAPTAIN AMERICA #35 [#584] (April 2008)

"The Death of Captain America Act 2, the Burden of Dreams: Part Five" (22 pages)

CREDITS: Ed Brubaker (writer), Butch Guice (pencils, co-inks), Mike Perkins (co-inks), Virtual Calligraphy's Joe Caramagna (letters), FrankD'Armata (colors), Molly Lazer (assoc editor), Tom Brevoort (editor), Steve Epting (c art)
FEATURE CHARACTER: Captain America
GUEST STARS: Falcon (last in Cap #33, '08), Black Widow, Tony Stark
SUPPORTING CAST: Sharon Carter (last bts in Cap #33, '08)
VILLAINS: Red Skull, Aleksander Lukin (also as Vladmir Morovin), Dr. Faustus (also in fb between Cap #33-34, '08), Sin (last in Cap #30, '07) & her Serpent Squad: Eel, Cobra, Viper (prev 3 last in Cap #29, '07 fb); Arnim Zola, RAID agents, Kronas soldiers (2 also in pfb as Kane-Meyer Securities force), Kronas water boy
OTHER CHARACTERS: Redwing (last in Cap #33, '08, next in Cap #38, '08), Sen. Gordon Wright (also in pfb), Roseanne McCarthy (reporter, on TV, 1st, next in Cap #37, '08), moving men (in fb), Cabinet Secretary, Senate security guard, administrative assistant, protestors, police
LOCATIONS/ITEMS: Faustus' abandoned upstate New York rehab clinic, Washington, DC inc Wright's office & Capitol, RAID upstate New York base inc hangar & Zola's lab; Kronas water bottles, protestor's Molotov cocktail, Cap's sleep gas grenade, Sin's guns
FLASHBACKS: Sen. Wright announces that he's hired Kane-Meyer Securities to police Washington, DC (p). Dr. Faustus abandons his rehab clinic.
SYNOPSIS: Falcon and Redwing track Faustus' movements to an abandoned rehab clinic in upstate New York. Meanwhile, the media continues to crucify SHIELD for their recent shooting of protestors. Elsewhere, Faustus assures Senator Wright that he'll be rewarded for his part in Red Skull's plan. James Barnes watches as protestors are policed by Kane-Meyer Securities and realizes Kronas is drugging the protestors. Meanwhile Lukin as "Morovin," negotiates new oil prices with the US, crippling the country further. When protestors riot against Kane-Meyer Securities, Captain America protects the protestors from the attacking security forces. Red Skull congratulates Faustus on engineering the riot. Black Widow tells Cap that a helicopter is landing on Capitol. Cap crashes in to find the Serpent Squad. Elsewhere, Arnim Zola begins to examine Sharon Carter.
NOTE: Includes recap/title page (1 page).

CAPTAIN AMERICA #36 [#585] (May 2008)

"The Death of Captain America Act 2, the Burden of Dreams: Part Six" (22 pages)

CREDITS: Ed Brubaker (writer), Butch Guice (art pgs 1-12), Mike Perkins (art pgs 13-22), Virtual Calligraphy's Joe Caramagna (letters), FrankD'Armata (colors), Molly Lazer (assoc editor), Tom Brevoort (editor), Steve Epting (c art)
FEATURE CHARACTER: Captain America (also in photo)
GUEST STARS: Black Widow (next bts in Cap #39, '08), Falcon, Tony Stark
SUPPORTING CAST: Sharon Carter
VILLAINS: Red Skull, Aleksander Lukin, Sin (next in Cap #39, '08) & her Serpent Squad: Cobra, Eel, Viper (both also in photo) (prev 3 last app); Crossbones (last in Cap #30, '07, next in Cap #600/2, '09), Captain America (William Burnside, last in Cap #236, '79 as Grand Director), Dr. Faustus, Arnim Zola, Kronos soldier (as Kane-Meyer Securities force, also in photo)
OTHER CHARACTERS: Sen. Gordon Wright (also in photo), Dick Cheney (US Vice president, bts, on phone w/Stark, last in AF #12, '05, last app), reporter (on TV), protestors, police
LOCATIONS/ITEMS: Washington, DC inc Capitol & Washington Monument, RAID upstate New York base, Steve's Brooklyn home; SHIELD Helicarrier & hovercar, Sin's & Crossbones' guns, Burnside's stasis unit, Red Skull mask
SYNOPSIS: As Captain America battles the Serpent Squad Crossbones joins the fight. Senator Wright watches, worried that Red Skull's plan is ruined. Meanwhile, Red Skull tells Faustus that Sharon is pregnant. Senator Wright is evacuated as Crossbones throws Cap out a window. Black Widow catches Cap on her hovercar and Cap shoots Crossbones. Cobra escapes with Sin. Cap races outside to try and talk down the riot like Steve would have, but is dismissed as a fraud. Later, the Skull releases doctored footage of Kane-Meyer Securities saving Senator Wright from the Serpent Squad. On the phone with the Vice president, Stark denies knowing anything about the new Cap. James Barnes and Black Widow begin to rekindle their relationship. Elsewhere, the need to protect her unborn child enables Sharon to break Faustus' programming and attempts an escape, but is stopped when she finds Steve Rogers in a stasis tube.
NOTE: Includes recap/title page (1 page).

CAPTAIN AMERICA #37 [#586] (June 2008)

"The Death of Captain America Act 3, the Man Who Bought America: Part One" (22 pages)

CREDITS: Ed Brubaker (writer), Steve Epting (art), Virtual Calligraphy's Joe Caramagna (letters), FrankD'Armata (colors), Molly Lazer (assoc editor), Tom Brevoort (editor), Butch Guice (c art)
FEATURE CHARACTERS: Captain America (Barnes, also in photo & fb as Bucky between Cap #3, '05 fb & YA Spec #1, '09 fb), Captain America (Rogers, in fb between Cap #3, '05 fb & Cap:Re #1, '09) (both also in Barnes' dream)
GUEST STARS: Clint Barton (last in NAv #39, '08, next in Av/Inv #2, '08), Tony Stark (next in SH #27, '08), Falcon
SUPPORTING CAST: Sharon Carter
VILLAINS: Red Skull (also in fb between Cap Ann., '01 fb & bts in Cap #12, '05 fb), Aleksander Lukin, Arnim Zola (voice only), Dr. Faustus, Captain America (Burnside), Kronos soldiers (others as Kane-Meyer Security force in pfb, 2 in photo)
OTHER CHARACTERS: Sen. Gordon Wright (only in pfb & photo), Roseanne McCarthy (on TV, last in Cap #35, '08), protestors (in pfb), American soldiers, French citizens (both in fb); Cobra, Eel (both in photo), Hydra agents (in Barnes' dream)
LOCATIONS/ITEMS: Paris, France (fb), RAID upstate New York base inc Zola's lab, Steve's Brooklyn home; SHIELD Helicarrier inc Stark's office, Kronos soldiers' guns, Red Skull mask
FLASHBACKS: Sen. Wright announces the creation of the Third Wing Party and his candidacy for President. Kane-Meyer Security force stops riots in Washington (p). August, 1944: Red Skull watches with loathing as Paris celebrates its liberation with Cap and Bucky.
SYNOPSIS: Red Skull and Dr. Faustus gloat over setting up Senator Wright as a Presidential contender and discuss their plans for the new Captain America. Meanwhile, Falcon expresses his disapproval over Stark thrusting James Barnes into the Captain America role. Stark suggests Falcon help him. That night, Clint Barton confronts James over being the new Cap and decides to give Barnes the chance to prove himself. Later, Falcon recruits James to rescue Sharon Carter. Meanwhile, Sharon tries to escape with the revived Steve Rogers, only to discover he's the Cap of the 1950s.
NOTE: Includes recap/title page (1 page).

CAPTAIN AMERICA #38 [#587] (July 2008)

"The Death of Captain America Act 3, the Man Who Bought America: Part Two" (22 pages)

CREDITS: Ed Brubaker (writer), Steve Epting (art), Mike Perkins (co-inks), Virtual Calligraphy's Joe Caramagna (letters), FrankD'Armata (colors), Molly Lazer (assoc. editor), Tom Brevoort (editor)
FEATURE CHARACTER: Captain America (also in photo)
GUEST STARS: Bucky (Monroe, only in rfb, Sharon's thoughts as Nomad & fb between CapC #77-77/2, '54), Falcon
SUPPORTING CAST: Sharon Carter
VILLAINS: Red Skull, Aleksander Lukin, Arnim Zola, Dr. Faustus (also in rfb) (all next in Cap #40, '08), Captain America (Burnside, also in rfb as Grand Director & fb between CapC #77-77/2, '54), AIM agents, Kronas soldiers
OTHER CHARACTERS: Redwing (last in Cap #35, '08), Roseanne McCarthy (on TV, last app), Sen. Gordon Wright; politicians, reporters (both in fb), National Force member, police, bystanders (prev 3 in rfb), Captain America (Rogers, in rfb & photo), Bucky (Winter, in Sharon's thoughts), Dwight Eisenhower (in photo)
LOCATIONS/ITEMS: Upstate New York inc RAID base & abandoned factory, Washington, DC; AIM ship & equipment, AIM agents' guns, Zola's blaster & spare body, Lukin's taser, Cap's motorcycle, Red Skull mask
FLASHBACKS: Grand Director sets himself on fire (Cap #236, '79). The Cap and Bucky of the '50s fight crime (YM #26/2, '54), receive a key to the city (1) and eventually go insane from improper use of the Super-Soldier Serum (Cap #155, '72 fb). Captain America battles the Grand Director and his National Force (Cap #232, '79).
SYNOPSIS: Sharon Carter prepares to shoot the 1950s Cap until Lukin knocks her out. Meanwhile, Captain America and Falcon find Arnim Zola and AIM agents clearing equipment from their abandoned factory. Wright continues to play on people's paranoia to drum up his poll numbers. Cap and Falcon attack Zola, and Cap finds himself wanting to make Falcon proud. Zola destroys the factory and escapes by sending his consciousness into another body. Falcon gets them clear in time. Elsewhere, Faustus begins programming the 1950s Cap, telling him the current Cap is an imposter who killed Jack Monroe.
NOTE: Includes recap/title page (1 page). Includes MK #20, '08 preview (4 pages).

CAPTAIN AMERICA #39 [#588] (August 2008)

"The Death of Captain America Act 3, the Man Who Bought America: Part Three" (22 pages)

CREDITS: Ed Brubaker (writer), Roberto De la Torre (art), Virtual Calligraphy's Joe Caramagna (letters), FrankD'Armata (colors), Molly Lazer (assoc editor), Tom Brevoort (editor), Steve Epting (c art)
FEATURE CHARACTER: Captain America (also in photo & pfb)
GUEST STARS: Black Widow (bts, on phone w/Falcon, last in Cap #36, '08, next in Cap #41, '08), Falcon (also in pfb)
SUPPORTING CAST: Sharon Carter
VILLAINS: Captain America (Burnside, also in photo), Sin (last in Cap #36, '08), Kronas soldiers (as Kane-Meyer Security force, some as political extremists), Kronas doctor
OTHER CHARACTERS: Redwing (only in pfb), Sen. Gordon Wright (also in photo) (both next in Cap #41, '08), reporters (1 on TV), Wright rally attendees
LOCATIONS/ITEMS: Chicago, IL, Minneapolis, MN inc Wright's hotel room, Steve's Brooklyn home, upstate New York inc abandoned factory (in pfb) & RAID base w/medlab; Kronas soldiers' guns, Zola's abandoned body, Sin's baton, Sharon's scalpel
FLASHBACK: Cap and Falcon find Zola's abandoned body (p).
SYNOPSIS: In Chicago, the 1950s Cap watches as extremists attack the campaigning Senator Wright. In Brooklyn, James Barnes and Sam Wilson spar until Black Widow calls, telling them to check the news. The 1950s Cap saves Senator Wright from the extremists, boosting Wright's popularity. Meanwhile in a RAID medlab, the injured Sin taunts Sharon, threatening to kill her when she's healed. James goes to Wright's next speech in Minneapolis hoping "Cap" will show, but he doesn't. Later, Sharon slips her restraints, knocks out their doctor, and takes Sin hostage with a scalpel. Meanwhile, Captain America investigates Wright's hotel room, finding it empty save for a murderous "Cap."
NOTE: Includes recap/title page (1 page).

CAPTAIN AMERICA #40 [#589] (September 2008)

"The Death of Captain America Act 3, the Man Who Bought America: Part Four" (22 pages)

CREDITS: Ed Brubaker (writer), Steve Epting (art), Virtual Calligraphy's Joe Caramagna (letters), FrankD'Armata (colors), Jeanine Schaefer (assoc editor), Tom Brevoort (editor)
FEATURE CHARACTER: Captain America
GUEST STAR: Falcon
SUPPORTING CAST: Sharon Carter
VILLAINS: Red Skull, Aleksander Lukin, Arnim Zola, Dr. Faustus (all last in Cap #38, '08), Captain America (Burnside), Sin, Kronas soldiers
LOCATIONS/ITEMS: Minneapolis, MN, upstate New York RAID base; Sharon's scalpel, Sin's knife, Kronas soldiers' guns, Red Skull mask
SYNOPSIS: Captain America fights the super-strong 1950s Cap on rooftops over Minneapolis. Red Skull, Dr. Faustus and Arnim Zola watch

the battle from afar as Sin frees herself from Sharon's grasp, Sharon weakened by the drugs in her system. Cap manages to unmask the 1950s Cap and is shocked to see he looks just like Steve Rogers. Sharon fights Sin, trying to save her unborn child. The 1950s Cap screams at Cap for killing Jack Monroe, and Cap unmasks, revealing he is the original Bucky. The 1950s Cap is confused until Barnes apologizes for Monroe's murder, which only sends the 1950s Cap into a rage. The 1950s Cap throws Cap off the building and Falcon saves him. Red Skull is upset to hear that Sin has stabbed Sharon in the stomach, ruining his plans.

NOTE: Includes recap/title page (1 page).

CAPTAIN AMERICA #41 [#590] (October 2008)

"The Death of Captain America Act 3, the Man who Bought America: Part Five" (22 pages)

CREDITS: Ed Brubaker (writer), Steve Epting (pencils, co-inks, c art), Rick Magyar (co-inks), Virtual Calligraphy's Joe Caramagna (letters), Frank D'Armata (colors), Jeanine Schaefer (assoc editor), Tom Brevoort (editor), Frank Cho (variant c art)

FEATURE CHARACTER: Captain America

GUEST STARS: Black Widow (last bts in Cap #39, '08), Falcon

SUPPORTING CAST: Sharon Carter

VILLAINS: Red Skull, Aleksander Lukin, Dr. Faustus (next in Cap #612, '11), Captain America (Burnside), Sin, Arnim Zola, AIM agents (Field Team Seven named), Kronas soldiers

OTHER CHARACTERS: Redwing (last in Cap #39, '08, next in Cap #600/2, '09), Sen. Gordon Wright (last in Cap #39, '08), Sen. Barack Obama (Democratic Presidential candidate), Sen. John McCain (Republican Presidential candidate) (both 1st), SHIELD agents, diner patrons, debate attendees, Secret Service

LOCATIONS/ITEMS: Motel w/ Sam & James' room, Greasy's Spoon (diner), upstate New York RAID base w/ Zola's lab & Sharon's cell, Albany, NY inc Wright's hotel room & convention center; AIM weapons inc electro-shock guns, Dr. Doom's chronal device & Time Platform, Sharon's SHIELD GPS transmitter, 4 SHIELD hovercars, SHIELD agents' guns, Kronas soldiers' guns, Sin's sniper rifle, Red Skull mask

SYNOPSIS: As Sam Wilson and James Barnes watch from a nearby motel room, AIM agents capture the confused the 1950s Cap; they plan to follow him to Red Skull. Meanwhile, Red Skull orders Arnim Zola to complete Dr. Doom's chronal device before it's too late. Dr. Faustus, seeing the Skull's plans falling apart, visits the imprisoned Sharon Carter and gives her SHIELD GPS transmitter. He spares her the grief of losing her unborn child by wiping her memory of ever being pregnant. En route to Red Skull's base, Captain America and Falcon are intercepted by the Black Widow, who tells them that Faustus tipped SHIELD off about the RAID base and about the Skull's plan for the Presidential debate in Albany. Zola completes Dr. Doom's Time Platform. As Zola learns that Faustus is missing, Falcon, Black Widow and SHIELD storm the RAID base. At the debate and upset at her father, Sin decides to kill Wright instead of the intended target. Cap arrives in time to save Wright.

NOTE: Includes recap/title page (1 page). Dr. Faustus shaves off his signature beard.

CAPTAIN AMERICA #42 [#591] (November 2008)

"The Death of Captain America Act 3, the Man who Bought America: Part Six" (20 pages)
"Epilogue One" (1 page)
"Epilogue Two" (3 pages)
"Epilogue Three" (1 page)

CREDITS: Ed Brubaker (writer), Steve Epting (art pgs 5-7, 9-11, 13-16, 20 & 25, c art), Luke Ross (pencils pgs 1-4, 8, 12, 17-19 & 21-24), Rick Magyar, Fabio Laguna (inks), Virtual Calligraphy's Joe Caramagna (letters), Frank D'Armata (colors), Jeanine Schaefer (assoc editor), Tom Brevoort (editor)

FEATURE CHARACTERS: Captain America (Barnes, also in CapDC #34, '08, next in Cap #43, '08 fb, Av/Inv #4-5, 7-8 & 12, '08-09, Cap #43 fb, SecInv #4, SecInv #6, Tb #125, all '08, SecInv:FL #4-5, '08-09, Av:In #19, '09, SecInv #7, '08, SecInv #8, '09 fb, NAv #48, NAv:Re #1 fb, bts in NAv:Re #1, NAv #49-50, Av:FCBD, all '09, MAv #21 & 23, '08, AoAtlas #3-5, W #73, W #74/2, all '09), Captain America (Rogers, bts, also & next in Cap:Re #1, '09 fb, next in Thor #11, '08, Cap:Re #1, '09, see NOTE)

GUEST STARS: Black Widow (next in CM #1, '08), Falcon (next in Cap #49, '09), Tony Stark (last in SH #27, '08, next in IM:DoS #21, '07)

SUPPORTING CAST: Sharon Carter (also in Cap:Re #1, '09 fb)

VILLAINS: Red Skull (also in Cap:Re #1, '09 fb, next in Cap #600/2, '09), Aleksander Lukin (also in Cap:Re #1, '09 fb, dies, last app), Captain America (Burnside, next in Cap #49, '09), Sin (next in Cap #600/2, '09), Arnim Zola (also in Cap:Re #1, '09 fb, next in Cap:Re #1, '09), Kronas soldiers (some die), AIM agents (some die)

OTHER CHARACTERS: Sen. Barack Obama (next as US President in ASM #583/2, '09), Sen. John McCain (last app) (both bts, in cars), Sen. Gordon Wright (last app) & his campaign staff, Secret Service (Yellow Dog 2 named), police, reporters, photographers; Dr. Faustus (on cover)

LOCATIONS/ITEMS: Albany, NY convention center inc parking lot, upstate New York RAID base inc Zola's lab, Steve's Brooklyn home, New York inc Times Square; Washington, DC (also on TV) inc Capitol & Wright's office, another of Zola's labs; Kronas soldiers' guns & knives, AIM agents' guns, Dr. Doom's chronal device & Time Platform, Zola's blaster, Sin's rocket launcher, Sharon's SHIELD GPS transmitter, Secret Service guns, SHIELD Helicarrier, Red Skull mask & robot body (1st)

SYNOPSIS: As the Presidential candidates are ushered to safety, Captain America attacks Sin and her Kronas soldiers, but Sin manages to escape to the roof. Meanwhile, Black Widow and Falcon storm the self-destructing RAID base as Red Skull and Arnim Zola connect Sharon

Carter to Dr. Doom's Time Platform. Cap fights through the Kronas soldiers. As a figure appears in the Time Platform, Sharon breaks free and shorts out Doom's chronal device, forcing Zola and the Skull to flee. Sin fires a rocket at the Presidential candidates. Sharon fatally shoots Aleksander Lukin and the 1950s Cap impales Zola. Cap stops Sin's rocket and saves the candidates. Sin is arrested and Cap recovers to the accolades of a cheering crowd. Falcon and Black Widow recover Sharon. Days later, Tony Stark tells Sam about Sharon's miscarriage and her inability to remember it. Black Widow convinces Senator Wright to withdraw from the Presidential race, and he resigns his Senate seat. The 1950s Cap wanders New York. Red Skull finds himself in one of Zola's biomechanical bodies, to his horror.
NOTE: Includes recap/title page (1 page). Cap:Re #1, '09 reveals that Steve Rogers is unlocked in time here.

CAPTAIN AMERICA #43 [#592] (December 2008)

"Time's Arrow – Part 1 of 3" (22 pages)

CREDITS: Ed Brubaker (writer), Luke Ross (pencils), Fabio Laguna (inks), Virtual Calligraphy's Joe Caramagna (letters), Frank D'Armata (colors), Jeanine Schaefer (assoc editor), Tom Brevoort (editor), Steve Epting (c art)
FEATURE CHARACTERS: Captain America (Barnes, also in photo, rfb & as Bucky and in fb1 between YA #6, '42 & Cap #46, '09 fb, also in fb2 between Cap #42, '08 & Av/Inv #4, '08, fb3 between Av/Inv #12, '09 & SecInv #4, '08), Captain America (Rogers, only in fb1 between Cap:SoL #4, '98 & Cap #46, '09 fb)
GUEST STARS: Black Widow (also in rfb, last in SecInv #8, '09 fb), Invaders: Human Torch (Hammond, only in fb1 between Cap:SoL #4, '98 & Cap #46, '09 fb), Sub-Mariner (bts in fb1, waiting in his Atlantean ship, between Cap:SoL #4, '98 & Cap #46, '09 fb)
SUPPORTING CAST: Sharon Carter (bts, doing well but refuses to return to SHIELD, next in Cap #49, '09)
VILLAINS: Batroc (last in SH #17, '07) & his Brigade, Man with No Face (in shadows, last in CapC #77/2, '54, chr last in Cap #45, '09 fb), Prof. Zhang Chin (1st in fb1, chr next in Cap #46, '09 fb), Wrecker (in fb3 between NAv #46, '08 & SecInv #6, '08), AIM agents (in fb2), Japanese soldiers (in fb1, 2 some as corpses, others die)
OTHER CHARACTERS: Gen. Douglas MacArthur (bts in fb, sent Invaders to Shanghai, between SubC #5/2, '42 & AllWin #8/2, '43), Ollie (Widow's UN contact, 1st), Shanghai citizens, Invaders' contact (both in fb1), UN security guard, Marty (UN guard's friend, bts on phone), police, waitress, bystanders; Luke Cage, Nick Fury, Corruptor (Jackson Day), Venom (MacDonald Gargan), Crossfire, Hulkling, Iron Fist, Iron Man, Ka-Zar, Skrull Queen Veranke (as Spider-Woman) & her Super-Skrulls (prev 11 in rfb), US soldiers (on cover)
LOCATIONS/ITEMS: Shanghai inc factory w/Chin's lab (all in fb1&4), Steve's Brooklyn home, New York inc Brooklyn Bridge, Chinese restaurant & UN Scientific Research Facility w/security checkpoint & archival storage room; Bucky's gun, Japanese soldiers' guns (both in fb1), AIM agents' guns (in fb2), Wrecker's crowbar (in fb3), Cap's motorcycle, Batroc's Brigade's weapons including electrical blaster rifle
FLASHBACKS: Shanghai, 1942: Disguised as German tourists, Captain America, Bucky, and the Human Torch raid a factory. As Cap and Torch battle Japanese soldiers Bucky finds and rescues 12-year-old scientific prodigy Prof. Zhang Chin (1). Cap battles AIM agents (2) and the Wrecker (3), and joins Earth's heroes against the recent Skrull invasion (SecInv #7, '08).
SYNOPSIS: Following a night of passion, Natasha Romanova and James Barnes discuss the super hero community's acceptance of James as the new Captain America. As James decides to go out to clear his head, Batroc robs a UN research facility. Hearing the police dispatch regarding the break-in, Barnes races there. Though he holds his own against Batroc, James is shot from behind with an electrical blaster by one of Batroc's men. Batroc notices Cap's shield under James' jacket before he escapes. Barnes changes into Cap before the police arrive. Later, Black Widow and Cap speak with Ollie, one of Natasha's UN contacts, who shows them the records archive Batroc raided. At a Chinese restaurant, Batroc gives his spoils and UN security camera photos of Barnes to his employer. The employer recognizes James as the Winter Soldier.
NOTE: Includes recap/title page (1 page).

CAPTAIN AMERICA #44 [#593] (January 2009)

"Time's Arrow – Part 2 of 3" (22 pages)

CREDITS: Ed Brubaker (writer), Luke Ross (pencils), Fabio Laguna, Rick Magyar (inks), Virtual Calligraphy's Joe Caramagna (letters), Frank D'Armata (colors), Jeanine Schaefer (assoc editor), Tom Brevoort (editor), Steve Epting (c art), Sal Buscema (variant c art)
FEATURE CHARACTER: Captain America (also as Winter Soldier in fb1-2 between BW:DO #2, '10 fb & Cap #45, '09 fb)
GUEST STAR: Black Widow
VILLAINS: Batroc & his Brigade (Griffin named), Prof. Zhang Chin (also in photo, only in fb1 between Cap #46, '09 fb & Cap #45, '09 fb), Man with No Face (also in fb1 between CapC #77/2, '54 & Cap #45, '09 fb), Vasily Karpov (in fb2 during Cap #11, '05 fb), Murphy (gun store owner) & his men
OTHER CHARACTERS: Human Torch (Hammond, corpse, bts in truck, last in Inv #9, '09), Ollie (last app), Dr. Penfield (UN scientist), UN soldiers (1 dies), Chinese soldiers (in fb1, all die); Josef Stalin (in photo), Mao Tse-Tung (as statue & in photo)
LOCATIONS/ITEMS: Beijing inc Chin's office (in fb1), Karpov's office (in fb2), New York inc parking facility, Murphy's gun store, Penfield's home, Chinatown w/Man with No Face's hotel room, Griffin's apartment; Chinese soldiers' guns, Winter Soldier's gun (both in fb1), Cap's motorcycle, Murphy's man's knife, Murphy's gun, Batroc's palm magnets, Batroc's Brigade's guns, UN biohazard transport truck
FLASHBACKS: Beijing, 1968: Winter Soldier kills guards as he closes in on his target, Prof. Chin, and interrupts Chin's recording decrying Chairman Mao's rejection of his ideas as too revolutionary. Winter Soldier hesitates when Chin recognizes him as Bucky. The Man with No Face arrives to defend Chin (1). Vasily Karpov orders Winter Soldier to kill Prof. Zhang Chin (2).
SYNOPSIS: Captain America and Black Widow meet with Ollie, who has been reassigned by the UN to Madripoor as punishment for involving

them in the heist investigation. Ollie feels the UN doesn't want Cap to know what Batroc stole. In civilian clothes, James interrogates gun store owner Murphy, a mercenary he met as Winter Soldier, and coerces information from him about Batroc's hired guns. Batroc forces a UN scientist to divulge information regarding their primary objective, then contacts his employer and assures him they have the information and that a proper trail was left for Cap. The next day, Batroc and his Brigade attack a UN convoy carrying their objective. Cap arrives to stop them, but finds himself in a two-pronged battle against Batroc and his employer, the latter Cap recognizes as Chin's guardian from Beijing.
NOTE: Includes recap/title page (1 page).

CAPTAIN AMERICA #45 [#594] (February 2009)

"Time's Arrow – Part 3 of 3" (22 pages)

CREDITS: Ed Brubaker (writer), Butch Guice (co-pencils, co-inks), Luke Ross (co-pencils), Rick Magyar, Mark Pennington (co-inks), Virtual Calligraphy's Joe Caramagna (letters), Frank D'Armata (colors), Jeanine Schaefer (assoc editor), Tom Brevoort (editor), Steve Epting (c art), Lee Bermejo (variant c art)
FEATURE CHARACTER: Captain America (also as Winter Soldier in fb between Cap #44, '09 fb & Cap #46, '09 fb)
GUEST STAR: Black Widow
VILLAINS: Batroc (next in X:TS&P #1/4, '11) & his Brigade, Prof. Zhang Chin (in fb between Cap #44, '09 fb & Cap #46, '09), Man with No Face (also in fb between Cap #44, '09 fb & Cap #43, '08)
OTHER CHARACTERS: Human Torch (Hammond, corpse, also in photo), 2 UN security guards, Chin's experimental subjects (in fb)
LOCATIONS/ITEMS: Beijing inc Chin's office & underground lab (in fb), New York inc UN Building w/archival storage room, Steve's Brooklyn home; Winter Soldier's rifle & pistol (in fb), Batroc's Brigade's guns, plastic explosive & helicopter, UN biohazard transport truck (destroyed), Torch's container, Chin's subject's containment tanks (fb)
FLASHBACK: Beijing, 1968: The Man with No Face attacks Winter Soldier. Winter Soldier shocks the intangible man with an electrical cable and escapes, soon finding himself in Chin's underground lab, where he discovers human test subjects in containment tanks.
SYNOPSIS: As Captain America fights the Man with No Face, Batroc and his Brigade blow the UN transport truck open and secure their objective. Meanwhile, Black Widow sneaks into the UN's records archives. Cap overpowers the Man with No Face by delivering a massive shock through his artificial arm. Black Widow learns what Batroc's objective is. Cap finds himself overwhelmed by Batroc, the Man with No Face, and gunfire from Batroc's getaway helicopter. Cap is unable to prevent Batroc's escape but Black Widow arrives and saves him from the Man with No Face. Cap discovers that Batroc has stolen the remains of Jim Hammond, the original Human Torch. Black Widow later tells James that the UN has been studying Hammond. Seething, James tells Natasha that Zhang Chin is likely the mastermind behind the theft.
NOTE: Includes recap/title page (1 page).

CAPTAIN AMERICA #46 [#595] (March 2009)

"Old Friends and Enemies Part 1 of 3" (22 pages)

CREDITS: Ed Brubaker (writer), Steve Epting (art), Virtual Calligraphy's Joe Caramagna (letters), Frank D'Armata (colors), Jeanine Schaefer (assoc editor), Tom Brevoort (editor), Marko Djurdjevic (variant c art)
FEATURE CHARACTER: Captain America (Barnes, also in photo & as Winter Soldier, also as Bucky in fb1 between Cap #43, '08 fb & Cap #5, '05 fb, also as Winter Soldier in fb2 between Cap #45, '09 fb & Cap #11, '05 fb), Captain America (Rogers, in fb1 between Cap #43, '08 fb & bts in Truth #4, '04)
GUEST STARS: Invaders: Human Torch (corpse, also in fb1 between Cap #43, '08 fb & Cap #5, '05 fb), Sub-Mariner (also in fb1 between bts in Cap #43, '08 fb & SubC #6, '42; last in InvIM #12, '09); Black Widow
VILLAINS: Prof. Zhang Chin (also in fb1 between Cap #43, '08 fb & Cap #44, '09 fb), Man with No Face
OTHER CHARACTERS: Sims (MI6 officer), Li (Chin's wife, in fb2, dies, also in photo), Japanese soldiers (in fb1), Chinese soldiers (in fb2, 2 die), bartender, bar patrons, Taiwanese soldiers; Hulk, Iron Man, Spider-Man, Thor, Wolverine (prev 5 on cover logo box only)
LOCATIONS/ITEMS: Taipei City inc government research facility w/Chin's lab & marina, Shanghai inc marina (fb1), Beijing inc Chin's quarters (fb2), Hong Kong inc bar & Black Widow's hotel room; Chin's lab equipment inc Torch's containment tank, holographic computer interface & Man With No Face's restoration chamber, Namor's Atlantean aircraft (also fb1), Japanese soldiers' guns (fb1), Bucky's gun (fb1), Chinese soldiers' guns (fb2), Winter Soldier's rifle (fb2) & pistol, Sims' drugged drink, Taiwanese soldiers' guns
FLASHBACKS: Shanghai, 1942: The Invaders rescue Chin from the Japanese and escape aboard Namor's aircraft. Chin is fascinated by the Human Torch (1). Beijing, 1968: Winter Soldier kills Chin's wife and two soldiers during his escape (2).

HUMAN TORCH
EST. 1939

SYNOPSIS: At his lab in Taipei City, Chin prepares Jim Hammond's corpse for his experiments, and assures his agent, the Man with No Face, that the new Captain America will come. En route to Taiwan aboard an Atlantean aircraft, Cap briefs Namor, the Sub-Mariner on the theft of Hammond's corpse and Chin's involvement. In Hong Kong, Black Widow gets information on Chin from Sims, an old MI6 ally. Cap and Namor sneak into Taipei City via the marina, taking out the military guards. Natasha peruses Chin's MI6 file at her hotel and is stunned to learn that Winter Soldier not only killed Chin's wife but is wanted by the Chinese for crimes against the state. Trading his Cap uniform for the garb of Winter Soldier, James breaks into a government research building.

NOTE: Includes recap/title page (1 page). Li's name is revealed in Cap #47, '09. Sims alludes that Chin engineered avian influenza, a claim Chin confirms in Cap #48, '09, and refers to Chin's nickname in the intelligence community, "Professor Pandemic."

CAPTAIN AMERICA #47 [#596] (April 2009)

"Old Friends and Enemies Part 2 of 3" (22 pages)

CREDITS: Ed Brubaker (writer), Butch Guice (art), Virtual Calligraphy's Joe Caramagna (letters), Frank D'Armata (colors), Jeanine Schaefer (assoc editor), Tom Brevoort (editor), Steve Epting (c art)
FEATURE CHARACTER: Captain America (as Winter Soldier)
GUEST STARS: Black Widow, Sub-Mariner
VILLAINS: Prof. Zhang Chin, Man with No Face
OTHER CHARACTERS: Chinese soldiers (2 die)
LOCATIONS/ITEMS: Taipei City inc Chin's lab, refinery & marina; soldiers' guns & powered exoskeletons, Black Widow's gun, 2 military cutters (destroyed), Cap's chains, jamming field clamp & note & GPS device, Chin's cattleprod, Namor's restraints

SYNOPSIS: The Man with No Face reports to Zhang Chin that Winter Soldier has been seen by multiple sources attacking government facilities. Chin orders their armored troops be dispatched to the Soldier's location. Meanwhile, Winter Soldier attacks a refinery. An annoyed Black Widow, En route to Taipei via speedboat with two military cutters in pursuit, calls him. As Winter Soldier tries to explain his actions, soldiers in powered exoskeletons capture him. Winter Soldier awakens chained in Chin's lab as Namor breaks into the building to rescue him, unaware the Man with No Face is behind him. As Chin greets Winter Soldier with a cattleprod, Black Widow finds Namor's ship with a GPS device keyed to his location, a note and Captain America's uniform and shield. Chin reveals that has created a viral weapon based on the Human Torch's artificial physiology; he demonstrates its power by killing two of his own men. Chin reveals the virus' next test subject: Namor.
NOTE: Includes recap/title page (1 page).

CAPTAIN AMERICA #48 [#597] (May 2009)

"Old Friends and Enemies Part 3 of 3" (22 pages)

CREDITS: Ed Brubaker (writer), Butch Guice, Luke Ross (art), Virtual Calligraphy's Joe Caramagna (letters), Frank D'Armata (colors), Jeanine Schaefer (assoc editor), Tom Brevoort (editor), Steve Epting (c art)
FEATURE CHARACTER: Captain America (also as Winter Soldier, also as Bucky on cover, next in Dp:SK #1, '09, MsM #41-42, '09, Cap #50, '09)
GUEST STARS: Black Widow (chr next in BW:DO #4, '10 fb, next in Cap #50, '09), Sub-Mariner (next in DR:Hood #2, '09)
VILLAINS: Zhang Chin, Man with No Face (both die, last app), Iron Patriot (Norman Osborn, HAMMER Director, last in WarM #10, '09, next in CB&MI13 #13, '09, see NOTE) & his Avengers (villains masquerading as heroes): Captain Marvel (Noh-Varr, Kree ex-soldier), "Hawkeye" (Bullseye), "Wolverine" (Daken, Wolverine's son) (prev 3 last in SavSH #4, '09, next in Thor #600, '09)), "Ms. Marvel" (Moonstone), "Spider-Man" (Venom, MacDonald Gargan) (both last in MAv #21, '09, next in Thor #600, '09), Ares (Greek god of war, last in WarM #5, '09, next in WarM #11, '10)
OTHER CHARACTERS: Human Torch (Hammond, corpse, also as statue, next in Torch #1, '09), Chinese & American soldiers, minister, memorial service attendees; Captain America (Rogers), Toro, German soldier (prev 3 on cover only)
LOCATIONS/ITEMS: Taipei City inc Chin's lab (destroyed), Arlington National Cemetery; Namor's holding tank & restraints, Cap's chains, Widow's gun w/electro-burst rounds, Chinese soldiers' guns, Torch Virus container & dispersal machinery, Chin's blaster, Namor's aircraft, Torch's casket & gravestone
SYNOPSIS: A chained Winter Soldier demands Namor's release as Zhang Chin exposes Namor to the Human Torch virus. Chin's plan is to unleash the virus on the world as a form of population control. Namor proves immune to the virus, which distracts Chin and the Man with No Face long enough for the arriving Black Widow to shatter Namor's holding tank with Captain America's shield. Black Widow subdues the Man with No Face with electro-burst shots, but Chin escapes. Winter Soldier, Black Widow and Namor plow through an oncoming horde of soldiers and make their way to Chin, who is activating the virus delivery system. Winter Soldier narrowly cleaves off the virus container with his shield. Chin dies from a heart attack during the battle, and Namor snaps the Man with No Face's neck. A week later, Jim Hammond is buried with full honors at Arlington National Cemetery. That night, Captain America secretly salutes his fallen friend.
NOTE: Includes recap/title page (1 page). Osborn took over SHIELD in SecInv #8, '09 and renamed it HAMMER in DAv #1, '09. His Avengers are the official American team, Hank Pym's are global, and Luke Cage's are outlaws.

CAPTAIN AMERICA #49 [#598] (June 2009)

"The Daughter of Time" (22 pages)

CREDITS: Ed Brubaker (writer), Luke Ross (pencils), Rick Magyar (inks), Virtual Calligraphy's Joe Caramagna (letters), Frank D'Armata (colors), Jeanine Schaefer (assoc editor), Tom Brevoort (editor), Steve Epting (c art)
FEATURE CHARACTER: Captain America (Rogers, also in Sharon's dream, only in fb2 between Cap #25, '07 fb & ToS #77/2, '66 fb)
GUEST STAR: Falcon (last in Cap #42, '08, next in Cap #600/2, '09)
SUPPORTING CAST: Sharon Carter (also in fb1 during Cap #25, '07 fb, fb3 between Cap #454, '96 & Cap #1, '98; last bts in Cap #43, '08, next in Cap #600/2, '09), Peggy Carter (also in fb2 between Cap #25, '07 fb & ToS #77/2, '66 fb, fb1 during Cap #25, '07 fb; last in Av Ann, '99 fb, last app)

VILLAIN: Captain America (Burnside, also in photo & as Steve Rogers, last in Cap #42, '08, next in Cap #600/2, '09)

OTHER CHARACTERS: Dave Cox (last bts in Cap #302, '85), Cody Cox-Morgan (last in Cap #300, '84) (both last app), American & German soldiers (both in fb2), Larkmoore residents & staff, bartender; Red Skull, Arnim Zola, US Marshall, bystanders (prev 4 in Sharon's dream); Redwing (only on cover)

LOCATIONS/ITEMS: Virginia inc Carter family Estate (also in fb1) inc bedroom, drawing room, kitchen, patio, closet, adjoining forest & Larkmoore Clinic (convalescent home) w/day room & Peggy's room, France (in fb2), cemetery (in fb3), bar, Dave's home w/bathroom; Peggy's scrapbook & war keepsakes (all in fb1), Peggy's rifle, soldiers' guns (both in fb2)

FLASHBACKS: Peggy Carter shows a young Sharon Carter her war scrapbook (1). Captain America and Peggy fight in war-torn France and share a kiss (2). Sharon visits her parents' graves (3).

SYNOPSIS: Sharon Carter visits her aunt Peggy, who now suffers from dementia and lives in a convalescent home. Meanwhile, Sam Wilson searches for the missing 1950s Cap. While exploring the grounds outside the Carter family Estate, Sharon finds Dave Cox on a hike. The two share dinner at Dave's home, and decide not to pursue a romantic relationship. The next morning, Sharon finds the c-section scar on her abdomen and remembers that she was pregnant. Sam finds a tearful Sharon at home and fills her in on the details. Posing as Steve Rogers, the 1950s Cap visits Peggy Carter and asks about "their" past. Sharon wakes from a nightmare and realizes that while she was strapped to Dr. Doom's Time Platform, she saw someone in the timestream...

CAPTAIN AMERICA #50 [#599] (July 2009)

"Days Gone By" (22 pages)

CREDITS: Ed Brubaker (writer), Luke Ross (pencils, co-inks), Rick Magyar (co-inks), Virtual Calligraphy's Joe Caramagna (letters), Frank D'Armata (colors), Jeanine Schaefer (assoc editor), Tom Brevoort (editor), Steve Epting (c art)

FEATURE CHARACTERS: Captain America (Barnes, also as Bucky in rfb & fb1 during MvPro #7, '10 fb, fb2 between Cap #5, '05 fb & CapC #23, '43, fb3 between CapC #48/3, '45 & CapC #46, '45, fb4 between Av/Inv #12, '09 fb & Cap #8, '05 fb; next in IHulk #601, FF #569, NAv #51-54, ASM #600 & 601/2, all '09, MAv #30-31, '09-10, SW #7, '10, NAv #55, '09, Utopia, '09, NAv #55-60, '09-10, BW:DO #1 & 3, '10, Cap #600/2, '09), Captain America (Rogers, only in fb2 between Cap #5, '05 fb & CapC #23, '43, in fb3 between CapC #48/3, '45 & CapC #46, '45)

GUEST STARS: Invaders: Human Torch (Hammond, in fb3 between Cap #5, '05 fb & Cap #616/6, '11), Toro (in fb3 between Cap #5, '05 fb & Cap:FA #1, '09 fb);   Luke Cage (last in MsM #42, '09, next in FF #569, '09) & his Avengers: Ronin (Clint Barton), Spider-Woman (both last in MsM #42, '09, next in NAv #51, '09), Mockingbird (last in WarM #10, '09, next in FF #569, '09), Ms. Marvel (last in MsM #46, '09, next in FF #569, '09), Spider-Man (last in MsM #43, '09, chr next in ASM #583/2, '09, next in ASM #590, '09), Wolverine (last in MsM #43, '09, next in DR:Elek #4, '09); Black Widow (last in Cap #48, '09, chr last in BW:DO #4, '10 fb, next in Tb #128, '09), Jessica Jones (between NAv #50-51, '09)

VILLAINS: Watchdogs, Master Man (Wilhelm Lohmer, in fb2 between Cap #5, '05 fb & Cap:ME #1, '94), Warrior Woman (Julia in fb2 between Inv #41, '79 & BP #21, '06 fb), German soldiers (in fb2) & spy (in fb3)

OTHER CHARACTERS: Danielle Cage (last in MsM #40, '09, next in NAv #51, '09), Sgt. Duffy (only in fb1 to 1st chr app before Cap #109, '69 fb), Maj. Samson (only app in fb1), inn's matron (bts, informed Master Man of Invaders' presence), German dogs (both in fb2), UK soldiers (in fb3), bystanders (others in rfb); Baron Zemo & his torturer, Vasily Karpov, Jack Monroe, Russian doctors & trainers, Winter Soldier's target (prev 7 in rfb)

LOCATIONS/ITEMS: Brooklyn inc Steve's home & Brooklyn Bridge, Camp Lehigh's brig (fb1), Poland inc inn (fb2), London inc Allied barracks (fb3), English Channel inc Zemo's secret base (rfb); Watchdogs' flight suits & rocket launchers, James' birthday cake, Bucky's machine gun (fb2), Zemo's drone plane, Winter Soldier's rifle (both rfb)

FLASHBACKS: 1941: Bucky spends his sixteenth birthday in Camp Lehigh's brig for disorderly conduct. Not knowing what else to do with him, Maj. Samson sends Bucky to England for special combat training (1). 1943: In occupied Poland, Toro gives away the Invaders' presence by ordering a birthday cake for Bucky. As they battle Master Man and Warrior Woman, Bucky thanks Toro (2). 1945: Cap and Bucky interrogate a German spy over Baron Zemo's recent actions in England, then leave to find a bar to celebrate Bucky's twentieth birthday (3). Zemo tortures Cap and Bucky (Cap #4, '05 fb). Cap falls from Zemo's drone plane (Av #4, '64 fb). Missing an arm, Bucky drifts in the English Channel (4). James Barnes receives an artificial arm and becomes Winter Soldier (Cap #11, '05 fb). Winter Soldier kills Jack Monroe (Cap #3, '05).

SYNOPSIS: Captain America battles the attacking Watchdogs, who feel he's only an imposter. Cap easily defeats them and returns home to a surprise birthday party held by his friends.

NOTE: Includes recap/title page (1 page).

2ND STORY: "Sentinel of Liberty" (14 pages)

CREDITS: Marcos Martin (writer, art), Virtual Calligraphy's Joe Caramagna (letters), Munsta Vicente (colors), Jeanine Schaefer (assoc editor), Tom Brevoort (editor)

FEATURE CHARACTERS: Captain America (Rogers), Captain America (Barnes, also as Bucky & Winter Soldier)

OTHER CHARACTERS: Avengers: Giant-Man, Hawkeye, Hercules, Hulk, Iron Man, Ms. Marvel, Quicksilver, Scarlet Witch, Sentry, She-Hulk, Thor, Wasp, Wonder Man, Luke Cage; Invaders: Human Torch, Spitfire, Sub-Mariner, Toro, Union Jack (Brian Falsworth); Baron Blood, Baron Strucker, Baron (Heinrich) Zemo, Baron (Helmut) Zemo, Batroc, Black Panther, Crossbones, Diamondback, Falcon, Flag-Smasher, Human Torch (Storm), Iron Fist (as Daredevil), Machinesmith, Madame Hydra, Master Man, MODOK, Mr. Fantastic, Nomad (Monroe), Patriot, Red Skull, Redwing, Sando, Sin, Spirit of '76, USAgent, Warrior Woman, Yellowjacket (Skrull), 4th Sleeper, William Burnside, Sharon Carter, Dum Dum Dugan, Prof. Erskine, Dr. Faustus, Nick Fury, Adolf Hitler, John F. Kennedy, Heinz Krueger, Aleksander Lukin, Arnim Zola, AIM agents, Hydra agents, Allied soldiers, Eskimos, bystanders

ITEMS: Cosmic Cube, Madbomb

SYNOPSIS: Steve Rogers becomes America's only Super-Soldier when Prof. Erskine is killed. As Captain America, he battles the Axis Powers with his partner Bucky and fights the Nazi war machine with his fellow Invaders. Cap is lost at the end of the war while trying to stop Zemo's drone plane. Time passes by while Cap is frozen, with three men taking his place as Captain America. Years later, Cap's wartime ally Namor, the Sub-Mariner finds his frozen body and the Avengers revive Cap. Over the years Cap battles enemies alongside friends, not knowing the Soviets have Bucky in their control as Winter Soldier. Cap loses the superhuman Civil War and is assassinated after his arrest. His former partner Bucky now keeps the dream alive as Captain America.

NOTE: A recap story celebrating the life and times of Captain America.

3ᴿᴰ STORY: "Passing the Torch!" (2 pages)

CREDITS: Fred Hembeck (writer, art, letters), Chris Giarrusso (colors), Jeanine Schaefer (assoc editor), Tom Brevoort (editor)

FEATURE CHARACTER: Acrobat (Carl Zante, as Captain America, also in own thoughts, last in Cap:SoL #11, '99, last app)

OTHER CHARACTER: Human Torch (Storm, in Acrobat's thoughts)

SYNOPSIS: The Acrobat recounts his time impersonating Captain America and his defeat by the Human Torch. He's now out of prison and hopes his interview for a job this afternoon goes well.

NOTE: Series continued in Cap #600, '09.

CAPTAIN AMERICA #600 (August 2009)

"Origin" (2 pages)

CREDITS: Steve Epting (c art), Alex Ross (variant c art), Jackson Guice (2ⁿᵈ printing c art)
NOTE: Reprinted from Cap:RW&B, '02. Includes contents page (1 page).

2ᴺᴰ STORY: "One Year After" (4 pages)
"Sharon Carter's Lament" (6 pages)
"The Other Steve Rogers" (4 pages)
"The Youth of Today" (6 pages)
"Crossbones and Sin" (6 pages)
"The Avengers Dilemma" (4 pages)
"The Red Skull's Delirium" (2 pages)
"The Vigilant" (8 pages)

CREDITS: Ed Brubaker (writer), Jackson Guice (art pgs 1-10, 27-30 & 33-40), David Aja (pgs 21-26), Howard Chaykin (art pgs 11-14), Rafael Albuquerque (art pgs 15-20), Mitchell Breitweiser (art pgs 31-32, co-colors), Virtual Calligraphy's Joe Caramagna, Christopher Eliopoulos (letters), Frank D'Armata, Edgar Delgado, Matt Hollingsworth (co-colors), Jeanine Schaefer (assoc editor), Tom Brevoort (editor)

FEATURE CHARACTERS: Captain America (Barnes, also as Bucky in rfb; next in Cap:Re #1, '09), Captain America (Rogers, only in photo, rfb & fb4 between AllWin #11/2, '43 & Av/Inv #1, '08, in fb5 between Cap #219, '78 fb & CD #8, '95 fb)

GUEST STARS: Luke Cage (last in NAv #60, '10, next in Cap:Who #1, '10) & his Avengers: Clint Barton (also as Hawkeye in rfb, last in NAv #60, '10, next in Cap:Re #4, '10), Jessica Drew (last in NAv #60, '10, next in DRL:Av #1, '09); Young Avengers: Hawkeye (Bishop), Hulkling (both only in pfb), Patriot (also in pfb) (prev 3 last in MAv #31, '10, next in Nomad #4, '10), Wiccan (also in pfb, bts, puts teleportation spell on Cage's Avengers, last in MAv #31, '10, next in Nomad #3, '10); Black Widow (last in Tb #136, '09, chr last in BW:DO #4, '10, next in Cap:Re #1, '09), Falcon (also in rfb, last in Cap #49, '09, next in Cap:Re #1, '09), Human Torch (Hammond, only in fb5 between CapC #36/2, '44 & AllSel #3/2, '44), Isaiah Bradley (also in rfb, last in FallSon:IM, '07, last app), Nick Fury (bts, supplies Sharon w/ memory restoration device, last in Tb #136, '09, next in Cap:Re #1, '09)

SUPPORTING CAST: Bucky (Rikki Barnes, girl from another world, last in OnsReb #5, '08, next in Nomad #1, '09), Bucky (Monroe, only in rfb & fb3 between Cap #155, '72 fb & MLG #1, '01 fb), Sharon Carter (also in fb1 during Cap #25, '07, last in Cap #49, '09, next in Cap:Re #1, '09)

VILLAINS: Red Skull (also in rfb & fb4 between AllSel #2, '43 & Av/Inv #9, '09, fb5 between Cap #220, '78 fb & AllWin #12/2, '44, fb6 between Cap/NF:OthW, '01 & Fury #1, '94; last in Cap #42, '08, next in Cap:Re #3, '09), Captain America (Burnside, also in rfb & fb2 between CapTW:AF, '09 fb & Cap #155, '72 fb, also in CapTW:AF, '09 fb, Cap #155, '72 fb, Cap #602, '10 fb, fb3 between Cap #155, '72 fb & MLG #1, '01 fb; last in Cap #49, '09, chr next in Cap #603, '10 fb, next in Cap #602, '10), Crossbones (also in photo, last in Cap #36, '08, next in Cap:Re #2, '09), Sin (last in Cap #42, '08, next in Cap:Re 2, '09), Iron Patriot (last in Tb #136, '09, next in Cap:Re #1, '09) & his Avengers: "Ms. Marvel" (Moonstone), Sentry (both last in NAv #60, '10, next in DRL:Av #1, '09); Adolf Hitler (only in fb6 between bts in FF #52, '02 fb & WarC #30, '54), Baron (Heinrich) Zemo (only in fb6 between FallSon:IM, '07 & Av #56, '68), Dr. Faustus' operative (also in fb1, only app), AIM agents (in pfb), Nazi soldiers (in rfb & fb6), 2 thieves, inmates

OTHER CHARACTERS: Redwing (also in rfb, last in Cap #41, '08, next in Nomad #2, '09), Faith Bradley (Isaiah Bradley's wife, last in BP #16, '06, last app), Paul Simon, Art Garfunkel (pop music duo, both bts, perform at vigil, only app), HAMMER prison guards (Max named), doctors (in fb2), government scientists (in fb3), US soldiers (in fb4), Bronx High School of Science vice-principal, janitor & students, News 4 reporter & her cameraman, waitress, bystanders, cat; Exiles: Angelo Baldini, Franz Cadavus, Gen. Jun Ching, Eric Gruning, Jurgen "Iron Hand"

Hauptmann, Ivan Kruski; Attuma, Baron (Helmut) Zemo, Dragon Man, Eternity, Kang, Mr. Hyde, Quicksilver, Scarlet Witch, Son of the Serpent, Super-Adaptoid, Swordsman, Ultron, Yellowjacket, criminals (prev 20 in rfb)

LOCATIONS/ITEMS: Germany inc Black Forest (fb4), Adolf Hitler's Eagle's Nest fortress at Berchtesgaden (fb5) & Schwarzebitte concentration camp (rfb), Manhattan federal courthouse (also rfb & fb1), New York Public Library, Central Park, Times Square, Dr. Faustus' operative's apartment, Bronx inc Bradley home & Bronx High School of Science, Steve's Brooklyn home (Avengers Hideout), southern US government lab (fb3), HAMMER Federal Holding Facility in Colorado inc Crossbones' cell & infirmary, Mirador, CA inc diner & Mirador Motel, Red Skull's base; Bucky's gun, Zemo's drone plane, Avengers submarine, original Cosmic Cube (all rfb), Nazi soldiers' guns (rfb & fb6), stasis chambers (fb3), Sharon's chronal pistol (also rfb & fb1) & tracker, Red Skull's guns (fb4-5) & robot body, HAMMER guards' guns, taser & tear gas, Fury's memory restoration device

FLASHBACKS: Cap and Bucky fight Nazi soldiers (ToS #68/2, '65). The Invaders swoop into action (Inv #16, '77 fb). Cap fails to save Bucky from Zemo's drone plane (Av #4, '64 fb). The Avengers revive Cap (Av #4, '64). Over the years, Cap fights alongside friends against all odds (montage) until under Dr. Faustus' control, Sharon Carter shoots Cap (Cap #25, '07) and hands the gun off to another of Faustus' enthralled operatives (1). The 1950s Cap has cosmetic surgery to look like Steve Rogers (2). The Cap and Bucky of the '50s fight crime (YM #26/2, '54). Scientists monitor the cryogenically frozen Cap and Bucky of the '50s (3). As Captain America, Isaiah Bradley fights Nazi soldiers at Schwarzbitte concentration camp (Truth #5, '03). The Young Avengers battle AIM agents (p). Cap fights Red Skull in the Black Forest (4) and joins Human Torch in attacking the Skull in Adolf Hitler's Eagle Nest fortress (5). Red Skull and the Exiles hold Cap captive (Cap #103-104, '68). Red Skull attacks Cap with the Cosmic Cube (Cap #115, '69). Hitler stops Red Skull from strangling Baron Zemo when he proposes a plan to exterminate Cap and Bucky (6).

SYNOPSIS: In New York, Sharon Carter tracks down the gun she used to shoot Captain America and is relieved to discover it's not an ordinary gun. In California, the 1950s Cap contemplates his past and subdues two men who try to steal his uniform and shield. In the Bronx, Rikki Barnes researches Elijah Bradley and tracks him down as the Patriot, hoping that he can introduce her to the new Cap. They talk, and Eli invites her to meet the Young Avengers. At a Colorado federal prison, Crossbones discovers that Sin is a fellow inmate and rampages towards her cell. As Luke Cage, Clint Barton and James Barnes work out at the Avengers Hideout, Black Widow convinces Barnes not to go the Captain America memorial vigil in costume. Later, Falcon meets up with Barnes, Natasha, Cage, Barton and Jessica Drew at the vigil. They have a teleportation spell from Wiccan to extract them quickly if necessary. Iron Patriot and his Avengers police the unauthorized vigil, even though they detect the outlaw Avengers, Osborn decides to do nothing except address the crowd and spin things to his advantage. Sharon arrives and announces that they can still save Steve Rogers.

NOTE: Story continued in Cap:Re #1, '09.

3RD STORY: "In Memorium" (12 pages)
CREDITS: Roger Stern (writer), Kalman Andrasofsky (art), Virtual Calligraphy's Joe Caramagna, Christopher Eliopoulos (letters), Marte Gracia (colors), Jeanine Schaefer (assoc editor), Tom Brevoort (editor)

FEATURE CHARACTER: Bernie Rosenthal (also in sketch, rfb & fb1 between Cap #267-268, '82, in fb2 during Cap #292, '84, also in fb3, last in Cap #443, '95, next in Cap #612, '11)

SUPPORTING CAST: Captain America (also as Steve Rogers in fb1 between FF #244, '82 fb & Cap #268, '82, fb2 during Cap #292, '84), Mike Farrel (also as Super-Patriot in rfb; as ashen remains, last in Cap #439, '95, last app) (both also in Bernie's thoughts), Josh Cooper (also in rfb; last in Cap #380, '90, last app) (all also in sketch & rfb), Nomad (Jack Monroe, only in fb2 during Cap #292, '84)

OTHER CHARACTERS: Sammy Bernstein, Harry Todd, Primus, Watchdog, Neo-Nazi protestors, US marshals (all in rfb), protestors (in rfb & fb7), Spider-Man (on coffee mug)

LOCATIONS/ITEMS: Santa Fe, NM inc Bernie's home & bluff; Bernie's jeep, sketches by Steve Rogers, Mike Farrel's urn

FLASHBACKS: Steve Rogers meets Bernie Rosenthal (Cap #248, '80). Steve and Josh Cooper help Bernie move into her apartment and Mike Farrel tells them Captain America is running for President (Cap #250, '80). After spending time with Steve (1), Bernie tells him she loves him (Cap #268, '82). Cap breaks up a fight at a Neo-Nazi rally and Bernie realizes Cap is Steve Rogers (Cap #275-276, '82). Cap and Bernie battle Primus (Cap #279, '83). Bernie watches Cap train (Cap #290, '84). Bernie bids goodbye to Cap as he and Nomad go out on patrol (2). Bernie tells Steve she's leaving for law school (Cap #316, '86). Steve and Bernie get reacquainted (Cap #380, '90). A Watchdog gets Cap to surrender by threatening Bernie (Cap #385, '91). Super-Patriot, Mike Farrel dies (Cap #439, '95). Bernie joins the crowd of people gathered outside the federal courthouse for Captain America's arraignment and is horrified (3) when Cap is shot (Cap #25, '07).

SYNOPSIS: Bernie Rosenthal and Josh Cooper reminisce about absent friends Steve Rogers and Mike Farrel, lamenting they weren't aware of Mike's brain tumor. As people set off fireworks to commemorate Captain America, Bernie and Josh scatter Mike's ashes.

4TH STORY: "The Persistence of Memorabilia" (10 pages)
CREDITS: Mark Waid (writer), Dale Eaglesham (art), Virtual Calligraphy's Joe Caramagna, Christopher Eliopoulos (letters), Paul Mounts (colors), Jeanine Schaefer (assoc editor), Tom Brevoort (editor)

FEATURE CHARACTER: Joseph Paglino (Captain America memorabilia collector, only app)

GUEST STARS: Captain America (also in comic art, poster, photo, rfb & fb1 between YA #7, '43 & CapC #26/3, '43, as Steve Rogers in fb2 between Av #104, '72 & Cap #153, '72), Tony Stark (last in ΩFlt #2, '07, next in MCP #4/4, '08)

VILLAINS: 2 suspects (in fb2), comic art bidder (see NOTE)

OTHER CHARACTERS: Bob Courtney (also in fb2 between Cap #152-153, '72, last in Cap #159, '73, last app), Mary (News 4 reporter) & her cameraman, 4th Infantry Division (some also in photo & fb1, others only in fb1, some as corpses), 4th Infantry veteran's wife, auction attendees (inc Stark's proxy), auctioneer, auction security, peace flag auction winners & their children, Marvel Comics & its stockholders (bts, canceled Captain America comic series), bidder's father (bts, sells publishing company to Paglino), Jenny (mentioned, Bayer & Rudinoff receptionist); Mr. Fantastic, police (both in rfb), Batroc, Red Skull's earth-based construct (both in comic art)

LOCATIONS/ITEMS: Guadalcanal (in fb2), New York (also in fb2) inc Bayer & Rudinoff publishing offices, Dayborne and Company auction house & police station, auction winners' homes, Stark's office; 4th Infantry's guns (in fb1), Captain America comic books (see NOTE), Cap's

Avengers ID, peace flag, comic art, police badge & Nomad costume

FLASHBACKS: Authorities arrest Captain America, ending the superhuman Civil War (CW #7, '07). During WWII, Captain America leads the 4th Infantry Division at Guadalcanal (1). Police officers Steve Rogers and Bob Courtney arrest two suspects (2).

SYNOPSIS: Joseph Paglino's collection of Captain America memorabilia goes up for auction and Cap fans buy objects to commemorate the fallen hero. Through a proxy, Tony Stark buys Cap's original Avengers ID for $2 million. Another bidder buys a collection of Cap comic art by Steve Rogers. He hopes to use his father's company to publish new comics showing Cap as a traitor. Paglino, having heard of the bidder's plan, buys the publishing company and tells off the bidder.

NOTE: One of the comic books shown in this story is CapC #1, '41. The Steve Rogers comic art is from ToS #81/2, '66 & ToS #85/2, '67 by Jack Kirby. The art bidder's name is not given, but is presumably Bayer or Rudinoff. Followed by "My Bulletin Board" (2 pages), a recollection of co-creating Captain America by Joe Simon.

5TH STORY: "Red Skull's Deadly Revenge!" (24 pages)

NOTE: Reprinted from CapC #16/4, '42. Followed by a cover gallery (9 pages), featuring cover reproductions of CapC #1-78, '41-'54, ToS #1-99, '59-'68 & Cap #100-600, '68-'09.

CAPTAIN AMERICA

CAPTAIN AMERICA #601 (September 2009)

"Red, White & Blue-Blood" (40 pages)

CREDITS: Ed Brubaker (writer), Gene Colan (art), Artmonkey's Dave Lanphear (letters), Dean White (colors), Jeanine Schaefer (assoc editor), Tom Brevoort (editor), Marko Djurdjevic (variant c art)

FEATURE CHARACTER: Captain America (Rogers, in photo, rfb & fb1 between Cap:Re #2, '09 & SpSM #17, '04 fb)

GUEST STARS: Nick Fury (last in Cap #24, '07, next voice only in Cap #25, '07), Union Jack (Brian Falsworth, bts in fb1, checked Baron Blood's tomb, between MSUn #9, '95 & SagaHT #2, '90)

SUPPORTING CAST: Winter Soldier (also as Bucky in fb1 between Inv #2, '10 fb & CapC #47, '45; last in WS:WK #1, '07, next in Cap #25, '07)

VILLAINS: Baron Blood (also in drawing, only in fb2 between Inv #9, '76 fb & Inv #7, '76, bts in fb1, still in his tomb, between Inv #2, '10 fb & UJack #2, '99 fb), Helmutt von Schuler (Nazi vampire, only app in fb2), Mary Arnett (actress & vampire, only app in fb1), Esme Ceorses (vampire child, only app in fb1-2)

OTHER CHARACTERS: Terry Foyle (musician, only app in fb1), Allied soldiers (in fb1, Frankie & Marty named, some also as vampires), Bastogne citizens (in fb1-2, some as corpses, inc Jews & Gypsies), crow, dogs (both in fb2); Gen. Phillips, Operation: Rebirth witnesses, Army recruits, bystanders (prev 4 in rfb), Goliath (Bill Foster), Iron Man, Ragnarok (Thor clone) (prev 3 in photo)

LOCATIONS/ITEMS: Fury's safehouse, Bastogne, Belgium (in fb1-2) inc USO camp w/Mary Arnett's room (fb), New York inc recruitment center & Operation: Rebirth (prev 3 in rfb); Bucky's gun, Allied solders' guns & tanks (all in fb1), German tanks (fb2), Winter Soldier's gun

FLASHBACKS: February, 1945: Captain America and Bucky stay with an injured soldier until he dies. Their suspicions are confirmed when the dead soldier comes back as a vampire. Bucky stakes him and Cap decapitates him. Cap and Bucky verify with Union Jack that Baron Blood is still in his tomb as actress Mary Arnett and musician Terry Foyle arrive for their USO show. Cap and Bucky interview an old woman whose house is guarded against vampires and learn that Nazi vampire Helmutt von Schuler is responsible for the vampires, but is no longer in the area. On their way back to camp another vampire attacks them, and the Allied soldiers learn of the vampire menace. Paranoia begins to get the better of the soldiers as they turn on themselves. Mary Arnett turns out to be a vampire, and after defeating her, Cap and Bucky learn that she spent time with child Esme Ceorses. Checking the graveyard, Cap learns that Esme died in 1941. Esme reveals she's been turning soldiers into vampires, so Cap and Bucky kill her (1). Steve Rogers hears of the Nazi war machine (Cap #25, '07 fb), is recruited by Gen. Phillips and becomes America's only Super-Soldier (Cap #109, '69 fb). Nazi soldiers arrive in Bastogne and round up the Jews and Gypsies. The commander, Helmutt von Schuler, is a vampire who attacks the local women. Baron Blood eventually takes von Schuler away (2).

SYNOPSIS: Nick Fury studies battles from the superhuman Civil War and reminisces with Winter Soldier about their time in WWII.

NOTE: Includes recap page (1 page). This issue takes place out of publication order.

CAPTAIN AMERICA: REBORN #1 of 6 (September 2009)

(30 pages)

CREDITS: Ed Brubaker (writer), Bryan Hitch (pencils), Butch Guice (inks), Virtual Calligraphy's Joe Caramagna (letters), Paul Mounts (colors), Jeanine Schaefer (assoc editor), Tom Brevoort (editor), John Cassaday, Alex Ross (variant c art), Joe Quesada (variant c pencils), Richard Isanove, Danny Miki (variant c inks), Laura Martin (variant c colors)

FEATURE CHARACTERS: Captain America (Rogers, past self between MvPro #4, '10 fb & Cap #255, '81 fb; between SecWs #17, '10 fb & Siege:Cap #1, '10 fb, also in SecWs #17, '10 fb, CapTW:AB #1, '09 fb, Order #7, '08 fb; between Cap

#37, '08 fb & Cap:DMR #2, '02 fb; also in rfb & fb1 between Cap&Crb #1, '11 fb & Cap #25, '07, fb2 during bts in Cap #42, '08), Captain America (Barnes, past self as Bucky between Cap #109, '69 fb & Siege:Cap #1, '10 fb; between Cap #37, '08 fb & Cap #26, '04 fb; also in pfb)

GUEST STARS: Invaders: Human Torch (Hammond, between Order #7, '08 fb & AWC #65/2, '90 fb), Toro (between MUni #1, '98 fb & AWC #65/2, '90 fb) (both bts in the past, report Nazi activity); Black Widow (also in pfb), Falcon (both last in Cap #600/2, '09), Wasp (Henry Pym, last in MDivas #3, '09 fb, see NOTE), Nick Fury (only in pfb, last in Cap #600/2, '09, next in Cap #602, '10), Vision (Jonas, last in FF #569, '09)

SUPPORTING CAST: Sharon Carter (also in rfb & fb1 during Cap #25, '07, fb2 during Cap #42, '08; last in Cap #600/2, '09)

VILLAINS: Norman Osborn (last in Cap #600/2, '09) & his Avengers: Ares, "Spider-Man" (Venom) (both last in NAv #60, '10); Arnim Zola (also in fb2 during Cap #42, '08; last in Cap #42, '08, next in Cap:Re #4, '10), Red Skull, Aleksander Lukin (both only in fb2 during Cap #42, '08), Nazi soldiers (bts in the past, running on cliffs), HAMMER agents

OTHER CHARACTERS: Sarah Rogers (in the past as corpse, after MvPro #4, '10 fb, last app), CAP (Conserve And Protect, deactivated robot, last in FF #557, '08, last app), US marshals (in rfb & fb1), US soldiers (in the past, many die), bystanders (in fb1), Sarah's doctor (in the past)

LOCATIONS/ITEMS: Normandy Beach, European town (both in past), Manhattan federal courthouse (in fb1), Red Skull's base (in fb2), Fury's secret rendezvous location (in pfb), HAMMER's Thunderbolts Mountain Base, Infinite Avengers Mansion inc Hank Pym's lab; military personnel carriers, US soldiers' rifles, German bomber & bombs (all in past), Dr. Doom's chronal device & Time Platform (both in fb2), Fury's Helicarrier schematics (in pfb), Sharon's chronal pistol, Ares' battleaxe, HAMMER agents' guns, HAMMER Helicarrier inc storage room, Cap's (Barnes) jet pack

FLASHBACKS: Cap is shot (Cap #25, '07) and Sharon Carter rushes to his side (1). While strapped to Dr. Doom's chronal device, Sharon sees Steve Rogers appear in the Time Platform. She breaks free and shorts out the device, unlocking Steve's spirit in time (2). James Barnes and Black Widow rendezvous with Nick Fury, who tells them that items confiscated from Red Skull's seized RAID base is held aboard a HAMMER Helicarrier (p).

SYNOPSIS: On June 6, 1944, Captain America leads US troops in the D-Day invasion of Normandy Beach. In the present, James Barnes as Captain America and Black Widow steal aboard a HAMMER Helicarrier in search of Red Skull's confiscated equipment. Meanwhile, Sharon Carter, Falcon and Vision have Hank Pym examine Sharon's chronal pistol. Aboard the HAMMER Helicarrier, Ares and Venom confront Cap and Black Widow. At Thunderbolts Mountain, Arnim Zola tells Norman Osborn that Steve Rogers is alive, but unlocked and lost in time. On D-Day, Cap surveys the casualties on Normandy Beach. As Bucky tells him the Human Torch and Toro have spotted nearby enemy activity, Cap finds himself at his mother's deathbed. Suddenly, Cap is on a battlefield and Bucky saves him from falling bombs. Confused, Steve begins to realize he's bouncing through the events of his life…

NOTE: For issues #1-3, the indicia name this series "Reborn" the indicia in issues #4-6 names it "Captain America: Reborn." Followed by preview for MvPro #1, '09 (6 pages). Henry Pym adopted the Wasp identity in SecInv:R #1, '09.

CAPTAIN AMERICA: REBORN #2 of 6 (October 2009)

(29 pages)

CREDITS: Ed Brubaker (writer), Bryan Hitch (pencils), Butch Guice (inks), Virtual Calligraphy's Joe Caramagna (letters), Paul Mounts (colors), Lauren Sankovitch, Jeanine Schaefer (assoc editors), Tom Brevoort (editor), John Cassaday, Jim Cheung, Tim Sale (variant c art), Laura Martin, Dave Stewart (variant c colors)

FEATURE CHARACTERS: Captain America (Rogers, past self between bts in Cap Ann '00 fb & Cap #255, '81 fb, also in Cap #215, '77 fb, ToS #63/2, '65, Cap #255, '81 fb, CapC #1, '41, Cap #109, '69 fb; between SecAv #12, '11 fb & Cap Ann '01 fb; between Inv #2, '10 fb & Cap #601, '09 fb; also in rfb), Captain America (Barnes)

GUEST STARS: Mr. Fantastic (last in Utopia, '09, next in Cap:Re #4, '10), Falcon, Vision (Jonas) (both bts, on recon mission), Black Widow, Wasp

SUPPORTING CAST: Sharon Carter (also in rfb)

VILLAINS: Norman Osborn (next in Cap:Re #4, '10) & his Avengers: Ares, "Spider-Man" (Venom) (both next in DRL:Av #1, '09); Crossbones, Sin (both last in Cap #600/2, '09); Heinz Kruger (as corpse between CapC #1, '41 & Cap #255, '81 fb), Master Man (between Cap #616/3, '11 fb & WX #14, '03 fb), Red Skull (bts, plotting to summon demonic forces, between bts in ToS #71/2, '65 & Cap Ann '01 fb), Nazi soldiers (prev

4 in the past), HAMMER agents

OTHER CHARACTERS: Franklin Roosevelt (between Cap Ann, '01 fb & MSUn #9, '95), Prof. Erskine (between Cap Ann '00 fb & Cap #255, '81 fb, also in Cap #215, '77 fb, ToS #63/2, '65, Cap #255, '81 fb, CapC #1, '41, Cap #109, '69 fb, Av:In Ann #1/4, '08), Operation: Rebirth personnel, US soldiers, US military officer, press reporters (all in the past), TV news reporters (voices only); US marshals (in rfb); Adolf Hitler (only on cover), Beast, Black Bolt, Black Panther (Shuri), Luke Cage, Cyclops, Daredevil, Deadpool, Emma Frost, Nick Fury, Molly Hayes, Hulk, Human Torch (Storm), Invisible Woman, Iron Man, Ms. Marvel, Nova, Pixie, Psylocke, Punisher, Red Hulk, Ronin, Sentry, Spider-Man, Spider-Woman, Storm, Sub-Mariner, Thing, Thor, War Machine, Wolverine, X-23 (prev 31 on variant cover only)

LOCATIONS/ITEMS: Operation: Rebirth, Red Skull's European keep, White House inc Oval Office (all in the past), Baxter Building inc Mr. Fantastic's lab, HAMMER high-security room; Super-Soldier Serum, Vita-Rays, Kruger's gun, Nazi soldiers' guns (all in the past), Ares' battleaxe, Black Widow's gun, Sharon's blood sample w/nano-particles, HAMMER agents' guns, HAMMER Helicarriers, Mr. Fantastic's bio-scanner, US military jets

FLASHBACK: Sharon tends to the dying Captain America (Cap:Re #1, '09 fb).

SYNOPSIS: 1944: Captain America and US troops fight Master Man and Nazi soldiers to stop Red Skull from summoning demonic forces to aid the Nazi war effort. Suddenly, Cap finds himself with Franklin Roosevelt, and the two hold a press conference. In the present, Ares and Venom defeat James Barnes as Captain America and Black Widow aboard the HAMMER Helicarrier. Henry Pym takes Sharon Carter to the Baxter Building, where Reed Richards finds something in her bloodstream similar to that discovered in Rogers' autopsy. Norman Osborn recruits the imprisoned Crossbones and Sin in arranging to have a reborn Cap with Red Skull's mind under his control. 1940: Steve Rogers asks Professor Erskine about time travel before entering Operation: Rebirth. Rogers drinks the Super-Soldier Serum and is bombarded with Vita-Rays, changing him into the first Super Soldier. Heinz Kruger shoots and kills Erskine and Steve retaliates, accidentally killing Kruger. Osborn tells the captive Barnes and Black Widow that he leaked to the press that Sharon shot Cap. Osborn tells Black Widow to get Sharon to turn herself in within twenty-four hours or Barnes will be killed.

NOTE: Back cover features a quote from Thomas Paine. Variant cover celebrates 70 years of Marvel Comics, as do all ongoing Marvel series this month.

(31 pages)

CREDITS: Ed Brubaker (writer), Bryan Hitch (pencils), Butch Guice (inks), Virtual Calligraphy's Joe Caramagna (letters), Paul Mounts (colors), Lauren Sankovitch (assoc editor), Tom Brevoort (editor), John Cassaday, Leinil Francis Yu (variant c art), Laura Martin (variant c colors)

FEATURE CHARACTERS: Captain America (Rogers, past self during Av #4, '64, also in FallSon:IM, '07; between Av #96, '72 & Cap:Re #4, '09 fb; also in photos), Captain America (Barnes)

GUEST STARS: Avengers: Iron Man, Thor, (both in the past during Av #96, '72; also in photo), Goliath (Clint Barton, in the past during Av #96, '72; also as Hawkeye in photo), Vision (Victor Shade, in the past between Av #96, '72 & off-panel in Cap:Re #4, '10 fb; also in photo); Falcon (also as "Redbird One", next in Cap:Re #5, '10), Sub-Mariner (also in the past during Av #4, '64, also in FallSon:IM, '07; last in DXM:Con #1, '09, next in DRL:X #1, '09), Wasp (Hank, also as "Insect Leader" & in photo as Giant-Man), Black Widow, Mr. Fantastic, Vision (Jonas)

SUPPORTING CAST: Sharon Carter (also in photo)

VILLAINS: Red Skull (last in Cap #600/2, '09), Crossbones, Sin, Thunderbolts: Ant-Man (Eric O'Grady, former SHIELD agent), Ghost (industrial saboteur), Scourge (Frank Simpson, cybernetically enhanced mercenary), Paladin (all between Tb #136-137, '09); Skrulls (in the past, 1 as Captain Marvel, see NOTE)

OTHER CHARACTERS: Firestar, Ms. Marvel, Scarlet Witch, Wasp (Janet) (all in photos), Eskimos (in the past), TV news reporter (voice only)

LOCATIONS/ITEMS: Arctic Ocean, space in Skrull Empire (both in the past), Infinite Avengers Mansion inc Captain America gallery & Hank Pym's lab, Red Skull's base; Skrull spaceships, block of ice (both in the past), displays inc medals, replica Cap shields & Cap's uniform, Cap's Arctic casket, Mr. Fantastic's scanner, Fantasti-Car, Thunderbolts aircraft, Red Skull's robot body & mask

SYNOPSIS: Frozen in a block of ice, Steve Rogers watches as an enraged Namor throws him into the sea. Reed Richards and Namor meet at Captain America's Arctic resting place to examine the corpse, only to observe Cap's body vanish. At Pym's lab, Sharon tells Black Widow and Vision that she should turn herself in to save James Barnes. Aboard a Thunderbolts craft piloted by Paladin, Ghost and Scourge taunt the captive Barnes. During the Avengers' first attack on a fleet of Skrull spaceships in the Kree-Skrull War, Captain America asks Vision to record a

message and to bury it deep within his memory storage. Falcon attacks the Thunderbolts craft and Ant-Man, hoping the Avengers will go easy on him in the future, frees Barnes. Falcon escapes with Barnes and they report to Pym, but Black Widow notices that Sharon is already gone. Sin and Crossbones meet Red Skull and give him a skull mask to partially disguise his robot body until they can transfer his mind into Steve Rogers' body.

NOTE: Back cover features a quote from Thomas Jefferson. Cap is surprised to see Captain Marvel in the past here as he is captive on the Skrull home world at this time; this must be a Skrull posing as Mar-Vell. Vision notes he regularly backs up his memory in the Avengers computer, explaining how he can retrieve data after he underwent several dismantlings and transplantations into new bodies over the years.

CAPTAIN AMERICA: REBORN #4 of 6 (January 2010)

(28 pages)

CREDITS: Ed Brubaker (writer), Bryan Hitch (pencils), Butch Guice (inks), Virtual Calligraphy's Joe Caramagna (letters), Paul Mounts (colors), Lauren Sankovitch (assoc editor), Tom Brevoort (editor), John Cassaday, Joe Kubert (variant c art), Laura Martin (variant c colors)

FEATURE CHARACTERS: Captain America (Rogers, past self between Cap:SoL #12, '99 & Cap #220, '78 fb, also in Cap:SoL #12, '99, Av #4, '64 fb, Cap:MoT #1, '11 fb, Cap #6, '05 fb; during Cap #110, '69; also in future vision, rfb & fb between Cap:Re #3, '09 fb & Av #96, '72; also in Cap:Re #6, '10 fb), Captain America (Barnes, past self as Bucky between Cap:SoL #12, '99 & Cap #220, '78 fb, also in Cap:SoL #12, '99, Av #4, '64 fb, Cap:MoT #1, '11 fb, Cap #6, '05 fb; also in rfb)

GUEST STARS: Mr. Fantastic (next in BP #9, '09), Ronin (Clint Barton, last in Cap #600/2, '09), Vision (Victor Shade, off-panel in fb between Cap:Re #3, '09 fb & Av #96, '72), Wasp (Hank, also as Giant-Man in rfb), Black Widow, Vision (Jonas)

SUPPORTING CAST: Bucky (Rick Jones, in the past during Cap #110, '69), Sharon Carter (also in rfb & future vision)

VILLAINS: Red Skull (also as Steve Rogers), Arnim Zola (last in Cap:Re #1, '09), Crossbones, Sin, Dr. Doom (also as statues, last in Utopia, '09, next in DrV #1, '09), Norman Osborn (last in Cap:Re #2, '09, next in Cap:Re #6, '10), Victoria Hand (Osborn's personal assistant & HAMMER second-in-command, last in NAv #60, '10, next in Cap:Re #6, '10), Baron (Heinrich) Zemo (in the past between Cap:SoL #12, '99 & Av #4, '64 fb) & his Nazi soldiers (in the past), Madame Hydra (in the past during Cap #110, '69) & her Hydra agents (in the past), HAMMER agents

OTHER CHARACTERS: Human Torch (Hammond), Iron Man, Master Man, Thor, Wasp (Janet), Skrulls, Allied soldiers, bystanders, police (all in rfb), Steve's & Sharon's children (in future vision), press reporters, birds

LOCATIONS/ITEMS: Zemo's English Channel base (in rfb & fb3), New York sewers (both in past), Infinite Avengers Mansion inc Hank Pym's lab, Latveria inc Doomstadt & palace, Manhattan inc Avengers Tower w/ HAMMER press room; Zemo's rifle & drone plane, Nazi soldiers' guns, motorcycle, Madame Hydra's whip, Hydra agents' guns (all in the past), Black Widow's gun, Cap's (Barnes) motorcycle, Crossbones' bandolier & rifle, Dr. Doom's chronal machine & servo-bots, HAMMER jet & Mobile Data Collector, HAMMER agents' guns, Red Skull's jet, robot body & mask, Ronin's bow & arrows, Sin's daggers, Zola's device for chronal machine

FLASHBACKS: Steve grows up in the Great Depression (Cap #25, '07 fb). Cap, Bucky and the Human Torch fight alongside Allied soldiers (Cap:SoL #2, '98 fb). Cap battles Master Man (Cap:Re #2, '09). Namor finds the frozen Cap (Cap:Re #3, '09). Sharon tends to the dying Cap (Cap:Re #1, '09 fb). The Avengers walk through a New York crowd (Av #8, '64). The Avengers battle the Skrulls (Cap:Re #3, '09). Cap and Sharon share a romantic moment (Cap #25, '07 fb). Steve and Sharon have children, but Sharon grows old and dies as Steve stays young (the future). During the Kree-Skrull War, Cap records a message saying that his consciousness is traveling throughout his life.

SYNOPSIS: Red Skull, Sin and Crossbones arrive in Latveria, where they meet Dr. Doom and Arnim Zola. In the past, Captain America and Rick Jones as Bucky battled Madame Hydra and her agents. In the Infinite Avengers Mansion, Reed Richards tells Hank Pym that the nano-particles in Sharon's blood are the key to Steve Rogers' return. This statement triggers a message in Vision's deep storage memory banks. Meanwhile, Ronin, James Barnes as Captain America and Black Widow attack a HAMMER Mobile Data Collector and question an operative within about Sharon's whereabouts. Vision's message confirms that Steve was cut loose in time when Sharon destroyed the Skull's chronal platform. Richards extrapolates that Sharon's blood contains chronal tracers. Osborn's assistant, Victoria Hand, arrives with the captive Sharon in Latveria, and Sharon is shocked to see the Skull alive. Carter and Red Skull are strapped into Doom's and Zola's chronal machine. In 1945, Cap and Bucky chase after Baron Zemo's drone plane. Just as the plane explodes Steve is pulled through time. He sees visions of his past and future as his body reconstitutes in the present. Steve Rogers stands up but with Red Skull's mind controlling it.

NOTE: Back cover features a quote from Thomas Paine.

(30 pages)

CREDITS: Ed Brubaker (writer), Bryan Hitch (pencils), Butch Guice (inks), Virtual Calligraphy's Joe Caramagna (letters), Paul Mounts (colors), Lauren Sankovitch (assoc editor), Tom Brevoort (editor), John Cassaday, David Finch (variant c art), Jason Keith, Laura Martin (variant c colors)

FEATURE CHARACTERS: Captain America (Rogers), Captain America (Barnes)

GUEST STARS: Wasp (next in MAv #34, '10), Black Widow, Falcon, Ronin, Vision (Jonas)

SUPPORTING CAST: Sharon Carter

VILLAINS: Red Skull (also as Steve Rogers & "Uncle Skull" in his consciousness), Crossbones, Sin, Arnim Zola, Super-MODOK Squadron (Military Organisms Designed Only for Killing, 1st), AIM agents, RAID agents

OTHER CHARACTERS: Manhattanites, Nazi soldiers (all in Red Skull's consciousness), bystanders

LOCATIONS/ITEMS: Washington, DC inc Lincoln Memorial w/reflecting pool & National Mall w/Smithsonian Museums & Washington Monument; AIM air transport & missiles, Avengers Quinjet, Black Widow's, Crossbones' & Super-MODOK Squadron's guns, Sin's daggers & guns, Ronin's katana, Zola's sub-particulate freezing device

SYNOPSIS: Steve Rogers finds himself inside Red Skull's consciousness. Aboard an AIM transport, Sharon Carter tries to reach Rogers, but the Skull maintains dominance over Steve's mind and body. Vision phases in to rescue Sharon, but Sin zaps him with one of Arnim Zola's weapons, freezing him at a sub-particulate level. Red Skull fires missiles at Ronin, Falcon, James Barnes as Captain America, Black Widow and Wasp, who pursue him in an Avengers Quinjet. The Quinjet is shot down and crashes in the National Mall in Washington, DC. As the Avengers emerge from the Quinjet, Rogers begins to fight against the Skull within his mind. Red Skull and Zola send Crossbones, the Super-Modok Squadron and RAID agents to attack the Avengers. As the battle rages on, Barnes decks Sin then fights the Skull in front of the Lincoln Memorial. Sin shoots Barnes and the Skull fells him. While Rogers continues to battle the Skull in his mindscape, Red Skull disarms Barnes by severing his cybernetic hand with his own shield.

NOTE: Back cover features a quote from Oscar Wilde. The Red Skull posters shown here are based on the 1917 Uncle Sam recruitment poster designed by James Montgomery Flagg.

(30 pages)

CREDITS: Ed Brubaker (writer), Bryan Hitch (pencils), Butch Guice (inks), Virtual Calligraphy's Joe Caramagna (letters), Paul Mounts (colors), Lauren Sankovitch (assoc editor), Tom Brevoort (editor), John Cassaday (variant c art), Joe Quesada (variant c pencils), Richard Isanove, Danny K. Miki (variant c inks), Laura Martin (variant c colors)

FEATURE CHARACTERS: Captain America (Rogers, also in fb during Cap:Re #4, '10, next in Cap:Who #1, '10), Captain America (Barnes, also as Winter Soldier in future vision, next in Cap:Who #1, '10)

GUEST STARS: Black Widow (also in future vision, next in Cap:Who #1, '10), Falcon (next in Nomad #2, '09), Ronin (next in NAv #55, '09), Vision (Jonas, next in MAv #34, '10)

SUPPORTING CAST: Sharon Carter (next in Cap:Who #1, '10)

VILLAINS: Red Skull (apparently dies, last app), Crossbones (next in Tb #144, '09), Sin (also in photo, chr next in Cap #613, '11 fb, next in Cap #606, '10), Arnim Zola (next in Inv #4, '11), Norman Osborn (last in Cap:Re #4, '10, next in DRL:Av #1, '09), Victoria Hand (last in Cap:Re #4, '10, next in DRL:SecWs #1, '10), Super-MODOK Squadron, AIM agents, RAID agents

OTHER CHARACTERS: Beast, Black Panther, Cyclops, Dr. Strange, Hulk, Human Torch (Storm), Invisible Woman, Iron Man, Mr. Fantastic, Quicksilver, Spider-Woman, Storm, Wolverine (all only on cover), Spider-Man, Thing, Thor, Luke Cage (prev 3 in future vision), bystanders

LOCATIONS/ITEMS: Brooklyn inc Brooklyn Bridge & Steve's home, Washington, DC inc Lincoln Memorial w/reflecting pool, Capitol & Washington Monument; AIM air transport & missiles, Black Widow's, Sin's, Crossbones' & Super-MODOK Squadron's guns, AIM agent's gun, Ronin's katana, Pym particle stream projector, HAMMER Helicarrier, Red Skull's mask & robot body

FLASHBACK: While being pulled through time, Steve Rogers sees dead friends scattered amidst a devastated New York.

SYNOPSIS: Wasp infiltrates the AIM transport and frees Sharon Carter. Steve Rogers regains control of his body, strikes Sin and reunites with James Barnes while Falcon, Black Widow and Ronin fight Crossbones and the Super-Modok Squadron on the National Mall. Wasp and Sharon rescue Vision from Arnim Zola as Red Skull finds himself once again in a Zola-made robot body. He tries to teleport away and Sharon stops him by zapping him with Pym particles, but the Skull grows to enormous size. Steve Rogers rallies the heroes and they defeat the MODOK Squadron as Sharon fires missiles at the giant Skull. The resulting explosion destroys the Skull's body and burns Sin's face. Sharon reunites with Rogers, who learns that Norman Osborn is running an Avengers team. That night, Victoria Hand reports on the incident to Osborn. In Brooklyn, Rogers reflects on the futures he saw while being pulled through time as his friends prepare a welcome back party for him.

NOTE: Back cover features a quote from John F. Kennedy. Story continued in Cap:Who #1, '10.

 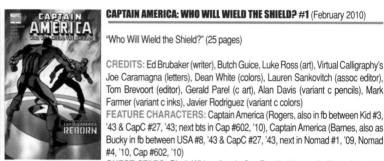

CAPTAIN AMERICA: WHO WILL WIELD THE SHIELD? #1 (February 2010)

"Who Will Wield the Shield?" (25 pages)

CREDITS: Ed Brubaker (writer), Butch Guice, Luke Ross (art), Virtual Calligraphy's Joe Caramagna (letters), Dean White (colors), Lauren Sankovitch (assoc editor), Tom Brevoort (editor), Gerald Parel (c art), Alan Davis (variant c pencils), Mark Farmer (variant c inks), Javier Rodriguez (variant c colors)

FEATURE CHARACTERS: Captain America (Rogers, also in fb between Kid #3, '43 & CapC #27, '43; next bts in Cap #602, '10), Captain America (Barnes, also as Bucky in fb between USA #8, '43 & CapC #27, '43, next in Nomad #1, '09, Nomad #4, '10, Cap #602, '10)

GUEST STARS: Black Widow (last in Cap:Re #6, '10, next in Nomad #1, '09), Luke Cage (last in Cap #600/2, '09, next in Tb #137, '09)

SUPPORTING CAST: Sharon Carter (last in Cap:Re #6, '10, next bts in Cap #602, '10)

VILLAINS: Mr. Hyde (last in DR:LL #3, '09, next in NAv #56, '09) & his men, Japanese soldiers (in fb)

OTHER CHARACTERS: Barack Obama (US President, last in SecWs #1, '09 fb, next in BP #7, '09), American soldiers (in fb), Presidential aide, Secret Service, bystanders; Abraham Lincoln, Franklin D. Roosevelt (both in photo), George Washington (in painting)

LOCATIONS/ITEMS: Brooklyn inc Steve's home, Brooklyn Bridge & Empire-Fulton Ferry State Park, White House inc Oval Office; Bucky's, American & Japanese soldiers' guns (fb), Cap's motorcycle

FLASHBACK: Captain America and Bucky battle alongside American soldiers in the Pacific. Afterwards, Bucky admires the way Cap is able to inspire the troops.

SYNOPSIS: James Barnes works on designs for a new uniform, ready to relinquish the mantle of Captain America back to Steve Rogers. Meanwhile, Steve tries to readjust to living again with Sharon's help. Black Widow convinces James to go out for one last hurrah and round up a Raft escapee. Steve suits up to get some air and, seeing Black Widow and Barnes leave, he follows them and watches their confrontation with Mr. Hyde. When Hyde tries to escape, Barnes spots Rogers and tosses him the shield. Rogers quickly defeats Hyde. Black Widow leaves them alone, and Rogers explains he's not ready to resume the role of Captain America yet, and asks Barnes to continue for a while. Later, the President pardons Steve Rogers for his crimes during the superhuman Civil War.

NOTE: Includes recap/title page (1 page).

CAPTAIN AMERICA #602 (March 2010)

"Two Americas" (22 pages)

CREDITS: Ed Brubaker (writer), Luke Ross (pencils, co-inks), Butch Guice (co-inks), Virtual Calligraphy's Joe Caramagna (letters), Dean White (colors), Lauren Sankovitch (assoc editor), Tom Brevoort (editor), Gerald Parel (c art)

FEATURE CHARACTERS: Captain America (Rogers, also in newsreel, bts, on vacation w/Sharon, next in Cap #616/3, '11 fb, MvPro #8, NAv Ann #3, DAv Ann #1, WoSM #8, InvIM #21-22 & 24, NAv #61-62, Siege #1, MAv #35, Siege #2, Siege:SecWs #1 fb, Av:In #34, Siege #3, NAv #63, Siege:Cap #1, all '10), Captain America (Barnes, also in photo, as trucker & as Bucky in newsreel)

GUEST STARS: Nick Fury (last in Cap:Re #1, '09 fb, next in DRL:SecWs #1, '09), Falcon (also as an IRS agent, last in Nomad #3, '10)

SUPPORTING CAST: Sharon Carter (bts, last in Cap:Who #1, '10, next in SecWs #17, '10 fb)

VILLAINS: Captain America (Burnside, also in pfb & fb1 to 1st chr app before Cap #155, '72 fb, fb2 during Cap #155, '72 fb; last in Cap #600/2, '09, chr last in Cap #603, '10 fb), Watchdogs (also in pfb), bank robbers (in pfb)

OTHER CHARACTERS: Boise police & residents (some in pfb) inc protest rally attendees, Barney Fleetway (Barney's owner) & his patrons, Plastic surgeon & his nurse (both in fb2)

LOCATIONS/ITEMS: Boise, ID (also in fb1 & pfb) inc "Barney's" & Foothills w/Watchdog compound w/Cap's command quarters, New York inc Fury's safehouse; Watchdogs' armor, guns & bomb, Avengers Quinjet, Cap's (Barnes) new robot arm (1st)

FLASHBACKS: As a child, William Burnside worships Captain America (1). As an adult, Burnside has cosmetic surgery to look like Steve Rogers (2). Burnside wanders through Boise, Idaho, angry at the economic depression that has hit his home town. He attacks some bank robbers and joins the Watchdogs (p).

SYNOPSIS: In the Idaho Foothills, police raid a Watchdog operation. Captain America arrives and fights off the police. Later, Nick Fury supplies James Barnes with a new robot arm and tells him of the 1950s Cap's activities. With Steve Rogers recuperating with Sharon Carter, Barnes decides to handle it. Cap and Falcon arrive in Boise and witness the townspeople holding an anti-tax rally, which gives James a plan. Later, posing as an IRS agent, Sam Wilson tells a local bar owner he's due for an audit. James intervenes and punches Sam, and he's quickly recruited by the Watchdogs. Later, the 1950s Cap, William Burnside, recognizes James Barnes at the Watchdog compound.

NOTE: Includes recap/title page (1 page).

2ND STORY: "Conjunction Part 1" (8 pages)

CREDITS: Sean McKeever (writer), David Baldeon (pencils), Sotocolor's N. Bowling (inks), Virtual Calligraphy's Joe Sabino (letters), Chris Sotomayor (colors), Lauren Sankovitch (assoc editor), Tom Brevoort (editor)

FEATURE CHARACTER: Nomad (Rikki Barnes, last in Nomad #4, '10)

GUEST STAR: Araña (Anya Corazon, student w/spider powers, last in Nomad #4, '10)

VILLAINS: Mad Dog, Professor Power (both last in Nomad #4, '10), Secret Empire (inc Number One, in shadows, last in Nomad #4, '10, next in Cap #605/2, '10)

OTHER CHARACTER: Rachel Baxter (Mad Dog's wife, only app)

LOCATIONS/ITEMS: New York inc sewers, Professor Power's cell; Nomad's photonic shield, Professor Power's attack drones

SYNOPSIS: Nomad waits near the Baxter residence for Mad Dog to make an appearance. When he does, Nomad tries to talk to him, but Araña mistakenly saves Nomad from Mad Dog. As the girls run after him, Rachel Baxter calls the Secret Empire and tells them that Nomad is following Mad Dog. After assuring Rachel that Mad Dog is not really her husband, Number One tells Professor Power that Nomad is on her way to him. Nomad and Araña confront Mad Dog in the sewers, but they're attacked by Professor Power's attack droids.

NOTE: Story continued from Nomad #4, '10.

CAPTAIN AMERICA #603 (April 2010)

"Two Americas Part Two of Four" (22 pages)

CREDITS: Ed Brubaker (writer), Luke Ross (pencils), Butch Guice (inks), Virtual Calligraphy's Joe Caramagna (letters), Dean White (colors), Lauren Sankovitch (assoc editor), Tom Brevoort (editor), Gerald Parel (c art)

FEATURE CHARACTER: Captain America (Barnes, also in pfb)

GUEST STAR: Falcon

VILLAINS: Captain America (Burnside, also in own thoughts & in fb between Cap #600/2, '09 & Cap #602, '10), Watchdogs (some also in pfb, 1 also as Captain America), bomb technician (1st, next in Cap #605, '10)

OTHER CHARACTERS: Redwing (bts, spots Watchdogs, last in Nomad #3, '10), Greyhound commuters, Boise residents (both in fb), Bucky (Monroe), Dwight Eisenhower (both in Burnside's thoughts)

LOCATIONS/ITEMS: Watchdog's Idaho Foothills compound inc training grounds (also in pfb), Cap's command quarters & barracks, Boise (also in fb) inc Front Street Hotel; Watchdogs' armor & guns, Bucky uniform, Falcon's shock-knuckles

FLASHBACKS: James Barnes undergoes Watchdog training (p). Burnside arrives in Boise.

SYNOPSIS: William Burnside is updated on James Barnes' Watchdog training, and he tells the Watchdogs to bring him in with the other new recruits. That night, Captain America and Falcon attack a Watchdog supply run. The next day, Barnes joins other recruits at the Watchdog compound. During the night James sneaks into Burnside's command quarters, but finds a decoy Cap waiting for him. An army of Watchdogs quickly surrounds him. In Boise, Burnside attacks Falcon and steals his flight harness, intending to use the Vibranium inside to fuel a bomb. NOTE: Includes recap/title page (1 page).

2ND STORY: "Conjunction Part 2" (8 pages)
CREDITS: Sean McKeever (writer), David Balden (pencils), Sotocolor's N. Bowling (inks), Virtual Calligraphy's Joe Sabino (letters), Chris Sotomayor (colors), Lauren Sankovitch (assoc editor), Tom Brevoort (editor)
FEATURE CHARACTER: Nomad
GUEST STAR: Araña
VILLAINS: Mad Dog, Professor Power, Secret Empire scientist
OTHER CHARACTERS: Bystanders, pigeon
LOCATIONS/ITEMS: New York inc sewers & internet café, Professor Power's cell, Secret Empire lab; Professor Power's attack drones, Nomad's photonic shield
SYNOPSIS: The attack droids escape with Mad Dog and Nomad yells at Araña for messing up her plan. Rikki looks on the internet for a lead on the Secret Empire, and later returns to the sewers. Meanwhile, the Secret Empire chastises Professor Power for letting Nomad escape again. In the sewers, Nomad finds Araña, who says she has a lead on the Secret Empire.

CAPTAIN AMERICA #604 (May 2010)

"Two Americas Part Three of Four" (22 pages)

CREDITS: Ed Brubaker (writer), Luke Ross (pencils), Butch Guice (inks), Virtual Calligraphy's Joe Caramagna (letters), Dean White (colors), Lauren Sankovitch (assoc editor), Tom Brevoort (editor), Gerald Parel (c art)
FEATURE CHARACTER: Captain America (Barnes, also as Bucky)
GUEST STAR: Falcon
VILLAINS: Captain America (Burnside), Watchdogs (Larry & Phil named)
OTHER CHARACTERS: Redwing (next in HFH #1, '11), David Price (train engineer, 1st)
LOCATIONS/ITEMS: Idaho Foothills inc Watchdog compound w/Cap's command quarters, Nevada, Colorado inc Hoover Dam; Watchdogs' armor, knife, explosives & guns, train, cargo plane
SYNOPSIS: William Burnside tells James Barnes to dress as Bucky, or he'll kill Falcon. Barnes grudgingly agrees. Later, Falcon wakes up in a train surrounded by Watchdogs. Redwing attacks, providing a distraction, and Falcon overpowers his captors. Falcon battles his way to the train's engine, where he discovers crates of explosives. The engineer tells him the controls are damaged and he can't stop the train. Meanwhile, Captain America and Bucky arrive at the Hoover Dam, which Cap plans to blow up as a rallying cry for America.
NOTE: Includes recap/title page (1 page).

2ND STORY: "Conjunction Part 3" (8 pages)
CREDITS: Sean McKeever (writer), David Baldeon (pencils), Sotocolor's N. Bowling (inks), Virtual Calligraphy's Joe Sabino (letters), Chris Sotomayor (colors), Lauren Sankovitch (assoc editor), Tom Brevoort (editor)
FEATURE CHARACTER: Nomad
GUEST STAR: Araña
VILLAINS: Mad Dog (last app), Professor Power
LOCATIONS/ITEMS: New York inc advertising office w/Secret Empire lab; gas
SYNOPSIS: Araña leads Nomad to an advertising agency's office and they break in. As Nomad checks the computers for Secret Empire activity Araña looks around for clues. The office suddenly slams its doors and Nomad is gassed while Mad Dog attacks Araña. Araña defeats Mad Dog, but Nomad is unconscious.

CAPTAIN AMERICA #605 (June 2010)

"Two Americas Conclusion" (22 pages)

CREDITS: Ed Brubaker (writer), Luke Ross (pencils), Butch Guice (inks), Virtual Calligraphy's Joe Caramagna (letters), Dean White (colors), Lauren Sankovitch (assoc editor), Tom Brevoort (editor), Gerald Parel (c art)
FEATURE CHARACTER: Captain America (Barnes, also as Bucky, next in DRL:Av #1, NAv Ann #3, DAv Ann #1, all '09, AvAtlas #1 & 4, '10, InvIM #17 & 19-22, '09, FoH:G, WWHs #1/2, IHulk #606-607, Hulk #21, IHulk #609, WWHs:W/C #1-2, Hulk #22, NAv #61-62, Siege #2, MAv #35, Av:In #34, Siege #3, NAv #63, Siege:Cap #1, all '10)
GUEST STAR: Falcon (next in Cap:FA #4, '11)
VILLAINS: Captain America (Burnside, apparently dies, last app), Watchdogs, bomb technician (last in Cap #603, '10, last app)
OTHER CHARACTERS: David Price (last app), Hoover Dam security, FBI agents, police
LOCATIONS/ITEMS: Colorado inc Hoover Dam, Nevada; Watchdogs' armor, helicopter, explosives, guns & bomb, train (destroyed), Falcon's hawk hook
SYNOPSIS: The Watchdogs attack the Hoover Dam's security guards as Bucky begs Captain America (Burnside) not to blow the structure up. Cap tells him the country is at war with itself and he has to rally it into sanity. A Watchdog tells Cap they've lost communication with their

train. Satisfied that Falcon is in charge of the situation, Barnes attacks Cap. On the train, Falcon interrogates a Watchdog, who tells him the vehicle is set to blow up a military installation as a distraction while Cap destroys the Hoover Dam. As Bucky battles Cap, Falcon sabotages the train and hitches a ride with the Watchdogs' pick-up helicopter. Bucky disables the remote for the Watchdogs' bomb and tries to reason with Cap. Enraged at his plan falling apart, Cap threatens to detonate manually, forcing Bucky to shoot him. He falls into the water, and the police subsequently fail to find Burnside's body. Falcon tells Barnes that despite their similar situations, he and Burnside are nothing alike.
NOTE: Includes recap/title page (1 page).

2ND STORY: "Conjunction Finale" (8 pages)
CREDITS: Sean McKeever (writer), David Baldeon (pencils), Sotocolor's N. Bowling (inks), Virtual Calligraphy's Joe Sabino (letters), Chris Sotomayor (colors), Lauren Sankovitch (assoc editor), Tom Brevoort (editor)
FEATURE CHARACTER: Nomad (also as Bucky in own dream, next in YA #1-6, '10-11)
GUEST STAR: Araña (next in ASM #635, '10)
VILLAINS: Professor Power (last app), Secret Empire's Number One (in shadows, last in Cap #602/2, '10, last app) & scientist
OTHER CHARACTERS: Night Nurse (last in NAv #58, '09, last app), Araña's classmates, Captain America, Falcon, terrorists (prev 3 in Nomad's dream)
LOCATIONS/ITEMS: Night Nurse's clinic, New York, Milton High School, Secret Empire lab; Nomad's note
SYNOPSIS: Nomad wakes up in the Night Nurse's clinic. Later, Nomad tracks Araña down at her school, apologizes for the way she treated her, and thanks her for saving her life. Meanwhile, Number One tells Professor Power that they're going to forget about Nomad and Professor Power is going to get a promotion within the Secret Empire. Later, Rikki Barnes enrolls at her friend Araña's school.

SIEGE: CAPTAIN AMERICA #1 (June 2010)

"Bear any Burden" (22 pages)

CREDITS: Christos N. Gage (writer), Federico Dallocchio (art), Dave Sharpe (letters), Giulia Brusco, Rob Schwager (colors), Rachel Pinnelas (asst editor), Bill Rosemann (editor), Marko Djurdjevic (c art)
FEATURE CHARACTERS: Captain America (Rogers, also in fb between Cap:Re #1, '09 & Cap #616/3, '11 fb; also in Siege #3, Siege:SecWs #1, Tb #143, Av:In #34, NAv #64, next in Av:In #35, Siege #3, Siege:Emb #4, NAv #64, Siege #4, DAv #16 fb, NAvFin #1, DAv #16, all '10, AvPr #1-5, '10-11, NAv #1, S:FallSun #1, Av #1, all '10, IM/Thor #1, '11, SecWs #17-19 fbs, AoH #1/3, bts in ASM #646, Av #1-6, EHAge #1/3, W:WX #11 & 13-15, UXM:HA #1, all '10, Av:Child #1-5, '10-11, Doomw #6, MK #9, SecAv #1 fb, IAmAv #3 fb, bts in IAm Av #3/3, IAmAv #5/2, SR:SSol #1-4, SecAv #1-4, MK #10, SecAv #5, AoH #4/4, all '10, Inv #1-5, '10-11, IHulk #613-615, '10, ChW #1-2, '10, ChW:DeAv #1, bts in ChW:DeAv #2, ChW:DeAv #3, all '11, IAmAv #2/4, bts in NAv #1, Tb #144 fb, EHAge #1/5, all '10, Tstrike #1-2 & 4-5, '11, Hawk&Mb #1 & 5-6, '10-11, AvAc #5, '10 fb, bts in X:TS&P #2/3, '11, Hulk #24, '10, Hulk #25-26 & 30 '10-11 fbs, Hulk #26-27, '10-11, Sland:MK #1 & 3, '10, Tb #150, Hulk #27-28, ASM #649, Task #3-4, all '11, bts in InvIM #26, '10, FF #588, '11, Av #8-12, '11, SecAv #6-7, '10-12, Klaws #4, SecAv #8-12, Cap&SecAv #1, bts in Widow #2, bts in NAv #8, Hawk:BS #1-2, all '11, Cap #606, '10), Captain America (Barnes, also in fb as Bucky between Cap:Re #1, '09 & Cap #616/3, '11 fb; also in Siege #3, Av:In #34, NAv #64, next in Siege #3-4, Siege:Emb #4, DAv #16 fb, NAvFin #1, Av:In #35, NAv #1, Av #1, AoH #1, Av #2-6, ASM #648, OMtL #5, W:WX #12-15, X:L #236, UXM #525, Doomw #6, IAmAv #5/2, all '10, Inv #1-5, '10-11, PoP #1-4, '10, ChW #1, '10, ChW :ChK #1, ChW #2, ChW:DeAv #1, bts in ChW:DeAv #2, ChW:DeAv #3, ChW #5, all '11, IAmAv #2/4, '10, BW #1-2 & 4-5, '10, Cap:FA #1-4, '10-11, YA #5, '10, Tstrike #2, '11, Hawk&Mb #1 & 5, '11, Sland #1, '10, IAmAv #5, '10, FF #584 & 588, '10-11, Cap&Falc #1, '11, Cap&Bat #1, '11, Cap #606, '10)
GUEST STARS: Luke Cage & his Avengers: Ronin (both last in NAv #63, next in Siege #3), Iron Fist (last in NAv #60, next in Siege #4), Ms. Marvel (last in Siege #3, next in Siege:SM #1); Young Avengers: Stature (last in Siege #3, next in Tb #141), Wiccan (during Siege #3); Stonewall (last in Av:In #34, next in Siege #3) (all '10)
VILLAINS: Hood (Parker Robbins), Griffin, Thunderball (off-panel) (all last in Siege #3, next in Thor #608), Crossfire (last in NAv #64, next in NAvFin #1), Iron Patriot (last in NAv #63, next in DW #83), Razorfist (last in NAv #63, also in Thor #608, NAv #64, next in NAv #64), Sentry (last in NAv #64, next in Av:In #34), Taskmaster (during Av:In #34) (all '10); German soldiers (off-panel in fb)
OTHER CHARACTERS: Jimmy (dad), Susie (mom), Madison & Kim (daughters), Asgardians
LOCATIONS/ITEMS: Ohlahoma inc Asgard & Broxton w/family home, Normandy Beach (fb); Bucky's machine gun (fb), Crossfire's gun, Jimmy's camera
FLASHBACK: June 6, 1944: Cap and Bucky storm Normandy Beach.
SYNOPSIS: During the Siege of Asgard, Broxton resident Jimmy takes photos of the battle, but his family is caught under debris when Sentry crashes Asgard. Captain America (Rogers) digs himself out as Crossfire prepares to shoot Captain America (Barnes). Together they defeat the villain, but Jimmy yells for help; he can't find his family. Together they find Jimmy's injured wife, but Razorfist is holding his daughters hostage. The Captains quickly defeat Razorfist and rush back to the battle in Asgard.
NOTE: Includes recap page (1 page). This and the covers of Siege:Loki #1, Siege:SecWs #1, Siege:SM #1 & Siege:YAv #1, all '10, combine to form one larger image. Story continued in Siege #4, '10, where Steve Rogers dismantles HAMMER and takes the SHIELD Directorship.

ABBREVIATION KEY

Below are the abbreviations used in this Index. A comprehensive list can be found at http://www.marvel.com/universe/index.

1st – in chronologies this usually refers to the first appearance. When it means another first, such as the first time a character is mentioned, a clarification (1st mention) is included.
Ann – Annual
app – appearance
bts – a behind the scenes appearance, where a character was not seen, but nonetheless impacted on the story in some way.
chr – chronologically. Differentiates between the real last and next appearances, and revised last and next appearances created by flashbacks and other continuity inserts.
dfb – during flashback. A flashback set within the issue it is presented in.
fb – flashback. An appearance set in a time frame earlier than the rest of a given issue's story.
GS – Giant size
HC – hardcover
inc – including
LOC – letter of comment
pfb – prior flashbacks. A flashback set just before the events in the main story.
prev – previous
rfb – reminder flashback. A flashback that reshows past events with no new content.
Spec – Special
TPB – trade paperback

AA – Amazing Adventures
ACap – Adventures of Captain America
AF – Amazing Fantasy
AFlt – Alpha Flight
AI:RIM – Age of Innocence: the Rebirth of Iron Man
AllSel – All-Select Comics
AllTrue – All-True Crime Cases
AllWin – All-Winners Comics

AmazMys – Amazing Mysteries
ANOH – All-New Official Handbook of the Marvel Universe
AntM – Irredeemable Ant-Man
AoAtlas – Agents of Atlas
AoH – Age of Heroes
Apache – Apache Skies
Arana – Araña: the Heart of the Spider
ASM – Amazing Spider-Man
AT – Astonishing Tales
Av – Avengers
Av&Tb– Avengers and the Thunderbolts (novel)
Av/Inv – Avengers/Invaders
Av/Tb – Avengers/Thunderbolts
Av/UF – Avengers/UltraForce
Av:C – Avengers: the Crossing
Av:Child – Avengers: the Children's Crusade
Av:EMH – Avengers: Earth's Mightiest Heroes
Av:FCBD – Free Comic Book Day: Avengers
Av:I – Avengers: Infinity
Av:In – Avengers: the Initiative
Av:KS – Avengers: the Korvac Saga
Av:TO – Avengers: the Terminatrix Objective
Av:Ts – Avengers: Timeslide
Av:UI – Avengers: the Ultron Imperative
Av:Vault – Avengers: Deathtrap, the Vault
AvA – Avengers Assemble
AvAc – Avengers Academy
AvAtlas – Avengers vs. Atlas
AvCl – Avengers Classic
AvCol – Avengers Collector's Edition
AvFin – Avengers Finale
AvFo – Avengers Forever
AvPr – Avengers Prime
AvS – Avengers Spotlight
AvStrike – Avengers Strikefile
AvUnp – Avengers Unplugged
AWC – Avengers West Coast
BG – Black Goliath
BK – Black Knight
Blackst – Blackstone the Magician
BlonPhan – Blonde Phantom Comics
BP – Black Panther

BW – Black Widow
BW:ColdW – Black Widow: the Coldest War
BW:DO – Black Widow: Deadly Origin
Bwulf – Blackwulf
C&D – Cloak and Dagger
C:Gene – Codename: Genetix
Cable&Dp – Cable & Deadpool
CallD:B – Call of Duty: the Brotherhood
Cap – Captain America
Cap&Bat – Captain America and Batroc
Cap&Crb – Captain America and Crossbones
Cap&Falc – Captain America and the Falcon
Cap&FT – Captain America and the First Thirteen
Cap&SecAv – Captain America and the Secret Avengers
Cap/CitV – Captain America & Citizen V
Cap/NF:BT – Captain America/Nick Fury: Blood Truce
Cap/NF:OthW – Captain America/Nick Fury: the Otherworld War
Cap:AmAv – Captain America: America's Avenger
Cap:DMR – Captain America: Dead Men Running
Cap:FA – Captain America: Forever Allies
Cap:Legend – Captain America: the Legend
Cap:ME – Captain America: the Medusa Effect
Cap:MoT – Captain America: Man Out of Time
Cap:P – Captain America: Patriot
Cap:Re – Captain America: Reborn
Cap:RW&B – Captain America: Red, White & Blue
Cap:SoL – Captain America: Sentinel of Liberty
Cap:Who – Captain America: Who Will Wield the Shield?
Cap:WPG – Captain America: What Price Glory?
CapBiB – Marvel Treasury Edition: Captain America's Bicentennial Battles
CapC – Captain America Comics

CapDC – Captain America Director's Cut
CapTW:AB – Captain America Theater of War: America the Beautiful
CapTW:AF – Captain America Theater of War: America First
CapTW:BA – Captain America Theater of War: a Brother in Arms
CapTW:OZP – Captain America Theater of War: Operation Zero Point
CapTW:PoD – Captain America Theater of War: Prisoners of Duty
CapTW:TSO – Captain America Theater of War: To Soldier On
CB – Captain Britain
CB&MI13 – Captain Britain and MI13
CD – ClanDestine
ChW – Chaos War
ChW:ChK – Chaos War: Chaos King
ChW:DeAv – Chaos War: Dead Avengers
CitV – Citizen V
CM – Captain Marvel
CoC – Marvel Super Hero Contest of Champions
CoC2 – Contest of Champions II
CoH – Code of Honor
Com – Comet Man
Comedy – Comedy Comics
ComMys – Complete Mystery
Conan – Conan the Barbarian
Consp – Conspiracy
CPU – Cosmic Powers Unlimited
Crimef – Crimefighters
CrimD – Crimson Dynamo
CW – Civil War
CW:BDR – Civil War: Battle Damage Report
CW:Choos – Civil War: Choosing Sides
CW:Conf – Civil War: the Confession
CW:FL – Civil War: Front Line
CW:In – Civil War: the Initiative
CW:WC – Civil War: War Crimes
CW:X – Civil War: X-Men
CW:YAv&Run – Civil War: Young Avengers & Runaways
CX – Classic X-Men
DarC – Daring Comics

DarMys – Daring Mystery Comics
DAv – Dark Avengers
Daz – Dazzler
DBCW – Daily Bugle Civil War Newspaper Special
DC – Damage Control
DC2 – Damage Control (vol. 2)
DCut – Die-Cut
DCvM – DC vs. Marvel
DD – Daredevil
DD&Cap – Daredevil & Captain America: Dead On Arrival
DDs – the Daredevils
DE:Ω – Double Edge: Omega
Def – Defenders
DF:Av – Domination Factor: Avengers
DF:FF – Domination Factor: Fantastic Four
DFSM – Deadly Foes of Spider-Man
Dhawk – Darkhawk
DHII – Death's Head II
DHKF – Deadly Hands of Kung Fu
Dhold – Darkhold
Dline – Deadline
Dlk – Deathlok
Doomw – Doomwar
Dp – Deadpool
Dp:SK – Deadpool: Suicide Kings
DR:Elek – Dark Reign: Elektra
DR:Hood – Dark Reign: the Hood
DR:LL – Dark Reign: Lethal Legion
DRL:Av – Dark Reign: the List - Avengers
DRL:SecWs – Dark Reign: the List - Secret Warriors
DRL:X – Dark Reign: the List - X-Men
DrS – Doctor Strange
DrV – Doctor Voodoo: Avenger of the Supernatural
DW – Dark Wolverine
DXM:Con – Dark X-Men: the Confession
EHAge – Enter the Heroic Age
Et – Eternals
Ex – Excalibur
Ex:P – Excalibur: the Possession
FallSon:Av – Fallen Son: the Death of Captain America - Avengers
FallSon:Cap – Fallen Son: the Death of Captain America - Captain America

FallSon:IM – Fallen Son: the Death of Captain America - Iron Man
FallSon:SM – Fallen Son: the Death of Captain America - Spider-Man
FallSon:W – Fallen Son: the Death of Captain America - Wolverine
FanFor – Fantastic Force
Fearlt:Book – Fear Itself: Book of the Skull
Fearlt:HF – Fear Itself: the Home Front
FF – Fantastic Four
FF/IM:Big – Fantastic Four/Iron Man: Big in Japan
FF:Foes – Fantastic Four: Foes
FF:WGCM – Fantastic Four: the World's Greatest Comics Magazine
FFU – Fantastic Four Unlimited
FFUnp – Fantastic Four Unplugged
FNSM – Friendly Neighborhood Spider-Man
FoH:G – Fall of the Hulks: Gamma
Fool – Foolkiller
FoS – Fury of SHIELD
Fury/13 – Fury/Agent 13
FW – Force Works
G&B – Gambit & Bishop
Galact – Galactus the Devourer
Gam – Gambit
GenX – Generation X
Godz – Godzilla
GotG – Guardians of the Galaxy
GR – Ghost Rider
GR/Cap – Ghost Rider/Captain America: Fear
GSAv – Giant-Size Avengers
GSAX – Giant-Size Astonishing X-Men
GSDef – Giant-Size Defenders
GSInv – Giant-Size Invaders
GSSVTU – Giant-Size Super-Villain Team-Up
GSX – Giant-Size X-Men
Hawk – Hawkeye
Hawk&Mb – Hawkeye & Mockingbird
Hawk:BS – Hawkeye: Blindspot
Hcat – Hellcat
Herc – Hercules
HFH – Heroes For Hire
HoM – House of M
HR – Heroes Reborn
HR:R – Heroes Reborn: the Return